Systematic Theology

By Charles Grandison Finney

This Edition Edited by Anthony Uyl

Woodstock, Ontario, Canada 2018

Systematic Theology

By Charles Grandison Finney (1792-1875)
This Edition Edited by Anthony Uyl

Lectures on Systematic Theology;
By the Rev. Charles G. Finney
Late President of Oberlin College and Professor of Theology
Originally Edited by Pres. J. H. Fairchild

What kind of philosophies do you have?
Let us know!

Visit our website: www.devotedpublishing.com
Contact us at: devotedpub@hotmail.com
Visit our shop on Facebook: Devoted Publishing

Published in Woodstock, Ontario, Canada 2018.

For bulk educational rates, please contact us at the above email address.

ISBN: 978-1-77356-268-1

Table of Contents

NOTE BY THE EDITOR

Two editions of President Finney's Lectures on Systematic Theology have been published -- the first in this country in 1846, the second in England in 1851, -- the English edition being somewhat more full than its predecessor. Both editions have been exhausted, and the book has disappeared from the market.

The present edition has been prepared from the English edition by a process of condensation, omitting, to some extent, restatements or repetitions of the argument, paragraphs of a hortatory character, and other parts not essential to the expression or elucidation of the doctrine.

Aside from these omissions, no changes have been made. No liberties have been taken with the author's style or thought. Every sentence is his own, and even in those parts where, in the judgment of the editor, the author's views are not elaborated with perfect consistency, as in the presentation of sin as selfishness, and in the lectures on sanctification, no attempt has been made to secure consistency, as might have been done by judicious omissions. The author was in the habit of thinking and speaking for himself while living, and no one can undertake to speak for him now that he is dead.

This condensed edition, it is believed, will not be less valuable, as an exponent of Mr. Finney's teaching, than the English edition, but even more valuable. Unnecessary bulk in a volume is a hindrance and discouragement to the reader. The topics will be found to be presented with all necessary fullness.

J. H. F.

OBERLIN COLLEGE, 1878.

PREFACE

BY REV. GEORGE REDFORD, D.D.,
[ORIGINAL] EDITOR OF THE ENGLISH EDITION.

THE Lectures of the Rev. Professor Finney, which are here given to the British public, were first delivered to the class of theological students at the Oberlin College, America, and subsequently published there. They were unknown in this country, except to a few of the Author's personal friends, until his arrival in England, about two years since. His name, however, was well known, and several of his works had been extensively read.

The Editor having had the pleasure and honor of forming a personal acquaintance with the Author soon after his arrival in this country, did not long remain ignorant of his Theological Lectures. After his first hasty perusal of them, he ventured strongly to recommend their publication, both for the sake of making the British churches better acquainted with the Author's doctrinal views, and also on account of the direct benefit which students, and other inquirers into the theory of gospel doctrines, would be likely to derive from a work so argumentative, and so unlike all the works on systematic and dogmatic theology known to the English schools. After due consultation and deliberation, the Author pressed upon the Editor the work of revision, and placed the Lectures in his hands, with the request that he would read them carefully, and suggest such alterations as he might deem desirable to adapt the work to the English reader; and then submit the whole to the Author's adoption or rejection.

This task the Editor undertook, and has performed in the best manner his time and ability would allow. The Author has carefully examined every part of his work again, and made such corrections and alterations as to him seemed needful. The Editor has merely performed the part of a friend, in suggesting such improvements as might make the Author's meaning better understood; but without interfering with that meaning, and without intending to give it an unqualified approbation. In fact, the Lectures have been to a considerable extent re-written by the Author, and in this edition proceed as strictly from his own pen, as in the American edition.

The Editor, however, would not have ventured to recommend the publication of these Lectures in this country, if he had not deemed them, as a whole, eminently deserving the attention and examination of British theologians. When they first came into his hands, they struck him as so pleasingly unlike all the other systems of dogmatic theology and moral philosophy it had ever been his lot to peruse, so thorough in their grappling with difficulties, and often so successful in the solution of them; so skillfully adjusted to modern metaphysical speculations, and so comprehensive of what is valuable in them; so manifestly the production of a masculine intellect and independent thinker, that he was not only pleased with the air of freshness and originality thrown over old themes of dry and elaborate discussion, but greatly benefited and instructed by some of the Author's views of important moral and theological questions. It may not be the same with all the Author's English readers; but assuredly few will rise from the perusal of the whole work without confessing that, at least, they have seen some points in a new and impressive light, have been constrained to think more closely of the opinions they hold, and in other respects have been benefited by the perusal.

As a contribution to theological science, in an age when vague speculation and philosophical theories are bewildering many among all denominations of Christians, this work will be considered by all competent judges to be both valuable and seasonable. Upon several important and difficult subjects the Author has thrown a clear and valuable light which will guide many a student through perplexities and difficulties which he had long sought unsuccessfully to explain. The Editor frankly confesses, that when a student he would gladly have bartered half the books in his library to have gained a single perusal of these Lectures; and he cannot refrain from expressing the belief, that no young student of theology will ever regret the purchase or perusal of Mr. Finney's Lectures.

One recommendation he begs respectfully to offer to all readers whether old or young; it is this: suspend your judgment of the Author and his theology until you have gone completely through his work. On many subjects, at the outset of the discussion, startling propositions may be found which will clash with your settled opinions; but if you will calmly and patiently await the Author's explanation, and observe how he qualifies some strong or novel assertions, you will most probably find in the issue, that you have less reason than you supposed to object to his statements.

In many respects Mr. Finney's theological and moral system will be found to differ both from the Calvinistic and Arminian. In fact, it is a system of his own, if not in its separate portions, yet in its construction; and as a whole is at least unique and compact; a system which the Author has wrought out for himself, with little other aid than what he has derived from the fount itself of heavenly truth, and his own clear and strong perception of the immutable moral principles and laws by which the glorious Author of the universe governs all his intellectual creatures.

There is one circumstance that will recommend the volume, and ought to recommend it, to impartial inquirers who are not bound to the words of any master save their Divine one; it is, that the Author in his youth was trained in none of the theological schools of his country, and had imbibed, therefore, no educational preference for one system more than another. He had been disciplined to argumentation, logic, and the laws of evidence, in a very different arena; and had advanced in the science of the Law before he had felt the truth of Christianity, or thought of studying its doctrines. His views, therefore, will be found more deserving of attention and examination, from the fact of his mental independence in the formation of them.

Should the work be read in a calm, devout, unprejudiced and liberal spirit, there can be no doubt that the reader will derive both pleasure and instruction. The earnestness, single-mindedness, deep piety, and eminent usefulness of the Author, both as a preacher and lecturer, justly entitle this production of his pen to the candid and patient investigation of English divines.

Apart from the peculiarities which will be observed, and the critical objections to which some will deem his theology justly liable, there can be no doubt that many will find in it a treasure of inestimable worth, a key to many perplexing enigmas, and a powerful reinforcement of their faith in the Christian verities. With at least the hope that such will be the effects of its publication in England, the Editor has cheerfully contributed his humble aid, and now commits the work to the blessing of Him by whose Word of Truth its real value must be finally tested.

G. R.

Worcester, (Eng.) 1851.

PREFACE BY THE AUTHOR

1. To a great extent, the truths of the blessed gospel have been hidden under a false philosophy. In my early inquiries on the subject of religion, I found myself wholly unable to understand either the oral or written instructions of uninspired religious teachers. They seemed to me to resolve all religion into states either of the intellect or of the sensibility, which my consciousness assured me were wholly passive or involuntary. When I sought for definitions and explanations, I felt assured that they did not well understand themselves. I was struck with the fact that they so seldom defined, even to themselves, their own positions. Among the words of most frequent use, I could find scarcely a single term intelligibly defined. I inquired in what sense the terms "regeneration," "faith," "repentance," "love," etc., were used, but could obtain no answer, at which it did not appear to me that both reason and revelation revolted. The doctrines of a nature, sinful per se, of a necessitated will, of inability, and of physical regeneration, and physical Divine influence in regeneration, with their kindred and resulting dogmas, embarrassed and even confounded me at every step. I often said to myself, "If these things are really taught in the Bible, I must be an infidel." But the more I read my Bible, the more clearly I saw that these things were not found there upon any fair principles of interpretation, such as would be admitted in a court of justice. I could not but perceive that the true idea of moral government had no place in the theology of the church; and, on the contrary, that underlying the whole system were the assumptions that all government was physical, as opposed to moral, and that sin and holiness are rather natural attributes, than moral, voluntary acts.

These errors were not stated in words, but I could not fail to see that they were assumed. The distinction between original and actual sin, and the utter absence of a distinction between physical and moral depravity, embarrassed me. Indeed, I was satisfied either that I must be an infidel, or that these were errors that had no place in the Bible. I was often warned against reasoning and leaning to my own understanding. I found that the discriminating teachers of religion were driven to confess that they could not establish the logical consistency of their system, and that they were obliged to shut their eyes and believe, when revelation seemed to conflict with the affirmations of reason. But this course I could not take. I found, or thought I found, nearly all the doctrines of Christianity embarrassed by the assumptions above named. But the Spirit of God conducted me through the darkness, and delivered me from the labyrinth and fog of a false philosophy, and set my feet upon the rock of truth, as I trust. But to this day I meet with those who seem to me to be in much confusion upon most of the practical doctrines of Christianity. They will admit, that sin and holiness must be voluntary, and yet speak of regeneration as consisting in anything but a voluntary change, and of Divine influence in regeneration, as anything but moral or persuasive. They seem not at all aware of what must follow from, and be implied in, the admission of the existence of moral government, and that sin and holiness must be free and voluntary acts and states of mind. In this work I have endeavored to define the terms used by Christian divines, and the doctrines of Christianity, as I understand them, and to push to their logical consequences the cardinal admissions of the more recent and standard theological writers. Especially do I urge, to their logical consequences, the two admissions that the will is free, and that sin and holiness are voluntary acts of mind. I will not presume that I have satisfied others upon the points I have discussed, but I have succeeded at least in satisfying myself. I regard the assertion, that the doctrines of theology cannot preserve a logical consistency throughout, as both dangerous and ridiculous.

2. My principal design in publishing Systematic Theology at first, was to furnish my pupils with a class or textbook, wherein many points and questions were discussed of great practical importance, but which have not, to my knowledge, been discussed in any system of theological instruction extant. I also hoped to benefit other studious and pious minds.

3. I have written for those who are willing to take the trouble of thinking and of forming opinions of their own on theological questions. It has been no part of my aim to spare my pupils or any one else the trouble of intense thought. Had I desired to do so, the subjects discussed would have rendered such an attempt abortive.

4. There are many questions of great practical importance, and questions in which multitudes are taking a deep interest at present, that cannot be intelligently settled without instituting fundamental inquiries involving the discussion of those questions that lie at the foundation of morality and religion.

5. Most of the subjects of dispute among Christians at the present day are founded in misconceptions upon the subjects discussed in the volume. If I have succeeded in settling the questions which I have discussed, we shall see, that in a future volume most of the subjects of disagreement among Christians at the present day can be satisfactorily adjusted with comparative ease.

6. What I have said on "Moral Law" and on the "Foundation of Moral Obligation" is the key to the whole subject. Whoever masters and understands these can readily understand all the rest. But he who will not possess himself of my meaning upon these subjects, will not understand the rest.

7. Let no one despair in commencing the book, nor stumble at the definitions, thinking that he can never understand so abstruse a subject. Remember that what follows is an expansion and an explanation by way of application, of what you find so condensed in the first pages of the book. My brother, sister, friend -- read, study, think, and read again. You were made to think. It will do you good to think; to develop your powers by study. God designed that religion should require thought, intense thought, and should thoroughly develop our powers of thought. The Bible itself is written in a style so condensed as to require much intense study. I do not pretend to so explain theology as to dispense with the labor of thinking. I have no ability and no wish to do so.

8. If any of my brethren think to convince me of error, they must first understand me, and show that they have read the book through, and that they understand it, and are candidly inquiring after truth and not "striving for masteries." If my brother is inquiring after truth, I will, by the grace of God, "hear with both ears, and then judge." But I will not promise to attend to all that cavillers may say, nor to notice what those impertinent talkers and writers may

say or write who must have controversy. But to all honest inquirers after truth I would say, Hail, my brother! Let us be thorough. Truth shall do us good.

9. It will be seen that the present volume contains only a part of a course of Systematic Theology. Should the entire course ever appear before the public, one volume will precede, and another succeed the present one. I published this volume first, because it contains all the points upon which I have been supposed to differ from the commonly received views. As a teacher of theology, I thought it due to the church and to the world, to give them my views upon those points upon which I had been accused of departing from the common opinions of Christians.

10. I have not yet been able to stereotype my theological views, and have ceased to expect ever to do so. The idea is preposterous. None but an omniscient mind can continue to maintain a precise identity of views and opinions. Finite minds, unless they are asleep or stultified by prejudice, must advance in knowledge. The discovery of new truth will modify old views and opinions, and there is perhaps no end to this process with finite minds in any world. True Christian consistency does not consist in stereotyping our opinions and views, and in refusing to make any improvement lest we should be guilty of change, but it consists in holding our minds open to receive the rays of truth from every quarter and in changing our views and language and practice as often and as fast, as we can obtain further information. I call this Christian consistency, because this course alone accords with a Christian profession. A Christian profession implies the profession of candor and of a disposition to know and obey all truth. It must follow, that Christian consistency implies continued investigation and change of views and practice corresponding with increasing knowledge. No Christian, therefore, and no theologian should be afraid to change his views, his language, or his practices in conformity with increasing light. The prevalence of such a fear would keep the world, at best, at a perpetual standstill, on all subjects of science, and consequently all improvements would be precluded.

Every uninspired attempt to frame for the church an authoritative standard of opinion which shall be regarded as an unquestionable exposition of the word of God, is not only impious in itself, but it is also a tacit assumption of the fundamental dogma of Papacy. The Assembly of Divines did more than to assume the necessity of a Pope to give law to the opinions of men; they assumed to create an immortal one, or rather to embalm their own creed, and preserve it as the Pope of all generations; or it is more just to say, that those who have adopted that confession of faith and catechism as an authoritative standard of doctrine, have absurdly adopted the most obnoxious principle of Popery, and elevated their confession and catechism to the Papal throne and into the place of the Holy Ghost. That the instrument framed by that assembly should in the nineteenth century be recognized as the standard of the church, or of an intelligent branch of it, is not only amazing, but I must say that it is most ridiculous. It is as absurd in theology as it would be in any other branch of science, and as injurious and stultifying as it is absurd and ridiculous. It is better to have a living than a dead Pope. If we must have an authoritative expounder of the word of God, let us have a living one, so as not to preclude the hope of improvement. "A living dog is better than a dead lion;" so a living Pope is better than a dead and stereotyped confession of faith, that holds all men bound to subscribe to its unalterable dogmas and its unvarying terminology.

11. I hold myself sacredly bound, not to defend these positions at all events, but on the contrary, to subject every one of them to the most thorough discussion, and to hold and treat them as I would the opinions of any one else; that is, if upon further discussion and investigation I see no cause to change, I hold them fast; but if I can see a flaw in any one of them, I shall amend or wholly reject it, as further light shall demand. Should I refuse or fail to do this, I should need to blush for my folly and inconsistency, for I say again, that true Christian consistency implies progress in knowledge and holiness, and such changes in theory and in practice as are demanded by increasing light.

On the strictly fundamental questions in theology, my views have not, for many years, undergone any change, except as I have clearer apprehensions of them than formerly, and should now state some of them, perhaps, in some measure, differently from what I should then have done.

THE AUTHOR

LECTURE I - MORAL LAW

Law, in a sense of the term both sufficiently popular and scientific for my purpose, is A RULE OF ACTION. In its generic signification, it is applicable to every kind of action, whether of matter or of mind--whether intelligent or unintelligent--whether free or necessary action.

Physical law is a term that represents the order of sequence, in all the changes that occur under the law of necessity, whether in matter or mind. I mean all changes whether of state or action, that do not consist in the states or actions of free will. Physical law is the law of the material universe. It is also the law of mind, so far as its states and changes are involuntary. All mental states or actions, which are not free and sovereign actions of will, must occur under, and be subject to, physical law. They cannot possibly be accounted for, except as they are ascribed to the law of necessity or force.

Moral law is a rule of moral action with sanctions. It is that rule to which moral agents ought to conform all their voluntary actions, and is enforced by sanctions equal to the value of the precept. It is the rule for the government of free and intelligent action, as opposed to necessary and unintelligent action. It is the law of liberty, as opposed to the law of necessity--of motive and free choice, as opposed to force of every kind. Moral law is primarily a rule for the direction of the action of free will, and strictly of free will only. But secondarily, and less strictly, it is the rule for the regulation of all those actions and states of mind and body, that follow the free actions of will by a law of necessity. Thus, moral law controls involuntary mental states and outward action only by securing conformity of the actions of free will to its precept.

The essential attributes of moral law, are,

1. Subjectivity. It is, and must be, an idea of reason developed in the mind of the subject. It is an idea, or conception, of that state of will, or course of action, which is obligatory upon a moral agent. No one can be a moral agent, or the subject of moral law, unless he has this idea developed; for this idea is identical with the law. It is the law developed or revealed within himself; and thus he becomes "a law to himself," his own reason affirming his obligation to conform to this idea, or law.

2. Objectivity. Moral law may be regarded as a rule of duty, prescribed by the supreme Lawgiver, and external to self. When thus contemplated, it is objective.

3. Liberty, as opposed to necessity. The precept must lie developed in the reason, as a rule of duty--a law of moral obligation--a rule of choice, or of ultimate intention, declaring that which a moral agent ought to choose, will, intend. But it does not, must not, can not possess the attribute of necessity in its relations to the actions of free will. It must not, cannot, possess an element or attribute of force, in any such sense as to render conformity of will to its precept unavoidable. This would confound it with physical law.

4. Fitness. It must be the law of nature, that is, its precept must prescribe and require just those actions of the will which are suitable to the nature and

relations of moral beings, and nothing more nor less; that is, the intrinsic value of the well-being of God and of the universe being given as the ground, and the nature and relations of moral beings as the condition of the obligation, the reason hereupon necessarily affirms the intrinsic propriety and fitness of choosing this good, and of consecrating the whole being to its promotion. This is what is intended by the law of nature. It is the law or rule of action imposed on us by God, in and by the nature which he has given us.

5. Universality. The conditions and circumstances being the same, it requires, and must require, of all moral agents, the same things, in whatever world they may be found.

6. Impartiality. Moral law is no respecter of persons--knows no privileged classes. It demands one thing of all, without regard to anything, except the fact that they are moral agents. By this it is not intended that the same course of outward conduct is required of all; but the same state of heart in all--that all shall have one ultimate intention--that all shall consecrate themselves to one end--that all shall entirely conform, in heart and life, to their nature and relations.

7. Practicability. That which the precept demands must be possible to the subject. That which demands a natural impossibility is not, and cannot be, moral law. The true definition of law excludes the supposition that it can, under any circumstances, demand an absolute impossibility. Such a demand could not be in accordance with the nature and relations of moral agents, and therefore practicability must always be an attribute of moral law. To talk of inability to obey moral law is to talk nonsense.

8. Independence. It is an eternal and necessary idea of the divine reason. It is the eternal, self-existent rule of the divine conduct, the law which the intelligence of God prescribes to himself. Moral law, as we shall see hereafter more fully, does not, and cannot originate in the will of God. It eternally existed in the divine reason. It is the idea of that state of will which is obligatory upon God, upon condition of his natural attributes, or, in other words, upon condition of his nature. As a law, it is entirely independent of his will just as his own existence is. It is obligatory also upon every moral agent, entirely independent of the will of God. Their nature and relations being given, and their intelligence being developed, moral law must be obligatory upon them, and it lies not in the option of any being to make it otherwise. Their nature and relations being given, to pursue a course of conduct suited to their nature and relations, is necessarily and self-evidently obligatory, independent of the will of any being.

9. Immutability. Moral law can never change, or be changed. It always requires of every moral agent a state of heart, and course of conduct, precisely suited to his nature and relations. Whatever his nature is, his capacity and relations are, entire conformity to just that nature, those capacities and relations, so far as he is able to understand them, is required at every moment, and nothing more nor less. If capacity is enlarged, the subject is not thereby rendered capable of works of supererogation--of doing more than the law demands; for the law still, as always, requires the full consecration of his whole being to the public interests. If by any means whatever, his ability is abridged, moral law, always and necessarily consistent with itself, still requires that what is left--nothing more or less--shall be consecrated to the same end as before. Whatever demands more or less than entire, universal, and constant conformity of heart and life, to the nature, capacity and relations of moral agents, be they

what they may, is not, and cannot be moral law. If therefore, the capacity is by any means abridged, the subject does not thereby become incapable of rendering full obedience; for the law still demands and urges, that the heart and life shall be fully conformed to the present, existing nature, capacity, and relations. Anything that requires more or less than this, cannot be moral law. Moral law invariably holds one language. It never changes its requirement. "Thou shalt love," or be perfectly benevolent, is its uniform and its only demand. This demand it never varies, and never can vary. It is as immutable as God is, and for the same reason. To talk of letting down, or altering moral law, is to talk absurdly. The thing is naturally impossible. No being has the right or the power to do so. The supposition overlooks the very nature of moral law. Moral law is not a statute, an enactment, that has its origin or its foundation in the will of any being. It is the law of nature, the law which the nature or constitution of every moral agent imposes on himself and which God imposes upon us because it is entirely suited to our nature and relations, and is therefore naturally obligatory upon us. It is the unalterable demand of the reason, that the whole being, whatever there is of it at any time, shall be entirely consecrated to the highest good of universal being, and for this reason God requires this of us, with all the weight of his authority.

10. Unity. Moral law proposes but one ultimate end of pursuit to God, and to all moral agents. All its requisitions, in their spirit, are summed up and expressed in one word, love or benevolence. This I only announce here. It will more fully appear hereafter. Moral law is a pure and simple idea of the reason. It is the idea of perfect, universal, and constant consecration of the whole being to the highest good of being. Just this is, and nothing more nor less can be, moral law; for just this, and nothing more nor less, is a state of heart and a course of life exactly suited to the nature and relations of moral agents, which is the only true definition of moral law.

11. Expediency. That which is upon the whole most wise is expedient. That which is upon the whole expedient is demanded by moral law. True expediency and the spirit of moral law are always identical. Expediency may be inconsistent with the letter, but never with the spirit of moral law. Law in the form of commandment is a revelation or declaration of that course which is expedient. It is expediency revealed, as in the case of the decalogue, and the same is true of every precept of the Bible, it reveals to us what is expedient. A revealed law or commandment is never to be set aside by our views of expediency. We may know with certainty that what is required is expedient. The command is the expressed judgment of God in the case, and reveals with unerring certainty the true path of expediency. When Paul says, "All things are lawful unto me, but all things are not expedient," we must not understand him as meaning that all things in the absolute sense were lawful to him, or that anything that was not expedient was lawful to him. But he doubtless intended, that many things were inexpedient that are not expressly prohibited by the letter of the law,--that the spirit of the law prohibited many things not expressly forbidden by the letter. It should never be forgotten that that which is plainly demanded by the highest good of the universe is law. It is expedient. It is wise. The true spirit of the moral law does and must demand it. So, on the other hand, whatever is plainly inconsistent with the highest good of the universe is illegal, unwise, inexpedient, and must be prohibited by the spirit of moral law. But let the thought be repeated, that the Bible precepts always reveal that which is

truly expedient, and in no case are we at liberty to set aside the spirit of any commandment upon the supposition that expediency requires it. Some have denounced the doctrine of expediency altogether, as at all times inconsistent with the law of right. These philosophers proceed upon the assumption that the law of right and the law of benevolence are not identical but inconsistent with each other. This is a common but fundamental mistake, which leads me to remark that--Law proposes the highest good of universal being as its end, and requires all moral agents to consecrate themselves to the promotion of this end. Consequently, expediency must be one of its attributes. That which is upon the whole in the highest degree useful to the universe must be demanded by moral law. Moral law must, from its own nature, require just that course of willing and acting that is upon the whole in the highest degree promotive of the public good,--in other words, that which is upon the whole in the highest degree useful, and therefore expedient. It has been strangely and absurdly maintained that right would be obligatory if it necessarily tended to and resulted in universal and perfect misery. Than which a more nonsensical affirmation was never made. The affirmation assumes that the law of right and of good-will are not only distinct, but may be antagonistic. It also assumes that that can be law that is not suited to the nature and relations of moral agents. Certainly it will not be pretended that that course of willing and acting that necessarily tends to, and results in, universal misery, can be consistent with the nature and relations of moral agents. Nothing is or can be suited to their nature and relations, that is not upon the whole promotive of their highest well-being. Expediency and right are always and necessarily at one. They can never be inconsistent. That which is upon the whole most expedient is right, and that which is right is upon the whole expedient.

12. Exclusiveness. Moral law is the only possible rule of moral obligation. A distinction is usually made between moral, ceremonial, civil and positive laws. This distinction is in some respects convenient, but is liable to mislead, and to create an impression that something can be obligatory, in other words can be law, that has not the attributes of moral law. Nothing can be law, in any proper sense of the term, that is not and would not be universally obligatory upon moral agents under the same circumstances. It is law because, and only because, under all the circumstances of the case, the course prescribed is fit, proper, suitable, to their natures, relations, and circumstances. There can be no other rule of action for moral agents but moral law, or the law of benevolence. Every other rule is absolutely excluded by the very nature of moral law. Surely there can be no law that is or can be obligatory upon moral agents but one suited to, and founded in their nature, relations, and circumstances. This is and must be the law of love or benevolence. This is the law of right, and nothing else is or can be. Every thing else that claims to be law, and to impose obligation upon moral agents, must be an imposition and "a thing of nought."

LECTURE II - MORAL GOVERNMENT

THE primary idea of government, is that of direction, guidance, control by, or in accordance with, rule or law.

All government is, and must be, either moral or physical; that is, all guidance and control must be exercised in accordance with either moral or physical law; for there can be no laws that are neither moral nor physical.

Physical government is control, exercised by a law of necessity or force, as distinguished from the law of free will, or liberty. It is the control of substance, as opposed to free will. The only government of which substance, as distinguished from free will, is capable, is and must be physical. This is true, whether the substance be material or immaterial, whether matter or mind. States and changes, whether of matter or mind, that are not actions of free will, must be subject to the law of necessity. They must therefore belong to the department of physical government. Physical government, then, is the administration of physical law, or the law of force.

Moral government consists in the declaration and administration of moral law. It is the government of free will by motives as distinguished from the government of substance by force. Physical government presides over and controls physical states and changes of substance or constitution, and all involuntary states and changes. Moral government presides over and controls, or seeks to control the actions of free will: it presides over intelligent and voluntary states and changes of mind. It is a government of motive, as opposed to a government of force--control exercised, or sought to be exercised, in accordance with the law of liberty, as opposed to the law of necessity. It is the administration of moral as opposed to physical law.

Moral government includes the dispensation of rewards and punishments; and is administered by means as complicated and vast as the whole of the works, and providence, and ways, and grace of God.

The fundamental reason of moral government.

Government must be founded in a good and sufficient reason, or it is not right. No one has a right to prescribe rules for, and control the conduct of another, unless there is some good reason for his doing so. There must be a necessity for moral government, or the administration of it is tyranny. Moral government is indispensable to the highest well-being of the universe of moral agents. The universe is dependent upon this as a means of securing the highest good. This dependence is a good and sufficient reason for the existence of moral government. Let it be understood, then, that moral government is a necessity of moral beings, and therefore right.

Our nature and circumstances demand that we should be under a moral government; because no community can perfectly harmonize in all their views and feelings, without perfect knowledge, or to say the least, the same degree of knowledge on all subjects on which they are called to act. But no community ever existed, or will exist, in which all possess exactly the same amount of knowledge, and where the members are, therefore, entirely agreed in all their thoughts, views, and opinions. But if they are not agreed in opinion, or have not exactly the same amount of knowledge, they will not, in every thing, harmonize, as it respects their courses of conduct. There must, therefore, be in every community, some standard or rule of duty, to which all the subjects of the community are to conform themselves. There must be some head or controlling mind, whose will shall be law, and whose decision shall be regarded as infallible, by all the subjects of the government. However diverse their intellectual attainments are, in this they must all agree, that the will of the lawgiver is right, and universally the rule of duty. This will must be authoritative, and not merely advisory. There must of necessity be a penalty attached to, and incurred by, every act of disobedience to this will. If disobedience be persisted in, exclusion from the privileges of the government is the lowest penalty that can consistently be inflicted. The good, then, of the universe imperiously requires that there should be a moral governor.

Whose right is it to govern?

We have just seen that the highest well-being of the universe demands, and is the end of moral government. It must, therefore, be his right and duty to govern, whose attributes, physical and moral, best qualify him to secure the end of government. To him all eyes and hearts should be directed, to fill this station, to exercise this control, to administer all just and necessary rewards and punishments. It is both his right and duty to govern.

That God is a moral governor, we infer--

1. From our own nature. From the very laws of our being, we naturally affirm our responsibility to him for our conduct. As God is our creator, we are naturally responsible to him for the right exercise of our powers. And as our good and his glory depend upon our conformity to the same rule to which he conforms his whole being, he is under a moral obligation to require us to be holy, as he is holy.

2. His natural attributes qualify him to sustain the relation of a moral governor to the universe.

3. His moral character also qualifies him to sustain this relation.

4. His relation to the universe as creator and preserver, when considered in connection with the necessity of government, and with his nature and attributes, confers on him the right of universal government.

5. His relation to the universe, and our relations to him and to each other, render it obligatory upon him to establish and administer a moral government over the universe. It would be wrong for him to create a universe of moral beings, and then refuse or neglect to administer over them a moral government, since government is a necessity of their nature and relations.

6. His happiness must demand it, as he could not be happy unless he acted in accordance with his conscience.

7. If God is not a moral governor he is not wise. Wisdom consists in the choice of the best ends, and in the use of the most appropriate means to accomplish those ends. If God is not a moral governor, it is inconceivable that he should have had any important end in view in the creation of moral beings, or that he should have chosen the best or any suitable means for the promotion of their happiness as the most desirable end.

8. The conduct or providence of God plainly indicates a design to exert a moral influence over moral agents.

9. His providence plainly indicates that the universe of mind is governed by moral laws, or by laws suited to the nature of moral agents.

10. If God is not a moral governor, the whole universe, so far as we have the means of knowing it, is calculated to mislead mankind in respect to this fundamental truth. All nations have believed that God is a moral governor.

11. We must disapprove the character of God, if we ever come to a knowledge of the fact that he created moral agents, and then exercised over them no moral government.

12. The Bible, which has been proved to be a revelation from God, contains a most simple and yet comprehensive system of moral government.

13. If we are deceived in respect to our being subjects of moral government, we are sure of nothing.

What is implied in the right to govern?

1. From what has just been said, it must be evident, that the right to govern implies the necessity of government, as a means of securing an intrinsically valuable end.

2. Also that the right to govern implies the duty, or obligation to govern. There can be no right, in this case, without corresponding obligation; for the right to govern is founded in the necessity of government, and the necessity of government imposes obligation to govern.

3. The right to govern, implies obligation, on the part of the subject, to obey. It cannot be the right, or duty, of the governor to govern, unless it is the duty of the subject to obey. The governor and subjects are alike dependent upon government, as the indispensable means of promoting the highest good. The governor and the subject must, therefore, be under reciprocal obligation, the one to govern, and the other to be governed, or to obey. The one must seek to govern, the other must submit to be governed.

4. The right to govern, implies the right and duty to dispense just and necessary rewards and punishments--distribute rewards proportioned to merit, and penalties proportioned to demerit, whenever the public interest demands their execution.

5. It implies obligation, on the part of the subject, cheerfully to acquiesce in any measure that may be necessary to secure the end of government, and in case of disobedience, to submit to merited punishment, and also, if necessary, to aid in the infliction of the penalty of law.

6. It implies obligation, on the part both of the ruler and the ruled, to be always ready, and when occasion arises, actually to make any personal and private sacrifice demanded by the higher public good--to cheerfully meet any emergency, and exercise any degree of self-denial, that can, and will, result in a good of greater value to the public than that sacrificed by the individual, or by any number of individuals, it always being understood, that present voluntary sacrifices shall have an ultimate reward.

7. It implies the right and duty to employ any degree of force, which is indispensable to the maintenance of order, the execution of wholesome laws, the suppression of insurrections, the punishment of rebels and disorganizers, and sustaining the supremacy of moral law. It is impossible that the right to govern should not imply this; and to deny this right, is to deny the right to govern. Should an emergency occur, in which a ruler had no right to use the indispensable means of securing order, and the supremacy of law, the moment this emergency occurred, his right to govern would, and must, cease: for it is

impossible that it should be his right to govern, unless it be at the same time, and for the same reason, his duty to govern; and it is absurd to say, that it is his right and duty to govern, and yet at the same time, that he has not a right to use the indispensable means of government. If it be asked, whether an emergency like the one under consideration is possible, and if so what might justly be regarded as such an emergency, I answer, that should circumstances occur under which the sacrifice necessary to sustain, would overbalance the good to be derived from the prevalence of government, this would create the emergency under consideration, in which the right to govern would cease.

The limits of this right.

The right to govern is, and must be, just co-extensive with the necessity of government. We have seen, that the right to govern is founded in the necessities of moral beings. In other words, the right to govern is founded upon the fact, that the highest good of moral agents cannot be secured, but by means of government. But to avoid mistake, and to correct erroneous impressions, which are sometimes entertained, I must show what is not the foundation of the right to govern. The boundary of the right must, as will be seen, depend upon the foundation of the right. The right must be as broad as the reason for it. If the reason of the right be mistaken, then the limits of the right cannot be ascertained, and must necessarily be mistaken also.

1. The right to govern the universe cannot be founded in the fact, that God sustains to it the relation of Creator. This is by itself no reason why he should govern it, unless it needs to be governed--unless some good will result from government. Unless there is some necessity for government, the fact that God created the universe can give him no right to govern it.

2. The fact that God is owner and sole proprietor of the universe is no reason why he should govern it. Unless either his own good or the good of the universe, or of both together, demand government, the relation of owner cannot confer the right to govern. Neither God, nor any other being, can own moral beings, in such a sense as to have a right to govern them, when government is wholly unnecessary, and can result in no good whatever to God, or to his creatures. Government, in such a case, would be perfectly arbitrary and unreasonable, and consequently an unjust, tyrannical and wicked act. God has no such right. No such right can, by possibility, in any case exist.

3. The right to govern cannot be founded in the fact, that God possesses all the attributes, natural and moral, that are requisite to the administration of moral government. This fact is no doubt a condition of the right; for without these qualifications he could have no right, however necessary government might be. But the possession of these attributes cannot confer the right independently of the necessity of government: for however well qualified he may be to govern, still, unless government is necessary to securing his own glory and the highest well-being of the universe, he has no right to govern it. Possessing the requisite qualifications is the condition, and the necessity of government is the foundation of the right to govern. More strictly, the right is founded in the intrinsic value of the interests to be secured by government, and conditioned upon the fact, that government is the necessary means of securing the end.

4. Nor is the right to govern conferred by the value of the interests to be secured, nor by the circumstance of the necessity of government merely, without respect to the condition just above mentioned. Did not God's natural

and moral attributes qualify him to sustain that relation better than any one else, the right could not be conferred on him by any other fact or relation.

5. The right to govern is not, and cannot be, an abstract right based on no reason whatever. The idea of this right is not an ultimate idea in such a sense, that our intelligence affirms the right without assigning any reason on which it is founded. The human intelligence cannot say that God has a right to govern, because he has such a right; and that this is reason enough, and all the reason that can be given. Our reason does not affirm that government is right because it is right; and that this is a first truth, and an ultimate idea. If this were so, then God's arbitrary will would be law, and no bounds could possibly be assigned to the right to govern. If God's right to govern be a first truth, an ultimate truth, fact, and idea, founded in no assignable reason, then he has the right to legislate as little, and as much, and as arbitrarily, as unnecessarily, as absurdly, and injuriously as possible, and no injustice is, or can be done; for he has, by the supposition, a right to govern, founded in no reason, and of course without any limit. Assign any other reason, as the foundation of the right to govern, than the value of the interests to be secured and the necessity of government, and you may search in vain for any limit to the right. But the moment the foundation and the condition of the right are discovered, we see instantly, that the right must be co-extensive with the reason upon which it is founded, or in other words, must be limited by, and only by the fact, that thus far, and no farther, government is necessary to the highest good of the universe. No legislation can be valid in heaven or earth--no enactments can impose obligation, except upon the condition, that such legislation is demanded by the highest good of the governor and the governed. Unnecessary legislation is invalid legislation. Unnecessary government is tyranny. It can, in no case be founded in right. It should, however, be observed, that it is often, and in the government of God universally true, that the sovereign, and not the subject, is to be the judge of what is necessary legislation and government. Under no government, therefore, are laws to be despised or rejected because we are unable to see at once their necessity, and hence their wisdom. Unless they are palpably unnecessary, and therefore unwise and unjust, they are to be respected and obeyed as a less evil than contempt and disobedience, though at present we are unable to see their wisdom. Under the government of God there can never be any doubt nor of course any ground for distrust and hesitancy as it respects the duty of obedience.

MORAL OBLIGATION

The idea of obligation, or of oughtness, is an idea of the pure reason. It is a simple, rational conception, and, strictly speaking, does not admit of a definition, since there are no terms more simple by which it may be defined. Obligation is a term by which we express a conception or idea which all men have, as is manifest from the universal language of men. All men have the ideas of right and wrong, and have words by which these ideas are expressed, and, perhaps, no idea among men more frequently reveals itself in words than that of oughtness or obligation. The term cannot be defined, for the simple reason that it is too well and too universally understood to need or even to admit of being expressed in any language more simple and definite than the word obligation itself.

The conditions of moral obligation.

There is a distinction of fundamental importance between the condition and the ground of obligation. The ground of obligation is the consideration which creates or imposes obligation, the fundamental reason of the obligation. Of this I shall inquire in its proper place. At present I am to define the conditions of obligation. But I must in this place observe that there are various forms of obligation. For example, obligation to choose an ultimate end of life as the highest good of the universe; obligation to choose the necessary conditions of this end, as holiness, for example; and obligation to put forth executive efforts to secure this end. The conditions of obligation vary with the form of obligation, as we shall fully perceive in the course of our investigations.

A condition of obligation in any particular form is a sine qua non of obligation in that particular form. It is that, without which, obligation in that form could not exist, and yet is not the fundamental reason of the obligation. For example, the possession of the powers of moral agency is a condition of the obligation to choose the highest good of being in general, as an ultimate end, or for its own sake. But the intrinsic value of this good is the ground of the obligation. This obligation could not exist without the possession of these powers; but the possession of these powers cannot of itself create the obligation to choose the good in preference to the ill of being. The intrinsic difference between the good and the ill of being is the ground of the obligation to will the one rather than the other. I will first define the conditions upon which all obligation depends, and without which obligation in no form can exist, and afterward proceed to point out the conditions of distinct forms of obligation.

1. Moral agency is universally a condition of moral obligation. The attributes of moral agency are intellect, sensibility, and free-will.

(1.) Intellect includes, among other functions which I need not name, reason, conscience, and self-consciousness. As has been said on a former occasion, reason is the intuitive faculty or function of the intellect. It gives by direct intuition the following among other truths: the absolute--for example, right and wrong; the necessary--space exists; the infinite--space is infinite; the perfect--God is perfect--God's law is perfect, etc. In short, it is the faculty that intuits moral relations and affirms moral obligation to act in conformity with perceived moral relations. It is that faculty that postulates all the à priori truths of science whether mathematical, philosophical, theological, or logical.

Conscience is the faculty or function of the intellect that recognizes the conformity or disconformity of the heart and life to the moral law as it lies revealed in the reason, and also awards praise to conformity, and blame to disconformity to that law. It also affirms that conformity to thc moral law deserves reward, and that disconformity deserves punishment. It also possesses a propelling or impulsive power, by which it urges the conformity, and denounces the nonconformity of will to moral law. It seems, in a certain sense, to possess the power of retribution.

Consciousness is the faculty or function of self-knowledge. It is the faculty that recognizes our own existence, mental actions, and states, together with the attributes of liberty or necessity, belonging to those actions or states.

"Consciousness is the mind in the act of knowing itself." By consciousness I know that I am--that I affirm that space is,--that I also affirm that the whole is equal to all its parts--that every event must have a cause, and many such like truths. I am conscious not only of these affirmations, but also that necessity is the law of these affirmations, that I cannot affirm otherwise than I do, in respect to this class of truths. I am also conscious of choosing to sit at my desk and write, and I am just as conscious that liberty is the law of this choice. That is, I am conscious of necessarily regarding myself as entirely free in this choice, and affirming my own ability to have chosen not to sit at my desk, and of being now able to choose not to sit and write. I am just as conscious of affirming the liberty or necessity of my mental states as I am of the states themselves. Consciousness gives us our existence and attributes, our mental acts and states, and all the attributes and phenomena of our being, of which we have any knowledge. In short, all our knowledge is given to us by consciousness. The intellect is a receptivity as distinguished from a voluntary power. All the acts and states of the intellect are under the law of necessity, or physical law. The will can command the attention of the intellect. Its thoughts, perceptions, affirmations, and all its phenomena are involuntary, and under a law of necessity. Of this we are conscious. Another faculty indispensable to moral agency is--

(2.) Sensibility. This is the faculty or susceptibility of feeling. All sensation, desire, emotion, passion, pain, pleasure, and, in short, every kind and degree of feeling, as the term feeling is commonly used, is a phenomenon of this faculty. This faculty supplies the chronological condition of the idea of the valuable, and hence of right and wrong, and of moral obligation. The experience of pleasure or happiness develops the idea of the valuable, just as the perception of body develops the idea of space. But for this faculty the mind could have no idea of the valuable, and hence of moral obligation to will the valuable, nor of right and wrong, nor of praise-worthiness and blame-worthiness.

Self-love is a phenomenon of this department of the mind. It consists in a constitutional desire of happiness, and implies a corresponding dread of misery. It is doubtless through, or by, this constitutional tendency that the rational idea of the intrinsic value of happiness or enjoyment is at first developed. Animals, doubtless, have enjoyment, but we have no evidence that they possess the faculty of reason in the sense in which I have defined the term. Consequently they have not, as we suppose, the rational conception of the intrinsic worth or value of enjoyment. They seek enjoyment from a mere impulse of their animal nature, without, as we suppose, so much as a conception of moral law, obligation, right or wrong.

But we know that moral agents have these ideas. Self-love is constitutional. Its gratification is the chronological condition of the development of the reason's idea of the intrinsically valuable to being. This idea develops that of moral law, or in other words, the affirmation that this intrinsic good ought to be universally chosen and sought for its own sake.

The sensibility, like the intellect, is a receptivity or purely a passive, distinguished from a voluntary faculty. All its phenomena are under the law of necessity. I am conscious that I cannot, by any direct effort, feel when and as I will. This faculty is so correlated to the intellect that when the intellect is intensely occupied with certain considerations, the sensibility is affected in a certain manner, and certain feelings exist in the sensibility by a law of necessity. I am conscious that when certain conditions are fulfilled, I necessarily have certain feelings, and that when these conditions are not fulfilled, I cannot be the subject of those feelings. I know by consciousness that my feelings and all the states and phenomena of the sensibility are only indirectly under the control of my will. By willing I can direct my intellect to the consideration of certain subjects, and in this way alone affect my sensibility, and produce a given state of feeling. So on the other hand, if certain feelings exist in the sensibility which I wish to suppress, I know that I cannot annihilate them by directly willing them out of existence, but by diverting my attention from the cause of them, they cease to exist of course and of necessity. Thus, feeling is only indirectly under the control of the will.

(3.) Moral agency implies the possession of free-will. By free-will is intended the power of choosing, or refusing to choose, in every instance, in compliance with moral obligation. Free-will implies the power of originating and deciding our own choices, and of exercising our own sovereignty, in every instance of choice upon moral questions--of deciding or choosing in conformity with duty or otherwise in all cases of moral obligation. That man cannot be under a moral obligation to perform an absolute impossibility, is a first truth of reason. But man's causality, his whole power of causality to perform or do anything, lies in his will. If he cannot will, he can do nothing. His whole liberty or freedom must consist in his power to will. His outward actions and his mental states are connected with the actions of his will by a law of necessity. If I will to move my muscles, they must move, unless there be a paralysis of the nerves of voluntary motion, or unless some resistance be opposed that overcomes the power of my volitions. The sequences of choice or volition are always under the law of necessity, and unless the will is free, man has no freedom; and if he has no freedom he is not a moral agent, that is, he is incapable of moral action and also of moral character. Free-will then, in the above defined sense, must be a condition of moral agency, and of course, of moral obligation.

As consciousness gives the rational affirmation that necessity is an attribute of the affirmations of the reason, and of the states of sensibility, so it just as unequivocally gives the reason's affirmation that liberty is an attribute of the actions of the will. I am as conscious of the affirmation that I could will differently from what I do in every instance of moral obligation, as I am of the affirmation that I cannot affirm, in regard to truths of intuition, otherwise than I do. I am as conscious of affirming that I am free in willing, as I am of affirming that I am not free or voluntary in my feelings and intuitions.

Consciousness of affirming the freedom of the will, that is, of power to will in accordance with moral obligation, or to refuse thus to will, is a necessary condition of the affirmation of obligation. For example, no man affirms, or can affirm, his obligation to undo all the acts of his past life, and to live his life over again. He cannot affirm himself to be under this obligation, simply because he cannot but affirm the impossibility of it. He cannot but affirm his obligation to repent and obey God in future, because he is conscious of affirming his ability to do this. Consciousness of the affirmation of ability to comply with any requisition, is a necessary condition of the affirmation of obligation to comply with that requisition. Then no moral agent can affirm himself to be under obligation to perform an impossibility.

2. A second condition of moral obligation is light, or so much knowledge of our moral relations as to develop the idea of oughtness. This implies--

(1.) The perception or idea of the intrinsically valuable.

(2.) The affirmation of obligation to will the valuable for its own sake. Before I can affirm my obligation to will, I must perceive something in that which I am required to will as an ultimate end, that renders it worthy of being chosen. I must have an object of choice. That object must possess, in itself, that which commends itself to my intelligence as worthy of being chosen.

All choice must respect means or ends. That is, everything must be willed either as an end or a means. I cannot be under obligation to will the means until I know the end. I cannot know an end, or that which can possibly be chosen as an ultimate end, until I know that something is intrinsically valuable. I cannot know that it is right or wrong to choose or refuse a certain end, until I know whether the proposed object of choice is intrinsically valuable or not. It is impossible for me to choose it, as an ultimate end, unless I perceive it to be intrinsically valuable. This is self-evident; for choosing it as an end is nothing else than choosing it for its intrinsic value. Moral obligation, therefore, always and necessarily implies the knowledge that the well-being of God and of the universe is valuable in itself, and the affirmation that it ought to be chosen for its own sake, that is, impartially and on account of its intrinsic value. It is impossible that the ideas of right and wrong should be developed until the idea of the valuable is developed. Right and wrong respect intentions, and strictly nothing else, as we shall see. Intention implies an end intended. Now that which is chosen as an ultimate end, is and must be chosen for its own sake or for its intrinsic value. Until the end is apprehended, no idea or affirmation of obligation can exist respecting it. Consequently, no idea of right or wrong in respect to that end can exist. The end must first be perceived. The idea of the intrinsically valuable must be developed. Simultaneously with the development of the idea of the valuable the intelligence affirms, and must affirm, obligation to will it, or, which is, strictly speaking, the same thing, that it is right to will it, and wrong not to will it.

It is impossible that the idea of moral obligation, or of right and wrong, should be developed upon any other conditions than those just specified. Suppose, for instance, it should be said that the idea of the intrinsically valuable is not necessary to the development of the idea of moral obligation, and of right and wrong. Let us look at it. It is agreed that moral obligation, and the ideas of right and wrong respect, directly, intentions only. It is also admitted that all intentions must respect either means or ends. It is also admitted that obligation to will means, cannot exist until the end is known. It is also admitted that the choice of an ultimate end implies the choice of a thing for its own sake, or because it is intrinsically valuable. Now, from these admissions, it follows that the idea of the intrinsically valuable is the condition of moral obligation, and also of the idea of moral obligation. It must follow also that the idea of the valuable must be the condition of the idea that it would be right to choose, or wrong not to choose, the valuable. It is, then, nonsense to affirm that the ideas of right and wrong are developed antecedently to the idea of the valuable. It is the same as to say that I affirm it to be right to will an end, before I have the idea of an end; or wrong not to will an end when as yet I have no idea or knowledge of any reason why it should be willed, or, in other words, while I have no idea of an ultimate end.

Let it be distinctly understood then, that the conditions of moral obligation, in the universal form of obligation to will the highest well-being of God and of the universe, for its own sake, are the possession of the powers, or faculties, and susceptibilities of a moral agent, and light or the development of the ideas of the valuable, of moral obligation, of right and wrong.

I have defined the conditions of obligation in its universal form, i. e. obligation to be benevolent, to love God and our neighbor, or to will the universal good of being for its intrinsic value. Obligation in this form is universal and always a unit, and has always the same conditions. But there are myriads of specific forms of obligation which relate to the conditions and means of securing this ultimate end. We shall have occasion hereafter fully to show that obligation respects three classes of the will's actions, viz. the choice of an ultimate end--the choice of the conditions and means of securing that end--and executive volitions or efforts put forth to secure the end. I have already shown that moral agency, with all that is implied in it, has the universal conditions of obligation to choose the highest good of being, as an ultimate end. This must be self-evident.

Obligation to choose the conditions of this end, the holiness of God and of all moral agents, for example, must be conditioned upon the perception that these are the conditions. In other words, the perception of the relation of these means to the end must be a condition of the obligation to will their existence. The perception of the relation is not the ground but simply the condition of obligation in this form. The relation of holiness to happiness as a condition of its existence, could not impose obligation to will the existence of holiness without reference to the intrinsic value of happiness, as the fundamental reason for willing it as a necessary condition and means. The ground of the obligation to will the existence of holiness, as a means of happiness, is the intrinsic value of happiness, but the perceived relation of holiness to happiness is a condition of the obligation. But for this perceived relation the obligation could not exist, yet the perceived relation could not create the obligation. Suppose that holiness is the means of happiness, yet no obligation to will holiness on account of this relation could exist but for the intrinsic value of happiness.

Conditions of obligation to put forth executive acts.

Having now defined the conditions of obligation in its universal form, and also in the form of obligation to choose the existence of holiness as a necessary means of happiness, I now proceed to point out the conditions of obligation to put forth executive volitions or efforts to secure holiness, and secure the highest good of being. Our busy lives are made up in efforts to secure some ultimate end, upon which the heart is set. The sense in which obligation extends to these executive volitions or acts I shall soon consider; at present I am concerned only to define the conditions of these forms of obligation. These forms of obligation, be it understood, respect volitions and consequent outward acts. Volitions, designed as executive acts, always suppose an existing choice of the end designed to be secured by them. Obligation to put forth executive efforts to secure an end must be conditioned upon the possibility, supposed necessity, and utility of such efforts. If the end chosen does not need to be promoted by any efforts of ours, or if such efforts are impossible to us, or if they are seen to be of no use, there can be no obligation to make them.

It is important, however, to observe that the utility of ultimate choice, or the choice of an object for its own sake, is not a condition of obligation in that form. Ultimate choice, or the choice of an object for its own sake, or for its intrinsic value, is not an effort designed to secure or obtain that object; that is, is not put forth with any such design. When the object which the mind perceives to be intrinsically valuable (as the good of being, for example), is perceived by the mind, it cannot but choose or refuse it. Indifference in this case is naturally impossible. The mind, in such circumstances, is under a necessity of choosing one way or the other. The will must embrace or reject it. The reason affirms the obligation to choose the intrinsically valuable for its own sake, and not because choosing it will secure it. Nor does the real choice of it imply a purpose or an obligation to put forth executive acts to secure it, except upon condition that such acts are seen to be necessary, and possible, and calculated to secure it.

Ultimate choice is not put forth with design to secure its object. It is only the will's embracing the object or willing it for its own sake. In regard to ultimate choice the will must choose or refuse the object entirely irrespectively of the tendency of the choice to secure the object. Assuming this necessity, the reason affirms that it is right, fit, suitable, or, which is the same thing, that the will ought, or is under obligation to choose, the good or valuable, and not refuse it, because of its intrinsic nature, and without regard to whether the choosing will secure the object chosen.

But executive acts, be it remembered, are, and must be put forth with design to secure their object, and of course, cannot exist unless the design exist, and the design cannot exist unless the mind assumes the possibility, necessity, and utility of such efforts.

LECTURE III - MORAL OBLIGATION

Man is a subject of moral obligation.

That man has intellect and sensibility, or the powers of knowing and feeling, has not, to my knowledge, been doubted. In theory, the freedom of the will in man has been denied. Yet the very deniers, have, in their practical judgment, assumed the freedom of the human will, as well, and as fully as the most staunch defenders of human liberty of will. Indeed, nobody ever did or can, in practice, call in question the freedom of the human will, without justly incurring the charge of insanity. By a necessity of his nature, every moral agent knows himself to be free. He can no more hide this fact from himself, or reason himself out of the conviction of its truth, than he can speculate himself into a disbelief of his own existence. He may, in speculation, deny either, but in fact he knows both. That he is, that he is free, are truths equally well known, and known precisely in the same way, namely, he intuits them--sees them in their own light, by virtue of the constitution of his being. I have said that man is conscious of possessing the powers of a moral agent. He has also the idea of the valuable, of right and of wrong; of this he is conscious. But nothing else is necessary to constitute man or any other being a subject of moral obligation, and the possession of these powers, together with sufficient light on moral subjects to develop the ideas just mentioned.

Man, by a law of necessity, affirms himself to be under moral obligation. He cannot doubt it. He affirms absolutely and necessarily, that he is praise-worthy or blame-worthy as he is benevolent or selfish. Every man assumes this of himself, and of all other men of sound mind. This assumption is irresistible, as well as universal.

The truth assumed then is not to be called in question. But if it be called in question in theory, it still remains, and must remain, while reason remains, a truth of certain knowledge, from the presence of which there is, and can be no escape. The spontaneous, universal, and irresistible affirmation that men of sound mind are praise-worthy or blame-worthy, as they are selfish or benevolent, shows beyond contradiction, that all men regard themselves, and others, as the subjects of moral obligation.

Extent of moral obligation.

By this is intended, to what acts and states of mind does moral obligation extend? This certainly is a solemn and a fundamentally important question. In the examination of this question, let us inquire first, to what acts and states of mind moral obligation cannot directly extend.

1. Not to external or muscular action. These actions are connected with the actions of the will, by a law of necessity. If I will to move my muscles, they must move, unless the nerves of voluntary motion are paralyzed, or some resistance is offered to muscular motion, that overpowers the strength of my will, or, if you please, of my muscles. It is generally understood and agreed that moral obligation does not directly extend to bodily or outward action.

2. Not to the states of the sensibility. I have already remarked that we are conscious, that our feelings are not voluntary, but involuntary states of mind. Moral obligation cannot, therefore, directly extend to them.

3. Not to states of the intellect. The phenomena of this faculty, we also know by consciousness, to be under the law of necessity. It is impossible that moral obligation should extend directly to any involuntary act or state of mind.

4. Not to unintelligent acts of will. There are many unintelligent volitions, or acts of will, to which moral obligation cannot extend, for example, the volitions of maniacs, or of infants, before the reason is at all developed. They must at birth, be the subjects of volition, as they have motion or muscular action. The volitions of somnambulists are also of this character. Purely instinctive volitions must also come under the category of unintelligent actions of will. For example: a bee lights on my hand, I instantly and instinctively shake him off. I tread on a hot iron, and instinctively move my foot. Indeed there are many actions of will which are put forth under the influence of pure instinct, and before the intellect can affirm obligation to will or not to will. These surely cannot have moral character, and of course moral obligation cannot extend to them.

We inquire in the second place, to what acts and states of mind moral obligation must directly extend.

1. To ultimate acts of will. These are and must be free. Intelligent acts of will, as has been before observed, are of three classes. First, the choice of some object for its own sake, i. e., because of its own nature, or for reasons found exclusively in itself, as, for example, the happiness of being. These are called ultimate choices, or intentions. Second, the choice of the conditions and means of securing the object of ultimate choice, as for example, holiness, as the conditions or means of happiness. Third, volitions, or executive efforts to secure the object of ultimate choice. Obligation must extend to these three classes of the actions of the will. In the most strict and proper sense it may be said, that obligation extends directly only to the ultimate intention.

The choice of an end necessitates the choice of the known conditions and means of securing this end. I am free to relinquish, at any moment, my choice of an end, but while I persevere in the choice, or ultimate intention, I am not free to refuse the known necessary conditions and means. If I reject the known conditions and means, I, in this act, relinquish the choice of the end. The desire of the end may remain, but the actual choice of it cannot, when the will knowingly rejects the known necessary conditions and means. In this case, the will prefers to let go the end, rather than to choose and use the necessary conditions and means. In the strictest sense the choice of known conditions and means, together with executive volitions, is implied in the ultimate intention or in the choice of an end.

When the good or valuable per se, is perceived by a moral agent, he instantly and necessarily, and without condition, affirms his obligation to choose it. This affirmation is direct and universal, absolute, or without condition. Whether he will affirm himself to be under obligation to put forth efforts to secure the good, must depend upon his regarding such acts as necessary, possible, and useful. The obligation, therefore, to put forth ultimate choice, is in the strictest sense direct, absolute and universal.

Obligation to choose holiness, (as the holiness of God,) as the means of happiness, is indirect in the sense that it is conditioned, first, upon the obligation to choose happiness as a good per se; and, second, upon the knowledge that holiness is the necessary means of happiness.

Obligation to put forth executive volitions is also indirect in the sense that it is conditioned; first, upon obligation to choose an object as an end; and, second, upon the necessity, possibility, and utility of such acts.

It should here be observed, that obligation to choose an object for its own sake, implies, of course, obligation to reject its opposite; and obligation to choose the conditions of an intrinsically valuable object for its own sake, implies obligation to reject the conditions or means of the opposite of this object. Also, obligation to use means to secure an intrinsically valuable object, implies obligation to use means, if necessary and possible, to prevent the opposite of this end. For example: Obligation to will happiness, for its intrinsic value, implies obligation to reject misery, as an intrinsic evil. Obligation to will the conditions of the happiness of being, implies obligation to reject the conditions of misery. Obligation to use means to promote the happiness of being, implies obligation to use means, if necessary and practicable, to prevent the misery of being.

Again, the choice of any object, either as an end, or a means, implies the refusal of its opposite. In other words, choice implies preference, refusing is properly only choice in an opposite direction. For this reason, in speaking of the actions of the will, it has been common to omit the mention of pilling, or refusing, since such acts are properly included in the categories of choices and volitions. It should also be observed that choice, or willing, necessarily implies an object chosen, and that this object should be such that the mind can regard it as being either intrinsically, or relatively valuable, or important. As choice must consist in an act, an intelligent act, the mind must have reason for choice. It cannot choose without a reason, for this is the same as to choose without an object of choice. A mere abstraction without any perceived or assumed, intrinsic, or relative importance, to any being in existence, cannot be an object of choice, either ultimate or executive. The ultimate reason which the mind has for choosing is in fact the object of choice; and where there is no reason there is no object of choice.

2. I have said, that moral obligation respects in the strictest sense and directly the intention only. I am now prepared to say still further, that this is a first truth of reason. It is a truth universally and necessarily assumed by all moral agents, their speculations to the contrary, in any wise, notwithstanding. This is evident from the following considerations:

(1.) Very young children know and assume this truth universally. They always deem it a sufficient vindication of themselves, when accused of any delinquency to say, "I did not mean to," or if accused of short coming, to say, "I meant or intended to have done it--I designed it." This, if true, they assume to be an all-sufficient vindication of themselves. They know that this, if believed, must be regarded as a sufficient excuse to justify them in every case.

(2.) Every moral agent necessarily regards such an excuse as a perfect justification, in case it be sincerely and truly made.

(3.) It is a saying as common as men are, and as true as common, that men are to be judged by their motives, that is, by their designs, intentions. It is impossible for us not to assent to this truth. If a man intend evil, though, perchance, he may do us good, we do not excuse him, but hold him guilty of the crime which he intended. So if he intend to do us good, and, perchance, do us evil, we do not, and cannot condemn him. For this intention and endeavor to do us good, we cannot blame him, although it has resulted in evil to us. He may be to blame for other things connected with the affair. He may have come to our help too late, and have been to blame for not coming when a different result would have followed; or he may have been blamable for not being better qualified for doing us good. He may have been to blame for many things connected with the transaction, but for a sincere, and of course hearty endeavor to do us good, he is not culpable, nor can he be, however it may result. If he honestly intended to do us good, it is impossible that he should not have used the best means in his power, at the time. This is implied in honesty of intention. And if he did this, reason cannot pronounce him guilty, for it must judge him by his intentions.

(4.) Courts of criminal law have always in every enlightened country assumed this as a first truth. They always inquire into the quo animo, that is, the intention, and judge accordingly.

(5.) The universally acknowledged truth that lunatics are not moral agents and responsible for their conduct, is but an illustration of the fact that the truth we are considering is regarded, and assumed, as a first truth of reason.

(6.) The Bible everywhere either expressly or impliedly recognizes this truth. "If there be a willing mind," that is, a right willing or intention, "it is accepted," etc. Again, "All the law is fulfilled in one word," "love." Now this cannot be true, if the spirit of the whole law does not directly respect intentions only. If it extends directly to thoughts, emotions, and outward actions, it cannot be truly said that love is the fulfilling of the law. This love must be good will, for how could involuntary love be obligatory? The spirit of the Bible everywhere respects the intention. If the intention is right, or if there be a willing mind, it is accepted as obedience. But if there be not a willing mind, that is, right intention, no outward act is regarded as obedience. The willing is always regarded by the scriptures as the doing. "If a man look on a woman, to lust after her," that is, with licentious intention, or willing, "he hath committed adultery with her already," etc. So on the other hand, if one intends to perform a service for God, which, after all, he is unable to perform, he is regarded as having virtually done it, and is rewarded accordingly. This is too obviously the doctrine of the Bible to need further elucidation.

3. We have seen that the choice of an end implies, and, while the choice continues, necessitates the choice of the known conditions and means of the end, and also the putting forth of volition to secure the end. If this is true, it follows that the choice of the conditions and means of securing an end, and also the volitions put forth as executive efforts to secure it, must derive their character from the ultimate choice or intention which gives them existence. This shows that moral obligation extends, primarily and directly, only to the ultimate intention or choice of an end, though really, but less directly, to the choice of the conditions and means, and also to executive volitions.

But I must distinguish more clearly between ultimate and proximate intentions, which discrimination will show, that in the most strict and proper sense, obligation belongs to the former, and only in a less strict and proper sense, to the latter.

An ultimate end, be it remembered, is an object chosen for its own sake.

A proximate end is an object chosen as a condition or means of securing an ultimate end.

An ultimate end is an object chosen because of its intrinsic nature and value.

A proximate end is an object chosen for the sake of the end, and upon condition of its relation as a condition or means of the end.

Example:--A student labors to get wages, to purchase books, to obtain an education, to preach the gospel, to save souls, and to please God. Another labors to get wages, to purchase books, to get an education, to preach the gospel, to secure a salary, and his own ease and popularity. In the first supposition he loves God and souls, and seeks, as his ultimate end, the happiness of souls, and the glory and gratification of God. In the last case supposed, he loves himself supremely, and his ultimate end is his own gratification. Now the proximate ends, or immediate objects of pursuit, in these two cases, are precisely alike, while their ultimate ends are entirely opposite. Their first, or nearest, end is to get wages. Their next end is, to obtain books; and so we follow them, until we ascertain their ultimate end, before we learn the moral character of what they are doing. The means they are using, i. e. their immediate objects or proximate ends of pursuit, are the same, but the ultimate ends at which they aim are entirely different, and every moral agent, from a necessary law of his intellect, must, as soon as he understands the ultimate end of each, pronounce the one virtuous, and the other sinful, in his pursuits. One is selfish and the other benevolent. From this illustration it is plain, that strictly speaking, moral character, and, of course, moral obligation, respect directly the ultimate intention only. We shall see, in the proper place, that obligation also extends, but less directly, to the use of means to obtain the end.

Our next inquiry is, to what acts and mental states moral obligation indirectly extends.

1. The muscles of the body are, directly, under the control of the will. I will to move, and my muscles must move, unless there be interposed some physical obstruction of sufficient magnitude to overcome the strength of my will.

2. The intellect is also directly under the control of the will. I am conscious that I can control and direct my attention as I please, and think upon one subject or another.

3. The sensibility, I am conscious, is only indirectly controlled by the will. Feeling can be produced only by directing the attention and thoughts to those subjects that excite feeling, by a law of necessity.

The way is now prepared to say--

1. That obligation extends indirectly to all intelligent acts of will, in the sense already explained.

2. That moral obligation extends indirectly, to outward or bodily actions. These are often required, in the word of God. The reason is, that, being connected with the actions of the will, by a law of necessity, if the will is right, the outward action must follow, except upon the contingencies just named; and therefore such actions may reasonably be required. But if the contingencies just named intervene, so that outward action does not follow the choice or intention, the Bible accepts the will for the deed, invariably. "If there be a willing mind, it is accepted according," etc.

3. Moral obligation extends, but less directly, to the states of the sensibility, so that certain emotions or feelings are required as outward actions are, and for the same reason, namely, the states of the sensibility are connected with the actions of the will, by a law of necessity. But when the sensibility is

exhausted, or when, for any reason, the right action of the will does not produce the required feelings, it is accepted upon the principle just named.

4. Moral obligation indirectly extends also to the states of the intellect; consequently the Bible, to a certain extent, and in a certain sense, holds men responsible for their thoughts and opinions. It everywhere assumes that if the heart be constantly right, the thoughts and opinions will correspond with the state of the heart, or will; "If any man will do his will, he shall know the doctrine whether it be of God." "If thine eye be single thy whole body shall be full of light." It is, however manifest, that the word of God everywhere assumes that, strictly speaking, all virtue and vice belong to the heart or intention. Where this is right, all is regarded as right; and where this is wrong, all is regarded as wrong. It is upon this assumption that the doctrine of total depravity rests. It is undeniable that the veriest sinners do many things outwardly which the law of God requires. Now unless the intention decides the character of these acts, they must be regarded as really virtuous. But when the intention is found to be selfish, then it is ascertained that they are sinful notwithstanding their conformity to the letter of the law of God.

The fact is, that moral agents are so constituted that it is impossible for them not to judge themselves, and others, by their subjective motives or intentions. They cannot but assume it as a first truth, that a man's character is as his intention is, and consequently, that moral obligation respects, directly, intention only.

5. Moral obligation then indirectly extends to everything about us, over which the will has direct or indirect control. The moral law, while, strictly, it legislates over intention only, yet in fact, in a sense less direct, legislates over the whole being, inasmuch as all our powers are directly or indirectly connected with intention, by a law of necessity. Strictly speaking, however, moral character belongs alone to the intention. In strict propriety of speech, it cannot be said that either outward action, or any state of the intellect, or sensibility, has a moral element or quality belonging to it. Yet in common language, which is sufficiently accurate for most practical purposes, we speak of thought, feeling, and outward action as holy or unholy. By this, however, all men really mean, that the agent is holy or unholy, is praise-worthy or blame-worthy in his exercises and actions, because they regard them as proceeding from the state or attitude of the will.

LECTURE IV - FOUNDATION OF MORAL OBLIGATION

In the discussion of this question, I will first state what is intended by the foundation, or ground, of obligation.

I shall use the terms ground and foundation as synonymous. Obligation must be founded on some good and sufficient reason. Be it remembered, that moral obligation respects moral action. That moral action is voluntary action. That properly speaking, obligation respects intentions only. That still more strictly, obligation respects only the ultimate intention. That ultimate intention or choice, which terms I use as synonymous, consists in choosing an object for its own sake, i. e. for what is intrinsic in the object, and for no reason that is not intrinsic in that object. That every object of ultimate choice must, and does, possess that in its own nature, the perception of which necessitates the rational affirmation, that it ought to be universally chosen, by moral agents, for its own sake, or, which is the same thing, because it is what it is, or, in other words still, because it is intrinsically valuable and not on account of its relations.

The ground of obligation, then, is that reason, or consideration, intrinsic in, or belonging to, the nature of an object, which necessitates the rational affirmation, that it ought to be chosen for its own sake. It is that reason, intrinsic in the object, which thus creates obligation by necessitating this affirmation. For example, such is the nature of the good of being that it necessitates the affirmation, that benevolence is a universal duty.

I will next call attention to some points of general agreement, and some principles essentially self-evident.

1. In the most strict and proper sense, moral obligation extends to moral actions only.

2. Strictly speaking, involuntary states of mind are not moral actions.

3. Intentions alone are, properly, moral actions.

4. In the most strict and proper sense, ultimate intentions alone are moral actions, ultimate intention being the choice of an object for its own sake, or for what is intrinsic in the object.

5. While, in the strictest sense, obligation respects only the ultimate intention, yet, in a less strict and proper sense, obligation extends to the choice of the conditions and means of securing an intrinsically valuable end, and also to executive acts put forth with design to secure such end: Hence there are different forms of obligation; for example, obligation to put forth ultimate choice--to choose the known necessary conditions and means--to put forth executive volitions, etc.

6. These different forms of obligation must have different conditions. For example, moral agency, including the possession of the requisite powers, together with the development of the ideas of the intrinsically valuable, of obligation, of right and wrong, is a condition of obligation in its universal form, namely, obligation to will the good of being in general, for its own sake; while

obligation to will the existence of the conditions and means to the end, or to put forth executive efforts to secure the end, have not only the conditions above named, but obligation in these forms must be conditional, also, upon the knowledge that there are conditions and means, and what they are, and also that executive efforts are necessary, possible, and useful.

7. The well-being of God, and of the universe of sentient existences, and especially of moral agents, is intrinsically important, or valuable, and all moral agents are under obligation to choose it for its own sake. Entire, universal, uninterrupted consecration to this end, or disinterested benevolence is the duty of all moral agents.

8. This consecration is really demanded by the law of God, as revealed in the two great precepts laid down by Christ, and this benevolence, when perfect, is in fact a compliance with the entire spirit of the law. This is right in itself, and consequently is always duty and always right, and that in all possible circumstances; and, of course, no obligation inconsistent with this can ever, in any case, exist. Reason and revelation agree in this; that the law of benevolence is the law of right, the law of nature, and no moral law, inconsistent with this, can exist.

9. Holiness, or obedience to moral law, or, in other words still, disinterested benevolence, is a natural, and of course necessary condition of the existence of that blessedness which is an ultimate or intrinsic good to moral agents, and ought to be chosen for that reason, i. e., that is a sufficient reason. Of course, the ground of obligation to choose holiness, and to endeavor to promote it in others, as a condition of the highest well-being of the universe, is the intrinsic nature of that good or well-being, and the relation of holiness to this end is a condition of the obligation to choose it, as a means to this end.

10. Truth, and conformity of heart and life to all known and practical truths, are conditions and means of the highest good of being. Of course, the obligation to conform to such truths is universal, because of this relation of truth, and of conformity to truth, to the highest good. The intrinsic value of the good must be the ground, and the relation only a condition, of the obligation.

11. God's ultimate end, in all he does, or omits, is the highest well-being of himself, and of the universe, and in all his acts and dispensations, his ultimate object is the promotion of this end. All moral agents should have the same end, and this comprises their whole duty. This intention or consecration to this intrinsically and infinitely valuable end, is virtue, or holiness, in God and in all moral agents. God is infinitely and equally holy in all things, because he does all things for the same ultimate reason, namely, to promote the highest good of being.

12. All God's moral attributes are only so many attributes of love or of disinterested benevolence; that is, they are only benevolence existing and contemplated in different relations. Creation and moral government, including both law and gospel, together with the infliction of penal sanctions, are only efforts of benevolence to secure the highest good.

13. He requires, both in his law and gospel, that all moral agents should choose the same end, and do whatever they do for its promotion; that is, this should be the ultimate reason for all they do. Consequently, all obligation resolves itself into an obligation to choose the highest good of God, and of being in general, for its own sake, and to choose all the known conditions and means of this end, for the sake of the end.

14. The intrinsic value of this end is the ground of this obligation, both as it respects God and all moral agents in all worlds. The intrinsic value of this end rendered it fit, or right, that God should require moral agents to choose it for its own sake; and of course, its intrinsic value, and not any arbitrary sovereignty, was, and is, his reason for requiring moral agents to choose it for its own sake.

15. Its known intrinsic value would, of itself, impose obligation on moral agents to choose it for its own sake, even had God never required it; or, if such a supposition were possible, had he forbidden it. Thus, disinterested benevolence is a universal and an invariable duty. This benevolence consists in willing the highest good of being, in general, for its own sake, or, in other words, in entire consecration to this good as the end of life. The intrinsic value of this good does, of its own nature, impose obligation upon all moral agents to will it for its own sake, and consecrate the whole being, without intermission, to its promotion.

Thus it is self-evident that moral character belongs to the ultimate intention, and that a man's character is as the end for which he lives, and moves, and has his being. Virtue consists in consecration to the right end, the end to which God is consecrated. This end is, and must be, by virtue of its own nature, the ground of obligation. That is, the nature of this end is such as to compel the reason of every moral agent to affirm, that it ought to be chosen for its own sake. This end is the good of being, and therefore disinterested benevolence, or good will, is a universal duty.

Now, with these facts distinctly kept in mind, let us proceed to the examination of the various conflicting and inconsistent theories of the ground of obligation.

Of the Will of God as the ground of obligation.

I will first consider the theory of those who hold that the sovereign will of God is the ground, or ultimate reason, of obligation. They hold that God's sovereign will creates, and not merely reveals and enforces, obligation. To this I reply:

1. That moral law legislates directly over voluntary action only--that moral obligation respects, primarily and strictly, the ultimate intention--that ultimate intention consists in choosing its object, for its own sake--that ultimate intention must find its reasons exclusively in its object--that the intrinsic nature and value of the object must impose obligation to choose it for its own sake--that therefore this intrinsic value is the ground, and the only possible ground, of obligation to choose it for its own sake. It would be our duty to will the highest good of God and of the universe, even did God not will that we should, or were he to will that we should not. How utterly unfounded then, is the assertion, that the sovereign will of God is the ground of obligation. Obligation to do what? Why to love God and our neighbor. That is to will their highest good. And does God's will create this obligation? Should we be under no such obligation, had he not commanded it? Are we to will this good, not for its own value to God and our neighbor, but because God commands it? The answer to these questions is too obvious to need so much as to be named. But what consistency is there in holding that disinterested benevolence is a universal duty, and at the same time that the sovereign will of God is the foundation of obligation; How can men hold, as many do, that the highest good of being ought to be chosen for its own sake -- that to choose it for its own sake is disinterested benevolence -- that its intrinsic value imposes obligation to choose it for its own sake, and

that this intrinsic value is therefore the ground of obligation, and yet that the will of God is the ground of obligation?

Why, if the will of God be the ground of obligation, then disinterested benevolence is sin. If the will of God does of itself create, and not merely reveal obligation, then the will, and not the interest and well-being of God, ought to be chosen for its own sake, and to be the great end of life. God ought to be consecrated to his own will, instead of his own highest good. Benevolence in God, and in all beings, must be sin, upon this hypothesis. A purely arbitrary will and sovereignty in God is, according to this theory, of more value than his highest well-being, and than that of the whole universe.

But observe,

Moral obligation respects ultimate intention, or the choice of an end.

The foundation, or fundamental reason for choosing a thing, is that which renders it obligatory to choose it.

This reason is the thing on which the choice ought to terminate, or the true end is not chosen.

Therefore the reason and the end are identical.

If, then, the will of God be the foundation of obligation, it must also be the ultimate end of choice.

But it is impossible for us to will or choose the divine willing as an ultimate end. God's willing reveals a law, a rule of choice, or of intention. It requires something to be intended as an ultimate end, or for its own intrinsic value. This end cannot be the willing, commandment, law, itself. Does God will that I should choose his willing as an ultimate end? This is impossible. It is a plain contradiction to say that moral obligation respects, directly, ultimate intention only, or the choice of an end, for its own intrinsic value, and yet, that the will of God is the foundation, or reason of the obligation. This is affirming at the same breath that the intrinsic value of the end which God requires me to choose, is the reason, or foundation of the obligation to choose it, and yet that this is not the reason, but that the will of God is the reason.

Willing can never be an end. God cannot will our willing as an end. Nor can he will his willing as an end. Willing, choosing, always, and necessarily, implies an end willed entirely distinct from the willing, or choice, itself. Willing, cannot be regarded, or willed, as an ultimate end, for two reasons:--

(1.) Because that on which choice or willing terminates, and not the choice itself, must be regarded as the end.

(2.) Because choice or willing is of no intrinsic value and of no relative value, aside from the end willed or chosen.

2. The will of God cannot be the foundation of moral obligation in created moral agents. God has moral character, and is virtuous. This implies that he is the subject of moral obligation, for virtue is nothing else than compliance with obligation. If God is the subject of moral obligation, there is some reason, independent of his own will, why he wills as he does; some reason, that imposes obligation upon him to will as he does. His will, then, respecting the conduct of moral agents, is not the fundamental reason of their obligation; but the foundation of their obligation must be the reason which induces God, or makes it obligatory on him, to will in respect to the conduct of moral agents, just what he does.

3. If the will of God were the foundation of moral obligation, he could, by willing it, change the nature of virtue and vice, which is absurd.

4. If the will of God were the foundation of moral obligation, he not only can change the nature of virtue and vice, but has a right to do so; for if there is nothing back of his will that is as binding upon him as upon his creatures, he has a right, at any time, to make malevolence a virtue, and benevolence a vice. For if his will is the ground of obligation, then his will creates right, and whatever he wills, or might will, is right simply and only because so he wills.

5. If the will of God be the foundation of moral obligation, we have no standard by which to judge of the moral character of his actions, and cannot know whether he is worthy of praise or blame. Upon the supposition in question, were God a malevolent being, and did he require all his creatures to be selfish, and not benevolent, he would be just ns virtuous and worthy of praise as now; for the supposition is, that his sovereign will creates right, and of course, will as he might, that would be right, simply because he willed it.

6. If the will of God is the foundation of moral obligation, he has no standard by which to judge of his own character, as he has no rule but his own will, with which to compare his own actions.

7. If the will of God is the foundation of moral obligation, he is not himself a subject of moral obligation. But,

8. If God is not a subject of moral obligation, he has no moral character; for virtue and vice are nothing else but conformity or non-conformity to moral obligation. The will of God, as expressed in his law, is the rule of duty to moral agents. It defines and marks out the path of duty, but the fundamental reason why moral agents ought to act in conformity to the will of God, is plainly not the will of God itself.

9. The will of no being can be law. Moral law is an idea of the divine reason, and not the willing of any being. If the will of any being were law, that being could not, by natural possibility, will wrong; for whatever he willed would be right, simply and only because he willed it.

10. But let us bring this philosophy into the light of divine revelation. "To the law and to the testimony; if it agree not therewith, it is because it hath no light in it."

The law of God, or the moral law, requires that God shall be loved with all the heart, and our neighbor as ourselves. Now it is manifest that the love required is not mere emotion, but that it consists in choice, willing, intention--i. e., in the choice of something on account of its own intrinsic value, or in the choice of an ultimate end. Now what is this end? What is that which we are to choose for its own intrinsic value? Is it the will or command of God? Are we to will as an ultimate end, that God should will that we should thus will? What can be more absurd, self-contradictory, and ridiculous than this? But again, what is this loving, willing, choosing, intending, required by the law? We are commanded to love God and our neighbor. What is this, what can it be, but to will the highest good or well-being of God and our neighbor? This is intrinsically and infinitely valuable. This must be the end, and nothing can possibly be law that requires the choice of any other ultimate end. Nor can that, by any possibility, be true philosophy, that makes anything else the reason or foundation of moral obligation.

But it is said that we are conscious of affirming our obligation to obey the will of God, without reference to any other reason than his will; and this, it is said, proves that his will is the foundation of obligation.

To this I reply, the reason does indeed affirm that we ought to will that which God commands, but it does not and cannot assign his will as the foundation of the obligation. His whole will respecting our duty, is summed up in the two precepts of the law. These, as we have seen, require universal good-will to being, or the supreme love of God and the equal love of our neighbor--that we should will the highest well-being of God and of the universe, for its own sake, or for its own intrinsic value. Reason affirms that we ought thus to will. And can it be so self-contradictory as to affirm that we ought to will the good of God and of the universe, for its own intrinsic value; yet not for this reason, but because God wills that we should will it? Impossible! But in this assertion, the objector has reference to some outward act, some condition or means of the end to be chosen, and not to the end itself. But even in respect to any act whatever, his objection does not hold good. For example, God requires me to labor and pray for the salvation of souls, or to do anything else. Now his command is necessarily regarded by me as obligatory, not as an arbitrary requirement, but as revealing infallibly the true means or conditions of securing the great and ultimate end, which I am to will for its intrinsic value. I necessarily regard his commandment as wise and benevolent, and it is only because I so regard it, that I affirm, or can affirm, my obligation to obey him. Should he command me to choose, as an ultimate end, or for its own intrinsic value, that which my reason affirmed to be of no intrinsic value, I could not possibly affirm my obligation to obey him. Should he command me to do that which my reason affirmed to be unwise and malevolent, it were impossible for me to affirm my obligation to obey him. This proves, beyond controversy, that reason does not regard his command as the foundation of the obligation, but only as infallible proof that that which he commands is wise and benevolent in itself, and commanded by him for that reason.

If the will of God were the foundation of moral obligation, he might command me to violate and trample down all the laws of my being, and to be the enemy of all good, and I should not only be under obligation, but affirm my obligation to obey him. But this is absurd. This brings us to the conclusion that he who asserts that moral obligation respects the choice of an end for its intrinsic value, and still affirms the will of God to be the foundation of moral obligation, contradicts his own admissions, the plainest intuitions of reason and divine revelation. His theory is grossly inconsistent and nonsensical. It overlooks the very nature of moral law as an idea of reason, and makes it to consist in arbitrary willing.

Paley's theory of Self-interest.

This theory, as every reader of Paley knows, makes self-interest the ground of moral obligation. Upon this theory I remark--

1. That if self-interest be the ground of moral obligation, then self-interest is the end to be chosen for its own sake. To be virtuous I must in every instance intend my own interest as the supreme good. Then, according to this theory, disinterested benevolence is sin. To live to God and the universe, is not right. It is not devotion to the right end. This theory affirms self-interest to be the end for which we ought to live. Then selfishness is virtue, and benevolence is vice. These are directly opposite theories. It cannot be a trifle to embrace the wrong view of this subject. If Dr. Paley was right, all are fundamentally wrong who hold the benevolence theory.

2. Upon this hypothesis, I am to treat my own interest as supremely valuable, when it is infinitely less valuable than the interests of God. Thus I am under a moral obligation to prefer an infinitely less good, because it is my own, to one of infinitely greater value that belongs to another. This is precisely what every sinner in earth and hell does.

3. But let us examine this theory in the light of the revealed law. If this philosophy be correct, the law should read, "Thou shalt love thyself supremely, and God and thy neighbor not at all." For Dr. Paley holds the only reason of the obligation to be self-interest. If this is so, then I am under an obligation to love myself alone, and never do my duty when I at all love God or my neighbor. He says, it is the utility of any rule alone which constitutes the obligation of it. (Paley's Moral Philos., book ii. chap. 6.) Again he says, "And let it be asked why I am obliged (obligated) to keep my word? and the answer will be, Because I am urged to do so by a violent motive, namely, the expectation of being after this life rewarded if I do so, or punished if I do not."--(Paley's Moral Philos., book ii. chap. 3.) Thus it would seem, that it is the utility of a rule to myself only, that constitutes the ground of obligation to obey it.

But should this be denied, still it cannot be denied that Dr. Paley maintains that self-interest is the ground of moral obligation. If this is so, i. e. if this be the foundation of moral obligation, whether Paley or any one else holds it to be true, then, undeniably, the moral law should read, "Thou shalt love thyself supremely, and God and thy neighbor subordinately;" or, more strictly, "Thou shalt love thyself as an end, and God and thy neighbor, only as a means of promoting thine own interest."

If this theory be true, all the precepts in the Bible need to be altered. Instead of the injunction, "Whatever you do, do it heartily unto the Lord," it should read, "Whatever you do, do it heartily unto yourself." Instead of the injunction, "Whether, therefore, ye eat or drink, or whatsoever ye do, do all to the glory of God," it should read, "Do all to secure your own interest." Should it be said that this school would say, that the meaning of these precepts is, Do all to the glory of God to secure your own interest thereby, I answer; This is a contradiction. To do it to or for the glory of God is one thing; to do it to secure my own interest is an entirely different and opposite thing. To do it for the glory of God, is to make his glory my end. But to do it to secure my own interest, is to make my own interest the end.

4. But let us look at this theory in the light of the revealed conditions of salvation. "Except a man forsake all that he hath he cannot be my disciple." If the theory under consideration be true, it should read: "Except a man make his own interest the supreme end of pursuit, he cannot be my disciple." Again, "If any man will come after me, let him deny himself and take up his cross," etc. This, in conformity with the theory in question, should read: "If any man will come after me, let him not deny himself, but cherish and supremely seek his own interest." A multitude of such passages might be quoted, as every reader of the Bible knows.

5. But let us examine this theory in the light of other scripture declarations. "It is more blessed to give than to receive." This, according to the theory we are opposing, should read, "It is more blessed to receive than to give." "Charity (love) seeketh not her own." This should read, "Charity seeketh her own." "No man (that is, no righteous man) liveth to himself." This should read, "Every (righteous) man liveth to himself."

6. Let this theory be examined in the light of the spirit and example of Christ. "Even Christ pleased not himself." This should read, if Christ was holy and did his duty, "Even Christ pleased himself, or which is the same thing, sought his own interest." "I seek not mine own glory, but the glory of him who sent me." This should read, "I seek not the glory of him who sent me, but mine own glory."

But enough; we cannot fail to see that this is a selfish philosophy, and the exact opposite of the truth of God.

The Utilitarian philosophy.

This maintains that the utility of an act or choice renders it obligatory. That is, utility is the foundation of moral obligation; that the tendency of an act, choice, or intention, to secure a good or valuable end, is the foundation of the obligation to put forth that choice or intention. Upon this theory I remark--

1. That utilitarians must hold, in common with others, that it is our duty to will the good of God and our neighbor for its own sake; and that the intrinsic value of this good creates obligation to will it, and to endeavor to promote it; that the tendency of choosing it, would be neither useful nor obligatory, but for its intrinsic value. How, then, can they hold that the tendency of choosing to secure its object, instead of the intrinsic value of the object, should be a ground of obligation. It is absurd to say that the foundation of the obligation to choose a certain end, is to be found, not in the value of the end itself, but in the tendency of the intention to secure the end. The tendency is valuable or otherwise, as the end is valuable or otherwise. It is, and must be, the value of the end, and not the tendency of an intention to secure the end, that constitutes the foundation of the obligation to intend.

2. We have seen that the foundation of obligation to will or choose any end as such, that is, on its own account, must consist in the intrinsic value of the end, and that nothing else whatever can impose obligation to choose anything as an ultimate end, but its intrinsic value. To affirm the contrary is to affirm a contradiction. It is the same as to say, that I ought to choose a thing as an end, and not yet as an end, that is, for its own sake, but for some other reason, to wit, the tendency of my choice to secure that end. Here I affirm at the same breath, that the thing intended is to be an end, that is, chosen for its own intrinsic value, and yet not as an end or for its intrinsic value, but for an entirely different reason, to wit, the tendency of the choice to secure it.

3. But the very announcement of this theory implies its absurdity. A choice is obligatory, because it tends to secure good. But why secure good rather than evil? The answer is, because good is valuable. Alt! here then we have another reason, and one which must be the true reason, to wit, the value of the good which the choice tends to secure. Obligation to use means to do good may, and must, be conditioned upon the tendency of those means to secure the end, but the obligation to use them is founded solely in the value of the end.

4. Does the law require us to love God and our neighbor, because loving God and our neighbor tends to the well-being either of God, our neighbor, or ourselves? Is it the tendency or utility of love that makes it obligatory upon us to exercise it? What! will good, not from regard to its value, but because willing good will do good! But why do good? What is this love? Here let it be distinctly remembered that the love required by the law of God is not a mere emotion or feeling, but willing, choosing, intending, in a word, that this love is nothing else than ultimate intention. What, then, is to be intended as an end, or

for its own sake? Is it the tendency of love, or the utility of ultimate intention, that is the end to be intended? It must be, if utilitarianism is true.

According to this theory, when the law requires supreme love to God, and equal love to our neighbor, the meaning is, not that we are to will, choose, intend the well-being of God and our neighbor for its own sake, or because of its intrinsic value, but because of the tendency of the intention to promote the good of God, our neighbor and ourselves. But let the tendency of love or intention be what it may, the utility of it depends upon the intrinsic value of that which it tends to promote. Suppose love or intention tends to promote its end, this is a useful tendency only because the end is valuable in itself. It is nonsense then to say that love to God and man, or an intention to promote their good, is required, not because of the value of their well-being, but because love tends to promote their well-being. This represents the law as requiring love, not to God and our neighbor as an end, but to tendency as an end. The law in this case should read thus: "Thou shalt love the utility or tendency of love with all thy heart," etc.

If the theory under consideration is true, this is the spirit and meaning of the law: "Thou shalt love the Lord and thy neighbor, that is, thou shalt choose their good, not for its own sake or as an end, but because choosing it tends to promote it." This is absurd; for, I ask again, why promote it but for its own value? If the law of God requires ultimate intention, it is a contradiction to affirm that the intention ought to terminate on its own tendency as an end.

5. But it is said that we are conscious of affirming obligation to do many things, on the ground, that those things are useful, or tend to promote good.

I answer, that we are conscious of affirming obligation to do many things upon condition of their tendency to promote good, but that we never affirm obligation to be founded on this tendency. I am under an obligation to use the means to promote good, not for the sake of its intrinsic value, but for the sake of the tendency of the means to promote it! This is absurd.

I say again, the obligation to use means may and must be conditionated upon perceived tendency, but never founded in this tendency. Ultimate intention has no such condition. The perceived intrinsic value imposes obligation without any reference to the tendency of the intention.

6. But suppose any utilitarian should deny that moral obligation respects ultimate intention only, and maintain that it also respects those volitions and actions that sustain to the ultimate end the relation of means, and therefore assert that the foundation of moral obligation in respect to all those volitions and actions, is their tendency to secure a valuable end. This would not at all relieve the difficulty of utilitarianism; for in this case tendency could only be a condition of the obligation, while the fundamental reason of the obligation would and must be, the intrinsic value of the end, which these may have a tendency to promote. Tendency to promote an end can impose no obligation. The end must be intrinsically valuable, and this alone imposes obligation to choose the end, and to use the means to promote it. Upon condition that anything is perceived to sustain to this end the relation of a necessary means, we are, for the sake of the end alone, under obligation to use the means.

LECTURE V - FOUNDATION OF MORAL OBLIGATION

The theory of Right as the foundation of obligation.

In the examination of this philosophy I must begin by defining terms. What is right? The primary signification of the term is straight. When used in a moral sense it means fit, suitable, agreeable to the nature and relations of moral agents. Right, in a moral sense, belongs to choice, intention, and is an intention straight with, or conformed to, moral law. The inquiry before us is, what is the ground of obligation to put forth choice or intention. Rightarians say that right is the ground of such obligation. This is the answer given to this question by a large school of philosophers and theologians. But what does this assertion mean? It is generally held by this school, that right, in a moral sense, pertains primarily and strictly to intentions only. They maintain, as I do, that obligation pertains primarily and strictly to ultimate choice or intentions, and less strictly to executive volitions, and to choice of the conditions and means of securing the object of ultimate choice. Now in what sense of the term right do they regard it as the ground of obligation?

Right is objective and subjective. Right in the objective sense of the term, has been recently defined to consist in the relation of intrinsic fitness existing between ultimate choice and its object. [1] For example, the nature or intrinsic value of the highest well-being of God and of the universe, creates the relation of intrinsic fitness between it and choice, and this relation, it is insisted, creates, or is the ground of, obligation.

Subjective right is synonymous with righteousness, uprightness, virtue. It consists in, or is an attribute of, that state of the will which is conformed to objective right or to moral law. It is a term that expresses the moral quality, element, or attribute of that ultimate intention which the law of God requires. In other words still, it is conformity of heart to the law of objective right; or, as I just said, it is more strictly the term that designates the moral character of that state of heart. Some choose to regard subjective right as consisting in this state of heart, and others insist that it is only an element, attribute, or quality of this state of heart, or of this ultimate intention. I shall not contend about words, but shall show that it matters not, so far as the question we are about to examine is concerned, in which of these lights subjective right is regarded, whether as consisting in ultimate intention conformed to law, or, as being an attribute, element, or quality of this intention.

The theory under consideration was held by the ancient Greek and Roman philosophers. It was the theory of Kant, and is now the theory of the transcendental school in Europe and America. Cousin, in manifest accordance with the views of Kant, states the theory in these words: "Do right for the sake of the right, or rather, will the right for the sake of the right. Morality has to do with the intentions."--(Enunciation of Moral Law--Elements of Psychology, p. 162.) Those who follow Kant, Cousin, and Coleridge state the theory either in the same words, or in words that amount to the same thing. They regard right as the foundation of moral obligation. "Will the right for the sake of the right." This must mean, will the right as an ultimate end, that is, for its own sake. Let us examine this very popular philosophy, first, in the light of its own principles, and secondly in the light of revelation.

The writer first above alluded to, has professedly given a critical definition of the exact position and teaching of rightarians. They hold, according to him, and I suppose he has rightly defined the position of that school, that subjective right is the ground of obligation. We shall see, hereafter, that subjective right, or righteousness, can never be a ground of moral obligation. We will here attend to the critically defined position of the rightarian who holds that the relation of intrinsic fitness existing between choice and an intrinsically valuable object, is the ground of obligation to choose that object.

Now observe, this writer strenuously maintains, that the reason for ultimate choice must be found exclusively in the object of such choice, in other words, that ultimate choice, is the choice of its object for its own sake, or for what is intrinsic in the object itself. He also affirms repeatedly, that the ground of obligation is, and must be, found exclusively in the object of ultimate choice, and also that the ground of obligation is the consideration, intrinsic in the object of choice, which compels the reason to affirm the obligation to choose it for its own sake. But all this as flatly as possible contradicts his rightarian theory, as above stated. If the ground of obligation to put forth ultimate choice is to be found, as it certainly must be, in the nature of the object of choice, and in nothing extrinsic to it, how can it consist in the relation of intrinsic fitness existing between the choice and its object? Plainly it cannot. This relation is not intrinsic in the object of choice.

Observe, the obligation is to choose the object of ultimate choice, not for the sake of the relation existing between the choice and its object, but exclusively for the sake of what is intrinsic in the object itself. The relation is not the object of choice, but the relation is created by the object of choice. Choice being what it is, the intrinsic nature or value of the object, as the good of being for example, creates both the relation of rightness and the obligation to choose the object for its own sake. That which creates the relation of objective rightness must, for the same reason, create the obligation, for it is absurd to say that the intrinsic value of the object creates the relation of rightness between itself and choice, and yet that it does not impose or create obligation to choose itself for its own sake.

It is self-evident then, that since the object ought to be chosen for the sake of its own nature, or for what is intrinsic in it, and not for the sake of the relation in question, the nature of the object, and not the relation, is, and must be, the ground of obligation.

But, the writer who has given the above defined position of the rightarians, says that "the intelligence, in judging an act to be right or wrong, does not take into the account the object nor the act by itself, but both together, in their intrinsic relations, as the ground of its affirmation."

But the nature of ultimate choice, and the nature of its object, the good of being, for example, with their intrinsic relations to each other, form a ground of obligation to choose--what? the choice, the object, and their intrinsic relations? No, but simply and only to choose the good for its own sake, or solely for the sake of what is intrinsic in it. Observe, it is often affirmed by this writer, that ultimate choice is the choice of an object for its own sake, or for what is intrinsic in the object itself. That the ground of obligation to put forth ultimate choice, must in every case, be intrinsic in the object of choice. But the object of choice in this case is the good of being, and not the nature of the choice and of the good of being, together with the intrinsic relation of rightness existing between them. The form of the obligation discloses the ground of it. The form of the obligation is to choose the good of being, i. e. the object of choice, for what is intrinsic in it. Then, the ground of the obligation must be, the intrinsic nature of the good, i. e. of the object of choice. The nature of choice, and the intrinsic relations of the choice, and the good, are conditions, but not the ground, of the obligation. Had this writer only kept in mind his own most critical definition of ultimate intention, his often repeated assertions that the ground of obligation must be, in every case, found intrinsically in the object of ultimate choice, and in nothing extraneous to it, he never could have made the statement we have just examined.

The duty of universal disinterested benevolence is universally and necessarily affirmed and admitted. But if the rightarian be the true theory, then disinterested benevolence is sin. According to this scheme, the right, and not the good of being, is the end to, and for which, God and all moral agents ought to live. According to this theory, disinterested benevolence can never be duty, can never be right, but always and necessarily wrong. I do not mean that the advocates of this theory see and avow this conclusion. But it is wonderful that they do not, for nothing is more self-evident. If moral agents ought to will the right for the sake of the right, or will good, not for the sake of the good, but for the sake of the relation of rightness existing between the choice and the good, then to will the good for its own sake is sin. It is not willing the right end. It is willing the good and not the right as an ultimate end. These are opposing theories. Both cannot be true. Which is the right to will, the good for its own sake, or the right? Let universal reason answer.

But let us examine this philosophy in the light of the oracles of God.

1. In the light of the moral law. The whole law is expressed by the great Teacher thus: "Thou shalt love the Lord thy God with all thy heart, and with all thy soul, with all thy might, and with all thy strength; and thy neighbor as thyself." Paul says: "All the law is fulfilled in one word--love: therefore love is the fulfilling of the law." Now it is admitted by this philosophy, that the love required by the law is not a mere emotion, but that it consists in willing, choice, intention; that it consists in the choice of an ultimate end, or in the choice of something for its own sake, or, which is the same thing, for its intrinsic value. What is this which the law requires us to will to God and our neighbor? Is it to will something to, or respecting, God and our neighbor, not for the sake of the intrinsic value of that something, but for the sake of the relation of rightness existing between choice and that something? This were absurd. Besides, what has this to do with loving God and our neighbor? To will the something, the good, for example, of God, and our neighbor, for the sake of the relation in question, is not the same as to love God and our neighbor, as it is not willing their good for its own sake. It is not willing their good, out of any regard to them, but solely out of regard to the relation of fitness existing between the willing and the object willed. Suppose it be said, that the law requires us to will the good, or highest blessedness of God and our neighbor, because it is right. This is a contradiction and an impossibility. To will the blessedness of God and

our neighbor, in any proper sense, is to will it for its own sake, or as an ultimate end. But this is not to will it because it is right. To will the good of God and our neighbor for its own sake, or its intrinsic value, is right. But to will it, not for the sake of its intrinsic value to them, but for the sake of the relations in question, is not right. To will the good because it is good, or the valuable because it is valuable, is right, because it is willing it for the right reason. But to will it, not for its value, but for the sake of the relation of fitness between the willing and the object, is not right, because it is not willing it for the right reason. The law of God does not, cannot, require us to love right more than God and our neighbor. What! right of greater value than the highest well being of God and of the universe? Impossible! It is impossible that the moral law should require anything else than to will the highest good of universal being as an ultimate end, i. e. for its own sake. It is a first truth of reason, that this is the most valuable thing possible or conceivable; and that could by no possibility be law, which should require anything else to be chosen as an ultimate end. According to this philosophy, the revealed law should read: "Thou shalt love the right for its own sake, with all thy heart and with all thy soul." The fact is, the law requires the supreme love of God, and the equal love of our neighbor. It says nothing, and implies nothing, about doing right for the sake of the right. Rightarianism is a rejection of the divine revealed law, and a substituting in its stead an entirely different rule of moral obligation: a rule that deifies right, that rejects the claim of God, and exalts right to the throne.

2. "Whether therefore ye eat or drink, or whatsoever ye do, do all to the glory of God." Does this precept require us to will the glory of God for its intrinsic or relative value, or for the sake of intrinsic fitness between the willing and its object? The glory and renown of God is of infinite value to him, and to the universe, and for this reason it should be promoted. The thing required here is doing, an executive act. The spirit of the requisition is this: Aim to spread abroad the renown or glory of God, as the means of securing the highest well-being of the universe. Why? I answer: for the sake of the intrinsic value of this well-being, and not for the sake of the relation of fitness existing between the willing and the object.

3. "Do good unto all men, as ye have opportunity." Here again, are we required to do the good, for the sake of the good, or for the sake of the relation of rightness, between the doing and the good? I answer: we are to do the good for the sake of the good.

4. Take the commands to pray and labor for the salvation of souls. Do such commandments require us to go forth to will or do the right for the sake of the right, or to will the salvation of souls for the intrinsic value of their salvation? When we pray and preach and converse, must we aim at right, must the love of right, and not the love of God and of souls influence us? When I am engaged in prayer, and travail night and day for souls, and have an eye so single to the good of souls and to the glory of God, and am so swallowed up with my subject as not so much as to think of the right, am I all wrong? Must I pray because it is right, and do all I do, and suffer all I suffer, not from good-will to God and man, but because it is right? Who does not know, that to intend the right for the sake of the right in all these things, instead of having an eye single to the good of being, would and must be anything rather than true religion?

5. Examine this philosophy in the light of the scripture declaration: "God so loved the world that he gave his only begotten Son, that whosoever believeth

in him might not perish, but have everlasting life." Now, are we to understand that God gave his Son, not from any regard to the good of souls for its own sake, but for the sake of the right? Did he will the right for the sake of the right? Did he give his Son to die for the right, for the sake of the right, or to die to render the salvation of souls possible, for the sake of the souls? Did Christ give himself to labor and die for the right, for the sake of the right, or for souls, from love to souls? Did prophets, and apostles, and martyrs, and have the saints in all ages, willed the right for the sake of the right, or have they labored and suffered and died for God and souls, from love to them?

6. But take another passage which is quoted in support of this philosophy: "Children, obey your parents in the Lord, for this is right." Now what is the spirit of this requirement? What is it to obey parents? Why, if as this philosophy holds, it must resolve itself into ultimate intention, what must the child intend for its own sake? Must he will good to God and his parents, and obey his parents as the means of securing the highest good, or must he will the right as an end, for the sake of the right, regardless of the good of God or of the universe? Would it be right to will the right for the sake of the right, rather than to will the good of the universe for the sake of the good, and obey his parents as a means of securing the highest good?

It is right to will the highest good of God and of the universe, and to use all the necessary means, and fulfil all the necessary conditions of this highest well-being. For children to obey their parents, is one of the means, and for this reason it is right, and upon no other condition can it be required. But it is said that children affirm their obligation to obey their parents, entirely irrespective of the obedience having any reference, or sustaining any relation, to the good of being. This is a mistake. The child, if he is a moral agent, and does really affirm moral obligation, not only does, but must perceive the end upon which his choice or intention ought to terminate. If he really makes an intelligent affirmation, it is and must be, that he ought to will an end; that this end is not, and cannot be the right, as has been shown. He knows that he ought to will his parents' happiness, and his own happiness, and the happiness of the world, and of God; and he knows that obedience to his parents sustains the relation of a means to this end; The fact is, it is a first truth of reason, that he ought to will the good of his parents, and the good of everybody. He also knows that obedience to his parents is a necessary means to this end. If he does not know these things, it is impossible for him to be a moral agent, to make any intelligent affirmation at all; and if he has any idea of obedience, it is, and must be, only such as animals have who are actuated wholly by hope, fear and instinct. As well might we say, that an ox or a dog, who gives indication of knowing, in some sense, that he ought to obey us, affirms moral obligation of himself, as to say this of a child in whose mind the idea of the good, or valuable to being is not developed. What! does moral obligation respect ultimate intention only; and does ultimate intention consist in the choice of something for its own intrinsic value, and yet is it true that children affirm moral obligation before the idea of the intrinsically valuable is at all developed? Impossible! But this objection assumes that children have the idea of right developed before the idea of the valuable. This cannot be. The end to be chosen must be apprehended by the mind, before the mind can have the idea of moral obligation to choose an end, or of the right or wrong of choosing or not choosing it. The development of the idea of the good or valuable, must precede the development of the ideas of right and of moral obligation.

Take this philosophy on its own ground, and suppose the relation of rightness existing between choice and its object to be the ground of obligation, it is plain that the intrinsically valuable object must be perceived, before this relation can be perceived. So that the idea of the intrinsically valuable must be developed, as a condition of the existence of the idea of the relation in question. The law of God, then, is not, and cannot be, developed in the mind of a child who has no knowledge or idea of the valuable, and who has, and can have, no reference to the good of any being, in obedience to his parents.

It is one thing to intend that, the intending of which is right, and quite another to intend the right as an end. For example, to choose my own gratification as an end, is wrong. But this is not choosing the wrong as an end. A drunkard chooses to gratify his appetite for strong drink as an end, that is, for its own sake. This is wrong. But the choice does not terminate on the wrong, but on the gratification. The thing intended is not the wrong. The liquor is not chosen, the gratification is not intended, because it is wrong, but notwithstanding it is wrong. To love God is right, but to suppose that God is loved because it is right, is absurd. It is to suppose that God is loved, not from any regard to God, but from a regard to right. This is an absurdity and a contradiction. To love or will the good of my neighbor, is right. But to will the right, instead of the good of my neighbor, is not right. It is loving right instead of my neighbor; but this is not right.

1. But it is objected, that I am conscious of affirming to myself that I ought to will the right. This is a mistake. I am conscious of affirming to myself, that I ought to will that, the willing of which is right, to wit, to will the good of God and of being. This is right. But this is not choosing the right as an end.

But it is still insisted, that we are conscious of affirming obligation to will, and do, many things, simply and only because it is right thus to will, and do, and in view of this rightness.

To this I reply, that the immediate reason for the act, thought of at the time, and immediately present to the mind, may be the rightness of the act, but in such cases the rightness is only regarded by the mind as a condition and never as the ground of obligation. The act must be ultimate choice, or the choice of conditions and means. In ultimate choice, surely, the mind can never affirm, or think of the relation of rightness between the choice and its object, instead of the intrinsic value of the object, as the ground of obligation. Nor can the mind think of the relation of rightness between the choice of conditions and means, and its object, as the ground of the obligation to choose them. It does, and must, assume, the value of the end, as creating both the obligation to choose, and the relation in question. The fact is, the mind necessarily assumes, without always thinking of this assumption, its obligation to will the good, for its own sake, together with all the known conditions and means. Whenever therefore it perceives a condition, or a means of good, it instantly and necessarily affirms obligation to choose it, or, which is the same thing, it affirms the rightness of such choice. The rightness of the choice may be, and often is the thing immediately thought of, but the assumption is, and must be, in the mind, that this obligation, and hence the rightness is created by the nature of the object to which this thing sustains the relation of a condition or a means.

2. But it is said again, "I am conscious of affirming to myself that I ought to will the good of being, because it is right." That is, to will the good of being, as a means, and the right as an end! which is making right the supreme good, and the good of being a means to that end. This is absurd. But to say, that I am conscious of affirming to myself my obligation to love or will the good of God and my neighbor, because it is right, is a contradiction. It is the same as to say, I ought to love, or intend the good of God and my neighbor, as an ultimate end, and yet not to intend the good of God and my neighbor, but intend the right.

3. But it is said, that "I ought to love God in compliance with, and out of respect to my obligation; that I ought to will it, because and for the reason that I am bound to will it." That is, that in loving God and my neighbor, I must intend to discharge or comply with my obligation; and this, it is said, is identical with intending the right. But ought my supreme object to be to discharge my duty--to meet obligation, instead of willing the well-being of God and my neighbor for its own sake? If my end is to do my duty, I do not do it. For what is my obligation? Why, to love, or will the good of God and my neighbor, that is, as an end, or for its own value. To discharge my obligation, then, I must intend the good of God and my neighbor, as an end. That is, I must intend that which I am under an obligation to intend. But I am not under an obligation to intend the right, because it is right, nor do my duty because it is my duty, but to intend the good of God and of my neighbor, because it is good. Therefore, to discharge my obligation, I must intend the good, and not the right--the good of God and my neighbor and not to do my duty. I say again, to intend the good, or valuable, is right but to intend the right is not right.

4. But it is said, that in very many instances, at least, I am conscious of affirming my moral obligation to do the right, without any reference to the good of being, when I can assign no other reason for the affirmation of obligation than the right. For example, I behold virtue; I affirm spontaneously and necessarily, that I ought to love that virtue. And this, it is said, has no reference to the good of being. Is willing the right for the sake of the right, and loving virtue, the same thing? But what is it to love virtue? Not a mere feeling of delight or complacency in it. It is agreed that moral obligation, strictly speaking, respects the ultimate intention only. What, then, do I mean by the affirmation that I ought to love virtue? What is virtue? It is ultimate intention, or an attribute of ultimate intention. But what is loving virtue? It consists in willing its existence. But it is said that I affirm my obligation to love virtue as an end, or for its own sake, and not from any regard to the good of being. This is absurd, and a contradiction. To love virtue, it is said, is to will its existence as an end. But virtue consists in intending an end. Now, to love virtue, it is said, is to will, intend its existence as an end, for its own sake. Then, according to this theory, I affirm my obligation to intend the intention of a virtuous being as an end, instead of intending the same end that he does. This is absurd; his intention is of no value, is neither naturally good nor morally good, irrespective of the end intended. It is neither right nor wrong, irrespective of the end chosen. It is therefore impossible to will, choose, intend the intention as an end, without reference to the end intended. To love virtue, then, is to love or will the end upon which virtuous intention terminates, namely, the good of being; or, in other words, to love virtue is to will its existence for the sake of the end it has in view, which is the same thing as to will the same end. Virtue is intending, choosing an end. Loving virtue is willing that the virtuous intention should

exist for the sake of its end. Take away the end, and who would or could will the intention? Without the end, the virtue, or intention, would not and could not exist. It is not true, therefore, that in the case supposed, I affirm my obligation to will, or intend, without any reference to the good of being.

5. But again, it is said, that when I contemplate the moral excellence of God, I affirm my obligation to love him solely for his goodness, without any reference to the good of being, and for no other reason than because it is right. But to love God because of his moral excellence, and because it is right, are not the same thing. It is a gross contradiction to talk of loving God for his moral excellence, because it is right. It is the same as to say, I love God for the reason that he is morally excellent, or worthy, yet not at all for this reason, but for the reason that it is right. To love God for his moral worth, is to will good to him for its own sake upon condition that he deserves it. But to will his moral worth because it is right, is to will the right as an ultimate end, to have supreme regard to right, instead of the moral worth, or the well-being of God.

But it may reasonably be asked, why should rightarians bring forward these objections? They all assume that moral obligation may respect something else than ultimate intention. Why, I repeat it, should rightarians affirm that the moral excellence of God is the foundation of moral obligation, since they hold that right is the foundation of moral obligation? Why should the advocates of the theory that the moral excellence of God is the foundation of moral obligation, affirm that right is the foundation, or that we are bound to love God for his moral excellence, because this is right? These are gross contradictions. Rightarians hold that disinterested benevolence is a universal duty; that this benevolence consists in willing the highest good of being in general, for its own sake; that this good, by virtue of its own nature, imposes obligation to choose it, for its own sake, and therefore, and for this reason, it is right thus to choose it. But notwithstanding all this, they most inconsistently affirm that right is universally the ground of obligation. Consistency must compel them to deny that disinterested benevolence ever is, or can be, duty and right, or to abandon the nonsensical dogma, that right is the ground of obligation. There is no end to the absurdities in which error involves its advocates, and it is singular to see the advocates of the different theories, each in his turn, abandon his own and affirm some other, as an objection to the true theory. It has also been, and still is, common for writers to confound different theories with each other, and to affirm, in the compass of a few pages, several different theories. At least this has been done in some instances.

Consistent rightarianism is a godless, Christless, loveless philosophy. This Kant saw and acknowledged. He calls it pure legality, that is, he understands the law as imposing obligation by virtue of its own nature, instead of the intrinsic value of the end, which the law requires moral agents to choose. He loses sight of the end, and does not recognize any end whatever. He makes a broad distinction between morality and religion. Morality consists, according to him, in the adoption of the maxim, "Do right for the sake of the right," or, "Act at all times upon a maxim fit for law universal." The adoption of this maxim is morality. But now, having adopted this maxim, the mind goes abroad to carry its maxim into practice. It finds God and being to exist, and sees it to be right to intend their good. This intending the good is religion, according to him. Thus, he says, ethics lead to or result in religion.--(See Kant, on Religion.) But we feel prompted to inquire whether, when we apprehend God and being, we are to will their well-being as an end, or for its own sake, or because it is right? If for its own sake, where then is the maxim, "Will the right for the sake of the right?" For if we are to will the good, not as an ultimate end, but for the sake of the right, then right is the end that is preferred to the highest well-being of God and of the universe. It is impossible that this should be religion. Indeed Kant himself admits that this is not religion.

But enough of this cold and loveless philosophy. As it exalts right above all that is called God, and subverts all the teachings of the Bible, it cannot be a light thing to be deluded by it. But it is remarkable and interesting to see Christian rightarians, without being sensible of their inconsistency, so often confound this philosophy with that which teaches that good-will to being constitutes virtue. Numerous examples of it occur everywhere in their writings, which demonstrate that rightarianism is with them only a theory that plays round the head but comes not near the heart."

Footnotes:

1. Mahan's Moral Philosophy.

LECTURE VI - FOUNDATION OF MORAL OBLIGATION

I now enter upon the discussion of the theory, that the goodness, or moral excellence of God is the foundation of moral obligation.

To this philosophy I reply,

1. That the reason of obligation, or that which imposes obligation, is identical with the end on which the intention ought to terminate. If, therefore, the goodness of God be the reason, or foundation of moral obligation, then the goodness of God is the ultimate end to be intended. But as this goodness consists in love or benevolence, it is impossible that it should be regarded or chosen, as an ultimate end; and to choose it were to choose the divine choice, to intend the divine intention as an ultimate end, instead of choosing what God chooses, and intending what he intends. Or if the goodness or moral excellence of God is to be regarded not as identical with, but as an attribute or moral quality of benevolence, then, upon the theory under consideration, a moral agent ought to choose a quality or attribute of the divine choice or intention as an ultimate end, instead of the end upon which the divine intention terminates. This is absurd.

2. It is impossible that virtue should be the foundation of moral obligation. Virtue consists in a compliance with moral obligation. But obligation must exist before it can be complied with. Now, upon this theory, obligation cannot exist until virtue exists as its foundation. Then this theory amounts to this: virtue is the foundation of moral obligation; therefore virtue must exist before moral obligation can exist. But as virtue consists in a conformity to moral obligation, moral obligation must exist before virtue can exist. Therefore neither moral obligation nor virtue, can ever by any possibility, exist. God's virtue must have existed prior to his obligation, as its foundation. But as virtue consists in compliance with moral obligation, and as obligation could not exist until virtue existed as its foundation; in other words, as obligation could not exist without the previous existence of virtue as its foundation, and as virtue could not exist without the previous existence of obligation, it follows, that neither God nor any other being could ever be virtuous, for the reason that he could never be the subject of moral obligation. Should it be said, that God's holiness is the foundation of our obligation to love him, I ask in what sense it can be so. What is the nature or form of that love, which his virtue lays us under an obligation to exercise? It cannot be a mere emotion of complacency, for emotions being involuntary states of mind and mere phenomena of the sensibility, are not strictly within the pale of legislation and morality. Is this love resolvable into benevolence or good-will? But why will good to God rather than evil? Why, surely, because good is valuable in itself. But if it is valuable in itself, this must be the fundamental reason for willing it as a possible good; and his virtue must be only a secondary reason or condition of the obligation to will his actual blessedness. But again, the foundation of moral

obligation must be the same in all worlds, and with all moral agents, for the simple reason that moral law is one and identical in all worlds. If God's virtue is not the foundation of moral obligation in him, which it cannot be, it cannot be the foundation of obligation in us, as moral law must require him to choose the same end that it requires us to choose. His virtue must be a secondary reason of his obligation to will his own actual blessedness, and the condition of our obligation to will his actual and highest blessedness, but cannot be the fundamental reason, that always being the intrinsic value of his well-being.

If this theory is true, disinterested benevolence is a sin. Undeniably benevolence consists in willing the highest well-being of God and the universe for its own sake, in devoting the soul anal all to this end. But this theory teaches us, either to will the moral excellence of God, for its own sake, or as an ultimate end, or to will his good and the good of the universe, not for its own sake, but because he is morally excellent. The benevolence theory regards blessedness as the end, and holiness or moral excellence only as a condition of the end. This theory regards moral excellence itself as the end. Does the moral excellence of God impose obligation to will his moral excellence for its own sake? If not, it cannot be a ground of obligation. Does his moral excellence impose obligation to will his highest good, and that of the universe, for its own sake? No, for this were a contradiction. For, be it remembered, no one thing can be a ground of obligation to choose any other thing, for its own sake. That which creates obligation to choose, by reason of its own nature, must itself be the identical object of choice; the obligation is to choose that object for its own sake.

If the divine moral excellence is the ground of obligation to choose, then this excellence must be the object of this choice, and disinterested benevolence is never right, but always wrong.

2. But for the sake of a somewhat systematic examination of this subject, I will--

(1.) Show what virtue, or moral excellence is.

(2.) That it cannot be the foundation of moral obligation.

(3.) Show what moral worth or good desert is.

(4.) That it cannot be the foundation of moral obligation.

(5.) Show what relation virtue, merit, and moral worth sustain to moral obligation.

(6.) Answer objections.

(1.) Show what virtue, or moral excellence is.

Virtue, or moral excellence, consists in conformity of will to moral law. It must either be identical with love or good-will, or it must be the moral attribute or element of good-will or benevolence.

(2.) It cannot be the foundation of moral obligation.

It is agreed, that the moral law requires love; and that, this term expresses all that it requires. It is also agreed that this love is good-will, or that it resolves itself into choice, or ultimate intention. It must, then, consist in the choice of an ultimate end. Or, in more common language, this love consists in the supreme devotion of heart and soul to God and to the highest good of being. But since virtue either consists in choice, or is an attribute of choice, or benevolence, it is impossible to will it as an ultimate end. For this would involve the absurdity of choosing choice, or intending intention, as an end, instead of choosing that as an end upon which virtuous choice terminates. Or, if virtue be regarded as the moral attribute of love or benevolence, to make it an ultimate end would be to make an attribute of choice an ultimate end, instead of that on which choice terminates, or ought to terminate. This is absurd.

(3.) Show what moral worth, or good desert is.

Moral worth, or good desert, is not identical with virtue, or obedience to moral law, but is an attribute of character, resulting from obedience. Virtue, or holiness, is a state of mind. It is an active and benevolent state of the will. Moral worth is not a state of mind, but is the result of a state of mind. We say that a man's obedience to moral law is valuable in such a sense that a holy being is worthy, or deserving of good, because of his virtue, or holiness. But this worthiness, this good desert, is not a state of mind, but, as I said, it is a result of benevolence. It is an attribute or quality of character, and not a state of mind.

(4.) Moral worth or good desert cannot be the foundation of moral obligation.

(a.) It is admitted, that good, or the intrinsically valuable to being, must be the foundation of moral obligation. The law of God requires the choice of an ultimate end. This end must be intrinsically valuable, for it is its intrinsic value that imposes obligation to will it. Nothing, then, can be the foundation of moral obligation but that which is a good, or intrinsically valuable in itself.

(b.) Ultimate good, or the intrinsically valuable, must belong to, and be inseparable from, sentient existences. A block of marble cannot enjoy, or be the subject of, good. That which is intrinsically good to moral agents, must consist in a state of mind. It must be something that is found within the field of consciousness. Nothing can be to them an intrinsic good, but that of which they can be conscious. By this it is not intended that everything of which they are conscious, is to them an ultimate good, or a good in any sense; but it is intended, that that cannot be to them an ultimate, or intrinsic good, of which they are not conscious. Ultimate good must consist in a conscious state of mind. Whatever conduces to the state of mind that is necessarily regarded by us as intrinsically good or valuable, is to us a relative good. But the state of mind alone is the ultimate good. From this it is plain, that moral worth, or good desert, cannot be the foundation of moral obligation, because it is not a state of mind, and cannot be an ultimate good. The consciousness of good desert, that is, the consciousness of affirming of ourselves good desert, is an ultimate good. Or, more strictly, the satisfaction which the mind experiences, upon occasion of affirming its good desert, is an ultimate good. But neither the conscious affirmation of good desert, nor the satisfaction occasioned by the affirmation, is identical with moral worth or good desert. Merit, moral worth, good desert, is the condition, or occasion, of the affirmation, and of the resulting conscious satisfaction, and is therefore a good, but it is not, and cannot be an ultimate, or intrinsic good. It is valuable; but not intrinsically valuable. Were it not that moral beings are so constituted, that it meets a demand of the intelligence, and therefore produces satisfaction in its contemplation, it would not be, and could not reasonably be regarded as a good in any sense. But since it meets a demand of the intelligence, it is a relative good, and results in ultimate good.

(5.) Show what relation moral excellence, worth, merit, desert, sustain to moral obligation.

(a.) We have seen, that neither of them can be the foundation of moral obligation; that neither of them has in it the element of the intrinsic, or ultimate good, or valuable; and that, therefore, a moral agent can never be under obligation to will or choose them as an ultimate end.

(b.) Worth, merit, good desert, cannot be a distinct ground, or foundation, of moral obligation, in such a sense as to impose obligation, irrespective of the intrinsic value of good. All obligation must respect, strictly, the choice of an object for its own sake, with the necessary conditions and means. The intrinsic value of the end is the foundation of the obligation to choose both it and the necessary conditions and means of securing it. But for the intrinsic value of the end there could be no obligation to will the conditions and means. Whenever a thing is seen to be a necessary condition or means of securing an intrinsically valuable end, this perceived relation is the condition of our obligation to will it. The obligation is, and must be, founded in the intrinsic value of the end, and conditionated upon the perceived relation of the object to the end. The intelligence of every moral agent, from its nature and laws, affirms, that the ultimate good and blessedness of moral beings is, and ought to be, conditionated upon their holiness and good desert. This being a demand of reason, reason can never affirm moral obligation to will the actual blessedness of moral agents, but upon condition of their virtue, and consequent good desert, or merit. The intelligence affirms that it is fit, suitable, proper, that virtue, good desert, merit, holiness, should be rewarded with blessedness. Blessedness is a good in itself, and ought to be willed for that reason, and moral agents are under obligation to will that all beings capable of good may be worthy to enjoy, and may, therefore, actually enjoy blessedness. But they are not under obligation to will that every moral being should actually enjoy blessedness, but upon condition of holiness and good desert. The relation that holiness, merit, good desert, etc., sustain to moral obligation, is this: they supply the condition of the obligation to will the actual blessedness of the being or beings who are holy. The obligation must be founded in the intrinsic value of the good we are to will to them. For it is absurd to say, that we are, or can be, under obligation to will good to them for its own sake, or as an ultimate end, and yet that the obligation should not be founded in the intrinsic value of the good. Were it not for the intrinsic value of their good, we should no sooner affirm obligation to will good to them than evil. The good or blessedness is the thing, or end, we are under obligation to will. But obligation to will an ultimate end cannot possibly be founded in anything else than the intrinsic value of the end. Suppose it should be said, that in the case of merit, or good desert, the obligation is founded in merit, and only conditioned on the intrinsic value of the good I am to will. This would be to make desert the end willed, and good only the condition, or means. This were absurd.

(c.) But again, to make merit the ground of the obligation, and the good willed only a condition, amounts to this: I perceive merit, whereupon I affirm my obligation to will--what? Not good to the deserving because of its value to him, nor from any disposition to see him enjoy blessedness for its own sake, but because of his merit. But what does he merit? Why, good, or blessedness. It is good, or blessedness, that I am to will to him, and this is the end I am bound to will; that is, I am to will his good, or blessedness, for its own intrinsic value. The obligation, then, must be founded in the intrinsic value of the end, that is, his well-being, or blessedness, and only conditioned upon merit.

(6.) I am to answer objections.

(a.) It is objected, that, if virtue is meritorious, if it merits, deserves anything, this implies corresponding obligation, and that merit, or desert, must impose, or be the ground of, the obligation to give that which is merited. But this objection is either a mere begging of the question, or it is sheer logomachy. It assumes that the words, desert and merit, mean what they cannot mean. Let the objector remember, that he holds that obligation respects ultimate intention. That ultimate intention must find the grounds of its obligation exclusively in its object. Now, if desert or merit is a ground of obligation, then merit or desert must be the object of the intention. Desert, merit, must be willed for its own sake. But is this the thing that is deserved, merited? Does a meritorious being deserve that his merit or desert should be willed for its own sake? Indeed, is this what he deserves? We understandingly speak of good desert, the desert of good and of evil; can a being deserve that his desert shall be chosen for its own sake? If not, then it is impossible that desert or merit should be a ground of obligation; for be it remembered, that whatever is a ground of obligation ought to be chosen for its own sake. But if good desert deserves good, it is self-evident that the intrinsic value of the good is the ground, and merit only a condition, of obligation to will the actual and particular enjoyment of the good by the meritorious individual. Thus merit changes merely the form of obligation. If an individual is wicked, I ought to will his good as valuable in itself, and that he should comply with the necessary conditions of happiness, and thereupon actually enjoy happiness. If he is virtuous, I am to will his good still for its intrinsic value; and, since he has complied with the conditions of enjoyment, that he actually enjoy happiness. In both cases, I am bound to will his good, and for the same fundamental reason, namely, its intrinsic value. Neither the fact nor the ground of obligation to will his good is changed by his virtue; the form only of the obligation is changed. I may be under obligation to will evil to a particular being, but in this case I am not bound to will the evil for its own sake, and therefore, not as an end or ultimate. I ought sometimes to will the punishment of the guilty, not for its own sake, but for the sake of the public good; and the intrinsic value of the good to be promoted is the ground of the obligation, and guilt or demerit is only a condition of the obligation in that form. If merit or desert be a ground of obligation, then merit or desert ought to be chosen for its own sake. It would follow from this, that ill desert ought to be chosen for its own sake, as well as good desert. But who will pretend that ill desert ought to be willed for its own sake? But if this is not, cannot be so, then it follows, that desert is not a ground of obligation, and that is not an object of ultimate choice, or of choice at all, only as a means to an end.

(b.) It is asserted, in support of the theory we are examining, that the Bible represents the goodness of God as a reason for loving him, or as a foundation of the obligation to love him.

To this I answer, the Bible may assign, and does assign the goodness of God as a reason for loving him, but it does not follow, that it affirms, or assumes, that this reason is the foundation, or a foundation of the obligation. The inquiry is, in what sense does the Bible assign the goodness of God as a reason for loving him? Is it that the goodness of God is the foundation of the obligation, or only a condition of the obligation to will his actual blessedness in particular? Is his goodness a distinct ground of obligation to love him? But what is this love that his goodness lays us under an obligation exercise to him? It is agreed, that it cannot be an emotion, that it must consist in willing something to him. It is said by some, that the obligation is to treat him as worthy. But I ask, worthy of what? Is he worthy of anything? If so, what is it? For this is the thing that I ought to will to him. Is he merely worthy that I should will his worthiness for its own sake? This must be, if his worthiness is the ground of obligation; for that which is the ground of obligation to choose must be the object of choice. Why, he is worthy of blessing, and honor, and praise. But these must all be embraced in the single word, love. The law has forever decided the point, that our whole duty to God is expressed by this one term. It has been common to make assertions upon the subject, that involve a contradiction of the Bible. The law of God, as revealed in the two precepts, "Thou shalt love the Lord thy God with all thy heart, and thy neighbor as thyself," covers the whole ground of moral obligation. It is expressly and repeatedly taught in the Bible, that love to God and our neighbor is the fulfilling of the law. It is, and must be admitted, that this love consists in willing something to God and our neighbor. What, then, is to be willed to them? The command is, "Thou shalt love thy neighbor as thyself." This says nothing about the character of my neighbor. It is the value of his interests, of his well-being, that the law requires me to regard. It does not require me to love my righteous neighbor merely, nor to love my righteous neighbor better than I do my wicked neighbor. It is my neighbor that I am to love. That is, I am to will his well-being, or his good, with the conditions and means thereof, according to its value. If the law contemplated the virtue of any being as a distinct ground of obligation, it could not read as it does. It must, in that case, have read as follows: If thou art righteous, and thy neighbor is as righteous as thou art, thou shalt love him as thyself. But if he is righteous and thou art not, thou shalt love him and not thyself. If thou art righteous, and he is not, thou shalt love thyself, and not thy neighbor." How far would this be from the gloss of the Jewish rabbies so fully rebuked by Christ, namely, "Ye have heard that it hath been said by them of old time, Thou shalt love thy neighbor, and hate thine enemy. But I say unto you, Love your enemies; bless them that curse you; do good to them that hate you; and pray for them that despitefully use and persecute you. For if ye love them that love you, what thank have ye? Do not even the publicans the same?" The fact is, the law knows but one ground of moral obligation. It requires us to love God and our neighbor. This love is good will. What else ought we to will, or can we possibly will to God and our neighbor, but their highest good, or well-being, with all the conditions and means thereof? This is all that can be of any value to them, and all that we can or ought to, will to them under any circumstances whatever. When we have willed this to them, we have done our whole duty to them. "Love is the fulfilling of the law." We owe them nothing more, absolutely. They can have nothing more. But this the law requires us to will to God and our neighbor, on account of the intrinsic value of their good, whatever their character may be; that is, this is to be willed to God and our neighbor, as a possible good, whether they are holy or unholy, simply because of its intrinsic value.

But while the law requires that this should be willed to all, as a possible and intrinsic good, irrespective of character; it cannot, and does not require us to will that God, or any moral agent in particular, shall be actually blessed, but upon condition that he be holy. Our obligation to the unholy, is to will that they might be holy, and perfectly blessed. Our obligation to the holy, is to will that they be perfectly blessed. As has been said, virtue only modifies the form, but does not change the ground of obligation. The Bible represents love to enemies as one of the highest forms of virtue: "God commendeth his love toward us, in that, while we were yet sinners, Christ died for us." But if love to enemies be a high and a valuable form of virtue, it must be only because the true spirit of the law requires the same love to them as to others, and because of the strong inducements not to love them. Who does not regard the virtue of the atonement as being as great as if it had been made for the friends, instead of the enemies of God? And suppose God were supremely selfish and unreasonably our enemy, who would not regard good-will exercised toward him as being as praiseworthy as it now is. Now if he were unjustly our enemy, would not a hearty good-will to him in such a case be a striking and valuable instance of virtue? In such a case we could not, might not, will his actual blessedness, but we might and should be under infinite obligation to will that he might become holy, and thereupon be perfectly blessed. We should be under obligation to will his good in such a sense, that should he become holy, we should will his actual blessedness, without any change in our ultimate choice or intention, and without any change in us that would imply an increase of virtue.

So of our neighbor: we are bound to will his good, even if he is wicked, in such a sense as to need no new intention or ultimate choice, to will his actual blessedness, should he become holy. We may be as holy in loving a sinner, and in seeking his salvation while he is a sinner, as in willing his good after he is converted and becomes a saint. God was as virtuous in loving the world, and seeking to save it while in sin, as he is in loving those in it who are holy. The fact is, if we are truly benevolent, and will the highest well-being of all, with the conditions and means of their blessedness, it follows of course, and of necessity, that when one becomes holy we shall love him with the love of complacency; that we shall, of course, will his actual blessedness, seeing that he has fulfilled the necessary conditions, and rendered himself worthy of blessedness. It implies no increase of virtue in God, when a sinner repents, to exercise complacency toward him. Complacency, as a state of will or heart, is only benevolence modified by the consideration or relation of right character in the object of it. God, prophets, apostles, martyrs, and saints, in all ages, are as virtuous in their self-denying and untiring labors to save the wicked, as they are in their complacent love to the saints.

This is the universal doctrine of the Bible. It is in exact accordance with the spirit and letter of the law. "Thou shalt love thy neighbor as thyself;" that is, whatever his character may be. This is the doctrine of reason, and accords with the convictions of all men. But if this is so, it follows that virtue is not a distinct ground of moral obligation, but only modifies the form of obligation. We are under obligation to will the actual blessedness of a moral being, upon condition of his holiness. We ought to will good or blessedness for its own value, irrespective of character; but we ought to will the enjoyment of it, by an individual, in particular, only upon condition of his holiness. Its intrinsic value is the foundation of the obligation, and his holiness changes not the fact, but form, of the obligation, and is the condition of the obligation to will his actual enjoyment of perfect blessedness in particular. When, therefore, the Bible calls on us to love God for his goodness, it does not and cannot mean to assign the fundamental reason, or foundation of the obligation to will his good; for it were absurd to suppose, that his good is to be willed, not for its intrinsic value, but because he is good. Were it not for its intrinsic value, we should as soon affirm our obligation to will evil as good to him. The Bible assumes the first truths of reason. It is a first truth of reason, that God's well-being is of infinite value, and ought to be willed as a possible good whatever his character may be; and that it ought to be willed as an actual reality upon condition of his holiness. Now the Bible does just as in this case might be expected. It asserts his actual and infinite holiness, and calls on us to love him, or to will his good, for that reason. But this is not asserting nor implying that his holiness is the foundation of the obligation to will his good in any such sense as that we should not be under obligation to will it with all our heart, and soul, and mind, and strength, as a possible good, whether he were holy or not. It is plain that the law contemplates only the intrinsic value of the end to be willed. It would require us to will the well-being of God with all our heart, etc., or as the supreme good, whatever his character might be. Were not this so, it could not be moral law. His interest would be the supreme and the infinite good, in the sense of the intrinsically and infinitely valuable, and we should, for that reason, be under infinite obligation to will that it might be, whether he were holy or sinful, and upon condition of his holiness, to will the actual existence of his perfect and infinite blessedness. Upon our coming to the knowledge of his holiness, the obligation is instantly imposed, not merely to will his highest well-being as a possible, but as an actually existing, good.

Again, it is impossible that goodness, virtue, good desert, merit, should be a distinct ground or foundation of moral obligation, in such a sense as to impose or properly to increase obligation. It has been shown that neither of these can be an ultimate good and impose obligation to choose itself as an ultimate end, or for its intrinsic value.

But if goodness or merit can impose moral obligation to will, it must be an obligation to will itself as an ultimate end. But this we have seen cannot be; therefore these things cannot be a distinct ground or foundation of moral obligation.

But again, the law does not make virtue, good desert, or merit, the ground of obligation, and require us to love them and to will them as an ultimate end; but to love God and our neighbor as an ultimate good. It does, no doubt, require us to will God's goodness, good desert, worthiness, merit, as a condition and means of his highest well-being, and of the well-being of the universe; but it is absurd to say that it requires us to will either of these things as an ultimate end, instead of his perfect blessedness, to which these sustain only the relation of a condition. Let it be distinctly understood that nothing can impose moral obligation but that which is an ultimate and an intrinsic good; for if it impose obligation, it must be an obligation to choose itself for what it is, in and of itself. All obligation must respect the choice either of an end or of means. Obligation to choose means is founded in the value of the end. Whatever, then, imposes obligation must be an ultimate end. It must possess that, in and of itself, that is worthy or deserving of choice as an intrinsic and ultimate good. This we have seen, virtue, merit, etc. cannot be; therefore they cannot be a foundation of moral obligation. But it is said they can increase obligation to love God and holy beings. But we are under infinite obligation to love God and to will his good with all our power, because of the intrinsic value of his well-being, whether he is holy or sinful. Upon condition that he is holy, we are under obligation to will his actual blessedness, but certainly we are under obligation to will it with no more than all our heart, and soul, and mind, and strength. But this we are required to do because of the intrinsic value of his blessedness, whatever his character might be. The fact is, we can do no more, and can be under obligation to do no more, than to will his good with all our power, and this we are bound to do for its own sake; and no more than this can we be under obligation to do, for any reason whatever. Our obligation is to will his good with all our strength, by virtue of its infinite value, and it cannot be increased by any other consideration than our increased knowledge of its value, which increases our ability.

(c.) But it is said that favors received impose obligation to exercise gratitude; that the relation of benefactor itself imposes obligation to treat the benefactor according to this relation.

Answer: I suppose this objection contemplates this relation as a virtuous relation, that is, that the benefactor is truly virtuous and not selfish in his benefaction. If not, then the relation cannot at all modify obligation.

If the benefactor has in the benefaction obeyed the law of love, if he has done his duty in sustaining this relation, I am under obligation to exercise gratitude toward him. But what is gratitude? It is not a mere emotion or feeling; for this is a phenomenon of the sensibility, and, strictly speaking, without the pale both of legislation and morality. Gratitude, when spoken of as a virtue and as that of which moral obligation can be affirmed, must be an act of will. An obligation to gratitude must be an obligation to will something to the benefactor. But what am I under obligation to will to a benefactor, but his actual highest well-being? If it be God, I am under obligation to will his actual and infinite blessedness with all my heart and with all my soul. If it be my neighbor, I am bound to love him as myself, that is, to will his actual well-being as I do my own. What else can either God or man possess or enjoy, and what else can I be under obligation to will to them? I answer, nothing else. To the law and to the testimony; if any philosophy agree not herewith, it is because there is no light in it. The virtuous relation of benefactor modifies obligation, just as any other and every other form of virtue does, and in no other way. Whenever we perceive virtue in any being, this supplies the condition upon which we are bound to will his actual highest well-being. He has done his duty. He has complied with obligation in the relation he sustains. He is truthful, upright, benevolent, just, merciful, no matter what the particular form may be in which the individual presents to me the evidence of his holy character. It is all precisely the same so far as my obligation extends. I any, independently of my knowledge of his character, under obligation to will his highest well-being for its own sake. That is, to will that he may fulfil all the conditions, and thereupon enjoy perfect blessedness. But I am not under obligation to will his actual enjoyment of blessedness until I have evidence of his virtue. This evidence, however I obtain it, by whatever manifestations of virtue in him or by whatever means, supplies the condition upon which I am under obligation to will his actual enjoyment or highest well-being. This is my whole obligation. It is all he can have, and all I can will to him. All objections of this kind, and indeed all possible objections to the true theory, and in support of the one I am examining, are founded in an erroneous view of the subject of moral obligation, or in a false and anti-scriptural philosophy that contradicts the law of God, and sets up another rule of moral obligation.

Again, if gratitude is a moral act, according to this objector, it is an ultimate intention, and as such must terminate on its object, and find its reasons or ground of obligation exclusively in its object. If this is so, then if the relation of benefactor is the ground of obligation to exercise gratitude, gratitude must consist in willing this relation for its own sake, and not at all in willing anything to the benefactor. This is absurd. It is certain that gratitude must consist in willing good to the benefactor, and not in willing the relation for its own sake, and that the ground of the obligation must be the intrinsic value of the good, and the relation only a condition of the obligation in the particular form of willing his enjoyment of good in particular. It is now said, in reply to this, that the "inquiry is not, what is gratitude? but, why ought we to exercise it?" But the inquiry is after the ground of the obligation; this, it is agreed, must be intrinsic in its object; and is it impertinent to inquire what the object is? Who can tell what is the ground of the obligation to exercise gratitude until he knows what the object of gratitude is, and consequently what gratitude is? The objector affirms that the relation of benefactor is a ground of obligation to put forth ultimate choice. Of course, according to him, and in fact, if this relation is the ground of the obligation, it is, and must be, the object chosen for its own sake. To exercise gratitude to a benefactor, then, according to this teaching is, not to will any good to him, nor to myself, nor to any being in existence, but simply to will the relation of benefactor for its own sake. Not for his sake, as a good to him. Not for my sake as a good to me, but for its own sake. Is not this a sublime philosophy?

(d.) But it is also insisted that when men attempt to assign a reason why they are under moral obligation of any kind, as to love God, they all agree in this, in assigning the divine moral excellence as the reason of that obligation.

I answer:--The only reason why any man supposes himself to assign the goodness of God as the foundation of the obligation to will good to him is, that he loosely confounds the conditions of the obligation to will his actual blessedness, with the foundation of the obligation to will it for its own sake, or as a possible good. Were it not for the known intrinsic value of God's highest well-being, we should as soon affirm our obligation to will evil as good to him, as has been said. But if the divine moral excellence were the foundation of moral obligation, if God were not holy and good, moral obligation could not exist in any case.

That every moral agent ought to will the highest well-being of God and of all the universe for its own sake, as a possible good, whatever their characters may be, is a truth of reason. Reason assigns and can assign no other reason for willing their good as an ultimate end than its intrinsic value; and to assign any other reason as imposing obligation to will it as an end, or for its own sake, were absurd and self-contradictory. Obligation to will it as an end and for its own sake, implies the obligation to will its actual existence in all cases, and to all persons, when the indispensable conditions are fulfilled. These conditions are seen to be fulfilled in God, and therefore upon this condition reason affirms obligation to will his actual and highest blessedness for its own sake, the intrinsic value being the fundamental reason of the obligation to will it as an end, and the divine goodness the condition of the obligation to will his highest blessedness in particular. Suppose that I existed and had the idea of blessedness and its intrinsic value duly developed, together with an idea of all the necessary conditions of it; but that I did not know that any other being than myself existed, and yet I knew their existence and blessedness possible; in this case I should be under obligation to will or wish that beings might exist and be blessed. Now suppose that I complied with this obligation, my virtue is just as real and as great as if I knew their existence, and willed their actual blessedness, provided my idea of its intrinsic value were as clear and just as if I knew their existence. And now suppose I came to the knowledge of the actual existence and holiness of all holy beings, I should make no new ultimate choice in willing their actual blessedness. This I should do of course, and, remaining benevolent, of necessity; and if this knowledge did not give me a higher idea of the value of that which I before willed for its own sake, the willing of the real existence of their blessedness would not make me a whit more virtuous than when I willed it as a possible good, without knowing that the conditions of its actual existence would ever, in any case, be fulfilled.

The Bible reads just as it might be expected to read, and just as we should speak in common life. It being a truth of reason that the well-being of God is of infinite value, and therefore ought to be willed for its own sake, it also being a truth that virtue is an indispensable condition of fulfilling the demands of his own reason and conscience, and of course of his actual blessedness, and of course also a condition of the obligation to will it, we might expect the Bible to exhort and require us to love God or will his actual blessedness, and mention his virtue as the reason or fulfilled condition of the obligation, rather than the intrinsic value of his blessedness as the foundation of the obligation. The foundation of the obligation, being a truth of reason, needs not to be a matter of revelation. Nor needs the fact that virtue is the condition of his blessedness, nor the fact that we are under no obligation to will his actual blessedness but upon condition of his holiness. But that in him this condition is fulfilled, needs to be impressed upon us, and therefore the Bible announces it as a reason or condition of the obligation to love him, that is, to will his actual blessedness.

God's moral excellence is naturally, and rightly, assigned by us as a condition, not the ground of obligation to receive his revealed will as our law. Did we not assume the rectitude of the divine will, we could not affirm our obligation to receive it as a rule of duty. This assumption is a condition of the obligation, and is naturally thought of when obligation to obey God is affirmed. But the intrinsic value and importance of the interest he requires us to seek, is the ground of the obligation.

(e.) Again: it is asserted that when men would awaken a sense of moral obligation they universally contemplate the moral excellence of God as constituting the reason of their obligation, and if this contemplation does not awaken their sense of obligation nothing else can or will.

I answer: -- The only possible reason why men ever do or can take this course, is that they loosely consider religion to consist in feelings of complacency in God, and are endeavoring to awaken these complacent emotions. If they conceive of religion as consisting in these emotions, they will of course conceive themselves to be under obligation to exercise them, and to be sure they take the only possible course to awaken both these and a sense of obligation to exercise them. But they are mistaken both in regard to their obligation and the nature of religion. Did they conceive of religion as consisting in good-will, or in willing the highest well-being of God and of the universe for its own sake, would they, could they, resort to the process in question, that is, the contemplation of the divine moral excellence, as the only reason for willing good to him, instead of considering the infinite value of those interests to the realization of which they ought to consecrate themselves?

If men often do resort to the process in question, it is because they love to feel and have a self-righteous satisfaction in feelings of complacency in God, and take more pains to awaken these feelings than to quicken and enlarge their benevolence. A purely selfish being may be greatly affected by the great goodness and kindness of God to him. I know a man who is a very niggard so far as all benevolent giving and doing for God and the world are concerned, who, I fear, resorts to the very process in question, and is often much affected with the goodness of God. He can bluster and denounce. all who do not feel as he does. But ask him for a dollar to forward any benevolent enterprise, and he will evade your request, and ask you how you feel, whether you are engaged in religion, etc.

But it may well be asked, why does the Bible and why do we, so often present the character of God and of Christ as a means of awakening a sense of moral obligation and of inducing virtue? Answer:--

It is to lead men to contemplate the infinite value of those interests which we ought to will. Presenting the example of God and of Christ, is the highest moral means that can be used. God's example and man's example is the most impressive and efficient way in which he can declare his views, and hold forth to public gaze the infinite value of those interests upon which all hearts ought to be set. For example, nothing can set the infinite value of the soul in a stronger light than the example of God the Father, Son, and Holy Ghost has done.

Nothing can beget a higher sense of obligation to will the glory of the Father and the salvation of souls, than the example of Christ. His example is his loudest preaching, his clearest, most impressive exhibition, not merely of his own goodness, but of the intrinsic and infinite value of the interest he sought and which we ought to seek. It is the love, the care, the self-denial, and the example of God, in his efforts to secure the great ends of benevolence, that hold those interests forth in the strongest light, and thus beget a sense of obligation to seek the same end. But let it be observed, it is not a contemplation of the goodness of God that awakens this sense of obligation, but the contemplation of the value of those interests which he seeks, in the light of his pains-taking and example; this quickens and gives efficiency to the sense of obligation to will what he wills. Suppose, for example, that I manifest the greatest concern and zeal for the salvation of souls; it would not be the contemplation of my goodness that would quicken in a bystander a sense of obligation to save souls, but my zeal, and life, and spirit would have the strongest tendency to arouse in him a sense of the infinite and intrinsic value of the soul, and thus quicken a sense of obligation. Should I behold multitudes rushing to extinguish a flaming house, it would not be a contemplation of their goodness, but the contemplation of the interests at stake, to the consideration of which their zeal would lead me, that would quicken a sense of obligation in me to hasten to lend my aid.

Revelation is concerned to impress the fact that God is holy, and of course calls on us, in view of his holiness, to love and worship him. But in doing this, it does not, cannot mean that his holiness is the foundation of the obligation to will his good as an ultimate end.

Our obligation, when viewed apart from his character, is to will or wish that God might fulfil all the conditions of perfect blessedness, and upon that condition, that he might actually enjoy perfect and infinite satisfaction. But seeing that he meets the demands of his own intelligence and the intelligence of the universe, and that he voluntarily fulfils all the necessary conditions of his highest well-being, our obligation is to will his actual and most perfect and eternal blessedness.

I am obliged to repeat much to follow the objector, because all his objections resolve themselves into one, and require to be answered much in the same way.

LECTURE VII - FOUNDATION OF MORAL OBLIGATION

I now come to consider the philosophy which teaches that moral order is the foundation of moral obligation.

But what is moral order? The advocates of this theory define it to be identical with the fit, proper, suitable. It is, then, according to them, synonymous with the right. Moral order must be, in their view, either identical with law or with virtue. It must be either an idea of the fit, the right, the proper, the suitable, which is the same as objective right; or it must consist in conformity of the will to this idea or law, which is virtue. It has been repeatedly shown that right, whether objective or subjective, cannot by any possibility be the end at which a moral agent ought to aim, and to which he ought to consecrate himself. If moral order be not synonymous with right in one of these senses, I do not know what it is; and all that I can say is, that if it be not identical with the highest well-being of God and of the universe, it cannot be the end at which moral agents ought to aim, and cannot be the foundation of moral obligation. But if by moral order, as the phraseology of some would seem to indicate, be meant that state of the universe in which all law is universally obeyed, and, as a consequence, a state of universal well-being, this theory is only another name for the true one. It is the same as willing the highest well-being of the universe, with the conditions and means thereof.

Or if it be meant, as other phraseology would seem to indicate, that moral order is a state of things in which either all law is obeyed, or in which the disobedient are punished for the sake of promoting the public good;--if this be what is meant by moral order, it is only another name for the true theory. Willing moral order, is only willing the highest good of the universe for its own sake, with the condition and means thereof.

But if by moral order be meant the fit, suitable, in the sense of law, physical or moral, it is absurd to represent moral order as the foundation of moral obligation. If moral order is the ground of obligation, it is identical with the object of ultimate choice. Does God require us to love moral order for its own sake? Is this identical with loving God and our neighbor? "Thou shalt will moral order with all thy heart, and with all thy soul!" Is this the meaning of the moral law? If this theory is right, benevolence is sin. It is not living to the right end.

Again it is maintained that the nature and relations of moral beings are the true foundation of moral obligation.

The advocates of this theory confound the conditions of moral obligation with the foundation of obligation. The nature and relations of moral agents to each other, and to the universe, are conditions of their obligation to will the good of being, but not the foundation of the obligation. What! the nature and relations of moral beings the foundation of their obligation to choose an ultimate end! Then this end must be their nature and relations. This is absurd.

Their nature and relations being what they are, their highest well-being is known to them to be of infinite and intrinsic value. But it is and must be the intrinsic value of the end, and not their nature and relations, that imposes obligation to will the highest good of the universe as an ultimate end.

If their nature and relations be the ground of obligation, then their nature and relations are the great object of ultimate choice, and should be willed for their own sakes, and not for the sake of any good resulting from their nature and relations. For, be it remembered, the ground of obligation to put forth ultimate choice must be identical with the object of this choice, which object imposes obligation by virtue of its own nature.

The natures and relations of moral beings are a condition of obligation to fulfil to each other certain duties. For example, the relation of parent and child is a condition of obligation to endeavor to promote each other's particular well-being, to govern and provide for, on the part of the parent, and to obey, etc., on the part of the child. But the intrinsic value of the good to be sought by both parent and child must be the ground, and their relation only the condition, of those particular forms of obligation. So in every possible case. Relations can never be a ground of obligation to choose, unless the relations be the object of the choice. The various duties of life are executive and not ultimate acts. Obligation to perform them is founded in the intrinsic nature of the good resulting from their performance. The various relations of life are only conditions of obligation to promote particular forms of good, and the good of particular individuals.

Writers upon this subject are often falling into the mistake of confounding the conditions with the foundation of moral obligation. Moral agency is a condition, but not the foundation of obligation. Light, or the knowledge of the intrinsically valuable to being, is a condition, but not the foundation of moral obligation. The intrinsically valuable is the foundation of the obligation; and light, or the perception of the intrinsically valuable, is only a condition of the obligation. So the nature and relations of moral beings are a condition of their obligation to will each other's good, and so is light, or a knowledge of the intrinsic value of their blessedness; but the intrinsic value is alone the foundation of the obligation. It is, therefore, a great mistake to affirm "that the known nature and relations of moral agents are the true foundation of moral obligation."

The next theory that demands attention is that which teaches that moral obligation is founded in the idea of duty.

According to this philosophy, the end at which a moral agent ought to aim, is duty. He must in all things "aim at doing his duty." Or, in other words, he must always have respect to his obligation, and aim at discharging it.

It is plain that this theory is only another form of stating the rightarian theory. By aiming, intending, to do duty, we must understand the advocates of this theory to mean the adoption of a resolution or maxim, by which to regulate their lives--the formation of a resolve to obey God--to serve God--to do at all times what appears to be right--to meet the demands of conscience--to obey the law--to discharge obligation, etc. I have expressed the thing intended in all these ways because it is common to hear this theory expressed in all these terms, and in others like them. Especially in giving instruction to inquiring sinners, nothing is more common than for those who profess to be spiritual guides to assume the truth of this philosophy, and give instructions accordingly.

These philosophers, or theologians, will say to sinners: Make up your mind to serve the Lord; resolve to do your whole duty, and do it at all times; resolve to obey God in all things--to keep all his commandments; resolve to deny yourselves--to forsake all sin--to love the Lord with all your heart and your neighbor as yourself. They often represent regeneration as consisting in this resolution or purpose.

Such-like phraseology, which is very common and almost universal among rightarian philosophers, demonstrates that they regard virtue or obedience to God as consisting in the adoption of a maxim of life. With them, duty is the great idea to be realized. All these modes of expression mean the same thing, and amount to just Kant's morality, which he admits does not necessarily imply religion, namely: "act upon a maxim at all times fit for law universal," and to Cousin's, which is the same thing, namely, "will the right for the sake of the right." Now I cannot but regard this philosophy on the one hand, and utilitarianism on the other, as equally wide from the truth, and as lying at the foundation of much of the spurious religion with which the church and the world are cursed. Utilitarianism begets one type of selfishness, which it calls religion, and this philosophy begets another, in some respects more specious, but not a whit the less selfish, God-dishonoring and soul-destroying. The nearest that this philosophy can be said to approach either to true morality or religion, is, that if the one who forms the resolution understood himself he would resolve to become truly moral instead of really becoming so. But this is in fact an absurdity and an impossibility, and the resolution-maker does not understand what he is about, when he supposes himself to be forming or cherishing a resolution to do his duty. Observe, he intends to do his duty. But to do his duty is to form and cherish an ultimate intention. To intend to do his duty is merely to intend to intend. But this is not doing his duty, as will be shown. He intends to serve God, but this is not serving God, as will also be shown. Whatever he intends, he is neither truly moral nor religious, until he really intends the same end that God does; and this is not to do his duty, nor to do right, nor to comply with obligation, nor to keep a conscience void of offence, nor to deny himself, nor any such like things. God aims at, and intends, the highest well-being of himself and the universe, as an ultimate end, and this is doing his duty. It is not resolving or intending to do his duty, but is doing it. It is not resolving to do right for the sake of the right, but it is doing right. It is not resolving to serve himself and the universe, but is actually rendering that service. It is not resolving to obey the moral law, but is actually obeying it. It is not resolving to love, but actually loving his neighbor as himself. It is not, in other words, resolving to be benevolent, but is being so. It is not resolving to deny self, but is actually denying self.

A man may resolve to serve God without any just idea of what it is to serve him. If he had the idea of what the law of God requires him to choose, clearly before his mind--if he perceived that to serve God, was nothing less than to consecrate himself to the same end to which God consecrates himself, to love God with all his heart and his neighbor as himself, that is, to will or choose the highest well-being of God and of the universe, as an ultimate end--to devote all his being, substance, time, and influence to this end;--I say, if this idea were clearly before his mind, he would not talk of resolving to consecrate himself to God--resolving to do his duty, to do right, to serve God, to keep a conscience void of offence, and such like things. He would see that such resolutions were totally absurd and a mere evasion of the claims of God. It has been repeatedly shown, that all virtue resolves itself into the intending of an ultimate end, or of the highest well-being of God and the universe. This is true morality, and nothing else is. This is identical with that love to God and man which the law of God requires. This then is duty. This is serving God. This is keeping a conscience void of offence. This is right, and nothing else is. But to intend or resolve to do this is only to intend to intend, instead of at once intending what God requires. It is resolving to love God and his neighbor, instead of really loving him; choosing to choose the highest well-being of God and of the universe, instead of really choosing it.

It is one thing for a man who actually loves God with all his heart and his neighbor as himself, to resolve to regulate all his outward life by the law of God, and a totally different thing to intend to love God or to intend his highest glory and well-being. Resolutions may respect outward action, but it is totally absurd to intend or resolve to form an ultimate intention. But be it remembered, that morality and religion do not belong to outward action, but to ultimate intentions. It is amazing and afflicting to witness the alarming extent to which a spurious philosophy has corrupted and is corrupting the church of God. Kant and Cousin and Coleridge have adopted a phraseology, and manifestly have conceived in idea a philosophy subversive of all true love to God and man, and teach a religion of maxims and resolutions instead of a religion of love. It is a philosophy, as we shall see in a future lecture, which teaches that the moral law or law of right, is entirely distinct from and may be opposite to the law of benevolence or love. The fact is, this philosophy conceives of duty and right as belonging to mere outward action. This must be, for it cannot be confused enough to talk of resolving or intending to form an ultimate intention. Let but the truth of this philosophy be assumed, in giving instructions to the anxious sinner, and it will immediately dry off his tears, and in all probability lead him to settle down in a religion of resolutions instead of a religion of love. Indeed this philosophy will immediately dry off, (if I may be allowed the expression,) the most genuine and powerful revival of religion, and run it down into a mere revival of a heartless, Christless, loveless philosophy. It is much easier to persuade anxious sinners to resolve to do their duty, to resolve to love God, than it is to persuade them really to do their duty, and really to love God with all their heart and with all their soul, and their neighbor as themselves.

We now come to the consideration of that philosophy which teaches the complexity of the foundation of moral obligation.

This theory maintains that there are several distinct grounds of moral obligation; that the highest good of being is only one of the grounds of moral obligation, while right, moral order, the nature and relations of moral agents, merit and demerit, truth, duty, and many such like things, are distinct grounds of moral obligation, but that each one of them can by itself impose moral obligation. The advocates of this theory, perceiving its inconsistency with the doctrine that moral obligation respects the ultimate choice or intention only, seem disposed to relinquish the position that obligation respects strictly only the choice of an ultimate end, and to maintain that moral obligation respects the ultimate action of the will. By ultimate action of the will they mean, if I understand them, the will's treatment of everything according to its intrinsic nature and character; that is treating every thing, or taking that attitude in respect to every thing known to the mind, that is exactly suited to what it is in and of itself. For example, right ought to be regarded and treated by the will as right because it is right. Truth ought to be regarded and treated as truth for its own sake, virtue as virtue, merit as merit, demerit as demerit, the useful as useful, the beautiful as beautiful, the good or valuable as valuable, each for its own sake; that in each case the action of the will is ultimate, in the sense that its action terminates on these objects as ultimates; in other words, that all those actions of the will are ultimate that treat things according to their nature and character, or according to what they are in and of themselves.

Now in respect to this theory I would inquire:--What is intended by the will's treating a thing, or taking that attitude in respect to it that is suited to its nature and character? Are there any other actions of will than volitions, choice, preference, intention? Are not all the actions of the will comprehended in these? If there are any other actions than these, are they intelligent actions? If so, what are those actions of will that consist neither in the choice of ends nor means, nor in volitions or efforts to secure an end? Can there be intelligent acts of will that neither respect ends nor means? Can there be moral acts of will when there is no choice or intention? If there is choice or intention, must not these respect an end or means? What then can be meant by ultimate action of will as distinguished from ultimate choice or intention? Can there be choice without an object of choice? If there is an object of choice, must not this object be chosen either as an end or as a means? If as an ultimate end, how does this differ from ultimate intention? If as a means, how can this be regarded as an ultimate action of the will? What can be intended by actions of will that are not acts of choice nor volition? I can conceive of no other. But if all acts of will must of necessity consist in willing or nilling, that is in choosing or refusing, which is the same as willing one way or another, in respect to all objects of choice apprehended by the mind, how can there be any intelligent act of the will that does not consist in, or that may not and must not, in its last analysis, be resolvable into, and be properly considered as the choice of an end, or of means, or in executive efforts to secure an end? Can moral law require any other action of will than choice and volition? What other actions of will are possible to us? Whatever moral law does require, it must and can only require choices and volitions. It can only require us to choose ends or means. It cannot require us to choose as an ultimate end anything that is not intrinsically worthy of choice--nor as a means any thing that does not sustain that relation.

Secondly, let us examine this theory in the light of the revealed law of God. The whole law is fulfilled in one word--love. Now we have seen that the will of God cannot be the foundation of moral obligation. Moral obligation must be founded in the nature of that which moral law requires us to choose. Unless there be something in the nature of that which moral law requires us to will that renders it worthy or deserving of choice, we can be under no obligation to will or choose it. It is admitted that the love required by the law of God must consist in an act of the will, and not in mere emotions. Now, does this love, willing, choice, embrace several distinct ultimates? If so, how can they all be expressed in one word--love? Observe, the law requires only love to God and our neighbor as an ultimate. This love or willing must respect and terminate on God and our neighbor. The law says nothing about willing right for the sake of the right, or truth for the sake of the truth, or beauty for the sake of beauty, or virtue for the sake of virtue, or moral order for its own sake, or the nature and relations of moral agents for their own sake; nor can any such thing be implied in the command to love God and our neighbor. All these and innumerable other things are, and must be, conditions and means of the highest well-being of God and our neighbor. As such, the law may, and doubtless does, in requiring us to will the highest well-being of God and our neighbor as an ultimate end, require us to will all these as the necessary conditions and means. The end which the revealed law requires us to will is undeniably simple as opposed to complex. It requires only love to God and our neighbor. One word expresses the whole of moral obligation. Now certainly this word cannot have a complex signification in such a sense as to include several distinct and ultimate objects of love, or of choice. This love is to terminate on God and our neighbor, and not on abstractions, nor on inanimate and insentient existences. I protest against any philosophy that contradicts the revealed law of God, and that teaches that anything else than God and our neighbor is to be loved for its own sake, or that anything else is to be chosen as an ultimate end than the highest well-being of God and our neighbor. In other words, I utterly object to any philosophy that makes anything obligatory upon a moral agent that is not expressed or implied in perfect good will to God, and to the universe of sentient existences. To the word and to the testimony; if any philosophy agree not therewith, it is because there is no light in it. The revealed law of God knows but one ground or foundation of moral obligation. It requires but one thing; and that is just that attitude of the will toward God and our neighbor that accords with the intrinsic value of their highest well-being; that God's moral worth shall be willed as of infinite value, as a condition of his own well-being, and that his actual and perfect blessedness shall be willed for its own sake, and because, or upon condition that he is worthy; that our neighbor's moral worth shall be willed as an indispensable condition of his blessedness, and that if our neighbor is worthy of happiness, his actual and highest happiness shall be willed. This law knows but one end which moral agents are under obligation to seek, and sets at nought all so-called ultimate actions of will that do not terminate on the good of God and our neighbor. The ultimate choice, with the choice of all the conditions and means of the highest well-being of God and the universe, is all that the revealed law recognizes as coming within the pale of its legislation. It requires nothing more and nothing less.

But there is another form of the complex theory of moral obligation that I must notice before I dismiss this subject.

This view admits and maintains that the good, that is, the valuable to being, is the only ground of moral obligation, and that in every possible case the valuable to being, or the good, must be intended as an end, as a condition of the intention being virtuous. In this respect it maintains that the foundation of moral obligation is simple, a unit. But it also maintains that there are several ultimate goods or several ultimates or things which are intrinsically good or valuable in themselves, and are therefore to be chosen for their own sake, or as an ultimate end; that to choose either of these as an ultimate end, or for its own sake, is virtue.

It admits that happiness or blessedness is a good, and should be willed for its own sake, or as an ultimate end, but it maintains that virtue is an ultimate good; that right is an ultimate good; that the just and the true are ultimate goods; in short, that the realization of the ideas of the reason, or the carrying out into concrete existence any idea of the reason, is an ultimate good. For instance: there were in the Divine Mind from eternity certain ideas of the good or valuable, the right, the just, the beautiful, the true, the useful, the holy. The realization of these ideas of the divine reason, according to this theory, was the end which God aimed at or intended in creation; he aimed at their realization as ultimates or for their own sake, and regarded the concrete realization of every one of these ideas as a separate and ultimate good: and so certain as God is virtuous, so certain it is, says this theory, that an intention on our part to realize these ideas for the sake of the realization is virtue. Then the foundation of moral obligation is complex in the sense that to will either the good or valuable, the right, the true, the just, the virtuous, the beautiful, the useful, etc., for its own sake, or as an ultimate end, is virtue; and there is more than one virtuous ultimate choice or intention. Thus any one of several distinct things may be intended as an ultimate end with equal propriety and with equal virtuousness. The soul may at one moment be wholly consecrated to one end, that is, to one ultimate good, and again to another; that is, sometimes it may will one good, and sometimes another good, as an ultimate end, and still be equally virtuous.

In the discussion of this subject I will inquire: In what does the supreme and ultimate good consist?

1. Good may be natural or moral. Natural good is synonymous with valuable. Moral good is synonymous with virtue. Moral good is in a certain sense a natural good, that is, it is valuable as a means of natural good; but the advocates of this theory affirm that moral good is valuable in itself.

2. Good may be absolute and relative. Absolute good is that which is intrinsically valuable. Relative good is that which is valuable as a means. It is not valuable in itself, but valuable because it sustains to absolute good the relation of a means to an end. Absolute good may also be a relative good, that is, it may tend to perpetuate and augment itself. Absolute good is also ultimate. Ultimate good is that good in which all relative good terminates--that good to which all relative good sustains the relation of a means or condition. Relative good is not intrinsically valuable, but only valuable on account of its relations.

The point upon which issue is taken, is, that enjoyment, blessedness, or mental satisfaction, is the only ultimate good.

It has been before remarked, and should be repeated here, that the intrinsically valuable must not only belong to, and be inseparable from, sentient beings, but that the ultimate or intrinsic absolute good must consist in a state of mind. It must be something to be found in the field of consciousness. Take away mind, and what can be a good per se; or what can be a good in any sense?

Again, it should be said that the ultimate and absolute good can not consist in a choice or in a voluntary state of mind. The thing chosen is, and must be the ultimate of the choice. Choice can never be chosen as an ultimate end. Benevolence then, or the love required by the law, can never be the ultimate and absolute good. It is admitted that blessedness, enjoyment, mental satisfaction, is a good, an absolute and ultimate good. All men assume it. All men seek enjoyment. That it is the only absolute and ultimate good, is a first truth. But for this there could be no activity--no motive to action--no object of choice. Enjoyment is in fact the ultimate good. It is in fact the result of existence and of action. It results to God from his existence, his attributes, his activity, and his virtue, by a law of necessity. His powers are so correlated that blessedness cannot but be the state of his mind, as resulting from the exercise of his attributes and the right activity of his will. Happiness, or enjoyment, results, both naturally and governmentally, from obedience to law both physical and moral. It also shows that government is not an end, but a means. It also shows that the end is blessedness, and the means obedience to law.

The ultimate and absolute good, in the sense of the intrinsically valuable, cannot be identical with moral law. Moral law, as we have seen, is an idea of the reason. Moral law and moral government must propose some end to be secured by means of law. Law cannot be its own end. It cannot require the subject to seek itself as an ultimate end. This were absurd. The moral law is nothing else than the reason's idea, or conception of that course of willing and acting that is fit, proper, suitable to, and demanded by the nature, relations, necessities, and circumstances of moral agents. Their nature, relations, circumstances, and wants being perceived, the reason necessarily affirms that they ought to propose to themselves a certain end, and to concentrate themselves to the promotion of this end, for its own sake, or for its own intrinsic value. This end cannot be law itself. The law is a simple and pure idea of the reason, and can never be in itself the supreme, intrinsic, absolute, and ultimate good.

Nor can obedience, or the course of acting or willing required by the law, be the ultimate end aimed at by the law or the lawgiver. The law requires action in reference to an end, or that an end should be willed; but the willing, and the end to be willed, cannot be identical. The action required, and the end to which it is to be directed, cannot be the same. Obedience to law cannot be the ultimate end proposed by law or government. The obedience is one thing, the end to be secured by obedience is and must be another. Obedience must be a means or condition; and that which law and obedience are intended to secure, is and must be the ultimate end of obedience. The law, or the law-giver, aims to promote the highest good, or blessedness of the universe. This must be the end of moral law and moral government. Law and obedience must be the means or conditions of this end. To deny this is to deny the very nature of moral law, and to lose sight of the true and only end of moral government. Nothing can be moral law, and nothing can be moral government, that does not propose the highest good of moral beings as its ultimate end. But if this is the end of law, and the end of government, it must be the end to be aimed at, or intended, by the ruler and the subject. And this end must be the foundation of moral obligation. The end must be good or valuable per se, or there can be no moral law requiring it to be sought or chosen as an ultimate end, nor any obligation to choose it as an ultimate end.

But what is intended by the right, the just, the true, etc., being ultimate goods and ends to be chosen for their own sake? These may be objective or subjective. Objective right, truth, justice, etc., are mere ideas, and cannot be good or valuable in themselves. Subjective right, truth, justice, etc., are synonymous with righteousness, truthfulness, and justness. These are virtue. They consist in an active state of the will, and resolve themselves into choice, intention. But we have repeatedly seen that intention can neither be an end nor a good in itself, in the sense of intrinsically valuable.

Again, constituted as moral agents are, it is a matter of consciousness that the concrete realization of the ideas of right, and truth, and justice, of beauty, of fitness, of moral order, and, in short, of all that class of ideas, is indispensable as the condition and means of their highest well-being, and that enjoyment or mental satisfaction is the result of realizing in the concrete those ideas. This enjoyment or satisfaction then is and must be the end or ultimate upon which the intention of God must have terminated, and upon which ours must terminate as an end or ultimate.

Again, the enjoyment resulting to God from the concrete realization of his own ideas must be infinite. He must therefore have intended it as the supreme good. It is in fact the ultimate good. It is in fact the supremely valuable.

Again, if there is more than one ultimate good, the mind must regard them all as one, or sometimes be consecrated to one and sometimes to another--sometimes wholly consecrated to the beautiful, sometimes to the just, and then again to the right, then to the useful, to the true, etc. But it may be asked, of what value is the beautiful, aside from the enjoyment it affords to sentient existences? It meets a demand of our being, and hence affords satisfaction. But for this in what sense could it be regarded as good? The idea of the useful, again, cannot be an idea of an ultimate end, for utility implies that something is valuable in itself to which the useful sustains the relation of a means, and is useful only for that reason.

Of what value is the true, the right, the just, etc., aside from the pleasure or mental satisfaction resulting from them to sentient existences? Of what value were all the rest of the universe, were there no sentient existences to enjoy it?

Suppose, again, that everything else in the universe existed just as it does, except mental satisfaction or enjoyment, and that there were absolutely no enjoyment of any kind in anything any more than there is in a block of granite, of what value would it all be? and to what, or to whom, would it be valuable? Mind, without susceptibility of enjoyment, can neither know nor be the subject of good or evil, any more than a slab of marble. Truth in that case could no more be a good to mind than mind could be a good to truth; light would no more be a good to the eye, than the eye a good to light. Nothing in the universe could give or receive the least satisfaction or dissatisfaction. Neither natural nor moral fitness nor unfitness could excite the least emotion or mental satisfaction. A block of marble might just as well be the subject of good as anything else, upon such a supposition.

Again, it is obvious that all creation, where law is obeyed, tends to one end, and that end is happiness or enjoyment. This demonstrates that enjoyment was the end at which God aimed in creation.

Again, it is evident that God is endeavoring to realize all the other ideas of his reason for the sake of, and as a means of, realizing that of the valuable to being. This, as a matter of fact, is the result of realizing in the concrete all those ideas. This must then have been the end intended.

It is nonsense to object that, if enjoyment or mental satisfaction be the only ground of moral obligation, we should be indifferent as to the means. This objection assumes that in seeking an end for its intrinsic value, we must be indifferent as to the way in which we obtain that end; that is, whether it be obtained in a manner possible or impossible, right or wrong. It overlooks the fact that from the laws of our own being it is impossible for us to will the end without willing also the indispensable, and therefore the appropriate, means; and also that we cannot possibly regard any other conditions or means of the happiness of moral agents as possible, and therefore as appropriate or right, but holiness and universal conformity to the law of our being. Enjoyment or mental satisfaction results from having the different demands of our being met. One demand of the reason and conscience of a moral agent is that happiness should be conditionated upon holiness. It is therefore naturally impossible for a moral agent to be satisfied with the happiness or enjoyment of moral agents, except upon the condition of their holiness.

But this class of philosophers insist that all the archetypes of the ideas of the reason are necessarily regarded by us as good in themselves. For example: I have the idea of beauty. I behold a rose. The perception of this archetype of the idea of beauty gives me instantaneous pleasure. Now it is said, that this archetype is necessarily regarded by me as a good. I have pleasure in the presence and perception of it, and as often as I call it to remembrance. This pleasure, it is said, demonstrates that it is a good to me; and this good is in the very nature of the object, and must be regarded as a good in itself. To this I answer, that the presence of the rose is a good to me, but not an ultimate good. It is only a means or source of pleasure or happiness to me. The rose is not a good in itself. If there were no eyes to see it, and no olfactories to smell it, to whom could it be a good? But in what sense can it be a good, except in the sense that it gives satisfaction to the beholder? The satisfaction, and not the rose, is and must be the ultimate good. But it is inquired, Do not I desire the rose for its own sake? I answer, Yes; you desire it for its own sake, but you do not, cannot choose it for its own sake, but to gratify the desire. The desires all terminate on their respective objects. The desire for food terminates on food; thirst terminates on drink, etc. These things are so correlated to these appetites that they are desired for their own sakes. But they are not and cannot be chosen for their own sakes or as an ultimate end. They are, and must be, regarded and chosen as the means of gratifying their respective desires. To choose them simply in obedience to the desire were selfishness. But the gratification is a good, and a part of universal good. The reason, therefore, urges and demands that they should be chosen as a means of good to myself. When thus chosen in obedience to the law of the intelligence, and no more stress is laid upon the gratification than in proportion to its relative value, and when no stress is laid upon it simply because it is my own gratification, the choice is holy. The perception of the archetypes of the various ideas of the reason will, in most instances, produce enjoyment. These archetypes, or, which is the same thing, the concrete realization of these ideas, is regarded by the mind as a good, but not as an ultimate good. The ultimate good is the satisfaction derived from the perception of them.

The perception of moral or physical beauty gives me satisfaction. Now moral and physical beauty are regarded by me as good, but not as ultimate good. They are relative good only. Were it not for the pleasure they give me, I could not in any way connect with them the idea of good. The mental eye might perceive order, beauty, physical and moral, or anything else; but these things would no more be good to the intellect that perceived them than their opposites. The idea of good or of the valuable could not in such a case exist, consequently virtue or moral beauty, could not exist. The idea of the good, or of the valuable, must exist before virtue can exist. It is and must be the development of the idea of the valuable, that develops the idea of moral obligation, of right and wrong, and consequently that makes virtue possible. The mind must perceive an object of choice that is regarded as intrinsically valuable, before it can have the idea of moral obligation to choose it as an end. This object of choice cannot be virtue or moral beauty, for this would be to have the idea of virtue or of moral beauty before the idea of moral obligation, or of right and wrong. This were a contradiction. The mind must have the idea of some ultimate good, the choice of which would be virtue, or concerning which the reason affirms moral obligation, before the idea of virtue, or of right or wrong, can exist. The development of the idea of the valuable, or of an ultimate good, must precede the possibility of virtue, or of the idea of virtue, of moral obligation, or of right and wrong. It is absurd to say that virtue is regarded as an ultimate good, when in fact the very idea of virtue does not and cannot exist until a good is presented, in view of which, the mind affirms moral obligation to will it for its own sake, and also affirms that the choice of it for that reason would be virtue.

So virtue or holiness is morally beautiful. Moral worth or excellence is morally beautiful. Beauty is an attribute or element of holiness, virtue, and of moral worth, or right character. But the beauty is not identical with holiness or moral worth, any more than the beauty of a rose, and the rose are identical. The rose is beautiful. Beauty is one of its attributes. So virtue is morally beautiful. Beauty is one of its attributes. But in neither case is the beauty a state of mind, and, therefore, it cannot be an ultimate good.

We are apt to say, that moral worth is an ultimate good; but it is only a relative good. It meets a demand of our being, and thus produces satisfaction. This satisfaction is the ultimate good of being. At the very moment we pronounce it a good in itself, it is only because we experience such a satisfaction in contemplating it. At the very time we erroneously say, that we consider it a good in itself, wholly independent of its results, we only say so, the more positively, because we are so gratified at the time, by thinking of it. It is its experienced results, that is the ground of the affirmation.

Thus we see:

1. That the utility of ultimate choice cannot be a foundation of obligation to choose, for this would be to transfer the ground of obligation from what is intrinsic in the object chosen to the useful tendency of the choice itself. As I have said, utility is a condition of obligation to put forth an executive act, but can never be a foundation of obligation; for the utility of the choice is not a reason found exclusively, or at all, in the object of choice.

2. The moral character of the choice cannot be a foundation of obligation to choose, for this reason is not intrinsic in the object of choice. To affirm that the character of choice is the ground of obligation to choose, is to transfer the ground of obligation to choose from the object chosen to the character of the choice itself; but this is a contradiction of the premises.

3. The relation of one being to another cannot be the ground of obligation of the one to will good to the other, for the ground of obligation to will good to another must be the intrinsic nature of the good, and not the relations of one being to another. Relations may be conditions of obligation to seek to promote the good of particular individuals; but in every case the nature of the good is the ground of the obligation.

4. Neither the relation of utility, nor that of moral fitness or right, as existing between choice and its object, can be a ground of obligation, for both these relations depend, for their very existence, upon the intrinsic importance of the object of choice; and besides, neither of these relations is intrinsic in the object of choice, as it must be to be a ground of obligation.

5. The relative importance or value of an object of choice can never be a ground of obligation to choose that object, for its relative importance is not intrinsic in the object. But the relative importance, or value, of an object may be

a condition of obligation to choose it, as a condition of securing an intrinsically valuable object, to which it sustains the relation of a means.

6. The idea of duty cannot be a ground of obligation; this idea is a condition, but never a foundation, of obligation, for this idea is not intrinsic in the object which we affirm it our duty to choose.

7. The perception of certain relations existing between individuals cannot be a ground, although it is a condition of obligation, to fulfil to them certain duties. Neither the relation itself, nor the perception of the relation, is intrinsic in that which we affirm ourselves to be under obligation to will or do to them; of course, neither of them can be a ground of obligation.

8. The affirmation of obligation by the reason, cannot be a ground, though it is a condition of obligation. The obligation is affirmed, upon the ground of the intrinsic importance of the object, and not in view of the affirmation itself.

9. The sovereign will of God is never the foundation, though it often is a condition of certain forms, of obligation. Did we know the intrinsic or relative value of an object, we should be under obligation to choose it, whether God required it or not.

The revealed will of God is always a condition of obligation, whenever such revelation is indispensable to our understanding the intrinsic or relative importance of any object of choice. The will of God is not intrinsic in the object which he commands us to will, and of course cannot be a ground of obligation.

10. The moral excellence of a being can never be a foundation of obligation to will his good; for his character is not intrinsic in the good we ought to will to him. The intrinsic value of that good must be the ground of the obligation, and his good character only a condition of obligation to will his enjoyment of good in particular.

Good character can never be a ground of obligation to choose anything which is not itself; for the reasons of ultimate choice must be found exclusively in the object of choice. Therefore, if character is a ground of obligation to put forth an ultimate choice, it must be the object of that choice.

11. Right can never be a ground of obligation, unless right be itself the object which we are under obligation to choose for its own sake.

12. Susceptibility for good can never be a ground, though it is a condition, of obligation to will good to a being. The susceptibility is not intrinsic in the good which we ought to will, and therefore cannot be a ground of obligation.

13. No one thing can be a ground of obligation to choose any other thing, as an ultimate; for the reasons for choosing anything, as an ultimate, must be found in itself, and in nothing extraneous to itself.

14. From the admitted fact, that none but ultimate choice or intention is right or wrong per se, and that all executive volitions, or acts, derive their character from the ultimate intention to which they owe their existence, it follows:--

(a.) That if executive volitions are put forth with the intention to secure an intrinsically valuable end, they are right; otherwise they are wrong.

(b.) It also follows, that obligation to put forth executive acts is conditioned, not founded, upon the assumed utility of such acts. Again--

(c.) It also follows, that all outward acts are right or wrong, as they proceed from a right or wrong intention.

(d.) It also follows that the rightness of any executive volition or outward act depends upon the supposed and intended utility of that volition, or act. Their utility must he assumed as a condition of obligation to put them forth, and, of course, their intended utility is a condition of their being right.

(e.) It also follows that, whenever we decide it to be duty to put forth any outward act whatever, irrespective of its supposed utility, and because we think it right, we deceive ourselves; for it is impossible that outward acts or volitions, which from their nature are always executive, should be either obligatory or right, irrespective of their assumed utility, or tendency to promote an intrinsically valuable end.

(f.) It follows also that it is a gross error to affirm the rightness of an executive act, as a reason for putting it forth, even assuming that its tendency is to do evil rather than good. With this assumption no executive act can possibly be right. When God has required certain executive acts, we know that they do tend to secure the highest good, and that, if put forth to secure that good, they are right. But in no case, where God has not revealed the path of duty, as it respects executive acts, or courses of life, are we to decide upon such questions in view of the rightness, irrespective of the good tendency of such acts or courses of life; for their rightness depends upon their assumed good tendency.

But it is said that a moral agent may sometimes be under obligation to will evil instead of good to others. I answer:--

It can never be the duty of a moral agent to will evil to any being for its own sake, or as an ultimate end. The character and governmental relations of a being may be such that it may be duty to will his punishment to promote the public good. But in this case good is the end willed, and misery only a means. So it may be the duty of a moral agent to will the temporal misery of even a holy being to promote the public interests. Such was the case with the sufferings of Christ. The Father willed his temporary misery to promote the public good. But in all cases when it is duty to will misery, it is only as a means or condition of good to the public, or to the individual, and not as an ultimate end.

LECTURE VIII - FOUNDATION OF MORAL OBLIGATION

THE PRACTICAL TENDENCY OF THE VARIOUS THEORIES

It has already been observed that this is a highly practical question, and one of surpassing interest and importance. I have gone through the discussion and examination of the several principal theories, for the purpose of preparing the way to expose the practical results of those various theories, and to show that they legitimately result in some of the most soul-destroying errors that cripple the church and curse the world.

1. I will begin with the theory that regards the sovereign will of God as the foundation of moral obligation.

One legitimate and necessary result of this theory is, a totally erroneous conception both of the character of God, and of the nature and design of his government. If God's will is the foundation of moral obligation, it follows that he is an arbitrary sovereign. He is not under law himself, and he has no rule by which to regulate his conduct, nor by which either himself or any other being can judge of his moral character. Indeed, unless he is subject to law, or is a subject of moral obligation, he has and can have, no moral character; for moral character always and necessarily implies moral law and moral obligation. If God's will is not itself under the law of his infinite reason, or, in other words, it is not conformed to the law imposed upon it by his intelligence, then his will is and must be arbitrary in the worst sense; that is, in the sense of having no regard to reason, or to the nature and relations of moral agents. But if his will is under the law of his reason, if he acts from principle, or has good and benevolent reasons for his conduct, then his will is not the foundation of moral obligation, but those reasons that lie revealed in the divine intelligence, in view of which it affirms moral obligation, or that he ought to will in conformity with those reasons. In other words, if the intrinsic value of his own well-being and that of the universe be the foundation of moral obligation; if his reason affirms his obligation to choose this as his ultimate end, and to consecrate his infinite energies to the realization of it; and if his will is conformed to this law it follows,--

(1.) That his will is not the foundation of moral obligation.

(2.) That he has infinitely good and wise reasons for what he wills, says, and does.

(3.) That he is not arbitrary, but always acts in conformity with right principles, and for reasons that will, when universally known, compel the respect and even admiration of every intelligent being in the universe.

(4.) That creation and providential and moral government, are the necessary means to an infinitely wise and good end, and that existing evils are only unavoidably incidental to this infinitely wise and benevolent arrangement, and, although great, are indefinitely the less of two evils. That is, they are an evil indefinitely less than no creation and no government would have been. It is conceivable, that a plan of administration might have been adopted that would have prevented the present evils; but if we admit that God has been governed by reason in the selection of the end he has in view, and in the use of means for its accomplishment, it will follow that the evils are less than would have existed under any other plan of administration; or at least, that the present system, with all its evils, is the best that infinite wisdom and love could adopt.

(5.) These incidental evils, therefore, do not at all detract from the evidence of the wisdom and goodness of God; for in all these things he is not acting from caprice, or malice, or an arbitrary sovereignty, but is acting in conformity with the law of his infinite intelligence, and of course has infinitely good and weighty reasons for what he does and suffers to be done--reasons so good and so weighty, that he could not do otherwise without violating the law of his own intelligence, and therefore committing infinite sin.

(6.) It follows also that there is ground for perfect confidence, love, and submission to his divine will in all things. That is, if his will is not arbitrary, but conformed to the law of his infinite intelligence, then it is obligatory, as our rule of action, because it reveals infallibly what is in accordance with infinite intelligence. We may always be entirely safe in obeying all the divine requirements, and in submitting to all his dispensations, however mysterious, being assured that they are perfectly wise and good. Not only are we safe in doing so, but we are under infinite obligation to do so; not because his arbitrary will imposes obligation, but because it reveals to us infallibly the end we ought to choose, and the indispensable means of securing it. His will is law, not in the sense of its originating and imposing obligation of its own arbitrary sovereignty, but in the sense of its being a revelation of both the end we ought to seek, and the means by which the end can be secured. Indeed this is the only proper idea of law. It does not in any case of itself impose obligation, but is only a revelation of obligation. Law is a condition, but not the foundation, of obligation. The will of God is a condition of obligation, only so far as it is indispensable to our knowledge of the end we ought to seek, and the means by which this end is to be secured. Where these are known, there is obligation, whether God has revealed his will or not.

The foregoing, and many other important truths, little less important than those already mentioned, and too numerous to be now distinctly noticed, follow from the fact that the good of being, and not the arbitrary will of God, is the foundation of moral obligation. But no one of them is or can be true, if his will be the foundation of obligation. Nor can any one, who consistently holds or believes that his will is the foundation of obligation, hold or believe any of the foregoing truths, nor indeed hold or believe any truth of the law or gospel. Nay, he cannot, if he be at all consistent, have even a correct conception of one truth of God's moral government. Let us see if he can.

(1.) Can he believe that God's will is wise and good, unless he admits and believes that it is subject to the law of his intelligence? If he consistently holds that the divine will is the foundation of moral obligation, he must either deny that his will is any evidence of what is wise and good, or maintain the absurdity, that whatever God wills is wise and good, simply for the reason that God wills it, and that if he willed the directly opposite of what he does, it would be equally wise and good. But this is an absurdity palpable enough to confound any one who has reason and moral agency.

(2.) If he consistently holds and believes that God's sovereign will is the foundation of moral obligation, he cannot regard him as having any moral character, for the reason, that there is no standard by which to judge of his willing and acting; for, by the supposition, he has no intelligent rule of action, and, therefore, can have no moral character, as he is not a moral agent, and can himself have no idea of the moral character of his own actions; for, in fact, upon the supposition in question, they have none. Any one, therefore, who holds that God is not a subject of moral law, imposed on him by his own reason, but, on the contrary, that his sovereign will is the foundation of moral obligation, must, if consistent, deny that he has moral character; and he must deny that God is an intelligent being, or else admit that he is infinitely wicked for not conforming his will to the law of his intelligence; and for not being guided by his infinite reason, instead of setting up an arbitrary sovereignty of will.

(3.) He who holds that God's sovereign will is the foundation of moral obligation, instead of being a revelation of obligation, if he be at all consistent, can neither have nor assign any good reason either for confidence in him, or submission to him. If God has no good and wise reasons for what he commands, why should we obey him? If he has no good and wise reasons for what he does, why should we submit to him?

Will it be answered, that if we refuse, we do it at our peril, and, therefore, it is wise to do so, even if he has no good reasons for what he does and requires? To this I answer that it is impossible, upon the supposition in question, either to obey or submit to God with the heart. If we can see no good reasons, but, on the other hand, are assured there are no good and wise reasons for the divine commands and conduct, it is rendered forever naturally impossible, from the laws of our nature, to render anything more than feigned obedience and submission. Whenever we do not understand the reason for a divine requirement, or of a dispensation of divine Providence, the condition of heart-obedience to the one and submission to the other, is the assumption that he has good and wise reasons for both. But assume the contrary, to wit, that he has no good and wise reasons for either, and you render heart-obedience, confidence, and submission impossible. It is perfectly plain, therefore, that he who consistently holds the theory in question, can neither conceive rightly of God, nor of anything respecting his law, gospel, or government, moral or providential. It is impossible for him to have an intelligent piety. His religion, if he have any, must be sheer superstition, inasmuch as he neither knows the true God, nor the true reason why he should love, believe, obey, or submit to him. In short, he neither knows, nor, if consistent, can know, anything of the nature of true religion, and has not so much as a right conception of what constitutes virtue.

But do not understand me as affirming, that none who profess to hold the theory in question have any true knowledge of God, or any true religion. No, they are happily so purely theorists on this subject, and so happily inconsistent with themselves, as to have, after all, a practical judgment in favor of the truth. They do not see the logical consequences of their theory, and of course do not embrace them, and this happy inconsistency is an indispensable condition of their salvation.

(4.) Another pernicious consequence of this theory is that those who hold it will of course give false directions to inquiring sinners. Indeed, if they be ministers, the whole strain of their instructions must be false. They must, if consistent, not only represent God to their hearers as an absolute and arbitrary sovereign, but they must represent religion as consisting in submission to arbitrary sovereignty. If sinners inquire what they must do to be saved, such teachers must answer in substance, that they must cast themselves on the sovereignty of a God whose law is solely an expression of his arbitrary will, and whose every requirement and purpose is founded in his arbitrary sovereignty. This is the God whom they must love, in whom they must believe, and whom they must serve with a willing mind. How infinitely different such instructions are from those that would be given by one who knew the truth. Such an one would represent God to an inquirer as infinitely reasonable in all his requirements, and in all his ways. He would represent the sovereignty of God as consisting, not in arbitrary will, but in benevolence or love, directed by infinite knowledge in the promotion of the highest good of being. He would represent his law, not as the expression of his arbitrary will, but as having its foundation in the self-existent nature of God, and in the nature of moral agents; as being the very rule which is agreeable to the nature and relations of moral agents; that its requisitions are not arbitrary, hut that the very thing, and only that, is required which is in the nature of things indispensable to the highest well-being of moral agents; that God's will does not originate obligation by any arbitrary fiat, but on the contrary, that he requires what he does, because it is obligatory in the nature of things; that his requirement does not create right, but that he requires only that which is naturally and of necessity right. These and many such like things would irresistibly commend the character of God to the human intelligence, as worthy to be trusted, and as a being to whom submission is infallibly safe and infinitely reasonable.

The fact is, the idea of arbitrary sovereignty is shocking and revolting, not only to the human heart, whether unregenerate or regenerate, but also to the human intelligence. Religion, based upon such a view of God's character and government, must be sheer superstition or gross fanaticism.

2. I will next glance at the legitimate results of the theory of the selfish school.

This theory teaches that our own interest is the foundation of moral obligation. In conversing with a distinguished defender of this philosophy, I requested the theorist to define moral obligation, and this was the definition given: "It is the obligation of a moral agent to seek his own happiness." Upon the practical bearing of this theory I remark,--

(1.) It tends directly and inevitably to the confirmation and despotism of sin in the soul. All sin, as we shall hereafter see, resolves itself into a spirit of self-seeking, or into a disposition to seek good to self, and upon condition of its relations to self, and not impartially and disinterestedly. This philosophy represents this spirit of self-seeking as virtue, and only requires that in our efforts to secure our own happiness, we should not interfere with the rights of others in seeking theirs. But here it may be asked, when these philosophers insist that virtue consists in willing our own happiness, and that, in seeking it, we are bound to have respect to the rights and happiness of others, do they mean that we are to have a positive, or merely a negative regard to the rights and happiness of others? If they mean that we are to have a positive regard to others' rights and happiness, what is that but giving up their theory, and holding the true one, to wit, that the happiness of each one shall be esteemed according to its intrinsic value, for its own sake? That is, that we should be disinterestedly benevolent? But if they mean that we are to regard our neighbor's happiness negatively, that is, merely in not hindering it, what is this but the most absurd thing conceivable? What! I need not care positively for my neighbor's happiness, I need not will it as a good in itself, and for its own value, and yet I must take care not to hinder it. But why? Why, because it is intrinsically as valuable as my own. Now, if this is assigning any good reason why I ought not to hinder it, it is just because it is assigning a good reason why I ought positively and disinterestedly to will it; which is the same thing as the true theory. But if this is not a sufficient reason to impose obligation, positively and disinterestedly, to will it, it can never impose obligation to avoid hindering it, and I may then pursue my own happiness in my own way without the slightest regard to that of any other.

(2.) If this theory be true, sinful and holy beings are precisely alike, so far as ultimate intention is concerned, in which we have seen all moral character consists. They have precisely the same end in view, and the difference lies exclusively in the means they make use of to promote their own happiness. That sinners are seeking their own happiness, is a truth of consciousness to them. If moral agents are under obligation to seek their own happiness as the supreme end of life, it follows, that holy beings do so. So that holy and sinful beings are precisely alike, so far as the end for which they live is concerned; the only difference being, as has been observed, in the different means they make use of to promote this end. But observe, no reason can be assigned, in accordance with this philosophy, why they use different means, only that they differ in judgment in respect to them; for, let it be remembered, that this philosophy denies that we are bound to have a positive and disinterested regard to our neighbor's interest; and, of course, no benevolent considerations prevent the holy from using the same means as do the wicked. Where, therefore, is the difference in their character, although they do use this diversity of means? I say again, there is none. If this difference be not ascribed to disinterested benevolence in one, and to selfishness in the other, there really is and can be no difference in character between them. According to this theory nothing is right in itself, but the intention to promote my own happiness; and anything is right or wrong as it is intended to promote this result or otherwise. For let it be borne in mind that, if moral obligation respects strictly the ultimate intention only, it follows that ultimate intention alone is right or wrong in itself, and all other things are right or wrong as they proceed from a right or wrong ultimate intention. This must be true.

Further, if my own happiness be the foundation of my moral obligation, it follows that this is the ultimate end at which I ought to aim, and that nothing is right or wrong in itself, in me, but this intention or its opposite; and furthermore, that everything else must be right or wrong in me as it proceeds from this, or from an opposite intention. I may do, and upon the supposition of the truth of this theory, I am bound to do, whatever will, in my estimation, promote my own happiness, and that, not because of its intrinsic value as a part of universal good, but because it is my own. To seek it as a part of universal happiness, and not because it is my own, would be to act on the true theory, or the theory of disinterested benevolence; which this theory denies.

(3.) Upon this theory I am not to love God supremely, and my neighbor as myself. If I love God and my neighbor, it is to be only as a means of promoting my own happiness, which is not loving them, but loving myself supremely.

(4.) This theory teaches radical error in respect both to the character and government of God; and the consistent defenders of it cannot but hold fundamentally false views in respect to what constitutes holiness or virtue, either in God or man. They do not and cannot know the difference between virtue and vice.

(5.) The teachers of this theory must fatally mislead all who consistently follow out their instructions. In preaching, they must, if consistent, appeal wholly to hope and fear. All their instructions must tend to confirm selfishness. All the motives they present, if consistent, tend only to stir up a zeal within them to secure their own happiness. If they pray, it will only be to implore the help of God to accomplish their selfish ends.

Indeed, it is impossible that this theory should not blind its advocates to the fundamental truths of morality and religion, and it is hardly conceivable that one could more efficiently serve the devil than by the inculcation of such a philosophy as this.

3. Let us in the next place look into the natural and, if its advocates are consistent, necessary results of utilitarianism.

This theory, you know, teaches that the utility of an action or of a choice, renders it obligatory. That is, I am bound to will good, not for the intrinsic value of the good; but because willing good tends to produce good--to choose an end, not because of the intrinsic value of the end, but because the willing of it tends to secure it. The absurdity of this theory has been sufficiently exposed. It only remains to notice its legitimate practical results.

(1.) It naturally, and I may say, necessarily diverts the attention from that in which all morality consists, namely, the ultimate intention. Indeed, it seems that the abettors of this scheme must have in mind only outward action, or at most executive volitions, when they assert that the tendency of an action is the reason of the obligation to put it forth. It seems impossible that they should assert that the reason for choosing an ultimate end should or could be the tendency of choice to secure it. This is so palpable a contradiction, that it is difficult to believe that they have ultimate intention in mind when they make the assertion. An ultimate end is ever chosen for its intrinsic value, and not because choice tends to secure it. How, then, is it possible for them to hold that the tendency of choice to secure an ultimate end is the reason of an obligation to make that choice? But if they have not their eye upon ultimate intention, when they speak of moral obligation, they are discoursing of that which is, strictly without the pale of morality. A consistent utilitarian, therefore, cannot conceive rightly of the nature of morality or virtue. He cannot consistently hold that virtue consists in willing the highest well-being of God and of the universe as an ultimate end, or for its own sake, but must, on the contrary, confine his ideas of moral obligation to volitions and outward actions, in which there is strictly no morality, and withal assign an entirely false reason for these, to wit, their tendency to secure an end, rather than the value of the end which they tend to secure.

This is the proper place to speak of the doctrine of expediency, a doctrine strenuously maintained by utilitarians, and as strenuously opposed by rightarians. It is this, that whatever is expedient is right, for the reason, that the expediency of an action or measure is the foundation of the obligation to put forth that action, or adopt that measure. It is easy to see that this is just equivalent to saying, that the utility of an action or measure is the reason of the obligation to put forth that action or to adopt that measure. But, as we have seen, utility, tendency, expediency, is only a condition of the obligation, to put forth outward action or executive volition, but never the foundation of the obligation--that always being the intrinsic value of the end to which the volition, action, or measure, sustains the relation of a means. I do not wonder that rightarians object to this, although I do wonder at the reason which, if consistent, they must assign for this obligation, to wit, that any action or volition, (ultimate intention excepted), can be right or wrong in itself, irrespective of its expediency or utility. This is absurd enough, and flatly contradicts the doctrine of rightarians themselves, that moral obligation strictly belongs only to ultimate intention. If moral obligation belongs only to ultimate intention, then nothing but ultimate intention can be right or wrong in itself. And every thing else, that is, all executive volitions and outward actions must be right or wrong, (in the only sense in which moral character can be predicated of them) as they proceed from a right or wrong ultimate intention. This is the only form in which rightarians can consistently admit the doctrine of expediency, viz., that it relates exclusively to executive volitions and outward actions. And this they can admit only upon the assumption that executive volitions and outward actions have strictly no moral character in themselves, but are right or wrong only as, and because, they proceed necessarily from a right or wrong ultimate intention. All schools that hold this doctrine, to wit, that moral obligation respects the ultimate intention only, must, if consistent, deny that any thing can be either right or wrong per se, but ultimate intention. Further, they must maintain, that utility, expediency, or tendency to promote the ultimate end upon which ultimate intention terminates, is always a condition of the obligation to put forth those volitions and actions that sustain to this end the relation of means. And still further, they must maintain, that the obligation to use those means must be founded in the value of the end, and not in the tendency of the means to secure it; for unless the end be intrinsically valuable, the tendency of means to secure it can impose no obligation to use them. Tendency, utility, expediency, then, are only conditions of the obligation to use any given means, but never the foundation of obligation. The obligation in respect to outward action is always founded in the value of the end to which this action sustains the relation of a means, and the obligation is conditionated upon the perceived tendency of the means to secure that end. Expediency can never have respect to the choice of an ultimate end, or to that in which moral character consists, to wit, ultimate intention. The end is to be chosen for its own sake. Ultimate intention is right or wrong in itself, and no questions of utility, expediency, or tendency, have any thing to do with the obligation to put forth ultimate intention, there being only one ultimate reason for this, namely, the intrinsic value of the end itself. It is true, then, that whatever is expedient is right, not for that reason, but only upon that condition. The inquiry then, Is it expedient? in respect to outward action, is always proper; for upon this condition does obligation to outward action turn. But in respect to ultimate intention, or the choice of an ultimate end, an inquiry into the expediency of this choice or intention is never proper, the obligation being founded alone upon the perceived and intrinsic value of the end, and the obligation being without any condition whatever, except the possession of the powers of moral agency, with the perception of the end upon which intention ought to terminate, namely, the good of universal being. But the mistake of the utilitarian, that expediency is the foundation of moral obligation, is fundamental, for, in fact, it cannot be so in any case whatever. I have said, and here repeat, that all schools that hold that moral obligation respects ultimate intention only, must, if consistent, maintain that perceived utility, expediency, etc., is a condition of obligation to put forth any outward action, or, which is the same thing, to use any means to secure the end of benevolence. Therefore, in practice or in daily life, the true doctrine of expediency must of necessity have a place. The railers against expediency, therefore, know not what they say nor whereof they affirm. It is, however, impossible to proceed in practice upon the utilitarian philosophy. This teaches that the tendency of an action to secure good, and not the intrinsic value of the good, is the foundation of the obligation to put forth that action. But this is too absurd for practice. For, unless the intrinsic value of the end be assumed as the foundation of the obligation to choose it, it is impossible to affirm obligation to put forth an action to secure that end. The folly and the danger of utilitarianism is, that it overlooks the true foundation of moral obligation, and consequently the true nature of virtue or holiness. A consistent utilitarian cannot conceive rightly of either.

The teachings of a consistent utilitarian must of necessity abound with pernicious error. Instead of representing virtue as consisting in disinterested benevolence, or in the consecration of the soul to the highest good of being in general, for its own sake, it must represent it as consisting wholly in using means to promote good:--that is, as consisting wholly in executive volitions and outward actions, which, strictly speaking, have no moral character in them. Thus consistent utilitarianism inculcates fundamentally false ideas of the nature of virtue. Of course it must teach equally erroneous ideas respecting the character of God--the spirit and meaning of his law--the nature of repentance--of sin--of regeneration--and, in short, of every practical doctrine of the Bible.

4. Practical bearings and tendency of rightarianism.

It will be recollected that this philosophy teaches that right is the foundation of moral obligation. With its advocates, virtue consists in willing the right for the sake of the right, instead of willing the good for the sake of the good, or more strictly, in willing the good for the sake of the right, and not for the sake of the good; or, as we have seen, the foundation of obligation consists in the relation of intrinsic fitness existing between the choice and the good. The right is the ultimate end to be aimed at in all things, instead of the highest good of being for its own sake. From such a theory the following consequences must flow. I speak only of consistent rightarianism.

(1.) If the rightarian theory is true, there is a law of right entirely distinct from, and opposed to, the law of love or benevolence. The advocates of this theory often assume, perhaps unwittingly, the existence of such a law. They speak of multitudes of things as being right or wrong in themselves, entirely independent of the law of benevolence. Nay, they go so far as to affirm it conceivable that doing right might necessarily tend to, and result in, universal misery; and that, in such a case, we should be under obligation to do right, or will right, or intend right, although universal misery should be the necessary result. This assumes and affirms that right has no necessary relation to willing the highest good of being for its own sake, or, what is the same thing, that the law of right is not only distinct from the law of benevolence, but may be directly opposed to it; that a moral agent may be under obligation to will as an ultimate end that which he knows will and must, by a law of necessity, promote and secure universal misery. Rightarians sternly maintain that right would be right, and that virtue would be virtue, although this result were a necessary consequence. What is this but maintaining that moral law may require moral agents to set their hearts upon and consecrate themselves to that which is necessarily subversive of the well-being of the entire universe? And what is this but assuming that that may be moral law that requires a course of willing and acting entirely inconsistent with the nature and relations of moral agents? Thus virtue and benevolence not only may be different but opposite things; and benevolence may be sin. This is not only opposed to our reason, but a more capital or mischievous error in morals or philosophy can hardly be conceived.

Nothing is or can be right, as an ultimate choice, but benevolence. Nothing can be moral law but that which requires that the highest well-being of God and of the universe should be chosen as an ultimate end. If benevolence is right, this must be self-evident. Rightarianism overlooks and misrepresents the very nature of moral law. Let any one contemplate the grossness of the absurdity that maintains, that moral law may require a course of willing that necessarily results in universal and perfect misery. What then, it may be asked, has moral law to do with the nature and relations of moral agents, except to mock, insult, and trample them under foot? Moral law is, and must be, the law of nature, that is, suited to the nature and relations of moral agents. But can that law be suited to the nature and relations of moral agents that requires a course of action necessarily resulting in universal misery? Rightarianism then, not only overlooks, but flatly contradicts, the very nature of moral law, and sets up a law of right in direct opposition to the law of nature.

(2.) This philosophy tends naturally to fanaticism. Conceiving as it does of right as distinct from, and often opposed to, benevolence, it scoffs or rails at the idea of inquiring what the highest good evidently demands. It insists that such and such things are right or wrong in themselves, entirely irrespective of what the highest good demands. Having thus in mind a law of right distinct from, and perhaps, opposed to benevolence, what frightful conduct may not this philosophy lead to? This is indeed the law of fanaticism. The tendency of this philosophy is illustrated in the spirit of many reformers, who are bitterly contending for the right, which, after all, is to do nobody any good.

(3.) This philosophy teaches a false morality and a false religion. It exalts right above God, and represents virtue as consisting in the love of right instead of the love of God. It exhorts men to will the right for the sake of the right, instead of the good of being for the sake of the good, or for the sake of being. It teaches us to inquire, How shall I do right? instead of, How shall I do good? What is right? instead of, What will most promote the good of the universe? Now that which is most promotive of the highest good of being, is right. To intend the highest well-being of God and of the universe, is right. To use the necessary means to promote this end, is right; and whatever in the use of means or in outward action is right, is so for this reason, namely, that it is designed to promote the highest well-being of God and of the universe. But rightarianism points out an opposite course. It says: Will right for the sake of the right, that is, as an end; and in respect to means, inquire not what is manifestly for the highest good of being, for with this you have nothing to do; your business is to will the right for the sake of the right. If you inquire how you are to know what is right, it does not direct you to the law of benevolence as the only standard, but it directs you to an abstract idea of right, as an ultimate rule, having no regard to the law of benevolence or love. It tells you that right is right, because it is right; and not that right is conformity to the law of benevolence, and right for this reason. Now certainly such teaching is radically false, and subversive of all sound morality and true religion.

(4.) As we have formerly seen, this philosophy does not represent virtue as consisting in the love of God, or of Christ, or our neighbor. Consistency must require the abettors of this scheme to give fundamentally false instructions to inquiring sinners. Instead of representing God and all holy beings as devoted to the public good, and instead of exhorting sinners to love God and their neighbor, this philosophy must represent God and holy beings as consecrated to right for the sake of the right; and must exhort sinners, who ask what they shall do to be saved, to will the right for the sake of the right, to love the right, to deify right, and fall down and worship it. There is much of this false morality and religion in the world and in the church. Infidels are great sticklers for this religion, and often exhibit as much of it as do some rightarian professors of religion. It is a severe, stern, loveless, Godless, Christless philosophy, and nothing but happy inconsistency prevents its advocates from manifesting it in this light to the world. The law of right, when conceived of as distinct from, or opposed to, the law of benevolence, is a perfect strait-jacket, an iron collar, a snare of death.

This philosophy represents all war, all slavery, and many things as wrong per se, without insisting upon such a definition of those things as necessarily implies selfishness. Any thing whatever is wrong in itself that includes and implies selfishness, and nothing else is or can be. All war waged for selfish purposes is wrong per se. But war waged for benevolent purposes, or war required by the law of benevolence, and engaged in with a benevolent design, is neither wrong in itself, nor wrong in any proper sense. All holding men in bondage from selfish motives is wrong in itself, but holding men in bondage in obedience to the law of benevolence is not wrong but right. And so it is with every thing else. Therefore, where it is insisted that all war and all slavery, or any thing else is wrong in itself, such a definition of things must be insisted on as necessarily implies selfishness. But consistent rightarianism will insist that all war, all slavery, and all of many other things, are wrong in themselves without regard to their being violations of the law of benevolence. This is consistent with such philosophy, but it is most false and absurd in fact. Indeed, any philosophy that assumes the existence of a law of right distinct from, and possibly opposed to, the law of benevolence, must teach many doctrines at war with both reason and revelation. It sets men in chase of a philosophical abstraction as the supreme end of life, instead of the concrete reality of the highest well-being of God and the universe. It preys upon the human soul, and turns into solid iron all the tender sensibilities of our being. Do but contemplate a human being supremely devoted to an abstraction, as the end of human life. He wills the right for the sake of the right. Or, more strictly, he wills the good of being, not from any regard to being, but because of the relation of intrinsic fitness or rightness existing between choice and its object. For this he lives, and moves, and has his being. What sort of religion is this? I wish not to be understood as holding, or insinuating, that professed rightarians universally, or even generally, pursue their theory to its legitimate boundary, or that they manifest the spirit that it naturally begets. No, I am most happy in acknowledging that with many, and perhaps with most of them, it is so purely a theory, that they are not greatly influenced by it in practice. Many of them I regard as the excellent of the earth, and I am happy to count them among my dearest and most valued friends. But I speak of the philosophy, with its natural results, when embraced not merely as a theory, but when adopted by the heart as the rule of life. It is only in such cases that its natural and legitimate fruits appear. Only let it be borne in mind that right is conformity to moral law, that moral law is the law of nature, or the law founded in the nature and relations of moral agents, the law that requires just that course of willing and action that tends naturally to secure the highest well-being of all moral agents, that requires this course of willing and acting for the sake of the end in which it naturally and governmentally results, and requires that this end shall be aimed at or intended by all moral agents as the supreme good and the only ultimate end of life;--I say, only let these truths be borne in mind, and you will never talk of a right, or a virtue, or a law, obedience to which necessarily results in universal misery; nor will you conceive that such a thing is possible.

5. Lastly, I come to the consideration of the practical bearings of what I regard as the true theory of the foundation of moral obligation, namely, that the intrinsic nature and value of the highest well-being of God and of the universe is the sole foundation of moral obligation.

Upon this philosophy I remark--

That if this be true, the whole subject of moral obligation is perfectly simple and intelligible; so plain, indeed, that "the wayfaring man, though a fool, cannot err therein."

Upon this theory, every moral agent knows in every possible instance what is right, and can never mistake his real duty.

His duty is to will this end with all the known conditions and means thereof. Intending this end with a single eye, and doing what appears to him, with all the light he can obtain, to be in the highest degree calculated to secure this end, he really does his duty. If in this case he is mistaken in regard to what is the best means of securing this end, still, with a benevolent intention, he does not sin. He has done right, for he has intended as he ought, and acted outwardly as he thought was the path of duty, under the best light he could obtain. This, then, was his duty. He did not mistake his duty; because it was duty to intend as he intended, and under the circumstances, to act as he acted. How else should he have acted?

If a moral agent can know what end he aims at or lives for, he can know, and cannot but know, at all times, whether he is right or wrong. All that upon this theory a moral agent needs to be certain of is, whether he lives for the right end, and this, if at all honest, or if dishonest, he really cannot but know. If he would ask, what is right or what is duty at any time, he need not wait for a reply. It is right for him to intend the highest good of being as an end. If he honestly does this, he cannot mistake his duty, for in doing this he really performs the whole of duty. With this honest intention, it is impossible that he should not use the means to promote this end, according to the best light he has; and this is right. A single eye to the highest good of God and the universe, is the whole of morality, strictly considered; and, upon this theory, moral law, moral government, moral obligation, virtue, vice, and the whole subject of morals and religion are the perfection of simplicity. If this theory be true, no honest mind ever mistook the path of duty. To intend the highest good of being is right and is duty. No mind is honest that is not steadily pursuing this end. But in the honest pursuit of this end there can be no sin, no mistaking the path of duty. That is and must be the path of duty that really appears to a benevolent mind to be so. That is, it must be his duty to act in conformity with his honest convictions. This is duty, this is right. So, upon this theory, no one who is truly honest in pursuing the highest good of being, ever did or can mistake his duty in any such sense as to commit sin.

I have spoken with great plainness, and perhaps with some severity, of the several systems of error, as I cannot but regard them, upon the most fundamental and important of subjects; not certainly from any want of love to those who hold them, but from a concern, long cherished and growing upon me, for the honor of truth and for the good of being. Should any of you ever take the trouble to look into this subject, in its length and breadth, and read the various systems, and take the trouble to trace out their practical results, as actually developed in the opinions and practices of men, you certainly would not be at a loss to account for the theological and philosophical fogs that so bewilder the world. How can it be otherwise, while such confusion of opinion prevails upon the fundamental question of morals and religion?

How is it, that there is so much profession and so little real practical benevolence in the world? Multitudes of professed Christians seem to have no conception that benevolence constitutes true religion; that nothing else does; and that selfishness is sin, and totally incompatible with religion. They live on in their self-indulgences, and dream of heaven. This could not be, if the true idea of religion, as consisting in sympathy with the benevolence of God, was fully developed in their minds.

I need not dwell upon the practical bearings of the other theories which I have examined; what I have said may suffice, as an illustration of the importance of being well-established in this fundamental truth. It is affecting to see what conceptions multitudes entertain in regard to the real spirit and meaning of the law and gospel of God, and, consequently, of the nature of holiness.

In dismissing this subject, I would remark, that any system of moral philosophy that does not correctly define a moral action, and the real ground of obligation, must be fundamentally defective. Nay, if consistent, it must be highly pernicious and dangerous. But let moral action be clearly and correctly defined, let the true ground of obligation be clearly and correctly stated; and let both these be kept constantly in view, and such a system would be of incalculable value. It would be throughout intelligible, and force conviction upon every intelligent reader. But I am not aware that any such system exists. So far as I know, they are all faulty, either in their definition of a moral action, and do not fasten the eye upon the ultimate intention, and keep it there as being the seat of moral character, and that from which the character of all our actions is derived; or they soon forget this, and treat mere executive acts as right or wrong, without reference to the ultimate intention. I believe they have all failed in not clearly defining the true ground of obligation, and, consequently, are faulty in their definition of virtue.

LECTURE IX - UNITY OF MORAL ACTION

CAN OBEDIENCE TO MORAL LAW BE PARTIAL?

1. What constitutes obedience to moral law?

We have seen in former lectures, that disinterested benevolence is all that the spirit of moral law requires; that is, that the love which it requires to God and our neighbor is good-willing, willing the highest good or well-being of God, and of being in general, as an end, or for its own sake; that this willing is a consecration of all the powers, so far as they are under the control of the will, to this end. Entire consecration to this end must of course constitute obedience to the moral law. The next question is: Can consecration to this end be real, and yet partial in the sense of not being entire, for the time being? This conducts us to the second proposition, namely,--

2. That obedience cannot be partial in the sense that the subject ever does, or can, partly obey and partly disobey at the same time.

That is, consecration, to be real, must be, for the time being, entire and universal. It will be seen that this discussion respects the simplicity of moral action, that is whether the choices of the will that have any degree of conformity to moral law, are always and necessarily wholly conformed or wholly disconformed to it. There are two distinct branches to this inquiry.

(1.) The one is, Can the will at the same time make opposite choices? Can it choose the highest good of being as an ultimate end, and at the same time choose any other ultimate end, or make any choices whatever inconsistent with this ultimate choice?

(2.) The second branch of this inquiry respects the strength or intensity of the choice. Suppose but one ultimate choice can exist at the same time, may not that choice be less efficient and intense than it ought to be? Let us take up these two inquiries in their order.

(1.) Can the will at the same time choose opposite and conflicting ultimate ends? While one ultimate end is chosen, can the will choose anything inconsistent with this end? In reply to the first branch of this inquiry I observe,

(a) That the choice of an ultimate end is, and must be, the supreme preference of the mind. Sin is the supreme preference of self-gratification. Holiness is the supreme preference of the good of being. Can then two supreme preferences co-exist in the same mind? It is plainly impossible to make opposite choices at the same time, that is, to choose opposite and conflicting ultimate ends.

(b) All intelligent choice, as has been formerly shown, must respect ends or means. Choice is synonymous with intention. If there is a choice or intention, of necessity something must be chosen or intended. This something must he chosen for its own sake, or as an end, or for the sake of something else to which it sustains the relation of a means. To deny this were to deny that the choice is intelligent. But we are speaking of no other than intelligent choice, or the choice of a moral agent.

(c) This conducts us to the inevitable conclusion--that no choice whatever can be made, inconsistent with the present choice of an ultimate end. The mind cannot choose one ultimate end, and choose at the same time another ultimate end. But if this cannot be, it is plain that it cannot choose one ultimate end, and at the same time, while in the exercise of that choice, choose the means to secure some other ultimate end, which other end is not chosen. But if all choice must necessarily respect ends or means, and if the mind can choose but one ultimate end at a time, it follows that, while in the exercise of one choice, or while in the choice of one ultimate end, the mind cannot choose, for the time being, anything inconsistent with that choice. The mind, in the choice of an ultimate end, is shut up to the necessity of willing the means to accomplish that end; and before it can possibly will means to secure any other ultimate end, it must change its choice of an end. If, for example, the soul chooses the highest well-being of God and the universe as an ultimate end, it cannot while it continues to choose that end, use or choose the means to effect any other end. It cannot, while this choice continues, choose self-gratification, or anything else as an ultimate end, nor can it put forth any volition whatever known to be inconsistent with this end. Nay, it can put forth no intelligent volition whatever that is not designed to secure this end. The only possible choice inconsistent with this end is the choice of another ultimate end. When this is done, other means can be used or chosen, and not before. This, then, is plain, to wit, that obedience to moral law cannot be partial, in the sense either that the mind can choose two opposite ultimate ends at the same time, or that it can choose one ultimate end, and at the same time use or choose means to secure any other ultimate end. It "cannot serve God and mammon." It cannot will the good of being as an ultimate end, and at the same time will self-gratification as an ultimate end. In other words, it cannot be selfish and benevolent at the same time. It cannot choose as an ultimate end the highest good of being, and at the same time choose to gratify self as an ultimate end. Until self-gratification is chosen as an end, the mind cannot will the means of self gratification. This disposes of the first branch of the inquiry.

(2.) The second branch of the inquiry respects the strength or intensity of the choice. May not the choice of an end be real, and yet have less than the required strength or intensity? The inquiry resolves itself into this: Can the mind honestly intend or choose an ultimate end, and yet not choose it with all the strength or intensity which is required, or with which it ought to choose it? Now what degree of strength is demanded? By what criterion is this question to be settled? It cannot be that the degree of intensity required is equal to the real value of the end chosen, for this is infinite. The value of the highest well-being of God and the universe is infinite. But a finite being cannot be under obligation to exert infinite strength. The law requires him only to exert his own strength. But does he, or may he not, choose the right end, but with less than all his strength? All his strength lies in his will; the question, therefore, is, may he not will it honestly, and yet at the same time withhold a part of the strength of his will? No one can presume that the choice can be acceptable unless it be honest. Can it be honest and yet less intense and energetic than it ought to be?

We have seen in a former lecture that the perception of an end is a condition of moral obligation to choose that end. I now remark that, as light in respect to the end is the condition of the obligation, so the degree of obligation cannot exceed the degree of light. That is, the mind must apprehend the valuable as a condition of the obligation to will it. The degree of the obligation must be just equal to the mind's honest estimate of the value of the end. The degree of the obligation must vary as the light varies. This is the doctrine of the Bible and of reason. If this is so, it follows that the mind is honest when, and only when, it devotes its strength to the end in view, with an intensity just proportioned to its present light, or estimate of the value of that end.

We have seen that the mind cannot will anything inconsistent with a present ultimate choice. If, therefore, the end is not chosen with an energy and intensity equal to the present light, it cannot be because a part of the strength is employed in some other choice. If all the strength is not given to this object, it must be because some part of it is voluntarily withholden. That is, I choose the end, but not with all my strength, or I choose the end, but choose not to choose it with all my strength. Is this an honest choice, provided the end appears to me to be worthy of all my strength? Certainly it is not honest.

But again: it is absurd to affirm that I choose an ultimate end, and yet do not consecrate to it all my strength. The choice of any ultimate end implies that that is the thing, and the only thing, for which we live and act; that we aim at, and live for nothing else, for the time being. Now what is intended by the assertion, that I may honestly choose an ultimate end, and yet with less strength or intensity than I ought? Is it intended that I can honestly choose an ultimate end, and yet not at every moment keep my will upon the strain, and will at every moment with the utmost possible intensity? If this be the meaning, I grant that it may be so. But I at the same time contend, that the law of God does not require that the will, or any other faculty, should be at every moment upon the strain, and the whole strength exerted at every moment. If it does, it is manifest that even Christ did not obey it. I insist that the moral law requires nothing more than honesty of intention, and assumes that honesty of intention will and must secure just that degree of intensity which from time to time, the mind in its best judgment sees to be demanded. The Bible everywhere assumes that sincerity or honesty of intention is moral perfection; that it is obedience to the law. The terms sincerity and perfection in scripture language are synonymous. Uprightness, sincerity, holiness, honesty, perfection, are words of the same meaning in Bible language.

Again, it seems to be intuitively certain that if the mind chooses its ultimate end, it must in the very act of choice consecrate all its time, and strength, and being, to that end; and at every moment, while the choice remains, choose and act with an intensity in precise conformity with its ability and the best light it has. The intensity of the choice, and the strenuousness of its efforts to secure the end chosen, must, if the intention be sincere, correspond with the view which the soul has of the importance of the end chosen. It does not seem possible that the choice or intention should be real and honest unless this is so. To will at every moment with the utmost strength and intensity, is not only impossible, but, were it possible to do so, could not be in accordance with the soul's convictions of duty. The irresistible judgment of the mind is, that the intensity of its action should not exceed the bound of endurance; that the energies of both soul and body should be so husbanded, as to be able to accomplish the most good upon the whole, and not in a given moment.

But to return to the question: does the law of God require simply uprightness of intention? or does it require not only uprightness, but also a certain degree of intensity in the intention? Is it satisfied with simple sincerity or uprightness of intention, or does it require that the highest possible intensity of choice shall exist at every moment? When it requires that we should love God with all the heart, with all the soul, with all the mind, and with all the strength, does it mean that all our heart, soul, mind, and strength, shall be consecrated to this end, and be used up, from moment to moment, and from hour to hour, according to the best judgment which the mind can form of the necessity and expediency of strenuousness of effort? or does it mean that all the faculties of soul and body shall be at every moment on the strain to the uttermost? Does it mean that the whole being is to be consecrated to, and used up for God with the best economy of which the soul is capable? or does it require that the whole being be not only consecrated to God, but be used up without any regard to economy, and without the soul's exercising any judgment or discretion in the case? In other words, is the law of God the law of reason, or of folly? Is it intelligible and just in its demands? or is it perfectly unintelligible and unjust? Is it a law suited to the nature, relations, and circumstances, of moral agents? or has it no regard to them? If it has no regard to either, is it, can it be, moral law, and impose moral obligation? It seems to me that the law of God requires that all our power, and strength, and being, be honestly and continually consecrated to God, and held, not in a state of the utmost tension, but that the strength shall be expended and employed in exact accordance with the mind's honest judgment of what is, at every moment, the best economy for God. If this be not the meaning and the spirit of the law, it cannot be law, for it could be neither intelligible nor just. Nothing else can be a law of nature. What! does, or can the command, "Thou shalt love the Lord thy God, with all thy heart, with all thy soul, with all thy might, and with all thy strength," require that every particle of my strength, and every faculty of my being, shall be in a state of the utmost possible tension? How long could my strength hold out, or my being last, under such a pressure as this? What reason, or justice, or utility, or equity, or wisdom, could there be in such a commandment as this? Would this be suited to my nature and relations? That the law does not require the constant and most intense action of the will, I argue for the following reasons:--

1. No creature in heaven or earth could possibly know whether he ever for a single moment obeyed it. How could he know that no more tension could possibly be endured?

2. Such a requirement would be unreasonable, inasmuch as such a state of mind would be unendurable.

3. Such a state of constant tension and strain of the faculties could be of no possible use.

4. It would be uneconomical. More good could be effected by a husbanding of the strength.

5. Christ certainly obeyed the moral law; and yet nothing is more evident than that his faculties were not always on the strain.

Every one knows that the intensity of the will's action depends, and must depend, upon the clearness with which the value of the object chosen is perceived. It is perfectly absurd to suppose that the will should, or possibly can, act at all times with the same degree of intensity. As the mind's apprehensions of truth vary, the intensity of the will's action must vary, or it does not act rationally, and consequently not virtuously. The intensity of the actions of the will, ought to vary as light varies, and if it does not, the mind is not honest. If honest, it must vary as light and ability vary.

That an intention cannot be right and honest in kind and deficient in the degree of intensity, I argue--

1. From the fact that it is absurd to talk of an intention right in kind, while it is deficient in intensity. What does rightness in kind mean? Does it mean simply that the intention terminates on the proper object? But is this the right kind of intention, when only the proper object is chosen, while there is a voluntary withholding of the required energy of choice? Is this, can this be, an honest intention? If so, what is meant by an honest intention? Is it honest, can it be honest, voluntarily to withhold from God and the universe what we perceive to be their due, and what we are conscious we might render? It is a contradiction to call this honest. In what sense then may, or can, an intention be acceptable in kind, while deficient in degree? Certainly in no sense, unless known and voluntary dishonesty can be acceptable. But again, let me ask, what is intended by an intention being deficient in degree of intensity? If this deficiency be a sinful deficiency, it must be a known deficiency. That is, the subject of it must know at the time that his intention is in point of intensity less than it ought to be, or that he wills with less energy than he ought; or, in other words, that the energy of the choice does not equal, or is not agreeable to, his own estimate of the value of the end chosen. But this implies an absurdity. Suppose I choose an end, that is, I choose a thing solely on account of its own intrinsic value. It is for its value that I choose it. I choose it for its value, but not according to its value. My perception of its value led me to choose it; and yet, while I choose it for that reason, I voluntarily withhold that degree of intensity which I know is demanded by my own estimate of the value of the thing which I choose! This is a manifest absurdity and contradiction. If I choose a thing for its value, this implies that I choose it according to my estimate of its value. Happiness, for example, is a good in itself. Now, suppose I will its existence impartially, that is, solely on account of its intrinsic value; now, does not this imply that every degree of happiness must be willed according to its real or relative value? Can I will it impartially, for its own sake, for and only for its intrinsic value, and yet not prefer a greater to a less amount of happiness? This is impossible. Willing it on account of its intrinsic value implies willing it according to my estimate of its intrinsic value. So, it must be that an intention cannot be sincere, honest, and acceptable in kind, while it is sinfully deficient in degree.

As holiness consists in ultimate intention, so does sin. And as holiness consists in choosing the highest well-being of God and the good of the universe, for its own sake, or as the supreme ultimate end of pursuit; so sin consists in willing, with a supreme choice or intention, self-gratification and self-interest. Preferring a less to a greater good, because it is our own, is selfishness. All selfishness consists in a supreme ultimate intention. By an ultimate intention, as I have said, is intended that which is chosen for its own sake as an end, and not as a means to some other end. Whenever a moral being prefers or chooses his own gratification, or his own interest, in preference to a higher good, because it is his own, he chooses it as an end, for its own sake, and as an ultimate end, not designing it as a means of promoting any other and higher end, nor because it is a part of universal good. Every sin, then, consists in an act of will. It consists in preferring self-gratification, or self-interest, to the authority of God, the glory of God, and the good of the universe. It is, therefore, and must be, a supreme ultimate choice, or intention. Sin and holiness, then, both consist in supreme, ultimate, and opposite choices, or intentions, and cannot by any possibility, co-exist.

Five suppositions may be made, and so far as I can see, only five, in respect to this subject.

1. It may be supposed, that selfishness and benevolence can co-exist in the same mind.

2. It may be supposed, that the same act or choice may have a complex character, on account of complexity in the motives which induce it.

3. It may be supposed, that an act or choice may be right, or holy in kind, but deficient in intensity or degree. Or--

4. That the will, or heart, may be right, while the affections, or emotions, are wrong. Or--

5. That there may be a ruling, latent, actually existing, holy preference, or intention, co-existing with opposing volitions.

Now, unless one of these suppositions is true, it must follow that moral character is either wholly right or wholly wrong, and never partly right and partly wrong at the same time. And now to the examination.

1. It may be supposed, that selfishness and benevolence can co-exist in the same mind.

It has been shown that selfishness and benevolence are supreme, ultimate, and opposite choices, or intentions. They cannot, therefore, by any possibility, co-exist in the same mind.

2. The next supposition is, that the same act or choice may have a complex character, on account of complexity in the motives. On this let me say:--

(1.) Motives are objective or subjective. An objective motive is that thing external to the mind that induces choice or intention. Subjective motive is the intention itself.

(2.) Character, therefore, does not belong to the objective motive, or to that thing which the mind chooses; but moral character is confined to the subjective motive, which is synonymous with choice or intention. Thus we say a man is to be judged by his motives, meaning that his character is as his intention is. Multitudes of objective motives or considerations, may have concurred, directly or indirectly, in their influence to induce choice or intention; but the intention or subjective motive is always necessarily simple and indivisible. In other words, moral character consists in the choice of an ultimate end, and this end is to be chosen for its own sake, else it is not an ultimate end. If the end chosen be the highest well-being of God and the good of the universe--if it be the willing or intending to promote and treat every interest in the universe, according to its perceived relative value, it is a right, a holy motive, or intention. If it be anything else, it is sinful. Now, whatever complexity there may have been in the considerations that led the way to this choice or intention, it is self-evident that the intention must be one, simple, and indivisible.

(3.) Whatever complexity there might have been in those considerations that prepared the way to the settling down upon this intention, the mind in a virtuous choice has, and can have, but one ultimate reason for its choice, and that is the intrinsic value of the thing chosen. The highest well-being of God, the good of the universe, and every good according to its perceived relative value, must be chosen for one, and only one reason, and that is the intrinsic value of the good which is chosen for its own sake. If chosen for any other reason, the choice is not virtuous. It is absurd to say, that a thing is good and valuable in itself, but may be rightly chosen, not for that but for some other reason--that God's highest well-being and the happiness of the universe are an infinite good in themselves, but are not to be chosen for that reason, and on their own account, but for some other reason. Holiness, then, must always consist in singleness of eye or intention. It must consist in the supreme disinterested choice, willing, or intending the good of God and of the universe, for its own sake. In this intention there cannot be any complexity. If there were, it would not be holy, but sinful. It is, therefore, sheer nonsense to say, that one and the same choice may have a complex character, on account of complexity of motive. For that motive in which moral character consists, is the supreme ultimate intention, or choice. This choice, or intention, must consist in the choice of a thing as an end, and for its own sake. The supposition, then, that the same choice or intention may have a complex character, on account of complexity in the motives, is wholly inadmissible.

If it be still urged, that the intention or subjective motive may be complex -- that several things may be included in the intention, and be aimed at by the mind -- and that it may, therefore, be partly holy and partly sinful -- I reply:--

(4.) If by this it be meant that several things may be aimed at or intended by the mind at the same time, I inquire what things?--It is true, that the supreme, disinterested choice of the highest good of being, may include the intention to use all the necessary means. It may also include the intention to promote every interest in the universe, according to its perceived relative value. These are all properly included in one intention; but this implies no such complexity in the subjective motive, as to include both sin and holiness.

(5.) If by complexity of intention is meant, that it may be partly disinterestedly benevolent, and partly selfish, which it must be to be partly holy and partly sinful, I reply, that this supposition is absurd. It has been shown that selfishness and benevolence consist in supreme, ultimate, and opposite choices or intentions. To suppose, then, that an intention can be both holy and sinful, is to suppose that it may include two supreme, opposite, and ultimate choices or intentions, at the same time; in other words, that I may supremely and disinterestedly intend to regard and promote every interest in the universe, according to its perceived relative value, for its own sake; and at the same time, may supremely regard my own self-interest and self-gratification, and in some things supremely intend to promote my selfish interests, in opposition to the interests of the universe and the commands of God. But this is naturally impossible. An ultimate intention, then, may be complex in the sense, that it may include the design to promote every perceived interest, according to its relative value; but it cannot, by any possibility, be complex in the sense that it includes selfishness and benevolence, or holiness and sin.

3. The third supposition is, that holiness may be right, or pure in kind, but deficient in degree. On this, I remark:--

(1.) We have seen that moral character consists in the ultimate intention.

(2.) The supposition, therefore, must be, that the intention may be right, or pure in kind, but deficient in the degree of its strength.

(3.) Our intention is to be tried by the law of God, both in respect to its kind and degree.

(4.) The law of God requires us to will, or intend the promotion of every interest in the universe, according to its perceived relative value, for its own sake; in other words, that all our powers shall be supremely and disinterestedly devoted to the glory of God, and the good of the universe.

(5.) This cannot mean, that any faculty shall at every moment be kept upon the strain, or in a state of utmost tension, for this would be inconsistent with natural ability. It would be to require a natural impossibility, and therefore be unjust.

(6.) It cannot mean that at all times, and on all subjects, the same degree of exertion shall be made; for the best possible discharge of duty does not always require the same degree or intensity of mental or corporeal exertion.

(7.) The law cannot, justly or possibly, require more than that the whole being shall be consecrated to God--that we shall fully and honestly will or intend the promotion of every interest, according to its perceived relative value, and according to the extent of our ability.

(8.) Now the strength or intensity of the intention must, and ought, of necessity, to depend upon the degree of our knowledge or light in regard to any object of choice. If our obligation is not to be graduated by the light we possess, then it would follow, that we may be under obligation to exceed our natural ability, which cannot be.

(9.) The importance which we attach to objects of choice, and consequently the degree of ardor or intenseness of the intention, must depend upon the clearness or obscurity of our views, of the real or relative value of the objects of choice.

(10.) Our obligation cannot be measured by the views which God has of the importance of those objects of choice. It is a well-settled and generally-admitted truth, that increased light increases responsibility, or moral obligation. No creature is bound to will any thing with the intenseness or degree of strength with which God wills it, for the plain reason, that no creature sees its importance or real value, as He does. If our obligation were to be graduated by God's knowledge of the real value of objects, we could never obey the moral law, either in this world or the world to come, nor could any being but God ever, by any possibility, meet its demands.

The fact is, that the obligation of every moral being must be graduated by his knowledge. If, therefore, his intention be equal in its intensity to his views or knowledge of the real or relative value of different objects, it is right. It is up to the full measure of his obligation; and if his own honest judgment is not to be made the measure of his obligation, then his obligation can exceed what he is able to know; which contradicts the true nature of moral law, and is, therefore, false.

If conscious honesty of intention, both as it respects the kind and degree of intention, according to the degree of light possessed, be not entire obedience to moral law, then there is no being in heaven or earth, who can know himself to be entirely obedient; for all that any being can possibly know upon this subject, is that he honestly wills or intends, in accordance with the dictates of his reason, or the judgment which he has of the real or relative value of the object chosen. No moral being can possibly blame or charge himself with any default, when he is conscious of honestly intending, willing, or choosing, and acting, according to the best light he has; for in this case he obeys the law, as he understands it, and, of course, cannot conceive himself to be condemned by the law.

Good-willing, or intending is, in respect to God, to be at all times supreme; and in respect to other beings, it is to be in proportion to the relative value of their happiness, as perceived by the mind. This is always to be the intention. The volitions, or efforts of the will to promote these objects, may vary, and ought to vary indefinitely in their intensity, in proportion to the particular duty to which, for the time being, we are called.

But further, we have seen that virtue consists in willing every good according to its perceived relative value, and that nothing short of this is virtue. But this is perfect virtue for the time being. In other words, virtue and moral perfection, in respect to a given act, or state of the will, are synonymous terms. Virtue is holiness. Holiness is uprightness. Uprightness is that which is just what, under the circumstances, it should be; and nothing else is virtue, holiness, or uprightness. Virtue, holiness, uprightness, moral perfection--when we apply these terms to any given state of the will--are synonymous. To talk, therefore, of a virtue, holiness, uprightness, justice, right in kind, but deficient in degree, is to talk sheer nonsense. It is the same absurdity as to talk of sinful holiness, an unjust justice, a wrong rightness, an impure purity, an imperfect perfection, a disobedient obedience.

Virtue, holiness, uprightness, etc., signify a definite thing, and never anything else than conformity to the law of God. That which is not entirely conformed to the law of God is not holiness. This must be true in philosophy, and the Bible affirms the same thing. "Whosoever shall keep the whole law, and yet offend in one point, he is guilty of all." The spirit of this text as clearly and as fully assumes and affirms the doctrine under consideration, as if it had been uttered with that design alone.

4. The next supposition is, that the will, or heart, may be right, while the affections or emotions are wrong. Upon this I remark:

(1.) That this supposition overlooks the very thing in which moral character consists. It has been shown that moral character consists in the supreme ultimate intention of the mind, and that this supreme, disinterested benevolence, good-willing or intention, is the whole of virtue. Now this intention originates volitions. It directs the attention of the mind, and therefore, produces thoughts, emotions, or affections. It also, through volition, produces bodily action. But moral character does not lie in outward actions, the movements of the arm, nor in the volition that moves the muscles; for that volition terminates upon the action itself. I will to move my arm, and my arm must move by a law of necessity. Moral character belongs solely to the intention that produced the volition that moved the muscles to the performance of the outward act. So intention produces the volition that directs the attention of the mind to a given object. Attention, by a natural necessity, produces thought, affection, or emotion. Now thought, affection, or emotion, are all connected with volition, by a natural necessity; that is, if the attention is directed to an object, corresponding thoughts and emotions must exist, as a matter of course. Moral character no more lies in emotion, than in outward action. It does not lie in thought, or attention. It does not lie in the specific volition that directed the attention; but in that intention, or design of the mind, that produced the volition, which directed the attention, which, again, produced the thought, which, again, produced the emotion. Now the supposition, that the intention may be right, while the emotions or feelings of the mind may be wrong, is the same as to say, that outward action may be wrong, while the intention is right. The fact is, that moral character is, and must be, as the intention is. If any feeling or outward action is inconsistent with the existing ultimate intention, it must be so in spite of the agent. But if any outward action or state of feeling exists, in opposition to the intention or choice of the mind, it cannot, by any possibility, have moral character. Whatever is beyond the control of a moral agent, he cannot be responsible for. Whatever he cannot control by intention, he cannot control at all. Everything for which he can possibly be responsible, resolves itself into his intention. His whole character, therefore, is, and must be, as his intention is. If, therefore, temptations, from whatever quarter they may come, produce emotions within him inconsistent with his intention, and which he cannot control, he cannot be responsible for them.

(2.) As a matter of fact, although emotions, contrary to his intentions, may, by circumstances beyond his control, be brought to exist in his mind; yet, by willing to divert the attention of the mind from the objects that produce them, they can ordinarily be banished from the mind. If this is done as soon as in the nature of the case it can be, there is no sin. If it is not done as soon as in the nature of the case it can be, then it is absolutely certain that the intention is not what it ought to be. The intention is to devote the whole being to the service of God and the good of the universe, and of course to avoid every thought, affection, and emotion, inconsistent with this. While this intention exists, it is certain that if any object be thrust upon the attention which excites thoughts and emotions inconsistent with our supreme ultimate intention, the attention of the mind will be instantly diverted from those objects, and the hated emotion hushed, if this is possible. For, while the intention exists, corresponding volitions must exist. There cannot, therefore, be a right state of heart or intention, while the emotions, or affections, of the mind are sinful. For emotions are in themselves in no case sinful, and when they exist against the will, through the force of temptation, the soul is not responsible for their existence. And, as I said, the supposition overlooks that in which moral character consists, and makes it to consist in that over which the law does not properly legislate; for love, or benevolence, is the fulfilling of the law.

But here it may be said, that the law not only requires benevolence, or good-willing, but requires a certain kind of emotions, just as it requires the performance of certain outward actions, and that therefore there may be a right intention where there is a deficiency, either in kind or degree of right emotion. To this I answer:--

Outward actions are required of men, only because they are connected with intention, by a natural necessity. And no outward action is ever required of us, unless it can be produced by intending and aiming to do it. If the effect does not follow our honest endeavors, because of any antagonistic influence, opposed to our exertions, which we cannot overcome, we have, by our intentions, complied with the spirit of the law, and are not to blame that the outward effect does not take place. Just so with emotions. All we have power to do, is, to direct the attention of the mind to those objects calculated to secure a given state of emotion. If, from any exhaustion of the sensibility, or from any other cause beyond our control, the emotions do not arise which the consideration of that subject is calculated to produce, we are no more responsible for the absence or weakness of the emotion than we should be for the want of power or weakness of motion in our muscles, when we willed to move them, provided that weakness was involuntary and beyond our control. The fact is, we cannot be blameworthy for not feeling or doing that which we cannot do or feel by intending it. If the intention then is what it ought to be for the time being, nothing can be morally wrong.

5. The last supposition is, that a latent preference, or right intention, may co-exist with opposing or sinful volitions. I formerly supposed that this could be true, but am now convinced that it cannot be true, for the following reasons:

(1.) Observe, the supposition is, that the intention or ruling preference may be right--may really exist as an active and virtuous state of mind, while, at the same time, volition may exist inconsistent with it.

(2.) Now what is a right intention? I answer: Nothing short of this -- willing, choosing, or intending the highest good of God and of the universe, and to promote this at every moment, to the extent of our ability. In other words -- right intention is supreme, disinterested benevolence. Now what are the elements which enter into this right intention?

(a.) The choice or willing of every interest according to its perceived intrinsic value.

(b.) To devote our entire being, now and forever, to this end. This is right intention. Now the question is, can this intention co-exist with a volition inconsistent with it? Volition implies the choice of something, for some reason. If it be the choice of whatever can promote this supremely benevolent end, and for that reason, the volition is consistent with the intention; but if it be the choice of something perceived to be inconsistent with this end, and for a selfish reason, then the volition is inconsistent with the supposed intention. But the question is, do the volition and intention co-exist? According to the supposition, the will chooses, or wills, something for a selfish reason, or something perceived to be inconsistent with supreme, disinterested benevolence. Now it is plainly impossible, that this choice can take place while the opposite intention exists. For this selfish volition is, according to the supposition, sinful or selfish; that is, something is chosen for its own sake, which is inconsistent with disinterested benevolence. But here the intention is ultimate. It terminates upon the object chosen for its own sake. To suppose, then, that benevolence still remains in exercise, and that a volition co-exists with it that is sinful, involves the absurdity of supposing, that selfishness and benevolence can co-exist in the same mind, or that the will can choose, or will, with a supreme preference or choice, two opposites at the same time. This is plainly impossible. Suppose I intend to go to the city of New York as soon as I possibly can. Now, if, on my way, I will to loiter needlessly a moment, I necessarily relinquish one indispensable element of my intention. In willing to loiter, or turn aside to some other object for a day, or an hour, I must of necessity, relinquish the intention of going as soon as I possibly can. I may not design finally to relinquish my journey, but I must of necessity relinquish the intention of going as soon as I can. Now, virtue consists in intending to do all the good I possibly can, or in willing the glory of God and the good of the universe, and intending to promote them to the extent of my ability. Nothing short of this is virtue. If at any time, I will something perceived to be inconsistent with this intention, I must, for the time being, relinquish the intention, as it must indispensably exist in my mind, in order to be virtue. I may not come to the resolution, that I will never serve God any more; but I must of necessity relinquish, for the time being, the intention of doing my utmost to glorify God, if at any time I put forth a selfish volition. For a selfish volition implies a selfish intention. I cannot put forth a volition intended to secure an end until I have chosen the end. Therefore a holy intention cannot co-exist with a selfish volition. It must be, therefore, that in every sinful choice, the will of a holy being must necessarily drop the exercise of supreme, benevolent intention, and pass into an opposite state of choice; that is, the agent must cease, for the time being, to exercise benevolence, and make a selfish choice. For, be it understood, that volition is the choice of a means to an end; and of course a selfish volition implies a selfish choice of an end.

Having briefly examined the several suppositions that can be made in regard to the mixed character of actions, I will now answer a few objections; after which, I will bring this philosophy, as briefly as possible, into the light of the Bible.

Objection. Does a Christian cease to be a Christian, whenever he commits a sin.? I answer:

1. Whenever he sins, he must, for the time being, cease to be holy. This is self-evident. Whenever he sins, he must be condemned; he must incur the penalty of the law of God. If he does not, it must be because the law of God is abrogated. But if the law of God be abrogated, he has no rule of duty; consequently, he can neither be holy nor sinful. If it be said that the precept is still binding upon him, but that, with respect to the Christian, the penalty is forever set aside, or abrogated, I reply, that to abrogate the penalty is to repeal the precept; for a precept without penalty is no law. It is only counsel or advice. The Christian, therefore, is justified no longer than he obeys, and must be condemned when he disobeys; or Antinomianism is true. Until he repents he cannot be forgiven. In these respects, then, the sinning Christian and the unconverted sinner are upon precisely the same ground.

2. In two important respects the sinning Christian differs widely from the unconverted sinner:

(1.) In his relations to God. A Christian is a child of God. A sinning Christian is a disobedient child of God. An unconverted sinner is a child of the devil. A Christian sustains a covenant relation to God; such a covenant relation as to secure to him that discipline which tends to reclaim and bring him back, if he wanders away from God. "If his children forsake my law, and walk not in my judgments; if they break my statutes and keep not my commandments; then will I visit their transgression with the rod, and their iniquity with stripes. Nevertheless my loving-kindness will I not utterly take from him, nor suffer my faithfulness to fail. My covenant will I not break, nor alter the thing that is gone out of my lips." Ps. lxxxix. 30-34.

(2.) The sinning Christian differs from the unconverted man, in the state of his sensibility. In whatever way it takes place, every Christian knows that the state of his sensibility in respect to the things of God, has undergone a great change. Now it is true, that moral character does not lie in the sensibility, nor in the will's obeying the sensibility. Nevertheless our consciousness teaches us, that our feelings have great power in promoting wrong choice on the one hand, and in removing obstacles to right choice on the other. In every Christian's mind there is, therefore, a foundation laid for appeals to the sensibilities of the soul, that gives truth a decided advantage over the will. And multitudes of things in the experience of every Christian, give truth a more decided advantage over his will, through the intelligence, than is the case with unconverted sinners.

Obj. Can a man be born again, and then be unborn? I answer:

If there were anything impossible in this, then perseverance would be no virtue. None will maintain, that there is anything naturally impossible in this, except it be those who hold to physical regeneration. If regeneration consist in a change in the ruling preference of the mind, or in the ultimate intention, as we shall see it does, it is plain, that an individual can be born again, and afterwards cease to be virtuous. That a Christian is able to apostatize, is evident, from the many warnings addressed to Christians in the Bible. A Christian may certainly fall into sin and unbelief, and afterwards be renewed, both to repentance and faith.

Obj. Can there be no such thing as weak faith, weak love, and weak repentance? I answer:

If you mean comparatively weak, I say, yes. But if you mean weak, in such a sense as to be sinful, I say, no. Faith, repentance, love, and every Christian grace, properly so called, do and must consist in acts of will, and resolve themselves into some modification of supreme, disinterested benevolence.

I shall, in a future lecture, have occasion to show the philosophical nature of faith. Let it suffice here to say, that faith necessarily depends upon the clearness or obscurity of the intellectual apprehension of truth. Faith, to be real or virtuous, must embrace whatever of truth is apprehended by the intelligence for the time being. Various causes may operate to divert the intelligence from the objects of faith, or to cause the mind to perceive but few of them, and those in comparative obscurity. Faith may be weak, and will certainly and necessarily be weak in such cases, in proportion to the obscurity of the views. And yet, if the will or heart confides so far as it apprehends the truth, which it must do to be virtuous at all, faith cannot be weak in such a sense as to be sinful; for if a man confides so far as he apprehends or perceives the truth, so far as faith is concerned he is doing his whole duty.

Again, faith may be weak in the sense, that it often intermits and gives place to unbelief. Faith is confidence, and unbelief is the withholding of confidence. It is the rejection of truth perceived. Faith is the reception of truth perceived. Faith and unbelief, then, are opposite states of choice, and can by no possibility co-exist.

Faith may be weak also in respect to its objects. The disciples of our Lord Jesus Christ knew so little of him, were so filled with ignorance and the prejudices of education, as to have very weak faith in respect to the Messiahship, power, and divinity of their blaster. He speaks of them as having but little confidence, and yet it does not appear that they did not implicitly trust him, so far as they understood him. And although, through ignorance, their faith was weak, yet there is no evidence, that when they had any faith at all they did not confide in whatever of truth they apprehended.

But did not the disciples pray, "Increase our faith?" I answer:

Yes. And by this they must have intended to pray for instruction; for what else could they mean? Unless a man means this, when he prays for faith, he does not know what he prays for. Christ produces faith by enlightening the mind. When we pray for faith we pray for light. And faith, to be real faith at all, must be equal to the light we have. If apprehended truth be not implicitly received and confided in, there is no faith, but unbelief. If it be, faith is what it ought to be, wholly unmixed with sin.

But did not one say to our Lord, "Lord, I believe, help thou my unbelief;" thus implying, that he was in the exercise both of faith and unbelief at the same time? I answer yes, but--

1. This was not inspiration.

2. It is not certain that he had any faith at all.

3. If he had, and prayed understandingly, he meant nothing more than to ask for an increase of faith, or for such a degree of light as to remove his doubts in respect to the divine power of Christ.

Again, it is objected that this philosophy contradicts Christian experience. To this I reply,

That it is absurd to appeal from reason and the Bible to empirical consciousness which must be the appeal in this case. Reason and the Bible plainly attest the truth of the theory here advocated. What experience is then to be appealed to, to set their testimony aside? Why, Christian experience, it is replied. But what is Christian experience? How shall we learn what it is? Why surely by appealing to reason and the Bible. But these declare that if a man offend in one point, he does and must, for the time being, violate the spirit of the whole law. Nothing is or can be more express than is the testimony of both reason and revelation upon this subject. Here, then, we have the unequivocal decision of the only court of competent jurisdiction in the case; and shall we befool ourselves by appealing from this tribunal to the court of empirical consciousness? Of what does that take cognizance? Why, of what actually passes in the mind; that is, of its mental states. These we are conscious of as facts. But we call these states Christian experience. How do we ascertain that they are in accordance with the law and gospel of God? Why only by an appeal to reason and the Bible. Here, then, we are driven back to the court from which we had before appealed, whose judgment is always the same.

Obj. But it is said, this theory seems to be true in philosophy, that is, the intelligence seems to affirm it, but it is not true in fact.

Answer. If the intelligence affirms it, it must be true, or reason deceives us. But if the reason deceives in this, it may also in other things. If it fails us here, it fails us on the most important of all questions. If reason gives false testimony, we can never know truth from error upon any moral subject. We certainly can never know what religion is or is not, if the testimony of reason can be set aside. If the reason cannot be safely appealed to, how are we to know what the Bible means? for it is the faculty by which we get at the truth of the oracles of God.

These are the principal objections to the philosophical view I have taken of the simplicity of moral action, that occur to my mind. I will now briefly advert to the consistency of this philosophy with the scriptures.

1. The Bible every where seems to assume the simplicity of moral action. Christ expressly informed his disciples, that they could not serve God and mammon. Now by this he did not mean, that a man could not serve God at one time and mammon at another; but that he could not serve both at the same time. The philosophy that makes it possible for persons to be partly holy and partly sinful at the same time, does make it possible to serve God and mammon at the same time, and thus flatly contradicts the assertion of our Saviour.

2. James has expressly settled this philosophy, by saying, that "Whosoever shall keep the whole law, and yet offend in one point, he is guilty of all." Here he must mean to assert, that one sin involves a breach of the whole spirit of the law, and is, therefore, inconsistent with any degree of holiness existing with it. Also, "Doth a fountain send forth at the same place sweet water and bitter? Can the fig-tree, my brethren, bear olive-berries? either a vine, figs? So can no fountain both yield salt-water and fresh," James iii. 11, 12. In this passage he clearly affirms the simplicity of moral action; for by the "the same place" he evidently means, the same time, and what he says is equivalent to saying, that a man cannot be holy and sinful at the same time.

3. Christ has expressly taught, that nothing is regeneration, or virtue, but entire obedience, or the renunciation of all selfishness. "Except a man forsake all that he hath, he cannot be my disciple."

4. The manner in which the precepts and threatenings of the Bible are usually given, shows that nothing is regarded as obedience, or virtue, but doing exactly that which God commands.

I might go to great lengths in the examination of scripture testimony, but it cannot be necessary, or in these lectures expedient. I must close this lecture with a few inferences and remarks.

1. It has been supposed by some, that the simplicity of moral action has been resorted to as a theory, by the advocates of entire sanctification in this life, as the only consistent method of carrying out their principle. To this I reply:--

(1.) That this theory is held in common, both by those who hold and those who deny the doctrine of entire sanctification in this life.

(2.) The truth of the doctrine of entire sanctification does not depend at all upon this philosophical theory for its support; but may be established by Bible testimony, whatever the philosophy of holiness may be.

2. Growth in grace consists in two things:--

(1.) In the stability or permanency of holy, ultimate intention.

(2.) In intensity or strength. As knowledge increases, Christians will naturally grow in grace, in both these respects.

3. The theory of the mixed character of moral actions, is an eminently dangerous theory, as it leads its advocates to suppose, that in their acts of rebellion there is something holy, or, more strictly, there is some holiness in them, while they are in the known commission of sin.

It is dangerous, because it leads its advocates to place the standard of conversion, or regeneration, exceedingly low--to make regeneration, repentance, true love to God, faith, etc., consistent with the known or conscious commission of present sin. This must be a highly dangerous philosophy. The fact is, regeneration, or holiness, under any form, is quite another thing than it is supposed to be, by those who maintain the philosophy of the mixed character of moral action. There can scarcely be a more dangerous error than to say, that while we are conscious of present sin, we are or can be in a state of acceptance with God.

4. The false philosophy of many leads them to adopt a phraseology inconsistent with truth; and to speak as if they were guilty of present sin, when in fact they are not, but are in a state of acceptance with God.

5. It is erroneous to say that Christians sin in their most holy exercises, and it is as injurious and dangerous as it is false. The fact is, holiness is holiness, and it is really nonsense to speak of a holiness that consists with sin.

6. The tendency of this philosophy is to quiet in their delusions those whose consciences accuse them of present sin, as if this could be true, and they, notwithstanding, in a state of acceptance with God.

7. The only sense in which obedience to moral law can be partial is, that obedience may be intermittent. That is, the subject may sometimes obey, and at other times disobey. He may at one time be selfish, or will his own gratification, because it is his own, and without regard to the well-being of God and his neighbor, and at another time will the highest well-being of God and the universe, as an end, and his own good in proportion to its relative value. These are opposite choices, or ultimate intentions. The one is holy; the other is sinful. One is obedience, entire obedience, to the law of God; the other is disobedience, entire disobedience, to that law. These, for aught we can see, may succeed each other an indefinite number of times, but co-exist they plainly cannot.

LECTURE X - OBEDIENCE ENTIRE

The government of God accepts nothing as virtue but obedience to the law of God.

But it may be asked, Why state this proposition? Was this truth ever called in question? I answer, that the truth of this proposition, though apparently so self-evident that to raise the question may reasonably excite astonishment, is generally denied. Indeed, probably nine-tenths of the nominal church deny it. They tenaciously hold sentiments that are entirely contrary to it, and amount to a direct denial of it. They maintain that there is much true virtue in the world, and yet that there is no one who ever for a moment obeys the law of God; that all Christians are virtuous, and that they are truly religious, and yet not one on earth obeys the moral law of God; in short, that God accepts as virtue that which, in every instance, comes short of obedience to his law. And yet it is generally asserted in their articles of faith, that obedience to moral law is the only proper evidence of a change of heart. With this sentiment in their creed, they will brand as a heretic, or as a hypocrite, any one who professes to obey the law; and maintain that men may be, and are pious, and eminently so, who do not obey the law of God. This sentiment, which every one knows to be generally held by those who are styled orthodox Christians, must assume that there is some rule of right, or of duty, besides the moral law; or that virtue, or true religion, does not imply obedience to any law. In this discussion. I shall,--

1. Attempt to show that there can be no rule of right or duty but the moral law; and,

2. That nothing can be virtue, or true religion, but obedience to this law, and that the government of God acknowledges nothing else as virtue or true religion.

1. There can be no rule of duty but the moral law. [2]

Upon this proposition I remark,--

(1.) That the moral law, as we have seen, is nothing else than the law of nature, or that rule of action which is founded, not in the will of God, but in the nature and relations of moral agents. It prescribes the course of action which is agreeable or suitable to our nature and relations. It is unalterably right to act in conformity with our nature and relations. To deny this, is palpably absurd and contradictory. But if this is right, nothing else can be right. If this course is obligatory upon us, by virtue of our nature and relations, no other course can possibly be obligatory upon us. To act in conformity with our nature and relations, must be right, and nothing, either more or less, can be right. If these are not truths of intuition, then there are no such truths.

(2.) God has never proclaimed any other rule of duty, and should he do it, it could not be obligatory. The moral law did not originate in his arbitrary will. He did not create it, nor can he alter it, or introduce any other rule of right among moral agents. Can God make anything else right than to love him with all the heart, and our neighbor as ourselves? Surely not. Some have strangely dreamed that the law of faith has superseded the moral law. But we shall see that moral law is not made void, but is established by the law of faith. True faith, from its very nature, always implies love or obedience to the moral law; and love or obedience to the moral law always implies faith. As has been said on a former occasion, no being can create law. Nothing is, or can be, obligatory on a moral agent, but the course of conduct suited to his nature and relations. No being can set aside the obligation to do this. Nor can any being render anything more than this obligatory. Indeed, there cannot possibly be any other rule of duty than the moral law. There can be no other standard with which to compare our actions, and in the light of which to decide their moral character. This brings us to the consideration of the second proposition, namely,--

2. That nothing can be virtue or true religion but obedience to the moral law.

That every modification of true virtue is only obedience to moral law, will appear, if we consider,--

(1.) That virtue is identical with true religion:

(2.) That true religion cannot properly consist in anything else, than the love to God and man, enjoined by the moral law:

(3.) That the Bible expressly recognizes love as the fulfilling of the law, and as expressly denies, that anything else is acceptable to God. "Therefore love is the fulfilling of the law." "Though I speak with the tongues of men and of angels, and have not charity (love), I am become as sounding brass or a tinkling cymbal. And though I have the gift of prophecy, and understand all mysteries and all knowledge; and though I have all faith, so that I could remove mountains, and have not charity, I am nothing. And though I bestow all my goods to feed the poor, and though I give my body to be burned, and have not charity (love), it profiteth me nothing." (1 Cor. xiii. 1-3) Love is repeatedly recognized in the Bible, not only as constituting true religion, but as being the whole of religion. Every form of true religion is only a form of love or benevolence.

Repentance consists in the turning of the soul from a state of selfishness to benevolence, from disobedience to God's law, to obedience to it.

Faith is the receiving of, or confiding in, embracing, loving, truth and the God of truth. It is only a modification of love to God and Christ. Every Christian grace or virtue, as we shall more fully see when we come to consider them in detail, is only a modification of love. God is love. Every modification of virtue and holiness in God is only love, or the state of mind which the moral law requires alike of him and of us. Benevolence is the whole of virtue in God, and in all holy beings. Justice, truthfulness, and every moral attribute, is only benevolence viewed in particular relations.

Nothing can be virtue that is not just what the moral law demands. That is, nothing short of what it requires can be, in any proper sense, virtue.

A common idea seems to be, that a kind of obedience is rendered to God by Christians which is true religion, and which, on Christ's account, is accepted of God, which after all comes indefinitely short of full or entire obedience at any moment; that the gospel has somehow brought men, that is. Christians, into such relations, that God really accepts from them an imperfect obedience, something far below what his law requires; that Christians are accepted and justified while they render at best but a partial obedience, and while they sin more or less at every moment. Now this appears to me, to be as radical an error as can well be taught. The subject naturally branches out into two distinct inquiries:--

(1.) Is it possible for a moral agent partly to obey, and partly to disobey, the moral law at the same time?

(2.) Can God, in any sense, justify one who does not yield a present and full obedience to the moral law?

The first of these questions has been fully discussed in the preceding lecture. We think that it has been shown, that obedience to the moral law cannot be partial, in the sense that the subject can partly obey, and partly disobey, at the same time.

We will now attend to the second question, namely,--

Can God, in any sense, justify one who does not yield a present and full obedience to the moral law? Or, in other words, Can he accept anything as virtue or obedience, which is not, for the time being, full obedience, or all that the law requires?

The term justification is used in two senses:

(a) In the sense of pronouncing the subject blameless:

(b) In the sense of pardon, acceptance, and treating one who has sinned, as if he had not sinned.

It is in this last sense, that the advocates of this theory hold, that Christians are justified, that is, that they are pardoned, and accepted, and treated as just, though at every moment sinning, by coming short of rendering that obedience which the moral law demands. They do not pretend that they are justified at any moment by the law, for that at every moment condemns them for present sin; but that they are justified by grace, not in the sense that they are made really and personally righteous by grace, but that grace pardons and accepts, and in this sense justifies them when they are in the present commission of an indefinite amount of sin; that grace accounts then righteous while, in fact, they are continually sinning; that they are fully pardoned and acquitted, while at the same moment committing sin, by coming entirely and perpetually short of the obedience which, under the circumstances the law of God requires. While voluntarily withholding full obedience, their partial obedience is accepted, and the sin of withholding full obedience is forgiven. God accepts what the shiner has a mind to give, and forgives what he voluntarily withholds. This is no caricature. It is, if I understand them, precisely what many hold. In considering this subject, I wish to propose for discussion the following inquiries, as of fundamental importance.

1. How much sin may we commit, or how much may we, at every moment, come short of full obedience to the law of God, and yet be accepted and justified?

This must be an inquiry of infinite importance. If we may wilfully withhold a part of our hearts from God, and yet be accepted, how great a part may we withhold? If we may love God with less than all our hearts, and our neighbor less than ourselves, and be accepted, how much less than supreme love to God, and equal love to our neighbor, will be accepted?

Shall we be told, that the least degree of true love to God and our neighbor will be accepted? But what is true love to God and our neighbor? This is the point of inquiry. Is that true love which is not what is required? If the least degree of love to God will be accepted, then we may love ourselves more than we love God, and yet be accepted. We may love God a little, and ourselves much, and still be in a state of acceptance with God. We may love God a little and our neighbor a little, and ourselves more than we love God and all our neighbors, and vet be in a justified state. Or shall we be told that God must be loved supremely? But what is intended by this? Is supreme love a loving with all the heart? But this is full and not partial obedience; yet the latter is the thing about which we are inquiring. Or is supreme love, not love with all the heart, but simply a higher degree of love than we exercise toward any other being? But how much greater must it be? Barely a little? How are we to measure it? In what scale are we to weigh, or by what standard are we to measure, our love, so as to know whether we love God a little more than any other being? But how much are we to love our neighbor, in order to our being accepted? If we may love him a little less than ourselves, how much less, and still be justified? These are certainly questions of vital importance. But such questions look like trifling. Yet why should they? If the theory I am examining be true, these questions must not only be asked, but they must admit of a satisfactory answer. The advocates of the theory in question are bound to answer them. And if they cannot, it is only because their theory is false. Is it possible that their theory should be true, and yet no one be able to answer such vital questions as these just proposed? If a partial obedience can be accepted, it is a momentous question, how partial, or how complete must that obedience be? I say again, that this is a question of agonizing interest. God forbid that we should be left in the dark here. But again,

2. If we are forgiven while voluntarily withholding a part of that which would constitute full obedience, are we not forgiven sin of which we do not repent, and forgiven while in the act of committing the sin for which we are forgiven?

The theory in question is that Christians never, at any time, in this world, yield a full obedience to the divine law; that they always withhold a part of their hearts from the Lord, and yet, while in the very act of committing this abominable sin of voluntarily defrauding God and their neighbor, God accepts their persons and their services, fully forgives and justifies them. What is this, but pardoning present and pertinacious rebellion! Receiving to favor a God-defrauding wretch! Forgiving a sin unrepented of and detestably persevered in! Yes, this must be, if it be true that Christians are justified without present full obedience. That surely must be a doctrine of devils, that represents God as receiving to favor a rebel who has one hand filled with weapons against his throne.

3. But what good can result to God, or the sinner, or to the universe, by thus pardoning and justifying an unsanctified soul? Can God be honored by such a proceeding? Will the holy universe respect, fear, and honor God for such a proceeding? Does it, can it, commend itself to the intelligence of the universe? Will pardon and justification save the sinner, while he yet continues to withhold a part, at least, of his heart from God, while he still cleaves to a part of his sins? Can heaven be edified, or hell confounded, and its cavils silenced, by such a method of justification?

4. But again: has God a right to pardon sin unrepented of;

Some may feel shocked at the question, and may insist that this is a question which we have no right to agitate. But let me inquire: Has God, as a moral governor, a right to act arbitrarily? Is there not some course of conduct which is suitable to him? Has he not given us intelligence on purpose that we may be able to see and judge of the propriety of his public acts? Does he not invite and require scrutiny? Why has he required an atonement for sin, and why has he required repentance at all? Who does not know that no executive magistrate has a right to pardon sin unrepented of? The lowest terms upon which any ruler can exercise mercy, are repentance, or, which is the same thing, a return to obedience. Who ever heard, in any government, of a rebel's being pardoned, while he only renounced a part of his rebellion? To pardon him while any part of his rebellion is persevered in, were to sanction by a public act that which is lacking in his repentance. It were to pronounce a public justification of his refusal to render full obedience.

5. But have we a right to ask forgiveness while we persevere in the sin of withholding a part of our hearts from him?

God has no right to forgive us, and we have no right to desire him to forgive us, while we keep back any part of the condition of forgiveness. While we persist in defrauding God and our neighbor, we cannot profess penitence and ask forgiveness without gross hypocrisy. And shall God forgive us while we cannot, without hypocrisy, even profess repentance? To ask for pardon, while we do not repent and cease from sin, is a gross insult to God.

6. But does the Bible recognize the pardon of present sin, and while unrepented of? Let the passage be found, if it can be, where sin is represented as pardoned or pardonable, unless repented of and fully forsaken. No such passage can be found. The opposite of this always stands revealed, expressly or impliedly, on every page of divine inspiration.

7. Does the Bible anywhere recognize a justification in sin? Where is such a passage to be found? Does not the law condemn sin, in every degree of it? Does it not unalterably condemn the sinner in whose heart the vile abomination is found? If a soul can sin, and yet not be condemned, then it must be because the law is abrogated, for surely, if the law still remains in force, it must condemn all sin. James most unequivocally teaches this: "If any man keep the whole law, and yet offend in one point, he is guilty of all." What is this but asserting, that if there could be a partial obedience, it would be unavailing, since the law would condemn for any degree of sin; that partial obedience, did it exist, would not be regarded as acceptable obedience at all? The doctrine, that a partial obedience, in the sense that the law is not at any time fully obeyed, is accepted of. God, is sheer antinomianism. What! a sinner justified while indulging in rebellion against God!

But it has been generally held in the church, that a sinner must intend fully to obey the law, as a condition of justification; that, in his purpose and intention, he must forsake all sin; that nothing short of perfection of aim or intention can be accepted of God. Now, what is intended by this language? We have seen in former lectures, that moral character belongs properly only to the intention. If, then, perfection of intention be an indispensable condition of justification, what is this, but an admission, after all, that full present obedience is a condition of justification? But this is what we hold, and they deny. What then can they mean? It is of importance to ascertain what is intended by the assertion, repeated by them thousands of times, that a sinner cannot be justified but upon condition that he fully purposes and intends to abandon all sin, and to live without sin; unless he seriously intends to render full obedience to all the commands of God. Intends to obey the law! What constitutes obedience to the law? Why, love, good-willing, good-intending. Intending to obey the law is intending to intend, willing to will, choosing to choose! This is absurd.

What then is the state of mind which is, and must be, the condition of justification? Not merely an intention to obey, for this is only an intending to intend, but intending what the law requires to be intended, to wit, the highest well-being of God and of the universe. Unless he intends this, it is absurd to say that he can intend full obedience to the law; that he intends to live without sin. The supposition is, that he is now sinning; that is, for nothing else is sin, voluntarily withholding from God and man their due. He chooses, wills, and intends this, and yet the supposition is, that at the same time he chooses, wills, intends, fully to obey the law. What is this but the ridiculous assertion, that he at the same time intends full obedience to the law, and intends not fully to obey, but only to obey in part, voluntarily withholding from God and man their dues.

But again, to the question, can man be justified while sin remains in him? Surely he cannot, either upon legal or gospel principles, unless the law be repealed. That he cannot be justified by the law, while there is a particle of sin in him, is too plain to need proof. But can he be pardoned and accepted, and then justified, in the gospel sense, while sin, any degree of sin, remains in him? Certainly not. For the law, unless it be repealed, continues to condemn him while there is any degree of sin in him. It is a contradiction to say, that he can both be pardoned, and at the same time condemned. But if he is all the time coming short of full obedience, there never is a moment in which the law is not uttering its curses against him. "Cursed is every one that continueth not in all things that are written in the book of the law to do them." The fact is, there never has been, and there never can be, any such thing as sin without condemnation. "Beloved, if our heart condemn us, God is greater than our heart;" that is, he much more condemns us. "But if our heart condemn us not, then have we confidence towards God." God cannot repeal the law. It is not founded in his arbitrary will. It is as unalterable and unrepealable as his own nature. God can never repeal nor alter it. He can, for Christ's sake, dispense with the execution of the penalty, when the subject has returned to full present obedience to the precept, but in no other case, and upon no other possible conditions. To affirm that he can, is to affirm that God can alter the immutable and eternal principles of moral law and moral government.

8. The next inquiry is, can there be such a thing as a partial repentance of sin? That is, does not true repentance imply a return to present full obedience to the law of God?

To repent is to change the choice, purpose, intention. It is to choose a new end,--to begin a new life,--to turn from self seeking to seeking the highest good of being,--to turn from selfishness to disinterested benevolence,--from a state of disobedience to a state of obedience. Certainly, if repentance means and implies anything, it does imply a thorough reformation of heart and life. A reformation of heart consists in turning from selfishness to benevolence. We have seen in a former lecture, that selfishness and benevolence cannot co-exist, at the same time, in the same mind. They are the supreme choice of opposite ends. These ends cannot both be chosen at the same time. To talk of partial repentance as a possible thing is to talk nonsense. It is to overlook the very nature of repentance. What! a man both turn away from, and hold on to sin at the same time! Serve God and mammon at one and the same time! It is impossible. This impossibility is affirmed both by reason and by Christ. But perhaps it will be objected, that the sin of those who render but a partial obedience, and whom God pardons and accepts, is not a voluntary sin. This leads to the inquiry:--

9. Can there be any other than voluntary sin?

What is sin? Sin is a transgression of the law. The law requires benevolence, good-willing. Sin is not a mere negation, or a not willing, but consists in willing self-gratification. It is a willing contrary to the commandment of God. Sin, as well as holiness, consists in choosing, willing, intending. Sin must be voluntary; that is, it must be intelligent and voluntary. It consists in willing, and it is nonsense to deny that sin is voluntary. The fact is, there is either no sin, or there is voluntary sin. Benevolence is willing the good of being in general, as an end, and, of course, implies the rejection of self-gratification, as an end. So sin is the choice of self-gratification, as an end, and necessarily implies the rejection of the good of being in general, as an end. Sin and holiness, naturally and necessarily, exclude each other. They are eternal opposites and antagonists. Neither can consist with the presence of the other in the heart. They consist in the active state of the will, and there can be no sin or holiness that does not consist in choice.

10. Must not present sin be sin unrepented of?

Yes, it is impossible for one to repent of present sin. To affirm that present sin is repented of, is to affirm a contradiction. It is overlooking both the nature of sin, and the nature of repentance. Sin is selfish willing; repentance is turning from selfish to benevolent willing. These two states of will, as has just been said, cannot possibly co-exist. Whoever, then, is at present falling short of full obedience to the law of God, is voluntarily sinning against God, and is impenitent. It is nonsense to say, that he is partly penitent and partly impenitent; that he is penitent so far as he obeys, and impenitent so far as he disobeys. This really seems to be the loose idea of many, that a man can be partly penitent, and partly impenitent at the same time. This idea, doubtless, is founded on the mistake, that repentance consists in sorrow for sin, or is a phenomenon of the sensibility. But repentance consists in a change of ultimate intention--a change in the choice of an end--a turning from selfishness to supreme disinterested benevolence. It is, therefore, plainly impossible for one to be partly penitent, and partly impenitent at the same time; inasmuch as penitence and impenitence consist in supreme opposite choices.

So then it is plain, that nothing is accepted as virtue under the government of God, but present full obedience to his law.

REMARKS.

1. If what has been said is true, we see that the church has fallen into a great and ruinous mistake, in supposing that a state of present sinlessness is a very rare, if not an impossible, attainment in this life. If the doctrine of this lecture be true, it follows that the very beginning of true religion in the soul, implies the renunciation of all sin. Sin ceases where holiness begins. Now, how great and ruinous must that error be, that teaches us to hope for heaven, while living in conscious sin; to look upon a sinless state, as not to be expected in this world; that it is a dangerous error to expect to stop sinning, even for an hour or a moment, in this world; and yet to hope for heaven!

2. How great and ruinous the error, that justification is conditionated upon a faith that does not purify the heart of the believer; that one may be in a state of justification who lives in the constant commission of more or less sin! This

error has slain more souls, I fear, than all the universalism that ever cursed the world.

3. We see that, if a righteous man forsake his righteousness, and die in his sin, he must sink to hell. Whenever a Christian sins he comes under condemnation, and must repent and do his first works, or be lost.

Footnotes:

2. See ante, p. 5.--Exclusiveness.

LECTURE XI - OBEDIENCE TO THE MORAL LAW

We have seen, that all the law requires is summarily expressed in the single word, love; that this word is synonymous with benevolence; that benevolence consists in the choice of the highest well-being of God and of the universe, as an end, or for its own sake; that this choice is an ultimate intention. In short, we have seen, that good-will to being in general is obedience to the moral law. Now the question before us is, what is not implied in this good-will, or in this benevolent ultimate intention?

Since the law of God, as revealed in the Bible, is the standard, and the only standard, by which the question in regard to what is not, and what is, implied in entire sanctification, is to be decided, it is of fundamental importance, that we understand what is, and what is not, implied in entire obedience to this law. Our judgment of our own state, or of the state of others, can never be relied upon, till these inquiries are settled. Christ was perfect, and yet so erroneous were the notions of the Jews, in regard to what constituted perfection, that they thought him possessed with a devil, instead of being holy, as he claimed to be. I will state then, what is not implied in entire obedience to the moral law, as I understand it. The law, as epitomized by Christ, "Thou shalt love the Lord thy God with all thy heart, and with all thy soul, and with all thy mind, and with all thy strength, and thy neighbor as thyself," -- I understand to lay down the whole duty of man to God, and to his fellow creatures. Now, the questions are, what is not, and what is, implied in perfect obedience to this law?

1. Entire obedience does not imply any change in the substance of the soul or body, for this the law does not require; and it would not be obligatory if it did, because the requirement would be inconsistent with natural justice, and, therefore, not law. Entire obedience is the entire consecration of the powers, as they are, to God. It does not imply any change in them, but simply the right use of them.

2. It does not imply the annihilation of any constitutional traits of character, such as constitutional ardor or impetuosity. There is nothing, certainly, in the law of God that requires such constitutional traits to be annihilated, but simply that they should be rightly directed in their exercise.

3. It does not imply the annihilation of any of the constitutional appetites or susceptibilities. It seems to be supposed by some, that the constitutional appetites and susceptibilities are in themselves sinful, and that a state of entire conformity to the law of God implies their entire annihilation. I have been not a little surprised to find, that some persons who, I had supposed, were far enough from embracing the doctrine of physical moral depravity, were, after all, resorting to this assumption, in order to set aside the doctrine of entire sanctification in this life. But let us appeal to the law. Does the law anywhere, expressly or impliedly, condemn the constitution of man, or require the annihilation of any thing that is properly a part of the constitution itself? Does it require the annihilation of the appetite for food, or is it satisfied merely with regulating its indulgence? In short, does the law of God any where require any

thing more than the consecration of all the powers, appetites, and susceptibilities of body and mind to the service of God?

4. Entire obedience does not imply the annihilation of natural affection, or natural resentment. By natural affection I mean, that certain persons may be naturally pleasing to us. Christ appears to have had a natural affection for John. By natural resentment I mean, that, from the laws of our being, we must resent or feel opposed to injustice or ill-treatment. Not that a disposition to retaliate or revenge ourselves is consistent with the law of God. But perfect obedience to the law of God does not imply that we should have no sense of injury and injustice, when we are abused. God has this, and ought to have it, and so has every moral being. To love your neighbor as yourself, does not imply, that if he injure you, you should feel no sense of the injury or injustice, but that you should love him and do him good, notwithstanding his injurious treatment.

5. It does not imply any unhealthy degree of excitement of the mind. Moral law is to be so interpreted as to be consistent with physical law. God's laws certainly do not clash with each other. And the moral law cannot require such a state of constant mental excitement as will destroy the physical constitution. It cannot require any more mental excitement than is consistent with all the laws, attributes, and circumstances of both soul and body. It does not imply that any organ or faculty is to be at all times exerted to the full measure of its capacity. This would soon exhaust and destroy any and every organ of the body. Whatever may be true of the mind, when separated from the body, it is certain, while it acts through a material organ, that a constant state of excitement is impossible. When the mind is strongly excited, there is of necessity a great determination of blood to the brain. A high degree of excitement cannot long continue, without producing inflammation of the brain, and consequent insanity. And the law of God does not require any degree of emotion, or mental excitement, inconsistent with life and health. Our Lord Jesus Christ does not appear to have been in a state of continual mental excitement. When he and his disciples had been in a great excitement for a time, they would turn aside, "and rest a while."

Who that has ever philosophized on this subject, does not know that the high degree of excitement which is sometimes witnessed in revivals of religion, must necessarily be short, or that the people must become deranged? It seems sometimes to be indispensable that a high degree of excitement should prevail for a time, to arrest public and individual attention, and draw off people from other pursuits, to attend to the concerns of their souls. But if any suppose that this high degree of excitement is either necessary or desirable, or possible to be long continued, they have not well considered the matter. And here is one grand mistake of the church. They have supposed that the revival consists mostly in this state of excited emotion, rather than in conformity of the human will to the law of God. Hence, when the reasons for much excitement have ceased, and the public mind begins to grow more calm, they begin immediately to say, that the revival is on the decline; when, in fact, with much less excited emotion, there may be vastly more real religion in the community. Excitement is often important and indispensable, but the vigorous actings of the will are infinitely more important. And this state of mind may exist in the absence of highly excited emotions.

Nor does it imply that the same degree of emotion, volition, or intellectual effort, is at all times required. All volitions do not need the same strength. They cannot have equal strength, because they are not produced by equally influential reasons. Should a man put forth as strong a volition to pick up an apple, as to extinguish the flames of a burning house? Should a mother, watching over her sleeping nursling, when all is quiet and secure, put forth as powerful volitions, as might be required to snatch it from the devouring flames? Now, suppose that she were equally devoted to God, in watching her sleeping babe, and in rescuing it from the jaws of death. Her holiness would not consist in the fact, that she exercised equally strong volitions, in both cases; but that in both cases the volition was equal to the accomplishment of the thing required to be done. So that persons may be entirely holy, and, yet continually varying in the strength of their affections, emotions, or volitions, according to their circumstances, the state of their physical system, and the business in which they are engaged.

All the powers of body and mind are to be held at the service and disposal of God. Just so much of physical, intellectual, and moral energy are to be expended in the performance of duty, as the nature and the circumstances of the case require. And nothing is further from the truth than that the law of God requires a constant, intense state of emotion and mental action, on any and every subject alike.

6. Entire obedience does not imply that God is to be at all times the direct object of attention and affection. This is not only impossible in the nature of the case, but would render it impossible for us to think of or love our neighbor as ourselves.

The law of God requires the supreme love of the heart. By this is meant that the mind's supreme preference should be of God--that God should be the great object of its supreme regard. But this state of mind is perfectly consistent with our engaging in any of the necessary business of life--giving to that business that attention, and exercising about it all those affections and emotions, which its nature and importance demand.

If a man love God supremely, and engage in any business for the promotion of his glory, if his eye be single, his affections and conduct, so far as they have any moral character, are entirely holy when necessarily engaged in the right transaction of his business, although, for the time being, neither his thoughts nor affections are upon God; just as a man, who is intensely devoted to his family, may be acting consistently with his supreme affection, and rendering them the most important and perfect service, while he does not think of them at all. The moral heart is the mind's supreme preference. The natural heart propels the blood through all the physical system. Now there is a striking analogy between this and the moral heart. And the analogy consists in this, that as the natural heart, by its pulsations, diffuses life through the physical system, so the moral heart, or the supreme governing preference, or ultimate intention of the mind, is that which gives life and character to man's moral actions. For example, suppose that I am engaged in teaching mathematics; in this, my ultimate intention is to glorify God in this particular calling. Now in demonstrating some of its intricate propositions, I am obliged, for hours together, to give the entire attention of my mind to that object. While my mind is thus intensely employed in one particular business, it is impossible that I should have any thoughts about God, or should exercise any direct affections, or emotions, or volitions, towards him. Yet if, in this particular calling, all selfishness is excluded, and my supreme design is to glorify God, my mind is in a state of entire obedience, even though, for the time being, I do not think of God.

It should be understood, that while the supreme preference or intention of the mind has such efficiency as to exclude all selfishness, and to call forth just that strength of volition, thought, affection, and emotion, that is requisite to the right discharge of any duty to which the mind may be called, the heart is in a right state. By a suitable degree of thought and feeling, to the right discharge of duty, I mean just that intensity of thought, and energy of action, that the nature and importance of the particular duty, to which, for the time being, I am called, demand, in my honest estimation.

In making this statement, I take it for granted, that the brain together with all the circumstances of the constitution are such that the requisite amount of thought, feeling, etc., are possible. If the physical constitution be in such a state of exhaustion, as to be unable to put forth that amount of exertion which the nature of the case might otherwise demand, even in this case, the languid efforts, though far below the importance of the subject, would be all that the law of God requires. Whoever, therefore, supposes that a state of entire obedience implies a state of entire abstraction of mind from everything but God, labors under a grievous mistake. Such a state of mind is as inconsistent with duty, as it is impossible, while we are in the flesh.

The fact is that the language and spirit of the law have been and generally are, grossly misunderstood, and interpreted to mean what they never did, or can, mean, consistently with natural justice. Many a mind has been thrown open to the assaults of Satan, and kept in a state of continual bondage and condemnation, because God was not, at all times, the direct object of thought, affection, and emotion; and because the mind was not kept in a state of perfect tension, and excited to the utmost at every moment.

7. Nor does it imply a state of continual calmness of mind. Christ was not in a state of continual calmness. The deep peace of his mind was never broken up, but the surface or emotions of his mind were often in a state of great excitement, and at other times, in a state of great calmness. And here let me refer to Christ, as we have his history in the Bible, in illustration of the positions I have already taken. For example, Christ had all the constitutional appetites and susceptibilities of human nature. Had it been otherwise, he could not have been "tempted in all points like as we are;" nor could he have been tempted in any point as we are, any further than he possessed a constitution similar to our own. Christ also manifested natural affection for his mother and for other friends. He also showed that he had a sense of injury and injustice, and exercised a suitable resentment when he was injured and persecuted. He was not always in a state of great excitement. He appears to have had his seasons of excitement and of calm--of labor and rest--of joy and sorrow, like other good men. Some persons have spoken of entire obedience to the law, as implying a state of uniform and universal calmness, and as if every kind and degree of excited feeling, except the feeling of love to God, were inconsistent with this state. But Christ often manifested a great degree of excitement when reproving the enemies of God. In short, his history would lead to the conclusion that his calmness and excitement were various, according to the circumstances of the case. And although he was sometimes so pointed and severe in his reproof, as to be accused of being possessed of a devil, yet his emotions and feelings were only those that were called for, and suited to the occasion.

8. Nor does it imply a state of continual sweetness of mind, without any indignation or holy anger at sin and sinners. Anger at sin is only a modification of love to being in general. A sense of justice, or a disposition to have the wicked punished for the benefit of the government, is only another of the modifications of love. And such dispositions are essential to the existence of love, where the circumstances call for their exercise. It is said of Christ, that he was angry. He often manifested anger and holy indignation. "God is angry with the wicked every day." And holiness, or a state of obedience, instead of being inconsistent with, always implies, the existence of anger, whenever circumstances occur which demand its exercise.

9. It does not imply a state of mind that is all compassion, and no sense of justice. Compassion is only one of the modifications of love. Justice, or willing the execution of law and the punishment of sin, is another of its modifications. God, and Christ, and all holy beings, exercise all those dispositions that constitute the different modifications of love, under every possible circumstance.

10. It does not imply that we should love or hate all men alike, irrespective of their value, circumstances, and relations. One being may have a greater capacity for well-being, and be of much more importance to the universe, than another. Impartiality and the law of love require us not to regard all beings and things alike, but all beings and things according to their nature, relations, circumstances, and value.

11. Nor does it imply a perfect knowledge of all our relations. Such an interpretation of the law as would make it necessary, in order to yield obedience, for us to understand all our relations, would imply in us the possession of the attribute of omniscience; for certainly there is not a being in the universe to whom we do not sustain some relation. And a knowledge of all these relations plainly implies infinite knowledge. It is plain that the law of God cannot require any such thing as this.

12. Nor does it imply freedom from mistake on any subject whatever. It is maintained by some that the grace of the gospel pledges to every man perfect knowledge, or at least such knowledge as to exempt him from any mistake. I cannot stop here to debate this question, but would merely say, the law does not expressly or impliedly require infallibility of judgment in us. It only requires us to make the best use we can of all the light we have.

13. It does not imply the same degree of knowledge we might have possessed, had we always improved our time in its acquisition. The law cannot require us to love God or man, as well as we might have been able to love them, had we always improved all our time in obtaining all the knowledge we could, in regard to their nature, character, and interests. If this were implied in the requisition of the law, there is not a saint on earth or in heaven that does, or ever can, perfectly obey. What is lost in this respect is lost, and past neglect can never be so remedied, that we shall ever be able to make up in our acquisitions of knowledge what we have lost. It will no doubt be true to all eternity, that we shall have less knowledge than we might have possessed, had we filled up all our time in its acquisition. We do not, cannot, nor shall we ever be able to, love God as well as we might have loved him, had we always applied our minds to the acquisition of knowledge respecting him. And if entire obedience is to be understood as implying that we love God as much as we should, had we all the

knowledge we might have had, then I repeat it, there is not a saint on earth or in heaven, nor ever will be, that is entirely obedient.

14. It does not imply the same amount of service that we might have rendered, had we never sinned. The law of God does not imply or suppose, that our powers are in a perfect state; that our strength of body or mind is what it would have been, had we never sinned. But it simply requires us to use what strength we have. The very wording of the law is proof conclusive, that it extends its demand only to the full amount of what strength we have. And this is true of every moral being, however great or small.

The most perfect development and improvement of our powers, must depend upon the most perfect use of them. And every departure from their perfect use, is a diminishing of their highest development, and a curtailing of their capabilities to serve God in the highest and best manner. All sin then does just so much towards crippling and curtailing the powers of body and mind, and rendering them, by just so much, incapable of performing the service they might otherwise have rendered.

To this view of the subject it has been objected, that Christ taught an opposite doctrine, in the case of the woman who washed his feet with her tears, when he said, "To whom much is forgiven, the same loveth much." But can it be that Christ intended to be understood as teaching, that the more we sin the greater will be our love, and our ultimate virtue? If this be so, I do not see why it does not follow that the more sin in this life, the better, if so be that we are forgiven. If our virtue is really to be improved by our sins, I see not why it would not be good economy, both for God and man, to sin as much as we can while in this world. Certainly Christ meant to lay down no such principle as this. He undoubtedly meant to teach that a person who was truly sensible of the greatness of his sins, would exercise more of the love of gratitude than would be exercised by one who had a less affecting sense of ill-desert.

15. Entire obedience does not imply the same degree of faith that might have been exercised but for our ignorance and past sin. We cannot believe anything about God of which we have neither evidence nor knowledge. Our faith must therefore be limited by our intellectual perceptions of truth. The heathen are not under obligation to believe in Christ, and thousands of other things of which they have no knowledge. Perfection in a heathen would imply much less faith than in a Christian. Perfection in an adult would imply much more and greater faith than in a child. And perfection in an angel would imply much greater faith than in a man, just in proportion as he knows more of God than man does. Let it be always understood, that entire obedience to God never implies that which is naturally impossible. It is naturally impossible for us to believe that of which we have no knowledge. Entire obedience implies, in this respect, nothing more than the heart's faith or confidence in all the truth that is perceived by the intellect.

16. Nor does it imply the conversion of all men in answer to our prayers. It has been maintained by some, that entire obedience implies the offering of prevailing prayer for the conversion of all men. To this I reply,--Then Christ did not obey, for he offered no such prayer. The law of God makes no such demands, either expressly or impliedly. We have no right to believe that all men will be converted in answer to our prayers, unless we have an express or implied promise to that effect. As, therefore, there is no such promise, we are

under no obligation to offer such a prayer. Nor does the non-conversion of the world imply, that there are no saints in the world who fully obey God's law.

It does not imply the conversion of any one for whom there is not an express or implied promise in the word of God. The fact that Judas was not converted in answer to Christ's prayer, does not prove that Christ did not fully obey.

Nor does it imply that all those things which are expressly or impliedly promised, will be granted in answer to our prayers; or, in other words, that we should pray in faith for them, if we are ignorant of the existence or application of those promises. A state of perfect love implies the discharge of all known duty. And nothing strictly speaking can be duty, of which the mind has no knowledge. It cannot, therefore, be our duty to believe a promise of which we are entirely ignorant, or the application of which to any specific object we do not understand.

If there is sin in such a case as this, it lies in the fact, that the soul neglects to know what it ought to know. But it should always be understood that the sin lies in this neglect to know, and not in the neglect of that of which we have no knowledge. Entire obedience is inconsistent with any present neglect to know the truth; for such neglect is sin. But it is not inconsistent with our failing to do that of which we have no knowledge. James says, "He that knoweth to do good and doeth it not, to him it is sin." "If ye were blind," says Christ, "ye should have no sin, but because ye say, We see, therefore your sin remaineth."

17. Entire obedience to the divine law does not imply, that others will of course regard our state of mind, and our outward life, as entirely conformed to the law.

It was insisted and positively believed by the Jews, that Jesus Christ was possessed of a wicked instead of a holy spirit. Such were their notions of holiness, that they no doubt supposed him to be actuated by any other than the Spirit of God. They especially supposed so on account of his opposition to the current orthodoxy, and to the ungodliness of the religious teachers of the day. Now, who does not see, that when the church is, in a great measure, conformed to the world, a spirit of holiness in any man would certainly lead him to aim the sharpest rebukes at the spirit and life of those in this state, whether in high or low places? And who does not see, that this would naturally result in his being accused of possessing a wicked spirit? And who does not know, that where a religious teacher finds himself under the necessity of attacking a false orthodoxy, he will certainly be hunted, almost as a beast of prey, by the religious teachers of his day, whose authority, influence, and orthodoxy are thus assailed?

18. Nor does it imply exemption from sorrow or mental suffering. It was not so with Christ. Nor is it inconsistent with our sorrowing for our own past sins, and sorrowing that we have not now the health, and vigor, and knowledge, and love, that we might have had, if we had sinned less; or sorrow for those around us--sorrow in view of human sinfulness, or suffering. These are all consistent with a state of joyful love to God and man, and indeed are the natural results of it.

19. Nor is it inconsistent with our living in human society--with mingling in the scenes, and engaging in the affairs of this world, as some have supposed. Hence the absurd and ridiculous notions of papists in retiring to monasteries, and convents--in taking the veil, and, as they say, retiring to a life of devotion.

Now I suppose this state of voluntary exclusion from human society, to be utterly inconsistent with any degree of holiness, and a manifest violation of the law of love to our neighbor.

20. Nor does it imply moroseness of temper and manners. Nothing is further from the truth than this. It is said of Xavier, than whom, perhaps, few holier men have ever lived, that "he was so cheerful as often to be accused of being gay." Cheerfulness is certainly the result of holy love. And entire obedience no more implies moroseness in this world than it does in heaven.

In all the discussions I have seen upon the subject of Christian holiness, writers seldom or never raise the distinct inquiry: What does obedience to the law of God imply, and what does it not imply? Instead of bringing everything to this test, they seem to lose sight of it. On the one hand, they include things that the law of God never required of man in his present state. Thus they lay a stumbling-block and a snare for the saints, to keep them in perpetual bondage, supposing that this is the way to keep them humble, to place the standard entirely above their reach. Or, on the other hand, they really abrogate the law, so as to make it no longer binding. Or they so fritter away what is really implied in it, as to leave nothing in its requirements, but a sickly, whimsical, inefficient sentimentalism, or perfectionism, which in its manifestations and results, appears to me to be anything but that which the law of God requires.

21. It does not imply that we always or ever aim at, or intend to do our duty. That is, it does not imply that the intention always, or ever, terminates on duty as an ultimate end. It is our duty to aim at or intend the highest well-being of God and the universe, as an ultimate end, or for its own sake. This is the infinitely valuable end at which we are at all times to aim. It is our duty to aim at this. While we aim at this, we do our duty, but to aim at duty is not doing duty.

Nor does it imply that we always think, at the time, of its being duty, or of our moral obligation to intend the good of being. This obligation is a first truth, and is always and necessarily assumed by every moral agent, and this assumption or knowledge is a condition of his moral agency. But it is not at all essential to virtue or true obedience to the moral law, that moral obligation should at all times be present to the thoughts as an object of attention.

Nor does it imply that the rightness or moral character of benevolence is, at all times, the object of the mind's attention. We may intend the glory of God and the good of our neighbor, without at all times thinking of the moral character of this intention. But the intention is not the less virtuous on this account. The mind unconsciously, but necessarily, assumes the rightness of benevolence, or of willing the good of being, just as it assumes other first truths, without being distinctly conscious of the assumption. It is not therefore, at all essential to obedience to the law of God, that we should at all times have before our minds the virtuousness or moral character of benevolence.

22. Nor does obedience to the moral law imply, that the law itself should be, at all times, the object of thought, or of the mind's attention. The law lies developed in the reason of every moral agent in the form of an idea. It is the idea of that choice or intention which every moral agent is bound to exercise. In other words, the law, as a rule of duty, is a subjective idea always and necessarily developed in the mind of every moral agent. This idea he always and necessarily takes along with him, and he is always and necessarily a law to himself. Nevertheless, this law or idea, is not always the object of the mind's

attention and thought. A moral agent may exercise good-will or love to God and man, without at the time being conscious of thinking, that this love is required of him by the moral law. Nay, if I am not mistaken, the benevolent mind generally exercises benevolence so spontaneously, as not, for much of the time, even to think that this love to God is required of him. But this state of mind is not the less virtuous on this account. If the infinite value of God's well-being and of his infinite goodness constrains me to love him with all my heart, can any one suppose that this is regarded by him as the less virtuous, because I did not wait to reflect, that God commanded me to love him, and that it was my duty to do so?

The thing upon which the intention must or ought to terminate is the good of being, and not the law that requires me to will it. When I will that end, I will the right end, and this willing is virtue, whether the law be so much as thought of or not. Should it be said that I may will that end for a wrong reason, and, therefore, thus willing it is not virtue; that unless I will it because of my obligation, and intend obedience to moral law, or to God, it is not virtue; I answer, that the objection involves an absurdity and a contradiction. I cannot will the good of God and of being, as an ultimate end, for a wrong reason. The reason of the choice and the end chosen are identical, so that if I will the good of being as an ultimate end, I will it for the right reason.

It is impossible to will God's good as an end, out of regard to his authority. This is to make his authority the end chosen, for the reason of a choice is identical with the end chosen. Therefore, to will anything for the reason that God requires it, is to will God's requirement as an ultimate end. I cannot, therefore, love God with any acceptable love, primarily, because he commands it. God never expected to induce his creatures to love him, or to will his good, by commanding them to do so.

23. Obedience to the moral law does not imply that we should practically treat all interests that are of equal value according to their value. For example, the precept, "Love thy neighbor as thyself," cannot mean that I am to take equal care of my own soul, and the soul of every other human being. This were impossible. Nor does it mean that I should take the same care and oversight of my own, and of all the families of the earth. Nor that I should divide what little of property, or time, or talent I have, equally among all mankind. This were--

(1.) Impossible.

(2.) Uneconomical for the universe. More good will result to the universe by each individual's giving his attention particularly to the promotion of those interests that are within his reach, and that are so under his influence that he possesses particular advantages for promoting them. Every interest is to be esteemed according to its relative value; but our efforts to promote particular interests should depend upon our relations and capacity to promote them. Some interests of great value we may be under no obligation to promote, for the reason that we have no ability to promote them, while we may be under obligation to promote interests of vastly less value, for the reason, that we are able to promote them. We are to aim at promoting those interests that we can most surely and extensively promote, but always in a manner that shall not interfere with others promoting other interests, according to their relative value. Every man is bound to promote his own, and the salvation of his family, not because they belong to self, but because they are valuable in themselves, and because they are particularly committed to him, as being directly within his reach. This is a principle everywhere assumed in the government of God, and I wish it to be distinctly borne in mind, as we proceed in our investigations, as it will, on the one hand, prevent misapprehension, and, on the other, avoid the necessity of circumlocution, when we wish to express the same idea; the true intent and meaning of the moral law, no doubt, is, that every interest or good known to a moral being shall be esteemed according to its intrinsic value, and that, in our efforts to promote good, we are to aim at securing the greatest practicable amount, and to bestow our efforts where, as it appears from our circumstances and relations, we can accomplish the greatest good. This ordinarily can be done, beyond all question, only by each one attending to the promotion of those particular interests which are most within the reach of his influence.

LECTURE XII - ATTRIBUTES OF LOVE

It has been shown that the sum and spirit of the whole law is properly expressed in one word--love. It has also been shown, that this love is benevolence or good willing; that it consists in choosing the highest good of God and of universal being, for its own intrinsic value, in a spirit of entire consecration to this as the ultimate end of existence. Although the whole law is fulfilled in one word--love, yet there are many things implied in the state of mind expressed by this term. It is, therefore, indispensable to a right understanding of this subject, that we inquire into the characteristics or attributes of this love. We must keep steadily in mind certain truths of mental philosophy. I will, therefore--

I. Call attention to certain facts in mental philosophy as they are revealed in consciousness.

1. Moral agents possess intellect, or the faculty of knowledge.

2 They also possess sensibility, and sensitivity, or in other words, the faculty or susceptibility of feeling.

3. They also possess will, or the power of choosing or refusing in every case of moral obligation.

These primary faculties are so correlated to each other, that the intellect or the sensibility may control the will, or the will may, in a certain sense, control them. That is, the mind is free to choose in accordance with the demands of the intellect, which is the law-giving faculty, or with the desires and impulses of the sensibility, or to control and direct them both. The will can directly control the attention of the intellect, and consequently its perceptions, thoughts, etc. It can indirectly control the states of the sensibility, or feeling faculty, by controlling the perceptions and thoughts of the intellect. We also know from consciousness, as was shown in a former lecture, that the voluntary muscles of the body are directly controlled by the will, and that the law which obliges the attention, the feelings, and the actions of the body to obey the decisions of the will, is physical law, or the law of necessity. The attention of the intellect and the outward actions are controlled directly, and the feelings indirectly, by the decisions of the will. The will can either command or obey. It can suffer itself to be enslaved by the impulses of the sensibility, or it can assert its sovereignty and control them. The will is not influenced by either the intellect or the sensibility, by the law of necessity or force; so that the will can always resist either the demands of the intelligence, or the impulses of the sensibility. But while they cannot lord it over the will, through the agency of any law of force, the will has the aid of the law of necessity or force by which to control them.

Again: We are conscious of affirming to ourselves our obligation to obey the law of the intellect rather than the impulses of the sensibility; that to act virtuously we must act rationally, or intelligently, and not give ourselves up to the blind impulses of our feelings.

Now, inasmuch as the love required by the moral law consists in choice, willing, intention, as before repeatedly shown; and inasmuch as choice, willing, intending, controls the states of the intellect and the outward actions directly, by a law of necessity, and by the same law controls the feelings or states of the sensibility indirectly, it follows that certain states of the intellect and of the sensibility, and also certain outward actions, must be implied in the existence of the love which the law of God requires. I say, implied in it, not as making a part of it, but as necessarily resulting from it. The thoughts, opinions, judgments, feelings, and outward actions must be moulded and modified by the state of the heart or will.

Here it is important to remark, that, in common language, the same word is often used to express either an action or attitude of the will, or a state of the sensibility, or both. This is true of all the terms that represent what are called the Christian graces or virtues, or those various modifications of virtue of which Christians are conscious, and which appear in their life and temper. Of this truth we shall be constantly reminded as we proceed in our investigations, for we shall find illustrations of it at every step of our progress.

Before I proceed to point out the attributes of benevolence, it is important to remark, that all the moral attributes of God and of all holy beings, are only attributes of benevolence. Benevolence is a term that comprehensively expresses them all. God is love. This term expresses comprehensively God's whole moral character. This love, as we have repeatedly seen, is benevolence. Benevolence is good-willing, or the choice of the highest good of God and the universe, as an end. But from this comprehensive statement, accurate though it be, we are apt to receive very inadequate conceptions of what really belongs to, as implied in, benevolence. To say that love is the fulfilling of the whole law; that benevolence is the whole of true religion; that the whole duty of man to God and his neighbor, is expressed in one word, love--these statements, though true, are so comprehensive as to need with all minds much amplification and explanation. Many things are implied in love or benevolence. By this is intended, that benevolence needs to be viewed under various aspects and in various relations, and its nature considered in the various relations in which it is called to act. Benevolence is an ultimate intention, or the choice of an ultimate end. But if we suppose that this is all that is implied in benevolence, we shall egregiously err. Unless we inquire into the nature of the end which benevolence chooses, and the means by which it seeks to accomplish that end, we shall understand but little of the import of the word benevolence. Benevolence has many attributes or characteristics. These must all harmonize in the selection of its end, and in its efforts to realize it. By this is intended that benevolence is not a blind, but the most intelligent, choice. It is the choice of the best possible end in obedience to the demand of the reason and of God, and implies the choice of the best possible means to secure this end. Both the end and the means are chosen in obedience to the law of God, and of reason. An attribute is a permanent quality of a thing. The attributes of benevolence are those permanent qualities which belong to its very nature. Benevolence is not blind, but intelligent, choice. It is the choice of the highest well-being of moral agents. It seeks this end by means suited to the nature of moral agents. Hence wisdom, justice, mercy, truth, holiness, and many other attributes, as we shall see, are essential elements, or attributes, of benevolence. To understand what true benevolence is, we must inquire into its attributes. Not everything that is called love has at all the nature of benevolence. Nor has all that is called benevolence any title to that appellation. There are various kinds of love. Natural affection is called love. Our preference of certain kinds of diet is called love. Hence we say we love fruit, vegetables, meat, milk, etc. Benevolence is also called love, and is the kind of love, beyond all question, required by the law of God. But there is more than one state of mind that is called benevolence. There is a constitutional or phrenological benevolence, which is often mistaken for, and confounded with, the benevolence which constitutes virtue. This so called benevolence is in truth only an imposing form of selfishness; nevertheless it is called benevolence. Many of its manifestations are like those of true benevolence. Care, therefore, should be taken, in giving religious instruction, to distinguish accurately between them. Benevolence, let it be remembered, is the obedience of the will to the law of reason and of God. It is willing good as an end, for its own sake, and not to gratify self. Selfishness consists in the obedience of the will to the impulses of the sensibility. It is a spirit of self-gratification. The will seeks to gratify the desires and propensities, for the pleasure of the gratification. Self-gratification is sought as an end, and as the supreme end. It is preferred to the claims of God and the good of being. Phrenological, or constitutional benevolence, is only obedience to the impulse of the sensibility--a yielding to a feeling of compassion. It is only an effort to gratify a desire. It is, therefore, as really selfishness, as is an effort to gratify any constitutional desire whatever.

It is impossible to get a just idea of what constitutes obedience to the divine law, and what is implied in it, without considering attentively the various attributes or aspects of benevolence, properly so called. Upon this discussion we are about to enter. But before I commence the enumeration and definition of these attributes, it is important further to remark that the moral attributes of God, as revealed in his works, providence, and word, throw much light upon the subject before us. Also the many precepts of the Bible, and the developments of benevolence therein revealed, will assist us much, as we proceed in our inquiries upon this important subject. As the Bible expressly affirms that love comprehends the whole character of God--that it is the whole that the law requires of man--that the end of the commandment is charity or love--we may be assured that every form of true virtue is only a modification of love or benevolence; that is, that every state of mind required by the Bible, and recognized as virtue, is, in its last analysis, resolvable into love or benevolence. In other words, every virtue is only benevolence viewed under certain aspects, or in certain relations. In other words still, it is only one of the elements, peculiarities, characteristics, or attributes of benevolence. This is true of God's moral attributes. They are, as has been said, only attributes of benevolence. They are only the essential qualities that belong to the very nature of benevolence, which are manifested and brought into activity wherever benevolence is brought into certain circumstances and relations. Benevolence is just, merciful, etc. Such is its nature, that in appropriate circumstances these qualities, together with many others, will manifest themselves in executive acts.[3] This is and must be true of every holy being.

II. I will now proceed to point out the attributes of that love which constitutes obedience to the law of God.

As I proceed I will call attention to the states of the intellect and of the sensibility, and also to the course of outward conduct implied in the existence of this love in any mind--implied in its existence as necessarily resulting from it by the law of cause and effect. These attributes are--

1. Voluntariness. That is to say, it is a phenomenon of the will. There is a state of the sensibility often expressed by the term love. Love may, and often does exist, as every one knows, in the form of a mere feeling or emotion. The term is often used to express the emotion of fondness or attachment, as distinct from a voluntary state of mind, or a choice of the will. This emotion or feeling, as we are all aware, is purely an involuntary state of mind. Because it is a phenomenon of the sensibility, and of course a passive state of mind, it has in itself no moral character. The law of God requires voluntary love or good-will, as has been repeatedly shown. This love consists in choice, intention. It is choosing the highest well-being of God and the universe of sentient beings as an end. Of course voluntariness must be one of its characteristics. The word benevolence expresses this idea.

If it consists in choice, if it be a phenomenon of the will, it must control the thoughts and states of the sensibility, as well as the outward action. This love, then, not only consists in a state of consecration to God and the universe, but also implies deep emotions of love to God and man. Though a phenomenon of the will, it implies the existence of all those feelings of love and affection to God and man, that necessarily result from the consecration of the heart or will to their highest wellbeing. It also implies all that outward course of life that necessarily flows from a state of will consecrated to this end. Let it be borne in mind, that where these feelings do not arise in the sensibility, and where this course of life is not, there the true love or voluntary consecration to God and the universe required by the law, is not. Those follow from this by a law of necessity. Those, that is, feelings or emotions of love, and a correct outward life, may exist without this voluntary love, as I shall have occasion to show in its proper place; but this love cannot exist without those, as they follow from it by a law of necessity. These emotions will vary in their strength, as constitution and circumstances vary, but exist they must, in some sensible degree, whenever the will is in a benevolent attitude.

2. Liberty is an attribute of this love. The mind is free and spontaneous in its exercise. It makes this choice when it has the power at every moment to choose self-gratification as an end. Of this every moral agent is conscious. It is a free, and therefore a responsible, choice.

3. Intelligence. That is, the mind makes choice of this end intelligently. It not only knows what it chooses, and why it chooses, but also that it chooses in accordance with the dictates of the intellect, and the law of God; that the end is worthy of being chosen, and that for this reason the intellect demands that it should be chosen, and also, that for its own intrinsic value it is chosen.

Because voluntariness, liberty, and intelligence are natural attributes of this love, therefore, the following are its moral attributes.

4. Virtue is an attribute of it. Virtue is a term that expresses the moral character of benevolence; it is moral rightness. Moral rightness is moral perfection, righteousness, or uprightness. The term marks or designates its relation to moral law, and expresses its conformity to it.

In the exercise of this love or choice, the mind is conscious of uprightness, or of being conformed to moral law or moral obligation. In other words, it is conscious of being virtuous or holy, of being like God, of loving what ought to be loved, and of consecration to the right end.

Because this choice is in accordance with the demands of the intellect, therefore the mind, in its exercise, is conscious of the approbation of that power of the intellect which we call conscience. The conscience must approve this love, choice, or intention.

Again: Because the conscience approves of this choice, therefore, there is and must be in the sensibility a feeling of happiness or satisfaction, a feeling of complacency or delight in the love that is in the heart or will. This love, then, always produces self-approbation in the conscience, and a felt satisfaction in the sensibility; and these feelings are often very acute and joyous, insomuch that the soul, in the exercise of this love of the heart, is sometimes led to rejoice with joy unspeakable and full of glory. This state of mind does not always and necessarily amount to joy. Much depends in this respect on the clearness of the intellectual views, upon the state of the sensibility, and upon the manifestation of Divine approbation to the soul. But where peace, or approbation of conscience, and consequently a peaceful state of the sensibility are not, this love is not. They are connected with it by a law of necessity, and must of course appear on the field of consciousness where this love exists. These, then, are implied in the love that constitutes obedience to the law of God. Conscious peace of mind, and conscious joy in God must be where true love to God exists.

5. Disinterestedness is another attribute of this love. By disinterestedness, it is not intended that the mind takes no interest in the object loved, for it does take a supreme interest in it. But this term expresses the mind's choice of an end for its own sake, and not merely upon condition that the good belongs to self. This love is disinterested in the sense that the highest well-being of God and the universe is chosen, not upon condition of its relation to self, but for its own intrinsic and infinite value. It is this attribute particularly that distinguishes this love from selfish love. Selfish love makes the relation of good to self the condition of choosing it. The good of God and of the universe, if chosen at all, is only chosen as a means or condition of promoting the highest good of self. But this love does not make good to self its end; but good to God and being in general, is its end.

As disinterestedness is an attribute of this love, it does not seek its own, but the good of others. "Charity (love) seeketh not her own." It grasps in its comprehensive embrace the good of being in general, and of course, of necessity, secures a corresponding outward life and inward feeling. The intellect will be employed in devising ways and means for the promotion of its end. The sensibility will be tremblingly alive to the good of all and of each; will rejoice in the good of others as in its own, and will grieve at the misery of others as in its own. It "will rejoice with them that do rejoice, and weep with them that weep." There will not, cannot be envy at the prosperity of others, but unfeigned joy, joy as real and often as exquisite as in its own prosperity. Benevolence enjoys everybody's good things, while selfishness is too envious at the good things of others even to enjoy its own. There is a Divine economy in benevolence. Each benevolent soul not only enjoys his own good things, but also enjoys the good things of all others so far as he knows their happiness. He drinks at the river of God's pleasure. He not only rejoices in doing good to others, but also in beholding their enjoyment of good things. He joys in God's joy, and in the joy of angels and of saints. Ile also rejoices in the good things of all sentient existences. He is happy in beholding the pleasure of the beasts of the field, the fowls of the air, and the fishes of the sea. He sympathizes with all joy and all suffering known to him; nor is his sympathy with the sufferings of others a feeling of unmingled pain. It is a real luxury to sympathize in the woes of others. He would not be without this sympathy. It so accords with his sense of propriety and fitness, that, mingled with the painful emotion, there is a sweet feeling of self-approbation; so that a benevolent sympathy with the woes of others is by no means inconsistent with happiness, and with perfect happiness. God has this sympathy. He often expresses and otherwise manifests it. There is, indeed, a mysterious and an exquisite luxury in sharing the woes of others. God and angels and all holy beings know what it is. Where this result of love is not manifested, there love itself is not. Envy at the prosperity, influence, or good of others, the absence of sensible joy in view of the good enjoyed by others, and of sympathy with the sufferings of others, prove conclusively that this love does not exist. There is an expansiveness, an ampleness of embrace, a universality, and a divine disinterestedness in this love, that necessarily manifests itself in the liberal devising of liberal things for Zion, and in the copious outpourings of the floods of sympathetic feeling, both in joys and sorrows, when suitable occasions present themselves before the mind.

6. Impartiality is another attribute of this love. By this term is not intended, that the mind is indifferent to the character of him who is happy or miserable; that it would be as well pleased to see the wicked as the righteous eternally and perfectly blessed. But it is intended that, other things being equal, it is the intrinsic value of their well-being which is alone regarded by the mind. Other things being equal, it matters not to whom the good belongs. It is no respecter of persons. The good of being is its end, and it seeks to promote every interest according to its relative value. Selfish love is partial. It seeks to promote self-interest first, and secondarily those interests that sustain such a relation to self as will at least indirectly promote the gratification of self. Selfish love has its favorites, its prejudices, unreasonable and ridiculous. Color, family, nation, and many other things of like nature, modify it. But benevolence knows neither Jew nor Greek, neither bond nor free, white nor black, Barbarian, Scythian, European, Asiatic, African, nor American, but accounts all men as men, and, by virtue of their common manhood, calls every man a brother, and seeks the interests of all and of each. Impartiality, being an attribute of this love, will of course manifest itself in the outward life, and in the temper and spirit of its subject. This love can have no fellowship with those absurd and ridiculous prejudices that are so often rife among nominal Christians. Nor will it cherish them for a moment in the sensibility of him who exercises it. Benevolence recognizes no privileged classes on the one hand, nor proscribed classes on the other. It secures in the sensibility an utter loathing of those discriminations, so odiously manifested and boasted of, and which are founded exclusively in a selfish state of the will. The fact that a man is a man, and not that he is of our party, of our complexion, or of our town, state, or nation--that he is a creature of God, that he is capable of virtue and happiness, these are the considerations that are seized upon by this divinely impartial love. It is the intrinsic value of his interests, and not that they are the interests of one connected with self, that the benevolent mind regards.

But here it is important to repeat the remark, that the economy of benevolence demands, that where two interests are, in themselves considered, of equal value, in order to secure the greatest amount of good, each one should bestow his efforts where they can be bestowed to the greatest advantage. For example: every man sustains such relations that he can accomplish more good by seeking to promote the interest and happiness of certain persons rather than of others; his family, his kindred, his companions, his immediate neighbors, and those to whom, in the providence of God, he sustains such relations as to give him access to them, and influence over them. It is not unreasonable, it is not partial, but reasonable and impartial, to bestow our efforts more directly upon them. Therefore, while benevolence regards every interest according to its relative value, it reasonably puts forth its efforts in the direction where there is a prospect of accomplishing the most good. This, I say, is not partiality, but impartiality; for, be it understood, it is not the particular persons to whom good can be done, but the amount of good that can be accomplished, that directs the efforts of benevolence. It is not because my family is my own, nor because their well-being is, of course, more valuable in itself than that of my neighbors' families, but because my relations afford me higher facilities for doing them good, I am under particular obligation to aim first at promoting their good. Hence the apostle says: "If any man provide not for his own, especially for those of his own household, he hath denied the faith, and is worse than an infidel." Strictly speaking, benevolence esteems every known good according to its intrinsic and relative value; but practically treats every interest according to the perceived probability of securing on the whole the highest amount of good. This is a truth of great practical importance. It is developed in the experience and observation of every day and hour. It is manifest in the conduct of God and of Christ, of apostles and martyrs. It is everywhere assumed in the precepts of the Bible, and everywhere manifested in the history of benevolent effort. Let it be understood, then, that impartiality, as an attribute of benevolence, does not imply that its effort to do good will be modified by relations and circumstances. But, on the contrary, this attribute implies, that the efforts to secure the great end of benevolence, to wit, the greatest amount of good to God and the universe, will be modified by those relations and circumstances that afford the highest advantages for doing good.

The impartiality of benevolence causes it always to lay supreme stress upon God's interests, because his well-being is of infinite value, and of course benevolence must be supreme to him. Benevolence, being impartial love, of course accounts God's interests and well-being, as of infinitely greater value than the aggregate of all other interests. Benevolence regards our neighbor's interests as our own, simply because they are in their intrinsic value as our own. Benevolence, therefore, is always supreme to God and equal to man.

7. Universality is another attribute of this love. Benevolence chooses the highest good of being in general. It excludes none from its regard; but on the contrary embosoms all in its ample embrace. But by this it is not intended, that it practically seeks to promote the good of every individual. It would if it could; but it seeks the highest practicable amount of good. The interest of every individual is estimated according to its intrinsic value, whatever the circumstances or character of each may be. But character and relations may and must modify the manifestations of benevolence, or its efforts in seeking to promote this end. A wicked character, and governmental relations and considerations, may forbid benevolence to seek the good of some. Nay, they may demand that positive misery shall be inflicted on some, as a warning to others to beware of their destructive ways. By universality, as an attribute of benevolence, is intended, that good-will is truly exercised towards all sentient beings, whatever their character and relations may be; and that, when the higher good of the greater number does not forbid it, the happiness of all and of each

will be pursued with a degree of stress equal to their relative value, and the prospect of securing each interest. Enemies as well as friends, strangers and foreigners as well as relations and immediate neighbors, will be enfolded in its sweet embrace. It is the state of mind required by Christ in the truly divine precept, "I say unto you, Love your enemies, pray for them that hate you, and do good unto them that despitefully use and persecute you." This attribute of benevolence is gloriously conspicuous in the character of God. His love to sinners alone accounts for their being to-day out of perdition. His aiming to secure the highest good of the greatest number, is illustrated by the display of his glorious justice in the punishment of the wicked. His universal care for all ranks and conditions of sentient beings, manifested in his works and providence, beautifully and gloriously illustrates the truth, that "his tender mercies are over all his works."

It is easy to see that universality must be a modification or attribute of true benevolence. It consists in good-willing, that is, in choosing the highest good of being as such, and for its own sake. Of course it must, to be consistent with itself, seek the good of all and of each, so far as the good of each is consistent with the greatest good upon the whole. Benevolence not only wills and seeks the good of moral beings, but also the good of every sentient existence, from the minutest animalcule to the highest order of beings. It of course produces a state of the sensibility tremblingly alive to all happiness and to all pain. It is pained at the agony of an insect, and rejoices in its joy. God does this, and all holy beings do this. Where this sympathy with the joys and sorrows of universal being is not, there benevolence is not. Observe, good is its end; where this is promoted by the proper means, the feelings are gratified. Where evil is witnessed, the benevolent spirit deeply and necessarily sympathizes.

Footnotes:

3. A recent writer has spoken contemptuously of "being," as he calls it, "sophisticated into believing, or rather saying, that faith is love, justice is love, humility is love." I would earnestly recommend to that and kindred writers, the study of the thirteenth chapter of the first Corinthians. They will there find a specimen of what they please to call sophistry. If it is "sophistry," or "excessive generalization," as other writers seem to regard it, to represent love as possessing the attributes which comprise the various forms of virtue, it surely is the "generalization" and "sophistry" of inspiration. Generalization was the great peculiarity of Christ's preaching His epitomizing all the commandments of God, and resolving the whole of obedience into love, is an illustration of this, and in no other way could he have exposed the delusion of those who obeyed the letter, but overlooked and outraged the spirit of the divine commandments. The same was true of the apostles, and so it is of every preacher of the gospel. Every outward act is only the expression of an inward voluntary state of mind. To understand ourselves or others, we must conceive clearly of the true spirit of moral law, and of heart-obedience to it.

LECTURE XIII - ATTRIBUTES OF LOVE

8. Efficiency is another attribute or characteristic of benevolence. Benevolence consists in choice, intention. Now we know from consciousness that choice or intention constitutes the mind's deepest source or power of action. If I honestly intend a thing, I cannot but make efforts to accomplish that which I intend, provided that I believe the thing possible. If I choose an end, this choice must and will energize to secure its end. When benevolence is the supreme choice, preference, or intention of the soul, it is plainly impossible that it should not produce efforts to secure its end. It must cease to exist, or manifest itself in exertions to secure its end, as soon as, and whenever the intelligence deems it wise to do so. If the will has yielded to the intelligence in the choice of an end, it will certainly obey the intelligence in pursuit of that end. Choice, intention, is the cause of all the outward activity of moral agents. They have all chosen some end, either their own gratification, or the highest good of being; and all the busy bustle of this world's teeming population, is nothing else than choice or intention seeking to compass its end.

Efficiency, therefore, is an attribute of benevolent intention. It must, it will, it does energize in God, in angels, in saints on earth and in heaven. It was this attribute of benevolence, that led God to give his only begotten Son, and that led the Son to give himself, "that whosoever believeth in him should not perish, but have everlasting life."

If love is efficient in producing outward action, and efficient in producing inward feelings; it is efficient to wake up the intellect, and set the world of thought in action to devise ways and means for realizing its end. It wields all the infinite natural attributes of God. It is the mainspring that moves all heaven. It is the mighty power that is heaving the mass of mind, and rocking the world like a smothered volcano. Look to the heavens above. It was benevolence that hung them out. It is benevolence that sustains those mighty rolling orbs in their courses. It was good-will endeavoring to realize its end that at first put forth creative power. The same power, for the same reason, still energizes, and will continue to energize for the realization of its end, so long as God is benevolent. And O! what a glorious thought, that infinite benevolence is wielding, and will forever wield, infinite natural attributes for the promotion of good! No mind but an infinite one can begin to conceive of the amount of good that Jehovah will secure. O blessed, glorious thought! But it is, it must be a reality, as surely as God and the universe exist. It is no vain imagination; it is one of the most certain, as well as the most glorious, truths in the universe. Mountains of granite are but vapor in comparison with it. But the truly benevolent on earth and in heaven will sympathize with God. The power that energizes in him, energizes in them. One principle animates and moves them all, and that principle is love, good-will to universal being. Well may our souls cry out, Amen, go on, God-speed the work; let this mighty power heave and wield universal mind, until all the ills of earth shall be put away, and until all that can be made holy are clothed in the garments of everlasting gladness.

Since benevolence is necessarily, from its very nature, active and efficient in putting forth efforts to secure its end, and since its end is the highest good of being, it follows that all who are truly religious will, and must, from the very nature of true religion, be active in endeavoring to promote the good of being. While effort is possible to a Christian, it is as natural to him as his breath. He has within him the very main-spring of activity, a heart set on the promotion of the highest good of universal being. While he has life and activity at all, it will, and it must, be directed to this end. Let this never be forgotten. An idle, an inactive, inefficient Christian is a misnomer. Religion is an essentially active principle, and when and while it exists, it must exercise and manifest itself. It is not merely good desire, but it is good-willing. Men may have desires, and hope and live on them, without making efforts to realize their desires. They may desire without action. If their will is active, their life must be. If they really choose an ultimate end, this choice must manifest itself. The sinner does and must manifest his selfish choice, and so likewise must the saint manifest his benevolence.

9. Complacency in holiness or moral excellence, is another attribute of benevolence. This consists in benevolence contemplated in its relations to holy beings.

This term also expresses both a state of the intelligence and of the sensibility. Moral agents are so constituted, that they necessarily approve of moral worth or excellence; and when even sinners behold right character, or moral goodness, they are compelled to respect and approve it, by a law of their intelligence. This they not infrequently regard as evidence of goodness in themselves. But this is doubtless just as common in hell as it is on earth. The veriest sinners on earth or in hell, have, by the unalterable constitution of their nature, the necessity imposed upon them, of paying intellectual homage to moral excellence. When a moral agent is intensely contemplating moral excellence, and his intellectual approbation is emphatically pronounced, the natural, and often the necessary result, is a corresponding feeling of complacency or delight in the sensibility. But this being altogether an involuntary state of mind, has no moral character. Complacency, as a phenomenon of will, consists in willing the highest actual blessedness of the holy being in particular, as a good in itself, and upon condition of his moral excellence.

This attribute of benevolence is the cause of a complacent state of the sensibility. It is true, that feelings of complacency may exist, when complacency of will does not exist. But complacency of feeling surely will exist, when complacency of will exists. Complacency of will implies complacency of conscience, or the approbation of the intelligence. When there is a complacency of intelligence and of will, there must follow, of course, complacency of the sensibility.

It is highly worthy of observation here, that this complacency of feeling is that which is generally termed love to God and to the saints, in the common language of Christians, and often in the popular language of the Bible. It is a vivid and pleasant state of the sensibility, and very noticeable by consciousness, of course. Indeed, it is perhaps the general usage now to call this phenomenon of the sensibility, love; and, for want of just discrimination, to speak of it as constituting religion. Many seem to suppose that this feeling of delight in, and fondness for, God, is the love required by the moral law. They are conscious of not being voluntary in it, as well they may be. They judge of their religious state, not by the end for which they live, that is, by their choice or intention, but by their emotions. If they find themselves strongly exercised with emotions of love to God, they look upon themselves as in a state well-pleasing to God. But if their feelings or emotions of love are not active, they of course judge themselves to have little or no religion. It is remarkable to what extent religion is regarded as a phenomenon of the sensibility, and as consisting in mere feelings. So common is it, indeed, that almost uniformly, when professed Christians speak of their religion, they speak of their feelings, or the state of their sensibility, instead of speaking of their conscious consecration to God, and the good of being.

It is also somewhat common for them to speak of their views of Christ, and of truth, in a manner that shows, that they regard the states of the intellect as constituting a part, at least, of their religion. It is of great importance that just views should prevail among Christians upon this momentous subject. Virtue, or religion, as has been repeatedly said, must be a phenomenon of the will. The attribute of benevolence which we are considering, that is, complacency of will in God, is the most common light in which the scriptures present it, and also the most common form in which it lies revealed on the field of consciousness. The scriptures often assign the goodness of God as a reason for loving him, and Christians are conscious of having much regard to his goodness in their love to him; I mean in their good-will to him. They will good to him, and ascribe all praise and glory to him, upon the condition that he deserves it. Of this they are conscious. Now, as was shown in a former lecture, in their love or good will to God, they do not regard his goodness as the fundamental reason for willing good to him. Although his goodness is that, which, at the time, most strongly impresses their minds, yet it must be that the intrinsic value of his well-being is assumed, and had in view by them, or they would no sooner will good than evil to him. In willing his good they must assume its intrinsic value to him, as the fundamental reason for willing it; and his goodness as a secondary reason or condition; but they are conscious of being much influenced in willing his good in particular, by a regard to his goodness. Should you ask the Christian why he loved God, or why he exercised good-will to him, he would probably reply, it is because God is good. But, suppose he should be further asked, why he willed good rather than evil to God; he would say, because good is good or valuable to him. Or, if he returned the same answer as before, to wit, because God is good, he would give this answer, only because he would think it impossible for any one not to assume and to know, that good is willed instead of evil, because of its intrinsic value. The fact is, the intrinsic value of well-being is necessarily taken along with the mind, and always assumed by it, as a first truth. When a virtuous being is perceived, this first truth being spontaneously and necessarily assumed, the mind thinks only of the secondary reason or condition, or the virtue of the being, in willing good to him.

Before I dismiss this subject, I must advert again to the subject of complacent love, as a phenomenon of the sensibility, and also as a phenomenon of the intellect. If I mistake not, there are sad mistakes, and gross and ruinous delusions, entertained by many upon this subject. The intellect, of necessity, perfectly approves of the character of God where it is apprehended. The intellect is so correlated to the sensibility, that, where it perceives in a strong light the divine excellence, or the excellence of the divine law, the sensibility is affected by the perception of the intellect, as a thing of course and of necessity; so that emotions of complacency and delight in the law, and in the divine character, may and often do glow and burn in the sensibility, while the will or heart is unaffected. The will remains in a selfish choice, while the intellect and the sensibility are strongly impressed with the perception of the Divine excellence. This state of the intellect and the sensibility is, no doubt, often mistaken for true religion. We have undoubted illustrations of this in the Bible, and similar cases of it in common life. "Yet they seek me daily, and delight to know my ways, as a nation that did righteousness, and forsook not the ordinance of their God: they ask of me the ordinances of justice, they take delight in approaching to God." Isaiah lviii. 2. "And, lo, thou art unto them as a very lovely song of one that hath a pleasant voice, and can play well on an instrument: for they hear thy words, but they do them not." Ezek. xxxiii. 32.

Nothing is of greater importance, than forever to understand, that religion is always and necessarily a phenomenon of the will; that it always and necessarily produces outward action and inward feeling; that, on account of the correlation of the intellect and sensibility, almost any and every variety of feeling may exist in the mind, as produced by the perceptions of the intellect, whatever the state of the will may be; that unless we are conscious of good-will, or of consecration to God and the good of being--unless we are conscious of living for this end, it avails us nothing, whatever our views and feelings may be.

And also it behooves us to consider that, although these views and feelings may exist while the heart is wrong, they will certainly exist when the heart is right; that there may be feeling, and deep feeling, when the heart is in a selfish attitude, yet, that there will and must be deep emotion and strenuous action, when the heart is right. Let it be remembered, that complacency, as a phenomenon of the will, is always a striking characteristic of true love to God; that the mind is affected and consciously influenced, in willing the actual and infinite blessedness of God, by a regard to his goodness. The goodness of God is not, as has been repeatedly shown, the fundamental reason for the good will, but it is one reason or a condition, both of the possibility of willing, and of the obligation to will, his blessedness in particular. It assigns to itself, and to others, his goodness as the reason for willing his good, rather than the intrinsic value of good; because this last is so universally, and so necessarily assumed, that it thinks not of mentioning it, taking it always for granted, that this will and must be understood.

10. Opposition to sin is another attribute or characteristic of true love to God.

This attribute certainly is implied in the very essence and nature of benevolence. Benevolence is good-willing, or willing the highest good of being as an end. Now there is nothing in the universe more destructive of this good than sin. Benevolence cannot do otherwise than be forever opposed to sin, as that abominable thing which it necessarily hates. It is absurd and a contradiction to affirm, that benevolence is not opposed to sin. God is love or benevolence. He must, therefore, be the unalterable opponent of sin--of all sin, in every form and degree.

But there is a state, both of the intellect and of the sensibility, that is often mistaken for the opposition of the will to sin. Opposition to all sin is, and must be, a phenomenon of the will, and on that ground, alone it becomes virtue. But it often exists also as a phenomenon of the intellect, and likewise of the sensibility. The intellect cannot contemplate sin without disapprobation. This disapprobation is often mistaken for opposition of heart, or of will. When the intellect strongly disapproves of, and denounces sin, there is naturally and necessarily a corresponding feeling of opposition to it in the sensibility, an emotion of loathing, of hatred, of abhorrence. This is often mistaken for opposition of the will, or heart. This is manifest from the fact, that often the most notorious sinners manifest strong indignation in view of oppression, injustice, falsehood, and many other forms of sin. This phenomenon of the sensibility and of the intellect, as I said, is often mistaken for a virtuous opposition to sin, which it cannot be unless it involve an act of the will.

But let it be remembered, that virtuous opposition to sin is a characteristic of love to God and man, or of benevolence. This opposition to sin cannot possibly co-exist with any degree of sin in the heart. That is, this opposition cannot co-exist with a sinful choice. The will cannot at the same time, be opposed to sin and commit sin. This is impossible, and the supposition involves a contradiction. Opposition to sin as a phenomenon of the intellect, or of the sensibility, may exist; in other words, the intellect may strongly disapprove of sin, and the sensibility may feel strongly opposed to certain forms of it, while at the same time, the will may cleave to self indulgence in other forms. This fact, no doubt, accounts for the common mistake, that we can, at the same time, exercise a virtuous opposition to sin, and still continue to commit it.

Many are, no doubt, laboring under this fatal delusion. They are conscious, not only of an intellectual disapprobation of sin in certain forms, but also, at times, of strong feelings of opposition to it. And yet they are also conscious of continuing to commit it. They, therefore conclude, that they have a principle of holiness in them, and also a principle of sin, that they are partly holy and partly sinful at the same time. Their opposition of intellect and of feeling, they suppose to be a holy opposition, when, no doubt, it is just as common in hell, and even more so than it is on earth, for the reason that sin is more naked there than it generally is here.

But now the inquiry may arise, how is it that both the intellect and the sensibility are opposed to it, and yet that it is persevered in? What reason can the mind have for a sinful choice, when urged to it neither by the intellect nor the sensibility? The philosophy of this phenomenon needs explanation. Let us attend to it.

I am a moral agent. My intellect necessarily disapproves of sin. My sensibility is so correlated to my intellect, that it sympathizes with it, or is affected by its perceptions and its judgments. I contemplate sin. I necessarily disapprove of it, and condemn it. This affects my sensibility. I loathe and abhor it. I nevertheless commit it. Now how is this to be accounted for? The usual method is by ascribing it to a depravity in the will itself, a lapsed or corrupted state of the faculty, so that it perversely chooses sin for its own sake. Although disapproved by the intellect, and loathed by the sensibility, yet such, it is said, is the inherent depravity of the will, that it pertinaciously cleaves to sin notwithstanding, and will continue to do so, until that faculty is renewed by the Holy Spirit, and a holy bias or inclination is impressed upon the will itself

But here is a gross mistake. In order to see the truth upon this subject, it is of indispensable importance to inquire what sin is.

It is admitted on all hands, that selfishness is sin. Comparatively few seem to understand that selfishness is the whole of sin, and that every form of sin may be resolved into selfishness, just as every form of virtue may be resolved into benevolence. It is not my purpose now to show that selfishness is the whole of sin. It is sufficient for the present to take the admission, that selfishness is sin. But what is selfishness? It is the choice of self-gratification as an end. It is the preference of our own gratification to the highest good of universal being. Self-gratification is the supreme end of selfishness. This choice is sinful. That is, the moral of this selfish choice is sin. Now, in no case, is or can sin be chosen for its own sake, or as an end. Whenever anything is chosen to gratify self, it is not chosen because the choice is sinful, but notwithstanding it is sinful. It is not the sinfulness of the choice upon which the choice fixes, as an end, or for its own sake, but it is the gratification to be afforded by the thing chosen. For example, theft is sinful. But the will, in an act of theft, does not aim at and terminate on the sinfulness of theft, but upon the gain or gratification expected from the stolen object. Drunkenness is sinful, but the inebriate does not intend or choose the sinfulness for its own sake, or as an end. He does not choose strong drink because the choice is sinful, but notwithstanding it is so. We choose the gratification, but not the sin, as an end. To choose the gratification as an end is sinful, but it is not the sin that is the object of choice. Our mother Eve ate the forbidden fruit. This eating was sinful. But the thing that she chose or intended, was not the sinfulness of eating, but the gratification expected from the fruit. It is not, it cannot in any case be true, that sin is chosen as an end, or for its own sake. Sin is only the quality of selfishness. Selfishness is the choice, not of sin as an end, or for its own sake, but of self-gratification; and this choice of self-gratification as an end is sinful. That is, the moral quality of the choice is sin. To say that sin is, or can be, chosen for its own sake, is untrue and absurd. It is the same as saying that a choice can terminate on an element, quality, or attribute, of itself; that the thing chosen is really an element of the choice itself.

But it is said, that sinners are sometimes conscious of choosing sin for its own sake, or because it is sin; that they possess such a malicious state of mind, that they love sin for its own sake; that they "roll sin as a sweet morsel under their tongue;" that "they eat up the sins of God's people as they eat bread;" that is, that they love their own sins and the sins of others, as they do their necessary food, and choose it for that reason, or just as they do their food; that they not only sin themselves with greediness, but also have pleasure in them that do the same. Now all this may be true, yet it does not at all disprove the position which I have taken, namely, that sin never is, and never can be chosen as an end, or for its own sake. Sin may be sought and loved as a means, but never as an end. The choice of food will illustrate this. Food is never chosen as an ultimate end; it never can be so chosen. It is always as a means. It is the gratification, or the utility of it, in some point of view, that constitutes the reason for choosing it. Gratification is always the end for which a selfish man eats. It may not be merely the present pleasure of eating which he alone or principally seeks. But, nevertheless, if a selfish man, he has his own gratification in view as an end. It may be that it is not so much a present, as a remote gratification he has in view. Thus he may choose food to give him health and strength to pursue some distant gratification, the acquisition of wealth, or something else that will gratify him.

It may happen that a sinner may get into a state of rebellion against God and the universe, of so frightful a character, that he shall take pleasure in willing, and in doing, and saying, things that are sinful, just because they are sinful and displeasing to God and to holy beings. But, even in this case, sin is not chosen as an end, but as a means of gratifying this malicious feeling. It is, after all, self-gratification that is chosen as an end, and not sin. Sin is the means, and self-gratification is the end.

Now we are prepared to understand how it is that both the intellect and sensibility can often be opposed to sin, and yet the will cleave to the indulgence. An inebriate is contemplating the moral character of drunkenness. He instantly and necessarily condemns the abomination. His sensibility sympathizes with the intellect. He loathes the sinfulness of drinking strong drink, and himself on account of it. He is ashamed, and were it possible, he would spit in his own face. Now, in this state, it would surely be absurd to suppose that he could choose sin, the sin of drinking, as an end, or for its own sake. This would be choosing it for an impossible reason, and not for no reason. But still he may choose to continue his drink, not because it is sinful, but notwithstanding it is so. For while the intellect condemns the sin of drinking strong drink, and the sensibility loathes the sinfulness of the indulgence, nevertheless there still exists so strong an appetite, not for the sin, but for the liquor, that the will seeks the gratification, notwithstanding the sinfulness of it. So it is, and so it must be, in every case where sin is committed in the face of the remonstrances of the intellect and the loathing of the sensibility. The sensibility loathes the sinfulness, but more strongly desires the thing the choice of which is sinful. The will in a selfish being yields to the strongest impulse of the sensibility, and the end chosen is, in no case, the sinfulness of the act, but the self-gratification. Those who suppose this opposition of the intellect, or of the sensibility, to be a holy principle, are fatally deluded. It is this kind of opposition to sin, that often manifests itself among wicked men, and that leads them to take credit for goodness or virtue, not an atom of which do they possess. They will not believe themselves to be morally and totally depraved, while they are conscious of so much hostility to sin within them. But they should understand, that this opposition is not of the will, or they could not go on in sin; that it is purely an involuntary state of mind, and has no moral character whatever. Let it be ever remembered, then, that a virtuous opposition to sin is always and necessarily an attribute of benevolence, a phenomenon of the will; and that it is naturally impossible, that this opposition of will should co-exist with the commission of sin.

As this opposition to sin is plainly implied in, and is an essential attribute of, benevolence, or true love to God, it follows, that obedience to the law of God cannot be partial, in the sense that we both love God and sin at the same time.

11. Compassion for the miserable is also an attribute of benevolence, or of pure love to God and man. This is benevolence viewed in its relations to misery and to guilt.

There is a compassion also which is a phenomenon of the sensibility. It may, and does often, exist in the form of an emotion. But this emotion being involuntary, has no moral character in itself. The compassion which is a virtue, and which is required of us as a duty, is a phenomenon of the will, and is of course an attribute of benevolence. Benevolence, as has been often said, is good-willing, or willing the highest happiness and well-being of God and the universe for its own sake, or as an end. It is impossible, therefore, from its own nature, that compassion for the miserable should not be one of its attributes. Compassion of will to misery is the choice or wish that it might not exist. Benevolence wills that happiness should exist for its own sake. It must, therefore, wish that misery might not exist. This attribute or peculiarity of benevolence consists in wishing the happiness of the miserable. Benevolence, simply considered, is willing the good or happiness of being in general. Compassion of will is a willing particularly that the miserable should be happy.

Compassion of sensibility is simply a feeling of pity in view of misery. As has been said, it is not a virtue. It is only a desire, but not willing; consequently does not benefit its object. It is the state of mind of which James speaks:--James ii. 15, 16: "If a brother or sister be naked, and destitute of daily food, and one of you say unto them, Depart in peace, be ye warmed and filled; notwithstanding ye give them not those things which are needful to the body, what doth it profit?" This kind of compassion may evidently co-exist with selfishness. But compassion of heart or will cannot; for it consists in willing the happiness of the miserable for its own sake, and of course impartially. It will, and from its very nature must, deny self to promote its end, whenever it wisely can, that is, when it is seen to be demanded by the highest general good. Circumstances may exist that render it unwise to express this compassion by actually extending relief to the miserable. Such circumstances forbid that God should extend relief to the lost in hell. But for their character and governmental relations, God's compassion would no doubt make immediate efforts for their relief.

Many circumstances may exist in which, although compassion would hasten to the relief of its object, yet, on the whole, the misery that exists is regarded as the less of two evils, and therefore, the wisdom of benevolence forbids it to put forth exertions to save its object.

But it is of the last importance to distinguish carefully between compassion, as a phenomenon of the sensibility, or as a mere feeling, and compassion considered as a phenomenon of the will. This, be it remembered, is the only form of virtuous compassion. Many, who, from the laws of their mental constitution, feel quickly and deeply, often take credit to themselves for being compassionate, while they seldom do much for the downtrodden and the miserable. Their compassion is a mere feeling. It says, "Be ye warmed and filled," but does not that for them which is needful. It is this particular attribute of benevolence that was so conspicuous in the life of Howard, Wilberforce, and many other Christian philanthropists.

It should be said, before I leave the consideration of this attribute, that the will is often influenced by the feeling of compassion. In this case, the mind is no less selfish in seeking to promote the relief and happiness of its object than it is in any other form of selfishness. In such cases, self-gratification is the end sought, and the relief of the suffering is only a means. Pity is stirred, and the sensibility is deeply pained and excited by the contemplation of misery. The will is influenced by this feeling, and makes efforts to relieve the painful emotion on the one hand, and to gratify the desire to see the sufferer happy on the other. This is only an imposing form of selfishness. We, no doubt, often witness displays of this kind of self-gratification. The happiness of the miserable is not in this case sought as an end, or for its own sake, but as a means of gratifying our own feelings. This is not obedience of will to the law of the intellect, but obedience to the impulse of the sensibility. It is not a natural and intelligent compassion, but just such compassion as we often see mere animals exercise. They will risk, and even lay down, their lives, to give relief to one of their number, or to a man who is in misery. In them this has no moral character. Having no reason, it is not sin for them to obey their sensibility; nay, this is a law of their being. This they cannot but do. For them, then, to seek their own gratification as an end is not sin. But man has reason; he is bound to obey it. He should will and seek the relief and the happiness of the miserable, for its own sake, or for its intrinsic value. When he seeks it for no higher reason than to gratify his feelings, he denies his humanity. He seeks it, not out of regard to the sufferer, but in self-defence, or to relieve his own pain, and to gratify his own desires. This in him is sin.

Many, therefore, who take to themselves much credit for benevolence, are, after all, only in the exercise of this imposing form of selfishness. They take credit for holiness, when their holiness is only sin. What is especially worthy of notice here, is, that this class of persons appear to themselves and others, to be all the more virtuous, by how much more manifestly and exclusively they are led on by the impulse of feeling. They are conscious of feeling deeply, of being more sincere and earnest in obeying their feelings. Every body who knows them can also see, that they feel deeply, and are influenced by the strength of their feelings, rather than by their intellect. Now, so gross is the darkness of most persons upon this subject, that they award praise to themselves and to others, just in proportion as they are sure that they are actuated by the depth of their feelings, rather than by their sober judgment.

But I must not leave this subject without observing, that when compassion exists as a phenomenon of the will, it will certainly also exist as a feeling of the sensibility. A man of a compassionate heart will also be a man of compassionate sensibility. He will feel and he will act. Nevertheless, his actions will not be the effect of his feelings, but will be the result of his sober judgment. Three classes of persons suppose themselves, and are generally supposed by others, to be truly compassionate. The one class exhibit much feeling of compassion; but their compassion does not influence their will, hence they do not act for the relief of suffering. These content themselves with mere desires and tears. They say, Be ye warmed and clothed, but give not the needed relief. Another class feel deeply, and give up to their feelings. Of course they are active and energetic in the relief of suffering. But being governed by feeling, instead of being influenced by their intellect, they are not virtuous, but selfish. Their compassion is only an imposing form of selfishness. A third class feel deeply, but are not governed by blind impulses of feeling. They take a rational view of the subject, act wisely and energetically. They obey their reason. Their feelings do not lead them, neither do they seek to gratify their feelings. But these last are truly virtuous, and altogether the most happy of the three. Their feelings are all the more gratified by how much less they aim at the gratification. They obey their intellect, and, therefore, have the double satisfaction of the applause of conscience, while their feelings are also fully gratified by seeing their compassionate desire accomplished.

LECTURE XIV - ATTRIBUTES OF LOVE

12. Mercy is also an attribute of benevolence. This term expresses a state of feeling, and represents a phenomenon of the sensibility. Mercy is often understood to be synonymous with compassion, but then it is not rightly understood.

Mercy, considered as a phenomenon of the will, is a disposition to pardon crime. Such is the nature of benevolence, that it will seek the good even of those who deserve evil, when this can be wisely done. It is "ready to forgive," to seek the good of the evil and unthankful, and to pardon when there is repentance. It is good-will viewed in relation to one who deserves punishment. Mercy, considered as a feeling or phenomenon of the sensibility, is a desire for the pardon or good of one who deserves punishment. It is only a feeling, a desire; of course it is involuntary, and has, in itself, no moral character.

Mercy will, of course, manifest itself in action, and in effort to pardon, or to procure a pardon, unless the attribute of wisdom prevent. It may be unwise to pardon, or to seek the pardon of a guilty one. In such cases, as all the attributes of benevolence must necessarily harmonize, no effort will be made to realize its end. It was this attribute of benevolence, modified and limited in its exercise by wisdom and justice, that energized in providing the means, and in opening the way, for the pardon of our guilty race.

As wisdom and justice are also attributes of benevolence, mercy can never manifest itself by efforts to secure its end, except in a manner and upon conditions that do not set aside justice and wisdom. No one attribute of benevolence is or can be exercised at the expense of another, or in opposition to it. The moral attributes of God, as has been said, are only attributes of benevolence, for benevolence comprehends and expresses the whole of them. From the term benevolence we learn, that the end upon which it fixes is good. And we must infer, too, from the term itself, that the means are unobjectionable; because it is absurd to suppose that good would be chosen because it is good, and yet that the mind that makes this choice should not hesitate to use objectionable and injurious means to obtain its end. This would be a contradiction, to will good for its own sake, or out of regard to its intrinsic value, and then choose injurious means to accomplish this end. This cannot be. The mind that can fix upon the highest well-being of God and the universe as an end, can never consent to use efforts for the accomplishment of this end that are seen to be inconsistent with it, that is, that tend to prevent the highest good of being.

Mercy, I have said, is the readiness of benevolence to pardon the guilty. But this attribute cannot go out in exercise, but upon conditions that consist with the other attributes of benevolence. Mercy as a mere feeling would pardon without repentance or condition; would pardon without reference to public justice. But viewed in connection with the other attributes of benevolence, we learn that, although a real attribute of benevolence, yet it is not and cannot be exercised, without the fulfilment of those conditions that will secure the consent of all the other attributes of benevolence. This truth is beautifully taught and illustrated in the doctrine and fact of atonement, as we shall see. Indeed, without consideration of the various attributes of benevolence, we are necessarily all in the dark, and in confusion, in respect to the character and government of God, the spirit and meaning of his law, the spirit and meaning of the gospel, our own spiritual state, and the developments of character around us. Without an acquaintance with the attributes of love or benevolence, we shall not fail to be perplexed--to find apparent discrepancies in the Bible and in the divine administration--and in the manifestation of Christian character, both as revealed in the Bible, and as exhibited in common life. For example: how universalists have stumbled for want of consideration upon this subject! God is love! Well, without considering the attributes of this love, they infer that if God is love, he cannot hate sin and sinners. If he is merciful, he cannot punish sinners in hell, etc. Unitarians have stumbled in the same way. God is merciful; that is, disposed to pardon sin. Well, then, what need of an atonement? If merciful he can and will pardon upon repentance without atonement. But we may inquire, if he is merciful, why not pardon without repentance? If his mercy alone is to be taken into view, that is, simply a disposition to pardon, that by itself would not wait for repentance. But if repentance is, and must be, a condition of the exercise of mercy, may there not be, nay, must there not be, other conditions of its exercise? If wisdom and public justice are also attributes of benevolence, and conditionate the exercise of mercy, and forbid that it should be exercised but upon condition of repentance, why may they not, nay, why must they not, equally conditionate its exercise upon such a satisfaction of public justice, as would secure as full and as deep a respect for the law, as the execution of its penalty would do? In other words, if wisdom and justice be attributes of benevolence, and conditionate the exercise of mercy upon repentance, why may and must they not also conditionate its exercise upon the fact of an atonement? As mercy is an attribute of benevolence, it will naturally and inevitably direct the attention of the intellect to devising ways and means to render the exercise of mercy consistent with the other attributes of benevolence. It will employ the intelligence in devising means to secure the repentance of the sinner, and to remove all the obstacles out of the way of its free and full exercise. It will also secure the state of feeling which is also called mercy, or compassion. Hence it is certain, that mercy will secure efforts to procure the repentance and pardon of sinners. It will secure a deep yearning in the sensibility over them, and energetic action to accomplish its end, that is, to secure their repentance and pardon. This attribute of benevolence led the Father to give his only-begotten and well-beloved Son, and it led the Son to give himself to die, to secure the repentance and pardon of sinners. It is this attribute of benevolence that leads the Holy Spirit to make such mighty and protracted efforts to secure the repentance of sinners. It is also this attribute that energized in prophets, and apostles, and martyrs, and saints of every age, to secure the conversion of the lost in sin. It is an amiable attribute. All its sympathies are sweet, and tender, and kind as heaven.

13. Justice is an attribute of benevolence.

This term also expresses a state or phenomenon of the sensibility. As an attribute of benevolence, it is the opposite of mercy, when viewed in its relations to crime. It consists in a disposition to treat every moral agent according to his intrinsic desert or merit. In its relations to crime, the criminal, and the public, it consists in a tendency to punish according to law. Mercy would pardon--justice would punish for the public good.

Justice, as a feeling or phenomenon of the sensibility, is a feeling that the guilty deserves punishment, and a desire that he may be punished. This is an involuntary feeling, and has no moral character. It is often strongly excited, and is frequently the cause of mobs and popular commotions. When it takes the control of the will, as it often does with sinners, it leads to what is popularly called lynching, and a resort to those summary methods of executing vengeance which are so appalling.

I have said that the mere desire has no moral character. But when the will is governed by this desire, and yields itself up to seek its gratification, this state of will is selfishness under one of its most odious and frightful forms. Under the providence of God, however, this form of selfishness, like every other in its turn, is overruled for good, like earthquakes, tornadoes, pestilence, and war, to purify the moral elements of society, and scourge away those moral nuisances with which communities are sometimes infested. Even war itself is often but an instance and an illustration of this.

Justice, as an attribute of benevolence, is virtue, and exhibits itself in the execution of the penalties of the law, and in support of public order, and in various other ways for the well-being of mankind. There are several modifications of this attribute. That is, it may and must be viewed under various aspects, and in various relations. One of these is public justice. This is a regard to the public interests, and secures a due administration of law for the public good. It will in no case suffer the execution of the penalty to be set aside, unless something be done to support the authority of the law and of the lawgiver. It also secures the due administration of rewards, and looks narrowly after the public interests, always insisting that the greater interest shall prevail over the lesser; that private interest shall never set aside or prejudice a public one of greater value. Public justice is modified in its exercise by the attribute of mercy. It conditionates the exercise of mercy, and mercy conditionates its exercise. Mercy cannot, consistently with this attribute, extend a pardon but upon conditions of repentance, and an equivalent being rendered to the government. So, on the other hand, justice is conditionated by mercy, and cannot, consistently with that attribute, proceed to take vengeance when the highest good does not require it, when punishment can be dispensed with without public loss. Thus these attributes mutually limit each other's exercise, and render the whole character of benevolence perfect, symmetrical, and heavenly.

Justice is reckoned among the sterner attributes of benevolence; but it is indispensable to the filling up of the entire circle of moral perfections. Although solemn and awful, and sometimes inexpressibly terrific in its exercise, it is nevertheless one of the glorious modifications and manifestations of benevolence. Benevolence without justice would be anything but morally lovely and perfect. Nay, it could not be benevolence. This attribute of benevolence appears conspicuous in the character of God as revealed in his law, in his gospel, and sometimes as indicated most impressively by his providence.

It is also conspicuous in the history of inspired men. The Psalms abound with expressions of this attribute. We find many prayers for the punishment of the wicked. Samuel hewed Agag in pieces; and David's writings abound in expressions that show, that this attribute was strongly developed in his mind; and the circumstances under which he was placed, often rendered it proper to express and manifest in various ways the spirit of this attribute. Many have stumbled at such prayers, expressions, and manifestations as are here alluded to. But this is for want of due consideration. They have supposed that such exhibitions were inconsistent with a right spirit. Oh, they say, how unevangelical! How un-Christ-like! How inconsistent with the sweet and heavenly spirit of Christ and of the gospel! But this is all a mistake. These prayers were dictated by the Spirit of Christ. Such exhibitions are only the manifestations of one of the essential attributes of benevolence. Those sinners deserved to die. It was for the greatest good that they should be made a public example. This the Spirit of inspiration knew, and such prayers, under such circumstances, are only an expression of the mind and will of God. They are truly the spirit of justice pronouncing sentence upon them. These prayers and suchlike things found in the Bible, are no vindication of the spirit of fanaticism and denunciation that so often have taken shelter under them. As well might fanatics burn cities and lay waste countries, and seek to justify themselves by an appeal to the destruction of the old world by flood, and the destruction of the cities of the plain by fire and brimstone.

Retributive justice is another modification of this attribute. This consists in a disposition to visit the offender with that punishment which he deserves, because it is fit and proper that a moral agent should be dealt with according to his deeds. In a future lecture I shall enlarge upon this modification of justice.

Another modification of this attribute is commercial justice. This consists in willing exact equivalents, and uprightness in business and all secular transactions. There are some other modifications of this attribute, but the foregoing may suffice to illustrate sufficiently the various departments over which this attribute presides.

This attribute, though stern in its spirit and manifestations, is nevertheless one of prime importance in all governments by moral agents, whether human or divine. Indeed, without it government could not exist. It is vain for certain philosophers to think to disparage this attribute, and to dispense with it altogether in the administration of government. They will, if they try the experiment, find to their cost and confusion, that no one attribute of benevolence can say to another, "I have no need of thee." In short, let any one attribute of benevolence be destroyed or overlooked, and you have destroyed its perfection, its beauty, its harmony, its propriety, its glory. You have, in fact, destroyed benevolence; it is no longer benevolence, but a sickly, and inefficient, and limping sentimentalism, that has no God, no virtue, no beauty, nor form, nor comeliness in it, that when we see it we should desire it.

This attribute stands by, nay, it executes law. It aims to secure commercial honesty. It aims to secure public and private integrity and tranquillity. It says to violence, disorder, and injustice, Peace, be still, and there must be a great calm. We see the evidences and the illustrations of this attribute in the thunderings of Sinai, and in the agony of Calvary. We hear it in the wail of a world when the fountains of the great deep were broken up, and when the windows of heaven were opened, and the floods descended, and the population of a globe was swallowed up. We see its manifestations in the descending torrent that swept over the cities of the plain; and lastly, we shall forever see its bright, but awful and glorious displays, in the dark and curling folds of that pillar of smoke of the torment of the damned, that ascends up before God forever and ever.

Many seem to be afraid to contemplate justice as an attribute of benevolence. Any manifestation of it among men, causes them to recoil and shudder as if they saw a demon. But let it have its place in the glorious circle of moral attributes; it must have--it will have--it cannot be otherwise. Whenever any policy of government is adopted, in family or state, that excludes the exercise of this attribute, all must be failure, defeat, and ruin.

Again: Justice being an attribute of benevolence, will prevent the punishment of the finally impenitent from diminishing the happiness of God and of holy beings. They will never delight in misery for its own sake; but they will take pleasure in the administration of justice. So that when the smoke of the torment of the damned comes up in the sight of heaven, they will, as they are represented, shout "Alleluia! the Lord God Omnipotent reigneth;" "Just and righteous are thy ways, thou King of saints!"

Before I pass from the consideration of this topic, I must not omit to insist, that where true benevolence is, there must be exact commercial justice, or business honesty and integrity. This is as certain as that benevolence exists. The rendering of exact equivalents, or the intention to do so, must be a characteristic of a truly benevolent mind. Impulsive benevolence may exist; that is, phrenological or constitutional benevolence, falsely so called, may exist to any extent, and yet justice not exist. The mind may be much and very often carried away by the impulse of feeling, so that a man may at times have the appearance of true benevolence, while the same individual is selfish in business, and overreaching in all his commercial relations. This has been a wonder and an enigma to many, but the case is a plain one. The difficulty is, the man is not just, that is, not truly benevolent. His benevolence is only an imposing species of selfishness. "He that hath an ear to hear, let him hear." His benevolence results from feeling, and is not true benevolence.

Again: Where benevolence is, the golden rule will surely be observed: "Whatsoever ye would that men should do to you, do ye even so to them." The justice of benevolence cannot fail to secure conformity to this rule. Benevolence is a just state of the will. It is a willing justly. It must then, by a law of necessity, secure just conduct. If the heart is just, the life must be.

This attribute of benevolence must secure its possessor against every species and degree of injustice; he cannot be unjust to his neighbor's reputation, his person, his property, his soul, his body, nor indeed be unjust in any respect to man or God. It will and must secure confession and restitution, in every case of remembered wrong, so far as this is practicable. It should be distinctly understood, that a benevolent or a truly religious man cannot be unjust. He may indeed appear to be so to others; but he cannot be truly religious or benevolent, and unjust at the same time. If he appears to be so in any instance, he is not and cannot be really so, if he is at the time in a benevolent state of mind. The attributes of selfishness, as we shall see in the proper place, are the direct opposite of those of benevolence. The two states of mind are as contrary as heaven and hell, and can no more co-exist in the same mind, than a thing can be and not be at the same time. I said, that if a man, truly in the exercise of benevolence, appears to be unjust in any thing, he is only so in appearance, and not in fact. Observe, I am speaking of one who is really at the time in a benevolent state of mind. He may mistake, and do that which would be unjust, did he see it differently and intend differently. Justice and injustice belong to the intention. No outward act can in itself be either just or unjust. To say that a man, in the exercise of a truly benevolent intention, can at the same time be unjust, is the same absurdity as to say, that he can intend justly and unjustly at the same time, and in regard to the same thing; which is a contradiction. It must all along be borne in mind, that benevolence is one identical thing, to wit, good-will, willing for its own sake the highest good of being and every known good according to its relative value. Consequently, it is impossible that justice should not be an attribute of such a choice. Justice consists in regarding and treating, or rather in willing, every thing just agreeably to its nature, or intrinsic and relative value and relations. To say, therefore, that present benevolence admits of any degree of present injustice, is to affirm a palpable contradiction. A just man is a sanctified man, is a perfect man, in the sense that he is at present in an upright state.

14. Veracity is another attribute of benevolence.

Veracity, as an attribute of benevolence, is that quality that adheres to truth. In the very act of becoming benevolent, the mind embraces truth, or the reality of things. Then veracity must be one of the qualities of benevolence. Veracity is truthfulness. It is the conformity of the will to the reality of things. Truth in statement is conformity of statement to the reality of things. Truth in action is action conformed to the nature and relations of things. Truthfulness is a disposition to conform to the reality of things. It is willing in accordance with the reality of things. It is willing the right end by the right means. It is willing the intrinsically valuable as an end, and the relatively valuable as a means. In short, it is the willing of every thing according to the reality or facts in the case.

Veracity, then, must be an attribute of benevolence. It is, like all the attributes, only benevolence viewed in a certain aspect or relation. It can not be distinguished from benevolence, for it is not distinct from it, but only a phase or form of benevolence. The universe is so constituted that if every thing proceeded and were conducted, and willed according to its nature and relations, the highest possible good must result. Veracity seeks the good as an end, and truth as a means to secure this end. It wills the good, and that it shall be secured only by means of truth. It wills truth in the end, and truth, in the means. The end is truly valuable, and chosen for that reason. The means are truth, and truth is the only appropriate or possible means.

Truthfulness of heart begets, of course, a state of the sensibility which we call the love of truth. It is a feeling of pleasure that spontaneously arises in the sensibility of one whose heart is truthful, in contemplating truth; this feeling is not virtue, it is rather a part of the reward of truthfulness of heart.

Veracity, as a phenomenon of the will, is also often called, and properly called, a love of the truth. It is a willing in accordance with objective truth. This is virtue, and is an attribute of benevolence. Veracity, as an attribute of the divine benevolence, is the condition of confidence in God as a moral governor. Both the physical and moral laws of the universe evince, and are instances and illustrations of the truthfulness of God. Falsehood, in the sense of lying, is naturally regarded by a moral agent with disapprobation, disgust, and abhorrence. Veracity is as necessarily regarded by him with approbation, and, if the will be benevolent, with pleasure. We necessarily take pleasure in contemplating objective truth, as it lies in idea on the field of consciousness. We also take pleasure in the perception and contemplation of truthfulness, in the concrete realization of the idea of truth. Veracity is morally beautiful. We are pleased with it just as we are with natural beauty, by a law of necessity, when the necessary conditions are fulfilled. This attribute of benevolence secures it against every attempt to promote the ultimate good of being by means of falsehood. True benevolence will no more, can no more, resort to falsehood as a means of promoting good, than it can contradict or deny itself. The intelligence affirms, that the highest ultimate good can be secured only by a strict adherence to truth. The mind cannot be satisfied with anything else. Indeed, to suppose the contrary is to suppose a contradiction. It is the same absurdity as to suppose, that the highest good could be secured only by the violation and setting aside of the nature and relations of things. Since the intellect affirms this unalterable relation of truth to the highest ultimate good, benevolence, or that attribute of benevolence which we denominate veracity or love of the truth, can no more consent to falsehood, than it can consent to relinquish the highest good of being as an end. Therefore, every resort to falsehood, every pious fraud, falsely so called, presents only a specious but real instance of selfishness. A moral agent cannot lie for God; that is, he cannot tell a sinful falsehood, thinking and intending thereby to please God. He knows, by intuition, that God cannot be pleased or truly served by a resort to lying. There is a great difference between concealing or withholding the truth for benevolent purposes, and telling a wilful falsehood. An innocent persecuted and pursued man, has taken shelter under my roof from one who pursued him to shed his blood. His pursuer comes and inquires after him. I am not under obligation to declare to him the fact that he is in my house. I may, and indeed ought to withhold the truth in this instance, for the wretch has no right to know it. The public and highest good demands that he should not know it. He only desires to know it for selfish and bloody purposes. But in this case I should not feel or judge myself at liberty to state a known falsehood. I could not think than this would ultimately conduce to the highest good. The person might go away deceived, or under the impression that his victim was not there. But he could not accuse me of telling him a lie. He might have drawn his own inference from my refusing to give the desired information. But even to secure my own life or the life of my friend, I am not at liberty to tell a lie. If it be said that lying implies telling a falsehood for selfish purposes, and that, therefore, it is not lying to tell a falsehood for benevolent purposes, I reply, that our nature is such that we can no more state a wilful falsehood with a benevolent intention, than we can commit a sin with a benevolent intention. We necessarily regard falsehood as inconsistent with the highest good of being, just as we regard sin as inconsistent with the highest good of being, or just as we regard holiness and truthfulness as the indispensable condition of the highest good of being. The correlation of the will and the intellect forbids the mistake that wilful falsehood is, or can be, the means or condition of the highest good. Universal veracity, then, will always characterize a truly benevolent man. While he is truly benevolent, he is, he must be, faithful, truthful. So far as his knowledge goes, his statements may be depended upon with as much safety as the statements of an angel. Veracity is necessarily an attribute of benevolence in all beings. No liar has, or can have, a particle of true virtue or benevolence in him.

LECTURE XV - ATTRIBUTES OF LOVE

15. Patience is another attribute of benevolence.

This term is frequently used to express a phenomenon of the sensibility. When thus used, it designates a calm and unruffled state of the sensibility or feelings, under circumstances that tend to excite anger or impatience of feeling. The calmness of the sensibility, or patience as a phenomenon of the sensibility, is purely an involuntary state of mind, and although it is a pleasing and amiable manifestation, yet it is not properly virtue. It may be, and often is, an effect of patience as a phenomenon of the will, and therefore an effect of virtue. But it is not itself virtue. This amiable temper may, and often does, proceed from constitutional temperament, and from circumstances and habits.

Patience as a virtue must be a voluntary state of mind. It must be an attribute of love or benevolence; for all virtue, as we have seen, and as the Bible teaches, is resolvable into love or benevolence. The Greek term, upomone, so often rendered patience in the New Testament, means perseverance under trials, continuance, bearing up under affliction, or privations, steadfastness of purpose in despite of obstacles. The word may be used in a good or in a bad sense. Thus a selfish man may patiently, that is perseveringly, pursue his end, and may bear up under much opposition to his course. This is patience as an attribute of selfishness, and patience in a bad sense of the term. Patience in the good sense, or in the sense in which I am considering it, is an attribute of benevolence. It is the quality of constancy, a fixedness, a bearing up under trials, afflictions, crosses, persecutions, or discouragements. This must be an attribute of benevolence. Whenever patience ceases, when it holds out no longer, when discouragement prevails, and the will relinquishes its end, benevolence ceases, as a matter of course.

Patience as a phenomenon of the will, tends to patience as a phenomenon of the sensibility. That is, the quality of fixedness and steadfastness in the intention naturally tends to keep down and allay impatience of temper. As, however, the states of the sensibility are not directly under the control of the will, there may be irritable or impatient feelings, when the heart remains steadfast. Facts or falsehoods may be suggested to the mind which may, in despite of the will, produce a ruffling of the sensibility, even when the heart remains patient. The only way in which a temptation, for it is only a temptation while the will abides firm to its purpose, I say the only way in which a temptation of this kind can be disposed of, is by diverting the attention from that view of the subject that creates the disturbance in the sensibility. I should have said before, that although the will controls the feelings by a law of necessity, yet, as it does not do so directly, but indirectly, it may, and does often happen, that feelings corresponding to the state of the will do not exist in the sensibility. Nay, for a time, a state of the sensibility may exist which is the opposite of the state of the will. From this source arise many, and indeed most, of our temptations. We could never be properly tried or tempted at all, if the feelings must always, by a law of necessity, correspond with the state of the will. Sin consists in willing to gratify our feelings or constitutional impulses, in opposition to the law of our reason. But if these desires and impulses could never exist in opposition to the law of the reason, and, consequently, in opposition to a present holy choice, then a holy being could not be tempted. He could have no motive or occasion to sin. If our mother Eve could have had no feelings of desire in opposition to the state of her will, she never could have desired the forbidden fruit, and of course would not have sinned. I wish now, to state distinctly what I should have said before, that the state or choice of the will does not necessarily so control the feelings, desires, or emotions, that these may never be strongly excited by Satan or by circumstances, in opposition to the will, and thus become powerful temptations to seek their gratification, instead of seeking the highest good of being. Feelings, the gratification of which would be opposed to every attribute of benevolence, may at times co-exist with benevolence, and be a temptation to selfishness; but opposing acts of will cannot co-exist with benevolence. All that can be truly said is, that as the will has an indirect control of the feelings, desires, appetites, passions, etc., it can suppress any class of feelings when they arise, by diverting the attention from their causes, or by taking into consideration such views and facts as will calm or change the state of the sensibility. Irritable feelings, or what is commonly called impatience, may be directly caused by ill health, irritable nerves, and by many things over which the will has no direct control. But this is not impatience in the sense of sin. If these feelings are not suffered to influence the will; if the will abides in patience; if such feelings are not cherished, and are not suffered to shake the integrity of the will; they are not sin. That is, the will does not consent to them, but the contrary. They are only temptations. If they are allowed to control the will, to break forth in words and actions, then there is sin; but the sin does not consist in the feelings, but in the consent of the will to gratify them. Thus, the apostle says, "Be ye angry, and sin not: let not the sun go down upon your wrath." That is, if anger arise in the feelings and sensibility, do not sin by suffering it to control your will. Do not cherish the feeling, and let not the sun go down upon it. For this cherishing it is sin. When it is cherished, the will consents and broods over the cause of it; this is sin. But if it be not cherished, it is not sin.

That the outward actions will correspond with the states and actions of the will, provided no physical obstacle be opposed to them, is a universal truth. But that feelings and desires cannot exist contrary to the states or decisions of the will, is not true. If this were a universal truth, temptation, as I have said, could not exist. The outward actions will be as the will is, always; the feelings, generally. Feelings corresponding to the choice of the will, will be the rule, and opposing feelings the exception. But these exceptions may and do exist in perfectly holy beings. They existed in Eve before she consented to sin, and had she resisted them she had not sinned. They doubtless existed in Christ, or he could not have been tempted in all points like as we are. If there be no desires or impulses of the sensibility contrary to the state of the will, there is not properly any temptation. The desire or impulse must appear on the field of consciousness, before it is a motive to action, and of course before it is a temptation to self-indulgence. Just as certainly then as a holy being may be tempted, and not sin, just so certain it is that emotions of any kind, or of any strength, may exist in the sensibility without sin. If they are not indulged, if the will does not consent to them, and to their indulgence or gratification, the soul is not the less virtuous for their presence. Patience as a phenomenon of the will must strengthen and gird itself under such circumstances, so that patience of will may be, and if it exist at all, must be, in exact proportion to the impatience of the sensibility. The more impatience of sensibility there is, the more patience of will there must be, or virtue will cease altogether. So that it is not always true, that virtue is strongest when the sensibility is most calm, placid, and patient. When Christ passed through his greatest conflicts, his virtue as a man was undoubtedly most intense. When in his agony in the garden, so great was the anguish of his sensibility, that he sweat as it were great drops of blood. This, he says, was the hour of the prince of darkness. This was his great trial. But did he sin? No, indeed. But why? Was he calm and placid as a summer's evening? As far from it as possible.

Patience, then, as an attribute of benevolence, consists, not in placid feeling, but in perseverance under trials and states of the sensibility that tend to selfishness. This is only benevolence viewed in a certain aspect. It is benevolence under circumstances of discouragement, of trial, or temptation. "This is the patience of the saints."

Before dismissing the subject of patience as an emotion, I would observe that, the steadfastness of the heart tends so strongly to secure patience, that if an opposite state of the sensibility is more than of momentary duration, there is strong presumption that the heart is not steadfast in love. The first risings of it will produce an immediate effort to suppress it. If it continues, this is evidence that the attention is allowed to dwell upon the cause of it. This shows that the will is in some sense indulging it.

If it so far influences the will as to manifest itself in impatient words and actions, there must be a yielding of the will. Patience, as an attribute of benevolence, is overcome. If the sensibility were perfectly and directly under the control of the will, the least degree of impatience would imply sin. But as it is not directly, but indirectly under the control of the will, momentary impatience of feeling, when it does not at all influence the will, and when it is not at all indulged, is not sure evidence of a sinful state of the will. It should always be borne in mind, that neither patience nor impatience, in the form of mere feeling, existing for any length of time, and in any degree, is in itself either holy on the one hand, or sinful on the other. All that can be said of these states of the sensibility is, that they indicate, as a general thing, the attitude of the will. When the will is for a long time steadfast in its patience, the result is great equanimity of temper, and great patience of feeling. This comes to be a law of the sensibility, insomuch that very advanced saints may, and doubtless do, experience the most entire patience of feeling for many years together. This does not constitute their holiness, but is a sweet fruit of it. It is to be regarded rather in the light of a reward of holiness, than as holiness itself.

16. Another attribute of benevolence is Meekness.

Meekness, considered as a virtue, is a phenomenon of the will. This term also expresses a state of the sensibility. When used to designate a phenomenon of the sensibility, it is nearly synonymous with patience. It designates a sweet and forbearing temper under provocation. Meekness, a phenomenon of the will, and as an attribute of benevolence, is the opposite both of resistance to injury and retaliation. It is properly and strictly forbearance under injurious treatment. This certainly is an attribute of God, as our existence and our being out of hell plainly demonstrate. Christ said of himself that he was "meek and lowly in heart;" and this surely was no vain boast. How admirably, and how incessantly did this attribute of his love manifest itself! The fifty-third chapter of Isaiah is a prophecy exhibiting this attribute in a most affecting light. Indeed, scarcely any feature of the character of God and of Christ is more strikingly exhibited than this. It must evidently be an attribute of benevolence. Benevolence is good-will to all beings. We are naturally forbearing toward those whose good we honestly and diligently seek. If our hearts are set upon doing them good, we shall naturally exercise great forbearance toward them. God has greatly commended his forbearance to us, in that, while we were yet his enemies, he forbore to punish us, and gave his Son to die for us. Forbearance is a sweet and amiable attribute. How affectingly it displayed itself in the hall of Pilate, and on the cross. "He is led as a lamb to the slaughter, and as a sheep before its shearers is dumb, so he opened not his mouth."

This attribute has in this world abundant opportunity to develop and display itself in the saints. There are daily occasions for the exercise of this form of virtue. Indeed, all the attributes of benevolence are called into frequent exercise in this school of discipline. This is indeed a suitable world in which to train God's children, to develop and strengthen every modification of holiness. This attribute must always appear where benevolence exists, and wherever there is an occasion for its exercise.

It is delightful to contemplate the perfection and glory of that love which constitutes obedience to the law of God. As occasions arise, we behold it developing one attribute after another, and there may be many of its attributes and modifications of which we have as yet no idea whatever. Circumstances will call them into exercise. It is probable, if not certain, that the attributes of benevolence were very imperfectly known in heaven previous to the existence of sin in the universe, and that but for sin many of these attributes would never have been manifested in exercise. But the existence of sin, great as the evil is, has afforded an opportunity for benevolence to manifest its beautiful phases, and to develop its sweet attributes in a most enchanting manner. Thus the divine economy of benevolence brings good out of so great an evil.

A hasty and unforbearing spirit is always demonstrative evidence of a want of benevolence, or of true religion. Meekness is, and must be, a peculiar characteristic of the saints in this world, where there is so much provocation. Christ frequently and strongly enforced the obligation to forbearance. "But I say unto you that ye resist not evil; but whosoever shall smite thee on thy right cheek, turn to him the other also. And if any man will sue thee at the law, and take away thy coat, let him have thy cloak also. And whosoever shall compel thee to go a mile, go with him twain." How beautiful!

17. Humility is another modification or attribute of love.

This term seems often to be used to express a sense of unworthiness, of guilt, of ignorance, and of nothingness, to express a feeling of ill-desert. It seems to be used in common language to express sometimes a state of the intelligence, when it seems to indicate a clear perception of our guilt. When used to designate a state of the sensibility, it represents those feelings of shame and unworthiness, of ignorance, and of nothingness, of which those are most deeply conscious who have been enlightened by the Holy Spirit, in respect to their true character.

But as a phenomenon of the will, and as an attribute of love, it consists in a willingness to be known and appreciated according to our real character.

Humility, as a phenomenon either of the sensibility or of the intelligence, may co-exist with great pride of heart. Pride is a disposition to exalt self, to get above others, to hide our defects, and to pass for more than we are. Deep conviction of sin, and deep feelings of shame, of ignorance, and of desert of hell, may co-exist with a great unwillingness to confess and be known just as we are, and to be appreciated just according to what our real character has been and is. There is no virtue in such humility. But humility, considered as a virtue, consists in the consent of the will to be known, to confess, and to take our proper place in the scale of being. It is that peculiarity of love that wills the good of being so disinterestedly, as to will to pass for no other than, we really are. This is an honest, a sweet, and amiable feature of love. It must, perhaps, be peculiar to those who have sinned. It is only love acting under or in a certain relation, or in reference to a peculiar set of circumstances. It would, under the same circumstances, develop and manifest itself in all truly benevolent minds. This attribute will render confession of sin to God and man natural, and even make it a luxury. It is easy to see that, but for this attribute, the saints could not be happy in heaven. God has promised to bring into judgment every work and every secret thing, whether it be good, or whether it be evil. Now while pride exists, it would greatly pain the soul to have all the character known; so that, unless this attribute really belongs to the saints, they would be ashamed at the judgment, and filled with confusion even in heaven itself. But this sweet attribute will secure them against that shame and confusion of face that would otherwise render heaven itself a hell to them. They will be perfectly willing and happy to be known and estimated according to their characters. This attribute will secure in all the saints on earth that confession of faults one to another, which is so often enjoined in the Bible. By this it is not intended, that Christians always think it wise and necessary to make confession of all their secret sins to man. But it is intended, that they will confess to those whom they have injured, and to all to whom benevolence demands that they should confess. This attribute secures its possessor against spiritual pride, against ambition to get above others. It is a modest and unassuming state of mind.

18. Self-denial is another attribute of love.

If we love any being better than ourselves, we of course deny ourselves when our own interests come in competition with his. Love is good-will. If I will good to others more than to myself, it is absurd to say that I shall not deny myself when my own inclinations conflict with their good. Now the love required by the law of God, we have repeatedly seen to be good will, or willing the highest good of being for its own sake, or as an end. As the interests of self are not at all regarded because they belong to self, but only according to their relative value, it must be certain, that self-denial for the sake of promoting the higher interests of God and of the universe, is and must be a peculiarity or attribute of love.

But again: the very idea of disinterested benevolence, and there is no other true benevolence, implies the abandonment of the spirit of self-seeking, or of selfishness. It is impossible to become benevolent, without ceasing to be selfish. In other words, perfect self-denial is implied in beginning to be benevolent. Self-indulgence ceases where benevolence begins. This must be. Benevolence is the consecration of our powers to the highest good of being in general as an end. This is utterly inconsistent with consecration to self-interest or self-gratification. Selfishness makes good to self the end of every choice.

Benevolence makes good to being in general the end of every choice. Benevolence, then, implies complete self-denial. That is, it implies that nothing is chosen merely because it belongs to self, but only because of its relative value, and in proportion to it.

I said there was no true benevolence, but disinterested benevolence; no true love, but disinterested love. There is such a thing as interested love or benevolence. That is, the good of others is willed, though not as an end, or for its intrinsic value to them, but as a means of our own happiness, or because of its relative value to us. Thus a man might will the good of his family, or of his neighborhood, or country, or of anybody, or anything that sustained such relations to self as to involve his own interests. When the ultimate reason of his willing good to others is, that his own may be promoted, this is selfishness. It is making good to self his end. This a sinner may do toward God, toward the church, and toward the interests of religion in general. This is what I call interested benevolence. It is willing good as an end only to self, and to all others only as a means of promoting our own good.

But again: when the will is governed by mere feeling in willing the good of others, this is only the spirit of self-indulgence, and is only interested benevolence. For example: the feeling of compassion is strongly excited by the presence of misery. The feeling is intense, and constitutes, like all the feelings, a strong impulse or motive to the will to consent to its gratification. For the time being, this impulse is stronger than the feeling of avarice, or any other feeling. I yield to it, and then give all the money I have to relieve the sufferer. I even take my clothes from my back, and give them to him. Now in this case, I am just as selfish as if I had sold my clothes to gratify my appetite for strong drink. The gratification of my feelings was my end. This is one of the most specious and most delusive forms of selfishness.

Again: when one makes his own salvation the end of prayer, of almsgiving, and of all his religious duties, this is only selfishness and not true religion, however much he may abound in them. This is only interested benevolence, or benevolence to self.

Again: from the very nature of true benevolence, it is impossible that every interest should not be regarded according to its relative value. When another interest is seen by me to be more valuable in itself, or of more value to God and the universe than my own, and when I see that, by denying myself, I can promote it, it is certain, if I am benevolent, that I shall do it. I cannot fail to do it, without failing to be benevolent. Benevolence is an honest and disinterested consecration of the whole being to the highest good of God and of the universe. The benevolent man will, therefore, and must, honestly weigh each interest as it is perceived in the balance of his own best judgment, and will always give the preference to the higher interest, provided he believes, that he can by endeavor, and by self-denial, secure it.

That self-denial is an attribute of the divine love, is manifested most gloriously and affectingly in God's gift of his Son to die for men. This attribute was also most conspicuously manifested by Christ, in denying himself, and taking up his cross, and suffering for his enemies. Observe, it was not for friends that Christ gave himself. It was not unfortunate nor innocent sufferers for whom God gave his Son, or for whom he gave himself. It was for enemies. It was not that he might make slaves of them that he gave his Son, nor from any selfish consideration whatever, but because he foresaw that, by making this sacrifice himself, he could secure to the universe a greater good than he should sacrifice. It was this attribute of benevolence that caused him to give his Son to suffer so much. It was disinterested benevolence alone that led him to deny himself, for the sake of a greater good to the universe. Now observe, this sacrifice would not have been made, unless it had been regarded by God as the less of two natural evils. That is, the sufferings of Christ, great and overwhelming as they were, were considered as an evil of less magnitude than the eternal sufferings of sinners. This induced him to make the sacrifice, although for his enemies. It mattered not whether for friends or for enemies, if so be he could, by making a less sacrifice, secure a greater good to them.

Let it be understood, that a self-indulgent spirit is never, and can never be, consistent with benevolence. No form of self-indulgence, properly so called, can exist where true benevolence exists. The fact is, self-denial must be, and universally is, wherever benevolence reigns. Christ has expressly made whole-hearted self-denial a condition of discipleship; which is the same thing as to affirm, that it is an essential attribute of holiness or love; that there cannot be the beginning of true virtue without it.

Again: much that passes for self-denial is only a specious form of self-indulgence. The penances and self-mortifications, as they are falsely called, of the superstitious, what are they after all but a self-indulgent spirit? A popish priest abstains from marriage to obtain the honor, and emoluments, and the influence of the priestly office here, and eternal glory hereafter. A nun takes the veil and a monk immures himself in a monastery; a hermit forsakes human society, and shuts himself up in a cave; a devotee makes a pilgrimage to Mecca, and a martyr goes to the stake. Now if these things are done with an ultimate reference to their own glory and happiness, although apparently instances of great self-denial, yet they are, in fact, only a spirit of self-indulgence and self-seeking. They are only following the strongest desire of good to self.

There are many mistakes upon this subject. For example: it is common for persons to deny self in one form, for the sake of gratifying self in another form. In one man avarice is the ruling passion. He will labor hard, rise early, and sit up late, eat the bread of carefulness and deny himself even the necessaries of life, for the sake of accumulating wealth. Every one can see, that this is denying self in one form merely for the sake of gratifying self in another form. Yet this man will complain bitterly of the self-indulgent spirit manifested by others, their extravagance and want of piety. One man will deny all his bodily appetites and passions, for the sake of a reputation with men. This is also an instance of the same kind. Another will give the fruit of his body for the sin of his soul--will sacrifice everything else to obtain an eternal inheritance, and be just as selfish as the man who sacrifices to the things of time, his soul and all the riches of eternity.

But it should be remarked, that this attribute of benevolence does and must secure the subjugation of all the propensities. It must, either suddenly or gradually, so far subdue and quiet them, that their imperious clamor must cease. They will, as it were, be slain, either suddenly or gradually, so that the sensibility will become, in a great measure, dead to those objects that so often and so easily excited it. It is a law of the sensibility--of all the desires and passions, that their indulgence develops and strengthens them, and their denial suppresses them. Benevolence consists in a refusal to gratify the sensibility, and in obeying the reason. Therefore it must be true, that this denial of the propensities will greatly suppress them; while the indulgence of the intellect and of the conscience will greatly develop them. Thus selfishness tends to stultify, while benevolence tends greatly to strengthen the intellect.

19. Condescension is another attribute of love.

This attribute consists in a tendency to descend to the poor, the ignorant, or the vile, for the purpose of securing their good. It is a tendency to seek the good of those whom Providence has placed in any respect below us, by stooping, descending, coming down to them for this purpose. It is a peculiar form of self-denial. God the Father, the Son, and the Holy Spirit, manifest infinite condescension in efforts to secure the well-being of sinners, even the most vile and degraded. This attribute is called by Christ lowliness of heart. God is said to humble himself, that is, to condescend, when he beholds the things that are done in heaven. This is true, for every creature is, and must forever be, infinitely below Him in every respect. But how much greater must that condescension be, that comes down to earth, and even to the lowest and most degraded of earth's inhabitants, for purposes of benevolence! This is a lovely modification of benevolence. It seems to be entirely above the gross conceptions of infidelity. Condescension seems to be regarded by most people, and especially by infidels, as rather a weakness than a virtue. Sceptics clothe their imaginary God with attributes in many respects the opposite of true virtue. They think it entirely beneath the dignity of God to come down even to notice, and much more to interfere with, the concerns of men. But hear the word of the Lord: "Thus saith the High and Lofty One, who inhabiteth eternity, whose name is Holy: I dwell in the high and holy place; with him also that is of a contrite and humble spirit, to revive the spirit of the humble, and to revive the heart of the contrite ones." And again, "Thus saith the Lord, the heaven is my throne and the earth is my footstool, where is the house that ye build unto me? and where is the place of my rest? For all those things hath my hand made, and all those things have been, saith the Lord. But to this man will I look, even to him that is poor and of a contrite spirit, and that trembleth at my word." Thus the Bible represents God as clothed with condescension as with a cloak.

This is manifestly an attribute both of benevolence and of true greatness. The natural perfections of God appear all the more wonderful, when we consider, that he can and does know and contemplate and control, not only the highest, but the lowest of all his creatures; that he is just as able to attend to every want and every creature, as if this were the sole object of attention with him. So his moral attributes appear all the more lovely and engaging when we consider that his "tender mercies are over all his works," "that not a sparrow falleth to the ground without him;" that he condescends to number the very hairs of the heads of his servants, and that not one of them can fall without him. When we consider that no creature is too low, too filthy, or too degraded for him to condescend to,--this places his character in a most ravishing light. Benevolence is good-will to all beings. Of course one of its characteristics must be condescension to those who are below us. This in God is manifestly infinite. He is infinitely above all creatures. For him to hold communion with them is infinite condescension.

This is an attribute essentially belonging to benevolence or love in all benevolent beings. With the lowest of moral beings it may have no other development, than in its relations to sentient existences below the rank of moral agents, for the reason, that there are no moral agents below them to whom they can stoop. God's condescension stoops to all ranks of sentient existences. This is also true with every benevolent mind, as to all inferiors. It seeks the good of being in general, and never thinks any being too low to have his interests attended to and cared for, according to their relative value. Benevolence cannot possibly retain its own essential nature, and yet be above any degree of condescension that can effect the greatest good. Benevolence does not, cannot know anything of that loftiness of spirit that considers it too degrading to stoop anywhere, or to any being whose interests need to be, and can be, promoted by such condescension. Benevolence has its end, and it cannot but seek this, and it does not, cannot think anything below it that is demanded to secure that end. O the shame, the infinite folly and madness of pride, and every form of selfishness! How infinitely unlike God it is! Christ could condescend to be born in a manger; to be brought up in humble life; to be poorer than the fox of the desert, or the fowls of heaven; to associate with fishermen; to mingle with and seek the good of all classes; to be despised in life, and die between two thieves on the cross. His benevolence "endured the cross and despised the shame." He was "meek and lowly in heart." The Lord of heaven and earth is as much more lowly in heart than any of his creatures, as he is above them in his infinity. He can stoop to anything but to commit sin. He can stoop infinitely low.

20. Stability is another attribute of benevolence. This love is not a mere feeling or emotion, that effervesces for a moment, and then cools down and disappears. But it is choice, not a mere volition which accomplishes its object, and then rests. It is the choice of an end, a supreme end. It is an intelligent choice--the most intelligent choice that can be made. It is considerate choice--none so much so; a deliberate choice, a reasonable choice, which will always commend itself to the highest perceptions and intuitions of the intellect. It is intelligent and impartial, and universal consecration to an end, above all others the most important and captivating in its influence. Now, stability must be a characteristic of such a choice as this. By stability, it is not intended that the choice may not be changed. Nor that it never is changed; but that when the attributes of the choice are considered, it appears as if stability, as opposed to instability, must be an attribute of this choice. It is a new birth, a new nature, a new creature, a new heart, a new life. These and such like are the representations of scripture. Are these representations of an evanescent state? The beginning of benevolence in the soul--this choice is represented as the death of sin, as a burial, a being planted, a crucifixion of the old man, and many such like things. Are these representations of what we so often see among professed Christians? Nay, verily. The nature of the change itself would seem to be a guarantee of its stability. We might reasonably suppose, that any other choice would be relinquished sooner than this; that any other state of mind would fail sooner than benevolence. It is vain to reply to this, that facts prove the contrary to be true. I answer what facts? Who can prove them to be facts? Shall we appeal to the apparent facts in the instability of many professors of religion; or shall we appeal to the very nature of the choice, and to the scriptures? To these doubtless. So far as philosophy can go, we might defy the world to produce an instance of choice which has so many chances for stability. The representations of scripture are such as I have mentioned above. What then shall we conclude of those effervescing professors of religion, who are soon hot and soon cold; whose religion is a spasm; "whose goodness is as the morning cloud and the early dew, which goeth away?" Why, we must conclude, that

they never had the root of the matter in them. That they are not dead to sin and to the world, we see. That they are not new creatures, that they have not the spirit of Christ, that they do not keep his commandments, we see. What then shall we conclude, but this, that they are stony-ground hearers?

21. Holiness is another attribute of benevolence. This term is used in the Bible, as synonymous with moral purity. In a ceremonial sense it is applied to both persons and things; to make holy and to sanctify are the same thing. To sanctify and to consecrate, or set apart to a sacred use, are identical. Many things were, in this sense, sanctified, or made holy, under the Jewish economy. The term holiness may, in a general sense, be applied to anything whatever which is set apart to a sacred use. It may be applied to the whole being of a moral agent, who is set apart to the service of God.

As an attribute of benevolence, it denotes that quality which leads it to seek to promote the happiness of moral agents, by means of conformity to moral law.

As a moral attribute of God, it is that peculiarity of his benevolence which secures it against all efforts to obtain its end by other means than those that are morally and perfectly pure. His benevolence aims to secure the happiness of the universe of moral agents, by means of moral law and moral government, and of conformity to his own subjective idea of right. In other words, holiness in God is that quality of his love that secures its universal conformity, in all its efforts and manifestations, to the Divine idea of right, as it lies in eternal development in the Infinite Reason. This idea is moral law. It is sometimes used to express the moral quality, or character of his benevolence generally, or to express the moral character of the Godhead. It sometimes seems to designate an attribute, and sometimes a quality of his moral attributes. Holiness is, doubtless, a characteristic, or quality of each and all of his moral attributes. They will harmonize in this, that no one of them can consent to do otherwise than conform to the law of moral purity, as developed and revealed in the Divine Reason.

That holiness is an attribute of God is everywhere assumed, and frequently asserted in the Bible. If an attribute of God, it must be an attribute of love; for God is love. This attribute is celebrated in heaven as one of those aspects of the divine character that give ineffable delight. Isaiah saw the seraphim standing around the throne of Jehovah, and crying one to another, "Holy! holy! holy!" John also had a vision of the worship of heaven, and says "They rest not day nor night, saying, Holy! holy! holy! Lord God Almighty." When Isaiah beheld the holiness of Jehovah, he cried out "Woe is me! I am undone. I am a man of unclean lips, and I dwell in the midst of a people of unclean lips; for mine eyes have seen the King, the Lord of hosts!" God's holiness is infinite, and it is no wonder that a perception of it should thus affect the prophet.

Finite holiness must forever feel itself awed in the presence of infinite holiness. Job says, "I have heard of thee by the hearing of the ear, but now mine eye seeth thee: wherefore I abhor myself, and repent in dust and ashes." There is no comparing finite with infinite. The time will never come when creatures can with open face contemplate the infinite holiness of Jehovah, without being like persons overcome with a harmony too intensely delightful to be calmly borne. Heaven seems not able to endure it without breaking forth into strains of inexpressible rapture.

The expressions of Isaiah and Job do not necessarily imply that at the time they were in a sinful state, but their expressions no doubt related to whatever of sin they had at any time been guilty of. In the light of Jehovah's holiness they saw the comparative pollution of their character taken as a whole. This view will always, doubtless, much affect the saints. This must be; and yet in another sense they may be, and are, as holy, in their measure as he is. They may be as perfectly conformed to what light or truth they have, as he is. This is doubtless what Christ intended when he said, "Be ye perfect, even as your Father which is in heaven is perfect." The meaning is, that they should live to the same end, and be as entirely consecrated to it as he is. This they must be, to be truly virtuous or holy in any degree. But when they are so, a full view of the holiness of God would confound and overwhelm them. If any one doubts this, he has not considered the matter in a proper light. He has not lifted up his thoughts, as he needs to do, to the contemplation of infinite holiness. No creature, however benevolent, can witness the divine benevolence without being overwhelmed with a clear vision of it. This is no doubt true of every attribute of the divine love. However perfect creature-virtue may be, it is finite, and, brought into the light of the attributes of infinite virtue, it will appear like the dimmest star in the presence of the sun, lost in the blaze of his glory. Let the most just man on earth or in heaven witness, and have a clear apprehension of, the infinite justice of Jehovah, and it would no doubt fill him with unutterable awe. So, could the most merciful saint on earth, or in heaven, have a clear perception of the divine mercy in its fulness, it would swallow up all thought and imagination, and, no doubt, overwhelm him. And so also of every attribute of God. Oh! when we speak of the attributes of Jehovah, we often do not know what we say. Should God unveil himself to us, our bodies would instantly perish. "No man," says he, "can see my face and live." When Moses prayed, "Show me thy glory," God condescendingly hid him in the cleft of a rock, and covering him with his hand, he passed by, and let Moses see only his back parts, informing him that he could not behold his face, that is, his unveiled glories, and live.

Holiness, or moral harmony of character is, then, an essential attribute of disinterested love. It must be so from the laws of our being, and from the very nature of benevolence. In man it manifests itself in great purity of conversation and deportment, in a great loathing of all impurity of flesh and spirit. Let no man profess piety who has not this attribute developed. The love required by the law of God is pure love. It seeks to make its object happy only by making him holy. It manifests the greatest abhorrence of sin and all uncleanness. In creatures it pants, and doubtless ever will pant and struggle, toward infinite purity or holiness. It will never find a resting place in such a sense as to desire to ascend no higher. As it perceives more and more of the fulness and infinity of God's holiness, it will no doubt pant and struggle to ascend the eternal heights where God sits in light too intense for the strongest vision of the highest cherub.

Holiness of heart or of will, produces a desire or feeling of purity in the sensibility. The feelings become exceedingly alive to the beauty of holiness and to the hatefulness and deformity of all spiritual, and even physical impurity. This is called the love of holiness. The sensibility becomes ravished with the great loveliness of holiness, and unutterably disgusted with the opposite. The least impurity of conversation or of action exceedingly shocks one who is holy. Impure thoughts, if suggested to the mind of a holy being, are instantly felt to be exceedingly offensive and painful. The soul heaves and struggles to cast them out as the most loathsome abominations.

LECTURE XVI - WHAT CONSTITUTES DISOBEDIENCE TO MORAL LAW?

In discussing this question, I will,

I. Show in what disobedience to moral law cannot consist.

1. It cannot consist in malevolence, or in the choice of evil or misery as an ultimate end. This will appear, if we consider, that the choice of an end implies the choice of it, not for no reason, but for a reason, and for its own intrinsic value, or because the mind prizes it on its own account. But moral agents are so constituted, that they cannot regard misery as intrinsically valuable. They cannot, therefore, choose it as an ultimate end, nor prize it on its own account.

2. Disobedience to moral law cannot consist in the constitution of soul or body. The law does not command us to have a certain constitution, nor forbid us to have the constitution with which we came into being.

3. It cannot consist in any unavoidable state, either of the sensibility or of the intelligence; for these, as we have seen, are involuntary, and are dependent upon the actings of the will.

4. It cannot consist in outward actions, independent of the design with which they are put forth; for these, we have seen, are controlled by the actions of the will, and, therefore, can have no moral character in themselves.

5. It cannot consist in inaction; for total inaction is to a moral agent impossible. Moral agents are necessarily active. That is, they cannot exist as moral agents without choice. They must, by a law of necessity, choose either in accordance with, or in opposition to, the law of God. They are free to choose in either direction, but they are not free to abstain from choice altogether. Choose they must. The possession of free-will, and the perception of opposing objects of choice, either exciting desire, or developing the rational affirmation of obligation to choose, render choice one way or the other inevitable. The law directs how they ought to choose. If they do not choose thus, it must be because they choose otherwise, and not because they do not choose at all.

6. It cannot consist in the choice of moral evil, or sin, as an ultimate end. Sin is but an element or attribute of choice or intention, or it is intention itself. If it be intention itself, then to make sin an end of intention, would be to make intention or choice terminate on itself, and the sinner must choose his own choice, or intend his own intention as an end: this is absurd.

7. Disobedience to moral law cannot consist in self-love. Self-love is simply the constitutional desire of happiness. It is altogether an involuntary state. It has, as a desire, no moral character, any more than has the desire of food. It is no more sinful to desire happiness, and properly to seek it, than it is wrong to desire food, and properly to seek that.

II. What disobedience to moral law must consist in.

Disobedience to God's law must consist in the choice of self-gratification as an end. In other words, it must consist essentially in committing the will, and through the will committing the whole being, to the indulgence of self-love, as the supreme and ultimate end of life. This is selfishness. In other words, it is seeking to gratify the desire of personal good, in a manner prohibited by the law of God.

It consists in choosing self-gratification as an end, or for its own sake, instead of choosing, in accordance with the law of the reason and of God, the highest well-being of God and of the universe as an ultimate end. In other words still, sin or disobedience to the moral law, consists in the consecration of the heart and life to the gratification of the constitutional and artificial desires, rather than in obedience to the law of the intelligence. Or, once more, sin consists in being governed by impulses of the sensibility, instead of being governed by the law of God, as it lies revealed in the reason.

That this is sin, and the whole of sin viewed in its germinating principles, will appear, if we consider:--

1. That this state of mind, or this choice, is the "carnal mind," or the minding of the flesh, which the apostle affirms to be "enmity against God." It is the universal representation of scripture, that sin consists in the spirit of self-seeking. This spirit of self-seeking is always in the Bible represented as the contrast or opposite of disinterested benevolence, or the love which the law requires. "Ephraim bringeth forth fruit to himself," is the sum of God's charges against sinners.

2. When we come to the consideration of the attributes of selfishness, it will be seen that every form of sin, not only may, but must resolve itself into selfishness, just as we have seen that every form of virtue does and must resolve itself into love or benevolence.

3. From the laws of its constitution, the mind is shut up to the necessity of choosing that, as an ultimate end, which is regarded by the mind as intrinsically good or valuable in itself. This is the very idea of choosing an end, to wit, something chosen for its own sake, or for what it is in and of itself, or, because it is regarded by the mind as intrinsically valuable to self, or to being in general, or to both.

4. Moral agents are, therefore, shut up to the necessity of willing the good of being, either partially or impartially, either good to self, or good to being in general. Nothing else can possibly be chosen as an end or for its own sake. Willing the good of being impartially, we have seen, is virtue. To will it partially is to will it, not for its own sake, except upon condition of its relation to self. That is, it is to will good to self. In other words, it is to will the gratification of self as an end, in opposition to willing the good of universal being as an end, and every good, or the good of every being, according to its intrinsic value.

5. But may not one will the good of a part of being as an end, or for the sake of the intrinsic value of their good? This would not be benevolence; for that, as we have seen, must consist in willing good for its own sake, and implies the willing of every good, and of the highest good of universal being. It would not be selfishness, as it would not be willing good to, or the gratification of, self. It would be sin, for it would be the partial love or choice of good. It would be loving some of my neighbors, but not all of them. It would, therefore, be sin, but not selfishness. If this can be, then there is such a thing possible, whether actual or not, as sin that does not consist in selfishness. But let us examine whether this supposition would not resolve itself into selfishness.

To say that I choose good for its own sake, or because it is valuable to being, that is, in obedience to the law of my reason, and of God, implies that I choose all possible good, and every good according to its relative value. If, then, a being chooses his own good, or the good of any being as an ultimate end, in obedience to the law of reason, it must be that he chooses, for the same reason, the highest possible good of all sentient being.

The partial choice of good implies the choice of it, not merely for its own sake, but upon condition of its relations to self, or to certain particular persons. Its relations conditionate the choice. When its relations to self conditionate the choice, so that it is chosen, not for its intrinsic value, irrespective of its relations, but for its relations to self, this is selfishness. It is the partial choice of good. If I choose the good of others besides myself, and choose good because of its relations to them, it must be either--

(1.) Because I love their persons with the love of fondness, and will their good for that reason, that is, to gratify my affection for them, which is selfishness; or--

(2.) Because of their relations to me, so that good to them is in some way a good to me, which also is selfishness; or

(3.) Upon condition that they are worthy, which is benevolence; for if I will good to a being upon condition that he is worthy, I must value the good for its own sake, and will it particularly to him, because he deserves it. This is benevolence, and not the partial choice of good, because it is obeying the law of my reason.

Again: If I will the good of any number of beings, I must do it in obedience to the law either of my intelligence and of God, or of my sensibility. But, if I will in obedience to the law of my intelligence, it must be the choice of the highest good of universal being. But if I will in obedience to the law or impulse of my sensibility, it must be to gratify my feelings or desires. This is selfishness.

Again: As the will must either follow the law of the reason and of God, or the impulses of the sensibility, it follows that moral agents are shut up to the necessity of being selfish or benevolent, and that there is no third way, because there is no third medium, through which any object of choice can be presented. The mind can absolutely know nothing as an object of choice, that is not recommended by one of these faculties. Selfishness, then, and benevolence, are the only two alternatives.

Let it be remembered, then, that sin is a unit, and always and necessarily consists in selfish ultimate intention, and in nothing else. This intention is sin; and thus we see that every phase of sin resolves itself into selfishness. This will appear more and more, as we proceed to unfold the subject of moral depravity.

LECTURE XVII - ATTRIBUTES OF SELFISHNESS

Formerly we considered the attributes of benevolence, and also what states of the sensibility and of the intellect, and also what outward actions, were implied in it, as necessarily resulting from it. We are now to take the same course with selfishness: and--

1. Voluntariness is an attribute of selfishness.

Selfishness has often been confounded with mere desire. But these things are by no means identical. Desire is constitutional. It is a phenomenon of the sensibility. It is a purely involuntary state of mind, and can in itself produce no action, nor can it, in itself, have moral character. Selfishness is a phenomenon of the will, and consists in committing the will to the gratification of the desires. The desire itself is not selfishness, but submitting the will to be governed by the desire, is selfishness. It should be understood, that no kind of mere desires, and no strength of mere desire, constitutes selfishness. Selfishness commences when the will yields to the desire, and seeks to obey it, in opposition to the law of the intelligence. It matters not what kind of desire it is; if it is the desire that governs the will, this is selfishness. It must be the will in a state of committal to the gratification of the desire.

2. Liberty is another attribute of selfishness.

That is, the choice of self-gratification is not necessitated by desire. But the will is always free to choose in opposition to desire. This every moral agent is as conscious of as of his own existence. The desire is not free, but the choice to gratify it is and must be free. There is a sense, as I shall have occasion to show, in which slavery is an attribute of selfishness, but not in the sense that the will chooses, by a law of necessity, to gratify desire. Liberty, in the sense of ability to make an opposite choice, must ever remain an attribute of selfishness, while selfishness continues to be a sin, or while it continues to sustain any relation to moral law.

3. Intelligence is another attribute of selfishness.

By this it is not intended that intelligence is an attribute or phenomenon of will, nor that the choice of self-gratification is in accordance with the demands of the intellect. But it is intended that the choice is made with the knowledge of the moral character that will be involved in it. The mind knows its obligation to make an opposite choice. It is not a mistake. It is not a choice made in ignorance of moral obligation to choose the highest good of being, as an end, in opposition to self-gratification. It is an intelligent choice in the sense, that it is a known resistance of the demands of the intellect. It is a known rejection of its claims. It is a known setting up of self-gratification, and preferring it to all higher interests.

4. Unreasonableness is another attribute of selfishness.

By this it is intended, that the selfish choice is in direct opposition to the demands of the reason. The reason was given to rule, that is, to affirm obligation, and thus announce the law of God. It affirms law and moral obligation. Obedience to moral law, as it is revealed in the reason, is virtue. Obedience to the sensibility in opposition to the reason, is sin. Selfishness consists in this. It is a dethroning of reason from the seat of government, and an enthroning of blind desire in opposition to it. Selfishness is always and necessarily unreasonable. It is a denial of that divine attribute that allies man to God, makes him capable of virtue, and is a sinking him to the level of a brute. It is a denial of his manhood, of his rational nature. It is a contempt of the voice of God within him, and a deliberate trampling down the sovereignty of his own intellect. Shame on selfishness! It dethrones human reason, and would dethrone the divine, and place mere blind lust upon the throne of the universe.

The very definition of selfishness implies that unreasonableness is one of its attributes. Selfishness consists in the will's yielding itself to the impulses of the sensibility, in opposition to the demands of the intelligence. Therefore, every act or choice of the will is necessarily altogether unreasonable. Sinners, while they continue such, never say nor do one thing that is in accordance with right reason. Hence the Bible says, that "madness is in their heart while they live." They have made an unreasonable choice of an end, and all their choices of means to secure their end are only a carrying out of their ultimate choice. They are, every one of them, put forth to secure an end contrary to reason. Therefore, no sinner, who has never been converted, has, even in a single instance, chosen otherwise than in direct opposition to reason. They are not merely sometimes unreasonable, but uniformly, and, while they remain selfish, necessarily so. The very first time that a sinner acts or wills reasonably, is when he turns to God, or repents and becomes a Christian. This is the first instance in which he practically acknowledges that he has reason. All previous to this, every one of the actions of his will and of his life, is a practical denial of his manhood, of his rational nature, of his obligation to God or his neighbor. We sometimes hear impenitent sinners spoken of as being unreasonable, and in such a manner as to imply that all sinners are not so. But this only favors the delusion of sinners by leaving them to suppose that they are not all of them, at all times, altogether unreasonable. But the fact is, that there is not, and there never can be, in earth or hell, one impenitent sinner who, in any instance, acts otherwise than in direct and palpable opposition to his reason. It had, therefore, been infinitely better for sinners if they had never been endowed with reason. They do not merely act without consulting their reason, but in stout and determined opposition to it.

Again: They act as directly in opposition to it as they possibly can. They not only oppose it, but they oppose it as much, and in as aggravated a manner, as possible. What can be more directly and aggravatedly opposed to reason than the choice which the sinner makes of an end? Reason was given him to direct him in regard to the choice of the great end of life. It gives him the idea of the eternal and the infinite. It spreads out before him the interests of God and of the universe as of absolutely infinite value. It affirms their value, and the infinite obligation of the sinner to consecrate himself to these interests; and it promises him endless rewards if he will do so. On the contrary, it lays before him the consequences of refusal. It thunders in his ear the terrible sanctions of the law. It points him to the coming doom that awaits his refusal to comply with its demands. But behold, in the face of all this, the sinner, unhesitatingly, in the face of these affirmations, demands, and threatenings, turns away and consecrates himself to the gratification of his desires with the certainty that he could not do greater despite to his own nature than in this most mad, most preposterous, most blasphemous choice. Why do not sinners consider that it is impossible for them to offer a greater insult to God, who gave them reason, or more truly and deeply to shame and degrade themselves, than they do in their beastly selfishness? Total, universal, and shameless unreasonableness, is the universal characteristic of every selfish mind.

5. Interestedness is another attribute of selfishness.

By interestedness is meant self-interestedness. It is not the disinterested choice of good, that is, it is not the choice of the good of being in general as an end, but it is the choice of self-good, of good to self. Its relation to self is the condition of the choice of this good. But for its being the good of self, it would not be chosen. The fundamental reason, or that which should induce choice, to wit, the intrinsic value of good, is rejected as insufficient; and the secondary reason, namely, its relation to self, is the condition of determining the will in this direction. This is really making self-good the supreme end. In other words, it is making self-gratification the end. Nothing is practically regarded as worthy of choice, except as it sustains to self the relation of a means of self-gratification.

This attribute of selfishness secures a corresponding state of the sensibility. The sensibility, under this indulgence, attains to a monstrous development, either generally, or in some particular directions. Selfishness is the committal of the will to the indulgence of the propensities. But from this it by no means follows, that all of the propensities will be indiscriminately indulged, and thereby greatly developed. Sometimes one propensity, and sometimes another, has the greatest natural strength, and thereby gains the ascendancy in the control of the will. Sometimes circumstances tend more strongly to the development of one appetite or passion than another. Whatever propensity is most indulged, will gain the greatest development. The propensities cannot all be indulged at once, for they are often opposed to each other. But they may all be indulged and developed in their turn. For example, the licentious propensities, and various other propensities, cannot be indulged consistently with the simultaneous indulgence of the avaricious propensities, the desire of reputation and of ultimate happiness. Each of these, and even all the propensities, may come in for a share, and in some instances may gain so equal a share of indulgence, as upon the whole to be about equally developed. But in general, either from constitutional temperament, or from circumstances, some one or more of the propensities will gain so uniform a control of the will, as to occasion its monstrous development. It may be the love of reputation; and then there will be at least a public decent exterior, more or less strict, according to the state of morals in the society in which the individual dwells. If it be amativeness that gains the ascendancy over the other propensities, licentiousness will be the result. If it be alimentiveness, then gluttony and Epicurism will be the result. The result of selfishness must be, to develop in general, or in particular, the propensities of the sensibility, and to beget a corresponding exterior. If avarice take the control of the will, we have the haggard and ragged miser. All the other propensities wither under the reign of this detestable one. Where the love of knowledge prevails, we have the scholar, the philosopher, the man of learning. This is one of the most decent and respectable forms of selfishness, but is nevertheless as absolutely selfishness as any other form. When compassion, as a feeling, prevails, we have, as a result, the philanthropist, and often the reformer; not the reformer in a virtuous sense, but the selfish reformer. Where love of kindred prevails, we often have the kind husband, the affectionate father, mother, brother, sister, and so on. These are the amiable sinners, especially among their own kindred. When the love of country prevails, we have the patriot, the statesman, and the soldier. The picture might be drawn at full length, but with these traits I must leave you to fill up the outline. I would only add, that several of these forms of selfishness so nearly resemble certain forms of virtue, as often to be confounded with them, and mistaken for them. Indeed, so far as the outward life is concerned, they are right, in the letter, but as they do not proceed from disinterestedly benevolent intention, they are only specious forms of selfishness.

6. Partiality is another attribute of selfishness. It consists in giving the preference to certain interests, on account of their being either directly the interests of self, or so connected with self-interest as to be preferred on that account. It matters not, whether the interest to which the preference is given be of greater or of less value, if so be it is preferred, not for the reason of its greater value, but because of its relation to self. In some instances the practical preference may justly be given to a less interest, on account of its sustaining such a relation to us that we can secure it, when the greater interest could not be secured by us. If the reason of the preference, in such case, be, not that it is self-interest, but an interest that can be secured while the greater cannot, the preference is a just one, and not partiality. My family, for example, sustain such relations to me, that I can more readily and surely secure their interests, than I can those of my neighbor, or of a stranger. For this reason I am under obligation to give the practical preference to the interests of my own family, not because they are my own, nor because their interests sustain such a relation to my own, but because I can more readily secure their interests than those of any other family.

The question in such a case turns upon the amount I am able to secure, and not on the intrinsic value merely. It is a general truth, that we can secure more readily and certainly the interests of those to whom we sustain certain relations; and therefore, God and reason point out these interests as particular objects of our attention and effort. This is not partiality but impartiality. It is treating interests as they should be treated.

But selfishness is always partial. If it gives any interest, whatever the preference, it is because of its relation to self. It always, and, continuing to be selfishness, necessarily, lays the greatest stress upon, and gives the preference to, those interests the promotion of which will gratify self.

Here care should be taken to avoid delusion. Oftentimes selfishness appears to be very disinterested and very impartial. For example: here is a man whose compassion, as a mere feeling or state of the sensibility, is greatly developed. He meets a beggar, an object that strongly excites his ruling passion. He empties his pockets, and even takes off his coat and gives it to him, and in his paroxysm he will divide his all with him, or even give him all. Now this would generally pass for most undoubted virtue, as a rare and impressive instance of moral goodness. But there is no virtue, no benevolence in it. It is a mere yielding of the will to the control of feeling, and has nothing in it of the nature of virtue. Innumerable examples of this might be adduced, as illustrations of this truth. It is only an instance and an illustration of selfishness.

It is the will seeking to gratify the feeling of compassion, which for the time is the strongest desire.

We constitutionally desire not only our own happiness, but also that of men in general, when their happiness in no way conflicts with our own. Hence selfish men will often manifest a deep interest in the welfare of those, whose welfare will not interfere with their own. Now, should the will be yielded up to the gratification of this desire, this would often be regarded as virtue. For example: a few years since much interest and feeling were excited in this country by the cause and sufferings of the Greeks, in their struggle for liberty; and since in the cause of the Poles. A spirit of enthusiasm appeared, and many were ready to give and do almost anything for the cause of liberty. They gave up their will to the gratification of this excited state of feeling. This, they may have supposed, was virtue; but it was not, nor was there a semblance of virtue about it, when it is once understood, that virtue consists in yielding the will to the law of the intelligence, and not to the impulse of excited feelings.

Some writers have fallen into the strange mistake of making virtue to consist in seeking the gratification of certain desires, because, as they say, these desires are virtuous. They make some of the desires selfish, and some benevolent. To yield the will to the control of the selfish propensities is sin; to yield to the control of the benevolent desires, such as the desire of my neighbor's happiness and of the public happiness, is virtue, because these are good desires, while the selfish desires are evil. Now this is, and has been, a very common view of virtue and vice. But it is fundamentally erroneous. None of the constitutional desires are good or evil in themselves; they are alike involuntary, and all alike terminate on their correlated objects. To yield the will to the control of any one of them, no matter which, is sin; it is following a blind feeling, desire, or impulse of the sensibility, instead of yielding to the demands of the intelligence, as the law affirming power. To will the good of my neighbor, or of my country, and of God, because of the intrinsic value of those interests, that is to will them as an end, and in obedience to the law of the reason, is virtue; but to will them to gratify a constitutional but blind desire, is selfishness and sin. The desires terminate on their respective objects; but the will, in this case, seeks the objects, not for their own sake, but because they are desired, that is, to gratify the desires. This is choosing them, not as an end, but as a means of self-gratification. This is making self-gratification the end after all. This must be a universal truth, when a thing is chosen merely in obedience to desire. The benevolence of these writers is sheer selfishness, and their virtue is vice.

The choice of any thing whatever, because it is desired, irrespective of the demands of the reason, is selfishness and sin. It matters not what it is. The very statement, that I choose a thing because I desire it, is only another form of saying, that I choose it for my own sake, or for the sake of appeasing the desire, and not on account of its own intrinsic value. All such choice is always and necessarily partial. It is giving one interest the preference over another, not because of its perceived intrinsic and superior value, but because it is an object of desire. If I yield to mere desire in any case, it must be to gratify the desire. This is, and in the case supposed must be, the end for which the choice is made. To deny this is to deny that the will seeks the object because it is desired. Partiality consists in giving one thing the preference of another for no good reason. That is, not because the intelligence demands this preference, but because the sensibility demands it. Partiality is therefore always and necessarily an attribute of selfishness.

7. Efficiency is another attribute of selfishness. Desire never produces action until it influences the will. It has no efficiency or causality in itself. It cannot, without the concurrence of the will, command the attention of the intellect, or move a muscle of the body. The whole causality of the mind resides in the will. In it resides the power of accomplishment.

Again: the whole efficiency of the mind, as it respects accomplishment, resides in the choice of an end, or in the ultimate intention. All action of the will, or all willing, must consist in choosing either an end, or the means of accomplishing an end. If there is choice, something is chosen. That something is chosen for some reason. To deny this is a denial that any thing is chosen. The ultimate reason for the choice and the thing chosen, are identical. This we have repeatedly seen.

Again: we have seen that the means cannot be chosen until the end is chosen. The choice of the end is distinct from the volitions or endeavors of the mind to secure the end. But although the choice of an end is not identical with the subordinate choices and volitions to secure the end, yet it necessitates them. The choice once made, secures or necessitates the executive volitions to secure the end. By this it is not intended that the mind is not free to relinquish its end, and of course to relinquish the use of the means to accomplish it; but only that, while the choice or intention remains, the choice of the end by the will is efficient in producing volitions to realize the end. This is true both of benevolence and selfishness. They are both choices of an end, and are necessarily efficient in producing the use of the means to realize this end. They are choices of opposite ends, and, of course, will produce their respective results.

The Bible represents sinners as having eyes full of adultery, and that cannot cease from sin; that while the will is committed to the indulgence of the propensities, they cannot cease from the indulgence. There is no way, therefore, for the sinner to escape from the commission of sin, but to cease to be selfish. While selfishness continues, you may change the form of outward manifestation, you may deny one appetite or desire for the sake of indulging another; but it is and must be sin still. The desire to escape hell, and to obtain heaven may become the strongest, in which case, selfishness will take on a most sanctimonious type. But if the will is following desire, it is selfishness still; and all your religious duties, as you call them, are only selfishness robed in the stolen habiliments of loving obedience to God.

Be it remembered, then, that selfishness is, and must be, efficient in producing its effects. It is cause; the effect must follow. The whole life, and activity of sinners is founded in it. It constitutes their life, or rather their spiritual death. They are dead in trespasses and in sins. It is in vain for them to dream of doing anything good, until they relinquish their selfishness. While this continues, they cannot act at all, except as they use the means to accomplish a selfish end. It is impossible, while the will remains committed to a selfish end, or to the promotion of self-interest or self-gratification, that it should use the means to promote a benevolent end. The first thing is to change the end, and then the sinner can cease from outward sin. Indeed, if the end be changed, many of the same acts which were before sinful will become holy. While the selfish end continues, whatever a sinner does, is selfish. Whether he eats, or drinks, or labors, or preaches, or, in short, whatever he does, is to promote some form of self-interest. The end being wrong, all is, and must be, wrong.

This is the philosophy of Christ. "Either make the tree good, and his fruit good; or else make the tree corrupt, and his fruit corrupt: for the tree is known by his fruit. A good man out of the good treasure of the heart bringeth forth good things: and an evil man out of the evil treasure bringeth forth evil things." Matt. xii. 33, 35. "Doth a fountain send forth at the same place sweet water and bitter? Can the fig-tree, my brethren, bear olive berries? either a vine figs? So can no fountain both yield salt water and fresh." James iii. 11, 12. "For a good tree bringeth not forth corrupt fruit; nether doth a corrupt tree bring forth good fruit. For every tree is known by his own fruit: for of thorns men do not gather figs, nor of a bramble bush gather they grapes. A good man out of the good treasure of his heart, bringeth forth that which is good; and an evil man out of the evil treasure of his heart, bringeth forth that which is evil; for out of the abundance of the heart his mouth speaketh." Luke vi. 43-45.

8. Opposition to benevolence or to virtue, or to holiness and true religion, is one of the attributes of selfishness.

Selfishness is not, in its relations to benevolence, a mere negation. It cannot be. It is the choice of self-gratification as the supreme and ultimate end of life. While the will is committed to this end, and benevolence, or a mind committed to an opposite end, is contemplated, the will cannot remain in a state of indifference to benevolence. It must either yield its preference of self-indulgence, or resist the benevolence which the intellect perceives. The will cannot remain in the exercise of this selfish choice, without as it were bracing and girding itself against that virtue, which it does not imitate. If it does not imitate it, it must be because it refuses to do so. The intellect does, and must, strongly urge the will to imitate benevolence, and to seek the same end. The will must yield or resist, and the resistance must be more or less resolute and determined, as the demands of the intellect are more or less emphatic. This resistance to benevolence or to the demands of the intellect in view of it, is what the Bible calls, hardening the heart. It is obstinacy of will, under the light and the presence of true religion, and the admitted claims of benevolence.

This opposition to benevolence or true religion, must be developed in specific action, whenever the mind apprehends true religion, or selfishness must be abandoned. Not only must this opposition be developed, or selfishness abandoned, under such circumstances, but it must be increased as true religion displays more and more of its loveliness. As the light from the radiant sun of benevolence is poured more and more upon the darkness of selfishness, the opposition of this principle of action must of necessity manifest itself in the same proportion, or selfishness must be abandoned. Thus selfishness remaining under light, must manifest more and more opposition, just in proportion as light increases, and the soul has less the color of an apology for its opposition.

This peculiarity of selfishness has always been manifested just in proportion as it has been brought into the light of true religion. This accounts for all the opposition that has been made to true religion since the world began. It also proves that where there are impenitent sinners, and they retain their impenitence, and manifest no hostility to the religion which they witness, that there is something defective in the professed piety which they behold; or at least they do not contemplate all the attributes of true piety. It also proves, that persecution will always exist where much true religion is manifested to those who hold fast their selfishness.

It is indeed true, that selfishness and benevolence are just as much opposed to each other, and just as much and as necessarily at war with each other, as God and Satan, as heaven and hell. There can never be a truce between them; they are essential and eternal opposites. They are not merely opposites, but they are opposite efficient causes. They are essential activities. They are the two, and the only two, great antagonistic principles in the universe of mind. Each is heaving and energizing like an earthquake to realize its end. A war of mutual and uncompromising extermination necessarily exists between them. Neither can be in the presence of the other, without repulsion and opposition. Each puts forth all its energy to subdue and overcome the other; and already selfishness has shed an ocean of the blood of saints, as well as the precious blood of the Prince of life. There is not a more gross and injurious mistake, than to suppose that selfishness ever, under any circumstances, becomes reconciled to benevolence. The supposition is absurd and contradictory; since for selfishness to become reconciled to benevolence, were the same thing as for selfishness to become benevolence. Selfishness may change the mode of attack or of its opposition, but its real opposition it can never change, while it retains its own nature and continues to be selfishness.

This opposition of the heart to benevolence often begets deep opposition of feeling. The opposition of the will engages the intellect in fabricating excuses, and cavils, and lies, and refuges, and often greatly perverts the thoughts, and excites the most bitter feelings imaginable toward God and toward the saints. Selfishness will strive to justify its opposition, and to shield itself against the reproaches of conscience, and will resort to every possible expedient to cover up its real hostility to holiness. It will pretend that it is not holiness, but sin that it opposes. But the fact is, it is not sin but holiness to which it stands forever opposed. The opposition of feeling is only developed when the heart is brought into a strong light, and makes deep and strong resistance. In such cases, the sensibility sometimes boils over with feelings of bitter opposition to God, and Christ, and all good.

The question is often asked, May not this opposition exist in the sensibility, and those feelings of hostility to God exist, when the heart is in a truly benevolent state? To this inquiry, I would reply: If it can, it must be produced by infernal or some other influence that misrepresents God, and places his character before the mind in a false light. Blasphemous thoughts may be suggested, and, as it were, injected into the mind. These thoughts may have their natural effect in the sensibility, and feelings of bitterness and hostility may exist without the consent of the will. The will may all the while be endeavoring to repel these suggestions, and divert the attention from such thoughts, yet Satan may continue to hurl his fiery darts, and the soul may be racked with torture under the poison of hell, which seems to be taking effect in the sensibility. The mind, at such times, seems to itself to be filled, so far as feeling is concerned, with all the bitterness of hell. And so it is, and yet it may be, that in all this there is no selfishness. If the will holds fast its integrity; if it holds out in the struggle, and where God is maligned and misrepresented by the infernal suggestions, it says with Job, "Although he slay me, yet will I trust in him," however sharp the conflict in such cases, we can look back and say, "We are more than conquerors through him that loved us." In such cases it is the selfishness of Satan, and not our own selfishness, that kindled up those fires of hell in our sensibility. "Blessed is the man that endureth temptation; for when he is tried he shall receive the crown of life."

9. Cruelty is another attribute of selfishness.

This term is often used to designate a state of the sensibility. It then represents that state of feeling which has a barbarous or savage pleasure in the misery of others.

Cruelty, as a phenomenon of the will or as an attribute of selfishness, consists, first, in a reckless disregard of the well-being of God and the universe, and secondly, in persevering in a course that must ruin the souls of the subjects of it, and, so far as they have influence, ruin the souls of others. What should we think of a man who was so intent on securing some petty gratification, that he would not give the alarm if a city were on fire, and the sleeping citizens in imminent danger of perishing in the flames? Suppose that sooner than deny himself some momentary gratification, he would jeopard many lives. Should we not call this cruelty? Now there are many forms of cruelty. Because sinners are not always brought into circumstances where they exercise certain forms of it, they flatter themselves that they are not cruel. But selfishness is always and necessarily cruel--cruel to the soul and highest interests of the subject of it; cruel to the souls of others, in neglecting to care and act for their salvation; cruel to God, in abusing him in ten thousand ways; cruel to the whole universe. If we should be shocked at the cruelty of him who should see his neighbor's house on fire, and the family asleep, and neglect to give them warning, because too self-indulgent to rise from his bed, what shall we say of the cruelty of one, who shall see his neighbor's soul in peril of eternal death, and yet neglect to give him warning?

Sinners are apt to possess very good dispositions, as they express it. They suppose they are the reverse of being cruel. They possess tender feelings, are often very compassionate in their feelings toward those who are sick and in distress, and who are in circumstances of any affliction. They are ready to do many things for them. Such persons would be shocked, should they be called cruel. And many professors would take their part, and consider them abused. Whatever else, it would be said, is an attribute of their character, surely cruelty is not. Now, it is true that there are certain forms of cruelty with which such persons are not chargeable. But this is only because God has so moulded their constitution, that they are not delighted with the misery of their fellow men. However, there is no virtue in their not being gratified at the sight of suffering, nor in their painstaking to prevent it while they continue selfish. They follow the impulses of their feelings, and if their temperament were such that it would gratify them to inflict misery on others--if this were the strongest tendency of their sensibility, their selfishness would instantly take on that type. But though cruelty, in all its lulus, is not common to all selfish persons, it is still true that some form of cruelty is practiced by every sinner. God says, "The tender mercies of the wicked are cruel." The fact that they live in sin, that they set an example of selfishness, that they do nothing for their own souls, nor for the souls of others; these are really most atrocious forms of cruelty, and infinitely exceed all those comparatively petty forms that relate to the miseries of men in this life.

10. Injustice is another attribute of selfishness.

Justice, as an attribute of benevolence, is that quality that disposes it to regard and treat every being and interest with exact equity.

Injustice is the opposite of this. It is that quality of selfishness which disposes it to treat the persons and interests of others inequitably, and a disposition to give the preference to self-interest, regardless of the relative value of the interests. The nature of selfishness demonstrates, that injustice is always and necessarily one of its attributes, and one that is universally and constantly manifested.

There is the utmost injustice in the end chosen. It is the practical preference of a petty self-interest over infinite interests. This is injustice as great as possible. This is universal injustice to God and man. It is the most palpable and most flagrant piece of injustice possible to every being in the universe. Not one known by him to exist who has not reason to bring against him the charge of most flagrant and shocking injustice. This injustice extends to every act and to every moment of life. He is never, in the least degree, just to any being in the universe. Nay, he is perfectly unjust. He cares nothing for the rights of others as such; and never, even in appearance, regards them except for selfish reasons. This, then, is, and can be, only the appearance of regarding them, while in fact, no right of any being in the universe is, or can be, respected by a selfish mind, any further than in appearance. To deny this is to deny his selfishness. He performs no act whatever but for one reason, that is, to promote his own gratification. This is his end. For the realization of this end every effort is made, and every individual act and volition put forth. Remaining selfish, it is impossible that he should act at all, but with reference directly or indirectly to this end. But this end has been chosen, and must be pursued, if pursued at all, in the most palpable and outrageous violation of the rights of God and of every creature in the universe. Justice demands that he should devote himself to the promotion of the highest good of God and the universe, that he should love God with all his heart, and his neighbor as himself. Every sinner is openly, and universally, and as perfectly, unjust as possible, at every moment of his impenitence.

It should, therefore, always be understood, that no sinner at any time is at all just to any being in the universe. All his paying of his debts, and all his apparent fairness and justice, are only a specious form of selfishness. He has, and, if a sinner, it is impossible that he should not have, some selfish reason for all he does, is, says, or omits. His entire activity is selfishness, and while he remains impenitent, it is impossible for him to think, or act, or will, or do, or be, or say, anything more or less than he judges expedient to promote his own interests. He is not just. Ho cannot be just, nor begin in any instance, or in the least degree, to be truly just, either to God or man, until he begins life anew, gives God his heart, and consecrates his entire being to promotion of the good of universal being. This, all this, justice demands. There is no beginning to be just, unless the sinner begins here. Begin and be just in the choice of the great end of life, and then you cannot but be just in the use of means. But be unjust in the choice of an end, and it is impossible for you, in any instance, to be otherwise than totally unjust in the use of means. In this case your entire activity is, and can be, nothing else than a tissue of the most abominable injustice.

The only reason why every sinner does not openly and daily practice every species of outward commercial injustice is, that he is so circumstanced that, upon the whole, he judges it not for his interest to practice this injustice. This is the reason universally, and no thanks to any sinner for abstaining, in any instance, from any kind or degree of injustice in practice, for he is only restrained and kept from it by selfish considerations. That is, he is too selfish to do it. His selfishness, and not the love of God or man, prevents. He may be prevented by a constitutional or phrenological conscientiousness, or sense of justice. But this is only a feeling of the sensibility, and, if restrained only by this, he is just as absolutely selfish as if he had stolen a horse in obedience to acquisitiveness. God so tempers the constitution as to restrain men, that is, that one form of selfishness shall prevail over and curb another. Approbativeness is, in most persons, so large, that a desire to be applauded by their fellow-men so modifies the developments of their selfishness, that it takes on a type of outward decency and appearance of justice. But this is no less selfishness than if it took on altogether a different type.

LECTURE XVIII - ATTRIBUTES OF SELFISHNESS

11. Falsehood, or lying, is another attribute of selfishness.

Falsehood may be objective or subjective. Objective falsehood is that which stands opposed to truth. Subjective falsehood is a heart conformed to error and to objective falsehood. Subjective falsehood is a state of mind, or an attribute of selfishness. It is the will in the attitude of resisting truth, and embracing error and lies. This is always and necessarily an attribute of selfishness.

Selfishness consists in the choice of an end opposed to all truth, and cannot but proceed to the realization of that end, in conformity with error or falsehood instead of truth. If at any time it seize upon objective truth, as it often does, it is with a false intention. It is with an intention at war with the truth, the nature, and the relations of things.

If any sinner, at any time, and under any circumstances, tell the truth, it is for a selfish reason; it is to compass a false end. He has a lie in his heart, and a lie in his right hand. He stands upon falsehood. He lives for it, and if he does not uniformly and openly falsify the truth, it is because objective truth is consistent with subjective falsehood. His heart is false, as false as it can be. It has embraced and sold itself to the greatest lie in the universe. The selfish man has practically proclaimed that his good is the supreme good; nay, that there is no other good but his own; that there are no other rights but his own, that all are bound to serve him, and that all interests are to yield to his. Now all this, as I said, is the greatest falsehood that ever was or can be. Yet this is the solemn practical declaration of every sinner. His choice affirms that God has no rights, that he ought not to be loved and obeyed, that he has no right to govern the universe, but that God and all beings ought to obey and serve the sinner. Can there be a greater, a more shameless falsehood than all this? And shall such an one pretend to regard the truth? Nay, verily. The very pretence is only an instance and an illustration of the truth, that falsehood is an essential element of his character.

If every sinner on earth does not openly and at all times falsify the truth, it is not because of the truthfulness of his heart, but for some purely selfish reason. This must be. His heart is utterly false. It is impossible that, remaining a sinner, he should have any true regard to the truth. He is a liar in his heart; this is an essential and an eternal attribute of his character. It is true that his intellect condemns falsehood and justifies truth, and that oftentimes through the intellect, a deep impression is or may be made on his sensibility, in favor of the truth; but if the heart is unchanged, it holds on to lies, and perseveres in the practical proclamation of the greatest lies in the universe, to wit, that God ought not to be trusted; that Christ is not worthy of confidence; that one's own interest is the supreme good; and that all interests ought to be accounted of less value than one's own.

12. Pride is another attribute of selfishness.

Pride is a disposition to exalt self above others, to get out of one's proper place in the scale of being, and to climb up over the heads of our equals or superiors. Pride is a species of injustice, on the one hand, and is nearly allied to ambition on the other. It is not a term of so extensive an import as either injustice or ambition. It sustains to each of them a near relation, but is not identical with either. It is a kind of self-praise, self-worship, self-flattery, self-adulation, a spirit of self-consequence, of self-importance. It is a tendency to exalt, not merely one's own interest, but one's person above others, and above God, and above all other beings. A proud being supremely regards himself. He worships and can worship no one but self. He does not, and remaining selfish, he cannot, practically admit that there is any one so good and worthy as himself. He aims at conferring supreme favor upon himself, and practically, admits no claim of any being in the universe to any good or interest, that will interfere with his own. He can stoop to give preference to the interest, the reputation, the authority of no one, no, not of God himself, except outwardly and in appearance. His inward language is, "Who is Jehovah, that I should bow down to him?" It is impossible that a selfish soul should be humble. Sinners are represented in the Bible as proud, as "flattering themselves in their own eyes."

Pride is not a vice distinct from selfishness, but is only a modification of selfishness. Selfishness is the root, or stock, in which every form of sin inheres. This it is important to show. Selfishness has been scarcely regarded by many as a vice, much less as constituting the whole of vice; consequently, when selfishness has been most apparent, it has been supposed and assumed that there might be along with it many forms of virtue. It is for this reason that I make this attempt to show what are the essential elements of selfishness. It has been supposed that selfishness might exist in any heart without implying every form of sin; that a man might be selfish and yet not proud. In short, it has been overlooked, that, where selfishness is, there must be every form of sin; that where there is one form of selfishness manifested, it is virtually a breach of every commandment of God, and implies, in fact, the real existence of every possible form of sin and abomination in the heart. My object is fully to develop the great truth that where selfishness is, there must be, in a state either of development or of undevelopment, every form of sin that exists in earth or hell; that all sin is a unit, and consists of some form of selfishness; and that where this is, all sin virtually is and must be.

The only reason that pride, as a form of selfishness, does not appear in all sinners, in the most disgusting forms, is only this, that their constitutional temperament, and providential circumstances, are such as to give a more prominent development to some other attribute of selfishness. It is important to remark, that where any one form of unqualified sin exists, there selfishness must exist, and there of course every form of sin must exist, at least in embryo, and waiting only for circumstances to develop it. When therefore, you see any form of sin, know assuredly that selfishness, the root, is there; and expect nothing else, if selfishness continues, than to see developed, one after another, every form of sin as the occasion shall present itself. Selfishness is a volcano, sometimes smothered, but which must have vent. The providence of God cannot but present occasions upon which its lava-tides will burst forth and carry desolation before them.

That all these forms of sin exist, has been known and admitted. But it does not appear to me, that the philosophy of sin has been duly considered by many. It is important that we should get at the fundamental or generic form of sin, that form which includes and implies all others, or, more properly, which constitutes the whole of sin. Such is selfishness. "Let it be written with the point of a diamond and engraved in the rock forever," that it may be known, that where selfishness is, there every precept of the law is violated, there is the whole of sin. Its guilt and ill desert must depend upon the light with which the selfish mind is surrounded. But sin, the whole of sin, is there. Such is the very nature of selfishness that it only needs the providential occasions, and to be left without restraint, and it will show itself to have embodied, in embryo, every form of iniquity.

13. Enmity against God is also an attribute of selfishness.

Enmity is hatred. Hatred may exist either as a phenomenon of the sensibility, or as a state or attitude of the will. Of course I am now to speak of enmity of heart or will. It is selfishness viewed in its relations to God. That selfishness is enmity against God will appear--

(1.) From the Bible. The apostle Paul expressly says that "the carnal mind (minding the flesh) is enmity against God." It is fully evident that the apostle, by the carnal mind, means obeying the propensities or gratifying the desires. But this, as I have defined it, is selfishness.

(2.) Selfishness is directly opposed to the will of God as expressed in his law. That requires benevolence. Selfishness is its opposite, and therefore enmity against the Lawgiver.

(3.) Selfishness is as hostile to God's government as it can be. It is directly opposed to every law, and principle, and measure of his government.

(4.) Selfishness is opposition to God's existence. Opposition to a government, is opposition to the will of the governor. It is opposition to his existence in that capacity. It is, and must be, enmity against the existence of the ruler, as such. Selfishness must be enmity against the existence of God's government, and as he does and must sustain the relation of Sovereign Ruler, selfishness must be enmity against his being. Selfishness will brook no restraint in respect to securing its end. There is nothing in the universe it will not sacrifice to self. This is true, or it is not selfishness. If then God's happiness, or government, or being, come into competition with it, they must be sacrificed, were it possible for selfishness to effect it. But God is the uncompromising enemy of selfishness. It is the abominable thing his soul hateth. He is more in the way of selfishness than all other beings. The opposition of selfishness to him is, and must be, supreme and perfect.

That selfishness is mortal enmity against God, is not left to conjecture, nor to a mere deduction or inference. God once took to himself human nature, and brought Divine benevolence into conflict with human selfishness. Men could not brook his presence upon earth, and they rested not until they had murdered him.

Enmity against any body or thing besides God, can be overcome more easily than against him. All earthly enmities can be overcome by kindness, and change of circumstances; but what kindness, what change of circumstances, can change the human heart, can overcome the selfishness or enmity to God that reigns there? Selfishness offers all manner and every possible degree of resistance to God. It disregards God's commands. It contemns his authority. It spurns his mercy. It outrages his feelings. It provokes his forbearance. Selfishness, in short, is the universal antagonist and adversary of God. It can no more be reconciled to his law, than it can cease to be selfish.

14. Intemperance is also a form or attribute of selfishness.

Selfishness is self-indulgence not sanctioned by the reason. It consists in the committal of the will to the indulgence of the propensities. Of course some one, or more, of the propensities must have taken the control of the will. Generally, there is some ruling passion or propensity, the influence of which becomes overshadowing, and overrules the will for its own gratification. Sometimes it is acquisitiveness or avarice, the love of gain; sometimes alimentiveness or Epicureanism; sometimes it is amativeness or sexual love; sometimes philoprogenitiveness or the love of our own children; sometimes self-esteem or a feeling of confidence in self; sometimes one and sometimes another of the great variety of the propensities, is so largely developed, as to be the ruling tyrant, that lords it over the will and over all the other propensities. It matters not which of the propensities, or whether their united influence gains the mastery of the will: whenever the will is subject to them, this is selfishness. It is the carnal mind.

Intemperance consists in the undue or unlawful indulgence of any propensity. It is, therefore, an essential element or attribute of selfishness. All selfishness is intemperance: of course it is an unlawful indulgence of the propensities. Intemperance has as many forms as there are constitutional and artificial appetites to gratify. A selfish mind cannot be temperate. If one or more of the propensities is restrained, it is only restrained for the sake of the undue and unlawful indulgence of another. Sometimes the tendencies are intellectual, and the bodily appetites are denied, for the sake of gratifying the love of study. But this is no less intemperance and selfishness, than the gratification of amativeness or alimentiveness. Selfishness is always, and necessarily, intemperate. It does not always or generally develop every form of intemperance in the outward life, but a spirit of self-indulgence must manifest itself in the intemperate gratification of some one or more of the propensities.

Some develop self-indulgence most prominently in the form of intemperance in eating; others in sleeping; others in lounging and idleness; others are gossippers; others love exercise, and indulge that propensity others study and impair health, and induce derangement, or seriously impair the nervous system. Indeed, there is no end to the forms which intemperance assumes, arising from the fact of the great number of propensities, natural and artificial, that in their turn seek and obtain indulgence.

It should be always borne in mind, that any form of self-indulgence, properly so called, is equally an instance of selfishness and wholly inconsistent with any degree of virtue in the heart. But it may be asked, are we to have no regard whatever to our tastes, appetites and propensities? I answer, we are to have no such regard to them, as to make their gratification the end for which we live, even for a moment. But there is a kind of regard to them which is lawful, and therefore, a virtue. For example: I am on a journey for the service and glory of God. Two ways are before me. One affords nothing to regale the senses; the other conducts me through variegated scenery, sublime mountain passes, deep ravines; beside bubbling brooks, and meandering rivulets; through beds of gayest flowers and woods of richest foliage; through aromatic groves and forests vocal with feathered songsters. The two paths are equal in distance, and in all respects that have a bearing upon the business I have in hand. Now, reason dictates and demands, that I should take the path that is most agreeable and suggestive of useful thoughts. But this is not being governed by the propensities, but by the reason. It is its voice which I hear and to which I listen, when I take the sunny path. The delights of this path are a real good. As such they are not to be despised or neglected. But if taking this path would embarrass and hinder the end of my journey, I am not to sacrifice the greater public good for a less one of my own. I must not be guided by my feelings, but by my reason and honest judgment in this and in every case of duty. God has not given us propensities to be our masters and to rule us, but to be our servants and to minister to our enjoyment, when we obey the biddings of reason and of God. They are given to render duty pleasant, and as a reward of virtue; to make the ways of wisdom pleasurable. The propensities are not, therefore, to be despised, nor is their annihilation to be desired. Nor is it true that their gratification is always selfish, but when their gratification is sanctioned and demanded by the intellect, as in the case just supposed, and in myriads of other cases that occur, the gratification is not a sin but a virtue. It is not selfishness but benevolence. But let it be remembered that the indulgence must not be sought in obedience to the propensity itself, but in obedience to the law of reason and of God. When reason and the will of God are not only not consulted, but even violated, it must be selfishness.

Intemperance, as a sin, does not consist in the outward act of indulgence, but in the inward disposition. A dyspeptic who can eat but just enough to sustain life, may be an enormous glutton at heart. He may have a disposition, that is, he may not only desire, but he may be willing, to eat all before him, but for the pain indulgence occasions him. But this is only the spirit of self-indulgence. He denies himself the amount of food he craves in order to gratify a stronger propensity, to wit, the dread of pain. So a man who was never intoxicated in his life, may be guilty of the crime of drunkenness every day. He may be prevented from drinking to inebriation only by a regard to reputation or health, or by an avaricious disposition. It is only because he is prevented by the greater power of some other propensity. If a man is in such a state of mind that he would indulge all his propensities without restraint, were it not that it is impossible, on account of the indulgence of some being inconsistent with the indulgence of the others, he is just as guilty as if he did indulge them all. For example: he has a disposition, that is a will, to accumulate property. He is avaricious in heart. He also has a strong tendency to luxury, to licentiousness, and prodigality. The indulgence of these propensities is inconsistent with the indulgence of avarice. But for this contrariety, he would in his state of mind indulge them all. He wishes to do so, but it is impossible. Now he is really guilty of all those forms of vice, and just as blameworthy as if he indulged in them.

Intemperance, as a crime, is a state of mind. It is the attitude of the will. It is an attribute of selfishness. It consists in the choice or disposition to gratify the propensities, regardless of the law of benevolence. This is intemperance; and so far as the mind is considered, it is the whole of it. Now, inasmuch as the will is committed to self-indulgence, and nothing but the contrariety there is between the propensities prevents the unlimited indulgence of them all, it follows, that every selfish person, or in other words every sinner, is chargeable in the sight of God with every species of intemperance, actual or conceivable.

His lusts have the reign. They conduct him whithersoever they list. He has sold himself to self-indulgence. If there is any form of self-indulgence that is not actually developed in him, no thanks to him. The providence of God has restrained the outward indulgence, while there has been in him a readiness to perpetrate any sin and every sin, from which he was not deterred by some overpowering fear of consequences.

15. Total moral depravity is implied in selfishness as one of its attributes. By this I intend that every selfish being is at every moment as wicked and as blameworthy as with his knowledge he can be.

It is affirmed, both by reason and revelation, that there are degrees of guilt; that some are more guilty than others; and that the same individual may be more guilty at one time than at another.

The same is true of virtue. One person may be more virtuous than another, when both are truly virtuous. And also the same person may be more virtuous at one time than at another, although he may be virtuous at all times. In other words, it is affirmed, both by reason and revelation, that there is such a thing as growth, both in virtue and vice.

It is matter of general belief, also, that the same individual, with the same degree of light or knowledge, is more or less praise or blameworthy, as he shall do one thing or another; or, in other words, as he shall pursue one course or another, to accomplish the end he has in view; or, which is the same thing, that the same individual, with the same knowledge or light, is more or less virtuous or vicious, according to the course of outward life which he shall pursue. This I shall attempt to show is human prejudice, and a serious and most injurious error.

It is also generally held that two or more individuals, having precisely the same degree of light or knowledge, and being both equally benevolent or selfish, may, nevertheless, differ in their degree of virtue or vice, according as they pursue different courses of outward conduct. This also, I shall attempt to show, is fundamental error.

We can arrive at the truth upon this subject only by clearly understanding how to measure moral obligation, and of course how to ascertain the degree of virtue and sin. The amount or degree of virtue or vice, or of praise-worthiness or blame-worthiness, is and must be decided by reference to the degree of obligation.

And here I would remind you--

(1.) That moral obligation is founded in the intrinsic value of the highest well-being of God and the universe: and--

(2.) That the conditions of the obligation are the possession of the powers of moral agency and light, or the knowledge of the end to be chosen.

(3.) Hence it follows that the obligation is to be measured by the mind's honest apprehension or judgment of the intrinsic value of the end to be chosen. That this, and nothing else, is the rule or standard by which the obligation, and, consequently, the guilt of violating it, is to be measured, will appear if we consider--

(1.) That the obligation cannot be measured by the infinity of God, apart from the knowledge of the infinite value of his interests. He is an infinite being, and his well-being must be of intrinsic and of infinite value. But unless this be known to a moral agent, he cannot be under obligation to will it as an ultimate end. If he knows it to be of some value, he is bound to choose it for that reason.

But the measure of his obligation must be just equal to the clearness of his apprehension of its intrinsic value.

Besides, if the infinity of God were alone, or without reference to the knowledge of the agent, the rule by which moral obligation is to be measured, it would follow, that obligation is in all cases the same, and of course that the guilt of disobedience would also in all cases be the same. But this, as has been said, contradicts both reason and revelation. Thus it appears, that moral obligation, and of course guilt, cannot be measured by the infinity of God, without reference to the knowledge of the agent.

(2.) It cannot be measured by the infinity of his authority, without reference to the knowledge of the agent, for the same reasons as above.

(3.) It cannot be measured by the infinity of his moral excellence, without reference, both to the infinite value of his interests, and of the knowledge of the agent; for his interests are to be chosen as an end, or for their own value, and without knowledge of their value there can be no obligation; nor can obligation exceed knowledge.

(4.) If, again, the infinite excellence of God were alone, or without reference to the knowledge of the agent, to be the rule by which moral obligation is to be measured, it would follow, that guilt in all cases of disobedience, is and must be equal. This we have seen cannot be.

(5.) It cannot be measured by the intrinsic value of the good, or wellbeing of God and the universe, without reference to the knowledge of the agent, for the same reason as above.

(6.) It cannot be measured by the particular course of life pursued by the agent. This will appear, if we consider that moral obligation has directly nothing to do with the outward life. It directly respects the ultimate intention only, and that decides the course of outward action or life. The guilt of any outward action cannot be decided by reference to the kind of action, without regard to the intention; for the moral character of the act must be found in the intention, and not in the outward act or life. This leads me to remark that

(7.) The degree of moral obligation, and of course the degree of the guilt of disobedience, cannot be properly estimated by reference to the nature of the intention, without respect to the degree of the knowledge of the agent. Selfish intention is, as we have seen, a unit, always the same; and if this were the standard by which the degree of guilt is to be measured, it would follow that it is always the same.

(8.) Nor can obligation, nor the degree of guilt, be measured by the tendency of sin. All sin tends to infinite evil, to ruin the sinner and from its contagious nature, to spread and ruin the universe. Nor can any finite mind know what the ultimate results of any sin may be, nor to what particular evil it may tend. As all sin tends to universal and eternal evil, if this were the criterion by which the guilt is to be estimated, all sin would be equally guilty, which cannot be.

Again: That the guilt of sin cannot be measured by the tendency of sin, is manifest from the fact, that moral obligation is not founded in the tendency of action or intention, but in the intrinsic value of the end to be intended. Estimating moral obligation, or measuring sin or holiness, by the mere tendency of actions, is the utilitarian philosophy, which we have shown to be false. Moral obligation respects the choice of an end, and is founded upon the intrinsic value of the end, and is not so much as conditionated upon the tendency of the ultimate choice to secure its end. Therefore, tendency can never be the rule by which obligation can be measured, nor, of course, the rule by which guilt can be estimated.

(9.) Nor can moral obligation be estimated by the results of a moral action or course of action. Moral obligation respects intention and respects results no further than they were intended. Much good may result, as from the death of Christ, without any virtue in Judas, but with much guilt. So, much evil may result, as from the creation of the world, without guilt in the Creator, but with great virtue. If moral obligation is not founded or conditionated on results, it follows that guilt cannot be duly estimated by results, without reference to knowledge and intention.

(10.) What has been said has, I trust, rendered it evident, that moral obligation is to be measured by the mind's honest apprehension or judgment of the intrinsic value of the end to be chosen, to wit, the highest well-being of God and the universe.

It should be distinctly understood, that selfishness involves the rejection of the interests of God and of the universe, for the sake of one's own. It refuses to will good, but upon condition that it belongs to self. It spurns God's interests and those of the universe, and seeks only self-interest as an ultimate end. It must follow, then, that the selfish man's guilt is just equal to his knowledge of the intrinsic value of those interests that he rejects. This is undeniably the doctrine of the Bible.

Acts xvii. 30, affords a plain instance. The apostle alludes to those past ages when the heathen nations had no written revelation from God, and remarks that "those times of ignorance God winked at." This does not mean that God did not regard their conduct as criminal in any degree, but it does mean that he regarded it as a sin of far less aggravation, than that which men would now commit, if they turned away when God commanded them all to repent. True, sin is never absolutely a light thing; but some sins incur small guilt, when compared with the great guilt of other sins. This is implied in the text quoted above.

James iv. 17.--"To him that knoweth to do good, and doeth it not, to him it is sin." This plainly implies that knowledge is indispensable to moral obligation; and even more than this is implied, namely, that the guilt of any sinner is always equal to the amount of his knowledge on the subject. It always corresponds to the mind's perception of the value of the end which should have been chosen, but is rejected. If a man knows he ought, in any given case, to do good, and yet does not do it, to him this is sin--the sin plainly lying in the fact of not doing good when he knew that he could do it, and being measured as to its guilt by the degree of that knowledge.

John ix. 41.--"Jesus said unto them, If ye were blind, ye should have no sin: but now ye say, We see; therefore, your sin remaineth." Here Christ asserts that men without knowledge would be without sin; and that men who have knowledge, and sin notwithstanding, are held guilty. This plainly affirms, that the presence of light or knowledge is requisite to the existence of sin, and obviously implies that the amount of knowledge possessed is the measure of the guilt of sin.

It is remarkable that the Bible everywhere assumes first truths. It does not stop to prove them, or even assert them--but seems to assume, that every one knows and will admit them. As I have been recently writing on moral government, and studying the Bible as to its teachings on this class of subjects, I have been often struck with this remarkable fact.

Luke xii. 47, 48.--"And that servant which knew his lord's will, and prepared not himself, neither did according to his will, shall be beaten with many stripes. But he that knew not, and did commit things worthy of stripes, shall be beaten with few stripes. For unto whomsoever much is given, of him shall be much required; and to whom men have committed much, of him will they ask the more." Here we have the doctrine laid down and the truth assumed, that men shall be punished according to knowledge. To whom much light is given, of him shall much obedience be required. This is precisely the principle, that God requires of men according to the light they have.

Selfishness is the rejection of all obligation. It is the violation of all obligation. The sin of selfishness is then complete; that is, the guilt of selfishness is as great as with its present light it can be. What can make it greater with present light? Can the course that it takes to realize its end mitigate its guilt? No; for whatever course it takes, it is for a selfish reason, and, therefore, it can in nowise lessen the guilt of the intention. Can the course it takes to realize its end without more light, increase the guilt of the sin? No; for the sin lies exclusively in having the selfish intention, and the guilt can be measured only by the degree of illumination or knowledge under which the intention is formed and maintained. The intention necessitates the use of the means; and whatever means the selfish person uses, it is for one and the same reason, to gratify himself. As I said in a former lecture, if the selfish man were to preach the gospel, it would be only because, upon the whole, it was most pleasing or gratifying to himself, and not at all for the sake of the good of being, as an end. If he should become a pirate, it would be for exactly the same reason, to wit, that this course is, upon the whole, most pleasing or gratifying to himself, and not at all for the reason that that course is evil in itself. Whichever course he takes, he takes it for precisely the same ultimate reason; and with the same degree of light it must involve the same degree of guilt. If light increase, his guilt must increase, but not otherwise. The proposition is, that every selfish being is, at every moment, as blame-worthy as with his present knowledge he can be. Which of these courses may tend ultimately to the most evil, no finite being can say, nor which shall result in the greatest evil. Guilt is not to be measured by unknown tendencies or results, but belongs to the intention; and its degree is to be measured alone by the mind's apprehension of the reason of the obligation violated, namely, the intrinsic value of the good of God and the universe, which selfishness rejects. Now, it should be remembered, that whichever course the sinner takes to realize his end, it is the end at which he aims. He intends the end. If he become a preacher of the gospel for a selfish reason, he has no right regard to the good of being. If he regards it at all, it is only as a means of his own good. So, if he becomes a pirate, it is not from malice, or a disposition to do evil for its own sake, but only to gratify himself. If he has any regard at all to the evil he may do, it is only to gratify himself that he regards it. Whether, therefore, he preach or pray, or rob and plunder upon the high seas, he does it only for one end, that is, for precisely the same ultimate reason; and of course his sinfulness is complete, in the sense that it can be varied only by varying light. This I know is contrary to common opinion, but it is the truth, and must be known; and it is of the highest importance that these fundamental truths of morality and of immorality should be held up to the minds of all.

Should the sinner abstain from any course of vice because it is wicked, it cannot be because he is benevolent, for this would contradict the supposition that he is selfish, or that he is a sinner. If, in consideration that an act or course is wicked, he abstains from it, it must be for a selfish reason. It may be in obedience to phrenological conscientiousness, or it may be from fear of hell, or of disgrace, or from remorse; at all events, it cannot but be for some selfish reason.

Total moral depravity is an attribute of selfishness, in the sense, that every selfish person is at all times just as wicked and blameworthy as with his present light he can be.

LECTURE XIX - SANCTIONS OF MORAL LAW, NATURAL AND GOVERNMENTAL

In the discussion of this subject, I shall show--

I. What constitute the sanctions of law.

1. The sanctions of law are the motives to obedience, the natural and the governmental consequences or results of obedience and of disobedience.

2. They are remuneratory, that is, they promise reward to obedience.

3. They are vindicatory, that is, they threaten the disobedient with punishment.

4. They are natural, that is, happiness is to some extent naturally connected with, and the necessary consequence of, obedience to moral law, and misery is naturally and necessarily connected with, and results from, disobedience to moral law, or from acting contrary to the nature and relations of moral beings.

5. Sanctions are governmental. By governmental sanctions are intended:

(1.) The favor of the government as due to obedience.

(2.) A positive reward bestowed upon the obedient by government.

(3.) The displeasure of government towards the disobedient.

(4.) Direct punishment inflicted by the government as due to disobedience.

All happiness and misery resulting from obedience or disobedience, either natural, or from the favor, or frown of government, are to be regarded as constituting the sanctions of law.

II. In what light sanctions are to be regarded.

1. Sanctions are to be regarded as an expression of the benevolent regard of the lawgiver for his subjects: the motives which he exhibits to induce in the subjects the course of conduct that will secure their highest well-being.

2. They are to be regarded as an expression of his estimation of the justice, necessity, and value of the precept to the subjects of his government.

3. They are to be regarded as an expression of the amount or strength of his desire to secure the happiness of his subjects.

4. They are to be regarded as an expression of his opinion in respect to the desert of disobedience.

The natural sanctions are to be regarded as a demonstration of the justice, necessity and perfection of the precept.

III. By what rule sanctions ought to be graduated.

1. We have seen that moral obligation is founded in the intrinsic value of the well-being of God and of the universe, and conditionated upon the perception of its value; and,

2. That guilt is always to be measured by the perceived value of the end which moral beings ought to choose.

3. The sanctions of law should be graduated by the intrinsic merit and demerit of holiness and sin.

IV. God's law has sanctions.

1. That sin, or disobedience to the moral law, is attended with, and results in, misery, is a matter of consciousness.

2. That virtue or holiness is attended with, and results in happiness, is also attested by consciousness.

3. Therefore that God's law has natural sanctions, both remuneratory and vindicatory, is a matter of fact.

4. That there are governmental sanctions added to the natural, must be true, or God, in fact, has no government but that of natural consequences.

5. The Bible expressly, and in every variety of form, teaches that God will reward the righteous and punish the wicked.

V. The perfection and duration of the remuneratory sanctions of the law of God.

1. The perfection of the natural reward is, and must be, proportioned to the perfection of virtue.

2. The duration of the remuneratory sanction must be equal to the duration of obedience. This cannot possibly be otherwise.

3. If the existence and virtue of man are immortal, his happiness must be endless.

4. The Bible most unequivocally asserts the immortality both of the existence and virtue of the righteous, and also that their happiness shall be endless.

5. The very design and end of government make it necessary that governmental reward should be as perfect and unending as virtue.

VI. Penal inflictions under the government of God must be endless.

Here the inquiry is, what kind of death is intended, where death is denounced against the transgressor, as the penalty of the law of God?

1. It is not merely natural death, for--

(1.) This would, in reality, be no penalty at all. But it would be offering a reward to sin. If natural death is all that is intended, and if persons, as soon as they are naturally dead, have suffered the penalty of the law, and their souls go immediately to heaven, the case stands thus: if your obedience is perfect and perpetual, you shall live in this world forever; but if you sin, you shall die and go immediately to heaven. "This would be hire and salary," and not punishment.

(2.) If natural death be the penalty of God's law, the righteous, who are forgiven, should not die a natural death.

(3.) If natural death be the penalty of God's law, there is no such thing as forgiveness, but all must actually endure the penalty.

(4.) If natural death be the penalty, then infants and animals suffer this penalty, as well as the most abandoned transgressors.

(5.) If natural death be the penalty, and the only penalty, it sustains no proportion whatever to the guilt of sin.

(6.) Natural death would be no adequate expression of the importance of the precept.

2. The penalty of God's law is not spiritual death.

(1.) Because spiritual death is a state of entire sinfulness.

(2.) To make a state of entire sinfulness the penalty of the law of God, would be to make the penalty and the breach of the precept identical.

(3.) It would be making God the author of sin, and would represent him as compelling the sinner to commit one sin as the punishment for another,--as forcing him into a state of total and perpetual rebellion, as the reward of his first transgression.

3. But the penal sanction of the law of God is endless death, or that state of endless suffering which is the natural and governmental result of sin or of spiritual death.

Before I proceed to the proof of this, I will notice an objection which is often urged against the doctrine of endless punishment. The objection is one, but it is stated in three different forms. This, and every other objection to the doctrine of endless punishment, with which I am acquainted, is levelled against the justice of such a governmental infliction.

(1.) It is said that endless punishment is unjust, because life is so short, that men do not live long enough in this world to commit so great a number of sins as to deserve endless punishment. To this I answer that it is founded in ignorance or disregard of a universal principle of government, viz., that one breach of the precept always incurs the penalty of the law, whatever that penalty is. The length of time employed in committing a sin, has nothing to do with its blameworthiness or guilt. It is the design which constitutes the moral character of the action, and not the length of the time required for its accomplishment. This objection takes for granted, that it is the number of sins, and not the intrinsic guilt of sin, that constitutes its blameworthiness, whereas it is the intrinsic desert or guilt of sin, as we shall soon see, that renders it deserving of endless punishment.

(2.) Another form of the objection is, that a finite creature cannot commit an infinite sin. But none but an infinite sin can deserve endless punishment: therefore endless punishments are unjust.

This objection takes for granted that man is so diminutive a creature, so much less than the Creator, that he cannot deserve his endless frown. Which is the greater crime, for a child to insult his playfellow, or his parent? Which would involve the most guilt, for a man to smite his neighbor and his equal, or his lawful sovereign? The higher the ruler is exalted above the subject in his nature, character, and rightful authority, the greater is the obligation of the subject to will his good, to render to him obedience, and the greater is the guilt of the transgression in the subject. Therefore, the fact that man is so infinitely below his Maker, does but enhance the guilt of his rebellion, and render him all the more worthy of his endless frown.

(3.) A third form of the objection is, that sin is not an infinite evil; and therefore, does not deserve endless punishment.

This objection may mean either, that sin would not produce infinite mischief if unrestrained, or that it does not involve infinite guilt. It cannot mean the first, for it is agreed on all hands, that misery must continue as long as sin does, and therefore, that sin unrestrained would produce endless evil. The objection, therefore, must mean, that sin does not involve infinite guilt. Observe, then, the point at issue is, what is the intrinsic demerit or guilt of sin? What does all sin in its own nature deserve? They who deny the justice of endless punishment, manifestly consider the guilt of sin as a mere trifle. They who maintain the justice of endless punishment, consider sin as an evil of immeasurable magnitude, and, in its own nature, deserving of endless punishment. Proof:--

Should a moral agent refuse to choose that as an ultimate end which is of no intrinsic value, he would thereby contract no guilt, because he would violate no obligation. But should he refuse to will the good of God and of his neighbor, he would violate an obligation, and of course contract guilt. This shows that guilt attaches to the violation of obligation, and that a thing is blameworthy because it is the violation of an obligation.

We have seen that sin is selfishness, that it consists in preferring self-gratification to the infinite interests of God and of the universe. We have also seen that obligation is founded in the intrinsic value of that good which moral agents ought to will to God and to the universe, and is equal to the affirmed value of that good. We have also seen that every moral agent, by a law of his own reason, necessarily affirms that God is infinite, and that the endless happiness and well-being of God and of the universe, is of infinite value. Hence it follows, that refusal to will this good is a violation of infinite or unlimited obligation, and, consequently involves unlimited guilt. It is as certain that the guilt of any sin is unlimited, as that obligation to will the good of God and of the universe is unlimited. To deny consistently that the guilt of sin is unlimited, it must be shown, that obligation to will good to God is unlimited. To maintain consistently this last, it must be shown, that moral agents have not the idea that God is infinite. Indeed, to deny that the guilt of sin is in any instance less than boundless, is as absurd as to deny the guilt of sin altogether.

Having shown that moral obligation is founded in the intrinsic value of the highest well-being of God and of the universe, that it is always equal to the soul's knowledge of the value of those interests, and having shown also, that every moral agent necessarily has the idea more or less clearly developed, that the value of those interests is infinite, it follows that the law is infinitely unjust, if its penal sanctions are not endless. Law must be just in two respects: the precept must be in accordance with the law of nature, and the penalty must be equal to the importance of the precept. That which has not these two peculiarities is not just, and therefore, is not and cannot be law. Either, then, God has no law, or its penal sanctions are endless. That the penal sanctions of the law of God are endless, is evident from the fact, that a less penalty would not exhibit as high motives as the nature of the case admits, to restrain sin and promote virtue. Natural justice demands that God should exhibit as high motives to secure obedience as the value of the law demands and the nature of the case admits.

The tendency of sin to perpetuate and aggravate itself, affords another strong inference, that the sinfulness and misery of the wicked will be eternal.

The fact, that punishment has no tendency to originate disinterested love in a selfish mind towards him who inflicts the punishment, also affords a strong presumption, that future punishment will be eternal.

But let us examine this question in the light of revelation.

The Bible, in a great many ways, represents the future punishment of the wicked as eternal, and never once represents it otherwise. It expresses the duration of the future punishment of the wicked by the same terms, and, in every way, forcibly as it expresses the duration of the future happiness of the righteous.

I will here introduce, without comment, some passages of scripture confirmatory of this last remark. "The hope of the righteous shall be gladness: but the expectation of the wicked shall perish."--Prov. x. 28. "When a wicked man dieth, his expectation shall perish; and the hope of unjust men perisheth."--Prov. xi. 7. "And many of them that sleep in the dust of the earth shall awake; some to everlasting life, and some to shame and everlasting contempt."--Dan. xii. 2. "Then shall he say also unto them on the left hand, Depart from me, ye cursed, into everlasting fire, prepared for the devil and his angels: for I was an hungered, and ye gave me no meat: I was thirsty, and ye gave me no drink. And these shall go away into everlasting punishment: but the righteous into life eternal."--Matt. xxv. 41, 42, 46. "And if thy hand offend thee, cut, it off: it is better for thee to enter into life maimed than having two hands to go into hell, into the fire that never shall be quenched; where their worm dieth not, and the fire is not quenched."--Mark ix. 43, 44. "Whose fan is in his hand, and he will thoroughly purge his floor; and will gather the wheat into his garner; but the chaff he will burn with fire unquenchable."--Luke iii. 17. "And besides all this, between us and you there is a great gulf fixed: so that they which would pass from hence to you, cannot; neither can they pass to us, that would come from thence."--Luke xvi. 26. "He that believeth on the Son hath everlasting life: and he that believeth not the Son shall not see life; but the wrath of God abideth on him."--John iii. 36. "And to you who are troubled, rest with us, when the Lord Jesus shall be revealed from heaven with his mighty angels, in flaming fire taking vengeance on them that know not God, and that obey not the gospel of our Lord Jesus Christ; who shall be punished with everlasting destruction from the presence of the Lord, and from the glory of his power."--2 Thess. i. 7-9. "And the angels which kept not their first estate, but left their own habitation, he hath reserved in everlasting chains, under darkness, unto the judgment of the great day. Even as Sodom and Gomorrah, and the cities about them, in like manner, giving themselves over to fornication, and going after strange flesh, are set forth for an example, suffering the vengeance of eternal fire. Raging waves of the sea, foaming out their own shame; wandering stars, to whom is reserved the blackness of darkness forever."--Jude 6, 7, 13. "And the third angel followed them, saying with a loud voice, If any man worship the beast and his image, and receive his mark in his forehead, or in his hand, the same shall drink of the wine of the wrath of God which is poured out without mixture into the cup of his indignation; and he shall be tormented with fire and brimstone in the presence of the holy angels, and in the presence of the Lamb: and the smoke of their torment ascendeth up forever and ever: and they have no rest day nor night, who worship the beast and his image, and whosoever receiveth the mark of his name."--Rev. xiv. 9-11. "And the devil that deceived them was cast into the lake of fire and brimstone, where the beast and the false prophet are, and shall be tormented day and night forever and ever."--Rev. xx. 10. But there is scarcely any end to the multitude of passages that teach directly, or by inference, both the fact and the endlessness of the future punishment of the wicked.

LECTURE XX - HUMAN GOVERNMENT

Human governments a part of the moral government of God.

In the discussion of this subject I will,--

I. Inquire into the ultimate end of God in creation.

We have seen in former lectures, that God is a moral agent, the self-existent and supreme; and is therefore himself, as ruler of all, subject to, and observant of, moral law in all his conduct. That is, his own infinite intelligence must affirm that a certain course of willing is suitable, fit, and right in him. This idea, or affirmation, is law to him; and to this his will must be conformed, or he is not good. This is moral law, a law founded in the eternal and self-existent nature of God. This law does, and must, demand benevolence in God. Benevolence is good-willing. God's intelligence must affirm that he ought to will good for its own intrinsic value. It must affirm his obligation to choose the highest possible good as the great end of his being. If God is good, the highest good of himself, and of the universe, must have been the end which he had in view in the work of creation. This is of infinite value, and ought to be willed by God. If God is good, this must have been his end. We have also seen,--

II. That providential and moral governments are indispensable means of securing the highest good of the universe.

The highest good of moral agents is conditionated upon their holiness. Holiness consists in conformity to moral law. Moral law implies moral government. Moral government is a government of moral law and of motives. Motives are presented by providential government; and providential government is, therefore, a means of moral government. Providential and moral government must be indispensable to securing the highest good of the universe.

III. Civil and family governments are indispensable to the securing of this end, and are, therefore, really a part of the providential and moral government of God.

In the discussion of this question I remark,

1. Human beings will not agree in opinion on any subject without similar degrees of knowledge. No human community exists, or ever will exist, the members of which will agree in opinion on all subjects. This creates a necessity for human legislation and adjudication, to apply the great principles of moral law to all human affairs. There are multitudes of human wants and necessities that cannot properly be met, except through the instrumentality of human governments.

2. This necessity will continue as long as human beings exist in this world. This is as certain as that the human body will always need sustenance and clothing; and that the human soul will always need instruction; and that the means of instruction will not come spontaneously, without expense and labor. It is as certain as that men of all ages and circumstances will never possess equal talents and degrees of information on all subjects. If all men were perfectly holy and disposed to do right, the necessity for human governments would not be set aside, because this necessity is founded in the ignorance of mankind,

though greatly aggravated by their wickedness. The decisions of legislators and judges must be authoritative, so as to settle questions of disagreement in opinion, and at once to bind and protect all parties.

The Bible presents human governments not only as existing, but as deriving their authority and right to punish evil-doers, and to protect the righteous, from God. But--

3. Human governments are plainly recognized in the Bible as a part of the moral government of God.

Dan. ii. 21. "He changeth the times and the seasons; he removeth kings, and setteth up kings: he giveth wisdom unto the wise, and knowledge to them that know understanding." Dan. iv. 17, 25. "This matter is by the degree of the watchers, and the demand by the word of the holy ones; to the intent that the living may know that the Most High ruleth in the kingdom of men, and giveth it to whomsoever he will, and setteth up over it the basest of men." "They shall drive thee from men, and thy dwelling shall be with the beasts of the field, and they shall make thee to eat grass as oxen, and they shall wet thee with the dew of heaven, and seven times shall pass over thee, till thou know that the Most High ruleth in the kingdom of men, and giveth it to whomsoever he will." Dan. v. 21. "He was driven from the sons of men; and his heart was made like the beasts, and his dwelling was with the wild asses: they fed him with grass like oxen, and his body was wet with the dew of heaven till he knew that the Most High God ruleth in the kingdom of men, and that he appointeth over it whomsoever he will." Rom. xiii. 1-7. "Let every soul be subject unto the higher powers. For there is no power but of God, the powers that be are ordained of God. Whosoever therefore resisteth the power, resisteth the ordinance of God: and they that resist shall receive to themselves damnation. For rulers are not a terror to good works but to the evil. Wilt thou then not be afraid of the power? Do that which is good, and thou shalt have praise of the same: for he is the minister of God to thee for good. But if thou do that which is evil, be afraid; for he beareth not the sword in vain; for he is the minister of God, a revenger to execute wrath upon him that doeth evil. Wherefore ye must needs be subject, not only for wrath but also for conscience' sake. For, for this cause pay ye tribute also: for they are God's ministers, attending continually upon this very thing. Render, therefore, to all their dues; tribute to whom tribute is due; custom to whom custom; fear to whom fear; honor to whom honor." Titus iii. 1. "Put them in mind to be subject to principalities and powers, to obey magistrates, to be ready to every good work." 1 Peter ii. 13, 14. "Submit yourselves to every ordinance of man for the Lord's sake: whether it be to the king, as supreme, or unto governors, as unto them that are sent by him for the punishment of evil doers, and for the praise of them that do well."

These passages prove conclusively, that God establishes human government, as parts of moral government.

4. It is the duty of all men to aid in the establishment and support of human government.

As the great law of benevolence, or universal good-willing, demands the existence of human governments, all men are under a perpetual and unalterable moral obligation to aid in their establishment and support. In popular or elective governments, every man having a right to vote, every human being who has moral influence, is bound to exert that influence in the promotion of virtue and happiness. And as human governments are plainly indispensable to the highest good of man, they are bound to exert their influence to secure a legislation that is in accordance with the law of God. The obligation of human beings to support and obey human governments, while they legislate upon the principles of the moral law, is as unalterable as the moral law itself.

5. I will answer objections.

Obj. 1. The kingdom of God is represented in the Bible as subverting all other kingdoms.

Ans. This is true, but all that can be meant by it is, that the time shall come when God shall be regarded as the supreme and universal sovereign of the universe, when his law shall be regarded as universally obligatory; when all kings, legislators, and judges shall act as his servants, declaring, applying, and administering the great principles of his law to all the affairs of human beings. Thus God will be the supreme sovereign, and earthly rulers will be governors, kings, and judges under him, and acting by his authority as revealed in the Bible.

Obj. 2. It is alleged that God only providentially establishes human governments, and that he does not approve of their selfish and wicked administration; that he only uses them providentially, as he does Satan, for the promotion of his own designs.

Ans. God nowhere commands mankind to obey Satan, but he does command them to obey magistrates and rulers. Rom. xiii. 1. "Let every soul be subject unto the higher powers; for there is no power but of God: the powers that be are ordained of God." 1 Pet. ii. 13, 14. "Submit yourselves to every ordinance of man for the Lord's sake: whether it be to the king as supreme; or unto governors, as unto them that are sent by him for the punishment of evil doers, and for the praise of them that do well."

He nowhere recognizes Satan as his servant, sent and set by him to administer justice and execute wrath upon the wicked; but he does this in respect to human governments. Rom. xiii. 2-6. "Whosoever therefore resisteth the power, resisteth the ordinance of God; and they that resist shall receive to themselves damnation. For rulers are not a terror to good works, but to the evil. Wilt thou then not be afraid of the power? Do that which is good, and thou shalt have praise of the same. For he is the minister of God to thee for good. But if thou do that which is evil, be afraid; for he beareth not the sword in vain: for he is the minister of God, a revenger to execute wrath upon him that doeth evil. Wherefore ye must needs be subject, not only for wrath, but also for conscience' sake. For, for this cause pay ye tribute also; for they are God's ministers, attending continually upon this very thing."

It is true indeed that God approves of nothing that is ungodly and selfish in human governments. Neither did he approve of what was ungodly and selfish in the scribes and Pharisees; and yet Christ said to his disciples, "The scribes and Pharisees sit in Moses' seat. Therefore, whatsoever things they command you, that observe and do; but do ye not after their works, for they say, and do not." Here the plain common-sense principle is recognized, that we are to obey when the requirement is not inconsistent with the moral law, whatever may he the character or the motive of the ruler. We are always to obey heartily as unto the Lord, and not unto men, and render obedience to magistrates for the honor and glory of God, and as doing service to him.

Obj. 3. It is said that Christians should leave human governments to the management of the ungodly, and not be diverted from the work of saving souls, to intermeddle with human governments.

Ans. To uphold and assist good government is not being diverted from the work of saving souls. The promotion of public and private order and happiness is one of the indispensable means of doing good and saving souls. It is nonsense to admit that Christians are under an obligation to obey human government, and still have nothing to do with the choice of those who shall govern.

Obj. 4. It is affirmed that we are commanded not to avenge ourselves, that "Vengeance is mine, and I will repay, saith the Lord." It is said, that if I may not avenge or redress my own wrongs in my own person, I may not do it through the instrumentality of human government.

Ans. It does not follow, that because you may not take it upon yourself to redress your own wrongs by a summary and personal infliction of punishment upon the transgressor, that therefore human governments may not punish them. All private wrongs are a public injury; and irrespective of any particular regard to your personal interest, magistrates are bound to punish crime for the public good. While God has expressly forbidden you to redress your own wrongs, by administering personal and private chastisement, he has expressly recognized the right, and made it the duty of public magistrates to punish crimes.

Obj. 5. It is alleged, that love is so much better than law, that where love reigns in the heart, law can be universally dispensed with.

Ans. This supposes that, if there is only love, there need be no rule of duty; no revelation, directing love in its efforts to secure the end upon which it terminates. But this is as untrue as possible. The objection overlooks the fact, that law is in all worlds the rule of duty, and that legal sanctions make up an indispensable part of that circle of motives that are suited to the nature, relations, and government of moral beings.

Obj. 6. It is asserted, that Christians have something else to do besides meddling with politics.

Ans. In a popular government, politics are an important part of religion. No man can possibly be benevolent or religious, to the full extent of his obligations, without concerning himself, to a greater or less extent, with the affairs of human government. It is true, that Christians have something else to do than to go with a party to do evil, or to meddle with politics in a selfish or ungodly manner. But they are bound to meddle with politics in popular governments, because they are bound to seek the universal good of all men; and this is one department of human interests, materially affecting all their higher interests.

Obj. 7. It is said that human governments are nowhere expressly authorized in the Bible.

Ans. This is a mistake. Both their existence and lawfulness are as expressly recognized in the above quoted scriptures as they can be. But if God did not expressly authorize them, it would still be both the right and the duty of mankind to institute human governments, because they are plainly demanded by the necessities of human nature. It is a first truth, that whatever is essential to the highest good of moral beings in any world, they have a right to pursue, and are bound to pursue according to the best dictates of reason and experience. So far, therefore, are men from needing any express authority to establish human governments, that no inference from the silence of scripture could avail to render their establishment unlawful. It has been shown, in these lectures on moral government, that moral law is a unit--that it is that rule of action which is in accordance with the nature, relations, and circumstances of moral beings--that whatever is in accordance with, and demanded by the nature, relations, and circumstances of moral beings, is obligatory on them. It is moral law, and no power in the universe can set it aside. Therefore, were the scriptures entirely silent (which they are not) on the subject of human governments, and on the subject of family government, as they actually are on a great many important subjects, this would be no objection to the lawfulness and expediency, necessity and duty of establishing human governments.

Obj. 8. It is said that human governments are founded in and sustained by force, and that this is inconsistent with the spirit of the gospel.

Ans. There cannot be a difference between the spirit of the Old and the New Testament, or between the spirit of the law and the gospel, unless God has changed, and unless Christ has undertaken to make void the law through faith, which cannot be. Rom. iii. 32. "Do we then make void the law through faith? God forbid: yea, we establish the law." Just human governments, and such governments only are contended for, will not exercise force, unless it is demanded to promote the highest public good. If it be necessary to this end, it can never be wrong. Nay, it must be the duty of human governments to inflict penalties, when their infliction is demanded by the public interest.

Obj. 9. It has been said by some persons, that church government is sufficient to meet the necessities of the world, without secular or state governments.

Ans. What! Church governments regulate commerce, make internal arrangements, such as roads, bridges, and taxation, and undertake to manage all the business affairs of the world! Preposterous and impossible! Church government was never established for any such end; but simply to regulate the spiritual, in distinction from the secular concerns of men--to try offenders and inflict spiritual chastisement, and never to perplex and embarrass itself with managing the business and commercial interests of the world.

Obj. 10. It is said, that were all the world holy, legal penalties would not be needed.

Ans. Were all men perfectly holy, the execution of penalties would not be needed; but still, if there were law, there must be penalties; and it would be both the right and the duty of magistrates to inflict them, whenever the needful occasion should call for their execution. But the state of the world supposed is not at hand, and while the world is what it is, laws must remain, and be enforced.

Obj. 11. It is asserted, that family government is the only form of government approved of God.

Ans. This is a ridiculous assertion, because God as expressly commands obedience to magistrates as to parents. He makes it as absolutely the duty of magistrates to punish crime, as of parents to punish their own disobedient children. The right of family government, though commanded by God, is not founded in the arbitrary will of God, but in the highest good of human beings; so that family government would be both necessary and obligatory, had God not commanded it. So the right of human government has not its foundation in the arbitrary will of God, but in the necessities of human beings. The larger the community the more absolute the necessity of government. If in the small circle of the family, laws and penalties are needed, how much more in the larger communities of states and nations. Now, neither the ruler of a family, nor any other human ruler, has a right to legislate arbitrarily, or enact, or enforce any other laws, than those that are demanded by the nature, relations, and circumstances of human beings. Nothing can be obligatory on moral beings, but that which is consistent with their nature, relations, and circumstances. But human beings are bound to establish family governments, state governments, national governments, and in short, whatever government may be requisite for the universal instruction, government, virtue, and happiness of the world, or any portion of it.

Christians therefore have something else to do than to confound the right of government with the abuse of this right by the ungodly. Instead of destroying human governments, Christians are bound to reform and uphold them. To attempt to destroy, rather than reform human governments, is the same in principle as is often aimed at, by those who are attempting to destroy, rather than to reform, the church. There are those who, disgusted with the abuses of Christianity practiced in the church, seem bent on destroying the church altogether, as the means of saving the world. But what mad policy is this!

It is admitted that selfish men need, and must feel the restraints of law; but yet it is contended that Christians should have no part in restraining them by law. But suppose the wicked should agree among themselves to have no law, and therefore should not attempt to restrain themselves, nor each other by law; would it be neither the right nor the duty of Christians to attempt their restraint, through the influence of wholesome government? It would be strange, that selfish men should need the restraints of law, and yet that Christians should have no right to meet this necessity, by supporting governments that will restrain them. It is right and best that there should be law. It is even absolutely necessary that there should be law. Universal benevolence demands it; can it then be wrong in Christians to have anything to do with it?

IV. Point out the limits or boundaries of the right of government.

Observe, the end of government is the highest good of human beings, as a part of universal good. All valid human legislation must propose this as its end, and no legislation can have any authority that has not the highest good of the whole for its end. No being can arbitrarily create law. All law for the government of moral agents must be moral law: that is, it must be that rule of action best suited to their natures and relations. All valid human legislation must be only declaratory of this one only law. Nothing else than this can by any possibility be law. God puts forth no enactments, but such as are declaratory of the common law of the universe; and should he do otherwise, they would not be obligatory. Arbitrary legislation can never be really obligatory.

The right of human government is founded in the intrinsic value of the good of being, and is conditionated upon its necessity, as a means to that end. So far as legislation and control are indispensable to this end, so far and no farther does the right to govern extend. All legislation and all constitutions not founded upon this basis, and not recognizing the moral law as the only law of the universe, are null and void, and all attempts to establish and enforce them are odious tyranny and usurpation. Human beings may form constitutions, establish governments, and enact statutes for the purpose of promoting the highest virtue and happiness of the world, and for the declaration and enforcement of moral law; and just so far human governments are essential to this end, but absolutely no farther.

It follows, that no government is lawful or innocent that does not recognize the moral law as the only universal law, and God as the Supreme Lawgiver and Judge, to whom nations in their national capacity, as well as all individuals, are amenable. The moral law of God is the only law of individuals and of nations, and nothing can be rightful government but such as is established and administered with a view to its support.

LECTURE XXI - HUMAN GOVERNMENT

V. I propose now to make several remarks respecting forms of government, the right and duty of revolution, etc.

1. The particular forms of state government must, and will, depend upon the virtue and intelligence of the people.

When virtue and intelligence are nearly universal, democratic forms of government are well suited to promote the public good. In such a state of society, democracy is greatly conducive to the general diffusion of knowledge on governmental subjects; and although, in some respects less convenient, yet in a suitable state of society, a democracy is in many respects the most desirable form of government.

God has always providentially given to mankind those forms of government that were suited to the degrees of virtue and intelligence among them. If they have been extremely ignorant and vicious, he has restrained them by the iron rod of human despotism. If more intelligent and virtuous, he has given them the milder form of limited monarchies. If still more intelligent and virtuous, he has given them still more liberty, and providentially established republics for their government. Whenever the general state of intelligence has permitted it, he has put them to the test of self-government and self-restraint, by establishing democracies.

If the world ever becomes perfectly virtuous, governments will be proportionally modified, and employed in expounding and applying the great principles of moral law.

2. That form of government is obligatory, that is best suited to meet the necessities of the people.

This follows as a self-evident truth, from the consideration, that necessity is the condition of the right of human government. To meet this necessity is the object of government; and that government is obligatory and best which is demanded by the circumstances, intelligence, and morals of the people.

Consequently, in certain states of society, it would be a Christian's duty to pray for and sustain even a military despotism; in a certain other state of society, to pray for and sustain a monarchy; and in other states, to pray for and sustain a republic; and in a still more advanced stage of virtue and intelligence, to pray for and sustain a democracy; if indeed a democracy is the most wholesome form of self government, which may admit of doubt. It is ridiculous to set up the claim of a Divine right for any given form of government. That form of government which is demanded by the state of society, and the virtue and intelligence of the people, has of necessity the Divine right and sanction, and none other has or can have.

3. Revolutions become necessary and obligatory, when the virtue and intelligence, or the vice and ignorance, of the people, demand them.

This is a thing of course. When one form of government fails to meet any longer the necessities of the people, it is the duty of the people to revolutionize. In such cases, it is vain to oppose revolution; for in some way the benevolence of God will bring it about. Upon this principle alone, can what is generally termed the American Revolution be justified. The intelligence and virtue of our Puritan forefathers rendered a monarchy an unnecessary burden, and a republican form of government both appropriate and necessary; and God always allows his children as much liberty as they are prepared to enjoy.

The stability of our republican institutions must depend upon the progress of general intelligence and virtue. If in these respects the nation falls, if general intelligence, public and private virtue, sink to that point below which self-control becomes practicably impossible, we must fall back into monarchy, limited or absolute; or into civil or military despotism; just according to the national standard of intelligence and virtue. This is just as certain as that God governs the world, or that causes produce their effects.

Therefore, it is the maddest conceivable policy, for Christians to attempt to uproot human governments, while they ought to be engaged in sustaining them upon the great principles of the moral law. It is certainly the grossest folly, if not abominable wickedness, to overlook either in theory or practice, these plain, common sense and universal truths.

4. In what cases are we bound to disobey human governments?

(1.) We may yield obedience, when the thing required does not involve a violation of moral obligation.

(2.) We are bound to obey when the thing required has no moral character in itself; upon the principle, that obedience in this case is a less evil than resistance and revolution. But--

(3.) We are bound in all cases to disobey, when human legislation contravenes moral law, or invades the rights of conscience.

VI. Apply the foregoing principles to the rights and duties of governments and subjects in relation to the execution of the necessary penalties of law:--the suppression of mobs, insurrections, rebellion; and also in relation to war, slavery, Sabbath desecration, etc.

1. It is plain that the right and duty to govern for the security and promotion of the public interests, implies the right and duty to use any means necessary to this result. It is absurd to say that the ruler has the right to govern, and yet that he has not a right to use the necessary means. Some have taken the ground of the inviolability of human life, and have insisted that to take life is wrong per se, and of course that governments are to be sustained without taking life. Others have gone so far as to assert, that governments have no right to resort to physical force to sustain the authority of law. But this is a most absurd philosophy, and amounts just to this:--The ruler has a right to govern while the subject is pleased to obey; but if the subject refuse obedience, why then the right to govern ceases: for it is impossible that the right to govern should exist when the right to enforce obedience does not exist. This philosophy is, in fact, a denial of the right to use the necessary means for the promotion of the great end for which all moral agents ought to live. And yet, strange to tell, this philosophy professes to deny the right to use force, and to take life in support of government, on the ground of benevolence, that is, that benevolence forbids it. What is this but maintaining that the law of benevolence demands that we should love others too much to use the indispensable means to secure their good? Or that we should love the whole too much to execute the law upon those who would destroy all good? Shame on such philosophy! It overlooks the foundation of moral obligation, and of all morality and religion. Just as if an

enlightened benevolence could forbid the due, wholesome, and necessary execution of law. This philosophy impertinently urges the commandment, "Thou shalt not kill," as prohibiting all taking of human life. But it may be asked, why say human life? The commandment, so far as the letter is concerned, as fully prohibits the killing of animals or vegetables as it does of men. The question is, what kind of killing does this commandment prohibit? Certainly not all killing of human beings, for in the next chapter the Jews were commanded to kill human beings for certain crimes. The ten commandments are precepts, and the Lawgiver, after laying down the precepts, goes on to specify the penalties that are to be inflicted by men for a violation of these precepts. Some of these penalties are death, and the penalty for the violation of the precept under consideration is death. It is certain that this precept was not intended to prohibit the taking of life for murder. A consideration of the law in its tenor and spirit renders it most evident that the precept in question prohibits murder, and the penalty of death is added by the lawgiver to the violation of this precept. Now how absurd and impertinent it is, to quote this precept in prohibition of taking life under the circumstances included in the precept!

Men have an undoubted right to do whatever is plainly indispensable to the highest good of man; and, therefore, nothing can, by any possibility be law, that should prohibit the taking of human life, when it becomes indispensable to the great end of government. This right is every where recognized in the Bible, and if it were not, still the right would exist. This philosophy that I am opposing, assumes that the will of God creates law, and that we have no right to take life, without an express warrant from him. But the facts are, that God did give to the Jews, at least, an express warrant and injunction to take life for certain crimes; and, if he had not, it would have been duty to do so whenever the public good required it. Let it be remembered, that the moral law is the law of nature, and that everything is lawful and right that is plainly demanded for the promotion of the highest good of being.

The philosophy of which I am speaking lays much stress upon what it calls inalienable rights. It assumes that man has a title or right to life, in such a sense, that he cannot forfeit it by crime. But the fact is, there are no rights inalienable in this sense. There can be no such rights. Whenever any individual by the commission of crime comes into such a relation to the public interest, that his death is a necessary means of securing the highest public good, his life is forfeited, and to take the forfeiture at his hands is the duty of the government.

2. It will be seen, that the same principles are equally applicable to insurrections, rebellions, etc. While government is right, it is duty, and while it is right and duty, because necessary as a means to the great end upon which benevolence terminates, it must be both the right and the duty of government, and of all the subjects, to use any indispensable means for the suppression of insurrections, rebellion, etc., as also for the due administration of justice in the execution of law.

3. These principles will guide us in ascertaining the right, and of course the duty of governments in relation to war.

Observe, war to be in any case a virtue, or to be less than a crime of infinite magnitude, must not only be honestly believed, by those who engage in it, to be demanded by the law of benevolence, but it must also be engaged in by them with an eye single to the glory of God, and the highest good of being. That war has been in some instances demanded by the spirit of the moral law, there can be no reasonable doubt, since God has sometimes commanded it, which he could not have done had it not been demanded by the highest good of the universe. In such cases, if those who were commanded to engage in war, had benevolent intentions in prosecuting it, as God had in commanding it, it is absurd to say that they sinned. Rulers are represented as God's ministers to execute wrath upon the guilty. If, in the providence of God, he should find it duty to destroy or to rebuke a nation for his own glory, and the highest good of being, he may beyond question command that they should be chastised by the hand of man. But in no case is war anything else than a most horrible crime, unless it is plainly the will of God that it should exist, and unless it be actually undertaken in obedience to his will. This is true of all, both of rulers and of subjects, who engage in war. Selfish war is wholesale murder. For a nation to declare war, or for persons to enlist, or in any way designedly to aid or abet, in the declaration or prosecution of war, upon any other conditions than those just specified, involves the guilt of murder.

There can scarcely be conceived a more abominable and fiendish maxim than "our country right or wrong." Recently this maxim seems to have been adopted and avowed in relation to the war of the United States with Mexico. It seems to be supposed by some, that it is the duty of good subjects to sympathize with, and support government in the prosecution of a war in which they have unjustly engaged, and to which they have committed themselves, upon the ground that since it is commenced it must be prosecuted as the less of two evils. The same class of men seem to have adopted the same philosophy in respect to slavery. Slavery, as it exists in this country, they acknowledge to be indefensible on the ground of right. It is a great evil and a great sin, but it must be let alone as the less of two evils. It exists, say they, and it cannot be abolished without disturbing the friendly relations and federal union of the States, therefore the institution must be sustained. The philosophy is this: war and slavery as they exist in this nation are unjust, but they exist, and to sustain them is duty, because their existence, under the circumstances, is the less of two evils.

Nothing can sanctify any crime but that which renders it no crime, but a virtue. But the philosophers, whose views I am examining, must, if consistent, take the ground, that since war and slavery exist, although their commencement was unjust and sinful, yet since they exist, it is no crime but a virtue to sustain them, as the least of two natural evils. But I would ask, to whom are they the least of two evils? To ourselves or to being in general? The least of two present, or of two ultimate evils? Our duty is not to calculate the evils in respect merely to ourselves, or to this nation and those immediately oppressed and injured, but to look abroad upon the world and the universe, and inquire what are the evils resulting, and likely to result, to the world, to the church, and to the universe, from the declaration and prosecution of such a war, and from the support of slavery by a nation professing what we profess--a nation boasting of liberty; who have drawn the sword and bathed it in blood in defence of the principle, that all men have an inalienable right to liberty; that they are born free and equal. Such a nation proclaiming such a principle, and fighting in the defence of it, standing with its proud foot on the neck of three millions of crushed and prostrate slaves! O horrible! This a less evil to the world than emancipation, or even than the dismemberment of our hypocritical union! "O shame, where is thy blush!" The prosecution of a war, unjustly engaged in, a less evil than repentance and restitution! It is impossible. Honesty is always and necessarily the best policy. Nations are bound by the same law as individuals. If they have done wrong, it is always duty, and honorable for them to repent, confess and make restitution. To adopt the maxim, "Our country right or wrong," and to sympathize with the government, in the prosecution of a war unrighteously waged, must involve the guilt of murder. To adopt the maxim, "Our union, even with perpetual slavery," is an abomination so execrable, as not to be named by a just mind without indignation.

4. The same principles apply to governmental sabbath desecration. The sabbath is plainly a divine institution, founded in the necessities of human beings. The letter of the law of the sabbath forbids all labor of every kind, and under all circumstances on that day. But, as has been said in a former lecture, the spirit of the law of the sabbath, being identical with the law of benevolence, sometimes requires the violation of the letter of the law. Both governments and individuals may do, and it is their duty to do, on the sabbath whatever is plainly required by the great law of benevolence. But nothing more, absolutely. No human legislature can nullify the moral law. No human legislation can make it right or lawful to violate any command of God. All human enactments requiring or sanctioning the violation of any command of God, are not only null and void, but they are a blasphemous usurpation and invasion of the prerogative of God.

5. The same principles apply to slavery. No human constitution or enactment can, by any possibility, be law, that recognizes the right of one human being to enslave another, in a sense that implies selfishness on the part of the slaveholder. Selfishness is wrong per se. It is, therefore, always and unalterably wrong. No enactment, human or divine, can legalize selfishness and make it right, under any conceivable circumstances. Slavery or any other evil, to be a crime, must imply selfishness. It must imply a violation of the command, "Thou shalt love thy neighbor as thyself." If it implies a breach of this, it is wrong invariably and necessarily, and no legislation, or any thing else, can make it right. God cannot authorize it. The Bible cannot sanction it, and if both God and the Bible were to sanction it, it could not be lawful. God's arbitrary will is not law. The moral law, as we have seen, is as independent of his will, as his own necessary existence is. He cannot alter or repeal it. He could not sanctify selfishness and make it right. Nor can any book be received as of divine authority that sanctions selfishness. God and the Bible quoted to sustain and sanctify slaveholding in a sense implying selfishness! 'Tis blasphemous! That slaveholding, as it exists in this country, implies selfishness, at least in almost all instances, is too plain to need proof. The sinfulness of slaveholding and war, in almost all cases, and in every case where the terms slaveholding and war are used in their popular signification, will appear irresistibly, if we consider that sin is selfishness, and that all selfishness is necessarily sinful. Deprive a human being of liberty who has been guilty of no crime; rob him of himself--his body--his soul--his time, and his earnings, to promote the interest of his master, and attempt to justify this on the principles of moral law! It is the greatest absurdity, and the most revolting wickedness.

LECTURE XXII - MORAL DEPRAVITY

In discussing the subject of human depravity, I shall,--

I. Define the term depravity.

The word is derived from the Latin de and pravus. Pravus means "crooked." De is intensive. Depravatus literally and primarily means "very crooked," not in the sense of original or constitutional crookedness, but in the sense of having become crooked. The term does not imply original mal-conformation, but lapsed, fallen, departed from right or straight. It always implies deterioration, or fall from a former state of moral or physical perfection.

Depravity always implies a departure from a state of original integrity, or from conformity to the laws of the being who is the subject of depravity. Thus we should not consider that being depraved, who remained in a state of conformity to the original laws of his being, physical and moral. But we justly call a being depraved, who has departed from conformity to those laws, whether those laws be physical or moral.

II. Point out the distinction between physical and moral depravity.

Physical depravity, as the word denotes, is the depravity of constitution, or substance, as distinguished from depravity of free moral action. It may be predicated of body or of mind. Physical depravity, when predicated of the body, is commonly and rightly called disease. It consists in a physical departure from the laws of health; a lapsed, or fallen state, in which healthy organic action is not sustained.

When physical depravity is predicated of mind, it is intended that the powers of the mind, either in substance, or in consequence of their connection with, and dependence upon, the body, are in a diseased, lapsed, fallen, degenerate state, so that the healthy action of those powers is not sustained.

Physical depravity, being depravity of substance as opposed to depravity of the actions of free-will, can have no moral character. It may as we shall see, be caused by moral depravity; and a moral agent may be blameworthy for having rendered himself physically depraved, either in body or mind. But physical depravity, whether of body or of mind, can have no moral character in itself, for the plain reason that it is involuntary, and in its nature is disease, and not sin. Let this be remembered.

Moral depravity is the depravity of free-will, not of the faculty itself, but of its free action. It consists in a violation of moral law. Depravity of the will, as a faculty, is, or would be, physical, and not moral depravity. It would be depravity of substance, and not of free, responsible choice. Moral depravity is depravity of choice. It is a choice at variance with moral law, moral right. It is synonymous with sin or sinfulness. It is moral depravity, because it consists in a violation of moral law, and because it has moral character.

III. Of what physical depravity can be predicated.

1. It can be predicated of any organized substance. That is, every organized substance is liable to become depraved. Depravity is a possible state of every organized body or substance in existence.

2. Physical depravity may be predicated of mind, as has already been said, especially in its connection with an organized body. As mind, in connection with body, manifests itself through it, acts by means of it, and is dependent upon it, it is plain that if the body become diseased, or physically depraved, the mind cannot but be affected by this state of the body, through and by means of which it acts. The normal manifestations of mind cannot, in such case, be reasonably expected. Physical depravity may be predicated of all the involuntary states of the intellect, and of the sensibility. That is, the actings and states of the intellect may become disordered, depraved, deranged, or fallen from the state of integrity and healthiness. This every one knows, as it is matter of daily experience and observation. Whether this in all eases is, and must be, caused by the state of the bodily organization, that is, whether it is always and necessarily to be ascribed to the depraved state of the brain and nervous system, it is impossible for us to know. It may, for aught we know, in some instances at least, be a depravity or derangement of the substance of the mind itself.

The sensibility, or feeling department of the mind, may be sadly and physically depraved. This is a matter of common experience. The appetites and passions, the desires and cravings, the antipathies and repellencies of the feelings fall into great disorder and anarchy. Numerous artificial appetites are generated, and the whole sensibility becomes a wilderness, a chaos of conflicting and clamorous desires, emotions and passions. That this state of the sensibility is often, and perhaps In some measure always, owing to the state of the nervous system with which it is connected, through and by which it manifests itself, there can be but little room to doubt. But whether this is always and necessarily so, no one can tell. We know that the sensibility manifests great physical depravity. Whether this depravity belong exclusively to the body, or to the mind, or to both in conjunction, I will not venture to affirm. In the present state of our knowledge, or of my knowledge, I dare not hazard an affirmation upon the subject. The human body is certainly in a state of physical depravity. The human mind also certainly manifests physical depravity. But observe, physical depravity has in no case any moral character, because it is involuntary.

IV. Of what moral depravity can be predicated.

1. Not of substance; for over involuntary substance the moral law does not directly legislate.

2. Moral depravity cannot be predicated of any involuntary acts or states of mind. These surely cannot be violations of moral law apart from the ultimate intention; for moral law legislates directly only over free, intelligent choices.

3. Moral depravity cannot be predicated of any unintelligent act of will, that is, of acts of will that are put forth in a state of idiocy, of intellectual derangement, or of sleep. Moral depravity implies moral obligation; moral obligation implies moral agency; and moral agency implies intelligence, or knowledge of moral relations. Moral agency implies moral law, or the development of the idea of duty, and a knowledge of what duty is.

4. Moral depravity can only be predicated of violations of moral law, and of the free volitions by which those violations are perpetrated. Moral law, as we have seen, requires love, and only love, to God and man, or to God and the

universe. This love, as we have seen, is goodwill, choice, the choice of an end, the choice of the highest well-being of God, and of the universe of sentient existences.

Moral depravity is sin. Sin is a violation of moral law. We have seen that sin must consist in choice, in the choice of self-indulgence or self-gratification as an end.

5. Moral depravity cannot consist in any attribute of nature or constitution, nor in any lapsed and fallen state of nature; for this is physical and not moral depravity.

6. It cannot consist in anything that is an original and essential part of mind, or of body; nor in any involuntary action or state of either mind or body.

7. It cannot consist in anything back of choice, and that sustains to choice the relation of a cause. Whatever is back of choice, is without the pale of legislation. The law of God, as has been said, requires good-willing only; and sure it is, that nothing but acts of will can constitute a violation of moral law. Outward actions, and involuntary thoughts and feelings, may be said in a certain sense to possess moral character because they are produced by the will. But, strictly speaking, moral character belongs only to choice, or intention.

It was shown in a former lecture, that sin does not, and cannot consist in malevolence, properly speaking, or in the choice of sin or misery as an end, or for its own sake. It was also shown, that all sin consists, and must consist in selfishness, or in the choice of self-gratification as a final end. Moral depravity then, strictly speaking, can only be predicated of selfish ultimate intention.

Moral depravity, as I use the term, does not consist in, nor imply a sinful nature, in the sense that the substance of the human soul is sinful in itself. It is not a constitutional sinfulness. It is not an involuntary sinfulness. Moral depravity, as I use the term, consists in selfishness; in a state of voluntary committal of the will to self-gratification. It is a spirit of self-seeking, a voluntary and entire consecration to the gratification of self. It is selfish ultimate intention; it is the choice of a wrong end of life; it is moral depravity, because it is a violation of moral law. It is a refusal to consecrate the whole being to the highest well-being of God and of the universe, and obedience to the moral law, and consecrating it to the gratification of self. Moral depravity sustains to the outward life, the relation of a cause. This selfish intention, or the will in this committed state, of course, makes efforts to secure its end, and these efforts make up the outward life of the selfish man. Moral depravity is sinfulness, not of nature but of voluntary state. It is a sinfully committed state of the will to self-indulgence. It is not a sinful nature but a sinful heart. It is a sinful ultimate aim, or intention. The Greek term amartia, rendered sin in our English Bible, signifies to miss the mark, to aim at the wrong end. Sin is a wrong aim, or intention. It is aiming at, or intending self-gratification as the ultimate and supreme end of life, instead of aiming, as the moral law requires, at the highest good of universal being, as the end of life.

V. Mankind are both physically and morally depraved.

1. There is, in all probability, no perfect health of body among all the ranks and classes of human beings that inhabit this world. The physical organization of the whole race has become impaired, and beyond all doubt has been becoming more and more so since intemperance of any kind was first introduced into our world. This is illustrated and confirmed by the comparative shortness of human life. This is a physiological fact.

2. As the human mind in this state of existence is dependent upon the body for all its manifestations, and as the human body is universally in a state of greater or less physical depravity or disease, it follows that the manifestations of mind thus dependent on a physically depraved organization, will be physically depraved manifestations. Especially is this true of the human sensibility. The appetites, passions, and propensities are in a state of most unhealthy development. This is too evident, and too much a matter of universal notoriety, to need proof or illustration. Every person of reflection has observed, that the human mind is greatly out of balance, in consequence of the monstrous development of the sensibility. The appetites, passions, and propensities have been indulged, and the intelligence and conscience stultified by selfishness. Selfishness, be it remembered, consists in a disposition or choice to gratify the propensities, desires, and feelings. This of course, and of necessity, produces just the unhealthy and monstrous developments which we daily see: sometimes one ruling passion or appetite lording it, not only over the intelligence and over the will, but over all the other appetites and passions, crushing and sacrificing them all upon the altar of its own gratification. See that bloated wretch, the inebriate! His appetite for strong drink has played the despot. His whole mind and body, reputation, family, friends, health, time, eternity, all, all are laid by him upon its filthy altar. There is the debauchee, the glutton, the gambler, the miser, and a host of others, each in his turn giving striking and melancholy proof of the monstrous development and physical depravity of the human sensibility.

3. That men are morally depraved is one of the most notorious facts of human experience, observation and history. Indeed, I am not aware that it has ever been doubted, when moral depravity has been understood to consist in selfishness.

The moral depravity of the human race is everywhere assumed and declared in the Bible, and so universal and notorious is the fact of human selfishness, that should any man practically call it in question--should he, in his business transactions, and in his intercourse with men, assume the contrary, he would justly subject himself to the charge of insanity. There is not a fact in the world more notorious and undeniable than this. Human moral depravity is as palpably evident as human existence. It is a fact everywhere assumed in all governments, in all the arrangements of society, and it has impressed its image, and written its name, upon every thing human.

VI. Subsequent to the commencement of moral agency, and previous to regeneration, the moral depravity of mankind is universal.

By this it is not intended to deny that, in some instances, the Spirit of God may, from the first moment of moral agency, have so enlightened the mind as to have secured conformity to moral law, as the first moral act. This may or may not be true. It is not my present purpose to affirm or to deny this, as a possibility, or as a fact.

But by this is intended, that every moral agent of our race is, from the dawn of moral agency to the moment of regeneration by the Holy Spirit, morally depraved, unless we except those possible cases just alluded to. The Bible exhibits proof of it--

1. In those passages that represent all the unregenerate as possessing one common wicked heart or character. "And God saw that the wickedness of man was great in the earth, and that every imagination of the thoughts of his heart

was only evil continually."--Gen. vi. 5. "This is an evil among all things that are done under the sun, that there is one event unto all: yea, also the heart of the sons of men is full of evil, and madness is in their heart while they live, and after that they go to the dead."--Eccl. ix. 3. "The heart is deceitful above all things and desperately wicked: who can know it?"--Jer. xvii. 9. "Because the carnal mind is enmity against God: for it is not subject to the law of God, neither indeed can be."--Rom. viii. 7.

2. In those passages that declare the universal necessity of regeneration. "Jesus answered and said unto him, Verily, verily, I say unto thee, Except a man be born again, he cannot see the kingdom of God."--John iii. 3.

3. Passages that expressly assert the universal moral depravity of all unregenerate moral agents of our race. "What then? are we better than they? No, in no wise: for we have before proved both Jews and Gentiles, that they are all under sin; as it is written, There is none righteous, no, not one. There is none that understandeth, there is none that seeketh after God. They are all gone out of the way, they are together become unprofitable; there is none that doeth good, no not one. Their throat is an open sepulchre; with their tongues they have used deceit; the poison of asps is under their lips: whose mouth is full of cursing and bitterness: their feet are swift to shed blood: destruction and misery are in their ways: and the way of peace have they not known: there is no fear of God before their eyes. Now we know that what things soever the law saith, it saith to them who are under the law: that every mouth may be stopped, and all the world may become guilty before God. Therefore by the deeds of the law there shall no flesh be justified in his sight; for by the law is the knowledge of sin."--Rom. iii. 9-20.

4. Universal history proves it. What is this world's history but the shameless chronicle of human wickedness?

5. Universal observation attests it. Who ever saw one unregenerate human being that was not selfish, that did not obey his feelings rather than the law of his intelligence, that was not under some form, or in some way, living to please self? Such an unregenerate human being, I may safely affirm, was never seen since the fall of Adam.

6. I may also appeal to the universal consciousness of the unregenerate. They know themselves to be selfish, to be aiming to please themselves, and they cannot honestly deny it.

VII. The moral depravity of the unregenerate moral agents of our race, is total.

By this is intended, that the moral depravity of the unregenerate is without any mixture of moral goodness or virtue, that while they remain unregenerate, they never in any instance, nor in any degree, exercise true love to God and to man. It is not intended, that they may not perform many outward actions, and have many inward feelings, that are such as the regenerate perform and experience: and such too as are accounted virtue by those who place virtue in the outward action. But it is intended, that virtue does not consist either in involuntary feelings or in outward actions, and that it consists alone in entire consecration of heart and life to God and the good of being, and that no unregenerate sinner previous to regeneration, is or can be, for one moment, in this state.

When virtue is clearly seen to consist in the heart's entire consecration to God and the good of being, it must be seen, that the unregenerate are not for one moment in this state. It is amazing, that some philosophers and theologians have admitted and maintained, that the unregenerate do sometimes do that which is truly virtuous. But in these admissions they necessarily assume a false philosophy, and overlook that in which all virtue does and must consist, namely, supreme ultimate intention. They speak of virtuous actions and of virtuous feelings, as if virtue consisted in them, and not in the intention.

Henry P. Tappan, for example, for the most part an able, truthful, and beautiful writer, assumes, or rather affirms, that volitions may be put forth inconsistent with, and contrary to the present choice of an end, and that consequently, unregenerate sinners, whom he admits to be in the exercise of a selfish choice of an end, may and do sometimes put forth right volitions, and perform right actions, that is, right in the sense of virtuous actions. But let us examine this subject. We have seen that all choice and all volition must respect either an end or means, that is, that everything willed or chosen, is willed or chosen for some reason. To deny this, is the same as to deny that anything is willed or chosen, because the ultimate reason for a choice and the thing chosen are identical. Therefore, it is plain, as was shown in a former lecture, that the will cannot embrace at the same time, two opposite ends; and that while but one end is chosen, the will cannot put forth volitions to secure some other end, which end is not yet chosen. In other words, it certainly is absurd to say, that the will, while maintaining the choice of one end, can use means for the accomplishment of another and opposite end.

When an end is chosen, that choice confines all volition to securing its accomplishment, and for the time being, and until another end is chosen, and this one relinquished, it is impossible for the will to put forth any volition inconsistent with the present choice. It therefore follows, that while sinners are selfish, or unregenerate, it is impossible for them to put forth a holy volition. They are under the necessity of first changing their hearts, or their choice of an end, before they can put forth any volitions to secure any other than a selfish end. And this is plainly the everywhere assumed philosophy of the Bible. That uniformly represents the unregenerate as totally depraved, and calls upon them to, repent, to make to themselves a new heart; and never admits directly, or by way of implication, that they can do anything good or acceptable to God, while in the exercise of a wicked or selfish heart.

LECTURE XXIII - MORAL DEPRAVITY

VIII. Let us consider the proper method of accounting for the universal and total moral depravity of the unregenerate moral agents of our race.

In the discussion of this subject, I will--

1. Endeavor to show how it is not to be accounted for.

In examining this part of the subject, it is necessary to have distinctly in view that which constitutes moral depravity. All the error that has existed upon this subject, has been founded in false assumptions in regard to the nature or essence of moral depravity. It has been almost universally true, that no distinction has been made between moral and physical depravity; and consequently, physical depravity has been confounded with and treated of, as moral depravity. This of course has led to vast confusion and nonsense upon this subject. Let the following fact, which has been shown in former lectures, be distinctly borne in mind.

That moral depravity consists in selfishness, or in the choice of self-interest, self-gratification, or self-indulgence, as an end.

Consequently it cannot consist,

(1.) In a sinful constitution, or in a constitutional appetency or craving for sin. This has been shown in a former lecture, on what is not implied in disobedience to the moral law.

(2.) Moral depravity is sin itself, and not the cause of sin. It is not something prior to sin, that sustains to it the relation of a cause, but it is the essence and the whole of sin.

(3.) It cannot be an attribute of human nature, considered simply as such, for this would be physical, and not moral depravity.

(4.) Moral depravity is not then to be accounted for by ascribing it to a nature or constitution sinful in itself. To talk of a sinful nature, or sinful constitution, in the sense of physical sinfulness, is to ascribe sinfulness to the Creator, who is the author of nature. It is to overlook the essential nature of sin, and to make sin a physical virus, instead of a voluntary and responsible choice. Both sound philosophy and the Bible, make sin to consist in obeying the flesh, or in the spirit of self-pleasing, or self-indulgence, or, which is the same thing, in selfishness--in a carnal mind, or in minding the flesh. But writers on moral depravity have assumed, that moral depravity was distinct from, and the cause of sin, that is, of actual transgression. They call it original sin, indwelling sin, a sinful nature, an appetite for sin, an attribute of human nature, and the like. We shall presently see what has led to this view of the subject.

I will, in the next place, notice a modern, and perhaps the most popular view of this subject, which has been taken by any late writer, who has fallen into the error of confounding physical and moral depravity. I refer to the prize essay of Dr. Woods, of Andover, Mass. He defines moral depravity to be the same as "sinfulness." He also, in one part of his essay, holds and maintains, that it is always and necessarily, voluntary. Still, his great effort is to prove that sinfulness or moral depravity, is an attribute of human nature. It is no part of my design to expose the inconsistency of holding moral depravity to be a voluntary state of mind, and yet a natural attribute, but only to examine the philosophy, the logic, and theory of his main argument. The following quotation will show the sense in which he holds moral depravity to belong to the nature of man. At page 54 he says:--

"The word depravity, relating as it here does to man's moral character, means the same as sinfulness, being the opposite of moral purity, or holiness. In this use of the word there is a general agreement. But what is the meaning of native, or natural? Among the variety of meanings specified by Johnson, Webster, and others, I refer to the following, as relating particularly to the subject before us.

"Native. Produced by nature. Natural, or such as is according to nature; belonging by birth; original. Natural has substantially the same meaning: produced by nature; not acquired.'--So Crabbe: Of a person we say, his worth is native, to designate it as some valuable property born with him, not foreign to him, or ingrafted upon him; but we say of his disposition, that it is natural, as opposed to that which is acquired by habit.' And Johnson defines nature to be the native state or properties of any thing, by which it is discriminated from others.' He quotes the definition of Boyle: Nature sometimes means what belongs to a living creature at its nativity, or accrues to it by its birth, as when we say a man is noble by nature, or a child is naturally froward." This,' he says, may be expressed by saying, the man was born so.'

"After these brief definitions, which come to nearly the same thing, I proceed to inquire, what are the marks or evidences which show anything in man to be natural, or native; and how far these marks are found in relation to depravity."

Again, page 66, he says:--

"The evil, then, cannot be supposed to originate in any unfavorable external circumstances, such as corrupting examples, or insinuating and strong temptations; for if we suppose these entirely removed, all human beings would still be sinners. With such a moral nature as they now have, they would not wait for strong temptations to sin. Nay, they would be sinners in opposition to the strongest motives to the contrary. Indeed, we know that human beings will turn those very motives which most powerfully urge to holiness, into occasions of sin. Now, does not the confidence and certainty with which we foretell the commission of sin, and of sin unmixed with moral purity, presuppose a full conviction in us, and a conviction resting upon what we regard as satisfactory evidence, that sin, in all its visible actings, arises from that which is within the mind itself, and which belongs to our very nature as moral beings? Have we not as much evidence that this is the case with moral evil as with any of our natural affections or bodily appetites?"

This quotation, together with the whole argument, shows that he considers moral depravity to be an attribute of human nature, in the same sense that the appetites and passions are.

Before I proceed directly to the examination of his argument, that sinfulness, or moral depravity, is an "attribute of human nature," I would premise, that an argument, or fact, that may equally well consist with either of two opposing theories, can prove neither. The author in question presents the following facts and considerations in support of his great position, that moral depravity, or sinfulness, is an attribute of human nature; and three presidents of colleges indorse the soundness and conclusiveness of the argument.

He proves his position--first from the "universality of moral depravity." To this I answer, that this argument proves nothing to the purpose, unless it be true, and assumed as a major premise, that whatever is universal among mankind, must be a natural attribute of man as such; that whatever is common to all men, must be an attribute of human nature. But this assumption is a begging of the question. Sin may be the result of temptation; temptation may be universal, and of such a nature as uniformly, not necessarily, to result in sin, unless a contrary result be secured by a Divine moral suasion. This I shall endeavor to show is the fact. This argument assumes, that there is but one method of accounting for the universality of human sinfulness. But this is the question in debate, and is not to be thus assumed as true.

Again: Selfishness is common to all unregenerate men. Is selfishness a natural attribute? We have seen, in a former lecture, that it consists in choice. Can choice be an attribute of human nature?

Again: This argument is just as consistent with the opposite theory, to wit, that moral depravity is selfishness. The universality of selfishness is just what might be expected, if selfishness consists in the committal of the will to the gratification of self. This will be a thing of course, unless the Holy Spirit interpose, greatly to enlighten the intellect, and break up the force of habit, and change the attitude of the will, already, at the first dawn of reason, committed to the impulses of the sensibility. If moral depravity is to be accounted for, as I shall hereafter more fully show, by ascribing it to the influence of temptation, or to a physically depraved constitution, surrounded by the circumstances in which mankind' first form their moral character, or put forth their first moral choices, universality might of course be expected to be one of its characteristics. This argument, then, agreeing equally well with either theory, proves neither.

His second argument is, that "Moral depravity developes itself in early life." Answer:--

This is just what might be expected upon the opposite theory. If moral depravity consist in the choice of self-gratification, it would of course appear in early life. So this argument agrees quite as well with the opposing theory, and therefore proves nothing. But--this argument is good for nothing, unless the following be assumed as a major premise, and unless the fact assumed be indeed a truth, namely, "Whatever is developed in early life, must be an attribute of human nature." But this again is assuming the truth of the point in debate. This argument is based upon the assumption that a course of action common to all men, and commencing at the earliest moment of their moral agency, can be accounted for only by ascribing it to an attribute of nature, having the same moral character as that which belongs to the actions themselves. But this is not true. There may be more than one way of accounting for the universal sinfulness of human actions from the dawn of moral agency. It may be ascribed to the universality and peculiar nature of temptation, as has been said.

His third argument is, that "Moral depravity is not owing to any change that occurs subsequent to birth." Answer:--

No, the circumstances of temptation are sufficient to account for it without supposing the nature to be changed. This argument proves nothing, unless it be true, that the peculiar circumstances of temptation under which moral agents act, from the dawn of moral agency, cannot sufficiently account for their conduct, without supposing a change of nature subsequent to birth. "What then, does this arguing prove?"

Again, this argument is just as consistent with the opposing theory, and therefore proves neither.

His fourth argument is, "That moral depravity acts freely and spontaneously." Answer:--

"The moral agent acts freely, and acts selfishly, that is, wickedly. This argument assumes, that if a moral agent acts freely and wickedly, moral depravity, or sin, must be an attribute of his nature. Or more fairly, if mankind universally, in the exercise of their liberty, act sinfully, sinfulness must be an attribute of human nature." But what is sin? Why sin is a voluntary transgression of law, Dr. Woods being judge. Can a voluntary transgression of law be denominated an attribute of human nature?

But again, this argument alleges nothing but what is equally consistent with the opposite theory. If moral depravity consist in the choice of self-gratification as an end, it would of course freely and spontaneously manifest itself. This argument then, is good for nothing.

His fifth argument is, "That moral depravity is hard to overcome, and therefore it must be an attribute of human nature." Answer:--

If it were an attribute of human nature, it could not be overcome at all, without a change of the human constitution. It is hard to overcome, just as selfishness naturally would be, in beings of a physically depraved constitution, and in the presence of so many temptations to self-indulgence. If it were an attribute of human nature, it could not be overcome without a change of personal identity. But the fact that it can be overcome without destroying the consciousness of personal identity, proves that it is not an attribute of human nature.

His sixth argument is, that "We can predict with certainty, that in due time it will act itself out." Answer:--

Just as might be expected. If moral depravity consists in selfishness, we can predict with certainty, that the spirit of self-pleasing will, in due time, and at all times, act itself out. We can also predict, without the gift of prophecy, that with a constitution physically depraved, and surrounded with objects to awaken appetite, and with all the circumstances in which human beings first form their moral character, they will seek universally to gratify themselves, unless prevented by the illuminations of the Holy Spirit. This argument is just as consistent with the opposite theory, and therefore proves neither.

It is unnecessary to occupy any more time with the treatise of Dr. Woods. I will now quote the standards of the Presbyterian church, which will put you in possession of their views upon this subject. At pp. 30, 31, of the Presbyterian Confession of Faith, we have the following: "By this sin, they (Adam and Eve) fell from their original righteousness and communion with God, and so became dead in sin, and wholly defiled in all the faculties and parts of soul and body. They being the root of all mankind, the guilt of this sin was imputed, and the same death in sin and corrupted nature conveyed to all their posterity, descending from them by ordinary generation. From this original corruption, whereby we are utterly indisposed, disabled, and made opposite to all good, and wholly inclined to all evil, do proceed all actual transgressions."

Again, pp. 152-154, Shorter Catechism. "Question 22. Did all mankind fall in that first transgression? Ans. The covenant being made with Adam as a public person, not for himself only, but for his posterity; all mankind descending from him by ordinary generation, sinned in him, and fell with him in that first transgression.

"Question 23. Into what estate did the fall bring mankind? Ans. The fall brought mankind into an estate of sin and misery.

"Question 24. What is sin? Ans. Sin is any want of conformity unto, or transgression of, any law of God, given as a rule to the reasonable creature.

"Question 25. Wherein consists the sinfulness of that estate whereinto man fell? Ans. The sinfulness of that estate whereinto man fell, consisteth in the guilt of Adam's first sin, the want of that righteousness wherein he was created, and the corruption of his nature, whereby he is utterly indisposed, disabled, and made opposite unto all that is spiritually good, and wholly inclined to all evil, and that continually, which is commonly called original sin, and from which do proceed all actual transgressions.

"Question 26. How is original sin conveyed from our first parents unto their posterity? Ans. Original sin is conveyed from our first parents unto their posterity by natural generation, so as all that proceed from them in that way, are conceived and born in sin."

These extracts show, that the framers and defenders of this confession of faith, account for the moral depravity of mankind by making it to consist in a sinful nature, inherited by natural generation from Adam. They regard the constitution inherited from Adam, as in itself sinful, and the cause of all actual transgression. They make no distinction between physical and moral depravity. They also distinguish between original and actual sin. Original sin is the sinfulness of the constitution, in which Adam's posterity have no other hand than to inherit it by natural generation, or by birth. This original sin, or sinful nature, renders mankind utterly disabled from all that is spiritually good, and wholly inclined to all that is evil. This is their account of moral depravity. This, it will be seen, is substantially the ground of Dr. Woods.

It has been common with those who confound physical with moral depravity, and who maintain that human nature is itself sinful, to quote certain passages of Scripture to sustain their position. An examination of these proof texts, must, in the next place, occupy our attention. But before I enter upon this examination, I must first call your attention to certain well settled rules of biblical interpretation.

(1.) Different passages must be so interpreted, if they can be, as not to contradict each other.

(2.) Language is to be interpreted according to the subject-matter of discourse.

(3.) Respect is always to be had to the general scope and design of the speaker or writer.

(4.) Texts that are consistent with either theory, prove neither.

(5.) Language is to be so interpreted, if it can be, as not to conflict with sound philosophy, matters of fact, the nature of things, or immutable justice.

Let us now, remembering and applying these plain rules of sound interpretation, proceed to the examination of those passages that are supposed to establish the theory of depravity I am examining.

Gen. v. 3.--"Adam lived an hundred and thirty years, and begat a son in his own likeness and after his own image, and called his name Seth." It is not very easy to see, why this text should be pressed into the service of those who hold that human nature is in itself sinful. Why should it be assumed that the likeness and image here spoken of was a moral likeness or image? But unless this be assumed, the text has nothing to do with the subject.

Again: it is generally admitted, that in all probability Adam was a regenerate man at the time and before the birth of Seth. Is it intended that Adam begat a saint or a sinner? If, as is supposed, Adam was a saint of God, if this text is anything to the purpose, it affirms that Adam begat a saint. But this is the opposite of that in proof of which the text is quoted.

Another text is, Job xiv. 4.--"Who can bring a clean thing out of an unclean? Not one." This text is quoted in support of the position of the Presbyterian Confession of Faith, that children inherit from their parents, by natural generation, a sinful nature. Upon this text, I remark, that all that can be made of it, even if we read it without regard to the translation or the context, is, that a physically depraved parent will produce a physically depraved offspring. That this is its real meaning, is quite evident, when we look into the context. Job is treating of the frail and dying state of man, and manifestly has in the text and context his eye wholly on the physical state, and not on the moral character of man. What he intends is; who can bring other than a frail, dying offspring from a frail dying parent? Not one. This is substantially the view that Professor Stuart takes of this text. The utmost that can be made of it is, that as he belonged to a race of sinners, nothing else could be expected than that he should be a sinner, without meaning to affirm anything in regard to the quo mode of this result.

Again: Job xv. 14.--"What is man that he should be clean, and he that is born of a woman that he should be righteous."

These are the words of Eliphaz, and it is improper to quote them as inspired truth. For God himself testifies that Job's friends did not hold the truth. But, suppose we receive the text as true, what is its import? Why, it simply asserts, or rather implies, the righteousness or sinfulness of the whole human race. It expresses the universality of human depravity, in the very common way of including all that are born of woman. This certainly says nothing, and implies nothing, respecting a sinful constitution. It is just as plain, and just as warrantable, to understand this passage as implying that mankind have become so physically depraved, that this fact, together with the circumstances under which they come into being, and begin their moral career, will certainly, (not necessarily,) result in moral depravity. I might use just such language as that found in this text, and, naturally enough, express by it my own views of moral depravity, to wit, that it results from a physically depraved constitution; and the circumstances of temptation under which children come into this world, and begin and prosecute their moral career; certainly this is the most that can be made of this text.

Again: Psalm li. 5.--"Behold, I was shapen in iniquity, and in sin did my mother conceive me."

Upon this I remark, that it would seem, if this text is to be understood literally, that the Psalmist intended to affirm the sinful state of his mother, at the time of his conception, and during gestation. But, to interpret these passages as teaching the constitutional sinfulness of man, is to contradict God's own definition of sin, and the only definition that human reason or common sense can receive, to wit, that "sin is a transgression of the law." This is, no doubt, the only correct definition of sin. But we have seen that the law does not legislate over substance, requiring men to have a certain nature, but over voluntary action only. If the Psalmist really intended to affirm, that the substance of his body was sinful from its conception, then he not only arrays himself against God's own definition of sin, but he also affirms sheer nonsense. The substance of an unborn child sinful! It is impossible! But what did the Psalmist mean? I answer: This verse is found in David's penitential psalm. He was deeply convinced of sin, and was, as he had good reason to be, much excited, and expressed himself, as we all do in similar circumstances, in strong language. His eye, as was natural and is common in such cases, had been directed back along the pathway of life up to the days of his earliest recollection. He remembered sins among the earliest acts of his recollected life. He broke out in the language of this text to express, not the anti-scriptural and nonsensical dogma of a sinful constitution, but to affirm in his strong, poetic language, that he had been a sinner from the commencement of his moral existence, or from the earliest moment of his capability of being a sinner. This is the strong language of poetry.

Some suppose that, in the passage in question, the Psalmist referred to, and meant to acknowledge and assert, his low and despicable origin, and to say, I was always a sinner, and my mother that conceived me was a sinner, and I am but the degenerate plant of a strange vine, without intending to affirm anything in respect to the absolute sinfulness of his nature.

Again, Ps. lviii. 3. "The wicked are estranged from the womb; they go astray as soon as they be born, speaking lies."

Upon this text I remark that it has been quoted at one time to establish the doctrine of a sinful nature, and at another to prove that infants commit actual sin from the very day and hour of their birth. But certainly no such use can be legitimately made of this text. It does not affirm anything of a sinful nature, but this has been inferred from what it does affirm, that the wicked are estranged from their birth. But does this mean, that they are really and literally estranged from the day and hour of their birth, and that they really go astray the very day they are born, speaking lies? This every one knows to be contrary to fact. The text cannot then be pressed to the letter. What then does it mean? It must mean, like the text last examined, that the wicked are estranged and go astray from the commencement of their moral agency. If it means more than this, it would contradict other plain passages of scripture. It affirms, in strong, graphic, and poetic language, the fact, that the first moral conduct and character of children is sinful. This is all that in truth it can assert; and it doubtless dates the beginning of their moral depravity at a very early period, and expresses it in very strong language, as if it were literally from the hour of birth. But when it adds, that they go astray, speaking lies, we know that this is not, and cannot be, literally taken, for, as every one knows, children do not speak at all from their birth. Should we understand the Psalmist as affirming, that children go astray as soon as they go at all, and speak lies as soon as they speak at all, this would not prove that their nature was in itself sinful, but might well consist with the theory that their physical depravity, together with their circumstances of temptation, led them into selfishness, from the very first moment of their moral existence.

Again, John iii. 6. "That which is born of the flesh is flesh, and that which is born of the Spirit is spirit."

Upon this I remark that it may, if literally taken, mean nothing more than this, that the body which is born of flesh is flesh, and that that which is born of the Spirit is spirit; that is, that this birth of which he was speaking was of the soul, and not of the body. But it may be understood to mean, that that which results from the influence of the flesh is flesh, in the sense of sin; for this is a common sense of the term flesh in the New Testament, and that which results from the Spirit, is spirit or spiritual, in the sense of holy. This I understand to be the true sense. The text when thus understood, does not at all support the dogma of a sinful nature or constitution, but only this, that the flesh tends to sin, that the appetites and passions are temptations to sin, so that when the will obeys them it sins. Whatever is born of the propensities, in the sense that the will yields to their control, is sinful. And, on the other hand, whatever is born of the Spirit, that is, whatever results from the agency of the Holy Spirit, in the sense that the will yields to Him, is holy.

Again, Eph. ii. 3. "By nature the children of wrath, even as others."

Upon this text I remark that it cannot, consistently with natural justice, be understood to mean, that we are exposed to the wrath of God on account of our nature. It is a monstrous and blasphemous dogma, that a holy God is angry with any creature for possessing a nature with which he was sent into being without his knowledge or consent. The Bible represents God as angry with men for their wicked deeds, and not for their nature.

It is common and proper to speak of the first state in which men universally are, as a natural state. Thus we speak of sinners before regeneration, as in a state of nature, as opposed to a changed state, a regenerate state, and a state of grace. By this we do not necessarily mean, that they have a nature sinful in itself, but merely that before regeneration they are universally and morally depraved, that this is their natural, as opposed to their regenerate state. Total moral depravity is the state that follows, and results from their first birth, and is in this sense natural, and in this sense alone, can it truly be said, that they are "by nature children of wrath." Against the use that is made of this text, and all this class of texts, may be arrayed the whole scope of scripture, that represents man as to blame, and to be judged and punished only for his deeds. The subject-matter of discourse in these texts is such as to demand that we should understand them as not implying, or asserting, that sin is an essential part of our nature.

LECTURE XXIV - MORAL DEPRAVITY

FURTHER EXAMINATION OF THE ARGUMENTS ADDUCED IN SUPPORT OF THE POSITION, THAT HUMAN NATURE IS IN ITSELF SINFUL

The defenders of the doctrine of constitutional sinfulness, or moral depravity, urge as an additional argument:--

That sin is a universal effect of human nature, and therefore human nature must be itself sinful. Answer:--

This is a non sequitur. Sin may be, and must be, an abuse of free agency; and this may be accounted for, as we shall see, by ascribing it to the universality of temptation, and does not at all imply a sinful constitution. But if sin necessarily implies a sinful nature, how did Adam and Eve sin? Had they a sinful nature to account for, and to cause their first sin? How did angels sin? Had they also a sinful nature? Either sin does not imply a sinful nature, or a nature in itself sinful, or Adam and angels must have had sinful natures before their fall.

Again: Suppose we regard sin as an event or effect. An effect only implies an adequate cause. Free, responsible will is an adequate cause in the presence of temptation, without the supposition of a sinful constitution, as has been demonstrated in the case of Adam and of angels. When we have found an adequate cause, it is unphilosophical to look for and assign another.

Again: it is said that no motive to sin could be a motive or a temptation, if there were not a sinful taste, relish, or appetite, inherent in the constitution, to which the temptation or motive is addressed. For example, the presence of food, it is said, would be no temptation to eat, were there not a constitutional appetency terminating on food. So the presence of any object could be no inducement to sin, were there not a constitutional appetency or craving for sin. So that, in fact, sin in action were impossible, unless there were sin in the nature. To this I reply,--

Suppose this objection be applied to the sin of Adam and of angels. Can we not account for Eve's eating the forbidden fruit without supposing that she had a craving for sin? The Bible informs us that her craving was for the fruit, for knowledge, and not for sin. The words are, "And when the woman saw that the tree was good for food, and that it was pleasant to the eyes, and a tree to be desired to make one wise, she took of the fruit thereof and did eat, and gave also unto her husband with her, and he did eat." Here is nothing of a craving for sin. Eating this fruit was indeed sinful; but the sin consisted in consenting to gratify, in a prohibited manner, the appetites, not for sin, but for food and knowledge. But the advocates of this theory say that there must be an adaptedness in the constitution, a something within answering to the outward motive or temptation, otherwise sin were impossible. This is true. But the question is, What is that something within, which responds to the outward motive? Is it a craving for sin? We have just seen what it was in the case of Adam and Eve. It was simply the correlation that existed between the fruit and their constitution, its presence exciting the desires for food and knowledge. This led to prohibited indulgence. But all men sin in precisely the same way. They consent to gratify, not a craving for sin, but a craving for other things, and the consent to make self-gratification an end, is the whole of sin.

The theologians whose views we are canvassing, maintain that the appetites, passions, desires, and propensities, which are constitutional and entirely involuntary, are in themselves sinful. To this I reply, that Adam and Eve possessed them before they fell. Christ possessed them, or he was not a man, nor, in any proper sense, a human being. No, these appetites, passions, and propensities, are not sinful, though they are the occasions of sin. They are a temptation to the will to seek their unlawful indulgence. When these lusts or appetites are spoken of as the "passions of sin," or as "sinful lusts or passions," it is not because they are sinful in themselves, but because they are the occasions of sin. It has been asked, Why are not the appetites and propensities to be regarded as sinful, since they are the prevalent temptations to sin? I reply,--

They are involuntary, and moral character can no more be predicated of them, on account of their being temptations, than it could of the fruit that was a temptation to Eve. They have no design to tempt. They are constitutional, unintelligent, involuntary; and it is impossible that moral character should be predicable of them. A moral agent is responsible for his emotions, desires, etc., so far as they are under the direct or indirect control of his will, and no further. He is always responsible for the manner in which he gratifies them. If he indulges them in accordance with the law of God, he does right. If he makes their gratification his end, he sins.

Again: the death and suffering of infants previous to actual transgression, is adduced as an argument to prove, that infants have a sinful nature. To this I reply,--

That this argument must assume, that there must be sin wherever there is suffering and death. But this assumption proves too much, as it would prove that mere animals have a sinful nature, or have committed actual sin. An argument that proves too much proves nothing.

Physical sufferings prove only physical, and not moral, depravity. Previous to moral agency, infants are no more subjects of moral government than brutes are; therefore, their sufferings and death are to be accounted for as are those of brutes, namely, by ascribing them to physical interference with the laws of life and health.

Another argument for a sinful constitution is, that unless infants have a sinful nature, they do not need sanctification to fit them for heaven. Answer:--

This argument assumes, that, if they are not sinful, they must be holy; whereas they are neither sinful or holy, until they are moral agents, and render themselves so by obedience or disobedience to the moral law. If they are to go to heaven, they must be made holy or must be sanctified. This objection assumes, that previous sinfulness is a condition of the necessity of being holy. This is contrary to fact. Were Adam and angels first sinful before they were sanctified? But it is assumed that unless moral agents are at first sinners, they do not need the Holy Spirit to induce them to be holy. That is, unless their nature is sinful, they would become holy without the Holy Spirit. But where do we ascertain this? Suppose that they have no moral character, and that their nature is neither holy nor sinful. Will they become holy without being enlightened by the Holy Spirit? Who will assert that they will?

That infants have a sinful nature has been inferred from the institution of circumcision so early as the eighth day after birth. Circumcision, it is truly urged, was designed to teach the necessity of regeneration, and by way of implication, the doctrine of moral depravity. It is claimed, that its being enjoined as obligatory upon the eighth day after birth, was requiring it at the earliest period at which it could be safely performed. From this it is inferred, that infants are to be regarded as morally depraved from their birth.

In answer to this I would say, that infant circumcision was doubtless designed to teach the necessity of their being saved by the Holy Spirit from the dominion of the flesh; that the influence of the flesh must be restrained, and the flesh circumcised, or the soul would be lost. This truth needed to be impressed on the parents, from the birth of their children. This very significant, and bloody, and painful rite, was well calculated to impress this truth upon parents, and to lead them from their birth to watch over the development and indulgence of their propensities, and to pray for their sanctification. Requiring it at so early a day was no doubt designed to indicate, that they are from the first under the dominion of their flesh, without however affording any inference in favor of the idea, that their flesh was in itself sinful, or that the action of their will at that early age was sinful. If reason was not developed, the subjection of the will to appetite could not be sinful. But whether this subjection of the will to the gratification of the appetite was sinful or not, the child must be delivered from it, or it could never be fitted for heaven, any more than a mere brute can be fitted for heaven. The fact, that circumcision was required on the eighth day, and not before, seems to indicate, not that they are sinners absolutely from birth, but that they very early become so, even from the commencement of moral agency.

Again: the rite must be performed at some time. Unless a particular day were appointed, it would be very apt to be deferred, and finally not performed at all. It is probable, that God commanded that it should be done at the earliest period at which it could be safely done, not only for the reasons already assigned, but to prevent its being neglected too long, and perhaps altogether: and perhaps, also, because it would be less painful and dangerous at that early age, when the infant slept most of the time. The longer it was neglected the greater would be the temptation to neglect it altogether. So painful a rite needed to be enjoined by positive statute, at, some particular time; and it was desirable on all accounts that it should be done as early as it safely could be. This argument, then, for native constitutional moral depravity amounts really to nothing.

Again: it is urged, that unless infants have a sinful nature, should they die in infancy, they could not be saved by the grace of Christ.

To this I answer, that, in this case they would not, and could not, as a matter of course, be sent to the place of punishment for sinners; because that were to confound the innocent with the guilty, a thing morally impossible with God.

But what grace could there be in saving them from a sinful constitution, that is not exercised in saving them from circumstances that would certainly result in their becoming sinners, if not snatched from them? In neither case do they need pardon for sin. Grace is unearned favor--a gratuity. If the child has a sinful nature, it is his misfortune, and not his crime. To save him from this nature is to save him from those circumstances that will certainly result in actual transgression, unless he is rescued by death and by the Holy Spirit. So if his nature is not sinful, yet it is certain that his nature and circumstances are such, that he will surely sin unless rescued by death or by the Holy Spirit, before he is capable of sinning. It certainly must be an infinite favor to be rescued from such circumstances, and especially to have eternal life conferred as a mere gratuity. This surely is grace. And as infants belong to a race of sinners who are all, as it were, turned over into the hands of Christ, they doubtless will ascribe their salvation to the infinite grace of Christ.

Again: is it not grace that saves us from sinning? What then is it but grace that saves infants from sinning, by snatching them away from circumstances of temptation? In what way does grace save adults from sinning, but by keeping them from temptation, or by giving them grace to overcome it? And is there no grace in rescuing infants from circumstances that are certain, if they are left in them, to lead them into sin?

All that can be justly said in either case is, that if infants are saved at all, which I suppose they are, they are rescued by the benevolence of God from circumstances that would result in certain and eternal death, and are by grace made heirs of eternal life. But after all, it is useless to speculate about the character and destiny of those who are confessedly not moral agents. The benevolence of God will take care of them. It is nonsensical to insist upon their moral depravity before they are moral agents, and it is frivolous to assert, that they must be morally depraved, as a condition of their being saved by grace.

We deny that the human constitution is morally depraved, because it is impossible that sin should be a quality of the substance of soul or body. It is, and must be, a quality of choice or intention, and not of substance. To make sin an attribute or quality of substance is contrary to God's definition of sin. "Sin," says the apostle, "is anomia," a "transgression of, or a want of conformity to, the moral law." That is, it consists in a refusal to love God and our neighbor, or, which is the same thing, in loving ourselves supremely.

To represent the constitution as sinful, is to represent God, who is the author of the constitution, as the author of sin. To say that God is not the direct former of the constitution, but that sin is conveyed by natural generation from Adam, who made himself sinful, is only to remove the objection one step farther back, but not to obviate it; for God established the physical laws that of necessity bring about this result.

But how came Adam by a sinful nature? Did his first sin change his nature? or did God change it as a penalty for sin? What ground is there for the assertion that Adam's nature became in itself sinful by the fall? This is a groundless, not to say ridiculous, assumption, and an absurdity. Sin an attribute of nature! A sinful substance! Sin a substance! Is it a solid, a fluid, a material, or a spiritual substance?

I have received from a brother the following note on this subject:--

"The orthodox creeds are in some cases careful to say that original sin consists in the substance of neither soul nor body. Thus Bretschneider, who is reckoned among the rationalists in Germany, says: The symbolical books very rightly maintained that original sin is not in any sense the substance of man, his body or soul, as Flacius taught,--but that it has been infused into human nature by Satan, and mixed with it, as poison and wine are mixed.'

"They rather expressly guard against the idea that they mean by the phrase man's nature,' his substance, but somewhat which is fixed in the substance. They explain original sin, therefore, not as an essential attribute of man, that is, a necessary and essential part of his being, but as an accident, that is, somewhat which does not subsist in itself, but as something accidental, which has come into human nature. He quotes the Formula Concordantiæ as saying: Nature does not denote the substance itself of man, but something which inheres fixed in the nature or substance.' Accident is defined, what does not subsist by itself, but is in some substance and can be distinguished from it."

Here, it seems, is sin by itself, and yet not a substance or subsistence--not a part or attribute of soul or body. What can it be? Does it consist in wrong action? No, not in action, but is an accident which inheres fixed in the nature of substance. But what can it be? Not substance, nor yet action. But if it be anything, it must be either substance or action. If it be a state of substance, what is this but substance in a particular state? Do these writers think by this subtlety and refinement to relieve their doctrine of constitutional moral depravity of its intrinsic absurdity?

I object to the doctrine of constitutional sinfulness, that it makes all sin, original and actual, a mere calamity, and not a crime. For those who hold that sin is an essential and inseparable part of our nature, to call it a crime, is to talk nonsense. What! a sinful nature the crime of him upon whom it is entailed, without his knowledge or consent? If the nature is sinful, in such a sense that action must necessarily be sinful, which is the doctrine of the Confession of Faith, then sin in action must be a calamity, and can be no crime. It is the necessary effect of a sinful nature. This cannot be a crime, since the will has nothing to do with it.

Of course it must render repentance, either with or without the grace of God, impossible, unless grace sets aside our reason. If repentance implies self-condemnation, we can never repent in the exercise of our reason. Constituted as we are, it is impossible that we should condemn ourselves for a sinful nature, or for actions that are unavoidable. The doctrine of original sin, or of a sinful constitution, and of necessary sinful actions, represents the whole moral government of God, the plan of salvation by Christ, and indeed every doctrine of the gospel, as a mere farce. Upon this supposition the law is tyranny, and the gospel an insult to the unfortunate.

It is difficult, and, indeed, impossible for those who really believe this doctrine to urge immediate repentance and submission on the sinner, feeling that he is infinitely to blame unless he instantly comply. It is a contradiction to affirm, that a man can heartily believe in the doctrine in question, and yet truly and heartily blame sinners for not doing what is naturally impossible to them. The secret conviction must be in the mind of such an one, that the sinner is not really to blame for being a sinner. For in fact, if this doctrine is true, he is not to blame for being a sinner, any more than he is to blame for being a human being. This the advocate of this doctrine must know. It is vain for him to set up the pretence that he truly blames sinners for their nature, or for their conduct that was unavoidable. He can no more do it, than he can honestly deny the necessary affirmations of his own reason. Therefore the advocates of this theory must merely hold it as a theory, without believing it, or otherwise they must in their secret conviction excuse the sinner.

This doctrine naturally and necessarily leads its advocates, secretly at least, to ascribe the atonement of Christ rather to justice than to grace--to regard it rather as an expedient to relieve the unfortunate, than to render the forgiveness of the inexcusable sinner possible. The advocates of the theory cannot but regard the case of the sinner as rather a hard one, and God as under an obligation to provide a way for him to escape a sinful nature, entailed upon him in spite of himself, and from actual transgressions which result from his nature by a law of necessity. If all this is true, the sinner's case is infinitely hard, and God would appear the most unreasonable and cruel of beings, if he did not provide for their escape. These convictions will, and must, lodge in the mind of him who really believes the dogma of a sinful nature. This, in substance, is sometimes affirmed by the defenders of the doctrine of original sin.

The fact that Christ died in the stead and behalf of sinners, proves, that God regarded them not as unfortunate, but as criminal and altogether without excuse. Surely Christ need not have died to atone for the misfortunes of men. His death was to atone for their guilt, and not for their misfortunes. But if they are without excuse for sin, they must be without a sinful nature that renders sin unavoidable. If men are without excuse for sin, as the whole law and gospel assume and teach, it cannot possibly be that their nature is sinful, for a sinful nature would be the best of all excuses for sin.

This doctrine is a stumbling-block both to the church and the world, infinitely dishonorable to God, and an abomination alike to God and the human intellect, and should be banished from every pulpit, and from every formula of doctrine, and from the world. It is a relic of heathen philosophy, and was foisted in among the doctrines of Christianity by Augustine, as every one may know who will take the trouble to examine for himself. This view of moral depravity that I am opposing, has long been the stronghold of Universalism. From it, the Universalists inveigh with resistless force against the idea that sinners should be sent to an eternal hell. Assuming the long-defended doctrine of original or constitutional sinfulness, they proceeded to show, that it would be infinitely unreasonable and unjust in God to send them to hell. What! create them with a sinful nature, from which proceed, by a law of necessity, actual transgressions, and then send them to an eternal hell for having this nature, and for transgressions that are unavoidable! Impossible! they say; and the human intellect responds, Amen.

From the dogma of a sinful nature or constitution also, has naturally and irresistibly flowed the doctrine of inability to repent, and the necessity of a physical regeneration. These too have been a sad stumbling-block to Universalists, as every one knows who is at all acquainted with the history of Universalism. They infer the salvation of all men, from the fact of God's benevolence and physical omnipotence! God is almighty, and he is love. Men are constitutionally depraved, and are unable to repent. God will not, cannot send them to hell. They do not deserve it. Sin is a calamity, and God can save them, and he ought to do so. This is the substance of their argument. And assuming the truth of their premises, there is no evading their conclusion. But the whole argument is built on "such stuff as dreams are made of." Strike out the erroneous dogma of a sinful nature, and the whole edifice of Universalism comes to the ground in a moment. We come now to consider--

2. The proper method of accounting for moral depravity.

We have more than once seen that the Bible has given us the history of the introduction of sin into our world; and that from the narrative, it is plain, that the first sin consisted in selfishness, or in consenting to indulge the excited constitutional propensities in a prohibited manner. In other words, it consisted in yielding the will to the impulses of the sensibility, instead of abiding by the law of God, as revealed in the intelligence. Thus the Bible ascribes the first sin of our race to the influence of temptation.

The Bible once, and only once, incidentally intimates that Adam's first sin has in some way been the occasion, not the necessary physical cause, of all the sins of men. Rom. v. 12-19. It neither says nor intimates anything in relation to the manner in which Adam's sin has occasioned this result. It only incidentally recognizes the fact, and then leaves it, just as if the quo modo was too obvious to need explanation. In other parts of the Bible we are informed how we are to account for the existence of sin among men. James says, that a man is tempted when he is drawn aside of his own lusts, (επιθυμιαι "desires") and enticed. That is, his lusts, or the impulses of his sensibility, are his tempters. When he or his will is overcome of these, he sins. Paul and other inspired writers represent sin as consisting in a carnal or fleshly mind, in the mind of the flesh, or in minding the flesh. It is plain that by the term flesh they mean what we understand by the sensibility, as distinguished from intellect, and that they represent sin as consisting in obeying, minding, the impulses of the sensibility. They represent the world, and the flesh, and Satan, as the three great sources of temptation. It is plain that the world and Satan tempt by appeals to the flesh, or to the sensibility. Hence, the apostles have much to say of the necessity of the destruction of the flesh, of the members, of putting off the old man with his deeds, etc. Now, it is worthy of remark, that all this painstaking, on the part of Inspiration, to intimate the source from whence our sin proceeds, and to apprise us of the proper method of accounting for it, and also of avoiding it, has probably been the occasion of leading certain philosophers and theologians who have not carefully examined the whole subject, to take a view of it which is directly opposed to the truth intended by the inspired writers. Because so much is said of the influence of the flesh over the mind, they have inferred that the nature and physical constitution of man is itself sinful. But the representations of Scripture are, that the body is the occasion of sin. The law in his members, that warred against the law of his mind, of which Paul speaks, is manifestly the impulse of the sensibility opposed to the law of the reason. This law, that is, the impulse of his sensibility, brings him into captivity, that is, influences his will, in spite of all his convictions to the contrary.

Moral depravity consists, remember, in the committal of the will to the gratification or indulgence of self--in the will's following, or submitting itself to be governed by, the impulses and desires of the sensibility, instead of submitting itself to the law of God revealed in the reason.

This definition of the thing shows how it is to be accounted for, namely: the sensibility acts as a powerful impulse to the will, from the moment of birth, and secures the consent and activity of the will to procure its gratification, before the reason is at all developed. The will is thus committed to the gratification of feeling and appetite, when first the idea of moral obligation is developed. This committed state of the will is not moral depravity, and has no moral character, until the idea of moral obligation is developed. The moment this idea is developed, this committal of the will to self-indulgence must be abandoned, or it becomes selfishness, or moral depravity. But, as the will is already in a state of committal, and has to some extent already formed the habit of seeking to gratify feeling, and as the idea of moral obligation is at first but feebly developed, unless the Holy Spirit interferes to shed light on the soul, the will, as might be expected, retains its hold on self-gratification. Here alone moral character commences, and must commence. No one can conceive of its commencing earlier.

This selfish choice is the wicked heart--the propensity to sin--that causes what is generally termed actual transgression. This sinful choice is properly enough called indwelling sin. It is the latent, standing, controlling preference of the mind, and the cause of all the outward and active life. It is not the choice of sin itself, distinctly conceived of, or chosen as sin, but the choice of self-gratification, which choice is sin.

Again: It should be remembered, that the physical depravity of our race has much to do with our moral depravity. A diseased physical system renders the appetites, passions, tempers, and propensities more clamorous and despotic in their demands, and of course constantly urging to selfishness, confirms and strengthens it. It should be distinctly remembered that physical depravity has no moral character in itself. But yet it is a source of fierce temptation to selfishness. The human sensibility is, manifestly, deeply physically depraved; and as sin, or moral depravity, consists in committing the will to the gratification of the sensibility, its physical depravity will mightily strengthen moral depravity. Moral depravity is then universally owing to temptation. That is, the soul is tempted to self-indulgence, and yields to the temptation, and this yielding, and not the temptation, is sin or moral depravity. This is manifestly the way in which Adam and Eve became morally depraved. They were tempted, even by undepraved appetite, to prohibited indulgence, and were overcome. The sin did not lie in the constitutional desire of food, or of knowledge, nor in the excited state of these appetites or desires, but in the consent of the will to prohibited indulgence. Just in the same way all sinners become such, that is, they become morally depraved, by yielding to temptation to self-gratification under some form. Indeed, it is impossible that they should become morally depraved in any other way. To deny this were to overlook the very nature of moral depravity.

To sum up the truth upon this subject in few words, I would say:--

1. Moral depravity in our first parents was induced by temptation addressed to the unperverted susceptibilities of their nature. When these susceptibilities became strongly excited, they overcame the will; that is, the human pair were over-persuaded, and fell under the temptation. This has been repeatedly said, but needs repetition in a summing up.

2. All moral depravity commences in substantially the same way. Proof:--

(1.) The impulses of the sensibility are developed, gradually, commencing from the birth, and depending on physical development and growth.

(2.) The first acts of will are in obedience to these.

(3.) Self-gratification is the rule of action previous to the development of reason.

(4.) No resistance is offered to the will's indulgence of appetite, until a habit of self-indulgence is formed.

(5.) When reason affirms moral obligation, it finds the will in a state of habitual and constant committal to the impulses of the sensibility.

(6.) The demands of the sensibility have become more and more despotic every hour of indulgence.

(7.) In this state of things, unless the Holy Spirit interpose, the idea of moral obligation will be but dimly developed.

(8.) The will of course rejects the bidding of reason, and cleaves to self-indulgence.

(9.) This is the settling of a fundamental question. It is deciding in favor of appetite, against the claims of conscience and of God.

(10.) Light once rejected, can be afterwards more easily resisted, until it is nearly excluded altogether.

(11.) Selfishness confirms, and strengthens, and perpetuates itself by a natural process. It grows with the sinner's growth, and strengthens with his strength; and will do so for ever, unless overcome by the Holy Spirit through the truth.

REMARKS

1. Adam, being the natural head of the race, would naturally, by the wisest constitution of things, greatly affect for good or evil his whole posterity.

2. His sin in many ways exposed his posterity to aggravated temptation. Not only the physical constitution of all men, but all the influences under which they first form their moral character, are widely different from what they would have been, if sin had never been introduced.

3. When selfishness is understood to be the whole of moral depravity, its quo modo, or in what way it comes to exist, is manifest. Clear conceptions of the thing will instantly reveal the occasion and manner.

4. The only difficulty in accounting for it, has been the false assumption, that there must be, and is, something lying back of the free actions of the will, which sustains to those actions the relation of a cause, that is itself sinful.

5. If holy Adam, and holy angels could fall under temptations addressed to their undepraved sensibility, how absurd it is to conclude, that sin in those who are born with a physically depraved constitution, cannot be accounted for, without ascribing it to original sin, or to a nature that is in itself sinful.

6. Without divine illumination, the moral character will of course be formed under the influence of the flesh. That is, the lower propensities will of course influence the will, unless the reason be developed by the Holy Spirit.

7. The dogma of constitutional moral depravity, is a part and parcel of the doctrine of a necessitated will. It is a branch of a grossly false and heathenish philosophy. How infinitely absurd, dangerous, and unjust, then, to embody it in a standard of Christian doctrine, to give it the place of an indispensable article of faith, and denounce all who will not swallow its absurdities, as heretics!

8. We are unable to say precisely at what age infants become moral agents, and of course how early they become sinners. Doubtless there is much difference among children in this respect. Reason is developed in one earlier than in another, according to the constitution and circumstances.

A thorough consideration of the subject, will doubtless lead to the conviction, that children become moral agents much earlier than is generally supposed. The conditions of moral agency are, as has been repeatedly said in former lectures, the possession of the powers of moral agency, together with the development of the ideas of the good or valuable, of moral obligation or oughtness--of right and wrong--of praise and blameworthiness. I have endeavored to show, in former lectures, that mental satisfaction, blessedness or happiness, is the ultimate good. Satisfaction arising from the gratification of the appetites, is one of the earliest experiences of human beings. This no doubt suggests or developer, at a very early period, the idea of the good or the valuable. The idea is doubtless developed, long before the word that expresses it is understood. The child knows that happiness is good, and seeks it in the form of self-gratification, long before the terms that designate this state of mind are at all understood. It knows that its own enjoyment is worth seeking, and doubtless very early has the idea, that the enjoyment of others is worth seeking, and affirms to itself, not in words, but in idea, that it ought to please its parents and those around it. It knows, in fact, though language is as yet unknown, that it loves to be gratified, and to be happy, that it loves and seeks enjoyment for itself, and doubtless has the idea that it ought not to displease and distress those around it, but that it ought to endeavor to please and gratify them. This is probably among the first ideas, if not the very first idea, of the pure reason that is developed, that is, the idea of the good, the valuable, the desirable; and the next must be that of oughtness, or of moral obligation, or of right and wrong, etc. I say again, these ideas are, and must be developed, before the signs or words that express them are at all understood, and the words would never be understood except the idea were first developed. We always find, at the earliest period at which children can understand words, that they have the idea of obligation, of right and wrong. As soon as these words are understood by them, they recognize them as expressing ideas already in their own minds, and which ideas they have had further back than they can remember. Some, and indeed most persons, seem to have the idea, that children affirm themselves to be under moral obligation, before they have the idea of the good; that they affirm their obligation to obey their parents before they know, or have the idea of the good or of the valuable. But this is, and must be a mistake. They may and do affirm obligation to obey their parents, before they can express in language, and before they would understand, a statement of the ground of their obligation. The idea, however, they have, and must have, or they could not affirm obligation.

9. Why is sin so natural to mankind? Not because their nature is itself sinful, but because the appetites and passions tend so strongly to self-indulgence. These are temptations to sin, but sin itself consists not in these appetites and propensities, but in the voluntary committal of the will to their indulgence. This committal of the will is selfishness, and when the will is once given up to sin, it is very natural to sin. The will once committed to self-indulgence as its end, selfish actions are in a sense spontaneous.

10. The constitution of a moral being as a whole, when all the powers are developed, does not tend to sin, but strongly in an opposite direction; as is manifest from the fact that when reason is thoroughly developed by the Holy Spirit, it is more than a match for the sensibility, and turns the heart to God.

The difficulty is, that the sensibility gets the start of reason, and engages the attention in devising means of self-gratification, and thus retards, and in a great measure prevents, the development of the ideas of the reason which were designed to control the will. It is this morbid development that the Holy Spirit is given to rectify, by so forcing truth upon the attention, as to secure the development of the reason. By doing this, he brings the will under the influence of truth. Our senses reveal to us the objects correlated to our animal nature and propensities. The Holy Spirit reveals God and the spiritual world, and all that class of objects that are correlated to our higher nature, so as to give reason the control of the will. This is regeneration and sanctification, as we shall see in its proper place.

LECTURE XXV - ATONEMENT

We come now to the consideration of a very important feature of the moral government of God; namely, the atonement.

In discussing this subject, I will--

I. Call attention to several well-established principles of government.

1. We have already seen that moral law is not founded in the mere arbitrary will of God or of any other being, but that it has its foundation in the nature and relations of moral agents, that it is that rule of action or of willing which is imposed on them by the law of their own intellect.

2. As the will of no being can create moral law, so the will of no being can repeal or alter moral law. It being just that rule of action that is agreeable to the nature and relations of moral agents, it is as immutable as those natures and relations.

3. There is a distinction between the letter and the spirit of moral law. The letter relates to the outward life or action; the spirit respects the motive or intention from which the act should proceed. For example: the spirit of the moral law requires disinterested benevolence, and is all expressed in one word--love. The letter of the law is found in the commandments of the decalogue, and in divers other precepts relating to outward acts.

4. To the letter of the law there may be many exceptions, but to the spirit of moral law there can be no exception. That is, the spirit of the moral law may sometimes admit and require, that the letter of the law shall be disregarded or violated; but the spirit of the law ought never to be disregarded or violated. For example: the letter of the law prohibits all labor on the sabbath day. But the spirit of the law often requires labor on the sabbath. The spirit of the law requires the exercise of universal and perfect love or benevolence to God and man, and the law of benevolence often requires that labor shall be done on the sabbath; as administering to the sick, relieving the poor, feeding animals; and in short, whatever, is plainly the work of necessity or mercy, in such a sense that enlightened benevolence demands it, is required by the spirit of moral law upon the sabbath, as well as all other days. This is expressly taught by Christ, both by precept and example. So again, the letter of the law says, "The soul that sinneth, it shall die;" but the spirit of the law admits and requires that upon certain conditions, to be examined in their proper place, the soul that sinneth shall live. The letter of the law is inexorable; it condemns and sentences to death all violators of its precepts, without regard to atonement or repentance. The spirit of moral law allows and requires that upon condition of satisfaction being made to public justice, and the return of the sinner to obedience, he shall live and not die.

5. In establishing a government and promulgating law, the lawgiver is always understood as pledging himself duly to administer the laws in support of public order, and for the promotion of public morals, to reward the innocent with his favor and protection, and to punish the disobedient with the loss of his protection and favor.

6. Laws are public property in which every subject of the government has an interest. Every obedient subject of government is interested to have law supported and obeyed, and wherever the law is violated, every subject of the government is injured, and his rights are invaded; and each and all have a right to expect the government duly to execute the penalties of law when it is violated.

7. There is an important distinction between retributive and public justice. Retributive justice consists in treating every subject of government according to his character. It respects the intrinsic merit or demerit of each individual, and deals with him accordingly. Public justice, in its exercise, consists in the promotion and protection of the public interests, by such legislation and such an administration of law, as is demanded by the highest good of the public. It implies the execution of the penalties of law where the precept is violated, unless something else is done that will as effectually secure the public interests. When this is done, public justice demands, that the execution of the penalty shall be dispensed with, by extending pardon to the criminal. Retributive justice makes no exceptions, but punishes without mercy in every instance of crime. Public justice makes exceptions, as often as this is permitted or required by the public good. Public justice is identical with the spirit of the moral law, and in its exercise, regards only the law. Retributive justice cleaves to the letter, and makes no exceptions to the rule, "The soul that sinneth, it shall die."

8. The design of legal penalties is to secure obedience to the precept. The same is also the reason for executing them when the precept is violated. The sanctions are to be regarded as an expression of the views of the lawgiver, in respect to the importance of his law; and the execution of penalties is designed and calculated to evince his sincerity in enacting, and his continued adherence to, and determination to abide by, the principles of his government as revealed in the law; his abhorrence of all crime; his regard to the public interests; and his unalterable determination to carry out, support and establish, the authority of his law.

9. It is a fact well established by the experience of all ages and nations, that the exercise of mercy, in setting aside the execution of penalties, is a matter of extreme delicacy and danger. The influence of law, as might be expected, is found very much to depend upon the certainty felt by the subjects that it will be duly executed. It is found in experience, to be true, that the exercise of mercy in every government where no atonement is made, weakens government, by begetting and fostering a hope of impunity in the minds of those who are tempted to violate the law. It has been asserted, that the same is true when an atonement has been made, and that therefore, the doctrines of atonement and consequent forgiveness tend to encourage the hope of impunity in the commission of sin, and for this reason, are dangerous doctrines, subversive of high and sound morality. This assertion I shall notice in its appropriate place.

10. Since the head of the government is pledged to protect and promote the public interests, by a due administration of law, if in any instance where the precept is violated, he would dispense with the execution of penalties, public justice requires that he shall see, that a substitute for the execution of law is provided, or that something is done that shall as effectually secure the influence of law, as the execution of the penalty would do. He cannot make exceptions to the spirit of the law. Either the soul that sinneth must die, according to the letter

of the law, or a substitute must be provided in accordance with the spirit of the law.

11. Whatever will as fully evince the lawgiver's regard for his law, his determination to support it, his abhorrence of all violations of its precepts, and withal guard as effectually against the inference, that violators of the precept might expect to escape with impunity, as the execution of the penalty would do, is a full satisfaction of public justice. When these conditions are fulfilled, and the sinner has returned to obedience, public justice not only admits, but absolutely demands, that the penalty shall be set aside by extending pardon to the offender. The offender still deserves to be punished, and, upon the principles of retributive justice, might be punished according to his deserts. But the public good admits and requires, that upon the above condition he should live; hence, public justice, in compliance with the public interests and the spirit of the law of love, spares and pardons him.

12. If mercy or pardon is to be extended to any who have violated law, it ought to be done in a manner and upon some conditions that will settle the question, and establish the truth, that the execution of penalties is not to be dispensed with merely upon condition of the repentance of the offender. In other words, if pardon is to be extended, it should be known to be upon a condition not within the power of the offender. Else he may know, that he can violate the law, and yet be sure to escape with impunity, by fulfilling the conditions of forgiveness, which are upon the supposition, all within his own power.

13. So, if mercy is to be exercised, it should be upon a condition that is not to be repeated. The thing required by public justice is, that nothing shall be done to undermine or disturb the influence of law. Hence it cannot consent to have the execution of penalties dispensed with, upon any condition that shall encourage the hope of impunity. Therefore, public justice cannot consent to the pardon of sin but upon condition of an atonement, and also upon the assumption that atonement is not to be repeated, nor to extend its benefits beyond the limits of the race for whom it was made, and that only for a limited time. If an atonement were to extend its benefits to all worlds, and to all eternity, it would nullify its own influence, and encourage the universal hope of impunity, in case the precepts of the law were violated. This would be indefinitely worse than no atonement; and public justice might as well consent to have mercy exercised, without any regard to securing the authority and influence of law.

II. The term. Atonement.

The English word atonement is synonymous with the Hebrew word cofer. This is a noun from the verb caufar, to cover. The cofer or cover was the name of the lid or cover of the ark of the covenant, and constituted what was called the mercy-seat. The Greek word rendered atonement is καταλλαγη. This means reconciliation to favor, or more strictly, the means or conditions of reconciliation to favor; from καταλλασσω, to "change, or exchange." The term properly means substitution. An examination of these original words, in the connection in which they stand, will show that the atonement is the governmental substitution of the sufferings of Christ for the punishment of sinners. It is a covering of their sins by his sufferings.

III. The teachings of natural theology, or the à priori affirmations of reason upon this subject.

The doctrine of atonement has been regarded as so purely a doctrine of revelation as to preclude the supposition, that reason could, à priori, make any affirmations about it. It has been generally regarded as lying absolutely without the pale of natural theology, in so high a sense, that, aside from revelation, no assumption could be made, nor even a reasonable conjecture indulged. But there are certain facts in this world's history, that render this assumption exceedingly doubtful. It is true, indeed, that natural theology could not ascertain and establish the fact, that an atonement had been made, or that it certainly would be made; but if I am not mistaken, it might have been reasonably inferred, the true character of God being known and assumed, that an atonement of some kind would be made to render it consistent with his relations to the universe, to extend mercy to the guilty inhabitants of this world. The manifest necessity of a divine revelation has been supposed to afford a strong presumptive argument, that such a revelation has been or will be made. From the benevolence of God, as affirmed by reason, and manifested in his works and providence, it has been, as I suppose, justly inferred, that he would make arrangements to secure the holiness and salvation of men, and as a condition of this result, that he would grant them a further revelation of his will than had been given in creation and providence. The argument stands thus:--

1. From reason and observation we know that this is not a state of retribution; and from all the facts in the case that lie open to observation, this is evidently a state of trial or probation.

2. The providence of God in this world is manifestly disciplinary, and designed to reform mankind.

3. These facts, taken in connection with the great ignorance and darkness of the human mind on moral and religious subjects, afford a strong presumption that the benevolent Creator will make to the inhabitants of this world who are so evidently yet in a state of trial, a further revelation of his will. Now, if this argument is good, so far as it goes, I see not why we may not reasonably go still further.

Since the above are facts, and since it is also a fact that when the subject is duly considered, and the more thoroughly the better, there is manifestly a great difficulty in the exercise of mercy without satisfaction being made to public justice; and since the benevolence of God would not allow him on the one hand to pardon sin at the expense of public justice, nor on the other to punish or execute the penalty of law, if it could be wisely and consistently avoided, these facts being understood and admitted, it might naturally have been inferred, that the wisdom and benevolence of God would devise and execute some method of meeting the demands of public justice, that should render the forgiveness of sin possible. That the philosophy of government would render this possible, is to us very manifest. I know, indeed, that with the light the gospel has afforded us, we much more clearly discern this, than they could who had no other light than that of nature. Whatever might have been known to the ancients, and those who have not the Bible, I think that when the facts are announced by revelation, we can see that such a governmental expedient was not only possible, but just what might have been expected of the benevolence of God. It would of course have been impossible for us, à priori, to have devised, or reasonably conjectured, the plan that has been adopted. So little was known or knowable on the subject of the trinity of God, without revelation, that natural theology could, perhaps, in its best estate, have taught nothing further than that, if it was possible, some governmental expedient would be resorted to, and was in contemplation, for the ultimate restoration of the sinning race, who were evidently spared hitherto from the execution of law, and placed under a system of discipline.

But since the gospel has announced the fact of the atonement, it appears that natural theology or governmental philosophy can satisfactorily explain it; that reason can discern a divine philosophy in it.

Natural theology can teach--

1. That the human race is in a fallen state, and that the law of selfishness, and not the law of benevolence, is that to which unconverted men conform their lives.

2. It can teach that God is benevolent, and hence that mercy must be an attribute of God; and that this attribute will be manifested in the actual pardon of sin, when this can be done with safety to the divine government.

3. Consequently that no atonement could be needed to satisfy any implacable spirit in the divine mind; that he was sufficiently and infinitely disposed to extend pardon to the penitent, if this could be wisely, benevolently, and safely done.

4. It can also abundantly teach, that there is a real and a great danger in the exercise of mercy under a moral government, and supremely great under a government so vast and so enduring as the government of God; that, under such a government, the danger is very great, that the exercise of mercy will be understood as encouraging the hope of impunity in the commission of sin.

5. It can also show the indispensable necessity of such an administration of the divine government as to secure the fullest confidence throughout the universe, in the sincerity of God in promulging his law with its tremendous penalty, and of his unalterable adherence to its spirit, and determination not to falter in carrying out and securing its authority at all events. That this is indispensable to the well-being of the universe, is entirely manifest.

6. Hence it is very obvious to natural theology, that sin cannot be pardoned unless something is done to forbid the otherwise natural inference that sin will be forgiven under the government of God upon condition of repentance alone, and of course upon a condition within the power of the sinner himself. It must be manifest, that to proclaim throughout the universe that sin would be pardoned universally upon condition of repentance alone, would be a virtual repeal of the divine law. All creatures would instantly perceive, that no one need to fear punishment, in any case, as his forgiveness was secure, however much he might trample on the divine authority, upon a single condition which he could at will perform.

7. Natural theology is abundantly competent to show, that God could not be just to his own intelligence, just to his character, and hence just to the universe, in dispensing with the execution of divine law, except upon the condition of providing a substitute of such a nature as to reveal as fully, and impress as deeply, the lessons that would be taught by the execution, as the execution itself would do. The great design of penalties is prevention, and this is of course the design of executing penalties. The head of every government is pledged to sustain the authority of law, by a due administration of rewards and punishments, and has no right in any instance to extend pardon, except upon conditions that will as effectually support the authority of law as the execution

of its penalties would do. It was never found to be safe, or even possible under any government, to make the universal offer of pardon to violators of law, upon the bare condition of repentance, for the very obvious reason already suggested, that it would be a virtual repeal of all law. Public justice, by which every executive magistrate in the universe is bound, sternly and peremptorily forbids that mercy shall be extended to any culprit, without some equivalent being rendered to the government; that is, without something being done that will fully answer as a substitute for the execution of penalties. This principle God fully admits to be binding upon him; and hence he affirms that he gave his Son to render it just in him to forgive sin. Rom. iii. 24-26: "Being justified freely by his grace, through the redemption that is in Christ Jesus, whom God hath set forth to be a propitiation through faith in his blood, to declare his righteousness for the remission of sins that are past, through the forbearance of God; to declare, I say, at this time, his righteousness; that he might be just, and the justifier of him which believeth in Jesus."

8. All nations have felt the necessity of expiatory sacrifices. This is evident from the fact that all nations have offered them.

9. The wisest heathen philosophers, who saw the intrinsic inefficacy of animal sacrifices, held that God could not forgive sin. This proves to a demonstration, that they felt the necessity of an atonement, or expiatory sacrifice. And having too just views of God and his government, to suppose that either animal, or merely human, sacrifices, could be efficacious under the government of God, they were unable to understand upon what principles sin could be forgiven.

10.Public justice required, either that an atonement should be made, or that the law should be executed upon every offender. By public justice is intended, that due administration of law, that shall secure in the highest manner which the nature of the case admits, private and public interests, and establish the order and well-being of the universe. In establishing the government of the universe, God had given the pledge, both impliedly and expressly, that he would regard the public interests, and by a due administration of the law, secure and promote, as far as possible, public and individual happiness.

11. Public justice could strictly require only the execution of law; for God had neither expressly nor impliedly given a pledge to do anything more for the promotion of virtue and happiness, than to administer due rewards to the righteous, and due punishment to the wicked. Yet an atonement, as we shall see, would more fully meet the necessities of government, and act as a more efficient preventive of sin, and a more powerful persuasive to holiness, than the infliction of the legal penalty would do.

12. An atonement was needed for the removal of obstacles to the free exercise of benevolence toward our race. Without an atonement, the race of man after the fall sustained to the government of God the relation of rebels and outlaws. And before God, as the great executive magistrate of the universe, could manifest his benevolence toward them, an atonement must be decided upon and made known, as the reason upon which his favorable treatment of them was conditionated.

13. An atonement was needed to promote the glory and influence of God in the universe. But more of this hereafter.

14. An atonement was needed to present overpowering motives to repentance.

15. An atonement was needed, that the offer of pardon might not seem like connivance at sin.

16. An atonement was needed to manifest the sincerity of God in his legal enactments.

17. An atonement was needed to make it safe to present the offer and promise of pardon.

18. Natural theology can inform us, that, if the lawgiver would or could condescend so much to deny himself, as to attest his regard to his law, and his determination to support it by suffering its curse, in such a sense as was possible and consistent with his character and relations, and so far forth as emphatically to inculcate the great lesson, that sin was not to be forgiven upon the bare condition of repentance in any case, and also to establish the universal conviction, that the execution of law was not to be dispensed with, but that it is an unalterable rule under his divine government, that where there is sin there must be inflicted suffering--this would be so complete a satisfaction of public justice, that sin might safely be forgiven.

IV. The fact of atonement.

This is purely a doctrine of revelation, and in the establishment of this truth appeal must be made to the scriptures alone.

1. The whole Jewish scriptures, and especially the whole ceremonial dispensation of the Jews, attest, most unequivocally, the necessity of an atonement.

2. The New Testament is just as unequivocal in its testimony to the same point.

I shall here take it as established, that Christ was properly "God manifest in the flesh," and proceed to cite a few out of the great multitude of passages, that attest the fact of his death, and also its vicarious nature; that is, that it was for us, and as a satisfaction to public justice for our sins, that his blood was shed. I will first quote a few passages to show that the atonement and redemption through it, was a matter of understanding and covenant between the Father and Son. "I have made a covenant with my chosen, I have sworn unto David my servant. Thy seed will I establish forever, and build up thy throne to all generations. Selah."--Ps. lxxxix. 3, 4. "Yet it pleased the Lord to bruise him; he hath put him to grief: when thou shalt make his soul an offering for sin he shall see his seed, he shall prolong his days, and the pleasure of the Lord shall prosper in his hand. He shall see of the travail of his soul, and shall be satisfied; by his knowledge shall my righteous servant justify many; for he shall bear their iniquities. Therefore will I divide him a portion with the great, and he shall divide the spoil with the strong; because he hath poured out his soul unto death: and he was numbered with the transgressors."--Isaiah liii. 10, 11, 12. "All that the Father giveth me shall come to me: and he that cometh to me I will in no wise cast out. For I came down from heaven, not to do mine own will, but the will of him that sent me. And this is the Father's will which hath sent me, that of all which he hath given me I should lose nothing, but should raise it up again at the last day."--John vi. 37, 38, 39. "I have manifested thy name unto the men which thou gavest me out of the world: thine they were, and thou gavest them me; and they have kept thy word. I pray for them: I pray not for the world, but for them which thou hast given me; for they are thine. And now I am no more in the world, but these are in the world, and I come to thee. Holy

Father, keep through thine own name those whom thou hast given me, that they may be one, as we are."--John xvii. 6, 9, 11.

I will next quote some passages to show, that, if sinners were to be saved at all, it must be through an atonement. "Neither is there salvation in any other: for there is none other name under heaven given among men whereby we must be saved."--Acts iv. 12. "Be it known unto you therefore, men and brethren, that through this man is preached unto you the forgiveness of sins: And by him all that believe are justified from all things, from which ye could not be justified by the law of Moses."--Acts xiii. 38, 39. "Now we know, that what things soever the law saith, it saith to them who are under the law; that every mouth may be stopped, and all the world may become guilty before God. Therefore, by the deeds of the law there shall no flesh be justified in his sight: for by the law is the knowledge of sin."--Rom. iii. 19, 20. "Knowing that a man is not justified by the works of the law, but by the faith of Jesus Christ, even we have believed in Jesus Christ, that we might be justified by the faith of Christ, and not by the works of the law: for by the works of the law shall no flesh be justified. I do not frustrate the grace of God: for if righteousness come by the law, then Christ is dead in vain."--Gal. ii. 16, 21. "For as many as are of the works of the law are under the curse: for it is written, Cursed is every one that continueth not in all things which are written in the book of the law to do them. But that no man is justified by the law in the sight of God, it is evident: for, The just shall live by faith. And the law is not of faith: but the man that doeth them shall live in them. For if the inheritance be of the law, it is no more of promise: but God gave it to Abraham by promise. Wherefore then serveth the law? It was added because of transgressions, until the seed should come to whom the promise was made; and it was ordained by angels in the hand of a mediator. Now a mediator is not a mediator of one, but God is one. Is the law, then, against the promises of God? God forbid, for if there had been a law given which could have given life, verily righteousness should have been by the law. Wherefore the law was our schoolmaster to bring us unto Christ, that we might be justified by faith."--Gal. iii. 10-12, 18-21, 24. "And almost all things are by the law purged with blood; and without shedding of blood is no remission. It was therefore necessary that the patterns of things in the heavens should be purified with these; but the heavenly things themselves with better sacrifices than these."--Heb. ix. 22, 23.

I will now cite some passages that establish the fact of the vicarious death of Christ, and redemption through his blood. "But he was wounded for our transgressions, he was bruised for our iniquities: the chastisement of our peace was upon him, and with his stripes we are healed. All we like sheep have gone astray; we have turned every one to his own way; and the Lord hath laid on him the iniquity of us all."--Isaiah liii. 5, 6. "Even as the Son of man came not to be ministered unto, but to minister, and to give his life a ransom for many."--Matt. xx. 28. "For this is my blood of the new testament which is shed for many for the remission of sins."--Matt. xxvi. 28. "And as Moses lifted up the serpent in the wilderness, even so must the Son of man be lifted up; that whosoever believeth in him should not perish, but have eternal life."--John iii. 14, 15. "I am the living bread which came down from heaven: if any man eat of this bread, he shall live for ever: and the bread that I will give is my flesh, which I will give for the life of the world."--John vi. 51. "Take heed therefore unto yourselves, and to all the flock over the which the Holy Ghost hath made you overseers, to feed the church of God, which he hath purchased with his own blood."--Acts xx. 28. "Being justified freely by his grace, through the redemption that is in Christ Jesus. To declare, I say, at this time, his righteousness: that he might be just, and the justifier of him which believeth in Jesus. For when we were yet without strength, in due time Christ died for the ungodly. For scarcely for a righteous man will one die: yet peradventure for a good man some would even dare to die. But God commendeth his love toward us, in that while we were yet sinners Christ died for us. Much more then, being now justified by his blood, we shall be saved from wrath through him. And not only so, but we also joy in God through our Lord Jesus Christ, by whom we have now received the atonement. Therefore, as by the offence of one, judgment came upon all men to condemnation; even so by the righteousness of one the free gift came upon all men unto justification of life. For as by one man's disobedience many were made sinners, so by the obedience of one shall many be made righteous."--Rom. iii. 24-26; v. 9-11, 18, 19. "purge out therefore the old leaven, that ye may be a new lump, as ye are unleavened. For even Christ our passover is sacrificed for us: for I delivered unto you first of all that which I also received, how that Christ died far our sins according to the scriptures."--1 Cor. v. 7: xv. 3. "I am crucified with Christ: nevertheless I live: yet not I, but Christ liveth in me: and the life which I now live in the flesh I live by the faith of the Son of God, who loved me, and gave himself for me. Christ hath redeemed us from the curse of the law, being made a curse for us: for it is written, Cursed is every one that hangeth on a tree. That the blessing of Abraham might come on the Gentiles through Jesus Christ; that we might receive the promise of the Spirit through faith."--Gal. ii. 20; iii. 13, 14. "But now in Christ Jesus ye who sometimes were far off are made nigh by the blood of Christ. And walk in love, as Christ also hath loved us, and hath given himself for us an offering and a sacrifice to God for a sweet smelling savour."--Eph. ii. 13; v. 2. "Neither by the blood of goats and calves, but by his own blood he entered in once into the holy place, having obtained eternal redemption for us. For if the blood of bulls and of goats, and the ashes of an heifer sprinkling the unclean, sanctifieth to the purifying of the flesh; how much more shall the blood of Christ, who through the eternal Spirit offered himself without spot to God, purge your conscience from dead works to serve the living God? And almost all things are by the law purged with blood; and without shedding of blood is no remission. It was therefore necessary that the patterns of things in the heavens should be purified with these, but the heavenly things themselves with better sacrifices than these. For Christ is not entered into the holy places made with hands, which are the figures of the true; but into heaven itself, now to appear in the presence of God for us. Nor yet that he should offer himself often, as the high priest entereth into the holy place every year with blood of others; for then must he often have suffered since the foundation of the world: but now once in the end of the world hath he appeared to put away sin by the sacrifice of himself. And as it is appointed unto men once to die, but after this the judgment: so Christ was once offered to bear the sins of many: and unto them that look for him shall he appear the second time without sin unto salvation."--Heb. ix. 12-14, 22-28. "By the which will we are sanctified through the offering of the body of Jesus Christ once for all. And every priest standeth daily ministering and offering oftentimes the same sacrifices, which can never take away sins: but this man, after he had offered one sacrifice for sins, for ever sat down on the right hand of God; from henceforth expecting till his enemies be made his footstool. For by one offering he hath perfected forever them that are sanctified."--Heb. x. 10-14. "Having therefore, brethren, boldness to enter into the holiest by the blood of Jesus, by a new and living way which he hath consecrated for us through the vail, that is to say, his flesh," etc.--Heb. x. 19, 20. "Forasmuch as ye know that ye were not redeemed with corruptible things, as silver and gold, from your vain conversation received by tradition from your fathers; but with the precious blood of Christ, as of a lamb without blemish and without spot."--1 Pet. i. 18, 19. "Who his own self bare our sins in his own body on the tree, that we being dead to sins should live unto righteousness; by whose stripes ye were healed."--1 Pet. ii. 24. "For Christ also hath once suffered for sins, the just for the unjust, that he might bring us to God, being put to death in the flesh, but quickened by the Spirit."--1 Peter iii. 18. "But if we walk in the light as he is in the light, we have fellowship one with another, and the blood of Jesus Christ his Son cleanseth us from all sin."--1 John i. 7. "And ye know that he was manifested to take away our sins; and in him is no sin."--1 John iii. 5. "In this was manifested the love of God toward us, because that God sent his only begotten Son into the world, that we might live through him. Herein is love, not that we loved God, but that he loved us, and sent his Son to be the propitiation for our sins."--1 John iv. 9, 10.

These, as every reader of the Bible must know, are only some of the passages that teach the doctrine of atonement and redemption by the death of Christ. It is truly wonderful in how many ways this doctrine is taught, assumed, and implied in the Bible. Indeed, it is emphatically the great theme of the Bible. It is expressed or implied upon nearly every page of divine inspiration.

V. The next inquiry is what constitutes the atonement.

The answer to this inquiry has been already, in part, unavoidably anticipated. Under this head I will show,--

1. That Christ's obedience to the moral law as a covenant of works, did not constitute the atonement.

(1.) Christ owed obedience to the moral law, both as God and man. He was under as much obligation to be perfectly benevolent as any moral agent is. It was, therefore, impossible for him to perform any works of supererogation; that is, so far as obedience to law was concerned, he could, neither as God nor as man, do anything more than fulfil its obligations.

(2.) Had he obeyed for us, he would not have suffered for us. Were his obedience to be substituted for our obedience, he need not certainly have both fulfilled the law for us, as our substitute, under a covenant of works, and at the same time have suffered as a substitute, in submitting to the penalty of the law.

(3.) If he obeyed the law as our substitute, then why should our own return to personal obedience be insisted upon as a sine quâ non of our salvation?

(4.) The idea that any part of the atonement consisted in Christ's obeying the law for us, and in our stead and behalf, represents God as requiring:--

(i.) The obedience of our substitute.

(ii.) The same suffering, as if no obedience had been rendered.

(iii.) Our repentance.

(iv.) Our return to personal obedience.

(v.) And then represents him as, after all, ascribing our salvation to grace. Strange grace this, that requires a debt to be paid several times over, before the obligation is discharged!

2. I must show that the atonement was not a commercial transaction.

Some have regarded the atonement simply in the light of the payment of a debt; and have represented Christ as purchasing the elect of the Father, and paying down the same amount of suffering in his own person that justice would have exacted of them. To this I answer--

(1.) It is naturally impossible, as it would require that satisfaction should be made to retributive justice. Strictly speaking, retributive justice can never be satisfied, in the sense that the guilty can be punished as much and as long as he deserves; for this would imply that he was punished until he ceased to be guilty, or became innocent. When law is once violated, the sinner can make no satisfaction. He can never cease to be guilty, or to deserve punishment, and no possible amount of suffering renders him the less guilty or the less deserving of punishment: therefore, to satisfy retributive justice is impossible.

(2.) But, as we have seen in a former lecture, retributive justice must have inflicted on him eternal death. To suppose, therefore, that Christ suffered in amount, all that was due to the elect, is to suppose that he suffered an eternal punishment multiplied by the whole number of the elect.

3. The atonement of Christ was intended as a satisfaction of public justice.

The moral law did not originate in the divine will, but is founded in his self-existence and immutable nature. He cannot therefore repeal or alter it. To the letter of the moral law there may be exceptions. God cannot repeal the precept, and just for this reason, he cannot set aside the spirit of the sanctions. For to dispense with the sanctions were a virtual repeal of the precept. He cannot, therefore, set aside the execution of the penalty when the precept has been violated, without something being done that shall meet the demands of the true spirit of the law. "Being justified freely by his grace through the redemption that is in Christ Jesus: whom God hath set forth to be a propitiation through faith in his blood, to declare his righteousness for the remission of sins that are past, through the forbearance of God; to declare, I say, at this time his righteousness: that he might be just, and the justifier of him which believeth in Jesus."--Rom. iii. 24-26. This passage assigns the reason, or declares the design, of the atonement, to have been to justify God in the pardon of sin, or in dispensing with the execution of law. Isa. xliii. 10-12: "Yet it pleased the Lord to bruise him; he hath put him to grief: when thou shalt make his soul an offering for sin, he shall see his seed, he shall prolong his days, and the pleasure of the Lord shall prosper in his hand. He shall see of the travail of his soul, and shall be satisfied: by his knowledge shall my righteous servant justify many; for he shall bear their iniquities. Therefore will I divide him a portion with the great, and he shall divide the spoil with the strong; because he hath poured out his soul unto death: and he was numbered with the transgressors: and he bare the sin of many, and made intercession for the transgressors."

I present several further reasons why an atonement in the case of the inhabitants of this world was preferable to punishment, or to the execution of the divine law. Several reasons have already been assigned, to which I will add the following, some of which are plainly revealed in the Bible; others are plainly inferrible from what the Bible does reveal; and others still are plainly inferrible from the very nature of the case.

(1.) God's great and disinterested love to sinners themselves was a prime reason for the atonement.

John iii. 16. "For God so loved the world, that he gave his only begotten Son, that whosoever believeth in him should not perish, but have everlasting life."

(2.) His great love to the universe at large must have been another reason, inasmuch as it is impossible that the atonement should not exert an amazing influence over moral beings, in whatever world they might exist, and where the fact of atonement should be known.

(3.) Another reason for substituting the sufferings of Christ in the place of the eternal damnation of sinners, is, that an infinite amount of suffering might be prevented. The relation of Christ to the universe rendered his sufferings so infinitely valuable and influential, as an expression of God's abhorrence of sin on the one hand, and his great love to his subjects on the other, that an infinitely less amount of suffering in him than must have been inflicted on sinners, would be equally, and no doubt vastly more, influential in supporting the government of God, than the execution of the law upon them would have been. Be it borne in mind, that Christ was the lawgiver, and his suffering in behalf of sinners is to be regarded as the lawgiver and executive magistrate suffering in the behalf and stead of a rebellious province of his empire. As a governmental expedient it is easy to see the great value of such a substitute; that on the one hand it fully evinced the determination of the ruler not to yield the authority of his law, and on the other, to evince his great and disinterested love for his rebellious subjects.

(4.) By this substitution, an immense good might be gained, the eternal happiness of all that can be reclaimed from sin, together with all the augmented happiness of those who have never sinned, that must result from this glorious revelation of God.

(5.) Another reason for preferring the atonement to the punishment of sinners must have been, that sin had afforded an opportunity for the highest manifestation of virtue in God: the manifestation of forbearance, mercy, self-denial, and suffering for enemies that were within his own power, and for those from whom he could expect no equivalent in return.

It is impossible to conceive of a higher order of virtues than are exhibited in the atonement of Christ. It was vastly desirable that God should take advantage of such an opportunity to exhibit his true character, and show to the universe what was in his heart. The strength and stability of any government must depend upon the estimation in which the sovereign is held by his subjects. It was therefore indispensable, that God should improve the opportunity, which sin had afforded, to manifest and make known his true character, and thus secure the highest confidence of his subjects.

(6.) In the atonement God consulted his own happiness and his own glory. To deny himself for the salvation of sinners, was a part of his own infinite happiness, always intended by him, and therefore always enjoyed. This was not selfishness in him, as his own well-being is of infinitely greater value than that of all the universe besides; he ought so to regard and treat it, because of its supreme and intrinsic value.

(7.) The atonement would present to creatures the highest possible motives to virtue. Example is the highest moral influence that can be exerted. If God, or any other being, would make others benevolent, he must manifest benevolence himself. If the benevolence manifested in the atonement does not subdue the selfishness of sinners, their case is hopeless.

(8.) The circumstances of his government rendered an atonement necessary; as the execution of law was not, as a matter of fact, a sufficient preventive of sin. The annihilation of the wicked would not answer the purposes of government. A full revelation of mercy, blended with such an exhibition of justice, was called for by the circumstances of the universe.

(9.) To confirm holy beings. Nothing could be more highly calculated to establish and confirm the confidence, love, and obedience of holy beings, than this disinterested manifestation of love to sinners and rebels.

(10.) To confound his enemies. How could anything be more directly calculated to silence all cavils, and to shut every mouth, and forever close up all opposing lips, than such an exhibition of love and willingness to make sacrifices for sinners?

(11.) The fact, that the execution of the law of God on rebel angels had not arrested, and could not arrest, the progress of rebellion in the universe, proves that something more needed to be done, in support of the authority of law, than would be done in the execution of its penalty upon rebels. While the execution of law may have a strong tendency to prevent the beginning of rebellion among loyal subjects, and to restrain rebels themselves; yet penal inflictions do not, in fact, subdue the heart, under any government, whether human or divine.

As a matter of fact, the law was only exasperating rebels, without confirming holy beings. Paul affirmed, that the action of the law upon his own mind, while in impenitence, was to beget in him all manner of concupiscence. One grand reason for giving the law was, to develop the nature of sin, and to show that the carnal mind is not subject to the law of God, neither indeed can be. The law was therefore given that the offence might abound, that thereby it might be demonstrated, that without an atonement there could be no salvation for rebels under the government of God.

(12.) The nature, degree, and execution of the penalty of the law, made the holiness and the justice of God so prominent, as to absorb too much of public attention to be safe. Those features of his character were so fully revealed, by the execution of his law upon the rebel angels, that to have pursued the same course with the inhabitants of this world, without the offer of mercy, might have had, and doubtless would have had, an injurious influence upon the universe, by creating more of fear than of love to God and his government. Hence, a fuller revelation of the love and compassion of God was necessary, to guard against the influence of slavish fear.

His taking human nature, and obeying unto death, under such circumstances, constituted a good reason for our being treated as righteous. It is a common practice in human governments, and one that is founded in the nature and laws of mind, to reward distinguished public service by conferring favors on the children of those who have rendered this service, and treating them as if they had rendered it themselves. This is both benevolent and wise. Its governmental importance, its wisdom and excellent influence, have been most abundantly attested in the experience of nations. As a governmental transaction, this same principle prevails, and for the same reason, under the government of God. All that are Christ's children and belong to him, are received for his sake, treated with favor, and the rewards of the righteous are bestowed upon them for his sake. And the public service which he has rendered to the universe, by laying down his life for the support of the divine government, has rendered it eminently wise, that all who are united to him by faith should be treated as righteous for his sake.

LECTURE XXVI - EXTENT OF ATONEMENT

VI. For whose benefit the atonement was intended.

1. God does all things for himself; that is, he consults his own glory and happiness, as the supreme and most influential reason for all his conduct. This is wise and right in him, because his own glory and happiness are infinitely the greatest good in and to the universe. He made the atonement to satisfy himself. "God so loved the world, that he gave his only begotten Son, that whosoever believeth in him should not perish, but have everlasting life." God himself, then, was greatly benefited by the atonement: in other words, his happiness has in a great measure resulted from its contemplation, execution, and results.

2. He made the atonement for the benefit of the universe. All holy beings are, and must be, benefited by it, from its very nature, as it gives them a higher knowledge of God than ever they had before, or ever could have gained in any other way. The atonement is the greatest work that he could have wrought for them, the most blessed and excellent, and benevolent thing he could have done for them. For this reason, angels are described as desiring to look into the atonement. The inhabitants of heaven are represented as being deeply interested in the work of atonement, and those displays of the character of God that are made in it. The atonement is then no doubt one of the greatest blessings that ever God conferred upon the universe of holy beings.

3. The atonement was made for the benefit particularly of the inhabitants of this world, from its very nature, as it is calculated to benefit all the inhabitants of this world; as it is a most stupendous revelation of God to man. (Its nature is adapted to benefit all mankind. All mankind can be pardoned, if they are rightly affected and brought to repentance by it, as well as any part of mankind.)

4. All do certainly receive many blessings on account of it. It is probable that, but for the atonement, none of our race, except the first human pair, would ever have had an existence.

5. All the blessings which mankind enjoy, are conferred on them on account of the atonement of Christ; that is, God could not consistently wait on sinners, and bless, and do all that the nature of the case admits, to save them, were it not for the fact of atonement.

6. That it was made for all mankind, is evident from the fact that it is offered to all indiscriminately.

7. Sinners are universally condemned for not receiving it.

8. If the atonement is not intended for all mankind, it is impossible for us not to regard God as insincere, in making them the offer of salvation through the atonement.

9. If the atonement was made only for a part, no man can know whether he has a right to embrace it, until by a direct revelation God has made known to him that he is one of that part.

10. If ministers do not believe that it was made for all men, they cannot heartily and honestly press its acceptance upon any individual, or congregation

in the world; for they cannot assure any individual, or congregation, that there is any atonement for him or them, any more than there is for Satan.

If to this it should be replied, that for fallen angels no atonement has been made, but for some men an atonement has been made, so that it may be true of any individual that it was made for him, and if he will truly believe, he will thereby have the fact revealed, that it was, in fact, made for him; I reply, What is a sinner to believe, as a condition of salvation? Is it merely that an atonement was made for somebody? Is this saving faith? Must he not embrace it, and personally and individually commit himself to it, and to Christ?--trust in it as made for him? But how is he authorized to do this upon the supposition that the atonement was made for some men only, and perhaps for him? Is it saving faith to believe that it was possibly made for him, and by believing this possibility, will he thereby gain the evidence that it was, in fact, made for him? No, he must have the word of God for it, that it was made for him. Nothing else can warrant the casting of his soul upon it. How then is "he truly to believe," or trust in the atonement, until he has the evidence, not merely that it possibly may have been, but that it actually was made for him? The mere possibility that an atonement has been made for an individual, is no ground of saving faith. What is he to believe? Why, that of which he has proof. But the supposition is, that he has proof only that it is possible that the atonement was made for him. He has a right, then, to believe it possible that Christ died for him. And is this saving faith? No, it is not. What advantage, then, has he over Satan in this respect. Satan knows that the atonement was not made for him; the sinner upon the supposition knows that, possibly, it may have been made for him; but the latter has really no more ground for trust and reliance than the former. He might hope, but he could not rationally believe.

But upon this subject of the extent of the atonement, let the Bible speak for itself: "The next day John seeth Jesus coming unto him, and saith, Behold the Lamb of God, which taketh away the sin of the world." "For God so loved the world, that he gave his only begotten Son, that whosoever believeth in him should not perish, but have everlasting life. For God sent not his Son into the world, to condemn the world: but that the world through him might be saved." "And said unto the woman, Now we believe, not because of thy saying; for we have heard him ourselves, and know that this is indeed the Christ, the Saviour of the world."--John i. 29; iii. 16, 17; iv. 42. "Therefore, as by the offence of one, judgment came upon all men to condemnation; even so, by the righteousness of one, the free gift came upon all men unto justification of life."--Rom. v. 18. "For the love of Christ constraineth us; because we thus judge, that if one died for all, then were all deed: and that he died for all, that they which live should not henceforth live unto themselves, but unto him which died for them, and rose again."--2 Cor. v. 14, 15, "Who gave himself a ransom for all, to be testified in due time." "For therefore we both labor and suffer reproach, because we trust in the living God, who is the Saviour of all men, especially of those that believe."--1 Tim. ii. 6; iv. 10. "And he is the propitiation for our sins; and not for ours only, but also for the sins of the whole world."--1 John ii. 2.

That the atonement is sufficient for all men, and, in that sense, general, as opposed to particular, is also evident from the fact, that the invitations and promises of the gospel are addressed to all men, and all are freely offered salvation through Christ. "Look unto me, and be ye saved, all the ends of the earth: for I am God and there is none else." "Ho! every one that thirsteth, come ye to the waters, and he that hath no money; come ye, buy and eat; yea, come, buy wine and milk without money and without price. Wherefore do ye spend money for that which is not bread, and your labor for that which satisfieth not? Hearken diligently unto me, and eat ye that which is good, and let your soul delight itself in fatness. Incline your ear, and come unto me: hear, and your soul shall live; and I will make an everlasting covenant with you, even the sure mercies of David."--Isa. xlv. 22; lv. 1-3. "Come unto me all ye that are weary and heavy laden, and I will give you rest. Take my yoke upon you, and learn of me; for I am meek and lowly in heart; and ye shall find rest unto your souls. For my yoke is easy, and my burden is light." "Again, he sent forth other servants, saying, Tell them which are bidden, Behold, I have prepared my dinner; my oxen and my fatlings are killed, and all things are ready; come unto the marriage."--Matt. xi. 28-30; xxii. 4. "And sent his servant at supper time to say to them that were bidden, Come, for all things are now ready."--Luke xiv. 17. "In the last day, the great day of the feast, Jesus stood and cried, saying, If any man thirst, let him come unto me, and drink."--John vii. 37. "Behold, I stand at the door, and knock; if any man hear my voice, and open the door, I will come in to him, and will sup with him, and he with me." "And the Spirit and the bride say, Come. And let him that heareth say, Come. And let him that is athirst come. And whosoever will, let him take the water of life freely."--Rev. iii. 20; xxii. 17.

Again: I infer that the atonement was made, and is sufficient, for all men, from the fact that God not only invites all, but expostulates with them for not accepting his invitations. "Wisdom crieth without; she uttereth her voice in the streets: she crieth in the chief place of concourse, in the openings of the gates; in the city she uttereth her words, saying, How long ye simple ones, will ye love simplicity? and the scorners delight in their scorning, and fools hate knowledge? Turn you at my reproof: behold I will pour out my Spirit unto you, I will make known my words unto you."--Prov. i. 20-23. "Come now, and let us reason together, saith the Lord: though your sins be as scarlet, they shall be white as snow, though they be red like crimson, they shall be as wool."--Isaiah i. 18. "Thus saith the Lord, thy Redeemer, the Holy One of Israel, I am the Lord thy God which teacheth thee to profit, which leadeth thee by the way that thou shouldest go. Oh that thou hadst hearkened to my commandments! then had thy peace been as a river, and thy righteousness as the waves of the sea."--Isaiah xlviii. 17, 18. "Say unto them, as I live, saith the Lord God, I have no pleasure in the death of the wicked; but that the wicked turn from his way and live; turn ye, turn ye from your evil ways; for why will ye die, O house of Israel?"--Ezek. xxxiii. 11. "Hear ye now what the Lord saith: Arise, contend thou before the mountains, and let the hills hear thy voice. Hear ye, O mountains, the Lord's controversy, and ye strong foundations of the earth; for the Lord hath a controversy with his people, and he will plead with Israel. O my people, what have I done unto thee? and wherein have I wearied thee? testify against me."--Micah vi. 1-3. "O Jerusalem, Jerusalem, thou that killest the prophets, and stonest them which are sent unto thee, how often would I have gathered thy children together, even as a hen gathereth her chickens under her wings, and ye would not!"--Matt. xxiii. 37.

Again: the same inference is forced upon us by the fact that God complains of sinners for rejecting his overtures of mercy: "Because I have called, and ye refused; I have stretched out my hand, and no man regarded."--Prov. i. 24. "But they refused to hearken, and pulled away the shoulder, and stopped their ears, that they should not hear. Yea, they made their hearts as an adamant stone, lest they should hear the law, and the words which the Lord of hosts hath sent in his Spirit by the former prophets: therefore came a great wrath from the Lord of hosts. Therefore it is come to pass; that as he cried and they would not hear: so they cried, and I would not hear, saith the Lord of hosts."--Zechariah vii. 11, 12, 13. "The kingdom of heaven is like unto a certain king which made a marriage for his son. And sent forth his servant to call them that were bidden to the wedding: and they would not come. Again, he sent forth other servants, saying, Tell them which are bidden, Behold I have prepared my dinner; my oxen and my fatlings are killed, and all things are ready; come unto the marriage. But they made light of it, and went their ways, one to his farm, another to his merchandise: and the remnant took his servants, and treated them spitefully, and slew them."--Matthew xxii. 2, 3, 4, 5, 6. "And sent his servant at supper-time to say to them that were bidden, Come; for all things are now ready. And they all with one consent began to make excuse. The first said unto him, I have bought a piece of ground, and I must needs go and see it: I pray thee have me excused. And another said, I have bought five yoke of oxen, and I go to prove them: I pray thee have me excused. And another said, I have married a wife; and therefore I cannot come."--Luke xiv. 17, 18, 19, 20. "And ye will not come to me, that ye might have life."--John v. 40. "Ye stiff-necked and uncircumcised in heart and ears, ye do always resist the Holy Ghost: as your fathers did, so do ye."--Acts vii. 51. "And as he reasoned of righteousness, temperance, and judgment to come, Felix trembled, and answered, Go thy way for this time; when I have a convenient season I will call for thee."--Acts xxiv. 25.

VII. I now proceed to answer objections.

1. Objection to the fact of atonement. It is said, that the doctrine of atonement represents God as unmerciful. To this I answer,

(1.) This objection supposes that the atonement was demanded to satisfy retributive instead of public justice.

(2.) The atonement was the exhibition of a merciful disposition. It was because God was disposed to pardon that he consented to give his own Son to die as the substitute of sinners.

(3.) The atonement is infinitely the most illustrious exhibition of mercy ever made in the universe. The mere pardon of sin, as an act of sovereign mercy, could not have been compared, had it been possible, with the merciful disposition displayed in the atonement itself.

2. It is objected that the atonement is unnecessary.

The testimony of the world and of the consciences of all men are against this objection. This is universally attested by their expiatory sacrifices. These, as has been said, have been offered by nearly every nation of whose religious history we have any reliable account. This shows that human beings are universally conscious of being sinners, and under the government of a sin-hating God; that their intelligence demands either the punishment of sinners, or that a substitute should be offered to public justice; that they all have the idea that substitution is conceivable, and hence they offer their sacrifices as expiatory. A heathen philosopher can answer this objection, and rebuke the folly of him who makes it.

3. It is objected, that it is unjust to punish an innocent being instead of the guilty.

(1.) Yes, it would not only be unjust, but it is impossible with God to punish an innocent moral agent at all. Punishment implies guilt. An innocent being may suffer, but he cannot be punished. Christ voluntarily "suffered, the just for the unjust." He had a right to exercise this self-denial; and as it was by his own voluntary consent, no injustice was done to any one.

(2.) If he had no right to make an atonement, he had no right to consult and promote his own happiness and the happiness of others; for it is said that "for the joy that was set before him, he endured the cross, despising the shame."

4. It is objected that the doctrine of atonement is utterly incredible.

To this I have replied in a former lecture; but will here again state, that it would be utterly incredible upon any other supposition, than that God is love. But if God is love, as the Bible expressly affirms that he is, the work of atonement is just what might be expected of him, under the circumstances; and the doctrine of atonement is, then the most reasonable doctrine in the universe.

5. It is objected to the doctrine of atonement, that it is of a demoralizing tendency.

There is a broad distinction between the natural tendency of a thing, and such an abuse of a good thing as to make it the instrument of evil. The best things and doctrines may be, and often are, abused, and their natural tendency perverted. Although the doctrine of the atonement may be abused, yet its natural tendency is the direct opposite of demoralizing. Is the manifestation of infinitely disinterested love naturally calculated to beget enmity? Who does not know that the natural tendency of manifested love is to excite love in return? Those who have the most cordially believed in the atonement, have exhibited the purest morality that has ever been in this world; while the rejecters of the atonement, almost without exception, exhibit a loose morality. This is, as might be expected, from the very nature and moral influence of atonement.

6. To a general atonement, it is objected that the Bible represents Christ as laying down his life for his sheep, or for the elect only, and not for all mankind.

(1.) It does indeed represent Christ as laying down his life for his sheep, and also for all mankind. 1 John ii. 2.--"And he is the propitiation for our sins; and not for ours only, but also for the sins of the whole world." John iii. 17--"For God sent not his Son into the world to condemn the world; but that the world through him might be saved." Heb. ii. 9.--"But we see Jesus, who was made a little lower than the angels for the suffering of death, crowned with glory and honor; that he, by the grace of God, should taste death for every man."

(2.) Those who object to the general atonement, take substantially the same course to evade this doctrine, that Unitarians do to set aside the doctrine of the Trinity and the Divinity of Christ. They quote those passages that prove the unity of God and the humanity of Christ, and then take it for granted that they have disproved the doctrine of the Trinity and Christ's Divinity. The asserters of limited atonement, in like manner, quote those passages that prove that Christ died for the elect and for his saints, and then take it for granted that he died for none else. To the Unitarian, we reply, we admit the unity of God and the humanity of Christ, and the full meaning of those passages of scripture which you quote in proof of these doctrines; but we insist that this is not the whole truth, but that there are still other passages which prove the doctrine of the

Trinity, and the Divinity of Christ. Just so to the asserters of limited atonement, we reply, we believe that Christ laid down his life for his sheep, as well as you; but we also believe that "he tasted death for every man." John iii. 16.--"For God so loved the world, that he gave his only begotten Son, that whosoever believeth in him should not perish, but have everlasting life."

7. To the doctrine of general atonement it is objected, that it would be folly in God to provide what he knew would be rejected; and that to suffer Christ to die for those who, he foresaw, would not repent, would be a useless expenditure of the blood and suffering of Christ.

(1.) This objection assumes that the atonement was a literal payment of a debt, which we have seen does not consist with the nature of the atonement.

(2.) If sinners do not accept it, in no view can the atonement be useless, as the great compassion of God, in providing an atonement and offering them mercy, will forever exalt his character, in the estimation of holy beings, greatly strengthen his government, and therefore benefit the whole universe.

(3.) If all men rejected the atonement, it would, nevertheless, be of infinite value to the universe, as the most glorious revelation of God that was ever made.

8. To the general atonement it is objected, that it implies universal salvation.

It would indeed imply this, upon the supposition that the atonement is the literal payment of a debt. It was upon this view of the atonement, that Universalism first took its stand. Universalists taking it for granted, that Christ had paid the debt of those for whom he died, and finding it fully revealed in the Bible that he died for all mankind, naturally, and if this were correct, properly, inferred the doctrine of universal salvation. But we have seen, that this is not the nature of atonement. Therefore, this inference falls to the ground.

9. It is objected that, if the atonement was not a payment of the debt of sinners, but general in its nature, as we have maintained, it secures the salvation of no one. It is true, that the atonement, of itself, does not secure the salvation of any one; but the promise and oath of God, that Christ shall have a seed to serve him, provide that security.

LECTURE XXVII - REGENERATION

In the examination of this subject I will--

I. Point out the common distinction between regeneration and conversion.

1. Regeneration is the term used by some theologians to express the divine agency in changing the heart. With them regeneration does not include and imply the activity of the subject, but rather excludes it. These theologians, as will be seen in its place, hold that a change of heart is first effected by the Holy Spirit while the subject is passive, which change lays a foundation for the exercise, by the subject, of repentance, faith, and love.

2. The term conversion with them expresses the activity and turning of the subject, after regeneration is effected by the Holy Spirit. Conversion with them does not include or imply the agency of the Holy Spirit, but expresses only the activity of the subject. With them the Holy Spirit first regenerates or changes the heart, after which the sinner turns or converts himself. So that God and the subject work each in turn. God first changes the heart, and as a consequence, the subject afterwards converts himself or turns to God. Thus the subject is passive in regeneration, but active in conversion.

When we come to the examination of the philosophical theories of regeneration, we shall see that the views of these theologians respecting regeneration result naturally and necessarily from their holding the dogma of constitutional moral depravity, which we have recently examined. Until their views on that subject are corrected, no change can be expected in their views of this subject.

II. The assigned reasons for this distinction.

1. The original term plainly expresses and implies other than the agency of the subject.

2. We need and must adopt a term that will express the Divine agency.

3. Regeneration is expressly ascribed to the Holy Spirit.

4. Conversion, as it implies and expresses the activity and turning of the subject, does not include and imply any Divine agency, and therefore does not imply or express what is intended by regeneration.

5. As two agencies are actually employed in the regeneration and conversion of a sinner, it is necessary to adopt terms that will clearly teach this fact, and clearly distinguish between the agency of God and of the creature.

6. The terms regeneration and conversion aptly express this distinction, and therefore should be theologically employed.

III. The objections to this distinction.

The original term γενναω, with its derivatives, may be rendered, (1.) To beget. (2.) To bear or bring forth. (3.) To be begotten. (4.) To be born, or brought forth.

2. Regeneration is, in the Bible, the same as the new birth.

3. To be born again is the same thing, in the Bible use of the term, as to have a new heart, to be a new creature, to pass from death unto life. In other words, to be born again is to have a new moral character, to become holy. To

regenerate is to make holy. To be born of God, no doubt expresses and includes the Divine agency, but it also includes and expresses that which the Divine agency is employed in effecting, namely, making the sinner holy. Certainly, a sinner is not regenerated whose moral character is unchanged. If he were, how could it be truly said, that whosoever is born of God overcometh the world, doth not commit sin, cannot sin, etc.? If regeneration does not imply and include a change of moral character in the subject, how can regeneration be made the condition of salvation? The fact is, the term regeneration, or the being born of God, is designed to express primarily and principally the thing done, that is, the making of a sinner holy, and expresses also the fact, that God's agency induces the change. Throw out the idea of what is done, that is, the change of moral character in the subject, and he would not be born again, he would not be regenerated, and it could not be truly said, in such a case, that God had regenerated him.

It has been objected, that the term really means and expresses only the Divine agency; and, only by way of implication, embraces the idea of a change of moral character and of course of activity in the subject. To this I reply--

(1.) That if it really expresses only the Divine agency, it leaves out of view the thing effected by Divine agency.

(2.) That it really and fully expresses not only the Divine agency, but also that which this agency accomplishes.

(3.) The thing which the agency of God brings about, is a new or spiritual birth, a resurrection from spiritual death, the inducing of a new and holy life. The thing done is the prominent idea expressed or intended by the term.

(4.) The thing done implies the turning or activity of the subject. It is nonsense to affirm that his moral character is changed without any activity or agency of his own. Passive holiness is impossible. Holiness is obedience to the law of God, the law of love, and of course consists in the activity of the creature.

(5.) We have said that regeneration is synonymous, in the Bible, with a new heart. But sinners are required to make to themselves a new heart, which they could not do, if they were not active in this change. If the work is a work of God, in such a sense, that He must first regenerate the heart or soul before the agency of the sinner begins, it were absurd and unjust to require hint to make to himself a new heart, until he is first regenerated.

Regeneration is ascribed to man in the gospel, which it could not be, if the term were designed to express only the agency of the Holy Spirit. "For though ye have ten thousand instructors in Christ, yet have ye not many fathers; for in Christ Jesus I have begotten you through the gospel."--1 Cor. iv. 15.

(6.) Conversion is spoken of in the Bible as the work of another than the subject of it, and cannot therefore have been designed to express only the activity of the subject of it.

(i.) It is ascribed to the word of God.--"The law of the Lord is perfect, converting the soul: the testimony of the Lord is sure, making wise the simple."--Ps. xix. 7.

(ii.) To man. "Brethren, if any of you do err from the truth, and one convert him; let him know, that he which converteth the sinner from the error of his way shall save a soul from death, and shall hide a multitude of sins."--James v. 19, 20.

Both conversion and regeneration are sometimes in the Bible ascribed to God, sometimes to man, and sometimes to the subject; which shows clearly that the distinction under examination is arbitrary and theological, rather than biblical.

The fact is, that both terms imply the simultaneous exercise of both human and Divine agency. The fact that a new heart is the thing done, demonstrates the activity of the subject; and the word regeneration, or the expression "born of the Holy Spirit," asserts the Divine agency. The same is true of conversion, or the turning of the sinner to God. God is said to turn him and he is said to turn himself. God draws him, and he follows. In both alike God and man are both active, and their activity is simultaneous. God works or draws, and the sinner yields or turns, or which is the same thing, changes his heart, or, in other words, is born again. The sinner is dead in trespasses and sins. God calls on him, "Awake thou that sleepest, and arise from the dead, and Christ shall give thee light."--Eph. v. 14. God calls; the sinner hears and answers, Here am I. God says, Arise from the dead. The sinner puts forth his activity, and God draws him into life; or rather, God draws, and the sinner comes forth to life.

(7.) The distinction set up is not only not recognized in the Bible, but is plainly of most injurious tendency, for two reasons:--

(i.) It assumes and inculcates a false philosophy of depravity and regeneration.

(ii.) It leads the sinner to wait to be regenerated, before he repents or turns to God. It is of most fatal tendency to represent the sinner as under a necessity of waiting to be passively regenerated, before he gives himself to God.

As the distinction is not only arbitrary, but anti-scriptural and injurious, and inasmuch as it is founded in, and is designed to teach a philosophy false and pernicious on the subject of depravity and regeneration, I shall drop and discard the distinction; and in our investigations henceforth, let it be understood, that I use regeneration and conversion as synonymous terms.

IV. What regeneration is not.

It is not a change in the substance of soul or body. If it were, sinners could not be required to effect it. Such a change would not constitute a change of moral character. No such change is needed, as the sinner has all the faculties and natural attributes requisite to render perfect obedience to God. All he needs is to be induced to use these powers and attributes as he ought. The words conversion and regeneration do not imply any change of substance, but only a change of moral state or of moral character. The terms are not used to express a physical, but a moral change. Regeneration does not express or imply the creation of any new faculties or attributes of nature, nor any change whatever in the constitution of body or mind. I shall remark further upon this point when we come to the examination of the philosophical theories of regeneration before alluded to.

V. What regeneration is.

It has been said that regeneration and a change of heart are identical. It is important to inquire into the scriptural use of the term heart. The term, like most others, is used in the Bible in various senses. The heart is often spoken of in the Bible, not only as possessing moral character, but as being the source of moral action, or as the fountain from which good and evil actions flow, and of course as constituting the fountain of holiness or of sin, or, in other words still, as comprehending, strictly speaking, the whole of moral character. "But those things which proceed out of the mouth come forth from the heart; and they defile the man. For out of the heart proceed evil thoughts, murders, adulteries, fornications, thefts, false witness, blasphemies."--Matt. xv. 18, 19. "O generation of vipers, how can ye, being evil, speak good things? for out of the abundance of the heart the mouth speaketh. A good man out of the good treasure of the heart bringeth forth good things: and an evil man out of the evil treasure bringeth forth evil things."--Matt. xii. 34, 35. When the heart is thus represented as possessing moral character, and as the fountain of good and evil, it cannot mean,--

1. The bodily organ that propels the blood.

2. It cannot mean the substance of the soul or mind itself: substance cannot in itself possess moral character.

3. It is not any faculty or natural attribute.

4. It cannot consist in any constitutional taste, relish, or appetite, for these cannot in themselves have moral character.

5. It is not the sensibility or feeling faculty of the mind: for we have seen, that moral character cannot be predicated of it. It is true, and let it be understood, that the term heart is used in the Bible in these senses, but net when the heart is spoken of as the fountain of moral action. When the heart is represented as possessing moral character, the word cannot be meant to designate any involuntary state of mind. For neither the substance of soul or body, nor any involuntary state of mind can, by any possibility, possess moral character in itself. The very idea of moral character implies, and suggests the idea of, a free action or intention. To deny this, were to deny a first truth.

6. The term heart, when applied to mind, is figurative, and means something in the mind that has some point of resemblance to the bodily organ of that name, and a consideration of the function of the bodily organ will suggest the true idea of the heart of the mind. The heart of the body propels the vital current, and sustains organic life. It is the fountain from which the vital fluid flows, from which either life or death may flow, according to the state of the blood. The mind as well as the body has a heart which, as we have seen, is represented as a fountain, or as an efficient propelling influence, out of which flows good or evil, according as the heart is good or evil. This heart is represented, not only as the source or fountain of good and evil, but as being either good or evil in itself, as constituting the character of man, and not merely as being capable of moral character.

It is also represented as something over which we have control, for which we are responsible, and which, in case it is wicked, we are bound to change on pain of death. Again: the heart, in the sense in which we are considering it, is that, the radical change of which constitutes a radical change of moral character. This is plain from Matthew xii. 34, 35, and xv. 18, 19, already considered.

7. Our own consciousness, then, must inform us that the heart of the mind that possesses these characteristics, can be nothing else than the supreme ultimate intention of the soul. Regeneration is represented in the Bible as constituting a radical change of character, as the resurrection from a death in sin, as the beginning of a new and spiritual life, as constituting a new creature, as a new creation, not a physical, but a moral or spiritual creation, as conversion, or turning to God, as giving God the heart, as loving God with all our heart, and our neighbor as ourselves. Now we have seen abundantly, that

moral character belongs to, or is an attribute of, the ultimate choice or intention of the soul.

Regeneration then is a radical change of the ultimate intention, and, of course, of the end or object of life. We have seen, that the choice of an end is efficient in producing executive volitions, or the use of means to obtain its end. A selfish ultimate choice is, therefore, a wicked heart, out of which flows every evil; and a benevolent ultimate choice is a good heart, out of which flows every good and commendable deed.

Regeneration, to have the characteristics ascribed to it in the Bible, must consist in a change in the attitude of the will, or a change in its ultimate choice, intention, or preference; a change from selfishness to benevolence; from choosing self-gratification as the supreme and ultimate end of life, to the supreme and ultimate choice of the highest wellbeing of God and of the universe; from a state of entire consecration to self-interest, self-indulgence, self-gratification for its own sake or as an end, and as the supreme end of life, to a state of entire consecration to God, and to the interests of his kingdom as the supreme and ultimate end of life.

VI. The universal necessity of regeneration.

1. The necessity of regeneration as a condition of salvation must be co-extensive with moral depravity. This has been shown to be universal among the unregenerate moral agents of our race. It surely is impossible, that a world or a universe of unholy or selfish beings should be happy. It is impossible that heaven should be made up of selfish beings. It is intuitively certain that without benevolence or holiness no moral being can be ultimately happy. Without regeneration, a selfish soul can by no possibility be fitted either for the employments, or for the enjoyments, of heaven.

2. The scriptures expressly teach the universal necessity of regeneration. "Jesus answered and said unto him, Verily, verily, I say unto thee, Except a man be born again, he cannot see the kingdom of God."--John iii. 3. "For in Christ Jesus neither circumcision availeth any thing, nor uncircumcision, but a new creature."--Gal. vi. 15.

VII. Agencies employed in regeneration.

1. The scriptures often ascribe regeneration to the Spirit of God. "Jesus answered, Verily, verily, I say unto thee, Except a man be born of water and of the Spirit, he cannot enter into the kingdom of God. That which is born of the flesh is flesh; and that which is born of the Spirit is spirit."--John iii. 5, 6. "Which were born, not of blood, nor of the will of the flesh, nor of the will of man, but of God."--John i. 15.

2. We have seen that the subject is active in regeneration, that regeneration consists in the sinner changing his ultimate choice, intention, preference; or in changing from selfishness to love or benevolence; or, in other words, in turning from the supreme choice of self-gratification, to the supreme love of God and the equal love of his neighbor. Of course the subject of regeneration must be an agent in the work.

3. There are generally other agents, one or more human beings concerned in persuading the sinner to turn. The Bible recognizes both the subject and the preacher as agents in the work. Thus Paul says: "I have begotten you through the gospel." Here the same word is used which is used in another case, where regeneration is ascribed to God.

Again an apostle says, "Ye have purified your souls by obeying the truth." Here the work is ascribed to the subject. There are then always two, and generally more than two agents employed in effecting the work. Several theologians have held that regeneration is the work of the Holy Spirit alone. In proof of this they cite those passages that ascribe it to God. But I might just as lawfully insist that it is the work of man alone, and quote those passages that ascribe it to man, to substantiate my position. Or I might assert that it is alone the work of the subject, and in proof of this position quote those passages that ascribe it to the subject. Or again, I might assert that it is effected by the truth alone, and quote such passages as the following to substantiate my position: "Of his own will begat He us with the word of truth, that we should be a kind of first-fruits of his creatures."--James i. 18. "Being born again, not of corruptible seed, but of incorruptible by the word of God, which liveth and abideth forever."--1 Peter i. 23.

It has been common to regard the third person as a mere instrument in the work. But the fact is, he is a willing, designing, responsible agent, as really so as God or the subject is.

If it be inquired how the Bible can consistently ascribe regeneration at one time to God, at another to the subject, at another to the truth, at another to a third person; the answer is to be sought in the nature of the work. The work accomplished is a change of choice, in respect to an end or the end of life. The sinner whose choice is changed, must of course act. The end to be chosen must be clearly and forcibly presented; this is the work of the third person, and of the Holy Spirit. The Spirit takes of the things of Christ and shows them to the soul. The truth is employed, or it is truth which must necessarily be employed, as an instrument to induce a change of choice.

VIII. Instrumentalities employed in the work.

1. Truth. This must, from the nature of regeneration, be employed in effecting it, for regeneration is nothing else than the will being duly influenced by truth.

2. There may be, and often are, many providences concerned in enlightening the mind, and in inducing regeneration. These are instrumentalities. They are means or instruments of presenting the truth. Mercies, judgments, men, measures, and in short all those things that conduce to enlightening the mind, are instrumentalities employed in effecting it.

Those who hold to physical or constitutional moral depravity must hold, of course, to constitutional regeneration; and, of course, consistency compels them to maintain that there is but one agent employed in regeneration, and that is the Holy Spirit, and that no instrument whatever is employed, because the work is, according to them, an act of creative power; that the very nature is changed, and of course no instrument can be employed, any more than in the creation of the world. These theologians have affirmed, over and over again, that regeneration is a miracle; that there is no tendency whatever in the gospel, however presented, and whether presented by God or man, to regenerate the heart. Dr. Griffin, in his Park Street Lectures, maintains that the gospel, in its natural and necessary tendency, creates and perpetuates only opposition to, and hatred of God, until the heart is changed by the Holy Spirit. He understands the carnal mind to be not a voluntary state, not a minding of the flesh, but the very nature and constitution of the mind; and that enmity against God is a part, attribute, or appetite of the nature itself. Consequently, he must deny the adaptability of the gospel to regenerate the soul. It has been proclaimed by this class of theologians, times without number, that there is no philosophical connection between the preaching of the gospel and the regeneration of sinners, no adaptedness in the gospel to produce that result; but, on the contrary, that it is adapted to produce an opposite result. The favorite illustrations of their views have been Ezekiel's prophesying over the dry bones, and Christ's restoring sight to the blind man by putting clay on his eyes. Ezekiel's prophesying over the dry bones had no tendency to quicken them, they say. And the clay used by the Saviour was calculated rather to destroy than to restore sight. This shows how easy it is for men to adopt a pernicious and absurd philosophy, and then to find, or think they find, it supported by the Bible. What must be the effect of inculcating the dogma, that the gospel has nothing to do with regenerating the sinner? Instead of telling him that regeneration is nothing else than his embracing the gospel, to tell him that he must wait, and first have his constitution recreated before he can possibly do anything but oppose God! This is to tell him the greatest and most abominable and ruinous of falsehoods. It is to mock his intelligence. What! call on him, on pain of eternal death, to believe; to embrace the gospel; to love God with all his heart, and at the same time represent him as entirely helpless, and constitutionally the enemy of God and of the gospel, and as being under the necessity of waiting for God to regenerate his nature, before it is possible for him to do otherwise than to hate God with all his heart!

IX. In regeneration the subject is both passive and active.

1. That he is active is plain from what has been said, and from the very nature of the change.

2. That he is, at the same time, passive, is plain from the fact that he acts, only when and as he is acted upon. That is he is passive in the perception of the truth presented by the Holy Spirit. I know that this perception is no part of regeneration. But it is simultaneous with regeneration. It induces regeneration. It is the condition and the occasion of regeneration. Therefore the subject of regeneration must be a passive recipient or percipient of the truth presented by the Holy Spirit, at the moment, and during the act of regeneration. The Spirit acts upon him through or by the truth: thus far he is passive. He closes with the truth: thus far he is active. What a mistake those theologians have fallen into who represent the subject as altogether passive in regeneration! This rids the sinner at once of the conviction of any duty or responsibility about it. It is wonderful that such an absurdity should have been so long maintained in the church. But while it is maintained, it is no wonder that sinners are not converted to God. While the sinner believes this, it is impossible, if he has it in mind, that he should be regenerated. He stands and waits for God to do what God requires him to do, and which no one can do for him. Neither God, nor any other being, can regenerate him, if he will not turn. If he will not change his choice, it is impossible that it should be changed. Sinners who have been taught thus and have believed what they have been taught, would never have been regenerated had not the Holy Spirit drawn off their attention from this error, and ere they were aware, induced them to close in with the offer of life.

X. What is implied in regeneration.

1. The nature of the change shows that it must be instantaneous. It is a change of choice, or of intention. This must be instantaneous. The preparatory

work of conviction and enlightening the mind may have been gradual and progressive. But when regeneration occurs, it must be instantaneous.

2. It implies an entire present change of moral character, that is, a change from entire sinfulness to entire holiness. We have seen that it consists in a change from selfishness to benevolence. We have also seen that selfishness and benevolence cannot co-exist in the same mind; that selfishness is a state of supreme and entire consecration to self; that benevolence is a state of entire and supreme consecration to God and the good of the universe. Regeneration, then, surely implies an entire change of moral character.

Again: the Bible represents regeneration as a dying to sin and becoming alive to God. Death in sin is total depravity. This is generally admitted. Death to sin and becoming alive to God, must imply entire present holiness.

3. The scriptures represent regeneration as the condition of salvation in such a sense, that if the subject should die immediately after regeneration, and without any further change, he would go immediately to heaven.

Again: the scriptures require only perseverance in the first love, as the condition of salvation, in ease the regenerate soul should live long in the world subsequently to regeneration.

4. When the scriptures require us to grow in grace, and in the knowledge of the Lord Jesus Christ, this does not imply that there is yet sin remaining in the regenerate heart which we are required to put away by degrees. But the spirit of the requirement must be, that we should acquire as much knowledge as we can of our moral relations, and continue to conform to all truth as fast as we know it. This, and nothing else, is implied in abiding in our first love, or abiding in Christ, living and walking in the Spirit.

LECTURE XXVIII - REGENERATION

XI. Philosophical theories of regeneration.

The principal theories that have been advocated, so far as my knowledge extends, are the following:--

1. The taste scheme. 2. The divine efficiency scheme. 3. The susceptibility scheme. 4. The divine moral suasion scheme.

1. The taste scheme.

This theory is based upon that view of mental philosophy which regards the mental heart as identical with the sensibility. Moral depravity, according to this school, consists in a constitutional relish, taste, or craving for sin. They hold the doctrine of original sin--of a sinful nature or constitution, as was shown in my lectures on moral depravity. The heart of the mind, in the estimation of this school, is not identical with choice or intention. They hold that it does not consist in any voluntary state of mind, but that it lies back of, and controls voluntary action, or the actions of the will. The wicked heart, according to them, consists in an appetency or constitutional taste for sin, and with them, the appetites, passions, and propensities of human nature in its fallen state, are in themselves sinful. They often illustrate their ideas of the sinful taste, craving, or appetite for sin, by reference to the craving of carnivorous animals for flesh.

A change of heart, in the view of this philosophy, must consist in a change of constitution. It must be a physical change, and wrought by a physical, as distinguished from a moral agency. It is a change wrought by the direct and physical power of the Holy Spirit in the constitution of the soul, changing its susceptibilities, implanting or creating a new taste, relish, appetite; craving for, or love of, holiness. It is, as they express it, the implantation of a new principle of holiness. It is described as a creation of a new taste or principle, as an infusion of a holy principle, etc. This scheme, of course, holds and teaches that, in regeneration, the subject is entirely passive. With this school, regeneration is exclusively the work of the Holy Spirit, the subject having no agency in it. It is an operation performed upon him, may be, while he is asleep, or in a fit of derangement, while he is entirely passive, or perhaps when at the moment he is engaged in flagrant rebellion against God. The agency by which this work is wrought, according to them, is sovereign, irresistible, and creative. They hold that there are of course no means of regeneration, as it is a direct act of creation. They hold the distinction already referred to and examined, between regeneration and conversion; that when the Holy Spirit has performed the sovereign operation and implanted the new principle, then the subject is active in conversion, or in turning to God.

They hold that the soul, in its very nature, is enmity against God; that therefore the gospel has no tendency to regenerate or convert the soul to God; but, on the contrary, that previous to regeneration by the sovereign and physical agency of the Holy Spirit, every exhibition of God made in the gospel, tends only to inflame and provoke this constitutional enmity.

They hold, that when the sinful taste, relish, or craving for sin is weakened, for they deny that it is ever wholly destroyed in this life, or while the soul continues connected with the body, and a holy taste, relish, or craving is implanted or infused by the Holy Spirit into the constitution of the soul, then, and not till then, the gospel has a tendency to turn or convert the sinner from the error of his ways.

As I have said, their philosophy of moral depravity is the basis of their philosophy of regeneration. It assumes the dogma of original sin, as taught in the Presbyterian Confession of Faith, and attempts to harmonize the philosophy of regeneration with that philosophy of sin, or moral depravity.

Upon this scheme or theory of regeneration, I remark,

(1.) That it has been sufficiently refuted in the lectures on moral depravity. If, as was then shown, moral depravity is altogether voluntary, and consists in selfishness, or in a voluntary state of mind, this philosophy of regeneration is of course without foundation.

(2.) It was shown in the lectures on moral depravity, that sin is not chosen for its own sake,--that there is no constitutional relish, taste, or craving for sin,--that in sinful choice, sin is not the end or object chosen, but that self-gratification is chosen, and that this choice is sinful. If this is so, then the whole philosophy of the taste scheme turns out to be utterly baseless.

The taste, relish, or craving, of which this philosophy speaks, is not a taste, relish or craving for sin, but for certain things and objects, the enjoyment of which is, to a certain extent, and upon certain conditions, lawful. But when the will prefers the gratification of taste or appetite to higher interests, this choice or act of will is sin. The sin never lies in the appetite, but in the will's consent to unlawful indulgence.

(3.) This philosophy confounds appetite or temptation to unlawful indulgence, with sin. Nay, it represents sin as consisting mostly, if not altogether, in that which is only temptation.

(4.) It throws the blame of unregeneracy upon God. If the sinner is passive, and has no agency in it; if it consists in what this philosophy teaches, and is accomplished in the manner which this theory represents, it is self-evident that God alone is responsible for the fact, that any sinner is unregenerate.

(5.) It renders holiness after regeneration physically necessary, just as sin was before, and perseverance also as physically necessary, and falling from grace as a natural impossibility. In this case holy exercises and living are only the gratification of a constitutional appetite, implanted in regeneration.

Let us consider next,--

2. The divine efficiency scheme or theory.

This scheme is based upon, or rather is only a carrying out of, an ancient heathen philosophy, bearing the same name. This ancient philosophy denies second causes, and teaches that what we call laws of nature are nothing else than the mode of divine operation. It denies that the universe would even exist for a moment, if the divine upholding were withdrawn. It maintains that the universe exists only by an act of present and perpetual creation. It denies that matter, or mind, has in itself any inherent properties that can originate laws or motions; that all action, whether of matter or mind, is the necessary result of direct divine irresistible efficiency or power; that this is not only true of the natural universe, but also of all the exercises and actions of moral agents in all worlds.

The abettors of the divine efficiency scheme of regeneration apply this philosophy especially to moral agents. They hold, that all the exercises and actions of moral agents in all worlds, and whether those exercises be holy or sinful, are produced by a divine efficiency, or by a direct act of Omnipotence; that holy and sinful acts are alike effects of an irresistible cause, and that this cause is the power and agency, or efficiency, of God.

This philosophy denies constitutional moral depravity, or original sin, and maintains that moral character belongs alone to the exercises or choices of the will; that regeneration does not consist in the creation of any new taste, relish, or craving, nor in the implantation or infusion of any new principles in the soul: but that it consists in a choice conformed to the law of God, or in a change from selfishness to disinterested benevolence; that this change is effected by a direct act of divine power or efficiency, as irresistible as any creative act whatever. This philosophy teaches, that the moral character of every moral agent, whether holy or sinful, is formed by an agency as direct, as sovereign, and as irresistible, as that which first gave existence to the universe; that true submission to God implies the hearty consent of the will to have the character thus formed, and then to be treated accordingly, for the glory of God.

To this theory I make the following objections:--

(1.) It tends to produce and perpetuate a sense of divine injustice. To create a character by an agency as direct and irresistible as that of the creation of the world itself, and then treat moral beings according to that character so formed, is wholly inconsistent with all our ideas of justice.

(2.) It contradicts human consciousness. I know it is said, that consciousness only gives our mental actions and states, but not the cause of them. This I deny, and affirm that consciousness not only gives us our mental actions and states, but it also gives us the cause of them; especially it gives the fact, that we ourselves are the sovereign and efficient causes of the choices and actions of our will. I am as conscious of originating in a sovereign manner my choices, as I am of the choices themselves. We cannot but affirm to ourselves, that we are the efficient causes of our own choices and volitions.

(3.) The philosophy in question, really represents God as the only agent, in any proper sense of that term, in the universe. If God produces the exercises of moral beings in the manner represented by this philosophy, then they are in fact no more agents than the planets are agents. If their exercises are all directly produced by the power of God, it is ridiculous to call them agents. What we generally call moral beings and moral agents, are no more so than the winds and the waves, or any other substance or thing in the universe.

(4.) If this theory be true, no being but God has, or can have, moral character. No other being is the author of his own actions.

(5.) This theory obliges its advocates, together with all other necessitarians, to give a false and nonsensical definition of free agency. Free agency, according to them, consists in doing as we will, while their theory denies the power to will, except as our willings are necessitated by God. But as we have seen in former lectures, this is no true account of freedom, or liberty. Liberty to execute my choices is no liberty at all. Choice is connected with its sequents by a law of necessity; and if an effect follow my volitions, that effect follows by necessity, and not freely. All freedom of will must, as was formerly shown, consist in the sovereign power to originate our own choices. If I am unable to will, I am unable to do any thing; and it is absurd to affirm, that a being is a moral or a free agent, who has not power to originate his own choices.

(6.) If this theory is true, the whole moral government of God is no government at all, distinct from, and superior to, physical government. It overlooks and virtually denies the fundamentally important distinction between moral and physical power, and moral and physical government. All power and all government, upon this theory, are physical.

(7.) This theory involves the delusion of all moral beings. God not only creates our volitions, but also creates the persuasion and affirmation that we are responsible for them.

3. The susceptibility scheme.

This theory represents, that the Holy Spirit's influences are both physical and moral; that he, by a direct and physical influence, excites the susceptibilities of the soul and prepares them to be affected by the truth; that he, thereupon, exerts a moral or persuasive influence by presenting the truth, which moral influence induces regeneration.

This philosophy maintains the necessity and the fact of a physical influence superadded to the moral or persuasive influence of the Holy Spirit as a sine quâ non of regeneration. It admits and maintains, that regeneration is effected solely by a moral influence, but also that a work preparatory to the efficiency of the moral influence, and indispensable to its efficiency, in producing regeneration, is performed by a direct and physical agency of the Holy Spirit upon the constitutional susceptibilities of the soul, to quicken and wake it up, and predispose it to be deeply and duly affected by the truth.

It is maintained by the defenders of this scheme, that the representations of the Bible upon the subject of the Holy Spirit's agency in regeneration, are such as to forbid the supposition, that his influence is altogether moral or persuasive, and such as plainly to indicate that he also exerts a physical agency, in preparing the mind to be duly affected by the truth.

In reply to this argument, I observe,--that I fear greatly to disparage the agency of the Holy Spirit in the work of man's redemption from sin, and would, by no means, resist or deny, or so much as call in question, any thing that is plainly taught or implied in the Bible upon this subject. I admit and maintain that regeneration is always induced and effected by the personal agency of the Holy Spirit. The question now before us relates wholly to the mode, and not at all to the fact, of divine agency in regeneration. Let this be distinctly understood, for it has been common for theologians of the old school, as soon as the dogma of a physical regeneration, and of a physical influence in regeneration, has been called in question, to cry out and insist that this is Pelagianism, and that it is a denial of divine influence altogether, and that it is teaching a self-regeneration, independent of any divine influence. I have been ashamed of such representations as these on the part of Christian divines, and have been distressed by their want of candor. It should, however, be distinctly stated that, so far as I know, the defenders of the theory now under consideration have never manifested this want of candor toward those who have called in question that part of their theory that relates to a physical influence.

Since the advocates of this theory admit that the Bible teaches that regeneration is induced by a divine moral suasion, the point of debate is simply, whether the Bible teaches that there is also a physical influence exerted by the

Holy Spirit, in exciting the constitutional susceptibilities. We will now attend to their proof texts. "Then opened he their understanding, that they might understand the scriptures."--Luke xxiv. 45. It is affirmed, that this text seems to teach or imply a physical influence in opening their understandings. But what do we mean by such language as this in common life? Language is to be understood according to the subject-matter of discourse. Here the subject of discourse is the understanding. But what can be intended by opening it? Can this be a physical prying, pulling, or forcing open any department of the constitution? Such language in common life would be understood only to mean, that such instruction was imparted as to secure a right understanding of the scriptures. Every one knows this, and why should we suppose and assume that anything more is intended here? The context plainly indicates that this was the thing, and the only thing done in this case. "Then he said unto them, O fools, and slow of heart to believe all that the prophets have spoken! Ought not Christ to have suffered these things, and to enter into his glory? And beginning at Moses and all the prophets, he expounded unto them in all the scriptures the things concerning himself.--And said unto them, thus it is written, and thus it behooved Christ to suffer, and to rise from the dead the third day."--Luke xxiv. 25-27, 46. From these verses it appears that he expounded the scriptures to them, when in the light of what had passed, and in the light of that measure of divine illumination which was then imparted to them, they understood the things which he explained to them. It does not seem to me, that this passage warrants the inference that there was a physical influence exerted. It certainly affirms no such thing. "And a certain woman named Lydia, a seller of purple, of the city of Thyatira, which worshipped God, heard us; whose heart the Lord opened, that she attended unto the things which were spoken of Paul."--Acts xvi. 14. Here is an expression similar to that just examined. Here it is said, "that the Lord opened the heart of Lydia, so that she attended," etc.; that is, the Lord inclined her to attend. But how? Why, say the advocates of this scheme, by a physical influence. But how does this appear? What is her heart that it should be pulled, or forced open? and what can be intended by the assertion, "that the Lord opened her heart?" All that can be meant is, that the Lord secured her attention, or disposed her to attend, and so enlightened her when she did attend, that she believed. Surely here is no assertion of a physical influence, nor, so far as I can see, any just ground for the inference, that such an influence was exerted. A moral influence can sufficiently explain all the phenomena; and any text that can equally well consist with either of two opposing theories, can prove neither.

Again: there are many passages that represent God as opening the spiritual eyes, and passages in which petitions are offered to God to do this. It is by this theory assumed that such passages strongly imply a physical influence. But this assumption appears to me unwarrantable. We are in the habit of using just such language, and speak of opening each other's eyes, when no such thing is intended or implied, as a physical influence, and when nothing more than a moral or persuasive influence is so much as thought of. Why then resort to such an assumption here? Does the nature of the case demand it? This I know is contended for by those who maintain a constitutional moral depravity. But this dogma has been shown to be false, and it is admitted to be so by those who maintain the theory now under consideration. Admitting, then, that the constitution is not morally depraved, should it be inferred that any constitutional change, or physical influence is needed to produce regeneration? I can see no sufficient reason for believing, or affirming, that a physical influence is demanded or exerted. This much I freely admit, that we cannot affirm the impossibility of such an influence, nor the impossibility of the necessity of such an influence. The only question with me is, does the Bible plainly teach or imply such an influence? Hitherto I have been unable to see that it does. The passages already quoted are of a piece with all that are relied upon in support of this theory, and as the same answer is a sufficient reply to them all, I will not spend time in citing and remarking upon them.

Again: a physical influence has been inferred from the fact, that sinners are represented as dead in trespasses and sins, as asleep, etc., etc. But all such representations are only declaratory of a moral state, a state of voluntary alienation from God. If the death is moral, and the sleep moral, why suppose that a physical influence is needed to correct a moral evil? Cannot truth, when urged and pressed by the Holy Spirit, effect the requisite change?

But a physical influence is also inferred from the fact, that truth makes so different an impression at one time from what it does at another. Answer: this can well enough be accounted for by the fact, that sometimes the Holy Spirit so presents the truth, that the mind apprehends it and feels its power, whereas at another time he does not.

But it is said, that there sometimes appears to have been a preparatory work performed by a physical influence pre-disposing the mind to attend to, and be affected by, the truth. Answer: there often is no doubt a preparatory work pre-disposing the mind to attend to, and be affected by, truth. But why assume that this is a physical influence? Providential occurrences may have had much to do with it. The Holy Spirit may have been directing the thoughts and communicating instructions in various ways, and preparing the mind to attend and obey. Who then is warranted in the affirmation that this preparatory influence is physical? I admit that it may be, but I cannot see either that it must be, or that there is any good ground for the assumption that it is.

4. The last theory to be examined is that of a Divine Moral Suasion.

This theory teaches--

(1.) That regeneration consists in a change in the ultimate intention or preference of the mind, or in a change from selfishness to disinterested benevolence; and

(2.) That this change is induced and effected by a divine moral influence; that is, that the Holy Spirit effects it with, through, or by the truth. The advocates of this theory assign the following as the principal reasons in support of it.

(1.) The Bible expressly affirms it. "Jesus answered, Verily, verily, I say unto thee, Except a man be born of water and of the Spirit, he cannot enter into the kingdom of God. That which is born of the flesh is flesh; and that which is born of the Spirit is spirit."--John iii. 5, 6. "Being born again, not of corruptible seed, but of incorruptible, by the word of God, which liveth and abideth for ever."--1 Pet. i. 23. "Of his own will begat he us with the word of truth, that we should be a kind Of first-fruits of his creatures."--James i. 18. "For though ye have ten thousand instructors in Christ, yet have ye not many fathers: for in Christ Jesus I have begotten you through the gospel."--1 Cor. iv. 15.

(2.) Men are represented as being sanctified by and through the truth. "Sanctify them through thy truth: thy word is truth."--John xvii. 17. "Now ye are clean through the word which I have spoken unto you."--John xv. 3.

(3.) The nature of regeneration decides the philosophy of it so far as this, that it must be effected by truth, addressed to the heart through the intelligence. The regenerate are conscious of having been influenced by the truth in turning to God. They are conscious of no other influence than light poured upon the intelligence, or truth presented to the mind.

When God affirms that he regenerates the soul with or by the truth, we have no right to infer that he does it in some other way. This he does affirm; therefore the Bible has settled the philosophy of regeneration. That he exerts any other than a moral influence, or the influence of divine teaching and illumination, is sheer assumption.

REMARKS

1. This scheme honors the Holy Spirit without disparaging the truth of God.

2. Regeneration by the Holy Spirit through the truth illustrates the wisdom of God. There is a deep and divine philosophy in regeneration.

3. This theory is of great practical importance. For if sinners are to be regenerated by the influence of truth, argument, and persuasion, then ministers can see what they have to do, and how it is that they are to be "workers together with God."

4. So also sinners may see, that they are not to wait for a physical regeneration or influence, but must submit to, and embrace, the truth, if they ever expect to be saved.

5. If this theory is true, sinners are most likely to be regenerated while sitting under the sound of the gospel, while listening to the clear exhibition of truth.

6. Ministers should lay themselves out, and press every consideration upon the attention of sinners, just as heartily and as freely, as if they expected to convert them themselves. They should aim at, and expect the regeneration of sinners, upon the spot, and before they leave the house of God.

7. Sinners must not wait for and expect physical omnipotence to regenerate them. The physical omnipotence of God affords no presumption that all men will be converted; for regeneration is not effected by physical power. God cannot do the sinner's duty, and regenerate him without the right exercise of the sinner's own agency.

8. This view of regeneration shows that the sinner's dependence upon the Holy Spirit arises entirely not of his own voluntary stubbornness, and that his guilt is all the greater, by how much the more perfect this kind of dependence is.

9. Physical regeneration, under every modification of it, is a stumbling-block. Original or constitutional sinfulness, physical regeneration, and all their kindred and resulting dogmas, are alike subversive of the gospel, and repulsive to the human intelligence; and should be laid aside as relics of a most unreasonable and confused philosophy.

LECTURE XXIX - EVIDENCES OF REGENERATION

I. Introductory remarks.

1. In ascertaining what are, and what are not, evidences of regeneration, we must constantly keep in mind what is not, and what is regeneration; what is not, and what is implied in it.

2. We must constantly recognize the fact, that saints and sinners have precisely similar constitutions and constitutional susceptibilities, and therefore that many things are common to both. What is common to both cannot, of course, he an evidence of regeneration.

3. That no state of the sensibility has any moral character in itself. That regeneration does not consist in, or imply, any physical change whatever, either of the intellect, sensibility, or the faculty of will.

4. That the sensibility of the sinner is susceptible of every kind and degree of feeling that is possible to saints.

5. The same is true of the consciences of both saints and sinners, and of the intelligence generally.

6. The inquiry is, What are evidences of a change in the ultimate intention? What is evidence that benevolence is the ruling choice, preference, intention of the soul? It is a plain question, and demands, and may have, a plain answer. But so much error prevails as to the nature of regeneration, and, consequently, as to what are evidences of regeneration, that we need patience, discrimination, and perseverance, and withal candor, to get at the truth upon this subject.

II. Wherein the experience and outward life of saints and sinners may agree.

It is plain that they may be alike, in whatever does not consist in, or necessarily proceed from, the attitude of their will; that is, in whatever is constitutional or involuntary. For example:--

1. They may both desire their own happiness. This desire is constitutional, and, of course, common to both saints and sinners.

2. They may both desire the happiness of others. This also is constitutional, and of course common to both saints and sinners. There is no moral character in these desires, any more than there is in the desire for food and drink. That men have a natural desire for the happiness of others, is evident from the fact that they manifest pleasure when others are happy, unless they have some selfish reason for envy, or unless the happiness of others is in some way inconsistent with their own. They also manifest uneasiness and pain when they see others in misery, unless they have some selfish reason for desiring their misery.

3. Saints and sinners may alike dread their own misery, and the misery of others. This is strictly constitutional, and has therefore no moral character. I have known that very wicked men, and men who had been infidels, when they were convinced of the truths of Christianity, manifested great concern about their families and about their neighbors; and, in one instance, I heard of an aged

man of this description who, when convinced of the truth, went and warned his neighbors to flee from the wrath to come, avowing at the same time his conviction, that there was no mercy for him, though he felt deeply concerned for others. Such like cases have repeatedly been witnessed. The case of the rich man in hell seems to have been one of this description, or to have illustrated the same truth. Although he knew his own case to be hopeless, yet he desired that Lazarus should be sent to warn his five brethren, lest they also should come to that place of torment. In this case and in the case of the aged man just named, it appears that they not only desired that others should avoid misery, but they actually tried to prevent it, and used the means that were within their reach to save them. Now it is plain that this desire took control of their will, and, of course, the state of the will was selfish. It sought to gratify desire. It was the pain and dread of seeing their misery, and of having them miserable, that led them to use means to prevent it. This was not benevolence, but selfishness.

Let it be understood, then, that as both saints and sinners constitutionally desire, not only their own happiness, but also the happiness of others, they may alike rejoice in the happiness and safety of others, and in converts to Christianity, and may alike grieve at the danger and misery of those who are unconverted. I well recollect, when far from home, and while an impenitent sinner, I received a letter from my youngest brother, informing me that he was converted to God. He, if he was converted, was, as I supposed, the first and the only member of the family who then had a hope of salvation. I was at the time, and both before and after, one of the most careless sinners, and yet on receiving this intelligence, I actually wept for joy and gratitude, that one of so prayerless a family was likely to be saved. Indeed, I have repeatedly known sinners to manifest much interest in the conversion of their friends, and express gratitude for their conversion, although they had no religion themselves. These desires have no moral character in themselves. In as far as they control the will, the will yielding to impulse instead of the law of the intelligence, this is selfishness.

4. They may agree in desiring the triumph of truth and righteousness, and the suppression of vice and error, for the sake of the bearings of these things on self and friends. These desires are constitutional and natural to both, under certain circumstances. When they do not influence the will, they have in themselves no moral character; but when they influence the will, their selfishness takes on a religious type. It then manifests zeal in promoting religion. But if desire, and not the intelligence, controls the will, it is selfishness notwithstanding.

5. Moral agents constitutionally approve of what i3 right and disapprove of what is wrong. Of course, both saints and sinners may both approve of and delight in goodness. I can recollect weeping at an instance of what, at the time, I supposed to be goodness, while at the same time, I was not religious myself. I have no doubt that wicked men, not only often are conscious of strongly approving the goodness of God, but that they also often take delight in contemplating it. This is constitutional, both as it respects the intellectual approbation, and also as it respects the feeling of delight. It is a great mistake to suppose that sinners are never conscious of feelings of complacency and delight in the goodness of God. The Bible represents sinners as taking delight in drawing near to him. "Yet they seek me daily, and delight to know my ways, as a nation that did righteousness, and forsook not the ordinance of their God: they ask of me the ordinances of justice; they take delight in approaching to God."--

Isa. lviii. 2. "And lo, thou art unto them as a very lovely song of one that hath a pleasant voice, and can play well on an instrument: for they hear thy words, but they do them not."--Ezek. xxxiii. 32. "For I delight in the law of God after the inward man."--Rom. vii. 22.

6. Saints and sinners may alike not only intellectually approve, but have feelings of deep complacency in, the characters of good men, sometimes good men of their own time and of their acquaintance, but more frequently good men either of a former age, or, if of their own age, 9f a distant country. The reason is this: good men of their own day and neighborhood are very apt to render them uneasy in their sins; to annoy them by their faithful reproofs and rebukes. This offends them, and overcomes their natural respect for goodness. But who has not observed the fact, that good and bad men unite in praising, admiring, and loving,--so far as feeling is concerned--good men of by-gone days, or good men at a distance, whose life and rebukes have annoyed the wicked in their own neighborhood? The fact is, that moral agents, from the laws of their being, necessarily approve of goodness wherever they witness it. Multitudes of sinners are conscious of this, and suppose that this is a virtuous feeling. It is of no use to deny, that they sometimes have feelings of love and gratitude to God, and of respect for, and complacency in good men. They often have these feelings, and to represent them as always having feelings of hatred and of opposition to God and to good men, is sure either to offend them, or to lead them to deny the truths of religion, if they are told that the Bible teaches this. Or, again, it may lead them to think themselves Christians, because they are conscious of such feelings as they are taught to believe are peculiar to Christians. Or again, they may think that, although they are not Christians, yet they are far from being totally depraved, inasmuch as they have so many good desires and feelings. It should never be forgotten, that saints and sinners may agree in their opinions and intellectual views and judgments. Many professors of religion, it is to be feared, have supposed religion to consist in desires and feelings, and have entirely mistaken their own character. Indeed, nothing is more common than to hear religion spoken of as consisting altogether in mere feelings, desires, and emotions. Professors relate their feelings, and suppose themselves to be giving an account of their religion. It is infinitely important, that both professors of religion and non-professors, should understand more than most of them do of their mental constitution, and of the true nature of religion. Multitudes of professors of religion have, it is to be feared, a hope founded altogether upon desires and feelings that are purely constitutional, arid therefore common to both saints and sinners.

7. Saints and sinners agree in this, that they both disapprove of, and are often disgusted with, and deeply abhor, sin: They cannot but disapprove of sin. Necessity is laid upon every moral agent, whatever his character may be, by the law of his being, to condemn and disapprove of sin. And often the sensibility of sinners, as well as of saints, is filled with deep disgust and loathing in view of sin. I know that representations the direct opposite of these are often made. Sinners are represented as universally having complacency in sin, as having a constitutional craving for sin, as they have for food and drink. But such representations are false and most injurious. They contradict the sinner's consciousness, and lead him either to deny his total depravity, or to deny the Bible, or to think himself regenerate. As was shown when upon the subject of moral depravity, sinners do not love sin for its own sake; yet they crave other

things, and this leads to prohibited indulgence, which indulgence is sin. But it is not the sinfulness of the indulgence that was desired. That might have produced disgust and loathing in the sensibility, if it had been considered even at the moment of the indulgence. For example: suppose a licentious man, a drunkard, a gambler, or any other wicked man, engaged in his favorite indulgence, and suppose that the sinfulness of this indulgence should be strongly set before his mind by the Holy Spirit. He might be deeply ashamed and disgusted with himself, and so much so as to feel a great contempt for himself, and feel almost ready, were it possible, to spit in his own face. And yet, unless this feeling becomes more powerful than the desire and feeling which the will is seeking to indulge, the indulgence will be persevered in, notwithstanding this disgust. If the feeling of disgust should for the time overmatch the opposing desire, the indulgence will be, for the time being, abandoned for the sake of gratifying or appeasing the feeling of disgust. But this is not virtue. It is only a change in the form of selfishness. Feeling still governs, and not the law of the intelligence. The indulgence is only abandoned for the time being, to gratify a stronger impulse of the sensibility. The will, will of course return to the indulgence again, when the feelings of fear, disgust, or loathing subside. This, no doubt, accounts for the multitudes of spurious conversions sometimes witnessed. Sinners are convicted, fears awakened, and disgust and loathing excited. These feelings for the time become stronger than their desires for their former indulgences, and consequently they abandon them for a time, in obedience, not to the law of God or of their intelligence, but in obedience to their fear, disgust, and shame. But when conviction subsides, and the consequent feelings are no more, these spurious converts "return like a dog to his vomit, and like a sow that was washed to her wallowing in the mire." It should be distinctly understood, that all these feelings of which I have spoken, and indeed any class or degree of mere feelings, may exist in the sensibility; and further, that these or any other feelings may, in their turn, control the will, and produce of course a corresponding outward life, and yet the heart be and remain all the while in a selfish state, or in a state of total depravity. Indeed, it is perfectly common to see the impenitent sinner manifest much disgust and opposition to sin in himself and in others, yet this is not principle in him; it is only the effect of present feeling. The next day, or perhaps hour, he will repeat his sin, or do that which, when beheld in others, enkindled his indignation.

8. Both saints and sinners approve of, and often delight in, justice. It is common to see in courts of justice, and on various other occasions, impenitent sinners manifest great complacency in the administration of justice, and the greatest indignation at, and abhorrence of, injustice. So strong is this feeling sometimes that it cannot be restrained, but will burst forth like a smothered volcano, and carry desolation before it. It is this natural love of justice, and abhorrence of injustice, common alike to saints and sinners, to which popular tumults and bloodshed are often to be ascribed. This is not virtue, but selfishness. It is the will giving itself up to the gratification of a constitutional impulse. But such feelings and such conduct are often supposed to be virtuous. It should always be borne in mind that the love of justice, and the sense of delight in it, and the feeling of opposition to injustice, are not only not peculiar to good men, but that such feelings are no evidence whatever of a regenerate heart. Thousands of instances might be adduced as proofs and illustrations of

this position. But such manifestations are too common to need to be cited, to remind any one of their existence.

9. The same remarks may be made in regard to truth. Both saints and sinners have a constitutional respect for, approbation of, and delight in truth. Who ever knew a sinner to approve of the character of a liar? What sinner will not resent it, to be accused or even suspected of lying? All men spontaneously manifest their respect for, complacency in, and approbation of truth. This is constitutional; so that even the greatest liars do not, and cannot, love lying for its own sake. They lie to gratify, not a love for falsehood on its own account, but to obtain some object which they desire more strongly than they hate falsehood. Sinners, in spite of themselves, venerate, respect, and fear a man of truth. They just as necessarily despise a liar. If they are liars, they despise themselves for it, just as drunkards and debauchees despise themselves for indulging their filthy lusts, and yet continue in them.

10. Both saints and sinners not only approve of, and delight in good men, when, as I have said, wicked men are not annoyed by them, but they agree in reprobating, disapproving, and abhorring wicked men and devils. Who ever heard of any other sentiment and feeling being expressed either by good or bad men, than of abhorrence and indignation toward the devil? Nobody ever approved, or can approve, of his character; sinners can no more approve of it than holy angels can. If he could approve of and delight in his own character, hell would cease to be hell, and evil would become his good. But no moral agent can, by any possibility, know wickedness and approve it. No man, saint or sinner, can entertain any other sentiments and feelings toward the devil, or wicked men, but those of disapprobation, distrust, disrespect, and often of loathing and abhorrence. The intellectual sentiment will be uniform. Disapprobation, distrust, condemnation, will always necessarily possess the minds of all who know wicked men and devils. And often, as occasions arise, wherein their characters are clearly revealed, and under circumstances favorable to such a result, the deepest feelings of disgust, of loathing, of indignation, and abhorrence of their wickedness, will manifest themselves alike among saints and sinners.

11. Saints and sinners may be equally honorable and fair in business transactions, so far as the outward act is concerned. They have different reasons for their conduct, but outwardly it may be the same. This leads to the remark,--

12. That selfishness in the sinner, and benevolence in the saint, may, and often do, produce, in many respects, the same results or manifestations. For example: benevolence in the saint, and selfishness in the sinner, may beget the same class of desires, to wit, as we have seen, desire for their own sanctification, and for that of others, to be useful, and to have others so; desires for the conversion of sinners, and many such like desires.

13. This leads to the remark, that, when the desires of an impenitent person for these objects become strong enough to influence the will, he may take the same outward course, substantially, that the saint takes in obedience to his intelligence. That is, the sinner is constrained by his feelings to do what the saint does from principle, or from obedience to the law of his intelligence. In this, however, although the outward manifestations be the same for the time being, yet the sinner is entirely selfish, and the saint benevolent. The saint is controlled by principle, and the sinner by impulse. In this case, time is needed to distinguish between them. The sinner not having the root of the matter in

him, will return to his former course of life, in proportion as his convictions of the truth and importance of religion subside, and his former feelings return; while the saint will evince his heavenly birth, by manifesting his sympathy with God, and the strength of principle that has taken possession of his heart. That is, he will manifest that his intelligence, and not his feelings, controls his will.

REMARKS

1. For want of these and such like discriminations, many have stumbled. Hypocrites have held on to a false hope, and lived upon mere constitutional desires and spasmodic turns of giving up the will, during seasons of special excitement, to the control of these desires and feelings. These spasms they call their waking up. But no sooner does their excitement subside, than selfishness again assumes its wonted forms. It is truly wonderful and appalling to see to what an extent this is true. Because, in seasons of special excitement they feel deeply, and are conscious of feeling, as they say, and acting, and of being entirely sincere in following their impulses, they have the fullest confidence in their good estate. They say they cannot doubt their conversion. They felt so and so, and gave themselves up to their feelings, and gave much time and money to promote the cause of Christ. Now this is a deep delusion, and one of the most common in Christendom, or at least one of the most common that is to be found among what are called revival Christians. This class of deluded souls do not see that they are, in such cases, governed by their feelings, and that if their feelings were changed, their conduct would be so, of course; that as soon as the excitement subsides, they will go back to their former ways, as a thing of course. When the state of feeling that now controls them has given place to their former feelings, they will of course appear as they used to do. This is, in few words, the history of thousands of professors of religion.

2. This has greatly stumbled the openly impenitent. Not knowing how to account for what they often witness of this kind among professors of religion, they are led to doubt whether there is any such thing as true religion.

Again: many sinners have been deceived just in the way I have pointed out, and have afterwards discovered that they had been deluded, but could not understand how. They have come to the conclusion that everybody is deluded, and that all professors are as much deceived as they are. This leads them to reject and despise all religion.

3. Some exercises of impenitent sinners, and of which they are conscious, have been denied for fear of denying total depravity. They have been represented as necessarily hating God and all good men; and this hatred has been represented as a feeling of malice and enmity towards God. Many impenitent sinners are conscious of having no such feelings; but, on the contrary, they are conscious of having at times feelings of respect, veneration, awe, gratitude, and affection towards God and good men. To this class of sinners, it is a snare and a stumbling-block to tell them, and insist, that they only hate God, and Christians, and ministers, and revivals; and to represent their moral depravity to be such, that they crave sin as they crave food, and that they necessarily have none but feelings of mortal enmity against God. Such representations either drive them into infidelity on the one hand, or to think themselves Christians on the other. But those theologians who hold the views of constitutional depravity of which we have spoken, cannot, consistently with

their theory, admit to these sinners the real truth, and then show them conclusively that in all their feelings which they call good, and in all their yielding to be influenced by them, there is no virtue; that their desires and feelings have in themselves no moral character, and that when they yield the will to their control, it is only selfishness.

The thing needed is a philosophy and a theology that will admit and explain all the phenomena of experience, and not deny human consciousness. A theology that denies human consciousness is only a curse and a stumbling-block. But such is the doctrine of universal constitutional moral depravity.

It is frequently true, that the feelings of sinners become exceedingly rebellious and exasperated, even to the most intense opposition of feeling toward God, and Christ, and ministers, and revivals, and toward everything of good report. If this class of sinners are converted, they are very apt to suppose, and to represent all sinners as having just such feelings as they had. But this is a mistake, for many sinners never had those feelings. Nevertheless, they are no less selfish and guilty than the class who have the rebellious and blasphemous feelings which I have mentioned. This is what they need to know. They need to understand definitely what sin is, and what it is not; that sin is selfishness; that selfishness is the yielding of the will to the control of feeling, and that it matters not at all what the particular class of feelings is, if feelings control the will, and not intelligence. Admit their good feelings, as they call them, and take pains to show them, that these feelings are merely constitutional, and have in themselves no moral character.

4. The ideas of depravity and of regeneration, to which I have often alluded, are fraught with great mischief in another respect. Great numbers, it is to be feared, both of private professors of religion and of ministers, have mistaken the class of feelings of which I have spoken, as common among certain impenitent sinners, for religion. They have heard the usual representations of the natural depravity of sinners, and also have heard certain desires and feelings represented as religion. They are conscious of these desires and feelings, and also, sometimes, when they are very strong, of being influenced in their conduct by them. They assume, therefore, that they are regenerate, and elected, and heirs of salvation. These views lull them asleep. The philosophy and theology that misrepresent moral depravity and regeneration thus, must, if consistent, also misrepresent true religion; and oh the many thousands that have mistaken the mere constitutional desires and feelings, and the selfish yielding of the will to their control, for true religion, and have gone to the bar of God with a lie in their right hand!

5. Another great evil has arisen out of the false views I have been exposing, namely:--

Many true Christians have been much stumbled and kept in bondage, and their comfort and their usefulness much abridged, by finding themselves, from time to time, very languid and unfeeling. Supposing religion to consist in feeling, if at any time the sensibility becomes exhausted, and their feelings subside, they are immediately thrown into unbelief and bondage. Satan reproaches them for their want of feeling, and they have nothing to say, only to admit the truth of his accusations. Having a false philosophy of religion, they judge of the state of their hearts by the state of their feelings. They confound their hearts with their feelings, and are in almost constant perplexity to keep their hearts right, by which they mean their feelings, in a state of great excitement.

Again: they are not only sometimes languid, and have no pious feelings and desires, but at others they are conscious of classes of emotions which they call sin. These they resist, but still blame themselves for having them in their hearts, as they say. Thus they are brought into bondage again, although they are certain that these feelings are hated, and not at all indulged, by them.

Oh, how much all classes of persons need to have clearly defined ideas of what really constitutes sin and holiness! A false philosophy of the mind, especially of the will, and of moral depravity, has covered the world with gross darkness on the subject of sin and holiness, of regeneration, and of the evidences of regeneration, until the true saints, on the one hand, are kept in a continual bondage to their false notions; and on the other, the church swarms with unconverted professors, and is cursed with many self-deceived ministers.

LECTURE XXX - EVIDENCES OF REGENERATION

III. Wherein saints and sinners must differ.

1. Let it be distinctly remembered, that all unregenerate persons, without exception, have one heart, that is, they are selfish. This is their whole character. They are universally and only devoted to self-gratification. Their unregenerate heart consists in this selfish disposition, or in this selfish choice. This choice is the foundation of, and the reason for, all their activity. One and the same ultimate reason actuates them in all they do, and in all they omit, and that reason is either presently or remotely, directly or indirectly, to gratify themselves.

2. The regenerate heart is disinterested benevolence. In other words, it is love to God and our neighbor. All regenerate hearts are precisely similar. All true saints, whenever they have truly the heart of the saints of God, are actuated by one and the same motive. They have only one ultimate reason for all they do, and suffer, or omit. They have one ultimate intention, one end. They live for one and the same object, and that is the same end for which God lives.

3. The saint is governed by reason, the law of God, or the moral law; in other words still, the law of disinterested and universal benevolence is his law. This law is not only revealed and developed in his intelligence, but it is written in his heart. So that the law of his intellect is the law of his heart. He not only sees and acknowledges what he ought to do and be, but he is conscious to himself, and gives evidence to others, whether they receive it and are convinced by it or not, that his heart, his will, or intention, is conformed to his convictions of duty. He sees the path of duty, and follows it. He knows what he ought to will, intend, and do, and does it. Of this he is conscious. And of this others may be satisfied, if they are observing, charitable, and candid.

4. The sinner is contrasted with this, in the most important and fundamental respects. He is not governed by reason and principle, but by feeling, desire, and impulse. Sometimes his feelings coincide with the intelligence, and sometimes they do not. But when they do so coincide, the will does not pursue its course out of respect or in obedience to the law of the intelligence, but in obedience to the impulse of the sensibility, which, for the time being, impels in the same direction as does the law of the reason. But for the most part the impulses of the sensibility incline him to worldly gratifications, and in an opposite direction to that which the intelligence points out. This leads him to a course of life that is too manifestly the opposite of reason, to leave any room for doubt as to what his true character is.

5. The saint is justified, and he has the evidence of it in the peace of his own mind. He is conscious of obeying the law of reason and of love. Consequently he naturally has that kind and degree of peace that flows from the harmony of his will with the law of his intelligence. He sometimes has conflicts with the impulses of feeling and desire. But unless he is overcome, these conflicts, though they may cause him inwardly, and, perhaps audibly, to groan, do not interrupt his peace. There are still the elements of peace within him. His

heart and conscience are at one, and while this is so, he has thus far the evidence of justification in himself. That is, he knows that God cannot condemn his present state. Conscious as he is of conformity of heart to the moral law, he cannot but affirm to himself, that the Lawgiver is pleased with his present attitude. But further, he has also within the Spirit of God witnessing with his spirit, that he is a child of God, forgiven, accepted, adopted. He feels the filial spirit drawing his heart to exclaim, Father, Father. He is conscious that he pleases God, and has God's smile of approbation.

He is at peace with himself, because he affirms his heart to be in unison with the law of love. His conscience does not upbraid, but smile. The harmony of his own being is a witness to himself, that this is the state in which he was made to exist. He is at peace with God, because he and God are pursuing precisely the same end, and by the same means. There can be no collision, no controversy between them. He is at peace with the universe, in the sense, that he has no and no malicious feelings or wish to gratify, in the injury of any one of the creatures of God. He has no fear, but to sin against God. He is not influenced on the one hand by the fear of hell, nor on the other by the hope of reward. He is not anxious about his own salvation, but prayerfully and calmly leaves that question in the hands of God, and concerns himself only to promote the highest glory of God, and the good of being. "Being justified by faith, he has peace with God through our Lord Jesus Christ." "There is now no condemnation to them that are in Christ Jesus, who walk not after the flesh, but after the Spirit."

6. The sinner's experience is the opposite of this. He is under condemnation, and seldom can so far deceive himself, even in his most religious moods, as to imagine that he has a consciousness of acceptance either with his own conscience or with God. There is almost never a time in which he has not a greater or less degree of restlessness and misgiving within. Even when he is most engaged in religion, as he supposes, ho finds himself dissatisfied with himself. Something is wrong. There is a struggle and a pang. He may not exactly see where and what the difficulty is. He does not, after all, obey reason and conscience, and is not governed by the law and will of God. Not having the consciousness of this obedience, his conscience does not smile. He sometimes feels deeply, and acts as he feels, and is conscious of being sincere in the sense of feeling what he says, and acting in obedience to deep feeling. But this does not satisfy conscience. He is more or less wretched after all. He has not true peace. Sometimes he has a self-righteous quiet and enjoyment. But this is neither peace of conscience nor peace with God. He, after all, feels uneasy and condemned, notwithstanding all his feeling, and zeal, and activity. They are not of the right kind. Hence they do not satisfy the conscience. They do not meet the demands of his intelligence. Conscience does not approve. He has not, after all, true peace. He is not justified; he cannot be fully and permanently satisfied that he is.

7. Saints are interested in, and sympathize with, every effort to reform mankind, and promote the interests of truth and righteousness in the earth.

The good of being is the end for which the saint really and truly lives. This is not merely held by him as a theory, as an opinion, as a theological or philosophical speculation. It is in his heart, and precisely for this reason he is a saint. He is a saint just because the theory, which is lodged in the head of both saint and sinner, has also a lodgment and reigning power in his heart, and consequently in his life.

As saints supremely value the highest good of being, they will, and must, take a deep interest in whatever is promotive of that end. Hence, their spirit is necessarily that of the reformer. To the universal reformation of the world they stand committed. To this end they are devoted. For this end they live, and move, and have their being. Every proposed reform interests them, and naturally leads them to examine its claims. The fact is, they are studying and devising ways and means to convert, sanctify, reform mankind. Being in this state of mind, they are predisposed to lay hold on whatever gives promise of good to man. True saints love reform. It is their business, their profession, their life to promote it; consequently they are ready to examine the claims of any proposed reform; candid and self-denying, and ready to be convinced, however much self-denial it may call them to. They have actually rejected self-indulgence, as the end for which they live, and are ready to sacrifice any form of self-indulgence, for the sake of promoting the good of men and the glory of God. The saint is truly and greatly desirous and in earnest, to reform all sin out of the world, and just for this reason is ready to hail with joy, and to try whatever reform seems, from the best light he can get, to bid fair to put down sin, and the evils that are in the world. Even mistaken men, who are honestly endeavoring to reform mankind, and denying their appetites, as many have done in dietetic reform, are deserving of the respect of their fellow men. Suppose their philosophy to be incorrect, yet they have intended well. They have manifested a disposition to deny themselves, for the purpose of promoting the good of others. They have been honest and zealous in this. Now no true saint can feel or express contempt for such reformers, however much mistaken they may be. No: his natural sentiments and feelings will be, and must be, the reverse of contempt or censoriousness in respect to them. If their mistake has been injurious, he may mourn over the evil, but will not, cannot, severely judge the honest reformer. War, slavery, licentiousness, and all such like evils and abominations, are necessarily regarded by the saint as great and sore evils, and he longs for their complete and final overthrow. It is impossible that a truly benevolent mind should not thus regard these abominations of desolation.

The saints in all ages have been reformers. I know it is said, that neither prophets, Christ, nor apostles, nor primitive saints and martyrs declaimed against war and slavery, etc. But they did. The entire instructions of Christ, and of apostles and prophets, were directly opposed to these and all other evils. If they did not come out against certain legalized forms of sin, and denounce them by name, and endeavor to array public sentiment against them, it is plainly because they were, for the most part, employed in a preliminary work. To introduce the gospel as a divine revelation; to set up and organize the visible kingdom of God on earth; to lay a foundation for universal reform, was rather their business, than the pushing forward of particular branches of reform. The overthrow of state idolatry, the great and universal sin of the world in that age; the labor of getting the world and the governments of earth to tolerate and receive the gospel as a revelation from the one only living and true God; the controversy with the Jews, to overthrow their objections to Christianity; in short, the great and indispensable and preliminary work of gaining for Christ and his gospel a hearing, and an acknowledgment of its divinity, was rather their work, the pushing of particular precepts and doctrines of the gospel to their legitimate results and logical consequences. This work once done, has left it for later saints to bring the particular truths, precepts, and doctrines of the blessed gospel to bear down every form of sin. Prophets, Christ, and his apostles, have left on the pages of inspiration no dubious testimony against every form of sin. The spirit of the whole Bible breathes from every page blasting and annihilation upon every unholy abomination, while it smiles upon everything of good report that promises blessings to man and glory to God. The saint is not merely sometimes a reformer; he is always so.

8. The sinner is never a reformer in any proper sense of the word. He is selfish and never opposed to sin, or to any evil whatever, from any such motive as renders him worthy the name of reformer. He sometimes selfishly advocates and pushes certain outward reforms; but as certain as it is that he is an unregenerate sinner, so certain is it, that he is not endeavoring to reform sin out of the world from any disinterested love to God or to man. Many considerations of a selfish nature may engage him at times in certain branches of reform. Regard to his reputation may excite his zeal in such an enterprise. Self-righteous considerations may also lead him to enlist in the army of reformers. His relation to particular forms of vice may influence him to set his face against them. Constitutional temperament and tendencies may lead to his engaging in certain reforms. For example, his constitutional benevolence, as phrenologists call it, may be such that from natural compassion he may engage in reforms. But this is only giving way to an impulse of the sensibility, and it is not principle that governs him. His natural conscientiousness may modify his outward character, and lead him to take hold of some branches of reform. But whatever other motives he may have, sure it is that he is not a reformer; for he is a sinner, and it is absurd to say that a sinner is truly engaged in opposing sin as sin. No, it is not sin that he is opposing, but he is seeking to gratify an ambitious, a self-righteous, or some other spirit, the gratification of which is selfishness.

But as a general thing, it is easy to distinguish sinners, or deceived professors from saints by looking steadfastly at their temper and deportment in their relations to reform. They are self-indulgent, and just for the reason that they are devoted to self-indulgence. Sometimes their self-indulgent spirit takes on one type, and sometimes another. Of course they need not be expected to ridicule or oppose every branch of reform, just because it is not every reformer that will rebuke their favorite indulgences, and call them to reform their lives. But as every sinner has one or more particular form of indulgence to which he is wedded, and as saints are devising and pushing reforms in all directions, it is natural that some sinners should manifest particular hostility to one reform, and some to another. Whenever a reform is proposed that would reform them out of their favorite indulgences, they will either ridicule it, and those that propose it, or storm and rail, or in some way oppose or wholly neglect it. Not so, and so it cannot be, with a true saint. He has no indulgence that he values when put in competition with the good of being. Nay, he holds his all and his life at the disposal of the highest good. Has he, in ignorance of the evils growing out of his course, used ardent spirits, wine, tobacco, ale, or porter? Has he held slaves; been engaged in any traffic that is found to be injurious; has he favored war through ignorance; or, in short, has he committed any mistake whatever? Let but a reformer come forth and propose to discuss the tendency of such things; let the reformer bring forth his strong reasons; and, from the very nature of true religion, the saint will listen with attention, weigh with candor, and suffer himself to be carried by truth, heart, and hand, and influence with the proposed reform, if it be worthy of support, how much soever it conflict with his former habits. This must be true, if he has a single eye to the good of being, which is the very characteristic of a saint.

9. The true saint denies himself. Self-denial must be his characteristic, just for the reason that regeneration implies this. Regeneration, as we have seen, consists in turning away the heart or will from the supreme choice of self-gratification, to a choice of the highest well-being of God and of the universe. This is denying self. This is abandoning self-indulgence, and pursuing or committing the will, and the whole being to an opposite end. This is the dethroning of self, and the enthroning of God in the heart. Self-denial does not consist, as some seem to imagine, in acts of outward austerity, in an ascetic and penance-doing course of starvation, and mere legal and outward retrenchment, in wearing a coat with one button, and in similar acts of "will worship and voluntary humility, and neglecting the body;" but self-denial consists in the actual and total renunciation of selfishness in the heart. It consists in ceasing wholly to live for self, and can be exercised just as truly upon a throne, surrounded with the paraphernalia of royalty, as in a cottage of logs, or as in rags, and in caves and dens of the earth.

The king upon his throne may live and reign to please himself. He may surround himself with all that can minister to his pleasure, his ambition, his pride, his lusts, and his power. He may live to and for himself. Self-pleasing, self-gratification, self-aggrandizement, may be the end for which be lives. This is selfishness. But he may also live and reign for God, and for his people. That is, he may be as really devoted to God, and render this as a service to God, as well as anything else. No doubt his temptation is great; but, nevertheless, he may be perfectly self-denying in all this. He may not do what he does for his own sake, nor be what he is, nor possess what he possesses for his own sake, but, accommodating his state and equipage to his relations, he may be as truly self-denying as others in the humbler walks of life. This is not an impossible, though, in all probability, a rare case. A man may as truly be rich for God as poor for him, if his relations and circumstances make it essential to his highest usefulness that he should possess a large capital. He is in the way of great temptation; but if this is plainly his duty, and submitted to for God and the world, he may have grace to be entirely self-denying in these circumstances, and all the more commendable, for standing fast under these circumstances.

So a poor man may be poor from principle, or from necessity. He may be submissive and happy in his poverty. He may deny himself even the comforts of life, and do all this to promote the good of being, or he may do it to promote his own interest, temporal or eternal, to secure a reputation for piety, to appease a morbid conscience, to appease his fears, or to secure the favor of God. In all things he may be selfish. He may be happy in this, because it may be real self-denial: or he may be murmuring at his poverty, may complain, and be envious at others who are not poor. He may be censorious, and think everybody proud and selfish who dresses better, or possesses a better house and equipage than he does. He may set up his views as a standard, and denounce as proud and selfish all who do not square their lives by his rule. This is selfishness, and these manifestations demonstrate the fact. A man, may forego the use of a coat, or a cloak, or a horse, or a carriage, or any and every comfort and convenience of life, and all this may proceed from either a benevolent or a selfish state of mind. If it be benevolence and true self-denial, it will be cheerfully and happily submitted to, without murmuring and repining, without censoriousness, and without envy towards others, without insisting that others shall do and be, just what he does and is. He will allow the judge his ermine, the king his robes of state, and the merchant his capital, and the husbandman his fields and his flocks, and will see the reasonableness and propriety of all this.

But if it be selfishness and the spirit of self-gratification instead of self-denial, he will be ascetic, caustic, sour, ill-natured, unhappy, severe, censorious, envious, and disposed to complain of, and pick at, the extravagance and self-indulgence of others.

Especially does the true saint deny his appetites and passions. His artificial appetites he denies absolutely, whenever his attention is called to the fact and the nature of the indulgence. The Christian is such just because he has become the master of his appetites and passions, has denied them, and consecrated himself to God. The sinner is a sinner just because his appetites and passions and the impulses of his desires are his masters, and he bows down to them, and serves them. They are his masters instead of his servants, as they are made to be. He is consecrated to them and not to God. But the saint has ceased to live to gratify his lusts. Has he been a drunkard, a rake, a tobacco user? Has he been in self-indulgent habits of any kind? He is reformed: old things are past away, and behold all things are become new. Has he still any habit the character of which he has either mistaken or not considered; such as smoking, chewing, or snuffing tobacco, using injurious stimulants of any kind, high and unwholesome living, extravagant dressing or equipage, retiring late at night and rising late in the morning, eating too much, or between meals, or in short, has there been any form of self-indulgence about him whatever? Only let his attention be called to it, he will listen with candor, be convinced by reasonable evidence, and renounce his evil habits without conferring with flesh and blood. All this is implied in regeneration, and must follow from its very nature. This also the Bible everywhere affirms to be true of the saints. "They have crucified the flesh with its affections and lusts." It should be forever remembered, that a self-indulgent Christian is a contradiction. Self-indulgence and Christianity are terms of opposition.

10. The sinner does not deny himself. He may not gratify all his desires, because the desires are often contradictory, and he must deny one for the sake of indulging another. Avarice may be so strong as to forbid his indulging in extravagance in eating, drinking, dressing, or equipage. His love of reputation may be so strong as to prevent his engaging in anything disgraceful, and so on. But self-indulgence is his law notwithstanding. The fear of hell, or his desire to be saved, may forbid his outward indulgence in any known sin. But still he lives, and moves, and has his being only for the sake of indulging himself. He may be a miser, and starve and freeze himself, and deny himself the necessaries of life; yet self-indulgence is his law. Some lusts he may and must control, as they may be inconsistent with others. But others he does not control. He is a slave. He bows down to his lusts and serves them. He is enslaved by his propensities, so that he cannot overcome them. This demonstrates that he is a sinner and unregenerate, whatever his station and profession may be. One who cannot, because he will not, conquer himself and his lusts--this is the definition of an unregenerate sinner. He is one over whom some form of desire, or lust, or

appetite, or passion has dominion. He cannot, or rather will not, overcome it. This one is just as certainly in sin, as that sin is sin.

11. The truly regenerate soul overcomes sin.

Let the Bible be heard upon this subject. "And hereby we do know that we know him, if we keep his commandments. He that saith I know him, and keepeth not his commandments, is a liar, and the truth is not in him."--1 John ii. 3, 4. "And every man that hath this hope in him purifieth himself, even as he is pure. Whosoever committeth sin transgresseth also the law: for sin is the transgression of the law. And ye know that he was manifested to take away our sins: and in him is no sin. Whosoever abideth in him sinneth not: whosoever sinneth hath not seen him, neither known him. Little children, let no man deceive you: he that doeth righteousness is righteous, even as he is righteous. He that committeth sin, is of the devil; for the devil sinneth from the beginning. For this purpose the Son of God was manifested, that he might destroy the works of the devil. Whosoever is born of God doth not commit sin; for his seed remaineth in him: and he cannot sin, because he is born of God. In this the children of God are manifest, and the children of the devil; whosoever cloth not righteousness is not of God, neither he that loveth not his brother."--1 John iii. 3-10. "Whosoever believeth that Jesus is the Christ, is born of God, and every one that loveth him that begat, loveth him also that is begotten of him. By this we know that we love the children of God, when we love God and keep his commandments. For this is the love of God, that we keep his commandments; and his commandments are not grievous. For whatsoever is born of God overcometh the world: and this is the victory that overcometh the world, even our faith."--1 John v. 1-4.

These passages, understood and pressed to the letter, would not only teach, that all regenerate souls overcome and live without sin, but also that sin is impossible to them. This last circumstance, as well as other parts of scripture, forbid us to press this strong language to the letter. But this much must be understood and admitted, that to overcome sin is the rule with every one who is born of God, and that sin is only the exception; that the regenerate habitually live without sin, and fall into sin only at intervals, so few and far between, that in strong language it may be said in truth they do not sin. This is surely the least which can be meant by the spirit of these texts, not to press them to the letter. And this is precisely consistent with many other passages of scripture, several of which I have quoted; such as these:--"Therefore, if any man be in Christ, he is a new creature: old things are passed away; behold, all things are become new."--2 Cor. v. 17. "For in Jesus Christ, neither circumcision availeth anything nor uncircumcision; but faith which worketh by love."--Gal. v. 6. "For in Christ Jesus neither circumcision availeth anything, nor uncircumcision, but a new creature."--Gal. vi. 15. "There is therefore now no condemnation to them which are in Christ Jesus, who walk not after the flesh, but after the Spirit. For the law of the Spirit of life in Christ Jesus hath made me free from the law of sin and death. For what the law could not do, in that it was weak through the flesh, God sending his own Son in the likeness of sinful flesh, and for sin, condemned sin in the flesh: that the righteousness of the law might be fulfilled in us, who walk not after the flesh, but after the Spirit."--Rom. viii. 1-4. "What shall we say then? Shall we continue in sin, that grace may abound? God forbid. How shall we that are dead to sin, live any longer therein? Know ye not, that so many of us as were baptized into Jesus Christ were baptized into his death? Therefore we are buried with him by baptism into death: that like as Christ was raised up from the dead by the glory of the Father, even so we also should walk in newness of life. For if we have been planted together in the likeness of his death, we shall be also in the likeness of his resurrection: knowing this, that our old man is crucified with him, that the body of sin might be destroyed, that henceforth we should not serve sin. For he that is dead is freed from sin. Now if we be dead with Christ, we believe that we shall also live with him; knowing that Christ being raised from the dead, dieth no more; death hath no more dominion over him. For in that he died, he died unto sin once: but in that he liveth, he liveth unto God. Likewise reckon ye also yourselves to be dead indeed unto sin, but alive unto God, through Jesus Christ our Lord. Let not sin therefore reign in your mortal body, that ye should obey it in the lusts thereof. Neither yield ye your members as instruments of unrighteousness unto sin: but yield yourselves unto God, as those that are alive from the dead, and your members as instruments of righteousness unto God. For sin shall not have dominion over you: for ye are not under the law, but under grace."--Rom. vi. 1-14.

The fact is, if God is true, and the Bible is true, the truly regenerate soul has overcome the world, the flesh, and Satan, and sin, and is a conqueror, and more than a conqueror. He triumphs over temptation as a general thing, and the triumphs of temptation over him are so far between, that it is said of him in the living oracles, that he does not, cannot sin. He is not a sinner, but a saint. He is sanctified; a holy person; a child and son of God. If at any time he is overcome, it is only to rise again, and soon return like the weeping prodigal. "The steps of a good man are ordered by the Lord: and he delighteth in his way. Though he fall he shall not be utterly cast down: for the Lord upholdeth him with his hand."--Psalm xxxvii. 23, 24.

12. The sinner is the slave of sin. The seventh of Romans is his experience in his best estate. When he has the most hope of himself, and others have the most hope of his good estate, he goes no further than to make and break resolutions. His life is but a death in sin. He has not the victory. He sees the right, but does it not. Sin is his master, to whom he yields himself a servant to obey. He only tries, as he says, to forsake sin, but does not in fact forsake it, in his heart. And yet because he is convicted, and has desires, and forms resolutions of amendment, he hopes he is regenerated. O, what a horrible delusion! Stop short with conviction, with the hope that he is already a Christian! Alas! how many are already in hell who have stumbled at this stumbling stone!

13. The subject of regeneration may know, and if honest he must know, for what end he lives. There is, perhaps, nothing of which he may be more certain than of his regenerate or unregenerate state; and if he will keep in mind what regeneration is, it would seem that he can hardly mistake his own character, so far as to imagine himself to be regenerate when he is not. The great difficulty that has been in the way of the regenerate soul's knowing his regeneration, and has led to so much doubt and embarrassment upon this subject, is that regeneration has been regarded as belonging to the sensibility, and hence the attention has been directed to the ever-fluctuating feelings for evidence of the change. No wonder that this has led conscientious souls into doubt and embarrassment. But let the subject of regeneration be disenthralled from a false philosophy, and let it be known that the new heart consists in supreme

disinterested benevolence, or in entire consecration to God, and then who cannot know for what end he lives, or what is the supreme preference or intention of his soul? If men can settle any question whatever beyond all doubt by an appeal to consciousness, it would seem that this must be the question. Hence the Bible enjoins it as an imperative duty to know ourselves, whether we are Christians. We are to know each other by our fruits. This is expressly given in the Bible as the rule of judgment in the case. The question is not so, much, What are the man's opinions? as, What does he live for? Does he manifest a charitable state of mind? Does he manifest the attributes of benevolence in the various circumstances in which he is placed? O, when shall the folly of judging men more by their opinions and feelings, than by the tenor of their lives cease? It seems difficult to rid men of the prejudice that religion consists in feelings and in experiences in which they are altogether passive. Hence they are continually prone to delusion upon the most momentous of all questions. Nothing can break this spell but the steady and thorough inculcation of the truth, in regard to the nature of regeneration.

LECTURE XXXI - NATURAL ABILITY

We next proceed to the examination of the question of man's ability or inability to obey the commandments of God. This certainly must be a fundamental question in morals and religion; and as our views are upon this subject, so, if we are consistent, must be our views of God, of his moral government, and of every practical doctrine of morals and religion. This is too obvious to require proof. The question of ability has truly been a vexed question. In the discussion of it, I shall consider the elder President Edwards as the representative of the common Calvinistic view of this subject, because he has stated it more clearly than any other Calvinistic author with whom I am acquainted. When, therefore, I speak of the Edwardean doctrine of ability and inability, you will understand me to speak of the common view of Calvinistic theological writers, as stated, summed up, and defended by Edwards.

In discussing this subject I will endeavor to show,--

I. President Edwards's notion of natural ability.

Edwards considers freedom and ability as identical. He defines freedom or liberty to consist in the power, opportunity, or advantage, that any one has, to do as he pleases. "Or, in other words, his being free from hindrance or impediment in the way of doing or conducting in any respect as he wills."--Works, vol. ii., page 38.

Again, page 39, he says, "One thing more I should observe concerning what is vulgarly called liberty; namely, that power and opportunity for one to do and conduct as he will, or according to his choice, is all that is meant by it; without taking into the meaning of the word anything of the cause of that choice; or at all considering how the person came to have such a volition; whether it was caused by some external motive, or internal habitual bias; whether it was determined by some internal antecedent volition, or whether it happened without a cause; whether it was necessarily connected with something foregoing, or not connected. Let the person come by his choice anyhow, yet if he is able, and there is nothing in the way to hinder his pursuing and exerting his will, the man is perfectly free, according to the primary and common notion of freedom." In the preceding paragraph, he says, "There are two things contrary to what is called liberty in common speech. One is, constraint; which is a person's being necessitated to do a thing contrary to his will: the other is, restraint, which is his being hindered, and not having power to do according to his will."

Power, ability, liberty, to do as you will, are synonymous with this writer. The foregoing quotations, with many like passages that might be quoted from the same author, show that natural liberty, or natural ability, according to him, consists in the natural and established connection between volition and its effects. Thus he says in another place, "Men are justly said to be able to do what they can do, if they will." His definition of natural ability, or natural liberty, as he frequently calls it, wholly excludes the power to will, and includes only the power or ability to execute our volitions. Thus it is evident, that natural ability, according to him, respects external action only, and has nothing to do with willing. When there is no restraint or hindrance to the execution of volition, when there is nothing interposed to disturb and prevent the natural and established result of our volitions, there is natural ability according to this school. It should be distinctly understood, that Edwards, and those of his school, hold that choices, volitions, and all acts of will, are determined, not by the sovereign power of the agent, but are caused by the objective motive, and that there is the same connection, or a connection as certain and as unavoidable between motive and choice, as between any physical cause and its effect: "the difference being," according to him, "not in the nature of the connection, but in the terms connected." Hence, according to his view, natural liberty or ability cannot consist in the power of willing or of choice, but must consist in the power to execute our choices or volitions. Consequently, this class of philosophers define free or moral agency to consist in the power to do as one wills, or power to execute one's purposes, choices, or volitions. That this is a fundamentally false definition of natural liberty or ability, and of free or moral agency, we shall see in due time. It is also plain, that the natural ability or liberty of Edwards and his school, has nothing to do with morality or immorality. Sin and holiness, as we have seen in a former lecture, are attributes of acts of will only. But this natural ability respects, as has been said, outward or muscular action only. Let this be distinctly borne in mind as we proceed.

II. This natural ability is no ability at all.

We know from consciousness that the will is the executive faculty, and that we can do absolutely nothing without willing. The power or ability to will is indispensable to our acting at all. If we have not the power to will, we have not power or ability to do anything. All ability or power to do resides in the will, and power to will is the necessary condition of ability to do. In morals and religion, as we shall soon see, the willing is the doing. The power to will is the condition of obligation to do. Let us hear Edwards himself upon this subject. Vol. ii. p. 156, he says, "The will itself, and not only those actions which are the effects of the will, is the proper object of precept or command. That is, such a state or acts of men's wills, are in many cases properly required of them by commands; and not only those alterations in the state of their bodies or minds that are the consequences of volition. This is most manifest; for it is the mind only that is properly and directly the subject of precepts or commands; that only being capable of receiving or perceiving commands. The motions of the body are matters of command only as they are subject to the soul, and connected with its acts. But the soul has no other faculty whereby it can, in the most direct and proper sense, consent, yield to, or comply with any command, but the faculty of the will; and it is by this faculty only that the soul can directly disobey or refuse compliance; for the very notions of consenting, yielding, accepting, complying, refusing, rejecting, etc., are, according to the meaning of terms, nothing but certain acts of will." Thus we see that Edwards himself held, that the will is the executive faculty, and that the soul can do nothing except as it wills to do it, and that for this reason a command to do is strictly a command to will. We shall see by and by, that he held also that the willing and the doing are identical, so far as moral obligation, morals, and religion are concerned. For the present, it is enough to say, whether Edwards or anybody else ever held it or not, that it is absurd and sheer nonsense to talk of an ability to do when there is no ability to will. Every one knows with intuitive certainty that he has no ability to do what he is unable to will to do. It is, therefore, the veriest folly to talk of a natural ability to do anything whatever, when we exclude from this ability the power to will. If there is no ability to will, there is, and can be no ability to do; therefore the natural ability of the Edwardean school is no ability at all.

Let it be distinctly understood, that whatever Edwards held in respect to the ability of man to do, ability to will entered not at all into his idea and definition of natural ability or liberty. But according to him, natural ability respects only the connection that is established by a law of nature between volition and its sequents, excluding altogether the inquiry how the volition comes to exist. This the foregoing quotations abundantly show. Let the impression, then, be distinct, that the Edwardean natural ability is no ability at all, and nothing but an empty name, a metaphysico-theological fiction.

III. What constitutes natural inability according to this school.

Edwards, vol. ii. p. 35, says, "We are said to be naturally unable to do a thing when we cannot do it if we will, because what is most commonly called nature, does not allow of it; or because of some impeding defect or obstacle that is extrinsic to the will; either in the faculty of understanding, constitution of body, or external objects." This quotation, together with much that might be quoted from this author to the same effect, shows that natural inability, according to him, consists in a want of power to execute our volitions. In the absence of power to do as we will, if the willing exists and the effect does not follow, it is only because we are unable to do as we will, and this is natural inability. We are naturally unable, according to him, to do what does not follow by a natural law from our volitions. If I will to move my arm, and the muscles do not obey volition, I am naturally unable to move my arm. So with anything else. Here let it be distinctly observed, that natural inability, as well as natural ability, respects and belongs only to outward action or doing. It has nothing to do with ability to will. Whatever Edwards held respecting ability to will, which will be shown in its proper place, I wish it to be distinctly understood that his natural inability had nothing to do with willing, but only with the effects of willing. When the natural effect of willing does not follow volition, its cause, here is a proper natural inability.

IV. This natural inability is no inability at all.

By this is intended that, so far as morals and religion are concerned, the willing is the doing, and therefore where the willing actually takes place, the real thing required or prohibited is already done. Let us hear Edwards upon this subject. Vol. ii. p. 164, he says, "If the will fully complies and the proposed effect does not prove, according to the laws of nature, to be connected with his volition, the man is perfectly excused; he has a natural inability to do the thing required. For the will itself, as has been observed, is all that can be directly and immediately required by command, and other things only indirectly, as connected with the will. If, therefore, there be a full compliance of will, the person has done his duty: and if other things do not prove to be connected with his volition, that is not criminally owing to him." Here, then, it is manifest, that the Edwardean notions of natural ability and inability have no connection with moral law or moral government, and, of course, with morals and religion. That the Bible everywhere accounts the willing as the deed, is most manifest. Both as it respects sin and holiness, if the required or prohibited act of the will takes place, the moral law and the lawgiver regard the deed as having been done, or the sin committed, whatever impediment may have prevented the natural effect from following. Here, then, let it be distinctly understood and remembered that Edwards's natural inability is, so far as morals and religion are concerned, no inability at all. An inability to execute our volitions, is in no case an inability to do our whole duty, since moral obligation, and of course, duty, respect strictly only acts of will. A natural inability must consist, as we shall see, in an inability to will. It is truly amazing that Edwards could have written the paragraph just quoted, and others to the same effect, without perceiving the fallacy and absurdity of his speculation--without seeing that the ability or inability about which he was writing, had no connection with morals or religion. How could he insist so largely that moral obligation respects acts of will only, and yet spend so much time in writing about an ability or inability to comply with moral obligation that respects outward action exclusively? This, on the face of it, was wholly irrelevant to the subject of morals and religion, upon which subjects he was professedly writing.

V. Natural ability is identical with freedom or liberty of will.

It has been, I trust, abundantly shown in a former lecture, and is admitted and insisted on by Edwards,--

1. That moral obligation respects strictly only acts of will.

2. That the whole of moral obligation resolves itself into an obligation to be disinterestedly benevolent, that is, to will the highest good of being for its own sake.

3. That willing is the doing required by the true spirit of the moral law. Ability, therefore, to will in accordance with the moral law, must be natural ability to obey God. But,--

4. This is and must be the only proper freedom of the will, so far as morals and religion, or so far as moral law is concerned. That must constitute true liberty of will that consists in the ability or power to will, either in accordance with, or in opposition to the requirements of moral law. Or in other words, true freedom or liberty of will must consist in the power or ability to will in every instance either in accordance with, or in opposition to, moral obligation. Observe, moral obligation respects acts of will. What freedom or liberty of will can there be in relation to moral obligation, unless the will or the agent has power or ability to act in conformity with moral obligation? To talk of a man's being free to will, or having liberty to will, when he has not the power or ability, is to talk nonsense. Edwards himself holds that ability to do, is indispensable to liberty to do. But if ability to do be a sine quâ non of liberty to do, must not the same be true of willing? That is, must not ability to will be essential to liberty to will? Natural ability and natural liberty to will, must then be identical. Let this be distinctly remembered, since many have scouted the doctrine of natural ability to obey God, who have nevertheless been great sticklers for the freedom of the will. In this they are greatly inconsistent. This ability is called a natural ability, because it belongs to man as a moral agent, in such a sense that without it he could not be a proper subject of command, of reward or punishment. That is, without this liberty or ability he could not be a moral agent, and a proper subject of moral government. He must then either possess this power in himself as essential to his own nature, or must possess power, or be able to avail himself of power to will in every instance in accordance with moral obligation. Whatever he can do, he can do only by willing; he must therefore either possess the power in himself directly to will as God commands, or he must be able by willing it to avail himself of power, and

to make himself willing. If he has power by nature to will directly as God requires, or by willing to avail himself of power so to will, he is naturally free and able to obey the commandments of God. Then let it be borne distinctly in mind, that natural ability, about which so much has been said, is nothing more nor less than the freedom or liberty of the will of a moral agent. No man knows what he says or whereof he affirms, who holds to the one and denies the other, for they are truly and properly identical.

VI. The human will is free, therefore men have power or ability to do all their duty.

1.The moral government of God everywhere assumes and implies the liberty of the human will, and the natural ability of men to obey God. Every command, every threatening, every expostulation and denunciation in the Bible implies and assumes this. Nor does the Bible do violence to the human intelligence in this assumption; for,--

2. The human mind necessarily assumes the freedom of the human will as a first truth.

First truths, let it be remembered, are those that are necessarily assumed by every moral agent. They are assumed always and necessarily by a law of the intelligence, although they may seldom be the direct objects of thought or attention. It is a universal law of the intelligence, to assume the truths of causality, the existence and the infinity of space, the existence and infinity of duration, and many other truths. These assumptions every moral agent always and necessarily takes with him, whether these things are matters of attention or not. And even should he deny any one or all of these first truths, he knows them to be true notwithstanding, and cannot but assume their truth in all his practical judgments. Thus, should any one deny the law and the doctrine of causality, as some in theory have done, he knows, and cannot but know,--he assumes, and cannot but assume, its truth at every moment. Without this assumption he could not so much as intend, or think of doing, or of any one else doing anything whatever. But a great part of his time, he may not, and does not, make this law a distinct object of thought or attention. Nor is he directly conscious of the assumption that there is such a law. He acts always upon the assumption, and a great part of his time is insensible of it. His whole activity is only the exercise of his own causality, and a practical acknowledgment of the truth, which in theory he may deny. Now just so it is with the freedom of the will, and with natural ability. Did we not assume our own liberty and ability, we should never think of attempting to do anything. We should not so much as think of moral obligation, either as it respects ourselves or others, unless we assumed the liberty of the human will. In all our judgments respecting our own moral character and that of others, we always and necessarily assume the liberty of the human will, or natural ability to obey God. Although we may not be distinctly conscious of this assumption, though we may seldom make the liberty of the human will the subject of direct thought or attention, and even though we may deny its reality, and strenuously endeavor to maintain the opposite, we, nevertheless, in this very denial and endeavor, assume that we are free. This truth never was, and never can be rejected in our practical judgments. All men assume it. All men must assume it. Whenever they choose in one direction, they always assume, whether conscious of the assumption or not, and cannot but assume, that they have power to will in the opposite direction. Did they not assume this, such a thing as election between two ways or objects would not be, and could not be, so much as thought of. The very ideas of right and wrong, of the praiseworthiness, and blameworthiness of human beings, imply the assumption, on the part of those who have these ideas, of the universal freedom of the human will, or of the natural ability of men as moral agents to obey God. Were not this assumption in the mind, it were impossible from its own nature and laws that it should affirm moral obligation, right or wrong, praiseworthiness or blameworthiness of men. I know that philosophers and theologians have in theory denied the doctrine of natural ability or liberty, in the sense in which I have defined it; and I know, too, that with all their theorizing, they did assume, in common with all other men, that man is free in the sense that he has liberty or power to will as God commands. I know that, but for this assumption, the human mind could no more predicate praiseworthiness or blameworthiness, right or wrong of man, than it could of the motions of a windmill. Men have often made the assumption in question without being aware of it, have affirmed right and wrong of human willing without seeing and understanding the conditions of this affirmation. But the fact is, that in all cases the assumption has lain deep in the mind as a first truth, that men are free in the sense of being naturally able to obey God: and this assumption is a necessary condition of the affirmation that moral character belongs to man.

VII. What constitutes moral inability, according to Edwards and those who hold with him.

I examine their views of moral inability first in order, because from their views of moral inability we ascertain more clearly what are their views of moral ability. Edwards regards moral ability and inability as identical with moral necessity. Concerning moral necessity, he says, vol. ii. pp. 32, 33, "And sometimes by moral necessity is meant that necessity of connection and consequence which arises from such moral causes as the strength of inclination or motives, and the connection which there is in many cases between these and such certain volitions and actions. And it is in this sense that I shall use the phrase moral necessity in the following discourse. By natural necessity, as applied to men, I mean such necessity as men are under through the force of natural causes, as distinguished from what are called moral causes, such as habits and dispositions of the heart, and moral motives and inducements. Thus men placed in certain circumstances are the subjects of particular sensations by necessity. They feel pain when their bodies are wounded; they see the objects presented before them in a clear light when their eyes are open: so they assent to the truth of certain propositions as soon as the terms are understood; as that two and two make four, that black is not white, that two parallel lines can never cross one another; so by a natural necessity men's bodies move downwards when there is nothing to support them. But here several things may be noted concerning these two kinds of necessity. 1. Moral necessity may be as absolute as natural necessity. That is, the effect may be as perfectly connected with its moral cause, as a natural effect is with its natural cause. Whether the will is in every case necessarily determined by the strongest motive, or whether the will ever makes any resistance to such a motive, or can ever oppose the strongest present inclination or not; if that matter should be controverted, yet I suppose none will deny, but that, in some cases, a previous bias and inclination, or the motive presented may be so powerful, that the act of the will may be certainly and indissolubly connected therewith. When motives or previous bias are very strong, all will allow that there is some difficulty in going against them. And if they were yet stronger, the difficulty would be still greater. And therefore if more were still added to their strength up to a certain degree, it might make the difficulty so great that it would be wholly impossible to surmount it, for this plain reason, because whatever power men may be supposed to have to surmount difficulties, yet that power is not infinite, and so goes not beyond certain limits. If a certain man can surmount ten degrees of difficulty of this kind, with twenty degrees of strength, because the degrees of strength are beyond the degrees of difficulty, yet if the difficulty be increased to thirty, or a hundred, or to a thousand degrees, and his strength not also increased, his strength will be wholly insufficient to surmount the difficulty. As therefore it must be allowed that there may be such a thing as a sure and perfect connection between moral causes and effects; so this only is what I call by the name of moral necessity." Page 35, he says: "What has been said of natural and moral necessity may serve to explain what is intended by natural and moral inability. We are said to be naturally unable to do a thing when we cannot do it if we will, because of some impeding defect or obstacle that is extrinsic to the will, either in the faculty of understanding, constitution of body, or external objects. Moral inability consists not in any of these things, but either in a want of inclination, or the want of sufficient motives in view, to induce and excite the act of the will, or the strength of apparent motives to the contrary. Or both these may be resolved into one, and it may be said in one word that moral inability consists in the opposition or want of inclination. For when a person is unable to will or choose such a thing, through a defect of motives or prevalence of contrary motives, it is the same thing as his being unable through the want of an inclination, or the prevalence of a contrary inclination in such circumstances, and under the influence of such views."

From these quotations, and much more that might be quoted to the same purpose, it is plain that Edwards, as the representative of his school, holds moral inability to consist, either in an existing choice or attitude of the will opposed to that which is required by the law of God, which inclination or choice is necessitated by motives in view of the mind, or in the absence of such motives as are necessary to cause or necessitate the state of choice required by the moral law, or to overcome an opposing choice. Indeed he holds these two to be identical. Observe, his words are, "Or these may be resolved into one, and it may be said in one word, that moral inability consists in opposition or want of inclination. For when a person is unable to will or choose such a thing, through a defect of motives, it is the same thing as his being unable through the want of an inclination, or the prevalence of a contrary inclination, in such circumstances and under the influence of such views," that is, in the presence of such motives. If there is a present prevalent contrary inclination, it is, according to him: 1. Because there are present certain reasons that necessitate this contrary inclination; and 2. Because there are not sufficient motives present to the mind to overcome these opposing motives and inclination, and to necessitate the will to determine or choose in the direction of the law of God. By inclination Edwards means choice or volition, as is abundantly evident from what he all along says in this connection. This no one will deny who is at all familiar with his writings.

It was the object of the treatise from which the above quotations have been made, to maintain that the choice invariably is as the greatest apparent good is.

And by the greatest apparent good he means, a sense of the most agreeable. By which he means, as he says, that the sense of the most agreeable, and choice or volition, are identical. Vol. ii., page 20, he says, "And therefore it must be true in some sense, that the will always is as the greatest apparent good is." "It must be observed in what sense I use the term good,' namely, as of the same import with agreeable. To appear good to the mind, as I use the phrase, is the same as to appear agreeable, or seem pleasing to the mind." Again, pp. 21, 22, he says: "I have rather chosen to express myself thus, that the will always is as the greatest apparent good is, or as what appears most agreeable, than to say that the will is determined by the greatest apparent good, or by what seems most agreeable; because an appearing most agreeable to the mind and the mind's preferring, seem scarcely distinct. If strict propriety of speech be insisted on, it may more properly be said, that the voluntary action, which is the immediate consequence of the mind's choice, is determined by that which appears most agreeable, than the choice itself." Thus it appears that the sense of the most agreeable, and choice or volition, according to Edwards, are the same things. Indeed, Edwards throughout confounds desire and volition, making them the same thing. Edwards regarded the mind as possessing but two primary faculties--the will and the understanding. He confounded all the states of the sensibility with acts of will. The strongest desire is with him always identical with volition or choice, and not merely that which determines choice. When there is a want of inclination or desire, or the sense of the most agreeable, there is a moral inability according to the Edwardean philosophy. This want of the strongest desire, inclination, or sense of the most agreeable, is always owing; 1. To the presence of such motives as to necessitate an opposite desire, choice, etc.; and 2. To the want of such objective motives as shall awaken this required desire, or necessitate this inclination or sense of the most agreeable. In other words, when volition or choice, in consistency with the law of God, does not exist, it is, 1. Because an opposite choice exists, and is necessitated by the presence of some motive; and 2. For want of sufficiently strong objective motives to necessitate the required choice or volition. Let it be distinctly understood and remembered, that Edwards held that motive, and not the agent, is the cause of all actions of the will. Will, with him, is always determined in its choice by motives as really as physical effects are produced by their causes. The difference with him in the connection of moral and physical causes and effects "lies not in the nature of the connection, but in the terms connected."

"That every act of the will has some cause, and consequently (by what has already been proved) has a necessary connection with its cause, and so is necessary by a necessity of connection and consequence, is evident by this, that every act of the will whatsoever is excited by some motive, which is manifest; because, if the mind, in willing after the manner it does, is excited by no motive or inducement, then it has no end which it proposes to itself, or pursues in so doing; it aims at nothing, and seeks nothing. And if it seeks nothing, then it does not go after anything, or exert any inclination or preference towards anything; which brings the matter to a contradiction; because for the mind to will something, and for it to go after something by an act of preference and inclination, are the same thing.

"But if every act of the will is excited by a motive, then that motive is the cause of the act. If the acts of the will are excited by motives, then motives are the causes of their being excited; or, which is the same thing, the cause of their existence. And if so, the existence of the acts of the will is properly the effect of their motives. Motives do nothing, as motives or inducements, but by their influence; and so much as is done by their influence is the effect of them. For that is the notion of an effect, something that is brought to pass by the influence of something else.

"And if volitions are properly the effects of their motives, then they are necessarily connected with their motives; every effect and event being, as was proved before, necessarily connected with that which is the proper ground and reason of its existence. Thus it is manifest that volition is necessary, and is not from any self-determining power in the will."--Vol. ii., pp. 86, 87.

Moral inability, then, according to this school, consists in a want of inclination, desire, or sense of the most agreeable, or the strength of an opposite desire or sense of the most agreeable. This want of inclination, etc., or this opposing inclination, etc., are identical with an opposing choice or volition. This opposing choice or inclination, or this want of the required choice, inclination, or sense of the most agreeable is owing, according to Edwards, 1. To the presence of such motives as to necessitate the opposing choice; and 2. To the absence of sufficient motives to beget or necessitate them. Here then we have the philosophy of this school. The will or agent is unable to choose as God requires in all cases, when, 1. There are present such motives as to necessitate an opposite choice; and, 2. When there is not such a motive or such motives in the view of the mind, as to determine or necessitate the required choice or volition; that is, to awaken a desire, or to create an inclination or sense of the agreeable stronger than any existing and opposing desire, inclination, or sense of agreeable. This is the moral inability of the Edwardeans.

VIII. Their moral inability to obey God consists in real disobedience and a natural inability to obey.

1. If we understand Edwardeans to mean that moral inability consists,--

(1.) In the presence of such motives as to necessitate an opposite choice; and,--

(2.) In the want or absence of sufficient motives to necessitate choice or volition, or, which is the same thing, a sense of the most agreeable, or an inclination, then their moral inability is a proper natural inability. Edwards says, he "calls it a moral inability, because it is an inability of will." But by his own showing, the will is the only executive faculty. Whatever a man can do at all, he can accomplish by willing, and whatever he cannot accomplish by willing he cannot accomplish at all. An inability to will then must be a natural inability. We are, by nature, unable to do what we are unable to will to do. Besides, according to Edwards, moral obligation respects strictly only acts of will, and willing is the doing that is prohibited or required by the moral law. To be unable to will then, is to be unable to do. To be unable to will as God requires, is to be unable to do what he requires, and this surely is a proper, and the only proper natural inability.

2. But if we are to understand this school, as maintaining that moral inability to obey God, consists in a want of the inclination, choice, desire, or sense of the most agreeable that God requires, or in an inclination or existing choice, volition, or sense of the most agreeable, which is opposed to the requirement of God, this surely is really identical with disobedience, and their moral inability to obey consists in disobedience. For, be it distinctly remembered, that Edwards holds, as we have seen, that obedience and

disobedience, properly speaking, can be predicated only of acts of will. If the required state of the will exists, there is obedience. If it does not exist, there is disobedience. Therefore, by his own admission and express holding, if by moral inability we are to understand a state of the will not conformed, or, which is the same thing, opposed to the law and will of God, this moral inability is nothing else than disobedience to God. A moral inability to obey is identical with disobedience. It is not merely the cause of future or present disobedience, but really constitutes the whole of present disobedience.

3. But suppose that we understand his moral inability to consist both in the want of an inclination, choice, volition, etc., or in the existence of an opposing state of the will, and also,--

(1.) In the presence of such motives as to necessitate an opposite choice, and,

(2.) In the want of sufficient motives to overcome the opposing state, and necessitate the required choice, volition, etc., then his views stand thus: moral inability to choose as God commands, consists in the want of this choice, or in the existence of an opposite choice, which want of choice, or, which is the same thing with him, which opposite choice is caused:--

(i.) By the presence of such motives as to necessitate the opposite choice, and,

(ii.) By the absence of such motives as would necessitate the required choice. Understand him which way you will, his moral inability is real disobedience, and is in the highest sense a proper natural inability to obey. The cause of choice or volition he always seeks, and thinks or assumes that he finds, in the objective motive, and never for once ascribes it to the sovereignty or freedom of the agent. Choice or volition is an event, and must have some cause. He assumes that the objective motive was the cause, when, as consciousness testifies, the agent is himself the cause. Here is the great error of Edwards. Edwards assumed that no agent whatever, not even God himself, possesses a power of self-determination, that the will of God and of all moral agents is determined, not by themselves, but by an objective motive. If they will in one direction or another, it is not from any free and sovereign self-determination in view of motives, but because the motives or inducements present to the mind, inevitably produce or necessitate the sense of the most agreeable, or choice. If this is not fatalism or natural necessity, what is?

IX. This pretended distinction between natural and moral inability is nonsensical.

What does it amount to? Why this:--

1. This natural inability is an inability to do as we will, or to execute our volitions.

2. This moral inability is an inability to will.

3. This moral inability is the only natural inability that has, or can have, anything to do with duty, or with morality and religion; or, as has been shown,--

4. It consists in disobedience itself. Present moral inability to obey is identical with present disobedience, with a natural inability to obey! It is amazing to see how so great and good a man could involve himself in a metaphysical fog, and bewilder himself and his readers to such a degree, that an absolutely senseless distinction should pass into the current phraseology, philosophy, and theology of the church, and a score of theological dogmas be

built upon the assumption of its truth. This nonsensical distinction has been in the mouth of the Edwardean school of theologians, from Edwards's day to the present. Both saints and sinners have been bewildered, and, I must say, abused by it. Men have been told that they are as really unable to will as God directs, as they were to create themselves; and when it is replied that this inability excuses the sinner, we are directly silenced by the assertion, that this is only a moral inability, or an inability of will, and therefore, that it is so far from excusing the sinner, that it constitutes the very ground, and substance, and whole of his guilt. Indeed! Men arc under moral obligation only to will as God directs. But an inability thus to will, consisting in the absence of such motives as would necessitate the required choice, or the presence of such motives as to necessitate an opposite choice, is a moral inability, and really constitutes the sinner worthy of an "exceeding great and eternal weight" of damnation! Ridiculous! Edwards I revere; his blunders I deplore. I speak thus of this Treatise on the Will, because, while it abounds with unwarrantable assumptions, distinctions without a difference, and metaphysical subtleties, it has been adopted as the text-book of a multitude of what are called Calvinistic divines for scores of years. It has bewildered the head, and greatly embarrassed the heart and the action of the church of God. It is time, high time, that its errors should be exposed, and so exploded, that such phraseology should be laid aside, and the ideas which these words represent should cease to be entertained.

X. What constitutes moral ability according to this school?

It is of course the opposite of moral inability. Moral ability, according to them, consists in willingness, with the cause of it. That is, moral ability to obey God consists in that inclination, desire, choice, volition, or sense of the most agreeable, which God requires together with its cause. Or it consists in the presence of such motives as do actually necessitate the above-named state or determination of the will. Or, more strictly, it consists in this state caused by the presence of these motives. This is as exact a statement of their views as I can make. According to this, a man is morally able to do as he does, and is necessitated to do, or, he is morally able to will as he does will, and as he cannot help willing. He is morally able to will in this manner, simply and only because he is caused thus to will by the presence of such motives as are, according to them, "indissolubly connected" with such a willing by a law of nature and necessity. But this conducts us to the conclusion,--

XI. Their moral ability to obey God is nothing else than real obedience and a natural inability to disobey.

Strictly, this moral ability includes both the state of will required by the law of God, and also the cause of this state, to wit, the presence of such motives as necessitate the inclination, choice, volition, or sense of the most agreeable, that God requires. The agent is able thus to will because he is caused thus to will. Or more strictly, his ability, and his inclination or willing, are identical. Or still further, according to Edwards, his moral ability thus to will and his thus willing, and the presence of the motives that cause this willing, are identical. This is a sublime discovery in philosophy; a most transcendental speculation! I would not treat these notions as ridiculous, were they not truly so, or if I could treat them in any other manner, and still do them anything like justice. If, where the theory is plainly stated, it appears ridiculous, the fault is not in me, but in the theory itself. I know it is trying to you, as it is to me, to connect anything ridiculous with so great and so revered a name as that of President Edwards. But if a blunder of his has entailed perplexity and error on the church, surely his great and good soul would now thank the hand that should blot out the error from under heaven.

Thus, when closely examined, this long established and venerated fog-bank vanishes away; and this famed distinction between moral and natural ability and inability, is found to be "a thing of nought."

XII. I will state what I consider to be the fundamental errors of Edwards and his school upon the subject of ability.

1. He denied that moral agents are the causes of their own actions. He started, of course, with the just assumption, that every event is an effect, and must have some cause. The choices and volitions of moral agents are effects of some cause. What is that cause? He assumed that every act of will must have been caused by a preceding one, or by the objective motive. By the reductio ad absurdum, he easily showed the absurdity of the first hypothesis, and consequently assumed the truth of the last. But how does he know that the sovereign power of the agent is not the cause? His argument against self-determination amounts to nothing; for it is, in fact, only a begging of the whole question. If we are conscious of anything, we are of the affirmation that we do, in fact, originate our own choices and volitions. Edwards, as really as any other man, believed himself to originate and be the proper cause of his own volitions. In his practical judgment be assumed his own causality, and the proper causality of all moral agents, or he never could have had so much as a conception of moral agency and accountability. But in theory, he adopted the capital error of denying the proper causality of moral agents. This error is fundamental. Every definition of a moral agent that denies or overlooks, his proper causality is radically defective. It drops out of the definition the very element that we necessarily affirm to be essential to liberty and accountability. Denying, as he did, the proper causality of moral agents, he was driven to give a false definition of free agency, as has been shown. Edwards rightly regarded the choices and volitions of moral agents as effects, but he looks in the wrong direction for the cause. Instead of heeding the affirmation of his own mind that causality, or the power of self-determination, is a sine quâ non of moral agency, he assumed, in theorizing, the direct opposite, and sought for the cause of choice and volition out of the agent, and in the objective motive; thus, in fact, denying the validity of the testimony of the pure reason, and reducing moral agents to mere machines. No wonder that so capital an error, and defended with so much ability, should have led one of his own sons into scepticism. But the piety of the president was stronger than even his powerful logic. Assuming a false major premise, his straightforward logic conducted him to the dogma of a universal necessity. But his well-developed reason, and deep piety of heart, controlled his practical judgment, so that few men have practically held the doctrines of accountability and retribution with a firmer grasp.

2. Edwards adopted the Lockean philosophy. He regarded the mind as possessing but two primary faculties, the understanding and the will. He considered all the desires, emotions, affections, appetites, and passions as voluntary, and as really consisting in acts of will. This confounding of the states of the sensibility with acts of the will, I regard as another fundamental error of his whole system of philosophy, so far as it respects the liberty of the will, or the doctrine of ability. Being conscious that the emotions, which he calls

affections, the desires, the appetites and passions, were so correlated to their appropriate objects, that they are excited by the presence or contemplation of them, and assuming them to be voluntary states of mind, or actions of the will, he very naturally, and with this assumption, necessarily and justly, concluded, that the will was governed or decided by the objective motive. Assuming as he did that the mind has but two faculties, understanding and will, and that every state of feeling and of mind that did not belong to the understanding, must be a voluntary state or act of will, and being conscious that his feelings, desires, affections, appetites and passions, were excited by the contemplation of their correlated objects, he could consistently come to no other conclusion than that the will is determined by motives, and that choice always is as the most agreeable is.

XIII. I will now present another scheme of inability and its philosophy.

1. This philosophy properly distinguishes between the will and the sensibility. It regards the mind as possessing three primary departments, powers, or susceptibilities, the intellect, the sensibility, and the will. It does not always call these departments or susceptibilities by these names, but if I understand them, the abetters of this philosophy hold to their existence, by whatever name they may call them.

2. This philosophy also holds, that the states of the intellect and of the sensibility are passive and involuntary.

3. It holds that freedom of will is a condition of moral agency.

4. It also teaches that the will is free, and consequently that man is a free moral agent.

5. It teaches that the will controls the outward life and the attention of the intellect, directly, and many of the emotions, desires, affections, appetites, and passions, or many states of the sensibility, indirectly.

6. It teaches that men have ability to obey God so far as acts of will are concerned, and also so far as those acts and states of mind are concerned that are under the direct or indirect control of the will.

7. But it holds that moral obligation may, and in the case of man at least, does extend beyond moral agency and beyond the sphere of ability; that ability or freedom of will is essential to moral agency, but that freedom of will or moral agency does not limit moral obligation; that moral agency and moral obligation are not co-extensive; consequently that moral obligation is not limited by ability or by moral agency.

8. This philosophy asserts that moral obligation extends to those states of mind that lie wholly beyond or without the sphere or control of the will; that it extends not merely to voluntary acts and states, together with all acts and states that come within the direct or indirect control of the will, but, as was said, it insists that those mental states that lie wholly beyond the will's direct or indirect control, come within the pale of moral legislation and obligation: and that therefore obligation is not limited by ability.

9. This philosophy seems to have been invented to reconcile the doctrine of original sin, in the sense of a sinful nature, or of constitutional moral depravity, with moral obligation. Assuming that original sin in this sense is a doctrine of divine revelation, it takes the bold and uncompromising ground already stated, namely, that moral obligation is not merely co-extensive with moral agency and ability, but extends beyond both into the region of those mental states that lie entirely without the will's direct or indirect control.

10. This bold assertion the abetters of this philosophy attempt to support by an appeal to the necessary convictions of men and to the authority of the Bible. They allege that the instinctive judgments of men, as well as the Bible, everywhere assume and affirm moral obligation and moral character of the class of mental states in question.

11. They admit that a physical inability is a bar to or inconsistent with moral obligation: but they of course deny that the inability to which they hold is physical.

XIV. This brings us to a brief consideration of the claims of this philosophy of inability.

1. It is based upon a petitio principii, or a begging of the question. It assumes that the instinctive or irresistible and universal judgments of men, together with the Bible, assert and assume that moral obligation and moral character extend to the states of mind in question. It is admitted that the teachings of the Bible are to be relied upon. It is also admitted that the first truths of reason, or what this philosophy calls the instinctive and necessary judgments of all men, must be true. But it is not admitted that the assertion in question is a doctrine of the Bible or a first truth of reason. On the contrary both are denied. It is denied, at least by me, that either reason or divine revelation affirms moral obligation or moral character of any state of mind, that lies wholly beyond both the direct and the indirect control of the will. Now this philosophy must not be allowed to beg the question in debate. Let it be shown, if it can be, that the alleged truth is either a doctrine of the Bible or a first truth of reason. Both reason and revelation do assert and assume, that moral obligation and moral character extend to acts of will, and to all those outward acts or mental states that lie within its direct or indirect control. "But further these deponents say not." Men are conscious of moral obligation in respect to these acts and states of mind, and of guilt when they fail, in these respects, to comply with moral obligation. But who ever blamed himself for pain, when, without his fault, he received a blow, or was seized with the tooth-ache, or a fit of bilious colic?

2. Let us inquire into the nature of this inability. Observe, it is admitted by this school that a physical inability is inconsistent with moral obligation--in other words, that physical ability is a condition of moral obligation. But what is a physical inability? The primary definition of the adjective physical, given by Webster, is, "pertaining to nature, or natural, objects." A physical inability then, in the primary sense of the term physical, is an inability of nature. It may be either a material or a mental inability; that is, it may be either an inability of body or mind. It is admitted by the school whose views we are canvassing, that all human causality or ability resides in the will, and therefore that there is a proper inability of nature to perform anything that does not come within the sphere of the direct or indirect causality of, or control of the will. It is plain, therefore, that the inability for which they contend must be a proper natural inability, or inability of nature. This they fully admit and maintain. But this they do not call a physical inability. But why do they not? Why, simply because it would, by their own admissions, overthrow their favorite position. They seem to assume that a physical inability must be a material inability. But where is the authority for such an assumption? There is no authority for it. A proper inability of nature must be a physical inability, as opposed to moral inability, or there is no meaning in language. It matters not at all whether the inability

belongs to the material organism, or to the mind. If it be constitutional, and properly an inability of nature, it is nonsense to deny that this is a physical inability, or to maintain that it can be consistent with moral obligation. It is in vain to reply that this inability, though a real inability of nature, is not physical but moral, because a sinful inability. This is another begging of the question.

The school whose views I am examining, maintain, that this inability is founded in the first sin of Adam. His first sin plunged himself and his posterity, descending from him by a natural law, into a total inability of nature to render any obedience to God. This first sin of Adam entailed a nature on all his posterity "wholly sinful in every faculty and part of soul and body." This constitutional sinfulness that belongs to every faculty and part of soul and body, constitutes the inability of which we are treating. But mark, it is not physical inability, because it is a sinful inability! Important theological distinction!--as truly wonderful, surely, as any of the subtleties of the Jesuits. But if this inability is sinful, it is important to inquire, Whose sin is it? Who is to blame for it? Why to be sure, we are told that it is the sin of him upon whom it is thus entailed by the natural law of descent from parent to child without his knowledge or consent. This sinfulness of nature, entirely irrespective of, and previous to any actual transgression, renders its possessor worthy of and exposed to the wrath and curse of God for ever. This sinfulness, observe, is transmitted by a natural or physical law from Adam, but it is not a physical inability. It is something that inheres in, and belongs to every faculty and part of soul and body. It is transmitted by a physical law from parent to child. It is, therefore, and must be a physical thing. But yet we are told that it cannot be a physical inability, because first, it is sinful, or sin itself; and, secondly, because a physical inability is a bar to, or inconsistent with, moral obligation. Here, then, we have their reasons for not admitting this to be a physical inability. It would in this case render moral obligation an impossibility; and, besides, if a, bar to moral obligation, it could not be sinful. But it is sinful, it is said, therefore it cannot be physical. But how do we know that it is sinful? Why, we are told, that the instinctive judgments of men, and the Bible everywhere affirm and assume it. We are told, that both the instinctive judgments of men and the Bible affirm and assume, both the inability in question and the sinfulness of it; "that we ought to be able, but are not;" that is, that we are so much to blame for this inability of nature entailed upon us without our knowledge or consent, by a physical necessity, as to deserve the wrath and curse of God for ever. We are under a moral obligation not to have this sinful nature. We deserve damnation for having it. To be sure, we are entirely unable to put it away, and had no agency whatever in its existence. But what of that? We are told, that "moral obligation is not limited by ability;" that our being as unable to change our nature as we are to create a world, is no reason why we should not be under obligation to do it, since "moral obligation does not imply ability of any kind to do what we are under obligation to do!" . . . . I was about to expose the folly and absurdity of these assertions, but hush! It is not allowable, we are told, to reason on this subject. We shall deceive ourselves if we listen to the "miserable logic of our understandings." We must fall back, then, upon the intuitive affirmations of reason and the Bible. Here, then, we are willing to lodge our appeal. The Bible defines sin to be a transgression of the law. What law have we violated in inheriting this nature? What law requires us to have a different nature from that which we possess? Does reason affirm that we are deserving of the wrath and curse of God for ever, for inheriting from Adam a sinful nature?

What law of reason have we transgressed in inheriting this nature? Reason cannot condemn us, unless we have violated some law which it can recognize as such. Reason indignantly rebukes such nonsense. Does the Bible hold us responsible for impossibilities? Does it require of us what we cannot do by willing to do it? Nay, verily; but it expressly affirms, that "if there be first a willing mind, it is accepted according to that a man hath, and not according to that he hath not." The plain meaning of this passage is, that if one wills as God directs, he has thereby met all his obligation; that he has done all that is naturally possible to him, and therefore nothing more is required. In this passage, the Bible expressly limits obligation by ability. This we have repeatedly seen in former lectures. The law also, as we have formerly seen, limits obligation by ability. It requires only that we should love the Lord with all our strength, that is, with all our ability, and our neighbor as ourselves.

Does reason hold us responsible for impossibilities, or affirm our obligation to do, or be, what it is impossible for us to do and be? No indeed! Reason never did and never can condemn us for our nature, and hold us worthy of the wrath and curse of God for possessing it. Nothing is more shocking and revolting to reason, than such assumptions as are made by the philosophy in question. This every man's consciousness must testify.

But is it not true that some, at least, do intelligently condemn themselves for their nature, and adjudge themselves to be worthy of the wrath and curse of God for ever for its sinfulness? The framers of the Westminster Confession of Faith made this affirmation in words, at least; whether intelligently or unintelligently, we are left to inquire. The reason of a moral agent condemning himself, and adjudging himself worthy of the wrath and curse of God for ever, for possessing a nature entailed on him by a natural law, without his knowledge or consent! This can never be.

But is it not true, as is affirmed, that men instinctively and necessarily affirm their obligation to be able to obey God, while they at the same time affirm that they are not able? I answer, no. They affirm themselves to be under obligation simply, and only, because deeply in their inward being lies the assumption that they are able to comply with the requirements of God. They are conscious of ability to will, and of power to control their outward life directly, and the states of the intellect and of their sensibility, either directly or indirectly, by willing. Upon this consciousness they found the affirmation of obligation, and of praise-worthiness and blame-worthiness in respect to these acts and states of mind. But for the consciousness of ability, no affirmation of moral obligation, or of praise-worthiness or blame-worthiness, were possible.

But do not those who affirm both their inability and their obligation, deceive themselves? I answer, yes. It is common for persons to overlook assumptions that lie, so to speak, at the bottom of their minds. This has been noticed in former lectures, and need not be here repeated.

It is true indeed that God requires of men, especially under the gospel, what they are unable to do directly in their own strength. Or more strictly speaking, he requires them to lay hold on his strength, or to avail themselves of his grace, as the condition of being what he requires them to be. With strict propriety, it cannot be said that in this, or in any case, he requires directly any more than we are able directly to do. The direct requirement in the case under consideration, is to avail ourselves of, or to lay hold upon his strength. This we have power to do. He requires us to lay hold upon his grace and strength, and thereby to rise to a higher knowledge of himself, and to a consequent higher state of holiness than would be otherwise possible to us. The direct requirement is to believe, or to lay hold upon his strength, or to receive the Holy Spirit, or Christ, who stands at the door, and knocks, and waits for admission. The indirect requirement is to rise to a degree of knowledge of God, and to spiritual attainments that are impossible to us in our own strength. We have ability to obey the direct command directly, and the indirect command indirectly. That is, we are able by virtue of our nature, together with the proffered grace of the Holy Spirit, to comply with all the requirements of God. So that in fact there is no proper inability about it.

But are not men often conscious of there being much difficulty in the way of rendering to God all that we affirm ourselves under obligation to render? I answer, yes. But strictly speaking, they must admit their direct or indirect ability, as a condition of affirming their obligation. This difficulty, arising out of their physical depravity, and the power of temptation from without, is the foundation or cause of the spiritual warfare of which the Scriptures speak, and of which all Christians are conscious. But the Bible abundantly teaches, that through grace we are able to be more than conquerors. If we are able to be this through grace, we are able to avail ourselves of the provisions of grace, so that there is no proper inability in the case. However great the difficulties may be, we are able through Christ to overcome them all. This we must and do assume as the condition of the affirmation of obligation.

LECTURE XXXII - GRACIOUS ABILITY

Grace is unmerited favor. Its exercise consists in bestowing that which, without a violation of justice, might be withheld.

Ability to obey God, as we have seen, is the possession of power adequate to the performance of that which is required. If, then, the terms are used in the proper sense, by a gracious ability must be intended that the power which men at present possess to obey the commands of God, is a gift of grace relatively to the command; that is, the bestowment of power adequate to the performance of the thing required, is a matter of grace as opposed to justice.

I. I will show what is intended by the term gracious ability.

The abettors of this scheme hold that by the first sin of Adam, he, together with all his posterity, lost all natural power and all ability of every kind to obey God; that therefore they were, as a race, wholly unable to obey the moral law, or to render to God any acceptable service whatever; that is, that they became, as a consequence of the sin of Adam, wholly unable to use the powers of nature in any other way than to sin. They were able to sin or to disobey God, but entirely unable to obey him; that they did not lose all power to act, but that they had power to act only in one direction, that is, in opposition to the will and law of God. By a gracious ability they intend, that in consequence of the atonement of Christ, God has graciously restored to man ability to accept the terms of mercy, or to fulfil the conditions of acceptance with God; in other words, that by the gracious aid of the Holy Spirit which, upon condition of the atonement, God has given to every member of the human family, all men are endowed with a gracious ability to obey God. By a gracious ability is intended, then, that ability or power to obey God, which all men now possess, not by virtue of their own nature or constitutional powers, but by virtue of the indwelling and gracious influence of the Holy Spirit, gratuitously bestowed upon man in consequence of the atonement of Christ. The inability, or total loss of all natural power to obey God into which men as a race fell by the first sin of Adam, they call original sin; perhaps more strictly, this inability is a consequence of that original sin into which man fell; which original sin itself consisted in the total corruption of man's whole nature. They hold, that by the atonement Christ made satisfaction for original sin, in such a sense that the inability resulting from it is removed, and that now men are by gracious aid able to obey and accept the terms of salvation. That is, they are able to repent and believe the gospel. In short, they are able, by virtue of this gracious ability, to do their duty, or to obey God. This, if I understand these theologians, is a fair statement of their doctrine of gracious ability.

II. This doctrine of a gracious ability is an absurdity.

The question is not whether, as a matter of fact, men ever do obey God without the gracious influence of the Holy Spirit. I hold that they do not. So the fact of the Holy Spirit's gracious influence being exerted in every case of human obedience, is not a question in debate between those who maintain, and those who deny the doctrine of gracious ability, in the sense above explained.

The question in debate is not whether men do, in any ease, use the powers of nature in the manner that God requires, without the gracious influence of the Holy Spirit, but whether they are naturally able so to use them. Is the fact, that they never do so use them without a gracious divine influence, to be ascribed to absolute inability, or to the fact that, from the beginning, they universally and voluntarily consecrate their powers to the gratification of self, and that therefore they will not, unless they are divinely persuaded, by the gracious influence of the Holy Spirit, in any case turn and consecrate their powers to the service of God? If this doctrine of natural inability and of gracious ability be true, it inevitably follows:--

1. That but for the atonement of Christ, and the consequent bestowment of a gracious ability, no one of Adam's race could ever have been capable of sinning. For in this case the whole race would have been wholly destitute of any kind or degree of ability to obey God. Consequently they could not have been subjects of moral government, and of course their actions could have had no moral character. It is a first-truth of reason, a truth everywhere and by all men necessarily assumed in their practical judgments, that a subject of moral government must be a moral agent, or that moral agency is a necessary condition of any one's being a subject of a moral government. And in the practical judgment of men, it matters not at all whether a being ever was a moral agent, or not. If by any means whatever he has ceased to be a moral agent, men universally and necessarily assume, that it is impossible for him to be a subject of moral government any more than a horse can be such a subject. Suppose he has by his own fault made himself an idiot or a lunatic; all men know absolutely, and in their practical judgment assume, that in this state he is not, and cannot be a subject of moral government. They know that in this state, moral character cannot justly be predicated of his actions. His guilt in thus depriving himself of moral agency may be exceeding great, and his guilt in thus depriving himself of moral agency may equal the sum of all the default of which it is the cause,--but be a moral agent, be under moral obligation, in this state of dementation or insanity, he cannot. This is a first-truth of reason, irresistibly and universally assumed by all men. If therefore Adam's posterity had by their own personal act cast away and deprived themselves of all ability to obey God, in this State they would have ceased to be moral agents, and consequently they could have sinned no more. But the case under consideration is not the one just supposed, but is one where moral agency was not cast away by the agent himself. It is one where moral agency was never, and never could have been possessed. In the case under consideration, Adam's posterity, had he ever had any, would never have possessed any power to obey God, or to do anything acceptable to him. Consequently, they never could have sustaincd to God the relation of subjects of his moral government. Of course they never could have had moral character; right or wrong, in a moral sense, never could have been predicated of their actions.

2. It must follow from this doctrine of gracious ability and natural inability, that mankind lost their freedom, or the liberty of will in the first sin of Adam; that both Adam himself, and all his posterity would and could have sustained to God only the relation of necessary, as opposed to free, agents, had not God bestowed upon them a gracious ability.

But that either Adam or his posterity lost their freedom or free agency by the first sin of Adam, is not only a sheer but an absurd assumption. To be sure

Adam fell into a state of total alienation from the law of God, and lapsed into a state of supreme selfishness. His posterity have unanimously followed his example. He and they have become dead in trespasses and sins. Now that this death in sin either consists in, or implies, the loss of free agency, is the very thing to be proved. But this cannot be proved. I have so fully discussed the subject of human moral depravity or sinfulness on a former occasion, as to render it unnecessary to enlarge upon it here.

3. Again, if it be true, as these theologians affirm, that men have only a gracious ability to obey God, and that this gracious ability consists in the presence and gracious agency of the Holy Spirit, it follows that, when the Holy Spirit is withdrawn from man, he is no longer a free agent, and from that moment he is incapable of moral action and of course can sin no more. Hence, should he live any number of years after this withdrawal, neither sin nor holiness, virtue nor vice, praiseworthiness nor blameworthiness could be predicated of his conduct. The same will and must be true of all his future eternity.

4. If the doctrine in question be true, it follows, that from the moment of the withdrawal of the gracious influence of the Holy Spirit, man is no longer a subject of moral obligation. It is from that moment absurd and unjust to require the performance of any duty of him. Nay to conceive of him as being any longer a subject of duty; to think or speak of duty as belonging to him, is as absurd as to think or speak of the duty of a mere machine. He has, from the moment of the withholding of a gracious ability, ceased to be a free and become a necessary agent, having power to act but in one direction. Such a being can by no possibility be capable of sin or holiness. Suppose he still possesses power to act contrary to the letter of the law of God; what then? This action can have no moral character, because, act in some way he must, and he can act in no other way. It is nonsense to affirm that such action can be sinful in the sense of blameworthy. To affirm that it can, is to contradict a first truth of reason. Sinners, then, who have quenched the Holy Spirit, and from whom he is wholly withdrawn, are no longer to be blamed for their enmity against God, and for all their opposition to him. They are, according to this doctrine, as free from blame as are the motions of a mere machine.

5. Again, if the doctrine in question be true, there is no reason to believe that the angels that fell from their allegiance to God ever sinned but once. If Adam lost his free agency by the fall, or by his first sin, there can be no doubt that the angels did so too. If a gracious ability had not been bestowed upon Adam, it is certain, according to the doctrine in question, that he never could have been the subject of moral obligation from the moment of his first sin, and consequently, could never again have sinned. The same must be true of devils. If by their first sin they fell into the condition of necessary agents, having lost their free agency, they have never sinned since. That is, moral character cannot have been predicable of their conduct since that event, unless a gracious ability has been bestowed upon them. That this has been done cannot, with even a show of reason, be pretended. The devils, then, according to this doctrine, are not now to blame for all they do to oppose God and to ruin souls. Upon the supposition in question, they cannot help it; and you might as well blame the winds and the waves for the evils which they sometimes do, as blame Satan for what he does.

6. If this doctrine be true, there is not, and never will be, any sin in hell, for the plain reason, that there are no moral agents there. They are necessary agents, unless it be true, that the Holy Spirit and a gracious ability be continued there. This is not, I believe, contended for by the abettors of this scheme. But if they deny to the inhabitants of hell freedom of the will, or, which is the same thing, natural ability to obey God, they must admit, or be grossly inconsistent, that there is no sin in hell, either in men or devils. But is this admission agreeable either to reason or revelation? I know that the abettors of this scheme maintain, that God may justly hold both men, from whom a gracious ability is withdrawn, and devils, responsible for their conduct, upon the ground that they have destroyed their own ability. But suppose this were true--that they had rendered themselves idiots, lunatics, or necessary as opposed to free agents, could God justly, could enlightened reason still regard them as moral agents, and as morally responsible for their conduct? No, indeed! God and reason may justly blame, and render them miserable, for annihilating their freedom or their moral agency, but to hold them still responsible for present obedience, were absurd.

7. We have seen that the ability of all men of sane mind to obey God, is necessarily assumed as a first truth, and that this assumption is from the very laws of mind, the indispensable condition of the affirmation, or even the conception, that they are subjects of moral obligation; that, but for this assumption, men could not so much as conceive the possibility of moral responsibility, and of praiseworthiness and blameworthiness. If the laws of mind remain unaltered, this is and always will be so. In the eternal world and in hell, men and devils must necessarily assume their own freedom or ability to obey God, as the condition of their obligation to do so, and, consequently of their being capable of sin or holiness. Since revelation informs us that men and devils continue to sin in hell, we know that there also it must be assumed as a first truth of reason, that they are free agents, or that they have natural ability to obey God.

8. But that a gracious ability to do duty or to obey God is an absurdity, will further appear, if we consider that it is a first truth of reason, that moral obligation implies moral agency, and that moral agency implies freedom of will; or in other words, it implies a natural ability to comply with obligation. This ability is necessarily regarded by the intelligence as the sine quâ non of moral obligation, on the ground of natural and immutable justice. A just command always implies an ability to obey it. A command to perform a natural impossibility would not, and could not, impose obligation. Suppose God should command human beings to fly without giving them power; could such a command impose moral obligation? No, indeed But suppose he should give them power, or promise them power, upon the performance of a condition within their reach; then he might in justice require them to fly, and a command to do so would be obligatory. But relatively to the requirement, the bestowment of power would not be grace, but justice. Relatively to the results or the pleasure of flying, the bestowment of power might be gracious. That is, it might be grace in God to give me power to fly, that I might have the pleasure and profit of flying; so that relatively to the results of flying, the giving of power might be regarded as an act of grace. But, if God requires me to fly as a matter of duty, he must in justice supply the power or ability to fly. This would in justice be a necessary condition of the command imposing moral obligation.

Nor would it at all vary the case if I had ever possessed wings, and by the abuse of them had lost the power to fly. In this case, considered relatively to the pleasure, and profit, and results of flying, the restoring of the power to fly might and would be an act of grace. But if God would still command me to fly, he must, as a condition of my obligation, restore the power. It is vain and absurd to say, as has been said, that in such a case, although I might lose the power of obedience, this could not alter the right of God to claim obedience. This assertion proceeds upon the absurd assumption that the will of God makes or creates law, instead of merely declaring and enforcing the law of nature. We have seen in former lectures, that the only law or rule of action that is, or can be obligatory on a moral agent, is the law of nature, or just that course of willing and acting, which is for the time being, suitable to his nature and relations. We have seen that God's will never makes or creates law, that it only declares and enforces it. If therefore, by any means whatever, the nature of a moral agent should be so changed that his will is no longer free to act in conformity with, or in opposition to, the law of nature, if God would hold him still obligated to obey, he must in justice, relatively to his requirement, restore his liberty or ability. Suppose one had by the abuse of his intellect lost the use of it, and become a perfect idiot, could he by any possibility be still required to understand and obey God? Certainly not. So neither could he be required to perform anything else that had become naturally impossible to him. Viewed relatively to the pleasure and results of obedience, the restoring of power would be an act of grace. But viewed relatively to his duty or to God's command, the restoring of power to obey is an act of justice and not of grace. To call this grace were to abuse language, and confound terms.

III. In what sense is a gracious ability possible?

1. Not, as we have just seen, in the sense that the bestowment of power to render obedience to a command possible, can be properly a gift of grace. Grace is undeserved favor, something not demanded by justice, that which under the circumstances might be withholden without injustice. It never can be just in any being to require that which under the circumstances is impossible. As has been said, relatively to the requirement and as a condition of its justice, the bestowment of power adequate to the performance of that which is commanded, is an unalterable condition of the justice of the command. This I say is a first truth of reason, a truth everywhere by all men necessarily assumed and known. A gracious ability to obey a command, is an absurdity and an impossibility.

2. But a gracious ability considered relatively to the advantages to result from obedience is possible. Suppose, for example, that a servant who supports himself and his family by his wages, should by his own fault render himself unable to labor and to earn his wages. His master may justly dismiss him, and let him go with his family to the poor-house. But in this disabled state his master cannot justly exact labor of him. Nor could he do so if he absolutely owned the servant. Now suppose the master to be able to restore to the servant his former strength. If he would require service of him, as a condition of the justice of this requirement, he must restore his strength so far at least as to render obedience possible. This would be mere justice. But suppose he restored the ability of the servant to gain support for himself and his family by labor. This, viewed relatively to the good of the servant, to the results of the restoration of his ability to himself and to his family, is a matter of grace.

Relatively to the right of the master in requiring the labor of the servant, the restoration of ability to obey is an act of justice. But relatively to the good of the servant, and the benefits that result to him from this restoration of ability, and making it once more possible for him to support himself and his family, the giving of ability is properly an act of grace.

Let this be applied to the ease under consideration. Suppose the race of Adam to have lost their free agency by the first sin of Adam, and thus to have come into a state in which holiness and consequent salvation were impossible. Now, if God would still require obedience of them, he must in justice restore their ability. And viewed relatively to his right to command, and their duty to obey, this restoration is properly a matter of justice. But suppose he would again place them in circumstances to render holiness and consequent salvation possible to them:-- viewed relatively to their good and profit, this restoration of ability is properly a matter of grace.

A gracious ability to obey, viewed relatively to the command to be obeyed, is impossible and absurd. But a gracious ability to be saved, viewed relatively to salvation, is possible. There is no proof that mankind ever lost their ability to obey, either by the first sin of Adam, or by their own sin. For this would imply, as we have seen, that they had ceased to be free, and had become necessary agents. But if they had, and God had restored their ability to obey, all that can be justly said in this case, is, that so far as his right to command is concerned, the restoration of their ability was an act of justice. But so far as the rendering of salvation possible to them is concerned, it was an act of grace.

3. But it is asserted, or rather assumed by the defenders of the dogma under consideration, that the Bible teaches the doctrine of a natural inability, and of a gracious ability in man to obey the commands of God. 1 admit, indeed, that if we interpret scripture without regard to any just rules of interpretation, this assumption may find countenance in the word of God, just as almost any absurdity whatever may do, and has done. But a moderate share of attention to one of the simplest and most universal and most important rules of interpreting language, whether in the Bible or out of it, will strip this absurd dogma of the least appearance of support from the word of God. The rule to which I refer is this, "That language is always to be interpreted in accordance with the subject-matter of discourse."

When used of acts of will, the term "cannot," interpreted by this rule, must not be understood to mean a proper impossibility. If I say, I cannot take five dollars for my watch, when it is offered to me, every one knows that I do not and cannot mean to affirm a proper impossibility. So when the angel said to Lot, "Haste thee, for I cannot do anything until thou be come thither," who ever understood him as affirming a natural or any proper impossibility? All that hc could have meant was, that he was not willing to do anything until Lot was in a place of safety. Just so when the Bible speaks of our inability to comply with the commands of God, all that can be intended is, that we are so unwilling that, without divine persuasion, we, as a matter of fact, shall not and will not obey. This certainly is the sense in which such language is used in common life. And in common parlance, we never think of such language, when used of acts of will, as meaning anything more than unwillingness, a state in which the will is strongly committed in an opposite direction.

When Joshua said to the children of Israel, "Ye cannot serve the Lord, for he is a holy God," the whole context, as well as the nature of the case, shows that he did not mean to affirm a natural, nor indeed any kind of impossibility. In the same connection, he requires them to serve the Lord, and leads them solemnly to pledge themselves to serve him. He undoubtedly intended to say, that with wicked hearts they could not render him an acceptable service, and therefore insisted on their putting away the wickedness of their hearts, by immediately and voluntarily consecrating themselves to the service of the Lord. So it must be in all cases where the term "cannot," and such-like expressions which, when applied to muscular action, would imply a proper impossibility, are used in reference to acts of will; they cannot, when thus used, be understood as implying a proper impossibility, without doing violence to every sober rule of interpreting language. What would be thought of a judge or an advocate at the bar of an earthly tribunal, who should interpret the language of a witness without any regard to the rule, "That language is to be understood according to the subject-matter of discourse." Should an advocate in his argument to the court or jury, attempt to interpret the language of a witness in a manner that made "cannot," when spoken of an act of will, mean a proper impossibility, the judge would soon rebuke his stupidity, and remind him that he must not talk nonsense in a court of justice; and might possibly add, that such nonsensical assertions were allowable only in the pulpit. I say again, that it is an utter abuse and perversion of the laws of language, so to interpret the Bible as to make it teach a proper inability in man to will as God directs. The essence of obedience to God consists in willing. Language, then, used in reference to obedience must, when properly understood, be interpreted in accordance with the subject-matter of discourse. Consequently, when used in reference to acts of will, such expressions as "cannot," and the like, can absolutely mean nothing more than a choice in an opposite direction.

But it may be asked, Is there no grace in all that is done by the Holy Spirit to make man wise unto salvation? Yes, indeed, I answer. And it is grace, and great grace, just because the doctrine of a natural inability in man to obey God is not true. It is just because man is well able to render obedience, and unjustly refuses to do so, that all the influence that God brings to bear upon him to make him willing, is a gift and an influence of grace. The grace is great, just in proportion to the sinner's ability to comply with God's requirements, and the strength of his voluntary opposition to his duty. If man were properly unable to obey, there could be no grace in giving him ability to obey, when the bestowment of ability is considered relatively to the command. But let man be regarded as free, as possessing natural ability to obey all the requirements of God, and all his difficulty as consisting in a wicked heart, or, which is the same thing, in an unwillingness to obey, then an influence on the part of God designed and tending to make him willing, is grace indeed. But strip man of his freedom, render him naturally unable to obey, and you render grace impossible, so far as his obligation to obedience is concerned.

But it is urged in support of the dogma of natural inability and of a gracious ability, that the Bible everywhere represents man as dependent on the gracious influence of the Holy Spirit for all holiness, and consequently for eternal life. I answer, it is admitted that this is the representation of the Bible, but the question is, in what sense is he dependent? Does his dependence consist in a natural inability to embrace the gospel and be saved? or does it consist in a voluntary selfishness--in an unwillingness to comply with the terms of salvation? Is man dependent on the Holy Spirit to give him a proper ability to obey God? or is he dependent only in such a sense that, as a matter of fact, he will not embrace the gospel unless the Holy Spirit makes him willing? The latter, beyond reasonable question, is the truth. This is the universal representation of scripture. The difficulty to be overcome is everywhere in the Bible represented to be the sinner's unwillingness alone. It cannot possibly be anything else; for the willingness is the doing required by God. "If there is first a willing mind, it is accepted according to that a man hath, and not according to that he hath not."

But it is said, if man can be willing of himself, what need of divine persuasion or influence to make him willing? I might ask, suppose a man is able but unwilling to pay his debts, what need of any influence to make him willing? Why, divine influence is needed to make a sinner willing, or to induce him to will as God directs, just for the same reason that persuasion, entreaty, argument, or the rod, is needed to make our children submit their wills to ours. The fact therefore that the Bible represents the sinner as in some sense dependent upon divine influence for a right heart, no more implies a proper inability in the sinner, than the fact that children are dependent for their good behavior, oftentimes, upon the thorough and timely discipline of their parents, implies a proper inability in them to obey their parents without chastisement.

The Bible everywhere, and in every way, assumes the freedom of the will. This fact stands out in strong relief upon every page of divine inspiration. But this is only the assumption necessarily made by the universal intelligence of man. The strong language often found in scripture upon the subject of man's inability to obey God, is designed only to represent the strength of his voluntary selfishness and enmity against God, and never to imply a proper natural inability. It is, therefore, a gross and most injurious perversion of scripture, as well as a contradiction of human reason, to deny the natural ability, or which is the same thing, the natural free agency of man, and to maintain a proper natural inability to obey God, and the absurd dogma of a gracious ability to do our duty.

REMARKS

1. The question of ability is one of great practical importance. To deny the ability of man to obey the commandments of God, is to represent God as a hard master, as requiring a natural impossibility of his creatures on pain of eternal damnation. This necessarily begets in the mind that believes it hard thoughts of God. The intelligence cannot be satisfied with the justice of such a requisition. In fact, so far as this error gets possession of the mind and gains assent, just so far it naturally and necessarily excuses itself for disobedience, or for not complying with the commandments of God.

2. The moral inability of Edwards is a real natural inability, and so it has been understood by sinners and professors of religion. When I entered the ministry, I found the persuasion of an absolute inability on the part of sinners to repent and believe the gospel, almost universal. When I urged sinners and professors of religion to do their duty without delay, I frequently met with stern opposition from sinners, professors of religion, and ministers. They desired me to say to sinners, that they could not repent, and that they must wait God's time, that is, for God to help them. It was common for the classes of persons just named to ask me, if I thought sinners could be Christians whenever they

pleased, and whether I thought that any class of persons could repent, believe, and obey God without the strivings and new-creating power of the Holy Spirit. The church was almost universally settled down in the belief of a physical moral depravity, and, of course, in a belief in the necessity of a physical regeneration, and also of course in the belief, that sinners must wait to be regenerated by divine power while they were passive. Professors also must wait to be revived, until God, in mysterious sovereignty, came and revived them. As to revivals of religion, they were settled down in the belief to a great extent, that man had no more agency in producing them than in producing showers of rain. To attempt to effect the conversion of a sinner, or to promote a revival, was an attempt to take the work out of the hands of God, to go to work in your own strength, and to set sinners and professors to do the same. The vigorous use of means and measures to promote a work of grace, was regarded by many as impious. It was getting up an excitement of animal feeling, and wickedly interfering with the prerogative of God. The abominable dogmas of physical moral depravity, or a sinful constitution, with a consequent natural, falsely called moral, inability, and the necessity of a physical and passive regeneration, had chilled the heart of the church, and lulled sinners into a fatal sleep. This is the natural tendency of such doctrines.

3. Let it be distinctly understood before we close this subject, that we do not deny, but strenuously maintain, that the whole plan of salvation, and all the influences, both providential and spiritual, which God exerts in the conversion, sanctification, and salvation, of sinners, is grace from first to last, and that I deny the dogma of a gracious ability, because it robs God of his glory. It really denies the grace of the gospel. The abettors of this scheme, in contending for the grace of the gospel, really deny it. What grace can there be, that should surprise heaven and earth, and cause "the angels to desire to look into it," in bestowing ability on those who never had any, and, of course, who never cast away their ability--to obey the requirements of God? According to them all men lost their ability in Adam, and not by their own act. God still required obedience of them upon pain of eternal death. Now he might, according to this view of the subject, just as reasonably command all men, on pain of eternal death, to fly, or to undo all that Adam had done, or perform any other natural impossibility, as to command them to be holy, to repent and believe the gospel. Now, I ask again, what possible grace was there, or could there be, in his giving them power to obey him? To have required the obedience without giving the power had been infinitely unjust. To admit the assumption, that men had really lost their ability to obey in Adam, and call this bestowment of ability for which they contend, grace, is an abuse of language, an absurdity, and a denial of the true grace of the gospel not to be tolerated. I reject the dogma of a gracious ability, because it involves a denial of the true grace of the gospel. I maintain that the gospel, with all its influences, including the gift of the Holy Spirit, to convict, convert, and sanctify the soul, is a system of grace throughout. But to maintain this, I must also maintain, that God might justly have required obedience of men without making these provisions for them. And to maintain the justice of God in requiring obedience, I must admit and maintain that obedience was possible to man.

Let it not be said then, that we deny the grace of the glorious gospel of the blessed God, nor that we deny the reality and necessity of the influences of the Holy Spirit to convert and sanctify the soul, nor that this influence is a gracious one; for all these we most strenuously maintain. But I maintain this upon the ground, that men are able to do their duty, and that the difficulty does not lie in a proper inability, but in a voluntary selfishness, in an unwillingness to obey the blessed gospel. I say again, that I reject the dogma of a gracious ability, as I understand its abettors to hold it, not because I deny, but solely because it denies the grace of the gospel. The denial of ability is really a denial of the possibility of grace in the affair of man's salvation. I admit the ability of man, and hold that he is able, but utterly unwilling to obey God. Therefore I consistently hold that all the influences exerted by God to make him willing, are of free grace abounding through Christ Jesus.

LECTURE XXXIII - THE NOTION OF INABILITY

PROPER METHOD OF ACCOUNTING FOR IT

I have represented ability, or the freedom of the will, as a first-truth of consciousness, a truth necessarily known to all moral agents. The inquiry may naturally arise, How then is it to be accounted for, that so many men have denied the liberty of the will, or ability to obey God? A recent writer thinks this denial a sufficient refutation of the affirmation, that ability is a first-truth of consciousness. It is important that this denial should be accounted for. That mankind affirm their obligation upon the real, though often latent and unperceived assumption of ability, there is no reasonable ground of doubt. I have said that first-truths are frequently assumed, and certainly known without being always the direct object of thought or attention; and also that these truths are universally held in the practical judgments of men, while they sometimes in theory deny them. They know them to be true, and in all their practical judgments assume their truth, while they reason against them, think they prove them untrue, and not unfrequently affirm, that they are conscious of an opposite affirmation. For example, men have denied, in theory, the law of causality, while they have at every moment of their lives acted upon the assumption of its truth. Others have denied the freedom of the will, who have, every hour of their lives, assumed, and acted, and judged, upon the assumption that the will is free. The same is true of ability, which, in respect to the commandments of God, is identical with freedom. Men have often denied the ability of man to obey the commandments of God, while they have always, in their practical judgments of themselves and of others, assumed their ability, in respect to those things that are really commanded by God. Now, how is this to be accounted for?

1. Multitudes have denied the freedom of the will, because they have loosely confounded the will with the involuntary powers--with the intellect and the sensibility. Locke, as is well known, regarded the mind as possessing but two primary faculties, the understanding and the will. President Edwards, as was said in a former lecture, followed Locke, and regarded all the states of the sensibility as acts of the will. Multitudes, nay the great mass of Calvinistic divines, with their hearers, have held the same views. This confounding of the sensibility with the will has been common for a long time. Now everybody is conscious, that the states of the sensibility, or mere feelings, cannot be produced or changed by a direct effort to feel thus or thus. Everybody knows from consciousness that the feelings come and go, wax and wane, as motives are presented to excite them. And they know also that these feelings are under the law of necessity and not of liberty; that is, that necessity is an attribute of these feelings, in such a sense, that under the circumstances, they will exist in spite of ourselves, and that they cannot be controlled by a direct effort to

control them. Everybody knows that our feelings, or the states of our sensibility can be controlled only indirectly, that is by the direction of our thoughts. By directing our thoughts to an object calculated to excite certain feelings, we know that, when the excitability is not exhausted, feelings correlated to that object will come into play, of course and of necessity. So when any class of feelings exist, we all know that by diverting the attention from the object that excites them, they subside of course, and give place to a class correlated to the new object that at present occupies the attention. Now, it is very manifest how the freedom of the will has come to be denied by those who confound the will proper with the sensibility. These same persons lave always known and assumed, that the actions of the will proper were free. Their error has consisted in not distinguishing in theory between the action of the proper will, and the involuntary states of the sensibility. In their practical judgments, and in their conduct, they have recognized the distinction which they have failed to recognize in their speculations and theories. They have every hour been exerting their own freedom, have been controlling directly their attention and their outward life, by the free exercise of their proper will. They have also, by the free exercise of the same faculty, been indirectly controlling the states of their sensibility. They have all along assumed the absolute freedom of the will proper, and have always acted upon the assumption, or they would not have acted at all, or even attempted to act. But since they did not in theory distinguish between the sensibility and the will proper, they denied in theory the freedom of the will. If the actions of the will be confounded with desires and emotions, as President Edwards confounded them, and as has been common, the result must be a theoretical denial of the freedom of the will. In this way we are to account for the doctrine of inability, as it has been generally held. It has not been clearly understood that moral law legislates directly, and, with strict propriety of speech, only over the will proper, and over the involuntary powers only indirectly through the will. It has been common to regard the law and the gospel of God, as directly extending their claims to the involuntary powers and states of mind; and, as was shown in a former lecture, many have regarded, in theory, the law as extending its claims to those states that lie wholly beyond, either the direct or indirect control of the will. Now, of course, with these views of the claims of God, ability is and must be denied. I trust we have seen in past lectures, that, strictly and properly speaking, the moral law restricts its claims to the actions of the will proper, in such a sense that, if there be a willing mind, it is accepted as obedience; that the moral law and the lawgiver legislate over involuntary states only indirectly, that is, through the will; and that the whole of virtue, strictly speaking, consists in good-will or disinterested benevolence. Sane minds never practically deny, or can deny, the freedom of the will proper, or the doctrine of ability, when they make the proper discriminations between the will and the sensibility, and properly regard moral law as legislating directly only over the will. It is worthy of all consideration, that those who have denied ability, have almost always confounded the will and the sensibility; and that those who have denied ability, have always extended the claims of moral law beyond the pale of proper voluntariness; and many of them even beyond the limits of either the direct or the indirect control of the will.

But the inquiry may arise, how it comes to pass that men have so extensively entertained the impression, that the moral law legislates directly over those feelings, and over those states of mind which they know to be involuntary? I answer, that this mistake has arisen out of a want of just discrimination between the direct and indirect legislation of the law, and of the lawgiver. It is true that men are conscious of being responsible for their feelings and for their outward actions, and even for their thoughts. And it is really true that they are responsible for them, in so far as they are under either the direct or indirect control of the will. And they know that these acts and states of mind are possible to them, that is, that they have an indirect ability to produce them. They, however, loosely confound the direct and indirect ability and responsibility. The thing required by the law directly and presently is benevolence or good-will. This is what, and all that, the law strictly, presently or directly requires. It indirectly requires all those outward and inward acts and states that are connected directly and indirectly with this required act of will, by a law of necessity; that is, that those acts and states should follow as soon as by a natural and necessary law they will follow from a right action of the will. When these feelings, and states, and acts do not exist, they blame themselves, generally with propriety, because the absence of them is in fact owing to a want of the required act of the will. Sometimes, no doubt, they blame themselves unjustly, not considering that, although the will is right, of which they are conscious, the involuntary state or act does not follow, because of exhaustion, or because of some disturbance in the established and natural connection between the acts of the will and its ordinary sequents. When this exhaustion or disturbance exists, men are apt, loosely and unjustly, to write bitter things against themselves. They often do the same in hours of temptation, when Satan casts his fiery darts at them, lodging them in the thoughts and involuntary feelings. The will repels them, but they take effect, for the time being, in spite of one's self, in the intellect and sensibility. Blasphemous thoughts are suggested to the mind, unkind thoughts of God are suggested, and in spite of one's self, these abominable thoughts awaken their correlated feelings. The will abhors them and struggles to suppress them, but for the time being, finds itself unable to do anything more than to fight and resist.

Now, it is very common for souls in this state to write the most bitter accusations against themselves. But should it be hence inferred that they really are as much in fault as they assume themselves to be? No, indeed! But why do ministers, of all schools, unite in telling such tempted souls, You are mistaken, my dear brother or sister, these thoughts and feelings, though exercises of your own mind, are not yours in such a sense that you are responsible for them? The thoughts are suggested by Satan, and the feelings are a necessary consequence. Your will resists them, and this proves that you are unable, for the time being, to avoid them. You are therefore not responsible for them while you resist them with all the power of your will, any more than you would be guilty of murder should a giant overpower your strength, and use your hand against your will to shoot a man. In such cases it is, so far as I know, universally true, that all schools admit that the tempted soul is not responsible or guilty for those things which it cannot help. The inability is here allowed to be a bar to obligation; and such souls are justly told by ministers, You are mistaken in supposing yourself guilty in this case. It is just as absurd, in the one case as in the other, to infer real responsibility from a feeling or persuasion of responsibility. To hold that men are always responsible, because they loosely think themselves to be so, is absurd. In cases of temptation, such as that just supposed, as soon as the attention is directed to the fact of inability to avoid those thoughts and feelings, and the mind is conscious of the will's resisting them, and of being unable to banish them, it readily rests in the assurance that it is not responsible for them. Its own irresponsibility in such cases appears self-evident to the mind, the moment the proper inability is considered, and the affirmation of irresponsibility attended to. Now if the soul naturally and truly regarded itself as responsible, when there is a proper inability and impossibility, the instructions above referred to could not relieve the mind. It would say, To be sure I know that I cannot avoid having these thoughts and feelings, any more than I can cease to be the subject of consciousness, yet I know I am responsible notwithstanding. These thoughts and feelings are states of my own mind, and no matter how I come by them, or whether I can control or prevent them or not. Inability, you know, is no bar to obligation; therefore, my obligation and my guilt remain. Woe is me, for I am undone. The idea, then, of responsibility, when there is in fact real inability, is a prejudice of education, a mistake.

The mistake, unless strong prejudice of education has taken possession of the mind, lies in overlooking the fact of a real and proper inability. Unless the judgment has been strongly biased by education, it never judges itself bound to perform impossibilities, nor even conceives of such a thing. Who ever held himself bound to undo what is past, to recall past time, or to substitute holy acts and states of mind in the place of past sinful ones? No one ever held himself bound to do this; first, because he knows it to be impossible; and secondly, because no one that I have heard of ever taught or asserted any such obligation; and therefore none have received so strong a bias from education as loosely to hold such an, opinion. But sometimes the bias of education is so great, that the subjects of it seem capable of believing almost anything, however inconsistent with the intuitions of the reason, and consequently in the face of the most certain knowledge. For example, President Edwards relates of a young woman in his congregation, that she was deeply convicted of being guilty for Adam's first sin, and deeply repented of it. Now suppose that this and like cases should be regarded as conclusive proof that men are guilty of that sin, and deserve the wrath and curse of God for ever for that sin; and that all men will suffer the pains of hell forever, except they become convinced of their personal guilt for that sin, and repent of it in dust and ashes! President Edwards's teaching on the subject of the relation of all men to Adam's first sin, it is well known, was calculated in a high degree to pervert the judgment upon that subject; and this sufficiently accounts for the fact above alluded to. But apart from education, no human being ever held himself responsible for, or guilty of, the first or any other sin of Adam, or of any other being, who existed and died before he himself existed. The reason is that all moral agents naturally know, that inability or a proper impossibility is a bar to moral obligation and responsibility; and they never conceive to the contrary, unless biased by a mystifying education that casts a fog over their primitive and constitutional convictions.

2. Some have denied ability because they have strangely held, that the moral law requires sinners to be, in all respects, what they might have been had they never sinned. That is, they maintain that God requires of them just as high and perfect a service as if their powers had never been abused by sin; as if they had always been developed by the perfectly right use of them. This they admit to be a natural impossibility; nevertheless they hold that God may justly require

it, and that sinners are justly bound to perform this impossible service, and that they sin continually in coming short of it. To this sentiment I answer, that it might be maintained with as much show of reason, and as much authority from the Bible, that God might and does require of all sinners to undo all their acts of sin, and to substitute holy ones in their places, and that he holds them as sinning every moment by the neglect to do this. Why may not God as well require one as the other? They are alike impossibilities originating in the sinner's own act or fault. If the sinner's rendering himself unable to obey in one case does not set aside the right of God to command, so does it not for the same reason in the other. If an inability resulting from the sinner's own act cannot bar the right of God to make the requisition in the one case, neither can it for the same reason in the other. But every one can see that God cannot justly require the sinner to recall past time, and to undo past acts. But why? No other reason can be assigned than that it is impossible. But the same reason, it is admitted, exists in its full extent in the other case. It is admitted that sinners, who have long indulged in sin, or who have sinned at all, are really as unable to render as high a degree of service as they might have done had they never sinned, as they are to recall past time, or to undo all their past acts of sin. On what ground, then, of reason or revelation does the assertion rest, that in one case an impossibility is a bar to obligation, and not in the other? I answer, there is no ground whatever for the assertion in question. It is a sheer and an absurd assumption, unsupported by any affirmation of reason, or any truth or principle of revelation.

But to this assumption I reply again, as I have done on a former occasion, that if it be true, it must follow, that no one on earth or in heaven who has ever sinned will be able to render as perfect a service as the law demands; for there is no reason to believe, that any being who has abused his powers by sin will ever in time or eternity be able to render as high a service as he might have done had he at every moment duly developed them by perfect obedience. If this theory is true, I see not why it does not follow that the saints will be guilty in heaven of the sin of omission. A sentiment based upon an absurdity in the outset, and resulting in such consequences as this, must be rejected without hesitation.

3. A consciousness of the force of habit, in respect to all the acts and states of body and mind, has contributed to the loose holding of the doctrine of inability. Every one who is at all in the habit of observation and self-reflection is aware, that for some reason we acquire a greater and greater facility in doing anything by practice or repetition. We find this to be true in respect to acts of will as really as in respect to the involuntary states of mind. When the will has been long committed to the indulgence of the propensities, and in the habit of submitting itself to their impulse, there is a real difficulty of some sort in the way of changing its action. This difficulty cannot really impair the liberty of the will. If it could, it would destroy, or so far impair, moral agency and accountability. But habit may, and, as every one knows, does interpose an obstacle of some sort in the way of right willing, or, on the other hand, in the way of wrong willing. That is, men both obey and disobey with greatest facility from habit. Habit strongly favors the accustomed action of the will in any direction. This, as I said, never does or can properly impair the freedom of the will, or render it impossible to act in a contrary direction: for if it could and should, the actions of the will, in that case, being determined by a law of

necessity in one direction, would have no moral character. If benevolence became a habit so strong that it were utterly impossible to will in an opposite direction, or not to will benevolently, benevolence would cease to be virtuous. So, on the other hand, with selfishness. If the will came to be determined in that direction by habit grown into a law of necessity, such action would and must cease to have moral character. But, as I said, there is a real conscious difficulty of some sort in the way of obedience, when the will has been long accustomed to sin. This is strongly recognized in the language of inspiration and in devotional hymns, as well as in the language of experience by all men. The language of scripture is often so strong upon this point, that, but for a regard to the subject-matter of discourse, we might justly infer a proper inability. For example, Jer. xiii. 23: "Can the Ethiopian change his skin, or the leopard his spots? then may ye also do good, that are accustomed to do evil." This and similar passages recognize the influence of habit. "Then may ye who are accustomed to do evil:" custom or habit is to be overcome, and, in the strong language of the prophet, this is like changing the Ethiop's skin or the leopard's spots. But to understand the prophet as here affirming a proper inability were to disregard one of the fundamental rules of interpreting language, namely, that it is to be understood by reference to the subject of discourse. The latter part of the seventh chapter of Romans affords a striking instance and an illustration of this. It is, as has just been said, a sound and most important rule of interpreting all language, that due regard be had to the subject-matter of discourse. When "cannot," and such like terms, that express an inability are applied to physical or involuntary actions or states of mind, they express a proper natural inability; but when they are used in reference to actions of free will, they express not a proper impossibility, but only a difficulty arising out of the existence of a contrary choice, or the law of habit, or both.

Much question has been made about the seventh of Romans in its relation to the subject of ability and inability. Let us, therefore, look a little into this passage, Romans vii. 15-23: "For that which I do, I allow not; for what I would, that do I not; but what I hate, that do I. If then I do that which I would not, I consent unto the law that it is good. Now then it is no more I that do it, but sin that dwelleth in me. For I know that in me (that is in my flesh) dwelleth no good thing; for to will is present with me; but how to perform that which is good I find not. For the good that I would I do not; but the evil which I would not, that I do. Now if I do that I would not, it is no more I that do it, but sin that dwelleth in me. I find then a law, that when I would do good, evil is present with me. For I delight in the law of God after the inward man. But I see another law in my members, warring against the law of my mind, and bringing me into captivity to the law of sin which is in my members." Now what did the apostle mean by this language? Did he use language here in the popular sense, or with strictly philosophical propriety? He says he finds himself able to will, but not able to do. Is he then speaking of a mere outward or physical inability? Does he mean merely to say, that the established connection between volition and its sequents was disturbed, so that he could not execute his volitions? This his language, literally interpreted, and without reference to the subject-matter of discourse, and without regard to the manifest scope and design of the writer, would lead us to conclude. But who ever contended for such an interpretation? The apostle used popular language, and was describing a very common experience. Convicted sinners and backslidden saints often make legal resolutions, and resolve upon obedience under the influence of legal motives, and without really becoming benevolent, and changing the attitude of their wills. They, under the influence of conviction, purpose selfishly to do their duty to God and man, and, in the presence of temptation, they constantly fail of keeping their resolutions. It is true, that with their selfish hearts, or in the selfish attitude of their wills; they cannot keep their resolutions to abstain from those inward thoughts and emotions, nor from those outward actions that result by a law of necessity from a selfish state or attitude of the will. These legal resolutions the apostle popularly calls willings. "To will is present with me, but how to do good I find not. When I would do good, evil is present with me, so that the good I would I do not, and the evil I would not, that I do. If then I do the evil I would not, it is no longer I that do it, but sin that dwelleth in me. I delight in the law of God after the inner man. But I see another law in my members warring against the law of my mind, and bringing me into captivity to the law of sin which is in my members," etc. Now, this appears to me to be descriptive of a very familiar experience of every deeply convicted sinner or backslider. The will is committed to the propensities, to the law in the members, or to the gratification of the impulses of the sensibility. Hence, the outward life is selfish. Conviction of sin leads to the formation of resolutions of amendment, while the will does not submit to God. These resolutions constantly fail of securing the result contemplated. The will still abides in a state of committal to self-gratification; and hence resolutions to amend in feeling or the outward life, fail of securing those results.

Nothing was more foreign from the apostle's purpose, it seems to me, than to affirm a proper inability of will to yield to the claims of God. Indeed, he affirms and assumes the freedom of his will. "To will," he says, "is present with me;" that is, to resolve. But resolution is an act of will. It is a purpose, a design. He purposed, designed to amend. To form resolutions was present with him, but how to do good he found not. The reason why he did not execute his purposes was, that they were selfishly made; that is, he resolved upon reformation without giving his heart to God, without submitting his will to God, without actually becoming benevolent. This caused his perpetual failure. This language, construed strictly to the letter, would lead to the conclusion, that the apostle was representing a case where the will is right, but where the established and natural connection between volition and its sequents is destroyed, so that the outward act did not follow the action of the will. In this case all schools would agree that the act of the will constitutes real obedience. The whole passage, apart from the subject-matter of discourse, and from the manifest design and scope of the writer, might lead us to conclude, that the apostle was speaking of a proper inability, and that he did not therefore regard the failure as his own fault. "It is no more I, but sin that dwelleth in me. O wretched man that I am," etc. Those who maintain that the apostle meant to assert a proper inability to obey, must also admit that he represented this inability as a bar to obligation, and regarded his state as calamitous, rather than as properly sinful. But the fact is, he was portraying a legal experience, and spoke of finding himself unable to keep selfish resolutions of amendment in the presence of temptation. His will was in a state of committal to the indulgence of the propensities. In the absence of temptation, his convictions, and fears, and feelings were the strongest impulses, and under their influence he would form resolutions to do his duty, to abstain from fleshly indulgences, etc. But as some other appetite or desire came to be more strongly excited, he yielded to that of course, and broke his former resolution. Paul writes as if speaking of himself, but was doubtless speaking as the representative of a class of persons already named. He found the law of selfish habit exceedingly strong, and so strong as to lead him to cry out, "O wretched man," etc. But this is not affirming a proper inability of will to submit to God.

4. All men who seriously undertake their own reformation find themselves in great need of help and support from the Holy Spirit, in consequence of the physical depravity of which I have formerly spoken, and because of the great strength of their habit of self-indulgence. They are prone, as is natural, to express their sense of dependence on the Divine Spirit in strong language, and to speak of this dependence as if it consisted in a real inability, when, in fact, they do not really consider it as a proper inability. They speak upon this subject just as they do upon any and every other subject, when they are conscious of a strong inclination to a given course. They say in respect to many things, "I cannot," when they mean only "I will not," and never think of being understood as affirming a proper inability. The inspired writers expressed themselves in the common language of men upon such subjects, and are doubtless to be understood in the same way. In common parlance, "cannot" often means "will not," and perhaps is used as often in this sense as it is to express a proper inability. Men do not misinterpret this language, and suppose it to affirm a proper inability, when used in reference to acts of will, except on the subject of obedience to God; and why should they assign a meaning to language when used upon this subject which they do not assign to it anywhere else?

But, as I said in a former lecture, under the light of the gospel, and with the promises in our hands, God does require of us what we should be unable to do and be, but for these promises and this proffered assistance. Here is a real inability to do directly in our own strength all that is required of us, upon consideration of the proffered aid. We can only do it by strength imparted by the Holy Spirit. That is, we cannot know Christ, and avail ourselves of his offices and relations, and appropriate to our own souls his fulness, except as we are taught by the Holy Spirit. The thing immediately and directly required, is to receive the Holy Spirit by faith to be our teacher and guide, to take of Christ's and show it to us. This confidence we are able to exercise. Who ever really and intelligently affirmed that he had not power or ability to trust or confide in the promise and oath of God?

Much that is said of inability in poetry, and in the common language of the saints, respects not the subjection of the will to God, but those experiences, and states of feeling that depend on the illuminations of the Spirit just referred to. The language that is so common in prayer and in the devotional dialect of the church, respects generally our dependence upon the Holy Spirit for such divine discoveries of Christ, as to charm the soul into a steadfast abiding in him. We feel our dependence upon the Holy Spirit so to enlighten us, as to break up for ever the power of sinful habit, and draw us away from our idols entirely and for ever.

In future lectures I shall have occasion to enlarge much upon the subject of our dependence upon Christ and the Holy Spirit. But this dependence does not consist in a proper inability to will as God directs, but, as I have said, partly in the power of sinful habit, and partly in the great darkness of our souls in respect to Christ and his mediatorial work and relations. All these together do not constitute a proper inability, for the plain reason, that through the right action of our will which is always possible to us, these difficulties can all be directly or indirectly overcome. Whatever we can do or be, directly or indirectly, by willing, is possible to us. But there is no degree of spiritual attainment required of us, that may not be reached directly or indirectly by right willing. Therefore these attainments are possible. "If any man," says Christ, "will do his will," that is, has an obedient will, "he shall know of the doctrine whether it be of God." "If thine eye be single," that is, if the intention or will is right, "thy whole body shall be full of light." "If any man love me, he will keep my words, and my Father will love him, and we will come and make our abode with him." The scriptures abound with assurances of light and instruction, and of all needed grace and help, upon condition of a right will or heart, that is, upon condition of our being really willing to obey the light, when and as fast as we receive it. I have abundantly shown on former occasions, that a right state of the will constitutes, for the time being, all that, strictly speaking, the moral law requires. But I said, that it also, though in a less strict and proper sense, requires all those acts and states of the intellect and sensibility which are connected by a law of necessity with the right action of the will. Of course, it also requires that cleansing of the sensibility, and all those higher forms of Christian experience that result from the indwelling of the Holy Spirit. That is, the law of God requires that these attainments shall be made when the means are provided and enjoyed, and as soon as, in the nature of the case, these attainments are possible. But it requires no more than this. For the law of God can never require absolute impossibilities. That which requires absolute impossibilities, is not and cannot be moral law. For, as was formerly said, moral law is the law of nature, and what law of nature would that be that should require absolute impossibilities? This would be a mockery of a law of nature. What! a law of nature requiring that which is impossible to nature, both directly and indirectly! Impossible.

LECTURE XXXIV - REPENTANCE AND IMPENITENCE

In the discussion of this subject I shall show,--

I. What repentance is not.

1. The Bible everywhere represents repentance as a virtue, and as constituting a change of moral character; consequently, it cannot be a phenomenon of the intelligence: that is, it cannot consist in conviction of sin, nor in any intellectual apprehension of our guilt or ill-desert. All the states or phenomena of the intelligence are purely passive states of mind, and of course moral character, strictly speaking, cannot be predicated of them.

2. Repentance is not a phenomenon of the sensibility: that is, it does not consist in a feeling of regret or remorse, of compunction or sorrow for sin, or of sorrow in view of the consequences of sin to self or to others, nor in any feelings or emotions whatever. All feelings or emotions belong to the sensibility, and are, of course, purely passive states of mind, and consequently can have no moral character in themselves.

It should be distinctly understood, and always borne in mind, that repentance cannot consist in any involuntary state of mind, for it is impossible that moral character, strictly speaking, should pertain to passive states.

II. What repentance is.

There are two Greek words which are translated by the English word, repent.

1. Metamelomai, "to care for," or to be concerned for one's self; hence to change one's course. This term seems generally to be used to express a state of the sensibility, as regret, remorse, sorrow for sin, etc. But sometimes it also expresses a change of purpose as a consequence of regret, or remorse, or sorrow; as in Matt. xxi. 29, "He answered and said, I will not; but afterwards he repented and went." It is used to represent the repentance of Judas, which evidently consisted of remorse and despair.

2. MetanoeO, "to take an after view:" or more strictly, to change one's mind as a consequence of, and in conformity with, a second and more rational view of the subject. This word evidently expresses a change of choice, purpose, intention, in conformity with the dictates of the intelligence.

This is no doubt the idea of evangelical repentance. It is a phenomenon of will, and consists in the turning or change of the ultimate intention from selfishness to benevolence. The term expresses the act of turning; the changing of the heart, or of the ruling preference of the soul. It might with propriety be rendered by the terms "changing the heart." The English word "repentance" is often used to express regret, remorse, sorrow, etc., and is used in so loose a sense as not to convey a distinct idea, to the common mind, of the true nature of evangelical repentance. A turning from sin to holiness, or more strictly, from a state of consecration to self to a state of consecration to God, is and must be the turning, the change of mind, or the repentance that is required of all sinners.

Nothing less can constitute a virtuous repentance, and nothing more can be required.

III. What is implied in repentance.

1. Such is the correlation of the will to the intellect, that repentance must imply reconsideration or after thought. It must imply self-reflection, and such an apprehension of one's guilt as to produce self-condemnation. That selfishness is sin, and that it is right and duty to consecrate the whole being to God and his service, are first truths, necessarily assumed by all moral agents. They are, however, often unthought of, not reflected upon. Repentance implies the giving up of the attention to the consideration and self-application of these first truths, and consequently implies conviction of sin, and guilt, and ill-desert, and a sense of shame and self-condemnation. It implies an intellectual and a hearty justification of God, of his law, of his moral and providential government, and of all his works and ways.

It implies an apprehension of the nature of sin, that it belongs to the heart, and does not essentially consist in, though it leads to, outward conduct; that it is an utterly unreasonable state of mind, and that it justly deserves the wrath and curse of God forever.

It implies an apprehension of the reasonableness of the law and commands of God, and of the folly and madness of sin. It implies an intellectual and a hearty giving up of all controversy with God upon all and every point.

It implies a conviction, that God is wholly right, and the sinner wholly wrong, and a thorough and hearty abandonment of all excuses and apologies for sin. It implies an entire and universal acquittal of God from every shade and degree of blame, a thorough taking of the entire blame of sin to self. It implies a deep and thorough abasement of self in the dust, a crying out of soul against self, and a most sincere and universal, intellectual, and hearty exaltation of God.

2. Such, also, is the connection of the will and the sensibility, that the turning of the will, or evangelical repentance, implies sorrow for sin as necessarily resulting from the turning of the will, together with the intellectual views of sin which are implied in repentance. Neither conviction of sin, nor sorrow for it, constitutes repentance. Yet from the correlation which is established between the intelligence, the sensibility, and the will, both conviction of sin, and sorrow for it, are implied in evangelical repentance, the one as necessarily preceding, and the other as often preceding, and always and necessarily resulting from repentance. During the process of conviction, it often happens, that the sensibility is hardened and unfeeling; or, if there is much feeling, it is often only regret, remorse, agony, and despair. But when the heart has given away, and the evangelical turning has taken place, it often happens that the fountain of the great deep in the sensibility is broken up, the sorrows of the soul are stirred to the very bottom, and the sensibility pours forth its gushing tides like an irresistible torrent. But it frequently happens, too, in minds less subject to deep emotion, that the sorrows do not immediately flow in deep and broad channels, but are mild, melting, tender, tearful, silent, subdued.

Self-loathing is another state of the sensibility implied in evangelical repentance. This state of mind may and often does, exist where repentance is not, just as outward morality does. But, like outward morality, it must exist where true repentance is. Self-loathing is a natural and a necessary consequence of those intellectual views of self that are implied in repentance. While the intelligence apprehends the utter, shameful guilt of self, and the heart yields to the conviction, the sensibility necessarily sympathizes, and a feeling of self-loathing and abhorrence is the inevitable consequence.

It implies a loathing and abhorrence of the sins of others, a most deep and thorough feeling of opposition to sin--to all sin, in self and everybody else. Sin has become, to the penitent soul, the abominable thing which it hates. It implies a holy indignation toward all sin and all sinners, and a manifest opposition to every form of iniquity.

3. Repentance also implies peace of mind. The soul that has full confidence in the infinite wisdom and love of God, in the atonement of Christ, and in his universal providence, cannot but have peace. And further, the soul that has abandoned all sin, and turned to God, is no longer in a state of warfare with itself and with God. It must have peace of conscience, and peace with God. It implies heart-complacency in God, and in all the holy. This must follow from the very nature of repentance.

It implies confession of sin to God and to man, as far as sin has been committed against men. If the heart has thoroughly renounced sin, it has become benevolent, and is of course disposed, as far as possible, to undo the wrong it has committed, to confess sin, and humble self on account of it, before God and our neighbor, whom we have injured. Repentance implies humility, or a willingness to be known and estimated according to our real character. It implies a disposition to do right, and to confess our faults to God and man, as far as man has a right to know them. Let no one who has refused, and still refuses or neglects to confess his sins to God, and those sins to men that have been committed against them, profess repentance unto salvation; but let him remember that God has said, "He that covereth his sins shall not prosper; but whoso confesseth and forsaketh them shall find mercy:" and again, "Confess your faults one to another, and pray one for another, that ye may be healed."

Repentance implies a willingness to make restitution, and the actual making of it as far as ability goes. He is not just, and of course is not penitent, who has injured his neighbor in his person, reputation, property, or in anything, and is unwilling to make restitution. And he is unwilling to make restitution who neglects to do so whenever he is able. It is impossible that a soul truly penitent should neglect to make all practicable restitution, for the plain reason that penitence implies a benevolent and just attitude of the will, and the will controls the conduct by a law of necessity.

Repentance implies reformation of outward life. This follows from reformation of heart by a law of necessity. It is naturally impossible that a penitent soul, remaining penitent, should indulge in any known sin. If the heart he reformed, the life must be as the heart is.

It implies a universal reformation of life, that is, a reformation extending to all outward sin. The penitent does not, and remaining penitent, cannot, reform in respect to some sins only. If penitent at all, he must have repented of sin as sin, and of course of all sin. If he has turned to God, and consecrated himself to God, he has of course ceased from sin, from all sin as such. Sin, as we have seen on a former occasion, is a unit, and so is holiness. Sin consists in selfishness, and holiness in disinterested benevolence: it is therefore sheer nonsense to say that repentance can consist with indulgence in some sins. What are generally termed little, as well as what are termed great sins, are alike rejected and abhorred by the truly penitent soul, and this from a law of necessity, he being truly penitent.

4. It implies faith or confidence in God in all things. It implies, not only the conviction that God is wholly right in all his controversy with sinners, but also that the heart has yielded to this conviction, and has come fully over to confide most implicitly in him in all respects, so that it can readily commit all interests for time and eternity to his hands. Repentance is a state of mind that implies the fullest confidence in all the promises and threatenings of God, and in the atonement and grace of Christ.

IV. What impenitence is not.

1. It is not a negation, or the mere absence of repentance. Some seem to regard impenitence as a nonentity, as the mere absence of repentance; but this is a great mistake.

2. It is not mere apathy in the sensibility in regard to sin, and a mere want of sorrow for it.

3. It is not the absence of conviction of sin, nor the consequent carelessness of the sinner in respect to the commandments of God.

4. It is not an intellectual self-justification, nor does it consist in a disposition to cavil at truth and the claims of God. These may and often do result from impenitence, but are not identical with it.

5. It does not consist in the spirit of excuse-making, so often manifested by sinners. This spirit is a result of impenitence, but does not constitute it.

6. Nor does it consist in the love of sin for its own sake, nor in the love of sin in any sense. It is not a constitutional appetite, relish, or craving for sin. If this constitutional craving for sin existed, it could have no moral character, inasmuch as it would be a wholly involuntary state of mind. It could not be the crime of impenitence.

V. What impenitence is.

1. It is everywhere in the Bible represented as a heinous sin, as in Matt. xi. 20-24: "Then began he to upbraid the cities wherein most of his mighty works were done, because they repented not. Woe unto thee, Chorazin! woe unto thee, Bethsaida! for if the mighty works which were done in you, had been done in Tyre and Sidon, they would have repented long ago in sackcloth and ashes. But I say unto you, it shall be more tolerable for Tyre and Sidon at the day of judgment than for you. And thou Capernaum, which art exalted unto heaven, shalt be brought down to hell; for if the mighty works which have been done in thee, had been done in Sodom, it would have remained until this day. But I say unto you, that it shall be more tolerable for the land of Sodom, in the day of judgment, than for thee." Here, as elsewhere, impenitence is represented as most aggravated wickedness.

2. Impenitence is a phenomenon of the will, and consists in the will's cleaving to self-indulgence under light. It consists in the will's pertinacious adherence to the gratification of self, in despite of all the light with which the sinner is surrounded. It is not, as has been said, a passive state nor a mere negation, nor the love of sin for its own sake; but it is an active and obstinate state of the will, a determined holding on to that course of self-seeking which constitutes sin, not from a love to sin, but for the sake of the gratification. This, under light, is of course, aggravated wickedness. Considered in this view, it is easy to account for all the woes and denunciations that the Saviour uttered against it. When the claims of God are revealed to the mind, it must necessarily

yield to them, or strengthen itself in sin. It must, as it were, gird itself up, and struggle to resist the claims of duty. This strengthening self in sin under light is the particular form of sin which we call impenitence. All sinners are guilty of it, because all have some light, but some are vastly more guilty of it than others.

VI. Notice some things that are implied in impenitence.

As it essentially consists in a cleaving to self-indulgence under light, it implies,--

1. That the impenitent sinner obstinately prefers his own petty and Momentary gratification to all the other and higher interests of God and the universe; that because these gratifications are his own, or the gratification of self, he therefore gives them the preference over all the infinite interests of all other beings.

2. It implies the deliberate and actual setting at naught, not only of the interests of God and of the universe, as of no value, but it implies also a total disregard, and even contempt, of the rights of all other beings. It is a practical denial that they have any rights or interests to be promoted.

3. It implies a rejection of the authority of God, and contempt for it, as well as a spurning of his law and gospel.

4. It implies a present justification of all past sin. The sinner who holds on to his self-indulgence, in the presence of the light of the gospel, really in heart justifies all his past rebellion.

5. Consequently present impenitence, especially under the light of the glorious gospel, is a heart-justification of all sin. It is taking sides deliberately with sinners against God, and is a virtual endorsing of all sins of earth and hell. This principle is clearly implied in Christ's teaching, Matt. xxiii. 34-36: "Wherefore, behold, I send unto you prophets, and wise men, and scribes; and some of them ye shall kill and crucify; and some of them shall ye scourge in your synagogues, and persecute them from city to city; that upon you may come all the righteous blood shed upon the earth, from the blood of righteous Abel unto the blood of Zacharias, son of Barachias, whom ye slew between the temple and the altar. Verily, I say unto you, All these things, shall come upon this generation."

6. Present impenitence, under all the light and experience which the sinner now has, involves the guilt of all his past sin. If he still holds on to it, he in heart justifies it. If he in heart justifies it, he virtually recommits it. If in the presence of accumulated light, he still persists in sin, he virtually endorses, recommits, and is again guilty of all past sin.

It implies a total want of confidence in God; want of confidence in his character and government; in his works and ways. It virtually charges God with usurpation, falsehood, and selfishness in all their odious forms. It is a making war on every moral attribute of God, and is utter enmity against him. It is mortal enmity, and would of course always manifest itself in sinners, as it did when Christ was upon the earth. When he poured the light upon them, they hardened themselves until they were ripe for murdering him. This is the true nature of impenitence. It involves the guilt of a mortal enmity against God.

VII. Notice some of the characteristics or evidences of impenitence.

1. A manifested indifference to the sins of men is evidence of an impenitent and sin-justifying state of mind. It is impossible that a penitent soul should not be deeply and heartily opposed to all sin; and if heartily opposed to

it, it is impossible that he should not manifest this opposition, for the heart controls the life by a law of necessity.

2. Of course a manifest heart-complacency in sin or in sinners is sure evidence of an impenitent state of mind. "He that will be the friend of the world is the enemy of God." Heart-complacency in sinners is that friendship with the world that is enmity against God.

3. A manifest want of zeal in opposing sin and in promoting reformation, is a sure indication of an impenitent state of mind. The soul that has been truly convinced of sin, and turned from sin to the love and service of God, cannot but manifest a deep interest in every effort to expel sin out of the world. Such a soul cannot but be zealous in opposing sin, and in building up and establishing righteousness in the earth.

4. A manifest want of sympathy with God in respect to his government, providential and moral, is an evidence of impenitence of heart. A penitent soul, as has been said, will and must of course justify God in all his ways. This is implied in genuine repentance. A disposition to complain of the strictness and rigor of God's commandments--to speak of the providence of God in a complaining manner, to murmur at its allotments, and repine at the circumstances in which it has placed a soul, is to evince an impenitent and rebellious state of mind.

5. A manifest want of confidence in the character, faithfulness, and promises of God, is also sure evidence of an impenitent state of mind. A distrust of God in any respect cannot consist with a penitent state of heart.

6. The absence of peace of mind is sure evidence of an impenitent state. The penitent soul must have peace of conscience, because penitence is a state of conscious rectitude. It also must have peace with God, in view of, and through confidence in, the atonement of Christ. Repentance is the turning from an attitude of rebellion against God, to a state of universal submission to his will, and approbation of it as wise and good. This must of course bring peace to the soul. When therefore there is a manifest want of peace, there is evidence of impenitence of heart.

7. Every unequivocal manifestation of selfishness is a conclusive evidence of present impenitence. Repentance, as we have seen, consists in the turning of the soul from selfishness to benevolence. It follows of course that the presence of selfishness, or a spirit of self-indulgence, is conclusive evidence of an impenitent state of mind. Repentance implies the denial of self; the denial or subjection of all the appetites, passions, and propensities to the law of the intelligence. Therefore a manifest spirit of self-indulgence, a disposition to seek the gratification of the appetites and passions, such as the subjection of the will to the use of tobacco, of alcohol, or to any of the natural or artificial appetites, under light, and in opposition to the law of the reason, is conclusive evidence of present impenitence. I say, "under light, and in opposition to the law of the reason." Such articles as those just named, are sometimes used medicinally, and because they are regarded as useful, and even indispensable to health under certain circumstances. In such cases their use may be a duty. But they are more frequently used merely to gratify appetite, and in the face of a secret conviction that they are not only unnecessary, but absolutely injurious. This is indulgence that constitutes sin. It is impossible that such indulgence should consist with repentance. Such a mind must be in impenitence, or there is no such thing as impenitence.

8. A spirit of self-justification is another evidence of impenitence. This manifestation must be directly the opposite of that which the truly penitent soul will make.

9. A spirit of excuse-making for neglect of duty is also a conclusive evidence of an impenitent heart. Repentance implies the giving up of all excuses for disobedience, and a hearty obedience in all things. Of course, where there is a manifest disposition to make excuses for not being what and all God requires us to be, it is certain that there is, and must be an impenitent state of mind. It is war with God.

10. A want of candor upon any moral subject relating to self, also betrays an impenitent heart. A penitent state of the will is committed to know and to embrace all truth. Therefore a prejudiced, uncandid state of mind must be inconsistent with penitence, and a manifestation of prejudice must evince present impenitence. An unwillingness to be searched, and to have all our words and ways brought into the light of truth, and to be reproved when we are in error, is a sure indication of an impenitent state of mind. "Every one that doeth evil hateth the light, neither cometh to the light, lest his deeds should be reproved. But he that doeth truth cometh to the light, that his deeds may be made manifest, that they are wrought in God."

11. Only partial reformation of life, also indicates that the heart has not embraced the whole will of God. When there is a disposition manifested to indulge in some sin, no matter how little, it is sure evidence of impenitence of heart. The penitent soul rejects sin as sin; of course every kind or degree of iniquity is put away, loathed, and abhorred. "Whoso keepeth the whole law and yet offends in one point, is guilty of all;" that is, if a man in one point unequivocally sins or disobeys God, it is certain that he truly from the heart obeys him in nothing. He has not an obedient state of mind. If he really had supreme respect to God's authority, he could not but obey him in all things. If therefore it be found, that a professor of penitence does not manifest the spirit of universal obedience; if in some things he is manifestly self-indulgent, it may be known that he is altogether yet in sin, and that he is still "in the gall of bitterness and in the bond of iniquity."

12. Neglect or refusal to confess and make restitution, so far as opportunity And ability are enjoyed, is also a sure indication of an unjust and impenitent state of mind. It would seem impossible for a penitent soul not at once to see and be impressed with the duty of making confession and restitution to those who have been injured by him. When this is refused or neglected, there must be impenitence. The heart controls the life by a law of necessity; when, therefore, there is a heart that confesses and forsakes sin, it is impossible that this should not appear in outward confession and restitution.

13. A spirit of covetousness, or grasping after the world, is a sure indication of impenitence. "Covetousness is idolatry." It is a hungering and thirsting after, and devotion to this world. Acquisitiveness indulged must be positive proof of an impenitent state of mind. If any man love the world, how dwelleth the love of God in him?

14. A want of interest in, and compassion for, sinners, is a sure indication of impenitence. If one has seen his own guilt and ruin, and has found himself sunk in the horrible pit and miry clay of his own abominations, and has found the way of escape, to feel deeply for sinners, to manifest a great compassion and concern for them, and a zeal for their salvation, is as natural as to breathe.

If this sympathy and zeal are not manifested, we may rely upon it that there is still impenitence. There is a total want of that love to God and souls that is always implied in repentance. Seest thou a professed convert to Christ whose compassions are not stirred, and whose zeal for the salvation of souls is not awakened? Be assured that you behold a hypocrite.

15. Spiritual sloth or indolence is another evidence of an impenitent heart. The soul that thoroughly turns to God, and consecrates itself to him, and wholly commits itself to promote his glory in the building up of his kingdom, will be, must be, anything but slothful. A disposition to spiritual idleness, or to lounging or indolence of any kind, is an evidence that the heart is impenitent. I might pursue this subject to an indefinite length; but what has been said must suffice for this course of instruction, and is sufficient to give you the clue by which you may detect the windings and delusions of the impenitent heart.

LECTURE XXXV - FAITH AND UNBELIEF

I. What evangelical faith is not.

1. The term faith, like most other words, has diverse significations, and is manifestly used in the Bible sometimes to designate a state of the intellect, in which case it means an undoubting persuasion, a firm conviction, an unhesitating intellectual assent. This, however, is not its evangelical sense. Evangelical faith cannot be a phenomenon of the intellect, for the plain reason that, when used in an evangelical sense, it is always regarded as a virtue. But virtue cannot be predicated of intellectual states, because these are involuntary, or passive states of mind. Faith is a condition of salvation. It is something which we are commanded to do upon pain of eternal death. But if it be something to be done--a solemn duty, it cannot be a merely passive state, a mere intellectual conviction. The Bible distinguishes between intellectual and saving faith. There is a faith of devils, and there is a faith of saints. James clearly distinguishes between them, and also between an antinomian and a saving faith. "Even so faith, if it hath not works, is dead, being alone. Yea, a man may say, thou hast faith, and I have works: show me thy faith without thy works, and I will show thee my faith by my works. Thou believest that there is one God; thou doest well: the devils also believe, and tremble. But wilt thou know, O vain man, that faith without works is dead? Was not Abraham our father justified by works, when he had offered Isaac his son upon the altar? Seest thou how faith wrought with his works, and by works was faith made perfect? And the scripture was fulfilled which saith, Abraham believed God, and it was imputed unto him for righteousness; and he was called the friend of God. Ye see then how that by works a man is justified, and not by faith only. Likewise also was not Rahab the harlot justified by works, when she had received the messengers, and had sent them out another way? For as the body without the spirit is dead, so faith without works is dead also."--James ii. 17-26. The distinction is here clearly marked, as it is elsewhere in the Bible, between intellectual and saving faith. One produces good works or a holy life; the other is unproductive. This shows that one is a phenomenon of the intellect merely, and does not of course control the conduct. The other must be a phenomenon of the will, because it manifests itself in the outward life. Evangelical faith, then, is not a conviction, a perception of truth. It does not belong to the intellect, though it implies intellectual conviction, yet the evangelical or virtuous element does not consist in it.

2. It is not a feeling of any kind; that is, it does not belong to, and is not a phenomenon of, the sensibility. The phenomena of the sensibility are passive states of mind, and therefore have no moral character in themselves. Faith, regarded as a virtue, cannot consist in any involuntary state of mind whatever. It is represented in the Bible as an active and most efficient state of mind. It works, and "works by love." It produces "the obedience of faith." Christians are said to be sanctified by the faith that is in Christ. Indeed the Bible, in a great variety of instances and ways, represents faith in God and in Christ as a

cardinal form of virtue, and as the mainspring of an outwardly holy life. Hence, it cannot consist in any involuntary state or exercise of mind whatever.

II. What evangelical faith is.

Since the Bible uniformly represents saving or evangelical faith as a virtue, we know that it must be a phenomenon of the will. It is an efficient state of mind, and therefore it must consist in the embracing of the truth by the heart or will. It is the will's closing in with the truths of the gospel. It is the soul's act of yielding itself up, or committing itself to the truths of the evangelical system. It is a trusting in Christ, a committing of the soul and the whole being to him, in his various offices and relations to men. It is a confiding in him, and in what is revealed of him, in his word and providence, and by his Spirit.

The same word that is so often rendered faith in the New Testament is also rendered commit; as in John ii. 24, "But Jesus did not commit himself unto them, because he knew all men." Luke xvi. 11, "If, therefore, ye have not been faithful in the unrighteous mammon, who will commit to your trust the true riches?" In these passages the word rendered commit is the same word as that which is rendered faith. It is a confiding in God and in Christ, as revealed in the Bible and in reason. It is a receiving of the testimony of God concerning himself, and concerning all things of which he has spoken. It is a receiving of Christ for just what he is represented to be in his gospel, and an unqualified surrender of the will, and of the whole being to him.

III. What is implied in evangelical faith?

1. It implies an intellectual perception of the things, facts, and truths believed. No one can believe that which he does not understand. It is impossible to believe that which is not so revealed to the mind, that the mind understands it. It has been erroneously assumed, that faith did not need light, that is, that it is not essential to faith that we understand the doctrines or facts that we are called upon to believe. This is a false assumption; for how can we believe, trust, confide, in what we do not understand? I must first understand what a proposition, a fact, a doctrine, or a thing is, before I can say whether I believe, or whether I ought to believe, or not. Should you state a proposition to me in an unknown tongue, and ask me if I believe it, I must reply, I do not, for I do not understand the terms of the proposition. Perhaps I should believe the truth expressed, and perhaps I should not; I cannot tell, until I understand the proposition. Any fact or doctrine not understood is like a proposition in an unknown tongue; it is impossible that the mind should receive or reject it, should believe or disbelieve it, until it is understood. We can receive or believe a truth, or fact, or doctrine no further than we understand it. So far as we do understand it, so far we may believe it, although we may not understand all about it. For example: I can believe in both the proper divinity and humanity of Jesus Christ. That he is both God and man, is a fact that I can understand. Thus far I can believe. But how his divinity and humanity are united I cannot understand. Therefore, I only believe the fact that they are united; the quo modo of their union I know nothing about, and I believe no more than I know. So I can understand that the Father, Son, and Holy Spirit are one God. That the Father is God, that the Son is God, that the Holy Spirit is God; that these three are Divine persons, I can understand as a fact. I can also understand that there is no contradiction or impossibility in the declared fact, that these three are one in their substratum of being; that is that they are one in a different sense from that in which they are three; that they are three in one sense, and one in another. I

understand that this may be a fact, and therefore I can believe it. But the quo modo of their union I neither understand nor believe: that is, I have no theory, no idea, no data on the subject, have no opinion, and consequently no faith, as to the manner in which they are united. Faith, then, in any fact or doctrine, implies that the intellect has an idea, or that the soul has an understanding, an opinion of that which the heart embraces or believes.

2. Evangelical faith implies the appropriation of the truths of the gospel to ourselves. It implies an acceptance of Christ as our wisdom, righteousness, sanctification, and redemption. The soul that truly believes, believes that Christ tasted death for every man, and of course for it. It apprehends Christ as the Saviour of the world, as offered to all, and embraces and receives him for itself. It appropriates his atonement, and his resurrection, and his intercession, and his promises to itself. Christ is thus presented in the gospel, not only as the Saviour of the world, but also to the individual acceptance of men. He is embraced by the world no further than he is embraced by individuals. He saves the world no further than he saves individuals. He died for the world, because he died for the individuals that compose the race. Evangelical faith, then, implies the belief of the truths of the Bible, the apprehension of the truths just named, and a reception of them, and a personal acceptance and appropriation of Christ to meet the necessities of the individual soul.

3. Evangelical faith implies an evangelical life. This would not be true if faith were merely an intellectual state or exercise. But since, as we have seen, faith is of the heart, since it consists in the committal of the will to Christ, it follows, by a law of necessity, that the life will correspond with the faith. Let this be kept in perpetual remembrance.

4. Evangelical faith implies repentance towards God. Evangelical faith particularly respects Jesus Christ and his salvation. It is an embracing of Christ and his salvation. Of course it implies repentance towards God, that is, a turning from sin to God. The will cannot be submitted to Christ, it cannot receive him as he is presented in the gospel, while it neglects repentance toward God; while it rejects the authority of the Father, it cannot embrace and submit to the Son.

5. Disinterested benevolence, or a state of good-will to being, is implied in evangelical faith; for that is the committal of the soul to God and to Christ in all obedience. It must, therefore, imply fellowship or sympathy with him in regard to the great end upon which his heart is set, and for which he lives. A yielding up of the will and the soul to him, must imply the embracing of the same end that he embraces.

6. It implies a state of the sensibility corresponding to the truths believed. It implies this, because this state of the sensibility is a result of faith by a law of necessity, and this result follows necessarily upon the acceptance of Christ and his gospel by the heart.

7. Of course it implies peace of mind. In Christ the soul finds its full and present salvation. It finds justification, which produces a sense of pardon and acceptance. It finds sanctification, or grace to deliver from the reigning power of sin. It finds all its wants met, and all needed grace proffered for its assistance. It sees no cause for disturbance, nothing to ask or desire that is not treasured up in Christ. It has ceased to war with God--with itself. It has found its resting-place in Christ, and rests in profound peace under the shadow of the Almighty.

8. It must imply the existence in the soul of every virtue, because it is a yielding up of the whole being to the will of God. Consequently, all the phases of virtue required by the gospel must be implied as existing, either in a developed or in an undeveloped state, in every heart that truly receives Christ by faith. Certain forms or modifications of virtue may not in all cases have found the occasions of their development, but certain it is, that every modification of virtue will manifest itself as its occasion shall arise, if there be a true and a living faith in Christ. This follows from the very nature of faith.

9. Present evangelical faith implies a state of present sinlessness. Observe, faith is the yielding and committal of the whole will, and of the whole being to Christ. This, and nothing short of this, is evangelical faith. But this comprehends and implies the whole of present, true obedience to Christ. This is the reason why faith is spoken of as the condition, and as it were, the only condition, of salvation. It really implies all virtue. Faith may be contemplated either as a distinct form of virtue, and as an attribute of love, or as comprehensive of all virtue. When contemplated as an attribute of love, it is only a branch of sanctification. When contemplated in the wider sense of universal conformity of will to the will of God, it is then synonymous with entire present sanctification. Contemplated in either light, its existence in the heart must be inconsistent with present sin there. Faith is an attitude of the will, and is wholly incompatible with present rebellion of will against Christ. This must be true, or what is faith?

10. Faith implies the reception and the practice of all known or perceived truth. The heart that embraces and receives truth as truth, and because it is truth, must of course receive all known truth. For it is plainly impossible that the will should embrace some truth perceived for a benevolent reason, and reject other truth perceived. All truth is harmonious. One truth is always consistent with every other truth. The heart that truly embraces one, will, for the same reason, embrace all truth known. If out of regard to the highest good of being, any one revealed truth is truly received, that state of mind continuing, it is impossible that all truth should not be received as soon as known.

IV. What unbelief is not.

1. It is not ignorance of truth. Ignorance is a blank; it is the negation or absence of knowledge. This certainly cannot be the unbelief everywhere represented in the Bible as a heinous sin. Ignorance may be a consequence of unbelief, but cannot be identical with it. We may be ignorant of certain truths as a consequence of rejecting others, but this ignorance is not, and, we shall see, cannot be unbelief.

2. Unbelief is not the negation or absence of faith. This were a mere nothing--a nonentity. But a mere nothing is not that abominable thing which the scriptures represent as a great and a damning sin.

3. It cannot be a phenomenon of the intellect, or an intellectual scepticism. This state of the intellect may result from the state of mind properly denominated unbelief, but it cannot be identical with it. Intellectual doubt or unbelief often results from unbelief properly so called, but unbelief, when contemplated as a sin, should never be confounded with theoretic or intellectual infidelity. They are as entirely distinct as any two phenomena of mind whatever.

4. It cannot consist in feelings or emotions of incredulity, doubt, or opposition to truth. In other words, unbelief as a sin cannot be a phenomenon of

the sensibility. The terra unbelief is sometimes used to express or designate a state of the intellect, and sometimes of the sensibility. It sometimes is used to designate a state of intellectual incredulity, doubt, distrust, scepticism. But when used in this sense, moral character is not justly predicable of the state of mind which the term unbelief represents.

Sometimes the term expresses a mere feeling of incredulity in regard to truth. But neither has this state of mind moral character; nor can it have, for the very good reason that it is involuntary. In short, the unbelief that is "so sorely denounced in the Bible, as a most aggravated abomination, cannot consist in any involuntary state of mind whatever.

V. What unbelief is.

The term, as used in the Bible, in those passages that represent it as a sin, must designate a phenomenon of will. It must be a voluntary state of mind. It must be the opposite of evangelical faith. Faith is the will's reception, and unbelief is the will's rejection, of truth. Faith is the soul's confiding in truth and in the God of truth. Unbelief is the soul's withholding confidence from truth and the God of truth. It is the heart's rejection of evidence, and refusal to be influenced by it. It is the will in the attitude of opposition to truth perceived, or evidence presented. Intellectual scepticism or unbelief, where light is proffered, always implies the unbelief of the will or heart. For if the mind knows, or supposes, that light may be had, on any question of duty, and does not make honest efforts to obtain it, this can be accounted for only by ascribing it to the will's reluctance to know the path of duty. In this case light is rejected. The mind has light so far as to know that more is proffered, but this proffered light is rejected. This is the sin of unbelief. All infidelity is unbelief in this sense, and infidels are so, not for want of light, but, in general, they have taken much pains to shut their eyes against it. Unbelief must be a voluntary state or attitude of the will, as distinguished from a mere volition, or executive act of the will. Volition may, and often does, give forth, through words and deeds, expressions and manifestations of unbelief. But the volition is only a result of unbelief, and not identical with it. Unbelief is a deeper and more efficient and more permanent state of mind than mere volition. It is the will in its profoundest opposition to the truth and will of God.

VI. Conditions of both faith and unbelief.

1. A revelation in some way to the mind, of the truth and will of God, must be a condition of faith and of unbelief. Be it remembered, that neither faith nor unbelief is consistent with total ignorance. There can be unbelief no further than there is light.

2. In respect to that class of truths which are discerned only upon condition of divine illumination, such illumination must be a condition both of faith and unbelief. It should be remarked, that when a truth has been once revealed by the Holy Spirit to the soul, the continuance of the divine light is not essential to the continuance of unbelief. The truth, once known and lodged in the memory, may continue to be resisted, when the agent that revealed it is withdrawn.

3. Intellectual perception is a condition of the heart's unbelief. The intellect must have evidence of truth as the condition of a virtuous belief of it. So the intellect must have evidence of the truth, as a condition of a wicked rejection of it. Therefore, intellectual light is the condition, both of the heart's faith and unbelief. By the assertion, that intellectual light is a condition of unbelief is intended, not that the intellect should at all times admit the truth in theory; but

that the evidence must be such, that by virtue of its own laws, the mind or intellect could justly admit the truth rejected by the heart. It is a very common case, that the unbeliever denies in words, and endeavors to refute in theory, that which he nevertheless assumes as true, in all his practical judgments.

VII. The guilt and ill-desert of unbelief.

We have seen, on a former occasion, that the guilt of sin is conditionated upon, and graduated by, the light under which it is committed. The amount of light is the measure of guilt, in every case of sin. This is true of all sin. But it is peculiarly manifest in the sin of unbelief; for unbelief is the rejection of light; it is selfishness in the attitude of rejecting truth. Of course, the amount of light rejected, and the degree of guilt in rejecting it, are equal. This is everywhere assumed and taught in the Bible, and is plainly the doctrine of reason.

The guilt of unbelief under the light of the gospel must be indefinitely greater, than when merely the light of nature is rejected. The guilt of unbelief, in cases where special divine illumination has been enjoyed, must be vastly and incalculably greater, than where the mere light of the gospel has been enjoyed, without a special enlightening of the Holy Spirit.

The guilt of unbelief in one who has been converted, and has known the love of God, must be greater beyond comparison, than that of an ordinary sinner. Those things that are implied in unbelief show that it must be one of the most provoking abominations to God in the universe. It is the perfection of all that is unreasonable, unjust, ruinous. It is infinitely slanderous and dishonorable to God, and destructive to man, and to all the interests of the kingdom of God.

VIII. Natural and governmental consequences of both faith and unbelief.

By natural consequences are intended consequences that flow from the constitution and laws of mind, by a natural necessity. By governmental consequences are intended those that result from the constitution, laws, and administration of moral government.

1. One of the natural consequences of faith is peace of conscience. When the will receives the truth, and yields itself up to conformity with it, the conscience is satisfied with its present attitude, and the man becomes at peace with himself. The soul is then in a state to really respect itself, and can, as it were, behold its own face without a blush. But faith in truth perceived is the unalterable condition of a man's being at peace with himself.

A governmental consequence of faith is peace with God:--

(1.) In the sense that God is satisfied with the present obedience of the soul. It is given up to be influenced by all truth, and this is comprehensive of all duty. Of course God is at peace with the soul, so far as its present obedience is concerned.

(2.) Faith governmentally results in peace with God, in the sense of being a condition of pardon and acceptance. That is, the penalty of the law for past sins is remitted upon condition of true faith in Christ. The soul not only needs present and future obedience, as a necessary condition of peace with self; but it also needs pardon and acceptance on the part of the government for past sins, as a condition of peace with God. But since the subject of justification or acceptance with God is to corn/ up as a distinct subject for consideration, I will not enlarge upon it here.

2. Self-condemnation is one of the natural consequences of unbelief. Such are the constitution and laws of mind, that it is naturally impossible for the

mind to justify the heart's rejection of truth. On the contrary, the conscience necessarily condemns such rejection, and pronounces judgment against it.

Legal condemnation is a necessary governmental consequence of unbelief. No just government can justify the rejection of known truth. But, on the contrary, all just governments must utterly abhor and condemn the rejection of truths, and especially those truths that relate to the obedience of the subject, and the highest well-being of the rulers and ruled. The government of God must condemn and utterly abhor all unbelief, as a rejection of those truths that are indispensable to the highest well-being of the universe.

3. A holy or obedient life results from faith by a natural or necessary law. Faith is an act of will which controls the life by a law of necessity. It follows of course that, when the heart receives or obeys the truth, the outward life must be conformed to it.

4. A disobedient and unholy life results from unbelief also by a law of necessity. If the heart rejects the truth, of course the life will not be conformed to it.

5. Faith will develop every form of virtue in the heart and life, as their occasions shall arise. It consists in the committing of the will to truth and to the God of truth. Of course as different occasions arise, faith will secure conformity to all truth on all subjects, and then every modification of virtue will exist in the heart, and appear in the life, as circumstances in the providence of God shall develop them.

6. Unbelief may be expected to develop resistance to all truth upon all subjects that conflict with selfishness; and hence nothing but selfishness in some form can restrain its appearing in any other and every other form possible or conceivable. It consists, be it remembered, in the heart's rejection of truth, and of course implies the cleaving to error. The natural result of this must be the development in the heart, and the appearance in the life, of every form of selfishness that is not prevented by some other form. For example, avarice may restrain amativeness, intemperance, and many other forms of selfishness.

7. Faith, governmentally results in obtaining help of God. God may and does gratuitously help those who have no faith. But this is not a governmental result or act in God. But to the obedient he extends his governmental protection and aid.

8. Faith lets God into the soul to dwell and reign there. Faith receives, not only the atonement and mediatorial work of Christ as a redeemer from punishment, but it also receives Christ as king to set up his throne, and reign in the heart. Faith secures to the soul communion with God.

9. Unbelief shuts God out of the soul, in the sense of refusing his reign in the heart. It also shuts the soul out from an interest in Christ's mediatorial work. This results not from an arbitrary appointment, but is a natural consequence. Unbelief shuts the soul out from communion with God.

These are hints at some of the natural and governmental consequences of faith and unbelief. They are designed not to exhaust the subject, but merely to call attention to topics which any one who desires may pursue at his pleasure. It should be here remarked, that none of the ways, commandments, or appointments of God are arbitrary. Faith is a naturally indispensable condition of salvation, which is the reason of its being made a governmental condition. Unbelief renders salvation naturally impossible: it must, therefore, render it governmentally impossible.

LECTURE XXXVI - JUSTIFICATION

Christ is represented in the gospel as sustaining to men three classes of relations.

1. Those which are purely governmental.
2. Those which are purely spiritual.
3. Those which unite both these.

We shall at present consider him as Christ our justification. I shall show,--

I. What gospel justification is not.

There is scarcely any question in theology that has been encumbered with more injurious and technical mysticism than that of justification.

Justification is the pronouncing of one just. It may be done in words, or, practically, by treatment. Justification must be, in some sense, a governmental act; and it is of importance to a right understanding of gospel justification, to inquire whether it be an act of the judicial, the executive, or the legislative department of government; that is, whether gospel justification consists in a strictly judicial or forensic proceeding, or whether it consists in pardon, or setting aside the execution of an incurred penalty, and is therefore properly either an executive or a legislative act. We shall see that the settling of this question is of great importance in theology; and as we view this subject, so, if consistent, we must view many important and highly practical questions in theology. This leads me to say,

That gospel justification is not to be regarded as a forensic or judicial proceeding. Dr. Chalmers and those of his school hold that it is. But this is certainly a great mistake, as we shall see. The term forensic is from forum, "a court." A forensic proceeding belongs to the judicial department of government, whose business it is to ascertain the facts and declare the sentence of the law. This department has no power over the law, but to pronounce judgment, in accordance with its true spirit and meaning. Courts never pardon, or set aside the execution of penalties. This does not belong to them, but either to the executive or to the lawmaking department. Oftentimes, this power in human governments is lodged in the head of the executive department, who is, generally at least, a branch of the legislative power of government. But never is the power to pardon exercised by the judicial department. The ground of a judicial or forensic justification invariably is, and must be, universal obedience to law. If but one crime or breach of law is alleged and proved, the court must inevitably condemn, and can in no such case justify, or pronounce the convicted just. Gospel justification is the justification of sinners; it is, therefore, naturally impossible, and a most palpable contradiction, to affirm that the justification of a sinner, or of one who has violated the law, is a forensic or judicial justification. That only is or can be a legal or forensic justification, that proceeds upon the ground of its appearing that the justified person is guiltless, or, in other words, that he has not violated the law, that he has done only what he had a legal right to do. Now it is certainly nonsense to affirm, that a sinner can be pronounced just in the eye of law; that he can be justified by deeds of law, or by the law at all. The law condemns him. But to be justified judicially or forensically, is to be pronounced just in the judgment of law. This certainly is an impossibility in respect to sinners. The Bible is as express as possible on this point. Romans iii. 20,--"Therefore by the deeds of the law there shall no flesh be justified in his sight: for by the law is the knowledge of sin."

It is proper to say here, that Dr. Chalmers and those of his school do not intend that sinners are justified by their own obedience to law, but by the perfect and imputed obedience of Jesus Christ. They maintain that, by reason of the obedience to law which Christ rendered when on earth, being set down to the credit of elect sinners, and imputed to them, the law regards them as having rendered perfect obedience in him, or regards them as having perfectly obeyed by proxy, and therefore pronounces them just, upon condition of faith in Christ. This they insist is properly a forensic or judicial justification. But this subject will come up more appropriately under another head.

II. What is gospel justification?

It consists not in the law pronouncing the sinner just, but in his being ultimately governmentally treated as if he were just; that is, it consists in a governmental decree of pardon or amnesty--in arresting and setting aside the execution of the incurred penalty of law--in pardoning and restoring to favor those who have sinned, and those whom the law had pronounced guilty, and upon whom it bad passed the sentence of eternal death, and rewarding them as if they had been righteous. In proof of this position, I remark,--

1. That this is most unequivocally taught in the Old Testament scriptures. The whole system of sacrifices taught the doctrine of pardon upon the conditions of atonement, repentance, and faith. This, under the old dispensation, is constantly represented as a merciful acceptance of the penitents, and never as a forensic or judicial acquittal or justification of them. The mercy-seat covered the law in the ark of the covenant. Paul informs us what justification was in the sense in which the Old Testament saints understood it, in Rom. iv. 6-8:--"Even also as David describeth the blessedness of the man to whom God imputeth righteousness without works, saying, Blessed are they whose iniquities are forgiven, and whose sins are covered. Blessed is the man to whom the Lord will not impute sin." This quotation from David shows both what David and what Paul understood by justification, to wit, the pardon and acceptance of the penitent sinner.

2. The New Testament fully justifies and establishes this view of the subject, as we shall abundantly see under another head.

3. Sinners cannot possibly be just in any other sense. Upon certain conditions they may be pardoned and treated as just. But for sinners to be forensically pronounced just, is impossible and absurd.

III. Conditions of justification.

In this discussion I use the term condition in the sense of a sine quâ non, a "not without which." This is its philosophical sense. A condition as distinct from a ground of justification, is anything without which sinners cannot be justified, which, nevertheless, is not the procuring cause or fundamental reason of their justification. As we shall see, there are many conditions, while there is but one ground, of the justification of sinners. The application and importance of this distinction we shall perceive as we proceed.

As has been already said, there can be no justification in a legal or forensic sense, but upon the ground of universal, perfect, and uninterrupted obedience to law. This is of course denied by those who hold that gospel justification, or the justification of penitent sinners, is of the nature of a forensic or judicial justification. They hold to the legal maxim, that what a man does by another he does by himself, and therefore the law regards Christ's obedience as ours, on the ground that ho obeyed for us. To this I reply,--

1. The legal maxim just repeated does not apply, except in cases where one acts in behalf of another by his own appointment, which was not the case with the obedience of Christ; and,--

2. The doctrine of an imputed righteousness, or that Christ's obedience to the law was accounted as our obedience, is founded on a most false and nonsensical assumption; to wit, that Christ owed no obedience to the law in his own person, and that therefore his obedience was altogether a work of supererogation, and might be made a substitute for our own obedience; that it might be set down to our credit, because he did not need to obey for himself.

I must here remark, that justification respects the moral law; and that it must be intended that Christ owed no obedience to the moral law, and therefore his obedience to this law, being wholly a work of supererogation, is set down to our account as the ground of our justification upon condition of faith in him. But surely this is an obvious mistake. We have seen, that the spirit of the moral law requires good-will to God and the universe. Was Christ under no obligation to do this? Nay, was he not rather under infinite obligation to be perfectly benevolent? Was it possible for him to be more benevolent than the law requires God and all beings to be? Did he not owe entire consecration of heart and life to the highest good of universal being? If not, then benevolence in him were no virtue, for it would not be a compliance with moral obligation. It was naturally impossible for him, and is naturally impossible for any being, to perform a work of supererogation; that is, to be more benevolent than the moral law requires him to be. This is and must be as true of God as it is of any other being. Would not Christ have sinned had he not been perfectly benevolent? If he would, it follows that he owed obedience to the law, as really as any other being. Indeed, a being that owed no obedience to the moral law must be wholly incapable of virtue, for what is virtue but obedience to the moral law?

But if Christ owed personal obedience to the moral law, then his obedience could no more than justify himself. It can never be imputed to us. He was bound for himself to love God with all his heart, and soul, and mind, and strength, and his neighbor as himself. He did no more than this. He could do no more. It was naturally impossible, then, for him to obey in our behalf.

There are, however, valid grounds and valid conditions of justification.

1. The vicarious suffering or atonement of Christ is a condition of justification, or of the pardon and acceptance of penitent sinners. It has been common either to confound the conditions with the ground of justification, or purposely to represent the atonement and work of Christ as the ground, as distinct from and opposed to a condition of justification. In treating this subject, I find it important to distinguish between the ground and conditions of justification and to regard the atonement and work of Christ not as a ground, but only as a condition of gospel justification. By the ground I mean the moving, procuring cause; that in which the plan of redemption originated as its source, and which was the fundamental reason or ground of the whole movement. This was the benevolence and merciful disposition of the whole Godhead, Father, Son, and Holy Spirit. This love made the atonement, but the

atonement did not beget this love. The Godhead desired to save sinners, but could not safely do so without danger to the universe, unless something was done to satisfy public, not retributive justice. The atonement was resorted to as a means of reconciling forgiveness with the wholesome administration of justice. A merciful disposition in the Godhead was the source, ground, mainspring, of the whole movement, while the atonement was only a condition or means, or that without which the love of God could not safely manifest itself in justifying and saving sinners.

Failing to make this distinction, and representing the atonement as the ground of the sinner's justification, has been a sad occasion of stumbling to many. Indeed, the whole questions of the nature, design, extent, and bearings of the atonement turn upon, and are involved in, this distinction. Some represent the atonement as not demanded by, nor as proceeding from the love or merciful disposition, but from the inexorable wrath of the Father, leaving the impression that Christ was more merciful, and more the friend of sinners than the Father. Many have received this impression from pulpit and written representations, as I well know.

Others, regarding the atonement as the ground as opposed to a condition of justification, have held the atonement to be the literal payment of the debt of sinners, and of the nature of a commercial transaction: a quid pro quo, a valuable consideration paid down by Christ, by suffering the same amount as was deserved by the whole number of the elect; thus negativing the idea of a merciful disposition in the Father, and representing him as demanding pay for discharging and saving sinners. Some of this class have held, that since Christ has died, the elect sinner has a right to demand his justification, on the ground of justice, that he may present the atonement and work of Christ, and say to the Father, "Here is the price; I demand the commodity." This class, of course, must hold to the limited nature of the atonement, or be universalists.

While others again, assuming that the atonement was the ground of justification in the sense of the literal payment of the debt of sinners, and that the scriptures represent the atonement as made for all men, have very consistently become universalists.

Others again have given up, or never held the view that the atonement was of the nature of the literal payment of a debt, and hold that it was a governmental expedient to reconcile the pardon of sin with a wholesome administration of justice: that it was sufficient for all as for a part of mankind: that it does not entitle those for whom it was made to a pardon on the score of justice, but that men are justified freely by grace through the redemption that is in Christ Jesus, and yet they inconsistently persist in representing the atonement as the ground, and not merely as a condition of justification.

Those who hold that the atonement and obedience of Christ were and are the ground of the justification of sinners, in the sense of the payment of their debt, regard all the grace in the transaction as consisting in the atonement and obedience of Christ, and exclude grace from the act of justification. Justification they regard as a forensic act. I regard the atonement of Christ as the necessary condition of safely manifesting the benevolence of God in the justification and salvation of sinners. A merciful disposition in the whole Godhead was the ground, and the atonement a condition of justification. Mercy would have saved without au atonement, had it been possible to do so.

That Christ's sufferings, and especially his death, were vicarious, has been abundantly shown in treating the subject of atonement. I need not repeat here what I said there. Although Christ owed perfect obedience to the moral law for himself, and could not therefore obey as our substitute, yet since he perfectly obeyed, he owed no suffering to the law or to the Divine government on his own account. He could therefore suffer for us. That is, he could, to answer governmental purposes, substitute his death for the infliction of the penalty of the law on us. He could not perform works of supererogation, but he could endure sufferings of supererogation, in the sense that he did not owe them for himself. The doctrine of substitution, in the sense just named, appears everywhere in both Testaments. It is the leading idea, the prominent thought, lying upon the face of the whole scriptures. Let the few passages that follow serve as specimens of the class that teach this doctrine:

Lev. xvii. 11. "For the life of the flesh is in the blood; and I have given it to you upon the altar, to make an atonement for your souls; for it is the blood that maketh an atonement for the soul."

Isa. liii. 5, 6, 11. "But he was wounded for our transgressions, he was bruised for our iniquities; the chastisement of our peace was upon him, and with his stripes we are healed. All we like sheep have gone astray; we have turned every one to his own way, and the Lord hath laid on him the iniquity of us all. He shall see of the travail of his soul, and shall be satisfied; by his knowledge shall my righteous servant justify many; for he shall bear their iniquities."

Matt. xx. 18. "Even as the Son of man came not to be ministered unto, but to minister, and to give his life a ransom for many."

Matt. xxvi. 28. "For this is my blood of the New Testament, which is shed for many for the remission of sins."

John iii. 14. "And as Moses lifted up the serpent in the wilderness, even so must the Son of man be lifted up: 15. That whosoever believeth in him should not perish, but have eternal life."

John vi. 51. "I am the living bread which came down from heaven; if any man eat of this bread, he shall live for ever; and the bread that I will give is my flesh, which I will give for the life of the world."

Acts xx. 28. "Take heed therefore unto yourselves, and to all the flock over the which the Holy Ghost hath made you overseers, to feed the church of God, which he hath purchased with his own blood."

Rom. iii. 24. "Being justified freely by his grace, through the redemption that is in Christ Jesus. 25. Whom God hath set forth to be a propitiation, through faith in his blood, to declare his righteousness for the remission of sins that are past, through the forbearance of God. 26. To declare, I say at this time his righteousness; that he might be just, and the justifier of him which believeth in Jesus."

Rom. v. 6. "For when we were yet without strength, in due time Christ died for the ungodly. 7. For scarcely for a righteous man will one die; yet peradventure for a good man some would even dare to die. 8. But God commendeth his love toward us, in that while we were yet sinners, Christ died for us. 9. Being now justified by his blood, we shall be saved from wrath through him. 11. And not only so, but we also joy in God, through our Lord Jesus Christ, by whom we have now received the atonement. 18. Therefore, as by the offence of one judgment came upon all men to condemnation, even so by the righteousness of one the free gift came upon all men unto justification of life. 19. For as by one man's disobedience many were made sinners, so by the obedience of one shall many be made righteous."

1 Cor. v. 7. "For even Christ our passover is sacrificed for us."

1 Cor. xv. 3. "Christ died for our sins according to the scriptures."

Gal. iii. 13. "Christ hath redeemed us from the curse of the law, being made a curse for us; for it is written, Cursed is every one that hangeth on a tree. 14. That the blessing of Abraham might come on the Gentiles through Jesus Christ; that we might receive the promise of the Spirit through faith."

Eph. ii. 13. "But now, in Christ Jesus, ye who sometimes were far off, are made nigh by the blood of Christ."

Heb. ix. 12. "Neither by the blood of goats and calves, but by his own blood, he entered in once into the holy place, having obtained eternal redemption for us. 13. For if the blood of bulls and of goats, and the ashes of an heifer sprinkling the unclean, sanctifieth to the purifying of the flesh; 14. How much more shall the blood of Christ, who through the eternal Spirit offered himself without spot to God, purge your conscience from dead works to serve the living God? 22. And almost all things are by the law purged with blood; and without shedding of blood is no remission. 23. It was therefore necessary that the patterns of things in the heavens should be purified with these; but the heavenly things themselves with better sacrifices than these. 24. For Christ is not entered into the holy places made with hands, which are the figures of the true: but into heaven itself, now to appear in the presence of God for us; 25. Nor yet that he should offer himself often, as the high priest entereth into the holy place every year with blood of others; 26. For then must he often have suffered since the foundation of the world; but now once in the end of the world hath he appeared to put away sin by the sacrifice of himself. 27. And as it is appointed unto men once to die, but after this the judgment; 28. So Christ was once offered to bear the sins of many."

1 Pet. i. 18. "Forasmuch as ye know that ye were not redeemed with corruptible things, as silver and gold, from your vain conversation received by tradition from your fathers: 19. But with the precious blood of Christ."

1 Pet. ii. 24. "Who his own self bare our sins in his own body on the tree, that we being dead to sins, should live unto righteousness; by whose stripes ye are healed."

1 John i. 7. "But if we walk in the light, we have fellowship one with another, and the blood of Jesus Christ his Son cleanseth us from all sin."

1 John iv. 9. "In this was manifested the live of God toward us, because that God sent his only-begotten Son into the world, that we might live through him. 10. Herein is love, not that we loved God, but that he loved us, and sent his Son to be the propitiation for our sins."

These and many such like passages establish the fact beyond question, that the vicarious atonement of Christ is a condition of our pardon and acceptance with God.

2. Repentance is also a condition of our justification. Observe, I here also use the term condition, in the sense of a "not without which," and not in the sense of a "that for the sake of which" the sinner is justified. It must be certain that the government of God cannot pardon sin without repentance. This is as truly a doctrine of natural as of revealed religion. It is self-evident that, until the sinner breaks off from sins by repentance or turning to God, he cannot be

justified in any sense. This is everywhere assumed, implied, and taught in the Bible. No reader of the Bible can call this in question, and it were a useless occupation of time to quote more passages.

3. Faith in Christ is, in the same sense, another condition of justification. We have already examined into the nature and necessity of faith. I fear that there has been much of error in the conceptions of many upon this subject. They have talked of justification by faith, as if they supposed that, by an arbitrary appointment of God, faith was the condition, and the only condition of justification. This seems to be the antinomian view. The class of persons alluded to speak of justification by faith; as if it were by faith, and net by Christ through faith, that the penitent sinner is justified; as if faith, and not Christ, were our justification. They seem to regard faith not as a natural, but merely as a mystical condition of justification; as bringing us into a covenant and mystical relation to Christ, in consequence of which his righteousness or personal obedience is imputed to us. It should never be forgotten that the faith that is the condition of justification, is the faith that works by love. It is the faith through and by which Christ sanctifies the soul. A sanctifying faith unites the believer to Christ as his justification; but be it always remembered, that no faith receives Christ as a justification, that does not receive him as a sanctification, to reign within the heart. We have seen that repentance, as well as faith, is a condition of justification. We shall see that perseverance in obedience to the end of life is also a condition of justification. Faith is often spoken of in scripture as if it were the sole condition of salvation, because, as we have seen, from its very nature it implies repentance and every virtue.

That faith is a naturally necessary condition of justification, we have seen. Let the following passages of scripture serve as examples of the manner in which the scriptures speak upon this subject.

Mark xvi. 15. "And he said unto them, Go ye into all the world, and preach the gospel to every creature. 16. He that believeth and is baptized, shall be saved; but he that believeth not, shall be damned."

John i. 12. "As many as received him, to them gave he power to become the sons of God, even to them that believe on his name."

John iii. 16. "For God so loved the world, that he gave his only-begotten Son, that whosoever believeth in him should not perish, but have everlasting life. 36. He that believeth on the Son hath everlasting life; and he that believeth not the Son shall not see life, but the wrath of God abideth on him."

John vi. 28. "Then said they unto him, What shall we do, that we might work the works of God? 29. Jesus answered and said unto them, This is the work of God, that ye believe on him whom he hath sent. 40. This is the will of him that sent me, that every one which seeth the Son, and believeth on him, may have everlasting life; and I will raise him up at the last day."

John viii. 24. "If ye believe not that I am he, ye shall die in your sins. 44. Ye are of your father the devil, and the lusts of your father ye will do; he was a murderer from the beginning, and abode not in the truth; because there is no truth in him. 47. He that is of God, heareth God's words; ye therefore hear them not, because ye are not of God."

John xi. 25. "Jesus said unto her, I am the resurrection and the life; he that believeth in me, though he were dead, yet shall he live; 26. And whosoever liveth, and believeth in me, shall never die."

Acts x. 43. "To him give all the prophets witness, that through his name, whosoever believeth in him shall receive remission of sins."

Acts xvi. 31. "Believe on the Lord Jesus Christ, and thou shalt be saved, and thy house."

Rom. iv. 5. "But to him that worketh not, but believeth on him that justifieth the ungodly, his faith is counted for righteousness."

Rom. x. 4. "For Christ is the end of the law for righteousness to every one that believeth."

Gal. ii. 16. "Knowing that a man is not justified by the works of the law, but by the faith of Jesus Christ, even we have believed in Jesus Christ, that we might be justified by the faith of Christ, and not by the works of the law; for by the works of the law shall no flesh be justified."

Heb. ii. 6. "Without faith it is impossible to please him; for he that cometh to God must believe that he is, and that he is a rewarder of them that diligently seek him."

1 John v. 10. "He that believeth on the Son of God hath the witness in himself; he that believeth not God hath made him a liar, because he believeth not the record that God gave of his Son. 11. And this is the record, that God hath given to us eternal life; and this life is in his Son. 12. He that hath the Son hath life; and he that hath not the Son of God, hath not life. 13. These things have I written unto you that believe on the name of the Son of God; that ye may know that ye have eternal life, and that ye may believe on the name of the Son of God."

4. Present sanctification, in the sense of present full consecration to God, is another condition, not ground, of justification. Some theologians have made justification a condition of sanctification, instead of making sanctification a condition of justification. But this we shall see is an erroneous view of the subject. The mistake is founded in a misapprehension of the nature both of justification and of sanctification. To sanctify is to set apart, to consecrate to a particular use. To sanctify anything to God is to set apart to his service, to consecrate it to him. To sanctify one's self is voluntarily to set one's self apart, to consecrate one's self to God. To be sanctified is to be set apart, to be consecrated to God. Sanctification is an act or state of being sanctified, or set apart to the service of God. It is a state of consecration to him. This is present obedience to the moral law. It is the whole of present duty, and is implied in repentance, faith, regeneration, as we have abundantly seen. Sanctification is sometimes used to express a permanent state of obedience to God, or of consecration. In this sense it is not a condition of present justification, or of pardon and acceptance. But it is a condition of continued and permanent acceptance with God. It certainly cannot be true, that God accepts and justifies the sinner in his sins. The Bible everywhere represents justified persons as sanctified, and always expressly, or impliedly, conditionates justification upon sanctification, in the sense of present obedience to God. 1 Cor. vi. 11; "And such were some of you: but ye are washed, but ye are sanctified, but ye are justified, in the name of the Lord Jesus, and by the Spirit of our God." This is but a specimen of the manner in which justified persons are spoken of in the Bible. Also, Rom. viii. 1; "There is therefore now no condemnation to them which are in Christ Jesus, who walk not after the flesh, but after the Spirit." They only are justified who walk after the Spirit. Should it be objected, as it may be, that the scripture often speaks of saints, or truly regenerate persons, as

needing sanctification, and of sanctification as something that comes after regeneration, and as that which the saints are to aim at attaining, I answer, that when sanctification is thus spoken of, it is doubtless used in the higher sense already noticed; to wit, to denote a state of being settled, established in faith, rooted and grounded in love, being so confirmed in the faith and obedience of the gospel, as to hold on in the way steadfastly, unmovably, always abounding in the work of the Lord. This is doubtless a condition of permanent justification, as has been said, but not a condition of present justification. By sanctification being a condition of justification, the following things are intended:

(1.) That present, full, and entire consecration of heart and life to God and his service, is an unalterable condition of present pardon of past sin, and of present acceptance with God.

(2.) That the penitent soul remains justified no longer than this full-hearted consecration continues. If he falls from his first love into the spirit of self-pleasing, he falls again into bondage to sin and to the law, is condemned, and must repent and do his "first work," must return to Christ, and renew his faith and love, as a condition of his salvation. This is the most express teaching of the Bible, as we shall fully see.

5. Perseverance in faith and obedience, or in consecration to God, is also an unalterable condition of justification, or of pardon and acceptance with God. By this language in this connection, you will of course understand me to mean, that perseverance in faith and obedience is a condition, not of present, but of final or ultimate acceptance and salvation.

Those who hold that justification by imputed righteousness is a forensic proceeding, take a view of final or ultimate justification, according with their view of the nature of the transaction. With them, faith receives an imputed righteousness, and a judicial justification. The first act of faith, according to them, introduces the sinner into this relation, and obtains for him a perpetual justification. They maintain that after this first act of faith it is impossible for the sinner to come into condemnation; that, being once justified, he is always thereafter justified, whatever he may do; indeed that he is never justified by grace, as to sins that are past, upon condition that he ceases to sin; that Christ's righteousness is the ground, and that his own present obedience is not even a condition of his justification, so that, in fact, his own present or future obedience to the law of God is, in no case, and in no sense, a sine quâ non of his justification, present or ultimate.

Now this is certainly another gospel from the one I am inculcating. It is not a difference merely upon some speculative or theoretic point. It is a point fundamental to the gospel and to salvation, if any one can be. Let us therefore see which of these is the true gospel.

I object to this view of justification:--

1. That it is antinomianism. Observe, they hold that upon the first exercise of faith, the soul enters into such a relation to Christ, that with respect to it the penalty of the divine law is for ever set aside, not only as it respects all past, but also as it respects all future acts of disobedience; so that sin does not thereafter bring the soul under the condemning sentence of the law of God. But a precept without a penalty is no law. Therefore, if the penalty is in their case permanently set aside or repealed, this is, and must be, a virtual repeal of the precept, for without a penalty it is only counsel, or advice, and no law.

2. But again: it is impossible that this view of justification should be true; for the moral law did not originate in the arbitrary will of God, and he cannot abrogate it either as to its precept or its penalty. He may for good and sufficient reasons dispense in certain cases with the execution of the penalty. But set it aside in such a sense, that sin would not incur it, or that the soul that sins shall not be condemned by it, he cannot--it is naturally impossible! The law is as unalterable and unrepealable, both as to its precept and its penalty, as the nature of God. It cannot but be, in the very nature of things, that sin in any being, in any world, and at any time, will and must incur the penalty of the moral law. God may pardon as often as the soul sins, repents and believes, but to prevent real condemnation where there is sin, is not at the option of any being.

3. But again; I object to the view of justification in question, that it is of course inconsistent with forgiveness or pardon. If justified by imputed righteousness, why pardon him whom the law accounts as already and perpetually, and perfectly righteous? Certainly it were absurd and impossible for the law and the law-giver judicially to justify a person on the ground of the perfect obedience of his substitute, and at the same time pardon him who is thus regarded as perfectly righteous. Especially must this be true of all sin committed subsequently to the first and justifying act of faith. If when once the soul has believed, it can no more come into condemnation, it certainly can no more be forgiven. Forgiveness implies previous condemnation, and consists in setting aside the execution of an incurred penalty.

4. If the view of justification I am opposing be true, it is altogether out of place for one who has once believed, to ask for the pardon of sin. It is a downright insult to God, and apostacy from Christ. It amounts according to their view of justification, to a denial of perpetual justification by imputed righteousness, and to an acknowledgment of being condemned. It must therefore imply a falling from grace, to pray for pardon after the soul has once believed.

5. But this view of justification is at war with the whole Bible. This everywhere represents Christians as condemned when they sin--teaches them to repent, confess, and pray for pardon--to betake themselves afresh to Christ as their only hope. The Bible, in almost every variety or manner, represents perseverance in faith, and obedience to the end, as a condition of ultimate justification and final salvation. Let the following passages serve as examples of the manner in which the Bible represents this subject:--

Ezek. xviii. 24. "But when the righteous turneth away from his righteousness, and committeth iniquity, and doeth according to all the abominations that the wicked man doeth, shall he live? All his righteousness that he hath done shall not be mentioned; in his trespass that he hath trespassed, and in his sin that he hath sinned, in them shall he die."

Ezek. xxxiii. 13. "When I shall say to the righteous, that he shall surely live; if he trust to his own righteousness, and commit iniquity, all his righteousness shall not be remembered; but for his iniquity that he hath committed, he shall die for it."

Matt. x. 22. "And ye shall be hated of all men for my name's sake; but he that endureth to the end shall be saved." [Matt. xxiv. 13.]

1 Cor. ix. 27. "But I keep under my body, and bring it into subjection; lest that by any means when I have preached to others, I myself should be a castaway."

1 Cor. x. 12. "Wherefore let him that thinketh he standeth, take heed lest he fall."

2 Cor. vi. 1. "We then, as workers together with him, beseech you also that ye receive not the grace of God in vain."

Col. i. 23. "If ye continue in the faith grounded and settled, and be not moved away from the hope of the gospel, which ye have heard, and which was preached to every creature which is under heaven; whereof I Paul am made a minister."

Heb. iv. 1. "Let us therefore fear, lest a promise being left us of entering into his rest, any of you should seem to come short of it. 11. Let us labor therefore to enter into that rest, lest any man fall after the same example of unbelief."

2 Pet. i. 10. "Wherefore the rather, brethren, give diligence to make your calling and election sure; for if ye do these things, ye shall never fall."

Rev. ii. 10. "Fear none of those things which thou shalt suffer. Behold, the devil shall cast some of you into prison, that ye may be tried; and ye shall have tribulation ten days. Be thou faithful unto death, and I will give thee a crown of life. 11. He that hath an ear, let him hear what the Spirit saith unto the churches; He that overcometh, shall not be hurt of the second death. 17. To him that overcometh will I give to eat of the hidden manna, and will give him a white stone, and in the stone a new name written, which no man knoweth, saving he that receiveth it. 26. And he that overcometh, and keepeth my words unto the end, to him will I give power over the nations; 27. And he shall rule them with a rod of iron; as the vessels of a potter shall they be broken to shivers; even as I received of my Father."

Observe, I am not here calling in question the fact, that all true saints do persevere in faith and obedience to the end; but am showing that such perseverance is a condition of salvation, or ultimate justification. The subject of the perseverance of the saints will come under consideration in its proper place.

6. The view of justification which I am opposing is contradicted by the consciousness of the saints. I think I may safely affirm that the saints in all time are very conscious of condemnation when they fall into sin. This sense of condemnation may not subject them to the same kind and degree of fear which they experienced before regeneration, because of the confidence they have that God will pardon their sin. Nevertheless, until they repent, and by a renewed act of faith lay hold on pardon and fresh justification, their remorse, shame, and consciousness of condemnation, do in fact, if I am not much deceived, greatly exceed, as a general thing, the remorse, shame, and sense of condemnation experienced by the impenitent. But if it be true, that the first act of faith brings the soul into a state of perpetual justification, so that it cannot fall into condemnation thereafter, do what it will, the experience of the saints contradicts facts, or, more strictly, their consciousness of condemnation is a delusion. They are not in fact condemned by the moral law as they conceive themselves to be.

7. If I understand the framers of the Westminster Confession of Faith, they regarded justification as a state resulting from the relation of an adopted child of God, which state is entered into by faith alone, and held that justification is not conditionated upon obedience for the time being, but that a person in this state may, as they hold that all in this life in fact do, sin daily, and even continually, yet without condemnation by the law, their sin bringing them only

under his fatherly displeasure, and subjecting them to the necessity of repentance, as a condition of his fatherly favor, but not as a condition of pardon or of ultimate salvation. They seem to have regarded the child of God as no longer under moral government, in such a sense that sin was imputed to him, this having been imputed to Christ, and Christ's righteousness so literally imputed to him that, do what he may, after the first act of faith he is accounted and treated in his person as wholly righteous. If this is not antinomianism, I know not what is; since they hold that all who once believe will certainly be saved, yet that their perseverance in holy obedience to the end is, in no case, a condition of final justification, but that this is conditionated upon the first act of faith alone. They support their positions with quotations from scripture about as much in point as is common for them. They often rely on proof-texts that, in their meaning and spirit, have not the remotest allusion to the point in support of which they are quoted. I have tried to understand the subject of justification as it is taught in the Bible, without going into labored speculations or to theological technicalities. If I have succeeded in understanding it, the following is a succinct and a true account of the matter:

The Godhead, in the exercise of his adorable love and compassion, sought the salvation of sinners, through and by means of the mediatorial death and work of Christ. This death and work of Christ were resorted to, not to create, but, as a result of, the merciful disposition of God and as a means of securing the universe against a misapprehension of the character and design of God in forgiving and saving sinners. To Christ, as Mediator between the Godhead and man, the work of justifying and saving sinners is committed. He is made unto sinners "wisdom, righteousness, sanctification, and redemption." In consideration of Christ's having by his death for sinners secured the subjects of the divine government against a misconception of his character and designs, God does, upon the further conditions of a repentance and faith that imply a renunciation of their rebellion and a return to obedience to his laws, freely pardon past sin, and restore the penitent and believing sinner to favor, as if he had not sinned, while he remains penitent and believing, subject however to condemnation and eternal death, unless he holds the beginning of his confidence steadfast unto the end. The doctrine of a literal imputation of Adam's sin to all his posterity, of the literal imputation of all the sins of the elect to Christ, and of his suffering for them the exact amount due to the transgressors, of the literal imputation of Christ's righteousness or obedience to the elect, and the consequent perpetual justification of all that are converted from the first exercise of faith, whatever their subsequent life may be--I say I regard these dogmas as fabulous, and better befitting a romance than a system of theology.

But it is said, that the Bible speaks of the righteousness of faith. "What shall we say then? That the Gentiles, which followed not after righteousness, have attained to righteousness, even the righteousness which is of faith."--Rom. ix. 30. "And be found in him, not having mine own righteousness, which is of the law, but that which is through the faith of Christ, the righteousness which is of God by faith."--Phil. iii. 9. These and similar passages are relied upon, as teaching the doctrine of an imputed righteousness; and such as these: "The Lord our righteousness;" "Surely, shall one say, in the Lord have I righteousness and strength." By "the Lord our righteousness," we may understand, either that we are justified, that is, that our sins are atoned for, and that we are pardoned and accepted by, or on account of the Lord, that is Jesus Christ; or we may understand that the Lord makes us righteous, that is, that he is our sanctification, or working in us to will and to do of his good pleasure; or both, that is, he atones for our sins, brings us to repentance and faith, works sanctification or righteousness in us, and then pardons our past sins, and accepts us. By the righteousness of faith, or of God by faith, I understand the method of making sinners holy, and of securing their justification or acceptance by faith, as opposed to mere works of law or self-righteousness. Dikaiosune, rendered righteousness, may be with equal propriety, and often is, rendered justification. So undoubtedly it should be rendered in 1 Cor. i. 30. "But of him are ye in Christ Jesus, who of God is made unto us wisdom, and righteousness, and sanctification, and redemption." The meaning here doubtless is, that he is the author and finisher of that scheme of redemption, whereby we are justified by faith, as opposed to justification by our own works. "Christ our righteousness" is Christ the author or procurer of our justification. But this does not imply that he procures our justification by imputing his obedience to us.

The doctrine of a literal imputation of Christ's obedience or righteousness is supported by those who hold it, by such passages as the following: Rom. iv. 5-8. "But to him that worketh not, but believeth on him that justifieth the ungodly, his faith is counted for righteousness. Even as David also describeth the blessedness of the man, unto whom God imputeth righteousness without works, saying, Blessed are they whose iniquities are forgiven, and whose sins are covered. Blessed is the man to whom the Lord will not impute sin." But here justification is represented only as consisting in forgiveness of sin, or in pardon and acceptance. Again, 2 Cor. v. 19, 21. "To wit, that God was in Christ, reconciling the world unto himself, not imputing their trespasses unto them; and hath committed unto us the word of reconciliation. For he hath made him to be sin for us who knew no sin; that we might be made the righteousness of God in him." Here again the apostle is teaching only his much loved doctrine of justification by faith, in the sense that upon condition or in consideration of the death and mediatorial interference and work of Christ, penitent believers in Christ are forgiven and rewarded as if they were righteous.

IV. Foundation of the justification of penitent believers in Christ. What is the ultimate ground or reason of their justification?

1. It is not founded in Christ's literally suffering the exact penalty of the law for them, and in this sense literally purchasing their justification and eternal salvation. The Westminster Confession of Faith affirms as follows: chapter on Justification section 3--"Christ by his obedience and death, did fully discharge the debt of all those that are thus justified, and did make a proper, real, and full satisfaction to his Father's justice in their behalf. Yet, inasmuch as he was given by the Father for them, and his obedience and satisfaction accepted in their stead, and both freely, not for anything in them, their justification is only of free grace, that both the exact justice and rich grace of God might be glorified in the justification of sinners." If the framers of this confession had made the distinction between the grounds and conditions of justification, so as to represent the gracious disposition that gave the Son, and that accepted his obedience and satisfaction in their stead, as the ground or moving cause, and the death and work of Christ as a condition or a means, as "that without which" the benevolence of God could not wisely justify sinners, their statement had been much improved. As it stands, the transaction is represented as a proper

quid pro quo, a proper full payment of the debt of the justified. All the grace consisted in giving his Son, and consenting to the substitution. But they deny that there is grace in the act of justification itself. This proceeds upon the ground of "exact justice." There is then according to this, no grace in the act of pardon and accepting the sinner as righteous. This is "exact justice," because the debt is fully cancelled by Christ. Indeed, "Christian, what do you think of this?" God has, in the act of giving his Son and in consenting to the substitution, exercised all the grace he ever will. Now your forgiveness and justification are, according to this teaching, placed on the ground of "exact justice." You have now only to believe and demand "exact justice." One act of faith places your salvation on the ground of "exact justice." Talk no more of the grace of God in forgiveness! But stop, let us see. What is to be understood here by exact justice, and by a real, full satisfaction to his Father's justice? I suppose all orthodox Christians to hold, that every sinner and every sin, strictly on the score of justice, deserves eternal death or endless suffering. Did the framers of this confession hold that Christ bore the literal penalty of the law for each of the saints? Or did they hold that by virtue of his nature and relations, his suffering, though indefinitely less in amount than was deserved by the transgressors, was a full equivalent to public justice, or governmentally considered, for the execution of the literal penalty upon the transgressors? If they meant this latter, I see no objection to it. But if they meant the former, namely, that Christ suffered in his own person the full amount strictly due to all the elect, I say,

(1.) That it was naturally impossible.

(2.) That his nature and relation to the government of God was such as to render it wholly unnecessary to the safe forgiveness of sin, that he should suffer precisely the same amount deserved by sinners.

(3.) That if, as their substitute, Christ suffered for them the full amount deserved by them, then justice has no claim upon them, since their debt is fully paid by the surety, and of course the principal is, in justice, discharged. And since it is undeniable that the atonement was made for the whole posterity of Adam, it must follow that the salvation of all men is secured upon the ground of "exact justice." This is the conclusion to which Huntington and his followers came. This doctrine of literal imputation, is one of the strongholds of universalism, and while his view of atonement and justification is held they cannot be driven from it.

(4.) If he satisfied justice for them, in the sense of literally and exactly obeying for them, why should his suffering be imputed to them as a condition of their salvation? Surely they could not need both the imputation of his perfect obedience to them, so as to be accounted in law as perfectly righteous, and also the imputation of his sufferings to them, as if he had not obeyed for them. Is God unrighteous? Does he exact of the surety, first, the literal and full payment of the debt, and secondly, perfect personal obedience for and in behalf of the sinner? Does he first exact full and perfect obedience, and then the same amount of suffering as if there had been no obedience? And this, too, of his beloved Son?

(5.) What Christian ever felt, or can feel in the presence of God, that he has a right to demand justification in the name of Christ, as due to him on the ground of "exact justice?" Observe, the framers of the Confession just quoted, studiously represent all the grace exercised in the justification of sinners, as confined to the two acts of giving his Son and accepting the substitution. This done, Christ fully pays the debt, fully and exactly satisfies his Father's justice. You now need not, must not conceive of the pardon of sin as grace or favor. To do this is, according to the teaching of this Confession, to dishonor Christ. It is to reject his righteousness and salvation. What think you of this? One act of grace in giving his Son, and consenting to the substitution, and all forgiveness, all accepting and trusting as righteous, is not grace, but "exact justice." To pray for forgiveness, as an act of grace, is apostacy from Christ. Christian! Can you believe this? No; in your closet, smarting under the sting of a recently committed sin, or broken down and bathed in tears, you cannot find it in your heart to demand "exact justice" at the hand of God, on the ground that Christ has fully and literally paid your debt. To represent the work and death of Christ as the ground of justification in this sense, is a snare and a stumbling-block. This view that I have just examined, contradicts the necessary convictions of every saint on earth. For the truth of this assertion I appeal to the universal consciousness of saints.

2. Our own works, or obedience to the law or to the gospel, are not the ground or foundation of our justification. That is, neither our faith, nor repentance, nor love, nor life, nor anything done by us or wrought in us, is the ground of our justification. These are conditions of our justification, in the sense of a "not without which," but not the ground of it. We are justified upon condition of our faith, but not for our faith; upon condition of our repentance, love, obedience, perseverance to the end, but not for these things. These are the conditions, but not the reason, ground, or procuring cause of our justification. We cannot be justified without them, neither are we or can we be justified by them. None of these things must be omitted on pain of eternal damnation. Nor must they be put in the place of Christ, upon the same penalty. Faith is so much insisted on in the gospel as the sine quâ non of our justification, that some seem disposed, or at least to be in danger of substituting faith in the place of Christ; of making faith instead of Christ the Savior.

3. Neither is the atonement, nor anything in the mediatorial work of Christ, the foundation of our justification, in the sense of the source, moving, or procuring cause. This, that is the ground of our justification, lies deep in the heart of infinite love. We owe all to that merciful disposition that performed the mediatorial work, and died the accursed death to supply an indispensable condition of our justification and salvation. To stop short in the act which supplied the condition, instead of finding the depths of a compassion as fathomless as infinity, as the source of the whole movement, is to fail in discrimination. The work, and death, and resurrection, and advocacy of Christ are indispensable conditions, are all-important, but not the fundamental reason of our justification.

4. Nor is the work of the Holy Spirit in converting and sanctifying the soul, the foundation of our justification. This is only a condition or means of bringing it about, but is not the fundamental reason.

5. But the disinterested and infinite love of God, the Father, Son, and Holy Spirit, is the true and only foundation of the justification and salvation of sinners. God is love, that is, he is infinitely benevolent. All he does, or says, or suffers, permits or omits, is for one and the same ultimate reason, namely, to promote the highest good of universal being.

6. Christ, the second person in the glorious Trinity, is represented in scripture, as taking so prominent a part in this work, that the number of offices

and relations which he sustains to God and man in it are truly wonderful. For example, he is represented as being,--King--Judge--Mediator--Advocate--Redeemer--surety--wisdom--righ teousness--sanctification--redemption--Prophet--Priest--passover, or Lamb of God--the bread and water of life--true God and eternal life--our life--our all in all--as the repairer of the breach--as dying for our sins--as rising for our justification--as the resurrection and the life--as bearing our griefs and carrying our sorrows--as he, by whose stripes we are healed--as the head of his people--as the bridegroom or husband of his church--as the shepherd of his flock--as the door by which they enter--as the way to salvation--as our salvation--as the truth--as being made sin for us--that we are made the righteousness of God in him--that in him dwells all the fulness of the Godhead--that in him all fulness dwells--all power in heaven and earth are said to be given to him--the true light that lighteth every man that cometh into the world--Christ in us the hope of glory--the true vine of which we are the branches--our brother--Wonderful--Counsellor--the mighty God--the everlasting Father--the prince of peace--the captain of salvation--the captain of the Lord's host.

These are among the official relations of Christ to his people, and to the great work of our justification. I shall have frequent occasion to consider him in some of these relations, as we proceed in this course of study. Indeed, the offices, relations, and works of Christ, are among the most important topics of Christian theology.

Christ is our Justification, in the sense that he carries into execution the whole scheme of redemption devised by the adorable Godhead. To him the scriptures everywhere direct the eyes of our faith and of our intelligence also. The Holy Spirit is represented not as glorifying himself, but as speaking of Jesus, as taking of the things of Christ and showing them to his people, as glorifying Christ Jesus, as being sent by Christ, as being the Spirit of Christ, as being Christ himself dwelling in the hearts of his people. But I must forbear at present. This subject of Christ's relations needs elucidation in future lectures.

REMARK

The relations of the old school view of justification to their view of depravity is obvious. They hold, as we have seen, that the constitution in every faculty and part is sinful. Of course, a return to personal, present holiness, in the sense of entire conformity to the law, cannot with them be a condition of justification. They must have a justification while yet at least in some degree of sin. This must be brought about by imputed righteousness. The intellect revolts at a justification in sin. So a scheme is devised to divert the eye of the law and of the lawgiver from the sinner to his substitute, who has perfectly obeyed the law. But in order to make out the possibility of his obedience being imputed to them, it must be assumed, that he owed no obedience for himself; than which a greater absurdity cannot be conceived. Constitutional depravity or sinfulness being once assumed, physical regeneration, physical sanctification, physical divine influence, imputed righteousness and justification, while personally in the commission of sin, follow of course.

LECTURE XXXVII - SANCTIFICATION

I. I will remind you of some points that have been settled in this course of study.

1. The true intent and meaning of the law of God has been, as I trust, ascertained in the lectures on moral government. Let this point if need be, be examined by reference to those lectures.

2. We have also seen, in those lectures, what is not, and what is implied in entire obedience to the moral law.

3. In those lectures, and also in the lectures on justification and repentance, it has been shown that nothing is acceptable to God, as a condition of justification, and of consequent salvation, but a repentance that implies a return to full obedience to the moral law.

4. It has also been shown, that nothing is holiness short of full obedience, for the time being, to the moral law.

5. It has also been shown, that regeneration and repentance consist in the heart's return to full obedience, for the time being, to this law.

6. We have also examined the doctrine of depravity, and seen, that moral depravity, or sin, consists in selfishness, and not at all in the constitution of men; that selfishness does not consist in the involuntary appetites, passions, and propensities, but that it consists alone in the committal of the will to the gratification of the propensities.

7. We have seen that holiness consists, not at all in the constitution of body or mind; but that it belongs, strictly, only to the will or heart, and consists in obedience of will to the law of God, as it lies revealed in the intellect; that it is expressed in one word, love; that this love is identical with the entire consecration of the whole being to the glory of God, and to the highest well-being of the universe; or in other words, that it consists in disinterested benevolence.

8. We have seen that all true saints, while in a state of acceptance with God, do actually render, for the time being, full obedience to all the known requirements of God; that is, that they do for the time being their whole duty--all that God, at this time, requires of them.

9. We have seen that this obedience is not rendered independent of the grace of God, but is induced by the indwelling spirit of Christ received by faith, and reigning in the heart. This fact will be more fully elucidated in this discussion than it has been in former lectures. A former lecture was devoted to it; but a fuller consideration of it remains to be entered upon hereafter.

II. Define the principal terms to be used in this discussion.

Here let me remark, that a definition of terms, in all discussions, is of prime importance. Especially is this true of this subject. I have observed that almost without an exception, those who have written on this subject dissenting from the views entertained here, do so upon the ground that they understand and define the terms sanctification and Christian perfection differently from what we do. Every one gives his own definition, varying materially from others, and from what we understand by the terms; and then he goes on professedly opposing the doctrine as inculcated here. Now this is not only utterly unfair, but palpably absurd. If I oppose a doctrine inculcated by another man, I am bound to oppose what he really holds. If I misrepresent his sentiments, "I fight as one that beateth the air." I have been amazed at the diversity of definitions that have been given to the terms Christian perfection, sanctification, etc.; and to witness the diversity of opinion as to what is, and what is not, implied in these terms. One objects wholly to the use of the term Christian perfection, because, in his estimation, it implies this, and that, and the other thing, which I do not suppose are at all implied in it. Another objects to our using the term sanctification, because that implies, according to his understanding of it, certain things that render its use improper. Now it is no part of my design to dispute about the use of words. I must however use some terms; and I ought to be allowed to use Bible language in its scriptural sense, as I understand it. And if I should sufficiently explain my meaning, and define the sense in which I use the terms, and the sense in which the Bible manifestly uses them, this ought to suffice. And I beg, that nothing more or less may be understood by the language I use, than I profess to mean by it. Others may, if they please, use the same terms, and give a different definition of them. But I have a right to hope and expect, if they feel called upon to oppose what I say, that they will bear in mind my definition of the terms, and not pretend, as some have done, to oppose my views, while they have only differed from me in their definition of the terms used, giving their own definition varying materially and, I might say, infinitely from the sense in which I use the same terms, and then arraying their arguments to prove, that according to their definition of it, sanctification is not really attainable in this life, when no one here or anywhere else, that I ever heard of pretended that, in their sense of the term, it ever was or ever will be, attainable in this life, and I might add, or in that which is to come.

Sanctification is a term of frequent use in the Bible. Its simple and primary meaning is a state of consecration to God. To sanctify is to set apart to a holy use--to consecrate a thing to the service of God. This is plainly both the Old and the New Testament use of the term. The Greek word hagiazo means to sanctify, to consecrate, or devote a person or thing to a particular, especially to a sacred, use. This word is synonymous with the Hebrew kaudash. This last word is used in the Old Testament to express the same thing that is intended by the Greek hagiazo, namely, to consecrate, devote, set apart, sanctify, purify, make clean or pure. Hagiasmos, a substantive from hagiazo, means sanctification, devotion, consecration, purity, holiness.

From the Bible use of these terms it is most manifest,--

1. That sanctification does not imply any constitutional change, either of soul or body. It consists in the consecration or devotion of the constitutional powers of body and soul to God, and not in any change wrought in the constitution itself.

2. It is also evident from the scriptural use of the term, that sanctification is not a phenomenon, or state of the intellect. It belongs neither to the reason, conscience, nor understanding. In short, it cannot consist in any state of the intellect whatever. All the states of this faculty are purely passive states of mind; and of course, as we have abundantly seen, holiness is not properly predicable of them.

3. It is just as evident that sanctification, in the scriptural and proper sense of the term, is not a mere feeling of any kind. It is not a desire, an appetite, a passion, a propensity, an emotion, nor indeed any kind or degree of feeling. It is not a state or phenomenon of the sensibility. The states of the sensibility are, like those of the intellect, purely passive states of mind, as has been repeatedly shown. They of course can have no moral character in themselves.

4. The Bible use of the term, when applied to persons, forbids the understanding of it, as consisting in any involuntary state or attitude of mind whatever.

5. The inspired writers evidently used the terms which are translated by the English word sanctify, to designate a phenomenon of the will, or a voluntary state of mind. They used the term hagiazo in Greek, and kaudash in Hebrew, to represent the act of consecrating one's self, or anything else to the service of God, and to the highest well-being of the universe. The term manifestly not only represents an act of the will, but an ultimate act or choice, as distinguished from a mere volition, or executive act of the will. Thus the terms rendered sanctified are used as synonymous with loving God with all the heart, and our neighbor as ourselves. The Greek hagiasmos, translated by the word sanctification, is evidently intended to express a state or attitude of voluntary consecration to God, a continued act of consecration; or a state of choice as distinct from a mere act of choice, an abiding act or state of choice, a standing and controlling preference of mind, a continuous committal of the will to the highest well-being of God and of the universe. Sanctification, as a state differing from a holy act, is a standing, ultimate intention, and exactly synonymous or identical with a state of obedience, or conformity to the law of God. We have repeatedly seen that the will is the executive or controlling faculty of the mind. Sanctification consists in the will's devoting or consecrating itself and the whole being, all we are and have, so far as powers, susceptibilities, possessions are under the control of the will, to the service of God, or, which is the same thing, to the highest interests of God and of being. Sanctification, then, is nothing more nor less than entire obedience, for the time being, to the moral law.

Sanctification may be entire in two senses: (1.) In the sense of present, full obedience, or entire consecration to God; and (2.) In the sense of continued, abiding consecration or obedience to God. Entire sanctification, when the terms are used in this sense, consists in being established, confirmed, preserved, continued in a state of sanctification or of entire consecration to God.

In this discussion, then, I shall use the term entire sanctification to designate a state of confirmed, and entire consecration of body, soul, and spirit, or of the whole being to God--confirmed, not in the sense, (1.) That a soul entirely sanctified cannot sin, but that as a matter of fact, he does not, and will not sin. (2.) Nor do I use the term entire sanctification as implying that the entirely sanctified soul is in no such danger of sinning as to need the thorough use and application of all the means of grace to prevent him from sinning, and to secure his continued sanctification. (3.) Nor, do I mean by entire sanctification, a state in which there will be no further struggle or warfare with temptation, or in which the Christian warfare will cease. This certainly did not cease in Christ to the end of life, nor will it with any being in the flesh. (4.) Nor do I use the term as implying a state in which no further progress in holiness is possible. No such state is, or ever will be, possible to any creature, for the plain reason, that all creatures must increase in knowledge; and increase of knowledge implies increase of holiness in a holy being. The saints will doubtless grow in grace or holiness to all eternity. (5.) Nor do I mean by the term entire sanctification, that the entirely sanctified soul will no longer need the continual grace and indwelling Spirit of Christ to preserve it from sin, and to secure its continuance in a state of consecration to God. It is amazing that such men as Dr. Beecher and others should suppose, that a state of entire consecration implies that the entirely sanctified soul no longer needs the grace of Christ to preserve it. Entire sanctification, instead of implying no further dependence on the grace of Christ, implies the constant appropriation of Christ by faith as the sanctification of the soul.

But since entire sanctification, as I understand the term, is identical with entire and continued obedience to the law of God, and since I have in lectures on moral government fully shown what is not, and what is, implied in full obedience to the law of God, to avoid much repetition in this place, I must refer you to what I have there said upon the topics just named.

III. Show what the real question now at issue is.

1. It is not whether a state of present full obedience to the divine law is attainable in this life. For this has, I trust, been clearly established in former lectures.

2. It is not whether a state of permanent, full obedience has been attained by all, or by any of the saints on earth.

3. But the true question at issue is, Is a state of entire, in the sense of permanent sanctification, attainable in this life?

If in this discussion I shall insist upon the fact, that this state has been attained, let it be distinctly understood, that the fact that the attainment has been made, is only adduced in proof of the attainability of this state; that it is only one of the arguments by which the attainability of this state is proved. Let it also be distinctly borne in mind, that if there should be in the estimation of any one a defect in the proof, that this state has been attained, still the integrity and conclusiveness of the other arguments in support of the attainability will not thereby be shaken. It is no doubt true, that the attainability of this state in this life may be abundantly established, entirely irrespective of the question whether this state has ever been attained.

The true question is, Is a state of entire, established, abiding consecration to God attainable in this life, in such a sense, that we may rationally expect or hope to become thus established in this life? Are the conditions of attaining this established state in the grace and love of God, such that we may rationally expect or hope to fulfil them, and thus become established, or entirely sanctified in this life? This is undoubtedly the true and the greatly important question to be settled.

IV. That entire sanctification is attainable in this life.

1. It is self-evident, that entire obedience to God's law is possible on the ground of natural ability. To deny this, is to deny that a man is able to do as well as he can. The very language of the law is such as to level its claims to the capacity of the subject, however great or small that capacity may be. "Thou shalt love the Lord thy God with all thy heart, with all thy soul, with all thy mind, and with all thy strength." Here then it is plain, that all the law demands, is the exercise of whatever strength we have, in the service of God. Now, as entire sanctification consists in perfect obedience to the law of God, and as the

law requires nothing more than the right use of whatever strength we have, it is, of course, forever settled, that a state of entire sanctification is attainable in this life, on the ground of natural ability.

This is generally admitted by those who are called moderate Calvinists. Or, perhaps I should say, it generally has been admitted by them, though at present some of them seem inclined to give up the doctrine of natural ability, and to take refuge in constitutional depravity, rather than admit the attainableness of a state of entire sanctification in this life. But let men take refuge where they will, they can never escape from the plain letter, and spirit, and meaning of the law of God. Mark with what solemn emphasis it says, "Thou shalt love the Lord thy God with all thy heart, with all thy soul, with all thy mind, and with all thy strength." This is its solemn injunction, whether it be given to an angel, a man, or a child. An angel is bound to exercise an angel's strength; a man, the strength of a man; and a child, the strength of a child. It comes to every moral being in the universe, just as he is, where he is, and requires, not that he should create new powers, or possess other powers than he has, but that such as his powers are, they should all be used with the utmost perfection and constancy for God.

2. The provisions of grace are such as to render its actual attainment in this life, the object of reasonable pursuit. It is admitted, that the entire sanctification of the church is to be accomplished. It is also admitted, that this work is to be accomplished, "through the sanctification of the Spirit and the belief of the truth." It is also universally agreed, that this work must be begun here; and also that it must be completed before the soul can enter heaven. This then is the inquiry,--Is this state attainable as a matter of fact before death?

BIBLE ARGUMENT

I come now to consider the question directly, and wholly as a Bible question, whether entire sanctification is in such a sense attainable in this life, as to make its attainment an object of rational pursuit.

1. It is evident from the fact, expressly stated, that abundant means are provided for the accomplishment of this end. Eph. iv. 15-19. "He that descended is the same also that ascended up far above all heavens, that he might fill all things. And he gave some, apostles; and some, prophets; and some, evangelists; and some, pastors and teachers; for the perfecting of the saints, for the work of the ministry, for the edifying of the body of Christ; till we all come in the unity of the faith, and of the knowledge of the Son of God, unto a perfect man, unto the measure of the stature of the fulness of Christ; that we henceforth be no more children tossed to and fro, and carried about with every wind of doctrine, by the sleight of men, and cunning craftiness, whereby they lie in wait to deceive; but speaking the truth in love, may grow up into him in all things, which is the head, even Christ; from whom the whole body fitly joined together and compacted by that which every joint supplieth, according to the effectual working in the measure of every part, maketh increase of the body, unto the edifying of itself in love." Upon this passage I remark:--

(1.) That what is here spoken of is plainly applicable only to this life. It is in this life that the apostles, evangelists, prophets, and teachers, exercise their ministry. These means therefore are applicable, and so far as we know, only applicable to this life.

(2.) The apostle here manifestly teaches, that these means are designed and adequate to perfecting the whole church as the body of Christ, "till we all come in the unity of the faith and of the knowledge of the Son of God, unto the measure of the stature of the fulness of Christ." Now observe,--

(3.) These means are for the perfecting of the saints, till the whole church, as a perfect man, "has come to the measure of the stature of the fulness of Christ." If this is not entire sanctification, what is? That this is to take place in this world is evident from what follows. For the apostle adds, "that we henceforth be no more tossed to and fro, and carried about with every wind of doctrine, by the sleight of men, and cunning craftiness, whereby they lie in wait to deceive."

(4.) It should be observed, that this is a very strong passage in support of the doctrine, inasmuch as it asserts that abundant means are provided for the sanctification of the church in this life. And as the whole includes all its parts, there must be sufficient provision for the sanctification of each individual.

(5.) If the work is ever to be effected, it is by these means. But these means are used only in this life. Entire sanctification then must take place in this life.

(6.) If this passage does not teach a state of entire sanctification, such a state is nowhere mentioned in the Bible. And if believers are not here said to be wholly sanctified by these means, and of course in this life, I know not that it is anywhere taught that they shall be sanctified at all.

(7.) But suppose this passage to be put into the language of a command, how should we understand it? Suppose the saints commanded to be perfect, and to "grow up to the measure of the stature of the fulness of Christ," could anything less than entire sanctification be understood by such requisitions? Then by what rule of sober criticism, I would inquire, can this language, used in this connection, mean anything less than I have supposed it to mean?

2. But let us look into some of the promises. It is not my design to examine a great number of scripture promises, but rather to show, that those which I do examine, fully sustain the positions I have taken. One is sufficient, if it be full and its application just, to settle this question for ever. I might occupy many pages in the examination of the promises, for they are exceedingly numerous, and full, and in point. But my design is at present to examine somewhat critically a few only out of the many. This will enable you to apply the same principles to the examination of the scripture promises generally.

(1.) I begin by referring you to the law of God, as given in Deut. x. 12. "And now, Israel, what doth the Lord thy God require of thee, but to fear the Lord thy God, to walk in all his ways, and to love him, and to serve the Lord thy God with all thy heart, and with all thy soul?" Upon this passage I remark:--

(i.) It professedly sums up the whole duty of man to God--to fear and love him with all the heart and all the soul.

(ii.) Although this is said of Israel, yet it is equally true of all men. It is equally binding upon all, and is all that God requires of any man in regard to himself.

(iii.) Continued obedience to this requirement is entire sanctification, In the sense in which I use those terms.

See Deut. xxx. 6. "And the Lord thy God will circumcise thine heart, and the heart of thy seed, to love the Lord thy God with all thine heart, and with all thy soul, that thou mayest live." Here we have a promise couched in the same language as the command just quoted. Upon this passage I remark:--

It promises just what the law requires. If the law requires a state of entire sanctification, or if that which the law requires is a state of entire sanctification, then this is a promise of entire sanctification. As the command is universally binding upon all and applicable to all, so this promise is universally applicable to all who will lay hold upon it. Faith is an indispensable condition of the fulfilment of this promise. It is entirely impossible that we should love God with all the heart, without confidence in him. God begets love in man in no other way than by so revealing himself as to inspire confidence, that confidence which works by love.

Now here there is no perceivable reason why we should not understand the language of the promise as meaning as much as the language of the command. This promise appears to have been designed to cover the whole ground of the requirement. Suppose the language in this promise to be used in a command, or suppose that the form of this promise were changed into that of a command;--suppose God should say as he does elsewhere, "Thou shalt love the Lord thy God with all thy heart and with all thy soul:" who would doubt that God designed to require a state of entire sanctification or consecration to himself? How then are we to understand it when used in the form of a promise? If his bountifulness equals his justice, his promises of grace must be understood to mean as much as the requirements of his justice. If he delights in giving as much as in receiving, his promises must mean as much as the language of his requirements.

This promise is designed to be fulfilled in this life. The language and connection imply this: "I will circumcise thy heart, and the heart of thy seed, to love the Lord thy God with all thy heart, and with all thy soul." This in some sense takes place in regeneration, but more than simple regeneration seems here to be promised. It is plain, I think, that this promise relates to a state of mind, and not merely to an exercise.

This promise as it respects the church, at some day, must be absolute and certain. So that God will undoubtedly, at some period, beget this state of mind in the church. But to what particular individuals and generation this promise will be fulfilled, must depend upon their faith in the promise.

(2.) See Jer. xxxi. 31-34: "Behold, the days come, saith the Lord, that I will make a new covenant with the house of Israel, and with the house of Judah; not according to the covenant that I made with their fathers, in the day that I took them by the hand, to bring them out of the land of Egypt, (which my covenant they brake, although I was a husband unto them, saith the Lord;) but this shall be the covenant that I will make with the house of Israel: After those days, saith the Lord, I will put my law in their inward parts, and write it in their hearts; and I will be their God, and they shall be my people. And they shall teach no more every man his neighbor, and every man his brother, saying, Know the Lord; for they shall all know me, from the least of them unto the greatest of them, saith the Lord; for I will forgive their iniquity, and I will remember their sin no more." Upon this passage, I remark:--

(i.) It was to become due, or the time when its fulfilment might be claimed and expected, was at the advent of Christ. This is unequivocally settled in Heb. viii. 8-12, where this passage is quoted at length, as being applicable to the gospel day.

(ii.) This is undeniably a promise of entire sanctification. It is a promise that the "law shall be written in the heart." It means that the very temper and spirit required by the law shall be begotten in the soul. Now, if the law requires entire sanctification or perfect holiness, this is certainly a promise of it; for it is a promise of all that the law requires. To say that this is not a promise of entire sanctification, is the same absurdity as to say, that perfect obedience to the law is not entire sanctification; and this last is the same absurdity as to say, that something more is our duty than what the law requires: and this again is to say, that the law is imperfect and unjust.

(iii.) A permanent state or entire sanctification is plainly implied in this promise. The reason for setting aside the first covenant was, that it was broken: "Which my covenant they brake." One grand design of the new covenant is, that it shall not be broken, for then it would be no better than the first. Permanency is implied in the fact, that it is to be engraven in the heart. Permanency is plainly implied in the assertion, that God will remember their sin no more. In Jer. xxxii. 39, 40, where the same promise is in substance repeated, you will find it expressly stated, that the covenant is to be "everlasting," and that he will so "put his fear in their hearts, that they shall not depart from him." Here permanency is as expressly promised as it can be.

Suppose the language of this promise to be thrown into the form of a command. Suppose God to say, "Let my law be within your hearts, and let it be in your inward parts, and let my fear be so within your hearts, that you shall not depart from me. Let your covenant with me be everlasting." If this language were found in a command, would any man in his senses doubt that it meant to require perfect and permanent sanctification? If not, by what rule of sober interpretation does he make it mean anything else, when found in a promise? It appears to be profane trifling, when such language is found in a promise, to make it mean less than it does when found in a command.

This promise as it respects the church, at some period of its history, is unconditional, and its fulfilment certain. But in respect to any particular individuals or generation of the church, its fulfilment is necessarily conditioned upon their faith. The church, as a body, have certainly never received this new covenant. Yet, doubtless, multitudes in every age of the Christian dispensation have received it. And God will hasten the time when it shall be so fully accomplished, that there shall be no need for one man to say to his brother, "Know the Lord, for all shall know him from the least to the greatest."

It should be understood, that this promise was made to the Christian church, and not at all to the Jewish church. The saints under the old dispensation had no reason to expect the fulfilment of this and kindred promises to themselves, because their fulfilment was expressly deferred until the commencement of the Christian dispensation.

It has been said, that nothing more is here promised than regeneration. But were not the Old Testament saints regenerated? Yet it is expressly said; that they received not the promises. Heb. xi. 13, 39, 40: "These all died in faith, not having received the promises, but having seen them afar off, and were persuaded of them, and embraced them, and confessed that they were strangers and pilgrims on the earth." And these all, having obtained a good report through faith, received not the promise; God having provided some better thing for us, that they without us should not be made perfect." Here we see that these promises were not received by the Old Testament saints. Yet they were regenerated.

It has also been said, that the promise implies no more than the final perseverance of the saints. But I would inquire, did not the Old Testament saints persevere? And yet we have just seen, that the Old Testament saints did not receive these promises in their fulfilment.

(3.) I will next examine the promise in Ezek. xxxvi. 25-27b: "Then will I sprinkle clean water upon you, and ye shall be clean; from all your filthiness, and from all your idols, will I cleanse you. A new heart also will I give you, and a new spirit will I put within you; and I will take away the stony heart out of your flesh, and I will give you an heart of flesh. And I will put my Spirit within you, and cause you to walk in my statutes, and ye shall keep my judgments and do them." Upon this I remark:--

(i.) It was written within nineteen years after that which we have just examined in Jeremiah. It plainly refers to the same time, and is a promise of the same blessing.

(ii.) It seems to be admitted, nor can it be denied, that this is a promise of entire sanctification. The language is very definite and full. "Then,"--referring to some future time, when it should become due, "will I sprinkle clean water upon you, and ye shall be clean." Mark, the first promise, "ye shall be clean." If to be "clean" does not mean entire sanctification, what does it mean?

The second promise is, "From all your filthiness and from all your idols will I cleanse you." If to be cleansed "from all filthiness and all idols," be not a state of entire sanctification, what is?

The third promise is, "A new heart also will I give you, and a new spirit will I put within you; I will take away the stony heart out of your flesh, and will give you an heart of flesh." If to have a "clean heart," a "new heart," a "heart of flesh," in opposition to a "heart of stone," be not entire sanctification, what is?

The fourth promise is, "I will put my Spirit within you, and cause you to walk in my statutes, and ye shall keep my judgments, and do them."

(iii.) Let us turn the language of these promises into that of command, and understand God as saying, "Make you a clean heart, a new heart, and a new spirit; put away all your iniquities, all your filthiness, and all your idols; walk in my statutes, and keep my judgments, and do them." Now what man, in the sober exercise of his reason, would doubt whether God meant to require a state of entire sanctification in such commands as these? The rules of legitimate interpretation would demand that we should so understand him.

If this is so, what is the fair and proper construction of this language, when found in a promise? I do not hesitate to say, that to me it is amazing, that any doubt should be left on the mind of any man whether, in these promises, God means as much as in his commands, couched in the same language: for example, see Ezek. xviii. 30, 31: "Repent, and turn yourselves from all your transgressions; so iniquity shall not be your ruin. Cast away from you all your transgressions, whereby ye have transgressed and make you a new heart and a new spirit; for why will ye die, O house of Israel?" Now, that the language in the promise under consideration, should mean as much as the language of this command, is demanded by every sober rule of interpretation. And who ever dreamed, that when God required his people to put away all their iniquities, he only meant that they should put away a part of them.

(iv.) This promise respects the church, and it cannot be pretended, that it has ever been fulfilled, according to its proper import, in any past age of the church.

(v.) As it regards the church, at a future period of its history, this promise is absolute, in the sense that it certainly will be fulfilled.

(vi.) It was manifestly designed to apply to Christians under the new dispensation, rather than to the Jews under the old dispensation. The sprinkling of clean water, and the outpouring of the Spirit, seems plainly to indicate, that the promise belonged more particularly to the Christian dispensation. It undeniably belongs to the same class of promises with that in Jer. xxvi. 31-34; Joel ii. 28, and many others, that manifestly look forward to the gospel-day as the time when they shall become due. As these promises have never been fulfilled, in their extent and meaning, their complete fulfilment remains to be realized by the church as a body. And those individuals, and that generation, will take possession of the blessing, who understand, and believe, and appropriate them to their own case.

(4.) I will next examine the promise in 1 Thess. v. 23, 24 "And the very God of peace sanctify you wholly; and I pray God your whole spirit, and soul, and body, be preserved blameless unto the coming of our Lord Jesus Christ. Faithful is he that calleth you, who also will do it." Upon this I remark:--

(i.) It is admitted, that this is a prayer for, and a promise of, entire sanctification.

(ii.) The very language shows, that both the prayer and the promise refer to this life, as it is a prayer for the sanctification of the body as well as the soul; also that they might be preserved, not after, but unto the coming of our Lord Jesus Christ.

(iii.) This is a prayer of inspiration, to which is annexed an express promise that God will do it.

(iv.) Its fulfilment is, from the nature of the case, conditioned upon our faith, as sanctification without faith is naturally impossible.

(v.) Now, if this promise, with those that have already been examined, does not, honestly interpreted, fully settle the question of the attainability of entire sanctification in this life, it is difficult to understand how anything can be settled by an appeal to scripture.

There are great multitudes of promises of the same import, to which I might refer you, and which, if examined in the light of the foregoing rules of interpretation, would be seen to heap up demonstration upon demonstration, that this is a doctrine of the Bible. Only examine them in the light of these plain, self-evident principles, and it seems to me, that they cannot fail to produce conviction.

Having examined a few of the promises in proof of the position that a state of entire sanctification is attainable in this life, I will now proceed to mention other considerations, in support of this doctrine.

3. The apostles evidently expected Christians to attain this state in this life. See Col. iii. 12. "Epaphras, who is one of you, a servant of Christ, saluteth you, always laboring fervently for you in prayers, that ye may stand perfect and complete in all the will of God." Upon this passage I remark,

(1.) It was the object of the efforts of Epaphras, and a thing which he expected to effect, to be instrumental in causing those Christians to be "perfect and complete in all the will of God."

(2.) If this language does not describe a state of entire, in the sense of permanent, sanctification, I know of none that would. If "to be perfect and complete in all the will of God," be not Christian perfection, what is?

(3.) Paul knew that Epaphras was laboring to this end, and with this expectation; and he informed the church of it, in a manner that evidently showed his approbation of the views and conduct of Epaphras.

That the apostles expected Christians to attain this state is further manifest, from 2 Cor. vii. 1: "Having therefore these promises, dearly beloved, let us cleanse ourselves from all filthiness of the flesh and spirit, perfecting holiness in the fear of God."

Now, does not the apostle speak in this passage, as if he really expected those to whom he wrote, "to perfect holiness in the fear of God? "Observe how strong and full the language is: "Let us cleanse ourselves from all filthiness of the flesh and spirit." If "to cleanse ourselves from ail filthiness of the flesh, and all filthiness of the spirit, and to perfect holiness," be not entire sanctification, what is? That he expected this to take place in this life, is evident from the fact, that he requires them to be cleansed from all filthiness of the flesh as well as of the spirit. This passage plainly contemplates a state as distinguished from an act of consecration or sanctification, that is, it evidently expresses the idea of entire, in the sense of continued, sanctification.

4. All the intermediate steps can be taken; therefore the end can be reached. There is certainly no point in our progress towards entire sanctification, where it can be said we can go no further. To this it has been objected, that though all the intermediate steps can be taken, yet the goal can never be reached in this life, just as five may be divided by three ad infinitum, without exhausting the fraction. Now this illustration deceives the mind that uses it, as it may the minds of those who listen to it. It is true, that you can never exhaust the fraction in dividing five by three, for the plain reason, that the division may be carried on ad infinitum. There is no end. You cannot, in this case, take all the intermediate steps, because they are infinite. But in the case of entire sanctification, all the intermediate steps can be taken: for there is an end, or state of entire sanctification, and that too at a point infinitely short of infinite.

5. That this state may be attained in this life, I argue from the fact, that provision is made against all the occasions of sin. Men sin only when they are tempted, either by the world, the flesh, or the devil. And it is expressly asserted, that, in every temptation, provision is made for our escape. Certainly, if it is possible for us to escape without sin, under every temptation, then a state of entire and permanent sanctification is attainable.

Full provision is made for overcoming the three great enemies of our souls, the world, the flesh, and the devil.

(1.) The world--"This is the victory that overcometh the world, even your faith." "Who is he that overcometh the world, but he that believeth that Jesus is the Christ."

(2.) The flesh--"If ye walk in the Spirit, ye shall not fulfil the lusts of the flesh."

(3.) Satan--"The shield of faith shall quench all the fiery darts of the wicked." And, "God shall bruise Satan under your feet shortly."

6. God is able to perform this work in and for us. Eph. iii. 14-19: "For this cause I bow my knees unto the Father of our Lord Jesus Christ, of whom the whole family in heaven and earth is named, that he would grant you according to the riches of his glory, to be strengthened with might by his Spirit in the inner man; that Christ may dwell in your hearts by faith; that ye, being rooted and grounded in love, may be able to comprehend with all saints what is the

breadth, and length, and depth, and height; and to know the love of Christ, which passeth knowledge, that ye might be filled with all the fulness of God." Upon this passage I remark,--

(1.) Paul evidently prays here for the entire sanctification of believers in this life. It is implied in our being "rooted and grounded in love," and being "filled with all the fulness of God," that we be as perfect in our measure and according to our capacity, as he is. If to be filled with the fulness of God, does not imply a state of entire sanctification, what does?

(2.) That Paul did not see any difficulty in the way of God's accomplishing this work, is manifest from what he says in the twentieth verse--"Now unto him that is able to do exceeding abundantly above all that we ask or think, according to the power that worketh in us," etc.

7. The Bible nowhere represents death as the termination of sin in the saints, which it could not fail to do, were it true, that they cease not to sin until death. It has been the custom of the church for a long time, to console individuals, in view of death, by the consideration, that it would be the termination of all their sin. And how almost universal has been the custom in consoling the friends of deceased saints, to mention this as a most important fact, that now they had ceased from sin! Now, if death is the termination of sin in the saints, and if they never cease to sin until they pass into eternity, too much stress never has been or can be laid upon that circumstance; and it seems utterly incredible, that no inspired writer should ever have noticed the fact. The representations of scripture are all directly opposed to this idea. It is said, "Blessed are the dead who die in the Lord, for they rest from their labors, and their works do follow them." Here it is not intimated that they rest from their sins, but from their good works in this life; such works as shall follow, not to curse, but to bless them. The representations of scripture are, that death is the termination of the saint's sufferings and labors of love in this world, for the good of men and the glory of God. But nowhere in the Bible is it intimated, that the death of a saint is the termination of his serving the devil.

The Bible representations of death are utterly inconsistent with its being an indispensable means of sanctification. Death is represented in the Bible as an enemy. But if death is the only condition upon which men are brought into a state of entire sanctification, its agency is as important and as indispensable as the influence of the Holy Ghost. When death is represented in the Bible as any thing else than an enemy, it is because it cuts short the sufferings of the saints, and introduces them into a state of eternal glory--not because it breaks them off from communion with the devil! How striking is the contrast between the language of the church and that of inspiration on this subject! The church is consoling the Christian in view of death, that it will be the termination of his sins--that he will then cease to serve the devil and his own lusts. The language of inspiration, on the other hand, is, that he will cease, not from wicked, but from good works, and labors and sufferings for God in this world. The language of the church is, that then he will enter upon a life of unalterable holiness--that he shall then, and not till then, be entirely sanctified. The language of inspiration is, that because he is sanctified, death shall be an entrance into a state of eternal glory.

8. Ministers are certainly bound to set up some definite standard, to which, as the ministers of God, they are to insist upon complete conformity. And now I would ask, what other standard can they and dare they set up than this? To

insist upon any thing less than this, is to turn pope and grant an indulgence to sin. But to set up this standard, and then inculcate that conformity to it is not, as a matter of fact, attainable in this life, is as absolutely to take the part of sin against God, as it would be to insist upon repentance in theory, and then avow that in practice it is not attainable. And here let me ask Christians what they expect ministers to preach? Do you think they have a right to connive at any sin in you, or to insist upon any thing else as a practicable fact, than that you should abandon every iniquity? I ask, by what authority can a minister preach any thing less? And how shall any minister dare to inculcate the duty as a theory, and yet not insist upon it as a practical matter, as something to be expected of every subject of God's kingdom.

9. A denial of this doctrine has the natural tendency to beget the very apathy witnessed in the church. Professors of religion go on in sin, without much conviction of its Wickedness. Sin unblushingly stalks abroad even in the church of God, and does not fill Christians with horror, because they expect its existence as a thing of course. Tell a young convert that he must expect to backslide, and he will do so of course, and with comparatively little remorse, because he looks upon it as a kind of necessity. And being led to expect it, you find him, in a few months after his conversion, away from God, and not at all horrified with his state. Just so, inculcate the idea among Christians, that they are not expected to abandon all sin, and they will of course go on in sin with comparative indifference. Reprove them for their sin, and they will say, "O, we are imperfect creatures; we do not pretend to be perfect, nor do we expect we ever shall be in this world." Many such answers as these will show you at once the God-dishonoring and soul-ruining tendency of a denial of this doctrine.

10. A denial of this doctrine prepares the minds of ministers to temporize, and wink at great iniquity in their churches. Feeling, as they certainly must, if they disbelieve this doctrine, that a great amount of sin in all believers is to be expected as a thing of course, their whole preaching, and spirit, and demeanor, will be such as to beget a great degree of apathy among Christians, in regard to their abominable sins.

11. If this doctrine is not true, how profane and blasphemous is the covenant of every church of every evangelical denomination. Every church requires its members to make a solemn covenant with God and with the church, in the presence of God and angels, and with their hands upon the emblems of the broken body and shed blood of the blessed Jesus, "to abstain from all ungodliness and every worldly lust, to live soberly, righteously, and godly, in this present world." Now, if the doctrine of the attainability of entire sanctification in this life is not true, what profane mockery is this covenant! It is a covenant to live in a state of entire sanctification, made under the most solemn circumstances, enforced by the most awful sanctions, and insisted upon by the minister of God distributing the bread and wine. Now what right has any minister on earth to require less than this? And again, what right has any minister on earth to require this, unless it is a practicable thing, and unless it is expected of him who makes the vow?

Suppose, when this covenant was proposed to a convert about to unite with the church, he should take it to his closet, and spread it before the Lord, and inquire whether it would be right for him to make such a covenant, and whether the grace of the gospel can enable him to fulfil it? Do you suppose the Lord Jesus would reply, that if he made that covenant, he certainly would, and must, as a matter of course, live in the habitual violation of it as long as he lives, and that his grace was not sufficient to enable him to keep it? Would he, in such a case, have any right to take upon himself this covenant? No, no more than he would have a right to lie to the Holy Ghost.

It has long been maintained by orthodox divines, that a person is not a Christian who does not aim at living without sin--that unless he aims at perfection, he manifestly consents to live in sin; and is therefore impenitent. It has been said, and I think truly, that if a man does not, in the fixed purpose of his heart, aim at total abstinence from sin, and at being wholly conformed to the will of God, he is not yet regenerated, and does not so much as mean to cease from abusing God. In Barnes' Notes upon 2 Cor. viii. 1, we have the following:-

"The unceasing and steady aim of every Christian should be perfection--perfection in all things--in the love of God, of Christ, of man; perfection of heart, and feeling, and emotion; perfection in his words, and plans, and dealings with men; perfection in his prayers, and in his submission to the will of God. No man can be a Christian who does not sincerely desire it, and who does not constantly aim at it. No man is a friend of God who can acquiesce in a state of sin, and who is satisfied and contented that he is not as holy as God is holy. And any man who has no desire to be perfect as God is, and who does not make it his daily and constant aim to be as perfect as God, may set it down as demonstrably certain that he has no true religion."

Now if this is so, I would ask how a person can aim at, and intend to do, what he knows to be impossible. Is it not a contradiction to say that a man can intend to do what he knows he cannot do? To this it has been objected, that if true, it proves too much--that it would prove that no man ever was a Christian who did not believe in this doctrine. To this I reply:--

A man may believe in what is really a state of entire sanctification, and aim at attaining it, although he may not call it by that name. This I believe to be the real fact with Christians; and they would much more frequently attain what they aim at, did they know how to appropriate the grace of Christ to their own circumstances. Mrs. President Edwards, for example, firmly believed that she could attain a state of entire consecration. She aimed at, and manifestly attained it, and yet, such were her views of constitutional depravity, that she did not call her state one of entire sanctification. It has been common for Christians to suppose, that a state of entire consecration is attainable; but while they believe in the sinfulness of their natures, they would not of course call even entire consecration, entire sanctification. Mrs. Edwards believed in, aimed at, and attained, entire consecration. She aimed at what she believed to be attainable, and she could aim at nothing more. She called it by the same name with her husband, who was opposed to the doctrine of Christian perfection, as held by the Wesleyan Methodists, manifestly on the ground of his notions of physical depravity. I care not what this state is called, if the thing be fully explained and insisted upon, together with the conditions of attaining it. Call it what you please, Christian perfection, heavenly mindedness, the full assurance of faith or hope, or a state of entire consecration; by all these I understand the same thing. And it is certain, that by whatever name it is called, the thing must be aimed at to be attained. The practicability of its attainment must be admitted, or it cannot be aimed at. And now I would humbly inquire, whether to preach any thing short of this is not to give countenance to sin?

12. Another argument in favor of this doctrine is, that the gospel, as a matter of fact, has often, not only temporarily, but permanently and perfectly, overcome every form of sin, in different individuals. Who has not seen the most beastly lusts, drunkenness, lasciviousness, and every kind of abomination, long indulged and fully ripe, entirely and forever slain by the power of the grace of God? Now how was this done? Only by bringing this sin fully into the light of the gospel, and showing the individual the relation which the death of Christ sustained to that sin.

Nothing is wanting to slay any and every form of sin, but for the mind to be fully baptized into the death of Christ, and to see the bearings of one's own sins upon the sufferings, and agonies, and death of the blessed Jesus. Let me state a fact to illustrate my meaning. An habitual and most inveterate smoker of tobacco, of my acquaintance, after having been plied with almost every argument to induce him to break the power of the habit and relinquish its use, in vain, on a certain occasion lighted his pipe, and was about to put it to his mouth, when the inquiry was started, Did Christ die to purchase this vile indulgence for me? The perceived relation of the death of Christ to this sin instantly broke the power of the habit, and from that day he has been free. I could relate many other facts more striking than this, where a similar view of the relation of a particular sin to the atonement of Christ, has, in a moment, not only broken the power of the habit, but destroyed entirely and forever, the appetite for similar indulgences. And in multitudes of cases when the appetite has not been entirely slain, the will has been endowed with abundant and abiding efficiency effectually to control it. If the most inveterate habits of sin, and even those that involve physical consequences, and have deeply debased the physical constitution, and rendered it a source of overpowering temptation to the mind, can be, and often have been, utterly broken up, and forever slain by the grace of God, why should it be doubted, that by the same grace a man can triumph over all sin, and that forever?

13. If this doctrine is not true, what is true upon the subject? It is certainly of great importance that ministers should be definite in their instructions; and if Christians are not expected to be wholly conformed to the will of God in this life, how much is expected of them? Who can say, Hitherto canst thou, must thou come, but no further? It is certainly absurd, not to say ridiculous, for ministers to be forever pressing Christians up to higher and higher attainments, saying at every step, you can and must go higher, and yet all along informing them, that they are expected to fall short of their whole duty, that they can as a matter of fact, be better than they are, far better, indefinitely better; but still it is not expected that they will do their whole duty. I have often been pained to hear men preach, who were afraid to commit themselves in favor of the whole truth; and who were yet evidently afraid of falling short in their instructions, of insisting that men should stand "perfect and complete in all the will of God." To be consistent they are evidently perplexed, and well they may be; for in truth there is no consistency in their views and teachings. If they do not inculcate, as a matter of fact, that men ought to do, and are expected to do, their whole duty, they are sadly at a loss to know what to inculcate. They have evidently many misgivings about insisting upon less than this, and still they fear to go to the full extent of apostolic teaching on this subject. And in their attempts to throw in qualifying terms and caveats, to avoid the impression, that they believe in the doctrine of entire sanctification, they place themselves in a

truly awkward position. Cases have occurred in which ministers have been asked, how far we may go, must go, and are expected to go, in dependence upon the grace of Christ, and how holy men may be, and are expected to be, and must be, in this life. They could give no other answer to this, than that they can be a great deal better than they are. Now this indefiniteness is a great stumbling-block to the church. It cannot be according to the teachings of the Holy Ghost.

14. The tendency of a denial of this doctrine is, to my mind, conclusive proof that the doctrine itself must be true. Many developments in the recent history of the church throw light upon this subject. Who does not see that the facts developed in the temperance reformation have a direct and powerful bearing upon this question? It has been ascertained, that there is no possibility of completing the temperance reformation, except by adopting the principle of total abstinence from all intoxicating drinks. Let a temperance lecturer go forth as an evangelist, to promote revivals on the subject of temperance--let him inveigh against drunkenness, while he admits and defends the moderate use of alcohol, or insinuates, at least, that total abstinence is not expected. or practicable. In this stage of the temperance reformation, every one can see that such a man can make no progress; that he would be employed like a child in building dams of sand to obstruct the rushing of mighty waters. It is as certain as that causes produce their effects, that no permanent reformation could be effected, without adopting and insisting on the total abstinence principle.

And now, if this is true, as it respects the temperance reformation, how much more so when applied to the subjects of holiness and sin. A man might, by some possibility, even in his own strength, overcome his habits of drunkenness, and retain what might be called the temperate use of alcohol. But no such thing is possible in a reformation from sin. There is no temperate indulgence in sin. Sin, as a matter of fact, is never overcome by any man in his own strength. If he admits into his creed the necessity of any degree of sin, or if he allows in practice any degree of sin, he becomes impenitent, consents to live in sin, and of course grieves the Holy Spirit, the certain result of which is a relapsing into a state of legal bondage to sin. And this is probably a true history of many professed Christians in the church. It is just what might he expected from the views and practice of the church upon this subject.

The secret of backsliding is, that reformations are not carried deep enough. Christians are not set with all their hearts to aim at a speedy deliverance from all sin, but on the contrary are left, and in many instances taught, to indulge the expectation that they shall sin as long as they live. I probably never shall forget the effect produced on my mind by reading, when a young convert, in the diary of David Brainerd, that he never expected to make any considerable attainments in holiness in this life. I can now easily see that this was a natural inference from the theory of physical sinfulness which he held. But not perceiving this at the time, I doubt not that this expression of his views had a very injurious effect upon me for many years. It led me to reason thus: if such a man as David. Brainerd did not expect to make much advancement in holiness in this life, it is vain for me to expect such a thing.

The fact is, if there be anything that is important to high attainments in holiness, and to the progress of the work of sanctification in this life, it is the adoption of the principle of total abstinence from sin. Total abstinence from sin must be every man's motto, or sin will certainly sweep him away as with a flood. That cannot possibly be a true principle in temperance, that leaves the causes which produce drunkenness to operate in their full strength. Nor can that be true in regard to holiness which leaves the root unextracted, and the certain causes of spiritual decline and backsliding at work in the very heart of the church. And I am fully convinced that until evangelists and pastors adopt, and carry out in practice, the principle of total abstinence from all sin, they will as certainly find themselves, every few months, called to do their work over again, as a temperance lecturer would who should admit the moderate use of alcohol.

Again, who does not know that to call upon sinners to repent, and at the same time to inform them that they will not, and cannot, and are not expected to repent, would for ever prevent their repentance? Suppose you say to a sinner, "You are naturally able to repent; but it is certain that you never will repent in this life, either with or without the Holy Spirit." Who does not see that such teaching would prevent his repentance as surely as he believed it? To say to a professor of religion, "You are naturally able to be wholly conformed to the will of God; but it is certain that you never will be, in this life, either in your own strength, or by the grace of God;" if this teaching be believed, it will just as certainly prevent his sanctification, as the other teaching would the repentance of the sinner. I can speak from experience on this subject. While I inculcated the common views, I was often instrumental in bringing Christians under great conviction, and into a state of temporary repentance and faith. But falling short of urging them up to a point where they would become so acquainted with Christ as to abide in him, they would of course soon relapse again into their former state. I seldom saw, and can now understand that I had no reason to expect to see, under the instructions which I then gave, such a state of religious principle, such steady and confirmed walking with God among Christians, as I have seen since the change in my views and instructions.

LECTURE XXXVIII - SANCTIFICATION

PAUL ENTIRELY SANCTIFIED

I might urge a great many other considerations, and as I have said, fill a book with scriptures, and arguments, and demonstrations, of the attainability of entire sanctification in this life.

But I forbear, and will present only one more consideration--a consideration which has great weight in some minds. It is a question of great importance, whether any actually ever did attain this state. Some who believe it attainable, do not consider it of much importance to show that it has actually been attained. Now I freely admit, that it may be attainable, even if it never has been attained. Yet it appears to me that as a source of encouragement to the church, it is of great importance whether, as a matter of fact, a state of entire and continued holiness has been attained in this life. This question covers much ground. But for the sake of brevity, I design to examine but one case, and see whether there is not reason to believe that, in one instance at least, it has been attained. The case to which I allude is that of the apostle Paul. And I propose to take up and examine the passages that speak of him, for the purpose of ascertaining whether there is evidence that he ever attained to this state in this life.

And here let me say that, to my own mind, it seems plain, that Paul and John, to say nothing of the other apostles, designed and expected the church to understand them as speaking from experience, and as having received of that fulness which they taught to be in Christ and in his gospel.

And I wish to say again and more expressly, that I do not rest the practicability of attaining a state of entire and continued holiness at all upon the question, whether any ever have attained it, any more than I would rest the question, whether the world ever will be converted, upon the fact whether it ever has been converted. I have been surprised, when the fact that a state of entire holiness has been attained, is urged as one argument among a great many to prove its attainability, and that too, merely as an encouragement to Christians to lay hold upon this blessing--that objectors and reviewers fasten upon this, as the doctrine of sanctification, as if by calling this particular question into doubt, they could overthrow all the other proof of its attainability. Now this is utterly absurd. When, then, I examine the character of Paul with this object in view, if it should not appear clear to you that he did attain this state, you are not to overlook the fact, that its attainability is settled by other arguments, on grounds entirely independent of the question, whether it has been attained or not; and that I merely use this as an argument, simply because to me it appears forcible, and fitted to afford great encouragement to Christians to press after this state.

I will first make some remarks in regard to the manner in which the language of Paul, when speaking of himself, should be understood; and then proceed to an examination of the passages which speak of his Christian character.

His character, as revealed in his life, demands that we should understand him to mean all that he says, when speaking in his own favor. The Spirit of inspiration would guard him against speaking too highly of himself. No man ever seemed to possess greater modesty, and to feel more unwilling to exalt his own attainments. If he considered himself as not having attained a state of entire sanctification, and as often, if not in all things, falling short of his duty, we may expect to find him acknowledging this in the deepest self-abasement. If he is charged with living in sin, and with being wicked in anything, we may expect him, when speaking under inspiration, not to justify, but unequivocally to condemn himself in those things, if he was really guilty.

Now, in view of these facts, let us examine those scriptures in which he speaks of himself, and is spoken of by others.

1 Thess. ii. 10: "Ye are witnesses, and God also, how holily, and justly, and unblamably, we behaved ourselves among you that believe." Here he unqualifiedly asserts his own holiness. This language is very strong, "How holily, justly, and unblamably." If to be holy, just, and unblamable, be not entire sanctification, what is? He appeals to the heart-searching God for the truth of what he says, and to their own observation, calling on God and on them also to bear witness, that he had been holy and without blame. Here we have the testimony of an inspired apostle, in the most unqualified language, asserting his own entire sanctification. Was he deceived? Can it be that he knew himself all the time to have been living in sin? If such language as this does not amount to an unqualified assertion, that he had lived among them without sin, what can be known by the use of human language?

2 Cor. vi. 3-7: "Giving no offence in anything, that the ministry be not blamed; but in all things approving ourselves as the ministers*of God, in much patience, in afflictions, in necessity, in distresses, in stripes, in imprisonments, in tumults, in labors, in watchings, in fastings; by pureness, by knowledge, by long-suffering, by kindness, by the Holy Ghost, by love unfeigned, by the word of truth, by the power of God, by the armor of righteousness on the right hand and on the left." Upon these verses I remark: Paul asserts that he gave no offence in anything, but in all things approved himself as a minister of God. Among other things, he did this "by pureness, by the Holy Ghost, by love unfeigned," and "by the armor of righteousness on the right hand and on the left." How could so modest a man as Paul speak of himself in this manner, unless he knew himself to be in a state of entire sanctification, and thought it of great importance that the church should know it?

2 Cor. i. 12: "For our rejoicing is this, the testimony of our conscience, that in simplicity and godly sincerity, not with fleshly wisdom, but by the grace of God, we have had our conversation in the world, and more abundantly to youward." This passage plainly implies the same thing, and was manifestly said for the same purpose--to declare the greatness of the grace of God as manifested in himself.

Acts xxiv. 16: "And herein do I exercise myself to have always a conscience void of offence toward God, and toward men." Paul doubtless at this time had an enlightened conscience. If an inspired apostle could affirm, that he "exercised himself to have always a conscience void of offence toward God and toward men," must he not have been in a state of entire sanctification?

2 Tim. i. 3: "I thank God, whom I serve from my forefathers with a pure conscience, that without ceasing I have remembrance of thee in my prayers night and day." Here again he affirms that he serves God with a pure conscience. Could this be, if he was often, and perhaps every day, as some suppose, violating his conscience?

Gal. ii. 20: "I am crucified with Christ; nevertheless I live; yet not I, but Christ liveth in me; and the life which I now live in the flesh, I live by the faith of the Son of God, who loved me, and gave himself for me." This does not assert, but strongly implies, that he lived without sin, and also that he regarded himself as dead to sin in the sense of being permanently sanctified.

Gal. vi. 14: "But God forbid that I should glory, save in the cross of our Lord Jesus Christ, by whom the world is crucified unto me, and I unto the world." This text also affords the same inference as above.

Phil. i. 21: "For to me to live is Christ, and to die is gain." Here the apostle affirms that for him to live was as if Christ lived in the church, that is, by his doctrine illustrated by his life, it was as if Christ lived again and preached his own gospel to sinners and to the church; or for him to live was to make Christ known as if Christ lived to make himself known. How could he say this, unless his example, and doctrine, and spirit, were those of Christ?

Acts xx. 26: "Wherefore I take you to record this day, that I am pure from the blood of all men." This passage, taken in its connection, shows clearly the impression that Paul desired to make upon the minds of those to whom he spake. It is certain that he could in no proper sense be "pure from the blood of all men," unless he had done his whole duty. If he had been sinfully lacking in any grace, or virtue, or labor, could he have said this? Certainly not.

1 Cor. ii. 16, 17: "Wherefore, I beseech you, be ye followers of me. For this cause have I sent unto you Timotheus, who is my beloved son, and faithful in the Lord, who shall bring you into remembrance of my ways which be in Christ, as I teach everywhere in every church." Here Paul manifestly sets himself up as an example to the church. How could Le do this if he were living in sin? He sent Timotheus to them to refresh their memories in regard to his doctrine and practice; implying that what he taught in every church he himself practiced.

1 Cor. xi. 1: "Be ye followers of me, even as I also am of Christ." Here Paul commands them to follow him "as he followed. Christ;" not so far as he followed Christ, as some seem to understand it, but to follow him because he followed Christ. How could he, in this unqualified manner, command the church to copy his example, unless he knew himself to be blameless?

Phil. iii. 17, 20: "Brethren, be followers together of me, and mark them which walk so as ye have us for an ensample. For our conversation is in heaven, from whence we also look for the Saviour, the Lord Jesus Christ." Here again, Paul calls upon the church to follow him, and particularly to notice those that copied his example, and assigns as the reason, "for our conversation is in heaven."

Phil. iii. 9: "Those things, which ye have both learned and received, and heard, and seen in me, do; and the God of peace shall be with you." The Philippians were commanded to "do those things which they had learned, and received, and seen in him." And then he adds, that if they do those things, the God of peace shall be with them. Now can it be, that he meant that they should understand anything less, than that he lived without sin among them?

I will next examine those passages which are supposed by some to imply that Paul was not in a state of entire sanctification.

Acts xv. 36-40: "And some days after, Paul said unto Barnabas, Let us go again and visit our brethren in every city where we have preached the word of the Lord, and see how they do. And Barnabas determined to take with them John whose surname was Mark. But Paul thought not good to take him with them, who departed from them from Pamphylia, and went not with them to the work. And the contention was so sharp between them, that they departed asunder one from the other; and so Barnabas took Mark, and sailed to Cyprus; and Paul chose Silas, and departed, being recommended by the brethren unto the grace of God."

This contention between Paul and Barnabas arose out of the fact, that John, who was a nephew of Barnabas, had once abruptly left them in their travels, it would seem, without any justifiable reason, and had returned home. It appears that the confidence of Barnabas in his nephew was restored. But Paul was not as yet satisfied of the stability of his character, and thought it dangerous to trust him as a travelling companion and fellow laborer. It is not intimated, nor can it fairly be inferred, that either of them sinned in this contention. If either was to be blamed, it seems that Barnabas was in fault, rather than Paul, inasmuch as he determined to take John with him, without having consulted Paul. And he persisted in this determination until he met with such firm resistance on the part of Paul, that he took John and sailed abruptly for Cyprus; while Paul choosing Silas as his companion, was recommended by the brethren to the grace of God, and departed. Now certainly there is nothing that we can discover in this transaction, that Paul, or any good man, or an angel, under the circumstances, needs to have been ashamed of. It does not appear, that Paul ever acted more from a regard to the glory of God and the good of religion, than in this transaction. And I would humbly inquire, what spirit is that which finds sufficient evidence in this case to charge an inspired apostle with rebellion against God?

Acts xxiii. 1-5: "And Paul, earnestly beholding the council, said, Men and brethren, I have lived in all good conscience before God until this day. And the high priest Ananias commanded them that stood by him to smite him on the mouth. Then said Paul unto him, God shall smite thee, thou whited wall: for sittest thou to judge me after the law, and commandest me to be smitten contrary to the law? And they that stood by said, Revilest thou God's high priest? Then said Paul, I wist not, brethren, that he was the high priest: for it is written, Thou shalt not speak evil of the ruler of thy people." In this case sinful anger has been imputed to Paul; but, so far as I can see, without any just reason. To my mind it seems plain, that the contrary is to be inferred. It appears, that Paul was not personally acquainted with the then officiating high priest. And he manifested the utmost regard to the authority of God in quoting from the Old Testament, "Thou shalt not speak evil of the ruler of thy people;" implying, that notwithstanding the abuse he had received, he should not have made the reply, had he known him to be the high priest.

Rom. vii. from the fourteenth to the twenty-fifth verse, has by many been supposed to be an epitome of Paul's experience at the time he wrote the epistle. Upon this I remark:--

1. The connection and drift of Paul's reasoning show, that the case of which he was speaking, whether his own or the case of some one else, was

adduced by him to illustrate the influence of the law upon the carnal mind. This is a case in which sin had the entire dominion, and overcame all his resolutions of obedience.

2. That his use of the singular pronoun, and in the first person, proves nothing in regard to the point, whether or not he was speaking of himself, for this is common with him, and with other writers, when using illustrations. He keeps up the personal pronoun, and passes into the eighth chapter; at the beginning of which, he represents himself, or the person of whom he is speaking, as being not only in a different, but in an exactly opposite state of mind. Now, if the seventh chapter contains Paul's experience, whose experience is this in the eighth chapter? Are we to understand them both as the experience of Paul? If so, we must understand him as first speaking of his experience before, and then after he was sanctified. He begins the eighth chapter by saying, "There is therefore now no condemnation to them who are in Christ Jesus, who walk not after the flesh, but after the Spirit;" and assigns as a reason, that "The law of the Spirit of life in Christ Jesus hath made me free from the law of sin and death." The law of sin and death was that law in his members, or the influence of the flesh, of which he had so bitterly complained in the seventh chapter. But now, it appears, that he has passed into a state in which he is made free from this influence of the flesh,--is emancipated and dead to the world and to the flesh, and in a state in which "there is no condemnation." Now, if there was no condemnation in the state in which he then was, it must have been, either because he did not sin, or, if he did sin, because the law did not condemn him; or because the law of God was repealed or abrogated. Now, if the penalty of the law was so set aside in his case, that he could sin without condemnation, this is a real abrogation of the law. But as the law was not, and could not be set aside, its penalty was not and could not be so abrogated, as not to condemn every sin. If Paul lived without condemnation, it must be because he lived without sin.

To me it does not appear that Paul speaks of his own experience in the seventh chapter of Romans, but that he merely supposes a case by way of illustration, and speaks in the first person, and in the present tense, simply because it was convenient and suitable to his purpose. His object manifestly was, in this and in the beginning of the eighth chapter, to contrast the influence of the law and of the gospel--to describe in the seventh chapter the state of a man who was living in sin, and every day condemned by the law, convicted and constantly struggling with his own corruptions, but continually overcome,--and in the eighth chapter to exhibit a person in the enjoyment of gospel liberty, where the righteousness of the law was fulfilled in the heart by the grace of Christ. The seventh chapter may well apply either to a person in a backslidden state, or to a convicted person who had never been converted. The eighth chapter can clearly be applicable to none but to those who are in a state of entire sanctification.

I have already said, that the seventh chapter contains the history of one over whom sin has dominion. Now, to suppose that this was the experience of Paul when he wrote the epistle, or of any one who was in the liberty of the gospel, is absurd and contrary to the experience of every person who ever enjoyed gospel liberty. And further, this is as expressly contradicted in the sixth chapter as it can be. As I said, the seventh chapter exhibits one over whom sin has dominion: but God says, in the sixth chapter and fourteenth verse, "For sin shall not have dominion over you; for ye are not under the law, but under grace." I remark finally upon this passage, that if Paul was speaking of himself in the seventh chapter of Romans, and really giving a history of his own experience, it proves nothing at all in regard to his subsequent sanctification; for the eighth chapter shows conclusively, that it was not his experience at the time he wrote the epistle. The fact that the seventh and eighth chapters have been separated since the translation was made, as I have before said, has led to much error in the understanding of this passage. Nothing is more certain, than that the two chapters were designed to describe not only different experiences, but experiences opposite to each other. And that both these experiences should belong to the same person at the same time, is manifestly impossible. If therefore Paul is speaking in this connection of his own experience, we are bound to understand the eighth chapter as describing his experience at the time he wrote the epistle; and the seventh chapter as descriptive of a former experience.

Now, therefore, if any one understands the seventh chapter as describing a Christian experience, he must understand it as giving the exercises of one in a very imperfect state; and the eighth chapter as descriptive of a soul in a state of entire sanctification. So that this epistle, instead of militating against the idea of Paul's entire sanctification, upon the supposition that he was speaking of himself, fully establishes the fact that he was in that state. What do those brethren mean who take the latter part of the seventh chapter as entirely disconnected from that which precedes and follows it, and make it tell a sad story on the subject of the legal and sinful bondage of an inspired apostle? What cannot be proved from the Bible in this way? Is it not a sound and indispensable rule of biblical interpretation, that a passage is to be taken in its connection, and that the scope and leading intention of the writer is to be continually borne in mind, in deciding upon the meaning of any passage? Why then, I pray, are the verses that precede, and those that immediately follow in the eighth chapter, entirely overlooked in the examination of this important passage?

Phil. iii. 10-15. "That I may know him, and the power of his resurrection, and the fellowship of his sufferings, being made conformable unto his death; if by any means I might attain unto the resurrection of the dead. Not as though I had already attained, either were already perfect; but I follow after, if that I may apprehend that for which also I am apprehended of Christ Jesus. Brethren, I count not myself to have apprehended; but this one thing I do, forgetting those things which are behind, and reaching forth unto those things which are before, I press toward the mark for the prize of the high calling of God in Christ Jesus. Let us therefore as many as be perfect, be thus minded: and if in anything ye be otherwise minded, God shall reveal even this unto you."

Here is a plain allusion to the Olympic games, in which men ran for a prize, and were not crowned until the end of the race, however well they might run. Paul speaks of two kinds of perfection here, one of which he claims to have attained, and the other he had not. The perfection which he had not attained, was that which he did not expect to attain until the end of his race, nor indeed until he had attained the resurrection from the dead. Until then he was not, and did not expect to be, perfect, in the sense that he should "apprehend all that for which he was apprehended of Christ Jesus." But all this does not imply that he was not living without sin, any more than it implies that Christ was living in sin when he said, "I must walk to-day and to-morrow, and the third day I shall be perfected." Here Christ speaks of a perfection which he had not attained.

Now it is manifest, that it was the glorified state to which Paul had not attained, and which perfection he was pressing after. But in the fifteenth verse, he speaks of another kind of perfection, which he professed to have attained. "Let us therefore," he says, "as many as be perfect, be thus minded;" that is, let us be pressing after this high state of perfection in glory, "if by any means we may attain unto the resurrection of the dead." The figure of the game should be kept continually in mind in the interpretation of this passage. The prize in those races was the crown. This was given only at the end of the race. And besides, a man was not crowned except he ran lawfully, that is, according to rule. Paul was running for the prize, that is the crown; not, as some suppose, for entire sanctification, but for a crown of glory. This he did not expect until he had completed his race. He exhorts those who were perfect, that is, those who were running lawfully or according to rule, to forget the things that were behind, and press to the mark, that is, the goal, for the prize, or the crown of glory, which the Lord the righteous judge, who was witnessing his race to award the crown to the victor, would give him at that day.

Now it is manifest to my mind, that Paul does not in this passage, teach expressly nor impliedly, that he was living in sin, but the direct opposite--that he meant to say, as he had said in many other places, that he was unblamable in respect to sin, but that he was aspiring after higher attainments, and meant to be satisfied with nothing short of eternal glory.

Again, Phil. iv. 11-13: "Not that I speak in respect of want: for I have learned, in whatsoever state I am, therewith to be content. I know both how to be abased, and I know how to abound: everywhere, and in all things, I am instructed, both to be fall and to be hungry, both to abound and to suffer need. I can do all things through Christ which strengtheneth me." Here Paul undoubtedly meant to affirm, not merely his abstract ability to do all his duty, but that he had learned by experience, that as a matter of fact and reality, he found himself able to do all things required of him.

In relation to the character of Paul, let me say:--If Paul was not sinless, he was an extravagant boaster, and such language used by any minister in these days would be considered as the language of an extravagant boaster. This setting himself up as an example so frequently and fully, without any caution or qualification, was highly dangerous to the interests of the church, if he was not in a state of entire sanctification.

His language in appealing to God, that in life and heart he was blameless, was blasphemous, unless he was really what he professed to be; and if he was what he professed to be, he was in a state of entire sanctification. It is doing dishonor to God, to maintain, under these circumstances, that Paul had not attained the blessing of entire sanctification. He nowhere confesses sin after he became an apostle, but invariably justifies himself, appealing to man and to God, for his entire integrity and blamelessness of heart and life. To maintain the sinfulness of this apostle, is to deny the grace of the gospel, and charge God foolishly. And I cannot but inquire, why is this great effort in the church to maintain that Paul lived in sin, and was never wholly sanctified till death?

Two things have appeared wonderful to me:

1. That so many professed Christians should seem to think themselves highly honoring God in extending the claims of the law, and yet denying that the grace of the gospel is equal to the demands of the law.

2. That so many persons seem to have an entirely self-righteous view of the subject of sanctification. With respect to the first of these opinions, much pains has been taken to extend to the utmost the claims of the law of God. Much has been said of its exceeding and infinite strictness, and the great length, and breadth, and height, and depth of its claims. Multitudes are engaged in defending the claims of the law, as if they greatly feared that the purity of the law would be defiled, its strictness and spirituality overlooked, and its high and holy claims set aside, or frittered down somehow to the level of human passion and selfishness. But while engaged in their zeal to defend the law, they talk and preach, and write, as if they supposed it indispensable, in order to sustain the high claims of the law, to deny the grace and power of the gospel, and its sufficiency to enable human beings to comply with the requisitions of the law. Thus they seem to me, unwittingly, to enter the lists against the grace of Christ, and with the utmost earnestness and even vehemence, to deny that the grace of Christ is sufficient to overcome sin, and to fulfil in us the righteousness of the law. Yes, in their zeal for the law they appear to me either to overlook, or flatly to deny, the grace of the gospel.

Now let the law be exalted. Let it be magnified and made honorable. Let it be shown to be strict, and pure, and perfect, as its Author; spread its claims over the whole field of human and angelic accountability; carry it like a blaze of fire to the deepest recess of every human heart; exalt it as high as heaven; and thunder its authority and claims to the depths of hell; stretch out its line upon the universe of mind; and let it, as it well may, and as it ought, thunder death and terrible damnation against every kind and degree of iniquity. Yet let it be remembered for ever, that the grace of the gospel is co-extensive with the claims of the law. Let no man, therefore, in his strife to maintain the authority of the law, insult the Saviour, exercise unbelief himself, or fritter away and drown the faith of the church, by holding out the profane idea, that the glorious gospel of the blessed God, sent home and rendered powerful by the efficacious application of the Holy Spirit, is not sufficient to fulfil in us "the righteousness of the law," and cause us "to stand perfect and complete in all the will of God."

With respect to the second thing which appears wonderful to me, namely, that so many seem to have an entirely self-righteous view of the doctrine of sanctification, let me say, that they seem afraid to admit, that any are entirely and perfectly sanctified in this life, lest they should flatter human pride, seeming to take it for granted, that, if any are entirely sanctified, they have whereof to glory, as if they had done something, and were in themselves better than others. Whereas, the doctrine of entire sanctification utterly abhors the idea of human merit, disclaims and repudiates it as altogether an abomination to God, and to the sanctified soul. This doctrine, as taught in the Bible, and as I understand it, is as far as possible from conniving in the least degree at the idea of anything naturally good in saints or sinners. It ascribes the whole of salvation and sanctification from first to last, not only till the soul is sanctified, but at every moment while it remains in that state, to the indwelling Spirit, and influence, and grace of Christ.

LECTURE XXXIX - SANCTIFICATION

V. The conditions of this attainment.

1. A state of entire sanctification can never be attained by an indifferent waiting of God's time.

2. Nor by any works of law, or works of any kind, performed in your own strength, irrespective of the grace of God. By this I do not mean, that, were you disposed to exert your natural powers aright, you could not at once obey the law in the exercise of your natural strength, and continue to do so. But I do mean, that as you are wholly indisposed to use your natural powers aright, without the grace of God, no efforts that you will actually make in your own strength, or independent of his grace, will ever result in your entire sanctification.

3. Not by any direct efforts to feel right. Many spend their time in vain efforts to force themselves into a right state of feeling. Now, it should be for ever understood, that religion does not consist in a mere feeling, emotion, or involuntary affection of any kind. Feelings do not result from a direct effort to feel. But, on the contrary, they are the spontaneous actings of the mind, when it has under its direct and deep consideration the objects, truths, facts, or realities, that are correlated to these involuntary emotions. They are the most easy and natural state of mind possible under such circumstances. So far from its requiring an effort to put them forth, it would rather, require an effort to prevent them, when the mind is intensely considering those objects and considerations which have a natural tendency to produce them. This is so true, that when persons are in the exercise of such affections, they feel no difficulty at all in their exercise, but wonder how any one can help feeling as they do. It seems to them so natural, so easy, and, I may say, so almost unavoidable, that they often feel and express astonishment, that any one should find it difficult to exercise the feelings of which they are conscious. The course that many persons take on the subject of religion, has often appeared wonderful to me. They make themselves, their own state and interests, the central point, around which their own minds are continually revolving. Their selfishness is so great, that their own interests, happiness, and salvation, fill their whole field of vision. And with their thoughts and anxieties, and whole souls, clustering around their own salvation, they complain of a hard heart, that they cannot love God, that they do not repent, and cannot believe. They manifestly regard love to God, repentance, faith, and all religion, as consisting in mere feelings. Being conscious that they do not feel right, as they express it, they are the more concerned about themselves, which concern but increases their embarrassment, and the difficulty of exercising what they call right affections. The less they feel, the more they try to feel--the greater efforts they make to feel right without success, the more are they confirmed in their selfishness, and the more are their thoughts glued to their own interests; and they are, of course, at a greater and greater distance from any right state of mind. And thus their selfish anxieties beget ineffectual efforts, and these efforts but deepen their anxieties. And if, in this state, death

should appear in a visible form before them, or the last trumpet sound, and they should be summoned to the solemn judgment, it would but increase their distraction, confirm, and almost give omnipotence to their selfishness, and render their sanctification morally impossible. It should never be forgotten, that all true religion consists in voluntary states of mind, and that the true and only way to attain to true religion, is to look at and understand the exact thing to be done, and then to put forth at once the voluntary exercise required.

4. Not by any efforts to obtain grace by works of law.

Should the question be proposed to a Jew, "What shall I do that I may work the work of God?" he would answer, Keep the law, both moral and ceremonial; that is, keep the commandments.

To the same inquiry an Arminian would answer, Improve common grace, and you will obtain converting grace; that is, use the means of grace according to the best light you have, and you will obtain the grace of salvation. In this answer it is not supposed, that the inquirer already has faith; but that he is in a state of unbelief, and is inquiring after converting grace. The answer, therefore, amounts to this; you must get converting grace by your impenitent works; you must become holy by your hypocrisy; you must work out sanctification by sin.

To this question, most professed Calvinists would make in substance the same reply. They would reject the language, while they retained the idea. Their direction would imply, either that the inquirer already has faith, or that he must perform some works to obtain it, that is, that he must obtain grace by works of law.

A late Calvinistic writer admits that entire and permanent sanctification is attainable, although he rejects the idea of the actual attainment of such a state in this life. He supposes the condition of attaining this state or the way to attain it, is by a diligent use of the means of grace, and that the saints are sanctified just so far as they make a diligent use of the means of sanctification. But as he denies, that any saints ever did or will use all the means with suitable diligence, he denies also, of course, that entire sanctification ever is attained in this life. The way of attaining it, according to his teaching, is by the diligent use of means. If then this writer were asked, "what shall I do that I may work the works of God?"--or in other words what shall I do to obtain entire and permanent sanctification? his answer, it seems, would be: "Use diligently all the means of grace;" that is, you must get grace by works, or, with the Arminian, improve common grace, and you will secure sanctifying grace. Neither an Arminian, nor a Calvinist, would formally direct the inquirer to the law, as the ground of justification. But nearly the whole church would give directions that would amount to the same thing. Their answer would be a legal and not a gospel answer. For whatever answer is given to this question, that does not distinctly recognize faith as the condition of abiding holiness in Christians, is legal. Unless the inquirer is made to understand, that this is the first, grand, fundamental duty, without the performance of which all virtue, all giving up of sin, all acceptable obedience, is impossible, he is misdirected. He is led to believe that it is possible to please God without faith, and to obtain grace by works of law. There are but two kinds of works--works of law, and works of faith. Now, if the inquirer has not the "faith that works by love," to set him upon any course of works to get it, is certainly to set him to get faith by works of law. Whatever is said to him that does not clearly convey the truth, that both justification and sanctification are by faith, without works of law, is law, and not gospel. Nothing before or without faith, can possibly be done by any one, but works of law. His first duty, therefore, is faith; and every attempt to obtain faith by unbelieving works, is to lay works at the foundation, and make grace a result. It is the direct opposite of gospel truth.

Take facts as they arise in every day's experience to show that what I have stated is true of almost all professors and non-professors. Whenever a sinner begins in good earnest to agitate the question, "What shall I do to be saved?" he resolves as a first duty, to break off from his sins, that is, in unbelief. Of course, his reformation is only outward. He determines to do better--to reform in this, that, and the other thing, and thus prepare himself to be converted. He does not expect to be saved without grace and faith, but he attempts to get grace by works of law. The same is true of multitudes of anxious Christians, who are inquiring what they shall do to overcome the world, the flesh, and the devil. They overlook the fact, that "this is the victory that overcometh the world, even our faith," that it is with "the shield of faith" they are to quench all the fiery darts of the wicked." They ask, Why am I overcome by sin? Why can I not get above its power? Why am I thus the slave of my appetites and passions, and the sport of the devil? They cast about for the cause of all this spiritual wretchedness and death. At one time, they think they have discovered it in the neglect of one duty; and at another time in the neglect of another. Sometimes they imagine they have found the cause to lie in yielding to one temptation, and sometimes in yielding to another. They put forth efforts in this direction, and in that direction, and patch up their righteousness on one side, while they make a rent in the other side. Thus they spend years in running round in a circle, and making dams of sand across the current of their own habitudes and tendencies. Instead of at once purifying their hearts by faith, they are engaged in trying to arrest the overflowing of the bitter waters of their own propensities. Why do I sin? they inquire; and casting about for the cause, they come to the sage conclusion, It is because I neglect such a duty, that is, because I do sin. But how shall I get rid of sin? Answer: By doing my duty, that is, by ceasing from sin. Now the real inquiry is, Why do they neglect their duty? Why do they commit sin at all? Where is the foundation of all this mischief? Will it be replied, the foundation of all this wickedness is the force of temptation--in the weakness of our hearts--in the strength of our evil propensities and habits? But all this only brings us back to the real inquiry again, How are these things to be overcome? I answer, by faith alone. No works of law have the least tendency to overcome our sins; but rather to confirm the soul in self-righteousness and unbelief.

The great and fundamental sin, which is at the foundation of all other sin, is unbelief. The first thing is, to give up that--to believe the word of God. There is no breaking off from one sin without this. "Whatsoever is not of faith is sin." "Without faith it is impossible to please God." Thus we see, that the backslider and convicted sinner, when agonizing to overcome sin, will almost always betake themselves to Works of law to obtain faith. They will fast, and pray, and read, and struggle, and outwardly reform, and thus endeavor to obtain grace. Now all this is vain and wrong. Do you ask, shall we not fast, and pray, and read, and struggle? Shall we do nothing but sit down in antinomian security and inaction? I answer, you must do all that God commands you to do; but begin where he tells you to begin, and do it in the manner in which he commands you to do it; that is, in the exercise of that faith that works by love. Purify your hearts by faith. Believe in the Son of God. And say not in your heart, "Who shall ascend into heaven, that is to bring Christ down from above; or who shall descend into the deep, that is, to bring up Christ again from the dead. But what saith it? The word is nigh thee, even in thy mouth, and in thy heart, that is, the word of faith which we preach." Now these facts show, that even under the gospel, almost all professors of religion, while they reject the Jewish notion of justification by works of law, have after all adopted a ruinous substitute for it, and suppose, that in some way they are to obtain grace by their works.

5. A state of entire sanctification cannot be attained by attempting to copy the experience of others. It is very common for convicted sinners, or for Christians inquiring after entire sanctification, in their blindness, to ask others to relate their experience, to mark minutely the detail of all their exercises, and then set themselves to pray for, and make direct efforts to attain the same class of exercises, not seeming to understand, that they can no more exercise feelings in the detail like others, than they can look like others. Human experiences differ as human countenances differ. The whole history of a man's former state of mind, comes in of course to modify his present and future experience; so that the precise train of feelings which may be requisite in your case, and which will actually occur, if you are ever sanctified, will not in all its details coincide with the exercises of any other human being. It is of vast importance for you to understand, that you can be no copyist in any true religions experience; and that you are in great danger of being deceived by Satan, whenever you attempt to copy the experience of others. I beseech you therefore to cease from praying for, or trying to obtain, the precise experience of any person whatever. All truly Christian experiences are, like human countenances, in their outline so much alike as to be readily known as the lineaments of the religion of Jesus Christ. But no further than this are they alike, any more than human countenances are alike.

But here let it be remembered, that sanctification does not consist in the various affections or emotions of which Christians speak, and which are often mistaken for, or confounded with, true religion; but that sanctification consists in entire consecration, and consequently it is all out of place for any one to attempt to copy the feelings of another, inasmuch as feelings do not constitute religion. The feelings of which Christians speak do not constitute true religion, but often result from a state of heart. These feelings may properly enough be spoken of as Christian experience, for although involuntary states of mind, they are experienced by true Christians. The only way to secure them is to set the will right, and the emotions will be a natural result.

6. Not by waiting to make preparations before you come into this state. Observe, that the thing about which you are inquiring, is a state of entire consecration to God. Now do not imagine that this state of mind must be prefaced by a long introduction of preparatory exercises. It is common for persons, when inquiring upon this subject with earnestness, to think themselves hindered in this progress by a want of this, or that, or the other exercise or state of mind. They look everywhere else but at the real difficulty. They assign any other, and every other but the true reason, for their not being already in a state of sanctification. The true difficulty is voluntary selfishness, or voluntary consecration to self-interest and self-gratification. This is the difficulty, and the only difficulty, to be overcome.

7. Not by attending meetings, asking the prayers of other Christians, or depending in any way upon the means of getting into this state. By this I do not intend to say, that means are unnecessary, or that it is not through the instrumentality of truth, that this state of mind is induced. But I do mean, that while you are depending upon any instrumentality whatever, your mind is diverted from the real point before you, and you are never likely to make this attainment.

8. Not by waiting for any particular views of Christ. When persons in the state of mind of which I have been speaking, hear those who live in faith describe their views of Christ, they say, Oh, if I had such views, I could believe; I must have these before I can believe. Now you should understand, that these views are the result and effect of faith in the promise of the Spirit, to take of the things of Christ and show them to you. Lay hold of this class of promises, and the Holy Spirit will reveal Christ to you, in the relations in which you need him from time to time. Take hold, then, on the simple promise of God. Take God at his word. Believe that he means just what he says; and this will at once bring you into the state of mind after which you inquire.

9. Not in any way which you may mark out for yourself. Persons in an inquiring state are very apt, without seeming to be aware of it, to send imagination on before them, to stake out the way, and set up a flag where they intend to come out. They expect to be thus and thus exercised--to have such and such peculiar views and feelings when they have attained their object. Now, there probably never was a person who did riot find himself disappointed in these respects. God says, "I will bring the blind by a way that they know not. I will lead them in paths that they have not known: I will make darkness light before them, and crooked things straight. These things will I do unto them, and not forsake them." This suffering your imagination to mark out your path is a great hindrance to you, as it sets you upon making many fruitless, and worse than fruitless attempts to attain this imaginary state of mind, wastes much of your time, and greatly wearies the patience and grieves the Spirit of God. While he is trying to lead you right to the point, you are hauling off from the course, and insisting, that this which your imagination has marked out is the way, instead of that in which he is trying to lead you. And thus in your pride and ignorance you are causing much delay, and abusing the long-suffering of God. He says, "This is the way, walk ye in it." But you say, no--this is the way. And thus you stand and parley and banter, while you are every moment in danger of grieving the Spirit of God away from you, and of losing your soul.

If there is anything in your imagination that has fixed definitely upon any particular manner, time, or place, or circumstance, you will, in all probability, either be deceived by the devil, or be entirely disappointed in the result. You will find, in all these particular items on which you had laid any stress, that the wisdom of man is foolishness with God--that your ways are not his ways, nor your thoughts his thoughts. "For as the heavens are higher than the earth, so are his ways higher than your ways and his thoughts higher than your thoughts." But,--

10. This state is to be attained by faith alone. Let it be for ever remembered, that "without faith it is impossible to please God," and "whatsoever is not of faith, is sin." Both justification and sanctification are by faith alone. Rom. iii. 30: "Seeing it is one God who shall justify the circumcision by faith, and the uncircumcision through faith;" and ch. v. 1:

"Therefore, being justified by faith, we have peace with God, through our Lord Jesus Christ." Also, ch. ix. 30, 31; "What shall we say then? That the Gentiles, who followed not after righteousness, have attained to righteousness, even the righteousness which is of faith. But Israel, who followed after the law of righteousness, hath not attained to the law of righteousness. Wherefore? Because they sought it not by faith, but, as it were, by the works of the law."

But let me by no means be understood as teaching sanctification by faith, as distinct from and opposed to sanctification by the Holy Spirit, or Spirit of Christ, or which is the same thing, by Christ our sanctification, living and reigning in the heart. Faith is rather the instrument or condition, than the efficient agent that induces a state of present and permanent sanctification. Faith simply receives Christ, as king, to live and reign in the soul. It is Christ, in the exercise of his different offices, and appropriated in his different relations to the wants of the soul, by faith, who secures our sanctification. This he does by Divine discoveries to the soul of his Divine perfections and fulness. The condition of these discoveries is faith and obedience. He says, John xiv. 21-23: "He that hath my commandments, and keepeth them, he it is that loveth me; and he that loveth me shall be loved of my Father, and I will love him, and will manifest myself to him. Judas saith unto him, (not Iscariot,) Lord, how is it that thou wilt manifest thyself unto us, and not unto the world? Jesus answered and said unto him, If a man love me, he will keep my words: and my Father will love him, and we will come unto him, and make our abode with him."

To ascertain the conditions of entire sanctification in this life, we must consider what the temptations are that overcome us. When first converted, we have seen, that the heart or will consecrates itself and the whole being to God. We have also seen, that this is a state of disinterested benevolence, or a committal of the whole being to the promotion of the highest good. We have also seen, that all sin is selfishness, or that all sin consists in the will's seeking the indulgence or gratification of self; that it consists in the will's yielding obedience to the propensities, instead of obeying God, as his law is revealed in the reason. Now, who cannot see what needs to be done to break the power of temptation, and let the soul go free? The fact is, that the department of our sensibility that is related to objects of time and sense, has received an enormous development, and is tremblingly alive to all its correlated objects, while, by reason of the blindness of the mind to spiritual objects, it is scarcely developed at all in its relations to them. Those objects are seldom thought of by the carnal mind, and when they are, they are only thought of. They are not clearly seen, and of course they are not felt.

The thought of God, of Christ, of sin, of holiness, of heaven, and hell, excites little or no emotion in the carnal mind. The carnal mind is alive and awake to earthly and sensible objects, but dead to spiritual realities. The spiritual world needs to be revealed to the soul. The soul needs to see and clearly apprehend its own spiritual condition, relations, wants. It needs to become acquainted with God and Christ, to have spiritual and eternal realities made plain, and present, and all-absorbing realities to the soul. It needs such discoveries of the eternal world, of the nature and guilt of sin, and of Christ, the remedy of the soul, as to kill or greatly mortify lust, or the appetites and passions in their relations to objects of time and sense, and thoroughly to develop the sensibility, in its relations to sin and to God, and to the whole circle of spiritual realities. This will greatly abate the frequency and power of temptation to self-gratification, and break up the voluntary slavery of the will. The developments of the sensibility need to be thoroughly corrected. This can only be done by the revelation to the inward man, by the Holy Spirit, of those great, and solemn, and overpowering realities of the "spirit land," that lie concealed from the eye of flesh.

We often see those around us whose sensibility is so developed, in some one direction, that they are led captive by appetite and passion in that direction, in spite of reason and of God. The inebriate is an example of this. The glutton, the licentious, the avaricious man, are examples of this kind. We sometimes, on the other hand, see, by some striking providence, such a counter development of the sensibility produced, as to slay and put down those particular tendencies, and the whole direction of the man's life seems to be changed; and outwardly, at least, it is so. From being a perfect slave to his appetite for strong drink, he cannot, without the utmost loathing and disgust, so much as hear the name of his once loved beverage mentioned. From being a most avaricious man he becomes deeply disgusted with wealth, and spurns and despises it. Now, this has been effected by a counter development of the sensibility; for, in the case supposed, religion has nothing to do with it. Religion does not consist in the states of the sensibility, nor in the will's being influenced by the sensibility; but sin consists in the will's being thus influenced. One great thing that needs to be done, to confirm and settle the will in the attitude of entire consecration to God, is to bring about a counter development of the sensibility, so that it will not draw the will away from God. It needs to be mortified or crucified to the world, to objects of time and sense, by so deep and clear, and powerful a revelation of self to self, and of Christ to the soul, as to awaken and develop all its susceptibilities in their relations to him, and to spiritual and divine realities. This can easily be done through and by the Holy Spirit, who takes of the things of Christ and shows them to us. He so reveals Christ, that the soul receives him to the throne of the heart, to reign throughout the whole being. When the will, the intellect, and the sensibility are yielded to him, he develops the intelligence, and the sensibility by clear revelations of himself, in all his offices and relations to the soul, confirms the will, mellows and chastens the sensibility, by these divine revelations to the intelligence.

We need the light of the Holy Spirit to teach us the character of God, the nature of his government, the purity of his law, the necessity and fact of atonement--to teach us our need of Christ in all his offices and relations, governmental, spiritual, and mixed. We need the revelation of Christ to our souls, in such power as to induce in us that appropriating faith, without which Christ is not, and cannot be, our salvation. We need to know Christ, for example, in such relations as the following:--

1. As King, to set up his government and write his law in our hearts; to establish his kingdom within us; to sway his sceptre over our whole being. As King he must be spiritually revealed and received.

2. As our Mediator, to stand between the offended justice of God and our guilty souls, to bring about a reconciliation between our souls and God. As Mediator he must be known and received.

3. As our Advocate or Paracletos, our next or best friend, to plead our cause with the Father, our righteous and all prevailing advocate to secure the triumph of our cause at the bar of God. In this relation he must be apprehended and embraced.

4. As our Redeemer, to redeem us from the curse of the law, and from the power and dominion of sin; to pay the price demanded by public justice for our release, and to overcome and break up forever our spiritual bondage. In this relation also we must know and appreciate him by faith.

5. As the propitiation for our sins, to offer himself as a propitiatory or offering for our sins. The apprehension of Christ as making an atonement for our sins seems to be indispensable to the entertaining of a healthy hope of eternal life. It certainly is not healthy for the soul to apprehend the mercy of God, without regarding the conditions of its exercise. It does not sufficiently impress the soul with a sense of the justice and holiness of God, with the guilt and desert of sin. It does not sufficiently awe the soul and humble it in the deepest dust, to regard God as extending pardon, without regard to the sternness of his justice, as evinced in requiring that sin should be recognized in the universe, as worthy of the wrath and curse of God, as a condition of its forgiveness. It is remarkable, and well worthy of all consideration, that those who deny the atonement make sin a comparative trifle, and seem to regard God's benevolence or love as good nature, rather than, as it is, "a consuming fire "to all the workers of iniquity. Nothing does or can produce that awe of God, that fear and holy dread of sin, that self-abasing, God-justifying spirit, that a thorough apprehension of the atonement of Christ will do. Nothing like this can beget that spirit of self-renunciation, of cleaving to Christ, of taking refuge in his blood. In these relations Christ must be revealed to us, and apprehended and embraced by us, as the condition of our entire sanctification.

It is the work of the Holy Spirit thus to reveal his death in its relations to our individual sins, and as related to our sins as individuals. The soul needs to apprehend Christ as crucified for us. It is one thing for the soul to regard the death of Christ merely as the death of a martyr, and an infinitely different thing, as every one knows, who has had the experience, to apprehend his death as a real and veritable vicarious sacrifice for our sins, as being truly a substitute for our death. The soul needs to apprehend Christ as suffering on the cross for it, or as its substitute; so that it can say, That sacrifice is for me, that suffering and that death are for my sins; that blessed Lamb is slain for my sins. If thus fully to apprehend and to appropriate Christ cannot kill sin in us, what can?

6. We also need to know Christ as risen for our justification. He arose and lives to procure our certain acquittal, or our complete pardon and acceptance with God. That he lives and is our justification we need to know, to break the bondage of legal motives, and to slay all selfish fear; to break and destroy the power of temptation from this source. The clearly convinced soul is often tempted to despondency and unbelief, to despair of its own acceptance with God, and it would surely fall into the bondage of fear, were it not for the faith of Christ as a risen, living, justifying Saviour. In this relation, the soul needs clearly to apprehend and fully to appropriate Christ in his completeness, as a condition of abiding in a state of disinterested consecration to God.

7. We need also to have Christ revealed to us as bearing our griefs and as carrying our sorrows. The clear apprehension of Christ, as being made sorrowful for us, and as bending under sorrows and griefs which in justice belonged to us, tends at once to render sin unspeakably odious, and. Christ infinitely precious to our souls. The idea of Christ our substitute, needs to be thoroughly developed in our minds. And this relation of Christ needs to be so clearly revealed to us, as to become an everywhere present reality to us. We

need to have Christ so revealed as to so completely ravish and engross our affections, that we would sooner die at once than sin against him. Is such a thing impossible? Indeed it is not. Is not the Holy Spirit able, and willing, and ready thus to reveal him, upon condition of our asking it in faith? Surely he is.

We need to apprehend. Christ as the one by whose stripes we are healed. We need to know him as relieving our pains and sufferings by his own, as preventing our death by his own, as sorrowing that we might eternally rejoice, as grieving that we might be unspeakably and eternally glad, as dying in unspeakable agony that we might die in deep peace and in unspeakable triumph.

8. "As being made sin for us." We need to apprehend him as being treated as a sinner, and even as the chief of sinners on our account, or for us. This is the representation of scripture, that Christ on our account was treated as if he were a sinner. He was made sin for us, that is, he was treated as a sinner, or rather as being the representative, or as it were the embodiment of sin for us. O! this the soul needs to apprehend--the holy Jesus treated as a sinner, and as if all sin were concentrated in him, on our account! We procured this treatment of him. He consented to take our place in such a sense as to endure the cross, and the curse of the law for us. When the soul apprehends this, it is ready to die with grief and love. O, how infinitely it loathes self under such an apprehension as this! In this relation he must not only be apprehended, but appropriated by faith.

We also need to apprehend the fact that "he was made sin for us, that we might be made the righteousness of God in him;" that Christ was treated as a sinner, that we might be treated as righteous; that we might also be made personally righteous by faith in him; that we might inherit and be made partakers of God's righteousness, as that righteousness exists and is revealed in Christ; that we might in and by him be made righteous as God is righteous. It needs to embrace and lay hold by faith upon that righteousness of God, which is brought home to saints in Christ, through the atonement and indwelling Spirit.

9. We also need Christ revealed to the inward being, as "head over all things to the church." All these relations are of no avail to our sanctification, only in so far forth as they are directly, and inwardly, and personally revealed to the soul by the Holy Spirit. It is one thing to have thoughts, and ideas, and opinions concerning Christ, and an entirely different thing to know Christ, as he is revealed by the Holy Spirit. All the relations of Christ imply corresponding necessities in us. When the Holy Spirit has revealed to us the necessity, and Christ as exactly suited to fully meet that necessity, and urged his acceptance in that relation, until we have appropriated him by faith, a great work is done. But until we are thus revealed to ourselves, and Christ is thus revealed to us and accepted by us, nothing is done more than to store our heads with notions or opinions and theories, while our hearts are becoming more and more, at every moment, like an adamant stone.

I have often feared, that many professed Christians knew Christ only after the flesh; that is, they have no other knowledge of Christ than what they obtain by reading and hearing about him, without any special revelation of him to the inward being by the Holy Spirit. I do not wonder, that such professors and ministers should be totally in the dark, upon the subject of entire sanctification in this life. They regard sanctification as brought about by the formation of holy habits, instead of resulting from the revelation of Christ to the soul in all his fulness and relations, and the soul's renunciation of self and appropriation of Christ in these relations. Christ is represented in the Bible as the head of the church. The church is represented as his body. He is to the church what the head is to the body. The head is the seat of the intellect, the will, and in short, of the living soul. Consider what the body would be without the head, and you may understand what the church would be without Christ. But as the church would be without. Christ, so each believer would be without Christ. But we need to have our necessities in this respect clearly revealed to us by the Holy Spirit, and this relation of Christ made plain to our apprehension. The utter darkness of the human mind in regard to its own spiritual state and wants, and in regard to the relations and fulness of Christ, is truly wonderful. His relations, as mentioned in the Bible, are overlooked almost entirely until our wants are discovered. When these are made known, and the soul begins in earnest to inquire after a remedy, it needs not inquire in vain. "Say not in thine heart, who shall ascend up to heaven? that is, to bring Christ down from above; or who shall descend into the deep? that is, to bring Christ again from the dead. But what saith it? The word is nigh thee, even in thy mouth, and in thy heart."

O how infinitely blind he is to the fulness and glory of Christ, who does not know himself and Christ as both are revealed by the Holy Spirit. When we are led by the Holy Spirit to look down into the abyss of our own emptiness--to behold the horrible pit and miry clay of our own habits, and fleshly, and worldly, and infernal entanglements; when we see in the light of God, that our emptiness and necessities are infinite; then, and not till then, are we prepared wholly to cast off self, and to put on Christ. The glory and fulness of Christ are not discovered to the soul, until it discovers its need of him. But when self, in all its loathsomeness and helplessness, is fully revealed, until hope is utterly extinct, as it respects every kind and degree of help in ourselves; and when Christ, the all and in all, is revealed to the soul as its all-sufficient portion and salvation, then, and not until then, does the soul know its salvation. This knowledge is the indispensable condition of appropriating faith, or of that act of receiving Christ, or that committal of all to him, that takes Christ home to dwell in the heart by faith, and to preside over all its states and actions. O, such a knowledge and such a reception and putting on of Christ is blessed. Happy is he who knows it by his own experience.

It is indispensable to a steady and implicit faith, that the soul should have a spiritual apprehension of what is implied in the saying of Christ, that all power was delivered unto him. The ability of Christ to do all, and even exceeding abundantly above all that we ask or think, is what the soul needs clearly to apprehend, in a spiritual sense that is, to apprehend it, not merely as a theory or as a proposition, but to see the true spiritual import of this saying. This is also equally true of all that is said in the Bible about Christ, of all his offices and relations. It is one thing to theorize, and speculate, and opine, about Christ, and an infinitely different thing to know him as he is revealed by the Holy Spirit. When Christ is fully revealed to the soul by the Comforter, it will never again doubt the attainability and reality of entire sanctification in this life.

When we sin, it is because of our ignorance of Christ. That is, whenever temptation overcomes us, it is because we do not know and avail ourselves of the relation of Christ that would meet our necessities. One great thing that needs to be done is, to correct the developments of our sensibility. The appetites and passions are enormously developed in their relations to earthly objects. In relation to things of time and sense, our propensities are greatly developed and are alive; but in relation to spiritual truths and objects, and eternal realities, we are naturally as dead as stones. When first converted, if we knew enough of ourselves and of Christ thoroughly to develop and correct the action of the sensibility, and confirm our wills in a state of entire consecration, we should not fall. In proportion as the law-work preceding conversion has been thorough, and the revelation of Christ at, or immediately subsequent to, conversion, full and clear, just in that proportion do we witness stability in converts. In most, if not in all instances, however, the convert is too ignorant of himself, and of course knows too little about Christ, to be established in permanent obedience. He needs renewed conviction of sin, to be revealed to himself, and to have Christ revealed to him, and be formed in him the hope of glory, before he will be steadfast, always abounding in the work of the Lord.

It must not be inferred, that the knowledge of Christ in all these relations is a condition of our coming into a state of entire consecration to God, or of present sanctification. The thing insisted on is, that the soul will abide in this state in the hour of temptation only so far forth as it betakes itself to Christ in such circumstances of trial, and apprehends and appropriates him by faith from time to time in those relations that meet the present and pressing necessities of the soul. The temptation is the 6c6itsion of revealing the necessity, and the Holy Spirit is always ready to reveal Christ in the particular relation suited to the newly-developed necessity. The perception and appropriation of him in this relation, under these circumstances of trial, is the sine quâ non of our remaining in the state of entire consecration.

The foregoing are some of the relations which Christ sustains to us as to our salvation. I could have enlarged greatly, as you perceive, upon each of these, and easily have swelled this part of our course of study to a large volume. I have only touched upon these relations, as specimens of the manner in which he is presented for our acceptance in the Bible, and by the Holy Spirit. Do not understand me as teaching, that we must first know Christ in all these relations, before we can be sanctified. The thing intended is, that coming to know Christ in these relations is a condition, or is the indispensable means, of our steadfastness or perseverance in holiness under temptation--that, when we are tempted, from time to time nothing can secure us against a fall, but the revelation of Christ to the soul in these relations one after another, and our appropriation of him to ourselves by faith. The gospel has directly promised, in every temptation to open a way of escape, so that we shall be able to bear it. The spirit of this promise pledges to us such a revelation of Christ, as to secure our standing, if we will lay hold upon him by faith, as revealed. Our circumstances of temptation render it necessary, that at one time we should apprehend Christ in one relation, and at another time in another. For example, at one time we are tempted to despair by Satan's accusing us of sin, and suggesting that our sins are too great to be forgiven. In this case we need a revelation and an appropriation of Christ, as having been made sin for us; that is, as having atoned for our sins--as being our justification or righteousness. This will sustain the soul's confidence and preserve its peace.

At another time we are tempted to despair of ever overcoming our tendencies to sin, and to give up our sanctification as a hopeless thing. Now we need a revelation of Christ as our sanctification, etc.

At another time the soul is harassed with the view of the great subtlety and sagacity of its spiritual enemies, and greatly tempted to despair on that account. Now it needs to know Christ as its wisdom.

Again, it is tempted to discouragement on account of the great number and strength of its adversaries. On such occasions it needs Christ revealed as the Mighty God, as its strong tower, its hiding place, its munition of rocks.

Again, the soul is oppressed with a sense of the infinite holiness of God, and the infinite distance there is between us and God, on account of our sinfulness and his infinite holiness, and on account of his infinite abhorrence of sin and sinners. Now the soul needs to know Christ as its righteousness, and as a mediator between God and man.

Again, the Christian's month is closed with a sense of guilt, so that he cannot look up, nor speak to God of pardon and acceptance. He trembles and is confounded before God. He lies along on his face, and despairing thoughts roll a tide of agony through his soul. He is speechless, and can only groan out his self-accusations before the Lord. Now as a condition of rising above this temptation to despair, he needs a revelation of Christ as his advocate, as his high priest, as ever living to make intercession for him. This view of Christ will enable the soul to commit all to him in this relation, and maintain its peace and hold on to its steadfastness.

Again, the soul is led to tremble in view of its constant exposedness to besetments on every side, oppressed with such a sense of its own utter helplessness in the presence of its enemies, as almost to despair. Now it needs to know Christ as the good shepherd, who keeps a constant watch over the sheep, and carries the lambs in his bosom. He needs to know him as a watchman and a keeper.

Again, it is oppressed with the sense of its own utter emptiness, and is forced to exclaim, I know that in me, that is, in my flesh, dwelleth no good thing. It sees that it has no life, or unction, or power, or spirituality in itself. Now it needs to know Christ as the true vine, from which it may receive constant and abundant spiritual nourishment. It needs to know him as the fountain of the water of life, and in those relations that will meet its necessities in this direction. Let these suffice, as specimens to illustrate what is intended by entire or permanent sanctification being conditioned on the revelation and appropriation of Christ in all the fulness of his official relations.

LECTURE XL - SANCTIFICATION

VI. Objections answered.

I will consider those passages of scripture which are by some supposed to contradict the doctrine we have been considering.

1 Kings viii. 46: "If they sin against thee, (for there is no man that sinneth not,) and thou be angry with them, and deliver them to the enemy, so that they carry them away captives unto the land of the enemy, far or near," etc. On this passage, I remark:--

1. That this sentiment in nearly the same language, is repeated in 2 Chron. vi. 26, and in Eccl. vii. 20, where the same original word in the same form is used.

2. These are the strongest passages I know of in the Old Testament, and the same remarks are applicable to the three.

3. I will quote, for the satisfaction of the reader, the note of Dr. Adam Clarke upon this passage, and also that of Barclay, the celebrated and highly spiritual author of "An Apology for the True Christian Divinity." And let me say, that they appear to me to be satisfactory answers to the objection founded upon these passages.

CLARKE: "If they sin against thee.'--This must refer to some general defection from truth; to some species of false worship, idolatry, or corruption of the truth and ordinances of the Most High; as for it, they are here stated to be delivered into the hands of their enemies, and carried away captive, which was the general punishment of idolatry, and what is called, [verse 47,] acting perversely and committing wickedness.

"If they sin against thee, for there is no man that sinneth not.' The second clause, as it is here translated, renders the supposition in the first clause, entirely nugatory; for, if there be no man that sinneth not, it is useless to say, if they sin; but this contradiction is taken away, by reference to the original ki yechetau lak, which should be translated, if they shall sin against thee; or should they sin against thee, ki ein adam asher lo yecheta; for there is no man that may not sin;' that is, there is no man impeccable, none infallible; none that is not liable to transgress. This is the true meaning of the phrase in various parts of the Bible, and so our translators have understood the original, for even in the thirty-first verse of this chapter, they have translated yecheta, if a man trespass; which certainly implies he might or might not do it; and in this way they have translated the same word, if a soul sin, in Lev. v. 1, and vi. 2; 1 Sam. ii. 25; 2 Chron. iv. 22; and in several other places. The truth is, the Hebrew has no mood to express words in the permissive or optative way, but to express this sense it uses the future tense of the conjugation kal.

"This text has been a wonderful strong-hold for all who believe that there is no redemption from sin in this life; that no man can live without committing sin; and that we cannot be entirely freed from it till we die.

"1. The text speaks no such doctrine; it only speaks of the possibility of every man's sinning; and this must be true of a state of probation.

"2. There is not another text in the divine records that is more to the purpose than this.

"3. The doctrine is flatly in opposition to the design of the gospel; for Jesus came to save his people from their sins, and to destroy the works of the devil.

"4. It is a dangerous and destructive doctrine, and should be blotted out of every Christian's creed. There are too many who are seeking to excuse their crimes by all means in their power; and we need not embody their excuses in a creed, to complete their deception, by stating that their sins are unavoidable."

BARCLAY: "Secondly,--Another objection is from two passages of scripture, much of one signification. The one is 1 Kings viii. 46: For there is no man that sinneth not.' The other is Eccl. vii. 20: For there is not a just man upon earth, that doeth good and sinneth not.'

"I answer,--

"1. These affirm nothing of a daily and continual sinning, so as never to be redeemed from it; but only that all have sinned, that there is none that doth not sin, though not always so as never to cease to sin; and in this lies the question. Yea, in that place of the Kings he speaks within two verses of the returning of such with all their souls and hearts, which implies a possibility of leaving off sin.

"2.There is a respect to be had to the seasons and dispensations; for if it should be granted that in Solomon's time there were none that sinned not, it will not follow that there are none such now, or that it is a thing not now attainable by the grace of God under the gospel.

"3. And lastly, this whole objection hangs upon a false interpretation; for the original Hebrew word may be read in the potential mood, thus,--There is no man who may not sin, as well as in the indicative; so both the old Latin, Junius, and Tremellius, and Vatablus have it, and the same word is so used, Ps. cxix. 11: Thy word have I hid in my heart, that I might not sin against thee'--in the potential mood, and not in the indicative: which being more answerable to the universal scope of the scriptures, the testimony of the truth, and the sense of almost all interpreters, doubtless ought to be so understood, and the other interpretation rejected as spurious."

Whatever may be thought of the views of these authors, to me it is a plain and satisfactory answer to the objection founded upon these passages, that the objection might be strictly true under the Old Testament dispensation, and prove nothing in regard to the attainability of a state of entire sanctification under the New. What! does the New Testament dispensation differ nothing from the Old in its advantages for the acquisition of holiness? If it be true, that no one under the comparatively dark dispensation of Judaism, attained a state of permanent sanctification, does that prove such a state is not attainable under the gospel? It is expressly stated in the Epistle to the Hebrews, that "the old covenant made nothing perfect, but the bringing in of a better hope did." Under the old covenant, God expressly promised that he would make a new one with the house of Israel, in "writing the law in their hearts," and in "engraving it in their inward parts." And this new covenant was to be made with the house of Israel, under the Christian dispensation. What then do all such passages in the Old Testament prove, in relation to the privileges and holiness of Christians under the new dispensation?

Whether any of the Old Testament saints did so far receive the new Covenant by way of anticipation, as to enter upon a state of permanent sanctification, it is not my present purpose to inquire. Nor will I inquire, whether, admitting that Solomon said in his day, that there was not a just man upon the earth that liveth and sinneth not, the same could with equal truth have been asserted of every generation under the Jewish dispensation. It is expressly asserted of Abraham, and multitudes of the Old Testament saints, that they "died in faith, not having received the promises." Now what can this mean? It cannot be, that they did not know the promises; for to them the promises were made. It cannot mean, that they did not receive Christ, for the Bible expressly asserts that they did--that "Abraham rejoiced to see Christ's day "that Moses, and indeed all the Old Testament saints, had so much knowledge of Christ as a Saviour to be revealed, as to bring them into a state of salvation. But still they did not receive the promise of the Spirit, as it is poured out under the Christian dispensation. This was the great thing all along promised, first to Abraham, or to his seed, which is Christ. Gal. iii. 14, 16: "That the blessing of Abraham might come on the Gentiles through Jesus Christ; that we might receive the promise of the Spirit through faith." "Now to Abraham and his seed were the promises made. He saith not, And to seeds, as of many; but as of one, and to thy seed, which is Christ;" and afterwards to the Christian church, by all the prophets. Acts ii. 16-21: "But this is that which was spoken by the prophet Joel; And it shall come to pass in the last days (saith God,) I will pour out of my Spirit upon all flesh, and your sons and your daughters shall prophesy, and your young men shall see visions, and your old men shall dream dreams; and on my servants, and on my handmaidens, I will pour out in those days of my Spirit; and they shall prophesy; and I will show wonders in heaven above and signs in the earth beneath; blood, and fire and vapor of smoke; the sun shall be turned into darkness, and the moon into blood, before the great and notable day of the Lord come; and it shall come to pass, that whosoever shall call on the name of the Lord shall be saved." Acts ii. 38, 39: "Then Peter said unto them, Repent, and be baptized every one of you in the name of Jesus Christ for the remission of sins, and ye shall receive the gift of the Holy Ghost. For the promise is unto you, and to your children, and to all that are afar off, even as many as the Lord our God shall call." Acts iii. 24, 26: "Yea, and all the prophets from Samuel, and those that follow after, as many as have spoken, have likewise foretold of these days." "Unto you first, God having raised up his Son Jesus, sent him to bless you, in turning away every one of you from his iniquities;" and lastly, by Christ himself, which he expressly styles "the promise" of the Father. Acts i. 4, 5: "And being assembled together with them, commanded them that they should not depart from Jerusalem, but wait for the promise of the Father, which, saith he, ye have heard of me. For John truly baptized with water; but ye shall be baptized with the Holy Ghost not many days hence." They did not receive the light and the glory of the Christian dispensation, nor the fulness of the Holy Spirit. And it is asserted in the Bible, "they without us," that is, without our privileges, "could not be made perfect."

The next objection is founded upon the Lord's Prayer. In this Christ has taught us to pray, "Forgive us our trespasses as we forgive those who trespass against us." Here it is objected, that if a person should become entirely sanctified, he could no longer use this clause of this prayer, which, it is said, was manifestly designed to be used by the church to the end of time. Upon this prayer I remark:--

1. Christ has taught us to pray for entire, in the sense of perpetual sanctification. "Thy will be done on earth, as it is done in heaven."

2. He designed, that we should expect this prayer to be answered, or that we should mock him by asking what we do not believe is agreeable to his will, and that too which we know could not consistently be granted; and that we are to repeat this insult to God as often as we pray.

3. The petition for forgiveness of our trespasses, it is plain, must apply to past sins, and not to sins we are committing at the time we make the prayer; for it would be absurd and abominable to pray for the forgiveness of a sin which we are then in the act of committing.

4. This prayer cannot properly be made in respect to any sin of which we have not repented; for it would be highly abominable in the sight of God, to pray for the forgiveness of a sin of which we did not repent.

5. If there be any hour or clay in which a man has committed no actual sin, he could not consistently make this prayer in reference to that hour or that day.

6. But at the very time, it would be highly proper for him to make this prayer in relation to all his past sins, and that too, although he may have repented of, and confessed them, and prayed for their forgiveness, a thousand times before. This does not imply a doubt, whether God has forgiven the sins of which we have repented; but it is only a renewal of our grief and humiliation for our sins, and a fresh acknowledgment of, and casting ourselves upon, his mercy. God may forgive when we repent, before we ask him, and while we abhor ourselves so much as to have no heart to ask for forgiveness; but his having forgiven us does not render the petition improper.

7. And although his sins may be forgiven, he ought still to confess them, to repent of them, both in this world and in the world to come. And it is perfectly suitable, so long as he lives in the world, to say the least, to continue to repent, and repeat the request for forgiveness. For myself, I am unable to see why this passage should be made a stumbling-block; for if it be improper to pray for the forgiveness of sins of which we have repented, then it is improper to pray for forgiveness at all. And if this prayer cannot be used with propriety in reference to past sins of which we have already repented, it cannot properly be used at all, except upon the absurd supposition, that we are to pray for the forgiveness of sins which we are now committing, and of which we have not repented. And if it be improper to use this form of prayer in reference to all past sins of which we have repented, it is just as improper to use it in reference to sins committed to-day or yesterday, of which we have repented.

Another objection is founded on James iii. 1, 2: "My brethren, be not many masters, knowing that we shall receive the greater condemnation. For in many things we offend all. If any man offend not in word, the same is a perfect man, and able also to bridle the whole body." Upon this passage I remark:--

1. The term rendered masters here, may be rendered teachers, critics, or censors, and be understood either in a good or bad sense. The apostle exhorts the brethren not to be many masters, because if they are so, they will incur the greater condemnation; "for," says he, "in many things we offend all." The fact that we all offend is here urged as a reason why we should not be many masters; which shows that the term masters is here used in a bad sense. "Be not many masters," for if we are masters, "we shall receive the greater condemnation," because we are all great offenders. Now I understand this to be the simple meaning of this passage; do not many (or any) of you become

censors, or critics, and set yourselves up to judge and condemn others. For inasmuch as you have all sinned yourselves, and we are all great offenders, we shall receive the greater condemnation, if we set ourselves up as censors. "For with what judgment ye judge, ye shall be judged, and with what measure ye mete, it shall be measured to you again."

2. It does not appear to me that the apostle designs to affirm anything at all of the present character of himself, or of those to whom he wrote; nor to have had the remotest allusion to the doctrine of entire sanctification, but simply to affirm a well-established truth in its application to a particular sin; that if they became censors, and injuriously condemned others, inasmuch as they had all committed many sins, they should receive the greater condemnation.

3. That the apostle did not design to deny the doctrine of Christian perfection or entire sanctification, as maintained in these lectures, seems evident from the fact, that he immediately subjoins, "If any man offend not in word, the same is a perfect man, and able also to bridle the whole body."

Another objection is founded on 1 John, i. 8: "If we say we have no sin, we deceive ourselves, and the truth is not in us." Upon this I remark:--

1. Those who make this passage an objection to the doctrine of entire sanctification in this life, assume that the apostle is here speaking of sanctification instead of justification; whereas an honest examination of the passage, if I mistake not, will render it evident that the apostle makes no allusion here to sanctification, but is speaking solely of justification. A little attention to the connection in which this verse stands will, I think, render this evident. But before I proceed to state what I understand to be the meaning of this passage, let us consider it in the connection in which it stands, in the sense in which they understand it who quote it for the purpose of opposing the sentiment advocated in these lectures. They understand the apostle as affirming, that, if we say we are in a state of entire sanctification and do not sin, we deceive ourselves, and the truth is not in us. Now if this were the apostle's meaning, he involves himself, in this connection, in two flat contradictions.

2. This verse is immediately preceded by the assertion that the "blood of Jesus Christ cleanseth us from all sin." Now it would be very remarkable, if immediately after this assertion the apostle should mean to say that it does not cleanse us from all sin, and if we say it does, we deceive ourselves; for he had just asserted, that the blood of Jesus Christ does cleanse us from all sin. If this were his meaning, it involves him in as palpable a contradiction as could be expressed.

3. This view of the subject then represents the apostle in the conclusion of the seventh verse, as saying, the blood of Jesus Christ his Son cleanseth us from all sin; and in the eighth verse, as saying, that if we suppose ourselves to be cleansed from all sin, we deceive ourselves, thus flatly contradicting what he had just said. And in the ninth verse he goes on to say, that "He is faithful and just to forgive us our sins, and to cleanse us from all unrighteousness;" that is, the blood of Jesus cleanseth us from all sin; but if we say it does, we deceive ourselves. "But if we confess our sins, he is faithful and just to forgive us our sins, and to cleanse us from all unrighteousness." Now, all unrighteousness is sin. If we are cleansed from all unrighteousness, we are cleansed from sin. And now suppose a man should confess his sin, and God should in faithfulness and justice forgive his sin, and cleanse him from all unrighteousness, and then he should confess and profess that God had done this; are we to understand, that

the apostle would then affirm that he deceives himself, in supposing that the blood of Jesus Christ cleanseth from all sin? But, as I have already said, I do not understand the apostle as affirming anything in respect to the present moral character of any one, but as speaking of the doctrine of justification.

This then appears to me to be the meaning of the whole passage. If we say that we are not sinners, that is, have no sin to need the blood of Christ; that we have never sinned, and consequently need no Saviour, we deceive ourselves. For we have sinned, and nothing but the blood of Christ cleanseth from sin, or procures our pardon and justification. And now, if we will not deny, but confess that we have sinned, "He is faithful and just to forgive us our sins, and to cleanse us from all unrighteousness." "But if we say we have not sinned, we make Min a liar, and his word is not in us."

These are the principal passages that occur to my mind, and those I believe upon which the principal stress has been laid, by the opposers of this doctrine. And as I do not wish to protract the discussion, I shall omit the examination of other passages.

There are many objections to the doctrine of entire sanctification, besides those derived from the passages of scripture which I have considered. Some of these objections are doubtless honestly felt, and deserve to be considered. I will therefore proceed to notice such of them as now occur to my mind.

1. It is objected, that the doctrine of entire and permanent sanctification in this life, tends to the errors of modern perfectionism. This objection has been urged by some good men, and I doubt not, honestly urged. But still I cannot believe that they have duly considered the matter. It seems to me, that one fact will set aside this objection. It is well known that the Wesleyan Methodists have, as a denomination, from the earliest period of their history, maintained this doctrine in all its length and breadth. Now if such is the tendency of the doctrine, it is passing strange that this tendency has never developed itself in that denomination. So far as I can learn, the Methodists have been in a great measure, if not entirely, exempt from the errors held by modern perfectionists. Perfectionists, as a body, and I believe with very few exceptions, have arisen out of those denominations that deny the doctrine of entire sanctification in this life.

Now the reason of this is obvious to my mind. When professors of religion, who have been all their life subject to bondage, begin to inquire earnestly for deliverance from their sins, they have found neither sympathy nor instruction, in regard to the prospect of getting rid of them in this life. Then they have gone to the Bible, and there found, in almost every part of it, Christ presented as a Saviour from their sins. But when they proclaim this truth, they are at once treated as heretics and fanatics by their brethren, until, being overcome of evil, they fall into censoriousness; and finding the church so decidedly and utterly wrong, in her opposition to this one great important truth, they lose confidence in their ministers and the church, and being influenced by a wrong spirit, Satan takes the advantage of them, and drives them to the extreme of error and delusion. This I believe to be the true history of many of the most pious members of the Calvinistic churches. On the contrary, the Methodists are very much secured against these errors. They are taught that Jesus Christ is a Saviour from all sin in this world. And when they inquire for deliverance, they are pointed to Jesus Christ as a present and all-sufficient Redeemer. Finding sympathy and instruction on this great and agonizing point, their confidence in their ministers and their brethren remains, and they walk quietly with them.

It seems to me impossible that the tendency of this doctrine should be to the peculiar errors of the modern perfectionists, and yet not an instance occur among all the Methodist ministers, or the thousands of their members, for one hundred years.

And here let me say, it is my full conviction, that there are but two ways in which ministers of the present day can prevent members of their churches from becoming perfectionists. One is, to suffer them to live so far from God, that they will not inquire after holiness of heart; and the other is, most fully to inculcate the glorious doctrine of entire consecration; and that it is the high privilege as well as the duty of Christians, to live in a state of entire consecration to God. I have many additional things to say upon the tendency of this doctrine, but at present this must suffice.

By some it is said to be identical with perfectionism; and attempts are made to show in what particulars antinomian perfectionism and our views are the same. On this I remark:--

(1.) It seems to have been a favorite policy of certain controversial writers for a long time, instead of meeting a proposition in the open field of fair and Christian argument, to give it a bad name, and attempt to put it down, not by force of argument, but by showing that it is identical with, or sustains a near relation to Pelagianism, Antinomianism, Calvinism, or some other ism, against which certain classes of minds are deeply prejudiced. In the recent controversy between what are called old and new school divines, who has not witnessed with pain the frequent attempts that have been made to put down the new school divinity, as it is called, by calling it Pelagianism, and quoting certain passages from Pelagius and other writers, to show the identity of sentiment that exists between them.

This is a very unsatisfactory method of attacking or defending any doctrine. There are no doubt, many points of agreement between Pelagius and all truly orthodox divines, and so there are many points of disagreement between them. There are also many points of agreement between modern perfectionists and all evangelical Christians, and so there are many points of disagreement between them and the Christian church in general. That there are some points of agreement between their views and my own, is no doubt true. And that we totally disagree in regard to those points that constitute their great peculiarities is, if I understand them, also true. But did I really agree in all points with Augustine, or Edwards, or Pelagius, or the modern perfectionists, neither the good nor the ill name of any of these would prove my sentiments to be either right or wrong. It would remain, after all, to show that those with whom I agreed were either right or wrong, in order, on the one hand, to establish that for which I contend, or on the other, to overthrow that which I maintain. It is often more convenient to give a doctrine or an argument a bad name, than it is soberly and satisfactorily to reply to it.

(2.) It is not a little curious, that we should be charged with holding the same sentiments with the perfectionists; while yet they seem to be more violently opposed to our views, since they have come to understand them, than almost any other persons whatever. I have been informed by one of their leaders, that he regards me as one of the master-builders of Babylon.

With respect to the modern perfectionists, those who have been acquainted with their writings, know that some of them have gone much farther from the truth than others. Some of their leading men, who commenced with them, and adopted their name, stopped far short of adopting some of their most abominable errors; still maintaining the authority and perpetual obligation of the moral law; and thus have been saved from going into many of the most objectionable and destructive notions of the sect. There are many more points of agreement between that class of perfectionists and the orthodox church, than between the church and any other class of them. And there are still a number of important points of difference, as every one knows who is possessed of correct information upon this subject.

I abhor the practice of denouncing whole classes of men for the errors of some of that name. I am well aware, that there are many of those who are termed perfectionists, who as truly abhor the extremes of error into which many of that name have fallen, as perhaps do any persons living.

2. Another objection is, that persons could not live in this world, if they were entirely sanctified. Strange! Does holiness injure a man? Does perfect conformity to all the laws of life and health, both physical and moral, render it impossible for a man to live? If a man break off from rebellion against God, will it kill him? Does there appear to have been anything in Christ's holiness inconsistent with life and health? The fact is, that this objection is founded in a gross mistake, in regard to what constitutes entire sanctification. It is supposed by those who hold this objection, that this state implies a continual and most intense degree of excitement, and many things which are not at all implied in it. I have thought, that it is rather a glorified than a sanctified state, that most men have before their minds, whenever they consider this subject.

When Christ was upon earth, he was in a sanctified but not in a glorified state. "It is enough for the disciple that he be as his Master." Now, what is there in the moral character of Jesus Christ, as represented in his history, that may not and ought not to be fully copied into the life of every Christian? I speak not of his knowledge, but of his spirit and temper. Ponder well every circumstance of his life that has come down to us, and say, beloved, what is there in it that may not, by the grace of God, be copied into your own? And think you, that a full imitation of him, in all that relates to his moral character, would render it impossible for you to live in the world?

3. Again, it is objected, that should we become entirely, in the sense of permanently, sanctified, we could not know it, and should not be able intelligently to profess it. I answer: All that a sanctified soul needs to know or profess is, that the grace of God in Christ Jesus is sufficient for him, so that he finds it to be true, as Paul did, that he can do all things through Christ who strengtheneth him, and that he does not expect to sin, but that on the contrary, he is enabled through grace "to reckon himself dead indeed unto sin, and alive unto God through Jesus Christ our Lord." A saint may not know that he shall never sin again; he may expect to sin no more, because of his confidence, not in his own resolutions, or strength, or attainments, but simply in the infinite grace and faithfulness of Christ. He may come to look upon, to regard, account, reckon himself, as being dead in deed and in fact unto sin, and as having done with it, and as being alive unto God, and to expect henceforth to live wholly to God, as much as he expects to live at all; and it may be true that he will thus live, without his being able to say that he knows that he is entirely, in the sense

of permanently, sanctified. This he need not know, but this he may believe upon the strength of such promises as 1 Thess. v. 23, 24: "And the very God of peace sanctify you wholly: and I pray God your whole spirit, and soul, and body, be preserved blameless unto the coming of our Lord Jesus Christ. Faithful is he that calleth you, who also will do it." It is also true, that a Christian may attain a state in which he will really fall no more into sin, as a matter of fact, while, at the same time, he may not be able to express even a thorough persuasion that he shall never fall again. All he may be able intelligently to say is: "God knoweth I hope to sin no more, but the event will show. May the Lord keep me; I trust that he will."

4. Another objection is, that the doctrine tends to spiritual pride. And is it true, indeed, that to become perfectly humble tends to pride? But entire humility is implied in entire sanctification. Is it true, that von must remain in sin, and of course cherish pride, in order to avoid pride? Is your humility more safe in your own hands, and are you more secure against spiritual pride, in refusing to receive Christ as your helper, than you would be in at once embracing him as a full Saviour?

I have seen several remarks in the papers of late, and have heard several suggestions from various quarters, which have but increased the fear which I have for sonic time entertained, that multitudes of Christians, and indeed many ministers, have radically defective views of salvation by faith in Jesus Christ. To the doctrine of entire sanctification in this life, as believed and taught by some of us, it has been frequently of late objected, that prayers offered in accordance with this belief, and by a sanctified soul, would savor strongly of spiritual pride and self-righteousness. I have seen this objection stated in its full force of late, in a religious periodical, in the form of a supposed prayer of a sanctified soul, the object of which was manifestly to expose the shocking absurdity, self-righteousness, and spiritual pride, of a prayer, or rather thanksgiving, made in accordance with a belief that one is entirely sanctified. Now, I must confess, that that prayer, together with objections and remarks which suggest the same idea, have created in my mind no small degree of alarm. I fear much that many of our divines, in contending for the doctrines of grace, have entirely lost sight of the meaning of the language they use, and have in reality but very little practical understanding of what is intended by salvation by grace, in opposition to salvation by works. If this is not the case, I know not how to account for their feeling, and for their stating such an objection as this to the doctrine of entire sanctification.

Now, if I understand the doctrine of salvation by grace, both sanctification and justification are wrought by the grace of God, and not by any works or merits of our own, irrespective of the grace of Christ through faith. If this is the real doctrine of the Bible, what earthly objection can there be to our confessing, professing, and thanking God for our sanctification, any more than for our justification? It is true, indeed, that in our justification our own agency is not concerned, while in our sanctification it is. Yet I understand the doctrine of the Bible to be, that both are brought about by grace through faith, and that we should no sooner be sanctified without the grace of Christ, than we should be justified without it. Now, who pretends to deny this? And yet if it is true, of what weight is that class of objections to which I have alluded? These objections manifestly turn upon the idea, no doubt latent and deep seated in the mind, that the real holiness of Christians, in whatever degree it exists, is, in some way, to be ascribed to some goodness originating in themselves, and not in the grace of Christ. But do let me ask, how is it possible that men who entertain, really and practically, right views upon this subject, can by any possibility feel, as if it must be proof conclusive of self-righteousness and Pharisaism, to profess and thank God for sanctification? Is it not understood on all hands, that sanctification is by grace, and that the gospel has made abundant provision for the sanctification of all men? This certainly is admitted by those who have stated this objection. Now, if this is so, which is the most honorable to God, to confess and complain that our sins triumph and gain dominion over us, or to be able truly and honestly to thank him for having given us the victory over our sins? God has said, "Sin shall not have dominion over you, for ye are not under the law, but under grace."

Now, in view of this and multitudes of kindred promises, suppose we come to God, and say: "O Lord, thou hast made these great and precious promises, but, as a matter of fact, they do not accord with our own experience. For sin does continually have dominion over us. Thy grace is not sufficient for us. We are continually overcome by temptation, notwithstanding thy promise, that in every temptation thou wilt make a way for us to escape. Thou hast said, the truth shall make us free, but we are not free. We are still the slaves of our appetites and lusts."

Now, which, I inquire, is the most honorable to God, to go on with a string of confessions and self-accusations, that are in flat contradiction to the promises of God, and almost, to say the least, a burlesque upon the grace of the gospel, or to be able, through grace, to confess that we have found it true in our own experience, that his grace is sufficient for us--that as our day is so our strength is, and that sin does not have dominion over us, because we are not under the law, but under grace?

To this I know it will be answered, that in this confessing of our sins we do not impeach the grace or faithfulness of God, inasmuch as all these promises are conditioned upon faith, and consequently, that the reason of our remaining in sin is to be ascribed to our unbelief, and is therefore no disparagement to the grace of Christ. But I beg that it may be duly considered, that faith itself is of the operation of God--is itself produced by grace; and therefore the fact of our being obliged to confess our unbelief is a dishonor to the grace of Christ. Is it honorable or dishonorable to God, that we should be able to confess that even our unbelief is overcome, and that we are able to testify from our own experience, that the grace of the gospel is sufficient for our present salvation and sanctification? There is no doubt a vast amount of self-righteousness in the church, which, while it talks of grace, really means nothing by it. For a man to go any farther than to hope that he is converted, seems to many minds to savor of self-righteousness. Now, why is this, unless they themselves entertain self-righteous notions in regard to conversion? Many persons would feel shocked to hear a man in prayer unqualifiedly thank God that he had been converted and justified. And they might just as well feel shocked at this, and upon precisely the same principle, as to feel shocked, if he should unqualifiedly thank God that he had been sanctified by his grace.

But again, I say, that the very fact that a man feels shocked to hear a converted or a sanctified soul unqualifiedly thank God for the grace received, shows that down deep in his heart lies concealed a self-righteous view of the way of salvation, and that in his mind all holiness in Christians is a ground of boasting; and that, if persons have become truly and fully sanctified, they really have a ground of boasting before God. I know not how else to account for this wonderful prejudice. For my own part, I do not conceive it to be the least evidence of self-righteousness, when I hear a man sincerely and heartily thank God for converting and justifying him by his grace. Nor should I feel either shocked, horrified, or disgusted, to hear a man thank God that he had sanctified him wholly by his grace. If in either or both cases I had the corroborative evidence of an apparently holy life, I should bless God, take courage, and feel like calling on all around to glorify God for such an instance of his glorious and excellent grace.

The feeling seems to be very general, that such a prayer or thanksgiving is similar, in fact, and in the principle upon which it rests, with that of the Pharisee noticed by our Saviour. But what reason is there for this assumption? We are expressly informed, that that was the prayer of a Pharisee. But the Pharisees were self-righteous, and expressly and openly rejected the grace of Christ. The Pharisee then boasted of his own righteousness, originated in and consummated by, his own goodness, and not in the grace of Christ. Hence he did not thank God, that the grace of Christ had made him unlike other men. Now, this prayer was designed to teach us the abominable folly of any man's putting in a claim to righteousness and true holiness, irrespective of the grace of God by Jesus Christ. But certainly this is an infinitely different thing from the thanksgiving of a soul, who fully recognizes the grace of Christ, and attributes his sanctification entirely to that grace. And I cannot see how a man, who has entirely divested himself of Pharisaical notions in respect to the doctrine of sanctification, can suppose these two prayers to be analogous in their principle and spirit.

LECTURE XLI - SANCTIFICATION

FURTHER OBJECTIONS ANSWERED

5. Again it is objected, that many who have embraced this doctrine, really are spiritually proud. To this I answer:

(1.) So have many who believed the doctrine of regeneration been deceived and amazingly puffed up with the idea that they have been regenerated when they have not been. But is this a good reason for abandoning the doctrine of regeneration, or any reason why the doctrine should not be preached?

(2.) Let me inquire, whether a simple declaration of what God has done for their souls, has not been assumed as of itself sufficient evidence of spiritual pride, on the part of those who embrace this doctrine, while there was in reality no spiritual pride at all? It seems next to impossible, with the present views of the church, that an individual should really attain this state, and profess to live without known sin in a manner so humble, as not, of course, to be suspected of enormous spiritual pride. This consideration has been a snare to some, who have hesitated and even neglected to declare what God had done for their souls, lest they should be accused of spiritual pride. And this has been a serious injury to their piety.

6. But again it is objected, that this doctrine tends to censoriousness. To this I reply:--

(1.) It is not denied, that some who have professed to believe this doctrine have become censorious. But this no more condemns this doctrine than it condemns that of regeneration: And that it tends to censoriousness, might just as well be urged against every acknowledged doctrine of the Bible, as against this doctrine.

(2.) Let any Christian do his whole duty to the church and the world in their present state, let him speak to them and of them as they really are, and he would of course incur the charge of censoriousness. It is therefore the most unreasonable thing in the world, to suppose that the church in its present state, would not accuse any perfect Christian of censoriousness. Entire sanctification implies the doing of all our duty. But to do all our duty, we must rebuke sin in high places and in low places. Can this be done with all needed severity, without in many cases giving offence, and incurring the charge of censoriousness? No, it is impossible; and to maintain the contrary would be to impeach the wisdom and holiness of Jesus Christ himself.

7. It is objected that the believers in this doctrine lower the standard of holiness to a level with their own experience. To this I reply, that it has been common to set up a false standard, and to overlook the true spirit and meaning of the law, and to represent it as requiring something else than what it does require; but this notion is not confined to those who believe in this doctrine. The moral law requires one and the same thing of all moral agents, namely, that they shall be universally and disinterestedly benevolent; in other words, that

they shall love the Lord their God with all their heart, and their neighbor as themselves. This is all that it does require of any. Whoever has understood the law as requiring less or more than this, has misunderstood it. Love is the fulfilling of the law. But I must refer the reader to what I have said upon this subject when treating of moral government.

The law, as we have seen on a former occasion, levels its claims to us as we are, and a just exposition of it, as I have already said, must take into consideration all the present circumstances of our being. This is indispensable to a right apprehension of what constitutes entire sanctification. There may be, as facts show, danger of misapprehension in regard to the true spirit and meaning of the law, in the sense that, by theorizing and adopting a false philosophy, one may lose sight of the deepest affirmations of his reason, in regard to the true spirit and meaning of the law; and I would humbly inquire, whether the error has not been in giving such an interpretation of the law, as naturally to beget the idea so prevalent, that, if a man should become holy, he could not live in this world? In a letter lately received from a beloved, and useful, and venerated minister of the gospel, while the writer expressed the greatest attachment to the doctrine of entire consecration to God, and said that he preached the same doctrine which we hold to his people every Sabbath, but by another name, still he added, that it was revolting to his feelings to hear any mere man set up the claim of obedience to the law of God. Now let me inquire, why should this be revolting to the feelings of piety? Must it not be because the law of God is supposed to require something of human beings in our state, which it does not and cannot require? Why should such a claim be thought extravagant, unless the claims of the living God be thought extravagant? If the law of God really requires no more of men than what is reasonable and possible, why should it be revolting to any mind to hear an individual profess to have attained to entire obedience? I know that the brother to whom I allude, would be almost the last man deliberately and knowingly to give any strained interpretation to the law of God; and yet, I cannot but feel that much of the difficulty that good men have upon this subject, has arisen out of a comparison of the lives of saints with a standard entirely above that which the law of God does or can demand of persons in all respects in our circumstances, or indeed of any moral agent whatever.

8. Another objection is, that, as a matter of fact, the grace of God is not sufficient to secure the entire sanctification of saints in this life. It is maintained, that the question of the attainability of entire sanctification in this life, resolves itself after all into the question, whether Christians are sanctified in this life? The objectors say, that nothing is sufficient grace that does not, as a matter of fact, secure the faith, and obedience, and perfection of the saints; and therefore that the provisions of the gospel are to be measured by the results; and that the experience of the church decides both the meaning of the promises, and the extent of the provisions of grace. Now to this I answer:--If this objection be good for anything in regard to entire sanctification, it is equally true in regard to the spiritual state of every person in the world. If the fact that men are not perfect, proves that no provision is made for their perfection, their being no better than they are proves, that there is no provision for their being any better than they are, or that they might not have aimed at being any better, with any rational hope of success. But who, except a fatalist, will admit any such conclusion as this? And yet I do not see but this conclusion is inevitable from

such premises. As well might an impenitent sinner urge, that the grace of the gospel is not, as a matter of fact, sufficient for him, because it does not convert him: as well might he resolve everything into the sovereignty of God, and say, the sovereignty of God must convert me, or I shall not be converted; and since I am not converted, it is because the grace of God has not proved itself sufficient to convert me. But who will excuse the sinner, and admit his plea, that the grace and provisions of the gospel are not sufficient for him?

Let ministers urge upon both saints and sinners the claims of God. Let them insist that sinners may, and can, and ought, immediately to become Christians, and that Christians can, and may, and ought to live wholly to God. Let them urge Christians to live without sin, and hold out the same urgency of command, and the same encouragement that the new school holds out to sinners; and we shall soon find that Christians are entering into the liberty of perfect love, as sinners have found pardon and acceptance. Let ministers hold forth the same gospel to all, and insist that the grace of the gospel is as sufficient to save from all sin as from a part of it; and we shall soon see whether the difficulty has not been, that the gospel has been hid and denied, until the churches have been kept weak through unbelief. The church has been taught not to expect the fulfilment of the promises to them; that it is dangerous error to expect the fulfilment to them, for example, of the promise in 1 Thess. v. 23, 24: "And the very God of peace sanctify you wholly; and I pray God your whole spirit, and soul, and body, be preserved blameless unto the coming of our Lord Jesus Christ. Faithful is he that calleth you, who also will do it." When God says he will sanctify us wholly, and preserve us blameless unto the coming of the Lord, masters in Israel tell us that to expect this is dangerous error.

9. Another objection to this doctrine is, that it is contrary to the views of some of the greatest and best men in the church: that such men as Augustine, Calvin, Doddridge, Edwards etc., were of a different opinion. To this I answer:-

(1.) Suppose they were; we are to call no man father, in such a Sense as to yield up to him the determination of our views of Christian doctrine.

(2.) This objection comes with a very ill grace from those who wholly reject the opinions of these divines on some of the most important points of Christian doctrine.

(3.) Those men all held the doctrine of physical moral depravity, which was manifestly the ground of their rejecting the doctrine of entire sanctification in this life. Maintaining, as they seem to have done, that the constitutional susceptibilities of body and mind were sinfully depraved, consistency of course led them to reject the idea, that persons could be entirely sanctified while in the body. Now, I would ask what consistency is there in quoting them as rejecting the doctrine of entire sanctification in this life, while the reason of this rejection in their minds, was founded in the doctrine of physical moral depravity, which notion is entirely denied by those who quote their authority?

10. But again; it is objected, that, if we should attain this state of continual consecration or sanctification, we could not know it until the day of judgment; and that to maintain its attainability is vain, inasmuch as no one can know whether he has attained it or not. To this I reply:--

(1.) A man's consciousness is the highest and best evidence of the present state of his own mind. I understand consciousness to be the mind's recognition of its own existence and exercises, and that it is the highest possible evidence to our own minds of what passes within us. Consciousness can of course testify only to our present sanctification; but,

(2.) With the law of God before us as our standard, the testimony of consciousness, in regard to whether the mind is conformed to that standard or not, is the highest evidence which the mind can have of a present state of conformity to that rule.

(3.) It is a testimony which we cannot doubt, any more than we can doubt our existence. How do we know that we exist? I answer, by our consciousness. How do I know that I breathe, or love, or hate, or sit, or stand, or lie down, or rise up, that I am joyful or sorrowful? In short, that I exercise any emotion, or volition, or affection of mind? How do I know that I sin, or repent, or believe? I answer, by my own consciousness. No testimony can be "so direct and convincing as this."

Now, in order to know that my repentance is genuine, I must know what genuine repentance is. So if I would know whether my love to God and man, or obedience to the law is genuine, I must have clearly before my mind the real spirit, and meaning, and bearing of the law of God. Having the rule before my mind, my own consciousness affords "the most direct and convincing evidence possible," whether my present state of mind is conformed to the rule. The Spirit of God is never employed in testifying to what my consciousness teaches, but in setting in a strong light before my mind the rule to which I am to conform my life. It is his province to make me understand, to induce me to love and obey the truth; and it is the province of consciousness to testify to my own mini whether I do or do not obey the truth, when I apprehend it. When God so presents the truth, as to give the mind assurance, that it understands his mind and will upon any subject, the mind's consciousness of its own state in view of that truth, is "the highest and most direct possible "evidence of whether it obeys or disobeys.

(4.) If a man cannot be conscious of the character of his own supreme or ultimate choice, in which choice his moral character consists, how can he know when, and of what, he is to repent? If he has committed sin of which he is not conscious, how is he to repent of it? And if he has a holiness of which he is not conscious, how could he feel that he has peace with God?

But it is said, that a man may violate the law, not knowing it, and consequently have no consciousness that he sinned, but that, afterwards, a knowledge of the law may convict him of sin. To this I reply, that if there was absolutely no knowledge that the thing in question was wrong, the doing of that thing was not sin, inasmuch as some degree of knowledge of what is right or wrong is indispensable to the moral character of any act. In such a case, there may be a sinful ignorance, which may involve all the guilt of those actions that were done in consequence of it; but that blameworthiness lies in that state of heart that has induced this, and not at all in the violation of the rule of which the mind was, at the time, entirely ignorant.

(5.) The Bible everywhere assumes, that we are able to know, and unqualifiedly requires us to know, what the moral state of our mind is. It commands us to examine ourselves, to know and to prove our own selves. Now, how can this be done, but by bringing our hearts into the light of the law of God, and then taking the testimony of our own consciousness, whether we are, or are not, in a state of conformity to the law? But if we are not to receive the testimony of our own consciousness, in regard to our present sanctification, are we to receive it in respect to our repentance, or any other exercise of our mind whatever? The fact is, that we may deceive ourselves, by neglecting to compare ourselves with the right standard. But when our views of the standard are right, and our consciousness bears witness of a felt, decided, unequivocal state of mind, we cannot be deceived any more than we can be deceived in regard to our own existence.

(6.) But it is said, our consciousness does not teach us what the power and capacities of our minds are, and that therefore if consciousness could teach us in respect to the kind of our exercises, it cannot teach us in regard to their degree, whether they are equal to the present capacity of our mind. To this I reply:--

Consciousness does as unequivocally testify whether we do or do not love God with all our heart, as it does whether we love him at all. How does a man know that he lifts as much as he can, or runs, or walks as fast as he is able? I answer, by his own consciousness. How does he know that he repents or loves with all his heart? I answer, by his own consciousness. This is the only possible way in which he can know it.

The objection implies that God has put within our reach no possible means of knowing whether we obey him or not. The Bible does not directly reveal the fact to any man, whether he obeys God or not. It reveals his duty, but does not reveal the fact whether he obeys. It refers for this testimony to his own consciousness. The Spirit of God sets our duty before us, but does not directly reveal to us whether we do it or not; for this would imply that every man is under constant inspiration.

But it is said, the Bible directs our attention to the fact, whether we outwardly obey or disobey, as evidence whether we are in a right state of mind or not. But I would inquire, How do we know whether we obey or disobey? How do we know anything of our conduct but by our consciousness? Our conduct, as observed by others, is to them evidence of the state of our hearts. But, I repeat it, our consciousness of obedience to God is to us the highest, and indeed the only, evidence of our true character.

If a man's own consciousness is not to be a witness, either for or against him, other testimony can never satisfy him of the propriety of God's dealing with him in the final judgment. There are cases of common occurrence, where the witnesses testify to the guilt or innocence of a man, contrary to the testimony of his own consciousness. In all such cases, from the very laws of his being, he rejects all other testimony: and let me add, that he would reject the testimony of God, and from the very laws of his being must reject it, if it contradicted his own consciousness. When God convicts a man of sin, it is not by contradicting his consciousness; but by placing the consciousness which he had at the time, in the clear strong light of his memory, causing him to discover clearly, and to remember distinctly what light he had, what thoughts, what convictions, what intention or design; in other words, what consciousness he had at the time. And this, let me add, is the way, and the only way, in which the Spirit of God can convict a man of sin, thus bringing him to condemn himself. Now, suppose that God should bear testimony against a man, that at such a time he did such a thing, that such and such were all the circumstances of the case; and suppose that at the same time the individual's consciousness unequivocally contradicts him. The testimony of God in this case could not satisfy the man's mind, nor lead him into a state of self-condemnation. The only possible way in which this state of mind could be induced, would be to annihilate his opposing consciousness, and to convict him simply upon the testimony of God.

(7.) Men may overlook what consciousness is. They may mistake the rule of duty, they may confound consciousness with a mere negative state of mind, or that in which a man is not conscious of a state of opposition to the truth. Yet it must forever remain true that, to our own minds, "consciousness must be the highest possible evidence" of what passes within us. And if a man does not by his own consciousness know whether he does the best that he can, under the circumstances--whether he has a single eye to the glory of God--and whether he is in a state of entire consecration to God--he cannot know it in any way whatever. And no testimony whatever, either of God or man, could, according to the laws of his being, satisfy him either as to conviction of guilt on the one hand, or self-approbation on the other.

(8.) Let me ask, how those who make this objection know that they are not in a sanctified state? Has God revealed it to them? Has he revealed it in the Bible? Does the Bible say to A. B., by name, You are not in a sanctified state? Or does it lay down a rule, in the light of which his own consciousness bears this testimony against him? Has God revealed directly by his Spirit, that he is not in a sanctified state, or does he hold the rule of duty strongly before the mind, and thus awaken the testimony of consciousness that he is not in this state? Now just in the same way consciousness testifies of those that are sanctified, that they are in this state. Neither the Bible nor the Spirit of God makes any new or particular revelation to them by name. But the Spirit of God bears witness to their spirits by setting the rule in a strong light before them. He induces that state of mind which conscience pronounces to be conformity to the rule. This is as far as possible from setting aside the judgment of God in the case; for conscience, under these circumstances, is the testimony of God, and the way in which he convinces of sin on the one hand, and of entire consecration on the other; and the decision of conscience is given to us in consciousness.

By some it is still objected, that consciousness alone is not evidence even to ourselves of our being, or not being, in a state of entire sanctification; that the judgment of the mind is also employed in deciding the true intent and meaning of the law, and is therefore as absolutely a witness in the case as consciousness is. "Consciousness," it is said, "gives us the exercises of our own mind, and the judgment decides whether these exercises are in accordance with the law of God." So then it is the judgment rather than the consciousness, that decides whether we are, or are not, in a state of entire sanctification; and therefore if, in our judgment of the law, we happen to be mistaken, than which nothing is more common, in such case we are utterly deceived if we think ourselves in a state of entire sanctification. To this I answer;--

It is indeed our judgment that decides upon the intent and meaning of the law. We may be mistaken in regard to its true application in certain cases, as it respects outward conduct, but let it be remembered, that neither sin nor holiness is to be found in the outward act. They both belong only to the ultimate intention. No man, as was formerly shown, can mistake his real duty. Every one knows, and cannot but know, that disinterested benevolence is his duty. This is, and nothing else is, his duty. This he can know, and about this he need not mistake. And sure it is, that if man can be certain of anything, he can be certain in respect to the end for which he lives, or in respect to his supreme ultimate intention.

I deny that it is the judgment which is to us the witness, in respect to the state of our own minds. There are several powers of the mind called into exercise, in deciding upon the meaning of, and in obeying, the law of God; but it is consciousness, alone that gives us these exercises. Nothing but consciousness can possibly give us any exercise of our own minds; that is, we have no knowledge of any exercise but by our own consciousness. Suppose then the judgment is exercised, the will is exercised, and all the involuntary powers are exercised. These exercises are revealed to us only and simply by consciousness; so that it remains an invariable truth, that consciousness is to us the only possible witness of what our exercises are, and consequently of the state of our own minds. When, therefore, I say, that by consciousness a man may know whether he is in a state of sanctification, I mean, that consciousness is the real and only evidence that we can have of being in this state.

This objection is based upon a misapprehension of that which constitutes entire or continued sanctification. It consists, as has been shown, in abiding consecration to God, and not as the objection assumes, in involuntary affections and feelings. When it is considered, that entire sanctification consists in an abiding good will to God and to being in general, in living to one end, what real impossibility can there be in knowing whether we are supremely devoted to this end, or supremely devoted to our own interest?

11. Again, it is objected, that if this state were attained in this life, it would be the end of our probation. To this I reply, that probation since the fall of Adam, or those points on which we are in a state of probation or trial, are--

(1.) Whether we will repent and believe the gospel.

(2.) Whether we will persevere in holiness to the end of life.

Some suppose, that the doctrine of the perseverance of the saints sets aside the idea of being at all in a state of probation after conversion. They reason thus: If it is certain that the saints will persevere, then their probation is ended; because the question is already settled, not only that they are converted, but that they will persevere to the end; and the contingency, in regard to the event, is indispensable to the idea of probation. To this I reply, that a thing may be contingent with man that is not at all so with God. With God, there is not, and never was any contingency, in the sense of uncertainty, with regard to the final destiny of any being. But with men almost all things are contingent. God knows with absolute certainty whether a man will be converted, and whether he will persevere. A man may know that he is converted, and may believe that by the grace of God he shall persevere. He may have an assurance of this in proportion to the strength of his faith. But the knowledge of this fact is not at all inconsistent with his idea of his continuance in a state of trial till the day of his death, inasmuch as his perseverance depends upon the exercise of his own voluntary agency; and also, because his perseverance is the condition of his final salvation.

In the same way some say, that if we have attained a state of entire or permanent sanctification, we can no longer be in a state of probation. I answer, that perseverance in this depends upon the promises and grace of God, just as the final perseverance of the saints does. In neither case can we have any other assurance of our perseverance, than that of faith in the promise and grace of God; nor any other knowledge that we shall continue in this state, than that which arises out of a belief in the testimony of God, that he will preserve us blameless until the coming of our Lord Jesus Christ. If this be inconsistent with our probation, I see not why the doctrine of the saint's perseverance is not equally inconsistent with it. If any one is disposed to maintain, that for us to have any judgment or belief grounded on the promises of God, in regard to our final perseverance, is inconsistent with a state of probation, all I can say is, that his views of probation are very different from my own, arid so far as I understand, from those of the church of God.

Again: there is a very high and important sense in which every moral being will remain on probation to all eternity. While under the moral government of God, obedience must for ever remain a condition of the favor of God. And continued obedience will for ever depend on the faithfulness and grace of God; and the only confidence we can ever have, either in heaven, or on earth, that we shall continue to obey, must be founded upon the faithfulness and truth of God.

Again: if it were true, that entering upon a state of permanent sanctification in this life, were, in some sense, an end of our probation, that would be no objection to the doctrine; for there is a sense in which probation often ends long before the termination of this life. Where, for example, for any cause God has left sinners to fill up the measure of their iniquity, withdrawing forever his Holy Spirit from them, and sealing them over to eternal death: this, in a very important sense, is the end of their probation, and they are as sure of hell as if they were already there. So on the other hand, when a person has received, after believing, the sealing of the Spirit unto the day of redemption, as an earnest of his inheritance, he may regard, and is bound to regard this as a solemn pledge on the part of God, of his final perseverance and salvation, and as no longer leaving the final question of his destiny in doubt.

Now it should be remembered, that in both these cases the result depends upon the exercise of the agency of the creature. In the case of the sinner given up of God, it is certain that he will not repent, though his impenitence is voluntary, and by no means a thing naturally necessary. So, on the other hand, the perseverance of the saints is certain, though not necessary. If in either case there should be a radical change of character, the result would differ accordingly.

12. Again: while it is admitted by some, that entire sanctification in this life is attainable, yet it is denied, that there is any certainty that it will be attained by any one before death; for it is said, that as all the promises of entire sanctification are conditioned upon faith, they therefore secure the entire sanctification of no one. To this I reply, that all the promises of salvation in the Bible are conditioned upon faith and repentance; and therefore it does not follow on this principle, that any person ever will be saved. What does all this arguing prove? The fact is, that while the promises of both salvation and sanctification, are conditioned upon faith, yet the promises that God will convert and sanctify the elect, spirit, soul and body, and preserve and save them, must be fulfilled, and will be fulfilled, by free grace drawing and securing the concurrence of freewill. With respect to the salvation of sinners, it is promised that Christ shall have a seed to serve him, and the Bible abounds with promises to Christ that secure the salvation of great multitudes of sinners. So the promises, that the church, as a body, at some period of her earthly history, shall be entirely sanctified, are, as it regards the church, unconditional, in the sense that they will assuredly be accomplished. But, as I have already

shown, as it respects individuals, the fulfilment of these promises must depend upon the exercise of faith. Both in respect to the salvation of sinners and the sanctification of Christians, God is abundantly pledged to bring about the salvation of the one and the sanctification of the other, to the extent of his promise to Christ.

13. It is also objected, that the sanctification of the saints depends upon the sovereignty of God. To this I reply, that both the sanctification of the saints and the conversion of sinners is, in some sense dependent upon the sovereign grace of God. But who except an antinomian would, for this reason, hesitate to urge it upon sinners to repent immediately and believe the gospel? Would any one think of objecting to the doctrine or the fact of repentance, that repentance and the conversion of sinners were dependent upon the sovereignty of God? And yet, if the sovereignty of God can be justly urged as a bar to the doctrine of entire sanctification, it may, for aught I see, with equal propriety be urged as a bar to the doctrine and fact of repentance. We have no controversy with any one upon the subject of entire sanctification, who will as fully and as firmly hold out the duty and the possibility, and the practical attainability, of entire sanctification, as of repentance and salvation. Let them both be put where the Bible puts them, upon the same ground, so far as the duty and the practicability of both are concerned. Suppose any one should assert, that it were irrational and dangerous for sinners to hope or expect to be converted, and sanctified, and saved, because all this depends upon the sovereignty of God, and they do not know what God will do. Who would say this? But why not as well say it, as make the objection to sanctification which we are now considering?

LECTURE XLII - SANCTIFICATION

REMARKS

1. There is an importance to be attached to the sanctification of the body, of which very few persons appear to be aware. Indeed, unless the bodily appetites and powers be consecrated to the service of God--unless we learn to eat, and drink, and sleep, and wake, and labor, and rest, for the glory of God, permanent sanctification as a practical thing is out of the question. It is plain, that very few persons are aware of the great influence which their bodies have over their minds, and of the indispensable necessity of bringing their bodies under, and keeping them in subjection.

Few people seem to keep the fact steadily in view, that unless their bodies be rightly managed, they will be so fierce and overpowering a source of temptation to the mind, as inevitably to lead it into sin. If they indulge themselves in a stimulating diet, and in the use of those condiments that irritate and rasp the nervous system, their bodies will be, of course and of necessity, the source of powerful and incessant temptation to evil tempers and vile affections. If persons were aware of the great influence which the body has over the mind, they would realize, that they cannot be too careful to preserve the nervous system from the influence of every improper article of food or drink, and preserve that system as they would the apple of their eye, from every influence that could impair its functions. No one who has opportunity to acquire information in regard to the laws of life and health, and the best means of sanctifying the whole spirit, soul, and body, can be guiltless if he, neglects these means of knowledge. Every man is bound to make the structure and laws of both body and mind the subject of as thorough investigation as his circumstances will permit, to inform himself in regard to what are the true principles of perfect temperance, and in what way the most can be made of all his powers of body and mind for the glory of God.

2. From what has been said in these lectures, the reason why the church has not been entirely sanctified is very obvious. As a body the church has not believed that such a state was attainable until near the close of life. And this is a sufficient reason, and indeed the most weighty of all reasons, for her not having attained it.

3. From what has been said, it is easy to see, that the true question in regard to entire sanctification in this life is: Is it attainable as a matter of fact? Some have thought the proper question to be: Are Christians entirely sanctified in this life? Now certainly this is not the question that needs to be discussed. Suppose it to be fully granted that they are not; this fact is sufficiently accounted for, by the consideration that they do not know or believe it to be attainable until the close of life. If they believed it to be attainable, it might no longer he true that they do not attain it. But if provision really is made for this attainment, it amounts to nothing, unless it be recognized and believed. The

thing needed then is, to bring the church to see and believe, that this is her high privilege and her duty. It is not enough, as has been shown, to say that it is attainable, simply on the ground of natural ability. This is as true of the devil, and the lost in hell, as of men in this world. Bat unless grace has put this attainment so within our reach, as that it may be aimed at with the reasonable prospect of success, there is, as a matter of fact, no more provision for our entire sanctification in this life, than for the devil's. As has been said, it seems to be trifling with mankind, merely to maintain the attainability of this state, on the ground of natural ability only, and at the same time to tell them, that they certainly never will exercise this ability unless disposed to do so by the grace of God; and furthermore, that it is a dangerous error for us to expect to receive grace from God to secure this result; that we might by natural possibility make this attainment, but it is irrational and dangerous error to expect or hope to make it, or hope to receive sufficient grace to secure it.

The real question is, Has grace brought this attainment so within our reach, that we may reasonably expect, by aiming at it, to experience it in this life? It is admitted, that on the ground of natural ability, both wicked men and devils have the power to be entirely holy. But it is also admitted that their indisposition to use this power aright is so complete, that as a matter of fact, they never will, unless influenced to do so by the grace of God. I insist therefore that the real question is, whether the provisions of the gospel are such, that did the church fully understand and lay hold upon the proffered grace, she might attain this state? Are we as fully authorized to offer this grace to Christians, as we are the grace of repentance and pardon to sinners? May we as consistently urge Christians to lay hold on sanctifying grace sufficient to keep them from all sin, as to urge sinners to lay hold of Christ for justification? May we insist upon the one as really and as honestly as the other?

4. We see how irrelevant and absurd the objection is, that as a matter of fact the church has not attained this state, and therefore it is not attainable. Why, if they have not understood it to be attainable, it no more disproves its attainableness, than the fact that the heathen have not embraced the gospel, proves that they will not when they know it. Within my memory it was thought to be dangerous to call sinners to repent and believe the gospel; and on the contrary, they were told by Calvinists, that they could not repent, that they must wait God's time; and it was regarded as a dangerous error for a sinner to think that he could repent. But who does not know, that the thorough inculcation of an opposite doctrine has brought scores of thousands to repentance? Now the same course needs to be pursued with Christians. Instead of being told, that it is dangerous to expect to be entirely sanctified in this life, they ought to be taught to believe at once, and take hold on the promises of perfect love and faith.

5. You see the necessity of fully preaching and insisting upon this doctrine, and of calling it by its true scriptural name. It is astonishing to see to what an extent there is a tendency among men to avoid the use of scriptural language, and to cleave to the language of such men as Edwards, and other great and good divines. They object to the terms perfection and entire sanctification, and prefer to use the terms entire consecration, and such other terms as have been common in the church.

Now, I would by no means contend about the use of words; but still it does appear to me to be of great importance, that we use scripture language, and insist upon men being "perfect as their Father in Heaven is perfect," and being "sanctified wholly, body, soul and spirit." This appears to me to be the more important for this reason, that if we use the language to which the church has been accustomed upon this subject, she will, as she has done, misunderstand us, and will not get before her mind that which we really mean. That this is so, is manifest from the fact, that the great mass of the church will express alarm at the use of the terms perfection and entire sanctification, who will neither express nor feel any such alarm, if we speak of entire consecration. This demonstrates, that they do not by any means understand these terms as meaning the same thing. And although I understand them as meaning precisely the same thing, yet I find myself obliged to use the terms perfection and entire sanctification to possess their minds of their real meaning. This is Bible language. It is unobjectionable language. And inasmuch as the church understands entire consecration to mean something less than entire sanctification or Christian perfection, it does seem to me of great importance, that ministers should use a phraseology which will call the attention of the church to the real doctrine of the Bible upon this subject. With great humility, I would submit the question to my beloved brethren in the ministry, whether they are not aware, that Christians have entirely too low an idea of what is implied in entire consecration, and whether it is not useful and best to adopt a phraseology in addressing them, that shall call their attention to the real meaning of the words which they use?

6. Young converts have not been allowed so much as to indulge the thought that they could live even for a day wholly without sin. They have as a general thing no more been taught to expect to live even for a day without sin, than they have been taught to expect immediate translation, soul and body, to heaven. Of course, they have not known that there was any other way than to go on in sin; and however shocking and distressing the necessity has appeared to them, in the ardor of their first love, still they have looked upon it as an unalterable fact, that to be in a great measure in bondage to sin is a thing of course while they live in this world. Now, with such an orthodoxy as this, with the conviction in the church and ministry so ripe, settled and universal, that the utmost that the grace of God can do for men in this world is to bring them to, repentance, and to leave them to live and die in a state of sinning and repenting, is it at all wonderful, that the state of religion should be as it really has been?

In looking over the results to Christians, of preaching the doctrine in question, I feel compelled to say, that so far as all observation can go, I have the same evidence that it is truth, and as such is owned and blessed of God to the elevation of the holiness of Christians, as I have, that those are truths which I have so often preached to sinners, and which have been blessed of God to their conversion. This doctrine seems as naturally calculated to elevate the piety of Christians, and as actually to result in the elevation of their piety, under the blessing of God, as those truths that I have preached to sinners were to their conversion.

7. Christ has been in a great measure lost sight of in some of his most important relations to mankind. He has been known and preached as a pardoning and justifying Saviour; but as an actually indwelling and reigning Saviour in the heart, he has been but little known. I was struck with a remark a few years since, of a brother whom I have from that time greatly loved, who had been for a time in a desponding state of mind, borne down with a great sense of his own vileness, but seeing no way of escape. At an evening meeting

the Lord so revealed himself to him, as entirely to overcome the strength of his body, and his brethren were obliged to carry him home. The next time I saw him, he exclaimed to me with a pathos I shall never forget, "Brother Finney, the church have buried the Saviour." Now it is no doubt true, that the church have become awfully alienated from Christ--have in a great measure lost a knowledge of what he is, and ought to be, to her; and a great many of her members, I have good reason to know, in different parts of the country, are saying with deep and overpowering emotion, "They have taken away my Lord, and I know not where they have laid him."

8. With all her orthodoxy, the church has been for a long time much nearer to Unitarianism than she has imagined. This remark may shock some of my readers, and you may think it savors of censoriousness. But, beloved, I am sure it is said in no such spirit. These are "the words of truth and soberness." So little has been known of Christ, that, if I am not entirely mistaken, there are multitudes in the orthodox churches, who do not know Christ, and who in heart are Unitarians, while in theory they are orthodox. They have never known Christ, in the sense of which I have spoken of him in these lectures.

I have been, for some years, deeply impressed with the fact, that so many professors of religion are coming to the ripe conviction that they never knew Christ. There have been in this place almost continual developments of this fact; and I doubt, whether there is a minister in the land who will present Christ as the gospel presents him, in all the fulness of his official relations to mankind, who will not be struck and agonized with developments that will assure him, that the great mass of professors of religion do not know the Saviour. It has been to my mind a painful and serious question, what I ought to think of the spiritual state of those who know so little of the blessed Jesus. That none of them have been converted, I dare not say. And yet, that they have been converted, I am afraid to say. I would not for the world "quench the smoking flax, or break the bruised reed," or say anything to stumble, or weaken the feeblest lamb of Christ; and yet my heart is sore pained, my soul is sick; my bowels of compassion yearn over the church of the blessed God. O, the dear church of Christ! What does she in her present state know of the gospel-rest, of that "great and perfect peace" which they have whose minds are stayed on God? The church in this place is composed, to a great extent, "of professors of religion from different parts of the world, who have come hither for educational purposes, and from religious considerations. And as I said, I have sometimes been appalled at the disclosures which the Spirit of God has made of the real spiritual state of many who have come here, and were considered by others before they came, and by themselves, as truly converted to God.

9. If I am not mistaken, there is an extensive feeling among Christians and ministers, that much that ought to be known and may be known of the Saviour, is not known. Many are beginning to find that the Saviour is to them "as a root out of a dry ground, having neither form nor comeliness;" that the gospel which they preach or hear is not to them "the power of God unto salvation" from sin; that it is not to them "glad tidings of great joy;" that it is not to them a peace-giving gospel; and many are feeling that if Christ has done for them all that his grace is able to do in this life, the plan of salvation is sadly defective; that Christ is not after all a Saviour suited to their necessities; that the religion which they have is not suited to the world in which they live; that it does not, cannot make them free, but leaves them in a state of perpetual bondage. Their

souls are agonized, and tossed to and fro without a resting-place. Multitudes also are beginning to see, that there are many passages, both in the Old and the New Testament, which they do not understand; that the promises seem to mean much more than they have ever realized; and that the gospel and the plan of salvation, as a whole, must be something very different from that which they have as yet apprehended. There are, if I mistake not, great multitudes all over the country, who are inquiring more earnestly than ever before, after a knowledge of that Jesus who is to save his people from their sins.

10. If the doctrine of these lectures is true, you see the immense importance of preaching it clearly and fully, in revivals of religion. When the hearts of converts are warm with their first love, then is the time to make them fully acquainted with their Saviour, to hold him up in all his offices and relations, so as to break the power of every sin--to lead them to break off forever from all self-dependence, and to receive Christ as a present, perfect, everlasting Saviour, so far as this can possibly be done with their limited experience.

11. Unless this course be taken, their backsliding is inevitable. You might as well expect to roll back the waters of Niagara with your hand, as to stay the tide of their former habitudes of mind, surrounded as they are with temptation, without a deep, and thorough, and experimental acquaintance with the Saviour. And if they are thrown upon their own watchfulness and resources, for strength against temptation, instead of being directed to the Saviour, they are certain to become discouraged, and fall into dismal bondage.

12. But, before I conclude these remarks, I must not omit to notice the indispensable necessity of a willingness to do the will of God, in order rightly to understand this doctrine. If a man is unwilling to give up his sins, to deny himself all ungodliness and every worldly lust, if he is unwilling to be set apart wholly and forever to the service of the Lord, he will either reject this doctrine altogether, or only intellectually admit it, without receiving it into his heart. It is an eminently dangerous state of mind to assent to this, or any other doctrine of the gospel, and not reduce it to practice.

13. Much evil has been done by those who have professedly embraced this doctrine in theory, and rejected it in practice. Their spirit and temper have been such as to lead those who saw them to infer, that the tendency of the doctrine itself was bad. And it is not to be doubted that some who have professed to have experienced the power of this doctrine in their hearts, have greatly disgraced religion, by exhibiting a very different spirit from that of an entirely sanctified one. But why in a Christian land should this be a stumbling block? When the heathen see persons from Christian nations who professedly adopt the Christian system, exhibit on their shores, and in their countries, the spirit which many of them do, they infer that this is the tendency of the Christian religion. To this our missionaries reply, that they are only nominal Christians, only speculative, not real believers. Should thousands of our church members go among them, they would have the same reason to complain; and might reply to the missionaries, these are not only nominal believers, but profess to have experienced the Christian religion in their own hearts. Now what would the missionaries reply? Why, to be sure, that they were professors of religion; but that they really did not know Christ, that they were deceiving themselves with a name to live, while in fact they were dead in trespasses and sins.

It has often been a matter of astonishment to me, that in a Christian land, it should be a stumbling-block to any, that some, or if you please, a majority of those who profess to receive and to have experienced the truth of this doctrine, should exhibit an unchristian spirit. What if the same objection should be brought against the Christian religion; against any and every doctrine of the gospel, that the great majority of all the professed believers and receivers of those doctrines were proud, worldly, selfish, and exhibited anything but a right spirit? This objection might be made with truth to the professed Christian church. But would the conclusiveness of such an objection be admitted in Christian lands? Who does not know the ready answer to all such objections as these, that the doctrines of Christianity do not sanction such conduct, and that it is not the real belief of them that begets any such spirit or conduct; that the Christian religion abhors all these objectionable things. And now suppose it should be replied to this, that a tree is known by its fruits, and that so great a majority of the professors of religion could not exhibit such a spirit, unless it were the tendency of Christianity itself to beget it. Who would not reply to this, that this state of mind and course of conduct of which they complain, is the natural state of man uninfluenced by the gospel of Christ; that, in these instances, on account of unbelief, the gospel has failed to correct what was already wrong, and that it needed not the influence of any corrupt doctrine to produce that state of mind? It appears to me, that these objectors against this doctrine, on account of the fact that some and perhaps many who have professed to receive it, have exhibited a wrong spirit, take it for granted that the doctrine produces this spirit, instead of considering that a wrong spirit is natural to men, and that the difficulty is that through unbelief, the gospel has failed to correct what was before wrong. They reason as if they supposed the human heart needed something to beget within it a bad spirit, and as if they supposed, that a belief in this doctrine had made men wicked; instead of recognizing the fact, that they were before wicked, and that through unbelief the gospel has failed to make them holy.

14. But let it not be understood, that I suppose or admit, that the great mass who have professed to have received this doctrine into their hearts, have exhibited a bad spirit. I must say, that it has been eminently otherwise, so far as my own observation extends. And I am fully convinced, that if I have ever seen Christianity and the spirit of Christ in the world, it has been exhibited by those, as a general thing, who have professed to receive this doctrine into their heart.

15. How amazingly important it is, that the ministry and the church should come fully to a right understanding and embracing of this doctrine. O, it will be like life from the dead! The proclamation of it is now regarded by multitudes as "good tidings of great joy." From every quarter, we get the gladsome intelligence, that souls are entering into the deep rest and peace of the gospel, that they are awaking to a life of faith and love--and that, instead of sinking down into antinomianism, they are eminently more benevolent, active, holy and useful than ever before; that they are eminently more prayerful, watchful, diligent, meek, sober-minded, and heavenly in all their lives. This is the character of those, to a very great extent, at least, with whom I have been acquainted, who have embraced this doctrine, and professed to have experienced its power. I say this for no other reason, than to relieve the anxieties of those who have heard very strange reports, and whose honest fears have been awakened in regard to the tendency of this doctrine.

16. Much pains have been taken to demonstrate, that our views of this subject are wrong. But in all the arguing to this end hitherto, there has been one

grand defect. None of the opponents of this doctrine have yet showed us "a more excellent way, and told us what is right." It is certainly impossible to ascertain what is wrong, on any moral subject, unless we have before us the standard of right. The mind must certainly be acquainted with the rule of right, before it can reasonably pronounce anything wrong; "for by the law is the knowledge of sin." It is therefore certainly absurd, for the opponents of the doctrine of entire sanctification in this life, to pronounce this doctrine wrong without being able to show us what is right. To what purpose, then, I pray, do they argue, who insist upon this view of the subject as wrong, while they do not so much as attempt to tell us what is right? It cannot be pretended, that the scriptures teach nothing upon this subject. And the question is, what do they teach? We therefore call upon the denouncers of this doctrine, and we think the demand reasonable, to inform us definitely, how holy Christians may be, and are expected to be in this life. And it should be distinctly understood, that until they bring forward the rule laid down in the scripture upon this subject, it is but arrogance to pronounce anything wrong; just as if they should pronounce anything to be sin without comparing it with the standard of right. Until they inform us what the scriptures do teach, we must beg leave to be excused from supposing ourselves obliged to believe, that what is taught in these lectures is wrong, or contrary to the language and spirit of inspiration. This is certainly a question that ought not to be thrown loosely aside, without being settled. The thing at which we aim is, to establish a definite rule, or to explain what we suppose to be the real and explicit teachings of the Bible upon this point. And we do think it absurd, that the opponents of this view should attempt to convince us of error, without so much as attempting to show what the truth upon this subject is. As if we could easily enough decide what is contrary to right, without possessing any knowledge of right. We therefore beseech our brethren, in discussing this subject, to show us what is right. And if this is not the truth, to show us a more excellent way, and convince us that we are wrong, by showing us what is right. For we have no hope of ever seeing that we are wrong, until we can see that something else than what is advocated in this discussion, is right.

17. But before I close my remarks upon this subject, I must not fail to state what I regard as the present duty of Christians. It is to hold their will in a state of consecration to God, and to lay hold on the promises for the blessing promised in such passages as 1 Thess. v. 23, 24:--"And the very God of peace sanctify you wholly, and I pray God your whole spirit, and soul, and body, be preserved blameless unto the coming of our Lord Jesus Christ; faithful is he that calleth you, who also will do it." This is present duty. Let them wait on the Lord in faith, for that cleansing of the whole being which they need, to confirm, strengthen, settle them. All they can do, and all that God requires them to do, is to obey him from moment to moment, and to lay hold of him for the blessing of which we have been speaking; and to be assured, that God will bring forth the answer in the best time and in the best manner. If you believe, the anointing that abideth will surely be secured in due time.

LECTURE XLIII - ELECTION

In discussing this subject,

I. I shall notice some points in which there is a general agreement among all denominations of Christians respecting the natural and moral attributes of God.

1. It is agreed that eternity is a natural attribute of God in the sense that he grows no older. He was just as old before the world or universe was made, as he is now, or as he will be at the day of judgment.

2. It is agreed that omniscience is an attribute of God, in the sense that he knows from a necessity of his infinite nature all things that are objects of knowledge.

3. That he has necessarily and eternally possessed this knowledge, so that he never has, and never can have, any accession to his knowledge. Every possible thing that ever was, or will be, or can be an object of knowledge, has been necessarily and eternally known to God. If this were not true, God would be neither infinite nor omniscient.

4. It is agreed also that God exercises an universal providence, embracing all events that ever did or ever will occur in all worlds. Some of these events he secures by his own agency, and others occur under his providence, in the sense that he permits or suffers them to occur rather than interpose to prevent them. They may be truly said to occur under his providence, because his plan of government in some sense embraces them all. He made provision to secure those that are good, that is, the holy intentions of moral agents, and to overrule for good those that are evil, that is, the selfish intentions of moral agents. These intentions are events, and may be said to occur under Divine Providence, because all events that do, or ever will, occur, are and must be foreseen results of God's own agency, or of the work of creation.

5. It is agreed that infinite benevolence is the sum of the moral attributes of God.

6. That God is both naturally and morally immutable; that in his natural attributes he is necessarily so, and in his moral attributes is certainly so.

7. It is agreed that all who are converted, sanctified and saved, are converted, sanctified, and saved by God's own agency; that is, God saves them by securing, by his own agency, their personal and individual holiness.

II. What the Bible doctrine of election is not.

1. The Bible doctrine of election is not that any are chosen to salvation, in such a sense, that they will or can be saved without repentance, faith, and sanctification.

2. Nor is it that some are chosen to salvation, in such a sense, that they will be saved irrespective of their being regenerated, and persevering in holiness to the end of life. The Bible most plainly teaches, that these are naturally indispensable conditions of salvation, and of course election cannot dispense with them.

3. Nor is it that any are chosen to salvation for, or on account of their own foreseen merits, or good works. 2 Tim. i. 9: "Who hath saved us, and called us with a holy calling, not according to our works, but according to his own purpose and grace, which was given us in Christ Jesus before the world began." The foreseen fact, that by the wisest governmental arrangement God could convert and sanctify and fit them for heaven, must have been a condition in the sense of a sine quâ non, of their election to salvation, but could not have been the fundamental reason for it, as we shall see. God did not elect them to salvation, for or on account of their foreseen good works, but upon condition of their foreseen repentance, faith and perseverance.

4. The Bible doctrine of election is not that God elected some to salvation, upon such conditions that it is really uncertain whether they will comply with those conditions, and be finally saved. The Bible does not leave the question of the final salvation of the elect as a matter of real uncertainty. This we shall see in its place. The elect were chosen to salvation, upon condition that God foresaw that he could secure their repentance, faith, and final perseverance.

III. What the Bible doctrine of election is.

It is, that all of Adam's race, who are or ever will be saved, were from eternity chosen by God to eternal salvation, through the sanctification of their hearts by faith in Christ. In other words, they are chosen to salvation by means of sanctification. Their salvation is the end--their sanctification is a means. Both the end and the means are elected, appointed, chosen; the means as really as the end, and for the sake of the end. The election of some individuals and nations to certain privileges, and to do certain things, is not the kind of election of which I treat at this time; but I am to consider the doctrine of election as it respects election unto salvation, as just explained.

IV. I am to prove the doctrine as I have stated it to be true.

1. It is plainly implied in the teaching of the Bible: the Bible everywhere assumes and implies the truth of this doctrine just as might be expected, since it so irresistibly follows from the known and admitted attributes of God. Instead of formally revealing it as a truth unknown to, or unknowable by, the human reason, the scriptures in a great variety of ways speak of the elect, of election, etc., as a truth known by irresistible inference from his known attributes. To deny it involves a denial of the attributes of God. I have been surprised at the labored and learned efforts to show that this doctrine is not expressly taught in the Bible. Suppose it were not, what then? Other truths are taught and reason irresistibly affirms truths, from which the doctrine of election, as I have stated it, must follow. It is common for the inspired writers to treat truths of this class in the same manner in which this is, for the most part, treated. Suppose it were possible so to explain every passage of scripture as that no one of them should unequivocally assert the doctrine in question, this would be to no purpose; the doctrine would still be irresistibly inferrible from the attributes of God. It would still be true, that the Bible assumes the truth of the doctrine, and incidentally speaks of it as a truth of reason, and as following of course from the attributes of God. It is thus treated throughout the entire scriptures. The Bible as really assumes the truth of this doctrine, as it does the existence of God. It asserts it just as it does the attributes of God. The learned and labored efforts to show that this doctrine is not expressly asserted in the Bible, are of no value, since it would follow as a certain truth from the attributes of God, and from the revealed facts, that some will be saved, and that God will save them, even had

the Bible been silent on the subject. I shall therefore only introduce a few passages for the purpose of showing that the inspired writers repeatedly recognize the truth of this doctrine, and thus preserve their own consistency. But I shall not attempt by labored criticism to prove it from scripture, for reasons just mentioned.

Matt. xx. 16: "So the last shall be first, and the first last, for many be called, but few chosen."

Matt. xxiv. 22: "And except those days should be shortened, there should no flesh be saved; but for the elect's sake those days shall be shortened."

John xiii. 18: "I speak not of you all; I know whom I have chosen."

John xv. 16: "Ye have not chosen me, but I have chosen you, and ordained you, that ye should go and bring forth fruit, and that your fruit should remain; that whatsoever ye shall ask of the Father in my name, he may give it you. 19. If ye were of the world, the world would love his own; but because ye are not of the world, but I have chosen you out of the world, therefore the world hateth you."

Rom. viii. 28: "And we know that all things work together for good to them that love God, to them who are the called according to his purpose. 29. For whom he did foreknow, he also did predestinate to be conformed to the image of his Son, that he might be the first-born among many brethren."

Rom. ix. 10: "And not only this, but when Rebecca had conceived by one, even by our father Isaac; 11. (For the children being not yet born, neither having done any good or evil, that the purpose of God according to election might stand, not of works, but of him that calleth.) 12. It was said unto her, The elder shall serve the younger. 13. As it is written, Jacob have I loved, but Esau have I hated. 14. What shall we say then? Is there unrighteousness with God? God forbid. 15. For he saith to Moses, I will have mercy on whom I will have mercy, and I will have compassion on whom I will have compassion."

Rom. xi. 5: "Even so at this present time also there is a remnant according to the election of grace. 7. What then? Israel hath not obtained that which he seeketh for, but the election hath obtained it, and the rest were blinded."

Eph. i. 4: "According as he hath chosen us in him before the foundation of the world, that we should be holy and without blame before him in love. 11. In whom also we have obtained an inheritance, being predestinated according to the purpose of him who worketh all things after the counsel of his own will."

1 Thess. i. 4: "Knowing, brethren beloved, your election of God."

1 Thess. v. 9: "For God hath not appointed us to wrath, but to obtain salvation by our Lord Jesus Christ."

2 Thess. ii. 13: "But we are bound to give thanks alway to God for. you, brethren beloved of the Lord, because God hath from the beginning chosen you to salvation through sanctification of the Spirit, and belief of the truth."

1 Pet. i. 2: "Elect according to the foreknowledge of God the Father, through sanctification of the Spirit, unto obedience and sprinkling of the blood of Jesus Christ."

Rev. xvii. 8: "The beast that thou sawest was, and is not; and shall ascend out of the bottomless pit, and go into perdition: and they that dwell on the earth shall wonder, (whose names were not written in the book of life from the foundation of the world,) when they behold the beast that was, and is not, and yet is." This doctrine is expressly asserted, or indirectly assumed and implied in every part of the Bible, and in ways and instances too numerous to be quoted in these lectures. The above are only specimens of the scripture treatment of this subject.

2. It is plainly the doctrine of reason.

(1.) It is admitted that God by his own agency secures the conversion, sanctification, and salvation of all that ever were or will be saved.

(2.) Whatever volitions or actions God puts forth to convert and save men, he puts forth designing to secure that end; that is, he does it in accordance with a previous design to do as and what he does. This must be an universal truth, to wit, that whatever God does for the salvation of men, he does with the design to secure the salvation of all who ever will be saved, or of all whose salvation he foresees that he can secure, and with the certain knowledge that he shall secure their salvation. He also does much for the non-elect, in the sense of using such means with them as might secure, and ought to secure, their salvation. But as he knows he shall not succeed in securing their salvation, on account of their voluntary and persevering wickedness, it cannot be truly said, that he uses these means with design to save them, but for other, and good, and wise reasons. Although he foresees, that he cannot secure their salvation, because of their wilful and persevering unbelief, yet he sees it important under his government to manifest a readiness to save them, and to use such means as he wisely can to save them, and such as will ultimately be seen to leave them wholly without excuse.

But with respect to those whom he foresees that he can and shall save, it must be true, since he is a good being, that be uses means for their salvation, with the design to save them. And since, as we have seen, he is an omniscient being, he must use these means, not only with a design to save them, but also with the certainty that he shall save them. With respect to them, he uses these means for the sake of this end; that is, for the sake of their salvation.

(3.) But if God ever chooses to save any human beings, he must always have chosen to do so, or else he has changed. If he now has, or ever will have, any design about it, he must always have had this design; for he never has, and never can have, any new design. If he ever does, or will, elect any human being to salvation, he must always have chosen or elected him, or he has, or will form some new purpose, which is inconsistent with his immutability.

(4.) If he will ever know who will be saved, he must always have known it, or he will obtain some new knowledge, which is contrary to his omniscience.

(5.) We are told by Christ, that at the day of judgment he will say to the righteous, "Come, ye blessed of my Father, inherit the kingdom prepared for you from the foundation of the world;" that is, from eternity. Now, has the Judge at that time any new knowledge or design respecting those individuals? Certainly not.

(6.) Since God of necessity eternally knew all about the elect that will ever be true, he must of necessity have chosen something in respect to them; for it is naturally impossible, that he should have had no choice about, or in respect to, them and their salvation.

(7.) Since God must of necessity from eternity have had some choice in respect to their salvation, it follows, that he must have chosen that they should be saved, or that he would not use such means as he foresaw would save them. If he chose not to use those means that he foresaw would save them, but afterwards saves them, he has changed, which is contrary to his immutability. If he always chose that they should be saved, this is the very thing for which we are contending.

(8.) It must therefore be true, that all whom God will ever save were from eternity chosen to salvation by him; and since he saves them by means of sanctification, and does this designedly, it must be that this also was eternally designed or intended by him.

To deny the doctrine of election, therefore, involves a denial of the attributes of God.

(9.) It must also be true, that God foreknew all that ever will be true of the non-elect, and must have eternally had some design respecting their final destiny. And also that he has from eternity had the same, and the only design that he ever will have in respect to them. But this will come up for consideration in its place.

V. What could not have been the reasons for election.

1. It is admitted that God is infinitely benevolent and wise. It must follow that election is founded in some reason or reasons; and that these reasons are good and sufficient; reasons that rendered it obligatory upon God to choose just as he did, in election. Assuming, as we must, that God is wise and good, we are safe in affirming that he could have had none but benevolent reasons for his election of some to eternal life in preference to others. Hence we are bound to affirm, that election was not based upon, nor does it imply partiality in God, in any bad sense of that term. Partiality in any being, consists in preferring one to another without any good or sufficient reason, or in opposition to good and sufficient reasons. It being admitted that God is infinitely wise and good, it follows, that he cannot be partial; that he cannot have elected some to eternal salvation and passed others by, without some good and sufficient reason. That is, he cannot have done it arbitrarily. The great objection that is felt and urged by opposers of this doctrine is, that it implies partiality in God, and represents him as deciding the eternal destiny of moral agents by an arbitrary sovereignty. But this objection is a sheer and altogether unwarrantable assumption. It assumes, that God could have had no good and sufficient reasons for the election. It has been settled, that good is the end upon which God set his heart; that is, the highest well being of himself and the universe of creatures. This end must be accomplished by means. If God is infinitely wise and good, he must have chosen the best practicable means. But he has chosen the best means for that end, and there can be no partiality in that.

In support of the assumption, that election implies partiality, and the exercise of an arbitrary sovereignty in God, it has been affirmed, that there might have been divers systems of means for securing the same end in every respect equal to each other; that is, that no reason existed for preferring any one, to many others; that therefore in choosing the present, God must have been partial, or must have exercised an arbitrary sovereignty. To this I answer:--

(1.) There is no ground for the assumption, that there are or can be divers systems of means of precisely equal value in all respects, in such a sense, that there could have been no good reason for preferring one to the other.

(2.) I reply, that if there were divers such systems, choosing the one, and not any other, would not imply preference. Choice of any one in such case must have proceeded upon the following ground; to wit, the value of the end demanded, that one should be chosen. There being no difference between the various systems of means, God chooses one without reference to the other, and makes no choice respecting it, any more than if it did not exist. He must choose one, he has no reason for preference, and consequently he cannot prefer one to the other. His benevolence leads him to choose one because the end demands it. He therefore takes any one of many exact equals, indifferently, without preferring it to any of the others. This implies no partiality in God in any bad sense of the term. For upon the supposition, he was shut up to the necessity of choosing one among many exact equals. If he is partial in choosing the one he does, he would have been equally so had he chosen any other. If this is partiality, it is a partiality arising out of the necessity of the case, and cannot imply anything objectionable in God.

That there is no preference in this case is plain, because there is no ground or reason for preference whatever, according to the supposition. But there can be no choice or preference, when there is absolutely no reason for the choice or preference. We have seen on a former occasion, that the reason that determines choice, or the reason in view of which, or in obedience to which, or for the sake of which, the mind chooses, and the object or end chosen, are identical. When there is absolutely no reason for a choice, there is absolutely no object of choice, nothing to choose, and of course there can be no choice. Choice must have an object; that is, choice must terminate upon something. If choice exists, something must be chosen. If there are divers systems of means, between which there is no possible ground of preference, there can absolutely be no such thing as preferring one to the other, for this would be the same as to choose without any object of choice, or without choosing anything, which is a contradiction.

If it be said, that there may be absolutely no difference in the system of means, so far as the accomplishment of the end is concerned, but that one may be preferred or preferable to another, on some other account, I ask on what other account? According to the supposition, it is only valued or regarded as an object of choice at all, because of its relation to the end. God can absolutely choose it only as a means, a condition, or an end; for all choice must respect these. The inquiry now respects means. Now, if as a means, there is absolutely no difference between diverse systems in their relation to the end, and the value of the end is the sole reason for choosing them, it follows, that to prefer one to another is a natural impossibility. But one must be chosen for the sake of the end, it matters not which; any one is taken indifferently so far as others are concerned. This is no partiality, and no exercise of arbitrary sovereignty in any objectionable sense.

But as I said, there is no ground for the assumption, that there are various systems of means for accomplishing the great end of benevolence in all respects equal. There must have been a best way, a best system, and if God is infinitely wise and good, he must have chosen that for that reason; and this is as far as possible from partiality. Neither we, nor any other creature may be able now to discover any good reasons for preferring the present to any other system, or for electing those who are elected, in preference to any other. Nevertheless, such reasons must have been apparent to the Divine mind, or no such election could have taken place.

2. Election was not an exercise of arbitrary sovereignty. By arbitrary sovereignty is intended the choosing and acting from mere will, without consulting moral obligation or the public good. It is admitted that God is infinitely wise and good. It is therefore impossible that he should choose or act

arbitrarily in any case whatever. He must have good and sufficient reasons for every choice and every act.

Some seem to have represented God, in the purpose or act of election, as electing some and not others, merely because he could or would, or in other words, to exhibit his own sovereignty, without any other reasons than because so he would have it. But it is impossible for God to act arbitrarily, or from any but a good and sufficient reason; that is, it is impossible for him to do so, and continue to be benevolent. We have said that God has one, and but one end in view; that is, he does, and says, and suffers all for one and the same reason, namely, to promote the highest good of being. He has but one ultimate end, and all his volitions are only efforts to secure that end. The highest well being of the universe, including his own, is the end on which his supreme and ultimate choice terminates. All his volitions are designed to secure this end, and in all things he is and must be directed by his infinite intelligence, in respect not only to his ultimate end, but also in the choice and use of the means of accomplishing this end. It is impossible that this should not be true, if he is good. In election then he cannot possibly have exercised any arbitrary sovereignty, but must have had the best of reasons for the election. His intelligence must have had good reasons for the choice of some and not of others to salvation, and have affirmed his obligation in view of those reasons to elect just as and whom he did. So good must the reasons have been, that to have done otherwise, would have been sin in him; that is, to have done otherwise would not have been wise and good.

3. Election was not based on a foreseen difference in the moral character of the elect and the non-elect, previous to regeneration. The Bible everywhere affirms, that, previous to regeneration, all men have precisely the same character, and possess one common heart or disposition, that this character is that of total moral depravity. God did not choose some to salvation because he foresaw that they would be less depraved and guilty, previous to regeneration, than the non-elect. Paul was one of the elect, yet he affirms himself to have been the chief of sinners. We often see, and this has been common in every age, the most outwardly abandoned and profligate converted and saved.

The reason of election is not found in the fact, that God foresaw that some would be more readily converted than others. We often see those who are converted hold out for a long time in great obstinacy and rebellion, while God brings to bear upon them a great variety of means and influences, and takes much more apparent pains to convert them than he does to convert many others who are, as well as those who are not, converted. There is reason to believe, that if the same means were used with those who are not converted that are used with those who are, many who are not converted would be. It may not be wise in God to use the same means for the non-elect, and if he should, they might, or might not be saved by them. God often uses means that to us seem more powerful to convert the non-elect than are used to convert many of the elect. This is fully implied in Matt. xi. 20-24. The fact is, he must have some reason aside from their characters for stubbornness or otherwise, for electing them to salvation.

VI. What must have been the reasons for election.

1. We have seen that God is infinitely wise and good. From the wisdom and goodness of God, it follows, that he must have chosen some good end, and must have had some plan, or system of means, to secure it. The end, we know,

is the good of being. The means, we know from reason and revelation, include election in the sense explained. It follows, that the fundamental reason for election was the highest good of the universe. That is, the best system of means for securing the great end of benevolence, included the election of just those who were elected, and no others. This has been done by the wisdom and benevolence of God. It follows, that the highest good demanded it. All choice must respect ends, or conditions and means. God has, and can have, but one ultimate end. All other choices or volitions must respect means. The choice or election of certain persons to eternal salvation, etc., must have been founded in the reason, that the great end of benevolence demanded it.

2. It is very easy to see, that under a moral government, it might be impossible so to administer law, as to secure the perpetual and universal obedience of all.

It is also easy to see, that under a remedial system, or system of grace, it might be impossible to secure the repentance and salvation of all. God must have foreseen all possible and actual results. He must have foreseen how many, and whom he could save by the wisest and best possible arrangement, all things considered. The perfect wisdom and benevolence of God being granted, it follows, that we are bound to regard the present system of means as the best, all things considered, that he could adopt for the promotion of the great end of his government, or the great end of benevolence. The fact, that the wisest and best system of government would secure the salvation of those who are elected, must have been a condition of their being elected. As God does everything for the same ultimate reason, it follows, that the intrinsic value of their salvation was his ultimate end, and that their salvation in particular must have been of greater relative value in promoting the highest good of the universe at large, and the glory of God, than would have been that of others; so that the intrinsic value of the salvation of those elected in particular, the fact that by the wisest arrangement he could save them in particular, and the paramount good to be promoted by it, must have been the reasons for election.

VII. When the election was made.

1. Not when the elect are converted. It is admitted, that God is omniscient, and has known all things from eternity as really and as perfectly as he ever will. It is also admitted, that God is unchangeable, and consequently has no new plans, designs, or choices. He must have had all the reasons he ever will have for election, from eternity, because he always has had all the knowledge of all events that he ever will have; consequently he always or from eternity chose in respect to all events just as he always will. There never can be any reason for change in the Divine mind, for he never will have any new views of any subject. The choice which constitutes election, then, must be an eternal choice.

2. Thus the scriptures represent it.

Eph. i. 4: "According as he hath chosen us in him before the foundation of the world, that we should be holy and without blame before him in love."

Eph. ii. 10: "For we are his workmanship, created in Christ Jesus unto good works, which God hath before ordained that we should walk in them."

2 Tim. i. 9: "Who hath saved us, and called us with a holy calling; not according to our works, but according to his own purpose and grace, which was given us in Christ Jesus before the world began."

Rev. xvii. 8: "The beast that thou sawest was, and is not, and shall ascend out of the bottomless pit, and go into perdition: and they that dwell on the earth shall wonder, (whose names were not written in the book of life from the foundation of the world,) when they behold the beast that was, and is not, and yet is."

This language means from eternity, beyond question.

3. But the question will arise, was election in the order of nature subsequent to, or did it precede the Divine foreknowledge. The answer to this plainly is, that in the order of nature what could be wisely done must have been foreseen before it was determined what should be done. And what should be done must, in the order of nature, have preceded the knowledge of what would be done. So that in the order of nature, foreknowledge of what could be wisely done preceded election, and foreknowledge of what would be done, followed or was subsequent to election. [4] In other words, God must have known whom he could wisely save, prior, in the order of nature, to his determination to save them. But his knowing who would be saved must have been, in the order of nature, subsequent to his election or determination to save them, and dependent upon that determination.

VIII. Election does not render means for the salvation of the elect unnecessary.

We have seen that the elect are chosen to salvation through the use of means. Since they are chosen to be saved by means, they cannot be saved in any other way or without them.

IX. Election is the only ground of hope in the success of means.

1. No means are of any avail unless God gives them efficiency.

2. If God gives them efficiency in any case, it is, and will be, in accordance with, and in execution of, his election.

3. It follows that election is the only ground of rational hope in the use of means to effect the salvation of any.

X. Election does not oppose any obstacle to the salvation of the non-elect.

1. God has taken care to bring salvation within the reach of all, and to make it possible to all.

2. He sincerely offers to save all, and does all to save all that he wisely can.

3. His saving some is no discouragement to others, but should rather encourage them to lay hold on eternal life.

4. The election of some is no bar to the salvation of others.

5. Those who are not elected may be saved, if they will but comply with the conditions, which they are able to do.

6. God sincerely calls, and ministers may sincerely call on the non elect to lay hold on salvation.

7. There is no injury or injustice done to the non-elect by the election of others. Has not God "a right to do what he will with his own?" If he offers salvation to all upon terms the most reasonable, and if he does all he wisely can for the salvation of all, shall some complain if God, in doing for all what be wisely can, secures the salvation of some and not of others?

XI. There is no injustice in election.

God was under obligation to no one--he might in perfect justice have sent all mankind to hell. The doctrine of election will damn no one: by treating the non-elect according to their deserts, he does them no injustice; and surely his exercising grace in the salvation of the elect, is no act of injustice to the non-elect; and especially will this appear to be true, if we take into consideration the fact, that the only reason why the non-elect will not be saved is, because they pertinaciously refuse salvation. He offers mercy to all. The atonement is sufficient for all. All may come, and are under an obligation to be saved. He strongly desires their salvation, and does all that he wisely can to save them. Why then should the doctrine of election be thought unjust? [5]

XII. This is the best that could be done for the inhabitants of this world.

It is reasonable to infer from the infinite benevolence of God, that his present government will secure a greater amount of good than could have been secured under any other mode of administration. This is as certain as that infinite benevolence must prefer a greater to a less good. To suppose that God would prefer a mode of administration that would secure a less good than could have been secured under some other mode, would manifestly be to accuse him of a want of benevolence. It is doubtless true that he could so vary the course of events as to save other individuals than those he does; to convert more in one particular neighborhood, or family, or nation, or at one particular time; or it may be a greater number upon the whole than he does. It would not follow that he does not secure the greater good upon the whole.

Suppose there is a man in this town, who has so strongly in trenched himself in error, that there is but one man in all the land who is so acquainted with his refuge of lies as to be able to answer his objections, and drive him from his hiding-places. Now, it is possible, that if this individual could be brought in contact with him, he might be converted; yet if he is employed in some distant part of the vineyard, his removal from that field of labor to this town, might not, upon the whole, be most for the glory of God's kingdom; and more might fail of salvation through his removal here, than would be converted by such removal. God has in view the good of his whole kingdom. He works upon a vast and comprehensive scale. He has no partialities for individuals, but moves forward in the administration of his government with his eye upon the general good, designing to secure the greatest amount of happiness within his kingdom that can be secured by the wisest possible arrangement, and administration of his government.

XIII. How we may ascertain our own election.

Those of the elect that are already converted, are known by their character and conduct. They have evidence of their election in their obedience to God. Those that are unconverted may settle the question each one for himself, whether he is elected or not, so as to have the most satisfactory evidence whether he is of that happy number. If you will now submit yourselves to God, you may have evidence that you are elected. But every hour you put off submission, increases the evidence that you are not elected.

Every sinner under the gospel has it within his power to accept or reject salvation. The elect can know their election only by accepting the offered gift. The non-elect can know their non-election only by the consciousness of a voluntary rejection of offered life. If any one fears that he is one of the non-elect, let him at once renounce his unbelief, and, cease to reject salvation, and the ground of fear and complaint instantly falls away.

INFERENCES AND REMARKS.

1. Foreknowledge and election are not inconsistent with free agency. The elect were chosen to eternal life, upon condition that God foresaw that in the perfect exercise of their freedom, they could be induced to repent and embrace the gospel.

2. You see why many persons are opposed to the doctrine of election, and try to explain it away; 1st., they misunderstand it, and 2nd, they deduce unwarrantable inferences from it. They suppose it to mean, that the elect will be saved at all events, whatever their conduct may be; and again, they infer from the doctrine that there is no possibility of the salvation of the non-elect. The doctrine, as they understand it, would be an encouragement to the elect to persevere in sin, knowing that their salvation was sure, and their inference would drive the non-elect to desperation, on the ground that for them to make efforts to be saved would be of no avail. But both the doctrine, as they understand it, and the inference, are false. For election does not secure the salvation of the elect irrespective of their character and conduct; nor, as we have seen, does it throw any obstacle in the way of the salvation of the non-elect.

3. This view of the subject affords no ground for presumption on the one hand, nor for despair upon the other. No one can justly say, If I am to be saved I shall be saved, do what I will. Nor can any one say, If I am to be damned I shall be damned, do what I will. But the question is left, so far as they are concerned, as a matter of entire contingency. Sinners, your salvation or damnation is as absolutely suspended upon your own choice, as if God neither knew nor designed anything about it.

4. This doctrine lays no foundation for a controversy with God. But on the other hand, it does lay a broad foundation for gratitude, both on the part of the elect and non-elect. The elect certainly have great reason for thankfulness, that they are thus distinguished. Oh, what a thought, to have your name written in the book of life, to be chosen of God an heir of eternal salvation, to be adopted into his family, to be destined to enjoy his presence, and to bathe your soul in the boundless ocean of his love for ever and ever! Nor are the non-elect without obligations of thankfulness. You ought to be grateful, if any of your brethren of the human family are saved. If all were lost, God would be just. And if any of this dying world receive the gift of eternal life, you ought to be grateful, and render everlasting thanks to God.

5. The non-elect often enjoy as great or greater privileges than the elect. Many men have lived and died under the sound of the gospel, have enjoyed all the means of salvation during a long life, and have at last died in their sins, while others have been converted upon their first hearing the gospel of God. Nor is this difference owing to the fact, that the elect always have more of the strivings of the Spirit than the non-elect. Many who die in their sins, appear to have had conviction for a great part of their lives; have often been deeply impressed with a strong sense of their sins and the value of their souls, but have strongly intrenched themselves under refuges of lies, have loved the world and hated God, and fought their way through all the obstacles that were thrown around them to hedge up their way to death, and have literally forced their passage to the gates of hell. Sin was their voluntary choice.

6. Why should the doctrine of election be made a stumbling-block in the way of sinners? In nothing else do they make the same use of the purposes and designs of God, as they do on the subject of religion; and yet, in everything else, God's purposes and designs are as much settled, and have as absolute an influence. God has as certainly designed the day and circumstances of your death, as whether your soul shall be saved. It is not only expressly declared in the Bible, but is plainly the doctrine of reason. What would you say if you

should be called in to see a neighbor who was sick; and, on inquiry, you should find he would neither eat nor drink, and that he was verily starving himself to death. On expostulating with him upon his conduct, suppose be should calmly reply, that he believed in the sovereignty of God, in foreknowledge, election and decrees; that his days were numbered, that the time and circumstances of his death were settled, that he could not die before his time, and that all efforts he could make would not enable him to live a moment beyond his time; and if you attempted to remonstrate against his inference, and such an abuse and perversion of the doctrine of decrees, he should accuse you of being a heretic, of not believing in divine sovereignty. Now, should you see a man on worldly subjects reasoning and acting thus, you would pronounce him insane. Should farmers, mechanics, and merchants, reason in this way in regard to their worldly business, they would be considered fit subjects for bedlam.

7. How forcibly the perversion and abuse of this doctrine illustrate the madness of the human heart, and its utter opposition to the terms of salvation I The fact that God foreknows, and has designs in regard to every other event, is not made an excuse for remaining idle, or worse than idle, on these subjects. But where men's duty to God is concerned, and here alone, they seize these scriptures, and wrest them to their own destruction. How impressively does this fact bring out the demonstration, that sinners want an excuse for disobeying God; that they desire an apology for living in sin; that they seek an occasion for making war upon their Maker.

8. I have said, that the question is as much open for your decision, that you are left as perfectly to the exercise of your freedom, as if God neither knew or designed anything in regard to your salvation. Suppose there was a great famine in New York city, and that John Jacob Astor alone had provisions in great abundance; that he was a benevolent and liberal-minded man, and willing to supply the whole city with provisions, free of expense; and suppose there existed a universal and most unreasonable prejudice against him, insomuch that when he advertised in the daily papers that his store-houses were open, that whosoever would, might come and receive provisions, without money and without price, they all, with one accord, began to make excuse, and obstinately refused to accept the offers. Now, suppose that he should employ all the cartmen to carry provisions around the city, and stop at every door. But still they strengthened each other's hands, and would rather die than be indebted to him for food. Many had said so much against him, that they were utterly ashamed to feel and acknowledge their dependence upon him. Others were so much under their influence as to be unwilling to offend them; and so strong was the tide of public sentiment, that no one had the moral courage to break loose from the multitude and accept of life. Now, suppose that Mr. Astor knew beforehand the state of the public mind, and that all the citizens hated him, and had rather die than be indebted to him for food. Suppose he also knew, from the beginning, that there were certain arguments that he could bring to bear upon certain individuals, that would change their minds, and that he should proceed to press them with these considerations, until they had given up their opposition, had most thankfully accepted his provisions, and were saved from death. Suppose he used all the arguments and means that he wisely could to persuade the rest, but that, notwithstanding all his benevolent efforts, they adhered to the resolution, and preferred death to submission to his proposals. Suppose, further, he had perfect knowledge from the beginning, of the issue of

this whole matter, would not the question of life and death be as entirely open for the decision of every individual as if he knew nothing about it?

9. Some may ask, Why does God use means with the non-elect, which he is certain they will not accept? I answer, because he designs that they shall be without excuse. He will demonstrate his willingness and their obstinacy before the universe. He will stop their mouths effectually in judgment by a full offer of salvation; and although he knows that their rejection of the offer will only enhance their guilt, and aggravate their deep damnation, still he will make the offer, as there is no other way in which to illustrate his infinite willingness to save them, and their perverse rejection of his grace.

10. Lastly, God requires you to give all diligence to make your calling and election sure. In choosing his elect, you must understand that he has thrown the responsibility of their being saved upon them; that the whole is suspended upon their consent to the terms; you are all perfectly able to give your consent and this moment to lay hold on eternal life. Irrespective of your own choice, no election could save you, and no reprobation can damn you. The "

Spirit and the Bride say Come: let him that heareth say, Come; let him that is athirst come; and whosoever will, let him take the water of life freely." The responsibility is yours. God does all that he wisely can, and challenges yon to show what more he could do that he has not done. If you go to hell, you must go stained with your own blood. God is clear, angels are clear. To your own Master you stand or fall; mercy waits; the Spirit strives; Jesus stands at the door and knocks. Do not then pervert this doctrine, and make it an occasion of stumbling, till you are in the depths of hell.

Footnotes:

4. I say, in the order of nature. With God all duration or time is present. In the order of time, therefore, all the divine ideas and purposes are cotemporaneous. But the divine ideas must sustain to each other a logical relation. In the above paragraph I have stated what must have been the logical order of the Divine ideas in regard to election. By the order of nature, is intended that connection and relation of ideas that must result from the nature of intellect.

5. To this paragraph it has been objected as follows:--"Can it be said, that the only reason why the non-elect are not saved is their rejection of salvation, etc? Is there not a reason back of this? God does not give that gracious influence in their case, which he does in the case of the elect. If the only reason why the non-elect are not saved is their pertinacious refusal, then it would follow that the only reason why the elect are saved, is their acceptance of salvation. If these two points are so, then why all this discussion about election to salvation, and the means to that end, and God's reason for electing? The whole matter would resolve itself into freewill, and God would stand quite independent of the issue in every case. Then would there be no such thing as election." The objection contains a non sequitur. I say, the only reason why the non-elect are not saved, is because they pertinaciously refuse salvation. But if this is true, he says, "it will follow that the only reason why the elect are saved, is their acceptance of salvation. But this does not follow. The non-elect

fail of salvation only because they resist all the grace that God can wisely bestow upon them. This grace they resist, and fail of salvation. It is no more reasonable to say, that God's not giving them more divine influence to convert, them "is a reason back of this," than it would be to say that his not having by a gracious influence, restrained them from sin altogether, is "a reason back of "their pertinacious resistance of grace. If the non-elect are lost, or fail of salvation only because they resist all the grace that God can wisely bestow, it would not follow that the only reason why the elect are saved, is because they accept, or yield to the same measure of gracious influence as that bestowed upon the non-elect, for it may be, and in many cases the fact is, that God does bestow more gracious influence on the elect, than on the non-elect, because he can wisely do so. Here then is a plain non sequitur. Observe, I am writing in the paragraph in question upon the justice of the divine proceeding. I say, that so far as this is concerned, he fails of salvation, not because God withholds the grace that he could wisely bestow, but only because he rejects the grace proffered, and all that can be wisely proffered. If I understand this objector, there is another non sequitur in his objection. I understand him to say, that upon the supposition that the elect and the non-elect have the same measure of gracious influence, and that the reason why the elect are saved, and the non-elect not saved is, that the elect yield to, and the non-elect resist this influence; the whole question resolves into free-will, and there is no election about it. If this is his meaning, as I think it must be, it is a plain non sequitur. Suppose God foresaw that this would be so, and in view of this foreseen fact elected those who he foresaw would yield both to the privileges and gracious influence to which he foresaw they would yield, and to salvation as a consequence of this influence and yielding. And suppose he foresaw that the non-elect, although ordained or elected to enjoy the same measure of gracious influence, would resist and reject salvation, and for this cause rejected or reprobated them in his eternal purpose. Would not this be election? To be sure, in this case the different results would turn upon the fact that the elect yielded, and the non-elect did not yield, to the same measure of gracious influence. But there would be an election of the one to eternal life, and a rejection of the other. I cannot see how this objector can say, that in this case there could be no election, unless in his idea of election there is the exercise of an arbitrary sovereignty. I suppose that God bestows on men unequal measures of gracious influence, but that in this there is nothing arbitrary; that, on the contrary, he sees the wisest and best reasons for this; that being in justice under obligation to none, he exercises his own benevolent discretion, in bestowing on all as much gracious influence as he sees to be upon the whole wise and good, and enough to throw the entire responsibility of their damnation upon them if they are lost. But upon some he foresaw that he could wisely bestow a sufficient measure of gracious influence to secure their voluntary yielding, and upon others he could not bestow enough in fact to secure this result, In accordance with this foreknowledge, he chose the elect to both the gracious influence and its results, eternal life. In all this there was nothing arbitrary or unjust. He does all for all that he wisely can. He does enough for all to leave them without excuse. If the non-elect would yield to that measure of gracious influence which he can and does bestow upon them, which is the best he can do without acting unwisely, and of course wickedly, they would be saved. To this they might yield. To this they ought to yield. God has no right to do more than he does for them, all things considered; and there is no reason of which they can justly complain why they are not saved. They can with no more reason complain of his not giving them more gracious influence than that he created them, or that he made them free agents, or that he did not restrain them from sin altogether, or do anything else which it had been unwise, and therefore wrong to have done. Nor is the fact that God does not bestow on them sufficient grace to secure their yielding and salvation, a "reason back of their obstinacy to which their not being saved is to be ascribed," any more than any one of the above-named things is such a reason. This objection proceeds upon the assumption, that election must be unconditional to be election at all--that election must be so defined, as to be the cause of the difference in the eternal state of the elect and non-elect. But I see not why election may not be conditioned upon the foreseen fact, that the wisest possible administration of moral government would secure the free concurrence of some, and not of others. What could be wisely done being foreseen, the purpose that so it should be done would be election. No man has a right to define the terms election and reprobation in such a sense, as to exclude all conditions, and then insist that conditional election is no election at all.

LECTURE XLIV - REPROBATION

In discussing this subject I shall endeavor to show,

I. What the true doctrine of reprobation is not.

1. It is not that the ultimate end of God in the creation of any was their damnation. Neither reason nor revelation confirms, but both contradict the assumption, that God has created or can create any being for the purpose of rendering him miserable as an ultimate end. God is love, or he is benevolent, and cannot therefore will the misery of any being as an ultimate end, or for its own sake. It is little less than blasphemy to represent God as creating any being for the sake of rendering him miserable, as an ultimate end of his creation.

2. The doctrine is not, that any will be lost or miserable to all eternity, do what they can to be saved, or in spite of themselves. It is not only a libel upon the character of God, but a gross misrepresentation of the true doctrine of reprobation, to exhibit God as deciding to send sinners to hell in spite of themselves, or notwithstanding their endeavors to please God and obtain salvation.

3. Nor is this the true doctrine of reprobation, to wit: that the purpose or decree of reprobation is the procuring cause of the destruction of reprobates. God may design to destroy a soul because of his foreseen wickedness; but his design to destroy him for this reason does not cause his wickedness, and consequently does not prove his destruction.

4. The doctrine is not, that any decree or purpose of reprobation throws any obstacles in the way of the salvation of any one. It is not that God has purposed the damnation of any one in such sense as that the decree opposes any obstacle to the salvation of any soul under heaven.

5. Nor is it that any one is sent to hell, except for his own voluntary wickedness and ill-desert.

6. Nor is it that any one will be lost who can be induced, by all the means that can be wisely used, to accept salvation, or to repent and believe the gospel.

7. Nor is it, nor does it imply, that all the reprobates might not be saved, if they would but comply with the indispensable conditions of salvation.

8. Nor does it imply, that the decree of reprobation presents or opposes any obstacle to their compliance with the necessary conditions of salvation.

9. Nor does it imply, that anything hinders or prevents the salvation of the reprobate, but their perverse perseverance in sin and rebellion against God, and their wilful resistance of all the means that can be wisely used for their salvation.

II. What the true doctrine of reprobation is.

The term reprobation, both in the Old and the New Testament, signifies refuse, cast away. Jer. vi. 30: "Reprobate silver shall men call them, because the Lord hath rejected them." The doctrine is, that certain individuals of mankind are, in the fixed purpose of God, cast away, rejected and finally lost.

III. This is a doctrine of reason.

By this is intended, that since the Bible reveals the fact, that some will be finally cast away and lost, reason affirms that if God casts them off, it must be in accordance with a fixed purpose on his part to do so, for their foreseen wickedness. If, as a matter of fact, they will be cast away and lost, it must be that God both knows and designs it. That is, he both knows that they will be cast away, and designs to cast them off for their foreseen wickedness. God can certainly never possess any new knowledge respecting their character and deserts, and since he is unchangeable, he can never have any new purpose respecting them.

Again, it follows from the doctrine of election. If God designs to save the elect, and the elect only, as has been shown, not for the reason, but upon condition of their foreseen repentance and faith in Christ, it must be that he designs, or purposes to cast away the wicked, for their foreseen wickedness. He purposes to do something with those whom he foresees will finally be impenitent. He certainly does not purpose to save them. What he will ever do with them, he now knows that he shall do with them. What be will intend to do with them he now intends to do with them, or he were not unchangeable. But we have seen that immutability or unchangeableness is an attribute of God. Therefore the present reprobation of those who will be finally cast away or lost, is a doctrine of reason.

The doctrine of reprobation is not the election of a part of mankind to damnation, in the same sense that the elect unto salvation are elected to be saved. The latter are chosen or elected, not only to salvation, but to holiness. Election, with those who are saved, extends not only to the end, salvation, but also to the conditions or means; to wit, the sanctification of the Spirit, and the belief of the truth. This has been shown. God has not only chosen them to salvation, but to be conformed to the image of his Son. Accordingly, he uses means with them, with the design to sanctify and save them. But he has not elected the reprobate to wickedness, and does not use means to make them wicked, with the ultimate design to destroy them. He knows, indeed, that his creating them, together with his providential dispensations, will be the occasion, not the cause, of their sin and consequent destruction. But their sin and consequent destruction are not the ultimate end God had in view in their creation, and in the train of providences that thus result. His ultimate end must in all cases be benevolent, or must be the promotion of good. Their sin and damnation are only an incidental result, and not a thing intended as an end, or for its own sake. God can have no pleasure, in either their sin or consequent misery for its own sake; but on the contrary, he must regard both as in themselves evils of enormous magnitude. He does not, and cannot therefore elect the reprobate to sin and damnation, in the same sense in which he elects the saints to holiness and salvation. The elect unto salvation he chooses to this end, from regard to, or delight in the end. But the reprobate he chooses to destroy, not for the sake of their destruction as an end, or from delight in it for its own sake; but he has determined to destroy them for the public good, since their foreseen sinfulness demanded it. He does not use means to make them sinful, or with this design; but his providence is directed to another end, which end is good; and the destruction of the reprobate is, as has been said, only an incidental and an unavoidable result. That is, God cannot wisely prevent this result.

IV. This is the doctrine of revelation.

That this view of the subject is sustained by divine revelation, will appear from a consideration of the following passages:--

Ex. ix. 16: "And in very deed for this cause have I raised thee up, for to shew in thee my power, and that my name may be declared throughout all the earth."

Prov. xvi. 5: "Every one that is proud in heart is an abomination to the Lord; though hand join in hand, he shall not be unpunished."

Mark iv. 11: "And he said unto them, unto you it is given to know the mystery of the kingdom of God, but unto them that are without, all these things are done in parables: 12. That seeing they may see, and not perceive, and hearing they may hear and not understand, lest at any time they should be converted, and their sins should be forgiven them."

Rom. ix. 17: "For the scripture saith unto Pharaoh, even for this same purpose have I raised thee up, that I might shew my power in thee, and that my name might be declared throughout all the earth. 22. What if God, willing to shew his wrath, and to make his power known, endured with much long-suffering the vessels of wrath fitted to destruction. 23. And that he might make known the riches of his glory on the vessels of mercy, which be had afore prepared unto glory. 24. Even us, whom he hath called, not of the Jews only, but also of the Gentiles?"

2 Cor. xiii. 56: "Examine yourselves, whether ye be in the faith; prove your own selves; know ye not your own selves, how that Jesus Christ is in you, except ye be reprobates? But I trust that ye shall know that we are not reprobates."

2 Peter ii. 12: "But these as natural brute beasts, made to be taken and destroyed, speak evil of the things that they understand not; and shall utterly perish in their own corruption."

Ezek. xviii. 23: "Have I any pleasure at all that the wicked should die? saith the Lord God; and not that he should return from his ways, and live? 32. For I have no pleasure in the death of him that dieth, saith the Lord God, wherefore turn yourselves, and live ye?"

Ezek. xxxiii. 11: "Say unto them, as I live, saith the Lord God, I have no pleasure in the death of the wicked, but that the wicked turn from his way and live; turn ye, turn ye, from your evil ways; for why will ye die, O house of Israel?"

2 Peter iii. 9: "The Lord is not slack concerning his promise, as some men count slackness, but is long-suffering to usward, not willing that any should perish, but that all should come to repentance."

These passages when duly considered are seen to teach:

1. That some men are reprobates, in the sense that God does not design to save, but to destroy them, and,--

2.That he does not delight in their destruction for its own sake; but would prefer their salvation, if under the circumstances in which his wisdom has placed them, they could be induced to obey him.

3. But that he regards their destruction as a less evil to the universe, than would be such a change in the administration and arrangements of his government as would secure their salvation. Therefore, for their foreseen wickedness and perseverance in rebellion, under circumstances the most favorable to their virtue and salvation, in which he can wisely place them, he is

resolved upon their destruction; and has already in purpose cast them off for ever.

V. Why sinners are reprobated or rejected.

This has been already substantially answered. But to avoid misapprehension upon a subject so open to cavil, I repeat:

1. That the reprobation and destruction of the sinner is not an end, in the sense that God delights in misery, and destroys sinners to gratify a thirst for destruction. Since God is benevolent, it is impossible that this should be.

2. It is not because of any partiality in God, or because he loves the elect, and hates the reprobate, in any sense implying partiality. His benevolence is disinterested, and cannot of course be partial.

3. It is not from any want of interest in, and desire to save them, on the part of God. This he often affirms, and abundantly attests by his dealings with them, and the provision he has made for their salvation.

4. But the reprobates are reprobated for their foreseen iniquities:--

Rom. i. 28: "And even as they did not like to retain God in their knowledge, God gave them over to a reprobate mind, to do those things which are not convenient."

Rom. ii. 6: "Who will render to every man according to his deeds: 7. To them who, by patient continuance in well-doing, seek for glory, honor, and immortality, eternal life; 8. But unto them that are contentious, and do not obey the truth, but obey unrighteousness, indignation and wrath; 9. Tribulation and anguish, upon every soul of man that doeth evil, of the Jew first, and also of the Gentile; 10. But glory, honor, and peace, to every man that worketh good; to the Jew first, and also to the Gentile: 11. For there is no respect of persons with God."

Ezek. xviii. 4: "Behold all souls are mine; as the soul of the father, so also the soul of the son is mine: the soul that sinneth, it shall die. 19. Yet say ye, Why? Doth not the son bear the iniquity of the father? When the son hath done that which is lawful and right, and hath kept all my statutes, and hath done them, he shall surely live. 20. The soul that sinneth, it shall die. The son shall not bear the iniquity of the father, neither shall the father bear the iniquity of the son: the righteousness of the righteous shall be upon him, and the wickedness of the wicked shall be upon him."

2 Cor. v. 10: "For we must all appear before the judgment-seat of Christ, that every one may receive the things done in the body, according to that he hath done, whether it be good or bad."

Gal. vi. 7: "Be not deceived, God is not mocked: for whatsoever a man soweth, that shall he also reap."

Eph. vi. 8: "Knowing that whatsoever good thing any man doeth, the same shall he receive of the Lord, whether he be bond or free."

Col. iii. 24: "Knowing that of the Lord ye shall receive the reward of the inheritance: for ye serve the Lord Christ."

Rev. xxii. 12: "And, behold, I come quickly; and my reward is with me, to give every man according as his work shall be."

Jer. vi. 30: "Reprobate silver shall men call them, because the Lord hath rejected them."

These passages show the teachings of inspiration on this subject. Be it remembered, then, that the reason why any are reprobated, is because they are unwilling to be saved; that is, they are unwilling to be saved on the terms upon which alone God can consistently save them. Ask sinners whether they are willing to be saved, and they all say, yes; and with perfect sincerity they may say this, if they can be saved upon their own terms. But when you propose to them the terms of salvation upon which the gospel proposes to save them; when they are required to repent and believe the gospel, to forsake their sins, and give themselves up to the service of God, they will with one consent begin to make excuse. Now, to accept these terms, is heartily and practically to consent to them. For them to say, that they are willing to accept salvation, while they actually do not accept it, is either to deceive themselves, or to utter an infamous falsehood. To be willing is to accept it; and the fact, that they do not heartily consent to, and embrace the terms of salvation, is demonstration absolute, that they are unwilling. Yes, sinners, the only terms on which you can possibly be saved, you reject. Is it not then an insult to God for you to pretend that you are willing? The only true reason why all of you are not Christians, is that you are unwilling. You are not made unwilling by any act of God, or because you are reprobate; but if you are reprobate, it is because you are unwilling.

But do any of you object and say, why does not God make us willing? Is it not because he has reprobated us, that he does not change our hearts and make us willing? No, sinner, it is not because he has reprobated you; but because you are so obstinate that he cannot, wisely, and in consistency with the public good, take such measures as will convert you. Here you are waiting for God to make you willing to go to heaven, and all the while you are diligently using the means to get to hell--yes, exerting yourself with greater diligence to get to hell, than it would cost to insure your salvation, if applied with equal zeal in the service of your God. You tempt God, and then turn round and ask him why he does not make you willing? Now, sinner, let me ask you, do you think you are a reprobate? If so, what do you think the reason is that has led the infinitely benevolent God to reprobate you? There must be some reason; what do you suppose it is? Did you ever seriously ask yourself, what is the reason that a wise and infinitely benevolent God has never made me willing to accept salvation? It must be for one of the following reasons: either--

(1.) He is a malevolent being, and wills your damnation for its own sake; or--

(2.) He cannot make you willing if he would; or--

(3.) You behave in such a manner in the circumstances in which you are, that, to his infinitely benevolent mind it appears unwise to take such a course as would bring you to repentance. Such a change in the administration of his government as would make you willing, would not, upon the whole, be wise.

Now, which of these do you think it is? You will not probably take the ground that he is malevolent, and desires your damnation because he delights in misery; nor will you, I suppose, take the ground that he could not convert you if he would, that is, if he thought it wise to do so.

The other, then, must be the reason, to wit: that your heart, and conduct, and stubbornness, are so abominable in his sight, that, every thing considered, he sees that to use such further means with you as to secure your conversion, would, on the whole, do more hurt than good to his kingdom. I have not time at present to agitate the question whether you, as a moral agent, could not resist any possible amount of moral influence that could be brought to bear upon you, consistently with your moral freedom.

Do you ask how I know that the reason why God does not make you willing is, that he sees that it would be unwise in him to do so? I answer, that it is an irresistible inference, from these two facts, that he is infinitely benevolent, and that he does not actually make you willing. I do not believe that God would neglect anything that he saw to be wise and benevolent, in the great matter of man's salvation. Who can believe that he could give his only-begotten and well-beloved Son to die for sinners, and then neglect any wise and benevolent means for their salvation? No, sinner, if you are a reprobate, it is because God foresaw that you would do just as you are doing; that you would be so wicked as to defeat all the efforts that he could wisely make for your salvation. What a variety of means he has used with you. At one time he has thrown you into the furnace of affliction; and when this has not softened you, he has turned round and loaded you with favors. He has sent you his word, he has striven by his Spirit, he has allured you by the cross; he has tried to melt you by the groanings of Calvary; and tried to drive you back from the way to death, by rolling in your ears the thunders of damnation. At one time clouds and darkness have been round about you; the heavens have thundered over your head; divine vengeance has hung out, all around your horizon, the portentous clouds of coming wrath. At another time mercy has smiled upon you from above like the noon-day sun, breaking through an ocean of storms. He urges every motive; he lays heaven, earth and hell, under perpetual contributions for considerations to move your stony heart. But you deafen your ears, and close your eyes, and harden your heart, and say, "Cause the holy one of Israel to cease from before us." And what is the inference from all this? How must all this end? "Reprobate silver shall men call them, because the Lord has rejected them."

VI. When sinners are reprobated.

1. In respect to the act of casting them off, they are cast away only when, and not until, the cup of their iniquity is full.

2. In respect to the purpose of reprobation, they are in the purpose of God reprobated or rejected from eternity. This follows irresistibly from the omniscience and immutability of God. He has certainly and necessarily had from eternity all the knowledge he ever can or will have of the character of all men, and must have designed from all eternity all things respecting them which he ever will design. This follows from his unchangeableness. If he ever does cast off sinners, he must do it designedly or undesignedly. He cannot do it without any design. He must therefore do it designedly. But if he does it designedly, it must be either that he eternally entertained this design, or that he has changed. But change of purpose or design is inconsistent with the moral immutability of God. Therefore the purpose of reprobation is eternal; or the reprobates were in the fixed purpose of God cast off and rejected from eternity.

VII. Reprobation is just.

Is it not just in God to let men have their own choice, especially when the highest possible motives are held out to them as inducements to choose eternal life. What! Is it not just to reprobate men when they obstinately refuse salvation--when every thing has been done that is consistent with infinite wisdom and benevolence to save them? Shall not men be willing to be either saved or lost? What shall God do with you? You are unwilling to be saved; why then should you object to being damned? If reprobation under these circumstances is not just, I challenge you, sinner, to tell what is just.

VIII. Reprobation is benevolent.

It was benevolent in God to create men, though he foresaw that they would sin and become reprobate. If he foresaw that, upon the whole, he could secure such an amount of virtue and happiness by means of moral government, as to more than counterbalance the sin and misery of those who would be lost, then certainly it was a dictate of benevolence to create them. The question was, whether moral beings should be created, and moral government established, when it was foreseen that a great evil would be the incidental consequence. Whether this would be benevolent or not, must turn upon the question, whether a good might be secured that would more than counterbalance the evil. If the virtue and happiness that could be secured by the administration of moral government, would greatly outmeasure the incidental evils arising out of a defection of a part of the subjects of this government, it is manifest that a truly benevolent mind would choose to establish the government, the attendant evils to the contrary notwithstanding. Now, if those who are lost deserve their misery, and bring it upon themselves by their own choice, when they might have been saved, then certainly in their damnation there can be nothing inconsistent with justice or benevolence. God must have a moral government, or there can be no such thing as holiness in the created universe. For holiness in a creature is nothing else than a voluntary conformity to the government of God.

Since the penalty of the law, although infinite, under the wisest possible administration of moral government, could not secure universal obedience; and since multitudes of sinners will not be reclaimed and saved by the gospel, one of three things must be done; either moral government must be given up; or the wicked must be annihilated, or they must be reprobated and sent to hell. Now, that moral government should be given up, will not be pretended; annihilation would not be just, inasmuch as it would not be an adequate expression of the abhorrence with which the divine ruler regards the violation of his law, and consequently it would not meet the demands of public justice. Now, as sinners really deserve eternal death, and as their punishment may be of real value to the universe, in creating a respect for the authority of God, and thus strengthening his government, it is plain that their reprobation and damnation is, for the general good, making the best use of the wicked that can be made.

Doubtless God views the loss of the soul as a great evil, and he always will look upon it as such, and would gladly avoid the loss of any soul, if it were consistent with the wisest administration of his government. How slanderous, injurious, and offensive to God it must be, then, to say, that he created sinners on purpose to damn them. He pours forth all the tender yearnings of a father over those whom he is obliged to destroy--"How shall I give thee up, Ephraim? How shall I deliver thee, Israel? How shall I make thee as Admah? How shall I set thee as Zeboim? My heart is turned within me, my repentings are kindled together." And now, sinner, can you find it in your heart to accuse the blessed God of a want of benevolence?" O ye serpents! ye generation of vipers! how can you escape the damnation of hell?"

IX. How it may be known who are reprobates.

It may be difficult for us to ascertain with certainty in this world, who are reprobates; but there are so many marks of reprobation given in the Bible, that by a sober and judicious investigation, we may form a pretty correct opinion, whether we or those around us are reprobates or not.

1. One evidence of reprobation is a long course of prosperity in sin. The Psalmist lays it down as such in Psa. xcii. 7: "When the wicked spring as the grass, and when all the workers of iniquity do flourish, it is that they shall be destroyed forever." God often gives the wicked their portion in this world, and lets them prosper and wax fat like a stalled ox, and then brings them forth to the slaughter. "The wicked are reserved unto the day of wrath." When therefore you see an individual for a long time prospering in his sins, there is great reason to fear that man is a reprobate. In this passage inspiration assumes the truth of the distinction between evidence and proof. The Psalmist does not mean to be understood as affirming a universal truth. He did not intend, that prosperity in sin was proof conclusive that the prosperous sinner is a reprobate. But the least that could have been intended was, that such prosperity in sin affords alarming evidence of reprobation. It may be called presumptive evidence.

2. Habitual neglect of the means of grace is a mark of reprobation. If men are to be saved at all, it is through the sanctification of the Spirit and belief of the truth; and it will probably be found to be true, that not one in ten thousand is saved of those who habitually absent themselves from places where God presents his claims. Sometimes, I know, a tract, or the conversation or prayer of some friend, may awaken an individual, and lead him to the house of God; but, as a general fact, if a man stays away from the means of grace, and neglects his Bible, it is a fearful sign of reprobation, and that he will die in his sins. He is voluntary in it, and he does not neglect the means of grace because he is reprobated, but was reprobated because God foresaw that he would take this course. Suppose a pestilence were prevailing, that was certain to prove fatal in every instance where the appropriate remedy was not applied. Now, if you wished to know whose days were numbered and finished, and who among the sick were certain to die with the disease, if you found any among them neglecting and despising the only appropriate remedy, you would know that they were the persons.

3. Those who have grown old in sin, are probably reprobates. It is a solemn and alarming fact, that a vast majority of those who give evidence of piety, are converted under twenty-five years of age. Look at the history of revivals, and see, even in those that have manifested the greatest power, how few aged persons have been converted. The men who are set upon the attainment of some worldly object, and determined to secure that before they will attend to religion, and yield to the claims of their Maker, expecting afterwards to be converted, are almost always disappointed. Such a cold calculation is odious in the sight of God. What! Take advantage of his forbearance, and say, that because he is merciful you will venture to continue in sin, till you have secured your worldly objects, and worn yourself out in the service of the devil, and thus turn your Maker off with the jaded remnant of your abused mortality! Yon need not expect God to set his seal of approbation upon such a calculation as this, and suffer you at last to triumph, and say, that you had served the devil as long as you pleased, and got to heaven at last.

4. Absence of chastisements is a sign of reprobation. God says in the epistle to the Hebrews: "My son, despise not thou the chastening of the Lord, nor faint when thou art rebuked of him; for whom the Lord loveth he chasteneth, and scourgeth every son whom he receiveth; if ye endure chastening, God dealeth with you as with sons; for what son is he whom the

Father chasteneth not; but if ye be without chastisement, whereof all are partakers, then are ye bastards, and not sons."

5. When men are chastened and not reformed by it, it is a mark of reprobation. A poet has said, "When pain can't bless, heaven quits us in despair." God says of such, "Why should ye be stricken any more? Ye will revolt more and more." When your afflictions are unsanctified, when you harden yourselves under his stripes, why should he not leave you to fill up the measure of your iniquity?

6. Embracing damnable heresies, is another mark of reprobation. Where persons seem to be given up to believe a lie, there is solemn reason for fearing that they are among that number upon whom God sends strong delusions, that they may believe a lie, and be damned, because they obey not the truth, but have pleasure in unrighteousness. Where you see persons giving themselves up to such delusions, the more certainly they believe them, the greater reason there is for believing that they are reprobates. The truth is so plain, that with the Bible in your hands, it is next to impossible to believe a fundamental heresy, without being given up to the judicial curse of God. It is so hard to believe a lie, with the truth of the Bible before you, that the devil cannot do it. If therefore you reject your Bible, and embrace a fundamental falsehood, you are more stupid and benighted than the devil is. When a man professes to believe a lie, almost the only hope of his salvation that remains, is, that he does not cordially believe it. Sinner, beware how you trifle with God's truth. How often have individuals begun to argue in favor of heresy, for the sake of argument, and because they loved debate, until they have finally come to believe their own lie, and are lost for ever.

X. Objections.

1. To the idea that God rejected the reprobate for their foreseen wickedness, it is replied that, Prov. xvi. 4: "The Lord hath made all things for himself; yea, even the wicked for the day of evil," teaches another doctrine; that this passage teaches, that God made the reprobates for the day of evil, or for the purpose of destroying them.

To this I reply, that if he did create them to destroy them, or with a design when he created them to destroy them, it does not follow that their destruction was an ultimate end, or a thing in which he delighted for its own sake. It must be true, as has been said, that he designed from eternity to destroy them, in view, and in consequence, of their foreseen wickedness; and of course, he designed their destruction when he created them. In one sense then, it was true, that he created them for the day of evil, that is, in the sense that he knew how they would behave, and designed as a consequence to destroy them when, and before, he created them. But this is not the same as his creating them for the sake of their destruction as an ultimate end. He had another and a higher ultimate end, which end was a benevolent one. He says "I have created all things for myself, even the wicked for the day of evil;" that is, he had some great and good end to accomplish by them, and by their destruction. He foresaw that he could use them for some good purpose, notwithstanding their foreseen wickedness; and even that he could overrule their sin and destruction to manifest his justice, and thus show forth his glory, and thereby strengthen his government. He must have foreseen that the good that might thus, from his overruling providence, result to himself and to the universe, would more than compensate for the evil of their rebellion and destruction; and therefore, and upon this condition, he created them, knowing that he should destroy and intending to destroy them. That destruction was not the ultimate end of their creation, must follow from such scriptures as the following:--

Ezek. xxxiii. 11: "Say unto them, As I live, saith the Lord God, I have no pleasure in the death of the wicked; but that the wicked turn from his way and live: turn ye, turn ye, from your evil ways; for why will ye die, O house of Israel?"

Ezek. xviii. 23: "Have I any pleasure at all that the wicked should die; saith the Lord God; and not that he should return from his ways and live?"

2 Peter iii. 9: "The Lord is not slack concerning his promise, as some men count slackness, but is long-suffering to usward, not willing that any should perish, but that all should come to repentance."

1 John iv. 8: "He that loveth not, knoweth not God, for God is love. 16. And we have known and believed the love that God hath to us. God is love; and he that dwelleth in love dwelleth in God, and God in him."

Heb. ii. 9: "But we see Jesus, who was made a little lower than the angels for the suffering of death, crowned with glory and honor; that he by the grace of God should taste death for every man."

2. Another objection to the doctrine of this lecture is founded on Rom. ix. 20-23: "Nay, but O man, who art thou that repliest against God? Shall the thing formed say to him that formed it, Why hast thou made me thus? Hath not the potter power over the clay, of the same lump to make one vessel unto honor, and another unto dishonor? What if God, willing to shew his wrath, and make his power known, endured with much long-suffering the vessels of wrath fitted to destruction; and that he might make known the riches of his glory on the vessels of mercy, which he had afore prepared unto glory?"

From this passage it has been inferred, that God creates the character and disposes of the destinies of both saints and sinners with as absolute and as irresistible a sovereignty as that exercised by the potter over his clay; that he creates the elect for salvation, and the reprobate for damnation, and forms the character of both so as to fit them for their respective destinies, with an absolutely irresistible and efficient sovereignty; that his ultimate end was in both cases his own glory, and that the value of the end justifies the use of the means, that is, of such means. To this I reply:--

(1.) That it is absurd and nonsensical, as we have abundantly seen, to talk of creating moral character, either good or bad, by an irresistible efficient sovereignty. This is naturally impossible, as it implies a contradiction. Moral character must be the result of proper, voluntary action, and the moral character of the vessels of wrath or of mercy neither is, nor can be, formed by any irresistible influence whatever.

(2.) It is not said nor implied in the passage under consideration, that the character of the vessels of wrath was created, or that God had any such agency in procuring their character, as he has in forming the character of the vessels of mercy. Of the vessels of wrath it is only said they are "fitted to destruction," that is, that their characters are adapted for hell; while of the vessels of mercy it is said "which he had afore prepared unto glory." The vessels of wrath are fitted, or had fitted themselves to destruction, under the light and influence that should have made them holy. The vessels of mercy God had, by the special grace and influence of the Holy Spirit, engaging and directing their voluntary agency, afore prepared for glory.

(3.) But the lump spoken of in the text contemplates, not the original creation of men, nor the forming or creating in them of a wicked character. But it manifestly contemplates them as already existing as the potter's clay exists; and not only as existing, but also as being sinners. God may reasonably proceed to form out of this lump vessels of wrath or of mercy, as seems wise and good unto him. He may appoint one portion to honor and another to dishonor, as is seen by him to be demanded by the highest good.

(4.) The passage under consideration cannot, in any event, be pressed into the service of those who would insist, that the destruction of the reprobate is chosen for its own sake, and therefore implies malevolence in God. Hear what it says: "What if God, willing to show his wrath, and make his power known, endured with much long-suffering the vessels of wrath fitted to destruction; and that he might make known the riches of his glory on the vessels of mercy, which he had afore prepared unto glory?" Here it appears, that he designed to show and make known his attributes. This cannot have been an ultimate, but must have been a proximate, end. The ultimate end must have been the highest glory of himself, and the highest good of the universe, as a whole. If God willed thus to make known his holiness and his mercy, for the purpose of securing the highest good of the universe, who has a right to say, What doest thou? or Why doest thou thus?

3. Another objection is, if God knew that they would be reprobate or lost, why did he create them? If he knew that such would be the result, and yet created them, it follows that he created them to destroy them. I reply:--

This objection has been already answered, but for the sake of perspicuity I choose here to answer it again.

From the admitted fact, that God knew when he created them just what their destiny would be, it does not follow that their destruction was the end for which he created them. He created them, not for their sin and destruction as an ultimate end, but for another and a good end, notwithstanding his foreknowledge of their sin and ultimate ruin.

4. It is further objected, that if God designed to make known his attributes, in the salvation of the vessels of mercy, and in the destruction of the vessels of wrath, he must have designed their characters as well as their end, inasmuch as their characters are indispensable conditions of this result.

I reply, that it is true, that the characters of both the vessels of wrath and of mercy must have been in some sense purposed or designed by God. But it does not follow that he designed them both in the same sense. The character of the righteous he designed to beget, or induce by his own agency; the character of the wicked he designed to suffer him to form for himself. He doubtless designed to suffer the one rather than to interfere, in such manner and form as would prevent sin, seeing as he did, that, hateful as it was in itself, it could be overruled for good. The other he designed to produce, or rather induce, both on account of the pleasure he has in holiness, and also for the sake of its bearings on the subject of it, and upon the universe.

5. To the doctrine of this lecture it is further objected, that if one is a reprobate it is of no use for him to try to be saved. If God knows what he will be in character, and designs his destruction, it is impossible that it should be otherwise than as God knows and designs, and therefore one may as well give up in despair first as last.

(1.) To such an objector I would say, you do not know that you are a reprobate, and therefore you need not despair.

(2.) If God designs to cast you off, though you cannot know this, it is only because he foresees that you will not repent and believe the gospel; or in other words, for your voluntary wickedness. He foreknows that you will be wicked simply because you will be, and not because his foreknowledge makes you so. Neither his foreknowledge respecting your character, nor his design to cast you off, in consequence of your character, has any agency in making you wicked. You are therefore perfectly free to obey and be saved, and the fact that you will not, is no reason why you should not.

(3.) You might just as reasonably make the same objection to every thing that takes place in the universe. Everything that did, or will, or can occur, is as infallibly known to God, as the fact of your wickedness and destruction is. He also has a fixed and eternal design about everything that ever did or will occur. He knows how long you will live, where you will live, and when and where you will die. His purposes respecting these and all other events are fixed, eternal, and unchangeable. Why, then, do you not live without food and say, I cannot make one hair black or white; I cannot die before my time, nor can I prolong my days beyond the appointed time, do what I will; therefore, I will take no care of my health? No; this would be unreasonable.

Why not also apply this objection to everything, and settle down in despair of ever doing or being anything, but what an irresistible fate makes you? The fact is, that the true doctrine, whether of election or reprobation, affords not the least countenance to such a conclusion. The foreknowledge and designs of God respecting our conduct or our destiny, do not in the least degree interfere with our free agency. We, in every case, act just as freely as if God neither knew nor designed anything about our conduct. Suppose the farmer should make the same objection to sowing his seed, and to doing anything to secure a crop; what would be thought of him? And yet he might with as much reason, since he can plead the foreknowledge and designs of God, as an excuse for doing nothing to secure his salvation. God as really knows now whether you will sow and whether you will have a crop, and has from eternity known this, as perfectly as he ever will. He has either designed that you shall, or that you shall not, have a crop this year, from all eternity; and it will infallibly come to pass just as he has foreseen and designed. Yet you are really just as free to raise a crop, or to neglect to do so, as if he neither knew nor designed anything about it.

The man who will stumble either at the doctrine of election or reprobation, as defined and maintained in these lectures, should, to be consistent, stumble at everything that takes place, and never try to accomplish anything whatever; because the designs and the foreknowledge of God extend equally to everything; and unless he has expressly revealed how it will be, we are left in the dark, in respect to any event, and are left to use means to accomplish what we desire, or to prevent what we dread, as if God knew and designed nothing about it.

6. But it is objected, that this is a discouraging doctrine, and liable to be a stumbling-block, and therefore should not be inculcated. I answer--

(1.) It is taught in the Bible, and plainly follows also from the attributes of God, as revealed in the reason. The scriptures that teach it are not less likely to be a snare and a stumbling-block, than are the definition and explanation of the doctrine.

(2.) The proper statement, explanation, and defence of the doctrines of election and reprobation, are important to a proper understanding of the nature and attributes of God.

(3.) The scriptures that teach these doctrines are often subjects of cavil, and sometimes of real difficulty. Religious teachers should, therefore, state these doctrines and explain them, so as to aid the inquirer after truth, and stop the mouths of gainsayers.

(4.) Again, these doctrines have often been so mis-stated and perverted as to make them amount to an iron system of fatalism. Many souls have heard or read these perversions, and greatly need to be enlightened upon the subject. It is therefore all the more important, that these truths should find a place in religious instruction. Let them be understood, properly stated, explained, and defended, and they can no more be a stumbling-block, than the fact of God's omniscience can be so.

LECTURE XLV - DIVINE SOVEREIGNTY

In this discussion I shall endeavor to show,

I. What is not intended by the term "sovereignty" when applied to God.

It is not intended, at least by me, that God, in any instance, wills or acts arbitrarily, or without good reasons; reasons so good and so weighty, that he could in no case act otherwise than he does, without violating the law of his own intelligence and conscience, and consequently without sin. Any view of divine sovereignty that implies arbitrariness on the part of the divine will, is not only contrary to scripture, but is revolting to reason, and blasphemous. God cannot act arbitrarily, in the sense of unreasonably, without infinite wickedness. For him to be arbitrary, in the sense of unreasonable, would be a wickedness as much greater than any creature is capable of committing, as his reason or knowledge is greater than theirs. This must be self-evident. God should therefore never be represented as a sovereign, in the sense that implies that he is actuated by self or arbitrary will, rather than by his infinite intelligence.

Many seem to me to represent the sovereignty of God as consisting in a perfectly arbitrary disposal of events. They seem to conceive of God as being wholly above and without any law or rule of action guiding his will by his infinite reason and conscience. They appear shocked at the idea of God himself being the subject of moral law, and are ready to inquire, Who gives law to God? They seem never to have considered that God is, and must be, a law unto himself; that he is necessarily omniscient, and that the divine reason must impose law on, or prescribe law to, the divine will. They seem to regard God as living wholly above law, and as disposed to have his own will at any rate, reasonable or unreasonable; to set up his own arbitrary pleasure as his only rule of action, and to impose this rule upon all his subjects. This sovereignty they seem to conceive of as controlling and disposing of all events, with an iron or adamantine fatality, inflexible, irresistible, omnipotent. "Who worketh all things after the counsel of his own will." This text they dwell much upon, as teaching that God disposes all events absolutely, not according to his own infinite wisdom and discretion, but simply according to his own will; and, as their language would often seem to imply, without reference at all to the universal law of benevolence. I will not say, that such is the view as it lies in their own mind; but only that from the language they use, such would seem to be their idea of divine sovereignty. Such, however, is not the view of this subject which I shall state and defend on the present occasion.

II. What is intended by divine sovereignty.

The sovereignty of God consists in the independence of his will, in consulting his own intelligence and discretion, in the selection of his end, and the means of accomplishing it. In other words, the sovereignty of God is nothing else than infinite benevolence directed by infinite knowledge. God consults no one in respect to what shall be done by him. He asks no leave to do and require what his own wisdom dictates. He consults only himself; that is, his own infinite intelligence. So far is he from being arbitrary in his sovereignty, in the sense of unreasonable, that he is invariably guided by infinite reason. He consults his own intelligence only, not from any arbitrary disposition, but because his knowledge is perfect and infinite, and therefore it is safe and wise to take counsel nowhere else. It were infinitely unreasonable, and weak, and wicked in God to ask leave of any being to act in conformity with his own judgment. He must make his own reason his rule of action. God is a sovereign, not in the sense that he is not under law, or that he is above all law, but in the sense that he is a law to himself; that he knows no law but what is given him by his own reason. In other words still, the sovereignty of God consists in such a disposal of all things and events, as to meet the ideas of his own reason, or the demands of his own intelligence. "He works all things after the counsel of his own will," in the sense that he formed and executes his own designs independently; in the sense that he consults his own infinite discretion; that is, he acts according to his own views of propriety and fitness. This he does, be it distinctly understood, without at all setting aside the freedom of moral agents. His infinite knowledge enabled him to select an end and means, that should consist with and include the perfect freedom of moral agents. The subjects of his moral government are free to obey or disobey, and take the consequences. But foreseeing precisely in all cases how they would act, he has laid his plan accordingly, so as to bring out the contemplated and desired results. In all his plans he consulted none but himself. But this leads me to say,--

III. That God is and ought to be an absolute and a universal sovereign.

By absolute, I mean, that his expressed will, in obedience to his reason, is law. It is not law because it proceeds from his arbitrary will, but because it is the revelation or declaration of the affirmations and demands of his infinite reason. His expressed will is law, because it is an infallible declaration of what is intrinsically fit, suitable, right. His will does not make the things that he commands, right, fit, proper, obligatory, in the sense, that should he require it, the opposite of what he now requires would be fit, proper, suitable, obligatory; but in the sense that we need no other evidence of what is in itself intrinsically proper, fit, obligatory, than the expression of his will. Our reason affirms, that what he wills must be right; not because he wills it, but that he wills it because it is right, or obligatory in the nature of things; that is, our reason affirms that he wills as he does, only upon condition, that his infinite intelligence affirms that such willing is intrinsically right, and therefore he ought to will or command just what he does.

He is a sovereign in the sense that his will is law, whether we are able to see the reason for his commands or not, because our reason affirms that he has and must have good and sufficient reasons for every command; so good and sufficient, that he could not do otherwise than require what he does, under the circumstances, without violating the law of his own intelligence. We therefore need no other reason for affirming our obligation to will and to do, than that God requires it; because we always and necessarily assume, that what God requires must be right, not because he arbitrarily wills it, but because he does not arbitrarily will it: on the contrary that he has, and must have in every instance, infinitely good and wise reasons for every requirement.

Some persons represent God as a sovereign, in the sense, that his arbitrary will is the foundation of obligation. But if this is so, he could in every instance render the directly opposite course from what he now requires, obligatory. But this is absurd. The persons just mentioned seem to think, that unless it be admitted that God's will is the foundation of obligation, it will follow that it does not impose obligation, unless he discloses the reasons for his requirements. But this is a great mistake. Our own reason affirms that God's expressed will is always law, in the sense that it invariably declares the law of nature, or discloses the decisions of his own reason.

God must and ought to be an absolute sovereign in the sense just defined. This will appear if we consider:--

1. That his end was chosen and means decided upon, when no being but himself existed, and of course, there was no one to consult but himself.

2. Creation and providence are only the results, and the carrying out of his plans settled from eternity.

3. The law of benevolence, as it existed in the divine reason, must have eternally demanded of him the very course he has taken.

4. His highest glory and the highest good of universal being demand that he should consult his own discretion, and exercise an absolute and a universal sovereignty, in the sense explained: Infinite wisdom and goodness ought of course to act independently in the promotion of their end. If infinite wisdom or knowledge is not to give law, what or who shall? If infinite benevolence shall not declare and enforce law, what or who shall? God's attributes and relations render it obligatory upon him to exercise just that holy sovereignty we have ascribed to him.

(1.) This sovereignty, and no other, he claims for himself.

Ps. cxv. 3: "But our God is in the heavens; he hath done whatsoever he hath pleased."

Ps. cxxxv. 6: "Whatsoever the Lord pleased, that did he in heaven, and in earth, in the seas, and all deep places."

Isa. lv. 10: "For as the rain cometh down, and the snow from heaven, and returneth not thither, but watereth the earth, and maketh it bring forth and bud, that it may give seed to the sower, and bread to the eater; 11. So shall my word be that goeth forth out of my mouth; it shall not return unto me void, but it shall accomplish that which I please, and it shall prosper in the thing whereto I sent it."

Matt. xi. 25: "At that time Jesus answered and said, I thank thee, O Father, Lord of heaven and earth, because thou hast hid these things from the wise and prudent, and hast revealed them unto babes. 26. Even so, Father, for so it seemed good in thy sight."

Rom. ix. 15: "For he saith to Moses, I will have mercy on whom I will have mercy, and I will have compassion on whom I will have compassion. 16. So then it is not of him that willeth, nor of him that runneth, but of God that showeth mercy. 17. For the scripture saith unto Pharaoh, Even for this same purpose have I raised thee up, that I might show my power in thee, and that my name might be declared throughout all the earth. 18. Therefore hath he mercy on whom he will have mercy, and whom he will he hardeneth."

Eph. i. 11: "In whom also we have obtained an inheritance, being predestinated according to the purpose of him who worketh all things after the counsel of his own will."

(2.) Again: God claims for himself all the prerogatives of an absolute and a universal sovereign, in the sense already explained. For example, he claims to be the rightful and sole proprietor of the universe.

1 Chron. xxix. 11: "Thine, O Lord, is the greatness, and the power, and the glory, and the victory, and the majesty; for all that is in the heaven and in the earth is thine; thine is the kingdom, O Lord, and thou art exalted as head above all."

Ps. 1. 10: "For every beast of the forest is mine, and the cattle upon a thousand hills; 11. I know all the fowls of the mountains; and the wild beasts of the field are mine. 12. If I were hungry, I would not tell thee, for the world is mine, and the fulness thereof."

Ps. xcv. 5: "The sea is his, and he made it, and his hands formed the dry land. 6. O come, let us worship, and bow down, let us kneel before the Lord our Maker; 7. For he is our God, and we are the people of his pasture, and the sheep of his hand."

Ps. c. 3: "Know ye that the Lord he is God, it is he that hath made us, and not we ourselves; we are his people, and the sheep of his pasture."

Ezek. xviii. 4: "Behold, all souls are mine; as the soul of the father, so also the soul of the son is mine; the soul that sinneth it shall die."

Rom. xiv. 8: "For whether we live, we live unto the Lord; and whether we die, we die unto the Lord; whether we live therefore, or die, we are the Lord' s."

(3.) Again: God claims to have established the natural or physical laws of the universe.

Ps. cxix. 90: "Thy faithfulness is unto all generations, thou hast established the earth, and it abideth. 91. They continue this day according to thine ordinances, for all are thy servants."

Prov. iii. 19: "The Lord by wisdom hath founded the earth, by understanding hath he established the heavens. 20. By his knowledge the depths are broken up, and the clouds drop down the dew."

Jer. xxxi. 35: "Thus saith the Lord, which giveth the sun for a light by day, and the stars for a light by night, which divideth the sea when the waves thereof roar; the Lord of hosts is his name."

Jer. xxxiii. 25: "Thus saith the Lord, if my covenant be not with day and night, and if I have not appointed the ordinances of heaven and earth; 26. Then will I cast away the seed of Jacob, and David my servant, so that I will not take any of his seed to be rulers over the seed of Abraham, Isaac, and Jacob; for I will cause their captivity to return, and have mercy on them."

(4.) God claims the right to exercise supreme authority.

1 Chron. xxix. 11: "Thine, O Lord, is the greatness and the power, and the glory, and the victory, and the majesty; for all that is in the heaven and the earth is thine; thine is the kingdom, O Lord, and thou art exalted as head above all."

Ps. xlvii. 7: "For God is the king of all the earth, sing ye praises with understanding."

Isa. xxxiii. 22: "For the Lord is our judge, the Lord is our lawgiver, the Lord is our king; he will save us."

(5.) God claims the right to exercise his own discretion in using such means, and in exerting such an agency as will secure the regeneration of men, or not, as it appears wise to him.

Deut. xxix. 4: "Yet the Lord hath not given you an heart to perceive, and eyes to see, and ears to hear, unto this day."

Jer. v. 14: "Wherefore thus saith the Lord God of hosts, Because ye speak this word, behold, I will make my words in thy mouth fire, and this people wood, and it shall devour them."

Matt. xiii. 10: "And the disciples came, and said unto him, Why speakest thou to them in parables? He answered and said unto them, Because it is given unto you to know the mysteries of the kingdom of heaven, but to them it is not given."

Rom. ix. 22: "What if God, willing to show his wrath, and to make his power known, endured with much long-suffering the vessels of wrath fitted to destruction. 23. And that he might make known the riches of his glory on the vessels of mercy, which he had afore prepared unto glory."

2 Tim. ii. 25: "In meekness instructing those that oppose themselves; if God peradventure will give them repentance to the acknowledging of the truth."

(6.) God claims the right to try his creatures by means of temptation.

Deut. xiii. 1: "If there arise among you a prophet, or a dreamer of dreams, and giveth thee a sign or a wonder, 2. And the sign or the wonder come to pass, whereof he spake unto thee, saying, let us go after other gods, which thou hest not known, and let us serve them; 3. "Thou shalt not hearken unto the words of that prophet, or that dreamer of dreams; for the Lord your God proveth you, to know whether ye love the Lord your God with all your heart and with all your soul."

1 Kings xxii. 20: "And the Lord said, Who shall persuade Ahab, that he may go up and fall at Ramoth-gilead? And one said on this manner, and another said on that manner. 21. And there came forth a spirit, and stood before the Lord, and said, I will persuade him. 22. And the Lord said unto him, Wherewith? And he said, I will go forth, and I will be a lying spirit in the mouth of all his prophets. And he said, Thou shalt persuade him, and prevail also; go forth, and do so."

Job ii. 3. "And the Lord said unto Satan, Hest thou considered my servant Job, that there is none like him in the earth, a perfect and an upright man, one that feareth God, and escheweth evil? And still he holdeth fast his integrity, although thou movedst me against him, to destroy him without cause. 7. So went Satan forth from the presence of the Lord, and smote Job with sore boils, from the sole of his foot unto his crown."

Matt. iv. 1: "Then was Jesus led up of the spirit into the wilderness to be tempted of the devil."

(7.) God also claims the right to use all creatures, and to dispose of all creatures and events, so as to fulfil his own designs.

2 Sam. vii. 14: "I will be his father, and he shall be my son; if he commit iniquity, I will chasten him with the rod of men, and with the stripes of the children of men."

2 Kings v. 1: "Now Naaman, captain of the host of the king of Syria, was a great man with his master, and honorable, because by him the Lord had given deliverance unto Syria; he was also a mighty man in valor, but he was a leper."

Job i. 15: "And the Sabeans fell upon them, and took them away; yea, they have slain the servants with the edge of the sword; and I am escaped alone to tell thee. 17. While he was yet speaking, there came also another, and said, The Chaldeans made out three bands, and fell upon the camels, and have carried them away; yea, and slain the servants with the edge of the sword; and I only am escaped to tell thee. And Job, said, Naked came I out of my mother' s womb, and naked shall I return thither; the Lord gave, and the Lord hath taken away; blessed be the name of the Lord."

Isa. x. 5: "O Assyrian, the rod of mine anger, and the staff in their hand is mine indignation: 6. I will send him against an hypocritical nation, and against the people of my wrath will I give him a charge, to take the spoil, and to take the prey, and to tread them down like the mire of the streets. 7. Howbeit he meaneth not so, neither doth his heart think so; but it is in his heart to destroy and cut off nations not a few. 12. Wherefore it shall come to pass, that when the Lord hath performed his whole work upon Mount Zion and on Jerusalem, I will punish the fruit of the stout heart of the king of Assyria, and the glory of his high looks. 15. Shall the axe boast itself against him that heweth therewith? or shall the saw magnify itself against him that shaketh it? as if the rod should shake itself against them that lift it up, or as if the staff should lift up itself, as if it were no wood."

Ezek. xxiv. 14: "And I will lay my vengeance upon Edom by the hand of my people Israel; and they shall do in Edom according to mine anger, and according to my fury; and they shall know my vengeance, saith the Lord God."

Hab. i. 6: "For, lo, I raise up the Chaldeans, that bitter and hasty nation, which shall march through the breadth of the land, to possess the dwelling-places that are not theirs. 12. Art thou not from everlasting, O Lord, my God, mine Holy One? We shall not die, O Lord, thou hast ordained them for judgment; and O mighty God, thou hast established them for correction."

(8.) God claims the right to take the life of his sinful subjects at his own discretion.

Gen. xxii. 2: "And he said, Take now thy son, thine only son Isaac, whom thou lovest, and get thee into the land of Moriah, and offer him there for a burnt-offering upon one of the mountains, which I will tell thee of."

Deut. xx. 16: "But of the cities of these people, which the Lord thy God doth give thee for an inheritance, thou shalt save alive nothing that breatheth. 17. But thou shalt utterly destroy them; namely, the Hittites, and the Amorites, the Canaanites, and the Perizzites, the Hivites, and the Jebusites, as the Lord thy God hath commanded thee: 18. That they teach you not to do after all their abominations, which they have done unto their gods; so should ye sin against the Lord your God."

1 Sam. xv. 3: "Now go and smite Amalek, and utterly destroy all that they have, and spare them not; but slay both man and woman, infant and suckling, ox and sheep, camel and ass."

(9.) God declares that he will maintain his own sovereignty.

Isa. xlii. 8: "I am the Lord; that is my name: and my glory will I not give to another, neither my praise to graven images."

Isa. xlviii. 11: "For mine own sake, even for mine own sake, will I do it: for how should my name be polluted? and I will not give my glory unto another."

These passages will disclose the general tenor of scripture upon this subject.

REMARKS

1. The Sovereignty of God is an infinitely amiable, sweet, holy, and desirable sovereignty. Some seem to conceive of it as if it were revolting and tyrannical. But it is the infinite opposite of this, and is the perfection of all that is reasonable, kind and good.

Isa. lvii. 15: "For thus saith the high and lofty One that inhabiteth eternity, whose name is holy: I dwell in the high and holy place, with him also that is of a contrite and humble spirit, to revive the spirit of the humble, and to revive the heart of the contrite ones. 16. For I will not contend for ever, neither will I be always wroth: for the spirit should fail before me, and the souls which I have made. 17. For the iniquity of his covetousness was I wroth, and smote him: I hid me, and was wroth, and he went on frowardly in the way of his heart. 18. I have seen his ways, and will heal him; I will lead him also, and restore comforts unto him, and to his mourners. 19. I create the fruit of the lips; Peace, peace to him that is far off, and to him that is near, saith the Lord; and I will heal him."

2. Many seem afraid to think or speak of God's sovereignty, and even pass over, with a very slight reading, those passages of scripture that so fully declare it. They think it unwise and dangerous to preach upon the subject, especially unless it be to deny or explain away the sovereignty of God. This fear in pious minds has no doubt originated in a misconception of the nature of this sovereignty. They have been led either by false teaching, or in some way, to conceive of the divine sovereignty as an iron and unreasonable despotism. That is, they have understood the doctrine of divine sovereignty to so represent God. They therefore fear and reject it. But let it be remembered and for ever understood, to the eternal joy and unspeakable consolation of all holy beings, that God's sovereignty is nothing else than infinite love directed by infinite knowledge, in such a disposal of events as to secure the highest wellbeing of the universe; that, in the whole details of creation, providence and grace, there is not a solitary measure of his that is not infinitely wise and good.

3. A proper understanding of God's universal agency and sovereignty, of the perfect wisdom and benevolence of every measure of his government, providential and moral, is essential to the best improvement of all his dispensations toward us, and to those around us. When it is understood, that God's hand is directly or indirectly in everything that occurs, and that he is infinitely wise and good, and equally wise and good in every single dispensation--that he has one end steadily and always, in view--that he does all for one and the same ultimate end--and that this end is the highest good of himself and of universal being;--I say, when these things are understood and considered, there is a divine sweetness in all his dispensations. There is then a divine reasonableness, and amiableness, and kindness, thrown like a broad mantle of infinite love over all his character, works and ways. The soul, in contemplating such a sacred, universal, holy sovereignty, takes on a sweet smile of delightful complacency, and feels secure, and reposes in perfect peace, surrounded and supported by the everlasting arms.

4. Many entertain most ruinous conceptions of divine sovereignty. They manifestly conceive of it as proceeding wholly independent of law, and of second causes, or means. They often are heard to use language that implies this. They say, "if it is God's will, you cannot hinder it. If God has begun the work, he will accomplish it." In fact, their language means nothing, unless they assume that in the dispensation of grace all is miracle. They often represent a thing as manifestly from God, or as providential, because it was, or appeared to be, so disconnected with appropriate means and instrumentalities. In other words it was quite miraculous.

Now, I suppose, that God's sovereignty manifests itself through and by means, or second causes, and appropriate instrumentalities. God is as much a sovereign in the kingdom of nature as of grace. Suppose farmers, mechanics, and shopkeepers should adopt, in practice, this absurd view of divine sovereignty of which I am speaking? Why, they would succeed about as well in raising crops and in transacting business, as those Christians and ministers who apply their views of sovereignty to spiritual matters, do in saving souls.

LECTURE XLVI - PURPOSES OF GOD

In discussing this subject I shall endeavor to show,

I. What I understand by the purposes of God.

Purposes, in this discussion, I shall use as synonymous with design, intention. The purposes of God must be ultimate and proximate. That is, God has and must have an ultimate end. He must purpose to accomplish something by his works and providence, which he regards as a good in itself, or as valuable to himself, and to being in general. This I call his ultimate end. That God has such an end or purpose, follows from the already established facts, that God is a moral agent, and that he is infinitely wise and good. For surely he could not be justly considered as either wise or good, had he no intrinsically valuable end which he aims to realize, by his works of creation and providence. His purpose to secure his great and ultimate end, I call his ultimate purpose. His proximate purposes respect the means by which he aims to secure his end. If he purposes to realize an end, he must of course purpose the necessary means for its accomplishment. The purposes that respect the means are what I call in this discussion, his proximate purposes.

II. Distinction between purpose and decree.

Purpose has just been defined, and the definition need not be repeated. The term decree is used in a variety of senses. The term is used in the Bible as synonymous--

1. With fore-ordination or determination, appointment.

Job xxviii. 10: "He putteth forth his hand upon the rock; he overturneth the mountains by the roots. 26. When he made a decree for the rain, and a way for the lightning of the thunder."

Ps. xi. 2: "I will declare the decree, the Lord hath said unto me, Thou art my son; this day have I begotten thee."

Ps. cxlviii. 6: "He hath also established them for ever and ever; he hath made a decree which shall not pass."

Prov. viii. 29: "When he gave to the sea his decree, that the waters should not pass his commandment; when he appointed the foundations of the earth."

Jer. v. 22: "Fear ye not me? saith the Lord: will ye not tremble at my presence, which have placed the sand for the bound of the sea, by a perpetual decree that it cannot pass it, and though the waves thereof toss themselves, yet can they not prevail; though they roar, yet can they not pass over it?"

Dan. iv. 24: "This is the interpretation, O king, and this is the decree of the Most High, which is come upon my lord the king."

2. It is used as synonymous with ordinance, statute, law.

Dan. vi. 7: "All the presidents of the kingdom, the governors, and the princes, the counsellors, and the captains, have consulted together to establish a royal statute, and to make a firm decree, that whosoever shall ask a petition of any god or man for thirty days, save of thee, O king, he shall be cast into the den of lions. 8. Now, O king, establish the decree, and sign the writing, that it be not changed, according to the law of the Medes and Persians, which altereth not. 26. I make a decree, that in every dominion of my kingdom men tremble and fear before the God of Daniel; for he is the living God, and steadfast for ever, and his kingdom that which shall not be destroyed, and his dominion shall be even unto the end."

This term has been generally used by theological writers as synonymous with fore-ordination, appointment. To decree, with these writers, is to appoint, ordain, establish, settle, fix, render certain. This class of writers also often confound decree with purpose, and use the word as meaning the same thing. I see no objection to using the term decree, in respect to a certain class of physical events, as synonymous with appointment, fore-ordination, fixing, rendering certain. But I think this use of it, applied, as it has been, to the actions of moral agents, is highly objectionable, and calculated to countenance the idea of fatality and necessity, in respect to the actions of men. It seems inadmissible to speak of God's decreeing the free actions of moral agents, in the sense of fixing, settling, determining fore-ordaining them as he fixes, settles, renders certain all physical events. The latter he has fixed or rendered certain by a law of necessity. The former, that is, free acts, although they may be, and are certain, yet they are not rendered so by a law of fate or necessity; or by an ordinance or decree that fixes them so, that it is not possible they should be otherwise.

In respect to the government of God, I prefer to use the term purpose, as I have said, to signify the design of God, both in respect to the end at which he aims, and the means he intends or purposes to use to accomplish it. The term decree I use as synonymous with command, law, or ordinance. The former I use as expressive of what God purposes or designs to do himself, and by his own agency, and also what he purposes or designs to accomplish by others. The latter I use as expressive of God's will, command, or law. He regulates his own conduct and agency in accordance with the former, that is, with his purposes. He requires his creatures to conform to the latter, that is, to his decrees or laws. We shall see, in its proper place, that both his purposes and his actions are conformed to the spirit of his decrees, or laws; that is, that he is benevolent in his purposes and conduct, as he requires his creatures to be. I distinguish what God purposes or designs to accomplish by others, and what they design. God's end or purpose is always benevolent. He always designs good. His creatures are often selfish, and their designs are often the direct opposite to the purpose of God, even in the same events. For example, see the following cases:--

Gen. xlv. 4: "And Joseph said unto his brethren, Come near to me, I pray you; and they came near. And he said, I am Joseph your brother, whom ye sold into Egypt. 5. Now therefore, be not grieved, nor angry with yourselves that ye sold me hither; for God did send me before you, to preserve life. 6. For these two years hath the famine been in the land, and yet there are five years, in the which there shall neither be earing nor harvest."

Gen. 1. 19: "And Joseph said unto them, Fear not; for am I in the place of God? 20. But as for you, ye thought evil against me, but God meant it unto good, to bring to pass, as it is this day, to save much people alive."

Isa. x. 5: "O Assyrian, the rod of mine anger, and the staff in their hand is mine indignation. 6. I will send him against a hypocritical nation, and against the people of my wrath will I give him a charge, to take the spoil, and to take the prey, and to tread them down like the mire of the streets. 7. Howbeit he meaneth not so, but it is in his heart to destroy, and cut off nations not a few.

12. Wherefore it shall come to pass, that when the Lord hath performed his whole work upon Mount Zion and on Jerusalem, I will punish the fruit of the stout heart of the king of Assyria, and the glory of his high looks."

Mark xv. 9: "But Pilate answered them, saying, Will ye that I release unto you the king of the Jews? 10. (For he knew that the chief priests had delivered him for envy)."

John iii. 16: "For God so loved the world, that he gave his only-begotten Son, that whosoever believeth in him should not perish, but have everlasting life."

Acts ii. 23: "Him, being delivered by the determinate counsel and fore-knowledge of God, ye have taken, and by wicked hands have crucified and slain."

III. There must be some sense in which God's purposes extend to all events.

1. This is evident from reason. His plans must, in some sense, include all actual events. He must foreknow all events by a law of necessity. This is implied in his omniscience. He must have matured and adopted his plan in view of, and with reference to, all events. He must have had some purpose or design respecting all events that he foresaw. All events transpire in consequence of his own creating agency; that is, they all result in some way directly or indirectly, either by his design or sufferance, from his own agency. He either designedly brings them to pass, or suffers them to come to pass without interposing to prevent them. He must have known that they would occur. He must have either positively designed that they should, or, knowing that they would result from the mistakes or selfishness of his creatures, negatively designed not to prevent them, or, he had no purpose or design about them. The last hypothesis is plainly impossible. He cannot be indifferent to any event. He knows all events, and must have some purpose or design respecting them.

2. The Bible abundantly represents God's purposes as in some sense extending to all events. For example:--

Deut. xxxii. 4: "He is the Rock, his work is perfect; for all his ways are judgment; a God of truth, and without iniquity; just and right is he."

Ps. civ. 24: "O Lord, how wonderful are thy works; in wisdom hast thou made them all; the earth is full of thy riches."

Job xiv. 5: "Seeing his days are determined, the number of his months are with thee; thou hast appointed his bounds that he cannot pass."

Isa. xiv. 26: "This is the purpose that is purposed upon the whole earth; and this is the hand that is stretched out upon all the nations."

Acts xvii. 26: "And hath made of one blood all nations of men for to dwell on all the face of the earth, and hath determined the times before appointed, and the bounds of their habitation."

Eph. i. 11: "In whom also we have obtained an inheritance, being predestinated according to the purpose of him who worketh all things after the counsel of his own will."

Acts ii. 23: "Him, being delivered by the determinate counsel and fore-knowledge of God, ye have taken, and by wicked hands have crucified and slain."

Acts iv. 27: "For of a truth against thy holy child Jesus, whom thou hast anointed, both Herod and Pontius Pilate, with the Gentiles, and the people of

Israel, were gathered together, 28. For to do whatsoever thy hand and thy counsel determined before to be done."

Acts xiii. 29: "And when they had fulfilled all that was written of him, they took him down from the tree, and laid him in a sepulchre."

Jude 4: "For there are certain men crept in unawares, who were before of old ordained to this condemnation, ungodly men, turning the grace of our God, into lasciviousness, and denying the only Lord God, and our Lord Jesus Christ."

Rev. xvii. 17: "For God hath put in their hearts to fulfil his will, and to agree, and give their kingdom unto the beast, until the words of God shall be fulfilled."

Acts xxxvii. 22: "And now I exhort you to be of good cheer; for there shall be no loss of any man' s life among you, but of the ship. 23. For there stood by me this night the angel of God, whose I am, and whom I serve, 24. Saying, Fear not Paul, thou must be brought before Cæsar; and, lo, God hath given thee all them that sail with thee. 30. And as the shipmen were about to flee out of the ship, when they had let down the boat into the sea, under color as though they would have cast anchors out of the foreship, 31. Paul said to the centurion and to the soldiers, except these abide in the ship, ye cannot be saved."

2 Thess. ii. 13: "But we are bound to give thanks alway to God for you, brethren, beloved of the Lord, because God hath from the beginning chosen you to salvation through sanctification of the Spirit, and belief of the truth."

1 Pet. i. 2: "Elect according to the foreknowledge of God the Father, through sanctification of the Spirit, unto obedience and sprinkling of the blood of Jesus Christ."

Ps. cxlvii. 8: "Who covereth the heaven with clouds, who prepareth rain for the earth, who maketh grass to grow upon the mountains. 9. He giveth to the beast his food, and to the young ravens which cry. 15. He sendeth forth his commandment upon earth; his word runneth very swiftly. 16. He giveth snow like wool; he scattereth the hoar-frost like ashes. 17. He casteth forth his ice like morsels; who can stand before his cold? 18. He sendeth out his word and melteth them, he causeth his winds to blow, and the waters flow."

Isa. xlv. 7: "I form the light, and create darkness; I make peace and create evil. I the Lord do all these things."

Dan. iv. 36: "And all the inhabitants of the earth are reputed as nothing; and he doeth according to his will in the army of heaven, and among the inhabitants of the earth, and none can stay his hand, or say unto him, What doest thou?"

Amos. iii. 6: "Shall a trumpet be blown in the city, and the people not be afraid? Shall there be evil in a city, and the Lord hath not done it?"

Matt. x. 29: "Are not two sparrows sold for a farthing? and one of them shall not fall on the ground without your Father."

Rom. xi. 36: "For of him, and through him, and to him, are all things."

Eph. i. 11: "In whom also we have obtained an inheritance, being predestinated according to the purpose of him who worketh all things after the counsel of his own will."

Matt. v. 45: "That ye may be the children of your Father which is in heaven; for he maketh his sun to rise on the evil and on the good, and sendeth rain on the just and on the unjust."

Matt. vi. 26: "Behold the fowls of the air, for they sow not, neither do they reap, nor gather into barns; yet your heavenly Father feedeth them. Are ye not much better than they? 28. And why take ye thought for raiment? Consider the lilies of the field, how they grow; they toil not, neither do they spin. 19. And yet I say unto you, that even Solomon in all his glory, was not arrayed like one of these. 30. Wherefore, if God so clothe the grass of the field, which to-day is, and to-morrow is cast into the oven, shall he not much more clothe you, O ye of little faith?"

Jer. x. 23: "O Lord, I know that the way of man is not in himself; it is not in man that walketh to direct his steps."

Jer. xviii. 6: "O house of Israel, cannot I do with you as this potter? saith the Lord. Behold, as the clay is in the potter' s hand, so are ye in mine hand, O house of Israel."

2 Cor. iii. 5: "Not that we are sufficient of ourselves to think anything, as of ourselves, but our sufficiency is of God."

Neh. ix. 5: "Thou, even thou, art Lord alone: thou hast made heaven, the heaven of heavens, with all their host, the earth, and all things that are therein, the seas, and all that is therein, and thou preservest them all; and the host of heaven worshippeth thee."

Ezek. xiv. 6: "And if the prophet be deceived when he hath spoken a thing, I the Lord have deceived that prophet; and I will stretch out my hand upon him, and will destroy him from the midst of my people Israel."

Luke x. 21: "In that hour Jesus rejoiced in spirit, and said, I thank thee, O Father, Lord of heaven and earth, that thou hast hid these things from the wise and prudent, and hast revealed them unto babes: even so, Father; for so it seemed good in thy sight."

John xii. 32: "Therefore they could not believe, because that Esaias said again, 40. He hath blinded their eyes, and hardened their heart; that they should not see with their eyes, nor understand with their heart, and be converted, and I should heal them. 41. These thing said Esaias, when he saw his glory, and spake of him."

Rom. ix. 18: "Therefore hath he mercy on whom he will have mercy, and whom he will he hardeneth."

2 Thess. ii. 10: "And with all deceivableness of unrighteousness in them that perish; because they received not the love of the truth, that they might be saved. 11. And for this cause God shall send them strong delusions, that they should believe a lie; 12. That they all might be damned who believed not the truth, but had pleasure in unrighteousness."

These passages will show the general tenor of scripture upon this subject.

IV. Different sense in which God purposes different events.

1. The great end of all his works and ways he must have purposed positively, that is, absolutely. This end, namely his own good and the highest good of the universe, he set his heart upon securing. This end he no doubt properly intended, or purposed to secure. This must have been his ultimate intention or purpose. This end was no doubt a direct object of choice.

2. God must no doubt also, in some sense, have purposed all the necessary means to this result. Such actions as tended naturally, or on account of their own nature, to this result, he must have purposed positively, in the sense that he delighted in them, and chose them because of their own nature, or of their natural relation to the great end he proposed to accomplish by them. Observe,

the end was an ultimate end, delighted in and chosen for its own sake. This end was the highest good or well-being of himself and the universe of sentient existences. This has been sufficiently shown in former lectures; and besides it follows of necessity from the nature and attributes of God. If this were not so, he would be neither wise nor good. Since he delighted in and chose the end for its own sake or value, and purposed it with a positive purpose, he must also have chosen and delighted in the necessary means. He must have created the universe, both of matter and of mind, and established its laws, with direct reference to, and for the sake of, the end he purposed to accomplish. The end was valuable in itself, and chosen for that reason. The necessary means were as really valuable as the end which depended upon them. This value, though real, because of their tendency and natural results, is not ultimate, but relative; that is, they are not, in the same sense that the end is, valuable in themselves; but they being the necessary means to this end, are as really valuable as the end that depends upon them. Thus our necessary food is not valuable in itself, but is the necessary means of prolonging our lives. Therefore, though not an ultimate good, yet it is a real good of as great value, as the end that naturally depends upon it. The naturally necessary means of securing a valuable end we justly esteem as equally valuable with the end, although this value is not absolute but relative. We are so accustomed to set a value on the means, equal to the estimated importance of the end to which they sustain the relation of necessary means, that we come loosely to regard and to speak of them as valuable in themselves, when in fact their value is not absolute but relative.

God must have purposed to secure, so far as he wisely could, obedience to the laws of the universe. These laws were established for the sake of the end to which they tended, and obedience to them must have been regarded by God as of real, though not ultimate, value, equal to that of the end, for the accomplishment of which they were ordained. He must have delighted in obedience to these laws for the sake of the end, and must have purposed to secure this obedience so far as he could in the nature of things; that is, in so far as he wisely could. Since moral law is a rule for the government of free moral agents, it is conceivable, that, in some cases, this law might be violated by the subjects of it, unless God resorted to means to prevent it, that might introduce an evil of greater magnitude than the violation of the law in the instances under consideration would be. It is conceivable, that, in some cases, God might be able so to overrule a violation of his laws, as upon the whole to secure a greater good than could be secured, by introducing such a change into the policy and measures of his administration, or so framing his administration, as to prevent altogether the violation of any law. In this case, he might regard the violation as the less of two evils, and suffer it rather than change the arrangements of his government. He might sincerely deplore and abhor these violations of law, and yet might see it not wise to prevent them, because the measures necessary to prevent them might result in an evil of still greater magnitude. He might purpose to suffer these violations, and take the trouble to overrule them, so far as was possible, for the promotion of the end he had in view, rather than interpose for their prevention. These violations he might not have purposed in any other sense than that he foresaw them, and purposed not to prevent them, but on the contrary to suffer them to occur, and to overrule them for good, so far as this was practicable. These events, or violations of law, have no natural tendency to promote the highest well-being of God and of the universe, but have in themselves a directly opposite tendency. Nevertheless, God could so overrule them as that these occurrences would be a less evil than that change would be that could have prevented them. Violations of law then, he might have purposed only to suffer, while obedience to law he might have designed to produce or secure.

3. We have seen, that God and men may have different motives in the same event, as in the case of the brethren of Joseph, already alluded to:--

Gen. xlv. 4: "And Joseph said unto his brethren, Come near to me, I pray you. And they came near. And he said, I am Joseph your brother, whom ye sold into Egypt. Now therefore be not grieved nor angry with yourselves that ye sold me hither; for God did send me before you to preserve life. 6. For these two years hath the famine been in the land; and yet there are five years, in the which there shall neither be earing nor harvest!"

As also in the case of the king of Assyria: Is. x. 5: "O Assyrian, the rod of mine anger, and the staff in their hand is mine indignation. 6. I will send him against a hypocritical nation, and against the people of my wrath will I give him a charge, to take the spoil, and to take the prey, and to tread them down like the mire of the streets. 7. Howbeit he meaneth not so, neither doth his heart think so; but it is in his heart to destroy and cut off nations not a few. 12. Wherefore it shall come to pass, that when the Lord hath performed his whole work upon mount Zion, and on Jerusalem, I will punish the fruit of the stout heart of the king of Assyria, and the glory of his high looks."

Also, John iii. 16: "For God so loved the world, that he gave his only begotten Son, that whosoever believeth in him should not perish, but have everlasting life."

Acts ii. 23. "Him being delivered by the determinate counsel and foreknowledge of God, ye have taken, and by wicked hands have crucified and slain."

These, and such like instances, show that wicked agents may, and often do, and when wicked always do, entertain a very different reason for their conduct from what God entertains in suffering it. They have a selfish end in view, or do what they do for a selfish reason. God, on the contrary, has a benevolent end in view in not interposing to prevent their sin; that is, he hates their sin as tending in itself, to destroy, or defeat the great end of benevolence. But foreseeing that the sin, notwithstanding its natural evil tendency, may be so overruled, as upon the whole to result in a less evil than the changes requisite to prevent it would, he benevolently prefers to suffer it rather than interpose to prevent it. He would, no doubt, prefer their perfect obedience, under the circumstances in which they are, but would sooner suffer them to sin, than so change the circumstances as to prevent it; the latter being, all things considered, the greater of two evils. God then always suffers his laws to be violated, because he cannot benevolently prevent it under the circumstances. He suffers it for benevolent reasons. But the sinner always has selfish reasons.

4. The Bible informs us, that God brings good out of evil, in the sense that he overrules sin to promote his own glory, and the good of being:--

Ps. lxxvi. 10. "Surely the wrath of man shall praise thee; the remainder of wrath shalt thou restrain."

Rom. iii. 5: "But if our unrighteousness commend the righteousness of God, what shall we say? Is God unrighteous who taketh vengeance? (I speak as a man.) 7. For if the truth of God hath more abounded through my lie unto his glory; why yet am I judged as a sinner? And not rather (as we be slanderously reported, and as some affirm that we say,) Let us do evil, that good may come? whose damnation is just."

Rom. v. 20: "Moreover, the law entered, that the offence might abound; but where sin abounded, grace did much more abound."

Rom. viii. 28: "And we know that all things work together for good to them that love God, to them who are the called according to his purpose."

5. The Bible also informs us that God does not aim at producing sin in creation and providence; that is, that he does not purpose the existence of sin in such a sense as to design to secure and promote it, in the administration of his government. In other words still, sin is not the object of a positive purpose on the part of God. It exists only by sufferance, and not as a thing which naturally tends to secure his great end, and which therefore he values on that account and endeavors to promote, as he does obedience to the law.

Jer. vii. 9. "Will ye steal, murder, and commit adultery, and swear falsely, and burn incense unto Baal, and walk after other gods whom ye know not? 10. And come and stand before me in this house, which is called by my name, and say, We are delivered to do all these abominations?"

1 Cor. xiv. 33: "For God is not the author of confusion, but of peace, as in all churches of the saints."

James i. 13: "Let no man say when he is tempted, I am tempted of God; for God cannot be tempted with evil, neither tempteth he any man; 14. But every man is tempted, when he is drawn away of his own lust, and enticed. 15. Then when lust hath conceived, it bringeth forth sin; and sin when it is finished, bringeth forth death. 16. Do not err, my beloved brethren. 17. Every good gift and every perfect gift is from above, and cometh down from the Father of lights, with whom is no variableness, neither shadow of turning."

James iii. 14: "But if ye have bitter envying and strife in your hearts, glory not, and lie not against the truth. 15. This wisdom descendeth not from above, but is earthly, sensual, devilish. 16. For where envying and strife is, there is confusion, and every evil work. 17. But the wisdom that is from above is first pure, then peaceable, and gentle, and easy to be entreated, full of mercy and good fruits, without partiality and hypocrisy."

1 John ii. 16: "For all that is in the world, the lust of the flesh, and the lust of the eyes, and the pride of life, is not of the Father, but is of the world."

Obedience to law is an object of positive purpose. God purposes to promote it, and uses means with that design. Sin occurs incidentally, so far as the purpose of God is concerned. It need not be, and doubtless is not, the object of positive design or purpose, but comes to pass because it cannot wisely be prevented. God uses means to promote obedience. But moral agents, in the exercise of their free agency, often disobey in spite of all the inducements to the contrary which God can wisely set before them. God never sets aside the freedom of moral agents to prevent their sinning, nor to secure their obedience. The Bible everywhere represents men as acting freely under the government and universal providence of God, and it represents sin as the result of, or as consisting in, an abuse of their freedom.

Gen. xlii. 21: "And they said one to another, We are verily guilty concerning our brother, in that we saw the anguish of his soul, when he besought us, and we would not hear; therefore is this distress come upon us."

Ex. viii. 32: "And Pharaoh hardened his heart at this time also, neither would he let the people go."

Ex. ix. 27: "And Pharaoh sent, and called for Moses and Aaron, and said unto them, I have sinned this time: the Lord is righteous, and I and my people are wicked."

Ex. x. 16: "Then Pharaoh called for Moses and Aaron in haste; and he said, I have sinned against the Lord your God, and against you. 17. Now therefore forgive, I pray thee, my sin only this once, and entreat the Lord your God, that he may take away from me this death only."

Deut. xxx. 19: "I call heaven and earth to record this day against you, that I have set before you life and death, blessing and cursing: therefore choose life, that both thou and thy seed may live."

Josh. xxiv. 15: "And if it seem evil unto you to serve the Lord, choose ye this day whom ye will serve; whether the gods which your fathers served that were on the other side of the flood, or the gods of the Amorites, in whose land ye dwell; but as for me and my house, we will serve the Lord."

2 Sam. xxiv. 1: "And again the anger of the Lord was kindled against Israel, and he moved David against them to say, Go, number Israel and Judah. 10. And David' s heart smote him after that he had numbered the people. And David said unto the Lord, I have sinned greatly in that I have done: and now, I beseech thee, O Lord, take away the iniquity of thy servant; for I have done very foolishly."

Prov. i. 10: "My son, if sinners entice thee, consent thou not. 29. For that they hated knowledge, and did not choose the fear of the Lord; 30. They would none of my counsel; they despised all my reproof; 31. Therefore shall they eat of the fruit of their own way, and be filled with their own devices."

Prov. xvi. 9: "A man' s heart deviseth his way, but the Lord directeth his steps."

The following things appear to be true in respect to the purposes of God, as taught both by reason and revelation:--

(1.) That God's purposes extend in some sense to all events.

(2.) That he positively purposes the highest good of being, as a whole as his end.

(3.) That he has ordained wise and wholesome laws as the necessary means of securing this end.

(4.) That he positively purposes to secure obedience to these laws in so far as he wisely can, and uses means with this design.

(5.) That he does not positively purpose to secure disobedience to his laws in any case, and use means with that design; but that he only purposes to suffer violations of his law rather than prevent them, because he foresees that, by his overruling power, he can prevent the violation from resulting in so great an evil as the change necessary to prevent it would do. Or in other words, he sees that he can secure a greater good upon the whole, by suffering the violation under the circumstances in which it occurs, than he could by interposing to prevent it. This is not the same thing as to say, that sin is the necessary means of the greatest good. For should all moral agents perfectly obey, under the identical circumstances in winch they disobey, this might, and doubtless would result in the highest possible good. But God, foreseeing that it were more conducive to the highest good of being to suffer some to sin, rather than so change the circumstances as to prevent it, purposed to suffer their sin, and overrule it for good; but he did not aim at producing it, and use means with that intent.

V. God's revealed will is never inconsistent with his secret purpose.

It has been common to represent sin as the necessary occasion, condition, or means of the greatest good, in such a sense, that upon the whole God secretly, but really prefers sin to holiness in every case where it exists; that while he has forbidden sin under all circumstances, upon pain of eternal death, yet because it is the necessary occasion, condition, or means of the greatest good, God really prefers its existence to holiness in every instance in which it exists. It has been said, sin exists. God does not therefore prevent it. But he could and would prevent it, if he did not upon the whole prefer it to holiness, in the circumstances in which it occurs. Its existence, then, it has been said, is proof conclusive that God secretly prefers its existence to holiness, in every case in which it occurs. But this is a non sequitur. It does not follow from the existence of sin, that God prefers sin to holiness in the circumstances in which it occurs; but it may be that he only prefers sin to such a change of circumstances as would prevent it. Suppose I require my son to do a certain thing. I know that he will do it, if I remain at home and see to it. But I know also, that if I go from home he will not do it. Now I might prefer that he should do as I command, and consider his disobedience as a great evil; still I might regard it as a less evil than for me to remain at home, and keep my eye upon him. I might have just reasons for supposing that, under the circumstances, a greater good could be secured upon the whole by my going from home, although his disobedience might be the consequence, than by remaining at home, and preventing his disobedience. Benevolence therefore might require me to go.

But should my son infer from my leaving him, under these circumstances, that I really, though secretly, preferred his disobedience to his obedience, under the identical circumstances in which I gave the command, would his inference be legitimate? No, indeed. All that he could justly infer from my leaving him, with the knowledge that he would disobey me if I did, would be, that although I regarded his disobedience as a great evil, yet I regarded remaining at home a greater.

Just so, it may be when sin exists. God is sincere in prohibiting it. He would greatly prefer that it should not exist. All that can be justly inferred from his not preventing it is, that, although he regards its existence as a great and real evil, yet upon the whole he regards it as a less evil, than would result from so great a change in the administration of his government as would prevent it. He is therefore entirely and infinitely sincere in requiring obedience, and in prohibiting disobedience, and his secret purpose is in strict keeping with his revealed will. Were the moral law universally obeyed, under the circumstances in which all moral agents exist, no one can say, that this would not be better for the universe, and more pleasing to God than disobedience is in the same circumstances. Nor is it fair to infer, that upon the whole, God must prefer sin to holiness, where it occurs, from the fact that he does not prevent it. As has been said, all that can justly be inferred from his not preventing it is, that under the circumstances he prefers not sin to holiness, but prefers to suffer the agent to sin and take the consequences, rather than introduce such changes in the policy and administration of his government as would prevent it. Or it may be said, that the present system is the best that infinite wisdom could devise and execute, not because of sin, but in spite of it, and notwithstanding sin is a real though incidental evil.

It is a palpable contradiction and an absurdity to affirm, that any being call sin, intending thereby to promote the greatest good. This will appear if we consider:--

1. That it is admitted on all hands, that benevolence is virtue.

2. That benevolence consists in willing good, or the highest good of being as an end.

3. That it is duty to will both the end and the necessary means to promote it.

4. That right and benevolence are always at one, that is, that which is benevolent must always be right, and can in no case be wrong.

5. That consequently it can never be sin to choose the highest good of being, with all the necessary occasions, conditions, and means of promoting it.

6. It is impossible therefore for a being to sin, or to consent to sin, as an occasion, condition, or means, or designing thereby to promote the highest good of being; for this design would be virtue, and not sin. Whether all virtue consists in benevolence, or not, still it must be admitted, that all forms of virtue must be consistent with benevolence, unless it be admitted, that there can be a law of right inconsistent with, and opposed to, the law of benevolence. But this would be to admit, that two moral laws might be opposed to each other; which would be to admit, that a moral agent might be under an obligation to obey two opposing laws at the same time, which is a contradiction. Thus it appears, that there can be no law of right opposed to, or separate from, the law of benevolence. Benevolence and right must then always be at one. If this be so, it follows, that whatever benevolence demands, cannot be wrong, but must be right. But the law of benevolence demands not only the choice of the highest good of being as an end, but also demands the choice of all the known necessary occasions, conditions, and means with a design to promote that end.

It is naturally impossible to sin, in using means designed and known to be necessary to the promotion of the end of benevolence. It is therefore naturally impossible to do evil, or to sin, that good may come, or with the design to promote good thereby.

Let those who hold that right and benevolence may be opposed to each other, and that a moral agent can sin with a benevolent intention, see what their doctrine amounts to, and get out of the absurdity as best they can. The fact is, if willing the highest good of being is always virtuous, it must always be right to will all the necessary occasions, conditions, and means to that end. It is therefore a contradiction to say that sin can be among the necessary and intended occasions, conditions, and means; that is, that any one could sin intending thereby to promote the highest good.

But it is not pretended by those who hold this dogma, that sin sustains to the highest good the same relations that holiness does. Holiness has a natural tendency to promote the highest good; but the supposition now under consideration is, that sin is hateful in itself, and that it therefore must dissatisfy and disgust all moral agents, and that its natural tendency is to defeat the end of moral government, and to prevent rather than promote the highest good; but that God foresees that, notwithstanding its intrinsically odious and injurious nature, he can so overrule it as to make it the condition, occasion, or instrument of the highest good of himself and of his universe, and that for this reason he really upon the whole is pleased that it should occur, and prefers its existence in every instance in which it does exist, to holiness in its stead. The supposition is, that sin is in its own nature infinitely odious and abominable to God, and perfectly odious to all holy moral agents, yet it is the occasion of calling into development and exercise such emotions and feelings in God and in holy beings, and such modifications of benevolence, its do really more than compensate for all the disgust and painful emotions that result to holy beings, and for all the remorse, agony, despair, and endless suffering, that result to sinners.

It is not supposed by any one that I know of, that sin naturally tends to promote the highest good at all, but only that God can, and does, so overrule and counteract its natural tendency, as to make it the occasion or condition of a greater good, than holiness would be in its stead. Now in reply to this, I would say, that I pretend not to determine to what extent God can, and will, overrule and counteract the naturally evil and injurious tendency of sin. It surely is enough to say that God prohibits it and that it is impossible for creatures to know that sin is the necessary occasion, or condition, or means of the highest good.

If sin is known by God to be the necessary occasion, condition, or means of the highest good of himself and of the universe, whatever it may be in itself, yet viewed in its relations, it must be regarded by him as of infinite value, since it is the indispensable condition of infinite good.' According to this theory, sin in every instance in which it exists, is and must be regarded by God as of infinitely greater value than holiness would be in its stead. He must then, upon the whole, have infinite complacency in it. But this leads me to attend to the principal arguments by which it is supposed this theory is maintained. It is said, for example:--

(1.) That the highest good of the universe of moral agents is conditionated upon the revelation of the attributes and character of God to them; that but for sin these attributes, at least some of them, could never have been revealed, inasmuch as without sin there would have been no occasion for their display or manifestation; that neither justice nor mercy, nor forbearance, nor self denial, nor meekness, could have found the occasions of their exercise or manifestation, had sin never existed.

To this I reply, that sin has indeed furnished the occasion for a glorious manifestation of the moral perfections of God. From this we see that God's perfections enable him greatly to overrule sin, and to bring good out of evil: but from this we are not authorized to infer, that God could not have revealed these attributes to his creatures without the existence of sin. Nor can we say, that these revelations would have been necessary to the highest perfection and happiness of the universe, had all moral agents perfectly and uniformly obeyed. When we consider what the moral attributes of God are, it is easy to see that there may be myriads of moral attributes in God of which no creature has, or ever will have, any knowledge; and the knowledge of which is not at all essential to the highest perfection and happiness of the universe of creatures. God's moral attributes are only his benevolence, existing and contemplated in its various relations to the universe of beings. Benevolence in any being must possess as many attributes as there are possible relations under which it can be contemplated, and should their occasions arise, these attributes would stand forth in exercise. It is not at all probable, that all of the attributes of benevolence, either in the Creator or in creatures, have yet found the occasions of their exercise, nor, perhaps, will they ever. As new occasions rise to all eternity, benevolence will develop new and striking attributes, and manifest itself under endless forms and varieties of loveliness. There can be no such thing as exhausting its capabilities of development.

In God benevolence is infinite. Creatures can never know all its attributes, nor approach any nearer to knowing all of them than they now are. There can be no end to its capabilities of developing in exercise new forms of beauty and loveliness. It is true, that God has taken occasion to show forth the glory of his benevolence through the existence of sin. He has seized the occasion, though mournful in itself, to manifest some of the attributes of his benevolence by the exercise of them. It is also true, that we cannot know how or by what means God could have revealed these attributes, if sin had not existed; and it is also true, that we cannot know that such a revelation was impossible without the existence of sin; nor that, but for sin, the revelation would have been necessary to the highest good of the universe.

God forbids sin, and requires universal holiness. He must be sincere in this. But sin exists. Shall we say that he secretly chooses that it should, and really, though secretly, prefers its existence to holiness, in, the circumstances in which it occurs? Or shall we assume, that it is an evil, that God regards it as such, but that he cannot wisely prevent it; that is, to prevent it would introduce a still greater evil? It is an evil, and a great evil, but still the less of two evils; that is, to suffer it to occur, under the circumstances, is a less evil than such a change of circumstances, as would prevent it, would be. This is all we can justly infer from its existence. This leaves the sincerity of God unimpeached, and sustains his consistency, and the consistency and integrity of his law. The opposite supposition represents God and the law as infinitely deceitful.

(2.) It has been said, that the Bible sustains the supposition, that sin is the necessary means of the highest good. I trust the passages that have been quoted, disprove this saying.

(3.) It is said, that to represent sin as not the means of the highest good, and God as unable to prevent it, is to represent God as unable to accomplish all his will; whereas he says, he will do all his pleasure, and that nothing is too hard for him.

I answer: God pleases to do only what is naturally possible, and he is well pleased to do that and nothing more. This he is able to do. This be will do. This he does. This is all he claims to be able to do; and this is all that in fact infinite wisdom and power can do.

(4.) But it is said, that if sin is an evil, and God can neither prevent nor overrule it, so as to make it a means of greater good than could be secured without it, he must be unhappy in view of this fact, because he cannot prevent it, and secure a higher good without it.

I answer: God neither desires nor wills to perform natural impossibilities. God is a reasonable being, and does not aim at nor desire impossibilities. He is well content to do as well as, in the nature of the case, is possible, and has no unreasonable regrets because he is not more than infinite, and that he cannot accomplish what is impossible to infinity itself. His good pleasure is, to secure all the good that is possible to infinity: with this he is infinitely well pleased.

Again: does not the objection, that the view of the subject here presented limits the divine power, lie with all its force against those who make this objection? To hold that sin is the necessary means or condition of the highest good, is to hold that God was unable to promote the highest good without resorting to such vile means as sin. Sin is an abomination in itself; and do not they, as really and as much limit the power of God, who maintain his inability to promote the highest good without it, as they do who hold, that he could not wisely so interfere with the free actions of moral agents as to prevent it? Sin exists. God abhors it. How is its existence to be accounted for? I suppose it to be an evil unavoidably incidental to that system of moral government which, notwithstanding the evil, was upon the whole the best that could be adopted. Others suppose that sin is the necessary means or condition of the greatest good; and account for its existence in this way:--that is, they suppose that God admits or permits its existence as a necessary occasion, condition, or means of the highest good; that he was not able to secure the highest good without it. The two explanations of the admitted fact that sin exists, differ in this:--

One method of explanation holds, that sin is the necessary occasion, condition, or means of the highest good; and that God actually, upon the whole, prefers the existence of sin to holiness, in every instance in which it exists; because, in those circumstances, it is a condition or means of greater good than could have been secured by holiness in its stead. This theory represents God as unable to secure his end by other means, or upon other conditions, than sin. The other theory holds, that God really prefers holiness to sin in every instance in which it occurs; that he regards sin as an evil, but that while he regards it as an evil, he suffers its existence as a less evil than such a change in the administration of his government as would prevent it, would be. Both theories must admit, that in some sense God could not wisely prevent it. Explain the fact of its existence as you will, it must be admitted, that in some sense God was not able to prevent it, and secure his end.

If it be said, that God could neither wisely prevent it, nor so overrule it as to make it the means or condition of the highest good, he must be rendered unhappy by its existence; I reply, that this must be equally true upon the other hypothesis. Sin is hateful, and its consequences are a great evil. These consequences will be eternal and indefinitely great. God must disapprove these consequences. If sin is the necessary condition or means of the greatest good, must not God lament that he cannot secure the good without a resort to such loathsome, and such horrible means? If his inability wisely to prevent it will interfere with and diminish his happiness, must not the same be true of his inability to secure the highest good, without such means as will prove the eternal destruction of millions?

VI. Wisdom and benevolence of the purposes of God.

We have seen that God is both wise and benevolent. This is the doctrine both of reason and of revelation. The reason intuitively affirms that God is, and is perfect. The Bible assumes that he is, and declares that he is perfect. Both wisdom and benevolence must be attributes of the infinite and perfect God. These attributes enter into the reason's idea of God. The reason could not recognize any being as God to whom these attributes did not belong. But if infinite wisdom and benevolence are moral attributes of God, it follows of course that all his designs or purposes are both perfectly wise and benevolent. God has chosen the best possible end, and pursues it in the use of the best practicable means. His purposes embrace the end and the means necessary to secure it, together with the best practicable disposal of the sin, which is the incidental result of his choosing this end and using these means; and they extend no further; they are all therefore perfectly wise and good.

VII. The immutability of the divine purposes.

We have seen that immutability is not only a natural, but also a moral attribute of God. The reason affirms, that the self-existent and infinitely perfect God is unchangeable in all his attributes. The ground of this affirmation it is not my purpose here to inquire into. It is sufficient here to say, what every one knows, that such is the affirmation of the reason. This is also everywhere assumed and taught in the Bible. God's moral attributes are not immutable in the sense of necessity, but only in the sense of certainty. Although God is not necessarily benevolent, yet he is as immutably so, as if he were necessarily so. If his benevolence were necessary, it would Dot be virtuous, for the simple reason that it would not be free. But being free, its immutability renders it all the more praiseworthy.

VIII. The purposes of God are a ground of eternal and joyful confidence.

That is, they may reasonably be a source of eternal comfort, joy, and peace. Selfish beings will not of course rejoice in them, but benevolent beings will and must. If they are infinitely wise and good, and sure to be accomplished, they must form a rational ground of unfailing confidence and joy. God says:--

Isa. xlvi. 10: "Declaring the end from the beginning, and from ancient times the things that are not yet done, saying, My counsel shall stand, and I will do all my pleasure."

Psa. xxxiii. 11: "The counsel of the Lord standeth for ever, the thoughts of his heart to all generations."

Prov. xix. 21: "There are many devices in a man' s heart, nevertheless, the counsel of the Lord, that shall stand."

Acts v. 39: "But if it be of God, ye cannot overthrow it, lest haply ye be found even to fight against God."

These, and many parallel passages are reasonably the source of perpetual confidence and joy to those who love God, and sympathize with him.

IX. The relation of God's purposes to his prescience or foreknowledge.

We have seen that God is omniscient, that is, that he necessarily and eternally knows whatever is, or can be, an object of knowledge. His purposes must also be eternal and immutable, as we have seen. In the order of time, therefore, his purposes and his foreknowledge must be coeval, that is, they must be co-eternal.

But in the order of nature, God's knowledge of what he could do, and what could be done, must have preceded his purposes: that is, he could not, so to speak, in the order of nature, have formed his purpose and made up his mind what to do, until he had considered what could be done, and what was best to be done. Until all possible ends, and ways, and means, were weighed and understood, it was of course impossible to make a selection, and settle upon the end with all the necessary means; and also settle upon the ways and means of overruling any evil, natural or moral, that might be seen to be unavoidably incidental to any system. Thus it appears, that, in the order of nature, fore-knowledge of what could be done, and what he could do, must have preceded the purpose to do. The purpose resulted from the prescience or fore-knowledge. He knew what he could do, before he decided what he would do. But, on the other hand, the purpose to do must, in the order of nature, have preceded the knowledge of what he should do, or of what would be done, or would come to pass as a result of his purpose. Viewed relatively to what he could do, and what could be done, the Divine prescience must in the order of nature have preceded the Divine purposes. But viewed relatively to what he would do, and what would be done, and would come to pass, the Divine purposes must, in the order of nature, have preceded the Divine prescience. But I say again, as fore-knowledge was necessarily eternal with God, his purposes must also have been eternal, and therefore, in the order of time, neither his prescience could have preceded his purposes, nor his purposes have preceded his prescience. They must have been cotemporaneous and co-eternal.

X. God's purposes are not inconsistent with, but demand the use of means both on his part, and on our part, to accomplish them.

The great end upon which he has set his heart necessarily depends upon the use of means, both moral and physical, to accomplish it. The highest well-being of the whole universe is his end. This end can be secured only by securing conformity to the laws of matter and of mind. Mind is influenced by motives, and hence moral and physical government are naturally necessary means of securing the great end proposed by the Divine mind.

Hence also results the necessity of a vast and complicated system of means and influences, such as we see spread around us on every hand. The history of the universe is but the history of creation, and of the means which God is using to secure his end, with their natural and incidental results. It has already been shown, that the Bible teaches that the purposes of God include and respect both means and ends. I will only add, that God's purposes do not render any event, dependent upon the acts of a moral agent, necessarily certain, or certain with a certainty of necessity. Although, as was before said, all events are certain with some kind of certainty, and would be and must be, if they are ever to conic to pass, whether God purposes them, or whether he foreknows them or not; yet no event, depending upon the will of a free agent, is, or can be, certain with a certainty of necessity. The agent could by natural possibility do otherwise than he will do, or than God purposes to suffer him to do, or wills that he shall do. God's purposes, let it be understood, are not a system of fatality. They leave every moral agent entirely free to choose and act freely. God knows infallibly how every creature will act, and has made all his arrangements accordingly, to overrule the wicked actions of moral agents on the one hand, and to produce or induce, the holy actions of others on the other hand. But be it remembered, that neither the Divine fore-knowledge nor the Divine purpose, in any instance, sets aside the free agency of the creature. He, in every instance, acts as freely and as responsibly, as if God neither knew nor purposed anything respecting his conduct, or his destiny.

God's purposes extend to all events in some sense, as has been shown. They extend as really to the most common events of life as to the most rare. But in respect to the every day transactions of life, men are not wont to stumble, and cavil, and say, Why, if I am to live, I shall live, whatever I may do to destroy my health and life; and if I am to die, I cannot live, do what I will. No, in these events they will not throw off responsibility, and cast themselves upon the purposes of God; but on the contrary, they are as much engaged to secure the end they have in view, as if God neither knew nor purposed anything about it. Why then should they do as they often do, in regard to the salvation of their souls, cast off responsibility, and settle down in listless inactivity, as if the purposes of God in respect to salvation were but a system of iron fatality, from which there is no escape? Surely "madness is in their hearts while they live." But let them understand, that, in thus doing, they sin against the Lord, and be sure their sin will find them out.

LECTURE XLVII - PERSEVERANCE OF SAINTS

In discussing this subject, I will,

I. Notice the different kinds of certainty.

Every thing must be certain with some kind of certainty. There is a way in which all things and events either have been, are, or will be. All events that ever did or will occur, were and are as really certain before as after their occurrence. To an omniscient mind their real certainty might and must have been known, as really before as after their occurrence. All future events, for example, will occur in some way, and there is no real uncertainty in fact, nor can there be any real uncertainty in the knowledge of God respecting them. They are really as certain before they come to pass as they will ever be, and they are as truly and perfectly known as certain by God as they ever will be. They are as truly present to the Divine fore-knowledge as they ever will be. Whatever of contingency and uncertainty there may be respecting them in some respects, yet, in point of fact, all events are certain, and there is no real uncertainty in respect to any event that ever did or will occur. This would be equally true, whether God or any other being knew how they would be or not. The fore-knowledge of God does not make them certain. He knows them to be certain simply because they are so. Omniscience is the necessary knowledge of all objects of knowledge, past, present, and future. But omniscience does not create objects of knowledge. It does not render events certain, but only knows how they certainly will be, because it is certain, not only that they will be, but how and when they will be. All the free actions of moral agents are as really certain before they occur, as they ever will be. And God must as truly know how they will be before they occur, as he does after they have occurred.

1. The first kind of certainty that I shall notice, is that of absolute necessity; that is, a certainty depending on no conditions whatever. This is the highest kind of certainty. It belongs to the absolute and the infinite, to the existence of space, duration, and to the existence of God; and in short to everything that is self-existent, infinite, and immutable in a natural sense; that is, to everything infinite that does not imply voluntariness. The natural attributes of God are certain by this kind of certainty, but his moral attributes, consisting as they do in a voluntary state of mind, though infinite and eternal, do not belong to this class.

2. A second kind of certainty is that of physical, but conditional necessity. To this class belong all those events that come to pass under the operation of physical law. These belong properly to the chain of cause and effect. The cause existing, the effect must exist. The event is rendered certain and necessary by the existence of its cause. Its certainty is conditionated upon its cause. The cause existing, the event must follow by a law of necessity, and the events would not occur of course, did not their causes exist. The causes being what they are, the events must be what they are. This class of events are as really certain as the foregoing class. By speaking of one of them as certain in a higher sense than the other, it is not intended, that one class is any more certain than

the other, but only that the certainty is of a different kind. For example, the first class are certain by a kind of certainty that does not, and never did depend on the will of any being whatever. There never was any possibility that these things should be otherwise than they are. This, it will be seen, must be true of space and duration, and of the existence and the natural attributes of God.

But all other things except the self-existent, the naturally immutable and eternal, are certain only as they are conditionated directly or indirectly upon the will of some being. For example, all the events of the physical universe were rendered certain by creation, and the establishing and upholding of those physical and necessary laws that cause these events. These are, therefore, certain by a conditioned, though physical necessity. There is no freedom or liberty in the events themselves; they occur necessarily, when their causes or conditions are supplied.

3. A third kind of certainty is that of a moral certainty. I call it a moral certainty, not because the class of events which belong to it are less certain than the foregoing, but because they consist in, or are conditionated upon, the free actions of moral agents. This class do not occur under the operation of a law of necessity, though they occur with certainty. There is no contingency predicable of the absolutely certain in the sense of absolute certainty above defined. The second class of certainties are contingent only in respect to their causes. Upon condition that the causes are certain, the events depending upon them are certain, without or beyond any contingency. This third class, though no less certain than the former two, are nevertheless contingent in the highest sense in which anything can be contingent. They occur under the operation of free will, and consequently there is not one of them that might not by natural possibility fail, or be otherwise than it is or will in fact be. This kind of certainty I call a moral certainty, as opposed to a physical certainty, that is, it is not a certainty of necessity in any sense; it is only a mere certainty, or a voluntary certainty, a free certainty, a certainty that might, by natural possibility in every case, be no certainty at all. But, on the contrary, the opposite might in every instance be certain by a natural possibility. God in every instance, knows how these events will be, as really as if they occurred by necessity; but his foreknowledge does not affect their certainty one way or the other. They might in every instance by natural possibility be no certainties at all, or be the opposite of what they are or will be, God's foreknowledge in anywise notwithstanding. God knows them to be certain, not because his knowledge has any influence of itself to necessitate them, but because they are certain in themselves. Because it is certain in itself that they will be, God knows that they will be. To this class of events belong all the free actions of moral agents. All events maybe traced ultimately to the action of God's free will; that is, God's free actions gave existence to the universe, with all its physical agencies and laws, so that all physical events are in some sense owing to, and result from the actions of free will. But physical events occur nevertheless under the immediate operation of a law of necessity. The class now under consideration depend not upon the operation of physical law as their cause. They are caused by the free agent himself. They find the occasions of their occurrence in the providential events with which moral agents are surrounded, and therefore may be traced indirectly, and more or less remotely, to the actions of the Divine will.

Concerning this class of events, I would further remark that they are not only contingent in such a sense, that they might in every case by natural possibility be other than they are, but there may be, humanly speaking, the utmost danger that they will be otherwise than they really will be, that is, there may be danger, and the utmost danger, in the only sense in which there can be in fact any danger that any event will be otherwise than what it turns out to be. All events being really certain, there is in fact no danger that any event whatever will turn out differently from what it does, in the sense that it is not certain how it will be. But since all acts of free will, and all events dependent on those acts, are contingent in the highest sense in which any event can in the nature of things be contingent; and in the sense that, humanly speaking, there may be millions of chances to one that they will be otherwise than they will in fact turn out to be,--we say of all this class of events, that there is danger that they may or may not occur.

Again: I remark in respect to this class of events, that God may foresee that so intricate is the labyrinth, and so complicated are the occasions of failure, that nothing but the utmost watchfulness and diligent use of means on his part, and on our part, can secure the occurrence of the event. Everything revealed in the Bible concerning the perseverance and final salvation of the saints, and everything that is true, and that God knows of the free actions and destinies of the saints, may be of this class. These events are nevertheless certain, and are known to God as certainties. Not one of them will, in fact, turn out differently from what he foresees that they will; and yet by natural possibility, they might every one of them turn out differently; and there may, in the only sense in which danger is predicable of anything, be the utmost danger that some or all of them will turn out differently from what they in fact will. These events are contingent in such a sense, that should the means fail to be used, or should any event in the whole chain of influences connected with their occurrence, be otherwise than it is, the end or event resulting, would or might be otherwise, than in fact it will be. They are, nevertheless, certain, every one of them, together with all the influences upon which each free act depends. Nothing is uncertain in respect to whether it will occur or not; and yet no free act, or event depending upon a free act, is certain, in the sense that it cannot by natural possibility be otherwise, nor in the sense that there may not be great danger, or, humanly speaking, a probability that it will be otherwise, and that, humanly speaking, there may not be many chances to one that it will be otherwise.

When I say, that any event may, by natural possibility, be otherwise than what it will in fact be, I mean, that the free agent has natural power in every instance to choose otherwise than he does or actually will choose. As an illustration of both the contingency and the certainty of this class of events, suppose a man about to attempt to cross Lake Erie on a wire, or to pass down the falls of Niagara in a bark canoe. The result of this attempt is really certain. God must know how it will be. But this result, though certain, is conditionated upon a multitude of things, each of which the agent has natural power to make otherwise than in fact he will. To secure his safe crossing, every volition must be just what and as it will be; but there is not one among them that might not, by natural possibility, be the opposite of what it will be.

Again, the case may be such, and the danger of failure so great, that nothing could secure the safe crossing, but a revelation from God that would inspire confidence, that the adventurer should in fact cross the lake, or venture down the falls safely: I say, this revelation of God might be indispensable to his safe crossing. Suppose it were revealed to a man under such circumstances, that he should actually arrive in safety; but the revelation was accompanied with the emphatic assurance, that the end depended upon the most diligent, cautious, and persevering use of means on his part, and that any failure in these would defeat the end. Both the revelation of the certainty of success, and the emphatic warning, might be indispensable to the securing of the end. Now, if the adventurer had confidence in the promise of success, he would have confidence in the caution not to neglect the necessary means, and his confidence in both might secure the desired result. But take an example from scripture:--

Acts xxvii. 21: "But after long abstinence, Paul stood forth in the midst of them, and said, Sirs, ye should have hearkened unto me, and not have loosed from Crete, and to have gained this harm and loss. 22. And now I exhort you to be of good cheer: for there shall be no loss of any man's life among you, but of the ship. For there stood by me this night the angel of God, whose I am, and whom I serve, 24. Saying, Fear not, Paul: thou must be brought before Cæsar: and lo, God hath given thee all them that sail with thee. 25. Wherefore, sirs, be of good cheer: for I believe God, that it shall be even as it was told me. 26. Howbeit we must be cast upon a certain island. 27. But when the fourteenth night was come, as we were driven up and down in Adria, about midnight the ship-men deemed that they drew near to some country; 28. And sounded, and found it twenty fathoms: and when they had gone a little further, they sounded again, and found it fifteen fathoms. 29. Then fearing lest we should have fallen upon rocks, they cast anchors out of the stern, and wished for the day. 30. And as the ship-men were about to flee out of the ship, when they had let down the boat into the sea, under color as though they would have cast anchors out of the fore-ship, 31. Paul said to the centurion and to the soldiers, Except these abide in the ship, ye cannot be saved." Here the end was foreknown and expressly foretold at first, without any condition expressed, though they plainly understood that the end was to be secured by means. Paul afterwards informed them, that if they neglected the means, the end would fail. Both the means and the end were certain in fact, and God therefore expressly revealed the certainty of the result, and afterwards by a subsequent revelation secured the use of the necessary means. Here was no uncertainty, in the sense that the thing might, in fact, turn out otherwise than it did, and yet it was uncertain in the sense that, by natural possibility, both the means and the end might fail.

I remark, again, in respect to events that are morally certain, that if they are greatly desired, they are not the more, but all the less, in danger of failing, by how much stronger the confidence is that they will occur, provided it be understood, that they are certain only by a moral certainty; that is, provided it be understood, that the event is conditioned upon the free acts of the agent himself.

Again: it is generally admitted, that hope is a condition of success in any enterprise; and if this is so, assurance of success, upon the proper conditions, cannot tend to defeat the end.

I remark, again, that there is a difference between real danger, and a knowledge or sense of danger. There may be as great and as real danger when we have no sense or knowledge of it, as when we have. And on the other hand, when we have the highest and the keenest sense of danger, there may be, in fact, no real danger; and indeed, as has been said, there never is any danger in the sense that anything will, as a matter of fact, turn out differently from what God foresees it will be.

Again: the fact that anything is revealed as certain, does not make it certain; that is, the revelation does not make it certain. It had been certain, had not this certainty been revealed, unless it be in cases where the revelation is a condition or means of the certainty revealed. An event may be really certain, and may be revealed as certain, and yet, humanly speaking, there may be millions of chances to one, that it will not be as it is revealed; that is, so far as human foresight can go, the probabilities may all be against it.

II. State what is not intended by the perseverance of the saints, as I hold the doctrine.

1. It is not intended that any sinner will be saved without complying with the conditions of salvation; that is, without regeneration, and persevering in obedience to the end of life, in a sense to be hereafter explained.

2. It is not intended that saints, or the truly regenerate, cannot fall from grace, and be finally lost, by natural possibility. It must be naturally possible for all moral agents to sin at any time. Saints on earth and in heaven can by natural possibility apostatize and fall, and be lost. Were not this naturally possible, there would be no virtue in perseverance.

3. It is not intended, that the true saints are in no danger of apostasy and ultimate damnation. For, humanly speaking, there may be, and doubtless is, the greatest danger in respect to many, if not of all of them, in the only sense in which danger is predicable of any event whatever, that they will apostatize, and be ultimately lost.

4. It is not intended, that there may not be, humanly speaking, myriads of chances to one, that some, or that many of them will fall and be lost. This may be, as we say, highly probable; that is, it may be probable in the only sense in which it is probable, that any event whatever may be different from what it will turn out to be.

5. It is not intended, that the salvation of the saints is possible, except upon condition of great watchfulness and effort, and perseverance on their part, and great grace on the part of God.

6. It is not intended, that their salvation is certain, in any higher sense than all their future free actions are. The result is conditioned upon their free actions, and the end can be no more certain than its means or conditions. If the ultimate salvation of the saints is certain, it is certain only upon condition, that their perseverance in obedience to the end of life is certain. Every act of this obedience is free and contingent in the highest sense in which contingency can be predicated of any thing whatever. It is also uncertain by the highest kind of uncertainty that can be predicated of any event whatever. Therefore there is and must be, as much real danger of the saints failing of ultimate salvation, as there is that any event whatever will be different from what it turns out to be.

But here it should be distinctly remembered, as was said, that there is a difference between a certainty and a knowledge of it. It is one thing for an event to be really certain, and another thing for us to have a knowledge of it as certain. Everything is really equally certain, but many things are not revealed to us as certain. Those that are revealed as certain, are no more really so than others, but with respect to future things, not in some way revealed to us, we know not how they will prove to be. The fact that a thing is revealed to us as certain does not make it certain, nor is it really any the less uncertain because it is revealed to us as certain, unless the revelation tends to secure the certainty. Suppose the ultimate salvation of all the saints is certain, and that this certainty is revealed to us; unless this revelation is the means of securing their salvation, they are in just as much real danger of ultimately failing of eternal life, as if no such revelation had been made. Notwithstanding the certainty of their salvation, and the fact that this certainty is revealed to them, there is just as much real, though unknown, certainty or uncertainty, in respect to any future event whatever, as there is in respect to this. All events are certain with some kind of certainty, and would be whether any being whatever knew the certainty or not. So all events, consisting in or depending upon the free acts of free agents, are really as uncertain as any event can be, and this is true whether the certainty is revealed or not. The salvation of the saints then, is not certain with any higher certainty than belongs to all future events that consist in, or are conditionated upon, the free acts of free will, though this certainty may be revealed to us in one case, and not in the other.

7. Of course the salvation of the saints is not certain by any kind or degree of certainty that affords the least ground of hope of impunity in a course of sin. "For if they are to be saved, they are to be saved upon condition of continuing in faith and obedience to the end of life."

Moreover, their salvation is no more certain than their future free obedience is. The certainty of future free obedience, and a knowledge of this certainty, cannot be a reason for not obeying, or afford encouragement to live in sin. So no more can the knowledge of the conditional and moral certainty of our salvation afford a ground for hope of impunity in a life of sin.

8. The salvation of the saints is not certain by any kind or degree of certainty that renders their salvation or their damnation any more impossible, than it renders impossible any future acts of sin or obedience. Consequently, it is not certain in such a sense as to afford the least encouragement for hope of salvation in sin, any more than a certainty that a farmer would raise a crop upon condition of his diligent, and timely, and persevering use of the appropriate means, would encourage him to neglect those means. If the farmer had a knowledge of the certainty with its conditions, it would be no temptation to neglect the means; but, on the other hand, this knowledge would operate as a powerful incentive to the required use of them. So neither can the knowledge of the certainty of the salvation of the saints, with the condition of it, be to them a temptation to live in sin; but, on the contrary, this knowledge must act as a powerful incentive to the exercise of confidence in God, and perseverance in holiness unto the end. So neither can the certainty that the necessary means will be used, afford any encouragement to neglect the use of them in the case of man's salvation, any more than the revealed certainty that a farmer will sow his field and have a crop, would encourage him to neglect to sow. The known certainty of both the means and the end, with an understanding of the moral nature of the certainty, has no natural tendency to beget presumption and neglect; but, on the contrary, to beget a diligent, and cheerful, and confident use of the necessary means.

III. Show what is intended by the doctrine in question.

It is intended, that all who are at any time true saints of God, are preserved by his grace and Spirit through faith, in the sense that subsequently to regeneration, obedience is their rule, and disobedience only the exception; and that being thus kept, they will certainly be saved with an everlasting salvation.

Before I proceed to the direct proof of the doctrine, a few remarks may be desirable.

1. I would remark, that I have felt greater hesitancy in forming and expressing my views upon this, than upon almost any other question in theology. I have read whatever I could find upon both sides of this question, and have uniformly found myself dissatisfied with the arguments on both sides. After very full and repeated discussion, I feel better able to make up and express an opinion upon the subject than formerly. I have at some periods of my ministry been nearly on the point of coming to the conclusion that the doctrine is not true. But I could never find myself able to give a satisfactory reason for the rejection of the doctrine. Apparent facts that have come under my observation have sometimes led me seriously to doubt the soundness of the doctrine; but I cannot see, and the more I examine the more unable I find myself to see, how a denial of it can be reconciled with the scriptures.

I shall give the substance of what I regard as the scripture proof of this doctrine, and beg the reader to make up his opinion for himself by a careful examination. Perhaps what has been satisfactory to my mind may not be so to the minds of others. Let no one believe this, or any other doctrine upon my authority, but "prove all things and hold fast that which is good."

2. I observe, that its truth cannot be inferred from the nature of regeneration. It is true, as was said, and as will be farther shown, that perseverance is an attribute or characteristic of Christian character; but this does not necessarily result from the nature of regeneration, but from the indwelling Spirit of Christ. It has been common for that class of writers and theologians, who hold what is called the Taste Scheme of regeneration, to infer the truth of this doctrine from the nature of the change that constitutes the new birth. In this they have been entirely consistent. If, as they suppose, regeneration consists in a change in the constitution of the mind, in the implanting or infusion of a new constitutional taste, relish, or appetite; if it consists in or implies a change back of all voluntary action, and such a change as to secure and necessitate a change of voluntary action; why, then it is consistent, to infer from such a change the perseverance of the saints, unless it can be made to appear that either God, or Satan, or voluntary sin, can change the nature back again. If, in regeneration, the nature is really changed, if there be some new appetite or taste implanted, some holy principle implanted or infused into the constitution, why, then it must follow, that they will persevere by a physical law of the new nature or constitution. I see not how, in this case, they could even be the subjects of temporary backsliding, unless the new appetite should temporarily fail, as does sometimes our appetite for food. But if this may be, yet if regeneration consists in or implies a new creation of something that is not voluntary, a creation of a new nature, instead of a new character, I admit, that perseverance might be reasonably inferred from the fact of such a change. But since I reject wholly this theory of regeneration, and maintain that it is wholly a voluntary change, I cannot consistently infer the final salvation of the saints from the nature of the change that occurs in regeneration. I have been struck with the inconsistency of those who hold the Taste Scheme of regeneration, and yet contend, not only for falling from a regenerate state, but also that the regenerate may and do fall into a state of entire depravity, every time they sin; that they fall from this state of physical or constitutional regeneration every time they commit sin, and must be regenerated or converted anew, or be lost. Now this is not reconcilable with the idea of the physical regeneration.

3. Nor can we infer the perseverance of the saints, with any justice, from their being, at their conversion, brought into a state of justification.

By perseverance some seem to mean, not that the saints do persevere or continue in obedience, but that they will be saved at any rate, whether they persevere in obedience or not. It was against this idea that such men as the Wesleys, and Fletcher, and their coadjutors fought so valiantly. They resisted justly and successfully the doctrine of perpetual justification, upon condition of one act of faith, and maintained that the saints as well as sinners are condemned whenever they sin. They also contended that there is no kind of certainty that all true saints will be saved. Since I have endeavored to refute the doctrine of a perpetual justification, conditioned upon the first act of faith, I cannot of course infer the final salvation of the saints from the nature of justification. Those who hold, that the first act of faith introduces the soul into a new relation of such a nature that, from thenceforth, it is not condemned by the law, do what it will, may justly infer from the nature of such a justification, that all who ever exercise faith will escape the penalty of the Divine law. But we have seen, that this is not the nature of gospel justification, and therefore we must not infer that all saints will be saved, from the mere fact that they have once believed and been justified.

LECTURE XLVIII - PERSEVERANCE OF THE SAINTS PROVED

The following considerations, taken together, seem to me to establish the truth of the doctrine in question beyond reasonable doubt.

1. God has from eternity resolved upon the salvation of all the elect. This we have seen. No one of this number will ever be lost. These are given to Christ from eternity, as a seed to serve him. The conversion, perseverance, and final salvation of the elect, we have seen to be secured. Their conversion, perseverance, and salvation, are secured by means of the grace of God in Christ Jesus, prevailing through the gospel, so to influence their free-will as to bring about this result. The instructions, promises, threatenings, warnings, expostulations of the Bible, with all the influences with which they are surrounded, are the instrumentalities by means of which the Holy Spirit converts, sanctifies, and saves them. At every step, as Fletcher acknowledges, "grace is beforehand with free will." God first comes to, and moves upon, the sinner; but the sinner does not come to and move, or attempt to move, God. God first draws, and the sinner yields. God calls and the sinner answers. The sinner would never approach God, did not God draw him.

Again: God calls effectually, but not irresistibly, before the sinner yields. He does not yield and answer to a slight call. Some indeed wait to be drawn harder, and to be called louder and longer than others; but no one, in fact, comes to God until effectually persuaded to do so; that is, until he is effectually hunted from his refuges of lies, and drawn with so great and powerful a drawing, as not to force, but to overcome, his reluctance or voluntary selfishness, and as to induce him to turn to God and to believe in Christ. That the sinner is wholly disinclined to obey, up to the very moment in which he is persuaded and induced to yield, there can be no doubt. His turning, as we have seen, is an act of his own, but he is induced to turn by the drawings of the Holy Spirit.

Every person who was ever truly converted knows, that his conversion is not to be ascribed to himself, in any other sense, than that he finally consented, being drawn and persuaded by the Holy Spirit. The glory belongs to God, for the sinner only yielded after, perhaps, protracted resistance, and never until after he was so convinced as to have no further excuse or apology for sin, nor until the Spirit, by means of truth, and argument, and persuasion, fairly overcame him, and constrained, not forced him to submit. This is a brief statement of the facts connected with the conversion of every soul that was ever converted to God. This is true of the conversion of all the elect of God; and if others besides the elect are ever converted, this is a true account of their conversion.

Again: the same is true of their perseverance in holiness, in every instance, in every act. The saints persevere, not by virtue of a constitutional change, but as a result of the abiding and indwelling influence of the Holy Spirit. "Free grace is always beforehand with free-will;" that is, the will never obeys, in any instance, nor for one moment, except as it is persuaded to do so as really as at the first. The work begun by the Holy Spirit is not carried on, except as the same Spirit continues to work in the saints to will and to do of his good pleasure. Saints do not begin in the Spirit, and then become perfect through or by the flesh. There is no holy exercise that is not as really to be ascribed to the grace and to the influence of the Holy Spirit, as is conversion itself.

The saints convert not themselves, in the sense that they turn or yield, until persuaded by the Holy Spirit. God converts them in the sense, that he effectually draws or persuades them. They turn themselves, in the sense that their turning is their own act. God turns them, in the sense that he induces or produces their turning. The same is true of their whole course of obedience in this life. The saints keep themselves, in the sense, that all obedience is their own; all their piety consists in their own voluntary obedience; but God keeps them, in the sense, that in every instance, and at every moment of obedience, he persuades, and enlightens, and draws them, insomuch, that he secures their voluntary obedience; that is, he draws and they follow. He persuades, and they yield to his persuasions. He works in them to will and to do, and they will and do. God always anticipates all their holy exercises, and persuades the saints to put them forth. This is so abundantly taught in the Bible, that to quote scripture to prove it were but to waste your time. The saints are not only said to be converted, but also sanctified, and kept by the power of God.

No saint then keeps himself, except in so far as he is kept by the grace, and Spirit, and power of God. There is therefore no hope for any saint, and no reason to calculate upon the salvation of any one, unless God prevails to keep him from falling away and perishing. All who ever are saved, or ever will be, are saved by and through free grace, prevailing over free will, that is, by free grace securing the voluntary concurrence of free will. This God does, and is sure to do, with all the elect. It was upon condition of the foreseen fact, that God could by the wisest administration of his government, secure this result, they were elected to eternal salvation, through sanctification of the Spirit, and belief of the truth. Now observe how the elect are saved. All the threatenings, warnings, and teachings of the Bible are addressed to them, as to all others. If there are any saints, at any time, who are not of the elect, the Bible nowhere notices any such persons, or speaks of them, as any less or more secure than the elect.

Again: the Bible nowhere represents or implies, that any but the elect are converted. It does not represent any but the elect as at any time coming in heart to Christ--as at any time regenerated or born of God. The Bible nowhere acknowledges two classes of saints, elect and non-elect. But, if there were two such classes, and the salvation of the elect was certain, as it really is, and that of the non-elect not certain, it is incredible that the Bible should not reveal this fact. Again: so far is the Bible from recognizing or implying any such distinction, that it everywhere implies the contrary. It divides mankind into two, and but two classes, and these it sets one over against the other. These are contrasted by the names, saint and sinner; people of God, and people of this world; children of God, and children of this world, or children of the devil; the elect and the reprobate, that is, the chosen and the rejected; the sanctified and the unsanctified; the regenerated and the unregenerated; the penitent and the impenitent. By whatever names they are called, it is manifest that the same classes and none others are meant. The elect of God is a common name for the saints or people of God. I cannot find in the Bible any evidence, that any were converted at any time, but the elect, or those whose salvation is sure. The elect are, or will be, every one of them certainly converted and saved. If any one chooses to contend that any other are ever converted, the burden of proof is upon him; let him prove it, if he can. But this he must prove, in order to establish the fact, that any truly regenerated persons are ever lost, for sure it is, that no one of the elect will ever be lost. But, since I am to take the affirmative, I must take the burden of showing, that none but the elect are recognized in the scriptures as saints; and as I am speaking only of the salvation of the saints, I shall take it for granted, that all those who were from eternity chosen to eternal salvation, through sanctification of the Spirit and belief of the truth, will certainly be saved.

Now, if it can be shown, that some saints have been really lost, it will follow, that some have been converted who were not of the elect. And, on the other hand, if it can be shown that no saint has been, or will be, finally lost; but, on the contrary, that all the true saints are, and will be, saved, it will follow that none but the elect are converted. For all who are, or will be, saved, are saved by God, and saved by design, and in accordance with an eternal design, and of course they were elected to salvation from eternity.

I have already said, that it is incredible that the Bible should read as it does, and that it should nowhere distinguish between elect and non-elect saints, if there is any such distinction. It cannot be said with justice, that the Bible purposely conceals from all saints the fact of their election, lest it should be a stumbling-block to them. This we have seen is not the fact, but on the contrary, that the elect, at least in some instances, have known that they were elect.

But it is said, that Peter exhorts the saints to "give all diligence to make their calling and election sure;" from which it is inferred, that they did not know that they were elect; and furthermore, that it might be that, although they were real saints, nevertheless they were not, at least all of them, of the elect. The words here referred to stand in the following connection:--

2 Pet. i. 1: "Simon Peter, a servant and an apostle of Jesus Christ, to them that have obtained like precious faith with us, through the righteousness of God and our Saviour Jesus Christ: 2. Grace and peace be multiplied unto you through the knowledge of God, and of Jesus our Lord; 3. According as his divine power has given unto us all things that pertain unto life and godliness, through the knowledge of him that hath called us to glory and virtue: 4. Whereby are given unto us exceeding great and precious promises; that by these ye might be partakers of the divine nature, having escaped the corruption that is in the world through lust. 5. And beside this, giving all diligence, add to your faith, virtue; and to virtue, knowledge; 6. And to knowledge, temperance; and to temperance, patience; and to patience, godliness; 7. And to godliness, brotherly kindness; and to brotherly kindness, charity. 8. For if these things be in you and abound, they make you that ye shall neither be barren nor unfruitful in the knowledge of our Lord Jesus Christ. 9. But he that lacketh these things is blind, and cannot see afar off, and hath forgotten that he was purged from his old sins. 10. Wherefore the rather, brethren, give diligence to make your calling and election sure: for if ye do these things, ye shall never fall." Upon this passage, I remark,--

That Peter addressed this epistle to all who had faith, that is, to all true Christians, as appears from the first verse. He addressed no one by name, but left it for every one to be sure that he had faith. He then proceeds to exhort them to grow in grace, assuring them that, if any one did not do so, he had forgotten that he was purged from his former sins; that is, if any one lacked that which he enjoined, it would prove that he had not true faith, or that he had backslidden. Then he adds, as in the 10th verse: "Wherefore the rather, brethren, give diligence to make your calling and election sure: for if ye do these things, ye shall never fall." The apostle plainly assumes:--

(1.) That the called and elected will be saved; to make their calling and election sure, was to make their salvation sure: and,

(2.) That none others are saved but the called and elected, for if others are saved, it were of no consequence whether they were of the called and elected or not, provided they were saved;

(3.) That he regarded none as Christians, or as at any time having true faith, but the called and elected; for he was not exhorting supposed impenitent sinners to become Christians, but supposed Christians to be sure of their calling and election. This shows that he regarded all Christians as of the called and elected. To be sure of their calling and election was to be sure of their salvation. The apostle did not certainly mean to exhort them to become of the number of the elect, for this number we have seen was settled from eternity; but by diligence and growth in grace to secure their salvation, or thus to prove or demonstrate their calling and election. He meant also to admonish them that, although called and elected, still their ultimate salvation was conditionated upon their diligent growth in grace, and perseverance in holiness to the end of life. He therefore exhorts them to make their calling and election sure, which is the same as to secure their salvation. He speaks of calling and election as indissolubly connected. Effectual calling either results from election, or election from calling. We have seen that election is eternal; therefore election cannot result from calling, but calling must result from election.

Again: Christians and saints, and the children and people of God, the disciples of Christ, and the elect, are to all appearance regarded throughout the Bible as the same class.

Again: Christ says, John vi. 37: "All that the Father giveth me shall come to me; and him that cometh to me I will in no wise cast out. 39. And this is the Father' s will which hath sent me, that of all which he hath given me I should lose nothing, but should raise it up again at the last day."

Here Jesus says, that all who are given to him by the Father shall come to him, and that of those that come to him, it is his Father's will that he should lose none, hut that he should raise them up, (that is, to eternal life,) at the last day. He does not say here, that none do come to him who are not given to him by the Father, but this is plainly implied, for he says, 37th. "All that the Father giveth me shall come to me; and him that cometh to me I will in no wise cast out." What he means by not casting them out, is plain from verse 39. That is, "It is the Father's will that of all that shall come to me I should lose nothing." By not casting them out, then, he intended that he should surely save them, that is, all that came to him. But if he saves them, they must have been given to Christ and have been elected, or they were not. If they were not elected, or given to Christ by the Father, they will never be saved, unless some are saved without God's designing or choosing to save them. If any are saved, God saves them, through or by Christ. If he saves them, he does it designedly, and not without design. But if he ever does, or will design it, he has from eternity designed it. So then, it appears, that all who come to Christ were given to him of the Father; and that he will lose none of them, but will raise them up at the last day. My object at present, however, is not to insist that no one that comes to Christ will be lost, but only that all who come to Christ are of the number that were given to him of the Father, or are of the elect.

Again: compare verses 37, 39, 44, 45. He says: John vi. 37: "All that the Father giveth me shall come to me, and him that cometh to me I will in no wise cast out. 39. And this is the Father' s will which hath sent me, that of all which he hath given me I should lose nothing, but should raise it up again at the last day. 44. No man can come to me except the Father which hath sent me, draw him, and I will raise him up at the last day. 45. It is written in the Prophets, And they shall be all taught of God. Every man therefore that hath heard, and hath learned of the Father, cometh unto me."

Here it appears that no one can come to Christ except he be drawn of the Father. Every one who is drawn by the Father with an effectual drawing, or every one who hears and learns of the Father comes to Christ, and no other. The Father draws none to Christ, but those whom he has given to Christ; for these, and these only, are the children of God. Isa. liv. 13: "And all thy children shall be taught of the Lord; and great shall be the peace of thy children." From these passages it appears that none come to Christ but those who are drawn by the Father, and that none are drawn by the Father but those whom he has given to his Son, or the elect; and that of those who are thus drawn to Christ, it is the Father's will that he should lose none, but that he should raise them up at the last day; that is, that he should save them. But observe, it is my particular object just now to establish the fact, that none come to Christ but those who are of the number that are given to Christ, and also that every one who is given to him shall come to him. These, and these only are effectually called or drawn of the Father. All are called in the sense of being earnestly and honestly invited, and all the divine persuasion is addressed to them that can wisely be addressed to them. But others, besides those given to the Son, are not, as a matter of fact, persuaded and effectually drawn, in a sense that secures the "concurrence of free will with free grace."

The same truth is strongly implied in many other passages in the teachings of Christ. For example, he says,--

John x. 1: "Verily, verily, I say unto you, he that entereth not by the door into the sheep-fold, but climbeth up some other way, the same is a thief and a robber. 2. But he that entereth in by the door is the shepherd of the sheep. 3. To him the porter openeth: and the sheep hear his voice; and he calleth his own sheep by name, and leadeth them out. 4. And when he putteth forth his own sheep, he goeth before them, and the sheep follow him: for they know his voice. 5. And a stranger will they not follow, but will flee from him: for they know not the voice of strangers. 6. This parable spake Jesus unto them: but they understood not what things they were which he spake unto them."

He then proceeds to expound the parable. He is the good shepherd having the care of his Father's sheep. He says:--

7. "Then said Jesus unto them again, Verily, verily, I say unto you, I am the door of the sheep. 8. All that ever came before me are thieves and robbers: but the sheep did not hear them. 9. I am the door; by me if any man enter in, he

shall be saved, and go in and out, and find pasture. 10. The thief cometh not, but for to steal, and to kill, and to destroy: I am come that they might have life, and that they might have it more abundantly. 11. I am the good shepherd: the good shepherd giveth his life for the sheep. 12. But he that is a hireling, and not the shepherd, whose own the sheep are not, seeth the wolf coming, and leaveth the sheep, and fleeth, and the wolf catcheth them, and scattereth the sheep. 13. The hireling fleeth, because he is a hireling, and careth not for the sheep. 14. I am the good shepherd, and know my sheep, and am known of mine. 15. As the Father knoweth me, even so know I the Father: and I lay down my life for the sheep. 16. And other sheep I have, which are not of this fold: them also I must bring, and they shall hear my voice; and there shall be one fold, and one shepherd. 17. Therefore doth my Father love me, because I lay down my life, that I might take it again."

He had other sheep which were not yet called--they were not of this fold--that is, they were not Jews, but Gentiles; these he must bring. To the unbelieving and cavilling Jews he said:--

John x. 26: "But ye believe not, because ye are not of my sheep, as I said unto you. 27. My sheep hear my voice, and I know them, and they follow me. 28. And I give unto them eternal life; and they shall never perish, neither shall any pluck them out of my hand. 29. My Father which gave them me, is greater than all; and none is able to pluck them out of my Father' s hand."

Here it is plainly implied, that all those were sheep who were given to him by the Father, and that all such would surely hear and know his voice and follow him, but those that were not of his sheep, or were not given him by the Father, would not believe. He says, verse 26: But ye believe not, because ye are not of my sheep, as I said unto you. What he here says amounts to this: all those are sheep who are given to me of my Father. All my sheep thus given, shall and will hear my voice, and follow me, and none others will. I do not notice in this place what he says of the certainty of their salvation, because my present object is only to show that those and those only come to Christ who are given to him of the Father, or are of the elect.

This same truth is either expressly taught, or strongly implied in a great many passages, and indeed it seems to me to be the doctrine of the whole Bible. Rom. viii. 28: "And we know that all things work together for good to them that love God, to them who are the called according to his purpose." Here they that love God are represented as identical with those "who are the called according to his purpose." In other words, they who love God are the called according to, or in consequence of their election. All that love God do so because they have been effectually called, according to the purpose or election of God. This passage seems to settle the question, especially when viewed in its connection, that all who ever love God are of the elect, and that they are prevailed upon to love God in conformity with their election.

We shall have occasion, by and by, to examine the connection in which this passage is found, for the purpose of showing that all who at any time truly come to love God, will be saved. I have only quoted this twenty-eighth verse here for the purpose of showing, not directly, that all that love God at any time will be saved, but that they are of the number of the elect, from which fact their ultimate salvation must be inferred.

It is plain that the apostles regarded regeneration as conclusive evidence of election. The manner in which they address Christians seems to me to put this beyond a doubt. Paul, in writing to the Thessalonians, 2 Thes. ii. 13, says, "But we are bound to give thanks alway to God for you, brethren beloved of the Lord, because God hath from the beginning chosen you to salvation through sanctification of the Spirit, and belief of the truth." Here the apostle speaks of all the brethren at Thessalonica as beloved of the Lord, and as being from eternity chosen to salvation. He felt called upon to give thanks to God for this reason, that God had chosen them to salvation from eternity. This he represents as true of the whole church: that is, doubtless, of all true Christians in the church. Indeed, the apostles everywhere speak as if they regarded all true saints as of the elect, and their saintship as evidence of their election. Peter, in writing to the Christians in his first letter, says:

1 Pet. i. 1: "Peter, an apostle of Jesus Christ, to the strangers scattered throughout Pontus, Galatia, Cappadocia, Asia, and Bithynia, 2. Elect according to the foreknowledge of God the Father, through sanctification of the Spirit unto obedience and sprinkling of the blood of Jesus Christ: Grace unto you, and peace, be multiplied. 3. Blessed be the God and Father of our Lord Jesus Christ, which, according to his abundant mercy, hath begotten us again unto a lively hope by the resurrection of Jesus Christ from the dead. 4. To an inheritance incorruptible, and undefiled, and that fadeth not away, reserved in heaven for you, 5. Who are kept by the power of God through faith unto salvation, ready to be revealed in the last time: 6. Wherein ye greatly rejoice, though now for a season, if need be, ye are in heaviness through manifold temptations; 7. That the trial of your faith, being much more precious than that of gold that perisheth, though it be tried with fire, might be found unto praise, and honor, and glory, at the appearing of Jesus Christ: 8. Whom having not seen ye love; in whom, though now ye see him not, yet believing, ye rejoice with joy unspeakable, and full of glory: 9. Receiving the end of your faith, even the salvation of your souls."

Here it is plain that Peter regarded all who had been born again to a lively hope, or who were regenerated, as elected, or as chosen to salvation. I might pursue this argument to an indefinite length, but I must attend to other considerations in support of the doctrine in question.

I will for the present close what I have to say under this particular branch of the argument, by reminding you that Christ has expressly asserted that no man can or does come to him except the Father draw him, and that the Father draws to him those--and by fair inference those only--whom he has given to Christ; and further, that it is the Father's will, that of those whom the Father had given to Christ, and drawn to him, Christ should lose none, but should raise them up at the last day. It is, I think, evident, that when Christ asserts it to be his Father's will, that of those whom the Father had given him he should lose none, but should raise them up at the last day, he intended to say, that his Father not merely desired and willed this, but that such was his design. That the Father designed to secure their salvation: This we shall more fully see in its proper place.

LECTURE XLIX - PERSEVERANCE PROVED

2. I REMARK, that God is able to preserve and keep the true saints from apostacy, in consistency with their liberty: 2 Tim. i. 12: "For the which cause I also suffer these things; nevertheless, I am not ashamed; for I know whom I have believed, and am persuaded that he is able to keep that which I have committed unto him against that day." Here the apostle expresses the fullest confidence in the ability of Christ to keep him: and indeed, as has been said, it is most manifest that the apostles expected to persevere and be saved only because they believed in the ability and willingness of God to keep them from falling. Again: Rom. xiv. 4: "Who art thou that judgest another man's servant; to his own master he standeth or falleth; yea, he shall be holden up, for God is able to make him stand." Again, Phil. iii. 21: "Who shall change our vile body, that it may be fashioned like unto his glorious body, according to the working whereby he is able even to subdue all things unto himself." Again, Eph. iii. 20: "Now unto him that is able to do exceeding abundantly above all that we ask or think, according to the power that worketh in us." Again, Jude 24: "Now unto him that is able to keep you from falling, and to present you faultless before the presence of his glory with exceeding joy." Again, 2 Cor. ix. 8: "And God is able to make all grace abound towards you; that ye, always having all sufficiency in all things, may abound to every good work." Eph. i. 18: The eyes of your understanding being enlightened; that ye may know what is the hope of his calling, and what the riches of the glory of his inheritance in the saints. 19. And what is the exceeding greatness of his power to usward who believe, according to the working of his mighty power, 20. Which he wrought in Christ, when he raised him from the dead, and set him at his own right hand in the heavenly places." Again, Heb. vii. 25: "Wherefore he is able to save them to the uttermost that come unto God by him, seeing he ever lived) to make intercession for them." These and many other passages prove beyond a doubt that God is able to preserve his saints.

3. God is not only able to keep all that conic to Christ, or all true Christians, but he is also willing. But Christ has settled this question, as we have seen.

John vi. 37: "All that the Father giveth me shall come to me, and him that cometh to me I will in no wise cast out. 38. For I came down from heaven, not to do my own will, but the will of him that sent me; 39. And this is the Father' s will which hath sent me, that of all which he hath given me I should lose nothing, but should raise it up again at the last day. 40. And this is the will of him that sent me, that every one which seeth the Son, and believeth on him, may have everlasting life; and I will raise him up at the last day."

Here, then, we have just seen these two points settled, namely, that God is able to save all saints, or all who at any time truly believe and come to Christ; and, that he is willing, or wills to do it. Now if he is both able and willing to keep and save all the saints, he certainly will do it.

But here I know it will be objected, that by this course of argument, the doctrine of universal salvation may be established. The Bible, it is said, represents God as both able and willing to save all men, and if his being both able and willing to save the saints, proves that they will all be saved, it follows that his being able and willing to save all men proves that all men will be saved. But the cases are not parallel; for God nowhere professes ability to save all men, but on the contrary, disclaims such ability, and professes to be unable to save all men; that is, he cannot, under the circumstances, wisely save them, nor can he wisely do any more for saints or sinners than he does. No passage can be found in the Bible, in which God asserts his ability to save all men. The passages that affirm that "God can do all things," and that "nothing is too hard for the Lord," and the like, cannot be understood as affirming God's ability to save all men. They do imply, that he has power to do whatever is an object of physical omnipotence; but to save sinners is not an object of physical power. Their salvation, if accomplished at all, must be brought about by a moral and persuasive influence, and not by the exercise of physical omnipotence. In the sense in which we can justly apply the terms ability and inability to this subject, God is really unable to do what it is unwise for him to do. He has an end in view. This end is the highest good and blessedness of universal being. This end can be accomplished only by the appropriate means, or upon certain conditions. These conditions include the perfect holiness of moral agents. If God cannot wisely use such means as will secure the conversion and sanctification of sinners, he cannot save them. That is, he is unable to save them. This he repeatedly professes to be unable to do.

Ezek. xviii. 23: "Have I any pleasure at all that the wicked should die, saith the Lord God; and not that he should return from his ways, and live? 32. For I have no pleasure in the death of him that dieth, saith the Lord God; wherefore turn yourselves, and live ye."

Ezek. xxxiii. 11. "Say unto them, As I live, saith the Lord God, I have no pleasure in the death of the wicked; but that the wicked turn from his way and live: turn ye, turn ye, from your evil ways; for why will ye die, O house of Israel?"

Isa. v. 4: "What could have been done more to my vineyard that I have not done in it? Wherefore, when I looked that it should bring forth grapes, brought it forth wild grapes?"

Hos. xi. 8: "How shall I give thee up, Ephraim? How shall I deliver thee, Israel? How shall I make thee as Admah? How shall I set thee as Zeboim? My heart is turned within me, my repentings are kindled together."

These are only specimens of the manner in which God speaks of his ability to save sinners, and to do more for the church or the world than he does. From such professions on the part of God, we are to understand him, as disclaiming ability to do more or otherwise than he does, in consistency with the highest good of being in general. Since the highest good of being in general is the end which he is aiming to secure, he "may justly be said to be unable to do whatever he cannot do in consistency with the use of those means that will secure this end." God, therefore, does not affirm his ability to save all men, but fully disclaims any such ability, and professes to do, and to be doing, all that he can to save them. He professes to be perfectly benevolent and infinitely wise, and to be doing all that infinite wisdom and benevolence can do for sinners and for all men, and complains, that all he can do does not save, and will not save many of them.

But with respect to the saints, he does expressly affirm his ability to keep them, in a sense that will secure their salvation. This we have seen. He does for them all that be wisely can, and does enough, as he expressly affirms, to secure their salvation. No one can attentively read and consider the passages relating to God's ability to save all men, and his ability to save his people, without perceiving, that the two cases are not parallel, but that in fact they are contrasts. He expressly affirms his ability to keep, to sanctify, and to save his elect children, whilst he repeatedly, either expressly, or by implication, disclaims ability to save all men.

Again: the Bible nowhere represents God as willing the salvation of all men, in the same sense in which it represents him as willing the salvation of Christians, or of his elect. Such passages as the following are specimens of God's professions of willingness to save all men.

1 Tim. ii. 4: "Who will have all men to be saved, and to come unto the knowledge of the truth."

John iii. 16. "For God so loved the world, that he gave his only-begotten Son, that whosoever believeth in him should not perish, but have everlasting life. 17. For God sent not his Son into the world to condemn the world; but that the world through him might be saved."

2 Peter iii. 9: "The Lord is not slack concerning his promise, as some men count slackness; but is long-suffering to usward, not willing that any should perish, but that all should come to repentance."

These and similar passages teach that God wills the salvation of all men, only in the sense of desiring it. This we know from the fact, that he nowhere intimates a willingness, in the sense of a design or intention, to save all men; but on the contrary, plainly reveals an opposite purpose or design; that is, he reveals the fact, that he cannot, shall not, and of course, does not, expect or design to save all men. By the profession of a willingness to save all men, we can therefore justly understand him to mean, only that he desires the salvation of all men, and that he would secure their salvation if he wisely could. This is all that we can understand him as affirming, unless we would accuse him of self-contradiction.

But he professes a willingness to save his elect, or in other words, all regenerate persons, or all believers in Christ, and all whoever will truly believe in him, in the sense of purposing or designing to save them. This is most manifest from the scriptures we have already examined, and this will still further appear from the passages to be examined.

We have seen that the Father has given a certain number to Christ, with express design to secure their salvation; that he has committed to him all the requisite power and influences to save them, and that they will actually be saved. Nothing like this can be found in the Bible, respecting any other class of men whatever. This objection, then, is without foundation, and the argument from the ability and willingness of God to save his saints, remains in full force and conclusiveness.

4. Again: Christ expressly prayed for all believers, and in a manner that secures their being kept and saved:--

John xvii. 2: "As thou hast given him power over all flesh, that he should give eternal life to as many as thou hast given him. 6. I have manifested thy name unto the men which thou gavest me out of the world; thine they were, and thou gavest them me; and they have kept thy word. 7. Now they have known that all things whatsoever thou hast given me are of thee;. 8. For I have given unto them the words which thou gavest me; and they have received them, and have known surely that I came out from thee, and they have believed that thou didst send me. 9. I pray for them; I pray not for the world, but for them which thou hast given me, for they are thine. 10. And all mine are thine, and thine are mine; and I am glorified in them. 11. And now I am no more in the world, but these are in the world, and I come to thee. Holy Father, keep through thine own name those whom thou hast given me, that they may be one, as we are. 12. While I was with them in the world, I kept them in thy name: those that thou gavest me I have kept, and none of them is lost, but the son of perdition, that the scripture might be fulfilled. 13. And now come I to thee; and these things I speak in the world, that they might have my joy fulfilled in themselves. 14. I have given them thy word; and the world hath hated them, because they are not of the world, even as I am not of the world. 20. Neither pray I for these alone, but for them also which shall believe on me through their word. 21. That they all may be one; as thou, Father, art in me, and I in thee, that they also may be one in us; that the world may believe that thou hast sent me. 22. And the glory which thou gavest me, I have given them; that they may be one, even as we are one. 23. I in them, and thou in me, that they may be made perfect in one, and that the world may know that thou hast sent me, and hast loved them as thou hast loved me. 24. Father, I will that they also whom thou hast given me, be with me where I am; that they may behold my glory, which thou hast given me; for thou lovedst me before the foundation of the world."

Now observe, that in this most affecting prayer Christ says,--

(1.) Verse 2. "As thou hast given him power over all flesh, that he should give eternal life to as many as thou hast given him." We have seen, that, in the 6th chapter of this book Christ expressly teaches, that all are given to him that come to him by the Father.

(2.) He proceeds to affirm, that he had in the exercise of this power kept in his Father's name all who had been given, and had come to him, and had lost none.

(3.) He asks the Father henceforth to keep them in his own name, as he was about to leave them, as to his bodily presence. He says, verse 15, "I pray not that thou shouldest take them out of the world, but that thou shouldest keep them from the evil." Again, he says, 20-24: "Neither pray I for these alone, but for them also which shall believe on me through their word. That they all may be one; as thou, Father, art in me, and I in thee, that they also may be one in us; that the world may believe that thou hast sent me. And the glory which thou gayest me I have given them; that they may be one, even as we are one. I in them, and thou in me, that they may be made perfect in one; and that the world may know that thou hast sent me, and hast loved them as thou hast loved me. Father, I will that they also whom thou hast given me be with me where I am; that they may behold my glory, which thou hast given me; for thou lovedst me before the foundation of the world."

Now, as surely as Christ's prayer is answered, all believers will be saved; that is, at least all who ever have believed, or ever will believe, subsequent to the offering of this prayer. But Christ's prayers are always answered.

To this it is objected, that a part of this same prayer is not answered, and of course never will be. It is said, for example, that in the 21st verse he prays for the union of all believers, which has been far enough from having been answered. The verse reads, "That they all may be one; as thou, Father, art in me, and I in thee, that they also may be one in us; that the world may believe that thou hast sent me." Here he explains the sense in which he prays that all believers may be one, not that they should be all of one denomination or creed, but that they should possess one and the same spirit; that the same spirit that united the Father and the Son, that is, the Holy Spirit, who is in the Father and the Son, might also be in all Christians. This is plainly his meaning; and that this is true of all real Christians, that they possess the Holy Spirit, or the Spirit that dwells in the Father and the Son, no one can doubt who understands and believes his Bible.

But it is objected again, that Christ prayed to be delivered from crucifixion, and his prayer was not answered.

I reply, that he did not pray for this, if at all, unqualifiedly. He says, if it be possible, nevertheless, not as I will, but as thou wilt." If it were the pains of the cross from which his soul shrunk in the garden, and from which he desired, if possible, to be excused, it is plain that he did not pray unqualifiedly to be delivered; but, on the contrary, submitted the question to the will of his Father. But in the prayer, in John 17, he made no such condition. He knew that in this case it was his Father's will to grant his request. Of this he had expressly informed his disciples, as we have seen; that is, that it was his Father's will to keep and save all who were given to Christ, and had been drawn by the Father to Christ. The Spirit of this petition accords precisely with his teaching upon the subject. He had taught before that all believers would be kept and saved, and that this was his Father's will; now, could he, either expressly or impliedly, in this prayer, put in the condition that was in the prayer just referred to, namely, "If it be thy will?" But, although what has been said is a full answer to the assertion that Christ's prayers were not always answered, it may be, for some minds, important to say, that it is far from being certain that Christ prayed to be delivered from crucifixion.

But be this as it may, we are to remember that Christ expressly affirms, that his Father always hears, that is, answers his prayers.

John. xi. 42: "And I knew that thou Nearest me always: but because of the people which stand by I said it, that they may believe that thou hast sent me."

Again, Paul says of Christ, Heb. vii. 25: "Wherefore he is able also to save them to the uttermost that come unto God by him, seeing he ever liveth to make intercession for them."

Here he asserts, that Christ is able to save unto the uttermost all that come unto God by him, seeing he always lives to make intercession for them. This, as plainly as possible, implies that his intercessions are all-prevailing. Indeed, as he is the mediator, they must be.

Now let us consider how far we have advanced in establishing the perseverance and final salvation of all believers.

(1.) We have seen, that all the elect to salvation will be saved.

(2.) That all true believers are of this number.

(3.) That God and Christ are able to keep them from apostasy, and save them.

(4.) That he is willing or wills to do it.

(5.) That Christ expressly prayed for the perseverance and final salvation of all believers.

(6.) That he prayed in express accordance with the revealed will of his Father; and--

(7.) That his prayers always prevail and are answered.

In Christ's prayer in John, chap. xvii., he expressly affirms that he did not pray for the world, that is, for all men. He prayed only for those whom the Father had given him. For these he prayed, not merely that God would save them upon condition of their perseverance, but that God would keep them from the evil that is in the world, and save them, and make them one, in the sense, that one Spirit should be in them all. He asked manifestly the same things for all that in future believe, that he asked for those who had already believed.

Should I proceed no further the argument is complete, and the proof conclusive. But since this doctrine is so abundantly taught, either expressly or impliedly, in the Bible, I proceed to the consideration of a number of other passages which will throw still further light on the subject.

5. Christ expressly and designedly teaches this doctrine.

John vi. 39: "And this is the Father' s will which hath sent me, that of all which he hath given me, I should lose nothing, but should raise it up again at the last day. 40. And this is the will of him that sent me, that every one which seeth the Son, and believeth on him, may have everlasting life: and I will raise him up at the last day. 47. Verily, verily, I say unto you, He that believeth on me hath everlasting life. 51. I am the living bread which came down from heaven. If any man eat of this bread, he shall live forever: and the bread that I will give is my flesh, which I will give for the life of the world."

Here he expressly teaches, as we have before seen, that it is his Father's will, that all believers, or all who at any time believe, (for this is plainly his meaning,) shall be saved; that he should lose none of them, but as we have seen, John xvii. 2, should give them eternal life. Then he claims ability to keep and save them agreeably to his Father's will. This, remember, respects all believers, or all who are given to Christ, who, we have learned, are the same persons.

Again: John x. 27: "My sheep hear my voice, and I know them, and they follow me: 28. And I give unto them eternal life; and they shall never perish, neither shall any pluck them out of my hand. 29. My Father which gave them me, is greater than all; and none is able to pluck them out of my Father' s hand."

The whole connection shows, that Christ intended to teach the certainty of the salvation of all his sheep, or of all the elect, or, which is the same, of all true believers. But, to this it is objected, that none are sheep any longer than they remain obedient, and therefore the assertion that he will save the sheep, does not secure those who at any time sin. But I reply, that Christ recognizes all the elect as his sheep, whether converted, or whether in a state of temporary backsliding, or not. He represents his sheep as hearing his voice, and as following him, and those who are not of his sheep as not hearing his voice, and as not following him, John x. 16: "And other sheep I have which are not of this fold: them also I must bring, and they shall hear my voice; and there shall be one fold, and one shepherd. 26. But ye believe not, because ye are not of my sheep, as I said unto you."

Again, Matt. xviii. 12: "How think ye? If a man have a hundred sheep, and one of them be gone astray, doth he not leave the ninety and nine, and goeth into the mountains, and seeketh that which is gone astray? 13. And if so be that he find it, verily I say unto you, he rejoiceth more of that sheep, than of the ninety and nine which went not astray. 14. Even so it is not the will of your Father which is in heaven, that one of these little ones should perish."

The design of this parable is to teach the doctrine I am defending. If not, what is its design? This is a full answer to the objection, that no one is recognized as a sheep who has gone astray.

But again, it is said, that although no one else can pluck the sheep out of the Father's hand, yet we can do it ourselves. I grant that we can by natural possibility; but this objection is good for nothing, for Christ expressly says, John x. 27: "My sheep hear my voice, and I know them, and they follow me: 28. And I give unto them eternal life; and they shall never perish, neither shall any pluck them out of my hand. 29. My Father, which gave them me, is greater than all; and none is able to pluck them out of my Father' s hand."

Not only is no one able to pluck them out of his Father's hand, but Christ gives unto them eternal life, and they shall never perish. This implies, that while they might or are able to apostatize and be lost, yet, as a matter of fact, they never will. What could be made out of all he says of himself as a shepherd in this passage, if, after all, he loses some of his sheep? Let any one ponder the whole chapter and see.

6. Another argument, in support of the doctrine under consideration, I deduce from the fact, that Paul, an inspired apostle, believed it.

Phil. i. 1: "Paul and Timotheus, the servants of Jesus Christ, to all the saints in Christ Jesus which are at Philippi, with the bishops and deacons; 2. Grace be unto you, and peace, from God our Father, and from the Lord Jesus Christ. 3. I thank my God upon every remembrance of you, 4. (Always in every prayer of mine for you all making request with joy,) 5. For your fellowship in the gospel, from the first day until now. 6. Being confident of this very thing, that he which hath begun a good work in you will perform it until the day of Jesus Christ.

Here the apostle represents himself as giving thanks for all the saints at Philippi, upon the ground of his confidence that he who had begun a good work in them would perform, or perfect it, until the day of Christ. His confidence did not rest in them, but in the faithfulness of Christ. He did not express a confidence, that they would of themselves persevere, but that he who had begun a good work in them, would carry it on: that is, that he would so work in them as to keep them, and as to secure their perseverance to the end. This he expected with respect to all the saints at Philippi. But if he believed this of all the saints at that place, it is plainly and fairly inferable that he believed it, simply because he expected this, as to all true saints. He does not intimate, that he expected this because of any peculiarity in their case,--that is, not because they were better than other saints, or that God would do more for them than for others. He seems plainly to have expressed this confidence, upon the ground of his expectation, that he who begins a good work in any saint, will carry it on and perfect it until the day of Christ. Should it be said, that Paul intended merely to express the conviction or opinion of a good man, that the Philippian saints would be saved, but that he did not intend to utter this as the voice of inspiration; I reply, that Paul plainly expresses a confidence that they would all be saved, and that God would perfect the work which he had begun. Now, how came he by this confidence? He was an inspired man. If inspiration had taught him that real saints do fall away and are lost, how could he consistently express so thorough a persuasion, that all the saints at Philippi would be saved? If Paul believed in the perseverance of the saints, it must be true, or he was deceived in respect to this important doctrine. But is it not safe to trust Paul's opinion of this doctrine? If any one is disposed to contend, that we cannot with strict justice infer that Paul believed the same in respect to God's perfecting the work in all saints, that he believed in respecting the Philippians, I will not contend with him with respect to this. It is, however, clear, that Paul no where in this epistle, nor elsewhere, intimates that he had higher expectations in regard to the salvation of the Philippians, than he had in respect to the salvation of all true saints. In writing to the churches, the apostles appear to have regarded and spoken of all true saints as the elect-children of God. They seem to represent the salvation of all such persons as certain, but always keeping in mind and holding forth, either expressly or by way of implication, the nature of this certainty, that it was conditioned upon the right and persevering use of their own agency. They consequently constantly endeavor to guard the churches against delusion, in regard to their being real saints, and admonish them to prove themselves in this respect, and also warn them against the supposition, that they can be saved, without actual perseverance in faith and obedience to the end of life.

7. The apostles seemed to regard the conversion of sinners as an evidence that God designed to save them, or that they were of the elect:--

Acts ii. 47: "Praising God, and having favor with all the people. And the Lord added to the church daily such as should be saved."

Acts xiii. 48. "And when the Gentiles heard this, they were glad and glorified the word of the Lord; and as many as were ordained to eternal life, believed."

In these passages as elsewhere, the conversion of sinners is spoken of as settling the question of their salvation. But if true saints do fall from grace and perish, why should the inspired writers so often express themselves, as if they regarded the regeneration of a person as an indication that he is one of the elect, and as securing his salvation?

So common is it for Christ and the apostles to speak of regeneration as settling the question of the salvation of those who are regenerated, that great multitudes have overlooked the fact, that there was any other condition of salvation insisted on in the Bible. When the jailor demanded of Paul and Silas what he should do to be saved, Paul replied to him, "Believe in the Lord Jesus Christ, and thou shalt be saved, and thy house."

Here, as is common in the Bible, faith is spoken of as if it were the sole condition of salvation. Repentance, faith, regeneration, etc., are often, as every student of the Bible knows, spoken of as if they were the only conditions of salvation. Now, it seems to me, that this could not, and ought not to be, if there is not a certain connection of some sort between real conversion and eternal salvation. It is true, the necessity of perseverance to the end is often mentioned and insisted upon in the Bible as a condition of salvation, just as might be expected when we consider the nature of the certainty in question. If there is not, however, a certain connection between true regeneration, or faith, or repentance and salvation, it seems to me incredible, that we should so often find faith, and repentance, and conversion spoken of as if they secured salvation.

Those who believe are represented as already having eternal life, as not coming into condemnation, but as having passed from death unto life. The following passages are specimens of the manner in which the scriptures speak upon this subject.

John i. 12: "But as many as received him, to them gave he power to become the sons of God, even to them that believe on his name; 13. Which were born, not of blood, nor of the will of the flesh, nor of the will of man, but of God."

John iii. 36: "He that believeth on the Son hath everlasting life and he that believeth not the Son shall not see life; but the wrath of God abideth on him. 16. For God so loved the world, that he gave his only begotten Son, that whosoever believeth in him should not perish, but have everlasting life. 18. He that believeth on him is not condemned; but he that believeth not is condemned already, because he hath not believed in the name of the only begotten Son of God."

John iv. 14: "But whosoever drinketh of the water that I shall give him, shall never thirst: but the water that I shall give him shall be in him a well of water springing up into everlasting life."

John v. 24: "Verily, verily, I say unto you, He that heareth my word, and believeth on him that sent me, hath everlasting life, and shall not come into condemnation; but is passed from death unto life."

John vi. 37: "All that the Father giveth me shall come to me; and him that cometh to me I will in no wise cast out. 40. And this is the will of him that sent me, That every one which seeth the Son, and believeth on him, may have everlasting life; and I will raise him up at the last day. 45. It is written in the prophets, And they shall be all taught of God. Every man therefore that hath heard, and hath learned of the Father, cometh unto me. 47. Verily, verily, I say unto you, He that believeth on me hath everlasting life."

Acts ii. 38: "Then Peter said unto them, Repent, and be baptized every one of you in the name of Jesus Christ, for the remission of sins; and ye shall receive the gift of the Holy Ghost."

Mark xvi. 15: "And he said unto them, Go ye into all the world, and preach the gospel to every creature. 16. He that believeth and is baptized shall be saved; but he that believeth not shall be damned."

Now it seems to me, that this numerous class of passages strongly imply that there is a certain connection of some sort between coming to Christ, receiving Christ, etc., and eternal life. Observe, I do not contend that perseverance in faith and obedience is not also a condition of salvation, but on the contrary, that it actually is. Nor do I contend that such like representations as the above, settle the question that all who at any time repent, believe, or come to Christ, will be saved. The thing which I here intend is, that this class of texts is just what we might expect, if the fact of regeneration were certainly connected with salvation, and just what it seems they ought not to be, in case this were not true.

To this it is objected, that many who attended on Christ' s ministry are represented from time to time as believing, of whom it is almost immediately said, that they turned back and walked no more with him. I answer, that the Bible manifestly recognizes different kinds of faith, such as an intellectual faith, a faith of miracles, and the faith of the heart. The following are specimens of the Bible treatment of this subject:

Acts viii. 13: "Then Simon himself believed also: and when he was baptized, he continued with Philip, and wondered, beholding the miracles and signs which were done. 21. Thou hast neither part nor lot in this matter: for thy heart is not right in the sight of God."

James ii. 19: "Thou believest that there is one God; thou doest well: the devils also believe and tremble."

These and many other passages manifestly speak of an intellectual faith, or of a simple conviction of the truth.

Matt. vii. 22, 23; 1 Cor. xiii. 1, 2, are specimens of the manner in which the faith of miracles is represented.

See Rom. x. 9, 10, 11; Acts viii. 37; Gal. v. 6. These and such like passages speak of evangelical faith, or the faith of the heart. When the multitude are spoken of as believing under Christ's instruction, or in view of his miracles, and then as going back and walking no more with him, we are doubtless to understand those passages as teaching simply, that they were at the time convinced of his Messiahship, and that they intellectually believed that he was what he professed to be. But their history seems to forbid the conclusion that they were truly regenerated, or that they had the true faith of the gospel.

Again: John speaks of those who openly apostatized as if they had mot been true Christians: 1 John ii. 19: "They went out from us, but they were not of us; for if they had been of us, they would no doubt have continued with us: but they went out, that they might be made manifest that they were not all of us." Observe the force of the expressions, "They went out from us, but they were not of us;" that is, were not truly Christians. Why does he say so? He assigns the reason for this assertion: "for if they had been of us, they would have continued with us, but they went out that they might be made manifest that they were not all of us." That is, a part of the professed disciples went out from the rest and returned to the world, that it might be made manifest who were and who were not Christians. I do not say, however, that this is indubitably taught in this passage; but it cannot be denied, that this is its most natural construction.

8. The inhabitants of heaven seem to believe that there is a certain connection between repentance and salvation.

Luke xv. 7: "I say unto you, that likewise joy shall be in heaven over one sinner that repenteth, more than over ninety and nine just persons which need no repentance."

Now surely this joy is premature, unless they expect the penitent to be saved. If, after all, there is an uncertainty about the result, in their estimation, and if it may be, or there is a probability, that the penitent will fall, and suffer a vastly more aggravated damnation than if he had never been enlightened, one would think that they would at least suspend their triumph until the result was known. To be sure they might rejoice, if the sinner broke off temporarily from his sin, and rejoice at the bare prospect of his salvation; but to me this passage reads just as it might be expected to read, if they regarded repentance as certainly connected with ultimate salvation.

Again: there are several parables that seem to take the perseverance of the saints for granted, or to assume its truth. The one immediately preceding the verse upon which I have just remarked is one of them.

Luke xv. 3: "And he spake this parable unto them saying: 4. What man of you, having a hundred sheep, if he lose one of them, doth not leave the ninety and nine in the wilderness, and go after that which is lost, until he find it? 5. And when he hath found it, he layeth it on his shoulders, rejoicing. 6. And when he cometh home, he calleth together his friends and neighbors, saying unto them, Rejoice with me; for I have found my sheep which was lost. 7. I say unto you, that likewise joy shall be in heaven over one sinner that repenteth, more than over ninety and nine just persons which need no repentance."

Now, why this joy at the return of a strayed or lost sheep, if there is no certainty, or scarcely any probability, that he will not stray again, and be finally lost with an aggravated destruction? Immediately following this is another parable of the same import.

Luke xv. 8: "Either what woman, having ten pieces of silver, if she lose one piece, doth not light a candle, and sweep the house, and seek diligently till she find it? 9. And when she hath found it, she calleth her friends and her neighbors together, saying, Rejoice with me; for I have found that which was lost. 10. Likewise, I say unto you, there is joy in the presence of the angels of God over one sinner that repenteth."

Here again it may be asked, why this great joy at finding the sinner, unless his conversion is to result in his salvation?

I do not quote these passages as proving the doctrine in question, but only as specimens of the class of passages that seem to assume the truth of the doctrine, and as being just what might be expected, if the doctrine is true, and just what might not be expected if the doctrine is not true.

To this it may be, and has been replied, that there are many passages that are just what we could not expect, if the perseverance of the saints were true. The following are relied upon as examples of this class:--

Heb. vi. 1: "Therefore, leaving the principles of the doctrine of Christ, let us go on unto perfection; not laying again the foundation of repentance from dead works, and of faith toward God; 2. Of the doctrine of baptisms, and of laying on of hands, and of resurrection of the dead, and of eternal judgment. 3. And this will we do if God permit. 4. For it is impossible for those who were once enlightened, and have tasted of the heavenly gift, and were made partakers of the Holy Ghost; 5. And have tasted of the good word of God, and the powers of the world to come; 6. If they shall fall away, to renew them again unto repentance; seeing they crucify to themselves the son of God afresh, and put him to an open shame."

Ez. xviii. 24: "But when the righteous turneth away from his righteousness, and committeth iniquity, and doeth according to all the abominations that the wicked man doeth, shall he live? All his righteousness that he hath done shall not be mentioned; in his trespass that he hath trespassed, and in his sin that he hath sinned, in them shall he die."

Ezek. xxxiii. 13: "When I shall say to the righteous, that he shall surely live; if he trust to his own righteousness and commit iniquity, all his righteousness shall not be remembered; but for his iniquity that he hath committed, he shall die for it."

Matt. x. 22: "And ye shall be hated of all men for my name's sake; but he that endureth to the end shall be saved."

John xv. 6: "If a man abide not in me, he is cast forth as a branch, and is withered; and men gather them, and cast them into the fire, and they are burned."

1 Cor. x. 12: "Wherefore let him that thinketh he standeth take heed lest he fall."

Heb. iii. 6: "But Christ as a Son over his own house; whose house are we, if we hold fast the confidence and the rejoicing of the hope firm unto the end. 12. Take heed, brethren, lest there be in any of you an evil heart of unbelief, in departing from the living God. 13. But exhort one another daily, while it is called to-day; lest any of you be hardened through the deceitfulness of sin. 14. For we are made partakers of Christ, if we hold the beginning of our confidence steadfast unto the end."

Heb. iv. 1: "Let us therefore fear, lest a promise being left us of entering into his rest, any of you should seem to come short of it. 11. Let us labor therefore to enter into that rest, lest any man fail after the same example of unbelief."

2 Peter i. 10: "Wherefore the rather, brethren, give diligence to make your calling and election sure: for if ye do these things, ye shall never fall."

In reply to this objection I remark, that instead of these passages being otherwise than might be expected if the doctrine in question were true, and therefore implying that the doctrine is not true, they are precisely what might be expected, if the doctrine as I have stated it, were true. If the certainty be but a moral certainty, even when the fact of conversion is settled beyond all doubt, or possibility of mistake, if the final salvation of the truly regenerate be as really conditioned upon perseverance as if there was no certainty about it; and if, moreover, the fact of conversion is seldom settled in this life beyond the possibility of mistake, then these passages, instead of implying any real uncertainty in regard to the final salvation of the saints, are just as and what might be expected, because they are just what is needed, upon the supposition, that the doctrine in question is true. They do not affirm that any true saints are, or will be, lost. They do imply the natural possibility, and, humanly speaking, the danger of such an event. They further imply, that without watchfulness and perseverance salvation is impossible. They also imply, that caution, warning, and threatening, are needed. They also imply, that some men, to say the least, are not certain of their own salvation, and that they do not certainly know that they are saints, beyond all possibility of mistake.

Now, these things that are fairly implied in this class of passages are really true: hence these passages just meet the necessities of the church, and are therefore just what might be expected when all the facts in the case are considered. I do not intend that this class of passages imply the truth of the doctrine under consideration, but that they are consistent with it, and might be expected, if the doctrine, as I have stated it, be true.

9. Regeneration is represented as securing perseverance in obedience:--

First, In those passages that make it the condition of salvation.

Secondly, In those passages that expressly affirm, that the truly regenerated do not, and cannot, live in sin.

1 John iii. 9: "Whosoever is born of God doth not commit sin; for his seed remaineth in him: and he cannot sin, because he is born of God."

1 John iv. 7: "Beloved, let us love one another: for love is of God; and every one that loveth is born of God, and knoweth God."

1 John v. 1: "Whosoever believeth that Jesus is the Christ is born of God: and every one that loveth him that begat, loveth him also that is begotten of him. 4. For whatsoever is born of God overcometh the world: and this is the victory that overcometh the world, even our faith. 18. We know that whosoever

is born of God sinneth not; but he that is begotten of God keepeth himself, and that wicked one toucheth him not."

These and similar passages expressly teach the persevering nature of true religion, through the indwelling of the Holy Spirit: in other words, they teach that the truly regenerate do not sin, in the sense at least of living in anything like habitual sin. They teach, that with all truly regenerate souls, holiness is at least the rule, and sin only the exception; that instead of its being true, that the regenerate souls live a great majority of their days subsequent to regeneration in sin, it is true that they so seldom sin, that in strong language it may be said in truth, they do not sin. This language so strongly and expressly teaches that perseverance is an unfailing attribute of Christian character, that but for the fact that other passages constrain us to understand these passages as strong language used in a qualified sense, we should naturally understand them as affirming that no truly regenerate soul does at any time sin. But since it is a sound rule of interpreting the language of an author, that he is, if possible, to be made consistent with himself; and since John, in other passages in this same epistle and elsewhere, represents that Christians, or truly regenerate persons, do sometimes sin; and since this is frequently taught in the Bible, we must understand these passages just quoted as only affirming a general and not a universal truth; that is, that truly regenerate persons do not sin anything like habitually, but that holiness is the rule with them, and sin only the exception. Certainly these passages cannot be reasonably understood as affirming and meaning less than this. I know that it has been said, that being born of God is used by John in these cases in a higher sense, and as meaning more than simple conversion or regeneration, as representing a higher state than can be predicated of all true Christians. But observe, he especially affirms that all who truly believe are born of God.

Again: Christ speaks as if he regarded those only as having truly believed who persevere in obedience. John viii. 31: "Then said Jesus to those Jews which believed on him, if ye continue in my word, then are ye my disciples indeed."

The parable of the sower appears to have been designed expressly to teach the persevering nature of true religion. Luke viii. 5: "A sower went out to sow his seed: and as he sowed, some fell by the way side, and it was trodden down, arid the fowls of the air devoured it. 6. And some fell upon a rock; and as soon as it was sprung up, it withered away, because it lacked moisture. 7. And some fell among thorns; and the thorns sprang up with it, and choked it. 8. And other fell on good ground, and sprang up, and bare fruit a hundred fold. And when he had said these things, he cried, He that hath ears to hear, let him hear. 11. Now the parable is this: The seed is the word of God. 12. Those by the way side arc they that hear; then cometh the devil, and taketh away the word out of their hearts, lest they should believe and be saved. 13. They on the rock are they, which, when they hear, receive the word with joy; and these have no met, which for a while believe, and in time of temptation fall away. 14. And that which fell among thorns are they, which when they have heard, go forth, and are choked with cares, and riches, and pleasures of this life, and bring no fruit to perfection. 15. But that on the good ground are they, which, in an honest and good heart, having heard the word, keep it, and bring forth fruit with patience."

If this parable was not designed to distinguish true religion from its counterfeits, and to illustrate the persevering nature of true religion, I do not know, and cannot conceive, what was its design. I need not enlarge upon it. Let any one read and consider the parable for himself.

Again: the parable of the leaven seems designed also to teach the progressive and persevering nature of true religion.

Matt. xiii. 33: "Another parable spake he unto them: the kingdom of heaven is like unto leaven, which a woman took and hid in three measures of meal, till the whole was leavened."

This parable I understand to represent or teach the aggressive nature of true faith and piety, as it exhibits itself both in the hearts and lives of individual Christians, and also as it progresses and extends itself in the world. It is in its nature persevering and aggressive, and when it once truly exists, it will through grace triumph. When I speak of the persevering nature of true religion, I do not mean, that religion as it exists in the hearts of the saints in this life would of itself, if unsupported by the grace and indwelling Spirit of God, prevail and triumph over its enemies; but the thing intended is, that through the faithfulness of God, he that has begun or shall begin a good work in any heart, will perfect it until the day of Jesus Christ. The persevering character of true religion is owing to the indwelling Spirit of God.

This leads me to remark again, that repentance is made the condition of receiving the Holy Spirit; and when this Spirit is received, it is with the express promise and pledge that he shall abide in the heart for ever.

John vii. 37: "In the last day, that great day of the feast, Jesus stood and cried, saying, If any man thirst let him come unto me and drink. He that believeth on me, as the Scripture hath said, out of his belly shall flow rivers of living water. 39. (But this spake he of the Spirit, which they that believe on him should receive; for the Holy Ghost was not yet given; because that Jesus was not yet glorified.")

Here we learn that water represents the Holy Spirit. This is abundantly taught in the Bible. Now let us hear what Christ said to the woman of Samaria.

John iv. 13: "Jesus answered and said unto her, Whosoever drinketh of this water shall thirst again. 14. But whosoever drinketh of the water that I shall give him, shall never thirst: but the water that I shall give him shall be in him a well of water springing up into everlasting life."

The prominent truth taught in this text is, that whosoever shall drink of this water shall never thirst. In this particular respect the Saviour contrasts it with the water of Jacob's well, and says, 13, 14: "Jesus answered and said unto her, Whosoever drinketh of this water shall thirst again: but whosoever drinketh of the water that I shall give him, shall never thirst; but the water that I shall give him shall be in him a well of water springing up into everlasting life." This Christ plainly states as a fact.

That is, he shall never perish for lack of this Spirit or water, but it shall abide in him, and spring up into eternal life. The Spirit shall remain in him, and secure him against falling and perishing. The fact that the Spirit shall abide with and in all who ever receive him, and shall prevail to secure their salvation, seems to be plainly taught in this passage.

Again, Rom. viii. 9: "But ye are not in the flesh, but in the Spirit, if so be that the Spirit of God dwell in you. Now if any man have not the Spirit of Christ, he is none of his. 10. And if Christ be in you, the body is dead because of sin; but the Spirit is life because of righteousness. 11. But if the Spirit of him that raised up Jesus from the dead dwell in you, he that raised up Christ from the dead shall also quicken your mortal bodies by his Spirit that dwelleth in you."

Here it is expressly declared, that none are Christians who have not the Holy Spirit, or Spirit of Christ, and that they who are Christ's do not walk after the flesh, but after the Spirit; that they who are Christ's have crucified, that is killed, the lusts of the flesh. This is the real character of all true saints. Such like passages, observe, are designed to distinguish true religion from its counterfeits, and to teach that perseverance in true obedience is a characteristic of all real saints.

10. Christ represents it as impossible to deceive the elect. Matt. xxiv. 24: We have seen that the elect unto salvation include all true Christians; that is, that all Christians are the elect children of God. They have come to Christ. Observe, the Saviour himself teaches, as we have seen:

(1.) That no one can come to, or believe in him, unless the Father draw him.

(2.) That the Father draws those, and only those to Christ, whom he has given to him.

(3.) That all whom the Father has given to him shall come to him, and of those that come to him he will lose none, but will raise them up at the last day.

John vi. 44: "No man can come to me except the Father which hath sent me, draw him; and I will raise him up at the last day. 45. It is written in the prophets, And they shall be all taught of God. Every man therefore that hath heard, and hath learned of the Father, cometh unto me. 39. All that the Father giveth me shall come to me; and him that cometh to me I will in no wise cast out. 38. For I came down from heaven not to do mine own will, but the will of him that sent me. 37. And this is the father's will which hath sent me, that of all which he hath given me I should lose nothing, but should raise it up again at the last day. 40. And this is the will of him that sent me, that every one which seeth the Son and believeth on him may have everlasting life; and I will raise him up at the last day."

False theories are represented as permitted to test the piety of true and false professors. 1 Cor. xi. 19: "For there must be also heresies among you, that they which are approved may be made manifest among you." Those that are of the elect, or are true children of God, will not follow heresies. Christ says, John x. 4, 6: "And when he putteth forth his own sheep, he goeth before them, and the sheep follow him; for they know his voice. 9. And a stranger will they not follow, but will flee from him: for they know not the voice of strangers. 27. My sheep hear my voice, and I know them, and they follow me. 28. And I give unto them eternal life; and they shall never perish, neither shall any pluck them out of my hand."

But those who are not true believers will not, and do not hear and know his voice, and follow him. John x. 26: "But ye believe not, because ye are not of my sheep, as I said unto you."

11. The eighth chapter of Romans seems to settle the question, or rather is of itself a clear proof of the doctrine we are examining. We need to read and ponder prayerfully the whole chapter, to apprehend distinctly the scope of the apostle's teaching upon this subject. He had in the seventh chapter been dwelling upon and portraying a legal experience. He begins this eighth chapter by asserting, Rom. viii. 1: "There is therefore now no condemnation to them which are in Christ Jesus, who walk not after the flesh, but after the Spirit. 2.

For the law of the Spirit of life in Christ Jesus hath made me free from the law of sin and death. 3. For what the law could not do, in that it was weak through the flesh, God sending his own Son in the likeness of sinful flesh, and for sin, condemned sin in the flesh; 4. That the righteousness of the law might be fulfilled in us, who walk not after the flesh but after the Spirit. 5. For they that are after the flesh do mind the things of the flesh; but they that are after the Spirit, the things of the Spirit. 6. For to be carnally minded is death; but to be spiritually minded is life and peace. 7. Because the carnal mind is enmity against God; for it is not subject to the law of God, neither indeed can be. 8. So then they that are in the flesh cannot please God. 9. But ye are not in the flesh, but in the Spirit, if so be that the Spirit of God dwell in you. Now, if any man have not the Spirit of Christ, he is none of his. 10. And if Christ be in you, the body is dead because of sin; but the Spirit is life, because of righteousness. 11. But if the Spirit of him that raised up Jesus from the dead dwell in you, he that raised up Christ from the dead shall also quicken your mortal bodies by his Spirit that dwelleth in you. 12. Therefore, brethren, we are debtors, not to the flesh, to live after the flesh. 13. For if ye live after the flesh, ye shall die; but if ye through the Spirit do mortify the deeds of the body, ye shall live. 14. For as many as are led by the Spirit of God, they are the sons of God. 15. For ye have not received the spirit of bondage again to fear; but ye have received the Spirit of adoption, whereby we cry, Abba, Father. 16. The Spirit itself beareth witness with our spirit, that we are the children of God: 17. And if children, then heirs; heirs of God and joint heirs with Jesus Christ: if so be that we suffer with him, that we may be also glorified together. 18. For I reckon, that the sufferings of this present time are not worthy to be compared with the glory which shall be revealed in us."

Here he describes the character of true believers as distinguished from mere legalists, of whom he had been speaking. True believers, he here asserts, are justified; they are in Christ Jesus; they walk not after the flesh, but after the Spirit; the righteousness of the law is fulfilled in them, that is, the law is written in their hearts; they have the Spirit of Christ, the Spirit of adoption; the Spirit witnesses with their spirit that they are the adopted children of God; "If children, then heirs, heirs of God and joint heirs with Christ;" the sufferings of this present time are not worthy to be compared to the glory that shall be revealed in them. Verse 24, he says: "For we are saved by hope; but hope that is seen, is not hope; for what a man seeth, why doth he yet hope for?"

He then proceeds to notice the ground of this hope: verses 26 and 27. "Likewise the Spirit also helpeth our infirmities; for we know not what we should pray for as we ought; but the Spirit itself maketh intercession for us with groanings which cannot be uttered. And he that searcheth the hearts knoweth what is the mind of the Spirit, because he maketh intercession for the saints according to the will of God." This, observe, he affirms to be true of all who are Christ's, or who are true believers. Of this Spirit he affirms the following things: (1.) That all Christians possess this Spirit. (2.) That this Spirit bears witness with the spirits of Christians that they are the children of God. (3.) That he makes intercession for the saints according to the will of God; that is, that he prays in them or excites them to pray, and to pray aright, for those things which it is the will of God to grant to them. He then in the 28th verse says, "And we know that all things work together for good to them that love God, to them who are the called according to his purpose." Here he represents those who love

God, and those who are the called according to his purpose, as the same persons; and affirms, that we know that all things shall work together for their good. This he notices as a second ground of hope. He next proceeds to state, how we know that all things work together for the good of those that love God: or, which he regards as the same thing, to those who are the elect, called according to the election or purpose of God. He says, verse 29, "For whom he did foreknow, he also did predestinate to be conformed to the image of his Son, that he might be the first-born among many brethren:" that is, we know it, because they are predestinated to be conformed to the image of his Son. Not if they will be, but to be, and therefore, all things must directly or indirectly contribute to this result. He then says, "Moreover, whom he did predestinate, them he also called; and whom he called, them he also justified; and whom he justified, them he also glorified." That is, furthermore, we know this, and have good ground of hope from the fact, that whom he did predestinate to be conformed to the image of his Son, them, that is the same persons, he also called; and whom, that is, the same persons whom he had predestinated to be conformed to the image of his Son and had called, them he also justified; and whom he predestinated, and called, and justified, them, that is, the same persons, he also glorified.

Here then, he concludes, is a firm foundation for the hope of which he had spoken, the grounds of which he had been pointing out. He accordingly proceeds to say in a spirit of triumph:--

Rom. viii. 31: "What shall we then say to these things? If God be for us, who can be against us? 32. He that spared not his own Son, but delivered him up for us all, how shall he not with him also freely give us all things? 33. Who shall lay anything to the charge of God's elect? It is God that justifieth. 34. Who is he that condemneth? It is Christ that died, yea rather, that is risen again, who is even at the right hand of God, who also maketh intercession for us."

Here he says, "if God be for us, who can be against us?" and then proceeds to point out several other considerations that enter into this ground of confidence. All who love God are his elect. God justifies them, and who is he that condemns them? God is for them, and who shall be against them? God freely gave his Son for all of them, how much more shall he freely give them all things? If he did not withhold his Son, surely he would withhold nothing else from them that was necessary to secure their salvation. Furthermore, it was Christ that died, and still more and rather, that had risen again, and maketh intercession for them. If these things are so, we may well inquire:--

Rom. viii. 35: "Who shall separate us from the love of Christ? Shall tribulation, or distress, or persecution, or famine, or nakedness, or peril, or sword? 36. (As it is written, For thy sake we are killed all the day long; we are accounted as sheep for the slaughter.)"

He then triumphantly affirms, verses 37-39: "Nay, in all these things we are more than conquerors, through him that loved us. For I am persuaded, that neither death, nor life, nor angels, nor principalities, nor powers, nor things present, nor things to come, nor height, nor depth, nor any other creature, shall be able to separate us from the love of God, which is in Christ Jesus our Lord."

If Paul in the eighth of Romans does not settle the question, that all true saints will be saved, how could it be settled? Let us in few words sum up the argument, as he here presents it:--

We are saved already in anticipation, or in hope; and only by hope, for as yet we have not received our crown. The grounds of this hope are, that we are in Christ Jesus, have the Spirit of Christ, Spirit of adoption. We walk not after the flesh, but after the Spirit. This Spirit witnesses that we are children and heirs of God. He makes intercession for us according to the will of God. We also know, that all things work together for good to them who love God, for they are the called according to his purpose. They who are called, that is, effectually called, are called in conformity with their predestination to be conformed to the image of God. Hence those who are thus predestinated are called, and justified, and glorified. Therefore, no one can lay anything to the charge of God's elect. God justifies, and who shall condemn them? Christ died for them, yea rather, has risen and makes intercession for them. God withheld not his Son, and of course will withhold from Christians nothing that is essential to secure their salvation. Wherefore he concludes, that nothing shall be able to separate us from the love of God.

I know that to this it has been replied, that although nothing else can separate us from the love of God, yet we may separate ourselves from his love.

To this I answer, true; we may, or can do so; but the question is, shall we, or will any of the elected and called do so? No, indeed; for this is the thing which the apostle intended to affirm, namely, the certainty of the salvation of all true saints. The apostle manifestly in this passage assumes, or affirms, that all who ever truly loved God are elect, or are chosen to be conformed to the image of his Son; and are called, and sanctified, and justified, in conformity with such predestination. If this is not his meaning, what is? If this is not his meaning, what ground of hope do we, after all, find in what he says? The apostle seems to have had the same thought in his mind in writing to the Hebrews.

Heb. vi. 17: "Wherein God willing more abundantly to show unto the heirs of promise the immutability of his counsel, confirmed it by an oath; 18. That by two immutable things, in which it was impossible for God to lie, we might have a strong consolation, who have fled for refuge to lay hold upon the hope set before us; 19. Which hope we have as an anchor of the soul, both sure and steadfast, and which entereth into that within the veil; 20. Whither the forerunner is for us entered, even Jesus, made a high-priest forever, after the order of Melchisedec."

There are a great many other passages of scripture, of the same import as those I have quoted in support of this doctrine, as every one knows who has taken the trouble to examine for himself. But I have pursued this investigation far enough. If what has been said fails to satisfy any mind, it is presumed that nothing which might be added would produce conviction. I will therefore, after replying to some further objections, conclude the discussion of this subject.

LECTURE L - PERSEVERANCE OF SAINTS

OBJECTIONS ANSWERED

1. It is said that the natural tendency of this doctrine condemns it; that it tends to beget and foster a carnal presumption in a life of sin, on the part of those who think themselves saints.

There is, I reply, a broad and obvious distinction between the abuse of a good thing or doctrine, and its natural tendency. The legitimate tendency of a thing or doctrine may be good, and yet it may be abused and perverted. This is true of the atonement, and the offer of pardon through Christ. These doctrines have been, and are, greatly objected to by Universalists and Unitarians, as having a tendency to encourage the hope of impunity in sin. It is said by them, that to hold out the idea that Christ has made an atonement for sin, and that the oldest and vilest sinners may be forgiven and saved, tends directly to immorality, and to encourage the hope of ultimate impunity in a life of sin--the hope that, after a sinful life, the sinner may at last repent and be saved.

Now, there is so much plausibility in this objection to the doctrine of pardon and atonement, that many sensible men have rejected those doctrines because of this objection. They have regarded the objection as unanswerable. But a close examination will show, that the objection against those doctrines is entirely without foundation; and not only so, but that the real natural tendency of those doctrines affords a strong presumptive argument in their favor.

The telling of a convinced and self-condemned sinner, that Christ has died for his sins, and offers freely and at once to forgive all the past, has no natural tendency to beget a spirit of perseverance in rebellion; but is on the contrary the readiest, and safest, and I may add, the only effectual method of subduing him, and bringing him to immediate repentance. But suppose, on the other hand, you tell him there is no forgiveness, that he must be punished for his sins at all events, what tendency has this to bring him to immediate and genuine repentance; to beget within him the love required by the law of God? Assuring him of punishment for all his sins, might serve to restrain outward manifestations of a sinful heart, but certainly it tends not to subdue selfishness, and to cleanse the heart; whereas the offer of mercy through the death of Christ, has a most sin-subduing tendency. It is such a manifestation to the sinner of God's great love to him, his real pity for him, and readiness to overlook and blot out the past, as tends to break down the stubborn heart into genuine repentance, and to beget the sincerest love to God. and Christ, together with the deepest self-loathing and self-abasement on account of sin. Thus the doctrines of the atonement and pardon through a crucified Redeemer, instead of being condemned by their legitimate tendency, are greatly confirmed thereby. These doctrines are no doubt liable to abuse, and so is every good thing; but is this a good reason for rejecting them? Our necessary food and drink may be abused, and often are, and so are all the most essential blessings of life. Should we reject them on this account?

It is admitted that the doctrines of atonement and forgiveness through Christ, are greatly abused by careless sinners and hypocrites; but is this a good reason for denying and withholding them from the convicted sinner, who is earnestly inquiring what he shall do to be saved? No indeed!

It is also admitted, that the doctrine of the perseverance of the saints is liable to abuse, and often is abused by the carnal and deceived professor; but is this a good reason for rejecting it, and for withholding its consolations from the tempted, tempest-tossed saint? By no means. Such are the circumstances of temptation from within and without, in which the saints are placed in this life, that when they are made really acquainted with themselves, and are brought to a proper appreciation of the circumstances in which they are, they have but little rational ground of hope, except what is found in this doctrine. The natural tendency and inevitable consequence of a thorough revelation of themselves to themselves, would be to beget despair, but for the covenanted grace and faithfulness of God. What saint who has ever been revealed to himself by the Holy Spirit, has not seen what Paul saw when he said, "In me, that is, in my flesh, dwelleth no good thing?" Who that has been made acquainted with himself, does not know that he never did, and never will take one step towards heaven, except as he is anticipated and drawn by the grace of God in Christ Jesus? Who that knows himself does not understand that he never would have been converted, but for the grace of God anticipating and exciting the first motions of his mind in a right direction? And what true saint does not know, that such are his former habitudes, and such the circumstances of trial under which he is placed, and such the downward tendency of his own soul that although converted, he shall not persevere for an hour, except the indwelling grace and Spirit of God shall hold him up, and quicken him in the path of holiness?

Where, I would ask, is the ground of hope for the saints as they exist in this world? Not in the fact that they have been physically regenerated, so that to fall is naturally impossible. Not in the fact that they have passed through any such change of nature as to secure their perseverance for an hour, if left to themselves. Not in the fact that they can or will sustain themselves for a day or a moment by their resolutions. Where then is their hope? There is not even a ground of probability, that any one of them will ever be saved, unless the doctrine in question be true, that is, unless the promised grace and faithfulness of God in Christ Jesus goes before, and from step to step secures their perseverance. But if this grace is promised to any saint, as his only ground of confidence, or even hope that he shall be saved, it is equally, and upon the same conditions, promised to all the saints. No one more than another can place the least reasonable dependence on anything, except the grace equally promised and vouchsafed to all. What does a man know of himself who hopes to be saved, and who yet does not depend wholly on promises of grace in Christ Jesus?

The natural tendency of true and thorough conviction of sin, and of such a knowledge of ourselves, as is essential to salvation, is to beget and foster despondency and despair; and, as I said, the soul in this condition. has absolutely little or no ground of hope of ultimate salvation, except that which this doctrine, when rightly understood, affords. However far he may have progressed in the way of life, he sees, when he thoroughly knows the truth, that he has progressed not a step, except as he has been drawn and inclined by the indwelling grace and Spirit of Christ; and that he shall absolutely go no further in the way to heaven, unless the same gracious influence is continued, in such a sense, and to such an extent, as to overcome all the temptations with which he is beset. His only hope is in the fact, that God has promised to keep and preserve him. Nothing but God's faithfulness to his Son procured the conversion of any saint. Nothing but this same faithfulness has procured his perseverance for a day, and nothing else can render the salvation of any soul at all probable. What can a man be thinking about, or what can he know of himself, who does not know this? Unless the same grace that secures the conversion of the saints, secures their perseverance to the end, there is no hope for them. It is true, that the promises to sinners and to saints are conditioned upon their faith, and upon the right exercise of their own agency; and it is also true, that grace secures the fulfilment of the conditions of the promises, in every instance in which they are fulfilled, or they never would be fulfilled.

We have seen that the promises of the Father to the Son secure the bestowment upon the saints of all grace to ensure their final salvation. It shocks and distresses me to hear professed Christians talk of being saved at all, except upon the ground of the anticipating, and persevering, and sin-overcoming, and hell-subduing grace of God in Christ Jesus. Why, I should as soon expect the devil to be saved, as that any saint on earth will be, if left, with all the promises of God in his hands, to stand and persevere without the drawings, and inward teachings, and over-persuading influences of the Holy Spirit. Shame on a theology that suspends the ultimate salvation of the saints upon the broken reed of their own resolutions in their best estate! Their firmest resolutions are nothing unless they are formed and supported by the influence of the Spirit of grace, going before, and exciting, and persuading to their formation and their continuance. This is everywhere taught in the Bible; and who that has considered the matter does not know, that this is the experience of every saint? Where, then, is the ground of hope, if the doctrine in question be denied?" If the foundation be destroyed, what shall the righteous do?" Where, then, is the evil tendency of this doctrine? It has naturally no evil tendency. Can the assurance of eternal salvation through the blood, and love, and grace of Christ, have a natural tendency to harden the heart of a child of God against his Father and his Saviour? Can the revealed fact, that he shall be more than a conqueror through Christ, beget in him a disposition to sin against Christ? Impossible! This doctrine, though liable to abuse by hypocrites, is nevertheless the sheet anchor of the saints in hours of conflict. And shall the children be deprived of the bread of life, because sinners will pervert the use of it to their own destruction? This doctrine is absolutely needful to prevent despair, when conviction is deep, and conflicts with temptation are sharp. Its natural tendency is to slay and keep down selfishness, to forestall selfish efforts and resolutions, and to sustain the confidence of the soul at all times. It tends to subdue sin, to humble the soul under a sense of the great love and faithfulness of God in Christ Jesus; to influence the soul to live upon Christ, and to renounce entirely and for ever all confidence in the flesh. Indeed, its tendency is the direct opposite of that asserted in the objection. It is the abuse, and not the natural tendency of this doctrine, against which this objection is urged. But the abuse of a doctrine is no reason why it should be rejected.

2. But it is said that real saints do sometimes fall into at least temporary backsliding, in which cases the belief of this doctrine tends to lull them into carnal security, and to prolong their backsliding, if not to embolden them to apostatize.

To this I reply that if real Christians do backslide, they lose for the time being their evidence of acceptance with God; and withal they know that in their present state they cannot be saved. This objection is leveled rather against that view of perseverance that says, "once in grace, always in grace;" that teaches the doctrine of perpetual justification upon condition of one act of faith. The doctrine as stated in these lectures, holds out no ground of hope to a backslider, except upon condition of return and perseverance to the end. Moreover, the doctrine as here taught is, that perseverance in holiness, in the sense, that, subsequent to regeneration holiness is at least the rule, and sin only the exception, is an attribute of Christian character. Every moment, therefore, a backslider remains in sin, he must have less evidence that he is a child of God.

But as I said, he loses confidence in his own Christianity, and in this state of backsliding he does not believe the doctrine of perseverance, as a doctrine of revelation. It is absurd to say, that while backslidden from God he still has faith in his word, and believes this doctrine as a Christian doctrine, and upon the strength of the testimony of God. He does not in this state really believe the doctrine, and therefore it is not the tendency of the doctrine when believed that harms him, but a gross abuse and perversion of it. But the perversion of a doctrine is no objection to it. The real tendency of the doctrine is to break the heart of the backslider, to exhibit to him the great love, and faithfulness, and grace of God which tend naturally to subdue selfishness, and to humble the heart. When backsliders are emboldened by this doctrine and rendered presumptuous, it is never by any other than a gross perversion and abuse of it.

Those who persist in such objections should reflect upon their own inconsistency, in making a manifest perversion and abuse of this doctrine an objection to it, when they hold other doctrines, equally liable to abuse and equally abused, in spite of such abuse. Let such persons see, that they are practically adopting a principle, and insisting upon its application in this case, which, if carried out, would set aside the whole gospel.

3. It is objected, that the Bible speaks of the saints as if there were real danger of their being lost. It requires them to spend the time of their sojourning here in fear, and abounds with cautions, and warnings, and threatenings, that are certainly out of place, and not at all to be regarded, if the salvation of the saints is a revealed certainty. How, it is inquired, can we fear, if God has revealed the certainty of our salvation? Is not fear in such a case a result of unbelief? Can God reveal to us the fact, that we shall certainly be saved, and then call on us or exhort us to fear that we shall not be saved? Can he require us to doubt his word and his oath? If God has revealed the certainty of the salvation of all true saints, can any saint fear that he shall not be saved without downright unbelief? and can God approve and even enjoin such fears? If a person is conscious of possessing the character ascribed to the true saints in the Bible, is he not bound upon the supposition that this doctrine is true, to have and to entertain the most unwavering assurance that he shall be saved? Has he any right to doubt it, or to fear that he shall not be saved?

I answer, that no true saint who has an evidence or an earnest of his acceptance with God, such as the true saint may have, has a right to doubt for a moment that he shall be saved, nor has he a right to fear, that he shall not be saved. I also add, that the Bible nowhere encourages, or calls upon the saints to fear, that they shall not be saved, or that they shall be lost. It calls on them to fear something else, to fear to sin or apostatize, lest they should be lost, but not that they shall sin and be lost. The following are specimens of the exhortations and warnings given to the saints:--

Matt. xxvi. 41. "Watch and pray, that ye enter not into temptation; the spirit indeed is willing, but the flesh is weak."

Mark xiii. 33: "Take ye heed, watch and pray; for ye know not when the time is. 34. For the Son of Man is as a man taking a far journey, who left his house, and gave authority to his servants, and to every man his work, and commanded the porter to watch. 35. Watch ye therefore; for ye know not when the master of the house cometh, at even, or at midnight, or at cock-crowing, or in the morning; 36. Lest, coming suddenly, he find you sleeping. 37. And what I say unto you, I say unto all, Watch."

Luke xii. 37: "Blessed are those servants, whom the Lord when he cometh, shall find watching; verily I say unto you, That he shall gird himself, and make them to sit down to meat, and will come forth and serve them."

1 Cor. x. 12: "Wherefore, let him that thinketh he standeth take heed lest he fall."

1 Cor. xix. 13: "Watch ye, stand fast in the faith, quit you like men, be strong."

Eph. v. 15: "See then that ye walk circumspectly, not as fools, but as wise, 16. Redeeming the time, because the days are evil."

Eph. vi. 10: "Finally, my brethren, be strong in the Lord and in the power of his might. 11. Put on the whole armor of God, that ye may be able to stand against the wiles of the devil."

Phil. i. 27: "Only let your conversation be as it becometh the gospel of Christ; that whether I come and see you, or else be absent, I may hear of your affairs, that ye stand fast in one spirit, with one mind striving together for the faith of the gospel; 28. And in nothing terrified by your adversaries; which is to them an evident token of perdition, but to you of salvation, and that of God."

1 Thess. v. 6: "Therefore, let us not sleep, as do others; but let us watch and be sober."

1 Tim. vi. 12: "Fight the good fight of faith, lay hold on eternal life, whereunto thou art also called, and halt professed a good profession before many witnesses."

2. Tim. ii. 3: "Thou therefore endure hardness, as a good soldier of Jesus Christ."

2 Tim. iv. 5: "But watch thou in all things, endure afflictions, do the work of an evangelist, make full proof of thy ministry."

1 Pet. iv. 7: "But the end of all things is at hand; be ye therefore sober, and watch unto prayer."

Matt. x. 22: "And ye shall be hated of all men for my name's sake; but he that endureth to the end shall be saved."

John xv. 6: "If a man abide not in me, he is cast forth as a branch, and is withered; and men gather them, and cast them into the fire, and they are burned."

Rom. ii. 6: "Who will render to every man according to his deeds; 7. To them who, by patient continuance in well-doing seek for glory, and honor, and immortality, eternal life."

1 Cor. ix. 27: "But I keep under my body, and bring it into subjection; lest that by any means, when I have preached to others, I myself should be a castaway."

2 Cor. vi. 1: "We, then, as workers together with him, beseech you also that ye receive not the grace of God in vain."

Col. i. 23: "If ye continue in the faith grounded and settled, and be not moved away from the hope of the gospel, which ye have heard, and which was preached to every creature which is under heaven: whereof I Paul am made a minister."

Heb. iii. 6: "But Christ as a Son over his own house; whose house are we, if we hold fast the confidence and the rejoicing of the hope firm unto the end. 12. Take heed, brethren, lest there be in any of you an evil heart of unbelief, in departing from the living God. 13. But exhort one another daily, while it is called to-day; lest any of you be hardened through the deceitfulness of sin. 14. For we are made partakers of Christ, if we hold the beginning of our confidence steadfast unto the end."

Heb. iv. 1: "Let us therefore fear, lest a promise being left us of entering into his rest, any of you should seem to come short of it. 11. Let us labor therefore to enter into that rest, lest any man fall after the same example of unbelief."

2 Pet i. 10: "Wherefore the rather, brethren, give diligence to make your calling and election sure; for if ye do these things, ye shall never fall."

Rev. ii. 10. "Fear none of those things which thou shalt suffer; behold, the devil shall cast some of you into prison, that ye may be tried; and ye shall have tribulation ten days; be thou faithful unto death, and I will give thee a crown of life. 11. He that hath an ear, let him hear what the Spirit saith unto the churches; he that overcometh shall not be hurt of the second death. 17. He that hath an ear, let him hear what the Spirit saith unto the churches: To him that overcometh will I give to eat of the hidden manna, and will give him a white stone, and in the stone a new name written, which no man knoweth, saving he that receiveth it. 26. And he that overcometh, and keepeth my words unto the end, to him will I give power over the nations."

Rev. xxi. 7: "He that overcometh shall inherit all things; and I will be his God, and he shall be my son."

1 Pet. i. 17: "And if ye call on the Father, who without respect of persons judgeth according to every man's work, pass the time of your sojourning here in fear."

I find no instance in the Bible in which the saints are enjoined or exhorted to fear that they shall actually be lost; but, on the contrary, this kind of fear is everywhere, in the word of God, discountenanced and rebuked, and the saints are exhorted to the utmost assurance that Christ will keep and preserve them to the end, and finally bestow on them eternal life. They are warned against sin and apostacy, and are informed that if they do apostatize they shall be lost. They are expressly informed, that their salvation is conditioned upon their perseverance in holiness to the end. They are also called upon to watch against sin and apostacy; to fear both, lest they should be lost.

Heb. iv. 1: "Let us therefore fear, lest a promise being left us of entering into his rest, any of you should seem to come short of it."

Heb. vi. 1: "Therefore, leaving the principles of the doctrine of Christ, let us go on unto perfection; not laying again the foundation of repentance from dead works, and of faith toward God, 2. Of the doctrine of baptism, and of laying on of hands, and of resurrection of the dead, and of eternal judgment. 3. And this will we do, if God permit. 4. For it is impossible for those who were once enlightened, and have tasted of the heavenly gift, and were made partakers of the Holy Ghost; 5. And have tasted the good word of God, and the powers of the world to come, 6. If they shall fall away, to renew them again unto repentance; seeing they crucify to themselves the Son of God afresh, and put him to an open shame."

Heb. iii. 12: "Take heed, brethren, lest there be in any of you an evil heart of unbelief, in departing from the living God. 13. But exhort one another daily, while it is called to-day; lest any of you be hardened through the deceitfulness of sin. 14. For we are made partakers of Christ, if we hold the beginning of our confidence steadfast unto the end."

They are required to fear to sin, but not to fear that they shall sin in any sense that implies any expectation of sinning. They are to fear to apostatize, but not to expect, or fear that they shall apostatize. They are to fear to be lost, but not that they shall be lost. To fear to sin lest we should be lost, is a very different thing from fearing that we shall sin and shall be lost. There is just as much need of our fearing to sin, and of fearing to be lost, as there would be if there were no certainty of our salvation. When we consider the nature of the certainty of the salvation of the saints, that it is only a moral and conditional certainty, we can see the propriety and the necessity of the warnings and threatenings which we find addressed to them in the Bible. The language of the Bible is just what it might be expected to be, in case the salvation of the saints were certain, with a moral and conditional certainty.

But again: this objection is based upon a gross error in respect to the philosophy of moral government. Moral law exists with its sanctions as really in heaven as on earth, and its sanctions have in heaven the very influence that they ought to have on earth. It is as true in heaven as on earth, that the soul that sinneth shall die. Now, can the sanctions of law exert no influence in heaven? I suppose no reasonable person will doubt the certainty, and the known certainty of the perseverance of all saints there. But if they are certain that they shall not sin and fall, can they not be the subjects of fear in any sense? I answer, yes. They are naturally able to sin, and may be sometimes placed under circumstances where they are tempted to selfishness. Indeed, the very nature of mind renders it certain, that the saints will always have need of watchfulness against temptation and sin.

Now, it is the design of the sanctions of law in all worlds to produce hope on the one hand, and fear on the other; in holy beings the hope of reward, and the fear to sin lest they should perish. This hope and fear in a being duly influenced by them, is not selfishness. It is madness and desperate wickedness not to be influenced by them. Our reason affirms that we ought to be influenced by them, that our own salvation is of infinite value, and that our damnation were an infinite evil. It therefore affirms that we ought to secure the one and to avoid the other. This is law both on earth and in heaven. This we are not to do selfishly, that is, to seek our own salvation, or to avoid our own damnation, exclusively or only, but to seek to save as many as possible; to love our neighbor as ourselves, and ourselves as our neighbor. In all worlds the sanctions of law ought to have their influence, and with holy beings they have. Holy beings are really subjects of fear to sin, and to be lost, and are the only beings who have the kind of fear which God requires, and which it is the design of the sanctions of law and of the gospel to inspire. What! Are we to be told that a certainty of safety is wholly inconsistent with every kind and degree of fear? What, then, is the use of law in heaven? Must a man on earth or in heaven doubt whether he shall have eternal life, in order to leave room for the influence of moral law, and of hope, and of fear, or in order to leave play for the motives of moral government? There is room for the same fear in heaven that ought to be on earth. No one has a right to expect to violate the precept, and thereby incur the penalty of law. But every one is bound to fear to do so. The penalty was never designed on earth, any more than it is in heaven, to beget a slavish fear, or a fear that we shall sin and be damned; but only a fear to sin and be damned. A fear to sin and to be lost, will, to all eternity, no doubt, be a means of confirming holy beings in heaven. The law will be the same there as here. Free agency will be the same there as here. Perseverance in holiness will be a condition of continued salvation there as really as here. There may, and doubtless will, be temptations there as well as here. They will, therefore, need there substantially the same motives to keep them that they need and have here. There will there be laws and conditions of continued bliss as here. There will be the same place, and in kind, if not in degree, the same occasion for fear there that there is here. I say again, that the objection we are considering, overlooks both the true philosophy of mind, and of the influence of the sanctions of moral law.

The objection we are considering is based upon the assumption that warnings, exhortation to fear, etc., are inconsistent with the revealed certainty of the salvation of the saints. But does not the Bible furnish abundant instances of warning in cases where the result is revealed as certain? The case of Paul's shipwreck is in point. This case has been once alluded to, but I recur to it for the sake of illustration in this place. God, by Paul, revealed the fact, that no life on board the ship should be lost. This he declared as a fact, without any revealed qualification or condition. But when the sailors, who alone knew how to manage the ship, were about to abandon her, Paul informs them that their abiding in the ship was a condition of their salvation from death. The means were really as certain as the end; yet the end was conditioned upon the means, and if the means failed, the end would fail. Therefore Paul appealed to their fears of death to secure them against neglecting the means of safety. He did not intend to excite in them a distrust of the promise of God, but only to apprise them of the conditional nature of the certainty of their safety which had been revealed to them, and thus cause them at once to fear to neglect the means, and to confide in the certainty of safety in the diligent use of them. But this is a case, be it understood, directly in point, and by itself affords a full answer to the objection under consideration. It is a case where a revealed certainty of the event was entirely consistent with warning and threatening. Nay, it is a case where the certainty, though real, was dependent upon the warning and threatening, and the consequent fear to neglect the means. This case is a full illustration of the revealed certainty of the ultimate salvation of the saints; and were there no other case in the Bible where warning and, threatening are addressed to those whose safety is revealed, this case would be a full answer to the assertion, that warnings and threatenings are inconsistent with revealed certainty. Paul feared to have the means of safety neglected, but he did not fear that they really would be, because he knew that they would not.

To the pertinency of this case as an illustration, it is objected, that the prophet pronounced the destruction of Nineveh in forty days to be certain, as really as Paul in this case revealed the certainty of the safety of all on board the ship; therefore, it is contended that Paul did not intend to reveal the result as certain, because when a revelation was made respecting the destruction of Nineveh, in just as unqualified terms, the event showed that it was not certain. To this I reply, that in the case of Jonah, it is manifest from the whole narrative that neither Jonah nor the Ninevites understood the event as unconditionally certain. Jonah expressly assigned to God his knowledge of the uncertainty of the event, as an excuse for not delivering his message. So the people themselves understood, that the event might not be certain, as their conduct abundantly shows. The difference in the two cases is just this: one was a real and a revealed certainty, and the other was neither. Why then should this case be adduced as setting aside that of the shipwreck? But it is said, that no condition was revealed in the one case more than in the other. Now so far as the history is recorded, no mention is made in the case of Nineveh, that Jonah intimated that there was any condition upon which the destruction of the city could be avoided: yet it is plain, that both Jonah and the Ninevites understood the threatening to be conditional, in the sense of the event's being uncertain. Jonah himself did not expect it with much certainty. But in the case of Paul, he expressly affirms, that he believed God that it should be as he had declared, that there should be the loss of no man's life, and he encouraged them to believe the same thing. Paul understood the end to be certain, though he knew, and soon informed them, that the certainty was a moral one, and conditioned upon the diligent use of means. The two cases are by no means parallel. It is true that Nineveh would have been destroyed, had they not used the appropriate means to prevent it; and the same is true of the ship's crew; and it is also true that, in both cases, it was really certain that the means would not be neglected; yet in one case, the certainty was really understood to be revealed, and was believed in, and not in the other. Now observe, the point to be illustrated by reference to this case of shipwreck. It is just this: Can a man have any fear, and can there be ground and need of caution and fear, where there is a real and revealed, and believed or known certainty? The objection I am answering is, that, if the salvation of the saints is certain, and revealed as such, and is believed to be certain, there is then no ground of fear, and no necessity or room for warning, threatening, etc. But this case of shipwreck is one in which all these things meet.

(1.) The event was certain, and of course the conditions were sure to be fulfilled.

(2.) The certainty was revealed.

(3.) It was believed. Yet,

(4.) There was warning, and threatening, and fear, to neglect the means.

But these things did not all meet in the case of Jonah and the Ninevites. In this case,

(1.) It was not certain that the city would be destroyed.

(2.) It was not understood to be revealed as certain.

(3.) It was not believed to be certain.

Why, then, I ask again, should these cases be taken as parallels?

Paul repeatedly speaks of his own salvation as certain, and yet in a manner that conditionates it upon his perseverance in faith and obedience to the end. He says:--

Phil. i. 19: "For I know that this shall turn to my salvation through your prayer, and the supply of the Spirit of Jesus Christ. 25. And having this confidence, I know I shall abide and continue with you all, for your furtherance and joy of faith."

2 Tim. iv. 18: "And the Lord shall deliver me from every evil work, and will preserve me unto his heavenly kingdom: to whom be glory forever and ever."

In this place it is plain, that he regarded his perseverance and ultimate salvation, by and through the grace of God, as certain. Paul everywhere, as every attentive reader of the Bible knows, renounces all hope but in the indwelling grace and Spirit of Christ. Still he felt confident of his salvation. But if he had no confidence in himself, on what was his confidence based? Again:--

2 Tim. i. 12: "For the which cause I also suffer these things: nevertheless I am not ashamed; for I know whom I have believed, and am persuaded that he is able to keep that which I have committed unto him against that day."

Here again Paul expresses the fullest confidence of his own salvation. He did not merely intend to say that Christ was able, if he was disposed, to keep that which he had committed to him, but he assumed his willingness and asserted his ability, as the ground of his confidence. That he here expressed entire confidence in his ultimate salvation, cannot reasonably be doubted. He did not say that he was persuaded that Christ was able to save him, if he persevered; but his confidence was founded in the fact, that Christ was able to secure his perseverance. It was because he was persuaded that Christ was able to keep him, that he had any assurance, and I might add even hope, of his own salvation. The same reason he assigned as the ground of confidence that others would be saved. To the Thessalonians he says, 2 Thess. iii. 3: "But the Lord is faithful, who shall establish you, and keep you from evil." Again, Jude says, ver. 24: "Now unto him that is able to keep you from falling, and to present you faultless before the presence of his glory with exceeding joy." Again, Peter says, of all the elect or saints, 1 Peter i. 5: "Who are kept by the power of God through faith unto salvation, ready to be revealed in the last time." Thus we see, that the ground of confidence with the apostles was, that God and Christ could and would keep them, not without their own efforts, but that he would induce them to be faithful, and so secure this result. The same was true of Christ, as is manifested in his last prayer for them. John xvii. 15, 16: "I pray not that thou shouldest take them out of the world, but that thou shouldest keep them from the evil. They are not of the world, even as I am not of the world." But the apostles frequently express their confidence, both in the certainty of their own salvation, and also in the salvation of those to whom they wrote. Paul says, 1 Cor. ix. 26, 27: "I therefore so run, not as uncertainly, so fight I, not as one that beateth the air: But I keep under my body, and bring it into subjection: lest that by any means, when I have preached to others, I myself should be a castaway." Here he expresses the fullest confidence that he shall win the crown, but at the same time recognizes the condition of his salvation, and informs us that he took care to fulfil it, lest he should be a castaway." He says, verse 26: "I therefore so run, not as uncertainly, so fight I, not as one who beateth the air." He alludes to the Olympic games, and in this connection says, verses 24 and 25: "Know ye not that they which run in a race run all, but one receiveth the prize? So run, that ye may obtain. And every man that striveth for the mastery is temperate in all things. Now they do it to obtain a corruptible crown, but we an incorruptible." He then adds, verses 26 and 27: "I therefore so run, not as uncertainly, so fight I not as one that beateth the air: But I keep under my body, and bring it into subjection; lest that by any means, when I have preached to others, I myself should be a castaway."

Of those who ran in these games, but one could win the prize. But not so in the Christian race: here all might win. In those games, because but one could possibly win, there was much uncertainty in respect to whether any one in particular could win the prize. In the Christian race there was no need of any such uncertainty. As it respected himself he says, "I therefore so run, not as uncertainly, so fight I, not as one that beateth the air:" that is, I do not run with any uncertainty or irresolution, because of uncertainty in respect to whether I shall win the prize. Nor do I fight as one that beateth the air, or as one who fights uncertainly or in vain; but while I have this confidence, I keep under my body. It has been denied that Paul intended to express a confidence in his salvation in this place; but this cannot be reasonably denied. He was speaking in this connection of the Christian race, and of the conditions of winning the victor's crown. He affirms that there was no real uncertainty whether he should win the crown. In the Olympic games there was uncertainty, because but one could win; but here no such ground of uncertainty existed; and, moreover, with him there was no real uncertainty at all, while at the same time he understood the conditional nature of the certainty, and kept under his body, etc. Can any one suppose that Paul really had any doubt in regard to his own ultimate salvation? Now observe, these passages in respect to Paul are not adduced to prove that all saints will be saved; nor that, if Paul was sure of his salvation, therefore all saints may be. To prove this is not my present design, but simply to show, that while Paul was sure, and had no doubt of his ultimate salvation, he yet feared to neglect the means. He was not disheartened in the Christian race with a sense of uncertainty, as they who ran in the Olympic games. He was not, as they might be, irresolute on account of their great uncertainty of winning. He expected to win, and yet he dared not neglect the conditions of winning. Nay, he expected to win, because he expected to fulfil the conditions; and he expected to fulfil the conditions, not because he had any confidence in himself, but because he confided in the grace and Spirit of God to secure his perseverance. Nevertheless, he kept under his body, and feared self-indulgence, lest he should be a castaway.

Paul affirms of the Thessalonians, that he knew their election of God. 1 Thess. i. 14: "Knowing, brethren beloved, your election of God." In both his epistles to this church, he often speaks of them in a manner that implies, that he regarded their salvation as certain, and yet he also frequently warns and exhorts them to faithfulness, and to guard against being deceived by false teachers, etc. 2 Thess. ii. 1-3: "Now we beseech you, brethren, by the coming of our Lord Jesus Christ, and by our gathering together unto him, that ye be not soon shaken in mind, or be troubled, neither by spirit nor by word, nor by letter as from us, as that the day of Christ is at hand. Let no man deceive you by any means; for that day shall not come, except there come a falling away first, and that man of sin be revealed, the son of perdition." He addresses the same strain of exhortation to them that he does to all Christians, and plies them with admonition and warning, just as might be expected, considering the moral and conditional nature of the certainty of their salvation.

In writing to the Philippians, he says, Phil. i. 6, 7: "Being confident of this very thing, that he which hath began a good work in you, will perform it until the day of Jesus Christ. Even as it is meet for me to think this of you all, because I have you in my heart; inasmuch as both in my bonds, and in the defence and confirmation of the gospel, ye are all partakers of my grace." Here he expresses the confidence of an inspired apostle, that Christ would secure their salvation. But yet in the 2d chapter, 12th and 13th verses, he says: "Wherefore, my beloved, as ye have always obeyed, not as in my presence only, but now much more in my absence, work out your own salvation with fear and trembling; For it is God which worketh in you, both to will and to do of his good pleasure." Here he warns them to work out their salvation with fear and trembling. There is no stronger passage than this, where the saints are exhorted to fear; and mark, this is addressed to the very persons of whom he had just said, i. 6: "Being confident of this very thing, that he which hath begun a good work in you, will perform it until the day of Jesus Christ." Almost at the same breath he expresses the confidence of an inspired apostle, that he who had begun a good work in them would carry it on until the day of Jesus Christ; that is, that he would surely save them; and at the same time exhorts them to "work out their salvation with fear and trembling." Paul also addresses the church at Ephesus as follows:--

Eph. i. 1: "Paul an apostle of Jesus Christ by the will of God, to the saints which are at Ephesus, and to the faithful in Christ Jesus: 2. Grace be to you, and peace, from God our Father, and from the Lord Jesus Christ: 3. Blessed be the God and Father of our Lord Jesus Christ, who hath blessed us with all spiritual blessings in heavenly places in Christ: 4. According as he hath chosen us in him before the foundation of the world, that we should be holy, and without blame before him in love: 5. Having predestinated us unto the adoption of children by Jesus Christ to himself, according to the good pleasure of his will, 6. To the praise of the glory of his grace, wherein he hath made us accepted in the Beloved. 7. In whom we have redemption through his blood, the forgiveness of sins, according to the riches of his grace; 8. Wherein he hath abounded toward us in all wisdom and prudence; 9. Having made known unto us the mystery of his will, according to his good pleasure which he hath purposed in himself: 10. That in the dispensation of the fulness of times, he might gather together in one all things in Christ, both which are in heaven and which are on earth, even in him: 11. In whom also we have obtained an inheritance, being predestinated according to the purpose of him who worketh all things after the counsel of his own will: 12. That we should be to the praise of his glory, who first trusted in Christ."

Now, let any one read the epistle through, and he will find, that these same elect persons are addressed throughout with precept, exhortation, and warning, just as all other saints throughout the Bible. To quote the instances of this were only to quote much of the epistle. Indeed this is the common usage of the inspired writers, to address the saints as the elect of God, as persons whose salvation was secure as a matter of fact, but whose salvation was after all conditionated upon their perseverance in holiness; and they hence proceed to warn, admonish, and exhort them, just as we might expect when we consider the nature of the certainty of which they were speaking.

But if it be still urged, that the fact of election is not revealed in any case to the individuals who compose the elect; that if the fact of election were revealed to any one, to him threatenings and warnings would be out of place; I reply, that this is only saying, that if certainty is revealed as such at any time, and in respect to anything, then warnings, and threatenings, and fears, are wholly out of place. But this is not true, as we have seen in the case of the shipwreck. Here the certainty was revealed to the individuals concerned, and accredited. Christ also revealed to his apostles the fact of their election, as we have seen, also to Paul. Can any one reasonably call in question the fact, that the apostles understood well their election of God, not only to the apostleship, but also to eternal life? Observe again, what Paul says in writing to the church at Ephesus, in the passage which has just been quoted.

Here he expressly recognizes himself as one of the elect, as he does elsewhere, and as the apostles always do, directly or by way of implication, and yet Paul and the other apostles did not feel that warning, and watchfulness, and fear to sin were at all out of place with them.

Job speaks as if the certainty of his salvation had been revealed to him. He says:

Job xix. 23: "For I know that my Redeemer liveth, and that he shall stand at the latter day upon the earth. 26. And though after my skin worms destroy this body, yet in my flesh shall I see God: 27. Whom I shall see for myself, and mine eyes shall behold, and not another; though my reins be consumed within me."

Can any one suppose that Job regarded threatenings, and warnings, and fear to sin, as out of place with him? It is generally admitted, that there is such a thing as the full assurance of faith or hope, or as attaining to the certain knowledge that salvation is secure to us. But would a saint who has made this attainment be less affected than others by all the threatenings, and warnings, and exhortations to fear, found in the Bible? Would such souls cease to tremble at the word of God? Would they cease to pass their time of sojourning here with fear? Would they cease to "work out their salvation with fear and trembling?" Would God no longer regard them as belonging to the class of persons mentioned in Isa. lxvi. 1: "For all those things hath mine hand made, and all those things have been, saith the Lord: but to this man will I look, even to him that is of a contrite spirit, and trembleth at my word?"

Christ prayed for the salvation of his apostles, in their presence, in such a manner as to leave no room for them to doubt their ultimate salvation, if they expected his prayers to be answered. He did the same with respect to all that should believe on him through their word. Now will you affirm, that they who are conscious of believing in Jesus, must cease to have confidence in the efficacy of his prayers, before they can feel the power, and propriety, and influence of warnings, and threatenings, and the various motives that are addressed to the elect of God to preserve them from falling? The supposition is preposterous. What Must we doubt the efficacy of his prayers, in order to credit and appreciate the force of his warnings? In fact, the more holy any one is, and the more certain he is of his eternal salvation, the more does sin become an object of loathing, of fear, and even of terror, to him. The more holy he is, the more readily he trembles at the word of God, and the more sensibly and easily he is affected by a contemplation of sin and divine wrath, the more awful and terrible these things appear to him, and the more solemnly do they affect him, although he has the fullest assurance that he shall never taste of either sin or hell. It is true, indeed, as we shall have occasion to remark hereafter, that in general, the Bible assumes that individuals are not sure of their salvation, and upon that assumption proceeds to warn them.

But still it is insisted that, if the end is certain, so are the means; and if one is revealed as certain, so is the other; and that therefore it is absurd, and implies unbelief, to fear that we shall neglect the means, or that either the end or means will fail. But as we have said, to fear to neglect the means, and to fear that we shall neglect them, are not the same. We are naturally able to neglect them, and there is just as much real danger of our neglecting them, as there would be if no revelation were made about it, unless the revelation of the certainty of their use be a means of securing the use of them. We are therefore to fear to neglect them. There is, in fact, as much real danger of our neglecting the means of our salvation, as there is that any event whatever will be different from what it turns out to be. There is no more real danger in one case than in the other; but in one case the certainty is revealed, and in the other not. Therefore, when the certainty is not revealed, it is reasonable to fear that the event will not be as we desire, and as it ought to be. But in the other,--that is, when the certainty is revealed, we have no right to fear that it will be otherwise than as revealed, nor to fear that the means will in fact be neglected; but in all such cases we should fear to neglect the means, as really and as much, as if no revelation of certainty had been made; just as Paul did in the case of his shipwreck.

Again, it is inquired, are we not to fear that any of the saints will be lost, and pray for them under the influence of this fear? I answer, no. The saints are the elect. None of God's elect will be lost. We are to pray for them as Christ prayed for his apostles, and as he prayed for all believers, not with the fear that they will be lost, for this were praying in unbelief; but we are to pray for all persons known to be saints, that they may persevere unto the end and be saved, with confidence that our prayer will be answered. But it is said, that Paul expressed doubts in regard to the salvation of the churches in Galatia. I answer, that he expressed no doubt in respect to their ultimate salvation; he says, "I desire to be present with you now, and to change my voice; for I stand in doubt of you." Gal. iv. 20. In the margin it reads, "I am perplexed for you." He says in the next chapter: "I have confidence in you through the Lord, that ye will be none otherwise minded; but he that troubleth you shall bear his judgment, whosoever he be." Gal. v. 10: Paul set himself zealously to reclaim these churches from error, and expresses full confidence of the result; and no where, that I see, intimates, that he doubted whether they would finally be saved.

But it is said still, that if the salvation of all the saints is secured, and this certainty is revealed, there is no real danger of their either neglecting the necessary means, or of their being lost, and therefore warnings, and threatenings, and fears are vain; and that the certainty being granted, it is irrational and impossible to fear, without doubting the truth of God; that certainty is certainty, and it matters not at all of what kind the certainty is; that if it be granted that the event is certain, all danger, and of course all cause of fear, is out of the question.

To this form of the objection I reply, that it proceeds upon the assumption, that there is no danger of the saints falling, if God has revealed the certainty of their ultimate salvation. But what do we mean by danger? It has already been said, that all events are certain, in the sense that it is and was from eternity as really certain that they will be, and how they will he; and that all their circumstances and conditions are, and eternally were, as certain as they ever will be. So that there never is any real danger, in the sense of uncertainty, that any event will be otherwise than it turns out in fact to be. By danger, then, is not meant that there is really any uncertainty in respect to how anything will be. But all that can properly be intended by danger is, that there is a natural possibility, and, humanly speaking, a probability, that it may be otherwise than as we desire; that this is probable in the sense that there is, humanly speaking, from the circumstances of the case, and so far as we can judge, from the course of events, a probability that a thing may not occur as we would have it.

Now, a natural possibility always exists in respect to the falling and final destruction of the saints; and in most cases at least, the circumstances are such that, humanly speaking, and aside from the grace of God, there is not only real danger, but a certainty that they will fail of eternal life. There are, humanly speaking, many chances to one that they will fall and be lost. Now, this danger is as real as if nothing of certainty had been revealed. The event would have been as certain without the revelation of the certainty as with it, unless it be true, which I suppose in many cases is the fact, that the revelation of the certainty helps to secure their perseverance.

But thus far I have replied to the objection, upon the assumption, that the certainty of the salvation of the saints is revealed, in the sense that individual saints may know the certainty of their own salvation. I have shown, as I trust, that admitting this to be true, yet the nature of the certainty leaves abundant room for the influence of a wholesome sense of danger, and for the feeling of hope and fear. But the fact is, that in but few cases comparatively does it appear, that the certainty is revealed to the individuals as such. The salvation of all true saints is revealed, as we have seen, and the characteristics of true saints are revealed in the Bible. So that it is possible for individual saints to possess a comfortable assurance of salvation, upon the knowledge that they are saints. And as was shown, it is doubtless true that in some cases, in the days of inspiration, and not improbably in some cases since the Bible was complete, individuals have had a direct revelation by the Holy Spirit that they were saints, and accepted of God.

But in the great majority of cases in all time hitherto, the saints have had no personal and clear revelation of their being saints, and no evidence of it, except what they gather from an experience that in their view accords with the Bible description of the character of the saints. When Peter addressed his epistles to the elect saints, for example, although he regarded the elect as certain of salvation, yet he did not distinguish and address individuals by name; but left it for them to be satisfied of their own election and saintship, by their own consciousness of possessing the character that belongs to the saints. He did not reveal to any one in particular the fact of his own election. This was for the most part true of all the letters written to the churches. Although they were addressed as a body, as elect, and as saints, yet from this they were not to infer, that they were all saints or elect, but were to learn that fact, and who were real saints, from their conscious character.

We have seen, in another place, that the Bible represents perseverance, in the sense already explained, as an attribute of Christian character; and therefore no one can have evidence that he is a saint, any farther than he is conscious of abiding in obedience. If saints do abide in the light, and have the assurance that they are saints, we have seen the sense in which they may be influenced by hope and fear, and the sense in which moral law with its sanctions may be useful to them. But when a saint shall backslide, he must lose the evidence of his being a saint, and then all the warnings and threatenings may take full effect upon him. He finds himself not persevering, and has of course to infer that he is not a saint; and the doctrine of the perseverance of the saints can be no comfort to him. It is in fact against him; for this doctrine is, that the saints do persevere; every day he lives in backsliding, it becomes less evident that he is a saint. The Bible is manifestly written, for the most part, upon the assumption, that individual saints do not certainly know their election, and the certainty of their own salvation. It therefore addresses them, as if there were real uncertainty in respect to their salvation; that is, as if, as individuals, they were not certain of salvation. It represents the salvation of real saints as certain, but represents many professed saints as having fallen, and warns them against presumption and self-deception, in the matter of their profession, privileges, and experience. It represents the danger of delusion as great, and exhorts them to examine and prove themselves, and see whether they are truly saints. The warnings found in the Bible are, for the most part, evidently of this kind; that is, they assume that individuals may deceive themselves, and presumptuously assume their own election, and saintship, and safety, from their privileges, relations, and experiences. Inspiration, therefore, proceeds to warn them, assuming that they do not know the certainty of their own individual salvation. We shall by and by have occasion to examine some passages that will illustrate and confirm this remark.

There is, therefore, I apprehend, no real difficulty in accounting for the manner in which the Bible is written, upon the supposition that the doctrine under consideration is true. But on the contrary, it appears to me, that the scriptures are just what might be expected, if the doctrine were true. When we consider the nature of the certainty in all cases, and also that the great mass of professed Christians have no certain revelation of their being real saints, that there is so much real danger of deception, in regard to our own characters, and that so many are and have been deceived;--I say, when we consider these things, there can be no difficulty in accounting for the manner in which both professors and real saints are addressed in the word of God.

LECTURE LI - PERSEVERANCE OF SAINTS

FURTHER OBJECTIONS ANSWERED

4. A fourth objection to this doctrine is, that if, by the perseverance of the saints is intended, that they live anything like lives of habitual obedience to God, then facts are against it.

To this objection I reply: that by the perseverance of the saints, as I use these terms, is intended that, subsequently to their regeneration, holiness is the rule of their lives, and sin only the exception. But it is said, that facts contradict this.

(1.) The case of king Saul is brought forward as an instance in point to sustain the objection.

To this I reply: that it is far from being clear that Saul was ever a truly regenerate man. He appears, in connection with his appointment to the throne of Israel, to have been the subject of divine illuminations, in so far as to be much changed in his views and deportment, and as to have had another heart, in so much that he prophesied, etc.; but it is nowhere intimated that he became a truly regenerate man, a truly praying child of God. Similar changes are not unfrequently witnessed in men, and changes evidently brought about by the illuminations of the Holy Spirit, where there is no good reason to believe that the subjects of them were truly regenerated. From the history of Saul, subsequent to the change of which we are speaking, we gather absolutely nothing that looks like true piety. His case therefore cannot properly be brought as an objection to the doctrine in question, for the plain reason, that evidence is wanting that he ever was a saint. His prophesying, as is evident from the connection in which it is spoken of, was merely speaking fervently upon religious subjects. He was so much enlightened, as to manifest for a time considerable excitement upon the subject of religion, and as to mingle with the schools of the prophets, and take an interest in their exercises. But this was only similar to what we often witness, when the end, and indeed when all the circumstances, duly considered, show clearly that true regeneration has not taken place. Who has not seen men have, for the time being, another, but not a holy, heart?

(2.) It is said, that David did not persevere in obedience, in the sense that obedience was his rule, and sin only the exception. To this I reply

(i.) It is not pretended that there is any doubt respecting the final salvation of David.

(ii.) That David did not persevere, in the sense above defined, wants proof. His Psalms, together with his whole history, show that he was a highly spiritual man. He was an eminent type of Christ, and, for a man in his circumstances, was a remarkable saint. To be sure, David practiced polygamy, and did many things that in us, under the light of the gospel, would be sin. But it should be considered, that David lived under a dispensation of comparative obscurity, and therefore many things which would now be unlawful and sinful, were not so in him. That David, with comparatively few exceptions, lived up to the light he had, cannot be reasonably called in question. He is said to have been a man after God's own heart. I know this is said of him as a king, but I know also that, as king this could not have been said of him, unless he had feared and served the Lord, and in the main lived up to the light with which he was surrounded.

(3.) It is also said, that Solomon king of Israel did not persevere, in the sense contended for in this discourse.

Of Solomon I would say, that he at one period of his life, for how long a time it does not appear, fell into grievous backsliding, and appears in some sense to have tolerated idolatry. His final apostacy has been inferred from the fact, that idolatry was practiced in Israel, after his supposed repentance; and until the end of his life, the people were allowed to offer sacrifices, and to burn incense in the high places, and therefore his repentance was not genuine.

To this I reply, that the same was true also during the reign of several of the pious kings who succeeded him, and is probably to be accounted for by the fact, that neither Solomon nor his successors had, far a considerable time, political power or influence enough to abolish idolatry altogether. The people were greatly divided in their religious views and worship. Many were the priests and devotees of the groves and high places, and multitudes of the high and more influential classes slave to their idols. It was a very difficult matter to put an effectual stop to idolatry, and perhaps was impossible in Solomon's day, and for a long time after. Solomon's idolatrous wives and concubines had doubtless exerted great influence in rendering idolatry popular with the people, and it was not until several generations had passed away, that the pious kings seem to have had sufficient political power to banish idolatry from the nation. Solomon's final apostacy, then, cannot be inferred from the fact, that idolatry continued to be practiced in the nation until long after his death. There is no reason to believe that he continued to practice it himself.

But, from the writings of Solomon, we may gather sufficient evidence that, in the general, he did not live a wicked life, though he fell into many grievous sins. His Ecclesiastes seems to have been written after he was reclaimed from backsliding, as appears from the fact, that the book contains many statements of his views and experiences while in his wanderings from God. It appears to me, that the book is inexplicable upon any other supposition. In his wanderings from God, as is common, he fell into great doubts and embarrassments in regard to the works and ways of God. He became sceptical, and in the book under consideration, he states the sceptical views that he had entertained. But the book, as a whole, contains conclusive evidence of piety at the time it was written. This probably will not be called in question.

(4.) Observation, it is said, conflicts with the doctrine in question. So far as human observation can go, I admit that this is so; that many persons seem to be born again, and to run well for a time, and afterwards fall, and apparently live and die in sin. But it should be remarked, that observation cannot be conclusive upon this subject, because we cannot certainly know, that any of the cases just alluded to are real conversions to God. Hence the objection fails of conclusiveness. Were it certainly known, that such persons were truly regenerated, and that afterwards they fall away and live in sin, and die in that state, it would follow, that the doctrine, at least in the form in which I have stated it, cannot be true. But this is not, and cannot be certainly known by observation. If, as I trust, it has been found to be true, in our examination, that the Bible plainly teaches the doctrine in question, in the form in which I have stated it, it must follow of course that observation cannot disprove it, for the reason that it is not a question that lies within the reach of observation, in such a sense as to admit of certainty, or of any such kind or degree of evidence as to shake the sure testimony of the Bible.

5. But an appeal is also made to consciousness to overthrow this doctrine. It is said, that the real saints, at least in some instances, know themselves to have lived a great part of their lives in sin, and even by far the greater part of their days subsequent to regeneration.

This objection or assertion may be answered substantially as was the last. It is true, indeed, that the saints may know themselves to have been regenerated; and it is also true, that many may think they know this when they are deceived. A man may know himself to be awake, but from this it does not follow that no one can think himself awake while he is asleep. But since upon examination, it has been found that the Bible plainly teaches the doctrine of the saints' perseverance, in the sense in which I have defined it, we must of course yield the objection founded on experience, and grant that such experiences can weigh nothing against the testimony of God. The objection of course cannot be conclusive; for it is not one of the nature that admits of no error or doubt. The Bible defines all the essential attributes of Christian character. Now, if upon examination, perseverance in the sense here insisted on is proved to be one of them, it is absurd to array against the doctrine the consciousness of not persevering. It is to assume that we, and not the Bible, can decide who is a Christian, and what arc the essential attributes of Christian character.

6. But it is also objected to the doctrine of the perseverance of the saints, that several passages of scripture plainly teach that some real saints have fallen away and been lost. I will therefore now proceed to the examination of those passages upon which the principal reliance is placed to disprove this doctrine. The first one which I shall notice is found in 1 Cor. x. 1: "Moreover, brethren, I would not that ye should be ignorant, how that all our fathers were under the cloud, and all passed through the sea; 2. And were all baptized unto Moses in the cloud and in the sea; 3. And did all eat of the same spiritual meat; 4. And did all drink the same spiritual drink; (for they drank of that spiritual rock that followed them, and that rock was Christ); 5. But with many of them God was not well pleased, for they were overthrown in the wilderness. 6. Now these things were our examples, to the intent we should not lust after evil things, as they also lusted. 7. Neither be ye idolaters, as were some of them, as it is written; The people sat down to eat and drink, and rose up to play. 8. Neither let us commit fornication as some of them committed, and fell in one day three and twenty thousand. 9. Neither let us tempt Christ, as some of them also tempted, and were destroyed of serpents. 10. Neither murmur ye, as some of them also murmured, and were destroyed of the destroyer. 11. Now all these things happened unto them for ensamples, and they are written for our admonition, upon whom the ends of the world are come. 12. Wherefore, let him that thinketh he standeth take heed lest he fall."

It is said of this passage, that the history of the Israelites is here introduced as a warning to real Christians; consequently, the apostle must have assumed, that those of the Israelites who fell were real saints, or there would have been no pertinency or force in his allusion. To this I reply, that the pertinency and force of the allusion appear to me to have been as follows. The Israelites composed the visible church of God. At the time mentioned, they were all professors of religion. All possessed great light and privileges compared with the rest of the world; they therefore felt confident of their acceptance with God, and of their consequent safety and salvation. But with many of them God was not well pleased. Some of them turned out to be idolaters and were destroyed. Now, says the apostle, let this be a warning to you. You are in like manner professors of religion. You are all members of the visible church of God to which the promises are made. You have great light and privileges when compared with the world at large. You may think yourselves to be altogether safe, and sure of final salvation. But remember, that the history of the ancient church is written for your benefit; and the destruction of those just alluded to, is recorded for your admonition. Be not high minded, but fear. Do not be presumptuous, because you are members in good standing in the visible church, and possess great light and privileges; but remember, that many before you, who were like you in these respects, have lost their souls; "Wherefore let him that thinketh he standeth take heed lest he fall."

If the apostle had intended to convey the impression that they were real saints that fell in the wilderness, and that real saints do fall away and are lost, he would no doubt have said, let him that standeth, instead of him that thinketh he standeth, take heed lest ho fall. The term rendered thinketh is represented by Robinson as correctly translated in this passage. The meaning of the apostle appears to have been this, that others who were, from their circumstances and fancied characters, very confident of their safety, had been finally cast off and lost; therefore, take heed to yourselves, lest being similarly situated, you in like manner deceive yourselves; and while you think that you stand, you should fall and perish.

But it may be said, that the apostle speaks of those as falling who had eaten of the spiritual meat, and drank of the rock Christ, and therefore must have been real saints. To this I reply, that the apostle does indeed use universal language, and speak of all the Israelites as doing these things; but who will soberly contend that he intended really to be understood as affirming, that all the Israelites that passed through the sea, etc., were true saints? What he says does not necessitate the conclusion that any of them were truly regenerated saints. They were all baptized unto Moses, that is, were all introduced into the covenant of which he was the mediator. They all ate of the same spiritual bread, that is, the manna on which the Lord fed them. They all drank of the spiritual rock; that is, of the water that gushed from the rock when Moses smote it with his rod, and which rock was a type of Christ, as was also the manna. Now, does the apostle mean to say, that all the Israelites understood the typical meaning of these waters, and this manna, and that they were all truly spiritual or regenerate persons? I think not. All that he intended appears to me to be, that all the church of the Jews at the time were so far partakers of the grace of Christ as to receive this baptism, and as to have this spiritual or typical bread and water, and also to enjoy great light and much miraculous instruction, but that, nevertheless, with many of them God was displeased. Their being baptized in their passage through the Red Sea, did not imply that they so understood and consented to it at the time, nor does the assertion that they ate the spiritual food, and drank of the spiritual rock, imply anything more than that they enjoyed these great and high privileges, and counted themselves as very secure in consequence of them. It is certainly straining the sense to make the apostle affirm, that all the Israelites were real saints who passed through the sea. Indeed, it is doubtful whether he intended to affirm the real piety of any of them. It was not essential to his purpose to do so.

In examining the class of passages adduced to prove that some real saints have fallen from grace and been lost, I am only concerned to show, that they do not by fair construction necessitate this conclusion. I may admit that, if the doctrine of perseverance were not found to be clearly taught in the Bible, the not unnatural construction of some of the class of texts in question might lead to the conclusion that some, yea many, real saints have been lost.

But, since, from the previous examination it has appeared, that the doctrine is plainly and unequivocally taught in the Bible, all that needs to be shown of the class of texts now under consideration is, that they do not, when fairly interpreted, really and unequivocally teach that some true saints have been lost. This showing will sufficiently vindicate the scriptures against the imputation of self-contradiction, in both affirming and denying the same doctrine. Observe, I am not called upon to show, that the passages in question cannot be so construed, and with considerable plausibility, as to make them contradict this doctrine; but all I am called upon to show in this place is, that they do not necessarily, by fair construction, contradict it; that they do not necessitate the admission either that the Bible contradicts itself, or that a different construction must be given to the passages that seem to teach this doctrine.

With these remarks I proceed to the examination of 2 Peter ii. 9-22: "The Lord knoweth how to deliver the godly out of temptations, and to reserve the unjust unto the day of judgment to be punished: but chiefly them that walk after the flesh in the lust of uncleanness, and despise government: presumptuous are they, self-willed; they are not afraid to speak evil of dignities. Whereas angels, which are greater in power and might, bring not railing accusation against them before the Lord. But these, as natural brute beasts, made to be taken and destroyed, speak evil of the things that they understand not; and shall utterly perish in their own corruption; and shall receive the reward of unrighteousness, as they that count it pleasure to riot in the day-time. Spots they are, and blemishes, sporting themselves with their own deceivings, while they feast with you; having eyes full of adultery, and that cannot cease from sin; beguiling unstable souls: a heart they have exercised with covetous practices; cursed children, which have forsaken the right way, and are gone astray, following the way of Balaam the son of Bosor, who loved the wages of unrighteousness; but was rebuked for his iniquity: the dumb ass speaking with man's voice, forbade the madness of the prophet. These are wells without water, clouds that are carried with a tempest; to whom the mist of darkness is reserved forever. For when they speak great swelling words of vanity, they allure through the lusts of the flesh, through much wantonness, those that were clean escaped from them who live in error. While they promise them liberty, they themselves are the servants of corruption: for of whom a man is overcome, of the same is he brought into bondage. For if after they have escaped the pollutions of the world, through the knowledge of the Lord and Saviour Jesus Christ, they are again entangled therein and overcome, the latter end is worse with them than the beginning. For it had been better for them not to have known the way of righteousness, than, after they have known it, to turn from the holy commandment delivered unto them. But it is happened unto them according to the true proverb, The dog is turned to his own vomit again; and the sow that was washed to her wallowing in the mire."

Now observe, the apostle calls the persons of whom he speaks "wells without water: clouds that are carried with a tempest:" that is, without rain. His whole description of them shows, that he is speaking of false professors or hypocrites. But it is inferred, that they are fallen saints, because it is said they have "forsaken the right way, and are gone astray after the error of Balaam," etc. But this does not necessarily imply that they were in heart ever in the right way, but that they have forsaken the right way, so far as the outward life is concerned: in which respect they had doubtless been in the right way, or they would not have been admitted to membership in the church.

But it is said of these false professors, that "they allure through lust and much wantonness those who were clean escaped from those who live in error." But neither does this necessitate the conclusion, that they had escaped in heart from those that lived in error, but merely that they had for the time being outwardly abandoned their idolatrous practices and companions, and had made a profession, and put on the form of Christianity.

But it is also said, verse 20-22: "For if after they have escaped the pollutions of the world, through the knowledge of the Lord and Saviour Jesus Christ, they are again entangled therein and overcome, the latter end is worse than the beginning. 21. For it had been better for them not to have known the way of righteousness, than, after they have known it, to turn from the holy commandment delivered unto them. 22. But it is happened unto them according to the true proverb, The dog is turned to his own vomit again; and the sow that was washed to her wallowing in the mire."

Neither does this necessitate the conclusion, that they had in heart escaped from the pollutions that are in the world, but merely that they had outwardly reformed. What is said in the last verse seems to favor this construction. Verse 22: "But it is happened unto them according to the true proverb, The dog is turned to his own vomit again; and the sow that was washed to her wallowing in the mire." That is, the dog has returned to his vomit, because he remains a dog, and is not changed; and the sow that is washed to her wallowing in the mire, because she is still a sow, and her washing has not changed her nature. So, the apostle would say, by returning to their former ways, do the persons in question show, that they have experienced no radical change; but on the contrary, that they are only like a washed sow, sinners still, who have been only outwardly cleansed, while within they are the same as ever. This appears to me to be all that can fairly be made out of this passage.

I will now attend to 1 Tim. i. 19, 20: "Holding faith and a good conscience, which some having put away, concerning faith have made shipwreck: of whom is Hymeneus and Alexander, whom I have delivered unto Satan, that they may learn not to blaspheme." Of this text I may say, that the apostle was writing to Timothy as an eminent religious teacher, and was giving him cautions respecting his influence in that relation. Hymeneus and Alexander, as we may infer from this, and which is still more plainly taught in other passages, were religious teachers, who had cast off or perverted the true faith or doctrine of the gospel, and thus made shipwreck. They had put away faith and a good conscience, and by so doing had made shipwreck of the true gospel. This passage does not teach that these men were true Christians, nor does it necessarily imply that any had been true saints who had gone with them. The expression, "some having put away," does not necessarily imply that they once had true faith and a good conscience, but only that they taught that which was inconsistent with either; or it may mean that they had rejected or refused both faith and a good conscience; that they practised and taught things inconsistent with either true faith, or with the true gospel, or with a good conscience, and had therefore run upon a rock, and wrecked their souls, and the souls of those who followed them. But this proves nothing in respect to their ever having been real saints.

The apostle was speaking in popular language, and represented things as they appeared to the observer. Thus we should speak of spurious converts. It certainly does not appear to me, that this passage would, without forced construction, warrant the conclusion that some real saints had been lost, even apart from those passages which, we have seen, seem unequivocally to teach the doctrine. Much less, when those passages are considered, are we, as I think we have seen, authorized so to construe this passage as to make it either contradict them, or to necessitate such a modification of their construction as is contended for by those who deny the doctrine in question. If the doctrine in question is not really taught in the Bible, we certainly should not believe it; but if it is, we must not lightly reject it. We need candidly to weigh each passage, and to understand, if we can, just what is the mind of God as therein revealed.

The case of Judas has been relied upon as an instance of utter apostacy, and of consequent destruction. It is said, that in the Psalms Judas is spoken of as the familiar friend of Christ in whom he trusted. Psalms xli. 9: "Yea, mine own familiar friend, in whom I trusted, which did eat of my bread, hath lifted up his heel against me."

There is no reason to believe that Ps. xli. primarily respected either Christ or Judas. Christ quotes the 9th verse, as is common in the New Testament, not because it was originally spoken of himself or of Judas, but because his case was like that of the Psalmist. In the passage in which Christ quotes these words, he directly negatives the idea of Judas being one of his true disciples. He says, John xiii. 18, "I speak not of you all; I know whom I have chosen; but that the scripture may be fulfilled, He that eateth bread with me hath lifted up his heel against me."

Here Christ plainly teaches, that ho to whom he applied these words, was not chosen in the sense of being chosen to salvation, or in the sense of his being a true saint. He says:--

John vi. 64: "But there are some of you who believe not. For Jesus knew from the beginning who they were that believed not, and who should betray him. 65. And he said, Therefore said I unto you, that no man can come unto me, except it were given him of my Father. 70. Jesus answered them, Have not I chosen you twelve, and one of you is a devil? 71. He spake of Judas Iscariot the son of Simon: for he it was that should betray him, being one of the twelve."

He had chosen twelve to follow him as pupils or disciples; but one of them he had known from the beginning to be a wicked man. In John xvii. 12: Christ says, "While I was with them in the world, I kept them in thy name: those that thou gavest me I have kept, and none of them is lost, but the son of perdition; that the scripture might be fulfilled." Christ has been represented as saying to his Father in this passage, that he had lost none that the Father had given him except the son of perdition, that is Judas. But this is not the meaning of the passage in Christ's prayer. He intended that of those that the Father had given him, he had lost none; but the son of perdition was lost that the scripture might be fulfilled.

The same form of expression is used in Luke iv. 27: "And many lepers were in Israel in the time of Eliseus the prophet; and none of them was cleansed, saving Naaman the Syrian. Here εἰ μὴ is used in the original as meaning not except, but as an adversative conjunction but. Naaman was not an Israelite, but a heathen. Christ here used the same form of expression as in John xvii. 12. In this passage in Luke it is plain, that he intended that the prophet was not sent to any Israelite, but to a heathen. This same form is also used, Matt. xii. 4: "How he entered into the house of God, and did eat the shew-bread, which was not lawful for him to eat, neither for them which were with him, but only for the priests."

Here the same form of expression in the original is used, as in John xvii. 12. "The plain meaning of this form in Matt. xii. 4: is but, not except. It was not lawful for David, nor for his companions to eat the shew-bread, but it was lawful for the priests to do so. So also, Acts xxi. 25: "As touching the Gentiles which believe, we have written and concluded that they observe no such thing, save only that they keep themselves from things offered unto idols, and from blood, and from strangled, and from fornication." Here the same form is used, and the plain meaning of the phraseology is just that which I am contending for, in the passage in Christ's prayer. Likewise, Rev. xxi. 27: "And there shall in no wise enter into it anything that defileth, neither whatsoever worketh abomination, or maketh a lie; but they which are written in the Lamb's book of life." Here again the same form of expression, and the same word in the original, are used in the sense now contended for. Nothing shall enter into the city that defileth, neither whatsoever worketh abomination or maketh a lie, but they which are written in the Lamb's book of life, shall enter in. So beyond reasonable doubt, Christ intended to say in his prayer to his Father: While I was with them in the world I kept them in thy name: those that thou gavest me I have kept and none of them is lost, that is, I have lost none of those whom thou hast given me; but the son of perdition is lost, according to the scriptures.

But it seems to me, that the context shows clearly what the Saviour intended by this form of expression. He says, verses 11 and 12: "And now I am no more in the world, but these are in the world, and I come to thee. Holy Father, keep through thine own name those whom thou hast given me, that they may be one as we are. While I was with them in the world, I kept them in thy name: those that thou gavest me I have kept, and none of them is lost, but the son of perdition; that the scripture might be fulfilled:" that is: "Do thou keep them in thine own name and lose none of them, for while I was with them I kept them in thy name, and lost none of them; but the son of perdition is lost." He evidently did not mean to say, I lost but one whom thou gavest me; or that he kept in his Father's name all except one of those whom the Father had given him. He says, 6: "I have manifested thy name unto the men which thou gavest me out of the world: thine they were, and thou gavest them me; and they have kept thy word. 7. Now they have known that all things, whatsoever thou hast given me, are of thee. 8. For I have given unto them the words which thou gavest me; and they have received them, and have known surely that I came out from thee, and they have believed that thou didst send me. 9. I pray for them: I pray not for the world, but for them which thou hast given me; for they are thine. 10. And all mine are thine, and thine are mine; and I am glorified in them. 11. And now I am no more in the world but these are in the world, and I come to thee. Holy Father, keep through thy own name those whom thou hast given me, that they may be one as we are. 12. While I was with them in the world, I kept them in thy name: those that thou gavest me I have kept, and none of them is lost, but the son of perdition; that the scripture might be fulfilled."

Here he plainly represents, that all who had been given him by the Father, had known and kept the word of God. They had believed and persevered, and Christ was glorified in them. Since he had kept them in his Father's name, and had lost none of them, he proceeds to pray, that now the Father will keep them in his own name. Let any one ponder well this passage from verses 6 to 12, and he will see, I trust, that this is a true view of the subject. At any rate this cannot be a proof text to establish the fact, that any have fallen from grace; for the plain reason, that the text can quite as naturally at least, and I think with much greater propriety, be quoted to sustain the doctrine which it is adduced to disprove. Again:--

Matt. xviii. 21: "Then came Peter to him, and said, Lord, how often shall my brother sin against me, and I forgive him? Till seven times? 22. Jesus saith unto him, I say not unto thee until seven times; but until seventy times seven. 23. Therefore is the kingdom of heaven likened unto a certain king, which would take account of his servants. 24. And when he had begun to reckon, one was brought unto him which owed him ten thousand talents. 25. But forasmuch as he had not to pay, his lord commanded him to be sold, and his wife and children, and all that he had, and payment to be made. 26. The servant therefore fell down and worshipped him, saying, Lord, have patience with me, and I will pay thee all. 27. Then the lord of that servant was moved with compassion, and loosed him, and forgave him the debt. 28. But the same servant went out, and found one of his fellow-servants, which owed him a hundred pence; and he laid hands on him, and took him by the throat, saying, Pay me that thou owest. 29. And his fellow-servant fell down at his feet, and besought him, saying, Have patience with me, and I will pay thee all. 30. And he would not; but went and cast him into prison, till he should pay the debt. 31. So when his fellow-servants saw what was done, they were very sorry, and came and told unto their lord all that was done. 32. Then his lord, after that he had called him, said unto him, O thou wicked servant, I forgave thee all that debt, because thou desiredst me: 33. Shouldest not thou also have had compassion on thy fellow-servant, even as I had pity on thee? 34. And his lord was wroth, and delivered him to the tormentors, till he should pay all that was due unto him. 35. So likewise shall my heavenly Father do also unto you, if ye from your hearts forgive not every one his brother their trespasses."

This has been adduced to prove that some do fall from grace, especially the 32d to the 34th verses. But from this whole passage it is evident, that what the Lord meant was to set in a strong light the necessity of a forgiving spirit, and that this is a condition of salvation. It is a parable designed to illustrate this truth, but does not assert as a fact, that any truly pardoned soul was ever lost; nor does it imply this, as any one may see who will duly weigh the whole parable. It does plainly imply, that a pardoned soul would be lost should he apostatize; but it does not imply that such a soul ever did apostatize.

I consider next, 1 Tim. v. 12: "Having damnation, because they have cast off their first faith." This passage stands in the following connection:--

1 Tim. v. 9: "Let not a widow be taken into the number under threescore years old, having been the wife of one man: 10. Well reported of for good works; if she have brought up children, if she have lodged strangers, if she have washed the saints' feet, if she have relieved the afflicted, if she have diligently followed every good work. 11. But the younger widows refuse, for when they have begun to wax wanton against Christ they will marry; 12. Having damnation, because they have cast off their first faith. 13. And withal they learn to be idle, wandering about from house to house; and not only idle, but tattlers also, and busy bodies, speaking things which they ought not."

The word rendered damnation in this passage is often rendered judgment and condemnation; and the meaning may be, that the younger widows were found to wax wanton and fall into condemnation, and for a time at least to disgrace their profession, by casting off their first faith; or it may mean, that they were apt to be found among those who renounced the profession of the true faith, which they at first professed. They were young widows, uneducated as heathen women were and are, and it could not be surprising that many of this class should make a spurious profession, and afterwards cast off their profession through wantonness, and disgrace their profession. The apostle, therefore, warns Timothy against too hasty a reception of them, or against having too early a confidence in the reality of their piety.

Again: it has been said, that from Christ's letters to the churches in Asia, recorded in Revelation, we learn that those churches, some of them at least, were in a state of apostacy from God; and that from the fact that the judgments of God annihilated those churches, there is reason to believe that the apostacy was complete and final, and their destruction certain. To this I reply, that those letters were written to churches as such, just as the prophets spoke of the Jewish church as such. The things which the prophets declare of the Jewish church were declared of them as a body of professed saints, some generations of whom had more, and some less, real piety. The prophets would rebuke one generation for their backsliding and apostacy, without meaning to represent that the particular individuals they addressed were ever true saints, but meaning only that the body as such was in a degenerate and apostate state, compared with what the body as such had been in former times. So Christ writes to the churches of Asia, and reproves them for their backslidden and apostate condition, asserts that they had fallen, had left their first love, etc., from which, however, we are not to infer, that he intended to say this of those who had been truly converted as individuals, but merely that those churches as bodies had fallen, and were now composed of members as a whole who were in the state of which he complained.

The churches of Asia were doubtless, when first gathered by the apostles and primitive ministers, full of faith, and zeal, and love. But things had changed. Many of the members had changed, and perhaps every member who had originally composed those churches was dead, previous to the time when these letters were written. However this may be, there had doubtless been great changes in the membership of those churches; and since they were evidently addressed as bodies, it cannot be fairly inferred, from what is said, that the same persons addressed had fallen from a state of high spirituality into backsliding of apostacy, but that that was true only of the then present membership, when compared with the former membership and state of the churches. These letters cannot be justly relied upon as disproving the doctrine in question; for the utmost that can be made of them is, that those churches as bodies were at the time in a state of declension.

The passages we have examined are, so far as I know, the principal ones upon which reliance has been placed to disprove the doctrine in question. I have read over attentively several times the views of Mr. Fletcher, in his Scripture Scales, and the passages quoted by him to disprove this doctrine. His chief reliance is manifestly upon the numerous passages that imply the possibility and danger of falling, rather than on any passages that unequivocally teach that any have fallen or will utterly fall. I am not aware that any respectable writer has laid much stress upon other passages than those I have examined, as expressly teaching, or unequivocally implying the fact of the fall and ruin of real saints. There may be such writers and such passages as those of which I speak; but if there are, I do not recollect to have seen them.

REMARKS

1. If the doctrine under consideration is not true, I cannot see upon what ground we can affirm, or even confidently hope, that many of our pious friends who have died have gone to heaven. Suppose they held on their way until the last hours of life. If we may not believe that the faithfulness of God prevailed to keep them through the last conflict, what reason have we to affirm that they were preserved from sin and apostacy in their last hours, and saved? If the sovereign grace of God do not protect them against the wiles and malice of Satan, in their feebleness, and in the wreck of their habitation of clay, what has become of them? I must confess that, if I did not expect the covenanted mercy and faithfulness of God to prevail, and to sustain the soul under such circumstances, I should have very little expectation that any would be saved. If I could have any confidence that Christians would stand fast while in health, aside from the truth of this doctrine, still I should expect that Satan would overcome them in the end, when they passed through the last great struggle. Who could then trust to the strength of his own purposes?

2. But I could no more hope, that myself or any one else, would persevere in holiness in our best estate, even for one day or hoar, if not kept by the power of God through faith, than I could hope to fly to heaven. As I have before said, there is no hope of any one's persevering, except in so far as free grace anticipates and secures the concurrence of free will. The soul must be called, and effectually called, and perpetually called, or it will not follow Christ for an hour. I say again, that by effectual calling, I do not mean an irresistible calling. I do not mean a calling that cannot, or that might not be resisted; but I do mean by an effectual calling, a calling that is not in fact resisted, a calling that does in fact secure the voluntary obedience of the soul. This is my only hope in respect to myself, or anybody else. This grace I regard as vouchsafed to me in the covenant of grace, or as a reward of Christ's obedience unto death. It is pledged to secure the salvation of those whom the Father has from eternity given to the Son. The Holy Spirit is given to them to secure their salvation, and I have no expectation that any others will ever be saved. But these, every one of them, will surely be saved. There is, there can be no hope for any others. Others are able to repent, but they will not. Others might be saved, if they would believe, and comply with the conditions of salvation, but they will not.

We have seen, that none come to Christ, except they are drawn of the Father, and that the Father draws to Christ those and those only whom he has given to Christ, and also, that it is the Father's design that of those whom he has given to Christ, he should lose none, but that he should raise them up at the last day. This is the only hope that any will be saved. Strike out this foundation, and what shall the righteous do? Strike out from the Bible the doctrine of God's covenanted faithfulness to Christ--the truth that the Father has given to him a certain number whose salvation he foresees that he could and should secure, and I despair of myself and of every body else. Where is any other ground of hope? I know not where.

END

www.ingramcontent.com/pod-product-compliance
Lightning Source LLC
Chambersburg PA
CBHW060321100426
42812CB00003B/839

* 9 7 8 1 7 7 3 5 6 2 6 8 1 *

Antony C. Sutton

LA TRILOGIE WALL STREET

Omnia Veritas

Antony C. Sutton
(1925-2002)

Économiste et essayiste américain d'origine britannique, chercheur à Stanford au sein de la fondation Hoover de 1968 à 1973. Il enseigna l'économie à l'UCLA. Il étudia à Londres, Göttingen et UCLA et fut titulaire d'un doctorat en sciences de l'Université de Southampton, en Angleterre.

LA TRILOGIE WALL STREET
Wall Street et la révolution bolchevique
Wall Street et Franklin D. Roosevelt
Wall Street et l'ascension d'Hitler

Wall Street and the Bolshevik Revolution (1974)
Wall Street and the Rise of Hitler (1976)
Wall Street and FDR (1976)

Traduit de l'américain par Omnia Veritas Limited

Publié par
Omnia Veritas Limited

www.omnia-veritas.com

ANTONY C. SUTTON

"Si quelqu'un l'emporte sur lui, deux lui résisteront, et un cordon triple ne se rompra pas rapidement" (Ecclésiaste 4:12).

Professeur Sutton (1925-2002).

Bien qu'il ait été un auteur prolifique, le professeur Sutton restera à jamais gravé dans les mémoires pour sa grande trilogie : *Wall St. et la révolution bolchévique, Wall St. et l'ascension d'Hitler, Wall St. et FDR.*

Le professeur Sutton a quitté l'Angleterre pluvieuse et nuageuse pour la Californie ensoleillée en 1957. Il était une voix qui pleurait dans le désert académique alors que la plupart des universités américaines avaient vendu leur âme pour l'argent de la Fondation Rockefeller.

Bien sûr, il est venu dans ce pays en croyant que c'était la terre des libertés et la patrie des braves.

ANTONY C. SUTTON est née à Londres en 1925 et a fait ses études dans les universités de Londres, de Gottingen et de Californie. Citoyen américain depuis 1962, il a été chercheur à la Hoover Institution for War, Revolution and Peace à Stanford, Californie, de 1968 à 1973, où il a réalisé la monumentale étude en trois volumes, *Western Technology and Soviet Economic Development.*

En 1974, le professeur Sutton a publié *National Suicide: Military Aid to the Soviet Union,* une étude à succès sur l'assistance technologique et financière occidentale, principalement américaine, fournie à l'URSS. *Wall Street et l'ascension d'Hitler* est son quatrième livre exposant le rôle des initiés des entreprises américaines dans le financement du socialisme international. Les deux autres livres de cette série sont *Wall Street et la révolution bolchévique* et *Wall Street et FDR.*

Le professeur Sutton a contribué à des articles dans *Human Events, The Review of the News, Triumph, Ordnance, National Review,* et de nombreuses autres revues.

WALL STREET ET LA RÉVOLUTION BOLCHÉVIQUE

"DEE-LIGHTED!"
WALL ST.
MORGAN
PERKINS
KARL MARX
ANDY

À ces libertaires russes inconnus, également connus sous le nom de Verts, qui en 1919 ont combattu les Rouges et les Blancs dans leur tentative d'obtenir une Russie libre et volontaire.

PRÉFACE

Depuis le début des années 20, de nombreux pamphlets et articles, et même quelques livres, ont cherché à établir un lien entre les "banquiers internationaux" et les "révolutionnaires bolchéviques". Ces tentatives ont été rarement étayées par des preuves solides, et jamais elles n'ont été argumentées dans le cadre d'une méthodologie scientifique. En effet, certaines des "preuves" utilisées dans ces efforts ont été frauduleuses, certaines n'ont pas été pertinentes, beaucoup ne peuvent être vérifiées. L'examen du sujet par des auteurs universitaires a été soigneusement évité, probablement parce que l'hypothèse heurte la dichotomie nette entre capitalistes et communistes (tout le monde sait, bien sûr, que ce sont des ennemis acharnés). En outre, comme beaucoup de choses qui ont été écrites frisent l'absurde, une solide réputation académique pourrait facilement être ruinée et ces travaux tournés en ridicule. Cela est en général une raison suffisante pour éviter le sujet.

Heureusement, le fichier décimal du Département d'État, en particulier la section 861.00, contient une documentation complète appuyant notre hypothèse. Lorsque les preuves contenues dans ces documents officiels sont fusionnées avec des preuves non officielles provenant de biographies, de documents personnels et même de sources historiques plus conventionnelles, une histoire vraiment fascinante émerge.

Nous constatons qu'il existait un lien entre *certains* banquiers internationaux de New York et de *nombreux* révolutionnaires, dont les bolcheviks. Ces banquiers - qui sont ici identifiés - avaient un intérêt financier dans le succès de la révolution bolchévique et l'encourageaient.

Les détails concernant les qui, pourquoi - et combien - constituent l'histoire racontée dans ce livre.

Mars 1974

Antony C. SUTTON

CHAPITRE I

LES ACTEURS DE LA SCÈNE RÉVOLUTIONNAIRE

Monsieur le Président : Je suis en sympathie avec la forme de gouvernement soviétique qui convient le mieux au peuple russe...

Lettre au président Woodrow Wilson (17 octobre 1918) de William Lawrence Saunders, président de l'Ingersoll-Rand Corp. et directeur de l'American International Corp ; et vice-président de la Banque de Réserve Fédérale de New York.

L'image d'illustration figurant au début de ce livre a été dessinée par le caricaturiste Robert Minor en 1911 pour le *St. Louis Post-Dispatch.* Minor était un artiste et un écrivain talentueux qui, en plus d'être un révolutionnaire bolchévique, s'est fait arrêter en Russie en 1915 pour subversion présumée, et a ensuite été soutenu par d'éminents financiers de Wall Street. La caricature de Minor montre un Karl Marx barbu et rayonnant, debout à Wall Street, le *socialisme* sous le bras et acceptant les félicitations des sommités financières J.P. Morgan, George W. Perkins, partenaire de Morgan, John D. Rockefeller, John D. Ryan de la National City Bank et Teddy Roosevelt - bien identifié par ses célèbres dents - en arrière-plan. Wall Street est décorée par des drapeaux rouges. Les acclamations de la foule et les chapeaux jetés en l'air suggèrent que Karl Marx devait être un type assez populaire dans le quartier financier de New York.

Robert Minor rêvait-il ? Au contraire, nous verrons que Minor était sur la bonne voie en décrivant une alliance enthousiaste passée entre Wall Street et le socialisme marxiste. Les personnages du dessin de Minor - Karl Marx (qui symbolise les futurs révolutionnaires Lénine et Trotsky), J. P. Morgan, John D. Rockefeller - et Robert Minor lui-même, jouent également un rôle important dans ce livre.

Les contradictions suggérées par la caricature de Minor ont été balayées sous le tapis de l'histoire parce qu'elles ne correspondent pas au concept généralement admis de la gauche et de la droite politiques. Les bolcheviks sont à l'extrémité gauche du spectre politique et les financiers de Wall Street sont à l'extrémité droite ; par conséquent, nous raisonnons implicitement, les deux groupes n'ont rien en commun et toute alliance entre les deux est absurde. Les facteurs contraires à cet arrangement conceptuel soigné sont généralement rejetés comme des observations bizarres ou des erreurs malheureuses. L'histoire moderne possède une telle dualité intrinsèque et il est certain que si trop de faits gênants ont été rejetés et balayés sous le tapis, il s'agit d'une histoire inexacte.

D'autre part, on peut observer que l'extrême droite et l'extrême gauche du spectre politique conventionnel sont toutes deux absolument collectivistes. Le national-socialisme (par exemple, le fasciste) et le socialisme international (par exemple, le communiste) recommandent tous deux des systèmes politico-économiques totalitaires basés sur le pouvoir politique brutal et sans entraves et sur la coercition individuelle. Les deux systèmes exigent un contrôle monopolistique de la société. Alors que le contrôle monopolistique des industries était autrefois l'objectif de J. P. Morgan et de J. D. Rockefeller, à la fin du XIXe siècle, les stratèges de Wall Street ont compris que le moyen le plus efficace d'obtenir un monopole incontesté était de "faire de la politique" et de faire travailler la société pour le compte des monopolistes - au nom du bien public et de l'intérêt général. Cette stratégie a été détaillée en 1906 par Frederick C. Howe dans ses *Confessions d'un Monopoliste.*[1] Howe, d'ailleurs, est aussi une figure de l'histoire de la révolution bolchévique.

Par conséquent, une autre façon de présenter les idées politiques et les systèmes politico-économiques serait de mesurer le degré de liberté individuelle par rapport au degré de contrôle politique centralisé. Dans un tel ordre de chose, l'État providence et le socialisme se trouvent au même bout du spectre. Nous voyons donc que les tentatives de contrôle monopolistique de la société peuvent revêtir des étiquettes différentes tout en possédant des caractéristiques communes.

Par conséquent, l'idée que tous les capitalistes sont les ennemis acharnés et inébranlables de tous les marxistes et socialistes, constitue un obstacle majeur à toute compréhension approfondie de l'histoire récente. Cette idée erronée est née avec Karl Marx et a sans aucun doute été utile à ses objectifs. En fait, cette idée est absurde. Il y a eu une alliance continue, bien que cachée, entre les capitalistes politiques internationaux et les socialistes révolutionnaires internationaux - à leur avantage mutuel. Cette alliance est passée inaperçue en grande partie parce que les historiens - à quelques exceptions notables près - ont un préjugé marxiste inconscient et sont donc enfermés dans l'impossibilité de l'existence d'une telle alliance. Le lecteur ouvert d'esprit doit prendre en compte deux indices : les capitalistes monopolistes sont les ennemis acharnés de la libre entreprise ; et, étant donné les faiblesses de la planification centrale socialiste, l'État socialiste totalitaire est un marché captif parfait pour les capitalistes monopolistes, si une alliance peut être conclue avec les fourrier du pouvoir socialiste. Supposons - et ce n'est qu'une hypothèse pour l'instant - que les capitalistes monopolistes américains soient capables de s'emparer d'une Russie socialiste par le biais d'une économie planifiée la réduisant ainsi au statut de colonie productiviste entre leurs mains ? Ne serait-ce pas là l'extension internationaliste logique, au XXe siècle, des

---

[1] "Ce sont les règles des grandes entreprises. Elles ont supplanté les enseignements de nos parents et se réduisent à une simple maxime : "Obtenez un monopole ; laissez la société travailler pour vous ; et rappelez-vous que la meilleure de toutes les affaires est la politique, car une subvention législative, une franchise, une subvention ou une exonération fiscale valent plus qu'un filon de Kimberly ou de Comstock, car elle ne nécessite aucun travail, ni mental ni physique, pour son exploitation" (Chicago : Public Publishing, 1906), p. 157.

monopoles de la compagnie des chemins de fer Morgan et du monopole pétrolier du consortium Rockefeller de la fin du XIXe siècle ?

Hormis Gabriel Kolko, Murray Rothbard et les révisionnistes, les historiens n'ont pas été attentifs à une telle combinaison d'événements. Les recherches historiques, à de rares exceptions près, ont été réduites à souligner la dichotomie entre capitalistes et socialistes. L'étude monumentale de George Kennan sur la Révolution russe maintient constamment la fiction d'un antagonisme[2] Wall Street-Bolchevik. L'ouvrage *Russia Leaves the War* fait une seule référence fortuite à la firme J.P. Morgan et aucune référence à la Guaranty Trust Company. Pourtant, les deux organisations sont mentionnées de manière évidente dans les dossiers du Département d'État, auxquels il est fréquemment fait référence dans ce livre, et toutes deux font partie du faisceau de preuves présenté ici. Ni le "banquier bolchévique" Olof Aschberg ni la Nya Banken de Stockholm ne sont mentionnés dans Kennan, mais tous deux ont pourtant joué un rôle central dans le financement bolchévique. De plus, dans des circonstances mineures mais cruciales, du moins pour *notre* argumentation, Kennan s'avère être en fait complètement dans l'erreur. Par exemple, Kennan indique que le directeur de la Federal Reserve Bank, William Boyce Thompson, a quitté la Russie le 27 novembre 1917. Cette date de départ rendrait physiquement impossible la présence de Thompson à Petrograd le 2 décembre 1917 pour transmettre une demande de financement d'un million de dollars à Morgan à New York. Thompson quitta en fait Petrograd le 4 décembre 1918, deux jours après avoir envoyé le câble à New York. Puis, Kennan déclare que le 30 novembre 1917, Trotsky a prononcé un discours devant le Soviet de Petrograd dans lequel il a observé : "Aujourd'hui, j'avais ici, au Smolny Institute, deux Américains étroitement liés aux éléments capitalistes américains". Selon Kennan, il est "difficile d'imaginer" qui ces deux Américains "auraient pu être, si ce n'est Robins et Gumberg". Mais en fait, Alexander Gumberg était russe, pas américain. De plus, comme Thompson était encore en Russie le 30 novembre 1917, les deux Américains qui ont rendu visite à Trotsky étaient plus que probablement Raymond Robins, un promoteur minier devenu bienfaiteur, et Thompson, de la Banque de Réserve Fédérale de New York.

La bolchevisation de Wall Street était connue dans les milieux bien informés dès 1919. Le journaliste financier Barron a enregistré une conversation avec le magnat du pétrole E. H. Doheny en 1919 et a spécifiquement nommé trois financiers éminents, William Boyce Thompson, Thomas Lamont et Charles R. Crane :

> À bord du S.S. Aquitania, vendredi soir, 1er février 1919.
> Il a passé la soirée avec les Dohenys dans leur suite. M. Doheny a dit : Si vous croyez en la démocratie, vous ne pouvez pas croire au socialisme. Le socialisme est le poison qui détruit la démocratie. La démocratie est synonyme d'opportunités pour tous. Le socialisme permet d'espérer qu'un homme peut quitter son travail et s'en sortir. Le bolchevisme est le véritable fruit du socialisme et si vous lisez les

---

[2] George F. Kennan, *Russia Leaves the War* (New York : Atheneum, 1967) ; et *Decision to Intervene, Soviet-American Relations, 1917-1920* (Princeton, N.J. : Princeton University Press, 1958).

> témoignages intéressants présentés devant la commission du Sénat vers la mi-janvier, qui ont montré tous ces pacifistes et artisans de paix comme des sympathisants allemands, socialistes et bolchéviques, vous verrez qu'une majorité des professeurs de collège aux États-Unis enseignent le socialisme et le bolchevisme et que cinquante-deux professeurs de collège faisaient partie de soi-disant comités de paix en 1914. Le président Eliot de Harvard enseigne le bolchevisme. Les pires bolchéviques des États-Unis ne sont pas seulement des professeurs d'université, dont le président Wilson fait partie, mais aussi des capitalistes et des épouses de capitalistes, et aucun d'entre eux ne semble savoir de quoi ils parlent. William Boyce Thompson enseigne le bolchevisme et il pourrait encore convertir Lamont de J.P. Morgan & Company. Vanderlip est un bolcheviste, tout comme Charles R. Crane. De nombreuses femmes rejoignent le mouvement et ni elles, ni leurs maris, ne savent ce que c'est, ni à quoi il mène. Henry Ford en est un autre, tout comme la plupart des cent historiens que Wilson a emmenés à l'étranger avec lui, dans l'idée stupide que l'histoire peut enseigner aux jeunes les démarcations appropriées des races, des peuples et des nations sur le plan géographique.[3]

En bref, c'est une histoire de la révolution bolchévique et de ses conséquences, mais une histoire qui s'écarte de l'approche conceptuelle habituelle du carcan des capitalistes contre les communistes. Notre histoire postule un partenariat entre le capitalisme monopoliste international et le socialisme révolutionnaire international pour leur bénéfice mutuel. Le coût humain final de cette alliance est retombé sur les épaules de chaque Russe et de chaque Américain. L'esprit d'entreprise a été discrédité et le monde a été propulsé vers une planification socialiste débilitante en raison de ces manœuvres monopolistiques dans le monde de la politique et de la révolution.

C'est aussi une histoire qui reflète la trahison de la Révolution russe. Les tsars et leur système politique corrompu ont été éjectés pour être remplacés par les nouveaux intermédiaires d'un autre système politique corrompu. Là où les États-Unis auraient pu exercer leur influence dominante pour faire naître une Russie libre, ils ont cédé aux ambitions de quelques financiers de Wall Street qui, pour leurs propres bénéfices, pouvaient accepter une Russie tsariste centralisée ou une Russie marxiste centralisée mais pas une Russie libre décentralisée. Et les raisons de ces affirmations se dévoileront au fur et à mesure que nous développerons l'histoire sous-jacente et, jusqu'à présent, inédite de la Révolution russe et de ses suites.[4]

---

[3] Arthur Pound et Samuel Taylor Moore, *They Told Barron* (New York : Harper & Brothers, 1930), pp. 13-14.

[4] Il existe une histoire parallèle, et également inconnue, en ce qui concerne le mouvement Makhanovite qui a combattu à la fois les "Blancs" et les "Rouges" pendant la guerre civile de 1919-20 (voir Voline, *The Unknown Revolution* [New York : Libertarian Book Club, 1953]). Il y avait aussi le mouvement "Vert", qui a combattu à la fois les Blancs et les Rouges. L'auteur n'a jamais vu une seule mention isolée des Verts dans l'histoire de la révolution bolchévique. Pourtant, l'Armée verte était forte d'au moins 700 000 hommes !

CHAPITRE II

TROTSKY QUITTE NEW YORK POUR ACCOMPLIR LA RÉVOLUTION

Vous aurez une révolution, une terrible révolution. Le cours qu'elle prendra dépendra en grande partie de ce que M. Rockefeller dira à M. Hague de faire. M. Rockefeller est un symbole de la classe dirigeante américaine et M. Hague est un symbole de ses outils politiques.

Léon Trotsky, dans le New York Times, 13 décembre 1938.
(Hague était un homme politique du New Jersey)

En 1916, l'année précédant la révolution russe, l'internationaliste Léon Trotsky est expulsé de France, officiellement en raison de sa participation à la conférence de Zimmerwald mais aussi sans doute à cause d'articles incendiaires écrits pour *Nashe Slovo*, un journal de langue russe imprimé à Paris. En septembre 1916, Trotsky a été poliment escorté à travers la frontière espagnole par la police française. Quelques jours plus tard, la police madrilène arrête l'internationaliste et le place dans une "cellule de première classe", coûtant une peseta par jour. Trotsky a ensuite été emmené à Cadix, puis à Barcelone pour être finalement placé à bord du navire à vapeur de la Compagnie transatlantique espagnole, le *Monserrat.* Trotsky et sa famille ont traversé l'océan Atlantique et ont débarqué à New York le 13 janvier 1917.

D'autres trotskistes ont également traversé l'Atlantique vers l'ouest. En effet, un groupe trotskiste a acquis une influence immédiate suffisante au Mexique pour rédiger la Constitution de Querétaro pour le gouvernement révolutionnaire de Carranza en 1917, donnant au Mexique la distinction douteuse d'être le premier gouvernement au monde à adopter une constitution de type soviétique.

Comment Trotsky, qui ne connaissait que l'allemand et le russe, a-t-il survécu dans l'Amérique capitaliste ? Selon son autobiographie, *Ma vie,* "Ma seule profession à New York était celle d'un socialiste révolutionnaire". En d'autres termes, Trotsky a écrit des articles occasionnels pour *Novy Mir,* la revue socialiste russe de New York. Pourtant, nous savons que l'appartement de la famille Trotsky à New York était équipé d'un réfrigérateur et d'un téléphone et, selon Trotsky, la famille voyageait occasionnellement en limousine avec chauffeur. Ce mode de vie a laissé les deux jeunes Trotsky perplexes. Lorsqu'ils entraient dans un salon de thé, les garçons demandaient anxieusement à leur mère : "Pourquoi le chauffeur n'entre-t-il pas ?[5] Le niveau de vie élégant est également en contradiction avec les revenus déclarés de Trotsky. Les seuls fonds que Trotsky admet avoir reçus en 1916 et 1917 sont de 310$, et, déclare Trotsky, "j'ai réparti les 310$ entre cinq émigrants qui retournaient en Russie". Pourtant, Trotsky avait payé une cellule de première classe en Espagne, la famille Trotsky avait voyagé à travers l'Europe jusqu'aux États-Unis, ils avaient acquis un excellent appartement à New York - en payant le loyer trois mois à l'avance - et ils avaient l'usage d'une limousine avec chauffeur. Tout cela grâce aux gains d'un révolutionnaire appauvri pour quelques articles dans le journal russophone à faible tirage du *Nashe Slovo* à Paris et du *Novy Mir à* New York !

Joseph Nedava estime les revenus de Trotsky en 1917 à 12 dollars par semaine, "complétés par quelques frais de conférence".[6] Trotsky a passé trois mois à New York en 1917, de janvier à mars, ce qui lui a permis de tirer 144 dollars de *Novy Mir* et, disons, 100 dollars de plus en frais de conférence, pour un total de 244 dollars. Sur ces 244 dollars, Trotsky a pu donner 310 dollars à ses amis, payer l'appartement à New York, subvenir aux besoins de sa famille - et récupérer les 10 000 dollars qui lui avaient été confisqués en avril 1917 par les autorités canadiennes de Halifax. Trotsky prétend que ceux qui ont dit qu'il avait d'autres sources de revenus sont des "calomniateurs" qui répandent des "calomnies stupides" et des "mensonges", mais à moins que Trotsky n'ait joué aux courses à l'hippodrome jamaïcain de New York, cela est tout bonnement impossible. Il est évident que Trotsky disposait d'une source de revenus non déclarée.

Quelle était cette source ? Dans *The Road to Safety*, l'auteur Arthur Willert dit que Trotsky gagnait sa vie en travaillant comme électricien pour les studios de cinéma Fox. D'autres écrivains ont cité d'autres occupations, mais rien ne prouve que Trotsky s'occupait contre rémunération autrement qu'en écrivant et en parlant.

La plupart des enquêtes se sont concentrées sur le fait vérifiable que lorsque Trotsky a quitté New York en 1917 pour Petrograd, afin d'organiser la phase bolchévique de la révolution, il est parti avec 10 000 dollars. En 1919, la commission Overman du Sénat américain a enquêté sur la propagande bolchévique financée par de l'argent allemand aux États-Unis et a incidemment touché à la source des 10 000 dollars de Trotsky. L'examen du colonel Hurban, attaché de Washington à la légation tchèque, par la commission Overman a donné les résultats suivants :

> **COL. HURBAN** : Trotsky a peut-être pris de l'argent à l'Allemagne, mais Trotsky le niera. Lénine ne le niera pas. Milioukov a prouvé qu'il avait reçu 10 000 dollars de certains Allemands pendant son séjour en Amérique. Milioukov avait la preuve, mais il l'a nié. Trotsky l'a fait, bien que Milioukov ait eu la preuve.
> **SÉNATEUR OVERMAN** : On a accusé Trotsky d'avoir obtenu 10 000$ ici.
> **COL. HURBAN** : Je ne me souviens pas combien c'était, mais je sais que c'était une question entre lui et Milioukov.

---

[5] Léon Trotsky, *My Life* (New York : Scribner's, 1930), chap. 22.

[6] Joseph Nedava, *Trotsky and the Jews* (Philadelphie : Jewish Publication Society of America, 1972), p. 163.

SÉNATEUR : Milioukov l'a prouvé, n'est-ce pas ?
COL. HURBAN : Oui, monsieur.
SÉNATEUR OVERMAN : Savez-vous d'où il les a obtenus ?
COL. HURBAN : Je me souviens que c'était 10 000 dollars ; mais ce n'est pas grave. Je vais parler de leur propagande. Le gouvernement allemand connaissait la Russie mieux que quiconque, et ils savaient qu'avec l'aide de ces gens, ils pouvaient détruire l'armée russe.
(À 17 h 45, la sous-commission s'ajourne jusqu'à demain, mercredi 19 février, à 10 h 30)[7]

Il est tout à fait remarquable que la commission se soit brusquement ajournée avant que la *source des* fonds de Trotsky ne soit inscrite au dossier du Sénat. Lorsque l'interrogatoire a repris le lendemain, Trotsky et ses 10 000 dollars n'intéressaient plus la commission Overman. Nous développerons plus tard les preuves concernant le financement des activités allemandes révolutionnaires aux États-Unis par les institutions financières de New York ; les origines des 10 000 dollars de Trotsky seront alors mises en lumière.

Un montant de 10 000 dollars d'origine allemande est également mentionné dans le télégramme officiel britannique adressé aux autorités navales canadiennes à Halifax, qui demandent que Trotsky et sa troupe en route pour la révolution soient débarqués du S.S. *Kristianiafjord* (voir plus loin). Nous apprenons également d'un rapport de la Direction britannique du renseignement[8] que Gregory Weinstein, qui en 1919 allait devenir un membre éminent du Bureau soviétique à New York, a collecté des fonds pour Trotsky à New York. Ces fonds provenaient d'Allemagne et étaient acheminés par le *Volkszeitung*, un quotidien germanophone de New York et subventionné par le gouvernement allemand.

Alors que les fonds de Trotsky sont officiellement déclarés allemands, Trotsky était activement engagé dans la politique américaine juste avant de quitter New York pour la Russie et la révolution. Le 5 mars 1917, les journaux américains ont fait leur une sur la possibilité croissante d'une guerre avec l'Allemagne ; le soir même, Trotsky a proposé une résolution lors de la réunion du parti socialiste du comté de New York "engageant les socialistes à encourager les grèves et à résister au recrutement en cas de guerre avec l'Allemagne".[9] Léon Trotsky a été qualifié par le *New York Times de* "révolutionnaire russe en exil". Louis C. Fraina, qui a coparrainé la résolution Trotsky, a ensuite - sous un pseudonyme - écrit un livre non critique sur l'empire financier Morgan intitulé *House of Morgan*[10]. La

[7] États-Unis, Sénat, *Brewing and Liquor Interests and German and Bolshevik Propaganda* (Sous-commission du pouvoir judiciaire), 65e Cong. 1919.

[8] Rapport spécial n° 5, *The Russian Soviet Bureau in the United States*, 14 juillet 1919, Scotland House, Londres Copie S.W.I. dans le fichier décimal du State Dept. américain, 316-23-1145.

[9] *New York Times*, 5 mars 1917.

[10] Lewis Corey, *House of Morgan: A Social Biography of the Masters of Money* (New York : G. W. Watt, 1930).

proposition Trotsky-Fraina a été rejetée par la faction Morris Hillquit, et le parti socialiste a ensuite voté contre la résolution.[11]

Plus d'une semaine plus tard, le 16 mars, au moment de la déposition du tsar, Léon Trotsky a été interviewé dans les bureaux de *Novy Mir*. L'interview contenait une déclaration prophétique sur la révolution russe :

> "... le comité qui a pris la place du ministère déchu en Russie ne représente pas les intérêts ou les buts des révolutionnaires, il sera probablement éphémère et se retirera en faveur d'hommes qui seraient plus sûrs de faire avancer la démocratisation de la Russie".[12]

Les "hommes qui seraient plus sûrs de faire avancer la démocratisation de la Russie", c'est-à-dire les mencheviks et les bolcheviks, étaient alors en exil à l'étranger et devaient d'abord retourner en Russie. Le "comité" temporaire a donc été baptisé "gouvernement provisoire", un titre, il faut le noter, qui a été utilisé dès le début de la révolution en mars et qui n'a pas été appliqué a posteriori par les historiens.

WOODROW WILSON PROCURE UN PASSEPORT À TROTSKY

Le président Woodrow Wilson fut le bon génie qui a fourni à Trotsky un passeport pour retourner en Russie afin de "faire avancer" la révolution. Ce passeport américain était accompagné d'un permis d'entrée en Russie et d'un visa de transit britannique. Jennings C. Wise, dans *Woodrow Wilson : Disciple de la Révolution*, fait le commentaire pertinent suivant : "Les historiens ne doivent jamais oublier que Woodrow Wilson, malgré les efforts de la police britannique, a permis à Léon Trotsky d'entrer en Russie avec un passeport américain".

Le président Wilson a facilité le passage de Trotsky en Russie au moment même où des bureaucrates prudents du Département d'État, préoccupés par l'entrée de tels révolutionnaires en Russie, tentaient unilatéralement de durcir les procédures de circulation. La délégation de Stockholm a envoyé un câble au Département d'État le 13 juin 1917, juste *après le passage de* Trotsky à la frontière finno-russe : "La délégation a informé confidentiellement les bureaux des passeports russe, anglais et français à la frontière russe de Tornio,

[11] Morris Hillquit. (anciennement Hillkowitz) avait été l'avocat de la défense de Johann Most, après l'assassinat du président McKinley, et en 1917, il était l'un des dirigeants du parti socialiste de New York. Dans les années 1920, Hillquit s'est imposé dans le monde bancaire new-yorkais en devenant directeur et avocat de l'International Union Bank. Sous le président Franklin D. Roosevelt, Hillquit a contribué à l'élaboration des codes de l'ARN pour l'industrie de l'habillement.

[12] *New York Times*, 16 mars 1917.

considérablement inquiets du passage de personnes suspectes porteuses de passeports américains".[13]

À ce câble, le Département d'État a répondu, le même jour, "Le ministère exerce un soin particulier dans la délivrance des passeports pour la Russie" ; le Département d'État a également autorisé des dépenses de la mission diplomatique pour établir un bureau de contrôle des passeports à Stockholm et pour engager un "citoyen américain absolument fiable" pour un emploi de vérification.[14] Mais l'oiseau s'était envolé. Le menchevik Trotsky et les bolcheviks de Lénine étaient déjà en Russie et se préparaient à "faire avancer" la révolution. Le piège à passeports mis en place n'a guère attrapé que des proies de second ordre. Par exemple, le 26 juin 1917, Herman Bernstein, un journaliste new-yorkais réputé qui se rendait à Petrograd pour représenter le *New York Herald,* fut retenu à la frontière et se vit refuser l'entrée en Russie. Un peu plus tard, à la mi-août 1917, l'ambassade de Russie à Washington a demandé au Département d'État (et l'État a accepté) "d'empêcher l'entrée en Russie de criminels et d'anarchistes... dont un certain nombre se sont déjà rendus en Russie".[15]

Par conséquent, en vertu du traitement préférentiel accordé à Trotsky, lorsque le S.S. *Kristianiafjord* a quitté New York le 26 mars 1917, Trotsky était à bord et détenait un passeport américain - et en compagnie d'autres révolutionnaires trotskystes, de financiers de Wall Street, de communistes américains et d'autres personnes intéressantes, dont peu s'étaient embarqués pour des affaires légitimes. Ce mélange de passagers a été décrit par Lincoln Steffens, le communiste américain :

> La liste des passagers était longue et mystérieuse. Trotsky était dans l'entrepont avec un groupe de révolutionnaires ; il y avait un révolutionnaire japonais dans ma cabine. Il y avait beaucoup de Hollandais qui rentraient de Java en toute hâte, les seuls innocents à bord. Les autres étaient des messagers de guerre, deux de Wall Street vers l'Allemagne.[16]

Lincoln Steffens, se trouvait notamment à bord en route pour la Russie à l'invitation expresse de Charles Richard Crane, un bailleur de fonds et ancien président de la commission des finances du parti démocrate. Charles Crane, vice-président de la Crane Company, avait organisé la Westinghouse Company en Russie, était membre de la mission Root en Russie et avait effectué pas moins de vingt-trois visites en Russie entre 1890 et 1930. Richard Crane, son fils, était l'assistant confidentiel de Robert Lansing, alors secrétaire d'État. Selon l'ancien ambassadeur en Allemagne William Dodd, Crane "a beaucoup contribué à la

---

[13] Fichier décimal du Département d'État américain, 316-85-1002.

[14] Ibid.

[15] Ibid, 861.111/315.

[16] Lincoln Steffens, *Autobiography* (New York : Harcourt, Brace, 1931), p. 764. Steffens était l'"intermédiaire" de Crane et Woodrow Wilson.

révolution de Kerensky qui a fait place au communisme".[17] Les commentaires de Steffens dans son journal sur les conversations à bord du S.S. *Kristianiafjord* sont donc très pertinents : "... tous s'accordent à dire que la révolution n'en est qu'à sa première phase, qu'elle doit se développer. Crane et les radicaux russes à bord du navire pensent que nous serons à Petrograd pour finaliser la révolution.[18]

Crane est rentré aux États-Unis lorsque la révolution bolchévique (c'est-à-dire "la révolution finalisée") a été accomplie et, bien que simple citoyen, il a reçu des rapports de première main sur les progrès de la révolution bolchévique au fur et à mesure que des câbles étaient reçus au Département d'État. Par exemple, un mémorandum, daté du 11 décembre 1917, est intitulé "Copie du rapport sur le soulèvement maximaliste pour M. Crane". Il provient de Maddin Summers, consul général des États-Unis à Moscou, et la lettre d'accompagnement de Summers se lit en partie comme suit :

> J'ai l'honneur de vous faire parvenir ci-joint une copie de ce rapport [ci-dessus] en demandant qu'il soit envoyé pour les informations confidentielles de M. Charles R. Crane. Il est supposé que le Département n'aura aucune objection à ce que M. Crane voie le rapport.[19]

En bref, le tableau improbable et déroutant qui se dégage est que Charles Crane, ami et bailleur de fonds de Woodrow Wilson et financier et homme politique de premier plan, a joué un rôle connu dans la "première" révolution et s'est rendu en Russie au milieu de l'année 1917 en compagnie du communiste américain Lincoln Steffens, qui était en contact à la fois avec Woodrow Wilson et Trotsky. Ce dernier était à son tour porteur d'un passeport délivré sur ordre de Wilson et de 10 000 dollars provenant de sources allemandes supposées. À son retour aux États-Unis une fois la "révolution finalisée", Crane a eu accès à des documents officiels concernant la consolidation du régime bolchévique : Il s'agit d'un schéma d'événements imbriqués - bien que déroutants - qui justifie une enquête plus approfondie et suggère, bien que sans fournir de preuves à ce stade, un certain lien entre le financier Crane et le révolutionnaire Trotsky.

LES DOCUMENTS DU GOUVERNEMENT CANADIEN SUR LA LIBÉRATION DE TROTSKY[20]

Les documents relatifs au bref séjour de Trotsky en détention canadienne sont désormais déclassifiés et disponibles dans les archives du gouvernement canadien.

---

[17] William Edward *Dodd, Ambassador Dodd's Diary, 1933-1938* (New York : Harcourt, Brace, 1941), pp. 42-43.

[18] Lincoln Steffens, *The Letters of Lincoln Steffens* (New York : Harcourt, Brace, 1941), p. 396.

[19] Fichier décimal du département d'État américain, 861.00/1026.

[20] Cette section est basée sur les dossiers du gouvernement canadien.

Selon ces archives, Trotsky a été arrêté par le personnel naval canadien et britannique du S.S. *Kristianiafjord* à Halifax, en Nouvelle-Écosse, le 3 avril 1917, inscrit comme prisonnier de guerre allemand, et interné à la maison d'arrêt pour prisonniers allemands d'Amherst, en Nouvelle-Écosse. Mme Trotsky, les deux garçons Trotsky et cinq autres hommes décrits comme des "socialistes russes" furent également interpelés et internés. Leurs noms sont consignés dans les dossiers canadiens sous le nom de : Nickita Muchin, Leiba Fisheleff, Konstantin Romanchanco, Gregor Teheodnovski, Gerchon Melintchansky et Leon Bronstein Trotsky (toutes les orthographes proviennent de documents canadiens originaux).

Le formulaire LB-1 de l'armée canadienne, sous le numéro de série 1098 (y compris les empreintes digitales), a été rempli pour Trotsky, avec la description suivante : "37 ans, exilé politique, journaliste de profession, né à Gromskty, Chuson, Russie, citoyen russe". Le formulaire a été signé par Léon Trotsky et son nom complet a été donné comme Léon Bromstein *(sic)* Trotsky.

Le groupe de Trotsky a été débarqué du S.S. *Kristianiafjord* sur instructions officielles reçues par télégramme du 29 mars 1917, depuis Londres, provenant vraisemblablement de l'Amirauté avec l'officier de contrôle naval, Halifax. Le câblogramme rapportait que Trotsky et son équipe se trouvaient sur le *"Christianiafjord" (sic)* et devaient être "interpelés et incarcérés en attendant les instructions". La raison donnée à l'officier de contrôle naval à Halifax était que "ce sont des socialistes russes qui partent dans le but d'entamer une révolution contre le gouvernement russe actuel pour laquelle Trotsky disposerait de 10.000 dollars fournis par les socialistes et les Allemands".

Le 1er avril 1917, l'officier de contrôle naval, le capitaine O. M. Makins, envoya une note confidentielle à l'officier général commandant à Halifax, selon laquelle il avait "examiné tous les passagers russes" à bord du S.S. *Kristianiafjord* et trouvé six hommes dans la section de seconde classe : "Ils sont tous socialistes déclarés, et bien qu'ils déclarent vouloir aider le nouveau gouvernement russe, ils pourraient bien être de mèche avec les socialistes allemands en Amérique, et très probablement constituer un gros problème pour le gouvernement russe à l'heure actuelle." Le capitaine Makins a ajouté qu'il allait débarquer le groupe, ainsi que la femme et les deux fils de Trotsky, afin de les placer en détention à Halifax. Une copie de ce rapport fut transmise de Halifax au chef de l'état-major général à Ottawa le 2 avril 1917.

Le document suivant dans les dossiers canadiens est daté du 7 avril, du chef de l'état-major général, Ottawa, au directeur des opérations d'internement, et accuse-réception d'un courrier précédent (qui ne figure pas dans les dossiers) sur l'internement des socialistes russes à Amherst, en Nouvelle-Écosse : ".... à ce propos, je dois vous informer de la réception d'un long télégramme hier du consul général de Russie à MONTRÉAL, protestant contre l'arrestation de ces hommes, car ils étaient en possession de passeports délivrés par le consul général de Russie à NEW YORK, aux États-Unis".

La réponse à ce télégramme de Montréal était que les hommes étaient incarcérés "parce qu'on les soupçonnait d'être allemands" et qu'ils ne seraient libérés qu'après avoir prouvé leur nationalité et leur loyauté envers les Alliés. Aucun télégramme du consul général de Russie à New York ne figure dans les dossiers canadiens, et l'on sait que ce bureau était réticent à délivrer des passeports russes aux exilés politiques russes. Cependant, il y a un télégramme dans les dossiers d'un procureur de New York, N. Aleinikoff, à R. M. Coulter, alors ministre adjoint des Postes du Canada. Le bureau du ministre des Postes du Canada n'avait aucun lien avec l'internement des prisonniers de guerre ou les activités militaires. En conséquence, ce télégramme avait le caractère d'une intervention personnelle et non officielle. Il se lit comme suit :

> DR. R. M. COULTER, Ministère des postes. OTTAWA Des exilés politiques russes retournant en Russie ont été détenus dans le camp d'Amherst à Halifax. Veuillez enquêter sur les causes de la détention et donner les noms de tous les détenus. Toute confiance au champion de la liberté que vous êtes pour intercéder en leur faveur. Câblez PCV SVP. NICHOLAS ALEINIKOFF

Le 11 avril, Coulter a câblé à Aleinikoff, "Télégramme reçu. Je vous écris cet après-midi. Vous devriez le recevoir demain soir. R. M. Coulter." Ce télégramme a été envoyé par le Canadian Pacific Railway Telegraph mais a été facturé au ministère des Postes. Normalement, un télégramme d'affaires privées est facturé au destinataire, car il ne s'agissait pas d'une affaire officielle. La réponse de Coulter à Aleinikoff est intéressante, car, après avoir confirmé que le groupe de Trotsky était bien détenu à Amherst, elle déclare qu'ils sont soupçonnés de faire de la propagande contre le gouvernement russe actuel et "sont supposés être des agents de l'Allemagne". Coulter ajoute ensuite : "... ils ne sont pas ce qu'ils prétendent" ; le groupe Trotsky est "... non pas détenu par le Canada, mais par les autorités impériales". Après avoir assuré à Aleinikoff que les détenus seraient bien traités, Coulter ajoute que toute information "en leur faveur" serait transmise aux autorités militaires. L'impression générale de la lettre est que, bien que Coulter soit sympathique et pleinement conscient des liens pro-allemands de Trotsky, il ne veut pas s'impliquer. Le 11 avril, Arthur Wolf envoie un télégramme à Coulter depuis le 134 East Broadway, à New York. Bien qu'envoyé de New York, ce télégramme, après avoir été accusé de réception, a également été transmis au ministère des Postes.

Cependant, la réaction de Coulter en dit davantage que la sympathie détachée qui transparaît dans sa lettre à Aleinikoff. Cette correspondance au nom de Trotsky doit être considérée à la lumière du fait que ces lettres provenaient de deux résidents américains de la ville de New York et concernaient une affaire militaire canadienne ou impériale d'importance internationale. En outre, Coulter, en tant que ministre des Postes adjoint, était un fonctionnaire canadien d'une certaine importance. Réfléchissez un instant à ce qui arriverait à quelqu'un qui interviendrait de la même manière dans les affaires américaines ! Dans l'affaire Trotsky, nous avons deux résidents américains qui correspondent avec un ministre des Postes canadien afin d'intervenir en faveur d'un révolutionnaire russe incarcéré.

L'action ultérieure de Coulter suggère également quelque chose de plus qu'une intervention occasionnelle. Après avoir pris connaissance des télégrammes Aleinikoff et Wolf, Coulter écrit au major général Willoughby Gwatkin du ministère de la Milice et de la Défense à Ottawa - un homme d'une grande influence dans l'armée canadienne - et joint des copies des télégrammes Aleinikoff et Wolf :

> Ces hommes ont été hostiles à la Russie à cause de la façon dont les Juifs ont été traités, et sont maintenant fortement en faveur de l'administration actuelle, pour autant que je sache. Ce sont tous deux des hommes responsables. Ce sont tous deux des hommes de bonne réputation, et je vous envoie leurs télégrammes pour ce qu'ils valent, et pour que vous puissiez les représenter auprès des autorités anglaises si vous le jugez bon.

De toute évidence, Coulter en sait - ou laisse entendre qu'il en sait - beaucoup sur Aleinikoff et Wolf. Sa lettre était en fait une recommandation adressée à Londres. Gwatkin était bien connu à Londres, et avait en fait été mis à disposition du Canada par le War Office[21] de Londres.[22]

Aleinikoff a ensuite envoyé une lettre à Coulter pour le remercier :

> pour l'intérêt que vous avez porté au sort des exilés politiques russes... Vous me connaissez, cher Dr Coulter, et vous connaissez aussi mon dévouement à la cause de la liberté russe... Heureusement, je connais M. Trotsky, M. Melnichahnsky et M. Chudnowsky... intimement.

On peut noter en passant que si Aleinikoff connaissait Trotsky "intimement", il savait probablement aussi que Trotsky avait déclaré son intention de retourner en Russie pour renverser le gouvernement provisoire et instaurer la "révolution finalisée". Dès réception de la lettre d'Aleinikoff, Coulter l'a immédiatement (16 avril) transmise au général de division Gwatkin, ajoutant qu'il avait fait connaissance avec Aleinikoff "en relation avec l'action du Département sur les documents américains en langue russe" et qu'Aleinikoff travaillait "sur les mêmes lignes que M. Wolf... qui était un prisonnier évadé de Sibérie".

Auparavant, le 14 avril, Gwatkin avait envoyé un mémorandum à son homologue naval du Comité interministériel militaire canadien répétant que les internés étaient des socialistes russes disposant de "10 000 dollars fournis par les socialistes et les Allemands". Le paragraphe de conclusion précisait "D'autre part, il y a ceux qui déclarent qu'un acte d'injustice flagrant a été commis." Puis le 16 avril, le vice-amiral C. E. Kingsmill, directeur du service naval, a pris l'intervention de Gwatkin au pied de la lettre. Dans une lettre au capitaine Makins, l'officier de contrôle de la marine à Halifax, il a déclaré : "Les autorités de la Milice demandent qu'une décision quant à leur (c'est-à-dire les six Russes) sort soit prise rapidement." Une copie de ces instructions a été transmise à Gwatkin qui, à son tour, en a informé le vice-ministre des Postes, le général Coulter. Trois

---

[21] Bureau de la Guerre. NdT.

[22] Les mémorandums de Gwatkin dans les dossiers du gouvernement canadien ne sont pas signés, mais paraphés avec une marque ou un symbole indéchiffrable. La marque a été identifiée comme étant celle de Gwatkin parce qu'une lettre de Gwatkin (celle du 21 avril) portant cette marque cryptique a été reconnue.

jours plus tard, Gwatkin a fait pression. Dans un mémorandum du 20 avril au secrétaire de la marine, il écrit : "Pouvez-vous dire, s'il vous plaît, si le bureau de contrôle naval a pris une décision ou non ?"

Le même jour (20 avril), le capitaine Makins a écrit à l'amiral Kingsmill pour lui expliquer les raisons de l'expulsion de Trotsky ; il a refusé de subir des pressions pour prendre une décision, déclarant : "Je vais envoyer un câble à l'amirauté pour l'informer que les autorités de la milice demandent une décision rapide quant à leur libération. Cependant, le lendemain, le 21 avril, Gwatkin écrivit à Coulter : "Nos amis les socialistes russes doivent être libérés ; et des dispositions sont prises pour leur passage en Europe." L'ordre donné à Makins de libérer Trotsky provient de l'Amirauté, à Londres. Coulter a reconnu l'information, "qui plaira énormément à nos correspondants de New York".

Si nous pouvons, d'une part, conclure que Coulter et Gwatkin étaient intensément intéressés par la libération de Trotsky, nous ne savons pas, d'autre part, pourquoi. Il y a peu de choses dans la carrière de Coulter ou de Gwatkin qui pourraient expliquer l'envie de libérer le menchevik Léon Trotsky.

Le Dr Robert Miller Coulter était un médecin de parents écossais et irlandais, un libéral, un franc-maçon et un Odd Fellow[23]. Il a été nommé vice-maître de poste du Canada en 1897. Son seul mérite est d'avoir été délégué à la Convention de l'Union postale universelle en 1906 et délégué en Nouvelle-Zélande et en Australie en 1908 pour le projet "All Red". All Red n'avait rien à voir avec les révolutionnaires rouges ; il s'agissait seulement d'un projet de navires à vapeur rapides tout rouge c'est-à-dire tout britannique entre la Grande-Bretagne, le Canada et l'Australie.

Le Major General Willoughby Gwatkin est issu d'une longue tradition militaire britannique (Cambridge puis Staff College). Spécialiste de la mobilisation, il a servi au Canada de 1905 à 1918. Au vu des seuls documents contenus dans les dossiers canadiens, on ne peut que conclure que leur intervention en faveur de Trotsky est un mystère.

LES SERVICES DE RENSEIGNEMENT MILITAIRE CANADIENS EXAMINENT TROTSKY

Nous pouvons aborder le cas de la libération de Trotsky sous un autre angle : Le renseignement canadien. Le lieutenant-colonel John Bayne MacLean, éminent éditeur et homme d'affaires canadien, fondateur et président de la MacLean Publishing Company, à Toronto, a dirigé de nombreuses revues professionnelles canadiennes, dont le *Financial Post*. MacLean était également associé de longue date aux services de renseignement de l'armée canadienne.[24]

---

[23] Société de bienfaisance, d'entraide et de solidarité, sur le mode maçonnique du Rotary club.

[24] H.J. Morgan, *Canadian Men and Women of the Times*, 1912, 2 vol. (Toronto : W. Briggs, 1898-1912).

En 1918, le colonel MacLean a écrit pour son propre magazine *MacLean's* un article intitulé "Pourquoi avons-nous laissé partir Trotsky ? Comment le Canada a perdu une occasion d'écourter la guerre".[25] L'article contenait des informations détaillées et inhabituelles sur Léon Trotsky, bien que la dernière moitié de l'article se perde en conjectures en évoquant des sujets à peine connexes. Nous avons deux indices sur l'authenticité de l'information. Tout d'abord, le colonel MacLean était un homme intègre qui jouissait d'excellentes relations dans les services de renseignement du gouvernement canadien. Deuxièmement, les documents gouvernementaux publiés depuis par le Canada, la Grande-Bretagne et les États-Unis confirment dans une large mesure la déclaration de MacLean. Certaines déclarations de MacLean restent à confirmer, mais les informations disponibles au début des années 70 ne sont pas nécessairement incompatibles avec l'article du colonel MacLean.

L'argument initial de MacLean est que "certains politiciens ou fonctionnaires canadiens sont les principaux responsables de la prolongation de la guerre [Première Guerre mondiale], des grandes pertes en vies humaines, des blessures et des souffrances de l'hiver 1917 et des grandes campagnes de 1918".

De plus, déclare MacLean, ces personnes faisaient (en 1919) tout leur possible pour empêcher le Parlement et le peuple canadien d'être informés sur les faits en question. Les rapports officiels, y compris ceux de Sir Douglas Haig, démontrent que sans la rupture avec la Russie en 1917, la guerre aurait été terminée un an plus tôt, et que "l'homme principalement responsable de la défection de la Russie était Trotsky... agissant selon les instructions allemandes".

Qui était Trotsky ? Selon MacLean, Trotsky n'était pas russe, mais allemand. Aussi étrange que cette affirmation puisse paraître, elle coïncide avec d'autres bribes d'informations des services de renseignement : à savoir que Trotsky parlait mieux l'allemand que le russe, et qu'il était l'exécutif russe du "Bund" allemand. Selon MacLean, Trotsky avait été "ostensiblement" expulsé de Berlin en août 1914[26]; il est finalement arrivé aux États-Unis où il a organisé les révolutionnaires russes, ainsi que les révolutionnaires de l'ouest du Canada, qui "étaient en grande partie des Allemands et des Autrichiens voyageant en tant que Russes". MacLean continue :

> À l'origine, les Britanniques ont découvert, par l'intermédiaire d'associés russes, que Kerensky,[27] Lénine et quelques dirigeants de moindre importance étaient pratiquement à la solde des Allemands dès 1915 et ils ont découvert en 1916 les liens avec Trotsky qui vivait alors à New York. À partir de ce moment, il fut surveillé de près par... l'équipe de déminage. Au début de 1916, un fonctionnaire allemand s'embarqua pour New York. Des agents des services de renseignements britanniques l'accompagnaient. Il fut retenu à Halifax, mais sur leurs instructions,

---

[25] Juin 1919, p. 66a-666. La bibliothèque publique de Toronto en possède un exemplaire ; le numéro de *MacLean's dans* lequel l'article du colonel MacLean a paru n'est pas facile à trouver et un résumé est fourni ci-dessous.

[26] Voir aussi Trotsky, *My Life*, p. 236.

[27] Voir l'annexe 3.

> on lui fit parvenir de nombreuses excuses pour le retard nécessaire. Après de nombreuses manœuvres, il arriva dans un petit bureau de journal sale dans les bidonvilles et y trouva Trotsky, à qui il donna d'importantes instructions. De juin 1916 à sa remise aux Britanniques, la brigade antiterroriste de New York n'a jamais perdu le contact avec Trotsky. Ils ont découvert que son vrai nom était Braunstein et qu'il était allemand et non russe.[28]

Une telle activité allemande dans les pays neutres est confirmée dans un rapport du Département d'État (316-9-764-9) décrivant l'organisation des réfugiés russes à des fins révolutionnaires.

Poursuivant, MacLean déclare que Trotsky et quatre associés ont navigué à bord du "S.S. *Christiania" (sic), et que* le 3 avril, ils ont fait leur rapport au "Capitaine Making" *(sic)* et ont été débarqués du navire à Halifax sous la direction du Lieutenant Jones. (En fait, un groupe de neuf personnes, dont six hommes, ont été débarqués du S.S. *Kristianiafjord.* Le nom de l'officier de contrôle naval à Halifax était le capitaine O. M. Makins, R.N. Le nom de l'officier qui a intercepté le groupe de Trotsky ne figure pas dans les documents du gouvernement canadien ; Trotsky a dit qu'il s'agissait de "Machen"). Encore une fois, selon MacLean, l'argent de Trotsky venait "de sources allemandes à New York". Aussi :

> En général, l'explication donnée est que la libération a été faite à la demande de Kerensky, mais des mois auparavant, des officiers britanniques et un Canadien servant en Russie, qui pouvait parler la langue russe, avaient signalé à Londres et à Washington que Kerensky était au service de l'Allemagne.[29]

Trotsky a été libéré "à la demande de l'ambassade britannique à Washington... [qui] agissait à la demande du Département d'État américain, qui agissait pour quelqu'un d'autre." Les fonctionnaires canadiens "ont été chargés d'informer la presse que Trotsky était un citoyen américain voyageant avec un passeport américain ; que sa libération était spécialement demandée par le Département d'État de Washington". De plus, écrit MacLean, à Ottawa, "Trotsky bénéficiait d'une forte influence clandestine. Son pouvoir était si grand que des ordres ont été donnés pour lui accorder toute l'attention nécessaire."

La thèse du reportage de MacLean est, de toute évidence, que Trotsky avait des relations intimes avec l'état-major allemand et travaillait probablement pour lui. Si de telles relations ont été établies à propos de Lénine - dans la mesure où Lénine a été subventionné et où son retour en Russie a été facilité par les Allemands - il semble certain que Trotsky a été aidé de la même manière. Les fonds de 10 000 dollars de Trotsky à New York provenaient de sources

---

[28] Selon son propre témoignage, Trotsky n'est arrivé aux États-Unis qu'en janvier 1917. Le vrai nom de Trotsky était Bronstein ; il a inventé le nom "Trotsky". "Bronstein" est allemand et "Trotsky" est polonais plutôt que russe. Son prénom est généralement "Leon" ; cependant, le premier livre de Trotsky, publié à Genève, porte l'initiale "N" et non "L".

[29] Voir l'annexe 3 ; ce document a été obtenu en 1971 auprès du ministère britannique des Affaires étrangères mais était apparemment connu de MacLean.

allemandes, et un document récemment déclassifié dans les dossiers du Département d'État américain se lit comme suit :

> 9 mars 1918 à : Consul américain, Vladivostok de Polk, Secrétaire d'État par intérim, Washington D.C.
> Pour vos informations confidentielles et une attention rapide : Voici la substance du message du 12 janvier de Von Schanz de la Banque Impériale Allemande à Trotsky, citant Consentement de la banque impériale à l'appropriation par le personnel général du crédit de cinq millions de roubles pour l'envoi du commissaire adjoint de la marine Kudrisheff en Extrême-Orient.

Ce message suggère une certaine liaison entre Trotsky et les Allemands en janvier 1918, époque à laquelle Trotsky proposait une alliance avec l'Ouest. Le Département d'État ne donne pas la provenance du télégramme, mais seulement qu'il provient de l'état-major du Collège de guerre. Le Département d'État a bien considéré que le message était authentique et a agi sur la base d'une authenticité supposée. Il est conforme au thème général de l'article du colonel MacLean.

LES INTENTIONS ET LES OBJECTIFS DE TROTSKY

Par conséquent, nous pouvons en déduire la séquence d'événements suivante : Trotsky a voyagé de New York à Petrograd avec un passeport fourni par l'intervention de Woodrow Wilson, et avec l'intention déclarée de "faire avancer" la révolution. Le gouvernement britannique a été la source immédiate de la libération de Trotsky en avril 1917, mais il se peut que des "pressions" aient été exercées. Lincoln Steffens, un communiste américain, a servi de lien entre Wilson et Charles R. Crane et entre Crane et Trotsky. En outre, alors que Crane n'avait aucune position officielle, son fils Richard était l'assistant confidentiel du secrétaire d'État Robert Lansing, et Crane senior recevait des rapports rapides et détaillés sur les progrès de la révolution bolchévique. De plus, l'ambassadeur William Dodd (ambassadeur américain en Allemagne à l'époque hitlérienne) a déclaré que Crane avait joué un rôle actif dans la phase Kerensky de la révolution ; les lettres de Steffens confirment que Crane ne voyait la phase Kerensky que comme une étape d'une révolution en cours.

Le point intéressant, cependant, n'est pas tant la communication entre des personnes dissemblables comme Crane, Steffens, Trotsky et Woodrow Wilson que l'existence d'au moins un certain accord sur la procédure à suivre - c'est-à-dire que le gouvernement provisoire était considéré comme "provisoire" et que la "révolution finalisée" devait suivre.

D'autre part, l'interprétation des intentions de Trotsky doit être prudente : il était adepte du double jeu. Les documents officiels montrent clairement des actions contradictoires. Par exemple, la Division des affaires d'Extrême-Orient du Département d'État américain a reçu le 23 mars 1918 deux rapports émanant de Trotsky ; l'un est contradictoire avec l'autre. Un rapport, daté du 20 mars et provenant de Moscou, a été publié dans le journal russe *Russkoe Slovo*. Le rapport citait une interview de Trotsky dans laquelle il déclarait que toute alliance avec les États-Unis était impossible :

> La Russie des Soviétiques ne peut pas s'aligner... avec l'Amérique capitaliste, car ce serait une trahison Il est possible que les Américains cherchent un tel rapprochement avec nous, poussés par leur antagonisme envers le Japon, mais en tout cas il ne peut être question d'une alliance de notre part, de quelque nature que ce soit, avec une nation bourgeoise.[30]

L'autre rapport, également originaire de Moscou, est un message daté du 17 mars 1918, trois jours plus tôt, et de l'ambassadeur Francis : "Trotsky demande cinq officiers américains comme inspecteurs de l'armée organisée pour la défense demande aussi des hommes et du matériel pour les opérations ferroviaires."[31]

Cette demande adressée aux États-Unis est bien sûr incompatible avec le rejet de toute "alliance".

Avant de quitter Trotsky, il convient de mentionner les procès-spectacles staliniens des années 1930 et, en particulier, les accusations et le procès de 1938 contre le "bloc antisoviétique de droite et trotskiste". Ces parodies forcées du processus judiciaire, rejetées presque unanimement en Occident, peuvent éclairer les intentions de Trotsky.

Le point essentiel de l'accusation stalinienne était que les trotskistes étaient des agents rémunérés du capitalisme international. K. G. Rakovsky, un des accusés de 1938, a dit, ou a été amené à dire, "Nous étions l'avant-garde de l'agression étrangère, du fascisme international, et pas seulement en URSS mais aussi en Espagne, en Chine et dans le monde entier". Les réquisitions du "tribunal" contiennent la déclaration suivante : "Il n'y a pas un seul homme au monde qui ait apporté autant de chagrin et de malheur aux gens que Trotsky. Il est le plus vil agent du fascisme..."[32]

S'il ne s'agit peut-être que d'insultes verbales couramment échangées entre les communistes internationaux des années 1930 et 1940, il convient également de noter que les fils conducteurs de l'autoaccusation sont conformes aux preuves présentées dans ce chapitre. De plus, comme nous le verrons plus tard, Trotsky a réussi à obtenir le soutien des capitalistes internationaux, qui, soit dit en passant, étaient également des partisans de Mussolini et d'Hitler.[33]

Tant que nous considérons tous les révolutionnaires internationaux et tous les capitalistes internationaux comme des ennemis implacables les uns des autres, nous passons à côté d'un point crucial : il y a effectivement eu une certaine coopération opérationnelle entre les capitalistes internationaux, y compris les

---

[30] Fichier décimal du département d'État américain, 861.00/1351.

[31] Fichier décimal du département d'État américain, 861.00/1341.

[32] *Rapport des procédures judiciaires dans l'affaire du "Bloc de droite et de trotskistes" antisoviétique* entendue devant le Collège militaire de la Cour suprême de l'URSS (Moscou : Commissariat du peuple à la justice de l'URSS, 1938), p. 293.

[33] Voir : Thomas Lamont des Morgans a été un des premiers partisans de Mussolini.

fascistes. Et il n'y a aucune raison a priori de rejeter Trotsky en tant que membre de cette alliance.

Cette réévaluation provisoire et limitée sera mise en lumière lorsque nous examinerons l'histoire de Michael Gruzenberg, le principal agent bolchévique en Scandinavie qui, sous le pseudonyme d'Alexander Gumberg, était également conseiller confidentiel de la Chase National Bank à New York et, plus tard, de Floyd Odium de l'Atlas Corporation. Ce double rôle était connu et accepté par les Soviétiques et ses employeurs américains. L'histoire de Gruzenberg est une histoire de révolution internationale alliée au capitalisme international.

Les observations du colonel MacLean selon lesquelles Trotsky exerçait "une forte influence clandestine" et que son "pouvoir était si grand que des ordres ont été donnés qu'il doit être pris en considération" ne sont pas du tout contradictoires avec l'intervention de Coulter-Gwatkin en faveur de Trotsky ; ou, d'ailleurs, avec ces événements ultérieurs, les accusations staliniennes dans les procès-spectacles trotskistes des années 1930. Elles ne sont pas non plus incompatibles avec l'affaire Gruzenberg. D'autre part, le seul lien direct connu entre Trotsky et la banque internationale est celui de son cousin Abram Givatovzo, qui était banquier privé à Kiev avant la révolution russe et à Stockholm après la révolution. Alors que Givatovzo professait l'anti-bolchevisme, il agissait en fait au nom des Soviétiques en 1918 dans les transactions monétaires.

Est-il possible qu'une toile internationale soit tissée à partir de ces événements ? Il y a d'abord Trotsky, un révolutionnaire internationaliste russe ayant des liens avec l'Allemagne, qui suscite l'assistance de deux supposés partisans du gouvernement du prince Lvov en Russie (Aleinikoff et Wolf, des Russes résidants à New York). Ces deux personnes déclenchent l'action d'un vice-maître de poste canadien libéral, qui à son tour intervient auprès d'un général de l'armée britannique de premier plan au sein de l'état-major canadien. Tous ces liens sont vérifiables.

En bref, les allégeances ne sont pas toujours ce qu'elles sont supposées, ou ce qu'elles paraissent être. Nous pouvons cependant supputer que Trotsky, Aleinikoff, Wolf, Coulter et Gwatkin, en agissant pour un objectif commun limité, avaient également un but commun plus élevé que l'allégeance nationale ou l'étiquette politique. Il n'y a pas de preuve absolue qu'il en soit ainsi. Il ne s'agit, pour l'instant, que d'une supposition logique basée sur des faits. Une loyauté plus élevée que celle forgée par un besoin immédiat commun aurait ainsi dépassé le cadre de l'amitié entre ces hommes, bien que cela mette l'imagination à rude épreuve lorsque nous réfléchissons à une telle combinaison de solidarité transnationale. Elle peut également avoir été favorisée par d'autres motifs. Le tableau est encore incomplet.

CHAPITRE III

LÉNINE ET L'AIDE ALLEMANDE À LA RÉVOLUTION BOLCHÉVIQUE

Ce n'est que lorsque les bolcheviks ont reçu de nous un flux constant de fonds par divers canaux et sous diverses étiquettes qu'ils ont pu construire leur organe principal, la Pravda, mener une propagande énergique et étendre sensiblement la base initialement étroite de leur parti.

Von Kühlmann, ministre des Affaires étrangères,
devant le kaiser, 3 décembre 1917

En avril 1917, Lénine et un groupe de 32 révolutionnaires russes, pour la plupart bolchéviques, ont pris le train de la Suisse à travers l'Allemagne, la Suède et Petrograd, en Russie. Ils étaient en route pour rejoindre Léon Trotsky afin de "compléter la révolution". Leur transit à travers l'Allemagne a été approuvé, facilité et financé par l'état-major allemand. Le transit de Lénine vers la Russie faisait partie d'un plan approuvé par le commandement suprême allemand, apparemment pas immédiatement connu du kaiser, pour aider à la désintégration de l'armée russe et ainsi éliminer la Russie de la Première Guerre mondiale. La possibilité que les bolcheviks puissent se retourner contre l'Allemagne et l'Europe n'a pas été envisagée par l'état-major allemand. Le général Hoffman a écrit : "Nous ne connaissions ni ne prévoyions le danger que représentait pour l'humanité le voyage des bolcheviks en Russie.[34]

Au plus haut niveau, l'officier politique allemand qui a approuvé le voyage de Lénine en Russie était le chancelier Theobald von Bethmann-Hollweg, un descendant de la famille bancaire Bethmann de Francfort, qui a atteint une grande prospérité au XIXe siècle. Bethmann-Hollweg est nommé chancelier en 1909 et, en novembre 1913, il fait l'objet du premier vote de censure jamais voté par le Reichstag allemand sur un chancelier. C'est Bethmann-Hollweg qui, en 1914, a déclaré au monde entier que la garantie allemande à la Belgique n'était qu'un "bout de papier". Pourtant, sur d'autres questions de guerre - comme le recours à la guerre sous-marine sans restriction - Bethmann-Hollweg était ambivalent ; en janvier 1917, il déclara au kaiser : "Je ne peux donner à Votre Majesté ni mon accord à la guerre sous-marine sans restriction ni mon refus." En 1917, Bethmann-Hollweg avait perdu le soutien du Reichstag et avait démissionné - mais pas avant

[34] Max Hoffman, *War Diaries and Other Papers* (Londres : M. Secker, 1929), 2:177.

d'avoir approuvé le transit des révolutionnaires bolchéviques vers la Russie. Les instructions de transit de Bethmann-Hollweg passèrent par le secrétaire d'État Arthur Zimmermann - qui était immédiatement sous les ordres de Bethmann-Hollweg et qui s'occupait des détails opérationnels quotidiens avec les ministres allemands à Berne et à Copenhague - au ministre allemand à Berne au début du mois d'avril 1917. Le kaiser lui-même n'a eu connaissance du mouvement révolutionnaire qu'après le passage de Lénine en Russie.

Si Lénine lui-même ne connaissait pas la source précise du financement, il savait certainement que le gouvernement allemand fournissait certains fonds. Il existait cependant des liens intermédiaires entre le ministère allemand des Affaires étrangères et Lénine, comme le montre ce qui suit :

LE TRANSFERT DE LÉNINE EN RUSSIE EN AVRIL 1917

Décision finale	BETHMANN-HOLLWEG (Chancelier)
Intermédiaire I	ARTHUR ZIMMERMANN (Secrétaire d'État)
Intermédiaire II	BROCKDORFF-RANTZAU (Ministre allemand à Copenhague)
Intermédiaire III	ALEXANDER ISRAEL HELPHAND (alias PARVUS)
Intermédiaire IV	JACOB FURSTENBERG (alias GANETSKY)
	LENIN, en Suisse

De Berlin, Zimmermann et Bethmann-Hollweg ont communiqué avec le ministre allemand à Copenhague, Brockdorff-Rantzau. À son tour, Brockdorff-Rantzau a été en contact avec Alexander Israel Helphand (plus connu sous son pseudonyme, Parvus), qui se trouvait à Copenhague.[35] Parvus était le lien avec Jacob Furstenberg, un Polonais descendant d'une famille riche mais plus connu sous son pseudonyme, Ganetsky. Et Jacob Furstenberg était le lien immédiat avec Lénine.

Bien que le Chancelier Bethmann-Hollweg ait été l'autorité finale pour le transfert de Lénine, et bien que Lénine ait probablement été au courant des origines allemandes de l'assistance, Lénine ne peut être qualifié d'agent allemand. Le ministère allemand des Affaires étrangères a estimé que les actions probables de Lénine en Russie étaient conformes à leurs propres objectifs de dissolution de la structure du pouvoir existant en Russie. Pourtant, les deux parties avaient également des objectifs cachés : L'Allemagne voulait un accès prioritaire aux marchés d'après-guerre en Russie, et Lénine avait l'intention d'établir une dictature marxiste.

L'idée d'utiliser les révolutionnaires russes de cette manière remonte à 1915. Le 14 août de cette année-là, Brockdorff-Rantzau écrit au sous-secrétaire d'État allemand au sujet d'une conversation avec Helphand (Parvus), et recommande vivement d'employer Helphand, "un homme extraordinairement important dont je pense que nous devons utiliser les pouvoirs inhabituels pendant toute la durée de

[35] Z. A. B. Zeman et W. B. Scharlau, *The Merchant of Revolution. The Life of Alexander Israel Helphand* (Parvus), 1867-1924 (New York : Oxford University Press, 1965).

la guerre... [36]" Le rapport contenait un avertissement : "Il serait peut-être risqué de vouloir utiliser les pouvoirs situés derrière Helphand, mais ce serait certainement un aveu de notre propre faiblesse si nous devions refuser leurs services par crainte de ne pas pouvoir les diriger."[37]

Les idées de Brockdorff-Rantzau sur la direction ou le contrôle des révolutionnaires sont parallèles, comme nous le verrons, à celles des financiers de Wall Street. C'est J.P. Morgan et l'American International Corporation qui ont tenté de contrôler les révolutionnaires nationaux et étrangers aux États-Unis pour leurs propres fins.

Un document ultérieur[38] expose les conditions exigées par Lénine, dont la plus intéressante est le point numéro sept, qui permet aux "troupes russes d'entrer en Inde" ; cela suggère que Lénine avait l'intention de poursuivre le programme tsariste expansionniste. Zeman mentionne également le rôle de Max Warburg dans la création d'une maison d'édition russe et annonce un accord datant du 12 août 1916, dans lequel l'industriel allemand Stinnes accepte de contribuer à hauteur de deux millions de roubles au financement d'une maison d'édition en Russie.[39]

En conséquence, le 16 avril 1917, un train de trente-deux personnes, dont Lénine, sa femme Nadezhda Krupskaya, Grigori Zinoviev, Sokolnikov et Karl Radek, quitta la gare centrale de Berne en direction de Stockholm. Lorsque le groupe a atteint la frontière russe, seuls Fritz Plattan et Radek se sont vu refuser l'entrée en Russie. Le reste a été autorisé à entrer. Plusieurs mois plus tard, ils sont suivis par près de 200 mencheviks, dont Martov et Axelrod.

Il est à noter que Trotsky, à New York à l'époque, disposait également des fonds dont on pouvait retracer les sources allemandes. En outre, Von Kuhlmann fait allusion à l'incapacité de Lénine à élargir la base de son parti bolchévique jusqu'à ce que les Allemands lui fournissent des fonds. Trotsky était un menchevik qui n'est devenu bolchévique qu'en 1917. Cela suggère que les fonds allemands étaient peut-être liés au changement d'étiquette du parti de Trotsky.

LES DOCUMENTS SISSON

Au début de 1918, Edgar Sisson, le représentant de Petrograd du Comité américain de l'information publique, a acheté un lot de documents russes prétendant prouver que Trotsky, Lénine et les autres révolutionnaires bolchéviques étaient non seulement à la solde du gouvernement allemand, mais aussi des agents de ce dernier.

---

[36] Z. A. B. Zeman, *L'Allemagne et la révolution en Russie, 1915-1918*. Documents provenant des archives du ministère allemand des Affaires étrangères (Londres : Oxford University Press, 1958).

[37] Ibid.

[38] Ibid, p. 6, doc. 6, rapportant une conversation avec l'intermédiaire estonien Keskula.

[39] Ibid, p. 92, n. 3.

Ces documents, appelés plus tard "documents Sisson", ont été expédiés aux États-Unis dans la plus grande hâte et le plus grand secret. À Washington, D.C., ils ont été soumis au National Board for Historical Service pour authentification. Deux éminents historiens, J. Franklin Jameson et Samuel N. Harper, ont témoigné de leur authenticité. Ces historiens ont divisé les documents de Sisson en trois groupes. En ce qui concerne le groupe I, ils ont conclu :

> Nous les avons soumis avec le plus grand soin à tous les tests applicables auxquels les étudiants en histoire sont habitués et... sur la base de ces investigations, nous n'hésitons pas à déclarer que nous ne voyons aucune raison de douter de l'authenticité de ces cinquante-trois documents.[40]

Les historiens étaient moins confiants quant au matériel du groupe II. Ce groupe n'a pas été rejeté comme étant des faux, mais il a été suggéré qu'il s'agissait de copies de documents originaux. Bien que les historiens n'aient fait "aucune déclaration de confiance" sur le groupe III, ils n'étaient pas prêts à rejeter les documents comme étant de véritables faux.

Les documents Sisson ont été publiés par la commission de l'information publique, dont le président était George Creel, un ancien collaborateur du mensuel pro-bolchéviques *The Masses*. La presse américaine en général a accepté les documents comme authentiques. L'exception notable était le *New York Evening Post, qui* appartenait à l'époque à Thomas W. Lamont, un associé de la firme Morgan. Alors que seuls quelques extraits avaient été publiés, le *Post* a contesté l'authenticité de tous les documents.[41]

Nous savons maintenant que les documents de Sisson étaient presque tous des faux : seules une ou deux des petites circulaires allemandes étaient authentiques. Même un examen superficiel de l'en-tête allemand suggère que les faussaires étaient des faussaires exceptionnellement négligents qui savaient le public américain particulièrement crédule. Le texte allemand était parsemé de termes frisant le ridicule : par exemple, *Bureau* au lieu du mot allemand *Büro ; Central* à la place du *Zentral allemand ;* etc.

Le fait que ces documents soient des faux est la conclusion d'une étude exhaustive de George Kennan[42] et d'études réalisées dans les années 1920 par le gouvernement britannique. Certains documents étaient basés sur des informations authentiques et, comme l'observe Kennan, ceux qui les ont falsifiés ont certainement eu accès à des informations d'une qualité inhabituelle. Par exemple, les documents 1, 54, 61 et 67 mentionnent que la Nya Banken à Stockholm a servi d'intermédiaire pour les fonds bolchéviques en provenance d'Allemagne. Ce rôle

[40] États-Unis, Committee on Public Information, *The German-Bolshevik Conspiracy,* War Information Series, no. 20, octobre 1918.

[41] *New York Evening Post,* 16-18 septembre, 21 ; 4 octobre 1918. Il est également intéressant, mais non concluant, que les bolcheviks aient eux aussi mis en doute l'authenticité des documents.

[42] George F. Kennan, "The Sisson Documents", *Journal of Modern History* 27-28 (1955-56) : 130-154.

a été confirmé par des sources plus fiables. Les documents 54, 63 et 64 mentionnent Furstenberg comme le banquier intermédiaire entre les Allemands et les Bolchéviques ; le nom de Furstenberg figure ailleurs dans des documents authentiques. Le document 54 de Sisson mentionne Olof Aschberg, et Olof Aschberg, selon ses propres déclarations, était le "banquier bolchévique". En 1917, Aschberg était le directeur de Nya Banken. D'autres documents de la série Sisson énumèrent des noms et des institutions, comme la Naptha-Industrial Bank allemande, la Disconto Gesellschaft, et Max Warburg, le banquier de Hambourg, mais les preuves tangibles sont plus difficiles à trouver. En général, les documents Sisson, bien qu'ils soient eux-mêmes des faux, sont néanmoins basés en partie sur des informations généralement authentiques.

Un aspect déroutant à la lumière de l'histoire de ce livre est que les documents ont été transmis à Edgar Sisson par Alexander Gumberg (alias Berg, de son vrai nom Michael Gruzenberg), l'agent bolchévique en Scandinavie et plus tard assistant confidentiel de la Chase National Bank et de Floyd Odium de la Atlas Corporation. Les bolchéviques, en revanche, ont répudié avec vigueur les documents de Sisson. Tout comme John Reed, le représentant américain à la direction de la troisième Internationale et dont le chèque de paie provenait du magazine *Metropolitan,* qui appartenait à J.P. Morgan.[43] Tout comme Thomas Lamont, l'associé de Morgan qui possédait le *New York Evening Post.* Il y a plusieurs explications possibles. Il est probable que les liens entre les intérêts de Morgan à New York et des agents tels que John Reed et Alexander Gumberg étaient très souples. Il pourrait s'agir *d'*une manœuvre de Gumberg visant à discréditer Sisson et Creel en mettant en circulation de faux documents ; ou peut-être Gumberg travaillait-il pour son propre intérêt.

Les documents de Sisson "prouvent" l'implication exclusive de l'Allemagne avec les bolcheviks. Ils ont également été utilisés pour "prouver" une théorie de conspiration judéo-bolchévique sur le modèle de celle des Protocoles de Sion. En 1918, le gouvernement américain a voulu unir l'opinion américaine derrière une guerre impopulaire avec l'Allemagne, et les Documents de Sisson ont "prouvé" de façon spectaculaire la complicité exclusive de l'Allemagne avec les Bolcheviks. Les documents ont également servi d'écran de fumée contre la connaissance par le public des événements qui seront décrits dans ce livre.

BRAS DE FER À WASHINGTON[44]

Un examen des documents du dossier décimal du Département d'État suggère que le Département d'État et l'ambassadeur Francis à Petrograd étaient assez bien informés des intentions et des progrès du mouvement bolchévique. Au cours de l'été 1917, par exemple, le Département d'État a voulu empêcher le départ des

---

[43] John Reed, *The Sisson Documents* (New York : Liberator Publishing, s.d.).

[44] Cette partie est basée sur la section 861.00 du fichier décimal du Département d'État américain, également disponible sous forme de liste 10 et 11 du microfilm 316 des Archives nationales.

États-Unis des "personnes nuisibles" (c'est-à-dire des révolutionnaires russes en transit) mais n'a pas pu le faire parce qu'ils utilisaient de nouveaux passeports russes et américains. Les préparatifs de la révolution bolchévique elle-même étaient bien connus au moins six semaines avant qu'elle ne se produise. Un rapport des dossiers du Département d'État indique, en ce qui concerne les forces de Kerensky, qu'il était "douteux que le gouvernement... puisse réprimer l'épidémie". La désintégration du gouvernement Kerensky a été signalée tout au long des mois de septembre et octobre, ainsi que les préparatifs bolchéviques en vue d'un coup d'État. Le gouvernement britannique a averti les résidents britanniques en Russie de partir au moins six semaines avant la phase bolchévique de la révolution.

Le premier rapport complet sur les événements de début novembre est parvenu à Washington le 9 décembre 1917. Ce rapport décrivait la nature discrète de la révolution elle-même, mentionnait que le général William V. Judson avait effectué une visite non autorisée à Trotsky, et signalait la présence d'Allemands à Smolny - le quartier général soviétique.

Le 28 novembre 1917, le président Woodrow Wilson ordonne de ne pas interférer avec la révolution bolchévique. Cette instruction répondait apparemment à une demande de l'ambassadeur Francis pour une conférence des Alliés, à laquelle la Grande-Bretagne avait déjà donné son accord. Le Département d'État a fait valoir qu'une telle conférence n'était pas pratique. Il y eut des discussions à Paris entre les Alliés et le colonel Edward M. House, qui les rapporta à Woodrow Wilson comme étant "des discussions longues et fréquentes au sujet de la Russie". Concernant une telle conférence, House déclara que l'Angleterre était "passivement disposée", la France "indifféremment contre" et l'Italie "activement disposée". Peu après, Woodrow Wilson approuva un câble rédigé par le secrétaire d'État Robert Lansing, qui apportait une aide financière au mouvement Kaledin (12 décembre 1917). Des rumeurs circulent également à Washington, selon lesquelles "des monarchistes travaillent avec les bolcheviks et ces derniers sont soutenus par divers événements et circonstances" ; le gouvernement Smolny est absolument sous le contrôle de l'état-major allemand ; et des rumeurs circulent ailleurs, selon lesquelles "beaucoup ou la plupart d'entre eux [c'est-à-dire les bolcheviks] viennent d'Amérique".

En décembre, le général Judson rendit à nouveau visite à Trotsky ; cette visite fut considérée comme un pas vers la reconnaissance par les États-Unis, bien qu'un rapport daté du 5 février 1918, de l'ambassadeur Francis à Washington, recommandait de ne pas la reconnaître. Un mémorandum émanant de Basil Miles à Washington soutenait que "nous devrions traiter avec toutes les autorités de Russie, y compris les bolcheviks". Et le 15 février 1918, le Département d'État a envoyé un câble à l'ambassadeur Francis à Petrograd, déclarant que le "Département souhaite que vous gardiez progressivement des contacts plus étroits et informels avec les autorités bolchéviques en utilisant des canaux qui éviteront toute reconnaissance officielle".

Le lendemain, le secrétaire d'État Lansing a transmis à l'ambassadeur de France à Washington, J. J. Jusserand, les informations suivantes "Il est déconseillé de prendre toute mesure qui pourrait contrarier à l'heure actuelle l'un des divers éléments du peuple qui contrôle maintenant le pouvoir en Russie... "[45]

Le 20 février, l'ambassadeur Francis a envoyé un câble à Washington pour signaler la fin prochaine du gouvernement bolchévique. Deux semaines plus tard, le 7 mars 1918, Arthur Bullard rapporta au Colonel House que l'argent allemand subventionnait les Bolcheviks et que cette subvention était plus importante que ce que l'on pensait. Arthur Bullard (du Comité américain de l'information publique) a fait valoir "nous devrions être prêts à aider tout gouvernement national honnête. Mais les hommes, l'argent ou le matériel envoyés aux dirigeants actuels de la Russie seront utilisés contre les Russes au moins autant que contre les Allemands".[46]

Un autre message de Bullard au colonel House a suivi : "Je déconseille vivement d'apporter une aide matérielle à l'actuel gouvernement russe. Des éléments sinistres semblent prendre le contrôle des Soviets."

Mais certaines forces contraires semblaient être à la manœuvre. Dès le 28 novembre 1917, le colonel House a envoyé un télégramme au président Woodrow Wilson depuis Paris pour lui dire qu'il était "extrêmement important" que les commentaires des journaux américains préconisant que "la Russie soit traitée comme un ennemi" soient "supprimés". Puis le mois suivant, William Franklin Sands, secrétaire exécutif de l'American International Corporation contrôlée par Morgan et ami de Basil Miles mentionné précédemment, a soumis un mémorandum qui décrivait Lénine et Trotsky comme faisant appel aux masses et qui exhortait les États-Unis à reconnaître la Russie. Même le socialiste américain Walling s'est plaint au Département d'État de l'attitude pro-soviétique de George Creel (du Comité américain de l'information publique), Herbert Swope et William Boyce Thompson (de la Banque de Réserve Fédérale de New York).

Le 17 décembre 1917, un journal moscovite publie un article sur l'attaque du colonel de la Croix-Rouge Raymond Robins et Thompson, alléguant un lien entre la révolution russe et les banquiers américains :

> Pourquoi s'intéressent-ils tant aux idées des Lumières ? Pourquoi l'argent a-t-il été donné aux révolutionnaires socialistes et non aux démocrates constitutionnels ? On pourrait supposer que ces derniers sont plus proches et plus chers au cœur des banquiers.

L'article poursuit en affirmant que cela est dû au fait que les capitaux américains considèrent la Russie comme un marché d'avenir et veulent donc y prendre pied. L'argent a été donné aux révolutionnaires parce que :

---

[45] Fichier décimal du département d'État américain, 861.00/1117a. Le même message a été transmis à l'ambassadeur italien.

[46] Voir les articles d'Arthur Bullard à l'université de Princeton.

> les travailleurs et les paysans arriérés font confiance aux révolutionnaires sociaux. Au moment où l'argent a été passé, les révolutionnaires sociaux étaient au pouvoir et il était supposé qu'ils resteraient au contrôle en Russie pendant un certain temps.

Un autre rapport, daté du 12 décembre 1917 et relatif à Raymond Robins, détaille la "négociation avec un groupe de banquiers américains de la mission de la Croix-Rouge américaine" ; la "négociation" portait sur un paiement de deux millions de dollars. Le 22 janvier 1918, Robert L Owen, président de la Commission du Sénat américain sur les banques et la monnaie et lié aux intérêts de Wall Street, envoie une lettre à Woodrow Wilson recommandant la reconnaissance de facto de la Russie, l'autorisation d'un chargement de marchandises dont la Russie a un besoin urgent, la nomination de représentants en Russie pour contrebalancer l'influence allemande et l'installation d'un contingent militaire.

Cette approche a été constamment soutenue par Raymond Robins en Russie. Par exemple, le 15 février 1918, un câble de Robins de Petrograd à Davison de la Croix-Rouge à Washington (et à transmettre à William Boyce Thompson) argumentait qu'il fallait soutenir l'autorité bolchévique le plus longtemps possible, et que la nouvelle Russie révolutionnaire se tournerait vers les États-Unis, car elle avait "rompu avec l'impérialisme allemand". Selon Robins, les bolcheviks voulaient l'aide et la coopération des États-Unis ainsi que la réorganisation des chemins de fer, car "par une assistance généreuse et des conseils techniques pour la réorganisation du commerce et de l'industrie, l'Amérique pourrait exclure totalement le commerce allemand pendant le reste de la guerre".

En bref, la lutte acharnée à Washington reflète une lutte entre, d'une part, les diplomates de la vieille école (comme l'ambassadeur Francis) et les fonctionnaires de niveau inférieur du ministère, et, d'autre part, les financiers comme Robins, Thompson et Sands avec des alliés comme Lansing et Miles au département d'État et le sénateur Owen au Congrès.

CHAPITRE IV

WALL STREET ET LA RÉVOLUTION MONDIALE

Ce sur quoi vous, les gauchistes, et nous, qui avons des points de vue opposés, divergeons, ce n'est pas tant la fin que les moyens, pas tant ce qui devrait être réalisé que la manière dont cela devrait, et peut, être réalisé...

Otto H. Kahn, directeur de l'American International Corp. et partenaire de Kuhn, Loeb & Co. s'adressant à la Ligue pour la Démocratie Industrielle, à New York, le 30 décembre 1924

Avant la Première Guerre mondiale, la structure financière et commerciale des États-Unis était dominée par deux conglomérats : Standard Oil, ou l'entreprise Rockefeller, et le complexe industriel Morgan - sociétés financières et de transport. Le jeu d'alliances entre Rockefeller et Morgan dominait non seulement Wall Street mais, par le biais de postes de directions imbriquées, la quasi-totalité du tissu économique des États-Unis.[47] Les intérêts de Rockefeller monopolisaient le pétrole et les industries connexes, et contrôlaient le trust du cuivre, le trust des fonderies et le gigantesque trust du tabac, en plus d'avoir une influence sur certaines propriétés de Morgan telles que l'U.S. Steel Corporation ainsi que sur des centaines de petits trusts industriels, des opérations de service public, des chemins de fer et des institutions bancaires. La National City Bank était la plus grande des banques gérant les intérêts de la Standard Oil-Rockefeller, mais le contrôle financier s'étendait à la United States Trust Company et à la Hanover National Bank ainsi qu'aux grandes compagnies d'assurance-vie - Equitable Life et Mutual of New York.

Les grandes entreprises de Morgan étaient dans l'acier, le transport maritime et l'industrie électrique ; elles comprenaient General Electric, le trust du caoutchouc et les chemins de fer. Comme Rockefeller, Morgan contrôlait des sociétés financières - la National Bank of Commerce et la Chase National Bank, la New York Life Insurance et la Guaranty Trust Company. Les noms J.P. Morgan et Guaranty Trust Company reviennent souvent dans ce livre. Au début du XXe siècle, la Guaranty Trust Company était dominée par les intérêts de Harriman. Lorsque l'aîné des Harriman (Edward Henry) est mort en 1909, Morgan et ses associés ont acheté la Guaranty Trust ainsi que la Mutual Life et la New York Life.

[47] John Moody, *The Truth about the Trusts* (New York : Moody Publishing, 1904).

En 1919, Morgan a également pris le contrôle de Equitable Life, et la Guaranty Trust Company a absorbé six autres sociétés de moindre importance. Ainsi, à la fin de la Première Guerre mondiale, le Guaranty Trust et le Bankers Trust étaient respectivement les premier et deuxième plus grands conglomérats des États-Unis, tous deux dominés par les intérêts de Morgan.[48]

Les financiers américains associés à ces groupes ont participé à des révolutions avant même 1917. L'intervention du cabinet d'avocats Sullivan & Cromwell de Wall Street dans la controverse du canal de Panama est enregistrée lors des audiences du Congrès en 1913. L'épisode est résumé par le membre du Congrès Rainey :

> Je soutiens que les représentants de ce gouvernement [États-Unis] ont rendu possible la révolution sur l'isthme de Panama. Sans l'intervention de ce gouvernement, une révolution n'aurait pas pu aboutir, et je soutiens que ce gouvernement a violé le traité de 1846. Je serai en mesure de prouver que la déclaration d'indépendance qui a été promulguée au Panama le 3 novembre 1903 a été conçue ici même à New York et apportée là-bas - préparée dans le bureau de Wilson (sic) Nelson Cromwell[49].

Le député Rainey a poursuivi en déclarant que seuls dix ou douze des plus grands révolutionnaires panaméens, plus "les officiers de la Panama Railroad & Steamship Co. qui étaient sous le contrôle de William Nelson Cromwell, de New York, et les fonctionnaires du département d'État à Washington", étaient au courant de la révolution imminente.[50] Le but de la révolution était de priver la Colombie, dont le Panama faisait alors partie, de 40 millions de dollars de revenus et d'acquérir le contrôle du canal de Panama.

L'exemple le mieux documenté de l'intervention de Wall Street dans la révolution est l'opération d'un cabinet d'affaires new-yorkais dans la révolution chinoise de 1912, qui était dirigée par Sun Yat-sen. Bien que les gains finaux de cette institution restent flous, l'intention et le rôle du groupe de financement new-yorkais sont entièrement documentés jusqu'aux montants d'argent, aux informations sur les sociétés secrètes chinoises affiliées et aux listes d'expédition des armements à acheter. Le consortium de banquiers new-yorkais en faveur de la révolution menée par Sun Yat-sen comprenait Charles B. Hill, un avocat du cabinet Hunt, Hill & Betts. En 1912, le cabinet était situé au 165 Broadway, New York, mais en 1917, il a déménagé au 120 Broadway (voir le chapitre 8 pour l'importance de cette adresse). Charles B. Hill était directeur de plusieurs filiales

---

[48] La J. P. Morgan Company a été fondée à Londres sous le nom de George Peabody and Co. en 1838. Elle n'a été constituée en société que le 21 mars 1940. La société a cessé d'exister en avril 1954 lorsqu'elle a fusionné avec la Guaranty Trust Company, alors sa plus importante filiale de banque commerciale, et est aujourd'hui connue sous le nom de Morgan Guarantee Trust Company of New York.

[49] États-Unis, Chambre, Commission des affaires étrangères, *L'histoire du Panama,* Audiences sur la résolution Rainey, 1913. p. 53.

[50] Ibid, p. 60.

de Westinghouse, dont Bryant Electric, Perkins Electric Switch et Westinghouse Lamp - toutes affiliées à Westinghouse Electric dont le bureau de New York était également situé au 120 Broadway. Charles R. Crane, organisateur des filiales de Westinghouse en Russie, a joué un rôle parfaitement identifié dans les première et deuxième phases de la révolution bolchévique.

Le travail du syndicat Hill de 1910 en Chine est consigné dans les papiers de Laurence Boothe à la Hoover Institution.[51] Ces documents contiennent plus de 110 articles connexes, y compris des lettres de Sun Yat-sen à l'attention de ses bailleurs de fonds américains. En échange de son soutien financier, Sun Yat-sen a promis au consortium Hill des concessions ferroviaires, bancaires et commerciales dans la nouvelle Chine révolutionnaire.

Un autre cas de révolution soutenu par les institutions financières de New York concerne celui du Mexique en 1915-16. Von Rintelen, un agent d'espionnage allemand aux États-Unis[52], a été accusé lors de son procès de mai 1917 à New York de tenter d'"ingérer" les États-Unis dans les affaires du Mexique et du Japon afin de détourner les munitions qui étaient alors destinées aux Alliés en Europe.[53] Le paiement des munitions qui ont été expédiées depuis les États-Unis au révolutionnaire mexicain Pancho Villa, a été effectué par l'intermédiaire de la Guaranty Trust Company. Le conseiller de Von Rintelen, Sommerfeld, a payé 380 000 dollars via la Guaranty Trust et la Mississippi Valley Trust Company à la Western Cartridge Company d'Alton, dans l'Illinois, pour les munitions expédiées à El Paso, pour être ensuite acheminées à Villa. C'était au milieu de l'année 1915. Le 10 janvier 1916, Villa assassine dix-sept mineurs américains à Santa Isabel et le 9 mars 1916, Villa effectue un raid sur Columbus, au Nouveau-Mexique, et tue dix-huit autres Américains.

L'implication de Wall Street dans ces raids à la frontière mexicaine a fait l'objet d'une lettre (6 octobre 1916) de Lincoln Steffens, un communiste américain, au colonel House, un "conseiller" de Woodrow Wilson :

> Mon cher colonel House :
> Juste avant mon départ de New York lundi dernier, on m'a dit de façon convaincante que "Wall Street" avait achevé les préparatifs d'un nouveau raid de bandits mexicains aux États-Unis : un raid si atroce et si bien planifié qu'il permettrait d'influer sur le cours des élections.[54]

Une fois au pouvoir au Mexique, le gouvernement Carranza a acheté des armes supplémentaires aux États-Unis. L'American Gun Company a passé un contrat

---

[51] Stanford, Calif. Voir également le *Los Angeles Times*, 13 octobre 1966.

[52] Plus tard codirecteur avec Hjalmar Schacht (le banquier d'Hitler) et Emil Wittenberg, de la Nationalbank für Deutschland.

[53] États-Unis, Sénat, commission des relations étrangères, *enquête sur les affaires mexicaines*, 1920.

[54] Lincoln Steffens, *The Letters of Lincoln Steffens* (New York : Harcourt, Brace, 1941, p. 386)

pour expédier 5000 Mauser et une licence d'expédition a été délivrée par le War Trade Board pour 15 000 fusils et 15 000 000 de munitions. L'ambassadeur américain au Mexique, Fletcher, "a catégoriquement refusé de recommander ou de sanctionner l'envoi de toute munition, fusil, etc. à Carranza".[55] Cependant, l'intervention du secrétaire d'État Robert Lansing a permis de réduire ce délai à un retard temporaire, et "en peu de temps... [l'American Gun Company] sera autorisée à effectuer l'expédition et à livrer."[56]

Les raids des forces de Villa et de Carranza sur les États-Unis ont été rapportés par le *New York Times* et désignés comme la "Révolution du Texas" (une sorte de répétition de la révolution bolchévique) et ont été entrepris conjointement par les Allemands et les Bolcheviks. Le témoignage de John A. Walls, procureur du district de Brownsville, Texas, devant le Comité d'automne 1919 a fourni des preuves documentaires du lien entre les intérêts bolchéviques aux États-Unis, l'activité allemande et les forces de Carranza au Mexique.[57] Par conséquent, le gouvernement Carranza, le premier au monde à disposer d'une constitution de type soviétique (rédigée par des trotskistes), était un gouvernement soutenu par Wall Street. La révolution de Carranza n'aurait probablement pas pu réussir sans les munitions américaines et Carranza ne serait pas resté au pouvoir aussi longtemps sans l'aide américaine.[58]

Une intervention similaire dans la révolution bolchévique de 1917 en Russie tourne autour du banquier et intermédiaire suédois Olof Aschberg. Logiquement, l'histoire commence par des prêts tsaristes prérévolutionnaires accordés par les grandes maisons bancaires de Wall Street.

BANQUIERS AMÉRICAINS ET PRÊTS TSARISTES

En août 1914, l'Europe est entrée en guerre. En vertu du droit international, les pays neutres (et les États-Unis l'étaient jusqu'en avril 1917) ne pouvaient pas contracter de prêts envers les pays belligérants. C'était une question de droit aussi bien que de moralité.

Lorsque la maison Morgan a émis des prêts de guerre pour la Grande-Bretagne et la France en 1915, J.P. Morgan a fait valoir qu'il ne s'agissait pas du tout de prêts de guerre mais simplement d'un moyen de faciliter le commerce international. Une telle distinction avait en effet été faite de manière détaillée par le président Wilson en octobre 1914 ; il expliqua que la vente d'obligations aux États-Unis pour des gouvernements étrangers était en fait un prêt d'épargne aux gouvernements belligérants et ne finançait pas la guerre. D'autre part, l'acceptation de bons du Trésor ou d'autres effets de dette en paiement d'articles

[55] États-Unis, Sénat, Commission des relations étrangères, *Investigation of Mexican Affairs*, 1920, pts. 2, 18, p. 681.

[56] Ibid.

[57] *New York Times*, 23 janvier 1919.

[58] États-Unis, Sénat, Commission des relations étrangères, op. cit. p. 795-96.

n'était qu'un moyen de faciliter le commerce et non de financer un effort de guerre.[59]

Des documents dans les dossiers du Département d'État démontrent que la National City Bank, contrôlée par les intérêts de Stillman et Rockefeller, et le Guaranty Trust, contrôlé par les intérêts de Morgan, ont conjointement levé des prêts substantiels pour la Russie belligérante avant l'entrée en guerre des États-Unis, et que ces prêts ont été levés alors que le Département d'État a fait remarquer à ces entreprises qu'ils étaient contraires au droit international. En outre, les négociations pour les prêts ont été entreprises par le biais des moyens de communication officiels du gouvernement américain sous le couvert du "Green Cipher"[60] décidé par le Département d'État. Vous trouverez ci-dessous des extraits des câbles du Département d'État qui permettront d'étayer le dossier.

Le 94 mai 1916, l'ambassadeur Francis à Petrograd envoie le câble suivant au Département d'État à Washington pour qu'il soit transmis à Frank Arthur Vanderlip, alors président de la National City Bank à New York. Le câble a été envoyé en Green Cipher et a été chiffré et déchiffré par les agents du Département d'État américain à Petrograd et à Washington aux frais des contribuables (dossier 861.51/110).

> 563, mai 94, 13 heures
> Pour la Vanderlip National City Bank New York. Cinq. Nos avis précédents ont renforcé le crédit. Nous approuvons le plan câblé en tant qu'investissement sûr plus une spéculation très attrayante en roubles. En raison de la garantie du taux de change avons placé le taux un peu au-dessus du marché actuel. En raison de l'opinion défavorable générée par un long retard sur leur propre responsabilité avons offert de souscrire vingt-cinq millions de dollars. Nous pensons qu'une grande partie du tout devrait être conservée par la banque et les institutions alliées. En ce qui concerne la clause de respect, les cautionnements douaniers deviennent un privilège pratique sur plus de cent cinquante millions de dollars par an, ce qui constitue une sécurité absolue et garantit le marché même en cas de défaut. Nous considérons que l'option de trois [ans ?] sur les obligations est très précieuse et c'est pourquoi le montant du crédit en roubles devrait être augmenté par groupe ou par distribution à des amis proches. American International devrait prendre le bloc et nous informerions le gouvernement. Un groupe de réflexion devrait être formé immédiatement pour prendre et émettre des obligations... il devrait obtenir une garantie de coopération totale. Je vous suggère de voir Jack personnellement, de faire tout ce qui est en votre pouvoir pour les faire fonctionner, sinon, coopérez avec la garantie d'un nouveau groupe. Les opportunités ici au cours des dix prochaines années sont très grandes, grâce au financement public et industriel, et si cette transaction est conclue, il faudra sans aucun doute la mettre en place. Dans votre réponse, gardez à l'esprit la situation du câble.

[59] États-Unis, Sénat, Audiences devant le Comité spécial chargé d'enquêter sur l'industrie des munitions, 73-74e Cong. 1934-37, pt. 25, p. 76-66.

[60] Le Code Vert, promulgué par le State Department à partir de 1910.

MacRoberts Rich à Francis, ambassadeur Américain[61]

Il y a plusieurs points à noter à propos du câble ci-dessus pour comprendre l'histoire qui suit. Tout d'abord, notez la référence à American International Corporation, une société de Morgan, une référence qui revient sans cesse dans cette histoire. Deuxièmement, "garantie" fait référence à la Guaranty Trust Company. Troisièmement, "MacRoberts" est Samuel MacRoberts, vice-président et directeur exécutif de la National City Bank.

Le 24 mai 1916, l'ambassadeur Francis a télégraphié un message de Rolph Marsh du Guaranty Trust à Petrograd au Guaranty Trust à New York, toujours dans le cadre du Green Cipher spécial et en utilisant de nouveau les installations du Département d'État. Ce câble se lit comme suit :

> 565, 24 mai, 18 heures
> pour la Guaranty Trust Company New York : Trois.
> Olof et soi-même considèrent que la nouvelle proposition prend soin d'Olof et aidera plutôt que de nuire à votre prestige. Une telle coopération est nécessaire si l'on veut accomplir de grandes choses ici. Vous devez absolument vous arranger avec la ville pour envisager et agir conjointement dans toutes les grandes propositions. Les avantages décidés pour les deux empêchent de jouer l'un contre l'autre. Les représentants de la ville souhaitent ici (par écrit) une telle coopération. La proposition à l'étude élimine notre option de crédit au nom, mais nous considérons tous deux le crédit en roubles avec l'option d'obligation dans les propositions. Le deuxième paragraphe offre une merveilleuse opportunité de profit, nous vous recommandons vivement de l'accepter. Veuillez m'envoyer un câble me donnant pleine autorité pour agir en relation avec la ville. Considérez notre proposition divertissante comme une situation satisfaisante pour nous et nous permet de faire de grandes choses. Encore une fois, je vous recommande vivement d'accepter un crédit de 25 millions de roubles. Pas de perte possible et des avantages spéculatifs décisifs. Recommandez encore une fois d'avoir le vice-président sur le terrain. L'effet sera décidément bon. L'avocat résident n'a pas le même prestige et le même poids. Cela passe par l'ambassade par une réponse codée de la même manière. Voir le câble sur les possibilités.
>
> Rolph Marsh. Francis, ambassadeur américain
> Note: — Message d'entrée en code vert. SALLE TÉLÉGRAPHIQUE[62]

"Olof" dans le câble était Olof Aschberg, banquier suédois et directeur de la Nya Banken à Stockholm. Aschberg s'était rendu à New York en 1915 pour s'entretenir avec la firme Morgan au sujet de ces prêts russes. En 1916, il se trouvait à Petrograd avec Rolph Marsh du Guaranty Trust et Samuel MacRoberts et Rich de la National City Bank (désignée comme "City" dans le câble) pour arranger des prêts pour le consortium Morgan-Rockefeller. L'année suivante, Aschberg, comme nous le verrons plus tard, sera connu sous le nom de "banquier

[61] Fichier décimal du Département d'État américain, 861.51/110 (316-116-682).

[62] Fichier décimal du Département d'État américain, 861.51/112.

bolchévique", et ses propres mémoires reproduisent les preuves de son droit au titre.

Les dossiers du Département d'État contiennent également une série de câbles entre l'ambassadeur Francis, le secrétaire d'État par intérim Frank Polk et le secrétaire d'État Robert Lansing concernant la légalité et l'opportunité de transmettre des câbles de la National City Bank et du Guaranty Trust aux frais de l'État. Le 25 mai 1916, l'ambassadeur Francis a envoyé les câbles suivants à Washington et s'est référé aux deux câbles précédents :

> 569, 25 mai, 13 heures
> Mes télégrammes 563 et 565 du 24 mai sont envoyés aux représentants locaux des institutions auxquelles ils s'adressent dans l'espoir de faciliter un prêt qui augmenterait largement le commerce international et bénéficierait grandement [aux relations diplomatiques ?] Les perspectives de succès sont prometteuses. Les représentants de Petrograd considèrent les conditions soumises comme très satisfaisantes mais craignent que ces représentations auprès de leurs institutions n'empêchent l'octroi de prêts à la consommation si le gouvernement ici présent prenait connaissance de ces propositions.
> Francis, ambassadeur américain.[63]

La raison fondamentale citée par Francis pour faciliter les câbles est "l'espoir de faciliter un prêt qui augmenterait largement le commerce international". La transmission de messages commerciaux utilisant les installations du Département d'État avait été interdite et, le 1er juin 1916, Polk a envoyé un câble à Francis :

> 842
> Compte tenu de la réglementation du ministère contenue dans sa circulaire d'instruction télégraphique du 15 mars[64] 1915 (cessation de l'acheminement des messages commerciaux), veuillez expliquer pourquoi les messages de vos 563, 565 et 575 doivent être communiqués.
> Ci-après, veuillez suivre attentivement les instructions du ministère.
> Agir. Polk
> 861.51/112/110

Puis, le 8 juin 1916, le secrétaire d'État Lansing a étendu l'interdiction et a clairement déclaré que les prêts proposés étaient illégaux :

> 860 Votre 563, 565, 24 mai, g : 569 25.1 pm Avant de délivrer des messages à Vanderlip et Guaranty Trust Company, je dois m'enquérir s'ils font référence à des prêts du gouvernement russe de quelque nature que ce soit. Si c'est le cas, je regrette que le ministère ne puisse pas prendre parti à leur transmission, car une telle action le soumettrait à des critiques justifiées en raison de la participation de ce gouvernement à une opération de prêt par un belligérant dans le but de poursuivre ses opérations hostiles. Une telle participation est contraire à la règle acceptée du

[63] Fichier décimal du Département d'État américain, 861.51/111.

[64] Écrit à la main entre parenthèses.

droit international selon laquelle les gouvernements neutres ne doivent pas prêter leur concours à l'obtention de prêts de guerre par des belligérants.

La dernière ligne du câble de Lansing, telle qu'elle a été écrite, n'a pas été transmise à Petrograd. La ligne se lisait ainsi : "Des dispositions ne peuvent-elles pas être prises pour envoyer ces messages par les canaux russes ?"

Comment pouvons-nous évaluer ces câbles et les parties concernées ?

Il est clair que les intérêts de Morgan-Rockefeller n'étaient pas entravés par le respect du droit international. Il y a une intention évidente dans ces câbles de fournir des prêts aux belligérants. Ces entreprises n'ont pas hésité à utiliser les installations du Département d'État pour mener les négociations. En outre, malgré les protestations, le Département d'État a permis aux messages de passer. Enfin, et ce qui est le plus intéressant pour les événements ultérieurs, Olof Aschberg, le banquier suédois, a été un participant et un intermédiaire de premier plan dans les négociations au nom de Guaranty Trust. Examinons donc de plus près le cas d'Olof Aschberg.

OLOF ASCHBERG EST À NEW YORK EN 1916

Olof Aschberg, le "banquier bolchévique" (ou "Bankier der Weltrevolution", comme on l'a appelé dans la presse allemande), était propriétaire de la Nya Banken, fondée en 1912 à Stockholm. Parmi ses codirecteurs figuraient des membres éminents de coopératives suédoises et des socialistes suédois, dont G. W. Dahl, K. G. Rosling et C. Gerhard Magnusson.[65] En 1918, la Nya Banken est placée sur la liste noire des Alliés pour ses opérations financières au profit de l'Allemagne. En réponse à cette liste noire, la Nya Banken changea de nom pour devenir Svensk Ekonomiebolaget. La banque est restée sous le contrôle d'Aschberg, qui en était le principal propriétaire. L'agent de la banque à Londres était la British Bank of North Commerce, dont le président était le comte Grey, ancien associé de Cecil Rhodes. Parmi les autres associés d'Aschberg, on trouve Krassin, qui, jusqu'à la révolution bolchévique (où il changea de couleur pour devenir un bolchévique de premier plan), était le directeur russe de Siemens-Schukert à Petrograd ; Carl Furstenberg, ministre des finances du premier gouvernement bolchévique ; et Max May, vice-président chargé des opérations à l'étranger pour le Guaranty Trust of New York. Olof Aschberg avait une telle estime pour Max May qu'une photo de May est incluse dans le livre d'Aschberg.[66]

Durant l'été 1916, Olof Aschberg était à New York pour représenter la Nya Banken auprès de Pierre Bark, le ministre tsariste des finances. Selon le *New York Times* (4 août 1916), la principale activité d'Aschberg à New York consistait à

---

[65] Olof Aschberg, *En Vandrande Jude Frän Glasbruksgatan* (Stockholm : Albert Bonniers Förlag, n.d.), pp. 98-99, qui est inclus dans *Memoarer (*Stockholm : Albert Bonniers Förlag, 1946). Voir également *Gästboken* (Stockholm : Tidens Förlag, 1955) pour d'autres informations sur Aschberg.

[66] Aschberg, p. 123.

négocier un prêt de 50 millions de dollars pour la Russie avec un groupe bancaire américain dirigé par la National City Bank de Stillman. Cette affaire a été conclue le 5 juin 1916 ; il en est résulté un crédit russe de 50 millions de dollars à New York au taux d'intérêt annuel de $7^{1/2}$% par an, et un crédit correspondant de 150 millions de roubles pour le groupe de la NCB en Russie. Le syndicat new-yorkais a ensuite fait volte-face et a émis des certificats à $6^{1/2}$% en son nom propre sur le marché américain pour un montant de 50 millions de dollars. Ainsi, le groupe NCB a réalisé un bénéfice sur le prêt de 50 millions de dollars à la Russie, l'a fait entrer sur le marché américain pour un autre bénéfice et a obtenu un crédit de 150 millions de roubles en Russie.

Lors de sa visite à New York au nom du gouvernement tsariste russe, Aschberg a fait quelques commentaires prophétiques concernant l'avenir de l'Amérique en Russie :

> L'ouverture au capital et à l'initiative américaine, avec le réveil apporté par la guerre, se fera à l'échelle du pays lorsque la lutte sera terminée. Il y a maintenant de nombreux Américains à Petrograd, des représentants d'entreprises commerciales, qui se tiennent au courant de la situation, et dès que le changement interviendra, un énorme floraison du commerce américain avec la Russie devrait voir le jour.[67]

OLOF ASCHBERG ET LA RÉVOLUTION BOLCHÉVIQUE

Pendant que cette opération de prêt tsariste était lancée à New York, Nya Banken et Olof Aschberg acheminaient des fonds du gouvernement allemand vers les révolutionnaires russes, qui allaient finalement faire tomber le "comité Kerensky" et instaurer le régime bolchévique.

Les preuves du lien intime d'Olof Aschberg avec le financement de la révolution bolchévique proviennent de plusieurs sources, certaines de plus grandes valeurs que d'autres. La Nya Banken et Olof Aschberg sont cités de manière évidente dans les documents de Sisson (voir chapitre trois) ; cependant, George Kennan a systématiquement analysé ces documents et a montré qu'ils étaient faux, bien qu'ils soient probablement basés en partie sur des documents authentiques. D'autres preuves proviennent du colonel B. V. Nikitine, responsable du contre-espionnage au sein du gouvernement Kerensky, et consistent en vingt-neuf télégrammes transmis de Stockholm à Petrograd, et vice versa, concernant le financement des bolcheviks. Trois de ces télégrammes concernent des banques - les télégrammes 10 et 11 concernent Nya Banken, et le télégramme 14 concerne la Banque russo-asiatique de Petrograd. Le télégramme 10 se lit comme suit :

> Gisa Furstenberg Saltsjobaden. Les fonds très faibles ne peuvent pas aider si vraiment urgent donner 500, car dernier paiement possible perte énorme – capital

[67] *New York Times*, 4 août 1916.

> initial irrécupérable - instruire Nya Banken câble 100 mille supplémentaires Sumenson.

Le télégramme 11 se lit comme suit :

> Kozlovsky Sergievskaya 81. Les premières lettres reçues - Nya Banken télégraphie par câble que Soloman utilisant l'agence télégraphique locale se réfère à Bronck Savelievich Avilov.

Fürstenberg était l'intermédiaire entre Parvus (Alexander I. Helphand) et le gouvernement allemand. À propos de ces transferts, Michael Futrell conclut :

> On a découvert qu'au cours des derniers mois, elle [Evegeniya Sumenson] avait reçu près d'un million de roubles de Furstenberg par l'intermédiaire de la Nya Banken à Stockholm, et que cet argent provenait de sources allemandes.[68]

Le télégramme 14 de la série Nikitine se lit comme suit : "Furstenberg Saltsjöbaden. Numéro 90 période cent mille dans Russo-Asiatique Sumenson." Le représentant américain pour la région russo-asiatique était la MacGregor Grant Company au 120 Broadway, New York City, et la banque était financée par Guaranty Trust aux États-Unis et la Nya Banken en Suède.

Une autre mention de la Nya Banken se trouve dans le document "Les accusations contre les bolcheviks", qui a été publié à l'époque de Kerensky. Il convient de noter en particulier dans ce document un document signé par Gregory Alexinsky, un ancien membre de la deuxième Douma d'État, qui fait référence à des transferts monétaires aux bolcheviks. Ce document se lit en partie comme suit :

> Selon les informations qui viennent d'être reçues, ces personnes de confiance à Stockholm étaient : le bolchévique Jacob Furstenberg, plus connu sous le nom de "Hanecki" (Ganetskii), et Parvus (Dr Helphand) ; à Petrograd : l'avocat bolchévique, M. U. Kozlovsky, une parente de Hanecki-Sumenson, qui se livrait à des spéculations avec Hanecki, et d'autres. Kozlovsky est le principal destinataire de l'argent allemand, qui est transféré de Berlin par la "Disconto-Gesellschaft" à la "Via Bank" de Stockholm, et de là à la Banque de Sibérie à Petrograd, où son compte présente actuellement un solde de plus de 2 000 000 de roubles. La censure militaire a mis au jour un échange ininterrompu de télégrammes de nature politique et financière entre les agents allemands et les dirigeants bolchéviques [Stockholm-Petrograd].[69]

En outre, le State Dept. conserve un message de l'ambassade des États-Unis à Christiania (Oslo, 1925), en Norvège, daté du 21 février 1918 et portant le code

---

[68] Michael Futrell, *Northern Underground* (Londres : Faber et Faber, 1963), p. 162.

[69] Voir Robert Paul Browder et Alexander F. Kerensky, *The Russian Provisional government, 1917* (Stanford, Calif. : Stanford University Perss, 1961), 3 : 1365. "Via Bank" est évidemment Nya Banken.

vert suivant "Suis informé que des fonds bolchéviques sont déposés à Nya Banken, Stockholm, Légation Stockholm conseillée. Schmedeman."[70]

Enfin, Michael Furtell, qui a interrogé Olof Aschberg juste avant sa mort, conclut que des fonds bolchéviques ont bien été transférés d'Allemagne par l'intermédiaire de la Nya Banken et Jacob Furstenberg sous forme de paiement de marchandises expédiées. Selon Futrell, Aschberg lui a confirmé que Furstenberg avait une affaire commerciale avec la Nya Banken et que Furstenberg avait également envoyé des fonds à Petrograd. Ces déclarations sont authentifiées dans les mémoires d'Aschberg (voir page 70). En résumé, Aschberg, par l'intermédiaire de sa Nya Banken, était sans aucun doute un canal pour les fonds utilisés dans la révolution bolchévique, et le Guaranty Trust était indirectement lié par son association avec Aschberg et sa participation dans la MacGregor Grant Co. de New York, agent de la Russo-Asiatic Bank, autre véhicule de transfert.

LA NYA BANKEN ET GUARANTY TRUST REJOIGNENT RUSKOMBANK

Plusieurs années plus tard, à l'automne 1922, les Soviétiques ont créé leur première banque internationale. Elle était basée sur un conglomérat qui comprenait les anciens banquiers privés russes et quelques nouveaux investissements de banquiers allemands, suédois, américains et britanniques. Connue sous le nom de Ruskombank (Foreign Commercial Bank ou Banque du commerce extérieur), elle était dirigée par Olof Aschberg ; son conseil d'administration était composé de banquiers privés tsaristes, de représentants de banques allemandes, suédoises et américaines et, bien sûr, de représentants de l'Union soviétique. La délégation américaine de Stockholm a fait rapport à Washington sur cette question et a noté, en référence à Aschberg, que "sa réputation est mauvaise. Il était mentionné dans le document 54 des documents de Sisson et dans la dépêche n° 138 du 4 janvier 1921 d'une délégation à Copenhague".[71]

Le consortium bancaire étranger impliqué dans la Ruskombank représentait principalement des capitaux britanniques. Il comprenait Russo-Asiatic

[70] Fichier décimal du Département d'État américain, 861.00/1130.

[71] Fichier décimal du Département d'État américain, 861.516/129, 28 août 1922. Un rapport du State Dept. de Stockholm, daté du 9 octobre 1922 (861.516/137), déclare à propos d'Aschberg : "J'ai rencontré M. Aschberg il y a quelques semaines et lors de la conversation qu'il a eue avec lui, il a déclaré en substance tout ce qui figurait dans ce rapport. Il m'a également demandé de lui demander s'il pouvait se rendre aux États-Unis et a donné comme références certaines des banques les plus importantes. À ce propos, je souhaite toutefois attirer l'attention du ministère sur le document 54 des documents de la Sisson, ainsi que sur de nombreuses autres dépêches que cette légation a écrites concernant cet homme pendant la guerre, dont la réputation et la position ne sont pas bonnes. Il travaille sans aucun doute en étroite collaboration avec les Soviétiques, et pendant toute la guerre il a été en étroite collaboration avec les Allemands" (U.S. State Dept. Decimal File, 861.516/137, Stockholm, 9 octobre 1922. Le rapport a été signé par Ira N. Morris).

Consolidated Limited, qui était l'un des plus grands créanciers privés de Russie, et qui s'est vu accorder 3 millions de livres par les Soviétiques pour compenser les dommages causés à ses propriétés en Union soviétique par la nationalisation. Le gouvernement britannique lui-même avait déjà acquis des intérêts substantiels dans les banques privées russes ; selon un rapport du Département d'État, "le gouvernement britannique est fortement investi dans le consortium en question".[72]

Le consortium a obtenu de vastes concessions en Russie et la banque avait un capital social de dix millions de roubles d'or. Un rapport du journal danois *National Titende* a déclaré que "des possibilités de coopération avec le gouvernement soviétique ont été créées là où cela aurait été impossible par des négociations politiques".[73] En d'autres termes, comme le dit le journal, les politiciens n'ont pas réussi à obtenir une coopération avec les Soviétiques, mais "il peut être considéré comme acquis que l'exploitation capitaliste de la Russie commence à prendre des formes plus définies".[74]

Début octobre 1922, Olof Aschberg rencontre à Berlin Emil Wittenberg, directeur de la Nationalbank fur Deutschland, et Scheinmann, directeur de la Banque d'État russe. Après avoir discuté de l'implication allemande dans la Ruskombank, les trois banquiers se sont rendus à Stockholm où ils ont rencontré Max May, vice-président de la Guaranty Trust Company. Max May a ensuite été désigné directeur de la division étrangère de la Ruskombank, en plus de Schlesinger, ancien directeur de la banque d'affaires de Moscou, Kalaschkin, ancien directeur de la Junker Bank, et Ternoffsky, ancien directeur de la banque sibérienne. La dernière banque avait été partiellement achetée par le gouvernement britannique en 1918. Le professeur Gustav Cassell de Suède a accepté d'être le conseiller de Ruskombank. Cassell a été cité dans un journal suédois *(Svenskadagbladet* du 17 octobre 1922) comme suit :

> Le fait qu'une banque ait maintenant été créée en Russie pour s'occuper de questions purement financières est un grand pas en avant, et il me semble que cette banque a été créée pour faciliter une nouvelle vie économique en Russie. Ce dont la Russie a besoin, c'est d'une banque pour gérer son commerce intérieur et extérieur. S'il doit y avoir des affaires entre la Russie et d'autres pays, il doit y avoir une banque pour les traiter. Ce pas en avant doit être soutenu à tous égards par d'autres pays, et lorsqu'on m'a demandé mon avis, j'ai déclaré que j'étais prêt à le donner. Je ne suis pas favorable à une politique négative et je pense qu'il faut saisir toutes les occasions de contribuer à une reconstruction positive. La grande question est de savoir comment ramener les échanges russes à la normale. C'est une question complexe qui nécessitera une enquête approfondie. Pour résoudre ce problème, je suis naturellement plus que disposé à prendre part aux travaux. Laisser la Russie à ses propres ressources et à son propre sort est une folie.[75]

---

[72] Ibid. 861.516/130, 13 septembre 1922.

[73] Ibid.

[74] Ibid.

[75] Ibid, 861.516/140, Stockholm, 23 octobre 1922.

L'ancien bâtiment de la Siberian Bank à Petrograd servait de siège social à la Ruskombank, dont les objectifs étaient de lever des prêts à court terme dans les pays étrangers, d'introduire ces capitaux étrangers en Union soviétique et, de manière générale, de faciliter le commerce extérieur russe. Il a ouvert ses portes le 1er décembre 1922 à Moscou et employait environ 300 personnes.

En Suède, la Ruskombank était représentée par la Svenska Ekonomibolaget de Stockholm, la Nya Banken d'Olof Aschberg sous un nouveau nom, et en Allemagne par la Garantie und Creditbank fur Den Osten de Berlin. Aux États-Unis, la banque était représentée par la Guaranty Trust Company de New York. Lors de l'ouverture de la banque, Olof Aschberg a commenté :

> La nouvelle banque s'occupera de l'achat de machines et de matières premières en Angleterre et aux États-Unis et donnera des garanties pour l'exécution des contrats. La question des achats en Suède ne s'est pas encore posée, mais il est à espérer que ce sera le cas plus tard.[76]

En rejoignant Ruskombank, Max May de Guaranty Trust a fait une déclaration similaire :

> Les États-Unis, étant un pays riche avec des industries bien développées, n'ont pas besoin d'importer quoi que ce soit de l'étranger, mais... ils sont très intéressés par l'exportation de leurs produits vers d'autres pays et considèrent la Russie comme le marché le plus approprié à cette fin, en prenant en considération les vastes exigences de la Russie dans tous les domaines de sa vie économique.[77]

May a déclaré que la Banque Commerciale Russe était "très importante" et qu'elle "financerait largement toutes les lignes des industries russes".

Dès le début, les opérations de la Ruskombank ont été limitées par le monopole soviétique du commerce extérieur. La banque avait des difficultés à obtenir des avances sur les marchandises russes déposées à l'étranger. Comme elles étaient transmises au nom des délégations commerciales soviétiques, une grande partie des fonds de la Ruskombank était bloquée dans des dépôts auprès de la Banque d'État russe. Finalement, au début de 1924, la Banque commerciale russe a fusionné avec le commissariat au commerce extérieur soviétique et Olof Aschberg a été démis de ses fonctions à la banque parce que, selon les allégations de Moscou, il avait fait un usage abusif des fonds bancaires. Son premier lien avec la banque était dû à son amitié avec Maxim Litvinov. Grâce à cette association, selon un rapport du Département d'État, Olof Aschberg a eu accès à d'importantes sommes d'argent afin d'effectuer des paiements sur des marchandises commandées par les Soviétiques en Europe :

> Ces sommes ont apparemment été placées dans l'Ekonomibolaget, une société bancaire privée, appartenant à M. Aschberg. Il est maintenant allégué qu'une grande

[76] Ibid, 861.516/147, 8 décembre 1922.

[77] Ibid, 861.516/144, 18 novembre 1922.

> partie de ces fonds a été utilisée par M. Aschberg pour faire des investissements pour son compte personnel et qu'il s'efforce maintenant de maintenir sa position dans la banque grâce à la possession de cet argent. Selon mon informateur, M. Aschberg n'a pas été le seul à profiter de ses opérations avec les fonds soviétiques, mais il a partagé les gains avec ceux qui sont responsables de sa nomination à la Banque de commerce russe, parmi lesquels Litvinoff.[78]

Ruskombank est alors devenue Vneshtorg, nom sous lequel elle est connue aujourd'hui.

Nous devons maintenant revenir sur nos pas et examiner les activités de l'associé new-yorkais d'Aschberg, la Guaranty Trust Company, pendant la Première Guerre mondiale, afin de jeter les bases d'un examen de son rôle dans l'ère révolutionnaire en Russie.

GUARANTY TRUST ET L'ESPIONNAGE ALLEMAND AUX ÉTATS-UNIS, 1914-1917[79]

Pendant la Première Guerre mondiale, l'Allemagne a collecté des fonds considérables à New York pour l'espionnage et les opérations secrètes en Amérique du Nord et du Sud. Il est important d'enregistrer le flux de ces fonds, car il provient des mêmes entreprises - Guaranty Trust et American International Corporation - qui étaient impliquées dans la révolution bolchévique et ses suites. Sans parler du fait (souligné au chapitre trois) que le gouvernement allemand a également financé les activités révolutionnaires de Lénine.

Un résumé des prêts accordés par les banques américaines aux intérêts allemands pendant la Première Guerre mondiale a été remis au Comité Overman du Sénat américain de 1919 par les services de renseignements militaires américains. Le résumé était basé sur la déposition de Karl Heynen, qui est venu aux États-Unis en avril 1915 pour assister le Dr Albert dans les affaires commerciales et financières du gouvernement allemand. Le travail officiel de Heynen était le transport de marchandises des États-Unis vers l'Allemagne en passant par la Suède, la Suisse et la Hollande. En fait, il était impliqué dans ces opérations secrètes jusqu'au cou.

Selon Heynen, les principaux emprunts allemands contractés aux États-Unis entre 1915 et 1918 ont été les suivants : Le premier prêt, de 400 000 dollars, a été accordé vers septembre 1914 par les banquiers d'affaires Kuhn, Loeb & Co. Une garantie de 25 millions de marks a été déposée auprès de Max M. Warburg à Hambourg, la filiale allemande de Kuhn, Loeb & Co. Le capitaine George B. Lester des services de renseignements militaires américains a déclaré au Sénat que la réponse de Heynen à la question "Pourquoi êtes-vous allé chez Kuhn, Loeb &

---

[78] Ibid, 861.316/197, Stockholm, 7 mars 1924.

[79] Cette section est basée sur les audiences de la commission Overman, États-Unis, Sénat, *intérêts des brasseries et des alcools et propagande allemande et bolchévique*, Audiences devant la sous-commission du pouvoir judiciaire, 65e Cong. 1919, 2:2154-74.

Co." était "nous considérions Kuhn, Loeb & Co. comme les banquiers naturels du gouvernement allemand et de la Reichsbank".

Le second prêt, de 1,3 million de dollars, ne provient pas directement des États-Unis mais a été négocié par John Simon, un agent de la Suedeutsche Disconto-Gesellschaft, afin d'obtenir des fonds pour effectuer des expéditions vers l'Allemagne.

Le troisième prêt a été accordé par la Chase National Bank (du groupe Morgan) pour un montant de trois millions de dollars. Le quatrième prêt a été accordé par la Mechanics and Metals National Bank pour un montant d'un million de dollars. Ces prêts ont financé des activités d'espionnage allemand aux États-Unis et au Mexique. Certains fonds ont été attribués à Sommerfeld, qui était conseiller auprès de Von Rintelen (un autre agent d'espionnage allemand) et qui a ensuite été associé à Hjalmar Schacht et Emil Wittenberg. Sommerfeld devait acheter des munitions destinées à être utilisées au Mexique. Il avait un compte auprès de la Guaranty Trust Company et, à partir de celui-ci, des paiements ont été effectués à la Western Cartridge Co. d'Alton, dans l'Illinois, pour des munitions qui ont été expédiées à El Paso pour être utilisées au Mexique par les bandits de Pancho Villa. Environ 400 000 dollars ont été dépensés pour les munitions, la propagande mexicaine et d'autres activités similaires.

Le comte Von Bernstorff, alors ambassadeur d'Allemagne, a raconté son amitié avec Adolf von Pavenstedt, un associé principal de la société Amsinck & Co, qui était contrôlée et, en novembre 1917, possédée par American International Corporation. American International figure en bonne place dans les chapitres suivants ; son conseil d'administration contient les noms clés de Wall Street : Rockefeller, Kahn, Stillman, du Pont, Winthrop, etc. Selon Von Bernstorff, Von Pavenstedt "connaissait intimement tous les membres de l'ambassade". Von Bernstorff[80] lui-même considérait Von Pavenstedt comme l'un des Allemands impériaux les plus respectés, "sinon le plus respecté de New York".[81] En effet, Von Pavenstedt a été "pendant de nombreuses années un chef de file du système d'espionnage allemand dans ce pays".[82] En d'autres termes, il ne fait aucun doute qu'Armsinck & Co, contrôlée par American International Corporation, était intimement associée au financement de l'espionnage allemand en temps de guerre aux États-Unis. Pour étayer la dernière déclaration de Von Bernstorff, il existe une photographie d'un chèque en faveur d'Amsinck & Co. daté du 8 décembre 1917 - quatre semaines seulement après le début de la révolution bolchévique en Russie - signé Von Papen (un autre opérateur d'espionnage allemand), et portant une vignette indiquant "frais de voyage sur Von W [c'est-à-dire Von Wedell]". French Strothers,[83] qui a publié la photographie, a déclaré que ce chèque est la preuve que

---

[80] Comte Von Bernstorff, *Mes trois années en Amérique* (New York : Scribner's, 1920), p. 261.

[81] Ibid.

[82] Ibid.

[83] French Strothers, *Fighting Germany's Spies* (Garden City, N.Y. : Doubleday, Page, 1918), p. 152.

Von Papen "est devenu complice après coup d'un crime contre les lois américaines" ; il fait également peser sur Amsinck & Co. une accusation similaire.

Paul Bolo-Pasha, un autre agent d'espionnage allemand, et un éminent financier français anciennement au service du gouvernement égyptien, est arrivé à New York en mars 1916 avec une lettre d'introduction à Von Pavenstedt. Par l'intermédiaire de ce dernier, Bolo-Pasha a rencontré Hugo Schmidt, directeur de la Deutsche Bank à Berlin et son représentant aux États-Unis. Un des projets de Bolo-Pasha était d'acheter des journaux étrangers afin d'orienter leurs éditoriaux en faveur de l'Allemagne. Les fonds pour ce programme ont été arrangés à Berlin sous forme de crédit par la Guaranty Trust Company, le crédit étant ensuite mis à la disposition d'Amsinck & Co. Adolf von Pavenstedt, d'Amsinck, a à son tour mis les fonds à la disposition de Bolo-Pasha.

En d'autres termes, la Guaranty Trust Company et Amsinck & Co, une filiale de l'American International Corporation, étaient toutes deux directement impliquées dans la mise en œuvre de l'espionnage allemand et d'autres activités aux États-Unis. Ces sociétés peuvent établir des liens avec chacun des principaux opérateurs allemands aux États-Unis - le Dr Albert, Karl Heynen, Von Rintelen, Von Papan, le comte Jacques Minotto (voir ci-dessous) et Paul Bolo-Pasha.

En 1919, la commission Overman du Sénat a également établi que Guaranty Trust avait un rôle actif dans le financement des efforts allemands de la Première Guerre mondiale d'une manière "non neutre". Le témoignage de l'officier de renseignement américain Becker le montre clairement :

> Dans cette mission, Hugo Schmidt [de la Deutsche Bank] a été très largement assisté par certaines institutions bancaires américaines. C'était alors que nous étions neutres, mais ils ont agi au détriment des intérêts britanniques, et je dispose de données considérables sur l'activité de la Guaranty Trust Co. à cet égard, et j'aimerais savoir si la commission souhaite que j'y revienne.
> **SÉNATEUR NELSON** : C'est une succursale de la City Bank, n'est-ce pas ?
> MR. BECKER : Non.
> **SÉNATEUR OVERMAN** : Si elle était contraire aux intérêts britanniques, elle n'était pas neutre, et je pense que vous feriez mieux de nous en informer.
> **SÉNATEUR KING** : S'agissait-il d'une transaction bancaire ordinaire ?
> **MR. BECKER** : Ce serait une question d'opinion. Il s'agissait de camoufler l'échange afin de le faire paraître comme un échange neutre, alors qu'il s'agissait en réalité d'une opération allemande à Londres. Grâce aux opérations auxquelles la Guaranty Trust Co. a principalement participé entre le 1er août 1914 et l'entrée en guerre de l'Amérique, la Deutsche Banke, dans ses succursales en Amérique du Sud, a réussi à négocier 4 670 000 livres sterling de change à Londres en temps de guerre.
> **SÉNATEUR OVERMAN** : Je pense que c'est suffisant.[84]

Ce qui est vraiment important, ce n'est pas tant que l'Allemagne ait reçu une aide financière, qui était illégale, mais que les directeurs de Guaranty Trust aient

[84] États-Unis, Sénat, Overman Committee, 2:2009.

aidé financièrement les Alliés au même moment. En d'autres termes, Guaranty Trust finançait les deux parties du conflit. Cela soulève la question de la moralité.

GARANTY TRUST, MINOTTO ET CAILLAUX[85]

Le comte Jacques Minotto est un fil conducteur très improbable mais vérifiable et persistant qui relie la révolution bolchévique en Russie aux banques allemandes, l'espionnage allemand de la Première Guerre mondiale aux États-Unis, la Guaranty Trust Company à New York, la révolution bolchévique française avortée et les procès d'espionnage Caillaux-Malvy qui y sont liés en France.

Jacques Minotto est né le 17 février 1891 à Berlin, d'un père autrichien descendant de la noblesse italienne et d'une mère allemande. Le jeune Minotto a fait ses études à Berlin, puis est entré à la Deutsche Bank à Berlin en 1912. Presque immédiatement, Minotto est envoyé aux États-Unis comme assistant de Hugo Schmidt, directeur adjoint de la Deutsche Bank et de son représentant à New York. Après un an à New York, Minotto est envoyé par la Deutsche Bank à Londres, où il circule dans les cercles politiques et diplomatiques les plus importants. Au début de la Première Guerre mondiale, Minotto retourne aux États-Unis et rencontre immédiatement l'ambassadeur allemand, le comte Von Bernstorff, après quoi il entre au service de la Guaranty Trust Company à New York. À la Guaranty Trust, Minotto était sous les ordres directs de Max May, directeur de son département des affaires étrangères et associé du banquier suédois Olof Aschberg. Minotto n'était pas un petit fonctionnaire de banque. Les interrogatoires des procès Caillaux à Paris en 1919 ont établi que Minotto travaillait directement sous les ordres de Max May. Le 25 octobre 1914, Guaranty Trust envoie Jacques Minotto en Amérique du Sud pour faire un rapport sur la situation politique, financière et commerciale. Comme il l'a fait à Londres, Washington et New York, Minotto s'est installé ici dans les plus hauts cercles diplomatiques et politiques. L'un des objectifs de la mission de Minotto en Amérique latine était d'établir le mécanisme par lequel le Guaranty Trust pourrait servir d'intermédiaire pour la collecte de fonds allemande mentionnée précédemment sur le marché monétaire de Londres, qui fut ensuite refusée à l'Allemagne en raison de la Première Guerre mondiale. Minotto retourna aux États-Unis, renouvela son association avec le comte Von Bernstorff et le comte Luxberg, puis, en 1916, tenta d'obtenir un poste au sein des services de renseignements de la marine américaine.

Il a ensuite été arrêté pour activités pro-allemandes. Lorsqu'il a été arrêté, Minotto travaillait à l'usine de Chicago de son beau-père Louis Swift, de Swift &

---

[85] Cette section s'appuie sur les sources suivantes (ainsi que sur celles qui sont citées ailleurs) : Jean Bardanne, *Le Colonel Nicolai : espion de génie* (Paris : Éditions Siboney, s.d.) ; Cours de Justice, *Affaire Caillaux, Loustalot et Comby : Procédure générale d'interrogatoires* (Paris, 1919), p. 349-50, 937-46 ; Paul Vergnet, *L'Affaire Caillaux* (Paris 1918), en particulier le chapitre intitulé "Marx de Mannheim" ; Henri Guernut, Emile Kahn et Camille M. Lemercier, *Études documentaires sur L'Affaire Caillaux* (Paris, s.d.), p. 1012-15 ; et George Adam, *Treason and Tragedy: An Account of French War Trials* (Londres : Jonathan Cape, 1929).

Co, des emballeurs de viande. Swift a constitué la garantie de la caution de 50 000 dollars nécessaire à la libération de Minotto, qui était représenté par Henry Veeder, l'avocat de Swift & Co. Louis Swift a lui-même été arrêté plus tard pour des activités pro-allemandes. Coïncidence intéressante et non négligeable, le "commandant" Harold H. Swift, frère de Louis Swift, était membre de la mission de la Croix-Rouge William Boyce Thompson à Petrograd en 1917 - c'est-à-dire l'un des groupes d'avocats et d'hommes d'affaires de Wall Street dont les liens intimes avec la révolution russe seront décrits plus tard. Helen Swift Neilson, sœur de Louis et Harold Swift, a été plus tard liée au Centre Abraham Lincoln "Unity", un groupe pro-communiste. Cela a établi un lien mineur entre les banques allemandes, les banques américaines, l'espionnage allemand et, comme nous le verrons plus tard, la révolution bolchévique.[86]

Joseph Caillaux était un célèbre (tristement célèbre selon certains) homme politique français. Il était également associé au comte Minotto dans les opérations de ce dernier en Amérique latine pour le compte de Guaranty Trust, et fut plus tard impliqué dans les célèbres affaires d'espionnage français de 1919, qui avaient des liens avec les bolchéviques. En 1911, Caillaux est devenu ministre des Finances et, plus tard dans la même année, Premier ministre de la France. John Louis Malvy devient sous-secrétaire d'État dans le gouvernement Caillaux. Quelques années plus tard, Madame Caillaux assassine Gaston Calmette, rédacteur en chef du *Figaro,* un journal parisien très connu. Le ministère public a accusé Madame Caillaux d'avoir assassiné Calmette pour empêcher la publication de certains documents compromettants. Cette affaire a entraîné le départ de Caillaux et de son épouse de France. Le couple se rend en Amérique latine et y rencontre le comte Minotto, l'agent de la Guaranty Trust Company qui était en Amérique latine pour établir des intermédiaires pour la finance allemande. Le comte Minotto est socialement lié au couple Caillaux à Rio de Janeiro et à Sao Paulo, au Brésil, à Montevideo, en Uruguay, et à Buenos Aires, en Argentine. En d'autres termes, le comte Minotto a été un compagnon constant du couple Caillaux pendant leur séjour en Amérique latine.[87] De retour en France, Caillaux et son épouse ont séjourné à Biarritz en tant qu'invités de Paul Bolo-Pasha, qui était, comme nous l'avons vu, également un opérateur d'espionnage allemand aux États-Unis et en France.[88] Plus tard, en juillet 1915, le comte Minotto arrive en France d'Italie, rencontre le couple Caillaux ; la même année, le couple Caillaux visite à nouveau Bolo-Pasha à Biarritz. En d'autres termes, en 1915 et 1916, Caillaux établit une relation sociale continue avec le comte Minotto et Bolo-Pasha, tous deux agents d'espionnage allemand aux États-Unis.

Le travail de Bolo-Pasha en France va permettre à l'Allemagne de gagner en influence dans les journaux parisiens *Le Temps* et le *Figaro.* Bolo-Pasha se rend

---

[86] Cette relation est traitée en détail dans le rapport en trois volumes de la commission Overman de 1919. Voir la bibliographie.

[87] Voir Rudolph Binion, *Defeated Leaders* (New York : Columbia University Press, 1960).

[88] George Adam, *Treason and Tragedy: An Account of French War Trials* (Londres : Jonathan Cape, 1929).

ensuite à New York, où il arrive le 24 février 1916. Il y négocie un prêt de deux millions de dollars et est associé à Von Pavenstedt, l'éminent agent allemand de la société Amsinck & Co.[89] Severance Johnson, dans *The Enemy Within*, a relié Caillaux et Malvy à la révolution bolchévique française avortée de 1918, et déclare que si la révolution avait réussi, "Malvy aurait été le Trotsky de France si Caillaux avait été son Lénine".[90] Caillaux et Malvy ont formé un parti socialiste radical en France en utilisant des fonds allemands et ont été traduits en justice pour ces efforts subversifs. Les interrogatoires du tribunal dans les procès d'espionnage français de 1919 introduisent des témoignages concernant les banquiers de New York et leurs relations avec ces opérateurs d'espionnage allemands. Ils exposent également les liens entre le comte Minotto et Caillaux, ainsi que la relation de la Guaranty Trust Company avec la Deutsche Bank et la coopération entre Hugo Schmidt de la Deutsche Bank et Max May de la Guaranty Trust Company. L'interrogatoire français (page 940) contient l'extrait suivant de la déposition du comte Minotto à New York (page 10, et traduit du français) :

> QUESTION : Sous les ordres de qui étiez-vous à Guaranty Trust ?
> RÉPONSE : Sous les ordres de M. Max May.
> QUESTION : Il était vice-président ?
> RÉPONSE : Il a été vice-président et directeur du ministère des Affaires étrangères.

Plus tard, en 1922, Max May est devenu directeur de la Ruskombank soviétique et a représenté les intérêts de Guaranty Trust dans cette banque. L'interrogatoire français établit que le comte Minotto, un agent d'espionnage allemand, était employé par la Guaranty Trust Company ; que Max May était son supérieur hiérarchique ; et que Max May était également étroitement associé au banquier bolchévique Olof Aschberg. En bref : Max May de la Guaranty Trust était lié à la collecte illégale de fonds et à l'espionnage allemand aux États-Unis pendant la Première Guerre mondiale ; il était lié indirectement à la révolution bolchévique et directement à la création de Ruskombank, la première banque internationale en Union soviétique.

Il est trop tôt pour tenter d'expliquer cette activité internationale apparemment incohérente, illégale et parfois immorale. En général, il y a deux explications plausibles : la première, une recherche implacable de profits ; la seconde - qui rejoint les propos d'Otto Kahn de la Kuhn, Loeb & Co. et de l'American International Corporation dans l'épigraphe de ce chapitre - la réalisation de buts socialistes, buts qui "devraient et peuvent être réalisés" par des moyens non socialistes.

---

[89] Ibid.

[90] *The Enemy Within* (Londres : George Allen & Unwin, 1920).

CHAPITRE V

LA MISSION DE LA CROIX-ROUGE AMÉRICAINE EN RUSSIE - 1917

Le pauvre M. Billings se croyait chargé d'une mission scientifique pour le secours de la Russie... En réalité, il n'était rien d'autre qu'une couverture - ce prétexte de mission de la Croix-Rouge n'était rien d'autre qu'un leurre.

Cornelius Kelleher, assistant de William Boyce Thompson
(dans *Russia Leaves the War*, de George F. Kennan,)

Le projet de Wall Street en Russie en 1917 a utilisé la mission de la Croix-Rouge comme véhicule opérationnel. Guaranty Trust et National City Bank avaient tous deux des représentants en Russie au moment de la révolution. Frederick M. Corse, de la succursale de la National City Bank à Petrograd, était attaché à la mission de la Croix-Rouge américaine, dont on parlera plus tard. Guaranty Trust était représenté par Henry Crosby Emery. Emery a été temporairement détenu par les Allemands en 1918, puis a représenté Guaranty Trust en Chine.

Jusqu'en 1915 environ, la personne la plus influente au siège national de la Croix-Rouge américaine à Washington, D.C., était Mlle Mabel Boardman. Promotrice active et énergique, Mlle Boardman avait été la force motrice de l'entreprise de la Croix-Rouge, bien que sa dotation ait été assurée par de riches et éminentes personnalités, dont J. P. Morgan, Mme E. H. Harriman, Cleveland H. Dodge et Mme Russell Sage. La campagne de collecte de fonds de 1910, par exemple, pour un montant de 2 millions de dollars, n'a réussi que parce qu'elle était soutenue par ces riches résidents de New York. En fait, la majeure partie de l'argent provenait de la ville de New York. J.P. Morgan lui-même a contribué à hauteur de 100 000 dollars et sept autres contributeurs de la ville de New York ont amassé 300 000 dollars. Une seule personne en dehors de New York a contribué à hauteur de plus de 10 000 dollars, il s'agit de William J. Boardman, le père de Mlle Boardman. Henry P. Davison a été président du Comité de collecte de fonds de New York en 1910 et est devenu plus tard président du Conseil de guerre de la Croix-Rouge américaine. En d'autres termes, pendant la Première Guerre mondiale, la Croix-Rouge dépendait fortement de Wall Street, et plus particulièrement de la firme Morgan.

La Croix-Rouge n'a pas pu faire face aux exigences de la Première Guerre mondiale et a été en fait reprise par ces banquiers new-yorkais. Selon John Foster Dulles, ces hommes d'affaires "considéraient la Croix-Rouge américaine comme un bras virtuel du gouvernement, ils envisageaient d'apporter une contribution incalculable à la victoire de la guerre".[91] Ce faisant, ils ont tourné en dérision la devise de la Croix-Rouge : "Neutralité et humanité".

En échange de la collecte de fonds, Wall Street a demandé la création du Conseil de guerre de la Croix-Rouge et, sur la recommandation de Cleveland H. Dodge, l'un des bailleurs de fonds de Woodrow Wilson, Henry P. Davison, un associé de la J.P. Morgan Company, en est devenu le président. La liste des administrateurs de la Croix-Rouge commence alors à prendre l'apparence du *Who's Who* des dirigeants d'entreprises new-yorkais : John D. Ryan, président de l'Anaconda Copper Company (voir frontispice) ; George W. Hill, président de l'American Tobacco Company ; Grayson M.P. Murphy, vice-président de la Guaranty Trust Company ; et Ivy Lee, expert en relations publiques pour les Rockefeller. Harry Hopkins, qui deviendra célèbre sous le président Roosevelt, devient l'assistant du directeur général de la Croix-Rouge à Washington, D.C.

La question d'une mission de la Croix-Rouge en Russie a été soulevée lors de la troisième réunion de ce Conseil de guerre reconstitué, qui s'est tenue dans le bâtiment de la Croix-Rouge, à Washington, D.C., le vendredi 29 mai 1917, à 11 heures. Le président Davison a été chargé d'étudier l'idée avec Alexander Legge de l'International Harvester Company. Par la suite, International Harvester, qui avait des intérêts considérables en Russie, a fourni 200 000 dollars pour aider au financement de la mission russe. Lors d'une réunion ultérieure, il fut fait savoir que William Boyce Thompson, directeur de la Banque de la Réserve Fédérale de New York, avait "offert de payer la totalité des frais de la commission" ; cette offre fut acceptée dans un télégramme : "Votre désir de payer les frais de la commission à la Russie est très apprécié et, de notre point de vue, très important."[92]

Les membres de la mission n'ont reçu aucune rémunération. Toutes les dépenses ont été payées par William Boyce Thompson et les 200 000 dollars d'International Harvester ont apparemment été utilisés en Russie pour des subventions politiques. Nous savons, grâce aux dossiers de l'ambassade américaine à Petrograd, que la Croix-Rouge américaine a donné 4000 roubles au Prince Lvoff, président du Conseil des ministres, pour "l'aide aux révolutionnaires" et 10 000 roubles en deux versements à Kerensky pour "l'aide aux réfugiés politiques".

MISSION DE LA CROIX-ROUGE AMÉRICAINE EN RUSSIE, 1917

En août 1917, la mission de la Croix-Rouge américaine en Russie n'avait qu'un lointain rapport avec sa maison-mère américaine, et devait vraiment être la mission de la Croix-Rouge la plus inhabituelle de l'histoire. Toutes les dépenses, y compris celles des uniformes - les membres étaient tous des colonels, des majors, des

[91] John Foster Dulles, *Croix-Rouge américaine* (New York : Harper, 1950).

[92] Procès-verbal du Conseil de guerre de la Croix-Rouge américaine (Washington, D.C., mai 1917)

capitaines ou des lieutenants - étaient payées de la poche de William Boyce Thompson. Un observateur contemporain a surnommé le groupe d'officiers "l'armée haïtienne" :

> La délégation de la Croix-Rouge américaine, une quarantaine de colonels, majors, capitaines et lieutenants, est arrivée hier. Elle est dirigée par le colonel (docteur) Billings de Chicago, et comprend le colonel William B. Thompson et de nombreux médecins et civils, tous avec des titres militaires ; nous avons surnommé l'unité "Haytian Army" parce qu'il n'y avait pas de soldats. Pour autant que je sache, ils ne sont venus remplir aucune mission clairement définie, en fait, le gouverneur Francis m'a dit il y a quelque temps qu'il avait insisté pour qu'ils ne soient pas autorisés à venir, car il y avait déjà trop de missions des différents alliés en Russie. Apparemment, cette Commission a imaginé qu'il y avait un besoin urgent de médecins et d'infirmières en Russie ; en fait, il y a actuellement un surplus de talents médicaux et d'infirmières, autochtones et étrangers dans le pays et de nombreux hôpitaux très vides dans les grandes villes.[93]

La mission ne comptait en fait que vingt-quatre personnes (et non quarante), ayant le grade militaire de lieutenant-colonel à lieutenant, et était complétée par trois aides-soignants, deux photographes de cinéma et deux interprètes, sans grade. Seuls cinq (sur vingt-quatre) étaient des médecins ; en outre, il y avait deux chercheurs médicaux. La mission est arrivée par train à Petrograd via la Sibérie en août 1917. Les cinq médecins et aides-soignants y restèrent un mois, et rentrèrent aux États-Unis le 11 septembre. Le Dr Frank Billings, chef nominal de la mission et professeur de médecine à l'université de Chicago, aurait été dégoûté par les activités ouvertement politiques de la majorité de la mission. Les autres médecins étaient William S. Thayer, professeur de médecine à l'université Johns Hopkins ; D. J. McCarthy, membre de l'Institut Phipps pour l'Étude et la Prévention de la Tuberculose, à Philadelphie ; Henry C. Sherman, professeur de chimie alimentaire à l'université de Columbia ; C. E. A. Winslow, professeur de bactériologie et d'hygiène à l'école de médecine de Yale ; Wilbur E. Post, professeur de médecine au Rush Medical College ; le Dr Malcolm Grow, du corps de réserve des médecins militaires de l'armée américaine ; et Orrin Wightman, professeur de médecine clinique à l'hôpital polyclinique de New York. George C. Whipple était inscrit comme professeur d'ingénierie sanitaire à l'université de Harvard, mais était en fait partenaire de la société new-yorkaise Hazen, Whipple & Fuller, consultants en ingénierie. Ceci est significatif, car Malcolm Pirnie - dont la liste est plus lointaine - était inscrit comme ingénieur sanitaire assistant et employé comme ingénieur par Hazen, Whipple & Fuller.

La majorité de la mission, telle que décrite dans le tableau ci-après, était composée d'avocats, de financiers et de leurs assistants, issus du secteur financier de New York. La mission a été financée par William B. Thompson, décrit dans la circulaire officielle de la Croix-Rouge comme "commissaire et directeur commercial ; directeur de la Banque fédérale américaine de New York". Thompson a amené avec lui Cornelius Kelleher, décrit comme un attaché de la

[93] Journal de Gibbs, 9 août 1917. Société historique de l'État du Wisconsin.

mission mais en réalité secrétaire de Thompson et ayant la même adresse - 14 Wall Street, New York City. La publicité pour la mission a été assurée par Henry S. Brown, de la même adresse. Thomas Day Thacher était avocat chez Simpson, Thacher & Bartlett, un cabinet fondé par son père, Thomas Thacher, en 1884, et très impliqué dans la réorganisation et les fusions des chemins de fer. Thomas, en tant que junior, a d'abord travaillé pour l'entreprise familiale, puis est devenu l'assistant du procureur américain sous la direction de Henry L. Stimson, et est retourné à l'entreprise familiale en 1909. Le jeune Thacher était un ami proche de Felix Frankfurter et devint plus tard l'assistant de Raymond Robins, également à la mission de la Croix-Rouge. En 1925, il est nommé juge de district sous le président Coolidge, devient solliciteur général sous Herbert Hoover, et est directeur du William Boyce Thompson Institute.

La mission de la Croix-Rouge américaine en Russie en 1919

Membres de la communauté financière de Wall Street et leurs affiliations	Médecins	Les aides-soignants, les interprètes, etc.
Andrews (Liggett & Myers Tobacco)	Billings (médecin)	Brooks (aide-soignant)
Barr (Chase National Bank)	Grandir (médecin)	Clark (aide-soignant)
Brown (a/s de William B. Thompson)	McCarthy (recherche médicale ; médecin)	Rocchia (ordonnée)
Cochran (McCann Co.)	Poste (médecin)	
Kelleher (c/o William B. Thompson)	Sherman (chimie alimentaire)	Travis (films)
Nicholson (Swirl & Co.)	Thayer (médecin)	Wyckoff (films)
Pirnie (Hazen, Whipple & Fuller)		
Redfield (Stetson, Jennings & Russell)	Wightman (médecine)	Hardy (justice)
Robins (promoteur minier)	Winslow (hygiène)	Corne (transport)
Swift (Swift & Co.)		
Thacher (Simpson, Thacher & Bartlett)		
Thompson (Banque de Réserve Fédérale de N.Y.)		
Wardwell (Stetson, Jennings & Russell)		
Whipple (Hazen, Whipple & Fuller)		
Corse (Banque nationale de la ville)		
Magnuson (recommandé par l'agent confidentiel du colonel Thompson)		

Alan Wardwell, également commissaire adjoint et secrétaire du président, était avocat au cabinet Stetson, Jennings & Russell du 15 Broad Street, à New York, et H. B. Redfield était le secrétaire juridique de Wardwell. Le major Wardwell était le fils de William Thomas Wardwell, trésorier de longue date de la Standard Oil du New Jersey et de la Standard Oil de New York. L'aîné Wardwell était l'un des signataires du célèbre accord de trust de Standard Oil, membre du comité chargé d'organiser les activités de la Croix-Rouge pendant la guerre hispano-américaine, et directeur de la banque d'épargne de Greenwich. Son fils Alan a été directeur non seulement de la Greenwich Savings, mais aussi de la Bank of New York et de Trust Co. et de la Georgian Manganese Company (avec W. Averell Harriman, directeur de Guaranty Trust). En 1917, Alan Wardwell est affilié à Stetson, Jennings & Russell et rejoint ensuite Davis, Polk, Wardwell, Gardner & Read (Frank L. Polk est secrétaire d'État par intérim pendant la période de la révolution bolchévique). La commission Overman du Sénat a noté que Wardwell était favorable au régime soviétique bien que Poole, le responsable du Département d'État sur place, ait noté que "le major Wardwell a de tous les Américains l'expérience la plus complète de la terreur" (316-23-1449). Dans les années 1920, Wardwell s'est engagé avec la Chambre de commerce russo-américaine dans la promotion des objectifs commerciaux soviétiques.

Le trésorier de la mission était James W. Andrews, auditeur de la compagnie de tabac Liggett & Myers de St. Robert I. Barr, un autre membre, était inscrit comme commissaire adjoint ; il était vice-président de la Chase Securities Company (120 Broadway) et de la Chase National Bank. William Cochran, du 61 Broadway, à New York, était responsable de la publicité. Raymond Robins, un promoteur minier, a été inclus comme commissaire adjoint et décrit comme "un économiste social". Enfin, la mission comprenait deux membres de Swift & Company de Union Stockyards, Chicago. Les Swifts ont été précédemment mentionnés comme étant liés à l'espionnage allemand aux États-Unis pendant la Première Guerre mondiale. Harold H. Swift, commissaire adjoint, était l'assistant du vice-président de Swift & Company ; William G. Nicholson travaillait également pour Swift & Company, Union Stockyards.

Deux personnes ont été ajoutées officieusement à la mission après son arrivée à Petrograd : Frederick M. Corse, représentant de la National City Bank à Petrograd ; et Herbert A. Magnuson, qui était "très fortement recommandé par John W. Finch, l'agent confidentiel en Chine du colonel William B. Thompson".[94]

Les documents Pirnie, déposés à la Hoover Institution, contiennent des informations de première main sur la mission. Malcolm Pirnie était un ingénieur employé par la firme Hazen, Whipple & Fuller, ingénieurs-conseils, de la 42e rue, à New York. Pirnie était un membre de la mission, figurant sur un manifeste en tant qu'ingénieur sanitaire adjoint. George C. Whipple, un associé de la firme, faisait également partie du groupe. Les documents de Pirnie comprennent un télégramme original de William B. Thompson, invitant l'ingénieur sanitaire adjoint Pirnie à le rencontrer, ainsi que Henry P. Davison, président du Conseil de guerre de la Croix-Rouge et associé de la firme J.P. Morgan, avant de partir pour la Russie. Le télégramme se lit comme suit :

---

94 Rapport de Billings à Henry P. Davison, 22 octobre 1917, archives de la Croix-Rouge américaine.

WESTERN UNION TELEGRAM New York, 21 juin 1917
À Malcolm Pirnie
J'aimerais beaucoup que vous dîniez avec moi au Metropolitan Club, Sixteenth Street and Fifth Avenue New York City, à huit heures demain soir, pour rencontrer M. H. P. Davison.
W. B. Thompson, 14 Wall Street

Les dossiers n'élucident pas pourquoi Davison, partenaire de Morgan, et Thompson, directeur de la Banque de la Réserve Fédérale - deux des financiers les plus en vue de New York - ont souhaité dîner avec un ingénieur sanitaire adjoint sur le point de partir pour la Russie. Les dossiers n'expliquent pas non plus pourquoi Davison n'a pas pu par la suite rencontrer le Dr Billings et la commission elle-même, ni pourquoi il était nécessaire d'informer Pirnie de son incapacité à le faire. Mais on peut supposer que la couverture officielle de la mission - les activités de la Croix-Rouge - était d'un intérêt nettement moindre que les activités de Thompson-Pirnie, quelles qu'elles aient pu être. Nous savons que Davison a écrit au Dr Billings le 25 juin 1917 :

Cher Docteur Billings :
C'est une déception pour moi et pour mes associés du Conseil de guerre de ne pas avoir pu rencontrer dans un organe les membres de votre Commission...

Une copie de cette lettre a également été envoyée à l'ingénieur sanitaire adjoint Pirnie avec une lettre personnelle du banquier Morgan Henry P. Davison, qui disait :

Mon cher M. Pirnie :
Vous comprendrez, j'en suis sûr, tout à fait la raison de la lettre adressée au Dr Billings, dont vous trouverez copie ci-jointe, et l'accepterez dans l'esprit dans lequel elle est envoyée...

Le but de la lettre de Davison au Dr Billings était de présenter des excuses à la commission et à Billings pour ne pas avoir pu les rencontrer. Nous pouvons alors être fondés à supposer que des arrangements plus approfondis ont été pris par Davison et Pirnie concernant les activités de la mission en Russie et que ces arrangements étaient connus de Thompson. La nature probable de ces activités sera décrite plus loin.[95]

La mission de la Croix-Rouge américaine (ou peut-être devrions-nous l'appeler la mission de Wall Street en Russie) a également employé trois interprètes russo-anglais : Le capitaine Ilovaisky, un bolchévique russe ; Boris Reinstein, un russo-américain, plus tard secrétaire de Lénine et chef du Bureau de

[95] Les documents de Pirnie nous permettent également de fixer exactement les dates auxquelles les membres de la mission ont quitté la Russie. Dans le cas de William B. Thompson, cette date est cruciale pour l'argumentation de ce livre : Thompson a quitté Petrograd pour Londres le 4 décembre 1917. George F. Kennan déclare que Thompson a quitté Petrograd le 27 novembre 1917 *(Russia Leaves the War*, p. 1140).

la propagande révolutionnaire internationale de Karl Radek, qui employait également John Reed et Albert Rhys Williams ; et Alexander Gumberg (alias Berg, de son vrai nom Michael Gruzenberg), qui était le frère de Zorin, un ministre bolchévique. Gumberg était également le principal agent bolchévique en Scandinavie. Il est ensuite devenu l'assistant confidentiel de Floyd Odlum de l'Atlas Corporation aux États-Unis, ainsi que le conseiller de Reeve Schley, vice-président de la Chase Bank.

Il faut le souligner en passant : Quelle a été l'utilité des traductions fournies par ces interprètes ? Le 13 septembre 1918, H. A. Doolittle, vice-consul américain à Stockholm, rendit compte au secrétaire d'État d'une conversation avec le capitaine Ilovaisky (qui était un "ami personnel proche" du colonel Robins de la mission de la Croix-Rouge) concernant une réunion entre le Soviet de Murman et les Alliés. La question d'inviter les Alliés à débarquer à Murman était en cours de discussion au Soviet, le major Thacher de la mission de la Croix-Rouge agissant pour les Alliés. Ilovaisky interpréta les vues de Thacher pour le compte du Soviétique. "Ilovaisky parlait assez longuement en russe, soi-disant en traduisant pour Thacher, mais en réalité pour Trotsky..."que" les États-Unis ne permettraient jamais un tel débarquement et demandant instamment la reconnaissance rapide des Soviétiques et de leur politique."[96] Apparemment, Thacher a soupçonné qu'il était mal traduit et a exprimé son indignation. Cependant, "Ilovaisky télégraphia immédiatement le contenu au quartier général bolchévique et, par l'intermédiaire de leur bureau de presse, fit apparaître dans tous les journaux qu'elle émanait des remarques du major Thacher et qu'elle représentait l'opinion générale de tous les représentants américains véritablement accrédités".[97]

Ilovaisky a raconté à Maddin Summers, consul général des États-Unis à Moscou, plusieurs cas où lui (Ilovaisky) et Raymond Robins de la mission de la Croix-Rouge avaient manipulé la presse bolchévique, notamment "en ce qui concerne le rappel de l'ambassadeur, M. Francis". Il a admis qu'ils n'avaient pas été scrupuleux, "mais qu'ils avaient agi selon leurs idées de droit, indépendamment de la manière dont ils auraient pu entrer en conflit avec la politique des représentants américains accrédités".[98]

Telle fut la mission de la Croix-Rouge américaine en Russie en 1917.

MISSION DE LA CROIX-ROUGE AMÉRICAINE EN ROUMANIE

En 1917, la Croix-Rouge américaine a également envoyé une mission d'assistance médicale en Roumanie, combattant alors les puissances centrales comme alliée de la Russie. Une comparaison de la mission de la Croix-Rouge américaine en Russie avec celle envoyée en Roumanie suggère que la mission de

---

96 Fichier décimal du département d'État américain, 861.00/3644.

97 Ibid.

98 Ibid.

la Croix-Rouge basée à Petrograd avait très peu de liens officiels avec la Croix-Rouge et encore moins avec l'assistance médicale. Alors que la mission de la Croix-Rouge en Roumanie a vaillamment défendu les deux principes d'"humanité" et de "neutralité" chers à la Croix-Rouge, la mission à Petrograd a fait fi de ces deux principes de manière flagrante.

La mission de la Croix-Rouge américaine en Roumanie a quitté les États-Unis en juillet 1917 et s'est installée à Jassy. La mission se composait de trente personnes sous la direction du président Henry W. Anderson, un avocat de Virginie. Sur ces trente personnes, seize étaient soit des médecins, soit des chirurgiens. En comparaison, sur les vingt-neuf personnes de la mission de la Croix-Rouge en Russie, trois seulement étaient des médecins, bien que quatre autres membres soient issus d'universités et spécialisés dans des domaines liés à la médecine. Tout au plus, sept personnes pouvaient être classées comme médecins avec la mission en Russie, contre seize avec la mission en Roumanie. Il y avait à peu près le même nombre d'aides-soignants et d'infirmières dans les deux missions. La comparaison significative, cependant, est que la mission roumaine ne disposait que de deux avocats, un trésorier et un ingénieur. La mission russe comptait quinze juristes et hommes d'affaires. Aucun des avocats ou médecins de la mission roumaine ne venait de la région de New York, mais tous, sauf un (un "observateur" du ministère de la Justice à Washington, D.C.), des avocats et hommes d'affaires de la mission russe venaient de cette région. Ce qui veut dire que plus de la moitié du total de la mission russe provenait du district financier de New York. En d'autres termes, la composition relative de ces missions confirme que la mission en Roumanie avait un but légitime - pratiquer la médecine - alors que la mission russe avait un objectif non médical et strictement politique. De par son personnel, elle pouvait être classée comme une mission commerciale ou financière, mais de par ses actions, elle était un groupe d'action politique subversif.

Personnel des missions de la Croix-Rouge américaine en Russie et en Roumanie, 1917

MISSION DE LA CROIX ROUGE AMÉRICAINE en		
Personnel	**Russie**	**Roumanie**
Médical (médecins et chirurgiens)	7	16
Les aides-soignants, les infirmières	7	10
Avocats et hommes d'affaires	15	4
TOTAL	29	30

SOURCES : Croix-Rouge américaine, Washington, D.C. Département d'État américain, ambassade de Petrograd, dossier de la Croix-Rouge, 1917.

La mission de la Croix-Rouge en Roumanie est restée à son poste à Jassy pendant le reste de l'année 1917 et jusqu'en 1918. Le personnel médical de la mission de la Croix-Rouge américaine en Russie - les sept médecins - démissionne par dégoût en août 1917, proteste contre les activités politiques du colonel Thompson et retourne aux États-Unis. Par conséquent, en septembre 1917, lorsque la mission roumaine a fait appel à Petrograd pour que des médecins et des infirmières américains viennent prêter main-forte dans les conditions de quasi-crise à Jassy, il n'y avait pas de médecins ou d'infirmières américains en Russie disponibles pour se rendre en Roumanie.

Alors que la majeure partie de la mission en Russie a occupé son temps dans des manœuvres politiques internes, la mission en Roumanie s'est lancée dans des travaux de secours dès son arrivée. Le 17 septembre 1917, un câble confidentiel de Henry W. Anderson, président de la mission en Roumanie, à l'ambassadeur américain Francis à Petrograd, demande une aide immédiate et urgente sous la forme de 5 millions de dollars pour faire face à une catastrophe imminente en Roumanie. S'ensuivit une série de lettres, de câbles et de communications d'Anderson à Francis, appelant à l'aide, sans succès.

Le 28 septembre 1917, Vopicka, ministre américain en Roumanie, envoie un long télégramme à Francis, pour qu'il le relaie à Washington, et répète l'analyse d'Anderson sur la crise roumaine et le danger d'épidémies - et pire encore - à l'approche de l'hiver :

> L'argent considérable et les mesures héroïques requises empêchent un désastre de grande envergure... Inutile d'essayer de gérer la situation sans quelqu'un ayant autorité et accès au gouvernement... Avec une organisation adéquate pour s'occuper du transport, recevoir et distribuer les fournitures.

Vopicka et Anderson avaient les mains liées, car toutes les fournitures et les transactions financières roumaines étaient traitées par la mission de la Croix-Rouge à Petrograd - et Thompson et son équipe de quinze avocats et hommes d'affaires de Wall Street avaient apparemment des questions plus importantes que les affaires de la Croix-Rouge roumaine. Rien dans les dossiers de l'ambassade de Petrograd au Département d'État américain n'indique que Thompson, Robins ou Thacher se soit préoccupé à un moment quelconque en 1917 ou 1918 de la situation urgente en Roumanie. Les communications en provenance de Roumanie ont été adressées à l'ambassadeur Francis ou à l'un de ses collaborateurs à l'ambassade, et parfois par l'intermédiaire du consulat à Moscou.

En octobre 1917, la situation en Roumanie a atteint le point de crise. Le 5 octobre, Vopicka a envoyé un câble à Davison à New York (via Petrograd) :

> Le problème le plus urgent ici... Effet désastreux redouté... Pourriez-vous organiser une expédition spéciale... Il faut se dépêcher ou il est trop tard.

Puis, le 5 novembre, Anderson a envoyé un câble à l'ambassade de Petrograd disant que les retards dans l'envoi de l'aide avaient déjà "coûté plusieurs milliers de vies". Le 13 novembre, Anderson a envoyé un télégramme à l'ambassadeur Francis concernant le manque d'intérêt de Thompson pour les conditions de vie en Roumanie :

> La société Thompson, qui a été sollicitée, a fourni des détails sur tous les envois reçus, mais n'a pas obtenu les mêmes... Lui a également demandé de me tenir au courant des conditions de transport, mais n'a reçu que très peu d'informations.

Anderson a alors demandé à l'ambassadeur Francis d'intercéder en sa faveur afin que les fonds destinés à la Croix-Rouge roumaine soient traités sur un compte séparé à Londres, directement sous les ordres d'Anderson et soustraits au contrôle de la mission de Thompson.

LE RÔLE DE THOMPSON DANS LA RUSSIE DE KERENSKY

Que faisait alors la mission de la Croix-Rouge ? Thompson a certainement acquis une réputation de mener une vie opulente à Petrograd, mais apparemment il n'a entrepris que deux grands projets dans la Russie de Kerensky : le soutien à un programme de propagande américain et le soutien au Prêt Liberté russe. Peu après son arrivée en Russie, Thompson rencontre Madame Breshko-Breshkovskaya et David Soskice, le secrétaire de Kerensky, et accepte de verser deux millions de dollars à un comité d'éducation populaire afin qu'il puisse "avoir sa propre presse et ... engager un personnel de conférenciers, avec des illustrations cinématographiques" (861.00/ 1032) ; ceci dans le but de faire de la propagande pour inciter la Russie à poursuivre la guerre contre l'Allemagne. Selon Soskice, "un paquet de 50 000 roubles" a été remis à Breshko-Breshkovskaya avec la déclaration suivante : "C'est à vous de le dépenser selon votre bon jugement". 2.100.000 roubles supplémentaires ont été déposés sur un compte bancaire courant. Une lettre de J.P. Morgan au Département d'État (861.51/190) confirme que Morgan a envoyé 425 000 roubles à Thompson à sa demande de prêt pour les Russian Liberty Loan ; J.P. transmet également l'intérêt de la firme Morgan concernant "la sagesse de faire une souscription individuelle par l'intermédiaire de M. Thompson" au Russian Liberty Loan. Ces sommes ont été transmises par l'intermédiaire de la succursale de la National City Bank à Petrograd.

THOMPSON DONNE UN MILLION DE DOLLARS AUX BOLCHEVIKS

Mais l'aide apportée aux bolcheviks par Thompson d'abord, puis, après le 4 décembre 1917, par Raymond Robins, est d'une importance historique plus grande.

La contribution de Thompson à la cause bolchévique a été rapportée dans la presse américaine contemporaine. Le *Washington Post* du 2 février 1918 contenait les paragraphes suivants :

> IL DONNE UN MILLION AUX BOLCHEVIKS
> W. B. Thompson, donateur de la Croix-Rouge, croit que le parti est mal représenté. New York, 2 février (1918). William B. Thompson, qui était à Petrograd de juillet

> à novembre dernier, a fait une contribution personnelle de 1 000 000 de dollars aux Bolcheviks dans le but de diffuser leur doctrine en Allemagne et en Autriche.
> M. Thompson a eu l'occasion d'étudier les conditions de vie en Russie en tant que chef de la mission de la Croix-Rouge américaine, dont les dépenses ont également été largement couvertes par ses contributions personnelles. Il estime que les bolcheviks constituent la plus grande puissance contre le pro-germanisme en Russie et que leur propagande a sapé les régimes militaristes des Empires généraux.
> M. Thompson dénigre les critiques américaines à l'égard des Bolcheviks. Il estime qu'ils ont été mal représentés et a apporté une contribution financière à la cause en pensant que cet argent sera bien dépensé pour l'avenir de la Russie ainsi que pour la cause des Alliés.

La biographie de Hermann Hagedorn, *Le Magnat : William Boyce Thompson et son époque (1869-1930)* reproduit une photographie d'un câblogramme de J.P. Morgan à New York à W. B. Thompson, "Care American Red Cross, Hotel Europe, Petrograd". Le télégramme est daté, montrant qu'il a été reçu à Petrograd "8-Dek 1917" (8 décembre 1917), et se lit comme suit :

> New York Y757/5 24W5 Nil - Votre deuxième câble reçu. Nous avons payé un million de dollars à la National City Bank selon les instructions - Morgan.

La succursale de la National City Bank à Petrograd avait été exemptée du décret de nationalisation bolchévique - la seule banque russe étrangère ou nationale à avoir été ainsi exemptée. Hagedorn affirme que ce million de dollars versé sur le compte de la BNC de Thompson a été utilisé à des "fins politiques".

LE PROMOTEUR MINIER SOCIALISTE RAYMOND ROBINS[99]

William B. Thompson quitte la Russie au début du mois de décembre 1917 pour rentrer chez lui. Il passe par Londres, où, en compagnie de Thomas Lamont de la firme J.P. Morgan, il rend visite au Premier ministre Lloyd George, un épisode que nous reprenons dans le chapitre suivant. Son adjoint, Raymond Robins, se voit confier la responsabilité de la mission de la Croix-Rouge en Russie. L'impression générale que le colonel Robins a présentée dans les mois qui ont suivi n'a pas échappé à la presse. Selon les termes du journal russe *Russkoe Slovo,* Robins "représente d'une part le travail américain et d'autre part le capital américain, qui s'efforce par le biais des Soviétiques de gagner leurs marchés russes".[100]

Raymond Robins a commencé sa vie comme directeur d'une société de phosphate de Floride. À partir de ce poste, il a développé un gisement de kaolin, puis a prospecté le Texas et les territoires indiens à la fin du XIXe siècle. En se déplaçant vers le nord, en Alaska, Robins a fait fortune lors de la ruée vers l'or du

---

99 Robins est l'orthographe correcte. Le nom est systématiquement orthographié "Robbins" dans les fichiers du département d'État.

100 Fichier décimal du Département d'État américain, 316-11-1265, 19 mars 1918.

Klondike. Puis, sans raison apparente, il se tourne vers le socialisme et le mouvement réformateur. En 1912, il est un membre actif du Parti progressiste de Roosevelt. Il a rejoint la mission de la Croix-Rouge américaine en Russie en 1917 en tant qu'"économiste social".

Il existe de nombreuses preuves, y compris les propres déclarations de Robins, que ses appels réformistes pour le bien social n'étaient guère plus que des couvertures pour l'acquisition d'un pouvoir et d'une richesse accrus, rappelant les suggestions de Frederick Howe dans *Confessions d'un Monopoliste*. Par exemple, en février 1918, Arthur Bullard se trouvait à Petrograd avec le Comité américain de l'information publique et s'était engagé à rédiger un long mémorandum pour le colonel Edward House. Ce mémorandum fut remis à Robins par Bullard pour commentaires et critiques avant d'être transmis à House à Washington, D.C. Les commentaires très peu socialistes et impérialistes de Robins étaient que le manuscrit était "exceptionnellement discriminatoire, clairvoyant et bien fait", mais qu'il avait une ou deux réserves - en particulier, que la reconnaissance des Bolcheviks était attendue depuis longtemps, qu'elle aurait dû être effectuée immédiatement, et que si l'U.S. a ainsi reconnu les bolcheviks : "Je crois que nous serions maintenant en mesure de contrôler les ressources excédentaires de la Russie et que nous aurions des agents de contrôle en tout point de la frontière".[101]

Ce désir de "contrôler les ressources excédentaires de la Russie" était également évident pour les Russes. Cela ressemble-t-il à un réformateur social de la Croix-Rouge américaine ou à un promoteur minier de Wall Street engagé dans l'exercice pratique de l'impérialisme financier ?

En tout cas, Robins n'a pas caché son soutien aux bolchéviques.[102] À peine trois semaines après le début de la phase bolchévique de la Révolution, Robins envoie un câble à Henry Davison au siège de la Croix-Rouge : "Veuillez insister auprès du président sur la nécessité de poursuivre nos relations avec le gouvernement bolchévique." Il est intéressant de noter que ce télégramme était en réponse à un autre télégramme donnant instruction à Robins que "le président souhaite que les représentants des États-Unis ne communiquent pas directement avec le gouvernement bolchévique".[103] Plusieurs rapports du Département d'État se sont plaints de la nature partisane des activités de M. Robins. Par exemple, le 27 mars 1919, Harris, le consul américain à Vladivostok, a commenté une longue conversation qu'il avait eue avec Robins et a protesté contre les inexactitudes flagrantes dans le rapport de ce dernier. Harris écrivit : "Robins m'a déclaré qu'aucun prisonnier de guerre allemand et autrichien n'avait rejoint l'armée bolchévique jusqu'en mai 1918. Robbins savait que cette déclaration était absolument fausse". Harris a ensuite fourni les détails des preuves dont disposait Robins.[104]

---

[101] Mme Bullard, Département d'État américain, fichier décimal, 316-11-1265.

[102] La *New World Review* (automne 1967, p. 40) commente Robins, notant qu'il était "en sympathie avec les objectifs de la Révolution, bien que capitaliste"

[103] Ambassade de Petrograd, dossier de la Croix-Rouge.

[104] Fichier décimal du département d'État américain, 861.00/4168.

Harris a conclu : "Robbins a délibérément déformé les faits concernant la Russie à l'époque et il le fait depuis".

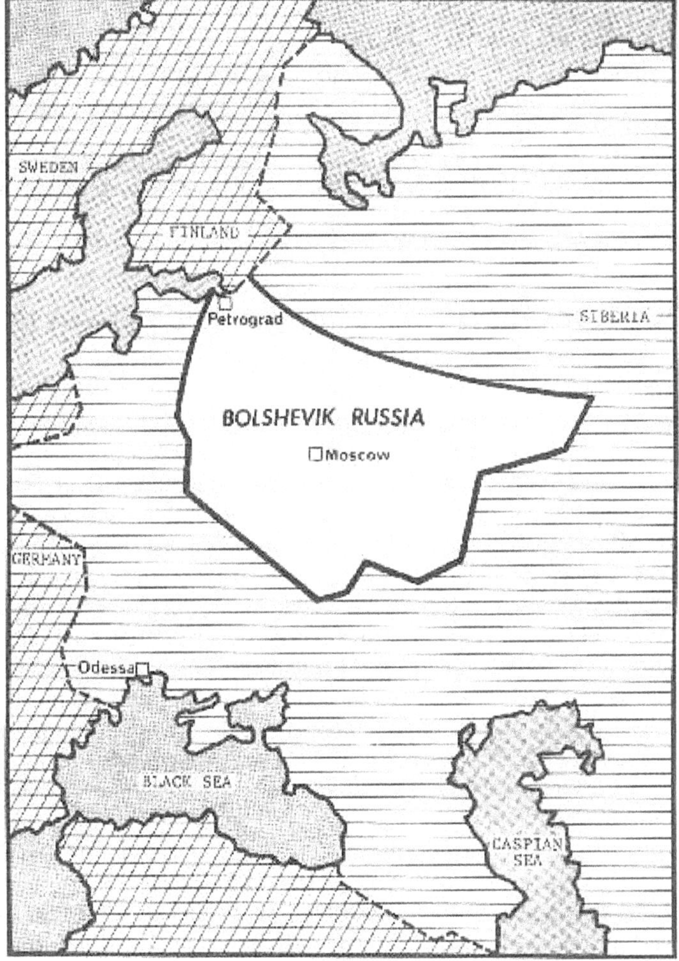

Limite de la zone contrôlée par les bolcheviks, en janvier 1918

À son retour aux États-Unis en 1918, Robins poursuit ses efforts en faveur des bolcheviks. Lorsque les dossiers du Bureau soviétique furent saisis par le Comité Lusk, on découvrit que Robins avait eu une "correspondance considérable" avec Ludwig Martens et d'autres membres du bureau. L'un des documents les plus intéressants saisis était une lettre de Santeri Nuorteva (alias Alexander Nyberg), le premier représentant soviétique aux États-Unis, adressée au "camarade Cahan", rédacteur en chef du *New York Daily Forward*. La lettre demandait aux fidèles du parti de préparer la voie à Raymond Robins :

(Au quotidien) AVANT le 6 juillet 1918
Cher camarade Cahan :
Il est de la plus haute importance que la presse socialiste lance immédiatement une campagne pour que le colonel Raymond Robins, qui vient de rentrer de Russie à la tête de la mission de la Croix-Rouge, soit entendu dans un rapport public au peuple américain. Le danger d'une intervention armée s'est considérablement accru. Les réactionnaires se servent de l'aventure tchécoslovaque pour provoquer une invasion. Robins dispose de tous les faits à ce sujet et sur la situation en Russie en général. Il adopte notre point de vue.
Je joins une copie de l'éditorial de Call qui présente une argumentation générale, ainsi que quelques faits concernant les Tchèques et les Slovaques.
Fraternellement,
PS&AU Santeri Nuorteva

LA CROIX-ROUGE INTERNATIONALE ET LA RÉVOLUTION

À l'insu de ses administrateurs, la Croix-Rouge a été utilisée de temps en temps comme véhicule ou couverture pour des activités révolutionnaires. L'utilisation des marques de la Croix-Rouge à des fins non autorisées n'est pas rare. Lorsque le tsar Nicolas a été déplacé de Petrograd à Tobolsk prétendument pour sa sécurité (bien que cette direction ait représenté un danger plutôt qu'une mise en sécurité), le train arborait les insignes de la Croix-Rouge japonaise. Les dossiers du Département d'État contiennent des exemples d'activités révolutionnaires sous couvert d'activités de la Croix-Rouge. Par exemple, un fonctionnaire russe de la Croix-Rouge (Chelgajnov) a été arrêté en Hollande en 1919 pour des actes révolutionnaires (316-21-107). Pendant la révolution bolchévique hongroise de 1918, dirigée par Bela Kun, des membres russes de la Croix-Rouge (ou des révolutionnaires opérant en tant que membres de la Croix-Rouge russe) ont été interpelés à Vienne et à Budapest. En 1919, l'ambassadeur des États-Unis à Londres a transmis par câble à Washington une nouvelle surprenante ; par l'intermédiaire du gouvernement britannique, il avait appris que "plusieurs Américains qui étaient arrivés dans ce pays dans l'uniforme de la Croix-Rouge et qui se disaient bolchéviques ... passaient par la France pour se rendre en Suisse afin de répandre la propagande bolchévique". L'ambassadeur a noté qu'environ 400 personnes de la Croix-Rouge américaine étaient arrivées à Londres en novembre et décembre 1918 ; un quart d'entre elles sont retournées aux États-Unis et "le reste a insisté pour se rendre en France". Le 15 janvier 1918, un rapport ultérieur indiquait qu'un rédacteur en chef d'un journal ouvrier de Londres avait été approché à trois reprises par trois responsables différents de la Croix-Rouge américaine qui proposaient de prendre des commissions pour les Bolcheviks en Allemagne. Le rédacteur en chef avait suggéré à l'ambassade américaine de surveiller le personnel de la Croix-Rouge américaine. Le département d'État américain a pris ces rapports au sérieux et Polk a envoyé des câbles pour obtenir des noms, déclarant : "Si c'est vrai, je considère que c'est de la plus haute importance" (861.00/3602 et /3627).

Pour résumer : l'image que nous nous faisons de la mission de la Croix-Rouge américaine en Russie en 1917 est loin d'être celle d'un humanitarisme neutre. La mission était en fait une mission des financiers de Wall Street pour influencer et ouvrir la voie au contrôle, par Kerensky ou les révolutionnaires bolchéviques, du marché et des ressources russes. Aucune autre explication n'est possible pour expliquer les actions de la mission. Cependant, ni Thompson ni Robins n'étaient bolchéviques. Ni même un socialiste convaincu. L'auteur est enclin à l'interprétation selon laquelle les appels socialistes de chaque homme étaient des couvertures pour des objectifs plus prosaïques. Chaque homme avait l'intention de faire du commerce, c'est-à-dire que chacun cherchait à utiliser le processus politique en Russie à des fins financières personnelles. La question de savoir si le peuple russe voulait des bolcheviks n'avait aucune importance. Que le régime bolchévique agisse contre les États-Unis - comme il l'a toujours fait par la suite - n'était pas un problème. Le seul objectif primordial était de gagner de l'influence politique et économique auprès du nouveau régime, quelle que soit son idéologie. Si William Boyce Thompson avait agi seul, sa fonction de directeur de la Banque de la Réserve Fédérale serait sans conséquence. Cependant, le fait que sa mission ait été dominée par des représentants des institutions de Wall Street soulève une question sérieuse - en fait, si la mission était une opération planifiée et préméditée par un groupe de Wall Street. Le lecteur en jugera de lui-même, au fur et à mesure que le reste de l'histoire se déroulera.

CHAPITRE VI

CONSOLIDATION ET EXPORTATION DE LA RÉVOLUTION

Le grand livre de Marx, Das Kapital, est à la fois un monument de raisonnement et un exposé de faits.

Lord Milner, membre du cabinet de guerre britannique, 1917, et directeur de la London Joint Stock Bank.

William Boyce Thompson est un nom inconnu dans l'histoire du XXe siècle, mais Thompson a joué un rôle crucial dans la révolution bolchévique.[105] En effet, si Thompson n'avait pas été en Russie en 1917, l'histoire ultérieure aurait pu suivre un tout autre cours. Sans l'aide financière et, plus important encore, l'aide diplomatique et de propagande apportée à Trotsky et à Lénine par Thompson, Robins et leurs associés new-yorkais, les bolcheviks auraient peut-être bien dépéri et la Russie serait devenue une société socialiste mais de type constitutionnel.

Qui était William Boyce Thompson ? Thompson était un promoteur d'actions minières, l'un des meilleurs dans une entreprise à haut risque. Avant la Première Guerre mondiale, il s'occupait des opérations boursières pour les intérêts du cuivre de Guggenheim. Lorsque les Guggenheim ont eu besoin de capitaux rapides pour une lutte boursière avec John D. Rockefeller, c'est Thompson qui a fait la promotion de Yukon Consolidated Goldfields devant un public sans méfiance pour lever un trésor de guerre de 3,5 millions de dollars. Thompson était le directeur du groupe Kennecott, une autre opération de Guggenheim, évaluée à 200 millions de dollars. C'est Guggenheim Exploration, d'autre part, qui a repris les options de Thompson sur la riche Nevada Consolidated Copper Company. Environ les trois quarts de la première société Guggenheim Exploration étaient contrôlés par la famille Guggenheim, la famille Whitney (propriétaire du magazine *Metropolitan*, qui employait le bolchévique John Reed), et John Ryan. En 1916, les intérêts de Guggenheim se sont réorganisés en Guggenheim Brothers et ont fait appel à William C. Potter, qui travaillait auparavant pour l'American Smelting and Refining Company de Guggenheim, mais qui était en 1916 le premier vice-président de Guaranty Trust.

[105] Pour une biographie, voir Hermann Hagedorn, *The Magnate: William Boyce Thompson and His Time (1869-1930)* (New York : Reynal & Hitchcock, 1935).

Ses compétences extraordinaires dans la mobilisation de capitaux pour des promotions minières risquées lui ont valu de se constituer une fortune personnelle et des postes de directeur dans les sociétés Inspiration Consolidated Copper Company, Nevada Consolidated Copper Company et Utah Copper Company - tous de grands producteurs de cuivre nationaux. Le cuivre est, bien sûr, un matériau majeur dans la fabrication des munitions. Thompson a également été directeur de la Chicago Rock Island & Pacific Railroad, de la Magma Arizona Railroad et de la Metropolitan Life Insurance Company. Et, fait particulièrement intéressant pour ce livre, Thompson était "l'un des plus gros actionnaires de la Chase National Bank". C'est Albert H. Wiggin, président de la Chase Bank, qui poussa Thompson à obtenir un poste dans le système de la Réserve Fédérale ; et en 1914, Thompson devint le premier directeur à plein temps de la Federal Reserve Bank of New York - la plus importante banque du système de la Réserve Fédérale.

En 1917, William Boyce Thompson était donc un opérateur financier disposant de moyens importants, d'une capacité démontrée, d'un flair pour la promotion et la mise en œuvre de projets capitalistes, et d'un accès facile aux centres du pouvoir politique et financier. C'est le même homme qui a d'abord soutenu Alexandre Kerensky, puis qui est devenu un ardent défenseur des Bolcheviks, en léguant un symbole survivant de ce soutien - un pamphlet de louanges en russe, "Pravda o Rossii i Bol'shevikakh".[106] (voir ci-dessous)

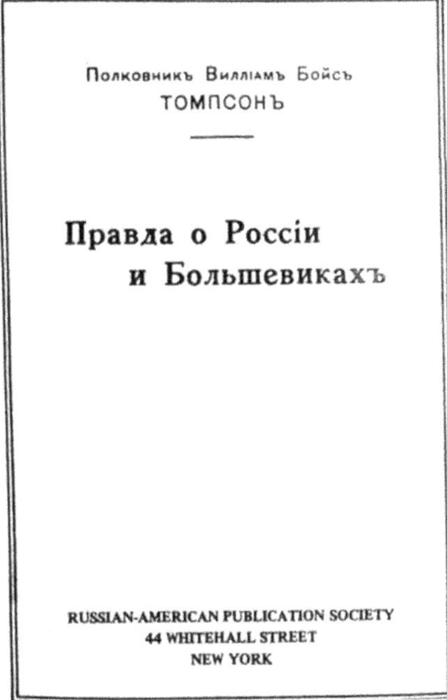
Полковникъ Вилліамъ Бойсъ
ТОМПСОНЪ

Правда о Россіи
и Большевикахъ

RUSSIAN-AMERICAN PUBLICATION SOCIETY
44 WHITEHALL STREET
NEW YORK

[106] Polkovnik' Villiam' Boic' Thompson', "Pravda o Rossii i Bol'shevikakh" (New York : Russian-American Publication Society, 1918). Colonel William Boyce Thompson "La verité sur les Russes et les Bolcheviks"

Avant de quitter la Russie au début du mois de décembre 1917, Thompson a remis la mission de la Croix-Rouge américaine à son adjoint Raymond Robins. Robins a ensuite organisé les révolutionnaires russes pour mettre en œuvre le plan de Thompson visant à répandre la propagande bolchévique en Europe (voir annexe 3). Un document du gouvernement français le confirme : "Il semble que le colonel Robins... ait pu envoyer une mission subversive de bolcheviks russes en Allemagne pour y lancer une révolution."[107] Cette mission a conduit à la révolte avortée des Spartakistes allemands en 1918. Le plan global comprenait également des objectifs pour larguer de la littérature bolchévique par avion ou pour la faire passer en contrebande à travers les lignes allemandes.

À la fin de 1917, Thompson se prépare à quitter Petrograd et à vendre la révolution bolchévique aux gouvernements européens et américains. Dans cette optique, Thompson envoie un câble à Thomas W. Lamont, un associé de la firme Morgan qui se trouve alors à Paris avec le colonel E. M. House. Lamont a consigné la réception de ce télégramme dans sa biographie :

> Au moment où la Mission de la Chambre achevait ses discussions à Paris en décembre 1917, j'ai reçu un câble d'arrestation de mon vieil ami d'école et d'affaires, William Boyce Thompson, qui était alors à Petrograd en charge de la Mission de la Croix-Rouge américaine dans cette ville.[108]

Lamont se rend à Londres et rencontre Thompson, qui a quitté Petrograd le 5 décembre, passe par Bergen, en Norvège, et arrive à Londres le 10 décembre. L'exploit le plus important de Thompson et Lamont à Londres fut de convaincre le cabinet de guerre britannique - alors résolument anti-bolchévique - que le régime bolchévique était là pour durer, et que la politique britannique devrait cesser d'être anti-bolchévique, devrait accepter les nouvelles réalités, et devrait soutenir Lénine et Trotsky. Thompson et Lamont quittent Londres le 18 décembre et arrivent à New York le 25 décembre 1917. Ils tentent le même processus de conversion aux États-Unis.

UNE CONSULTATION AVEC LLOYD GEORGE

Les documents secrets du cabinet de guerre britannique sont maintenant disponibles et valident l'argument utilisé par Thompson pour orienter le gouvernement britannique vers une politique pro-bolchévique. Le Premier ministre de Grande-Bretagne était David Lloyd George. Les machinations privées et politiques de Lloyd George rivalisaient avec celles d'un homme politique de Tammany Hall - pourtant, de son vivant et pendant des décennies après, les

---

[107] John Bradley, *Allied Intervention in Russia* (Londres : Weidenfeld et Nicolson, 1968.)

[108] Thomas W. Lamont, *Across World Frontiers* (New York : Harcourt, Brace, 1959), p. 85. Voir aussi p. 94-97 pour les coups de sein massifs suite à l'échec du président Wilson à agir rapidement pour se lier d'amitié avec le régime soviétique. Corliss Lamont, son fils, est devenu un [gauchiste national de première ligne aux États-Unis

biographes n'ont pas pu, ou n'ont pas voulu, les appréhender. En 1970, *The Mask of Merlin*, de Donald McCormick, a levé le voile sur ce secret. McCormick montre qu'en 1917, David Lloyd George s'était enlisé "trop profondément dans les mailles des intrigues internationales en matière d'armement pour être un agent libre" et qu'il était redevable à Sir Basil Zaharoff, un marchand d'armes international, dont la fortune considérable a été faite en vendant des armes aux deux camps au cours de plusieurs guerres.[109] Zaharoff exerçait un énorme pouvoir en coulisses et, selon McCormick, était consulté sur les politiques de guerre par les dirigeants alliés. À plus d'une reprise, les rapports indiquent que McCormick, Woodrow Wilson, Lloyd George et Georges Clemenceau se sont rencontrés dans la maison de Zaharoff à Paris. McCormick note que "les hommes d'État et les dirigeants alliés étaient obligés de le consulter avant de planifier toute grande attaque". Les services de renseignement britanniques, selon McCormick, "ont découvert des documents qui incriminaient des serviteurs de la Couronne en tant qu'agents secrets de Sir Basil Zaharoff *au vu et au su de Lloyd George.*[110] " En 1917, Zaharoff était lié aux bolcheviks ; il cherchait à détourner des munitions des anti-bolcheviks et était déjà intervenu en faveur du régime bolchevik à Londres et à Paris.

À la fin de 1917, alors - à l'époque où Lamont et Thompson sont arrivés à Londres - le Premier ministre Lloyd George était redevable aux puissants intérêts internationaux en matière d'armement qui étaient alliés aux Bolcheviks et qui fournissaient de l'aide pour étendre le pouvoir des Bolcheviks en Russie. Le Premier ministre britannique qui rencontra William Thompson en 1917 n'était pas alors un agent libre ; Lord Milner était la puissance en coulisses et, comme l'épigraphe de ce chapitre le suggère, favorablement inclinée vers le socialisme et Karl Marx.

Les documents "secrets" du Cabinet de guerre donnent le "compte-rendu du Premier ministre sur une conversation avec M. Thompson, un Américain revenu de Russie",[111] et le rapport fait par le Premier ministre au Cabinet de guerre après sa rencontre avec Thompson.[112] Le document du cabinet indique ce qui suit :

> Le Premier ministre a rapporté une conversation qu'il avait eue avec un M. Thompson - un voyageur américain et un homme aux moyens considérables - qui venait de rentrer de Russie, et qui avait donné une impression des affaires de ce pays quelque peu différente de ce que l'on croyait généralement. L'essentiel de ses remarques était que la Révolution était là pour durer ; que les Alliés ne s'étaient pas montrés suffisamment sympathiques à la Révolution ; et que MM. Trotsky et

---

[109] Donald McCormick, *The Mask of Merlin* (Londres : MacDonald, 1963 ; New York : Holt, Rinehart et Winston, 1964), p. 208. La vie personnelle de Lloyd George le laisserait certainement exposé au chantage.

[110] Ibid. Les italiques de McCormick.

[111] Documents du Cabinet de guerre britannique, non. 302, sec. 2 (Public Records Office, Londres).

[112] Le mémorandum écrit que Thompson a soumis à Lloyd George et qui a servi de base à la déclaration du cabinet de guerre est disponible auprès de sources d'archives américaines et est imprimé dans son intégralité à l'annexe 3.

> Lénine n'étaient pas à la solde de l'Allemagne, ce dernier étant un professeur assez distingué. M. Thompson avait ajouté qu'il considérait que les Alliés devaient mener en Russie une propagande active, menée par une forme quelconque de Conseil Allié composé d'hommes spécialement sélectionnés ; en outre, il estimait que dans l'ensemble, compte tenu de la nature du gouvernement russe de facto, les différents gouvernements alliés n'étaient pas représentés de façon appropriée à Petrograd. Selon M. Thompson, il était nécessaire que les Alliés se rendent compte que l'armée et le peuple russes étaient sortis de la guerre, et que les Alliés auraient à choisir entre une Russie neutre amie ou hostile.
> La question a été débattue de savoir si les Alliés ne devraient pas modifier leur politique à l'égard du gouvernement russe de facto, les Bolcheviks étant, selon M. Thompson, anti-allemands. À cet égard, Lord Robert Cecil a attiré l'attention sur les conditions de l'armistice entre les armées allemande et russe, qui prévoyait notamment des échanges commerciaux entre les deux pays et la création d'une commission d'achat à Odessa, le tout étant évidemment dicté par les Allemands. Lord Robert Cecil estime que les Allemands s'efforceront de poursuivre l'armistice jusqu'à ce que l'armée russe soit complètement neutralisée.
> Sir Edward Carson a lu une communication, signée par M. Trotzki, qui lui avait été envoyée par un sujet britannique, le directeur de la branche russe de la Vauxhall Motor Company, qui venait de rentrer de Russie [Paper G.T. - 3040]. Ce rapport indiquait que la politique de M. Trotzki était, en tout cas ostensiblement, une politique d'hostilité à l'organisation de la société civilisée plutôt que pro-allemande. D'autre part, il était suggéré qu'une telle attitude n'était en aucun cas incompatible avec le fait que Trotzki était un agent allemand, dont l'objectif était de ruiner la Russie afin que l'Allemagne puisse faire ce qu'elle souhaitait dans ce pays.

Après avoir entendu le rapport de Lloyd George et les arguments à l'appui, le cabinet de guerre décide de suivre Thompson et les bolcheviks. Milner avait un ancien consul britannique en Russie - Bruce Lockhart - prêt et attendant dans les coulisses. Lockhart a été informé et envoyé en Russie avec pour instruction de travailler de manière informelle avec les Soviétiques.

La minutie du travail de Thompson à Londres et la pression qu'il a pu exercer sur la situation sont suggérées par les rapports ultérieurs qui sont parvenus entre les mains du cabinet de guerre, provenant de sources authentiques. Ces rapports donnent une vision de Trotsky et des bolcheviks tout à fait différente de celle présentée par Thompson, et pourtant ils ont été ignorés par le cabinet. En avril 1918, le général Jan Smuts rapporte au cabinet de guerre son entretien avec le général Nieffel, le chef de la mission militaire française qui vient de rentrer de Russie :

> Trotski (sic)... est une crapule accomplie qui n'est peut-être pas pro-allemande, mais qui est tout à fait pro-Trotski et pro-révolutionnaire et à qui on ne peut faire confiance en aucune façon. Son influence se manifeste par la façon dont il en est venu à dominer Lockhart, Robins et le représentant français. Il [Nieffel] conseille

> une grande prudence dans ses rapports avec Trotski, dont il admet qu'il est le seul homme vraiment compétent en Russie.[113]

Quelques mois plus tard, Thomas D. Thacher, avocat de Wall Street et autre membre de la mission américaine de la Croix-Rouge en Russie, était à Londres. Le 13 avril 1918, Thacher écrit à l'ambassadeur américain à Londres qu'il a reçu une demande de H. P. Davison, un associé de Morgan, "pour s'entretenir avec Lord Northcliffe" au sujet de la situation en Russie et pour se rendre ensuite à Paris "pour d'autres conférences". Lord Northcliffe est malade et Thacher part avec un autre partenaire de Morgan, Dwight W. Morrow, laissant un mémorandum qui sera soumis à Northcliffe à son retour à Londres.[114] Non seulement ce mémorandum contenait des suggestions explicites sur la politique russe qui soutenaient la position de Thompson, mais il déclarait même que "l'aide la plus complète devait être apportée au gouvernement soviétique dans ses efforts pour organiser une armée révolutionnaire volontaire". Les quatre principales propositions de ce rapport Thacher sont les suivantes :

> Tout d'abord... les Alliés doivent décourager l'intervention japonaise en Sibérie.
> En second lieu, il faut apporter toute l'aide possible au gouvernement soviétique dans ses efforts pour organiser une armée révolutionnaire volontaire.
> Troisièmement, les gouvernements alliés devraient apporter leur soutien moral au peuple russe dans ses efforts pour élaborer son propre système politique sans la domination d'une quelconque puissance étrangère...
> Quatrièmement, jusqu'à ce qu'un conflit ouvert éclate entre le gouvernement allemand et le gouvernement soviétique de Russie, les agences allemandes auront la possibilité de pénétrer pacifiquement en Russie à des fins commerciales. Tant qu'il n'y aura pas de rupture ouverte, il sera probablement impossible d'empêcher entièrement ce commerce. Des mesures devraient donc être prises pour entraver, dans la mesure du possible, le transport de céréales et de matières premières de Russie vers l'Allemagne.[115]

LES INTENTIONS ET LES OBJECTIFS DE THOMPSON

Pourquoi un éminent financier de Wall Street, et directeur de la Banque de la Réserve Fédérale, voudrait-il organiser et aider les révolutionnaires bolchéviques ? Pourquoi non pas un mais plusieurs associés de Morgan travaillant de concert voudraient-ils encourager la formation d'une "armée révolutionnaire

---

113 Le mémorandum complet se trouve dans le fichier décimal du département d'État américain, 316-13-698.

114 Documents du Cabinet de guerre, 24/49/7197 (G.T. 4322) Secret, 24 avril 1918.

115 Lettre reproduite intégralement à l'annexe 3. Il convient de noter que nous avons identifié Thomas Lamont, Dwight Morrow et H. P. Davison comme étant étroitement impliqués dans le développement de la politique à l'égard des Bolcheviks. Tous étaient associés dans le cabinet J.P. Morgan. Thacher faisait partie du cabinet d'avocats Simpson, Thacher & Bartlett et était un ami proche de Felix Frankfurter.

volontaire" soviétique - une armée censée se consacrer au renversement de Wall Street, comprenant Thompson, Thomas Lamont, Dwight Morrow, la firme Morgan et tous leurs associés ?

Thompson était au moins franc quant à ses objectifs en Russie : il voulait maintenir la Russie en guerre contre l'Allemagne (pourtant, il a fait valoir devant le Cabinet de guerre britannique que la Russie était de toute façon sortie de la guerre) et conserver la Russie comme marché pour les entreprises américaines de l'après-guerre. Le mémorandum de Thompson à Lloyd George de décembre 1917 décrit ces objectifs. Le mémorandum[116] commence ainsi : "La situation russe est perdue et la Russie est entièrement ouverte à l'exploitation allemande sans opposition..." et conclut : "Je crois qu'un travail intelligent et courageux empêchera encore l'Allemagne d'occuper le terrain à elle seule et donc d'exploiter la Russie aux dépens des Alliés." Par conséquent, c'est l'exploitation commerciale et industrielle de la Russie par l'Allemagne que craignait Thompson (ce qui se reflète également dans le mémorandum Thacher) et qui a amené Thompson et ses amis de New York à conclure une alliance avec les Bolcheviks. D'ailleurs, cette interprétation se reflète dans une déclaration quasi-humoristique faite par Raymond Robins, l'adjoint de Thompson, à Bruce Lockhart, l'agent britannique :

> Vous entendrez dire que je suis le représentant de Wall Street ; que je suis le serviteur de William B. Thompson pour lui procurer le cuivre de l'Altaï ; que je me suis déjà procuré 500 000 acres des meilleures terres à bois de Russie ; que j'ai déjà pris le chemin de fer transsibérien ; qu'on m'a donné le monopole du platine de Russie ; que cela explique mon travail pour le compte de l'Union soviétique... Vous allez entendre ce discours. Maintenant, je ne pense pas que ce soit vrai, Monsieur le Commissaire, mais supposons que ce soit vrai. Supposons que je sois ici pour capturer la Russie pour le compte de Wall Street et des hommes d'affaires américains. Supposons que vous soyez un loup britannique et que je sois un loup américain, et que, lorsque cette guerre sera terminée, nous nous dévorerons mutuellement pour le marché russe ; faisons-le en toute franchise, à la manière d'un homme, mais supposons en même temps que nous soyons des loups assez intelligents, et que nous sachions que si nous ne chassons pas ensemble à cette heure, le loup allemand nous dévorera tous les deux, et alors mettons-nous au travail.[117]

Dans cette optique, examinons les motivations personnelles de Thompson. Thompson était un financier, un promoteur, et, bien que sans intérêt préalable pour la Russie, il avait personnellement financé la mission de la Croix-Rouge en Russie et utilisé la mission comme un véhicule de certaines manœuvres politiques. De l'ensemble du tableau, nous pouvons déduire que les motivations de Thompson étaient principalement financières et commerciales. Plus précisément, Thompson s'intéressait au marché russe et à la façon dont ce marché pouvait être influencé, détourné et capturé pour être exploité après la guerre par un ou plusieurs syndicats

---

[116] Voir l'annexe 3.

[117] États-Unis, Sénat, *Propagande bolchévique*, Audiences devant une sous-commission de la Commission du pouvoir judiciaire, 65e Cong. 1919, p. 802.

de Wall Street. Il est certain que Thompson considérait l'Allemagne comme un ennemi, mais moins comme un ennemi politique que comme un ennemi économique ou commercial. L'industrie et les banques allemandes étaient les véritables ennemis. Pour déjouer les plans de l'Allemagne, Thompson était prêt à parier sur tout pouvoir politique qui lui permettrait d'atteindre son objectif. En d'autres termes, Thompson était un impérialiste américain qui luttait contre l'impérialisme allemand, et cette lutte fut habilement reconnue et exploitée par Lénine et Trotsky.

Les preuves confirment cette approche apolitique. Au début du mois d'août 1917, William Boyce Thompson a déjeuné à l'ambassade américaine de Petrograd avec Kerensky, Terestchenko et l'ambassadeur américain Francis. Au cours du déjeuner, Thompson montra à ses invités russes un câble qu'il venait d'envoyer au bureau new-yorkais de J.P. Morgan demandant le transfert de 425 000 roubles pour couvrir une souscription personnelle au nouveau "Russian Liberty Loan". Thompson a également demandé à Morgan d'"informer mes amis que je recommande ces obligations comme le meilleur investissement de guerre que je connaisse". Je serai heureux de m'occuper de leur achat ici sans compensation" ; il a ensuite proposé de prendre personnellement vingt pour cent d'un syndicat new-yorkais achetant cinq millions de roubles du prêt russe. Sans surprise, Kerensky et Terestchenko ont indiqué qu'ils étaient "très satisfaits" du soutien de Wall Street. Et l'ambassadeur Francis, par câble, a rapidement informé le Département d'État que la commission de la Croix-Rouge "travaillait harmonieusement avec moi" et qu'elle aurait "un excellent effet".[118] D'autres auteurs ont raconté comment Thompson a tenté de convaincre les paysans russes de soutenir Kerensky en investissant un million de dollars de son propre argent et des fonds du gouvernement américain du même ordre de grandeur dans des activités de propagande. Par la suite, le Comité sur l'éducation civique dans la Russie libre, dirigé par la "grand-mère" révolutionnaire Breshkovskaya, avec David Soskice (secrétaire privé de Kerensky) comme cadre, a créé des journaux, des bureaux de presse, des imprimeries et des bureaux de conférenciers pour promouvoir l'appel : "Combattez le kaiser et sauvez la révolution". Il est à noter que la campagne de Kerensky, financée par Thompson, avait le même appel : "Maintenez la Russie dans la guerre" - tout comme son soutien financier aux bolcheviks. Le lien commun entre le soutien de Thompson à Kerensky et son soutien à Trotsky et Lénine était : "continuez la guerre contre l'Allemagne" et gardez l'Allemagne hors de Russie.

En bref, derrière et en dessous des aspects militaires, diplomatiques et politiques de la Première Guerre mondiale, une autre bataille faisait rage, à savoir une manœuvre pour l'hégémonie économique mondiale de l'après-guerre par des opérateurs internationaux ayant une force et une influence considérables. Thompson n'était pas un bolchévique ; il n'était même pas pro-bolchévique. Il n'était pas non plus pro-Kerensky. Il n'était même pas non plus pro-Américain. *Sa motivation première était la conquête du marché russe de l'après-guerre.* C'était un objectif commercial, et non idéologique. L'idéologie pouvait influencer

[118] Fichier décimal du Département d'État américain, 861.51/184.

des opérateurs révolutionnaires comme Kerensky, Trotsky, Lénine et autres, mais pas les financiers.

Le mémorandum de Lloyd George démontre l'impartialité de Thompson que ce soit pour Kerensky ou les bolcheviks : "Après le renversement du dernier gouvernement Kerensky, nous avons aidé matériellement la diffusion de la littérature bolchévique, en la distribuant par des agents et par des avions à l'armée allemande".[119] Ce texte a été écrit à la mi-décembre 1917, cinq semaines seulement après le début de la révolution bolchévique, et moins de quatre mois après que Thompson ait exprimé son soutien à Kerensky lors d'un déjeuner à l'ambassade américaine.

THOMPSON RETOURNE AUX ÉTATS-UNIS

Thompson est ensuite rentré au pays et a fait une tournée aux États-Unis avec un plaidoyer public pour la reconnaissance des Soviétiques. Dans un discours prononcé devant le Rocky Mountain Club de New York en janvier 1918, Thompson demande d'apporter de l'aide au gouvernement bolchévique naissant et, s'adressant à un public composé en grande partie d'Occidentaux, évoque l'esprit des pionniers américains :

> Ces hommes n'auraient pas hésité très longtemps à reconnaître le gouvernement ouvrier de Russie et à lui apporter toute l'aide et la sympathie possibles, car en 1819 et dans les années qui ont suivi, nous avions des gouvernements bolchéviques... et de rudement bons gouvernements alors ![120]

Il est difficile de comparer l'expérience pionnière de notre frontière occidentale à l'extermination impitoyable de l'opposition politique alors en cours en Russie. Pour Thompson, cette conquête était sans doute considérée comme similaire à celle des stocks miniers qu'il avait faite par le passé. Quant aux personnes présentes dans l'auditoire de Thompson, nous ne savons pas ce qu'elles pensaient ; cependant, personne n'a soulevé de défi. L'orateur était un directeur respecté de la Banque de Réserve Fédérale de New York, un millionnaire autodidacte (et cela compte beaucoup aux USA). Et après tout, n'était-il pas tout juste revenu de Russie ? Mais tout n'était pas rose. Le biographe de Thompson, Hermann Hagedorn, a écrit que Wall Street était "stupéfait" que ses amis aient été "choqués" et qu'il ait "dit qu'il avait perdu la tête, qu'il était devenu lui-même bolchévique".[121]

Alors que Wall Street se demandait s'il était effectivement "devenu bolchévique", Thompson a trouvé de la sympathie parmi ses collègues du conseil d'administration de la Banque de Réserve Fédérale de New York. Le codirecteur

---

[119] Voir l'annexe 3.

[120] Inséré par le sénateur Calder dans le *procès-verbal du Congrès,* 31 janvier 1918, p. 1409.

[121] Hagedorn, op. tit., p. 263.

W. L. Saunders, président de l'Ingersoll-Rand Corporation et administrateur de la FRB, écrivit au président Wilson le 17 octobre 1918, déclarant qu'il était "en sympathie avec la forme de gouvernement soviétique" ; en même temps, il déclinait toute arrière-pensée telle que "se préparer maintenant à obtenir le contrôle du commerce du monde après la guerre".[122]

Parmi les collègues de Thompson, le plus intéressant est George Foster Peabody, vice-président de la Banque de la Réserve Fédérale de New York et ami proche du socialiste Henry George. Peabody avait fait fortune dans la manipulation des chemins de fer, tout comme Thompson avait fait fortune dans la manipulation des actions du cuivre. Peabody s'est alors déclaré en faveur de la nationalisation des chemins de fer par le gouvernement et a ouvertement adopté la socialisation.[123] Comment Peabody a-t-il concilié le succès de son entreprise privée avec la promotion de la propriété publique ? Selon son biographe Louis Ware, "son raisonnement lui a fait comprendre qu'il était important que cette forme de transport soit exploitée comme un service public plutôt qu'au profit d'intérêts privés". Ce raisonnement de haute voltige ne sonne guère juste. Il serait plus exact de dire qu'étant donné l'influence politique dominante de Peabody et de ses collègues financiers à Washington, ils pourraient plus facilement éviter les rigueurs de la concurrence grâce au contrôle des chemins de fer par le gouvernement. Grâce à leur influence politique, ils pouvaient manipuler le pouvoir de police de l'État pour obtenir ce qu'ils n'avaient pas pu gagner, ou ce qui était trop coûteux, dans le cadre d'une entreprise privée. En d'autres termes, le pouvoir de police de l'État était un moyen de maintenir un monopole privé. C'était exactement ce que Frederick C. Howe avait proposé. L'idée d'une Russie socialiste planifiée de manière centralisée a dû plaire à Peabody. Pensez-y - un monopole d'État gigantesque ! Et Thompson, son ami et collègue directeur, avait le dessus sur ceux qui dirigeaient l'opération ![124]

LES AMBASSADEURS NON OFFICIELS : ROBINS, LOCKHART ET SADOUL

Les bolcheviks, pour leur part, ont correctement évalué à Petrograd le manque de sympathie des représentants des trois grandes puissances occidentales : les États-Unis, la Grande-Bretagne et la France. Les États-Unis étaient représentés par l'ambassadeur Francis, sans que ce dernier dissimule son antipathie à l'égard de la révolution. La Grande-Bretagne était représentée par Sir James Buchanan, qui

---

[122] Fichier décimal du département d'État américain, 861.00/3005.

[123] Louis Ware, *George Foster Peabody* (Athènes : University of Georgia Press, 1951).

[124] Si cet argument semble trop farfelu, le lecteur devrait consulter Gabriel Kolko, *Railroads and Regulation 1877-1916* (New York : W. W. Norton, 1965), qui décrit comment les pressions en faveur du contrôle gouvernemental et de la formation de l'Interstate Commerce Commission sont venues des *propriétaires des chemins de fer, et* non des agriculteurs et des utilisateurs des services ferroviaires.

avait des liens étroits avec la monarchie tsariste et était soupçonné d'avoir aidé à la phase Kerensky de la révolution. La France était représentée par l'ambassadeur Maurice Paléologue, ouvertement anti-bolchévique. Au début de 1918, trois autres personnalités font leur apparition ; elles deviennent des représentants de facto de ces pays occidentaux et évincent les représentants officiellement reconnus.

Raymond Robins a repris la mission de la Croix-Rouge de W. B. Thompson au début du mois de décembre 1917, mais il s'est davantage préoccupé des questions économiques et politiques que de l'obtention de secours et d'assistance pour la Russie frappée par la misère. Le 26 décembre 1917, Robins envoie un câble à Henry Davison, partenaire de Morgan et temporairement directeur général de la Croix-Rouge américaine : "Veuillez insister auprès du Président sur la nécessité de poursuivre nos relations avec le gouvernement bolchévique."[125] Le 23 janvier 1918, Robins a envoyé un télégramme à Thompson, alors à New York :

> Le gouvernement soviétique est aujourd'hui plus fort que jamais. Son autorité et son pouvoir ont été considérablement renforcés par la dissolution de l'Assemblée constituante... On ne peut pas insister trop fortement sur l'importance d'une reconnaissance rapide de l'autorité bolchévique... Sisson approuve ce texte et vous demande de montrer ce câble à Creel. Thacher et Wardwell sont d'accord.[126]

Plus tard en 1918, à son retour aux États-Unis, Robins a soumis au secrétaire d'État Robert Lansing un rapport contenant ce paragraphe d'introduction :

> "Coopération économique américaine avec la Russie ; la Russie accueillera favorablement l'aide américaine à la reconstruction économique."[127]

Les efforts persistants de Robins en faveur de la cause bolchévique lui ont donné un certain prestige dans le camp bolchévique, et peut-être même une certaine influence politique. L'ambassade américaine à Londres a affirmé en novembre 1918 que "Salkind doit sa nomination, en tant qu'ambassadeur bolchévique en Suisse, à un Américain... qui n'est autre que M. Raymond Robins".[128] À peu près à cette époque, des rapports ont commencé à filtrer à Washington, selon lesquels Robins était lui-même un bolchévique ; par exemple, le suivant de Copenhague, daté du 3 décembre 1918 :

> Confidentiel. Selon une déclaration faite par Radek à George de Patpourrie, ancien consul général d'Autriche et de Hongrie à Moscou, le colonel Robbins [*sic*], ancien directeur de la mission de la Croix-Rouge américaine en Russie, est actuellement à

---

[125] C. K. Cumming et Waller W. Pettit, *Russian-American Relations, Documents and Papers* (New York : Harcourt, Brace & Howe, 1920), doe. 44.

[126] Ibid, doc. 54.

[127] Ibid, doc. 92.

[128] Fichier décimal du département d'État américain, 861.00/3449. Mais voir Kennan, *Russia Leaves the War*, pp. 401-5.

> Moscou pour négocier avec le gouvernement soviétique et sert d'intermédiaire entre les Bolcheviks et leurs amis aux États-Unis. Certains milieux semblent penser que le colonel Robbins est lui-même un bolchévique, tandis que d'autres soutiennent qu'il ne l'est pas, mais que ses activités en Russie sont contraires aux intérêts des gouvernements associés.[129]

Des documents dans les dossiers du Bureau soviétique à New York, et saisis par le Comité Lusk en 1919, confirment que Robins et sa femme étaient étroitement associés aux activités bolchéviques aux États-Unis et à la formation du Bureau soviétique à New York.[130]

Le gouvernement britannique a établi des relations non officielles avec le régime bolchévique en envoyant en Russie un jeune agent russophone, Bruce Lockhart. Lockhart était, en fait, l'homologue de Robins ; mais contrairement à Robins, Lockhart avait des contacts directs avec son ministère des Affaires étrangères. Lockhart n'a pas été choisi par le ministre des Affaires étrangères ou le ministère ; tous deux ont été consternés par cette nomination. Selon Richard Ullman, Lockhart a été "sélectionné pour sa mission par Milner et Lloyd George eux-mêmes..." Maxim Litvinov, agissant en tant que représentant soviétique non officiel en Grande-Bretagne, a écrit pour Lockhart une lettre d'introduction à Trotsky ; il y qualifie l'agent britannique "d'homme tout à fait honnête qui comprend notre position et sympathise avec nous."[131]

Nous avons déjà noté les pressions exercées sur Lloyd George pour qu'il adopte une position pro-bolchévique, en particulier celles de William B. Thompson, et celles indirectement exercées par Sir Basil Zaharoff et Lord Milner. Milner était, comme l'épigraphe de ce chapitre le suggère, extrêmement prosocialiste. Edward Crankshaw a décrit succinctement la dualité de Milner.

> Certains des passages [dans Milner] sur l'industrie et la société... sont des passages que n'importe quel socialiste serait fier d'avoir écrit. Mais ils n'ont pas été écrits par un socialiste. Ils ont été écrits par "l'homme qui a fait la guerre des Boers". Certains des passages sur l'impérialisme et le fardeau de l'homme blanc pourraient avoir été écrits par un conservateur pur et dur. Ils ont été écrits par l'étudiant de Karl Marx.[132]

Selon Lockhart, le directeur socialiste de la banque Milner était un homme qui lui inspirait "la plus grande affection et l'adoration des héros". Lockhart[133] raconte

---

[129] Ibid, 861.00 3333.

[130] Voir le chapitre 7.

[131] Richard H. Ullman, *Intervention and the War* (Princeton, N.J. : Princeton University Press, 1961), t). 61.

[132] Edward Crankshaw, *L'idée abandonnée : Une étude o ! Vicomte Milner* (Londres : Longmans Green, 1952), p. 269.

[133] Robert Hamilton Bruce Lockhart, *agent britannique* (New York : Putnam's, 1933), p. 119.

comment Milner a personnellement parrainé sa nomination russe, l'a poussée au niveau du cabinet, et après sa nomination a parlé "presque quotidiennement" avec Lockhart. Tout en ouvrant la voie à la reconnaissance des bolcheviks, Milner a également encouragé le soutien financier de leurs opposants en Russie du Sud et ailleurs, comme l'a fait Morgan à New York. Cette double politique est conforme à la thèse selon laquelle le *modus operandi* des internationalistes politisés - tels que Milner et Thompson - était de placer l'argent de l'État sur tout cheval révolutionnaire ou contre-révolutionnaire qui semblait être un gagnant possible. Les internationalistes, bien sûr, réclamaient tout bénéfice ultérieur. L'indice se trouve peut-être dans l'observation de Bruce Lockhart selon laquelle Milner était un homme qui "croyait en un État hautement organisé".[134]

Le gouvernement français a nommé un sympathisant encore plus ouvertement bolchévique, Jacques Sadoul, un vieil ami de Trotsky.[135]

En résumé, les gouvernements alliés ont neutralisé leurs propres représentants diplomatiques à Petrograd et les ont remplacés par des agents non officiels plus ou moins sympathiques aux bolchéviques.

Les rapports de ces ambassadeurs non officiels étaient en contradiction directe avec les appels à l'aide adressés à l'Occident depuis l'intérieur de la Russie. Maxim Gorky a protesté contre la trahison des idéaux révolutionnaires par le groupe Lénine-Trotsky, qui avait imposé la main de fer d'un État policier en Russie :

> Nous, les Russes, constituons un peuple qui n'a jamais encore travaillé librement, qui n'a pas encore eu la chance de développer tous son potentiel et ses talents. Et quand je pense que la révolution nous donne la possibilité de travailler librement, d'avoir une joie multiforme de créer, mon cœur se remplit d'espoir et de joie, même en ces jours maudits qui sont entachés de sang et d'alcool.
>
> C'est là que commence la ligne de ma séparation décidée et irréconciliable contre les actions insensées des Commissaires du peuple. Je considère que le Maximalisme dans les idées est très utile pour l'âme russe sans limites ; sa tâche est de développer dans cette âme de grands et audacieux besoins, de susciter l'esprit de combat et l'activité si nécessaire, de promouvoir l'initiative dans cette âme indolente et de lui donner forme et vie en général.
>
> Mais le Maximalisme pratique des anarcho-communistes et des visionnaires du Smolny est ruineux pour la Russie et, surtout, pour la classe ouvrière russe. Les commissaires du peuple traitent la Russie comme un matériau d'expérimentation. Le peuple russe est pour eux ce que le cheval est pour les savants bactériologues qui inoculent au cheval le typhus afin que la lymphe antityphus se développe dans son sang. Aujourd'hui, les commissaires tentent une telle expérience prédestinée à l'échec sur le peuple russe sans penser que le cheval tourmenté et à moitié affamé peut mourir.
>
> Les réformateurs du Smolny ne se soucient pas de la Russie. Ils sacrifient de sang-froid la Russie au nom de leur rêve de révolution mondiale et européenne. Et aussi longtemps que je le pourrai, je ferai comprendre au prolétaire russe ceci : "On te

[134] Ibid, p. 204.

[135] See Jacques Sadoul, *Notes sur la révolution bolchévique* (Paris: Éditions de la sirène, 1919).

> conduit à la destruction". Ton peuple est utilisé comme cobaye dans une expérience inhumaine".

Contrairement aux rapports des ambassadeurs officieux sympathiques, les rapports des représentants diplomatiques de l'ancienne ligne sont également contraires. Le câble suivant de la légation américaine à Berne, en Suisse, est typique des nombreux messages qui sont parvenus à Washington au début de 1918 - en particulier après l'expression du soutien de Woodrow Wilson aux gouvernements bolchéviques :

> Pour Polk. Le message du Président au Consul de Moscou n'a pas été compris ici et les gens se demandent pourquoi le Président exprime son soutien aux Bolcheviks, au vu de la rapine, du meurtre et de l'anarchie de ces bandes.[136]

Le soutien continu de l'administration Wilson aux bolcheviks a conduit à la démission de De Witt C. Poole, le chargé d'affaires américain compétent d'Arkhangelsk (Russie) :

> Il est de mon devoir d'expliquer franchement au ministère la perplexité dans laquelle m'a plongé la déclaration de politique russe adoptée par la conférence de paix, le 22 janvier, sur proposition du président. Cette annonce reconnaît très volontiers la révolution et confirme une fois de plus l'absence totale de sympathie pour toute forme de contre-révolution qui a toujours été une note clé de la politique américaine en Russie, mais elle ne contient pas un seul [mot] de condamnation pour l'autre ennemi de la révolution - le gouvernement bolchévique.[137]

Ainsi, même dans les premiers jours de 1918, la trahison de la révolution libertaire avait été notée par des observateurs aussi aguerris que Maxim Gorky et De Witt C. Poole. La démission de Poole a ébranlé le Département d'État, qui a témoigné de "la plus grande réticence quant à votre désir de démissionner" et a déclaré qu'"il sera nécessaire de vous remplacer de manière naturelle et normale afin d'éviter des effets graves et peut-être désastreux sur le moral des troupes américaines dans le district d' Arkhangelsk qui pourraient entraîner la perte de vies américaines".[138]

Ainsi, non seulement les gouvernements alliés ont neutralisé leurs propres représentants gouvernementaux, mais les États-Unis ont ignoré les appels de l'intérieur et de l'extérieur de la Russie à cesser de soutenir les Bolcheviks. Le soutien influent des Soviétiques est venu en grande partie de la zone financière de New York (peu de soutien efficace a émané des révolutionnaires américains). Il

---

[136] Fichier décimal du Département d'État américain, 861.00/1305, 15 mars 1918.

[137] Ibid, 861.00/3804.

[138] Ibid.

provenait en particulier de l'American International Corporation, une société contrôlée par Morgan.

EXPORTER LA RÉVOLUTION : JACOB H. RUBIN

Nous sommes maintenant en mesure de comparer deux cas - qui ne sont en aucun cas les seuls - où les citoyens américains Jacob Rubin et Robert Minor ont aidé à exporter la révolution en Europe et dans d'autres régions de Russie.

Jacob H. Rubin était un banquier qui, selon ses propres termes, "a aidé à former le gouvernement soviétique d'Odessa".[139] Rubin était président, trésorier et secrétaire de Rubin Brothers au 19 West 34th Street, New York City. En 1917, il est associé à l'Union Bank of Milwaukee et à la Provident Loan Society of New York. Les administrateurs de la Provident Loan Society comprenaient des personnes mentionnées ailleurs comme ayant un lien avec la révolution bolchévique : P. A. Rockefeller, Mortimer L. Schiff et James Speyer.

Par un procédé quelconque - dont il n'est que vaguement rendu compte dans son livre *I Live to Tell*[140] - Rubin se trouvait à Odessa en février 1920 et a fait l'objet d'un message de l'amiral McCully au département d'État (daté du 13 février 1920, 861.00/6349). Ce message indiquait que Jacob H. Rubin de l'Union Bank, Milwaukee, était à Odessa et souhaitait rester avec les bolcheviks - "Rubin ne souhaite pas partir, a offert ses services aux bolcheviks et semble sympathiser avec eux". Rubin a ensuite retrouvé son chemin vers les États-Unis et a témoigné devant la commission des affaires étrangères de la Chambre des représentants en 1921 :

> J'avais été avec les gens de la Croix-Rouge américaine à Odessa. J'étais là quand l'armée rouge a pris possession d'Odessa. À cette époque, j'étais favorable au gouvernement soviétique, car j'étais socialiste et j'étais membre de ce parti depuis 20 ans. Je dois admettre que, dans une certaine mesure, j'ai contribué à la formation du gouvernement soviétique d'Odessa.[141]

Tout en ajoutant qu'il avait été arrêté en tant qu'espion par le gouvernement Denikin de Russie du Sud, nous n'en apprenons guère plus sur Rubin. En revanche, nous en savons beaucoup plus sur Robert Minor, qui a été pris sur le fait et libéré par un mécanisme rappelant la libération de Trotsky d'un camp de prisonniers de guerre de Halifax.

---

[139] États-Unis, Chambre, Commission des affaires étrangères, *Conditions en Russie,* 66e cong., 3e sess. 1921.

[140] Jacob H. Rubin, *I Live to Tell: The Russian Adventures of an American Socialist* (Indianapolis : Bobbs-Merrill, 1934).

[141] États-Unis, Chambre, commission des affaires étrangères, op. cit.

EXPORTER LA RÉVOLUTION : ROBERT MINOR

Le travail de propagande bolchévique en Allemagne,[142] financé et organisé par William Boyce Thompson et Raymond Robins, a été mis en œuvre sur le terrain par des citoyens américains, sous la supervision du Commissariat du peuple aux affaires étrangères de Trotsky :

> L'une des premières innovations de Trotsky au ministère des Affaires étrangères avait été d'instituer un Bureau de presse sous la direction de Karl Radek et un Bureau de la propagande révolutionnaire internationale sous la direction de Boris Reinstein, dont les assistants étaient John Reed et Albert Rhys Williams, et l'ensemble de ces dispositifs était dirigé contre l'armée allemande.
> Un journal allemand, *Die Fackel* (*La Torche*), était imprimé à raison d'un demi-million d'exemplaires par jour et envoyé par train spécial aux comités centraux de l'armée à Minsk, Kiev et dans d'autres villes, qui les distribuaient à leur tour à d'autres points du front.[143]

Robert Minor était un agent du bureau de propagande de Reinstein. Les ancêtres de Minor ont joué un rôle important dans les débuts de l'histoire américaine. Le général Sam Houston, premier président de la République du Texas, était apparenté à la mère de Minor, Routez Houston. Les autres parents étaient Mildred Washington, la tante de George Washington, et le général John Minor, directeur de campagne de Thomas Jefferson. Le père de Minor était un avocat de Virginie qui avait émigré au Texas. Après des années difficiles avec peu de clients, il est devenu juge à San Antonio.

Robert Minor était un dessinateur de talent et un socialiste. Il a quitté le Texas pour venir dans l'Est. Certaines de ses contributions ont été publiées dans *Masses*, une revue pro-bolchévique. En 1918, Minor est caricaturiste au sein de l'équipe du *Philadelphia Public Ledger*. Minor a quitté New York en mars 1918 pour couvrir la révolution bolchévique. Pendant son séjour en Russie, Minor rejoint le Bureau de la propagande révolutionnaire internationale de Reinstein (voir schéma), aux côtés de Philip Price, correspondant du *Daily Herald* et du *Manchester Guardian*, et de Jacques Sadoul, ambassadeur français non officiel et ami de Trotsky.

D'excellentes données sur les activités de Price, Minor et Sadoul ont survécu sous la forme d'un rapport spécial secret de Scotland Yard (Londres), n° 4, intitulé "The Case of Philip Price and Robert Minor", ainsi que dans des rapports figurant dans les dossiers du Département d'État, à Washington.[144] Selon ce rapport de Scotland Yard, Philip Price était à Moscou au milieu de l'année 1917, avant la

[142] Voir George G. Bruntz, *Allied Propaganda and the Collapse of the German Empire in 1918* (Stanford, Calif. : Stanford University Press, 1938), p. 144-55 ; voir aussi ici p. 82.

[143] John W. Wheeler-Bennett, *The Forgotten Peace* (New York : William Morrow, 1939).

[144] Il existe une copie de ce rapport de Scotland Yard dans le fichier décimal du ministère américain des Affaires étrangères, 316-23-1184 9.

révolution bolchévique, et a admis "être impliqué jusqu'au cou dans le mouvement révolutionnaire". Entre la révolution et l'automne 1918 environ, Price a travaillé avec Robert Minor au sein du Commissariat aux affaires étrangères.

L'ORGANISATION DU TRAVAIL DE PROPAGANDE ÉTRANGÈRE EN 1918

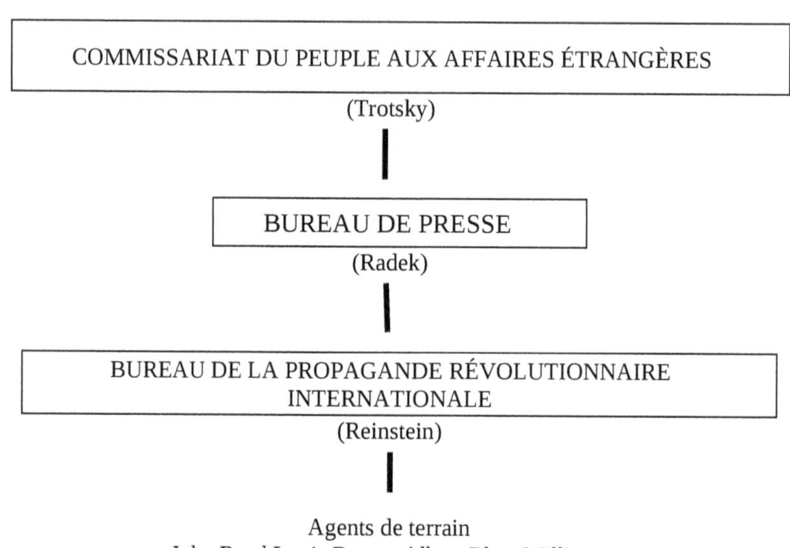

Agents de terrain
John Reed Louis Bryant Albert Rhys Williams
Robert Minor Philip Price Jacques Sadoul

En novembre 1918, Minor et Price quittent la Russie et se rendent en Allemagne.[145] Leur propagande a été utilisée pour la première fois sur le front russe de Murman ; des tracts ont été largués par des avions bolchéviques parmi les troupes britanniques, françaises et américaines - selon le programme de William Thompson.[146] La décision d'envoyer Sadoul, Price et Minor en Allemagne a été prise par le Comité exécutif central du Parti communiste. En Allemagne, leurs activités ont été portées à la connaissance des services de renseignement britanniques, français et américains. Le 15 février 1919, le lieutenant J. Habas de l'armée américaine fut envoyé à Düsseldorf, alors sous le contrôle d'un groupe révolutionnaire spartakiste ; il se fit passer pour un déserteur de l'armée américaine et offrit ses services aux Spartakistes. Habas fit la connaissance de Philip Price et de Robert Minor et suggéra d'imprimer des pamphlets pour les distribuer aux troupes américaines. Le rapport de Scotland Yard relate que Price et Minor avaient déjà écrit plusieurs pamphlets pour les troupes britanniques et américaines, que Price avait traduit en anglais certains des ouvrages de Wilhelm

[145] Joseph North, *Robert Minor : Artist and Crusader* (New York : International Publishers, 1956).

[146] Des échantillons des tracts de propagande de Minor sont toujours dans les fichiers du Département d'État américain. Voir p. 197-200 sur Thompson.

Liebknecht et que tous deux travaillaient sur d'autres tracts de propagande. Habas rapporte que Minor et Price ont déclaré avoir travaillé ensemble en Sibérie pour imprimer un journal bolchévique en anglais destiné à être distribué par avion aux troupes américaines et britanniques.[147]

Le 8 juin 1919, Robert Minor est arrêté à Paris par la police française et remis aux autorités militaires américaines à Coblence. Simultanément, les Spartakistes allemands sont arrêtés par les autorités militaires britanniques dans la région de Cologne. Par la suite, les Spartakistes ont été condamnés pour conspiration en vue de provoquer une mutinerie et une sédition au sein des forces alliées. Price est arrêté mais, comme Minor, il est rapidement libéré. Cette libération précipitée a été constatée au Département d'État :

> Robert Minor a maintenant été libéré, pour des raisons qui ne sont pas tout à fait claires, puisque les preuves contre lui semblent avoir été suffisantes pour obtenir une condamnation. Cette libération aura un effet malheureux, car on pense que Minor était intimement lié à l'IWW en Amérique.[148]

Le mécanisme par lequel Robert Minor a obtenu sa libération est consigné dans les dossiers du Département d'État. Le premier document pertinent, daté du 12 juin 1919, provient de l'ambassade américaine à Paris et est adressé au secrétaire d'État à Washington, D.C., et porte la mention URGENT ET CONFIDENTIEL.[149] Le ministère français des Affaires étrangères a informé l'ambassade que le 8 juin, Robert Minor, "un correspondant américain", avait été arrêté à Paris et remis au quartier général de la troisième armée américaine à Coblence. Des documents trouvés sur Minor apparaissent "pour confirmer les rapports fournis sur ses activités". Il semble donc établi que Minor a noué des relations à Paris avec les partisans avoués du bolchevisme". L'ambassade considère Minor comme un "homme particulièrement dangereux". Des enquêtes sont menées auprès des autorités militaires américaines ; l'ambassade estime que cette question relève de la seule compétence des militaires, de sorte qu'elle n'envisage aucune action bien que des instructions soient bienvenues.

Le 14 juin, le juge R. B. Minor à San Antonio, Texas, a télégraphié à Frank L. Polk au Département d'État :

> La presse rapporte que mon fils Robert Minor est détenu à Paris pour des raisons inconnues. Je vous prie de faire tout votre possible pour le libérer. Je vous renvoie aux sénateurs du Texas. R. P. Minor, juge de district, San Antonio, Texas.[150]

Polk a télégraphié au juge Minor que ni le Département d'État ni le Département de la Guerre n'avaient d'informations sur la détention de Robert

---

[147] Voir l'annexe 3.

[148] Fichier décimal du Département d'État américain, 316-23-1184.

[149] Ibid, 861.00/4680 (316-22-0774).

[150] Ibid, 861.00/4685 (/783).

Minor, et que l'affaire était maintenant devant les autorités militaires à Coblence. Fin juin, le Département d'État a reçu un message "urgent et strictement confidentiel" de Paris rapportant une déclaration du Bureau des renseignements militaires (Coblence) concernant la détention de Robert Minor : "Minor a été arrêté à Paris par les autorités françaises à la demande des services de renseignements militaires britanniques et immédiatement remis au quartier général américain à Coblence".[151] Il a été accusé d'avoir écrit et diffusé de la littérature révolutionnaire bolchévique, qui avait été imprimée à Düsseldorf, auprès des troupes britanniques et américaines dans les zones qu'elles occupaient. Les autorités militaires avaient l'intention d'examiner les accusations portées contre Minor et, si elles étaient fondées, de le juger en cour martiale. Si les accusations n'étaient pas fondées, elles avaient l'intention de remettre Minor aux autorités britanniques, "qui avaient initialement demandé que les Français le leur remettent".[152] Le juge Minor au Texas a contacté indépendamment Morris Sheppard, sénateur américain du Texas, et Sheppard a contacté le colonel House à Paris. Le 17 juin 1919, le colonel House envoya au sénateur Sheppard ce qui suit :

> L'ambassadeur américain et moi-même suivons le cas de Robert Minor. Je suis informé qu'il est détenu par les autorités militaires américaines à Cologne sur la base d'accusations graves, dont la nature exacte est difficile à découvrir. Néanmoins, nous prendrons toutes les mesures possibles pour assurer une juste considération à son égard.[153]

Le sénateur Sheppard et le membre du Congrès Carlos Bee (14e district, Texas) ont tous deux fait part de leur intérêt au Département d'État. Le 27 juin 1919, le membre du Congrès Bee a demandé des facilités pour que le juge Minor puisse envoyer à son fils 350 dollars et un message. Le 3 juillet, le sénateur Sheppard a écrit à Frank Polk, déclarant qu'il était "très intéressé" par l'affaire Robert Minor, et se demandant si l'État pouvait s'assurer de son statut, et si Minor était bien sous la juridiction des autorités militaires. Puis, le 8 juillet, l'ambassade de Paris envoie un télégramme à Washington : "Confidentiel. Minor a été libéré par les autorités américaines... et est retourné aux États-Unis sur le premier bateau disponible". Cette libération soudaine a intrigué le Département d'État, et le 3 août, le secrétaire d'État Lansing a envoyé un câble à Paris : "Secret. En référence aux précédents, je suis très désireux d'obtenir les raisons de la libération de Minor par les autorités militaires".

À l'origine, les autorités de l'armée américaine avaient voulu que les Britanniques jugent Robert Minor, car "ils craignaient que la politique n'intervienne aux États-Unis pour empêcher une condamnation si le prisonnier était jugé par une cour martiale américaine". Cependant, le gouvernement britannique a fait valoir que Minor était un citoyen américain, que les preuves

[151] Fichier décimal du Département d'État américain, 861.00/4688 (/788).

[152] Ibid.

[153] Ibid, 316-33-0824.

montraient qu'il avait préparé une propagande contre les troupes américaines en première instance, et que, par conséquent - c'est ce que le chef d'état-major britannique a suggéré - Minor devrait être jugé devant un tribunal américain. Le chef d'état-major britannique a estimé qu'il était "de la plus haute importance d'obtenir une condamnation si possible".[154]

Les documents du bureau du chef d'état-major de la troisième armée concernent les détails internes de la libération de Minor.[155] Un télégramme du 23 juin 1919 du Major General Harbord, chef d'état-major de la Troisième Armée (plus tard président du conseil d'administration d'International General Electric, dont le centre exécutif, par coïncidence, se trouvait également au 120 Broadway), au général commandant la Troisième Armée, déclarait que le commandant en chef John J. Pershing "ordonne que vous suspendiez l'action dans l'affaire contre Minor en attendant d'autres ordres". Il existe également un mémorandum signé par le Brigadier Général W. A. Bethel dans le bureau du juge-avocat, daté du 28 juin 1919, portant la mention "Secret et Confidentiel", et intitulé "Robert Minor, en attente de jugement par une commission militaire au quartier général de la 3e Armée". Le mémo passe en revue les poursuites judiciaires contre Minor. Parmi les points soulevés par Bethel, on peut noter que les Britanniques étaient manifestement réticents à traiter le cas Minor parce qu'"ils craignent l'opinion américaine en cas de procès d'un Américain pour un délit de guerre en Europe", même si le délit de fatigue dont Minor est accusé est aussi grave "qu'un homme puisse commettre". C'est une déclaration significative ; Minor, Price, et Sadoul mettaient en œuvre un programme conçu par le directeur de la Banque de la Réserve Fédérale Thompson, un fait confirmé par le propre mémorandum de Thompson (voir annexe 3). Thompson (et Robins) n'étaient-ils donc pas, dans une certaine mesure, soumis aux mêmes accusations ?

Après avoir interrogé Siegfried, le témoin contre Minor, et examiné les preuves, Bethel a commenté :

> Je crois sincèrement que Minor est coupable, mais si j'étais au tribunal, je ne dirais pas qu'il est coupable sur la base des preuves dont je dispose maintenant - le témoignage d'un seul homme qui agit comme un détective et un informateur n'est pas suffisant.

Bethel poursuit en déclarant que l'on saurait dans une semaine ou dans dix jours si une corroboration substantielle du témoignage de Siegfried était disponible. S'il est disponible, "je pense que Minor devrait être jugé", mais "si la corroboration ne peut être obtenue, je pense qu'il serait préférable de classer l'affaire".

---

[154] Fichier décimal du département d'État américain, 861.00/4874.

[155] Bureau du chef d'état-major de l'armée américaine, Archives nationales, Washington, D.C.

Cette déclaration du Béthel a été relayée sous une forme différente par le général Harbord dans un télégramme du 5 juillet au général Malin Craig (chef d'état-major de la troisième armée, Coblence) :

> En ce qui concerne l'affaire contre Minor, à moins que d'autres témoins que Siegfried n'aient été localisés à ce moment, C en C[156] ordonne que l'affaire soit abandonnée et Minor libéré. Veuillez prendre acte et indiquer les mesures à suivre.

La réponse de Craig au général Harbord (5 juillet) indique que Minor a été libéré à Paris et ajoute : "Ceci est conforme à ses propres souhaits et convient à nos objectifs". Craig ajoute également que d'autres témoins avaient été entendus.

Cet échange de télégrammes suggère une certaine hâte à abandonner les charges contre Robert Minor, et la hâte suggère la pression. Il n'y a pas eu de tentative significative pour développer des preuves. L'intervention du colonel House et du général Pershing au plus haut niveau à Paris et le télégramme du colonel House au sénateur Morris Sheppard donnent du poids aux rapports des journaux américains selon lesquels la Chambre et le président Wilson sont tous deux responsables de la libération précipitée de Minor sans procès.[157]

Minor retourne aux États-Unis et, comme Thompson et Robins avant lui, fait une tournée aux États-Unis pour promouvoir les merveilles de la Russie bolchévique.

En résumé, nous constatons que le directeur de la Federal Reserve Bank, William Thompson, a été actif dans la promotion des intérêts bolchéviques de plusieurs manières - production d'un pamphlet en russe, financement d'opérations bolchéviques, discours, organisation (avec Robins) d'une mission révolutionnaire bolchévique en Allemagne (et peut-être en France), et avec le partenaire de Morgan, Lamont, influence Lloyd George et le British War Cabinet afin de provoquer un changement dans la politique britannique. De plus, Raymond Robins a été cité par le gouvernement français pour avoir organisé des bolcheviks russes pour la révolution allemande. Nous savons que Robins travaillait de manière non déguisée pour les intérêts soviétiques en Russie et aux États-Unis. Enfin, nous constatons que Robert Minor, l'un des propagandistes révolutionnaires utilisés dans le programme de Thompson, a été libéré dans des circonstances suggérant une intervention des plus hauts niveaux du gouvernement américain.

De toute évidence, ce n'est qu'une fraction d'un tableau beaucoup plus vaste. Ce ne sont pas des événements accidentels ou aléatoires. Ils constituent un schéma cohérent et continu sur plusieurs années. Ils suggèrent une forte influence au sommet de plusieurs gouvernements.

---

[156] Commandant en Chef, NdT.

[157] États-Unis, Sénat, *Congressional Record*, octobre 1919, p. 6430, 6664-66, 7353-54 ; et *New York Times*, 11 octobre, 1919. Voir également *Sacramento Bee*, 17 juillet 1919.

CHAPITRE VII

LES BOLCHEVIKS RETOURNENT À NEW YORK

> Martens est très en vue. Il ne semble y avoir aucun doute sur ses liens avec la société Guarantee [sic], bien qu'il soit surprenant qu'une entreprise aussi grande et influente ait des relations avec une entreprise bolchévique.
>
> Rapport de Scotland Yard Intelligence, Londres, 1919[158]

Après les premiers succès de la révolution, les Soviétiques n'ont pas perdu de temps pour tenter, par l'intermédiaire d'anciens résidents américains, d'établir des relations diplomatiques avec les États-Unis et des moyens de propagande dans ce pays. En juin 1918, le consul américain à Harbin envoie un câble à Washington :

> Albert R. Williams, porteur du passeport 52913 ; le 15 mai 1917, en route pour les États-Unis en vue d'y établir un bureau d'information pour le compte du gouvernement soviétique, duquel il a une autorisation écrite. Dois-je accorder un visa ?[159]

Washington a refusé le visa et Williams a donc échoué dans sa tentative d'y établir un bureau d'information. Williams a été suivi par Alexander Nyberg (alias Santeri Nuorteva), un ancien immigrant finlandais aux États-Unis en janvier 1912, qui est devenu le premier représentant soviétique opérationnel aux États-Unis. Nyberg était un propagandiste actif. En fait, en 1919, il était, selon J. Edgar Hoover (dans une lettre au Comité américain des affaires étrangères), "le précurseur de LCAK Martens et avec Gregory Weinstein l'individu le plus actif de la propagande officielle bolchévique aux États-Unis".[160]

Nyberg n'a pas eu beaucoup de succès en tant que représentant diplomatique ou, finalement, en tant que propagandiste. Les dossiers du Département d'État enregistrent une interview de Nyberg par le bureau des conseillers, datée du *29*

---

[158] Copie dans le fichier décimal du département d'État américain, 316-22-656.

[159] Ibid, 861.00/1970.

[160] États-Unis, Chambre, Commission des affaires étrangères, *Conditions en Russie*, 66e cong., 3e sess. 1921, p. 78.

janvier 1919. Nyberg était accompagné de H. Kellogg, décrit comme "un citoyen américain, diplômé de Harvard", et, plus surprenant encore, d'un certain M. McFarland, avocat de l'organisation Hearst. Les archives du Département d'État montrent que Nyberg a fait "de nombreuses déclarations erronées concernant l'attitude à l'égard du gouvernement bolchévique" et a affirmé que Peters, le chef de la police terroriste de Petrograd, n'était qu'un "poète au grand cœur". Nyberg a demandé au ministère d'envoyer un câble à Lénine, "sur la théorie qu'il pourrait être utile pour faire aboutir la conférence proposée par les Alliés à Paris".[161] Le message proposé, un appel décousu à Lénine pour qu'il soit accepté au niveau international lors de la conférence de Paris, ne fut pas envoyé.[162]

DESCENTE DE POLICE SUR LE BUREAU SOVIÉTIQUE À NEW YORK

Alexander Nyberg (Nuorteva) a ensuite été licencié et remplacé par le Bureau soviétique, qui a été établi au début de 1919 dans le World Tower Building, 110 West 40 Street, New York City. Le bureau était dirigé par un citoyen allemand, Ludwig C. A. K. Martens, qui est généralement considéré comme le premier ambassadeur de l'Union soviétique aux États-Unis et qui, jusqu'à cette époque, était vice-président de Weinberg & Posner, une société d'ingénierie située au 120 Broadway, New York City. La raison pour laquelle "l'ambassadeur" et ses bureaux étaient situés à New York plutôt qu'à Washington D.C. n'a pas été expliquée ; cela suggère que le commerce plutôt que la diplomatie était son objectif premier. Quoi qu'il en soit, le bureau a rapidement publié un appel aux échanges entre la Russie et les États-Unis. L'industrie s'était effondrée et la Russie avait un besoin urgent de machines, de matériel ferroviaire, de vêtements, de produits chimiques, de drogues - en fait, de tout ce qui est utilisé par une civilisation moderne. En échange, les Soviétiques offraient de l'or et des matières premières. Le Bureau soviétique a alors procédé à l'établissement de contrats avec des entreprises américaines, en ignorant les faits de l'embargo et de la non-reconnaissance. En même temps, il apportait un soutien financier au parti communiste américain naissant.[163]

Le 7 mai 1919, le Département d'État a mis fin à l'intervention des entreprises au nom du Bureau (mentionné ailleurs) et a répudié Ludwig Martens, le Bureau soviétique et le gouvernement bolchévique de Russie. Cette réfutation officielle n'a pas dissuadé les chasseurs d'ordre avides de l'industrie américaine. Lorsque les bureaux du Bureau soviétique furent perquisitionnés le 12 juin 1919 par des représentants du Comité Lusk de l'État de New York, des dossiers de lettres adressées à des hommes d'affaires américains et provenant de ceux-ci,

[161] Fichier décimal du Département d'État américain, 316-19-1120.

[162] Ibid.

[163] Voir Benjamin Gitlow, U.S., House, *Un-American Propaganda Activities* (Washington, 1939), vol. 7-8, p. 4539.

représentant près d'un millier d'entreprises, furent mis au jour. Le "Special Report No. 5 (Secret)" de la Direction des renseignements du ministère britannique de l'Intérieur, publié par Scotland Yard à Londres le 14 juillet 1919 et rédigé par Basil H. Thompson, se fondait sur ces documents saisis ; le rapport en faisait état :

> ... Dès le début, Martens et ses associés ont tout mis en œuvre pour susciter l'intérêt des capitalistes américains et il y a tout lieu de croire que le Bureau a reçu le soutien financier de certaines sociétés d'exportation russes, ainsi que de la société Guarantee [*sic*], bien que cette dernière ait nié l'allégation selon laquelle elle finançait l'organisation de Martens.[164]

Thompson note que le loyer mensuel des bureaux du Bureau soviétique est de 300$ et que les salaires des employés s'élèvent à environ 4000$. Les fonds de Martens pour payer ces factures provenaient en partie de coursiers soviétiques - tels que John Reed et Michael Gruzenberg - qui apportaient des diamants de Russie pour les vendre aux États-Unis, et en partie de sociétés commerciales américaines, dont la Guaranty Trust Company de New York. Les rapports britanniques résumaient les dossiers saisis par les enquêteurs de Lusk dans les bureaux du bureau, et ce résumé mérite d'être cité dans son intégralité :

(1) Une intrigue se prépare au moment où le président se rend pour la première fois en France pour que l'administration utilise Nuorteva comme intermédiaire avec le gouvernement soviétique russe, en vue de sa reconnaissance par l'Amérique. On s'efforça d'y faire participer le colonel House, et il existe une longue et intéressante lettre adressée à Frederick C. Howe, sur laquelle Nuorteva semblait s'appuyer pour obtenir son soutien et sa sympathie. D'autres documents relient Howe à Martens et Nuorteva.

(2) Il existe un dossier de correspondance avec Eugène Debs.

(3) Une lettre d'Amos Pinchot à William Kent de la Commission tarifaire américaine dans une enveloppe adressée au sénateur Lenroot, présente Evans Clark "maintenant au Bureau de la République soviétique de Russie". "Il veut vous parler de la reconnaissance de Kolchak et de la levée du blocus, etc.

(4) Un rapport à Felix Frankfurter, daté du 27 mai 1919, parle de la virulente campagne de diffamation du gouvernement russe.

(5) Il existe une correspondance considérable entre un colonel et Mme Raymond Robbins *[sic]* et Nuorteva, tant en 1918 qu'en 1919. En juillet 1918, Mme Robbins a demandé à Nuorteva des articles pour "Life and Labour", l'organe de la National Women's Trade League. En février et mars 1919, Nuorteva essaya, par l'intermédiaire de Robbins, d'être invitée à témoigner devant la commission Overman. Il voulait également que Robbins dénonce les documents de Sisson.

(6) Dans une lettre de la Jansen Cloth Products Company, New York, à Nuorteva, datée du 30 mars 1918, E. Werner Knudsen dit qu'il comprend que

---

164 Copie dans le fichier décimal du département d'État américain, 316-22-656. Confirmation de l'implication de Guaranty Trust dans des rapports de renseignement ultérieurs.

Nuorteva a l'intention de prendre des dispositions pour l'exportation de denrées alimentaires à travers la Finlande et qu'il offre ses services. Nous disposons d'un dossier sur Knudsen, qui a transmis des informations à destination et en provenance de l'Allemagne via le Mexique concernant les transports maritimes britanniques.[165]

Ludwig Martens, poursuit le rapport des services de renseignement, était en contact avec tous les dirigeants de la "gauche" aux États-Unis, y compris John Reed, Ludwig Lore et Harry J. Boland, le rebelle irlandais. Une campagne vigoureuse contre Alexandre Kolchak en Sibérie avait été organisée par Martens. Le rapport conclut :

> L'organisation de [Martens] est une arme puissante pour soutenir la cause bolchévique aux États-Unis et... il est en contact étroit avec les promoteurs de troubles politiques sur tout le continent américain.

La liste du personnel de Scotland Yard employé par le Bureau soviétique à New York coïncide assez étroitement avec une liste similaire dans les dossiers du Comité Lusk à Albany, New York, qui sont aujourd'hui ouverts à l'inspection publique.[166] Il y a une différence essentielle entre les deux listes : l'analyse britannique incluait le nom "Julius Hammer" alors que Hammer a été omis du rapport du Comité Lusk.[167] Le rapport britannique caractérise Julius Hammer comme suit :

> Dans Julius Hammer, Martens a un véritable bolchevik et un ardent partisan de la gauche, venu de Russie il n'y a pas longtemps. Il a été l'un des organisateurs du mouvement de gauche à New York, et s'exprime lors de réunions sur la même plateforme avec des leaders de la gauche tels que Reed, Hourwich, Lore et Larkin.

Il existe également d'autres preuves du travail de Hammer en faveur des Soviétiques. Une lettre de la National City Bank, New York, adressée au département du Trésor américain indique que les documents reçus par la banque

---

[165] Sur Frederick C. Howe, voir p. 16, 177, pour une première déclaration sur la manière dont les financiers utilisent la société et ses problèmes à leurs propres fins ; sur Felix Frankfurter, plus tard juge à la Cour suprême, voir l'annexe 3 pour une première lettre de Frankfurter à Nuorteva ; sur Raymond Robins, voir p. 100.

[166] La liste du personnel du Comité Lusk au sein du Bureau soviétique est imprimée à l'annexe 3. Cette liste comprend Kenneth Durant, assistant du colonel House, Dudley Field Malone, nommé par le président Wilson comme collecteur des douanes du port de New York, et Morris Hillquit, l'intermédiaire financier entre le banquier new-yorkais Eugène Boissevain d'une part, et John Reed et l'agent soviétique Michael Gruzenberg d'autre part.

[167] Julius Hammer est le père d'Armand Hammer, qui est aujourd'hui président de l'Occidental Petroleum Corp. de Los Angeles.

de Martens ont été "attestés par un Dr Julius Hammer pour le directeur par intérim du département financier" du Bureau soviétique.[168]

La famille Hammer a entretenu des liens étroits avec la Russie et le régime soviétique de 1917 à nos jours. Armand Hammer est aujourd'hui en mesure d'acquérir les contrats soviétiques les plus lucratifs. Jacob, grand-père d'Armand Hammer, et Julius sont nés en Russie. Armand, Harry et Victor, fils de Julius, sont nés aux États-Unis et sont citoyens américains. Victor était un artiste connu ; son fils - également appelé Armand - et sa petite-fille sont citoyens soviétiques et résident en Union soviétique. Armand Hammer est président de l'Occidental Petroleum Corporation et a un fils, Julian, qui est directeur de la publicité et des publications de l'Occidental Petroleum.

Julius Hammer était un membre éminent et un financier de l'aile gauche du Parti socialiste. Lors de son congrès de 1919, Hammer a fait partie, avec Bertram D. Wolfe et Benjamin Gitlow, du comité directeur qui a donné naissance au Parti communiste des États-Unis.

En 1920, Julius Hammer a été condamné à trois ans et demi à quinze ans de prison à Sing Sing pour avortement criminel. Lénine a suggéré - avec justification - que Julius était "emprisonné sous l'accusation de pratiquer des avortements illégaux mais en fait à cause du communisme".[169] D'autres membres du parti communiste américain furent condamnés à la prison pour sédition ou déportés en Union soviétique. Les représentants soviétiques aux États-Unis ont fait des efforts acharnés mais infructueux pour obtenir la libération de Julius et de ses collègues du parti.

Un autre membre éminent du Bureau soviétique était le secrétaire adjoint, Kenneth Durant, un ancien assistant du colonel House. En 1920, Durant a été identifié comme un messager soviétique. L'annexe 3 reproduit une lettre à Kenneth Durant qui a été saisie par le ministère américain de la Justice en 1920 et qui décrit les relations étroites de Durant avec la hiérarchie soviétique. Elle a été insérée dans le compte-rendu des audiences d'une commission de la Chambre en 1920, avec le commentaire suivant :

> **M. NEWTON** : C'est un courrier intéressant pour cette commission de savoir quelle était la nature de cette lettre, et j'ai une copie de la lettre que je veux faire insérer dans le dossier en rapport avec le témoignage du témoin.
> **M. MASON** : Cette lettre n'a jamais été montrée au témoin. Il a dit qu'il n'avait jamais vu la lettre, qu'il avait demandé à la voir, et que le ministère avait refusé de la lui montrer. Nous ne mettrons aucun témoin à la barre et ne lui demanderons pas de témoigner sur une lettre sans la voir.
> **M. NEWTON** : Le témoin a déclaré qu'il avait une telle lettre, et il a témoigné qu'ils l'ont trouvée dans son manteau dans le coffre, je crois. Cette lettre était adressée à M. Kenneth Durant, et elle contenait une autre enveloppe qui était également scellée. Elle a été ouverte par les fonctionnaires du gouvernement et une copie photostatique en a été faite. La lettre, je peux dire, est signée par un homme du nom de *"Bill"*. Elle fait spécifiquement référence à l'argent soviétique déposé à

---

[168] Voir l'annexe 3.

[169] V. I. Lénine, *Polnoe Sobranie Sochinenii*, 5e éd. (Moscou, 1958), 53:267.

> Christiania, en Norvège, dont une partie a été remise ici aux fonctionnaires du gouvernement soviétique de ce pays.[170]

Kenneth Durant, qui agissait comme courrier soviétique dans le transfert des fonds, était trésorier du Bureau soviétique et attaché de presse et éditeur de la *Russie soviétique,* l'organe officiel du Bureau soviétique. Durant était issu d'une famille aisée de Philadelphie. Il a passé la plus grande partie de sa vie au service des Soviétiques, d'abord en charge du travail de publicité au Bureau soviétique puis, de 1923 à 1944, comme responsable du bureau soviétique de Tass aux États-Unis. J. Edgar Hoover a décrit Durant comme "à tout moment... particulièrement actif dans les intérêts de Martens et du gouvernement soviétique".[171]

Felix Frankfurter - plus tard juge de la Cour Suprême - était également très présent dans les dossiers du Bureau soviétique. Une lettre de Frankfurter à l'agent soviétique Nuorteva est reproduite à l'annexe 3 et suggère que Frankfurter avait une certaine influence sur le bureau.

En bref, le Bureau soviétique n'aurait pas pu être créé sans l'aide influente des États-Unis. Une partie de cette assistance est venue de nominations influentes spécifiques au sein du personnel du Bureau soviétique et une autre partie est venue de sociétés commerciales extérieures au Bureau, des sociétés qui étaient réticentes à faire connaître publiquement leur soutien.

DES ENTREPRISES ALLIÉES AU BUREAU SOVIÉTIQUE

Le 1er février 1920, la première page du *New York Times* comportait un encadré indiquant que Martens allait être arrêté et déporté en Russie. Au même moment, Martens était recherché comme témoin pour comparaître devant un sous-comité de la commission des relations étrangères du Sénat qui enquêtait sur les activités soviétiques aux États-Unis. Après avoir fait profil bas pendant quelques jours, Martens comparaît devant la commission, revendique le privilège diplomatique et refuse de rendre les documents "officiels" en sa possession. Puis, après une vague de publicité, Martens a "cédé", a remis ses papiers et a admis avoir mené des activités révolutionnaires aux États-Unis dans le but ultime de renverser le système capitaliste.

Martens s'est vanté auprès des médias et du Congrès que les grandes entreprises, dont les emballeurs de Chicago, aidaient les Soviétiques :

> En accord avec Martens, au lieu de se contenter de faire de la propagande parmi les radicaux et le prolétariat, il a consacré la plupart de ses efforts à gagner aux côtés de la Russie les intérêts des grandes entreprises et des industries de ce pays, les emballeurs, l'United States Steel Corporation, la Standard Oil Company et d'autres

[170] États-Unis, Chambre des représentants, Commission des affaires étrangères, *Conditions en Russie,* 66e Congrès, 3e session, 1921, p. 75. "Bill" était William Bobroff, agent soviétique.

[171] Ibid, p. 78.

> grandes entreprises engagées dans le commerce international. Martens a affirmé que la plupart des grandes maisons de commerce du pays l'aidaient dans son effort pour obtenir la reconnaissance du gouvernement soviétique par le gouvernement.[172]

Cette revendication a été développée par A. A. Heller, attaché commercial au Bureau soviétique :

> "Parmi les personnes qui nous aident à obtenir la reconnaissance du département d'État, on trouve les grands emballeurs de Chicago, Armour, Swift, Nelson Morris et Cudahy.... Parmi les autres entreprises, on trouve... l'American Steel Export Company, la Lehigh Machine Company, l'Adrian Knitting Company, l'International Harvester Company, l'Aluminum Goods Manufacturing Company, l'Aluminum Company of America, l'American Car and Foundry Export Company, M.C.D. Borden & Sons."[173]

Le *New York Times* a confirmé ces affirmations et a rapporté les commentaires des entreprises citées. "Je n'ai jamais entendu parler de cet homme [Martens] de ma vie", a déclaré G. F. Swift, Jr, responsable du département export de Swift & Co. "Je suis certain que nous n'avons jamais eu de relations d'aucune sorte avec lui."[174] Le *Times* a ajouté que O. H. Swift, le seul autre membre de la firme qui pouvait être contacté, "a également nié toute connaissance de Martens ou de son bureau à New York." La déclaration de Swift était au mieux évasive. Lorsque les enquêteurs du Comité Lusk ont saisi les dossiers du Bureau soviétique, ils ont trouvé une correspondance entre le bureau et presque toutes les sociétés nommées par Martens et Heller. La "liste des entreprises qui ont proposé de faire des affaires avec le Bureau soviétique russe", compilée à partir de ces dossiers, comprenait une entrée (page 16), "Swift and Company, Union Stock Yards, Chicago, Ill. En d'autres termes, Swift avait été en communication avec Martens malgré son démenti au *New York Times.*

Le *New York Times* a contacté United States Steel et a rapporté que "le juge Elbert H. Gary a déclaré hier soir que la déclaration du représentant soviétique ici présent n'était pas fondée et qu'il avait eu des relations avec l'United States Steel Corporation". C'est techniquement correct. L'United States Steel Corporation n'est pas répertoriée dans les dossiers soviétiques, mais la liste contient (page 16) une filiale, "United States Steel Products Co., 30 Church Street, New York City".

La liste du comité Lusk contient les informations suivantes sur les autres entreprises mentionnées par Martens et Heller : Standard Oil - ne figure pas sur la liste. Armour & Co., emballeur de viande - répertoriés comme "Armour Leather" et "Armour & Co. Union Stock Yards, Chicago". Morris Go., emballeur de viande, est listé à la page 13. Cudahy - listé à la page 6. American Steel Export Co. - listée à la page 2 comme étant située au Woolworth Building ; elle avait offert de commercer avec l'URSS. Lehigh Machine Co. - non répertoriée. Adrian Knitting

---

[172] *New York Times*, 17 novembre 1919.

[173] Ibid.

[174] Ibid.

Co. - citée à la page 1. International Harvester Co. - citée à la page 11. La société Aluminum Goods Manufacturing - citée à la page 1. Aluminum Company of America - non répertoriée. American Car and Foundry Export - la société la plus proche est "American Car Co. - Philadelphie". M.C.D. Borden 8c Sons - société située au 90 Worth Street, page 4.

Puis, le samedi 21 juin 1919, Santeri Nuorteva (Alexander Nyberg) a confirmé dans une interview à la presse le rôle d'International Harvester :

> **Q** : [par un journaliste du *New York* Times] : Quelle est votre activité ?
> **R** : Directeur des achats en Russie soviétique.
> **Q** : Qu'avez-vous fait pour y parvenir ?
> **R** : Je me suis adressé aux fabricants américains.
> **Q** : Nommez-les.
> **R** : L'International Harvester Corporation en fait partie.
> **Q** : Qui avez-vous vu ?
> **R** : M. Koenig.
> **Q** : Êtes-vous allé le voir ?
> **R** : Oui.
> **Q** : Donnez plus de noms.
> **R** : Je suis allé voir tellement de gens, environ 500 personnes, et je ne me souviens pas de tous les noms. Nous avons des dossiers dans le bureau qui les divulguent.[175]

En bref, les affirmations de Heller et Martens concernant leurs nombreux contacts entre certaines entreprises américaines ont été étayées par les dossiers du Bureau soviétique. D'autre part, pour leurs propres raisons, ces entreprises semblaient peu désireuses de confirmer leurs activités.

LES BANQUIERS EUROPÉENS AIDENT LES BOLCHEVIKS

Outre Guaranty Trust et le banquier privé Boissevain à New York, certains banquiers européens ont apporté une aide directe pour maintenir et développer l'emprise bolchévique sur la Russie. Un rapport de 1918 du département d'État de notre ambassade à Stockholm détaille ces transferts financiers. Le département a félicité son auteur, déclarant que ses "rapports sur les conditions en Russie, la propagation du bolchevisme en Europe et les questions financières... se sont avérés très utiles pour le département. Le ministère est très satisfait de votre capacité à gérer les affaires de la légation".[176] Selon ce rapport, l'un de ces "banquiers bolchéviques" agissant au nom du régime soviétique émergent était Dmitri Rubenstein, de l'ancienne banque russo-française de Petrograd. Rubenstein, un associé du célèbre Grigori Raspoutine, avait été emprisonné à Petrograd avant la révolution en relation avec la vente de la deuxième compagnie d'assurance-vie russe. Le directeur et gestionnaire américain de la deuxième compagnie d'assurance-vie russe était John MacGregor Grant, qui était situé au 120

[175] *New York Times*, 21 juin 1919.

[176] Fichier décimal du Département d'État américain, 861.51/411, 23 novembre 1918.

Broadway, New York City. Grant était également le représentant à New York de la Banque Russo-Asiatique de Putiloff. En août 1918, Grant est inscrit (pour des raisons inconnues) sur la "liste des suspects" du Bureau des renseignements militaires.[177] Cela peut s'expliquer par le fait qu'Olof Aschberg, au début de 1918, a déclaré avoir ouvert un crédit étranger à Petrograd "avec la John MacGregor Grant Co, société d'exportation, qu'il [Aschberg] finance en Suède et qui est financée en Amérique par la Guarantee *[sic]* Trust Co".[178] Après la révolution, Dmitri Rubenstein s'installe à Stockholm et devient l'agent financier des bolcheviks. Le Département d'État a noté que, bien que Rubenstein ne soit "pas un bolchévique, il a été sans scrupules dans sa recherche du gain", et on soupçonne qu'il pourrait effectuer la visite envisagée en Amérique dans l'intérêt des bolchéviques et pour le compte de ceux-ci.[179]

Un autre "banquier bolchévique" de Stockholm était Abram Givatovzo, beau-frère de Trotsky et Lev Kamenev. Le rapport du Département d'État a affirmé que si Givatovzo prétendait être "très anti-bolchévique", il avait en fait reçu "de grosses sommes" des bolcheviks par courrier pour financer des opérations révolutionnaires. Givatovzo faisait partie d'un syndicat qui comprenait Denisoff de l'ancienne banque sibérienne, Kamenka de l'Asoff Don Bank et Davidoff de la Banque du commerce extérieur. Ce syndicat a vendu les actifs de l'ancienne banque sibérienne au gouvernement britannique.

Un autre banquier privé tsariste, Gregory Lessine, s'est occupé des affaires bolchéviques par l'intermédiaire de la société Dardel and Hagborg. D'autres "banquiers bolchéviques" nommés dans le rapport sont Stirrer et Jakob Berline, qui contrôlait auparavant, par l'intermédiaire de sa femme, la banque Petrograd Nelkens. Isidor Kon a été utilisé par ces banquiers comme agent.

Le plus intéressant de ces banquiers européens opérant au nom des bolcheviks était Gregory Benenson, ancien président à Petrograd de la Russian and English Bank - une banque qui comptait dans son conseil d'administration Lord Balfour (secrétaire d'État aux Affaires étrangères en Angleterre) et Sir I. M. H. Amory, ainsi que S. H. Cripps et H. Guedalla. Benenson se rend à Petrograd après la révolution, puis à Stockholm. Il est venu, a déclaré un fonctionnaire du département d'État, "en apportant à ma connaissance dix millions de roubles avec lui, car il me les a offerts à un prix élevé pour l'utilisation de notre ambassade Arkhangelsk". Benenson avait un accord avec les bolcheviks pour échanger soixante millions de roubles contre 1,5 million de livres sterling.

En janvier 1919, les banquiers privés de Copenhague qui étaient associés aux institutions bolchéviques ont été alarmés par des rumeurs selon lesquelles la police politique danoise avait signalé la délégation soviétique et les personnes en contact avec les bolcheviks pour les expulser du Danemark. Ces banquiers et la délégation ont tenté à la hâte de retirer leurs fonds des banques danoises - en particulier, sept

[177] Ibid, 316-125-1212.

[178] États-Unis, Département d'État, Relations extérieures des États-Unis : 1918, Russie, 1:373.

[179] U.S. State Dept. Decimal File, 861.00/4878, July,' 21, 1919.

millions de roubles de la Revisionsbanken.[180] De plus, des documents confidentiels ont été cachés dans les bureaux de la compagnie d'assurance Martin Larsen.

Par conséquent, nous pouvons identifier une sorte d'assistance des banquiers capitalistes à l'Union soviétique. Certains étaient des banquiers américains, d'autres des banquiers tsaristes exilés et vivant en Europe, et d'autres encore des banquiers européens. Leur objectif commun était le profit, et non l'idéologie politique.

Les aspects discutables du travail de ces "banquiers bolchéviques", comme on les appelait, s'inscrivent dans le cadre des événements contemporains en Russie. En 1919, des troupes françaises, britanniques et américaines combattaient les troupes soviétiques dans la région d'Arkhangelsk. Lors d'un affrontement en avril 1919, par exemple, les pertes américaines se sont élevées à un officier, cinq hommes tués et neuf disparus.[181] En effet, à un moment donné en 1919, le général H. Bliss, commandant américain dans la région d'Arkhangelsk, a confirmé la déclaration britannique selon laquelle "les troupes alliées dans les districts de Mourmansk et d'Arkhangelsk étaient en danger d'extermination à moins qu'elles ne soient rapidement renforcées".[182] Des renforts étaient alors en route sous le commandement du Brigadier Général W. P. Richardson.

En bref, alors que Guaranty Trust et des entreprises américaines de premier plan aidaient à la formation du Bureau soviétique à New York, les troupes américaines étaient en conflit avec les troupes soviétiques en Russie du Nord. En outre, ces conflits étaient quotidiennement rapportés dans le *New York Times*, vraisemblablement lu par ces banquiers et hommes d'affaires. De plus, comme nous le verrons au chapitre dix, les cercles financiers qui soutenaient le Bureau soviétique à New York ont également formé à New York les "United Americans" - une organisation virulemment anticommuniste qui prédisait une révolution sanglante, une famine massive et la panique dans les rues de New York.

---

[180] Ibid, 316-21-115/21.

[181] *New York Times*, 5 avril 1919.

[182] Ibid.

CHAPITRE VIII

120 BROADWAY, NEW YORK CITY

William B. Thompson, qui était à Petrograd de juillet à novembre dernier, a fait une contribution personnelle de 1 000 000 de dollars aux Bolcheviks dans le but de diffuser leur doctrine en Allemagne et en Autriche...

Washington Post, 2 février 1918

À mesure que je rassemblais du matériel de recherche pour ce livre, un seul endroit et une seule adresse dans le quartier de Wall Street se sont peu à peu imposés : 120 Broadway, New York City. Ce livre aurait pu être écrit en ne mentionnant que des personnes, des entreprises et des organisations situées au 120 Broadway en 1917. Bien que cette méthode de recherche eut été forcée et non naturelle, elle n'aurait exclu qu'une partie relativement petite de l'histoire.

Le bâtiment original du 120 Broadway a été détruit par un incendie avant la Première Guerre mondiale. Par la suite, le site a été vendu à l'Equitable Office Building Corporation, organisé par le général T. Coleman du Pont, président de la Compagnie des poudres du Pont de Nemours.[183] Un nouveau bâtiment a été achevé en 1915 et la compagnie d'assurance Equitable Life a réintégré son ancien site. Au passage, il faut noter un intéressant emboîtement dans l'histoire d'Equitable. En 1916, le caissier du bureau de Berlin de la compagnie Equitable Life était William Schacht, le père de Hjalmar Horace Greeley Schacht - qui deviendra plus tard le banquier et le génie financier d'Hitler. William Schacht était un citoyen américain, il a travaillé trente ans pour Equitable en Allemagne, et possédait une maison à Berlin connue sous le nom de "Equitable Villa". Avant de rejoindre Hitler, le jeune Hjalmar Schacht a été membre du Conseil des travailleurs et des soldats (soviétique) de Zehlendoff ; il l'a quitté en 1918 pour rejoindre le conseil d'administration de la Nationalbank fur Deutschland. Son codirecteur à la DONAT était Emil Wittenberg, qui, avec Max May de la Guaranty Trust Company de New York, était directeur de la première banque internationale soviétique, la Ruskombank.

[183] Par une bizarrerie, les documents de constitution du Equitable Office Building ont été rédigés par Dwight W. Morrow, plus tard associé de Morgan, mais alors membre du cabinet d'avocats Simpson, Thacher & Bartlett. Le cabinet Thacher a apporté deux membres à la mission de la Croix-Rouge américaine en Russie en 1917 (voir chapitre 5).

En tout cas, le bâtiment du 120 Broadway était en 1917 connu sous le nom de Equitable Life Building. C'est un grand bâtiment, bien qu'il ne soit pas le plus grand immeuble de bureaux de la ville de New York, qui occupe une zone d'un seul tenant à l'angle de Broadway et de Pine, et qui compte trente-quatre étages. Le Bankers Club était situé au trente-quatrième étage. La liste des locataires de 1917 reflète en effet l'implication américaine dans la révolution bolchévique et ses suites. Par exemple, le siège du deuxième district de la Réserve Fédérale - la région de New York - de loin le plus important des districts de la Réserve Fédérale, était situé au 120 Broadway. Les bureaux de plusieurs directeurs individuels de la Banque de la Réserve Fédérale de New York et, plus important encore, de l'American International Corporation, se trouvaient également au 120 Broadway. En revanche, Ludwig Martens, nommé par les Soviétiques comme le premier "ambassadeur" bolchévique aux États-Unis et chef du Bureau soviétique, était en 1917 le vice-président de Weinberg & Posner - et avait également des bureaux au 120 Broadway.[184]

Cette concentration est-elle un accident ? La contiguïté géographique a-t-elle une signification ? Avant de tenter de proposer une réponse, nous devons changer de cadre de référence et abandonner le spectre gauche-droite de l'analyse politique.

Avec un manque de perception presque unanime, le monde universitaire a décrit et analysé les relations politiques internationales dans le contexte d'un conflit incessant entre le capitalisme et le communisme, et l'adhésion rigide à cette formule marxiste a déformé l'histoire moderne. De temps en temps, on lance des remarques étranges selon lesquelles la polarité est effectivement fausse, mais elles sont rapidement envoyées dans les limbes. Par exemple, Carroll Quigley, professeur de relations internationales à l'université de Georgetown, a fait le commentaire suivant sur la Maison de Morgan :

> Il y a plus de cinquante ans, la firme Morgan a décidé d'infiltrer les mouvements politiques de gauche aux États-Unis. Cela a été relativement facile à faire, car ces groupes étaient privés de fonds et désireux de faire entendre leur voix pour atteindre le peuple. Wall Street fournissait les deux. Le but n'était pas de détruire, mais de dominer ou de prendre le contrôle...[185]

Le commentaire du professeur Quigley, apparemment basé sur des documents confidentiels, a tous les ingrédients d'une bombe historique s'il peut être étayé. Nous suggérons que la firme Morgan a infiltré non seulement la gauche nationale, comme l'a noté Quigley, mais aussi la gauche étrangère - c'est-à-dire le mouvement bolchévique et la Troisième Internationale. De plus, par

[184] La société John MacGregor Grant, agent de la Banque Russo-Asiatique (impliquée dans le financement des bolcheviks), se trouvait au 120 Broadway - et était financée par la Guaranty Trust Company.

[185] Carroll Quigley, *Tragedy and Hope* (New York : Macmillan, 1966), p. 938. Quigley écrivait en 1965, ce qui situe le début de l'infiltration vers 1915, une date qui correspond aux preuves présentées ici.

l'intermédiaire d'amis du Département d'État américain, Morgan et des intérêts financiers alliés, en particulier la famille Rockefeller, ont exercé une puissante influence sur les relations américano-russes depuis la Première Guerre mondiale jusqu'à aujourd'hui. Les preuves présentées dans ce chapitre suggèrent que deux des véhicules opérationnels pour infiltrer ou influencer les mouvements révolutionnaires étrangers se trouvaient au 120 Broadway : le premier, la Banque de Réserve Fédérale de New York, fortement liée aux personnes nommées par Morgan ; le second, l'American International Corporation contrôlée par Morgan. De plus, il y avait un lien important entre la Federal Reserve Bank of New York et l'American International Corporation - C. A. Stone, le président d'American International, était également un directeur de la Federal Reserve Bank.

L'hypothèse provisoire est donc que cette concentration inhabituelle à une seule adresse était le reflet d'actions délibérées menées par des entreprises et des personnes spécifiques et que ces actions et événements ne peuvent être analysés dans le spectre habituel de l'antagonisme politique gauche-droite.

AMERICAN INTERNATIONAL CORPORATION

L'American International Corporation (AIC) a été formée à New York le 22 novembre 1915 par les intérêts de J.P. Morgan, avec une participation importante de la National City Bank de Stillman et des intérêts de Rockefeller. Le bureau général de l'AIC se trouvait au 120 Broadway. La charte de la société l'autorisait à exercer tout type d'activité, à l'exception des activités bancaires et des services publics, dans n'importe quel pays du monde. L'objectif déclaré de la société était de développer les entreprises nationales et étrangères, d'étendre les activités américaines à l'étranger et de promouvoir les intérêts des banquiers, des entreprises et des ingénieurs américains et étrangers.

Frank A. Vanderlip a décrit dans ses mémoires la création d'American International et l'engouement suscité à Wall Street par son potentiel commercial.[186] L'idée originale est née d'une discussion entre Stone & Webster - les entrepreneurs ferroviaires internationaux qui "étaient convaincus qu'il n'y avait pas beaucoup plus de construction ferroviaire à faire aux États-Unis" - et Jim Perkins et Frank A. Vanderlip de la National City Bank (NCB).[187] L'autorisation initiale de capital était de 50 millions de dollars et le conseil d'administration représentait les principaux acteurs du monde financier new-yorkais. Vanderlip rapporte qu'il a écrit ce qui suit au président de la NCB, Stillman, enthousiasmé par l'énorme potentiel de l'American International Corporation :

> James A. Farrell et Albert Wiggin ont été invités [à faire partie du conseil d'administration] mais ont dû consulter leurs comités avant d'accepter. Je pense aussi à demander à Henry Walters et Myron T. Herrick. M. Herrick est vivement

[186] Frank A. Vanderlip, *From Farm Boy to Financier* (New York : A. Appleton-Century, 1935).

[187] Ibid, p. 267.

> contesté par M. Rockefeller, mais M. Stone le veut et je suis convaincu qu'il serait particulièrement désirable en France. Le tout s'est déroulé dans la douceur et la réception a été marquée par un enthousiasme qui m'a surpris, même si j'étais fermement convaincu que nous étions sur la bonne voie.
> J'ai vu James J. Hill aujourd'hui, par exemple. Il a dit au début qu'il ne pouvait pas envisager d'étendre ses responsabilités, mais après que j'ai fini de lui dire ce que nous prévoyons de faire, il a dit qu'il serait heureux de faire partie du conseil d'administration, qu'il prendrait une grande quantité d'actions et qu'il voulait surtout une participation importante dans la City Bank et m'a chargé de lui acheter les actions au marché.
> J'ai parlé avec Ogden Armour à ce sujet pour la première fois aujourd'hui. Il s'est assis dans un silence parfait pendant que je racontais l'histoire, et, sans poser une seule question, il a dit qu'il intégrerait le conseil et voulait 500 000 dollars d'actions.
> M. Coffin [de General Electric] est un autre homme retiré de tout, mais il est "devenu si enthousiaste à ce sujet qu'il était prêt à faire partie du conseil d'administration et à offrir la coopération la plus active.
> Je me sentais très bien d'avoir Sabin. Le Guaranty Trust est le concurrent le plus actif que nous ayons dans ce domaine et il est très utile de les faire entrer dans le giron de la société de cette manière. Ils ont été particulièrement enthousiastes chez Kuhn, Loeb. Ils veulent prendre jusqu'à 2 500 000$. Il y avait vraiment une sacrée concurrence pour savoir qui devait entrer au conseil, mais comme j'avais parlé avec Kahn et l'avais invité en premier, il a été décidé qu'il devait continuer. Il est peut-être le plus enthousiaste de tous. Ils veulent un demi-million d'actions pour le château de Sir Ernest[188] à qui ils ont transmis le plan et ils ont reçu de lui son approbation.
> J'ai expliqué toute l'affaire au conseil d'administration [de la City Bank] mardi et n'ai reçu que des commentaires favorables.[189]

Tout le monde convoitait les actions de l'AIC. Joe Grace (de W. R. Grace & Co.) voulait 600 000 dollars en plus de sa participation dans la National City Bank. Ambrose Monell voulait 500 000$. George Baker voulait 250 000$. Et "William Rockefeller a essayé, en vain, de me convaincre de le mettre à terre pour 5 000 000$ de la commune."[190]

En 1916, les investissements de l'AIC à l'étranger s'élevaient à plus de 23 millions de dollars et en 1917 à plus de 27 millions de dollars. La société a établi des représentations à Londres, Paris, Buenos Aires et Pékin, ainsi qu'à Petrograd, en Russie. Moins de deux ans après sa création, AIC opérait à grande échelle en Australie, Argentine, Uruguay, Paraguay, Colombie, Brésil, Chili, Chine, Japon, Inde, Ceylan, Italie, Suisse, France, Espagne, Cuba, Mexique et d'autres pays d'Amérique centrale.

---

188 Sir Ernest Cassel, éminent financier britannique.

189 Ibid, pp. 268-69. Il convient de noter que plusieurs noms mentionnés par Vanderlip apparaissent ailleurs dans ce livre : Rockefeller, Armour, Guaranty Trust et (Otto) Kahn ont tous eu un lien plus ou moins étroit avec la révolution bolchévique et ses conséquences.

190 Ibid, p. 269.

American International possédait plusieurs filiales, avait des intérêts importants dans d'autres sociétés et exploitait d'autres entreprises aux États-Unis et à l'étranger. La Allied Machinery Company of America a été fondée en février 1916 et la totalité du capital social a été reprise par American International Corporation. Le vice-président de l'American International Corporation était Frederick Holbrook, ingénieur et ancien directeur de la Holbrook Cabot & Rollins Corporation. En janvier 1917, la Grace Russian Company est créée, les copropriétaires étant W. R. Grace & Co. et la San Galli Trading Company de Petrograd. L'American International Corporation avait un investissement substantiel dans la Grace Russian Company et, par l'intermédiaire de Holbrook, un poste de direction interdépendant.

L'AIC a également investi dans la United Fruit Company, qui a participé aux révolutions d'Amérique centrale dans les années 1920. L'American International Shipbuilding Corporation, détenue à 100% par AIC, a signé des contrats importants pour des navires de guerre avec l'Emergency Fleet Corporation : un contrat portait sur cinquante navires, suivi d'un autre contrat pour quarante navires, puis d'un autre encore pour soixante cargos. American International Shipbuilding a été le principal bénéficiaire des contrats attribués par la Emergency Fleet Corporation du gouvernement américain. Une autre société exploitée par AIC était G. Amsinck & Co. de New York ; le contrôle de la société a été acquis en novembre 1917. Amsinck était la source de financement de l'espionnage allemand aux États-Unis (voir page 66). En novembre 1917, l'American International Corporation a créé la Symington Forge Corporation, une importante entreprise publique de forgeage d'obus, dont elle était propriétaire à 100%. En conséquence, l'American International Corporation avait des intérêts importants dans les contrats de guerre aux États-Unis et à l'étranger. Elle avait, en un mot, un intérêt direct dans la poursuite de la Première Guerre mondiale.

Les directeurs d'American International et de certaines de leurs associations l'étaient (en 1917) :

J. OGDEN ARMOUR Abattoirs de Armour & Company, Chicago ; directeur de la National City Bank de New York ; et mentionné par A. A. Heller en relation avec le Bureau soviétique.

GEORGE JOHNSON BALDWIN Of Stone & Webster, 120 Broadway. Pendant la Première Guerre mondiale, Baldwin a été président du conseil d'administration de l'American International Shipbuilding, vice-président senior de l'American International Corporation, directeur de G. Amsinck (Von Pavenstedt d'Amsinck était un trésorier allemand spécialisé dans l'espionnage aux États-Unis, voir page 65), et administrateur de la Fondation Carnegie, qui a financé le plan de Marburg pour que le socialisme international soit contrôlé en coulisses par la finance mondiale (voir plus loin).

C. A. COFFIN Président de General Electric (bureau exécutif : 120 Broadway), président du comité de coopération de la Croix-Rouge américaine.

W. E. COREY (14 Wall Street) Directeur de l'American Bank Note Company, de la Mechanics and Metals Bank, de la Midvale Steel and Ordnance et de l'International Nickel Company ; puis directeur de la National City Bank.

ROBERT DOLLAR Magnat de la marine marchande de San Francisco, qui a tenté au nom des Soviétiques d'importer des roubles d'or tsaristes aux États-Unis en 1920, en violation de la réglementation américaine.

PIERRE S. DU PONT De la famille du Pont.

PHILIP A. S. FRANKLIN Directeur de la National City Bank.

J.P. GRACE Directeur de la National City Bank.

R. F. HERRICK Directeur, New York Life Insurance ; ancien président de l'American Bankers Association ; administrateur de la Carnegie Foundation.

OTTO H. KAHN Associé à Kuhn, Loeb. Le père de Kahn est arrivé en Amérique en 1948, "après avoir participé à la révolution allemande infructueuse de cette année-là". Selon J. H. Thomas (socialiste britannique, financé par les Soviétiques), "le visage d'Otto Kahn est tourné vers la lumière".

H. W. PRITCHETT Administrateur de la Fondation Carnegie.

PERCY A. ROCKEFELLER Fils de John D. Rockefeller ; marié à Isabel, fille de J. A. Stillman de la National City Bank.

JOHN D. RYAN Directeur des sociétés d'exploitation du cuivre, de la National City Bank et de la Mechanics and Metals Bank. (Voir le frontispice de ce livre).

W. L. SAUNDERS Directeur de la Banque de Réserve Fédérale de New York, 120 Broadway, et président de Ingersoll-Rand. Selon la *National Cyclopaedia* (26:81) : "Tout au long de la guerre, il a été l'un des conseillers les plus fiables du président." Voir page 15 pour son point de vue sur les Soviétiques.

J. A. STILLMAN Président de la National City Bank, après le décès de son père (J. Stillman, président de la NCB) en mars 1918.

C. A. STONE Directeur (1920-22) de la Federal Reserve Bank of New York, 120 Broadway ; président de Stone & Webster, 120 Broadway ; président (1916-23) de l'American International Corporation, 120 Broadway.

T. N. VAIL Président de la National City Bank of Troy, New York

F. A. VANDERLIP Président de la National City Bank.

E. S. WEBSTER Of Stone & Webster, 120 Broadway.

A. H. WIGGIN Directeur de la Banque de Réserve Fédérale de New York au début des années 1930.

BECKMAN WINTHROPE Directeur de la National City Bank.

WILLIAM WOODWARD Directeur de la Federal Reserve Bank of New York, 120 Broadway, et de la Hanover National Bank.

L'imbrication des vingt-deux directeurs de l'American International Corporation avec d'autres institutions est significative. La National City Bank avait pas moins de dix administrateurs au conseil d'administration d'AIC ; Stillman de la NCB était à l'époque un intermédiaire entre les intérêts de Rockefeller et de Morgan, et les intérêts de Morgan et de Rockefeller étaient directement représentés au sein d'AIC. Kuhn, Loeb et les du Ponts avaient chacun un administrateur. Stone & Webster avait trois directeurs. Pas moins de quatre directeurs d'AIC (Saunders, Stone, Wiggin, Woodward) étaient directeurs de la Federal Reserve Bank of New York ou devaient plus tard en devenir membres. Nous avons noté dans un chapitre précédent que William Boyce Thompson, qui a apporté des fonds et son prestige considérable à la révolution bolchévique, était également un directeur de la Federal Reserve Bank of New York - la direction de la FRB de New York ne comptait que neuf membres.

L'INFLUENCE DE L'AIC SUR LA RÉVOLUTION

Après avoir identifié les directeurs de l'AIC, nous devons maintenant identifier leur influence révolutionnaire.

Alors que la révolution bolchévique s'installe en Russie centrale, le secrétaire d'État Robert Lansing demande l'avis de l'American International Corporation sur la politique à mener à l'égard du régime soviétique. Le 16 janvier 1918 - à peine deux mois après la prise de pouvoir à Petrograd et à Moscou, et avant qu'une fraction de la Russie ne passe sous le contrôle des bolcheviks - William Franklin Sands, secrétaire exécutif de l'American International Corporation, a soumis au secrétaire d'État Lansing le mémorandum demandé sur la situation politique russe. La lettre d'accompagnement de Sands, adressée au 120 Broadway, commence :

> À l'honorable secrétaire d'État du 16 janvier 1918
> Washington D.C.
> Monsieur,
> J'ai l'honneur de vous faire parvenir ci-joint le mémorandum que vous m'avez demandé de vous présenter sur ma vision de la situation politique en Russie.
> Je l'ai divisé en trois parties : une explication des causes historiques de la Révolution, racontée aussi brièvement que possible ; une suggestion quant à la politique et un exposé des différentes branches de l'activité américaine à l'œuvre actuellement en Russie.[191]

Bien que les bolcheviks n'aient eu qu'un contrôle précaire en Russie - et qu'ils aient même failli le perdre au printemps 1918 - Sands écrit que déjà (janvier 1918) les États-Unis ont trop tardé à reconnaître "Trotzky". Il ajoutait : "Tout le terrain perdu devrait être regagné maintenant, même au prix d'un léger triomphe personnel pour Trotzky".[192]

Les entreprises situées au 120 Broadway ou à proximité :

American International Corp 120 Broadway
National City Bank 55 Wall Street
Bankers Trust Co Bldg 14 Wall Street
Bourse de New York 13 Wall Street/12 Broad

---

[191] Fichier décimal du Stale Dept. américain, 861.00/961.

[192] Mémorandum de Sands à Lansing, p. 9.

L'immeuble Morgan au coin de Wall & Broad
Banque de la Réserve Fédérale de NY 120 Broadway
Equitable Building 120 Broadway
Bankers Club 120 Broadway
Simpson, Thather & Bartlett 62 Cedar St
William Boyce Thompson 14 Wall Street
Immeuble Hazen, Whipple & Fuller, 42e rue
Chase National Bank 57 Broadway
McCann Co 61 Broadway
Stetson, Jennings & Russell 15 Broad Street
Guggenheim Exploration 120 Broadway
Weinberg & Posner 120 Broadway
Bureau soviétique 110 West 40th Street
John MacGregor Grant Co 120 Broadway
Stone & Webster 120 Broadway
General Electric Co 120 Broadway
Plan Morris de NY 120 Broadway
Sinclair Gulf Corp 120 Broadway
Guaranty Securities 120 Broadway
Guaranty Trust 140 Broadway

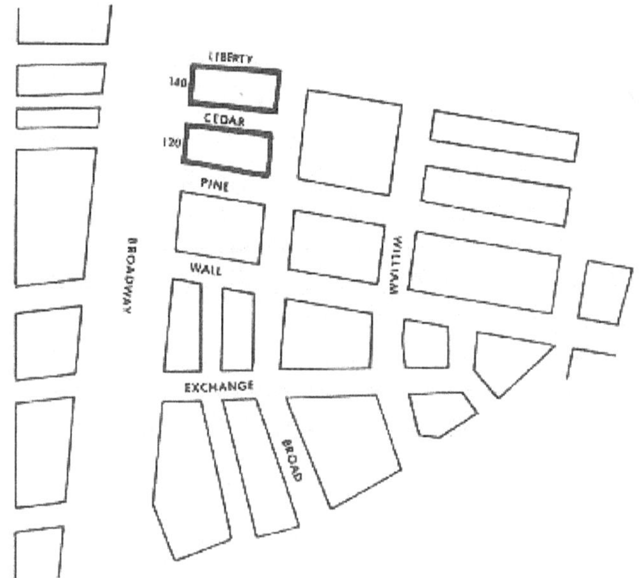

Carte de la région de Wall Street indiquant l'emplacement des bureaux

Sands élabore ensuite la manière dont les États-Unis pourraient rattraper le temps perdu, établit un parallèle entre la révolution bolchévique et "notre propre révolution", et conclut : "J'ai toutes les raisons de croire que les plans de l'administration pour la Russie recevront tout le soutien possible du Congrès, et l'appui chaleureux de l'opinion publique américaine".

En bref, Sands, en tant que secrétaire exécutif d'une société dont les directeurs étaient les plus prestigieux de Wall Street, a apporté un soutien énergique aux bolcheviks et à la révolution bolchévique, et ce quelques semaines après le début de la révolution. Et en tant que directeur de la Federal Reserve Bank of New York, Sands venait de verser un million de dollars aux Bolcheviks - un tel soutien des intérêts bancaires aux Bolcheviks était on ne peut plus cohérent.

De plus, William Sands d'American International était un homme aux relations et à l'influence vraiment peu communes au sein du Département d'État.

La carrière de Sands a alterné entre le Département d'État et Wall Street. À la fin du XIXe et au début du XXe siècle, il a occupé divers postes diplomatiques aux États-Unis. En 1910, il a quitté le département pour rejoindre la société bancaire de James Speyer afin de négocier un prêt équatorien, et pendant les deux années suivantes, il a représenté la Central Aguirre Sugar Company à Porto Rico. En 1916, il est en Russie pour un "travail de la Croix-Rouge" - en fait une "mission spéciale" de deux hommes avec Basil Miles - et revient pour rejoindre l'American International Corporation à New York.[193]

Au début de 1918, Sands est devenu le destinataire connu et prévu de certains "traités secrets" russes. Si l'on en croit les dossiers du Département d'État, il semble que Sands était également un coursier, et qu'il avait déjà eu accès à des documents officiels - avant, c'est-à-dire, à des fonctionnaires du gouvernement américain. Le 14 janvier 1918, deux jours seulement avant que Sands n'écrive son mémo sur la politique à l'égard des bolcheviks, le secrétaire d'État Lansing a fait envoyer le câble suivant en Green Cipher à la légation américaine à Stockholm : "D'importants documents officiels que Sands devait apporter ici ont été laissés à la légation. Les avez-vous transmis ? Lansing". La réponse du 16 janvier de Morris à Stockholm est la suivante : "Votre 460 14 janvier, à 17 heures. Ces documents ont été transmis au département dans la valise numéro 34 le 28 décembre". À ces documents est joint un autre mémo, signé "BM" (Basil Miles, un associé de Sands) : "M. Phillips. Ils n'ont pas donné à Sands la première tranche des traités secrets qu'il a apportés de Petrograd à Stockholm."[194]

Si l'on met de côté la question de savoir pourquoi un simple citoyen serait porteur de traités secrets russes et la question du contenu de ces traités secrets (probablement une première version des documents dits de Sisson), on peut au moins en déduire que le secrétaire exécutif de l'AIC s'est rendu de Petrograd à

---

193 William Franklin Sands a écrit plusieurs livres, dont *Undiplomatic Memoirs* (New York : McGraw-Hill, 1930), une biographie couvrant les années jusqu'en 1904. Plus tard, il a écrit *Our Jungle Diplomacy* (Chapel Hill : University of North Carolina Press, 1941), un traité peu remarquable sur l'impérialisme en Amérique latine. Ce dernier ouvrage n'est remarquable que par un point mineur à la page 102 : la volonté d'imputer une aventure impérialiste particulièrement peu recommandable à Adolf Stahl, un banquier new-yorkais, tout en soulignant inutilement que Stahl était "d'origine juive allemande". En août 1918, il publie en *Asie* un article intitulé "Sauver la Russie", pour expliquer le soutien au régime bolchévique.

194 Tout ce qui précède figure dans le fichier décimal du département d'État américain, 861.00/969.

Stockholm à la fin de 1917 et qu'il devait en effet être un citoyen privilégié et influent pour avoir accès aux traités secrets.[195]

Quelques mois plus tard, le 1er juillet 1918, Sands écrivit au secrétaire au Trésor McAdoo pour lui suggérer de créer une commission pour "l'assistance économique à la Russie". Il insistait sur le fait que puisqu'il serait difficile pour une commission gouvernementale de "fournir le mécanisme" d'une telle assistance, "il semble donc nécessaire de faire appel aux intérêts financiers, commerciaux et industriels des États-Unis pour fournir un tel mécanisme sous le contrôle du commissaire en chef ou de tout autre fonctionnaire choisi par le président à cette fin".[196] En d'autres termes, Sands avait manifestement l'intention que toute exploitation commerciale de la Russie bolchévique inclue le 120 Broadway.

LA BANQUE DE RÉSERVE FÉDÉRALE DE NEW YORK

Le mémorandum de constitution de la Banque de Réserve Fédérale de New York a été déposé le 18 mai 1914. Elle prévoyait trois administrateurs de classe A représentant les banques membres du district, trois administrateurs de classe B représentant le commerce, l'agriculture et l'industrie, et trois administrateurs de classe C représentant le Conseil de la Réserve Fédérale. Les premiers administrateurs ont été élus en 1914 ; ils ont procédé à la mise en place d'un programme énergique. Au cours de la première année d'organisation, la Banque de la Réserve Fédérale de New York a tenu pas moins de 50 réunions.

De notre point de vue, ce qui est intéressant, c'est l'association entre, d'une part, les directeurs de la Banque de Réserve Fédérale (dans le district de New York) et de l'American International Corporation et, d'autre part, la Russie soviétique émergente.

En 1917, les trois directeurs de classe A étaient Franklin D. Locke, William Woodward et Robert H. Treman. William Woodward était administrateur de l'American International Corporation (120 Broadway) et de la Hanover National Bank, contrôlée par Rockefeller. Ni Locke ni Treman n'entrent dans notre histoire. Les trois directeurs de classe B en 1917 étaient William Boyce Thompson, Henry R. Towne et Leslie R. Palmer. Nous avons déjà noté l'importante contribution en espèces de William B. Thompson à la cause bolchévique. Henry R. Towne était président du conseil d'administration du Plan Morris de New York, situé au 120 Broadway ; son siège fut ensuite occupé par Charles A. Stone de l'American International Corporation (120 Broadway) et de Stone & Webster (120 Broadway). Leslie R. Palmer n'entre pas dans notre histoire. Les trois réalisateurs de classe C étaient Pierre Jay, W. L. Saunders et George Foster Peabody. On ne sait rien de Pierre Jay, si ce n'est que son bureau était au 120 Broadway et qu'il ne

[195] L'auteur ne peut s'abstenir de comparer le traitement des chercheurs universitaires. En 1973, par exemple, l'auteur s'est encore vu refuser l'accès à certains dossiers du Département d'État datant de 1919.

[196] Fichier décimal du Département d'État américain, 861.51/333.

semblait important qu'en tant que propriétaire de la Brearley School, Ltd. William Lawrence Saunders était également directeur de l'American International Corporation ; il a ouvertement avoué, comme nous l'avons vu, des sympathies pro-bolchéviques, les révélant dans une lettre au président Woodrow Wilson. George Foster Peabody était un socialiste actif.

En bref, sur les neuf directeurs de la Banque de la Réserve Fédérale de New York, quatre étaient physiquement installés au 120 Broadway et deux étaient alors liés à l'American International Corporation. Et au moins quatre membres du conseil d'administration de l'AIC ont été à un moment ou à un autre directeurs de la FRB de New York. Nous pourrions qualifier tout cela d'important, mais nous ne considérons pas nécessairement qu'il s'agit d'un élément primordial.

L'ALLIANCE INDUSTRIELLE AMÉRICANO-RUSSE

La proposition de William Franklin Sands de créer une commission économique pour la Russie n'a pas été adoptée. Au lieu de cela, un véhicule privé a été mis en place pour exploiter les marchés russes et le soutien accordé auparavant aux bolcheviks. Un groupe d'industriels du 120 Broadway a formé le Syndicat Industriel Américano-russe Inc. pour développer et favoriser ces opportunités. Le soutien financier de la nouvelle entreprise provient des frères Guggenheim, 120 Broadway, précédemment associés à William Boyce Thompson (fonderie et raffinage américains contrôlés par Guggenheim, et les sociétés de cuivre de Kennecott et de l'Utah) ; de Harry F. Sinclair, président de la Sinclair Gulf Corp, également 120 Broadway ; et de James G. White de la J. G. White Engineering Corp, 43 Exchange Place - l'adresse du syndicat industriel américano-russe.

À l'automne 1919, l'ambassade des États-Unis à Londres a envoyé un câble à Washington au sujet de MM. Lubovitch et Rossi "représentant le syndicat industriel américano-russe Incorporated Quelle est la réputation et l'attitude du ministère à l'égard du syndicat et des individus ?[197]

À ce câble, le fonctionnaire du Département d'État Basil Miles, ancien associé de Sands, a répondu :

> ... Les hommes mentionnés ainsi que leur société sont de bonne réputation et sont soutenus financièrement par les intérêts de White, Sinclair et Guggenheim dans le but de faciliter des relations d'affaires avec la Russie.[198]

On peut donc conclure que les intérêts de Wall Street avaient des idées bien précises sur la manière dont le nouveau marché russe allait être exploité.

[197] Fichier décimal du Département d'État américain, 861.516 84, 2 septembre 1919.

[198] Ibid.

L'assistance et les conseils offerts au nom des bolcheviks par les parties intéressées à Washington et ailleurs ne devaient pas rester lettre morte.

JOHN REED : LE RÉVOLUTIONNAIRE DE L'ESTABLISHMENT

Outre l'influence d'American International au sein du Département d'État, il existe une relation intime - que l'AIC a elle-même appelée "contrôle" - avec un bolchévique connu : John Reed. Reed était un auteur prolifique et très lu de l'époque de la Première Guerre mondiale, qui a contribué au magazine *Masses* d'orientation bolchévique et à la revue *Metropolitan*, contrôlée par Morgan[199]. Le livre de Reed sur la révolution bolchévique, *Ten Days That Shook the World*, comporte une introduction de Nikolaï Lénine, et est devenu le travail de Reed le plus connu et le plus lu. Aujourd'hui, le livre se lit comme un commentaire superficiel des événements actuels, est entrecoupé de proclamations et de décrets bolchéviques, et est imprégné de cette ferveur mystique qui, comme le savent les bolchéviques, suscitera des sympathisants étrangers. Après la révolution, Reed est devenu un membre américain du comité exécutif de la Troisième Internationale. Il est mort du typhus en Russie en 1920.

La question cruciale qui se présente ici ne concerne pas le ténor pro-bolchevik connu Reed et ses activités, mais la manière dont Reed disposait de toute la confiance de Lénine ("Voici un livre que je voudrais voir publié à des millions d'exemplaires et traduit dans toutes les langues", commentait Lénine dans *Ten Days*), qui était membre de la Troisième Internationale, et qui possédait un laissez-passer du Comité militaire révolutionnaire (N° 955, émis le 16 novembre 1917) lui permettant d'entrer à tout moment à l'Institut Smolny (le quartier général de la révolution) en tant que représentant de la "presse socialiste américaine", était aussi - malgré cela - une marionnette sous le "contrôle" des intérêts financiers de Morgan par le biais de l'American International Corporation. Il existe des preuves documentaires de cette apparente contradiction (voir ci-dessous et annexe 3).

Complétons l'arrière-plan. Des articles pour le *Metropolitan* et *Masses* ont permis à John Reed de toucher un large public pour ses reportages sur les révolutions bolchéviques mexicaine et russe. Le biographe de Reed, Granville Hicks, a suggéré, dans *John Reed*, qu'il "était... le porte-parole des bolcheviks aux États-Unis". D'autre part, le soutien financier de Reed de 1913 à 1918 est venu en grande partie du *Metropolitan* - propriété de Harry Payne Whitney, un directeur du Guaranty Trust, une institution citée dans chaque chapitre de ce livre - et aussi du banquier privé et marchand new-yorkais Eugène Boissevain, qui a canalisé les fonds vers Reed à la fois directement et par le biais du journal pro-bolchéviques *Masses*. En d'autres termes, le soutien financier de John Reed est venu de deux éléments supposés concurrents dans le spectre politique. Ces fonds étaient destinés

---

[199] Les autres contributeurs au journal *Masses* mentionnés dans ce livre sont le journaliste Robert Minor, président du Comité de la marionnette de l'information publique américaine, George Creel, Carl Sandburg, poète et historien, et Boardman Robinson, artiste.

à l'écriture et peuvent être classés comme suit : paiements du *Metropolitan* à partir de 1913 pour des articles ; paiements de *Masses* à partir de 1913, dont les revenus provenaient au moins en partie d'Eugène Boissevain. Une troisième catégorie doit être mentionnée : Reed a reçu quelques paiements mineurs et apparemment sans lien avec le commissaire de la Croix-Rouge Raymond Robins à Petrograd. Il a vraisemblablement aussi reçu des sommes moins importantes pour des articles écrits pour d'autres revues, et des droits d'auteur sur des livres ; mais aucune preuve n'a été trouvée concernant le montant de ces paiements.

JOHN REED ET LE MAGAZINE *METROPOLITAN*

Le *Metropolitan* a soutenu les causes de l'establishment contemporain, notamment la préparation à la guerre. Le magazine appartenait à Harry Payne Whitney (1872-1930), qui a fondé la Navy League et était associé dans la firme J.P. Morgan. À la fin des années 1890, Whitney est devenu directeur de l'American Smelting and Refining et de la Guggenheim Exploration. À la mort de son père en 1908, il devient directeur de nombreuses autres sociétés, dont la Guaranty Trust Company. Reed a commencé à écrire pour le *Metropolitan* en juillet 1913 et a contribué à une demi-douzaine d'articles sur les révolutions mexicaines : "Avec Villa au Mexique", "Les causes derrière la révolution mexicaine", "Si nous entrons au Mexique", "Avec Villa en marche", etc. Reed a sympathisé avec le révolutionnaire Pancho Villa. Vous vous souvenez du lien entre le Guaranty Trust et les fournitures de munitions à Villa.

En tout état de cause, *Metropolitan* était la principale source de revenus de Reed. Selon le biographe Granville Hicks, "L'argent signifiait principalement du travail pour le *Metropolitan* et accessoirement des articles et des histoires pour d'autres magazines rémunérateurs". Mais le fait d'être employé par le *Metropolitan* n'empêchait pas Reed d'écrire des articles critiques à l'égard des intérêts de Morgan et Rockefeller. L'un de ces articles, "Prendre la République à la gorge" *(Masses*, juillet 1916), retraçait les relations entre les industries de munitions, le lobby de la préparation à la sécurité nationale, les directions interdépendantes des intérêts de Morgan et Rockefeller, "et montrait qu'elles dominaient à la fois les sociétés de préparation et la toute nouvelle American International Corporation, organisée pour l'exploitation des pays en voie de développement".[200]

En 1915, John Reed a été arrêté en Russie par les autorités tsaristes, et le *Metropolitan* est intervenu auprès du Département d'État en faveur de Reed. Le 21 juin 1915, H. J. Whigham écrit au secrétaire d'État Robert Lansing pour l'informer que John Reed et Boardman Robinson (également arrêté et collaborateur de *Masses)* étaient en Russie "avec une commande du magazine *Metropolitan* pour écrire des articles et faire des illustrations dans le domaine oriental de la guerre". Whigham a souligné qu'aucun d'eux n'avait "le désir ou

---

[200] Granville Hicks, *John Reed, 1887-1920* (New York : Macmillan, 1936), p. 215.

l'autorité d'interférer avec les opérations d'une quelconque puissance belligérante". La lettre de Whigham continue :

> Si M. Reed a porté des lettres de recommandation de Bucarest à des personnes en Galice d'un état d'esprit anti-russe, je suis sûr que cela a été fait innocemment avec la simple intention de rencontrer le plus de gens possible...

Whigham fait remarquer au secrétaire Lansing que John Reed était connu à la Maison Blanche et avait apporté "une certaine assistance" à l'administration sur les affaires mexicaines ; il conclut : "Nous avons la plus haute estime pour les grandes qualités de Reed en tant qu'écrivain et penseur et nous sommes très inquiets pour sa sécurité."[201] La lettre de Whigham ne provient pas, notons-le, d'un journal de l'establishment en faveur d'un écrivain bolchévique ; elle provient d'un journal de l'establishment en faveur d'un écrivain bolchévique pour *Masses* et autres feuilles révolutionnaires similaires, un écrivain qui a également été l'auteur d'attaques tranchantes ("L'éthique involontaire du grand capital : une fable pour pessimistes", par exemple) sur les mêmes intérêts Morgan qui possédaient *Metropolitan.*

La preuve du financement par le banquier privé Boissevain est incontestable. Le 23 février 1918, la légation américaine à Christiania, en Norvège, envoie un câble à Washington au nom de John Reed pour qu'il soit remis au chef du parti socialiste, Morris Hillquit. Le câble précisait en partie "Dites à Boissevain qu'il peut compter sur lui mais avec précaution." Une note confidentielle de Basil Miles dans les dossiers du Département d'État, datée du 3 avril 1918, déclare : "Si Reed rentre à la maison, autant qu'il ait de l'argent. Je comprends que les alternatives sont l'expulsion par la Norvège ou une expulsion dans les formes. Si c'est le cas, cette dernière semble préférable". Cette note de protection est suivie d'un télégramme daté du 1er avril 1918, et à nouveau de la légation américaine à Christiania : "John Reed demande d'urgence à Eugène Boissevain, 29 Williams Street, New York, de virer 300,00$ au bénéfice de la légation.[202] Ce télégramme a été relayé à Eugène Boissevain par le Département d'État le 3 avril 1918.

Reed a apparemment reçu ses fonds et est arrivé sain et sauf aux États-Unis. Le document suivant dans les dossiers du Département d'État est une lettre de John Reed à William Franklin Sands, datée du 4 juin 1918 et écrite depuis Croton On Hudson, New York. Dans cette lettre, Reed affirme qu'il a rédigé un mémorandum pour le Département d'État, et appelle Sands à user de son influence pour obtenir la restitution des documents ramenés de Russie. Reed conclut : "Pardonnez-moi de vous déranger, mais je ne sais pas vers qui me tourner, et je ne peux pas me permettre un autre voyage à Washington". Par la suite, Frank Polk, secrétaire d'État par intérim, a reçu une lettre de Sands concernant la restitution des papiers de John Reed. La lettre de Sands, datée du 5 juin 1918, provenant du 120

---

[201] Fichier décimal du département d'État américain, 860d.1121 R 25/4.

[202] Ibid, 360d.1121/R25/18. Selon Granville Hicks dans *John Reed,* "Masses ne pouvait pas payer ses dépenses [Reed]. Finalement, des amis du magazine, notamment Eugene Boissevain, ont réuni l'argent" (p. 249).

Broadway, est ici reproduite dans son intégralité ; elle contient des déclarations très explicites sur le contrôle exercé par Reed :

> 120 BROADWAY NEW YORK
> 5 juin 1918
> Mon cher M. Polk :
> Je prends la liberté de vous faire parvenir un appel de John ("Jack") Reed pour l'aider, si possible, à obtenir la restitution des papiers qu'il a apportés de Russie dans le pays.
> J'ai eu une conversation avec M. Reed à son arrivée, au cours de laquelle il a esquissé certaines tentatives du gouvernement soviétique pour amorcer un développement constructif, et a exprimé le désir de mettre à la disposition de notre gouvernement toutes les observations qu'il avait faites ou les informations qu'il avait obtenues grâce à sa relation avec Léon Trotzky. Je lui ai suggéré de rédiger un mémorandum à ce sujet pour vous, et j'ai promis de téléphoner à Washington pour vous demander de lui accorder un entretien à cette fin. Il a ramené avec lui une masse de documents qui lui ont été retirés pour être examinés et, à ce sujet, il souhaitait également parler à une personne en position d'autorité, afin d'offrir volontairement au gouvernement les informations qu'ils pourraient contenir et de demander la restitution de ceux dont il a besoin pour son travail dans les journaux et les magazines.
> Je ne pense pas que M. Reed soit un "bolchevik" ou un "anarchiste dangereux", comme je l'ai entendu dire. C'est un journaliste à sensation, sans aucun doute, mais c'est tout. Il ne cherche pas à embarrasser notre gouvernement, et pour cette raison a refusé la "protection" qui lui a été offerte par Trotzky, si j'ai bien compris, lorsqu'il est retourné à New York pour faire face à l'accusation portée contre lui dans le procès intenté à "Masses". Cependant, il est apprécié des bolchéviques de Petrograd et, par conséquent, tout ce que notre police peut faire qui ressemble à de la "persécution" sera ressenti à Petrograd, ce que je considère comme indésirable, car inutile. *Il peut être manipulé et contrôlé bien mieux par d'autres moyens que par la police.*
> Je n'ai pas vu le mémorandum qu'il a remis à M. Bullitt - je *voulais qu'il me laisse le voir d'abord et peut-être le modifier,* mais il n'a pas eu l'occasion de le faire.
> J'espère que vous ne me considérerez pas comme un intrus dans cette affaire ou comme un intervenant dans des affaires qui ne me concernent pas. Je pense qu'il est sage de ne pas offenser les dirigeants bolchéviques tant que cela ne sera pas nécessaire - si cela devait devenir nécessaire - et il n'est pas sage de considérer chacun comme un personnage suspect, voire dangereux, qui a eu des relations amicales avec les bolchéviques en Russie. *Je pense qu'il est préférable de tenter d'utiliser de telles personnes à nos propres fins dans le développement de notre politique envers la Russie, si cela est possible.* La conférence que Reed a été empêché par la police de donner à Philadelphie (il a perdu son sang-froid, est entré en conflit avec la police et a été arrêté) est la seule conférence sur la Russie que j'aurais payé pour entendre, si je n'avais pas déjà vu ses notes sur le sujet. Elle portait sur un sujet qui pourrait bien être un point de contact avec le gouvernement soviétique, à partir duquel on pourrait commencer un travail constructif !
> *Ne pouvons-nous pas l'utiliser,* au lieu de l'aigrir et d'en faire un ennemi ? Il n'est pas bien équilibré, mais il est, sauf erreur de ma part, *susceptible d'être guidé discrètement et pourrait être très utile.*
>
> Bien à vous, William Franklin Sands
> L'honorable Frank Lyon Polk

Conseiller pour le Département d'État Washington, D.C.
WFS:AO pièce jointe[203]

L'importance de ce document démontre la réalité de l'intervention directe d'un officier (secrétaire exécutif) de l'American International Corporation au nom d'un bolchévique connu. Réfléchissez à quelques déclarations de Sands à propos de Reed : "Il peut être manipulé et contrôlé bien mieux par d'autres moyens que par la police" ; et, "Ne pouvons-nous pas l'utiliser, au lieu de l'aigrir et d'en faire un ennemi ? ... il est, à moins que je ne me trompe beaucoup, susceptible de recevoir des conseils discrets et pourrait être très utile". De toute évidence, l'American International Corporation considérait John Reed comme un agent ou un agent potentiel qui pouvait être, et avait probablement déjà été, placé sous son contrôle. Le fait que Sands ait été en mesure de demander l'édition d'un mémorandum de Reed (pour Bullitt) suggère qu'un certain degré de contrôle avait déjà été établi.

Notez ensuite l'attitude potentiellement hostile de Sands à l'égard des bolcheviks - et son intention à peine voilée de les provoquer : "Je pense qu'il est sage de ne pas offenser les dirigeants bolchéviques à moins et *jusqu'à ce qu'il soit nécessaire de le faire* - si cela devait devenir nécessaire..." (italique ajouté).

Il s'agit d'une lettre extraordinaire au nom d'un agent soviétique, émanant d'un citoyen américain privé dont le Département d'État avait sollicité et continuait de demander les conseils.

Un mémorandum ultérieur, daté du 19 mars 1920, dans les dossiers de l'État, fait état de l'arrestation de John Reed par les autorités finlandaises à Abo, et de la possession par Reed de passeports anglais, américains et allemands. Reed, voyageant sous le pseudonyme de Casgormlich, transportait des diamants, une importante somme d'argent, de la littérature de propagande soviétique et des films. Le 21 avril 1920, la légation américaine à Helsingfors envoie un câble au Département d'État :

> Je transmets par la prochaine valise les copies certifiées des lettres d'Emma Goldman, Trotsky, Lénine et Sirola trouvées en possession de Reed. Le ministère des Affaires étrangères a promis de fournir un compte rendu complet de la procédure judiciaire.

Une fois de plus, Sands est intervenu : "Je connaissais personnellement M. Reed.[204]" Et, comme en 1915, le magazine *Metropolitan* est également venu au secours de Reed. Le 15 avril 1920, H. J. Whigham écrit à Bainbridge Colby au Département d'État : "J'ai entendu dire que John Reed risquait d'être exécuté en Finlande. J'espère que le Département d'État pourra prendre des mesures immédiates pour qu'il soit jugé comme il se doit. Demande une action rapide et

---

[203] Fichier décimal du Département d'État américain, 360. D. II21.R/20/221/2, /R25 (John Reed). La lettre a été transférée par M. Polk aux archives du Département d'État le 2 mai 1935. Tous les italiques ont été ajoutés.

[204] Ibid, 360d.1121 R 25/72.

urgente".[205] Ceci s'ajoutait à un télégramme du 13 avril 1920 de Harry Hopkins, qui était destiné à la célébrité sous le président Roosevelt :

> Comprendre que le Département d'État a des informations sur Jack Reed arrêté par la Finlande, sera exécuté. Un de ses amis, ainsi que les vôtres et sa femme, vous demandent instamment de prendre rapidement des mesures pour empêcher l'exécution et obtenir la libération de Jack Reed. Sommes sûrs de pouvoir compter sur votre intervention immédiate et efficace.[206]

John Reed a ensuite été libéré par les autorités finlandaises.

Ce récit paradoxal sur l'intervention en faveur d'un agent soviétique peut avoir plusieurs explications. Une hypothèse qui correspond à d'autres preuves concernant Wall Street et la révolution bolchévique est que John Reed était en fait un agent des intérêts de Morgan - peut-être seulement à moitié conscient de son double rôle - que ses écrits anticapitalistes entretenaient le précieux mythe selon lequel tous les capitalistes sont en guerre perpétuelle avec tous les révolutionnaires socialistes. Carroll Quigley, comme nous l'avons déjà noté, a rapporté que les intérêts Morgan soutenaient financièrement les organisations révolutionnaires nationales et les écrits anticapitalistes.[207] Et nous avons présenté dans ce chapitre des preuves documentaires irréfutables que les intérêts de Morgan exerçaient également le contrôle d'un agent soviétique, intercédant en son nom et, plus important encore, intervenant généralement en faveur des intérêts soviétiques auprès du gouvernement américain. Ces activités étaient centrées à une seule adresse : 120 Broadway, New York City.

---

[205] Ibid.

[206] Elle a été adressée à Bainbridge Colby, ibid, 360d.1121 R 25/30. Une autre lettre, datée du 14 avril 1920 et adressée au secrétaire d'État depuis le 100 Broadway, New York, était de W. Bourke Cochrane ; elle plaidait également pour la libération de John Reed.

[207] Quigley, op. cit.

CHAPITRE IX

LE GUARANTY TRUST S'INSTALLE EN RUSSIE

Le gouvernement soviétique souhaite que la Guarantee Trust Company devienne l'agent fiscal aux États-Unis pour toutes les opérations soviétiques et envisage l'achat de l'Eestibank par les Américains en vue de lier complètement les fortunes soviétiques aux intérêts financiers américains.

William H. Coombs, sous les ordres de l'ambassade des États-Unis à Londres, le 1er juin 1920 (fichier décimal du département d'État américain, 861.51/752).

("Eestibank" était une banque estonienne)

En 1918, les Soviétiques ont été confrontés à un ensemble ahurissant de problèmes internes et externes. Ils n'occupaient qu'une fraction de la Russie. Pour maîtriser le reste, ils avaient besoin d'armes étrangères, de nourriture importée, de soutien financier extérieur, de reconnaissance diplomatique et - surtout - de commerce extérieur. Pour obtenir la reconnaissance diplomatique et le commerce extérieur, les Soviétiques avaient d'abord besoin d'une représentation à l'étranger, et la représentation nécessitait à son tour un financement en or ou en devises étrangères. Comme nous l'avons déjà vu, la première étape a été d'établir le Bureau soviétique à New York sous la direction de Ludwig Martens. En même temps, des efforts ont été faits pour transférer des fonds aux États-Unis et en Europe pour l'achat de biens nécessaires. Ensuite, une influence a été exercée aux États-Unis pour obtenir la reconnaissance ou les licences d'exportation nécessaires pour expédier des marchandises en Russie.

Les banquiers et les avocats de New York ont apporté une aide importante - et parfois cruciale - pour chacune de ces tâches. Lorsque le professeur George V. Lomonossoff, l'expert technique russe du Bureau soviétique, a eu besoin de transférer des fonds de l'agent soviétique principal en Scandinavie, un éminent avocat de Wall Street est venu à son aide - en utilisant les canaux officiels du Département d'État et le secrétaire d'État en exercice comme intermédiaire. Lorsque l'or a dû être transféré aux États-Unis, ce sont American International Corporation, Kuhn, Loeb & Co. et Guaranty Trust qui ont demandé les facilités et ont utilisé leur influence à Washington pour faciliter le processus. Et lorsqu'il s'agit de reconnaissance, nous trouvons des entreprises américaines qui supplient le Congrès et le public d'approuver le régime soviétique.

De peur que le lecteur ne déduise - trop hâtivement - de ces affirmations que Wall Street était effectivement teintée de rouge, ou que des drapeaux rouges flottaient dans la rue (voir le dessin en début d'ouvrage), nous présentons également dans un chapitre ultérieur des preuves que la firme J.P. Morgan a financé l'amiral Kolchak en Sibérie. Alexandre Kolchak combattait les bolcheviks, pour installer sa propre marque de régime autoritaire. La firme a également contribué à l'organisation anticommuniste d'United Americans.

WALL STREET VIENT EN AIDE AU PROFESSEUR LOMONOSSOFF

Le cas du professeur Lomonossoff est une histoire détaillée de l'aide apportée par Wall Street au premier régime soviétique. À la fin de 1918, George V. Lomonossoff, membre du Bureau soviétique à New York et plus tard premier commissaire soviétique des chemins de fer, s'est retrouvé bloqué aux États-Unis sans fonds. À cette époque, les fonds bolchéviques se voyaient refuser l'entrée aux États-Unis ; en effet, il n'y avait aucune reconnaissance officielle du régime. Lomonossoff a fait l'objet d'une lettre du 24 octobre 1918 du ministère américain de la Justice au Département d'État.[208] Cette lettre faisait référence aux attributs bolchéviques de Lomonossoff et à ses discours pro-bolchéviques. L'enquêteur concluait : "Le professeur Lomonossoff n'est pas un bolchévique, bien que ses discours constituent un soutien sans équivoque à la cause bolchévique". Pourtant, Lomonossoff a réussi à tirer les ficelles au plus haut niveau de l'administration pour faire transférer 25 000 dollars de l'Union soviétique par l'intermédiaire d'un agent d'espionnage soviétique en Scandinavie (qui sera lui-même plus tard l'assistant confidentiel du préfet Schley, un vice-président de la Chase Bank). Tout cela avec l'aide d'un membre d'un éminent cabinet d'avocats de Wall Street ![209]

Les preuves sont présentées en détail parce que les détails eux-mêmes mettent en évidence la relation étroite entre certains intérêts qui, jusqu'à présent, étaient considérés comme des ennemis acharnés. La première indication du problème de Lomonossoff est une lettre datée du 7 janvier 1919, adressée par Thomas L. Chadbourne de Chadbourne, Babbitt & Wall of 14 Wall Street (même adresse que celle de William Boyce Thompson) à Frank Polk, secrétaire d'État par intérim. Notez la salutation amicale et la référence occasionnelle à Michael Gruzenberg, alias Alexander Gumberg, agent soviétique en chef en Scandinavie et plus tard assistant de Lomonossoff :

> Cher Frank : Vous avez eu la gentillesse de me dire que si je pouvais vous informer de l'état des 25 000 dollars de fonds personnels appartenant à M. et Mme Lomonossoff, vous mettriez en route les mécanismes nécessaires pour les obtenir ici pour eux.

---

[208] Fichier décimal du département d'État américain, 861.00/3094.

[209] Cette section est tirée de la *propagande américaine,* du Sénat, de la Russie, des auditions devant une sous-commission de la Commission des relations étrangères, 66e Cong., 2d sess. 1920.

> J'ai communiqué avec M. Lomonossoff à ce sujet, et il me dit que M. Michael Gruzenberg, qui s'est rendu en Russie pour M. Lomonossoff avant les difficultés entre l'ambassadeur Bakhmeteff et M. Lomonossoff, lui a transmis les informations concernant cet argent par l'intermédiaire de trois Russes récemment arrivés de Suède, et M. Lomonossoff pense que l'argent est détenu à l'ambassade de Russie à Stockholm, Milmskilnad Gaten 37. Si l'enquête du Département d'État devait révéler que ce n'est pas l'endroit où l'argent est déposé, l'ambassade russe à Stockholm pourrait alors donner l'adresse exacte de M. Gruzenberg, qui pourrait lui fournir les informations appropriées concernant cet argent. M. Lomonossoff ne reçoit pas de lettres de M. Gruzenberg, bien qu'il soit informé qu'elles ont été écrites : aucune de ses lettres à M. Gruzenberg n'a été remise, il en est également informé. Pour cette raison, il est impossible d'être plus précis que je ne l'ai été, mais j'espère que quelque chose pourra être fait pour soulager son embarras et celui de sa femme par manque de fonds, et il n'a besoin que d'un peu d'aide pour obtenir cet argent qui leur appartient pour les aider de ce côté-ci de l'eau.
> Je vous remercie d'avance pour tout ce que vous pouvez faire et je vous prie de rester, comme toujours,
>
> Bien à vous, Thomas L. Chadbourne.

En 1919, à l'époque où cette lettre a été écrite, Chadbourne était un homme à un dollar par an à Washington, conseiller et directeur du War Trade Board américain, et directeur de l'U.S. Russian Bureau Inc, une société-écran officielle du gouvernement américain. Auparavant, en 1915, Chadbourne avait organisé la Midvale Steel and Ordnance pour tirer profit des affaires en temps de guerre. En 1916, il est devenu président du Comité des finances démocrates, puis directeur de Wright Aeronautical et de Mack Trucks.

La raison pour laquelle Lomonossoff ne recevait pas de lettres de Gruzenberg est qu'elles étaient, selon toute probabilité, interceptées par l'un des nombreux gouvernements qui s'intéressent de près aux activités de ce dernier.

Le 11 janvier 1919, Frank Polk a câblé la légation américaine à Stockholm :

> Le ministère reçoit des informations selon lesquelles 25 000$, des fonds personnels de... Veuillez vous renseigner auprès de la légation russe, de manière informelle et personnelle, pour savoir si ces fonds sont détenus de cette manière. Dans le cas contraire, vérifiez l'adresse de M. Michael Gruzenberg, qui serait en possession d'informations à ce sujet. Département non concerné officiellement, se contentant d'entreprendre des enquêtes au nom d'un ancien fonctionnaire russe dans ce pays.
>
> Polk, par intérim

Dans cette lettre, Polk semble ignorer les connexions bolchéviques de Lomonossoff, et le qualifie d'"ancien fonctionnaire russe dans ce pays". Quoi qu'il en soit, Polk a reçu dans les trois jours une réponse de Morris à la légation américaine à Stockholm :

> 14 janvier, 15 heures 3492. Votre n° 1443 du 12 janvier, 15 heures.
> Somme de 25 000$ de l'ancien président de la commission russe des moyens de communication aux États-Unis non connue de la légation russe ; on ne peut pas non plus obtenir l'adresse de M. Michael Gruzenberg.
>
> Morris

Apparemment, Frank Polk a ensuite écrit à Chadbourne (la lettre n'est pas incluse dans la source) et a indiqué que l'État ne pouvait trouver ni Lomonossoff ni Michael Gruzenberg. Chadbourne a répondu le 21 janvier 1919 :

> Cher Frank : Merci beaucoup pour votre lettre du 17 janvier. Je crois savoir qu'il existe deux légations russes en Suède, l'une soviétique et l'autre Kerensky, et je suppose que votre enquête a été dirigée vers la légation soviétique, puisque c'est l'adresse que je vous ai donnée dans ma lettre, à savoir Milmskilnad Gaten 37, Stockholm.
> L'adresse de Michael Gruzenberg est la suivante : Holmenkollen Sanitarium, Christiania, Norvège, et je pense que la légation soviétique pourrait tout savoir sur les fonds par l'intermédiaire de M. Gruzenberg si elle communique avec lui.
> Je vous remercie d'avoir pris cette peine et vous assure de ma profonde reconnaissance,
>
> Bien à vous, Thomas L. Chadbourne

Il convient de noter qu'un avocat de Wall Street avait l'adresse de M. Gruzenberg, principal agent bolchévique en Scandinavie, à une époque où le secrétaire d'État par intérim et la légation américaine de Stockholm n'avaient aucune trace de cette adresse ; la légation n'a pas pu non plus la retrouver. Chadbourne a également présumé que les Soviétiques étaient le gouvernement officiel de la Russie, bien que ce gouvernement ne soit pas reconnu par les États-Unis, et la position officielle du gouvernement de Chadbourne au sein du War Trade Board exigerait qu'il le sache.

Frank Polk a ensuite câblé la légation américaine à Christiania, en Norvège, avec l'adresse de Michael Gruzenberg. On ignore si Polk savait qu'il transmettait l'adresse d'un agent d'espionnage, mais son message était le suivant

> À la légation américaine, Christiania. Le 25 janvier 1919. On rapporte que Michael Gruzenberg se trouve au sanatorium de Holmenkollen. Est-il possible de le localiser et de savoir s'il a des informations concernant la disposition d'un fonds de 25 000 dollars appartenant à l'ancien président de la mission russe des moyens de communication aux États-Unis, le professeur Lomonossoff.
>
> Polk, par intérim

Le représentant américain (Schmedeman) à Christiania connaissait bien Gruzenberg. En effet, le nom avait figuré dans des rapports de Schmedeman à Washington concernant les activités pro-soviétiques de Gruzenberg en Norvège. Schmedeman a répondu :

> 29 janvier, 20 heures 1543. Important. Votre télégramme du 25 janvier, n° 650.
> Avant de partir aujourd'hui pour la Russie, Michael Gruzenberg a informé notre attaché naval que lorsqu'il était en Russie il y a quelques mois, il avait reçu, à la demande de Lomonossoff, 25 000 dollars de l'Institut Expérimental Ferroviaire Russe, dont le professeur Lomonossoff était président. Gruzenberg affirme qu'aujourd'hui il a envoyé un télégramme à l'avocat de Lomonossoff à New York, Morris Hillquitt [sic], pour lui dire que lui, Gruzenberg, est en possession de l'argent, et qu'avant de le transmettre, il attend de nouvelles instructions des États-

> Unis, demandant dans le télégramme que Lomonossoff se fasse rembourser ses frais de subsistance et ceux de sa famille par Hillquitt en attendant la réception de l'argent.[210]
> Comme le ministre Morris se rendait à Stockholm dans le même train que M. Gruzenberg, ce dernier a déclaré qu'il donnerait des conseils supplémentaires à M. Morris à ce sujet.
>
> Schmedeman

Le ministre américain s'est rendu avec M. Gruzenberg à Stockholm où il a reçu le câble suivant de Polk :

> Il est rapporté par légation à Christiania que Michael Gruzenberg, a pour le professeur G. Lomonossoff, la... somme de 25 000$, reçue de l'Institut expérimental des chemins de fer russes. Si vous pouvez le faire sans être impliqué avec les autorités bolchéviques, le département sera heureux pour vous de faciliter le transfert de cet argent au Prof. Lomonossoff dans ce pays. Merci de bien vouloir répondre.
>
> Polk, par intérim

Ce câble donna des résultats, car le 5 février 1919, Frank Polk écrivit à Chadbourne au sujet d'un "dangereux agitateur bolchévique", Gruzenberg :

> Mon cher Tom : J'ai un télégramme de Christiania indiquant que Michael Gruzenberg a les 25 000 dollars du professeur Lomonossoff, qu'il les a reçus de l'Institut expérimental des chemins de fer russes et qu'il a envoyé un câble à Morris Hillquitt [sic], à New York, pour qu'il fournisse au professeur Lomonossoff de l'argent pour ses frais de subsistance jusqu'à ce que le fonds en question puisse lui être transmis. Comme Gruzenberg vient d'être expulsé de Norvège en tant que dangereux agitateur bolchévique, il a peut-être eu des difficultés à télégraphier depuis ce pays. Je crois savoir qu'il est maintenant parti à Christiania, et bien que cela soit quelque peu en dehors de la ligne de conduite du ministère, je serai heureux, si vous le souhaitez, de voir si je peux demander à M. Gruzenberg de remettre l'argent au professeur Lomonossoff de Stockholm, et j'y télégraphie à notre ministre pour savoir si cela peut être fait.
>
> Très sincèrement vôtre, Frank L. Polk

Le télégramme de Christiania mentionné dans la lettre de Polk se lit comme suit :

> 3 février, 18 heures, 3580. Important. Le 12 janvier, le numéro 1443, 10 000 dollars ont été déposés à Stockholm à mon ordre pour être transmis au professeur Lomonossoff par Michael Gruzenberg, un des anciens représentants des bolcheviks en Norvège. Avant d'accepter cet argent, je l'ai informé que je communiquerais avec vous et que je demanderais si vous souhaitez que cet argent soit transmis à Lomonossoff. Je demande donc des instructions quant à ma ligne de conduite.

---

[210] Morris Hillquit était l'intermédiaire entre le banquier new-yorkais Eugène Boissevain et John Reed à Petrograd.

Morris

Par la suite, Morris, à Stockholm, a demandé des instructions pour l'élimination d'une traite de 10 000 dollars déposée dans une banque de Stockholm. Sa phrase "[ceci] a été mon seul lien avec l'affaire" suggère que Morris était conscient que les Soviétiques pouvaient, et probablement allaient, réclamer ce transfert monétaire officiellement accéléré, puisque cette action impliquait l'approbation par les États-Unis de tels transferts monétaires. Jusqu'alors, les Soviétiques avaient été obligés de faire entrer clandestinement de l'argent aux États-Unis.

> 16 heures, 12 février 3610, Routine.
> En ce qui concerne mon numéro 3580 du 3 février, 18 heures, et votre numéro 1501 du 8 février, 19 heures. Je ne sais pas si vous souhaitez que je transfère par votre intermédiaire les 10 000 dollars mentionnés par le professeur Lomonossoff. Le fait que Gruzenberg m'ait informé qu'il avait déposé cet argent à l'ordre de Lomonossoff dans une banque de Stockholm et qu'il ait informé la banque que cette traite pourrait être envoyée en Amérique par mon intermédiaire, à condition que je l'ordonne, a été mon seul lien avec l'affaire. Veuillez me donner vos instructions.
> Morris

Suit une série de lettres sur le transfert des 10 000 dollars du bureau de l'A.B. Nordisk Resebureau à Thomas L. Chadbourne au 520 Park Avenue, New York, par l'intermédiaire du Département d'État. La première lettre contient des instructions de Polk, sur les modalités du transfert ; la deuxième, de Morris à Polk, contient 10 000 dollars ; la troisième, de Morris à A/B Nordisk Resebureau, demande une traite ; la quatrième est une réponse de la banque avec un chèque ; et la cinquième est l'accusé de réception.

> Votre 12 février, 16 heures, n° 3610.
> L'argent peut être transmis directement à Thomas L. Chadbourne, 520 Park Avenue, New York City,
> Polk, par intérim
>
> * * * * *
>
> Dispatch, n° 1600, 6 mars 1919 :
> L'Honorable Secrétaire d'État, Washington
> Monsieur : Me référant à mon télégramme, n° 3610 du 12 février, et à la réponse du ministère, n° 1524 du 19 février, concernant la somme de 10 000 dollars pour le professeur Lomonossoff, j'ai l'honneur de vous faire parvenir ci-joint une copie d'une lettre que j'ai adressée le 25 février à A. B. Nordisk Resebureau, les banquiers auprès desquels cet argent a été déposé ; une copie de la réponse de A. B. Nordisk Resebureau, datée du 26 février ; et une copie de ma lettre à A. B. Nordisk Resebureau, datée du 27 février.
> Il ressort de cette correspondance que la banque souhaitait que cet argent soit transmis au professeur Lomonossoff. Je leur ai cependant expliqué, comme on le verra dans ma lettre du 27 février, que j'avais reçu l'autorisation de le transmettre directement à M. Thomas L. Chadbourne, 520 Park Avenue, New York City. Je joins également à la présente une enveloppe adressée à M. Chadbourne, dans

laquelle sont joints une lettre à son intention ainsi qu'un chèque de 10 000 dollars émis par la National City Bank of New York.
J'ai l'honneur d'être, monsieur, votre serviteur obéissant,

Ira N. Morris

* * * * *

A. B. Nordisk Reserbureau,
No. 4 Vestra Tradgardsgatan, Stockholm.
Messieurs : Dès réception de votre lettre du 30 janvier, indiquant que vous aviez reçu 10 000 dollars à verser au professeur G. V. Lomonossoff, à ma demande, j'ai immédiatement télégraphié à mon gouvernement pour lui demander s'il souhaitait que cet argent soit transmis au professeur Lomonossoff. Je reçois aujourd'hui une réponse m'autorisant à transmettre l'argent directement à M. Thomas L. Chadbourne, à l'ordre du professeur Lomonossoff. Je serai heureux de la transmettre conformément aux instructions de mon gouvernement.
Je le suis, messieurs,

Très sincèrement, à vous, Ira N. Morris

* * * * *

M. I. N. Morris,
Ministre américain, Stockholm
Marché conclu, Monsieur : Nous vous prions d'accuser réception de votre faveur d'hier concernant le paiement de 10 000 dollars - au professeur G. V. Lomonossoff, et nous avons par la présente le plaisir d'inclure un chèque dudit montant à l'ordre du professeur G. V. Lomonossoff, que nous croyons comprendre que vous avez l'amabilité de transmettre à ce monsieur. Nous serons heureux d'avoir votre reçu pour ce montant, mais nous vous prions de bien vouloir rester,
Bien à vous, respectueusement,

A. B. Nordisk Reserbureau

E. Molin

* * * * *

A. B. Nordisk Resebureau, Stockholm
Messieurs : Je vous prie d'accuser réception de votre lettre du 26 février, accompagnée d'un chèque de 10 000 dollars à l'ordre du professeur G. V. Lomonossoff. Comme je vous l'ai indiqué dans ma lettre du 25 février, j'ai été autorisé à faire parvenir ce chèque à M. Thomas L. Chadbourne, 520 Park Avenue, New York City, et je le ferai parvenir à ce monsieur dans les prochains jours, sauf indication contraire de votre part.

Très sincèrement, à vous, Ira N. Morris

Suit alors un mémorandum interne du Département d'État et l'accusé de réception de Chadbourne :

M. Phillips à M. Chadbourne, le 3 avril 1919.
Monsieur le Président : Se référant à une correspondance antérieure concernant une remise de dix mille dollars de A. B. Norsdisk Resebureau au professeur G. V. Lomonossoff, dont vous avez demandé la transmission par l'intermédiaire de la légation américaine à Stockholm, le ministère vous informe qu'il a reçu une dépêche du ministre américain à Stockholm en date du 6 mars 1919, portant sur la lettre ci-jointe qui vous est adressée, accompagnée d'un chèque du montant visé, tiré à l'ordre du professeur Lomonossoff.
Je suis, monsieur, votre serviteur obéissant

William Phillips, secrétaire d'État par intérim.

Pièce jointe : lettre cachetée adressée à M. Thomas L. Chadbourne, accompagnée de 1 600 exemplaires de la Suède.
* * * * *
Réponse de M. Chadbourne, 5 avril 1919.
Monsieur, je vous prie d'accuser réception de votre lettre du 3 avril, à laquelle est jointe une lettre qui m'est adressée et qui contient un chèque de 10 000 dollars tiré à l'ordre du professeur Lomonossoff, chèque que je dois remettre aujourd'hui.
Je vous prie de rester, avec beaucoup de respect,
Très sincèrement, le vôtre, Thomas L. Chadbourne

Par la suite, la légation de Stockholm s'est enquise de l'adresse de Lomonossoff aux États-Unis et a été informée par le département d'État que "pour autant que le département sache, le professeur George V. Lomonossoff peut être joint aux soins de M. Thomas L. Chadbourne, 520 Park Avenue, New York City".

Il est évident que le Département d'État, pour des raisons soit d'amitié personnelle entre Polk et Chadbourne, soit d'influence politique, a senti qu'il devait se joindre à eux et servir de collecteur de fonds pour un agent bolchévique - tout juste expulsé de Norvège. Mais pourquoi un cabinet d'avocats de l'establishment prestigieux s'intéresserait-il de si près à la santé et au bien-être d'un émissaire bolchévique ? Peut-être un rapport contemporain du Département d'État en donne-t-il la réponse :

> Martens, le représentant bolchévique, et le professeur Lomonossoff comptent sur le fait que Bullitt et son parti feront un rapport favorable à la mission et au président concernant les conditions en Russie soviétique et que, sur la base de ce rapport, le gouvernement des États-Unis sera favorable à l'idée de traiter avec le gouvernement soviétique comme le propose Martens. Le 29 mars 1919.[211]

TOUTES LES CONDITIONS SONT RÉUNIES POUR L'EXPLOITATION COMMERCIALE DE LA RUSSIE

C'est l'exploitation commerciale de la Russie qui excite Wall Street, et Wall Street n'a pas perdu de temps pour préparer son programme. Le 1er mai 1918 - une date propice pour les révolutionnaires rouges - la Ligue américaine d'Aide et de Coopération avec la Russie fut créée, et son programme approuvé lors d'une conférence tenue dans le Senate Office Building, à Washington, D.C. Les dirigeants et le comité exécutif de la ligue représentaient quelques factions superficiellement dissemblables. Son président était le Dr Frank J. Goodnow, président de l'université Johns Hopkins. Les vice-présidents étaient les toujours actifs William Boyce Thompson, Oscar S. Straus, James Duncan et Frederick C. Howe, qui a écrit *Confessions of a Monopolist*, le livre détaillants les instructions par lesquelles les monopoles pouvaient contrôler la société. Le trésorier était George P. Whalen, vice-président de la Vacuum Oil Company. Le Congrès était représenté par le sénateur William Edgar Borah et le sénateur John Sharp

[211] Fichier décimal du département d'État américain, 861.00/4214a.

Williams, de la commission sénatoriale des relations étrangères ; le sénateur William N. Calder et le sénateur Robert L. Owen, président de la commission bancaire et monétaire. Les membres de la Chambre étaient Henry R. Cooper et Henry D. Flood, président de la commission des affaires étrangères de la Chambre. Les entreprises américaines étaient représentées par Henry Ford, Charles A. Coffin, président du conseil d'administration de la General Electric Company, et M. A. Oudin, alors directeur étranger de la General Electric. George P. Whalen représentait la Vacuum Oil Company, et Daniel Willard était président de la Baltimore & Ohio Railroad. L'élément le plus ouvertement révolutionnaire était représenté par Mme Raymond Robins, dont le nom s'est révélé plus tard être bien en vue dans les dossiers du Bureau soviétique et lors des audiences de la Commission Lusk ; Henry L. Slobodine, décrit comme un "éminent socialiste patriote" ; et Lincoln Steffens, un communiste national de renom.

En d'autres termes, il s'agissait d'un comité exécutif hybride ; il représentait des éléments révolutionnaires nationaux, le Congrès des États-Unis et des intérêts financiers très impliqués dans les affaires russes.

Le comité exécutif a approuvé un programme qui mettait l'accent sur la création d'une division russe officielle au sein du gouvernement américain "dirigée par des hommes forts". Cette division s'assurerait le concours d'universités, d'organisations scientifiques et d'autres institutions pour étudier la "question russe", coordonnerait et unirait les organisations au sein des États-Unis "pour la sauvegarde de la Russie", mettrait en place un "comité spécial de renseignement pour l'enquête sur la question russe" et, de manière générale, étudierait et enquêterait elle-même sur ce qui était considéré comme la "question russe". Le comité exécutif a ensuite adopté une résolution soutenant le message du président Woodrow Wilson au congrès soviétique à Moscou et la ligue a confirmé son propre soutien à la nouvelle Russie soviétique.

Quelques semaines plus tard, le 20 mai 1918, Frank J. Goodnow et Herbert A. Carpenter, représentant la ligue, font appel au secrétaire d'État adjoint William Phillips et lui font comprendre la nécessité de créer une "division officielle du gouvernement russe pour coordonner toutes les questions russes". Ils m'ont demandé [écrit Phillips] s'ils devaient aborder cette question avec le président".[212]

Phillips en fit directement rapport au secrétaire d'État et, le lendemain, écrivit à Charles R. Crane à New York pour lui demander son avis sur la Ligue américaine d'aide et de coopération avec la Russie. Phillips a demandé à Crane : "Je voudrais vraiment avoir votre avis sur la façon dont nous devrions traiter la ligue... Nous ne voulons pas semer le trouble en refusant de coopérer avec eux. D'un autre côté, c'est un comité homosexuel et je ne comprends pas bien."[213]

Début juin, le Département d'État a reçu une lettre de William Franklin Sands, de l'American International Corporation, adressée au secrétaire d'État Robert Lansing. Sands proposait que les États-Unis nomment un administrateur en Russie plutôt qu'une commission, et estimait que "la suggestion d'une force militaire

[212] Ibid, 861.00/1938.

[213] Ibid.

alliée en Russie à l'heure actuelle me semble très dangereuse".[214] Sands a souligné la possibilité de commerce avec la Russie et que cette possibilité pourrait être avancée "par un administrateur bien choisi jouissant de la pleine confiance du gouvernement" ; il a indiqué que "M. Hoover" pourrait jouer ce rôle.[215] La lettre a été transmise à Phillips par Basil Miles, un ancien associé de Sands, avec l'expression : "Je pense que le secrétaire trouverait utile de la lire".

Au début du mois de juin, le War Trade Board, subordonné au Département d'État, a adopté une résolution, et un comité du conseil comprenant Thomas L. Chadbourne (un contact du professeur Lomonossoff), Clarence M. Woolley et John Foster Dulles a soumis un mémorandum au Département d'État, demandant instamment l'examen des moyens "d'instaurer des relations commerciales plus étroites et plus amicales entre les États-Unis et la Russie". Le conseil a recommandé une mission en Russie et a rouvert la question de savoir si celle-ci devait résulter d'une invitation du gouvernement soviétique.

Puis, le 10 juin, M. A. Oudin, directeur étranger de la General Electric Company, a exprimé son point de vue sur la Russie et s'est clairement prononcé en faveur d'un "plan constructif d'assistance économique" de la Russie.[216] En août 1918, Cyrus M. McCormick de International Harvester écrivit à Basil Miles au Département d'État et loua le programme du président pour la Russie, que McCormick considérait comme "une occasion en or".[217]

Par conséquent, nous trouvons au milieu de l'année 1918 un effort concerté d'une partie des entreprises américaines - manifestement prête à ouvrir le commerce - pour tirer profit de sa propre position privilégiée vis-à-vis des Soviétiques.

L'ALLEMAGNE ET LES ÉTATS-UNIS SE BATTENT POUR FAIRE DES AFFAIRES EN RUSSIE

En 1918, cette assistance au régime bolchévique embryonnaire était justifiée par la volonté de vaincre l'Allemagne et d'empêcher l'exploitation de la Russie par l'Allemagne. Ce fut l'argument utilisé par W. B. Thompson et Raymond Robins pour envoyer des révolutionnaires bolchéviques et des équipes de propagande en Allemagne en 1918. Cet argument a également été utilisé par Thompson en 1917 lors d'une conférence avec le Premier ministre Lloyd George sur l'obtention du soutien britannique au régime bolchévique naissant. En juin 1918, l'ambassadeur Francis et son équipe sont revenus de Russie et ont exhorté le président Wilson "à reconnaître et à aider le gouvernement soviétique de

[214] Ibid, 861.00/2003.

[215] Ibid.

[216] Ibid, 861.00/2002.

[217] Ibid.

Russie".[218] Ces rapports faits par le personnel de l'ambassade au Département d'État ont été divulgués à la presse et largement imprimés. On prétendait surtout qu'un retard dans la reconnaissance de l'Union soviétique aiderait l'Allemagne "et contribuerait au plan allemand pour favoriser la réaction et la contre-révolution".[219] Des statistiques exagérées ont été citées pour appuyer la proposition - par exemple, que le gouvernement soviétique représentait quatre-vingt-dix pour cent du peuple russe "et que les dix pour cent restants sont l'ancienne classe propriétaire et dirigeante... Naturellement, ils sont mécontents".[220] Un ancien fonctionnaire américain aurait déclaré : "Si nous ne faisons rien - c'est-à-dire si nous laissons les choses dériver - nous contribuons à affaiblir le gouvernement soviétique russe. Et cela fait le jeu de l'Allemagne.[221]" Il a donc été recommandé qu'"une commission armée de crédits et de bons conseils commerciaux pourrait être d'une grande aide".

Entre-temps, la situation économique était devenue critique en Russie et le Parti communiste et ses planificateurs ont compris qu'il était inévitable d'embrasser le capitalisme. Lénine a cristallisé cette prise de conscience devant le dixième congrès du parti communiste russe :

> Sans l'aide du capital, il nous sera impossible de conserver le pouvoir prolétarien dans un pays incroyablement ruiné où la paysannerie, elle aussi ruinée, constitue l'écrasante majorité - et, bien sûr, pour cette aide, le capital nous exterminera à cent pour cent. C'est ce que nous devons comprendre. Donc, soit ce type de relations économiques, soit rien[222]

Ensuite, Léon Trotsky aurait déclaré : "Ce dont nous avons besoin ici, c'est d'un organisateur comme Bernard M. Baruch".[223]

La prise de conscience par les Soviétiques de l'imminence de son effondrement économique suggère que les entreprises américaines et allemandes ont été attirées par la possibilité d'exploiter le marché russe pour les marchandises nécessaires ; les Allemands, en fait, ont commencé très tôt en 1918. Les premiers accords conclus par le Bureau soviétique à New York indiquent que le soutien financier et moral apporté par les Américains aux Bolcheviks a porté ses fruits sous la forme de contrats.

La plus grosse commande en 1919-20 a été passée à Morris & Co, les abattoirs de Chicago, pour cinquante millions de livres de produits alimentaires, d'une valeur d'environ 10 millions de dollars. La famille Morris était apparentée à la

---

[218] Ibid, M 316-18-1306.

[219] Ibid.

[220] Ibid.

[221] Ibid.

[222] V. 1. Lénine, Rapport au dixième congrès du parti communiste russe (bolchévique), 15 mars 1921.

[223] William Reswick, *I Dreamt Revolution* (Chicago : Henry Regnery, 1952), p. 78.

famille Swift. Helen Swift, plus tard liée au Abraham Lincoln Center "Unity", était mariée à Edward Morris et était également le frère de Harold H. Swift, un "major" de la mission de la Croix-Rouge de Thompson en Russie en 1917.

CONTRATS CONCLUS EN 1919 PAR LE BUREAU SOVIÉTIQUE AVEC LES ENTREPRISES AMÉRICAINES			
Date du contrat	***Entreprise***	***Biens vendus***	***Valeur***
7 juillet 1919	Milwaukee Shaper Co.*	Machines	$45,071
30 juillet 1919	Kempsmith Mfg. Co.*	Machines	$97,470
10 mai 1919	F. Mayer Boot & Shoe*	Boots	$1,201,250
Août 1919	Steel Sole Shoe & Co.*	Boots	$58,750
23 juillet 1919	Eline Berlow, N.Y.	Boots	$3,000,000
24 juillet 1919	Fischmann & Co.	Vêtements	$3,000,000
29 septembre 1919	Weinberg & Posner	Machines	$3,000,000
27 octobre 1919	LeHigh Machine Co.	Presses d'imprimerie	$4,500,000
22 janvier 1920	Morris & Co. Chicago	50 millions de livres de produits alimentaires	$10,000,000
*Plus tard, par l'intermédiaire de la société Bobroff Foreign Trade and Engineering Co. de Milwaukee.			
SOURCE : États-Unis, Sénat, *Propagande russe,* auditions devant une sous-commission de la commission des relations étrangères, 66e cong., 2e sess. 1920, p. 71.			

Ludwig Martens était auparavant vice-président de Weinberg & Posner, situé au 120 Broadway, New York City, et cette entreprise a reçu une commande de 3 millions de dollars.

L'OR SOVIÉTIQUE ET LES BANQUES AMÉRICAINES

L'or était le seul moyen pratique par lequel l'Union soviétique pouvait payer ses achats à l'étranger et les banquiers internationaux étaient tout à fait disposés à faciliter les expéditions d'or soviétique. Les exportations d'or russe, principalement des pièces d'or impériales, ont commencé au début de 1920, vers la Norvège et la Suède. Elles étaient transbordées en Hollande et en Allemagne pour d'autres destinations mondiales, y compris les États-Unis.

En août 1920, une cargaison de pièces d'or russes a été reçue à la Den Norske Handelsbank en Norvège comme garantie de paiement de 3000 tonnes de charbon par la Niels Juul and Company aux États-Unis pour le compte du gouvernement soviétique. Ces pièces ont été transférées à la Norges Bank pour y être conservées. Les pièces ont été examinées et pesées, il a été constaté qu'elles avaient été frappées avant le déclenchement de la guerre en 1914, et qu'il s'agissait donc de véritables pièces de monnaie impériales russes.[224]

224 Fichier décimal du département d'État américain, 861.51/815.

Peu après ce premier épisode, la Robert Dollar Company de San Francisco a reçu sur son compte de Stockholm des lingots d'or, évalués à trente-neuf millions de couronnes suédoises ; l'or "portait le cachet de l'ancien gouvernement du tsar de Russie". L'agent de la Dollar Company à Stockholm a demandé à la société American Express des facilités pour expédier l'or aux États-Unis. American Express a refusé de s'occuper de l'envoi. Robert Dollar, il convient de noter, était un directeur de l'American International Company ; l'AIC était donc liée à la première tentative d'expédition d'or directement vers l'Amérique.[225]

Simultanément, il a été rapporté que trois navires avaient quitté Reval sur la mer Baltique avec de l'or soviétique destiné aux États-Unis. Le S.S. *Gauthod a* chargé 216 boîtes d'or sous la supervision du professeur Lomonossoff - qui retourne maintenant aux États-Unis. Le S.S. *Carl Line* a chargé 216 boîtes d'or sous la supervision de trois agents russes. Le S.S. *Ruheleva* était chargé de 108 boîtes d'or. Chaque boîte contenait trois caniches d'or d'une valeur de soixante mille roubles d'or chacune. Le tout a été suivi d'une expédition sur le S.S. *Wheeling Mold.*

Kuhn, Loeb & Company, agissant apparemment au nom de la Guaranty Trust Company, s'est alors renseigné auprès du Département d'État sur l'attitude officielle à l'égard de la réception de l'or soviétique. Dans un rapport, le département a exprimé son inquiétude, car si l'or était refusé, "il reviendrait probablement au ministère de la Guerre, ce qui entraînerait une responsabilité gouvernementale directe et un embarras accru".[226] Le rapport, rédigé par Merle Smith en conférence avec Kelley et Gilbert, soutient que, à moins que le possesseur n'ait une connaissance précise en la matière, il serait impossible de refuser l'acceptation. Il est prévu de demander aux États-Unis de faire fondre l'or dans le bureau d'analyse, et il est alors décidé de télégraphier à Kuhn, Loeb & Company qu'aucune restriction ne sera imposée à l'importation de l'or soviétique aux États-Unis.

L'or est arrivé au New York Assay Office et a été déposé non pas par Kuhn, Loeb & Company - mais par la Guaranty Trust Company de New York. La Guaranty Trust s'est alors renseignée auprès du Conseil de la Réserve Fédérale, qui à son tour s'est renseigné auprès du Trésor américain, concernant l'acceptation et le paiement. Le surintendant du New York Assay Office a informé le Trésor que les quelque sept millions de dollars d'or ne portaient aucune marque d'identification et que "les barres déposées ont déjà été fondues dans des barres de monnaie américaine". Le Trésor a suggéré que le Conseil de la Réserve Fédérale détermine si la Guaranty Trust Company avait agi "pour son propre compte ou pour le compte d'un tiers en présentant l'or", et en particulier "si un transfert de crédit ou une opération de change a résulté ou non de l'importation ou du dépôt de l'or".[227]

[225] Ibid, 861.51/836.

[226] Ibid, 861.51,/837, 4 octobre 1920.

[227] Ibid, 861.51/837, 24 octobre 1920.

Le 10 novembre 1920, A. Breton, un vice-président du Guaranty Trust, écrivit au secrétaire adjoint Gilbert du département du Trésor pour se plaindre que Guaranty n'avait pas reçu du bureau d'analyse l'avance immédiate habituelle contre les dépôts de "métal jaune laissé avec eux pour la réduction". La lettre indique que Guaranty Trust avait reçu des assurances satisfaisantes que les barres étaient le produit de la fonte de pièces françaises et belges, bien qu'elle ait acheté le métal en Hollande. La lettre demande au Trésor d'accélérer le paiement de l'or. En réponse, le Trésor a fait valoir qu'il "n'achète pas l'or soumis à la Monnaie des États-Unis ou aux bureaux d'analyse dont on sait ou on soupçonne qu'il est d'origine soviétique", et compte tenu des ventes d'or soviétique connues en Hollande, l'or soumis par la Guaranty Trust Company a été considéré comme un "cas douteux, avec des suggestions d'origine soviétique". Elle a suggéré que la Guaranty Trust Company pouvait retirer l'or du bureau d'analyse à tout moment, ou qu'elle pouvait "présenter au Trésor, à la Banque de Réserve Fédérale de New York ou au Département d'État les preuves supplémentaires nécessaires pour laver l'or de tout soupçon d'origine soviétique".[228]

Il n'y a pas de dossier concernant le règlement final de cette affaire, mais on peut supposer que la Guaranty Trust Company a été payée pour l'envoi. Il est évident que ce dépôt d'or devait mettre en œuvre l'accord fiscal conclu au milieu des années 1920 entre la Guaranty Trust et le gouvernement soviétique, en vertu duquel la société est devenue l'agent soviétique aux États-Unis (voir l'épigraphe de ce chapitre).

Il a été déterminé plus tard que l'or soviétique était également envoyé à la Monnaie suédoise. La Monnaie suédoise "fait fondre l'or russe, le teste et appose le timbre de la Monnaie suédoise à la demande des banques suédoises ou d'autres sujets suédois qui détiennent l'or".[229] Et au même moment, Olof Aschberg, chef de la Svenska Ekonomie A/B (l'intermédiaire soviétique et filiale de Guaranty Trust), offrait "des quantités illimitées d'or russe" par l'intermédiaire de banques suédoises.[230]

En bref, nous pouvons relier American International Corporation, l'influent professeur Lomonossoff, Guaranty Trust et Olof Aschberg (que nous avons déjà identifié) aux premières tentatives d'importation d'or soviétique aux États-Unis.

MAX MAY DE GUARANTY TRUST DEVIENT DIRECTEUR DE RUSKOMBANK

L'intérêt de Guaranty Trust pour la Russie soviétique a été renouvelé en 1920 sous la forme d'une lettre de Henry C. Emery, directeur adjoint du département des affaires étrangères de Guaranty Trust, à De Witt C. Poole au département

[228] Ibid, 861.51/853, 11 novembre 1920.

[229] Ibid, 316-119, 1132.

[230] Ibid, 316-119-785. Ce rapport contient davantage de données sur les transferts d'or russe par d'autres pays et intermédiaires. Voir aussi 316-119-846.

d'État. La lettre est datée du 21 janvier 1920, quelques semaines avant qu'Allen Walker, le directeur du ministère des Affaires étrangères, ne participe activement à la formation de la virulente organisation anti-soviétique United Americans (voir page 165). Emery posait de nombreuses questions sur la base juridique du gouvernement soviétique et du secteur bancaire en Russie et demandait si le gouvernement soviétique était le gouvernement de facto en Russie.[231] "Révolte avant 1922 planifiée par les Rouges", affirmaient les Américains Unis en 1920, mais Guaranty Trust avait entamé des négociations avec ces mêmes Rouges et agissait en tant qu'agent soviétique aux États-Unis au milieu de l'année 1920.

En janvier 1922, le secrétaire au commerce Herbert Hoover, est intervenu auprès du Département d'État pour un programme de Guaranty Trust visant à établir des relations d'échange avec la "Nouvelle Banque d'État à Moscou". Ce projet, écrivait Herbert Hoover, "ne serait pas critiquable si l'on stipulait que toutes les sommes entrant en leur possession devaient être utilisées pour l'achat de marchandises civiles aux États-Unis" ; et après avoir affirmé que ces relations semblaient être conformes à la politique générale, Hoover ajoutait : "Il pourrait être avantageux d'organiser ces transactions de manière à ce que nous sachions ce qu'est le mouvement au lieu des opérations désintégrées actuelles". Bien sûr, de telles "opérations désintégrées" sont conformes aux opérations d'un marché libre, mais cette approche a été rejetée par Herbert Hoover qui a préféré canaliser l'échange par des sources spécifiées et contrôlables à New York. Le secrétaire d'État Charles E. Hughes a exprimé son aversion pour le système Hoover-Guaranty Trust, qui, selon lui, pouvait être considéré comme une reconnaissance de facto des Soviétiques alors que les crédits étrangers acquis pouvaient être utilisés au détriment des États-Unis. Une réponse sans engagement a été envoyée par l'État à Guaranty Trust. Cependant, Guaranty va de l'avant (avec le soutien d'Herbert Hoover), participe à la formation de la première banque internationale soviétique, et Max May de Guaranty Trust devient chef du département des affaires étrangères de la nouvelle Ruskombank.

---

[231] Ibid, 861.516/86.

CHAPITRE X

J.P. MORGAN DONNE UN COUP DE MAIN À L'ENNEMI

Je ne m'assiérais pas pour déjeuner avec un Morgan - sauf peut-être pour apprendre quelque chose sur ses motivations et ses attitudes.
William E. Dodd, *Journal de l'ambassadeur Dodd, 1933-1938*

Notre histoire a jusqu'à présent tourné autour d'une seule grande maison financière - la Guaranty Trust Company, le plus grand trust financier des États-Unis et contrôlée par la firme J.P. Morgan. Guaranty Trust a utilisé Olof Aschberg, le banquier bolchévique, comme intermédiaire en Russie avant et après la révolution. Guaranty était un bailleur de fonds de Ludwig Martens et de son bureau soviétique, les premiers représentants soviétiques aux États-Unis. Et au milieu des années 1920, Guaranty était l'agent fiscal soviétique aux États-Unis ; les premières expéditions d'or soviétique aux États-Unis remontaient également à Guaranty Trust.

Cette activité pro-bolchévique a un revers surprenant : Guaranty Trust est l'un des fondateurs de United Americans, une organisation antisoviétique virulente qui menaçait bruyamment l'invasion rouge en 1922, affirmait que 20 millions de dollars de fonds soviétiques étaient en route pour financer la révolution rouge, et prévoyait la panique dans les rues et la famine massive à New York. Cette duplicité soulève, bien sûr, de sérieuses questions sur les intentions de Guaranty Trust et de ses directeurs. Le fait de traiter avec les Soviétiques, voire de les soutenir, peut s'expliquer par une avidité apolitique ou simplement par le souci du profit. D'autre part, la diffusion d'une propagande destinée à créer la peur et la panique tout en encourageant les conditions qui engendrent la peur et la panique est un problème beaucoup plus grave. Elle suggère une dépravation morale totale. Examinons d'abord de plus près les Américains unis anticommunistes.

LES AMÉRICAINS UNIS POUR COMBATTRE LE COMMUNISME[232]

[232] *New York Times*, 21 juin 1919.

En 1920, l'organisation United Americans a été fondée. Elle était limitée aux citoyens des États-Unis et prévue pour cinq millions de membres, "dont le seul but serait de combattre les enseignements des socialistes, des communistes, de l'I.W.W., des organisations russes et des syndicats paysans radicaux".

En d'autres termes, les Américains unis devaient combattre toutes les institutions et tous les groupes considérés comme anticapitalistes.

Les officiers de l'organisation préliminaire mise en place pour construire les États-Unis étaient Allen Walker de la Guaranty Trust Company ; Daniel Willard, président de la Baltimore & Ohio Railroad ; H. H. Westinghouse, de la Westinghouse Air Brake Company ; et Otto H. Kahn, de Kuhn, Loeb & Company et American International Corporation. Ces pontes de Wall Street étaient soutenus par divers présidents d'université, dont Newton W. Gilbert (ancien gouverneur des Philippines). De toute évidence, les Américains Unis étaient, à première vue, exactement le type d'organisation que les capitalistes de l'establishment devaient financer et rejoindre. Sa formation n'aurait pas dû apporter de grande surprise.

D'autre part, comme nous l'avons déjà vu, ces financiers étaient également très impliqués dans le soutien au nouveau régime soviétique en Russie - bien que ce soutien se soit fait en coulisses, enregistré uniquement dans les dossiers du gouvernement, et n'ait pas été rendu public pendant 50 ans. Dans le cadre de United Americans, Walker, Willard, Westinghouse et Kahn jouaient un double jeu. Otto H. Kahn, l'un des fondateurs de l'organisation anticommuniste, a été rapporté par le socialiste britannique J. H. Thomas comme ayant son "visage vers la lumière". Kahn a écrit la préface du livre de Thomas. En 1924, Otto Kahn s'adressa à la Ligue pour la démocratie industrielle et professa des objectifs communs avec ce groupe socialiste militant (voir page 49). La Baltimore & Ohio Railroad (l'employeur de Willard) a participé activement au développement de la Russie dans les années 1920. Westinghouse en 1920, l'année de la fondation de United Americans, exploitait une usine en Russie qui avait été exemptée de la nationalisation. Et le rôle de Guaranty Trust a déjà été minutieusement décrit.

UNITED AMERICANS DÉVOILE DES "RÉVÉLATIONS SURPRENANTES" SUR LES ROUGES

En mars 1920, le *New York Times* a fait la une d'un reportage détaillé sur l'invasion des États-Unis par les Rouges en l'espace de deux ans, une invasion qui devait être financée par 20 millions de dollars de fonds soviétiques "obtenus par le meurtre et le vol de la noblesse russe".[233]

Il a été révélé que les Américains avaient fait une enquête sur les "activités radicales" aux États-Unis, et ce dans le cadre de son rôle d'organisation formée pour "préserver la Constitution des États-Unis avec la forme représentative de gouvernement et le droit de possession individuelle que prévoit la Constitution".

---

[233] Ibid, 28 mars 1920.

En outre, l'enquête, a-t-on proclamé, a reçu le soutien du conseil d'administration, "notamment d'Otto H. Kahn, d'Allen Walker de la Guaranty Trust Company, de Daniel Willard" et d'autres. Le sondage affirmait que :

> les dirigeants gauchistes sont persuadés d'effectuer une révolution dans les deux ans, que le début doit être fait à New York avec une grève générale, que les dirigeants rouges ont prédit beaucoup d'effusions de sang et que le gouvernement soviétique russe a contribué à hauteur de 20 000 000$ au mouvement radical américain.

Les cargaisons d'or soviétiques destinées au Guaranty Trust au milieu des années 1920 (540 boîtes de trois caniches chacune) valaient environ 15 000 000$ (à 20$ l'once troy), et d'autres cargaisons d'or par l'intermédiaire de Robert Dollar et Olof Aschberg ont porté le total à très près de 20 millions de dollars. Les informations sur l'or soviétique destinées au mouvement radical ont été qualifiées de "tout à fait fiables" et ont été "remises au gouvernement". Les Rouges, affirmait-on, prévoyaient d'affamer New York pour qu'elle se soumette dans les quatre jours :

> En attendant, les Rouges comptent sur une panique financière dans les prochaines semaines pour faire avancer leur cause. Une telle panique provoquerait la détresse des ouvriers et les rendrait ainsi plus susceptibles d'adhérer à la doctrine de la révolution.

Le rapport des Américains a grossièrement surestimé le nombre de radicaux aux États-Unis, en avançant d'abord des chiffres comme deux ou cinq millions, puis en se contentant de 3 465 000 membres dans quatre organisations radicales. Le rapport conclut en soulignant la possibilité d'une effusion de sang et cite "Skaczewski, président de l'Association internationale de l'édition, sinon le Parti communiste, [qui] s'est vanté que... le moment était venu où les communistes allaient détruire complètement la forme actuelle de la société".

En bref, les Américains ont publié un rapport sans preuves à l'appui, destiné à faire paniquer l'homme de la rue : le point important est bien sûr que c'est le même groupe qui était chargé de protéger et de subventionner, voire d'aider, les Soviétiques pour qu'ils puissent entreprendre ces mêmes plans.

CONCLUSIONS CONCERNANT UNITED AMERICANS

S'agit-il d'un cas où la main droite ne sait pas ce que fait la main gauche ? Probablement pas. Nous parlons de chefs d'entreprise, d'entreprises éminemment performantes d'ailleurs. Donc, United Americans était probablement une ruse pour détourner l'attention du public - et des autorités - des efforts souterrains déployés pour pénétrer le marché russe.

United Americans est le seul exemple documenté connu de cet écrivain d'une organisation qui aide le régime soviétique et qui est également au premier plan de l'opposition aux Soviétiques. Il ne s'agit nullement d'une ligne de conduite incohérente, et les recherches futures devraient au moins se concentrer sur les aspects suivants :

(a) Existe-t-il d'autres exemples de doubles allégeances commis par des groupes influents généralement connus sous le nom d'établissement ?

(b) Ces exemples peuvent-ils être étendus à d'autres domaines ? Par exemple, existe-t-il des preuves que des conflits du travail ont été provoqués par ces groupes ?

(c) Quel est le but ultime de ces tactiques d'encadrement dialectique ? Peuvent-elles être liées à l'axiome marxiste : la thèse contre l'antithèse permet la synthèse ? C'est une énigme de savoir pourquoi le mouvement marxiste attaquerait le capitalisme de front si son objectif était un monde communiste et s'il acceptait vraiment la dialectique. Si l'objectif est un monde communiste - c'est-à-dire si le communisme est la synthèse souhaitée - et que le capitalisme est la thèse, alors quelque chose d'autre que le capitalisme ou le communisme doit être l'antithèse. Le capitalisme pourrait-il donc être la thèse et le communisme l'antithèse, l'objectif des groupes révolutionnaires et de leurs partisans étant de synthétiser ces deux systèmes en un système mondial non encore décrit ?

MORGAN ET ROCKEFELLER AIDENT KOLCHAK

Parallèlement à ces efforts pour aider le Bureau soviétique et les Américains unis, la firme J.P. Morgan, qui contrôlait le Guaranty Trust, apportait une aide financière à l'un des principaux opposants des bolcheviks, l'amiral Alexandre Kolchak en Sibérie. Le 23 juin 1919, le membre du Congrès Mason a présenté la résolution 132 de la Chambre des Représentants donnant instruction au Département d'État "de faire une enquête sur tous et sur chacun des rapports de presse" accusant les détenteurs d'obligations russes d'avoir usé de leur influence pour obtenir le "maintien des troupes américaines en Russie" afin d'assurer le paiement continu des intérêts sur les obligations russes. Selon une note de dossier de Basil Miles, un associé de William F. Sands, le membre du Congrès Mason a accusé certaines banques de tenter d'obtenir la reconnaissance de l'amiral Kolchak en Sibérie pour obtenir le paiement d'anciennes obligations russes.

Puis en août 1919, le secrétaire d'État, Robert Lansing, reçut de la National City Bank of New York, influencée par le Rockefeller, une lettre demandant un commentaire officiel sur un projet de prêt de 5 millions de dollars à l'amiral Kolchak ; et de J.P. Morgan & Co. et d'autres banquiers, une autre lettre demandant l'avis du ministère concernant un projet de prêt supplémentaire de 10 millions de livres sterling à Kolchak par un consortium de banquiers britanniques et américains.[234]

Le secrétaire Lansing informa les banquiers que les États-Unis n'avaient pas reconnu Kolchak et que, bien que prêt à lui apporter son aide, "le ministère ne pensait pas pouvoir assumer la responsabilité d'encourager de telles négociations

[234] Fichier décimal du Département d'État américain, 861.51/649.

mais que, néanmoins, il semblait n'y avoir aucune objection au prêt à condition que les banquiers le jugent opportun".[235]

Par la suite, le 30 septembre, Lansing a informé le consul général américain à Omsk que le "prêt a depuis suivi son cours normal".[236] Deux cinquièmes ont été souscrits par des banques britanniques et trois cinquièmes par des banques américaines. Les deux tiers du total devaient être dépensés en Grande-Bretagne et aux États-Unis et le tiers restant là où le gouvernement Kolchak le souhaitait. Le prêt était garanti par de l'or russe (celui de Kolchak) qui était expédié à San Francisco. Le calendrier des exportations d'or soviétiques décrit précédemment suggère que la coopération avec les Soviétiques sur les ventes d'or a été déterminée dans la foulée de l'accord de prêt d'or de Kolchak.

Les ventes d'or soviétiques et le prêt Kolchak suggèrent également que la déclaration de Carroll Quigley selon laquelle les intérêts de Morgan ont infiltré la gauche intérieure s'appliquait aussi aux mouvements révolutionnaires et contre-révolutionnaires d'outre-mer. L'été 1919 fut une période de revers militaires soviétiques en Crimée et en Ukraine et cette image négative a peut-être incité les banquiers britanniques et américains à se réconcilier avec les forces anti-bolchéviques. La raison évidente serait d'avoir un pied dans tous les camps, et donc d'être dans une position favorable pour négocier des concessions et des affaires après que la révolution ou la contre-révolution ait réussi et qu'un nouveau gouvernement se soit stabilisé. Comme l'issue d'un conflit ne peut être constatée dès le départ, l'idée est de parier sur tous les chevaux de la course à la révolution. Ainsi, une aide a été apportée d'une part aux Soviétiques et d'autre part à Kolchak - alors que le gouvernement britannique soutenait Denikin en Ukraine et que le gouvernement français est allé au secours des Polonais.

À l'automne 1919, le journal berlinois *Berliner Zeitung am Mittak* (8 et 9 octobre) a accusé la firme Morgan de financer le gouvernement de la Russie occidentale et les forces russo-allemandes dans la Baltique qui combattent les bolcheviks - tous deux alliés à Kolchak. La firme Morgan a vigoureusement nié cette accusation : "Cette firme n'a eu aucune discussion ou réunion avec le gouvernement ouest-russe ou avec quiconque prétendant le représenter, à aucun moment."[237] Mais si l'accusation de financement était inexacte, il y a des preuves de collaboration. Les documents trouvés par les services de renseignement du gouvernement letton parmi les papiers du colonel Bermondt, commandant de l'Armée Volontaire Occidentale, confirment "les relations prétendument existantes entre l'agent londonien de Kolchak et le réseau industriel allemand qui était à l'arrière de Bermondt".[238]

---

[235] Ibid, 861.51/675

[236] Ibid, 861.51/656

[237] Ibid, 861.51/767 - lettre de J. P. Morgan au Département d'État, 11 novembre 1919. Le financement lui-même était un canular (voir le rapport d'AP dans les dossiers du Département d'État à la suite de la lettre de Morgan).

[238] Ibid, 861.51/6172 et /6361.

En d'autres termes, nous savons que J.P. Morgan, les banquiers de Londres et de New York ont financé Kolchak. Il existe également des preuves qui relient Kolchak et son armée à d'autres armées anti-bolchéviques. Et il semble évident que les cercles industriels et bancaires allemands finançaient l'armée anti-bolchévique russe dans la Baltique. Il est évident que les fonds des banquiers n'ont pas de drapeau national.

CHAPITRE XI

L'ALLIANCE DES BANQUIERS ET DE LA RÉVOLUTION

Le nom de Rockefeller n'évoque pas un révolutionnaire, et mon mode de vie a favorisé une attitude prudente et circonspecte qui frise le conservatisme. Je ne suis pas connu pour soutenir des causes perdues...

John D. Rockefeller III, *La deuxième révolution américaine*
(New York : Harper & Row. 1973)

RÉSUMÉ DES PREUVES

Les preuves déjà publiées par George Katkov, Stefan Possony et Michael Futrell a établi que le retour en Russie de Lénine et de son parti de bolcheviks exilés, suivi quelques semaines plus tard par un parti de mencheviks, a été financé et organisé par le gouvernement allemand.[239] Les fonds nécessaires ont été transférés en partie par l'intermédiaire de la Nya Banken à Stockholm, propriété d'Olof Aschberg, et le double objectif allemand était : (a) soustraire la Russie de la guerre, et (b) contrôler le marché russe de l'après-guerre.[240]

Nous sommes maintenant allés au-delà de ces preuves pour établir une relation de travail continue entre le banquier bolchévique Olof Aschberg et la Guaranty Trust Company, contrôlée par Morgan, à New York, avant, pendant et après la révolution russe. À l'époque tsariste, Aschberg était l'agent de Morgan en Russie et le négociateur des prêts russes aux États-Unis ; en 1917, Aschberg était l'intermédiaire financier des révolutionnaires ; et après la révolution, Aschberg est devenu directeur de Ruskombank, la première banque internationale soviétique, tandis que Max May, un vice-président de la Guaranty Trust contrôlée par Morgan, est devenu directeur et chef du département des affaires étrangères de Ruskom-

239 Michael Futrell, *Northern Underground* (Londres : Faber et Faber, 1963) ; Stefan Possony, *Lénine : The Compulsive Revolutionary* (Londres : George Allen & Unwin, 1966) ; et George Katkov, "German Foreign Office Documents on Financial Support to the Bolsheviks in 1917", *International Affairs 32* (Royal Institute of International Affairs, 1956).

240 Ibid. et surtout Katkov.

bank. Nous avons présenté des preuves documentaires d'une relation de travail continue entre la Guaranty Trust Company et les Bolcheviks. Les directeurs de Guaranty Trust en 1917 sont énumérés à l'annexe 1.

De plus, il existe des preuves de transferts de fonds de banquiers de Wall Street vers des activités révolutionnaires internationales. Par exemple, il y a la déclaration (étayée par un télégramme) de William Boyce Thompson - un directeur de la Federal Reserve Bank of New York, un actionnaire important de la Chase Bank contrôlée par Rockefeller et un associé financier des Guggenheim et des Morgan - selon laquelle il (Thompson) a contribué à la révolution bolchévique à hauteur d'un million de dollars à des fins de propagande. Un autre exemple est celui de John Reed, le membre américain du comité exécutif de la Troisième Internationale, qui a été financé et soutenu par Eugène Boissevain, un banquier privé de New York, et qui était employé par le magazine *Metropolitan* de Harry Payne Whitney. Whitney était à l'époque directeur de Guaranty Trust. Nous avons également établi que Ludwig Martens, le premier "ambassadeur" soviétique aux États-Unis, était (selon le chef des services secrets britanniques Sir Basil Thompson) soutenu par des fonds de la Guaranty Trust Company. En retraçant le financement de Trotsky aux États-Unis, nous sommes arrivés à des sources allemandes, encore à identifier, à New York. Bien que nous ne connaissions pas les sources allemandes précises des fonds de Trotsky, nous savons que Von Pavenstedt, le principal responsable de l'espionnage allemand aux États-Unis, était également associé principal de la société Amsinck & Co. Amsinck était la propriété de l'omniprésente American International Corporation - également contrôlée par la firme J.P. Morgan.

De plus, des entreprises de Wall Street, dont Guaranty Trust, ont été impliquées dans les activités révolutionnaires de Carranza et Villa au Mexique pendant la guerre. Nous avons également identifié des preuves documentaires concernant. le financement par un syndicat de Wall Street de la révolution menée par Sun Yat-sen de 1912 en Chine, une révolution aujourd'hui saluée par les communistes chinois comme le précurseur de la révolution de Mao en Chine. Charles B. Hill, avocat new-yorkais négociant avec Sun Yat-sen au nom de ce syndicat, était directeur de trois filiales de Westinghouse, et nous avons découvert que Charles R. Crane de Westinghouse en Russie était impliqué dans la révolution russe.

Outre la finance, nous avons identifié d'autres preuves, peut-être plus significatives, de l'implication de Wall Street dans la cause bolchévique. La mission de la Croix-Rouge américaine en Russie était une entreprise privée de William B. Thompson, qui a publiquement apporté un soutien partisan aux bolcheviks. Les documents du Cabinet de guerre britannique actuellement disponibles indiquent que la politique britannique a été détournée vers le régime de Lénine et Trotsky par l'intervention personnelle de Thompson auprès de Lloyd George en décembre 1917. Nous avons reproduit les déclarations du directeur Thompson et du vice-président William Lawrence Saunders, tous deux de la Banque de Réserve Fédérale de New York, qui étaient fortement favorables aux bolcheviks. John Reed n'était pas seulement financé par Wall Street, mais bénéficiait d'un soutien constant pour ses activités, jusqu'à l'intervention au Département d'État de William Franklin Sands, secrétaire exécutif de l'American

International Corporation. Dans l'affaire de la sédition de Robert Minor, il y a de fortes indications et quelques preuves circonstancielles que le colonel Edward House est intervenu pour faire libérer Minor. L'importance de l'affaire Minor réside dans le fait que le programme de William B. Thompson pour la révolution bolchévique en Allemagne était le programme même que Minor mettait en œuvre lorsqu'il a été arrêté en Allemagne.

Certains agents internationaux, par exemple Alexander Gumberg, ont travaillé pour Wall Street et les bolcheviks. En 1917, Gumberg a été le représentant d'une entreprise américaine à Petrograd, a travaillé pour la mission de la Croix-Rouge américaine de Thompson, est devenu l'agent principal des bolcheviks en Scandinavie jusqu'à sa déportation de Norvège, puis est devenu l'assistant confidentiel du préfet Schley de la Chase Bank à New York et plus tard de Floyd Odium de la Atlas Corporation.

Cette activité au nom des bolcheviks est en grande partie issue d'une adresse unique : 120 Broadway, New York City. Les preuves de cette observation sont exposées, mais aucune raison concluante n'est donnée pour expliquer la concentration inhabituelle de l'activité à une seule adresse, si ce n'est qu'il semble s'agir de la contrepartie étrangère de l'affirmation de Carroll Quigley selon laquelle J.P. Morgan a infiltré la gauche nationale. Morgan a également infiltré la gauche internationale.

La Banque de Réserve Fédérale de New York se trouve au 120 Broadway. Le véhicule de cette activité pro-bolchévique était l'American International Corporation - au 120 Broadway. Les vues de l'AIC sur le régime bolchévique ont été questionnées par le secrétaire d'État Robert Lansing quelques semaines seulement après le début de la révolution, et Sands, secrétaire exécutif de l'AIC, pouvait à peine contenir son enthousiasme pour la cause bolchévique. Ludwig Martens, le premier ambassadeur soviétique, avait été vice-président de Weinberg & Posner, qui était également situé au 120-Broadway. La Guaranty Trust Company était à côté, au 140 Broadway, mais la Guaranty Securities Co. était au 120 Broadway. En 1917, Hunt, Hill & Betts se trouvait au 120 Broadway, et Charles B. Hill de cette société était le négociateur dans les affaires de Sun Yat-sen. La société John MacGregor Grant, financée par Olof Aschberg en Suède et Guaranty Trust aux États-Unis, et qui figurait sur la liste noire des services de renseignements militaires, était située au 120 Broadway. Les Guggenheim et le cœur exécutif de General Electric (également intéressé par American International) se trouvaient au 120 Broadway. Il n'est donc pas surprenant que le Bankers Club se trouvât également au 120 Broadway, au dernier étage (le trente-quatrième).

Il est significatif que le soutien aux bolcheviks n'ait pas cessé avec la consolidation de la révolution ; par conséquent, ce soutien ne peut pas s'expliquer entièrement par la guerre avec l'Allemagne. Le syndicat américano-russe formé en 1918 pour obtenir des concessions en Russie était soutenu par les intérêts de White, Guggenheim et Sinclair. Les directeurs des sociétés contrôlées par ces trois financiers étaient Thomas W. Lamont (Guaranty Trust), William Boyce Thompson (Banque de la Réserve Fédérale) et Harry Payne Whitney (Guaranty Trust), l'employeur de John Reed. Cela suggère fortement que le syndicat a été formé pour tirer profit du soutien apporté à la cause bolchévique pendant la période révolutionnaire. Et puis nous avons découvert que Guaranty Trust a soutenu financièrement le Bureau soviétique à New York en 1919.

Le premier signal vraiment concret que le soutien politique et financier précédent portait ses fruits est apparu en 1923 lorsque les Soviétiques ont créé leur première banque internationale, Ruskombank. L'associé de Morgan, Olof Aschberg, est devenu le directeur nominal de cette banque soviétique ; Max May, un vice-président de Guaranty Trust, est devenu directeur de Ruskom-bank, et la Ruskombank a rapidement nommé la Guaranty Trust Company comme agent américain.

L'EXPLICATION DE L'ALLIANCE CONTRE NATURE

Quel motif explique cette coalition de capitalistes et de bolcheviks ?

La Russie était alors - et est aujourd'hui - le plus grand marché inexploité du monde. En outre, la Russie, à l'époque comme aujourd'hui, constituait la plus grande menace concurrentielle potentielle pour la suprématie industrielle et financière américaine. (Un coup d'œil sur une carte du monde suffit pour mettre en évidence la différence géographique entre la vaste étendue terrestre de la Russie et celle plus petite des États-Unis). Wall Street avait des frissons lorsqu'il visualisait la Russie comme un deuxième super géant industriel américain.

Mais pourquoi permettre à la Russie de devenir un concurrent et un défi à la suprématie américaine ? À la fin du XIXe siècle, Morgan/Rockefeller et Guggenheim avaient démontré leurs tendances monopolistiques. Dans *Railroads and Regulation 1877-1916,* Gabriel Kolko a montré comment les propriétaires des chemins de fer, et non les agriculteurs, voulaient que l'État contrôle les chemins de fer afin de préserver leur monopole et d'abolir la concurrence. L'explication la plus simple de nos preuves est donc qu'un syndicat de financiers de Wall Street a élargi l'horizon de leurs ambitions monopolistiques et a facilité les opérations à l'échelle mondiale. *Le gigantesque marché russe devait être converti en un marché captif et en une colonie technique exploitée par quelques financiers américains puissants et les sociétés qu'ils contrôlaient.* Ce que l'Interstate Commerce Commission et la Federal Trade Commission, sous la houlette de l'industrie américaine, pouvaient réaliser pour cette industrie dans le pays, un gouvernement socialiste planifié pouvait le réaliser à l'étranger - avec le soutien et les incitations appropriés de Wall Street et de Washington, D.C.

Enfin, de peur que cette explication ne semble trop radicale, rappelez-vous que c'est Trotsky qui a nommé les généraux tsaristes pour consolider l'Armée rouge ; que c'est Trotsky qui a appelé les officiers américains à contrôler la Russie révolutionnaire et à intervenir en faveur des Soviétiques ; que c'est Trotsky qui a écrasé d'abord l'élément libertaire dans la révolution russe, puis les ouvriers et les paysans ; et que l'histoire écrite ignore totalement l'Armée verte de 700 000 hommes composée d'ex-bolcheviks, furieux de la trahison de la révolution, qui a combattu les Blancs *et* les Rouges. En d'autres termes, nous suggérons que la révolution bolchévique était une alliance de statistiques : des révolutionnaires étatiques et des financiers étatiques alignés contre les véritables éléments révolutionnaires libertaires en Russie.[241]

La question qui se pose maintenant aux lecteurs est la suivante : ces banquiers étaient-ils aussi des bolcheviks secrets ? Non, bien sûr que non. Les financiers étaient sans idéologie. Ce serait une erreur d'interprétation de supposer que l'aide aux bolcheviks était motivée par l'idéologie, au sens strict du terme. Les financiers étaient motivés par le pouvoir et ont donc aidé tout instrument politique qui leur permettrait d'accéder au pouvoir : Trotsky, Lénine, le tsar, Kolchak, Dénikine - tous ont reçu une aide, plus ou moins. Tous, c'est-à-dire, sauf ceux qui voulaient une société individualiste vraiment libre.

L'aide n'a pas non plus été limitée aux Bolcheviks étatiques et aux contre-Bolcheviks étatiques. John P. Diggins, dans *Mussolini and fascism: The View from America*,[242] a noté à propos de Thomas Lamont du Guaranty Trust que de tous les chefs d'entreprise américains, celui qui a le plus vigoureusement soutenu la cause du fascisme était Thomas W. Lamont. Chef du puissant réseau bancaire J.P. Morgan, Lamont a été en quelque sorte un consultant en affaires pour le gouvernement de l'Italie fasciste.

Lamont a obtenu un prêt de 100 millions de dollars pour Mussolini en 1926, à un moment particulièrement crucial pour le dictateur italien. On peut aussi se rappeler que le directeur de Guaranty Trust était le père de Corliss Lamont, un communiste national. Cette approche impartiale des deux systèmes totalitaires, le communisme et le fascisme, ne s'est pas limitée à la famille Lamont. Par exemple, Otto Kahn, directeur de l'American International Corporation et de Kuhn, Loeb & Co, était convaincu que "les capitaux américains investis en Italie trouveront sécurité, encouragement, opportunité et récompense".[243] C'est ce même Otto Kahn qui, en 1924, a déclaré à la Ligue socialiste de la démocratie industrielle que ses objectifs étaient les mêmes que les siens. Ils ne différaient - selon Otto Kahn - que sur les moyens d'atteindre ces objectifs.

Ivy Lee, l'homme des relations publiques de Rockefeller, a fait des déclarations similaires, et a été responsable de la vente du régime soviétique au public américain crédule à la fin des années 1920. Nous avons également observé que Basil Miles, responsable du bureau russe au département d'État et ancien associé de William Franklin Sands, était décidément utile aux hommes d'affaires qui défendaient les causes bolchéviques ; mais en 1923, le même Miles a écrit un article profasciste, "Les chemises noires de l'Italie et les affaires".[244] "Le succès des fascistes est une expression de la jeunesse italienne", écrivait Miles tout en glorifiant le mouvement fasciste et en applaudissant son estime pour le monde des affaires américain.

---

241 Voir aussi Voline (V.M. Eichenbaum), *Nineteen-Seventeen: The Russian Revolution Betrayed* (New York : Libertarian Book Club, n.d.).

242 Princeton, N.J. : Princeton University Press, 1972.

243 Ibid, p. 149.

244 *Nation's Business*, février 1923, p. 22-23.

LE PLAN MARBURG

Le plan Marburg, financé par le vaste héritage d'Andrew Carnegie, a été réalisé dans les premières années du XXe siècle. Il suggère une préméditation pour ce genre de schizophrénie superficielle, qui masque en fait un programme intégré d'acquisition de pouvoir : "Et si Carnegie et sa richesse illimitée, les financiers internationaux et les socialistes pouvaient s'organiser en un mouvement pour contraindre à la formation d'une ligue pour imposer la paix".[245]

Les gouvernements du monde, selon le plan de Marburg, devaient être socialisés tandis que le pouvoir ultime resterait entre les mains des financiers internationaux "pour contrôler ses conseils et faire respecter la paix [et ainsi] fournir une solution adaptée pour tous les maux politiques de l'humanité".[246]

Cette idée a été imbriquée avec d'autres éléments ayant des objectifs similaires. Lord Milner en Angleterre fournit l'exemple d'intérêts bancaires transatlantique reconnaissant les vertus et les possibilités du marxisme. Milner était un banquier, influent dans la politique britannique en temps de guerre, et pro-marxiste.[247] À New York, le club socialiste "X" a été fondé en 1903. Il comptait parmi ses membres non seulement le communiste Lincoln Steffens, le socialiste William English Walling et le banquier communiste Morris Hillquit, mais aussi John Dewey, James T. Shotwell, Charles Edward Russell et Rufus Weeks (vice-président de la New York Life Insurance Company). La réunion annuelle de l'Economic Club à l'hôtel Astor, à New York, a été marquée par la présence d'orateurs socialistes. En 1908, lorsque A. Barton Hepburn, président de la Chase National Bank, était président de l'Economic Club, l'orateur principal était Morris Hillquit, déjà cité, qui "eut l'occasion de prêcher le socialisme à une assemblée qui représentait la richesse et les intérêts financiers".[248]

De ces germes improbables est né le mouvement internationaliste moderne, qui comprenait non seulement les financiers Carnegie, Paul Warburg, Otto Kahn, Bernard Baruch et Herbert Hoover, mais aussi la Fondation Carnegie et son excroissance de l'*International Conciliation*. Les administrateurs de Carnegie étaient, comme nous l'avons vu, des membres importants du conseil d'administration de l'American International Corporation. En 1910, Carnegie a fait don de 10 millions de dollars pour fonder la Carnegie Endowment for International Peace, et parmi les membres du conseil d'administration figuraient Elihu Root (Mission Root en Russie, 1917), Cleveland H. Dodge (un bailleur de fonds du président Wilson), George W. Perkins (partenaire de Morgan), G. J. Balch (AIC et Amsinck), R. F. Herrick (AIC), H. W. Pritchett (AIC) et d'autres personnalités de Wall Street. Woodrow Wilson a subi la puissante influence de ce

---

[245] Jennings C. Wise, *Woodrow Wilson: Disciple of Revolution* (New York : Paisley Press, 1938), p.45.

[246] Ibid, p.46.

[247] Voir p. 89.

[248] Morris Hillquit, *Loose Leaves from a Busy Life* (New York : Macmillan, 1934), p. 81.

groupe d'internationalistes, dont il était d'ailleurs financièrement redevable. Comme l'a écrit Jennings C. Wise, "Les historiens ne doivent jamais oublier que Woodrow Wilson... a permis à Leon Trotsky d'entrer en Russie avec un passeport américain."[249]

Mais Léon Trotsky s'est également déclaré internationaliste. Nous avons remarqué avec un certain intérêt ses relations d'internationaliste de haut niveau, ou du moins ses amis, au Canada. Trotsky n'était alors ni pro-russe, ni pro-allié, ni pro-allemand, comme beaucoup ont essayé de le faire croire. Trotsky était *pour la* révolution mondiale, *pour la* dictature mondiale ; il était, en un mot, un internationaliste.[250] Les bolchéviques et les banquiers ont alors ce point commun important : l'internationalisme. La révolution et la finance internationale ne sont pas du tout contradictoires si le résultat de la révolution est d'établir une autorité plus centralisée. La finance internationale préfère traiter avec les gouvernements centraux. La dernière chose que la communauté bancaire souhaite est une libre économie et un pouvoir décentralisé, car ces éléments amoindrissent leur pouvoir.

Il s'agit donc d'une explication qui correspond aux preuves. Cette poignée de banquiers et de promoteurs n'était ni bolchévique, ni communiste, ni socialiste, ni démocrate, ni même américaine. Ces hommes voulaient avant tout des marchés, de préférence des marchés internationaux captifs - et un monopole du marché mondial captif comme but ultime. Ils voulaient des marchés qui pouvaient être exploités de manière monopolistique sans craindre la concurrence des Russes, des Allemands ou de quiconque - y compris les hommes d'affaires américains en dehors du cercle des initiés. Ce groupe fermé était apolitique et amoral. En 1917, il avait un objectif unique : la consolidation d'un marché captif en Russie, le tout présenté sous couvert d'une ligue pour faire respecter la paix et protégé intellectuellement par celle-ci.

Wall Street a en effet atteint son objectif. Les entreprises américaines contrôlées par ce syndicat devaient plus tard poursuivre la construction de l'Union soviétique, et sont aujourd'hui en bonne voie pour faire entrer le complexe militaro-industriel soviétique dans l'ère de l'informatique.

Aujourd'hui, l'objectif est toujours d'actualité. John D. Rockefeller l'explique dans son livre *The Second American Revolution*, dont la première page comporte une étoile à cinq branches.[251] Le livre contient un plaidoyer nu pour l'humanisme, c'est-à-dire un plaidoyer selon lequel notre première priorité est de travailler pour les autres. En d'autres termes, un plaidoyer pour le collectivisme. L'humanisme, c'est le collectivisme. Il est remarquable que les Rockefeller, qui ont promu cette idée humaniste pendant un siècle, n'aient pas cédé leur PROPRE patrimoine à d'autres... Il est vraisemblablement implicite dans leur recommandation que nous devons tous travailler pour les Rockefeller. Le livre de Rockefeller promeut le

[249] Wise, op. cit. p. 647

[250] Leon Trotsky, *The Bolsheviki and World Peace* (New York : Boni & Liveright, 1918).

[251] En mai 1973, la Chase Manhattan Bank (dont le président est David Rockefeller) ouvre un bureau à Moscou, au 1 Karl Marx Square. Le bureau de New York est situé au 1 Chase Manhattan Plaza.

collectivisme sous les apparences d'un "conservatisme prudent" et du "bien public". Il s'agit en fait d'un plaidoyer pour la poursuite du soutien antérieur de Morgan-Rockefeller aux entreprises collectivistes et à la subversion massive des droits individuels.

En bref, le bien public a été, et est encore aujourd'hui, utilisé comme un moyen et une excuse pour s'agrandir par un cercle élitiste qui plaide pour la paix mondiale et la décence humaine. Mais tant que le lecteur regardera l'histoire du monde en termes d'un conflit marxiste inexorable entre le capitalisme et le communisme, les objectifs d'une telle alliance entre la finance internationale et la révolution internationale resteront insaisissables. Il en sera de même pour l'absurdité de la promotion du bien public par ces pillards. Si ces alliances échappent encore au lecteur, alors il devrait réfléchir au fait évident que ces mêmes intérêts et promoteurs internationaux sont toujours prêts à déterminer ce que d'autres personnes devraient faire, mais qu'ils ne sont manifestement pas disposés à être les premiers à renoncer à leur propre richesse et à leur propre pouvoir. Leurs bouches sont ouvertes, leurs poches sont fermées.

Cette technique, utilisée par les monopolistes pour escroquer la société, a été exposée au début du XXe siècle par Frederick C. Howe dans *The Confessions of a Monopolist.*[252] D'abord, dit Howe, la politique est une partie nécessaire des affaires. Pour contrôler les industries, il est nécessaire de contrôler le Congrès et les régulateurs et donc de faire travailler la société pour vous, le monopoliste. Ainsi, selon Howe, les deux principes d'un monopolisateur qui réussit sont : "Premièrement, laissez la société travailler pour vous ; et deuxièmement, faites de la politique une affaire comme les autres".[253] Ce sont, selon Howe, les "règles de base du big business".

Y a-t-il des preuves que cet objectif magnifiquement ambitieux était également connu du Congrès et du monde universitaire ? Il est certain que la possibilité était connue et rendue publique. En témoigne par exemple le témoignage d'Albert Rhys Williams, un commentateur avisé de la révolution, devant la commission Overman du Sénat :

> ... il est probablement vrai que sous le gouvernement soviétique, la vie industrielle se développera peut-être beaucoup plus lentement que sous le système capitaliste habituel. Mais pourquoi un grand pays industriel comme l'Amérique souhaiterait-il la création et la concurrence conséquente d'un autre grand rival industriel ? Les intérêts de l'Amérique à cet égard ne sont-ils pas conformes au rythme lent de développement que la Russie soviétique se projette ?
> **SÉNATEUR WOLCOTT** : Alors votre argument est qu'il serait dans l'intérêt de l'Amérique de faire réprimer la Russie ?
> **M. WILLIAMS** : Non réprimé...
> **SÉNATEUR WOLCOTT** : Vous dites. Pourquoi l'Amérique devrait-elle vouloir que la Russie devienne un concurrent industriel à ses côtés ?
> **M. WILLIAMS** : C'est parler d'un point de vue capitaliste. L'intérêt de l'Amérique n'est pas, je pense, d'avoir un autre grand rival industriel, comme

[252] Chicago : Public Publishing, s.d.

[253] Ibid.

l'Allemagne, l'Angleterre, la France et l'Italie, lancé sur le marché en concurrence. Je pense qu'un autre gouvernement que le gouvernement soviétique augmenterait peut-être le rythme ou le taux de développement de la Russie, et nous aurions un autre rival. Bien sûr, il s'agit là d'un débat d'un point de vue capitaliste.
SÉNATEUR WOLCOTT : Vous présentez donc ici un argument qui, selon vous, pourrait plaire au peuple américain, à savoir que si nous reconnaissons le gouvernement soviétique de Russie tel qu'il est constitué, nous reconnaîtrons un gouvernement qui ne pourra pas nous concurrencer dans l'industrie pendant de nombreuses années ?
M. WILLIAMS : C'est un fait.
SÉNATEUR WOLCOTT : C'est un argument selon lequel, sous le gouvernement soviétique, la Russie n'est pas en mesure, depuis de nombreuses années du moins, d'approcher les rendements de l'Amérique sur le plan industriel ?
M. WILLIAMS : Absolument.[254]

Et dans cette déclaration franche d'Albert Rhys Williams se trouve l'indice fondamental de l'interprétation révisionniste de l'histoire russe au cours du dernier demi-siècle.

Wall Street, ou plutôt le complexe Morgan-Rockefeller représenté au 120 Broadway et au 14 Wall Street, souhaitait quelque chose de très proche de l'argument de Williams. Wall Street s'est battue à Washington pour les bolcheviks. Il a réussi. Le régime totalitaire soviétique a survécu. Dans les années 1930, des entreprises étrangères, principalement du groupe Morgan-Rockefeller, ont construit les plans quinquennaux. Elles ont continué à construire la Russie, économiquement et militairement.[255] D'autre part, Wall Street n'a vraisemblablement pas prévu la guerre de Corée et la guerre du Vietnam - au cours desquelles 100 000 Américains et d'innombrables alliés ont perdu la vie à cause des armements soviétiques construits avec cette même technologie américaine importée. Ce qui semblait être une politique clairvoyante, et sans doute profitable, pour un syndicat de Wall Street, est devenu un cauchemar pour des millions de personnes en dehors du cercle du pouvoir élitiste et de la classe dirigeante.

---

[254] États-Unis, Sénat, *Propagande bolchévique*, auditions devant une sous-commission de la Commission du pouvoir judiciaire, 65e Cong., pp. 679-80. Voir aussi, à la page 107, le rôle de Williams au sein du Bureau de presse de Radek.

[255] Voir Antony C. Sutton, *Western Technology and Soviet Economic Development*, 3 vols. (Stanford, Californie : Hoover Institution, 1968, 1971, 1973) ; voir aussi *National Suicide: Military Aid to the Soviet Union* (New York : Arlington House, 1973).

ANNEXE I

DIRECTEURS DES GRANDES BANQUES, ENTREPRISES ET INSTITUTIONS MENTIONNÉES DANS CE LIVRE (EN 1917-1918)

AMERICAN INTERNATIONAL CORPORATION (120 Broadway)

J. Armure Ogden
G. J. Baldwin
C. A. Cercueil
W. E. Corey
Robert Dollar
Pierre S. du Pont
Philip A. S. Franklin
J. P. Grace
R. F. Herrick
Otto H. Kahn
H. W. Pritchett
Percy A. Rockefeller
John D. Ryan
W.L. Saunders
J.A. Stillman
C.A. Stone
T.N. Vail
F.A. Vanderlip
E.S. Webster
A.H. Wiggin
Beckman Winthrop
William Woodward

CHASE NATIONAL BANK

J. N. Hill
A. B. Hepburn
S. H. Miller
C. M. Schwab
H. Bendicott
Guy E. Tripp
Newcomb Carlton
D.C. Jackling
E.R. Tinker
A.H. Wiggin
John J. Mitchell

EQUITABLE TRUST COMPANY (37-43 Wall Street)

Charles B. Alexander
Albert B. Boardman
Robert.C. Clowry
Howard E. Cole
Henry E. Cooper
Paul D. Cravath Hunter
Franklin Wm. Cutcheon
Bertram Cutler
Thomas de Witt Cuyler
Frederick W. Fuller
Henry E. Huntington
Edward T. Jeffrey
Otto H. Kahn
Alvin W. Krech
James W. Lane
S. Marston
Charles G. Meyer
George Welwood Murray
Henry H. Pierce
Winslow S. Pierce

Robert Goelet
Carl R. Gray
Charles Hayden
Bertram G. Work
Lyman Rhoades
Walter C. Teagle
Henry Rogers Winthrop

CONSEIL CONSULTATIF FÉDÉRAL (1916)

Daniel G. Wing, Boston, District n° 1
J. P. Morgan, New York, District n° 2
Levi L. Rue, Philadelphie, District n° 3
W. S. Rowe, Cincinnati, District n° 4
J. W. Norwood, Greenville, S.C., District n° 5
C. A. Lyerly, Chattanooga, district n° 6
J. B. Forgan, Chicago, Président, District n° 7
Frank O. Watts, St. Louis, district n° 8
C. T. Jaffray, Minneapolis, District n° 9
E. F. Swinney, Kansas City, District n° 10
T. J. Record, Paris, District n° 11
Herbert Fleishhacker, San Francisco, District n° 12

FEDERAL RESERVE BANK OF NEW YORK (120 Broadway)

William Woodward (1917)
Robert H. Treman (1918) — Classe A
Franklin D. Locke (1919)

Charles A. Stone (1920)
Wm. B. Thompson (1918) — Classe B
L. R. Palmer (1919)

Pierre Jay (1917)
George F. Peabody (1919) — Classe C
William Lawrence Saunders (1920)

CONSEIL DE LA RÉSERVE FÉDÉRALE

William G. M'Adoo
Charles S. Hamlin (1916)
Paul M. Warburg (1918)
John Skelton Williams
Adolf C. Miller (1924)
Frédéric A. Delano (1920)
W.P.G. Harding (1922)

GUARANTY TRUST COMPANY (140 Broadway)

Alexander J. Hemphill (Président)
Charles H. Allen
A. C. Bedford Grayson
Edward J. Berwind
W. Murray Crane
T. de Witt Cuyler
James B. Duke
Caleb C. Dula
Robert W. Goelet
Edgar L. Marston
M-P Murphy
Charles A. Peabody
William C. Potter
John S. Runnells
Thomas F. Ryan
Charles H. Sabin
John W. Spoor

Daniel Guggenheim
W. Averell Harriman
Albert H. Harris
Walter D. Hines
Augustus D. Julliard
Thomas W. Lamont
William C. Lane
Albert Straus
Harry P. Whitney
Thomas E. Wilson
Comité de Londres :
Arthur J. Fraser (Président)
Cecil F. Parr
Robert Callander

NATIONAL CITY BANK

P. A. S. Franklin
J.P. Grace
G. H. Dodge
H. A. C. Taylor
R. S. Lovett
F. A. Vanderlip
G. H. Miniken
E. P. Swenson
Frank Trumbull
Edgar Palmer
P.A. Rockefeller
James Stillman
W. Rockefeller
J. O. Armure
J.W. Sterling
J.A. Stillman
M.T. Pyne
E.D. Bapst
J.H. Post
W.C. Procter

NATIONALBANK FÜR DEUTSCHLAND

(Comme en 1914, Hjalmar Schacht l'a intégrée en 1918)
Emil Wittenberg
Hjalmar Schacht
Martin Schiff
Franz Rintelen
Hans Winterfeldt
Th Marba
Paul Koch

SINCLAIR CONSOLIDATED OIL CORPORATION (120 Broadway)

Harry F. Sinclair
H. P. Whitney
Wm. E. Corey
Wm. B. Thompson
James N. Wallace
Edward H. Clark
Daniel C. Jackling
Albert H. Wiggin

J. G. WHITE ENGINEERING CORPORATION

James Brown
Douglas Campbell
G. C. Clark, Jr.
Bayard Dominick, Jr.
A. G. Hodenpyl
T. W. Lamont
Marion McMillan
J. H. Pardee
G. H. Walbridge
E. N. Chilson
A. N. Connett
C.E. Bailey
J.G. White
Gano Dunn
E.G. Williams
A.S. Crane
H.A. Lardner
G.H. Kinniat
A.F. Kountz
R.B. Marchant
Henry Parsons

ANNEXE II

LA THÉORIE DE LA CONSPIRATION JUIVE DE LA RÉVOLUTION BOLCHÉVIQUE

Il existe une littérature abondante en anglais, en français et en allemand qui reflète l'argument selon lequel la révolution bolchévique est le résultat d'une "conspiration juive" ; plus précisément, une conspiration des banquiers mondiaux juifs. En général, le contrôle du monde est considéré comme l'objectif ultime ; la révolution bolchévique n'était qu'une phase d'un programme plus vaste qui est censé refléter une lutte religieuse séculaire entre le christianisme et les "forces des ténèbres".

L'argument et ses variantes peuvent être trouvés dans les endroits les plus surprenants et auprès de personnes tout à fait différentes. En février 1920, Winston Churchill a écrit un article - rarement cité aujourd'hui - pour le *London Illustrated Sunday Herald* intitulé "Sionisme contre bolchevisme". Dans cet article, Churchill concluait qu'il était "particulièrement important... que les Juifs nationaux de chaque pays qui sont loyaux à leur terre d'adoption se manifestent à chaque occasion... et prennent une part importante dans toutes les mesures visant à combattre la conspiration bolchévique". Churchill trace une ligne entre les "Juifs nationaux" et ce qu'il appelle les "Juifs internationaux". Il soutient que les "Juifs internationaux pour la plupart athées" ont certainement joué un "très grand" rôle dans la création du bolchevisme et dans l'avènement de la révolution russe. Il affirme (contrairement à la réalité) qu'à l'exception de Lénine, "la majorité" des figures de proue de la révolution étaient juives, et ajoute (également contrairement à la réalité) que dans de nombreux cas, les intérêts juifs et les lieux de culte juifs ont été exemptés par les bolcheviks de leur politique de saisie. Churchill appelle les Juifs internationaux une "sinistre confédération" issue des populations persécutées des pays où les Juifs ont été martyrisés en raison de leur race. Winston Churchill fait remonter ce mouvement à Spartacus-Weishaupt, se poursuivant avec Trotsky, Bela Kun, Rosa Luxemburg et Emma Goldman, et porte des accusations : "Cette conspiration mondiale pour le renversement de la civilisation et pour la reconstitution de la société sur la base d'un développement arrêté, d'une malveillance envieuse et d'une égalité impossible, n'a cessé de s'étendre".

Churchill soutient ensuite que ce groupe conspirateur de Spartacus-Weishaupt a été le moteur de tous les mouvements subversifs du XIXe siècle. Tout en soulignant que le sionisme et le bolchevisme sont en concurrence pour l'âme du peuple juif, Churchill (en 1920) se préoccupe du rôle du juif dans la révolution bolchévique et de l'existence d'une conspiration juive mondiale.

Autre auteur bien connu dans les années 1920, Henry Wickham Steed décrit dans le deuxième volume de son ouvrage *Through 30 Years 1892-1922* (p. 302) comment il a tenté de porter le concept de conspiration juive à l'attention du colonel Edward M. House et du président Woodrow Wilson. Un jour de mars 1919, Wickham Steed a appelé le colonel House et l'a trouvé perturbé par les récentes critiques de Steed concernant la reconnaissance des bolcheviks par les États-Unis. Steed a fait remarquer à House que Wilson serait discrédité parmi les nombreux peuples et nations d'Europe et "a insisté sur le fait que, à son insu, les principaux acteurs étaient Jacob Schiff, Warburg et d'autres financiers internationaux, qui souhaitaient avant tout soutenir les bolchéviques juifs afin de garantir un terrain pour l'exploitation allemande et juive de la Russie".[256] Selon Steed, le colonel House a plaidé pour l'établissement de relations économiques avec l'Union soviétique.

La collection de documents sur la conspiration juive la plus accablante à première vue se trouve probablement dans le fichier décimal du Département d'État (861.00/5339). Le document central est celui intitulé "Bolchevisme et judaïsme", daté du 13 novembre 1918. Le texte se présente sous la forme d'un rapport, qui indique que la révolution en Russie a été conçue "en février 1916" et "il a été constaté que les personnes et entreprises suivantes étaient engagées dans ce travail destructeur" :

(1) Jacob Schiff	Juif
(2) Kuhn, Loeb & Company	Entreprise juive
Gestion : Jacob Schiff	Juif
Felix Warburg	Juif
Otto H. Kahn	Juif
Mortimer L. Schiff	Juif
Jérôme J. Hanauer	Juif
(3) Guggenheim	Juif
(4) Max Breitung	Juif
(5) Isaac Seligman	Juif

Le rapport poursuit en affirmant qu'il ne fait aucun doute que la révolution russe a été lancée et conçue par ce groupe et qu'en avril 1917

> Jacob Schiff a fait une annonce publique et c'est grâce à son influence financière que la révolution russe a été accomplie avec succès. Au printemps 1917, Jacob Schiff a commencé à financer Trotsky, un juif, dans le but d'accomplir une révolution sociale en Russie.

Le rapport contient d'autres informations diverses sur le financement de Trotsky par Max Warburg, le rôle du syndicat de Rhénanie-Westphalie et Olof

[256] Voir l'annexe 3 pour le rôle réel de Schiff.

Aschberg de la Nya Banken (Stockholm) avec Jivotovsky. L'auteur anonyme (en fait employé par le War Trade Board américain)[257] affirme que les liens entre ces organisations et leur financement de la révolution bolchévique montrent comment "le lien entre les multimillionnaires juifs et les prolétaires juifs a été forgé". Le rapport énumère ensuite un grand nombre de bolcheviks qui étaient également juifs, puis décrit les actions de Paul Warburg, Judas Magnes, Kuhn, Loeb & Company et Speyer & Company.

Le rapport se termine par une pique à "la juiverie internationale" et place l'argument dans le contexte d'un conflit judéo-chrétien étayé par des citations des Protocoles des Sages de Sion. Ce rapport est accompagné d'une série de câbles entre le Département d'État à Washington et l'ambassade américaine à Londres concernant les démarches à entreprendre avec ces documents :[258]

> 5399 Grande-Bretagne, TEL. 3253 13 heures ; 16 octobre 1919 Dans le dossier confidentiel Secret for Winslow de Wright. Aide financière au bolchevisme et à la révolution bolchévique en Russie de la part d'éminents Juifs américains : Jacob Schiff, Felix Warburg, Otto Kahn, Mendell Schiff, Jerome Hanauer, Max Breitung et un des Guggenheim. Document de source française en possession des autorités policières britanniques. Demande confirmation des faits.
>
> * * * * *
>
> 17 octobre Grande-Bretagne TEL. 6084, midi r c-h 5399 Top secret. Wright pour Winslow. Aide financière à la révolution bolchévique en Russie de la part d'éminents Juifs d'Amérique. Pas de preuve, mais enquête. Demande aux autorités britanniques de suspendre la publication au moins jusqu'à la réception du document par le ministère des Affaires étrangères.
>
> * * * * *
>
> 28 novembre Grande-Bretagne TEL. 6223 R 5 pro. 5399
> POUR WRIGHT. Document concernant l'aide financière accordée aux bolchéviques par d'éminents juifs américains. Rapports - identifiés comme étant la traduction française d'une déclaration rédigée à l'origine en anglais par un citoyen russe en Amérique etc. Semble imprudent de donner la moindre publicité.

Il a été convenu de supprimer ce matériel et les dossiers concluent : "Je pense que nous devons étouffer le tout".

Un autre document portant la mention "Top secret" est joint à ce lot de matériel. La provenance de ce document est inconnue ; il s'agit peut-être d'un document du FBI ou du renseignement militaire. Il examine une traduction des Protocoles des réunions des Sages de Sion, et conclut :

---

[257] L'auteur anonyme était un Russe employé par le War Trade Board américain. L'un des trois directeurs de l'U.S. War Trade Board à cette époque était John Foster Dulles.

[258] Fichier décimal du département d'État américain, 861.00/5399.

> À cet égard, une lettre a été envoyée à M. W., à laquelle était joint un mémorandum de notre part concernant certaines informations de l'attaché militaire américain selon lesquelles les autorités britanniques avaient intercepté des lettres de divers groupes de Juifs internationaux exposant un plan de domination mondiale. Des copies de ces documents nous seront très utiles.

Cette information a apparemment été élaborée et un rapport ultérieur des services de renseignement britanniques porte l'accusation catégorique :

> RÉSUMÉ : Il est désormais clairement établi que le bolchevisme est un mouvement international contrôlé par les Juifs ; des communications sont en cours entre les dirigeants d'Amérique, de France, de Russie et d'Angleterre en vue d'une action concertée.[259]

Toutefois, aucune des déclarations ci-dessus ne peut être étayée par des preuves empiriques solides. L'information la plus significative est contenue dans le paragraphe selon lequel les autorités britanniques possédaient "des lettres interceptées de divers groupes de Juifs internationaux exposant un projet de domination mondiale". Si de telles lettres existent effectivement, alors elles fourniraient une justification (ou pas) à une hypothèse actuellement non fondée : à savoir que la révolution bolchévique et d'autres révolutions sont l'œuvre d'une conspiration juive mondiale.

Par ailleurs, lorsque les déclarations et les affirmations ne sont pas étayées par des preuves tangibles et lorsque les tentatives de dénicher des preuves tangibles ramènent en cercle au point de départ - en particulier lorsque tout le monde cite tout le monde - nous devons rejeter l'histoire comme étant fallacieuse. *Il n'existe aucune preuve concrète que les Juifs ont été impliqués dans la révolution bolchévique parce qu'ils étaient juifs.* Il se peut en effet qu'une plus grande proportion de Juifs ait été impliquée, mais étant donné le traitement tsariste des Juifs, à quoi d'autre pouvions-nous nous attendre ? Il y avait probablement beaucoup d'Anglais ou de personnes d'origine anglaise dans la Révolution américaine qui combattaient les tuniques rouges. Et alors ? Cela fait-il de la Révolution américaine une conspiration anglaise ? La déclaration de Winston Churchill selon laquelle les Juifs ont joué un "très grand rôle" dans la Révolution bolchévique n'est étayée que par des preuves déformées. La liste des Juifs impliqués dans la révolution bolchévique doit être mise en balance avec les listes de non-Juifs impliqués dans la révolution. Lorsque cette approche scientifique est adoptée, la proportion de juifs bolchéviques étrangers impliqués tombe à moins de vingt pour cent du nombre total de révolutionnaires - et ces juifs ont pour la plupart été déportés, assassinés ou envoyés en Sibérie dans les années qui ont suivi. La Russie moderne a en fait maintenu un antisémitisme de type tsariste.

Il est significatif que des documents dans les dossiers du Département d'État confirment que le banquier d'affaires Jacob Schiff, souvent cité comme source de

---

[259] Grande-Bretagne, Directorate of Intelligence, *A Monthly Review of the Progress of Revolutionary Movements Abroad,* no. 9, 16 juillet 1913 (861.99/5067).

fonds pour la révolution bolchévique, était en fait contre le soutien au régime bolchévique.[260] Cette position, comme nous le verrons, était en contradiction directe avec la promotion des bolchéviques par Morgan-Rockefeller.

La persistance avec laquelle le mythe de la conspiration juive a été mis en avant suggère qu'il pourrait bien s'agir d'un dispositif délibéré visant à détourner l'attention des véritables problèmes et des causes réelles. Les preuves fournies dans ce livre suggèrent que les banquiers new-yorkais qui étaient également juifs ont eu des rôles relativement mineurs dans le soutien aux bolcheviks, alors que les banquiers new-yorkais qui étaient également des Gentils (Morgan, Rockefeller, Thompson) ont eu des rôles majeurs.

Quelle meilleure façon de détourner l'attention des *véritables* opérateurs que de faire usage du croque-mitaine médiéval de l'antisémitisme ?

[260] Voir l'annexe 3.

ANNEXE III

DOCUMENTS SÉLECTIONNÉS DANS LES ARCHIVES GOUVERNEMENTALES DES ÉTATS-UNIS ET DE LA GRANDE-BRETAGNE

Note : Certains documents comprennent plusieurs papiers qui forment un groupe apparenté.

DOCUMENT N°1 Câble de l'Ambassadeur Francis à Petrograd au Département d'État américain et lettre correspondante du Secrétaire d'État Robert Lansing au Président Woodrow Wilson (17 mars 1917)

DOCUMENT N°2 Document du Foreign Office britannique (octobre 1917) affirmant que Kerensky était à la solde du gouvernement allemand et aidait les bolcheviks

DOCUMENT N°3 Jacob Schiff de Kuhn, Loeb & Company et sa position sur les régimes Kerensky et Bolchevik (novembre 1918)

DOCUMENT N°4 Mémorandum de William Boyce Thompson, directeur de la Federal Reserve Bank of New York, au Premier ministre britannique David Lloyd George (décembre 1917)

DOCUMENT N°5 Lettre de Felix Frankfurter à l'agent soviétique Santeri Nuorteva (9 mai 1918)

DOCUMENT N°6 Personnel du Bureau soviétique, New York, 1920 ; liste tirée des dossiers du Comité Lusk de l'État de New York

DOCUMENT N°7 Lettre de la National City Bank au Trésor américain se référant à Ludwig Martens et au Dr Julius Hammer (15 avril 1919)

DOCUMENT N°8 Lettre de l'agent soviétique William (Bill) Bobroff à Kenneth Durant (3 août 1920)

DOCUMENT N°9 Mémo faisant référence à un membre de la firme J. P. Morgan et au directeur de la propagande britannique Lord Northcliffe (13 avril 1918)

DOCUMENT N°10 Mémo du Département d'État (29 mai 1922) concernant General Electric Co.

DOCUMENT N°1

Câble de l'ambassadeur Francis à Petrograd au Département d'État à Washington, D.C., daté du 14 mars 1917, et relatant la première étape de la Révolution russe (861.00/273).

> Petrograd 14 mars 1917, 15e anniversaire, 2h30 du matin.
> Secrétaire d'État, Washington
> 1287. Impossible d'envoyer un câblogramme depuis le onze. Les révolutionnaires ont le contrôle absolu à Petrograd et font des efforts acharnés pour préserver l'ordre, ce qui réussit sauf dans de rares cas. Aucun télégramme depuis votre 1251 du 9, reçu le 11 mars. Le gouvernement provisoire s'est organisé sous l'autorité de la Douma qui a refusé d'obéir à l'ordre d'ajournement de l'empereur. Rodzianko, président de la Douma, donne des ordres sous sa propre signature. Le ministère aurait démissionné. Les ministres trouvés sont conduits devant la Douma, ainsi que de nombreux officiers russes et autres hauts fonctionnaires. La plupart sinon tous les régiments ordonnés à Petrograd ont rejoint les révolutionnaires après leur arrivée. La colonie américaine est en sécurité. Aucune connaissance de blessures sur des citoyens américains.
>
> FRANCIS,
> Ambassadeur américain

Dès réception du câble précédent, Robert Lansing, secrétaire d'État, en a mis le contenu à la disposition du président Wilson (861.00/273) :

> PERSONNEL ET CONFIDENTIEL
> Mon cher Monsieur le Président :
> Je vous joins un télégramme très important qui vient d'arriver de Petrograd, ainsi qu'une coupure de presse du New York WORLD de ce matin, dans laquelle se trouve une déclaration de Signor Scialoia, ministre sans portefeuille du cabinet italien, qui est significative au vu du rapport de M. Francis. Ma propre impression est que les Alliés sont au courant de cette affaire et je suppose qu'ils sont favorables aux révolutionnaires puisque le parti de la Cour a été, tout au long de la guerre, secrètement pro-allemand.
>
> Fidèlement à vous, ROBERT LANSING
> Annexe : Le président, la Maison Blanche

COMMENTAIRE

La phrase significative de la lettre de Lansing-Wilson est la suivante : "Ma propre impression est que les Alliés sont au courant de cette affaire et je présume qu'ils sont favorables aux révolutionnaires puisque le parti de la Cour a été, tout au long de la guerre, secrètement pro-allemand". On se souviendra (chapitre deux) que l'ambassadeur Dodd a affirmé que Charles R. Crane, de Westinghouse et de la Crane Co. à New York et conseiller du président Wilson, était impliqué dans cette première révolution.

DOCUMENT N°2

Mémorandum du ministère britannique des Affaires étrangères, dossier FO 371/ 2999 (La guerre - Russie), 23 octobre 1917, n° de dossier. 3743.

DOCUMENT
Personnel (et) secret.
Des rumeurs inquiétantes nous sont parvenues de plusieurs sources, selon lesquelles Kerensky est à la solde de l'Allemagne et que lui et son gouvernement font tout leur possible pour affaiblir (et) désorganiser la Russie, afin d'arriver à une situation où il ne serait pas possible d'aller plus loin qu'une paix séparée. Estimez-vous qu'il y a un motif pour de telles insinuations et que le gouvernement, en s'abstenant de toute action efficace, permet délibérément aux éléments bolchéviques de se renforcer ?
S'il s'agissait de corruption, nous pourrions être compétitifs si l'on savait comment et par quels agents cela pourrait se faire, bien que ce ne soit pas une pensée agréable.

COMMENTAIRE

Fait référence à l'information selon laquelle Kerensky était financé par l'Allemagne.

DOCUMENT N°3

Il se compose de quatre parties :

(a) Câble de l'ambassadeur Francis, le 27 avril 1917, à Petrograd, à Washington, D.C., demandant la transmission d'un message d'éminents banquiers juifs russes à d'éminents banquiers juifs de New York et demandant leur souscription au Kerensky Liberty Loan (861.51/139).
(b) Réponse de Louis Marshall (10 mai 1917) représentant les Juifs américains ; il décline l'invitation tout en exprimant son soutien à l'American Liberty Loan (861.51/143).
(c) Lettre de Jacob Schiff de Kuhn, Loeb (25 novembre 1918) au Département d'État (M. Polk) relayant un message du banquier juif russe Kamenka appelant à l'aide des Alliés *contre* les Bolcheviks ("parce que le gouvernement bolchévique ne représente pas le peuple russe").
(d) Câble de Kamenka relayé par Jacob Schiff.

DOCUMENTS
(a) Secrétaire d'État à Washington.
1229, vingt-septième.
Veuillez remettre les documents suivants à Jacob Schiff, au juge Brandies [*sic*], *au* professeur Gottheil, à Oscar Strauss [sic], au rabbin Wise, à Louis Marshall et à Morgenthau :
"Nous, les Juifs russes, avons toujours cru que la libération de la Russie signifiait aussi notre libération. Étant profondément dévoués à notre pays, nous avons implicitement fait confiance au gouvernement provisoire. Nous savons que la puissance économique illimitée de la Russie et ses immenses ressources naturelles et l'émancipation que nous avons obtenue nous permettront de participer au

développement du pays. Nous croyons fermement que la fin victorieuse de la guerre grâce à l'aide de nos alliés et des États-Unis est proche.
Le gouvernement temporaire émet maintenant un nouveau prêt public et nous estimons que notre prêt de soutien au devoir national est hautement vital pour la guerre et la liberté. Nous sommes sûrs que la Russie dispose d'un pouvoir inébranlable de crédit public et qu'elle supportera facilement une charge financière nécessaire. Nous avons formé un comité spécial de juifs russes pour le prêt de soutien, composé de représentants des milieux financiers, industriels et commerciaux et d'hommes publics de premier plan.
Nous vous informons ici et nous demandons à nos frères au-delà des mers de soutenir la liberté de la Russie qui est devenue une affaire d'humanité et de civilisation mondiale. Nous vous suggérons de former un comité spécial et de nous informer des mesures que vous pouvez prendre pour soutenir le prêt de liberté du comité juif. Boris Kamenka, Président, Baron Alexander Gunzburg, Henry Silosberg".

FRANCIS

* * * * *

(b) Monsieur le Secrétaire :
Après avoir rapporté à nos associés le résultat de l'entretien que vous avez bien voulu accorder à M. Morgenthau, à M. Straus et à moi-même, concernant l'opportunité de demander des souscriptions au prêt de la liberté russe, comme cela est demandé dans le télégramme du baron de Gunzbourg et de MM. Kamenka et Silosberg de Petrograd, que vous nous avez récemment communiqué, nous avons conclu d'agir strictement sur vos conseils. Il y a quelques jours, nous avons promis à nos amis de Petrograd une réponse rapide à leur appel à l'aide. Nous vous serions donc très reconnaissants de bien vouloir nous faire parvenir le télégramme suivant, à condition que vous en approuviez les termes :
"*Boris Kamenka,*
Banque Don Azov, Petrograd.
Notre département d'État, que nous avons consulté, considère que toute tentative actuelle de garantir des souscriptions publiques ici pour tout prêt étranger est déconseillée ; la concentration de tous les efforts pour le succès des prêts de guerre américains étant essentielle, ce qui permet à notre gouvernement de fournir des fonds à ses alliés à des taux d'intérêt plus bas que ce qui serait possible autrement. Nos énergies pour aider la cause russe le plus efficacement possible doivent donc nécessairement être dirigées vers l'encouragement des souscriptions au Liberty Loan américain. Schiff, Marshall, Straus, Morgenthau, Wise, Gonheil".
Vous êtes bien entendu libre d'apporter à la phraséologie de ce câblogramme suggéré toute modification que vous jugerez souhaitable et qui indiquera que notre incapacité à répondre directement à la demande qui nous a été faite est due à notre souci de rendre nos activités plus efficaces.
Puis-je vous demander de m'envoyer une copie du câblogramme tel qu'il a été transmis, avec un relevé des coûts afin que le ministère puisse être remboursé rapidement.
Je suis, avec le plus grand respect, fidèlement vôtre, [sgd.] Louis Marshall. Le secrétaire d'État de Washington, D.C.

* * * * *

(c) Cher M. Polk :

Permettez-moi de vous envoyer une copie d'un télégramme reçu ce matin et qui, pour des raisons de régularité, devrait, je pense, être porté à la connaissance du secrétaire d'État ou de vous-même, pour toute considération que l'on pourrait juger utile de lui accorder.
M. Kamenka, l'expéditeur de ce télégramme, est l'un des hommes les plus influents de Russie et a été, me dit-on, conseiller financier du gouvernement du Prince Lvoff et du gouvernement Kerensky. Il est président de la Banque de Commerce de l'Azov Don de Petrograd, l'une des plus importantes institutions financières de Russie, mais a dû, vraisemblablement, quitter la Russie avec l'avènement de Lénine et de ses "camarades".
Permettez-moi de profiter de cette occasion pour vous saluer sincèrement, vous et Mme Polk, et pour exprimer l'espoir que vous êtes à nouveau en parfaite forme et que Mme Polk et les enfants sont en bonne santé.

Fidèlement à vous, Jacob H. Schiff
M. Frank L. Polk Conseiller du Département d'État de Washington, D.C.
MM-Encl. [Daté du 25 novembre 1918]

* * * * *

(d) Traduction :
Le triomphe complet de la liberté et du droit me fournit une nouvelle occasion de vous répéter ma profonde admiration pour la noble nation américaine. J'espère voir maintenant des progrès rapides de la part des Alliés pour aider la Russie à rétablir l'ordre. J'attire également votre attention sur l'urgente nécessité de remplacer en Ukraine les troupes ennemies au moment même de leur retraite afin d'éviter la dévastation bolchévique. Une intervention amicale des Alliés serait partout accueillie avec enthousiasme et considérée comme une action démocratique, car le gouvernement bolchévique ne représente pas le peuple russe. Je vous ai écrit le 19 septembre. Salutations cordiales.

Kamenka

COMMENTAIRE

C'est une série importante, car elle réfute l'histoire d'une conspiration bancaire juive derrière la révolution bolchévique. Il est clair que Jacob Schiff de Kuhn, Loeb n'était pas intéressé à soutenir le prêt de la liberté de Kerensky et Schiff s'est donné la peine d'attirer l'attention du Département d'État sur les plaidoyers de Kamenka pour une intervention alliée contre les Bolcheviks. De toute évidence, Schiff et son collègue banquier Kamenka, contrairement à J.P. Morgan et John D. Rockefeller, étaient aussi mécontents des bolcheviks qu'ils l'avaient été des tsars.

DOCUMENT N°4

Description

Mémorandum de William Boyce Thompson (directeur de la Federal Reserve Bank of New York) à Lloyd George (Premier ministre de Grande-Bretagne), décembre 1917.

PREMIÈREMENT :

La situation russe est perdue et la Russie est entièrement ouverte à l'exploitation allemande sans opposition, à moins qu'un revirement radical de politique ne soit immédiatement entrepris par les Alliés.

DEUXIÈMEMENT :

En raison de leur diplomatie à courte vue, les Alliés n'ont rien accompli de bénéfique depuis la Révolution, et ont fait beaucoup de tort à leurs propres intérêts.

TROISIÈMEMENT :

Les représentants alliés à Petrograd n'ont pas compris avec sympathie le désir du peuple russe d'atteindre la démocratie. Nos représentants ont d'abord été officiellement liés au régime du tsar. Naturellement, ils ont été influencés par cet environnement.

QUATRIÈMEMENT :

D'autre part, les Allemands ont mené une propagande qui les a sans doute aidés matériellement à détruire le gouvernement, à démanteler l'armée et à anéantir le commerce et l'industrie. Si cela continue sans opposition, cela peut aboutir à l'exploitation complète du grand pays par l'Allemagne contre les Alliés.

CINQUIÈMEMENT :

Je fonde mon opinion sur une étude minutieuse et intime de la situation tant à l'extérieur qu'à l'intérieur des cercles officiels, lors de mon séjour à Petrograd entre le 7 août et le 29 novembre 1917.

SIXIÈMEMENT :

"Que peut-on faire pour améliorer la situation des Alliés en Russie" ?

Le personnel diplomatique, tant britannique qu'américain, devrait être transformé en homme d'esprit démocratique et capable de soutenir les aspirations démocratiques.

Il faudrait mettre en place un comité non officiel puissant, dont le siège serait à Petrograd, pour fonctionner en quelque sorte en arrière-plan, dont l'influence en matière de politique serait reconnue et acceptée par les responsables DIPLOMATIQUES, CONSULAIRES et MILITAIRES des Alliés. Ce comité devrait être composé d'un personnel tel qu'il soit possible de lui confier de larges pouvoirs discrétionnaires. Il entreprendrait vraisemblablement des travaux par divers canaux dont la nature deviendra évidente au fur et à mesure de l'avancement de la tâche. Il viserait à répondre à toutes les nouvelles conditions qui pourraient se présenter.

SEPTIÈMEMENT :

Il est maintenant impossible de définir complètement le champ d'action de ce nouveau comité allié. Je peux peut-être aider à mieux comprendre son utilité et son service éventuels en faisant brièvement référence au travail que j'ai commencé et qui est maintenant entre les mains de Raymond Robins, qui est bien connu du colonel Buchan - un travail qui, à l'avenir, devra sans aucun doute être quelque peu modifié et complété afin de répondre à de nouvelles conditions. Mon travail a été effectué principalement par un "Comité d'éducation civique" russe aidé par Madame Breshkovsky, la grand-mère de la Révolution. Elle était assistée par le Dr David Soskice, le secrétaire privé du Premier ministre de l'époque, M. Kerensky (aujourd'hui de Londres), par Nicolas Basil Tchaïkovski, qui fut un temps président de la Société coopérative des paysans, et par d'autres révolutionnaires sociaux importants qui constituaient l'élément salvateur de la démocratie entre l'extrême "droite" de la classe officielle et propriétaire, et l'extrême "gauche" incarnant les éléments les plus radicaux des partis socialistes. L'objectif de cette commission, tel qu'il est énoncé dans un message télégraphique de Mme Breshkovsky au président Wilson, peut être déduit de cette citation : "Une éducation généralisée est nécessaire pour faire de la Russie une démocratie ordonnée. Nous prévoyons d'apporter cette éducation au soldat dans le camp, à l'ouvrier dans l'usine, au paysan dans le village". Ceux qui ont participé à ce travail se sont rendu compte que pendant des siècles, les masses avaient été sous la coupe de l'autocratie qui leur avait donné non pas une protection mais une oppression ; qu'une forme de gouvernement démocratique en Russie ne pouvait être maintenue que PAR LA DESTRUCTION DE L'ARMÉE ALLEMANDE ; PAR LA VICTOIRE SUR L'AUTOCRATIE ALLEMANDE. La Russie libre, non préparée à de grandes responsabilités gouvernementales, sans éducation ni formation, pouvait-elle espérer cohabiter longtemps avec l'Allemagne impériale, son voisin immédiat ? Certainement pas. La Russie démocratique deviendrait rapidement le plus grand butin de guerre que le monde ait jamais connu.

Le Comité a conçu un centre éducatif dans chaque régiment de l'armée russe, sous forme de Clubs de soldats. Ces clubs furent organisés aussi rapidement que possible, et des conférenciers furent employés pour s'adresser aux soldats. Les conférenciers étaient en réalité des enseignants, et il faut rappeler qu'il y a 90% des soldats de Russie qui ne savent ni lire ni écrire. Au moment de l'épidémie bolchévique, beaucoup de ces conférenciers étaient sur le terrain, faisant bonne impression et obtenant d'excellents résultats. Ils étaient 250 dans la seule ville de Moscou. Le Comité a envisagé d'avoir au moins 5000 de ces conférenciers. Nous avions en cours de publication de nombreux journaux de la classe "A B C", imprimant du matériel dans le style le plus simple, et nous en aidions une centaine d'autres. Ces journaux portaient l'appel au patriotisme, à l'unité et à la coordination dans les foyers des ouvriers et des paysans.

Après le renversement du dernier gouvernement Kerensky, nous avons aidé matériellement à la diffusion de la littérature bolchévique, en la distribuant par des agents et des avions à l'armée allemande. Si la suggestion est recevable, il serait bon de se demander s'il ne serait pas souhaitable que cette même littérature bolchévique soit envoyée en Allemagne et en Autriche à travers les fronts occidental et italien.

HUITIÈMEMENT :

La présence d'un petit nombre de troupes alliées à Petrograd aurait certainement fait beaucoup pour empêcher le renversement du gouvernement Kerensky en novembre. Je voudrais suggérer à votre considération, si les conditions actuelles se maintiennent, la concentration de tous les employés des gouvernements britannique et français à Petrograd, et si la nécessité s'en fait sentir, elle pourrait être transformée en une force assez efficace. Il serait peut-être même souhaitable de verser une petite somme à une force russe. Il existe également un grand nombre de volontaires recrutés en Russie, dont beaucoup font partie de l'intelligentzia du "Centre", et qui ont fait un travail splendide dans les tranchées. Ils pourraient être aidés comme il se doit.

NEUVIÈMEMENT :

Si vous demandez un programme supplémentaire, je dois dire qu'il est impossible de le donner maintenant. Je crois qu'un travail intelligent et courageux empêchera encore l'Allemagne d'occuper le terrain à elle seule et d'exploiter ainsi la Russie aux dépens des Alliés. Il y aura de nombreuses façons de rendre ce service, qui deviendront évidentes au fur et à mesure de l'avancement des travaux.

COMMENTAIRE

Suite à ce mémorandum, le cabinet de guerre britannique a changé sa politique en faveur d'un bolchevisme tiède. Notez que Thompson admet avoir distribué de la littérature bolchévique par ses agents. La confusion sur la date à laquelle Thompson a quitté la Russie (il déclare le 29 novembre dans ce document) est dissipée par les papiers de Pirnie à la Hoover Institution. Il y a eu plusieurs changements de plans de voyage et Thompson était toujours en Russie au début du mois de décembre. Le mémorandum a probablement été rédigé à Petrograd fin novembre.

DOCUMENT N°5

DESCRIPTION

Lettre du 9 mai 1918 de Felix Frankfurter (alors assistant spécial du secrétaire à la Guerre) à Santeri Nuorteva (alias Alexander Nyberg), agent bolchévique aux États-Unis. Inscrit comme document n° 1544 dans les dossiers du Comité Lusk, New York :

DOCUMENT

WASHINGTON DEPARTEMENT DE GUERRE 9 mai 1918

Mon cher M. Nhorteva [sic] :

Merci beaucoup pour votre lettre du 4. Je savais que vous comprendriez le caractère purement amical et totalement non officiel de notre entretien, et j'apprécie les mesures rapides que vous avez prises pour corriger votre lettre à Sirola*. Soyez assuré que rien ne s'est passé qui diminue mon intérêt pour les questions que vous présentez. Bien au contraire. Je suis très intéressé par** les considérations que vous avancez et par le point de vue que vous défendez. Les questions*** en jeu sont des intérêts qui signifient beaucoup pour le monde entier. Pour y répondre de manière adéquate, nous avons besoin de toutes les connaissances et de toute la sagesse que nous pouvons obtenir****.

Cordialement vôtre, Felix Frankfurter

Santeri Nuorteva, Esq.

* Yrjo Sirola était un bolchévique et commissaire en Finlande.

** Texte original, "continuellement reconnaissant envers vous".

*** Texte original, "intérêts".

**** Texte original ajouté "ces jours-ci".

COMMENTAIRE

Cette lettre de Frankfurter a été écrite à Nuorteva/Nyberg, un agent bolchévique aux États-Unis, à une époque où Frankfurter occupait un poste officiel d'assistant spécial du secrétaire à la guerre Baker au ministère de la guerre.

Apparemment, Nyberg était prêt à modifier une lettre adressée au commissaire "Sirola" selon les instructions de Frankfurter. Le Comité Lusk a acquis le projet original de Francfort, y compris les modifications de Francfort, et non la lettre reçue par Nyberg.

LE BUREAU SOVIÉTIQUE EN 1920

Position	Nom	Citoyenneté	Né	Ancien emploi
Représentant de l'URSS	Ludwig C.A.K. MARTENS	Allemand	Russie	V-P de Weinberg & Posner Engineering (120 Broadway)
Directeur de bureau	Gregory WEINSTEIN	Russe	Russie	Journaliste
Secrétaire	Santeri NUORTEVA	En finnois	Russie	Journaliste
Secrétaire adjoint	Kenneth DURANT	ÉTATS-UNIS	ÉTATS-UNIS	(1) Comité américain de l'information publique (2) Ancien assistant du colonel House
Secrétaire particulier de NUORTEVA	Dorothy KEEN	ÉTATS-UNIS	ÉTATS-UNIS	Lycée
Traducteur	Mary MODELL	Russe	Russie	L'école en Russie
Commis au dossier	Alexander COLEMAN	ÉTATS-UNIS	ÉTATS-UNIS	Lycée
Téléphoniste	Blanche ABUSHEVITZ	Russe	Russie	Lycée
Préposé au bureau	Nestor KUNTZEVICH	Russe	Russie	—
Expert militaire	Lieutenant-colonel Boris Tagueeff Roustam BEK	Russe	Russie	Critique militaire sur le *Daily Express* (Londres)

Département commercial

Position	Nom	Citoyenneté	Né	Ancien emploi
Directeur	A. HELLER	Russe	ÉTATS-UNIS	International Oxygen Company
Secrétaire	Ella TUCH	Russe	ÉTATS-UNIS	Les entreprises américaines
Greffier	Rose HOLLAND	ÉTATS-UNIS	ÉTATS-UNIS	Ligue scolaire Gary
Greffier	Henrietta MEEROWICH	Russe	Russie	Travailleur social
Greffier	Rose BYERS	Russe	Russie	École
Statisticien	Vladimir OLCHOVSKY	Russe	Russie	Armée russe

Département de l'information

Position	Nom	Citoyenneté	Né	Ancien emploi
Directeur	Evans CLARK	ÉTATS-UNIS	ÉTATS-	Université de Princeton

			UNIS	
Greffier	Nora G. SMITHMAN	ÉTATS-UNIS	ÉTATS-UNIS	Expédition Ford pour la paix
Steno	Etta FOX	ÉTATS-UNIS	ÉTATS-UNIS	Conseil du commerce de guerre
—	Wilfred R. HUMPHRIES	ROYAUME-UNI	—	Croix-Rouge américaine

Département technique

Directeur	Arthur ADAMS	Russe	ÉTATS-UNIS	—

Département de l'éducation

Directeur	William MALISSOFF	Russe	ÉTATS-UNIS	Université de Columbia

Département médical

Directeur	Leo A. HUEBSCH	Russe	ÉTATS-UNIS	Médecin
	D. H. DUBROWSKY	Russe	ÉTATS-UNIS	Médecin

Département juridique

Directeur	Morris HILLQUIT Avocat retenu : Charles RECHT Dudley Field MALONE George Cordon BATTLE	En lituanien	—	—

Département de l'économie et des statistiques

Directeur	Isaac A. HOURWICH	Russe	ÉTATS-UNIS	Bureau américain du recensement
	Eva JOFFE	Russe	ÉTATS-UNIS	Commission nationale sur le travail des enfants
Steno	Elizabeth GOLDSTEIN	Russe	ÉTATS-UNIS	Étudiant

Rédaction de la Russie soviétique

Rédacteur en chef	Jacob w. HARTMANN	ÉTATS-UNIS	ÉTATS-UNIS	Collège de la ville de New York

Steno	Ray TROTSKY	Russe	Russie	Étudiant
Traducteur	Théodore BRESLAUER	Russe	Russie	—
Greffier	Vaste IVANOFF	Russe	Russie	—
Greffier	David OLDFIELD	Russe	Russie	—
Traducteur	J. BLANKSTEIN	Russe	Russie	—

SOURCE : États-Unis, Chambre, *Conditions en Russie* (Commission des affaires étrangères), 66e Cong., 3e sess. (Washington, D.C., 1921). Voir également la liste britannique dans le fichier décimal du département d'État américain, 316-22- 656, qui porte également le nom de Julius Hammer.

DOCUMENT N°7

DESCRIPTION

Lettre de la National City Bank of New York au Trésor américain, 15 avril 1919, concernant Ludwig Martens et son associé, le Dr Julius Hammer (316-118).

DOCUMENT

La Banque nationale de la ville de New York

New York, le 15 avril 1919

Honorable Joel Rathbone,

Secrétaire adjoint au Trésor Washington, D.C.

Cher M. Rathbone :

Je vous prie de bien vouloir nous remettre ci-joint des photographies de deux documents que nous avons reçus ce matin par courrier recommandé d'un M. L. Martens qui prétend être le représentant aux États-Unis de la République socialiste fédérative soviétique de Russie, et en présence d'un Dr Julius Hammer pour le directeur par intérim du département financier.

Vous verrez dans ces documents qu'il nous est demandé de verser tous les fonds en dépôt chez nous au nom de M. Boris Bakhmeteff, prétendu ambassadeur de Russie aux États-Unis, ou au nom de toute personne, comité ou mission censé agir au nom du gouvernement russe sous la subordination de M. Bakhmeteff ou directement.

Nous serions très heureux de recevoir de votre part tout conseil ou instruction que vous pourriez nous donner à ce sujet.

Avec tout le respect que je vous dois, J. H. Carter, vice-président.

JHC:M Pièce jointe

COMMENTAIRES

L'importance de cette lettre est liée à l'association de longue date (1917-1974) de la famille Hammer avec les Soviétiques.

DOCUMENT N°8

DESCRIPTION

Lettre datée du 3 août 1920 du courrier soviétique "Bill" Bobroff à Kenneth Durant, ancien aide du Colonel House. Extrait de Bobroff par le ministère américain de la Justice.

DOCUMENT
Bureau d'enquête du ministère de la Justice,
15 Park Row, New York City, N. Y., 10 août 1920
Directeur du bureau d'enquête
Département de la justice des États-Unis, Washington, D.C.
Cher Monsieur : Confirmant la conversation téléphonique avec M. Ruch aujourd'hui, je vous transmets ci-joint des documents originaux provenant des effets de B. L. Bobroll, du navire à vapeur *Frederick VIII.*
La lettre adressée à M. Kenneth Durant, signée par Bill, datée du 3 août 1920, ainsi que la traduction de "Pravda", 1er juillet 1920, signée par Trotzki, et des copies de télégrammes ont été trouvées à l'intérieur de l'enveloppe bleue adressée à M. Kenneth Durant, 228 South Nineteenth Street, Philadelphia, Pa. Cette enveloppe bleue était à son tour scellée à l'intérieur de l'enveloppe blanche jointe.
La plupart des effets de M. Bobroff consistaient en catalogues de machines, spécifications, correspondance concernant l'expédition de divers équipements, etc. vers les ports russes. M. Bobroff a été interrogé de près par l'agent Davis et les autorités douanières, et un rapport détaillé sera envoyé à Washington.

Bien sincèrement à vous,
G. F. Lamb, surintendant de division

LETTRE À KENNETH DURANT

Cher Kenneth : Merci pour votre lettre de bienvenue. Je me suis senti très isolé et enfermé, un sentiment qui a été fortement accentué par les expériences récentes. J'ai été bouleversé par l'incapacité à imposer une attitude différente à l'égard du Bureau et à vous faire parvenir des fonds d'une manière ou d'une autre. Vous envoyer 5000 dollars par câble, comme cela a été fait la semaine dernière, n'est qu'une triste plaisanterie. J'espère que la proposition de vendre de l'or en Amérique, à propos de laquelle nous avons câblé récemment, sera bientôt trouvée réalisable. Hier, nous avons câblé en vous demandant si vous pouviez vendre 5.000.000 de roubles à un minimum de 45 cents, le taux actuel du marché étant de 51,44 cents. Cela rapporterait au moins 2.225.000 dollars. L'entreprise a actuellement besoin de 2 000 000$ pour payer la société Niels Juul & Co. à Christiania, pour la première partie du transport de charbon d'Amérique vers Vardoe, Mourmansk et Arkhangelsk. Le premier navire s'approche de Vardoe et le second a quitté New York vers le 28 juillet. Au total, la société Niels Juul & Co, ou plutôt la Norges' Bank, du Christiania, détiennent sur leur compte et le nôtre 11 000 000 de roubles d'or, qu'ils ont eux-mêmes apportés de Reval au Christiania, en garantie de notre commande de charbon et du tonnage nécessaire, mais les offres d'achat de cet or qu'ils ont pu obtenir jusqu'à présent sont très médiocres, la meilleure étant de 575 dollars par kilo, alors que le taux offert par la Monnaie américaine ou le Département du Trésor est actuellement de 644,42 dollars, et compte tenu de l'importance de la somme en jeu, il serait dommage de la laisser occasionner de trop lourde perte. J'espère qu'avant d'en arriver là, vous aurez pu réaliser la vente, et en même temps obtenir un quart de million de dollars ou plus pour le bureau. Si nous ne pouvons pas, d'une manière ou d'une autre, payer les

2 000 000$ de Christiania, qui étaient dus il y a quatre jours, dans un délai très court, Niels Juul & Co. aura le droit de vendre notre or qu'elle détient maintenant au meilleur prix possible à l'époque, qui, comme indiqué plus haut, est assez bas.
Nous ne savons pas encore comment se déroulent les négociations canadiennes. Nous croyons savoir que Nuorteva a remis les ficelles à Shoen lorsque l'arrestation de N. semblait imminente. Nous ne savons pas encore où se trouve Nuorteva. Nous pensons qu'après son retour forcé en Angleterre depuis Esbjerg, au Danemark, Sir Basil Thomson l'a fait embarquer à bord d'un navire à vapeur pour Reval, mais nous n'avons pas encore eu de nouvelles de Reval qu'il était arrivé là-bas, et nous aurions certainement des nouvelles de Goukovski ou de N. lui-même. Humphries a vu Nuorteva à Esbjerg, et est lui-même en difficulté avec la police danoise à cause de cela. Tous ses liens sont recherchés ; son passeport lui a été retiré : il s'est présenté deux fois à l'examen et il semble qu'il aura de la chance s'il échappe à la déportation. Il y a deux semaines, Nuorteva est arrivé à Esbjerg, à 300 miles d'ici, mais n'ayant pas de visa danois, les autorités danoises lui ont refusé le droit de débarquer et il a été transféré sur un bateau à vapeur qui devait appareiller à 8 heures le lendemain matin. En déposant 200 couronnes, il a pu bénéficier d'une permission de débarquement de quelques heures. Voulant obtenir Copenhague par télégramme interurbain et n'ayant pratiquement plus d'argent, il mit une fois de plus en gage sa montre en or pour 25 couronnes, prenant ainsi contact avec Humphries qui, en une demi-heure, sauta à bord du train de nuit, dormit par terre et arriva à Esbjerg à 7h30. Humphries a trouvé le Nuorteva, a obtenu la permission du capitaine de monter à bord, a eu 20 minutes avec N., puis a dû aller à terre et le bateau a pris la mer. Humphries a ensuite été invité au bureau de police par deux hommes en civil, qui avaient observé la procédure. Il a été interrogé de près, son adresse a été prise, puis relâché, et cette nuit-là, il a pris le train pour rentrer à Copenhague. Il envoya des télégrammes à Ewer, du *Daily Herald*, Shoen, et à Kliskho, au 128 New Bond Street, les pressant d'être sûrs et de rencontrer le bateau de Nuorteva, afin que N. ne puisse plus être emporté, mais on ne sait pas encore ce qui s'est passé. Le gouvernement britannique a vigoureusement nié qu'il avait l'intention de l'envoyer en Finlande. Moscou a menacé d'exercer des représailles s'il lui arrivait quelque chose. Entre-temps, l'enquête sur H. a commencé. La police l'a convoqué à son hôtel, lui a demandé de se rendre au quartier général (mais il n'a pas été arrêté), et nous croyons savoir que son cas est maintenant devant le ministre de la Justice. Quelle que soit l'issue finale, Humphries commente la courtoisie raisonnable dont il a fait preuve, en la comparant à la férocité des raids des Rouges en Amérique.
Il a découvert qu'au quartier général des détectives, on connaissait certains de ses lettres et télégrammes.
J'ai été intéressé par votre commentaire favorable sur l'interview de Krassin de Tobenken (vous ne mentionnez pas celle de Litvinoff), car j'ai dû me battre comme un démon avec L. pour obtenir les opportunités pour Tobenken. Par l'intermédiaire de T. qui est arrivé avec une lettre de Nuorteva, comme l'a fait également Arthur Ruhl, L. a brusquement refusé en moins d'une minute la demande que T. faisait pour entrer en Russie, ne prendrait guère le temps de l'entendre, disant qu'il était impossible de permettre à deux correspondants du même journal d'entrer en Russie. Il a donné un visa au Ruhl, en grande partie à cause d'une promesse faite l'été dernier au Ruhl par L. Ruhl est ensuite parti à Reval, là pour attendre la permission que L. avait câblée en demandant à Moscou de donner. Tobenken, un homme nerveux, presque brisé à cause de son refus, est resté ici. Je me suis rendu compte de l'erreur que le jugement rapide avait commise et j'ai commencé à le faire changer. Pour faire court, je l'ai amené à Reval avec une lettre de L à Goukovsky. Entre-temps, Moscou a refusé Ruhl, malgré le visé de L. L. était furieux de l'affront

fait à son visé, et insistait pour qu'il soit honoré. Ce fut le cas, et le Ruhl se prépara à partir. Soudain, Moscou fit savoir au Ruhl qu'il révoquait l'autorisation et à Litvinoff que des informations étaient parvenues à Moscou selon lesquelles le Ruhl était au service du Département d'État. Au moment où nous écrivons ces lignes, Tobenken et Ruhl sont tous deux à Reval, bloqués.
J'ai parlé ce matin à L. du bateau qui part demain et du courrier B. disponible, je lui ai demandé s'il avait quelque chose à écrire à Martens, je lui ai proposé de le prendre en sténo pour lui, mais non, il a dit qu'il n'avait rien à écrire et que je pourrais peut-être envoyer des doubles de nos récents télégrammes à Martens.
Kameneff est passé par ici sur un destroyer britannique en route pour Londres, et ne s'est pas arrêté du tout ici, et Krassin est parti directement de Stockholm. Des négociations, alliées et polonaises, et de la situation générale, vous en savez autant que nous ici. Les négociations de L avec les Italiens ont finalement abouti à l'établissement d'une représentation mutuelle. Notre représentant, Vorovsky, s'est déjà rendu en Italie et leur représentant, M. Gravina, est en route pour la Russie. Nous venons d'envoyer deux chargements de blé russe en Italie depuis Odessa.
Transmettez mes salutations aux personnes de votre entourage que je connais. Avec tous mes vœux de réussite.

Bien à vous, Bill

Le lot de lettres que vous avez envoyé - 5 Cranbourne Road, Charlton cum Hardy, Manchester, n'est pas encore arrivé.
La recommandation de L. à Moscou, depuis que M. a demandé à s'installer au Canada, est que M. y soit nommé, et que N., après avoir passé quelques semaines à Moscou pour faire connaissance, soit nommé représentant en Amérique.
L. critique vivement le bureau pour avoir donné trop facilement des visées et des recommandations. Il a manifestement été surpris et furieux lorsque B. est arrivé ici avec des contrats obtenus à Moscou sur la base de lettres que lui avait données M. Le message ultérieur de M. n'est manifestement pas parvenu à Moscou. Je ne sais pas ce que L. a l'intention de faire à ce sujet. Je suggérerais que M. chiffre sa recommandation à L. dans cette affaire. L. n'aurait rien à voir avec B. ici. Une situation gênante pourrait se créer.
L. a également mis en avant la recommandation de Rabinoff.
Deux enveloppes, M. Kenneth Durant, 228 South Nineteenth Street, Philadelphie, Pennsylvanie, États-Unis.

SOURCE : Fichier décimal du Département d'État américain, 316-119-458/64.

NOTE : IDENTIFICATION DES PERSONNES

William (Bill) L. BOBROFF : Courrier et agent soviétique. Dirigeait la Bobroff Foreign Trading and Engineering Company de Milwaukee. Invente le système de vote utilisé dans la législature du Wisconsin.

Kenneth DURANT : Aide au colonel House ; voir le texte.

SHOEN : employé de la société International Oxygen Co. qui appartient à Heller, un éminent financier et communiste.

EWER : Agent soviétique, reporter au *Daily Herald de Londres*.

KLISHKO : agent soviétique en Scandinavie

NUORTEVA Aussi connut sous le nom d'Alexander Nyberg, premier représentant soviétique aux États-Unis ; voir le texte.

Sir Basil THOMPSON : Chef des services de renseignements britanniques

"L" : LITVINOFF.

"H" : Wilfred Humphries, associé à Martens et Litvinoff, membre de la Croix-Rouge en Russie.

KRASSIN : Commissaire bolchévique au commerce et au travail, ancien chef de Siemens-Schukert en Russie.

COMMENTAIRES

Cette lettre suggère l'existence de liens étroits entre Bobroff et Durant.

DOCUMENT N°9

DESCRIPTION

Mémorandum faisant référence à une demande de Davison (partenaire de Morgan) à Thomas Thacher (avocat de Wall Street associé aux Morgans) et transmis à Dwight Morrow (partenaire de Morgan), 13 avril 1918.

DOCUMENT

L'hôtel Berkeley, Londres

13 avril 1918.

L'honorable Walter H. Page,

Ambassadeur américain en Angleterre, Londres.

Cher Monsieur :

Il y a quelques jours, j'ai reçu une demande de M. H. P. Davison, président du Conseil de guerre de la Croix-Rouge américaine, de s'entretenir avec Lord Northcliffe au sujet de la situation en Russie, puis de se rendre à Paris pour d'autres conférences. En raison de la maladie de Lord Northcliffe, je n'ai pas pu m'entretenir avec lui, mais je pars avec M. Dwight W. Morrow, qui séjourne actuellement à l'hôtel Berkeley, pour un mémorandum sur la situation que M. Morrow soumettra à Lord Northcliffe à son retour à Londres.

Pour votre information et celle du Service, je vous joins, ci-joint, une copie du mémorandum.

Respectueusement à vous,

Thomas D. Thacher.

COMMENTAIRE

Lord Northcliffe vient d'être nommé directeur de la propagande. Ceci est intéressant à la lumière du fait que William B. Thompson subventionne la propagande bolchévique et de ses liens avec les intérêts de Morgan-Rockefeller.

DOCUMENT N°10

DESCRIPTION

Ce document est un mémorandum de D.C. Poole, Division des affaires russes du Département d'État, au secrétaire d'État concernant une conversation avec M. M. Oudin de General Electric.

> DOCUMENT
> 29 mai 1922
> Monsieur le Secrétaire :
> M. Oudin, de la General Electric Company, m'a informé ce matin que sa société estime que le moment approche pour entamer des conversations avec Krassin concernant une reprise des affaires en Russie. Je lui ai dit que le ministère estime que la voie à suivre par les entreprises américaines dans cette affaire est une question de jugement commercial et que le ministère n'interviendra certainement pas pour empêcher une entreprise américaine de reprendre ses activités en Russie sur toute base que l'entreprise jugerait praticable.
> Il a déclaré que des négociations sont actuellement en cours entre la General Electric Company et l'Allgemeine Elektrizitats Gesellschaft pour une reprise de l'accord de travail qu'ils avaient avant la guerre. Il s'attend à ce que l'accord qui sera conclu comprenne une disposition relative à la coopération de la Russie.
> Respectueusement, DCP D.C. Poole

COMMENTAIRE

Il s'agit d'un document important dans la mesure où il concerne la reprise prochaine des relations avec la Russie par une importante société américaine. Il illustre le fait que l'initiative est venue de la société, et non du Département d'État, et qu'aucune considération n'a été donnée à l'effet du transfert de technologie de General Electric à un ennemi autoproclamé. Cet accord avec GE était la première étape d'une série de transferts techniques majeurs qui ont directement entraîné la mort de 100 000 Américains et d'innombrables alliés.

WALL STREET ET FRANKLIN D. ROOSEVELT

CHAPITRE I

LES ROOSEVELT ET LES DELANO

La vérité est, comme vous et moi le savons, qu'un pouvoir financier issu des grands centres urbains contrôle le gouvernement depuis l'époque d'Andrew Jackson - et l'administration de W.W.[261] *ne fait pas exception. Le pays connaît une répétition de la lutte de Jackson avec la Banque des États-Unis – seulement cette fois sur une base beaucoup plus importante.*

Le président Franklin Delano Roosevelt au colonel Edward Mandell House, 21 novembre 1933, *F.D.R.: His Personal Letters* (New York : Duell, Sloan and Pearce 1950), p. 373.

Ce livre[262] dépeint Franklin Delano Roosevelt comme un financier de Wall Street qui, durant son premier mandat de président des États-Unis, a reflété les objectifs des pouvoirs financiers concentrés dans l'establishment commercial de New York. Étant donné la longue association historique - depuis la fin du XVIIIe siècle - des familles Roosevelt et Delano avec la finance new-yorkaise et la propre carrière de FDR de 1921 à 1928 en tant que banquier et spéculateur au 120 Broadway et au 55 Liberty Street, un tel thème ne devrait pas surprendre le lecteur. D'autre part, les biographes de FDR, Schlesinger, Davis, Freidel, et les commentateurs de Roosevelt, par ailleurs précis, semblent éviter de pénétrer très loin dans les liens enregistrés et documentés entre les banquiers de New York et FDR. Nous avons l'intention d'exposer les faits tels qu'ils sont enregistrés dans les dossiers des lettres de FDR. Ces faits ne sont nouveaux que dans le sens où ils n'ont pas été publiés auparavant ; ils sont facilement accessibles à la recherche dans les archives et l'examen de ces informations suggère une réévaluation du rôle de FDR dans l'histoire du 20ème siècle.

Il est peut-être toujours bon sur le plan politique de se présenter devant l'électorat américain comme un critique, sinon un ennemi déclaré, de la coterie bancaire internationale. Sans aucun doute, Franklin D. Roosevelt, ses partisans et ses biographes dépeignent FDR comme un chevalier blanc brandissant l'épée de

[261] W.W. est Woodrow Wilson.

[262] Un volume précédent, Antony C. Sutton, *Wall Street et la révolution bolchévique* a exploré les liens entre les financiers de Wall Street et la révolution bolchévique. En grande partie, compte tenu des décès et des nouveaux visages, ce livre se concentre sur le même segment de l'establishment financier new-yorkais.

la juste vengeance contre les barons voleurs dans les gratte-ciel du centre-ville de Manhattan. Par exemple, la campagne présidentielle Roosevelt de 1932 a systématiquement attaqué le président Herbert Hoover pour sa prétendue association avec des banquiers internationaux et pour avoir cédé aux exigences des grandes entreprises. En témoigne l'échec de FDR au plus profond de la Grande Dépression, lors du soutien public de Hoover aux affaires et à l'individualisme, prononcé dans le discours de campagne à Columbus, Ohio, le 20 août 1932 :

> En évaluant la situation à l'aube d'une matinée froide, que constatons-nous ? Nous constatons que les deux tiers de l'industrie américaine sont concentrés dans quelques centaines de sociétés et qu'elles sont en fait gérées par cinq personnes au maximum.
> Plus de la moitié de l'épargne du pays est investie dans des actions et des obligations d'entreprises, et fait le bonheur de la bourse américaine.
> On trouve moins de trois douzaines de banques privées et de filiales de banques commerciales qui dirigent les flux de capitaux américains.
> En d'autres termes, nous trouvons un pouvoir économique concentré entre quelques mains, l'exact opposé de l'individualisme dont parle le président.[263]

Cette déclaration fait apparaître Franklin Delano Roosevelt comme un autre Andrew Jackson, contestant le monopole des banquiers et leur mainmise sur l'industrie américaine. Mais FDR était-il aussi un outil des banquiers de Wall Street, comme on peut le déduire de sa lettre au colonel Edward House, citée dans l'introduction de ce chapitre ?

Il est clair que si, comme Roosevelt l'a écrit à House, "un pouvoir financier dans les grandes villes a contrôlé le gouvernement depuis l'époque d'Andrew Jackson", alors ni Hoover ni Roosevelt n'ont fait preuve d'honnêteté intellectuelle dans leur présentation des problèmes au public américain. Les questions de fond portaient vraisemblablement sur l'identité de ce "pouvoir financier" et sur la manière dont il maintenait son "contrôle" du gouvernement américain.

Pour mettre temporairement de côté cette question intrigante, l'image historique omniprésente de FDR est celle d'un président se battant au nom de l'homme de la rue, au milieu du chômage et de la dépression financière provoquée par les spéculateurs des grandes entreprises alliés à Wall Street. Nous constaterons, au contraire, que cette image déforme la vérité dans la mesure où elle dépeint FDR comme un ennemi de Wall Street ; cela est simplement dû au fait que la plupart des historiens qui enquêtent sur les méfaits de Wall Street ont été réticents à appliquer à Franklin D. Roosevelt les mêmes normes de probité qu'aux autres dirigeants politiques. Ce qui est un péché pour Herbert Hoover ou même pour le candidat démocrate à la présidence de 1928, Al Smith, est présumé être une vertu dans le cas de FDR. Prenez Ferdinand Lundberg dans *The Rich and the*

263 *The Public Papers and Addresses of Franklin D. Roosevelt*, Volume 1 (New York : Random House, 1938), p. 679.

Super-Rich[264]. Lundberg se penche également sur les Présidents et Wall Street et fait l'affirmation suivante :

> En 1928, Al Smith a reçu le soutien principal, financier et émotionnel, de son confrère catholique John J. Raskob, Premier ministre des Du Ponts. Si Smith avait gagné, il aurait été bien moins catholique qu'un président des Du Ponts.[265]

Or les Du Ponts ont effectivement contribué de manière importante à la campagne présidentielle démocratique d'Al Smith en 1928. Ces contributions sont examinées en détail dans ce volume au chapitre 8, "Wall Street achète le New Deal", et cette affirmation ne peut être contestée. Lundberg se penche ensuite sur l'adversaire de Smith, Herbert Hoover, et écrit :

> Hoover, le républicain, était une marionnette de J. P. Morgan ; Smith, son opposant démocratique, était dans la poche des Du Ponts, dont J. P. Morgan & Company était le banquier.

Lundberg omet les détails financiers, mais les Du Ponts et Rockefeller sont certainement cités dans les enquêtes du Congrès comme les plus grands contributeurs à la campagne Hoover de 1928. Mais Wall Street a retiré son soutien à Herbert Hoover en 1932 et est passé à FDR. Lundberg omet de mentionner ce retrait critique et crucial. Pourquoi Wall Street est-elle passée à FDR ? Parce que, comme nous le verrons plus tard, Herbert Hoover n'adoptera pas le plan Swope créé par Gerard Swope, président de longue date de General Electric. En revanche, FDR a accepté le plan devenu la loi nationale de relance industrielle de FDR. Ainsi, alors que Hoover était redevable à Wall Street, FDR l'était beaucoup plus. Arthur M. Schlesinger Jr. dans *The Crisis of the Old Orde*: *1919-1933* est plus proche du sujet que n'importe quel historien de l'establishment, mais comme d'autres Rooseveltophiles, il ne parvient pas à porter les faits à leurs conclusions ultimes et logiques. Schlesinger note qu'après l'élection de 1928, le Parti démocrate avait une dette de 1,6 million de dollars et que "deux des principaux créanciers, John J. Raskob et Bernard Baruch, étaient des millionnaires démocrates philanthropes, prêts à aider le parti à se maintenir jusqu'en 1932".[266] John J. Raskob a été vice-président de Du Pont et également de General Motors, la plus grande entreprise des États-Unis. Bernard Baruch était, de son propre aveu, au cœur même de la spéculation de Wall Street. Schlesinger ajoute qu'en échange de la bienveillance de Wall Street, "ils s'attendaient naturellement à avoir une influence sur l'organisation et la politique du parti".[267] Malheureusement, Arthur Schlesinger, qui (contrairement à la plupart des biographes de Roosevelt) a le doigt sur le cœur même du problème, laisse tomber la question pour poursuivre avec

[264] New York : Lyle Stuart, 1968.

[265] Ibid, p. 172.

[266] Boston : Riverside Press, 1957, p. 273.

[267] Ibid.

une discussion sur les superficialités de la politique - les conventions, les hommes politiques, les concessions mutuelles et les affrontements occasionnels qui masquent les réalités sous-jacentes. Il est évident que la main sur le porte-monnaie décrète en fin de compte quelles politiques sont mises en œuvre, quand et par qui.

On peut trouver une attitude protectrice similaire pour FDR dans la biographie en quatre volumes de Frank Freidel, *Franklin D. Roosevelt*[268]. En évoquant l'échec retentissant de la Banque des États-Unis juste avant Noël 1930, Freidel passe sous silence la négligence de FDR alors qu'il était gouverneur de l'État de New York. La Banque des États-Unis comptait 450 000 déposants, dont 400 000 comptes avaient moins de 400 dollars. En d'autres termes, la Banque des États-Unis était la banque d'un petit homme. Un rapport du sénateur Robert Moses sur l'état d'un précédent échec bancaire - City Trust- a été ignoré par le gouverneur F. D. Roosevelt, qui a nommé une autre commission qui a produit des recommandations plus modérées pour la réforme bancaire. Freidel pose la question :

> Pourquoi n'a-t-il pas réussi à faire adopter une loi de réforme qui aurait empêché la débâcle de la Banque des États-Unis ? Ce sont des questions pointues que les critiques de Roosevelt ont posées à l'époque et plus tard.[269]

Freidel conclut que la réponse réside dans la "confiance personnelle de FDR dans la communauté bancaire". Pourquoi FDR avait-il cette confiance totale ? Parce que, écrit Freidel :

> Herbert Lehman était l'un des banquiers de Wall Street les plus solides et les plus libéraux sur le plan politique ; en matière bancaire, Roosevelt semble avoir suivi l'exemple de Lehman, qui était de coopérer autant que possible avec les titans de la banque.[270]

Cela revient à dire que si votre banquier est un libéral et qu'il perd votre argent, c'est normal, car après tout, il est un libéral et un partisan de FDR. Mais d'un autre côté, si votre banquier perd votre argent et qu'il n'est ni un libéral ni un partisan de FDR, alors c'est un escroc et il doit payer le prix de ses péchés.

La biographie en quatre volumes de Freidel ne comporte qu'un seul chapitre sur FDR en tant qu'"homme d'affaires", ce qui est le plus grand espace accordé par un grand biographe de FDR. Même Freidel réduit des entreprises importantes à un simple paragraphe. Par exemple, alors que l'entreprise American

[268] Cette série est : Frank Freidel, Franklin D. Roosevelt : *The Apprenticeship* (1952), Freidel, Franklin D. Roosevelt : *The Ordeal* (1954), Franklin D. Roosevelt : *The Triumph* (1956), Freidel, Franklin D. Roosevelt, *Launching The New Deal* (1973). Les quatre volumes ont été publiés à Boston par Little, Brown.

[269] Freidel, *The Triumph*, op. cit. p. 187.

[270] Ibid, p. 188.

Investigation Corporation n'est pas nommée, une entreprise associée, General Air Service, est mentionnée, mais rejetée avec un paragraphe :

> En 1923, avec Owen D. Young, Benedict Crowell (qui avait été secrétaire adjoint à la guerre sous Wilson) et d'autres notables, il organisa le General Air Service pour faire fonctionner des dirigeables remplis d'hélium entre New York et Chicago.[271]

Nous verrons que le General Air Service (et surtout l'American Investigation Corporation non mentionnée) a été bien plus que ce que ce paragraphe indique. En particulier, l'examen de l'expression "et autres notables" de Freidel suggère que FDR avait des relations et travaillait en coopération avec certains membres importants de Wall Street.

Pourquoi Schlesinger, Freidel et d'autres biographes de FDR moins connus évitent la question et se montrent réticents à poursuivre les pistes ? Tout simplement parce que, si l'on examine les faits, Roosevelt était une création de Wall Street, une partie intégrante de la fraternité bancaire new-yorkaise, et avait à cœur les intérêts pécuniaires de l'établissement financier.

Lorsque l'information est présentée en détail, il est absurde de penser que Wall Street hésiterait une seconde à accepter Roosevelt comme candidat bienvenu à la présidence : il était l'un des leurs, alors que l'homme d'affaires Herbert Hoover avait travaillé à l'étranger pendant 20 ans avant d'être rappelé par Woodrow Wilson pour prendre en charge l'administration alimentaire pendant la Première Guerre mondiale.

Pour être précis, Franklin D. Roosevelt a été, à un moment ou à un autre dans les années 1920, vice-président de la Fidelity & Deposit Company (120 Broadway) ; président d'une association professionnelle de l'industrie, l'American Construction Council (28 West 44th Street) ; associé de Roosevelt & O'Connor (120 Broadway) ; associé de Marvin, Hooker & Roosevelt (52 Wall Street) ; président de United European Investors, Ltd. (7 Pine Street) ; un administrateur de International Germanic Trust, Inc. (dans le Standard Oil Building au 26 Broadway) ; un administrateur de Consolidated Automatic Merchandising Corporation, une organisation de papier ; un administrateur de la Georgia Warm Springs Foundation (120 Broadway) ; un administrateur de l'American Investigation Corporation (37-39 Pine Street) ; un administrateur de Sanitary Postage Service Corporation (285 Madison Avenue) ; le président de la General Trust Company (15 Broad Street) ; un administrateur de Photomaton (551 Fifth Avenue) ; un administrateur de Mantacal Oil Corporation (Rock Springs, Wyoming) ; et un constituant du Federal International Investment Trust.

C'est une liste assez juste de postes de direction. Elle vaut certainement à FDR le titre de Wall Streeter[272] *par excellence*. La plupart de ceux qui travaillent dans "la rue" n'atteignent jamais, et ne rêvent probablement même pas d'atteindre, un record de 11 mandats d'administrateur de sociétés, deux partenariats juridiques et la présidence d'une importante association professionnelle.

---

[271] Freidel, *The Ordeal*, op. cit. p. 149.

[272] Néologisme conservé, car intraduisible, NdT.

En sondant ces postes de direction et les activités qui y sont associées, nous constatons que Roosevelt était un banquier et un spéculateur, les deux occupations qu'il a dénoncées avec insistance lors de l'élection présidentielle de 1932. En outre, si les activités bancaires et spéculatives ont des rôles légitimes dans une société libre - elles sont en effet essentielles pour un système monétaire sain -, elles peuvent toutes deux faire l'objet d'abus. La correspondance de FDR dans les dossiers déposés à la bibliothèque de FDR à Hyde Park apporte la preuve - et on lit avec le cœur lourd - que FDR était associé aux éléments les moins recommandables de la banque et de la spéculation de Wall Street, et on ne peut arriver à aucune autre conclusion que celle indiquant que FDR a utilisé l'arène politique, et non le marché impartial, pour faire ses profits.[273]

Il n'est donc pas surprenant que les groupes de Wall Street qui ont soutenu Al Smith et Herbert Hoover, tous deux fortement liés à la communauté financière, aient également soutenu Franklin D. Roosevelt. En fait, à la croisée des chemins politiques en 1932, lorsque le choix se posait entre Herbert Hoover et FDR, Wall Street a choisi Roosevelt et a laissé tomber Hoover.

Compte tenu de ces informations, comment expliquer la carrière de FDR à Wall Street ? Et les services qu'il a rendus à Wall Street en créant, en partenariat avec Herbert Hoover, les associations professionnelles des années 20 si ardemment recherchées par la fraternité bancaire ? Ou l'amitié de FDR avec les principaux opérateurs de Wall Street, John Raskob et Barney Baruch ? Pour mettre tout cela en perspective, il faut remonter dans l'histoire et examiner le passé des familles Roosevelt et Delano, qui sont associées au secteur bancaire new-yorkais depuis le XVIIIe siècle.

---

[273] Cela soulève une question légitime concernant la portée de ce livre et la pertinence des preuves. L'auteur s'intéresse uniquement à l'établissement de la relation entre Wall Street et FDR et aux conclusions à tirer de cette relation. Par conséquent, les épisodes qui se sont produits en 1921, alors que FDR était à Wall Street, mais qui n'étaient pas directement liés à ses activités financières, sont omis. Par exemple, en 1921, la commission sénatoriale des affaires navales a publié un rapport contenant 27 conclusions, presque toutes critiques à l'égard de FDR, et posant de graves questions morales. La première conclusion du rapport du Sénat est la suivante "Que des actes immoraux et obscènes ont été pratiqués sur instructions ou suggestions, par un certain nombre de soldats de la marine américaine, en uniforme ou non, dans le but de recueillir des preuves contre des pervers sexuels, et que l'autorisation d'utiliser ces hommes comme opérateurs ou détectives a été donnée oralement et par écrit au lieutenant Hudson par le secrétaire adjoint Franklin D. Roosevelt, avec la connaissance et le consentement de Josephus Daniels, secrétaire de la marine. Les 26 conclusions connexes et le rapport minoritaire sont contenus dans le Sénat américain, Commission des affaires navales, 67e Congrès, 1ère session, Conditions immorales présumées à la station d'entraînement naval de Newport (R.I.) (Washington : Government Printing Office, 1921). Cependant, si la conduite de FDR dans la marine américaine a pu être inexcusable et peut ou non refléter sa fibre morale, cette conduite n'est pas pertinente pour ce livre, et ces incidents sont omis. Il convient également de noter que, lorsque la correspondance de FDR est d'une importance capitale pour l'argumentation de ce livre, il est d'usage de citer des passages textuellement, sans paraphrase, pour permettre au lecteur de faire ses propres interprétations.

LA FAMILLE DELANO ET WALL STREET

La famille Delano est fière de faire remonter ses ancêtres aux Actii, une famille romaine de 600 avant J.-C. Elle est également fière de Franklin Delano Roosevelt. En effet, les Delano affirment que l'influence des Delano a été le facteur prédominant dans l'œuvre de la vie de FDR et explique ses extraordinaires réalisations. Quoi qu'il en soit, il ne fait aucun doute que le côté Delano de la famille lie FDR à de nombreux autres dirigeants et autres hommes politiques. Selon l'histoire de la famille Delano,[274] "Franklin partageait une ascendance commune avec un tiers de ses prédécesseurs à la Maison Blanche". Les présidents liés au FDR du côté des Delano sont John Adams, James Madison, John Quincy Adams, William Henry Harrison, Zachary Taylor, Andrew Johnson, Ulysses S. Grant, Benjamin Harrison et William Howard Taft. Du côté de la famille Roosevelt, FDR est apparenté à Theodore Roosevelt et Martin Van Buren, qui ont épousé Mary Aspinwall Roosevelt. L'épouse de George Washington, Martha Dandridge, faisait partie des ancêtres de FDR, et Daniel Delano prétend que Winston Churchill et Franklin D. Roosevelt étaient "des cousins au huitième degré".[275] Cela fait presque des États-Unis une nation dirigée par une famille royale, une mini-monarchie.

Le lecteur doit porter son propre jugement sur les affirmations généalogiques de Delano ; cet auteur n'a pas la capacité d'analyser les relations familiales confuses et complexes qui sont en jeu. Plus précisément et sans aucun doute, les Delano étaient actifs à Wall Street dans les années 1920 et 1930 et bien avant. Les Delano ont joué un rôle de premier plan dans le développement des chemins de fer aux États-Unis et à l'étranger. Lyman Delano (1883-1944) était un important dirigeant de chemin de fer et le grand-père maternel de Franklin D. Roosevelt. Comme FDR, Lyman a commencé sa carrière dans le secteur des assurances, avec la Northwestern Life Insurance de Chicago, puis deux ans chez Stone & Webster.[276] Pendant la plus grande partie de sa vie professionnelle, Lyman Delano a siégé au conseil d'administration de l'Atlantic Coast Line Railroad, en tant que président en 1920 et en tant que président du conseil d'administration de 1931 à 1940. Lyman Delano a également été directeur (avec W. Averell Harriman) de l'Aviation Corporation, de la Pan American Airways, de la P & O Steamship Lines et d'une demi-douzaine de compagnies de chemin de fer.

Un autre Delano de Wall Street était Moreau Delano, associé de Brown Brothers & Co. (après 1933, il a absorbé Harriman & Co. pour devenir Brown Brothers, Harriman) et directeur de Cuban Cane Products Co. et de l'American Bank Note Company.

Le Delano le plus célèbre de Wall Street était "l'oncle préféré" de FDR (selon Elliott Roosevelt), Frederic Adrian Delano (1863-1953), qui a commencé sa

---

274 Daniel W. Delano, Jr, *Franklin Roosevelt and the Delano Influence* (Pittsburgh, Pa. : Publications Nudi, 1946), p. 53.

275 Ibid, p. 54.

276 Voir Sutton, *Wall Street et la révolution bolchévique*, op. cit.

carrière avec la Chicago, Burlington and Quincy Railroad et a ensuite assumé la présidence de la Wheeling & Lake Erie Railroad, de la Wabash Railroad et, en 1913, de la Chicago, Indianapolis and Louisville Railway. "Oncle Fred" fut consulté en 1921 à un moment critique de l'attaque de paralysie de FDR, trouva rapidement le Dr Samuel A. Levine pour un diagnostic urgent, et organisa le train privé spécial pour transporter FDR du Maine à New York alors qu'il entamait la longue et difficile route vers la guérison.[277]

En 1914, Woodrow Wilson a nommé oncle Fred membre du conseil de la Réserve Fédérale. Les liens intimes de Delano avec la fraternité bancaire internationale sont illustrés par une lettre confidentielle du banquier central Benjamin Strong à Fred Delano demandant des données confidentielles de la FRB :[278]

> (Personnel)
> 11 décembre 1916
> Mon cher Fred : Serait-il possible que tu me transmettes, à titre strictement confidentiel, les chiffres obtenus par le Contrôleur financier concernant les avoirs des banques nationales en titres étrangers ? Je serais très influencé dans mon opinion sur la situation actuelle si je pouvais obtenir ces chiffres, qui seraient traités avec la confiance que vous suggérez.
> Si jamais le moment arrive où vous pouvez vous éclipser pendant une semaine environ pour vous reposer un peu, pourquoi ne pas aller à Denver et me rendre visite ? Il y a mille choses dont j'aimerais discuter avec vous.
>
> Fidèlement à vous,
> Benjamin Strong
> L'honorable F. A. Delano
> Conseil de la Réserve Fédérale, Washington, D.C.

Après la Première Guerre mondiale, Frédéric Delano s'est consacré à ce qu'on appelle par euphémisme le service public, tout en poursuivant ses activités commerciales. En 1925, Delano est président du Comité international de la Société des Nations sur la production d'opium ; en 1927, il est président de la Commission sur l'aménagement du territoire à New York ; il devient alors actif dans le parrainage de la Commission des parcs nationaux. En 1934, FDR nomme l'oncle Fred Delano président de la Commission de planification des ressources nationales. Le comité industriel du Conseil de planification des ressources nationales, que Frederic Delano a probablement contribué à choisir, était une heureuse petite coterie de planificateurs socialistes, dont Laughlin Currie, Leon Henderson, Isador Lublin (éminent dans le transfert de technologie industrielle vers l'URSS avant la guerre de Corée), et Mordecai Ezekiel.

---

[277] Elliott Roosevelt et James Brough, *An untold Story: Les Roosevelt de Hyde Park* (New York : Putnam's, 1973), p. 142, 147-8.

[278] Sénat des États-Unis, Audiences devant la Commission spéciale chargée d'enquêter sur l'industrie des munitions, 74e Congrès, deuxième session, partie 25, *World War Financing and United States Industrial Expansion 1914-1915, J. P. Morgan & Company* (Washington : Government Printing Office, 1937), p. 10174, pièce n° 3896.

Le conseiller du Conseil était Beardsley Ruml.

Puis, de 1931 à 1936, alors qu'il participe à des projets de planification socialistes, Delano est également président du conseil d'administration de la Banque de la Réserve Fédérale de Richmond, en Virginie. En bref, Frédéric Delano était à la fois capitaliste et planificateur.

Delano a laissé quelques écrits dont nous pouvons tirer quelques concepts de ses idées politiques. Nous y trouvons un soutien à la thèse selon laquelle les plus grands partisans de la réglementation gouvernementale sont les hommes d'affaires qui doivent être réglementés, bien que Delano prévienne que la nationalisation des chemins de fer par le gouvernement peut aller trop loin :

> La propriété publique des chemins de fer est un vœu pieux qui, bien que souvent évoqué, n'est pas exigé par le public. Si la propriété publique des chemins de fer survint, c'est parce que les propriétaires des chemins de fer la préfèrent à la réglementation gouvernementale, et ce sera un jour triste pour la république lorsque la réglementation sera portée à un tel point que les propriétaires des chemins de fer ne seront plus disposés à accepter les responsabilités de la direction.[279]

Cependant, dans un autre livre, écrit environ 20 ans plus tard, Delano est beaucoup plus réceptif à la planification gouvernementale :

> Un grand problème rencontré par la planification est celui de l'éducation des gens. Si le public réalisait seulement que des efforts ciblés peuvent apporter des gains sociaux et que le temps nécessaire pour accomplir la plupart des choses par la planification vient avant que la nécessité d'apporter des changements ne se manifeste, les autres problèmes de la planification pourraient être plus facilement résolus.[280]

Plus loin :

> La brève classification ci-dessus du problème posé par la planification sert de base pour indiquer la nécessité d'un contrôle social direct et indirect.

Très peu de gens connaissent vraiment la meilleure utilisation des terres pour leur propre avantage, sans parler de la planification de leur utilisation pour le bien commun. Les institutions ont beaucoup fait pour apprendre aux agriculteurs à planifier les exploitations individuelles, et pourtant, beaucoup d'exploitations dans ce pays sont mal organisées.[281]

En bref, le côté Delano de la famille a entrepris des entreprises capitalistes et a des intérêts à Wall Street qui remontent au XIXe siècle. Dans les années 1930,

---

[279] Frederic A. Delano, Nos chemins de fer sont-ils équitablement traités ? Discours devant le Comité économique du Club de New York, 29 avril 1913, p. 11.

[280] Frederic A. Delano, Et l'an 2000 ? Comité mixte des bases de son Land Policy, s.d., pp. 138-9.

[281] Ibid, p. 141.

cependant, Frédéric Delano avait abandonné l'initiative capitaliste pour la planification socialiste.

LA FAMILLE ROOSEVELT ET WALL STREET

Franklin Delano Roosevelt descendait également du côté des Roosevelt de l'une des plus anciennes familles de banquiers des États-Unis. L'arrière-grand-père de FDR, James Roosevelt, a fondé la Bank of New York en 1784 et en a été le président de 1786 à 1791. La banque d'investissement Roosevelt & Son of New York City a été fondée en 1797. Dans les années 1930, George E. Roosevelt, le cousin de FDR, a été le cinquième membre de la famille en succession directe à la tête de l'entreprise. Les racines bancaires new-yorkaises de la famille Roosevelt s'étendent donc sans interruption jusqu'à la fin du XVIIIe siècle. Dans le domaine industriel, James Roosevelt a construit la première raffinerie de sucre américaine à New York dans les années 1740, et Roosevelt avait encore des liens avec le raffinage du sucre cubain dans les années 1930. Le père de FDR, également appelé James Roosevelt, est né à Hyde Park, New York, en 1828 dans cette vieille et distinguée famille. Ce James Roosevelt a obtenu son diplôme de la faculté de droit de Harvard en 1851, est devenu directeur de la Consolidated Coal Company du Maryland et, comme les Delano dans les années qui ont suivi, a été associé au développement des transports, d'abord en tant que directeur général de la Cumberland & Pennsylvania Railroad, puis en tant que président de la Louisville, New Albany & Chicago Railroad, de la Susquehanna Railroad Co, Champlain Transportation Co, Lake George Steamboat Co et New York & Canada Railroad Co. James Roosevelt a également été vice-président et directeur de la Delaware & Hudson Canal Co. et président de la Maritime Canal Company of Nicaragua, mais surtout organisateur de la Southern Railway Security Company, créée en 1871 et l'un des premiers holdings de sécurité à avoir été constitué pour acheter et consolider des chemins de fer. La Southern Railway Security Company était un projet de consolidation ou de cartellisation similaire dans son principe monopolistique aux associations commerciales formées par Franklin D. Roosevelt dans les années 1920 et à la National Recovery Act, autre projet de cartellisation, du New Deal. La deuxième femme de James Roosevelt était Sara, fille de Warren Delano, et leur fils était Franklin Delano Roosevelt, futur président des États-Unis.

Franklin a fait ses études à Groton et à Harvard, puis il est allé à la faculté de droit de Columbia. Selon son fils Elliott,[282] FDR "n'a jamais obtenu de diplôme, mais il a pu passer son examen du barreau de l'État de New York".[283] Le premier emploi de FDR a été dans l'ancien cabinet d'avocats Carter, Ledyard and Milburn, situé dans le centre-ville, dont le principal client était J. Pierpont Morgan. En trois ans, FDR a gravi les échelons, passant de postes de recherche juridique mineurs à la cour municipale et aux divisions de l'amirauté du cabinet. Notons au passage que, lorsque FDR s'est rendu pour la première fois à Washington D.C. en 1916

[282] Elliott Roosevelt, *An Untold Story*, op. cit. p. 43.

[283] Ibid, p. 67.

pour devenir secrétaire adjoint de la marine, c'est Thomas W. Lamont - banquier international et le plus influent des associés de Morgan - qui a loué la maison de FDR à New York.[284]

Il y avait d'autres Roosevelt à Wall Street. George Emlen Roosevelt (1887-1963) était un cousin de Franklin et de Theodore Roosevelt. En 1908, George Emlen est devenu membre de la société bancaire familiale Roosevelt & Son. En janvier 1934, après l'adoption de la loi bancaire de 1933 de FDR, la société a été scindée en trois unités individuelles : Roosevelt & Son, avec laquelle George Roosevelt est resté associé principal, Dick & Merle-Smith, et Roosevelt & Weigold. George Emlen Roosevelt était un financier de premier plan dans le secteur ferroviaire, impliqué dans pas moins de 14 réorganisations de chemins de fer, ainsi que dans des postes d'administrateur dans plusieurs sociétés importantes, dont la Guaranty Trust Company contrôlée par Morgan,[285] la Chemical Bank et la Bank for Savings à New York. La liste complète des postes d'administrateur de George Emlen à 1930 nécessite six pouces de petits caractères dans le Poor's *Directory of Directors*.

Un autre Roosevelt associé à Morgan était Theodore Roosevelt, 26ème président des États-Unis et petit-fils de Cornelius Roosevelt, l'un des fondateurs de la Chemical National Bank. Comme Clinton Roosevelt, dont nous parlerons plus tard, Théodore a été membre de l'Assemblée de l'État de New York de 1882 à 1884 ; il a été nommé membre de la Commission de la fonction publique américaine en 1889, commissaire de police de la ville de New York en 1895 et secrétaire adjoint de la marine en 1897 ; il a été élu vice-président en 1900 pour devenir président des États-Unis lors de l'assassinat du président McKinley en 1901. Theodore Roosevelt est réélu président en 1904, pour devenir le fondateur du Parti progressiste, soutenu par l'argent et l'influence de J. P. Morgan, et lance ainsi les États-Unis sur la voie de l'État providence. La plus longue section de la plate-forme du Parti progressiste était celle consacrée aux "affaires" et se lit en partie :

> Nous demandons donc une réglementation nationale forte des sociétés interétatiques. L'entreprise est un élément essentiel du commerce moderne. La concentration des entreprises modernes, dans une certaine mesure, est à la fois inévitable et nécessaire pour l'efficacité des entreprises nationales et internationales.

La seule différence vraiment significative entre cette déclaration soutenue par Morgan et l'analyse marxiste est que Karl Marx considérait la concentration des grandes entreprises comme inévitable plutôt que "nécessaire". Pourtant, le Parti

---

[284] Voir Sutton, *Wall Street et la révolution bolchévique*, pour de nombreuses citations de l'ouvrage de Thomas Lamont des liens avec la révolution bolchévique en 1917, alors qu'il résidait dans la maison louée de FDR à New York.

[285] Il est important de noter, alors que nous développons l'histoire de FDR à Wall Street, que Guaranty La confiance est importante dans la première révolution bolchévique de Sutton.

progressiste de Roosevelt qui s'est penché sur la réglementation des entreprises a été financé par Wall Street, notamment par l'International Harvester Corporation, contrôlée par Morgan, et par les partenaires de J. P. Morgan. Selon les mots de Kolko :

> Les documents financiers du parti pour 1912 mentionnent C. K. McCormick, M. et Mme Medill McCormick, Mme Katherine McCormick, Mme A. A. McCormick, Fred S. Oliver et James H. Pierce. Les dons les plus importants pour les Progressistes proviennent cependant de Munsey, Perkins, du Willard Straight de la Morgan Company, de Douglas Robinson, de W. E. Roosevelt et de Thomas Plant.[286]

Il existe bien sûr une longue tradition politique de Roosevelt, centrée sur l'État de New York et le gouvernement fédéral de Washington, qui est parallèle à cette tradition de Wall Street. Nicholas Roosevelt (1658-1742) était en 1700 membre de l'Assemblée de l'État de New York. Isaac Roosevelt (1726-1794) était membre du Congrès provincial de New York. James I. Roosevelt (1795-1875) a été membre de l'Assemblée de l'État de New York en 1835 et 1840 et membre de la Chambre des représentants des États-Unis entre 1841 et 1843. Clinton Roosevelt (1804-1898), l'auteur d'un programme économique de 1841 remarquablement similaire au New Deal de Franklin Roosevelt (voir chapitre 6) était membre de l'Assemblée de l'État de New York en 1835. Robert Barnwell Roosevelt (1829-1906) a été membre de la Chambre des représentants des États-Unis en 1871-73 et ministre américain aux Pays-Bas en 1888-1890. Puis, bien sûr, comme nous l'avons noté, il y a eu le président Theodore Roosevelt. Franklin a poursuivi la tradition politique de Theodore Roosevelt en tant que sénateur de l'État de New York (1910-1913), secrétaire adjoint de la marine (1913-1920), gouverneur de l'État de New York (1928-1930), puis président (1933-1945).

Pendant que FDR était en fonction, d'autres Roosevelt ont assumé des fonctions mineures. Theodore Roosevelt, Jr. (1887-1944) fut membre de l'Assemblée de l'État de New York de 1919 à 1921, puis continua le quasi-monopole de la marine Roosevelt en tant que secrétaire adjoint de la marine de 1921 à 1924, gouverneur de Porto Rico de 1922 à 1932 et gouverneur général des Philippines de 1932 à 1933. Nicolas Roosevelt a été vice-gouverneur des Philippines en 1930. D'autres Roosevelt ont poursuivi cette tradition politique depuis l'époque du New Deal.

Une alliance de Wall Street et du monde politique est implicite dans cette tradition Roosevelt. Les politiques mises en œuvre par les nombreux Roosevelt ont eu tendance à accroître l'intervention de l'État dans les affaires, ce qui est souhaitable pour certains éléments du monde des affaires. L'euphémisme de "service public" est une couverture pour l'utilisation du pouvoir policier de l'État à des fins personnelles, une thèse sur laquelle nous devons nous pencher. Si la tradition Roosevelt avait été celle d'un *laissez-faire* sans compromis, d'un retrait

---

[286] Gabriel Kolko, *The Triumph of Conservatism* (Londres : Free Press, 1963), p. 202. Willard Straight était le propriétaire de *The New Republic*.

de l'État des affaires plutôt que d'une intervention dans les activités économiques, notre évaluation serait nécessairement différente. Cependant, depuis au moins Clinton Roosevelt en 1841 jusqu'à Franklin D. Roosevelt, le pouvoir politique accumulé par le clan Roosevelt a été utilisé pour réglementer les affaires dans le but de restreindre la concurrence, d'encourager le monopole et donc de saigner le consommateur dans l'intérêt d'une élite financière. De plus, nous devons considérer l'observation transmise par Franklin D. Roosevelt à Edward House et citée dans l'épigraphe de ce chapitre, selon laquelle "un pouvoir financier dans les grands centres a contrôlé le gouvernement depuis l'époque d'Andrew Jackson". Par conséquent, il est pertinent de conclure ce chapitre introductif par les observations de 1943 de William Allen White, un éditeur honnête s'il en est, qui a fait l'une des meilleures critiques sur cet établissement financier dans le contexte de la Seconde Guerre mondiale ; ceci, il faut le noter, après dix ans de FDR et au sommet du pouvoir politique de Roosevelt :

> On ne peut pas se déplacer à Washington sans se heurter au fait que nous menons deux guerres : une guerre étrangère et une guerre intérieure.
>
> La guerre intérieure est dans les différents conseils de guerre. Toutes les grandes industries de produits de base de ce pays sont organisées au niveau national et beaucoup d'entre elles, peut-être la plupart, font partie de grandes organisations nationales, de cartels, d'accords, qui fonctionnent des deux côtés du front de bataille.
>
> Ici, à Washington, chaque industrie est intéressée à se sauver elle-même. Elle veut sortir de la guerre avec toute son organisation intacte, légalement ou illégalement.
>
> On est surpris de trouver des hommes représentant de grands trusts ou accords de marchandises ou des syndicats plantés dans les différents conseils de guerre. Il est idiot de dire que ce sont les New Dealers qui dirigent ce spectacle. Il est dirigé en grande partie par des propriétaires absents de richesses industrielles fusionnées, des hommes qui, directement ou par l'intermédiaire de leurs employeurs, contrôlent de petits blocs minoritaires, étroitement organisés, qui manipulent les usines physiques de ces trusts.
>
> La plupart de ces magnats de la gestion sont des Américains décents et patriotes. Ils ont de grands talents. Si vous les approchez neuf cas sur dix, ils sont des gentlemen chrétiens aimables et courtois.
>
> Mais dans la dixième relation, où elle touche leur propre organisation, ils sont complètement fous, impitoyables, sans respect de Dieu ou de l'homme, paranoïaques, en fait, aussi mauvais qu'Hitler dans leurs agissements.
>
> Ils sont déterminés à sortir victorieux de cette guerre pour leurs propres actionnaires - ce qui n'est pas surprenant. Il est également compréhensible qu'Hitler souhaite à tout prix sortir victorieux de cette guerre pour le peuple allemand.
>
> Mais cette attitude des hommes qui contrôlent les grandes industries de matières premières, et qui se proposent de les diriger selon leur propre jugement et leur propre morale, ne donne pas une belle image aux yeux de l'homme du commun.
>
> Ces combinaisons internationales de capital industriel sont des animaux troglodytes féroces, dotés d'une puissance énorme et sans considération sociale d'aucune sorte. Ils planent comme un vieux reptile silurien sur notre décente civilisation plus ou

moins chrétienne, comme de grands dragons en ces temps modernes où les dragons sont censés avoir disparu.[287]

[287] Citation de George Seldes, *One Thousand Americans* (New York : Boni & Gaer, 1947), p. 149-150.

CHAPITRE II

LA POLITIQUE DANS LE SECTEUR DES OBLIGATIONS[288]

Je vais profiter de notre vieille amitié et vous demander si vous pouvez m'aider à obtenir des garanties et des contrats de la part des autorités de Brooklyn.
Franklin D. Roosevelt au membre du Congrès J. A. Maher, 2 mars 1922.

Au début de 1921, Franklin D. Roosevelt devient vice-président de la Fidelity & Deposit Company du Maryland et directeur résident du bureau new-yorkais de la société au 120 Broadway. Fidelity & Deposit of Maryland était une compagnie d'assurance bien établie, spécialisée dans les polices de cautionnement et de garantie exigées dans les contrats du gouvernement et des entreprises, ainsi que dans toute une série d'emplois individuels allant de secrétaire d'un syndicat à employé de maisons de courtage. En fait, il existe un potentiel d'activité de cautionnement partout où un entrepreneur ou un employé peut violer une confiance fiduciaire ou ne pas exécuter un contrat, comme dans les projets de construction. En bref, le cautionnement est un domaine spécialisé de l'assurance couvrant le risque de non-conformité. En 1921, Fidelity & Deposit était la quatrième plus grande société de cautionnement des États-Unis, mais à ne pas confondre avec la Fidelity and Casualty Company de New York, une autre compagnie d'assurance, qui comptait d'ailleurs W. Emlen Roosevelt, le cousin de FDR, dans son conseil d'administration.

Pourquoi Van-Lear Black, propriétaire du Baltimore Sun et président du conseil d'administration de Fidelity & Deposit, a-t-il engagé le novice en assurance Franklin D. Roosevelt comme vice-président de l'important bureau de New York ? Il est presque certain qu'il a engagé FDR parce que l'activité de cautionnement est inhabituellement dépendante de l'influence politique. En lisant les dossiers des lettres de Fidelity & Deposit de 1921 à 1928, nous constatons que le prix ou le service n'apparaissent que rarement comme des éléments concurrentiels dans le domaine du cautionnement. Les principales armes concurrentielles sont "Qui connaissez-vous ?" et "Quelle est votre politique ? En d'autres termes, la politique est un substitut au marché. La politique était le point

[288] Ce chapitre est basé sur les documents de FDR à Hyde Park, New York : en particulier le Groupe 14, dossier intitulé "Fidelity & Deposit Co. of Maryland, Correspondance de FDR en tant que Vice-Président, 1921-1928".

fort de FDR et Van-Lear Black connaissait son monde de la caution lorsqu'il a acquis FDR. Il est important de noter la nature politique de l'activité de liaison, car les biographes de FDR ont, dans certains cas, suggéré que FDR, novice en affaires, était relativement inutile à Van-Lear Black. Par exemple, Frank Freidel écrit :

> Il est impossible de déterminer si Van-Lear Black l'a engagé parce qu'il s'agissait d'un geste commercial intelligent ou simplement pour collectionner une célébrité. Le pire que Wall Street ait pu reprocher à Roosevelt est que la société a gaspillé les vingt-cinq mille dollars par an qu'elle lui versait en salaire.[289]

Quels étaient alors les rôles de la politique et des politiciens dans le commerce des liens dans l'État de New York dans les années 1920 ?

LES POLITICIENS SONT LES SIGNATAIRES DES OBLIGATIONS D'ÉTAT

La nature politique omniprésente de l'activité de cautionnement se reflète dans une coupure de presse contemporaine, mais anonyme, trouvée dans les dossiers des lettres de FDR et soigneusement marquée par FDR lui-même. L'extrait fait référence à des fonctionnaires du gouvernement de l'État de New York qui négocient des contrats d'État tout en agissant en tant que membres de sociétés privées émettant des obligations et vendant des cautionnements à des entrepreneurs de l'État. Le journal a judicieusement dirigé la rubrique "All Under One Roof" et a rapporté que Daniel P. O'Connell, membre de la société d'émission d'obligations d'Albany O'Connell Brothers & Corning et simultanément responsable des affaires publiques de la ville et du comté d'Albany, s'efforçait d'exercer une influence sur l'émission de ses obligations dans tout l'État, au grand dam des auteurs d'obligations concurrents :

> Alors qu'auparavant Daniel P. était quelque peu occupé à s'occuper des obligations de divers et divers électeurs, il fera désormais tout son possible, dit-on, pour soumettre ses obligations à d'autres personnes, en particulier aux entrepreneurs qui font des affaires avec la ville et le comté.
>
> Son arrivée dans le monde de l'écriture a été aussi bienvenue qu'une tempête de neige le serait pour une mariée rougissante par un matin de juin lumineux et ensoleillé. On dit que les assureurs locaux, démocrates comme républicains, qui s'occupent depuis de nombreuses années de la rédaction de cautionnements d'entrepreneurs, n'apprécient pas l'arrivée de Daniel P dans leur domaine, tout en admirant peut-être son ambition et sa démonstration de courage et ce genre de

---

[289] Freidel, *The Ordeal*, op. cit. p. 138. Freidel est injuste envers Roosevelt. Aucune preuve n'est donnée de la critique de Wall Street à l'égard de cette nomination. Les critiques sont peu probables, étant donné la nature politique de l'entreprise, le fait que sa connaissance du monde de la politique était la force de FDR, et sa longue tradition de connivence avec les élites de "Wall Street".

> choses ; et dans les cercles politiques de l'État, on dit que Royal K. Fuller, commissaire d'État du Bureau des canaux et des voies navigables, craint que si Daniel P. réussit dans le domaine local [ce sera] à son détriment (à celui de M. Fuller), ou plutôt au détriment de l'entreprise de cautionnement avec laquelle il est lié et au profit de laquelle, dit-on, il utilise l'influence de sa position.

L'écrivain et titulaire d'une charge publique, M. O'Connell, a ensuite écrit des lettres de sollicitation à tous les entrepreneurs de la ville et du comté d'Albany pour leur faire savoir qu'il travaillait dans le secteur des cautions du bâtiment de la Caisse d'épargne de la ville, qui appartient d'ailleurs au maire d'Albany, M. Hackett, et qui se trouve être le siège de l'organisation démocratique du comté d'Albany. La lettre de M. O'Connell aux entrepreneurs de l'État s'est terminée par l'appel :

> Je vous serais reconnaissant de bien vouloir donner à ce bureau la possibilité de vous servir. Un appel téléphonique ou une lettre qui m'est adressé à ce bureau recevra une attention rapide.

Il est important de noter cette utilisation dominante et apparemment acceptable de la fonction et de l'influence politiques pour faire son propre nid. À la lumière des preuves ci-dessous, cela suggère que FDR ne faisait que suivre les mœurs contemporaines de son environnement. L'utilisation de la politique pour obtenir des contrats de cautionnement se reflète dans les dossiers de lettres de FDR et constitue essentiellement la seule façon dont il a obtenu des contrats de cautionnement alors qu'il était vice-président de Fidelity & Deposit Company. Bien entendu, ses lettres de sollicitation d'affaires auprès des autres Roosevelt de Wall Street sont tout à fait légitimes. Nous trouvons par exemple une lettre adressée à "Cher cousin Emlen" (W. Emlen Roosevelt de Roosevelt & Son, 30 Pine Street) datée du 10 mars 1922 pour s'enquérir de l'obtention du cautionnement prévu pour la Buffalo, Rochester and Pittsburgh Railway Company, cautionnement alors rédigé par la National Surety Company, une société concurrente. Emlen répondit rapidement le 16 mars qu'il "a pu parler au président de l'affaire". Cela a dû stimuler l'imagination de FDR, car le 16 mars 1922, il écrivit à "Dear George" (George E. Roosevelt), également chez Roosevelt & Son, pour s'enquérir de la caution globale souscrite par la société elle-même pour sa propre protection.

Les syndicats étaient une cible particulière de FDR pour les entreprises ; comme chaque secrétaire et trésorier de section syndicale est tenu d'avoir une caution, c'était un domaine lucratif. Le 13 décembre 1921, le secrétaire général et trésorier E. C. Davison de l'Association internationale des machinistes écrivait à FDR :

> Nous réalisons désormais l'essentiel de notre activité de cautionnement avec votre société, ce qui a été influencé dans une large mesure par votre intermédiaire.

Puis, le 26 janvier 1922, Joseph F. Valentine, président de l'Union internationale des mouleurs d'Amérique du Nord, a écrit à FDR qu'il appréciait au plus haut point tous les efforts de FDR en faveur de l'union alors qu'il était secrétaire adjoint de la marine et :

> Je souhaite donner à la Fidelity and Deposit Company of Maryland la plus grande part possible de nos activités... dès que nos obligations existantes seront arrivées à échéance, ce sera un plaisir personnel de voir votre société s'occuper de nos affaires à l'avenir.

Les responsables syndicaux à Washington et ailleurs ont rapidement demandé à leurs sections locales de détourner les affaires vers leur vieil ami FDR et de les éloigner des autres sociétés de cautionnement. À leur tour, les responsables syndicaux locaux ont été prompts à faire rapport sur leurs actions de détournement, les informations étant à leur tour rapidement transmises à FDR. Par exemple, le président de l'Association internationale des chaudronniers a écrit au secrétaire Berres du département des métiers de la métallurgie, A. F. of L., à Washington, D.C :

> ... Vous pouvez être assurés que tout ce que je peux faire pour rendre service à M. Roosevelt dans ses nouvelles fonctions sera un plaisir pour moi, et c'est pourquoi j'écris aujourd'hui à M. Roosevelt.

Naturellement, FDR a exploité ses vieux amis politiques au maximum et avec un souci du détail louable. Dans un discours de vente daté du 2 mars 1922, adressé au membre du Congrès J. A. Maher, FDR a écrit deux lettres, pas une seule. La première lettre se lisait en partie :

> Howe [Louis Howe, le bras droit de FDR] m'a raconté sa conversation téléphonique avec vous et je propose une lettre plus formelle à des fins de clarification. C'est une petite note amicale, de peur que vous ne pensiez que je suis devenu soudainement formel depuis que j'ai adopté Wall Street comme adresse professionnelle.
> Venez me voir. Je sais que cela vous fera du bien d'entendre le langage que le Frère Berres et d'autres personnes liées au Bureau du travail utilisent à l'égard de l'administration actuelle en général et des membres du Congrès en particulier. S'il arrive que la Madame ne soit pas entendue à votre arrivée, je répéterai certains des extraits les plus cités.

FDR a joint au député Maher une lettre plus formelle, qu'il faut évidemment montrer aux amis de Maher, et qui indique précisément ce qu'il veut : "des obligations de fidélité et de contrats de la part des pouvoirs en place à Brooklyn :"

> Je vais profiter de notre vieille amitié et vous demander si vous pouvez m'aider à obtenir des garanties de fidélité et de contrat de la part des autorités de Brooklyn. Il existe un grand nombre de cautionnements nécessaires dans le cadre du travail du gouvernement de la ville, en plus des cautionnements personnels que chaque fonctionnaire municipal doit donner, et j'espère que certains de mes vieux amis

> seront prêts à se souvenir de moi. Malheureusement, je ne peux pas aborder cette question avec eux pour l'instant, mais comme tous mes amis sont vos amis, je pense que si vous en avez le temps et l'envie, vous pouvez m'aider réellement. Je vous assure que cette faveur ne sera pas oubliée de sitôt.

Nous verrons plus tard dans quelle mesure cette approche a été couronnée de succès pour la F & D.

INFLUENCE POLITIQUE ET ATTRIBUTION DE CONTRATS

Les contacts et les influences politiques de FDR étaient bien sûr bien connus au sein de Fidelity & Deposit, et il a été appelé à plusieurs reprises par d'autres membres de la firme à utiliser son expertise politique et son crédit personnel pour générer des affaires obligataires, même en dehors de New York. Cela peut être illustré par une lettre datée du 23 août 1928 du directeur de F & D, F. A. Price, responsable du bureau de Chicago, concernant les affaires des politiciens locaux de Chicago. Price a écrit "Cher Franklin" avec le message que, depuis la mort du leader politique de Chicago George Brennan, plusieurs noms avaient été proposés comme leaders de la machine locale du parti démocrate. Avant sa mort, Brennan a demandé que M. L. Igoe lui succède, écrit Price à FDR :

> Vous avez sans doute pris contact avec lui pendant votre séjour à Houston et, au cas où vous le connaîtriez personnellement, j'aimerais que vous me remettiez une lettre de présentation aussi solide que possible.

M. Price a noté que récemment, lors de son séjour à Baltimore, il a discuté avec le président de la société F & D, Charles Miller, de "l'idée de conclure un accord avec le nouveau leader démocratique de l'Illinois". C'est dans cette optique que je souhaite que la lettre d'introduction". Comme la politique des machines à Chicago est connue pour ses normes éthiques peu élevées, il ne faut guère d'imagination pour visualiser le type d'accord que Price suggérait et que FDR a utilisé son nom et son influence pour faire avancer.

Cette amitié personnelle ne suffisait pas pour obtenir des contrats de cautionnement et une certaine édulcoration est mise en évidence dans une lettre sur la situation politique de New York datée du 23 septembre 1925, adressée à "My Dear Mr. Roosevelt" par John Griffin, responsable de la division des contrats du bureau de New York. Cette lettre traite des interconnexions complexes entre les bureaux politiques de New York et le secteur du courtage en obligations. La lettre se lit en partie comme suit :

> La grande victoire de Walker sur Hylan va, bien sûr, donner un nouveau souffle à la situation des courtiers en obligations. Sinnott & Canty, de qui nous avons pu obtenir des obligations au début de l'administration Hylan et qui n'a pas été très favorisé dans la dernière partie, sera sans doute hors-jeu et soit Charles F. Murphy, Jr, Hyman & McCall, Jim Hoey, soit un homme nommé McLaughlin, un frère du surintendant des banques, sera le favori. À mon avis, notre lien le plus fort passera

> par Al Smith avec Charlie Murphy, McCall ou McLaughlin, car Hoey a sa propre compagnie, la Columbia Casualty Company.
> Peut-être Murphy reçoit-il de la National Surety Company, ou de la société avec laquelle il fait actuellement affaire, une commission plus importante que celle que nous pourrions être prêts à lui donner pour ses affaires directes, mais un mot à son oreille, par votre intermédiaire et, bien sûr, par celui du gouverneur et peut-être de Jimmie Walker, nous placerait au moins sous la clause de la nation la plus favorisée ou [pour] toute division de ces obligations, comme vous le savez, toutes doivent être divisées entre deux ou plusieurs sociétés.
> Je connais tous ces gens assez bien et favorablement, mais une simple amitié personnelle ne suffira pas.

Une lecture méticuleuse de cette lettre interne à la société suggère que les pots-de-vin étaient le moyen habituel d'obtenir des affaires de cautionnement des agences gouvernementales de New York ; notez le paragraphe, "Peut-être que Murphy reçoit de la National Surety Company, ou de la société à laquelle il donne des affaires maintenant, une commission plus importante que celle que nous pourrions être prêts à donner pour ses affaires directes. La phrase de conclusion, "... une simple amitié personnelle ne suffira pas" raisonne de façon inquiétante.

La politisation de l'activité de cautionnement, si évidente à Chicago et à New York, s'étendit également à l'arène des contrats du gouvernement fédéral à Washington D.C. Le 5 mai 1926, le second vice-président de F & D, F. A. Bach, à Baltimore, écrivit à FDR un rapport d'environ $1^{1/4}$ de dollars ; un bâtiment du Bureau des vétérans d'un million de dollars dont la construction était prévue pour le printemps :

> Cher Franklin,
> Parmi les autres projets du Bureau des anciens combattants ce printemps, il y en a un qui implique environ un million et quart de dollars à Bedford, Massachusetts, et j'espère secrètement que grâce à une influence telle que celle de connaître Mme Rogers, représentante du Massachusetts, nous aurons peut-être une chance d'obtenir une part de cette affaire, bien que, bien sûr, le plus gros projet sera à North Port, Long Island.

De même, à un contact dans une "entreprise détenant des contrats de la marine", FDR a écrit :

> Une référence occasionnelle dans une lettre d'un de mes vieux amis du département de la marine à l'attribution de quelques pièces de canons de 8 pouces à votre société m'a rappelé les relations très agréables que nous avons entretenues pendant mon mandat de secrétaire adjoint à la marine, et je me demandais si vous auriez envie de laisser ma société rédiger certaines des garanties de contrat que vous êtes obligés de donner au gouvernement de temps en temps. J'aimerais beaucoup que l'un de nos représentants nous appelle.

Louis Howe, le bras droit de FDR, travaillait également dans les bureaux de F & D, négociait activement des obligations et n'était pas du tout en retard dans la prospection. La lettre de Howe à Homer Ferguson de la Newport News

Shipbuilding Company en décembre 1921 note que la société a fait des offres pour la construction du navire Leviathan et remercie Ferguson pour le cautionnement :

> Si par hasard le fait qu'il s'agisse de l'entreprise de M. Roosevelt vous a influencé pour l'attribution de ce prix, cela ferait énormément plaisir à M. Roosevelt si vous pouviez lui écrire une petite ligne à cet effet.

Ces méthodes politiques de faire des affaires sont, bien sûr, très éloignées du marché concurrentiel des manuels universitaires. Il serait naïf de penser que la préférence politique et l'amitié personnelle n'ont aucun rôle, ou seulement un rôle mineur, dans les relations d'affaires. En examinant les activités obligataires de FDR, il est toutefois difficile d'imaginer une autre activité dans laquelle la politique joue un rôle aussi global que dans les activités de cautionnement et de garantie dans les années 20. La moralité des pots-de-vin et de l'utilisation de la fonction politique pour générer des affaires personnelles est discutable, et la légalité est certainement douteuse. La perte d'efficacité économique et la perte pour la société dans son ensemble qui en résulte sont beaucoup moins évidentes. Si l'achat et la vente de ces obligations sont déterminés par le prix et les performances passées - et la connaissance personnelle peut être un facteur légitime pour juger des performances passées - alors le marché apportera un maximum d'avantages économiques et d'efficacité à la société. Dans une atmosphère commerciale politisée, ces facteurs de concurrence impartiale sont éliminés, l'efficacité économique est perdue et les avantages sont réduits. Nous avons, en effet, un microcosme d'une économie socialiste dans laquelle toutes les décisions sont politisées au détriment de la société dans son ensemble. En bref, les opérations de cautionnement de FDR étaient, dans une certaine mesure, antisociales.

D'autres lettres des dossiers Roosevelt donnent un aperçu authentique des coulisses de la politique de l'époque de 1920, des manigances qui ont si souvent dégénéré en corruption pure et simple. En témoigne une lettre de FDR datée du 11 juillet 1928 adressée au premier vice-président George L. Radcliffe à Baltimore, concernant la manière dont John J. Raskob est devenu président du Comité national démocrate. Raskob était vice-président de Du Pont et de General Motors et, par conséquent, il était membre de l'establishment de Wall Street au même titre que les autres :

> Lors d'une réunion hier soir, le gouverneur [Smith] a définitivement choisi John J. Raskob comme président du Comité national. Il a dit qu'il voulait un organisateur et un homme qui mettrait le Parti Démocrate en faveur des intérêts commerciaux du pays. Mon premier jugement est qu'il s'agit d'une grave erreur, car il est catholique ; deuxièmement, il est encore plus mouillé que Smith, cherchant à obtenir l'abrogation du dix-huitième amendement ; et troisièmement, il est à la tête de la plus grande organisation commerciale du monde. Je crains qu'il ne chasse définitivement une foule de personnes dans le sud et l'ouest, et dans l'est rural, qui ne sont pas particulièrement favorables à Smith, mais qui jusqu'à aujourd'hui se sont retranchées du Parti.

> Je ne connais pas très bien Raskob, mais j'espère avoir une conférence avec lui d'ici quelques jours, et je mentionnerai entre autres la possibilité de V. L. B. [Van-Lear Black].

Plus loin dans ce livre, nous évoquerons les énormes fonds versés au Parti démocrate par Raskob et les contreparties pour les grandes entreprises : le New Deal et l'Administration nationale de redressement (NRA).

Le 24 août 1927, une autre lettre adressée à George Radcliffe décrit la manière dont l'industrie obligataire peut se résumer au nom de James Beha, alors surintendant des assurances dans l'État de New York. Cette citation confirme le fait que les industries "réglementées" ne sont rien d'autre que des dispositifs politiques destinés à tenir en échec une concurrence indésirable et que les régulateurs peuvent se remplir les poches et agir au nom de l'industrie prétendument réglementée :

> Vic Cullen[290] et moi venons d'avoir une discussion au sujet de la directrice Beha. Vic dit qu'il pense qu'il y a un mouvement initié par Joyce, pour faire entrer Beha au National dans une certaine mesure et Cullen fait ce qui me semble être une suggestion des plus valables. C'est que Beha pourrait devenir le dirigeant de l'association de cautionnement. Nous aimons tous Beha et lui faisons confiance ; c'est un homme de courage et d'indépendance, et je ne peux pas penser à quelqu'un de plus apte pour occuper ce poste. Bien sûr, cela coûterait un salaire élevé - je pense qu'il est de 35 000 dollars par an - mais ce montant, réparti entre tous les membres, ne représente qu'une goutte d'eau dans la mer.
> Si vous pensez bien à cette suggestion, Cullen et moi pensons tous deux que vous êtes l'homme, plutôt que l'un ou l'autre d'entre nous, à approcher les dirigeants de l'U.S. F. & G. et d'un ou deux autres de manière informelle et confidentielle.

D'autre part, il y a eu des tentatives à New York pour éliminer les abus dans le domaine de la caution. L'une de ces tentatives a été celle de l'architecte d'État Sullivan W. Jones, qui a tenté d'éliminer l'obligation de cautionnement imposée par l'État. Le gouverneur Al Smith a d'abord été amené à étendre son approbation au plan Jones. C'est ainsi que R.H. Towner, du 160 Broadway, envoya rapidement une lettre à FDR pour lui dire que le plan Jones serait désastreux et que (si) "le gouverneur Smith (s'est) égaré, certains de ses amis devraient le remettre sur le droit chemin". La réponse rapide de FDR à Towner a été la suivante : "J'espère voir le gouverneur dans les deux prochaines semaines et je lui parlerai alors comme un oncle néerlandais du plan Jones". Nous ne lisons plus rien dans les dossiers de FDR sur la suppression des cautions obligatoires dans l'État de New York.

Le fait que le bureau de F & D ait fait preuve d'une grande fermeté à l'égard de ses propres intérêts se reflète même dans des questions relativement mineures : par exemple, aucune association commerciale de New York n'a pu obtenir de soutien financier pour F & D. Le 5 août 1926, une demande d'abonnement du Better Business Bureau de New York a suscité une réponse froide de F & D. FDR

[290] Cullen était directeur du bureau de production de New York.

a transmis la lettre au vice-président Cullen pour qu'il prépare une "réponse appropriée", et Cullen a rapidement refusé le Better Business Bureau. Ce refus a été appuyé par le président Charles R. Miller à Baltimore, "je ne suis pas très enthousiaste à l'idée d'apporter une contribution au Better Business Bureau à cette époque....". Puis la Merchants Association of New York a écrit à FDR le 23 mai 1925 au sujet de l'adhésion de F & D à leur association. Une fois de plus, Cullen soutient que "la Merchants Association ne nous apporte absolument aucun avantage". Aucune loi n'exige l'adhésion à de meilleures associations d'entreprises, mais ces refus font naître des appels sociaux suspects de la part de ces non-adhérents.

LA RÉCOMPENSE POUR FIDELITY & DEPOSIT COMPANY

Cette brève revue de la carrière de Franklin D. Roosevelt de 1921 à 1928 en tant que vice-président de la Fidelity & Deposit Company à New York suggère le chemin philosophique que Roosevelt a suivi pendant les deux décennies suivantes. L'activité de cautionnement était essentiellement politique, et FDR en politique était comme un poisson dans l'eau. Les contacts politiques établis pendant son service en tant que secrétaire adjoint de la marine ont été utilisés au maximum, de nouveaux contacts politiques, encouragés par la direction de F & D à Baltimore, ont été établis, et FDR a eu sept ans pour pratiquer cet art de la politique dans les affaires. Les résultats de F & D furent exceptionnellement bons. Les affaires se sont développées, dans une certaine mesure peut-être parce que presque tous les accords ont eu lieu dans les années 1920, mais presque certainement dans une large mesure à cause des activités politiques de FDR. Entre le 1er janvier 1923 et le 1er janvier 1924, Fidelity & Deposit a enregistré un gain de 3 millions de dollars dans l'année et s'est hissée à la troisième place des sociétés de cautionnement, devançant de beaucoup la société américaine Fidelity and Casualty Co, son concurrent évincé. Voici les chiffres :

Obligations de sociétés de cautionnement dans l'État de New York

	1er janvier 1923	**1er janvier 1924**	**Gain/perte**
Fidelity & Deposit Co.	$ 7,033,100	$10,184,600	+$3,151,500
National Surety Co.	$14,993,000	$15,677,550	+ 684,550
Fidelity & Casualty Co. Surety Co. de New York	$ 3,211,900	$ 3,215,150	+ 3,250
Aetna Casualty & Surety Co.	$ 5,517,200	4,799,500	- – 717,700
U.S. Fidelity & Casualty Co.	$ 8,064,500	$ 6,817,000	- – 1,247,500
American Surety Co.	$13,263,125	$12,127,400	- – 1,125,725

Le bureau de Fidelity & Deposit au 120 Broadway était la base d'opérations de FDR dans les années 1920, mais l'activité de cautionnement, aussi fructueuse soit-elle, n'était pas la seule activité commerciale de FDR. D'autres activités intéressantes seront examinées dans les chapitres suivants. Ces sept années passées dans une atmosphère d'affaires politiquement chargée - un microcosme d'une société socialiste, car les sociétés socialistes sont également des économies gérées politiquement - ont sans aucun doute eu une influence déterminante sur les approches ultérieures de FDR pour résoudre les problèmes économiques nationaux. Ce fut la première exposition de FDR au monde des affaires. Ce n'était pas une exposition aux éléments du marché concurrentiel que sont le prix et la qualité des produits ; c'était une exposition au monde des affaires sur la base des questions "Qui connaissez-vous ?" et "Quelles sont vos politiques ? - en fin de compte, les bases les plus inefficaces et les moins rentables possibles pour l'entreprise commerciale.

CHAPITRE III

FDR LE SPÉCULATEUR INTERNATIONAL

L'un des aspects les plus moralement préjudiciables de l'inflation a été le "sac de l'Allemagne" qui s'est produit au plus fort de l'inflation [1923]. Quiconque possédait des dollars ou des livres sterling était roi en Allemagne. Quelques dollars américains permettaient à un homme de vivre comme un millionnaire. Les étrangers affluaient dans le pays, achetant les trésors familiaux, les domaines, les bijoux et les œuvres d'art à des prix incroyablement bas.

Marjori Palmer, *1918-1923 Hyperinflation allemande,* (New York : Traders Press, 1967)

Franklin D. Roosevelt a été l'organisateur et le président de plusieurs entreprises financières internationales spéculatives reliant l'Allemagne et les États-Unis, et en particulier d'une entreprise visant à profiter de la ruineuse hyperinflation allemande de 1922-23. En 1922, FDR est devenu président et a été l'un des organisateurs de United European Investors, Ltd. avec une charte canadienne, mais basé au 160 Broadway, New York. En 1927, FDR a également été l'organisateur de l'International Germanic Trust Company, Inc. et du Federal International Investment Trust, qui n'ont jamais vu le jour. La plus importante de ces entreprises spéculatives dans le monde de la finance internationale était de loin la United European Investors, Ltd, créée pour accumuler les marks allemands déposés aux États-Unis et pour réinvestir ces marks en Allemagne en achetant des biens à des Allemands démunis. Pour bien comprendre la portée et la signification de United European et pour suivre les activités de l'International Germanic Trust Company, il faut faire un bref rappel des conditions financières allemandes au début des années 1920.

L'HYPERINFLATION ALLEMANDE DE 1922-23

Lionel Robbins, l'éminent économiste britannique, a décrit l'inflation allemande de 1922-23 :

> C'était la chose la plus colossale de ce genre dans l'histoire : et après probablement la Grande Guerre elle-même, elle doit porter la responsabilité de nombre des difficultés politiques et économiques de notre génération. Elle a détruit la richesse

> des éléments les plus solides de la société allemande : et a laissé derrière elle un déséquilibre moral et économique, un terreau fertile pour les catastrophes qui ont suivi. Hitler est l'enfant adoptif de l'inflation.[291]

Le traité de Versailles a imposé une charge de réparation massive à l'Allemagne vaincue, un pays déjà financièrement affaibli par la première guerre mondiale, avec des dépenses déficitaires et une réduction territoriale d'après-guerre, avec des ressources naturelles réduites en conséquence. Les réparations ont un effet sur la balance des paiements similaire à celui des importations. Elles nécessitent soit une imposition, soit des dépenses déficitaires pour compenser la fuite. Si l'on suit le cours des dépenses déficitaires, le résultat sera inflationniste, et c'est la voie qu'a suivie l'Allemagne.

L'Allemagne a été obligée par les Alliés de réparer tous les dommages causés à la propriété privée, sauf en Russie, et de payer tous les frais des troupes alliées sur le sol allemand, mais aucune limite maximale n'a été fixée aux demandes. L'Allemagne devait immédiatement remettre 100 milliards de marks d'or, avec des paiements d'un milliard de marks d'or par an après 1921. Le plan de paiement final élaboré lors de l'"Ultimatum de Londres" en mai 1921 reflétait ces conditions sévères et impossibles et constituait donc une incitation claire à gonfler pour supprimer le fardeau des paiements directs.

Ce qui est extraordinaire dans le programme de réparation, c'est l'identité des soi-disant experts chargés de prendre les dispositions de réparation, créant incidemment le chaos monétaire et social auquel Lionel Robbins a fait allusion. Le Comité des Réparations de 1923 avait pour membres américains le Brigadier Général Charles G. Dawes et Owen D. Young de la General Electric Company.

Le Comité d'experts du Plan Young de 1928 comprend, du côté américain, Owen D. Young et J.P. Morgan, avec Thomas N. Perkins et Thomas W. Lamont comme suppléants. Du côté allemand, les membres étaient Hjalmar Schacht et A. Voegler, avec C. Melchior et L. Kastl comme suppléants.

En bref, les éléments de General Electric-Morgan qui ont joué un rôle important dans la révolution bolchévique, et comme nous le verrons également dans le New Deal, étaient les négociateurs d'un plan généralement considéré comme l'une des causes principales du déclenchement de la Seconde Guerre mondiale - et accessoirement d'un plan dans lequel ces mêmes financiers, ainsi que Franklin Delano Roosevelt, devaient faire des bénéfices.

Il est également intéressant de noter que les hommes d'affaires du côté allemand des négociations sur les réparations ont été associés à la montée du national-socialisme en Allemagne.

Witness Hallgarten raconte dans son essai *Adolf Hitler et l'industrie lourde allemande* :

---

[291] Constantino Bresciani-Turroni, *The Economics of Inflation: a Study of Currency Depreciation in Post War Germany, 1914-1923* (Londres : Allen & Unwin, 1937), "Foreword", p. 5.

> ... en novembre 1918, un groupe des plus éminents hommes d'affaires du Reich, comprenant Stinnes, Albert Voegler (alors directeur de la Gelsenkirchen Mining Co., Ltd.), Carl Friedrich von Siemens, Felix Deutsche (de la German General Electric), le directeur Mankiewitz de la Deutsche Bank, et le directeur Salomonsohn, de la Diskontogesellschaft, finança le mouvement d'un précurseur d'Hitler, un certain Dr Eduard Stadtler, qui exigeait la création d'un État national-socialiste allemand.[292]

Le point pertinent est que le Felix Deutsche mentionné était un directeur de General Electric allemand et les représentants américains des réparations comprenaient Owen D. Young de General Electric, tandis que l'Albert Voegler mentionné par Hallgarten était le représentant allemand dans les négociations du Plan Young.

Le tableau suivant illustre la dépréciation du mark allemand en une monnaie de papier sans valeur en raison de cette charge de réparation imposée par ces hommes :

Le mark allemand en termes de[293]

Date	Change (1913=1.00)	Prix de gros en Allemagne
Janvier 1913	1.0	1.0
Janvier 1920	15.4	12.6
Janvier 1921	15.4	14.4
Janvier 1922	45.7	36.7
Juillet 1922	117.0	101.0
L'inflation s'est accélérée après la création de la société United European Investors, Ltd, dont Franklin D. Roosevelt est le président et John von Berenberg Gossler le membre du conseil consultatif allemand :		
Janvier 1923	4,279.0	2,785.0
Juillet 1923	84,150.0	74,787.0
Août 1923	1,100,100.0	944,041.0
L'inflation est devenue totalement incontrôlable après la destitution du chancelier Wilhelm Cuno, qui est revenu en tant que président de l'HAPAG, et des co-directeurs John von Berenberg Gossler et Max Warburg :		
Septembre 1923	23,540,000.0	23,949,000.0
Octobre 1923	6,014,300,000.0	7,095,500,000.0
Novembre 1923	1,000,000,000,000.0	750,000,000,000.0

Les politiques qui ont conduit à la ruineuse inflation allemande ont été initiées sous le Chancelier Wilhelm Cuno, qui était, juste avant de devenir Chancelier, le président de la Hamburg-America Line (HAPAG). Deux des codirecteurs de Cuno à la HAPAG étaient Max Warburg, banquier de Hambourg et frère de Paul

---

292 George W. F. Hallgarten, *Adolf Hitler and German Heavy Industry* dans *Journal of Economic History*, été 1952, p. 224.

293 Source : Annuaire statistique du Reich allemand.

Warburg, membre du conseil consultatif du système de la Réserve Fédérale aux États-Unis, et John von Berenberg Gossler, membre du conseil consultatif allemand de la société United European Investors, Ltd. de Franklin D. Roosevelt.

Cuno a été démis de ses fonctions de chancelier allemand en août 1923, mais on notera dans le tableau que l'inflation était déjà hors de contrôle et qu'en novembre de cette année-là, le mark s'était déprécié jusqu'à zéro. Il convient de souligner que Wilhelm Cuno était chancelier en 1922-23, lorsque le mark se dépréciait rapidement, et que Cuno venait d'un milieu d'affaires qui était capable et désireux de tirer un avantage pécuniaire et personnel de l'inflation allemande.

Cette terrifiante inflation monétaire et l'effondrement final du mark allemand en 1923 ont ruiné la classe moyenne allemande et ont profité à trois groupes : quelques grands hommes d'affaires allemands, quelques hommes d'affaires étrangers qui étaient en mesure de tirer profit de l'inflation, et le mouvement hitlérien croissant. En tant que président de United European Investors, Ltd, Franklin D. Roosevelt faisait partie de ces hommes d'affaires étrangers qui profitaient de la misère de l'Allemagne pour leur propre profit.

L'HISTOIRE DE WILLIAM SCHALL

Malheureusement, il y a une perspective plus profonde à cette question de ce que l'on pourrait appeler un groupe élitiste s'attaquant au malheur du monde. Dans le précédent volume de cette série, *Wall Street et la révolution bolchévique,* nous avons identifié des liens personnels entre les financiers de Wall Street et les révolutionnaires bolchéviques. Certains de ces mêmes liens personnels peuvent être étendus à FDR et United European Investors. Les liens établis avec précision impliquaient auparavant l'ambassadeur allemand de l'époque aux États-Unis, le comte von Bernstorff, et son ami Adolf von Pavenstedt, associé principal de la société Amsinck & Co, qui a été "pendant de nombreuses années un trésorier en chef du système d'espionnage allemand dans ce pays".[294] Amsinck & Co. était contrôlée par J. P. Morgan, John D. Rockefeller et d'autres intérêts financiers new-yorkais par le biais de l'American International Corporation. Avec la Guaranty Trust Company, l'American International Corporation constituait les points centraux du financement de l'espionnage allemand et bolchévique aux États-Unis et en Amérique du Nord pendant la Première Guerre mondiale. Adolf von Pavenstedt et Edmund Pavenstedt, les deux associés d'Amsinck, étaient également membres d'une autre maison financière, Müller, Schall & Company. Et c'est chez Müller, Schall qu'en 1922 nous trouvons Franklin D. Roosevelt et son entreprise United European Investors, Ltd.

Après la révélation publique, en 1918, des liens entre Amsinck & Co. et l'espionnage allemand, les intérêts allemands dans Müller, Schall & Co. ont été représentés par Edmund S. Payne, un avocat de New York. Müller, Schall & Co.

[294] Voir Sutton, *Wall Street et la révolution bolchévique*, op. cit., p. 64-67, et Johann-Heinrich von Bernstorff, *Mes trois années en Amérique* (New York : Scribner's, 1920), p. 261.

fut formellement liquidée, et une "nouvelle" société - William Schall & Co. - prit place à la même adresse, 45 William Street, New York City. Le nouveau cabinet, créé en janvier 1918, comprenait les deux associés initiaux, William Schall et Carl Müller, qui étaient désormais rejoints par John Hanway de Harris, Forbes & Co, Frank M. Welty, vice-président de l'American Colonial Bank of Puerto Rico, et l'avocat Edmund S. Payne, associé du cabinet Rounds, Hatch, Dillingham & Debevoise, qui représentait les intérêts allemands de l'ancienne société Müller, Schall & Co.

Les Pavenstedt étaient également "fortement intéressés par les propriétés sucrières de Porto Rico et possédaient et contrôlaient la Central Los Canos".[295] William Schall était président de la Colonial Bank of Puerto Rico et président de la South Puerto Rico Sugar Company. De même, la famille Roosevelt avait des intérêts dans l'industrie sucrière des Caraïbes depuis la fin du XVIIIe siècle, et George Emlen Roosevelt était en 1918 directeur de la Cuban Cane Products Co. à New York. Il est donc concevable qu'à travers cet intérêt commun pour le sucre des Caraïbes, les Pavenstedt et les Roosevelt se soient connus. Quoi qu'il en soit, c'est le groupe Schall-Pavenstedt, qui faisait auparavant partie de l'opération allemande d'espionnage aux États-Unis, qui a fusionné en 1921-22 avec Franklin D. Roosevelt et plusieurs entrepreneurs financiers douteux pour former la société United European Investors, Ltd. afin de profiter du fardeau écrasant de l'inflation allemande.

UNITED EUROPEAN INVESTORS LTD

Le groupe organisateur initial de United European Investors Ltd. était composé de William Schall et Franklin D. Roosevelt, mentionnés ci-dessus, rejoints par A. R. Roberts, Charles L. Gould et Harvey Fisk & Sons. Les 60 000 actions privilégiées émises étaient détenues par Harvey Fisk & Sons (25 000 dollars), Franklin D. Roosevelt (10 000 dollars) et Schall, Roberts et Gould (5000 dollars chacun). En bref, FDR était le plus grand actionnaire individuel privilégié du groupe de constitution en société.

United European Investors, Ltd. s'est vu accorder une charte canadienne inhabituelle qui conférait à la société des pouvoirs uniques, notamment le droit de promouvoir les échanges et le commerce entre le Canada et tout autre pays, d'acquérir des titres de propriété, de souscrire ou de négocier des obligations, des actions et des parts, d'agir en tant que courtier et agent, d'assumer toutes sortes de fonctions en matière d'achat, d'échange et de transfert d'actions et de parts, de prêter de l'argent, d'exercer toute activité, "manufacturière ou autre", et d'acheter et de vendre des biens. En fait, à la lecture de la charte, il est difficile de visualiser toute activité qui ne pourrait être exercée en vertu de ses nombreuses clauses.[296]

---

[295] Paul Haber, *The House of Roosevelt* (New York : Authors Publishing Co., 1936), p. 71.

[296] La copie de la charte de l'U.E.I. dans les dossiers de FDR comporte un amendement de A. B. Copp, secrétaire d'État canadien, qui interdit la construction de chemins de fer et l'émission de monnaie de papier.

Le stock de capital a été divisé en deux segments : 60 000 dollars canadiens divisés en 60 000 actions privilégiées et 60 000 actions ordinaires, libellées en 10 000 marks allemands. L'objectif de la société, comme l'a indiqué la presse contemporaine, était d'investir les nombreux milliards de marks allemands alors détenus aux États-Unis et au Canada dans des biens immobiliers allemands :

Une fois que les marks sont investis dans des biens immobiliers en Allemagne, les fonds doivent commencer à rapporter immédiatement et ne peuvent pas disparaître, car ils sont représentés par la propriété de biens corporels, et l'on peut toujours profiter d'une éventuelle augmentation de la valeur d'échange. Par rapport à cela, la détention de devises ou de traites en marks est une opération des plus dangereuses et les fonds sont soit inutilisés, soit très peu rémunérés. En outre, si la cotation de la monnaie s'approchait du point de disparition, il ne resterait plus rien de tangible pour les détenteurs de marks ou de traites. Le capital de la société sera investi dans des biens immobiliers améliorés, des hypothèques, le financement de marchandises en transit et la participation à des entreprises industrielles et commerciales rentables.[297]

La référence au tableau précédent, qui enregistre la dépréciation du mark allemand (page 39), confirme la remarquable rapidité de United European Investors, Ltd. En juillet 1922, le mark, avec 1913 comme base 100, était à 117 en devises. Cela reflète un taux d'inflation élevé du mark, mais rien qui le distingue de l'inflation dans de nombreux autres pays. Pourtant, la brochure de l'Union européenne mentionne expressément la possibilité que le mark "s'approche du point de disparition", ce qu'il a fait un an plus tard, en novembre 1923.

L'investissement proprement dit de l'U.E.I. a été réalisé en Allemagne par un conseil consultatif allemand qui occupait un bureau à Hambourg dirigé par le sénateur August Lattman, ancien associé de la société G. Amsinck & Company de New York (voir page 41). Le deuxième membre de ce conseil allemand était le sénateur John von Berenberg Gossler, directeur de la société bancaire hambourgeoise Berenberg, Gossler & Co. Berenberg, Gossler était également membre du conseil d'administration de la ligne Hambourg-Amérique (HAPAG) ; les autres membres étaient Wilhelm Cuno, alors chancelier de l'Allemagne et responsable de la politique économique de son pays, et Max Warburg, frère de Paul Warburg, membre du conseil de la Réserve Fédérale des États-Unis.

Dans une lettre datée du 11 novembre 1922 à l'U.E.I., le conseil consultatif allemand a enregistré ses investissements initiaux : "Tous les investissements réalisés jusqu'à présent sont des actions industrielles de première classe." Cependant, le prospectus publié aux États-Unis mettait l'accent sur les investissements dans l'immobilier, et sur ce point, le conseil allemand écrivait :

> En ce qui concerne l'investissement dans les hypothèques, nous comprenons votre point de vue mais nous reviendrons éventuellement sur la question au cas où nous serions en mesure de vous proposer des hypothèques avec une clause or qui pourrait

[297] Ceci est extrait d'un communiqué de presse marqué "De l'honorable Franklin D. Roosevelt" dans les dossiers de FDR.

être possible, et nous exclurions tout risque supplémentaire au cas où la marque diminuerait encore.

Il n'est fait mention nulle part dans le fichier United European Investors de l'achat de biens immobiliers ou de tout autre bien corporel mentionné dans la charte de la société et les annonces publiques.

Les investissements réalisés par le conseil au cours des années suivantes étaient des actions de sociétés allemandes. En outre, les prix des investissements étaient cités de manière inhabituelle, non pas en marks allemands ou en chiffres absolus de quelque nature que ce soit, mais en pourcentage d'augmentation, vraisemblablement par rapport à une base de 1913, ce qui a permis au conseil allemand d'écrire à New York : "les actions que vous avez achetées jusqu'à présent ont considérablement augmenté avec la dépréciation du mark".

Parmi ces parts et le pourcentage d'augmentation cité, par exemple :

Deutsche Maschinen A.G.	achetée à 1350%, maintenant cotée à 1805%.
Société Générale d'électricité	achetée à 740% et maintenant cotée à 5000%.
La dynamique du prix Nobel	achetée à 1119% maintenant cotée à 3975%

Le conseil allemand n'a pas mentionné le fait que la dépréciation du mark en termes de dollar américain avait été supérieure à l'avance des prix des actions qu'ils avaient achetées, tels que cotés en marks allemands. En fait, les allégations de hausse des prix des actions étaient illusoires. Un auteur précédent l'a décrit de la manière suivante : "une manipulation pure et simple, manifestement destinée à rebuter les autres détenteurs de marks allemands pour les inciter à investir dans une société capable de réaliser de tels miracles".[298]

Le conseil d'administration de New York ne s'est toutefois pas inquiété de cette situation. Lors de la réunion ordinaire du conseil d'administration du 15 janvier 1923, Franklin D. Roosevelt a ouvert la réunion et George W. Muller en a assuré le secrétariat. Il a alors été enregistré que la valeur des investissements en actions allemandes effectués jusqu'alors par la société était de plus ou moins 73 millions de marks, et cet investissement était actuellement coté à 420 millions de marks.

Dans les dossiers de FDR, on trouve une lettre intéressante du professeur Homer B. Vanderblue, professeur d'économie d'entreprise à l'université de Harvard, qui demande des explications sur le programme d'investissement de l'U.E.I. La lettre était adressée à FDR, en tant que président de la société, mais Edmund S. Paine y a répondu en déclarant que l'idée initiale d'investir dans des biens corporels, tels que des biens immobiliers, s'était avérée irréalisable, car elle "entraînerait des frais généraux très lourds en raison de la nécessité de supervision et d'exploitation", et qu'il avait donc été décidé de n'investir que dans des actions

[298] Haber, *The House of Roosevelt*, op. cit., p. 81-2.

allemandes "représentant la propriété indirecte d'actifs corporels". Paine a ajouté que la théorie se justifiait à un "degré remarquable :"

> En prenant comme test les premiers 60.000.000 de marks investit par la société, nous constatons que l'appréciation du prix des titres a quelque peu dépassé la dépréciation de la valeur d'échange du mark. En d'autres termes, les titres achetés pourraient probablement être vendus aujourd'hui à un prix en marks qui rapporterait un peu plus en dollars que ce qu'auraient pu obtenir les détenteurs de marks s'ils les avaient vendus au moment de l'investissement malgré le fait que la valeur de leurs marks ait énormément baissé.

Cependant, Paine affirme le contraire, un "Statement of Conditions as of January 31 1923" (Déclaration des conditions au 31 janvier 1923) trouvé dans les dossiers de FDR indique que la valeur comptable par action ordinaire à cette époque était de 2,62 dollars par action, alors que la valeur comptable moyenne au moment de l'investissement était de 2,64 dollars - en d'autres termes, une légère baisse.

Lors de la réunion des directeurs du 19 septembre 1923, il a été confirmé que la valeur totale des investissements était d'environ 120 000 dollars, et en mai 1925, c'était encore approximativement le montant enregistré dans la trésorerie. Cependant, dans les années qui ont suivi la stabilisation du mark, les conditions se sont améliorées et une déclaration datée du 12 mai 1926 indique une valeur nette de 147 098,07 dollars, avec 17 275 actions en circulation, et qui est alors égale à 8,50 dollars par action. Le 21 mai 1926, la société a proposé d'acheter toutes les actions offertes dans les 90 jours à 7,50$ l'action. En mai 1926, FDR a démissionné de son poste de président et a accepté l'offre de 7,50$ par unité pour ses 1005 actions ordinaires.

Les détenteurs américains de marks allemands qui ont investi dans des investisseurs européens unis ont-ils gagné ou perdu sur leur investissement ? Si nous supposons qu'ils ont conservé leurs actions jusqu'en 1926 et ont accepté l'offre de la société à 7,50 dollars par unité d'action ordinaire, puis ont acheté au prix d'émission de 10 000 marks allemands en septembre 1922 (date de l'offre), ils auraient perdu considérablement. En septembre 1922, le taux de change du dollar était de 1,00$ pour 764 marks allemands. Ainsi, une action de 10 000 marks équivaudrait à 13 dollars par action, et une action détenue de 1922 à 1926 aurait subi une perte d'environ 5,50 dollars par action ; d'autre part, un actionnaire aurait évité une dépréciation totale et la perte de tous ses fonds en raison de sa détention.

ENQUÊTE SUR UNITED EUROPEAN INVESTORS, LTD.

L'élément Roberts-Gould qui a rejoint FDR et Schall au Conseil de l'U.E.I. avait une mauvaise réputation dans "le milieu". En fait, Roberts et Gould faisaient l'objet d'une enquête pour activités criminelles présumées. En juillet 1922, alors que United European en était aux premiers stades de son incorporation, un certain M. Crary, un ancien enquêteur de la Mercantile Agency de Proudfoot - l'agence d'investigation de premier plan utilisée par les prestigieuses entreprises de Wall

Street - a approché la secrétaire de FDR, Mlle Le Hand. M. Crary a transmis à "Missy" des informations sur ce qu'il a appelé une "bande d'escrocs ayant des bureaux au 7 Pine Street" et dont la plaque sur la porte portait l'inscription "United European Investors, Ltd." Missy Le Hand a transmis l'information au bras droit de FDR, Louis Howe, qui à son tour a soulevé le problème avec l'ancien partenaire de Schall, Müller. De Müller et d'autres sources, Howe a appris que Roberts et Gould faisaient partie de cette prétendue "bande d'escrocs" qui, selon Crary, "se livraient à toutes sortes de promotions douteuses et ... il est certain qu'ils comptent parmi leurs membres un ancien détenu sous un faux nom à la réputation des plus douteuses".[299] Lorsque le nom de United European Investors, Ltd. a été affiché sur la porte de leur bureau au 7 Pine Street, l'enquêteur Crary, qui surveillait régulièrement le bureau depuis un an, a commencé à sonder discrètement Roberts et Gould. Bien que Roberts n'ait jamais été dans le bureau du 7 Pine Street, Crary a découvert que Gould "avait l'habitude d'utiliser ce bureau depuis au moins un an, et était considéré comme l'un de leurs (c'est-à-dire celui des escrocs) amis éprouvés". L'association de Gould avec "les escrocs" a rendu Crary méfiant, car, bien que l'agence Proudfoot ait précédemment donné à Gould "un dossier assez propre", elle l'avait également placé dans "la classe des promoteurs professionnels".

L'enquête de Crary a été entreprise au nom des propriétaires de l'immeuble du 7 Pine Street, "qui ont l'intention de se débarrasser de tout le monde en peu de temps". C'est au cours de l'enquête que l'Agence Proudfoot est tombée sur une circulaire mentionnant le nom de Franklin D. Roosevelt comme président de United European Investors, Ltd. et de William Schall comme banquier. Les preuves mises au jour par l'Agence Proudfoot ont été confirmées à Louis Howe par un certain M. Hanway, membre de la société de courtage en valeurs mobilières Harris, Forbes. M. Hanway a déclaré qu'il avait "été mis au courant des activités de Gould pendant plusieurs années, et qu'il se méfiait tellement de lui qu'il l'a amené à faire tous les efforts possibles pour éviter de rencontrer Schall dès le début".

De plus, l'Agence Proudfoot soupçonnait que Gould avait tenté d'obtenir des informations confidentielles de leur part et que Gould agissait comme "un espion pour les escrocs afin de découvrir quelles étaient les connaissances de Proudfoot & Company sur leurs affaires tordues".

Toutes ces informations ont été dûment rapportées par Howe dans une lettre ("Cher patron") à FDR (29 juillet 1922). La plupart des hommes d'affaires confrontés à un partenaire de ce calibre abandonneraient probablement toute opération proposée par United European Investors, mais le mémorandum de Howe à FDR ne recommande rien de tel. Il se lit en partie comme suit :

> Mes recommandations sont les suivantes : Que Gould et Roberts soient invités à trouver immédiatement de nouveaux bureaux, de préférence dans une église ou un autre endroit respectable. Qu'on se débarrasse de Roberts, qui est de toute façon un

[299] Informations extraites de la lettre Howe-FDR du 29 juin 1922 dans les dossiers de United European Investors, Ltd.

> sauvage de la publicité, et qui n'a aucune fonction importante dans ce jeu, et qu'on surveille de près Gould. Si M. Crary présente effectivement la circulaire, je déclencherai un tel tapage que son utilisation sera suspendue jusqu'à ce que nous soyons prêts à faire une annonce officielle. Je pense qu'il serait sage d'insister pour que je sois nommé membre du conseil d'administration pendant l'été, d'autant plus que Jenks et Rogers seront tous deux absents la plupart du temps et que certains veulent surveiller chaque action entreprise.

En d'autres termes, Howe suggère que les précautions contre les doubles allégeances seront suffisantes et que le meilleur moyen d'y parvenir est de nommer Louis Howe au conseil d'administration.

Quoi qu'il en soit, le plan se déroule comme prévu ; Roberts devient secrétaire de l'U.E.I., et Gould, présumé espion des escrocs, conserve son rôle de promoteur actif et continue de rendre compte périodiquement à FDR par lettre de l'évolution de leurs efforts de collecte de fonds. Le 20 juillet, avant que Howe ne rapporte à FDR le contenu de l'enquête Proudfoot, Gould avait écrit à FDR depuis le Southern Hotel de Baltimore au sujet de ses entretiens avec Edward Clark & Co, les banquiers de Baltimore, dont le partenaire Herbert Clark connaissait FDR depuis l'époque où ils étaient à Harvard. Puis, le 13 août 1923, Gould écrivit à FDR depuis le Canadian Club de New York pour relayer les télégrammes reçus de William Schall en Europe et conclut :

> J'ai été désolé d'apprendre que vous étiez à nouveau sujet à des difficultés. Vous en faites probablement trop, il ne faut pas essayer d'aller trop vite après une telle maladie. En tout cas, j'espère avoir le plaisir de vous voir avant mon retour en Europe début septembre.

Rien n'indique que FDR ait communiqué de quelque façon que ce soit avec Gould, et la lettre suivante dans les dossiers est de Gould à FDR, datée du 14 septembre 1923 et également écrite par le Canadian Club de New York. Cette lettre critiquait les "banquiers jaloux dont nous avons fait échouer les plans, et dont les projets ont été entravés. Si nous n'avions pas publié cette lettre aujourd'hui, nous aurions échoué".

Gould conclut alors : "Merci pour la grande et noble manière dont vous nous avez soutenu, et je pense personnellement que c'est votre attitude forte qui fait de notre projet une réussite totale", ajoutant que lorsqu'il (Gould) a appelé les grandes banques et les trust à présenter "leur proposition", il a trouvé que "votre nom [FDR] a été applaudi à tout rompre, car vous étiez le maître d'œuvre pour assurer le bon fonctionnement de l'aide au malheureux investisseur américain", et que si FDR avait pu entendre ces commentaires de la part des "plus grandes maisons financières", cela lui aurait donné "une grande satisfaction".

Sur la base de ces lettres, nous devons conclure que FDR a sciemment conclu un accord commercial avec des personnes dont la réputation était pour le moins douteuse, et que cet accord commercial a été maintenu après que des preuves de malversations aient été portées à la connaissance de FDR par Missy Le Hand et Louis Howe.

Seules des preuves superficielles que l'ensemble de l'opération United European Investors a été conçue par Roosevelt existent. Lorsque Gould dit à FDR que son "nom a été applaudi comme étant l'esprit maître", il est raisonnable de supposer que Gould flattait Roosevelt pour ses propres fins. Il n'y a vraiment aucune preuve, ni dans les dossiers ni ailleurs, que les antécédents et les connaissances financières de Roosevelt étaient suffisants pour élaborer un plan aussi ingénieux que celui de l'U.E.I.

LE CHANCELIER WILHELM CUNO ET LA HAPAG

La dépréciation désastreuse du mark allemand, qui était la raison d'être de United European Investors, s'est concentrée sur la période allant du milieu de l'année 1922 à novembre 1923. Le tableau indique comment l'inflation est devenue complètement incontrôlable après la mi-1922. Le Chancelier allemand entre la mi-1922 et août 1923 était Wilhelm Cuno (1876-1933). Cuno était à l'origine un fonctionnaire, toujours actif dans la politique, et en novembre 1917 il a été élu directeur de la ligne Hambourg-Amérique (HAPAG).

Lorsque Ballin, le président de la HAPAG, se suicida en 1918, Cuno en devint le président. Après le 10 mai 1921, Karl Wirth était chancelier allemand et Walter Rathenau, président de la General Electric (A.E.G.), était ministre des réparations. S'ensuivit une série d'événements dramatiques. Le ministre allemand des Finances Matthias Erzberger a été assassiné le 26 août 1921. En janvier 1922, Rathenau devient ministre des Affaires étrangères et le 24 juin 1922, il est également assassiné. En octobre 1922, Friedrich Ebert est nommé Chancelier du Reich et Wilhelm Cuno de la HAPAG est nommé Chancelier allemand. La dépréciation du mark se produit sous Cuno et culmine avec la crise financière et sa destitution en août 1923. Cuno revient à la présidence de la ligne Hambourg-Amérique. On peut noter au passage la prédominance des présidents d'entreprises dans la politique contemporaine : par exemple, Rathenau de la General Electric allemande et Cuno de la HAPAG. Owen D. Young, de General Electric aux États-Unis, a également été le créateur du plan Young pour les réparations allemandes, et le président de General Electric (A.E.G.) allemand, Rathenau, était ministre des réparations allemandes en 1922. Ces nominations sont généralement expliquées sur la base du principe du "meilleur homme pour le poste" mais, compte tenu des preuves présentées dans le dernier chapitre sur la politique dans le domaine des cautionnements, nous pouvons à juste titre exprimer notre scepticisme quant à cette explication. Il est beaucoup plus probable que les Youngs, les Cunos, les Rathenaus - et les Roosevelt - mélangeaient les affaires et la politique pour leur propre gain pécuniaire. Malheureusement, si nous devons laisser sans réponse la question clé de savoir dans quelle mesure ces groupes élitistes ont utilisé l'appareil d'État à leurs propres fins, il est clair que, lorsque nous examinons l'histoire de Wilhelm Cuno, nous revenons à Franklin D. Roosevelt et à la formation de United European Investors, Ltd. Cuno, sous les auspices duquel la grande inflation allemande a fait rage, était directeur de la Hamburg-America Line ; John von Berenberg Gossler, le conseiller de United European Investors en Allemagne, était également membre du conseil d'administration de cette société.

En résumé, Cuno et Gossler faisaient partie du même conseil d'administration à la HAPAG. La politique de Cuno était essentiellement responsable de l'inflation allemande de 1922-23, tandis que son co-directeur Gossler, en coopération avec Franklin D. Roosevelt, tirait profit de ces mêmes politiques d'inflation. Cela fait réfléchir.

L'INTERNATIONAL GERMANIC TRUST COMPANY

L'International Germanic Trust Company, fondée en 1927, a été motivée, selon ses promoteurs, par une demande d'institutions bancaires américaines en Europe centrale. Parmi les organisateurs du trust, approuvés par le département bancaire de l'État de New York, figuraient Franklin D. Roosevelt, Herman A. Metz, directeur de I.G. Farben, James A. Beha, surintendant des assurances de l'État de New York, et E. Roland Harriman de la société bancaire internationale W. A. Harriman & Co. Le président de l'International Germanic Company associée et président du comité exécutif de la société était Harold G. Aron, qui avait eu plus que sa part de procès concernant la promotion des actions. Les bureaux principaux de l'International Germanic Trust se trouvaient au rez-de-chaussée du 26 Broadway, le Standard Oil Building à New York. Le capital autorisé se composait de 30 000 actions pour un capital de 3 millions de dollars et un excédent de 2 millions de dollars. Dans sa demande au département bancaire, la société était représentée par le sénateur Robert F. Wagner ; bien que ne figurant pas parmi les organisateurs, le vieil ami de FDR, James A. Beha, surintendant des assurances pour l'État de New York, devint membre du conseil d'administration.

Les objectifs de la société, tels qu'ils ont été énoncés par son président, Harold G. Aron, étaient les suivants :

> Il semble qu'il y ait un réel besoin d'une institution de taille et de soutien suffisants, pour remplacer les institutions qui existaient avant la guerre et qui étaient principalement concernées par le financement des relations commerciales entre l'Amérique et le monde des affaires d'Europe centrale. Par l'intermédiaire de ses fondateurs, la société aura et développera des relations tant avec les Américains d'origine allemande dans tout le pays qu'avec les entreprises et les institutions bancaires en Allemagne. La société a l'intention de mettre particulièrement l'accent sur le développement de ses départements des affaires étrangères et des trusts, et de fournir une agence fiscale efficace dans la liquidation prévue des biens et des trusts allemands encore sous la garde du gouvernement.
>
> Dès le départ, la société sera assurée du soutien d'organisations et de sociétés importantes dans ce pays, et le petit déposant, à New York et ailleurs, sera le bienvenu. Elle s'efforcera de distribuer ses actions à grande échelle et en quantités relativement faibles. Il n'y aura pas de vote des trusts ni de contrôle individuel ou collectif.

Roosevelt a participé à l'introduction en bourse de la société proposée. Un télégramme daté du 7 avril 1927 de Julian Gerrard, président de la société, à FDR lui demandait de télégraphier à Frank Warder, surintendant des banques de l'État de New York, pour lui faire savoir que lui (Roosevelt) était intéressé par la société.

Il était prévu que cette intervention permettrait de rattraper le retard dans l'octroi de la charte. Les réunions du conseil d'administration se sont tenues dans le Standard Oil Building, dans le bureau de FDR et dans le Bankers Club, ce dernier étant situé au 120 Broadway. La première réunion du comité d'organisation se tient au Bankers Club le vendredi 27 mai 1927 ; bien que FDR ne puisse y assister, il écrit à Julian M. Gerrard : "Quelles sont les nouvelles de la société ? Le 15 août 1927, FDR demande à nouveau à Gerrard : "Comment se déroule le travail d'organisation et que fait-on en ce qui concerne les souscriptions d'actions ?

Une partie considérable des dossiers de lettres FDR de cette promotion est constituée de demandes d'emploi, de participation dans l'entreprise proposée ou de faveurs connexes. Par exemple, la National Park Bank of New York a écrit au FDR le 26 juillet 1927 qu'elle était intéressée par la création de la Société internationale germanique et qu'elle serait heureuse "qu'un de nos agents s'adresse à cet organisme, en donnant des détails sur nos installations". En d'autres termes, la National Park Bank était à la recherche d'une activité de dépôt. FDR a promis de s'adresser au comité d'organisation de la nouvelle société. Puis, le 12 août 1927, Basil O'Connor, partenaire de Roosevelt, lui a laissé un mot : "Cher Franklin, sur la Germanic Bank, voyez si vous pouvez m'obtenir 100 actions." L'émission d'actions elle-même a été fortement sursouscrite. Il était prévu d'émettre 30 000 actions, mais le total des demandes au 12 septembre dépassait 109 000 actions, et au 20 septembre, les demandes dépassaient 200 000 actions provenant d'environ 1900 personnes. Le 3 octobre 1927, le trust a notifié à FDR que son allocation était de 120 actions à 170 dollars par action et qu'elle devait être souscrite avant le 5 octobre. Le télégramme ajoutait que l'émission était fortement sursouscrite et cotée à 187 offres, 192 demandes, ce qui donnerait à FDR un bénéfice sur une revente immédiate. Ce télégramme de Howe ajoutait : "Je voudrais dix de vos actions pour Grace, si vous êtes d'accord."

FDR a été dûment élu membre du conseil d'administration et a notifié le 4 novembre 1927 que la première réunion du conseil se tiendrait le vendredi 11 novembre au Bankers Club au 120 Broadway. Cependant, Basil O'Connor, le partenaire juridique de Roosevelt, a apparemment eu la frousse ou a reçu des informations défavorables sur la promotion parce qu'il a écrit à FDR le 14 novembre :

> Je ne sais pas quelle est notre position actuelle dans ce domaine, mais si c'est comme lorsque je me suis séparé, je me sens très mal. La proposition ne nous a pas aidés à établir d'autres relations bancaires sur lesquelles j'ai travaillé pendant un an et, franchement, elle a toutes les caractéristiques que Gerrard (sic) pense pouvoir "vous faire marcher".

O'Connor a suggéré que FDR devrait démissionner du conseil d'administration parce que "jusqu'à présent, j'ai pu dire que nous n'avons pas d'affiliation bancaire, c'était faux. Je ne peux pas dire cela maintenant". Apparemment, FDR n'a pas immédiatement suivi ce conseil, car le 19 janvier 1928, il a été informé de sa réélection au poste d'administrateur pour l'année à venir, mais dans une lettre datée du 27 janvier 1928, FDR a écrit à Gerrard ce qui suit :

> Cher Julian,
> Plus je considère ma fonction de directeur et la société internationale germanique, plus je suis enclin à penser que c'est quelque peu futile. Je vous ai déjà fait part de mes sentiments et de ceux de mon partenaire en ce qui concerne les relations extérieures de l'un ou l'autre d'entre nous, qui se limitent à assister à des réunions occasionnelles et rien de plus. Il m'est bien sûr quelque peu difficile d'assister aux réunions du 26 Broadway compte tenu des étapes, mais, franchement, j'ai le sentiment qu'en conservant mon poste d'administrateur, je n'accomplis pas grand-chose, ni pour moi, ni pour le trust, ni pour la société internationale germanique.

FDR lui a alors offert sa démission. Il est à noter que les raisons de cette démission étaient les suivantes : "Je n'accomplis pas grand-chose, ni pour moi, ni pour le trust". Compte tenu de la réputation plutôt peu glorieuse des promoteurs, cette explication est un peu faible.

CHAPITRE IV

FDR LE PROMOTEUR D'ENTREPRISE

Les mailles de nos lois bancaires ont été tissées de manière si lâche qu'elles permettent à ces criminels les plus vils de tous, qui dilapident les fonds de centaines de petits déposants dans une spéculation imprudente à des fins privées, de se livrer sans frein à leur activité prédatrice. L'ensemble de la loi bancaire doit être révisé et le département bancaire a besoin immédiatement de moyens d'inspection beaucoup plus adéquats.

Franklin Delano Roosevelt, message annuel à la législature de l'État de New York, 1er janvier 1930.

Outre les entreprises spéculatives flottantes dans le domaine de la finance internationale, FDR a été intimement impliqué dans les émissions nationales, dont au moins une était d'une certaine importance. La plus importante de ces entreprises a été organisée par un groupe éminent comprenant Owen D. Young de General Electric (l'éternel Young du plan Young pour les réparations allemandes décrit dans le dernier chapitre) et S. Bertron de Bertron Griscom, banquiers d'affaires à New York. Ce syndicat a créé l'American Investigation Corporation en 1921. En 1927 suivirent Photomaton, Inc. et en 1928 la Sanitary Postage Service Corporation. Puis Roosevelt devient directeur de CAMCO, Consolidated Automatic Merchandising Corporation, mais seulement brièvement, démissionnant lors de son élection au poste de gouverneur de l'État de New York. Comme nous l'avons lu dans l'épigraphe ci-dessus, en 1930, FDR a eu des doutes quant à la possibilité de jouer avec l'argent des autres.

AMERICAN INVESTIGATION CORPORATION

Les scientifiques et les ingénieurs allemands ont commencé très tôt à utiliser avec succès des véhicules ou des dirigeables plus légers que l'air pour le transport de passagers et de marchandises. Dès 1910, l'Allemagne a exploité des services réguliers de transport de passagers par dirigeable. Les brevets pour les dirigeables ont été saisis pendant la première guerre mondiale par le gouvernement américain en vertu de la loi de 1917 sur le commerce avec l'ennemi, et après la guerre, la Commission des réparations a interdit à l'Allemagne de construire des dirigeables. Cela a laissé le champ libre aux entreprises américaines. Les opportunités offertes par le travail allemand et les restrictions de développement en Allemagne ont été observées par un groupe de financiers de Wall Street : S.R. Bertron de Bertron,

Griscom & Co. (40 Wall Street) et, ce qui n'est pas surprenant, puisqu'il était intimement impliqué dans les réparations allemandes, par Owen D. Young de General Electric (120 Broadway). Ce groupe était particulièrement intéressé par les possibilités de développement rentable du transport par dirigeable aux États-Unis. Le 10 janvier 1921, alors que FDR déballe ses valises dans les bureaux de la Fidelity & Deposit Company au 120 Broadway, il reçoit une lettre de Bertron dont voici un extrait :

> Mon cher M. Roosevelt :
> Représentant ici le petit groupe d'hommes éminents qui s'intéressent de plus en plus à la question du transport aérien, j'ai eu une longue conférence avec des responsables de l'armée à Washington la semaine dernière à ce sujet. On me dit que vous, en tant que secrétaire adjoint de la marine, connaissez bien ce sujet et j'aimerais beaucoup en discuter avec vous....

FDR et Bertron se sont rencontrés pour discuter du transport aérien au cours d'un déjeuner à l'Association du centre-ville. On peut supposer que Bertron a renseigné Roosevelt sur les développements techniques jusqu'à cette époque. Nous savons d'après les dossiers qu'il y a également eu une réunion entre Owen D. Young, S.R. Bertron, et l'ingénieur-attorney Fred S. Hardesty, représentant les détenteurs de brevets allemands, qui avaient de bonnes relations à Washington où les brevets saisis étaient sous la garde du dépositaire des biens étrangers et n'avaient pas encore été libérés.

Cette deuxième réunion a donné lieu à un accord préliminaire daté du 19 janvier 1921, connu sous le nom d'accord Hardesty-Owen-Bertron, qui prévoyait la voie à suivre pour développer l'exploitation de dirigeables commerciaux aux États-Unis. Un syndicat a ensuite été formé par Owen-Bertron pour "étudier toutes les phases de la navigation aérienne, la législation requise et les méthodes de collecte de fonds". Hardesty et ses associés ont remis au syndicat toutes leurs données et tous leurs droits en échange d'un remboursement de leurs frais de 20 000 dollars engagés jusqu'à cette date et d'une participation au syndicat. Le rôle de FDR était celui de collecteur de fonds, en utilisant ses nombreux contacts politiques à travers les États-Unis. Le 17 mai 1921, Bertron écrit à FDR qu'il a essayé de collecter des fonds auprès de personnes à Saint-Louis, Cincinnati et Chicago, tandis que Stanley Fahnestock, un associé de son cabinet, a fait le tour de la Californie et de Chicago. Lewis Stevenson, un autre membre du syndicat, était à l'œuvre parmi ses contacts dans le Middle-West. Bertron a donc fait appel à FDR pour une série de présentations personnelles à des contributeurs potentiels :

> Stevenson a hâte que vous le recommandiez auprès de Edward Hurley, E. F. Carey et Charles Piez, que vous connaissez tous. Il aimerait également écrire à Edward Hines, R.P. Lamont et H.C. Chatfield-Taylor. Je crains qu'il ne s'agisse d'une tâche importante. Ferez-vous de votre mieux ?

FDR a pris acte de la demande de Bertron, selon laquelle il envoyait des lettres à Stevenson "pour le présenter à Edward Hurley et à Charles Piez et E.F. Carey". J'ai bien peur de ne pas connaître les autres". Charles Piez, président de la Link-

Belt Company à Chicago, s'est excusé de sa participation en déclarant que "... je pratique l'économie la plus rigide, faisant la sourde oreille aux perspectives les plus attrayantes et les plus séduisantes", et en citant la "forme déplorable" de l'industrie. (Ce plaidoyer en faveur de la pauvreté a été soutenu par la lettre de Piez à FDR, sur un vieux papier à lettre, avec la nouvelle adresse imprimée par-dessus l'ancienne, laissant à peine deviner un président d'une grande société comme la Link-Belt Company). Edward N. Hurley a écrit qu'il n'était "pas très actif dans le monde des affaires", mais quand il sera à New York, "je vais me faire un devoir de faire appel à vous et de raviver le passé".

Le 1er juin, Lewis Stevenson a rendu compte à Roosevelt de ses progrès en matière de collecte de fonds dans le Middle-West. Il a confirmé que Piez était à court d'argent et que Hurley voulait parler plus tard, mais que Carey pourrait avoir un certain intérêt :

> Charles Swift, Thomas Wilson, tous deux emballeurs, étudient actuellement la proposition, tout comme Potter Palmer, Chauncey McCormick et une douzaine d'autres. Depuis que j'ai obtenu le contrat de Marshall Field, j'ai ajouté à notre liste C. Bai Lehme, une fonderie de zinc aux moyens très importants ; M. Wrigley, membre junior de la grande entreprise de chewing-gum ; John D. Black, de Winston, Strawn & Shaw ; B.M. Winston et Hampton Winston, de Winston & Company, et Lawrence Whiting, président de la nouvelle banque Boulevard Bridge. Peu à peu, je rassemble un groupe conséquent, mais je dois avouer qu'il s'agit d'un travail décourageant, lent et difficile. D'après mon expérience, je peux convaincre un individu de la faisabilité de ce projet, mais dès qu'il en discute avec ses amis, qui ne savent rien de la proposition, ils développent dans son esprit un doute sérieux que je dois combattre à nouveau. Grâce à mes observations à l'étranger, je suis fermement convaincu qu'il est possible d'en faire un succès.

Stevenson a conclu en demandant une lettre de présentation à l'éminent avocat de Chicago, Levy Meyer. Il est clair qu'à la fin du mois de juin 1921, Stevenson avait incité un certain nombre d'éminents citoyens de Chicago, dont Marshall Field, Philip N. Wrigley et Chauncey McCormick, à signer avec diligence.

En ce qui concerne FDR, ses lettres de vente sur ce projet feraient honneur à un vendeur professionnel. En témoigne sa lettre au colonel Robert R. McCormick, de l'empire des journaux de Chicago :

> Cher Bert :
> Comme vous êtes une personne à l'esprit progressiste, je demande à M. Lewis G. Stevenson de vous parler d'un sujet qui, à première vue, peut sembler une idée parfaitement folle. Mais il s'agit en réalité de quelque chose de très différent et tout ce que je peux vous dire, c'est que bon nombre d'entre nous ici présents, comme Young de la General Electric Company, Bertron de Bertron Griscom & Co, et un certain nombre d'autres citoyens parfaitement respectables ont manifesté suffisamment d'intérêt pour approfondir la question. Tout cela concerne l'établissement de lignes commerciales pour les dirigeables aux États-Unis...

Des lettres similaires ont été adressées à Chauncey McCormick, Frank S. Peabody de Peabody Coal et Julius Rosenwald de Sears, Roebuck. Ces initiatives ont été suivies de dîners personnels. Par exemple, le 21 avril 1921, FDR a écrit à Frank Peabody :

> ... est-il possible que vous puissiez dîner avec M. Bertron, M. Snowden Fahnestock et plusieurs autres d'entre nous à l'Union Club lundi soir prochain à 19h30 ? Bertron revient tout juste de l'autre côté de l'Atlantique et a des données très intéressantes concernant ces dirigeables commerciaux, qui ont fait leurs preuves en Allemagne.

FDR a ajouté que le groupe "promettra de ne pas vous retenir contre votre gré". Ce à quoi un Peabody réticent a télégraphié : "Impossible d'être là, n'aurait pas du tout peur d'être retenu, aurait énormément apprécié vous rendre visite".

À Edsel B. Ford, FDR écrit : "J'envoie cette note de M. G. Hall Roosevelt, mon beau-frère, qui connaît bien toute l'affaire." G. Hall Roosevelt, qui travaillait par hasard pour General Electric en tant que chef de division, s'est révélé être un négociateur habile, mais pas suffisamment pour rallier Ford dès les premiers échanges.

Toutefois, le 18 février 1922, l'American Investigation Corporation avait établi une liste très saine d'abonnés, comme le confirme la liste partielle suivante[300]:

Nom	**Affiliation**	**Lieu**
W.E. Boeing	Président, Boeing Airplane Co.	Seattle
Edward H. Clark	Président, Homestake Mining Co.	New York
Benedict Crowell	Crowell & Little Construction Co.	Cleveland
Arthur V. Davis	Président, Aluminum Co. of America	Pittsburgh
L.L. Dunham	Equitable Building Association	New York
Snowden A. Fahnestock	Bertron, Griscom & Co.	New York
Marshall Field, III	Capitaliste	Chicago
E.M. Herr	Président, Westinghouse Electric & Mfg. Co.	Pittsburg
J.R. Lovejoy	Vice-président de la General Electric Company	New York
John R. McCune	Président, Union National Bank	Pittsburgh
Samuel McRoberts	Capitaliste	New York
R.B. Mellon	Président, Mellon National Bank	Pittsburgh
W.L. Mellon	Président, Gulf Oil Co.	Pittsburgh
Theodore Pratt	Standard Oil Company	New York
Franklin D. Roosevelt	Vice-président, Fidelity & Deposit Co.	New York
Philip N. Wrigley	Vice-président, Wm. Wrigley Co.	Chicago
Owen D. Young	Vice-président de General Electric Co.	New York

Le premier conseil d'administration était composé de Samuel McRoberts[301], vice-président de la National City Bank, de William B. Joyce, président de la National Surety Company - l'un des concurrents de FDR dans le domaine du cautionnement et des obligations - et de Benedict Crowell, ancien secrétaire adjoint à la guerre et président du conseil d'administration de la société de

---

[300] Liste datée du 18 février 1922 dans les dossiers de FDR.

[301] Samuel McRoberts figure en bonne place dans Sutton, *Wall Street et la révolution bolchévique*, op. cit.

construction Crowell & Little Construction de Cleveland. Snowden A. Fahnestock de Bertron, Griscom était le fils du financier new-yorkais Gibson Fahnestock et un associé de la société de courtage en valeurs mobilières Fahnestock & Company. Le frère de Gibson, William Fahnestock, associé dans la même société, était directeur de plusieurs grandes sociétés, dont Western Union et, avec Allen Dulles, de la Gold Dust Corporation. David Goodrich, un autre souscripteur, était président du conseil d'administration de la B.F. Goodrich Company et administrateur de l'American Metals Company of New Mexico.

Il convient de noter avec soin que cette entreprise était une entreprise privée où le risque et les récompenses étaient pris par des capitalistes expérimentés et clairvoyants. Le financement de cette entreprise ne peut faire l'objet d'aucune critique ; la critique porte sur la manière dont elle a acquis son principal actif, les brevets allemands.

Le rapport du président pour l'année 1922, publié le 8 janvier 1923, résume les réalisations de l'A.I.C. jusqu'à cette date.

La Commission allemande des réparations a refusé d'autoriser la construction de grands dirigeables en Allemagne, et il y a eu un retard dans l'achèvement et l'essai du nouvel appareil conçu par le Bureau américain des mines pour la fabrication économique de gaz hélium, mais on a estimé que l'A.I.C. était à quelques mois du moment de faire appel au public pour un soutien financier. Selon ce rapport, la première étape des travaux avait été conclue par la signature, le 11 mars 1922, d'un contrat entre l'American Investigation Corporation et la Schuette-Lanz Company, par lequel l'American Investigation Corporation obtenait les droits de brevet mondiaux sur les conceptions et les méthodes de construction des dirigeables rigides de la Schuette. Le contrat prévoyait des paiements échelonnés et comprenait un accord avec Schuette-Lanz soit pour construire un dirigeable, soit pour fournir les services des experts chargés d'entreprendre la construction aux États-Unis.

La société avait "définitivement déterminé, par l'intermédiaire du Département d'État, que la Commission des réparations et le Conseil des ambassadeurs ne consentiraient pas à la construction en Allemagne du navire de grande taille envisagé par l'American Investigation Corporation", et le Dr Schuette a donc été prié de se rendre aux États-Unis pour parvenir à un accord définitif. L'objectif ultime, poursuit le rapport, est l'implantation de l'industrie des dirigeables aux États-Unis et "ne perdons pas de vue ; néanmoins, que l'obtention du premier navire en provenance d'Allemagne à moindre coût et construit par les meilleurs experts est hautement souhaitable".

L'importance d'assurer un approvisionnement en hélium pour les dirigeables a été mise en évidence par la destruction du R. 38 britannique et des dirigeables italiens *Roma*. Après consultation du Helium Board et du chimiste en chef du Bureau des Mines, une décision sur la question de l'hélium a été reportée jusqu'à l'achèvement de l'appareil amélioré que le Bureau était en train de concevoir pour la production d'hélium commercial. Selon les termes de l'accord entre l'American Investigation Corporation et l'ingénieur Hardesty et ses associés de Washington, en plus des 20 000 dollars fournis pour couvrir leurs travaux avant la création de l'American Investigation Corporation, certaines dépenses réelles devaient être remboursées pour l'aide à organiser la société. L'accord final était toutefois subordonné à la signature d'un contrat concernant la part que M. Hardesty et ses associés devaient recevoir dans l'American Investigation Corporation et dans l'une de ses filiales en échange de leur travail de promotion : il exigeait surtout que les brevets allemands détenus au nom du public américain par l'Alien Property Custodian soient remis à l'A.I.C.

POLITIQUE, BREVETS ET DROITS D'ATTERRISSAGE

Par conséquent, le syndicat A.I.C. avait un obstacle majeur à surmonter avant de pouvoir commencer à travailler sur le développement commercial des dirigeables aux États-Unis. Cet obstacle politique - acquérir les droits sur les brevets de construction de dirigeables Schuette-Lanz - a nécessité l'assistance politique avisée de FDR. Ces brevets étaient allemands, mais sous le contrôle du gouvernement américain. Selon la loi américaine, les biens étrangers saisis ne peuvent être cédés que par vente aux enchères et par appel d'offres. Cependant, nous trouvons dans le rapport du président de l'A.I.C. du 26 mai 1922 que l'A.I.C. était alors "le propriétaire des brevets actuels de Schuette-Lanz" et qu'elle répertoriait 24 brevets et 6 demandes de brevets provenant d'Allemagne, 6 demandes provenant d'Angleterre, et 13 brevets et 6 demandes provenant des États-Unis. Le rapport se poursuit : "Aux États-Unis, 7 brevets sont soumis à la restitution par l'Alien Property Custodian. Par le biais de cessions de dépôt, tous les nouveaux brevets américains sont délivrés directement à l'A.I.C.". Comment, alors, le syndicat A.I.C. a-t-il obtenu les brevets allemands détenus en fiducie par les États-Unis ? C'est particulièrement important, car il n'existe aucune trace d'enchères ou d'appels d'offres. Le rapport de l'A.I.C. ne contient que des notes :

> Les intérêts de l'A.I.C. ont été protégés par la collaboration à la rédaction des contrats et des assignations de M. J. Pickens Neagle (Solicitor of the Navy Department) Franklin Roosevelt, M. Howe et Blackwood Brothers.

Cela soulève certainement la question de la légitimité d'un avocat du département de la marine des États-Unis agissant au nom d'un syndicat d'intérêt privé. Les brevets allemands ont été délivrés par le gouvernement américain pour l'A.I.C. grâce à l'intervention personnelle de Franklin D. Roosevelt. Voyons comment il s'y est pris.

Franklin D. Roosevelt était l'ancien secrétaire adjoint de la marine, l'un des Roosevelt à occuper ce poste, et avait donc de bons contacts politiques au sein du département de la marine. Au milieu de l'année 1921, FDR a commencé à enquêter auprès de ses anciens amis de la Marine sur deux questions : (1) la position des brevets Schuette et (2) la possibilité d'acquérir un usage privé pour le syndicat A.I.C. de la base navale de Lakehurst pour les dirigeables A.I.C. Le 4 mai 1921, l'amiral R.R. Byrd, au Bureau des opérations navales, a répondu à une invitation à visiter le domaine de FDR à Campobello. Neuf mois plus tard, le 23 mai 1922, le commandant E.S. Land, du Bureau des opérations aéronautiques de la marine, a également pris acte d'une invitation à visiter FDR lors de sa prochaine visite à

New York. Land a ajouté qu'il "semble peu probable que je me rende à New York au cours des trois ou quatre prochaines semaines. Si vous pouviez me conseiller quant à la nature de vos demandes, je pourrais peut-être vous donner quelques informations dans le sens souhaité".

FDR a répondu au commandant de la Force terrestre dans une lettre portant la mention "*Personnel*", mais envoyée au département de la Marine, en précisant que sa demande ne pouvait être faite par téléphone ou par lettre. FDR a ensuite brièvement passé en revue la position de l'A.I.C. et a déclaré que la compagnie "est sur le point de procéder à la construction et à l'exploitation proprement dite de dirigeables", mais qu'elle avait besoin d'en savoir plus sur le programme du gouvernement américain pour ce type d'embarcations : "Je ne cherche pas d'informations confidentielles, mais simplement des faits que je suis sûr de pouvoir obtenir sans trop de difficultés si je pouvais me rendre moi-même à Washington".

Cette information est, écrit FDR à Land, "pour le bien de la cause en général", et il a ensuite proposé de prendre en charge les frais du commandant Land s'il se rendait à New York. Cette offre n'a apparemment pas eu beaucoup de succès, car le 1er juin, FDR a de nouveau demandé l'information et a poussé encore plus loin : "Au fait, y aurait-il une objection à ce que nous obtenions une copie du contrat du Zeppelin ? Théoriquement, ce sont tous des documents publics".

En dernière analyse, c'est Pickens Neagle, du bureau du juge-avocat général de la marine, qui a été le principal artisan de l'obtention des brevets allemands requis pour l'A.I.C. ; Neagle se rendait manifestement utile à FDR dans d'autres domaines également. Le 15 mai 1922, FDR écrivit à Neagle au sujet de Hardesty, l'ingénieur-avocat qui s'occupait des négociations sur les brevets à Washington :

> M. Fahnestock et moi-même avons approuvé sans conteste la très modeste somme que Hardesty a mise à votre disposition, [Neagle] et je suis sûr que les directeurs l'approuveront lors de leur réunion, qui ne tardera pas.

Le Navy Solicitor Neagle y a répondu le 16 juin pour donner à FDR des informations sur d'éventuelles affaires de cautionnement :

> J'ai honte de mentionner une chose aussi minime que la caution qui accompagnerait un contrat de 29 000 dollars, mais les choses sont très ennuyeuses dans le domaine des marchés publics en ce moment. La Midvale Steel and Ordnance Company vient de recevoir un contrat pour des pièces forgées de 8 pouces, pour un montant total inférieur à 29 000 dollars. La caution sera d'un montant égal à quelque chose comme 15 à 20% du montant du contrat.

De nouveau, le 9 août 1922, Neagle écrivit à Louis Howe et fit référence aux documents de la marine de FDR, qui étaient apparemment en train de subir l'examen habituel au sein du département avant d'être remis à FDR. Le problème de FDR était d'empêcher les documents de "passer entre les mains d'employés du service des archives ou de personnes curieuses ayant peu de sens des responsabilités". Le Département de la Marine ne voulait pas communiquer les documents sans examen approprié, même après l'intervention personnelle de Neagle. Neagle écrit à FDR :

> Je ne voyais pas comment je pourrais amener M. Curtis à changer d'avis sur le sujet, alors je l'ai laissé dans cet état avec la réserve cependant que vous serez bientôt ici vous-même et que vous le secouerez peut-être.

Le dossier à ce jour suggère que Pickens Neagle, avocat au bureau du Juge-avocat général de la Marine, travaillait plus pour le compte de FDR que pour le contribuable et le ministère de la Marine. Le contenu de ce dossier se déplace ensuite vers la tentative d'acquisition de l'utilisation des brevets allemands pour l'A.I.C. ; ces lettres ne sont plus sur du papier à lettres de la marine, mais sur du papier ordinaire, sans adresse imprimée, mais signées par Neagle. Le 16 février 1922, une lettre de Neagle à Howe relate que :

> notre bureau de l'arrière. (sic) est retourné au Bureau de l'Aéronautique qui a suggéré une forme de contrat avec un avenant disant que la station pourrait être louée à l'A.I.C. et que les employés [de la Marine] seraient mis à pied pour que la société les emploie.

Neagle a ajouté que, bien que les officiers de la marine ne puissent pas diriger et superviser les employés de l'A.I.C., ils pourraient être détachés dans l'industrie privée pour apprendre le métier de constructeur de dirigeables. Cette information privée est suivie d'une lettre officielle de Neagle à Fahnestock de l'A.I.C. (qui porte maintenant sa casquette officielle de Solicitor dans la marine américaine) pour confirmer le fait que la marine était prête à louer la station et l'usine de Cape May, une autorisation révocable sans préavis. Un autre, daté du 6 janvier 1923, rapporte que Hardesty a signé un contrat qui "devrait être acceptable pour la société".

Il est clair que les brevets Schuette ont été transférés sans enchères publiques ni appels d'offres, mais par un accord privé entre le gouvernement américain et des avocats agissant au nom d'une société privée. Il s'agit d'une violation de la loi sur le commerce avec l'ennemi.

Les dossiers font également état d'un autre employé du ministère de la Marine qui s'est précipité au secours de FDR. Une lettre datée du 31 mars 1923 de M.N. McIntyre, chef du bureau des nouvelles de la marine, à Louis Howe, suggère que l'A.I.C. s'empare du "dirigeable allemand en construction pour la marine", ainsi que l'accès à la base navale de Lakehurst. McIntyre est d'une franchise rafraîchissante sur sa proposition d'assistance politique : Si vous me faites connaître votre position sur la proposition de Lakehurst, je peux peut-être faire quelque chose pour aider à "graisser la patte". Il en va de même pour l'autre proposition".

Nous pouvons établir à partir des dossiers que FDR et son syndicat ont pu faire appel à des sources d'information et d'assistance au sein du Département de la Marine. Comment précisément l'A.I.C. a-t-elle alors pris le contrôle des brevets Schuette-Lanz ? Il s'agissait prétendument de biens publics dont il fallait se défaire par voie d'appel d'offres. Le rapport Hardesty de février 1921 explique le statut juridique des brevets et jette plus de lumière sur leur transfert.

Les brevets avaient été saisis par le gardien des biens des étrangers et jusqu'alors, ils n'avaient fait l'objet de licences que pour les ministères de la Guerre et de la Marine. Une demande a été soumise le 10 janvier 1921 par Fred Hardesty, indiquant qu'une société (vraisemblablement l'A.I.C.) devait être créée et qu'elle avait besoin des brevets, mais Hardesty a nié "que les brevets eux-mêmes aient une grande valeur intrinsèque". En d'autres termes, Hardesty marchait sur une corde raide. L'A.I.C. avait absolument besoin des brevets pour se protéger des étrangers. En même temps, affirme Hardesty, les brevets n'avaient pas vraiment de grande valeur. Ils sont nécessaires, écrit-il au gardien des biens des étrangers, "pour nous constituer un rempart moral contre l'agression des parties extérieures". Hardesty a fait valoir que l'intérêt public était vital et qu'il serait "heureux de recevoir des informations sur la valeur qui a été fixée pour les brevets, si leur valeur a été évaluée, et sur les conditions auxquelles ils pourraient nous être vendus".

À cette lettre est joint, dans les dossiers de FDR, un "Memorandum pour M. Hardesty" sur les brevets de Johann Schuette qui semble avoir été délivré par l'Office de conservation des biens étrangers. Le mémorandum confirme le fait que les brevets étaient détenus en vertu de la loi de 1917 sur le commerce avec l'ennemi, que le seul droit restant au détenteur allemand était le droit de réclamer la restitution, et que ces revendications doivent être réglées selon les instructions du Congrès. Il est peu probable, indique le mémorandum, que les brevets soient vendus par le dépositaire des biens étrangers mais, si les brevets étaient mis en vente, "il y aurait peu ou pas de concurrence, car il y a probablement très peu de sociétés existantes ou proposées qui envisagent de les utiliser, et que par conséquent les prix proposés ne seraient pas très élevés". Le mémorandum aborde ensuite le cœur du problème auquel l'A.I.C. est confrontée :

> L'A.P.C. ne vend des brevets, autres que ceux destinés au gouvernement, qu'à des citoyens américains lors d'une vente publique au plus offrant après annonce publique, sauf décision contraire du président. L'achat de biens auprès de l'A.P.C. pour un donneur d'ordre non déclaré ou pour la revente à une personne non citoyenne des États-Unis, ou au profit d'une personne non citoyenne des États-Unis est interdit sous peine de sanctions sévères.

Cela laisse ouverte la possibilité que le ministre de la guerre ou le ministre de la marine puisse recommander une vente immédiate au président "dans le cadre d'une politique commerciale saine et dans l'intérêt du public".

Le syndicat a ensuite tenté de suivre la voie présidentielle, apparemment avec succès. Le 4 février 1921, FDR à New York écrivait à Hardesty à Washington :

> "Je suis d'accord avec vous pour dire que nous devrions faire quelque chose immédiatement en ce qui concerne les brevets Schuette, et au moins faire l'essai avant que l'administration actuelle ne se retire."

Ensuite, un mémorandum des services reproduit dans les dossiers indique que le 9 et le 17 février 1921, FDR s'est rendu à Washington et a au moins rencontré le gardien des biens étrangers. Par la suite, Schuette a donné une procuration à Hardesty, et les brevets ont été restitués par le gardien des biens étrangers, mais pas immédiatement. Les dossiers de FDR ne contiennent pas de documents originaux signés sur la mainlevée, mais seulement des ébauches de documents, mais comme les brevets ont finalement été remis à l'A.I.C., on peut supposer que ces ébauches de travail sont raisonnablement proches du document final signé. Un document signé par le dépositaire des biens étrangers et le titulaire du brevet allemand Johann Schuette est rédigé comme suit :

> Il est en outre entendu et convenu par et entre les parties aux présentes que le ou les prix auxquels les brevets de Johann Schuette énumérés ci-dessus peuvent être vendus à l'American Investigation Corporation par l'Alien Property Custodian sont et seront considérés uniquement comme une valeur nominale desdits brevets fixée et convenue par et entre les parties aux présentes et la valeur réelle de ceux-ci ; et que ledit agent doit donner, exécuter et remettre au Alien Property Custodian une décharge sans réserve de la part dudit Johann Schuette et de son agent et de leurs héritiers, ayants droit et représentants légaux de toutes les réclamations, demandes, etc.

Il ressort clairement de ce document (1) que le dépositaire des biens étrangers a vendu les brevets à A.I. C., (2) qu'il n'a facturé à A.I.C. qu'un "prix nominal", (3) qu'il n'y a pas eu d'appel d'offres pour les brevets et (4) que l'ancien détenteur allemand Schuette a obtenu un droit directement ou indirectement. Ces quatre actions semblent être contraires aux exigences de la loi de 1917 sur le commerce avec l'ennemi, même si les procédures (1) et (2) étaient soumises à l'autorité présidentielle.

Par la suite, le 9 mai 1922, un contrat a été établi entre American Investigation Corporation et Johann Schuette. Il prévoyait le versement de 30 000 dollars en espèces à Schuette, ainsi que 220 000 dollars supplémentaires payables par mensualités, le dernier paiement devant être effectué au plus tard le 1er juillet 1923. En cas de défaut de paiement par l'A.I.C., tous les droits sur les brevets seraient remis à Schuette. Une allocation de stock était accordée à Schuette, qui devait à son tour fournir une coopération et une assistance technique à l'A.I.C. Il y a également dans les dossiers de FDR une note interne qui semble être écrite sur la machine à écrire normalement utilisée pour les lettres de FDR ; il s'agit donc peut-être d'une note rédigée soit par FDR, soit plus probablement par Louis Howe. Ce mémorandum résumait la stratégie de l'A.I.C. Il énumère "ce que nous avons à vendre" et répond à cette question comme suit :

> 1. Les brevets Schuette-Lanz, décrits comme fondamentaux et nécessaires par les ingénieurs de Ford travaillant également sur la construction de dirigeables.
> 2. Un contrat provisoire à la marine par lequel plus d'un million de dollars de construction d'une usine et d'un hangar de construction sont

économisés. C'est notre propriété, car le contrat proposé est en échange d'une licence d'utilisation des brevets Schuette par la Marine.

En d'autres termes, l'A.I.C. a non seulement pu acquérir les brevets sans appel d'offres dans les coulisses des manœuvres politiques, mais a également acquis le droit de les revendre à la marine. C'est le genre d'accord dont la plupart des pauvres contribuables ne rêvent même pas, bien qu'ils en paient la facture au final.

3. Toutes les données, dessins et essais des brevets de Schuette-Lanz.
4. Un arrangement pour la production d'hélium.
5. Une liste d'actionnaires composée d'hommes à l'esprit public et aux moyens considérables.

Cela n'était pas suffisant, car la section suivante est intitulée "Ce dont nous avons besoin" et énumère (1) les fonds et (2) le travail. Le mémo propose ensuite une fusion des travaux de l'A.I.C. avec ceux des ingénieurs de Ford.

Nous pouvons résumer comme suit l'accord conclu par FDR avec l'American Investigation Corporation :

Tout d'abord, l'A.I.C. a pu, grâce à l'intervention personnelle de Franklin D. Roosevelt, obtenir des brevets saisis à titre de cadeau ou à un prix symbolique. La loi exigeait que ces brevets saisis soient offerts à un appel d'offres public et non à l'avantage de l'ancien propriétaire allemand. En pratique, ils ont été restitués à huis clos à la suite d'un accord privé entre FDR et le gardien des biens étrangers, éventuellement avec l'intervention du président, bien qu'aucune trace de cette assistance n'ait pu être trouvée. Ces brevets, précédemment décrits comme étant sans valeur, ont ensuite fait l'objet d'un contrat impliquant le paiement de 250 000 dollars au citoyen allemand Schuette et le principal actif d'une société visant à promouvoir la construction de dirigeables aux États-Unis. À première vue, les documents contenus dans les dossiers indiquent une violation de la loi tant par FDR que par le dépositaire des biens étrangers.

Deuxièmement, ces brevets semblent avoir été délivrés au profit indirect d'une partie étrangère, une procédure soumise à des sanctions sévères en vertu de la loi.

Troisièmement, l'A.I.C. a pu obtenir l'utilisation d'installations de la marine d'une valeur d'un million de dollars et des informations officielles au sein du département de la marine.

Quatrièmement, le seul risque pris par les opérateurs de Wall Street était de mettre sur pied l'entreprise. Les brevets ont été obtenus nominalement, les fonds provenaient de l'extérieur de New York, et l'expertise était allemande ou celle de la Ford Motor Company. Franklin Delano Roosevelt a fourni le levier politique pour mettre en place un accord qui, à première vue, était illégal et certainement très éloigné de la notion de "confiance publique" que FDR et ses associés aimaient promouvoir dans leurs écrits et leurs discours.

FDR DANS LE SECTEUR DES DISTRIBUTEURS AUTOMATIQUES

Les ventes de machines à timbrer automatiques ont commencé en 1911, mais n'ont pas vraiment été des débouchés efficaces avant le développement de la machine Shermack dans les années 1920. En 1927, la Sanitary Postage Stamp Corporation a été créée pour commercialiser les machines Shermack pour la distribution automatique de timbres-poste, auparavant vendus dans les magasins sous forme de timbres en vrac qui, selon la documentation commerciale de l'entreprise, exposaient l'utilisateur à la transmission de maladies. Le conseil d'administration de la société était composé de l'inventeur Joseph J. Shermack, Edward S. Steinam, J.A. de Camp (120 Broadway), du banquier George W. Naumburg, A.J. Sach, Nathan S. Smyth et Franklin D. Roosevelt.

En avril 1927, la société vendait environ 450 installations de machines par semaine. Selon une lettre écrite par FDR à A.J. Sach, vice-président de la société, il y avait de gros problèmes avec les collections ; en fait, on n'avait pas eu de nouvelles de dix emplacements de timbres depuis plus de six mois, et les liquidités étaient insuffisantes. FDR a fait une suggestion éminemment sensée : les vendeurs devraient arrêter de vendre pendant une semaine et consacrer le temps ainsi libéré à la collecte de l'argent. En dehors de ces suggestions occasionnelles, le rôle de FDR dans le domaine des timbres-poste sanitaires était minime. Henry Morgenthau, Jr. l'a fait participer à l'origine et a même payé la souscription initiale de 812,50 dollars pour les 100 premières actions de FDR : "Vous pouvez m'envoyer un chèque de la même somme à votre convenance." FDR a envoyé son chèque le jour même. Les sponsors ont émis 3000 actions ordinaires de FDR "en contrepartie des services que vous avez rendus", évidemment pour utiliser son nom comme appât pour les investisseurs.

FDR démissionne à la fin de 1928 lors de son élection au poste de gouverneur de New York.

FDR a également été directeur de CAMCO (Consolidated Automatic Merchandising Corporation), mais n'a jamais pris une part active à son introduction en bourse. CAMCO était une holding destinée à prendre plus de 70% du capital social en circulation d'un certain nombre de sociétés, dont la Sanitary Postage Stamp Corporation, et est remarquable parce que le conseil d'administration comprenait non seulement FDR, mais aussi Saunders Norwell, qui de 1926 à 1933 a été président de la Remington Arms Company. En 1933, Remington Arms a été vendue à la société Du Pont. Au chapitre 10, nous allons examiner l'affaire Butler, une tentative avortée d'installer une dictature à la Maison Blanche. Remington Arms et Du Pont sont tous deux cités dans le témoignage supprimé de la commission d'enquête du Congrès. Pourtant, en 1928, nous trouvons FDR et Saunders Norvell comme co-directeurs de CAMCO.

LA FONDATION GEORGIA WARM SPRINGS

La lutte personnelle et très louable de FDR pour retrouver l'usage de ses jambes après une attaque de polio en 1921 l'a conduit à fréquenter la station thermale de Georgia Warm Springs. Reprenant des forces, FDR a décidé de convertir ces sources, abandonnées et presque inutilisées, en une proposition commerciale pour aider d'autres victimes de la polio.

Malheureusement, l'origine précise des principaux fonds utilisés pour développer Georgia Warm Springs ne peut être déterminée à partir des fichiers FDR tels qu'ils existent aujourd'hui. Le dossier FDR sur Georgia Warm Springs est relativement maigre, et il est très peu probable qu'il contienne tous les documents relatifs au développement du projet. Le dossier donne l'impression d'avoir été examiné avant d'être transmis aux archives de Hyde Park. Il n'existe aucune trace publique du financement de Georgia Warm Springs. Étant donné les finances personnelles serrées de FDR pendant les années 1920, il est peu probable que les fonds proviennent de ses ressources personnelles. Nous avons des preuves de l'existence de trois sources de financement. Premièrement, il est plus que probable que sa mère, Mme James Roosevelt, en était une. En fait, Eleanor Roosevelt a écrit à FDR : "Ne vous laissez pas aller à dépenser trop d'argent et n'obligez pas maman à en investir beaucoup, car si elle perdait, elle ne s'en remettrait jamais ![302] Deuxièmement, Edsel B. Ford aurait apporté des fonds pour construire l'enceinte de la piscine, mais n'était pas administrateur de la fondation. Troisièmement, et c'est le plus important, la propriété d'origine appartenait à l'entreprise socialiste George Foster Peabody. Selon le fils de FDR, Elliott Roosevelt, il y avait une hypothèque personnelle importante sur la propriété elle-même, et cette caution était probablement détenue par Peabody :

> Le 29 avril 1926, il acquiert la propriété abandonnée, où Loyless s'endette de plus en plus. Au plus fort de ses obligations en tant que nouveau propriétaire, Père avait précisément investi 201 667,83 dollars dans le lieu sous la forme d'une créance privée, qui ne fut complètement remboursé qu'après sa mort, et ensuite seulement à partir d'une assurance vie qu'il avait souscrite en faveur de Warm Springs. Les 200 000 dollars et plus représentaient plus des deux tiers de tout ce qu'il possédait. C'est la seule fois qu'il a pris un risque aussi monumental. Mère était terrifiée à l'idée que si cela allait dans le sens de tant de ses entreprises, aucun de nous ne pourrait aller à l'université, un destin que j'étais, pour ma part, plus que prêt à affronter.[303]

Il est significatif qu'Elliott Roosevelt signale l'existence d'un prêt privé de 200 000 dollars qui n'a pas été remboursé avant la mort de FDR. Il est d'ailleurs raisonnable de supposer que les fonds ont été mis en place par une partie ou la totalité des administrateurs. Cela place FDR dans la même position que Woodrow Wilson, redevable à ses créanciers de Wall Street. Comme ces administrateurs étaient parmi les hommes les plus puissants de Wall Street, l'accusation selon laquelle FDR était "sous l'emprise des banquiers" est parfaitement plausible.

Il est donc raisonnable de supposer que les fonds pour Georgia Warm Springs ont été mis en place, ou étaient sous le contrôle des administrateurs de la Fondation Georgia Warm Springs et de la réserve Meriweather associée. Les administrateurs

---

[302] Elliott Roosevelt, *The Untold Story*, op. cit. p. 232.

[303] Ibid.

de la fondation en 1934 et leurs principales affiliations commerciales sont énumérés ci-dessous :

Fondation Georgia Warm Springs : Administrateurs en 1934[304]

Nom de l'administrateur[305]	**Affiliations principales**
Franklin D. Roosevelt	Président des États-Unis d'Amérique
Basil O'Connor	Avocat, 120 Broadway, ancien partenaire juridique de FDR
Jeremiah Milbank	Directeur, Chase National Bank of N.Y.
James A. Moffett	Vice-président et directeur de la Standard Oil du New Jersey
George Foster Peabody	Propriétaire initial de la propriété et détenteur de la note sur les sources chaudes de Géorgie
Leighton McCarthy	Administrateur de Aluminum, Ltd (filiale canadienne d'ALCOA)
Eugene S. Wilson	Président, American Telephone & Telegraph (195 Broadway)
William H. Woodin	Secrétaire du Trésor sous FDR
Henry Pope	Directeur de la société Link-Belt
Cason J. Callaway	Président de Callaway Mills, Inc. de New York

Les administrateurs de Georgia Warm Springs lient évidemment FDR à Wall Street. Les plus éminents d'entre eux sont Eugene Smith Wilson (1879-1973), vice-président de l'American Telephone and Telegraph du 195 Broadway, à New York. Wilson a également occupé des postes d'administrateur dans de nombreuses autres compagnies de téléphone, dont Northwestern and Southwestern Bell et la Wisconsin Telephone Company. En 1919, il est avocat pour la Western Electric, puis devient conseiller juridique pour A.T.&T. avant d'être nommé vice-président en 1920. Wilson a longtemps été associé à la campagne contre la polio, s'est associé à Franklin D. Roosevelt et, au milieu des années 1930, a été membre du comité d'investissement de la Georgia Warm Springs Foundation. Parmi ses collègues d'A.T.&T., on trouve John W. Davis, qui apparaît dans l'affaire Butler (voir chapitre 10).

Un autre des administrateurs de Georgia Warm Springs était James A. Moffett, vice-président de la Standard Oil du New Jersey. Walter Teagle, de la même société, était l'un des principaux administrateurs de la NRA.

L'administrateur Jeremiah Milbank était directeur de la Chase National Bank, contrôlée par Rockefeller et la Equitable Trust Company.

L'administrateur William H. Woodin a été directeur de la Federal Reserve Bank of New York de 1926 à 1931 et a été nommé secrétaire au Trésor par Franklin D. Roosevelt après avoir fortement soutenu la candidature de FDR aux

---

[304] Extrait d'une lettre datée du 5 mars 1932 de Fred Botts, directeur commercial de Warm Springs, à FDR à la Maison Blanche.

[305] Parmi les administrateurs figuraient également Frank C. Root, de Greenwich, au Connecticut, Keith Morgan, de New York, et Arthur Carpenter, administrateur résident.

élections de 1932. Woodin démissionne dans les six mois, mais pour des raisons de santé, et non par manque d'intérêt pour le poste de trésorier.

L'administrateur George Peabody a été identifié dans le volume précédent[306] et a été associé de façon importante à la révolution bolchévique de 1917 en Russie et à la Banque de Réserve Fédérale de New York.

306 Sutton, *Wall Street et la révolution bolchévique*, op. cit.

CHAPITRE V

LA GENÈSE DU SOCIALISME D'ENTREPRISE

Alors que la société lutte pour la liberté, ces hommes célèbres qui se sont mis à sa tête sont imprégnés de l'esprit des XVIIe et XVIIIe siècles. Ils ne pensent qu'à soumettre l'humanité à la tyrannie philanthropique de leurs propres inventions sociales.

Frederic Bastiat, *The Law,* (New York : Fondation pour l'éducation économique, 1972), p. 52

Nous avons décrit la carrière de sept ans de Franklin D. Roosevelt à Wall Street, qui s'est terminée par son élection au poste de gouverneur de New York en 1928. Cette description est tirée des dossiers de lettres de FDR. Pour éviter toute erreur d'interprétation, des parties de ces lettres ont été reproduites textuellement et en détail. Sur la base de ces lettres, il ne fait aucun doute que FDR a utilisé son influence politique presque exclusivement pour obtenir des contrats de cautionnement alors qu'il était vice-président de Fidelity & Deposit Co ; que des liens financiers et politiques internationaux importants et douteux ont fait surface dans le cas de United European Investors et de International Germanic Trust ; et que ses associés intimes allaient d'Owen D. Young, président de General Electric, un membre de l'établissement financier élitiste, à des hommes décrits par un agent de l'Agence Proudfoot comme une "bande d'escrocs".

Il y a un thème récurrent dans la méthode de travail de FDR : il a utilisé la voie politique à un degré extraordinaire. En d'autres termes, FDR a utilisé à des fins personnelles le pouvoir de police de l'État tel qu'il est mis en œuvre par les organismes de réglementation, par la réglementation gouvernementale et par les fonctionnaires du gouvernement par son intercession, par exemple, auprès du gardien des biens étrangers, de la marine américaine, du système de la Réserve Fédérale et du surintendant des assurances de l'État de New York. Tous ces contacts politiques établis dans le cadre de sa fonction publique ont donné à FDR son avantage concurrentiel dans le monde des affaires. Il s'agit de dispositifs politiques, et non de dispositifs nés du marché libre. Ce sont des dispositifs reflétant la coercition politique, et non un échange volontaire sur le marché.

Les quatre chapitres suivants de la deuxième partie de ce livre développent ce thème de la politisation de l'entreprise commerciale. Tout d'abord, nous jetons un filet plus large pour formuler la thèse du socialisme d'entreprise et identifier certains socialistes d'entreprise éminents, principalement associés à FDR. Ensuite, nous remontons dans le temps jusqu'aux années 1840, jusqu'à l'un des ancêtres de FDR, l'homme d'affaires new-yorkais Clinton Roosevelt et sa première version de la NRA. Ce schéma est comparé au War Industries Board de Baruch en 1917, au fonctionnement du système de la Réserve Fédérale et au Roosevelt-Hoover American Construction Council des années 20. Enfin, dans le dernier chapitre de cette partie, nous détaillons l'investissement financier de Wall Street dans le New Deal.

LES ORIGINES DU SOCIALISME D'ENTREPRISE

Le vieux John D. Rockefeller et ses compagnons capitalistes du XIXe siècle étaient convaincus d'une vérité absolue : aucune grande richesse monétaire ne pouvait être accumulée selon les règles impartiales d'une société sur la base du libre-échange concurrentiel. La seule voie sûre vers l'acquisition d'une richesse massive était le monopole : chassez vos concurrents, réduisez la concurrence, éliminez la libre concurrence et, surtout, obtenez la protection de l'État pour votre industrie grâce à des politiciens et à une réglementation gouvernementale en votre faveur. Ce dernier processus aboutit à un monopole légal, et un monopole légal mène toujours à l'accumulation d'une vaste richesse.

Ce schéma de baron voleur est aussi, sous différentes étiquettes, le plan socialiste. La différence entre un monopole d'État corporatif et un monopole d'État socialiste n'est essentiellement que l'identité du groupe qui contrôle la structure du pouvoir. L'essence du socialisme est le contrôle monopolistique par l'État à l'aide de planificateurs engagés et de fonctionnaires aux ordres. D'un autre côté, Rockefeller, Morgan et leurs amis du monde des affaires cherchent à acquérir et à contrôler leur monopole et à maximiser leurs profits en exerçant une influence sur l'appareil politique de l'État ; bien que cela nécessite encore des planificateurs et des propagandistes universitaires, il s'agit d'un processus discret et bien plus subtil que la propriété de l'État sous le socialisme. Le succès du stratagème de Rockefeller a notamment consisté à attirer l'attention du public sur des controverses historiques largement superficielles et non pertinentes, telles que le mythe d'une lutte entre capitalistes et communistes, et à faire soutenir soigneusement les forces politiques par les grandes entreprises. Nous appelons ce phénomène de monopole légal des entreprises - le contrôle du marché acquit en utilisant l'influence politique - le "socialisme d'entreprise".

La description la plus lucide et la plus franche du socialisme d'entreprise, de ses mœurs et de ses objectifs se trouve dans une brochure de Frederick Clemson Howe de 1906, *Confessions of a Monopolist*.[307]

---

307 Frederic C. Howe, *Confessions of a Monopolist* (Chicago : Public Publishing Co. 1906). Le commanditaire du livre de Howe est le même éditeur qui a publié en 1973 un ouvrage faisant l'apologie du collectivisme de John D. Rockefeller III intitulé *The Second American Revolution*.

Le rôle de Frederick Howe dans la révolution bolchévique de 1917 et ses conséquences a été décrit dans *Wall Street et la révolution bolchévique*[308]. Howe apparaît également dans le New Deal de Roosevelt en tant que conseiller des consommateurs au sein de l'Administration de l'ajustement agricole. L'intérêt de Howe pour la société et ses problèmes s'étend donc au début du XXe siècle, de son association avec Newton D. Baker, plus tard secrétaire à la Guerre, au communiste Lincoln Steffens. En tant que commissaire spécial des États-Unis, Howe a fait des études sur la propriété municipale des services publics en Angleterre et, en 1914, il a été nommé par le président Wilson au poste de commissaire américain à l'immigration.

Quel est le secret de la création de grandes richesses ? Howe répond à la question comme suit :

> "M. Rockefeller peut penser qu'il a gagné ses centaines de millions grâce à l'économie, en économisant sur ses factures de gaz, mais ce n'est pas le cas. Il a simplement réussi à faire travailler les gens du monde entier pour lui....".[309]

En bref, le socialisme d'entreprise est intimement lié à l'idée de faire fonctionner la société pour le bénéfice de quelques-uns.

FAIRE EN SORTE QUE LA SOCIÉTÉ FONCTIONNE AU BÉNÉFICE EXCLUSIF DE QUELQUES-UNS

C'est le thème important du livre de Howe, exprimé à maintes reprises, avec des exemples détaillés du système "laissez les autres travailler pour vous" à l'œuvre. Comment M. Rockefeller et ses collègues monopolistes ont-ils fait en sorte que le monde entier travaille pour eux ? C'est ainsi que cela s'est passé, selon Howe :

> C'est l'histoire de quelque chose qui ne sert à rien - à faire payer l'autre. Cette histoire de faire payer l'autre, d'obtenir quelque chose pour rien, explique la soif de franchises, de droits miniers, de privilèges tarifaires, de contrôle des chemins de fer, d'évasion fiscale. Toutes ces choses sont synonymes de monopole, et tout monopole repose sur la législation.
>
> Et les lois sur les monopoles naissent dans la corruption. Le mercantilisme de la presse, ou de l'éducation, voire de la charité, fait partie du prix à payer pour les privilèges spéciaux créés par la loi. Le désir de quelque chose pour rien, de faire payer l'autre, de monopoliser une ressource sous une forme ou une autre, est la cause de la corruption. Le monopole et la corruption sont une cause et l'effet qui en découle.
>
> Ensemble, ils travaillent au Congrès, au sein du Commonwealth, ainsi que dans nos municipalités. Il en est toujours ainsi. Il en a toujours été ainsi. Le privilège donne

[308] Sutton, *Wall Street et la révolution bolchévique*, op. cit.

[309] Howe, op. cit. p. 145.

> naissance à la corruption, tout comme l'égout empoisonné engendre la maladie. L'égalité des chances, une entente équitable et sans faveurs, les échanges directs ne sont jamais corrompus. Ils ne finissent pas dans les prétoires ni devant les salles du Conseil. Car ces activités signifient travail pour travail, valeur pour valeur, quelque chose pour quelque chose. C'est pourquoi le petit homme d'affaires, le marchand en gros et au détail, l'employé et le fabricant ne sont pas les hommes d'affaires dont les activités corrompent le processus politique.[310]

L'opposé de Howe à ce système de monopole corrompu est décrit comme "travail pour travail, valeur pour valeur, quelque chose pour quelque chose". Mais ces valeurs sont aussi les marques de fabrique essentielles d'un système de marché, c'est-à-dire un système purement concurrentiel, où les prix de compensation du marché sont établis par l'interaction impartiale de l'offre et de la demande sur le marché. Un tel système impartial ne peut, bien entendu, être influencé ou corrompu par l'interventionnisme politique. Le système économique monopolistique basé sur la corruption et les privilèges décrits par Howe est une économie gérée politiquement. C'est aussi un système de travail forcé déguisé, appelé par Ludwig von Mises le système *Zwangswirtschaft*, un système de contrainte. C'est cet élément de compulsion qui est commun à toutes les économies gérées politiquement : le Nouvel Ordre d'Hitler, l'État corporatif de Mussolini, la Nouvelle Frontière de Kennedy, la Grande Société de Johnson et le Fédéralisme créatif de Nixon. La contrainte a également été un élément de la réaction d'Herbert Hoover à la grande dépression et, de façon beaucoup plus évidente, du New Deal de Franklin D. Roosevelt et de la National Recovery Administration.

C'est cet élément de contrainte qui permet à quelques-uns - ceux qui détiennent le monopole légal et en tirent profit - de vivre en société au détriment du plus grand nombre. Ceux qui contrôlent ou tirent profit des franchises législatives et de la réglementation et qui influencent en même temps les bureaucraties gouvernementales déterminent les règles et les règlements pour protéger leur richesse actuelle, profiter de la richesse des autres et empêcher les nouveaux venus de s'enrichir par leur entreprise. Par exemple, pour que les choses soient claires, la Commission du Commerce Interétatique, créée en 1880, existe pour restreindre la concurrence dans le secteur des transports, et non pour obtenir les meilleures conditions possibles pour les expéditeurs. De même, le Conseil de l'Aéronautique Civile existe pour protéger l'industrie aéronautique nationale, et non le voyageur aérien. Pour un exemple actuel, parmi des centaines, voir la saisie par la CAB en juillet 1974 d'un DC-10 de Philippines Air Lines (PAL) à l'aéroport de San Francisco. Quel péché la PAL avait-elle commis ? La compagnie aérienne a simplement remplacé un DC-10, pour lequel la CAB n'avait pas accordé d'autorisation, par un DC-8. Qui a gagné ? Les compagnies aériennes américaines, en raison de la diminution de la concurrence. Qui a perdu ? Le voyageur s'est vu refuser des sièges et un choix d'équipement. Les doutes sur le camp dans lequel se trouvait le CAB ont été dissipés par un article paru quelques semaines plus tard dans le *Wall Street Journal* (13 août 1974) intitulé "Le CAB est un partisan

---

[310] Howe, op. cit., pp. V-VI.

enthousiaste des mesures visant à améliorer le service des compagnies aériennes et à augmenter les tarifs". Cet article contenait une perle du vice-président de la CAB, Whitney Gillilland : "Nous avons trop mis l'accent sur le confort des passagers dans le passé." Gillilland a ajouté que la CAB doit être plus tolérante envers les avions pleins de capacités, "même si cela peut signifier que quelqu'un doit attendre un jour pour prendre un vol."

En bref, les agences de régulation sont des dispositifs permettant d'utiliser le pouvoir de police de l'État pour protéger les industries favorisées des assauts de la concurrence, pour protéger leurs inefficacités et pour maximiser leurs profits. Et, bien sûr, ces dispositifs sont défendus avec véhémence par leurs bénéficiaires : les hommes d'affaires réglementés ou, comme nous les appelons, "les socialistes d'entreprise".

Ce système de contrainte légale est l'expression moderne de la maxime de Frédéric Bastiat selon laquelle le socialisme est un système où chacun tente de vivre aux dépens des autres. Par conséquent, le socialisme d'entreprise est un système dans lequel les quelques personnes qui détiennent les monopoles légaux du contrôle financier et industriel profitent au détriment de tous les autres membres de la société.

Dans l'Amérique moderne, l'illustration la plus significative du fait que la société dans son ensemble travaille pour quelques-uns est la loi de 1913 sur la Réserve Fédérale. Le système de la Réserve Fédérale est, en effet, un monopole bancaire privé, qui n'est pas responsable devant le Congrès ou le grand public des contribuables, mais qui exerce un contrôle monopolistique légal sur la masse monétaire, sans se laisser ni entraver, ni même contrôler par le General Accounting Office.[311] C'est la manipulation irresponsable de la masse monétaire par ce Système de la Réserve Fédérale qui a provoqué l'inflation des années 20, la dépression de 1929, et donc la présumée nécessité d'un New Deal par Roosevelt. Dans le prochain chapitre, nous examinerons de plus près le système de la Réserve Fédérale et ses initiateurs. Pour l'instant, examinons de plus près les arguments avancés par les financiers philosophes de Wall Street pour justifier leur credo "faire fonctionner la société au bénéfice de quelques-uns".

LES SOCIALISTES D'ENTREPRISE PLAIDENT LEUR CAUSE

Nous pouvons remonter le cours de productions intellectuelles par lesquelles d'éminents financiers ont poussé à la planification et au contrôle national pour leur propre bénéfice et qui a finalement évolué vers le New Deal de Roosevelt.

Dans les années qui ont suivi la publication des *Confessions d'un monopoliste* de Howe en 1906, les financiers de Wall Street ont apporté des contributions littéraires sous forme de livres, aucune aussi spécifique que celle de Howe, mais toutes en faveur des institutions juridiques qui accorderaient le monopole souhaité et le contrôle qui en découle. À partir de ces livres, nous pouvons retracer les idées du New Deal et la base théorique sur laquelle le socialisme d'entreprise s'est plus

[311] Un audit très limité du système de la Réserve Fédérale a été voté par le Congrès en 1974.

tard justifié. Deux thèmes sont communs dans ces efforts intellectuels de Wall Street. Premièrement, que l'individualisme, l'effort individuel et l'initiative individuelle sont dépassés et que la concurrence "destructrice", généralement appelée "concurrence aveugle" ou "concurrence sauvage" est dépassée, non désirée et destructrice des idéaux humains. Deuxièmement, nous pouvons identifier un thème qui découle de cette attaque contre l'individualisme et la concurrence, à savoir que de grands avantages découlent de la coopération, que la coopération fait progresser la technologie et que la coopération empêche le "gaspillage des énergies concurrentes". Ces philosophes financiers concluent ensuite que les associations commerciales et, en fin de compte, la planification économique - en d'autres termes, la "coopération" forcée - sont un objectif primordial pour les hommes d'affaires modernes responsables et éclairés.

Ces thèmes de la coopération et du rejet de la concurrence s'expriment de différentes manières et avec des degrés de lucidité variables. Les hommes d'affaires ne sont pas des écrivains persuasifs. Leurs livres ont tendance à être turgescents, superficiellement égoïstes et quelque peu lourdement pédants. Quelques exemples de ce type montreront cependant comment les socialistes d'entreprise de Wall Street ont fait valoir leurs arguments.

Bernard Baruch était l'éminent socialiste d'entreprise dont nous examinerons les idées dans le prochain chapitre. Après Baruch et les Warburg, dont nous parlerons également dans le chapitre suivant, l'écrivain le plus prolifique suivant est l'influent banquier Otto Kahn de Kuhn, Loeb & Co.

Kahn se distingue par son soutien à la révolution bolchévique et à Benito Mussolini, soutien qu'il a concrétisé par des expressions totalitaires telles que "Le pire ennemi de la démocratie n'est pas l'autocratie mais la liberté effrénée".[312] En ce qui concerne le socialisme, Otto Kahn a déclaré à de nombreuses reprises sa sympathie pour ses objectifs. Par exemple, son discours devant la Ligue socialiste de la démocratie industrielle en 1924 comprenait ce qui suit :

> Permettez-moi de souligner que des mesures telles que, par exemple, l'impôt progressif sur le revenu, les négociations collectives des employés, la journée de huit heures, la surveillance et la réglementation gouvernementales des chemins de fer et des monopoles ou semi-monopoles naturels similaires, sont approuvées par le sens de la justice des entreprises, à condition que l'application de ces mesures soit maintenue dans les limites du raisonnable, et qu'elles ne soient pas abrogées par les entreprises si elles en avaient la possibilité.
>
> Ce sur quoi vous, les radicaux, et nous, qui avons des points de vue opposés, divergeons, ce n'est pas tant la fin que les moyens, pas tant ce qui devrait être réalisé que la manière dont cela devrait et peut être réalisé, en croyant comme nous, que se repaître d'utopie est non seulement inutile et inefficace, mais constitue une entrave et retarde les progrès vers la réalisation d'améliorations possibles.
>
> Avec tout le respect que je vous dois, j'ose suggérer que le radicalisme tend trop souvent à s'adresser davantage à la perfection théorique qu'à l'amélioration concrète ; aux griefs fantômes, ou aux griefs du passé, qui ont perdu leur réalité,

[312] Otto H. Kahn, *Frenzied Liberty*: *The Myth of a Rich Man's War*, discours à l'université du Wisconsin, 14 janvier 1918, p. 8.

> plutôt qu'aux questions réelles du jour ; aux slogans, aux dogmes, aux professions, plutôt qu'aux faits.[313]

Un certain nombre de ces financiers philosophes de Wall Street étaient administrateurs de la Brookings Institution à Washington D.C., responsable de nombreux guides politiques pour parvenir à ce système dont ils rêvaient. Robert S. Brookings, fondateur de la Brookings Institution, est généralement qualifié d'économiste, mais Brookings lui-même a écrit : "Je n'ai certainement pas droit à ce titre professionnel. J'écris seulement en tant que personne qui, grâce à une longue expérience commerciale de plus de soixante ans, a eu beaucoup à faire avec la fabrication et la distribution...".[314] Dans son rôle d'homme d'affaires tel qu'il se décrit lui-même, Brookings a publié trois livres : *Industrial Ownership*, *Economic Democracy*, et *The Way Forward*. Dans ces trois livres, Brookings soutient que l'économie politique classique, telle qu'elle se reflète dans le travail d'Adam Smith et de son école :

> bien que logiquement convaincante, était en fait incomplète en ce sens qu'elle ne tenait pas compte du développement moral et intellectuel de l'homme et de sa dépendance à l'égard du nationalisme pour son expression, si habilement présenté plus tard par Adam Müller et Frederick List, ni de l'influence économique de la production mécanique sur le rapport entre le capital et le travail.[315]

Par conséquent, mais sans présenter ses preuves, Brookings rejette les idées de libre entreprise d'Adam Smith et accepte les idées étatistes de la Liste - qui se reflètent d'ailleurs dans l'État corporatif hitlérien. Du rejet de la libre entreprise, Brookings déduit assez facilement un système "moral" rejetant le marché et y substituant une approximation de la théorie marxiste de la valeur du travail. Par exemple, Brookings écrit :

> Un système sain de moralité économique exige donc qu'au lieu de payer au travail un simple salaire de marché, le minimum nécessaire pour assurer ses services, le capital reçoive le salaire de marché nécessaire pour assurer ses services, et que le solde aille au travail et au public consommateur.[316]

À partir de cet argument quasi marxiste, Brookings construit, de manière assez vague et sans soutien détaillé, les grandes lignes des propositions nécessaires pour combattre les "maux" du système de marché dominant. Parmi ces propositions, "La première est la révision des lois antitrust de manière à permettre une

[313] Otto H. Kahn, *Of Many Things*, (New York : Boni & Liveright, 1925), p. 175.

[314] R. S. Brookings, *Economic Democracy*, (New York : Macmillan, 1929), p. xvi.

[315] Ibid, pp. XXI-XXII.

[316] R. S. Brookings, *Industrial Ownership* (New York : Macmillan, 1925), p. 28.

coopération étendue".[317] Selon Brookings, cela aurait deux effets : faire progresser la recherche et le développement et aplanir le cycle économique. Brookings ne précise pas comment ces objectifs découlent de la "coopération", mais il cite longuement Herbert Hoover pour étayer son argument, et en particulier l'article de Hoover, "Si les entreprises ne le font pas, le gouvernement le fera".[318]

Puis, comme tout bon socialiste, Brookings conclut : "Les entreprises gérées efficacement n'ont rien à craindre d'une supervision publique intelligente conçue pour protéger le public et le commerce contre des minorités captives et intraitables."[319] Ceci est nécessaire, car, comme Brookings le soutient ailleurs, les statistiques indiquent que la plupart des entreprises fonctionnent de manière inefficace, "Nous savons donc par triste expérience que la concurrence aveugle ou effrénée n'a pas réussi à apporter sa contribution raisonnable par le biais des revenus à nos besoins économiques nationaux".[320]

En 1932, Brookings est sorti de sa coquille dans *The Way Forward* pour s'exprimer encore plus ouvertement sur l'évolution du communisme soviétique :

> La condamnation verbale du communisme, aujourd'hui très populaire aux États-Unis, ne nous mènera nulle part. La différence entre le capitalisme et le communisme repose sur un point. Le capitalisme peut-il s'adapter à cette nouvelle ère ? Peut-il sortir de son ancien individualisme, dominé par la recherche égoïste du profit, et créer ainsi une nouvelle ère coopérative avec une planification et un contrôle sociaux, afin de servir, mieux qu'il ne l'a fait jusqu'à présent, le bien-être de tous les peuples ? S'il le peut, il peut survivre. S'il ne le peut pas, une certaine forme de communisme sera imposée à nos enfants. Soyez-en sûrs ![321]

Et dans le même livre, Brookings a de bons mots à dire sur un autre système de travail forcé, le fascisme italien :

> Bien que l'Italie soit une autocratie sous la dictature du Duce, chaque intérêt économique du pays se voit offrir la possibilité de discuter et de négocier afin qu'ils puissent, d'un commun accord, arriver à un juste compromis de leurs différends. Le gouvernement n'autorisera cependant, ni par le biais de blocages ni par des grèves, aucune interférence avec la productivité de la nation, et si, en dernière analyse, les groupes ne parviennent pas à se mettre d'accord entre eux, le gouvernement par l'intermédiaire de son ministre ou du tribunal des prudhommes, détermine la solution de tous les problèmes. Mais en Italie comme ailleurs, l'autocratie du capital

[317] Ibid, p. 44.

[318] The *Nation's Business*, 5 juin 1924, p. 7-8.

[319] Brookings, *Industrial Ownership*, op. cit. p. 56.

[320] Brookings, *Economic Democracy*, op. cit. p. 4.

[321] R. S. Brookings, *The Way Forward* (New York : Macmillan, 1932), p. 6.

> semble exister, et le sentiment général des classes ouvrières est que le gouvernement favorise le patronat.[322]

Ce qui domine alors dans les écrits de Brookings, c'est sa prédilection pour tout système social, communisme, fascisme, appelez-le comme vous voulez, qui réduit l'initiative et l'effort individuels et les remplace par la planification et le fonctionnement collectifs. Ce qui n'est pas dit par Brookings et ses collègues philosophes financiers, c'est l'identité des quelques personnes qui dirigent ce collectif de travail forcé.

Il est implicite dans leurs arguments que les opérateurs du système seront les socialistes d'entreprise eux-mêmes.

Des propositions purement théoriques de Brookings, nous pouvons passer à celles de George W. Perkins, qui a combiné des propositions parallèles avec quelques moyens efficaces, mais peu moraux, de les mettre en pratique.

George W. Perkins a été le constructeur énergique de la grande compagnie d'assurance-vie de New York. Perkins était également, avec Kahn et Brookings, l'expert des maux causés par la concurrence et des grands avantages à tirer d'une coopération ordonnée des affaires commerciales. Perkins a prêché ce thème collectiviste dans le cadre d'une série de conférences données par des hommes d'affaires à l'université de Columbia en décembre 1907. Son discours n'a guère eu de succès ; le biographe John Garraty affirme que lorsqu'il fut terminé :

> ... Le président de l'université Colombia, Nicholas Murray Butler, s'est empressé de partir sans un mot de félicitations, croyant manifestement, selon Perkins, qu'il avait involontairement invité un dangereux radical à Morningside Heights. Car Perkins avait attaqué certains des concepts de base de la concurrence et de la libre entreprise.[323]

Garraty résume la philosophie d'entreprise de Perkins :

> Le principe fondamental de la vie est la coopération plutôt que la concurrence - telle est l'idée que Perkins a développée dans son exposé. La concurrence est cruelle, gaspilleuse, destructrice, dépassée ; la coopération, inhérente à toute théorie d'un univers bien ordonné, est humaine, efficace, inévitable et moderne.[324]

Là encore, comme dans le cas de Brookings, nous trouvons des propositions pour "l'élimination du gaspillage" et pour plus de "planification" dans la gestion des ressources matérielles et humaines et le concept selon lequel les grandes entreprises ont des "responsabilités envers la société" et sont plus susceptibles d'agir équitablement envers les travailleurs que les petites entreprises. Ces phrases

---

[322] Ibid, p. 8.

[323] John A. Garraty, *Right hand man: The Life of George W. Perkins,* (New York : Harper & Row, n.d.), p. 216.

[324] Ibid.

à forte connotation sont, bien sûr, impressionnantes - surtout si la New York Life Insurance avait été à la hauteur de ses sermons de bienveillance sociale. Malheureusement, lorsque nous approfondissons notre enquête, nous trouvons des preuves de méfaits de la part de New York Life Insurance et une enquête conduite par l'État de New York, qui a découvert un mode opératoire résolument antisocial concernant le comportement des entreprises de New York Life. En 1905-06, le comité Armstrong (le comité mixte de l'Assemblée législative de l'État de New York chargé d'enquêter sur l'assurance-vie) a découvert que la New York Life Insurance Company avait été un contributeur régulier du Comité national républicain en 1896, 1900 et 1904. Il ne fait aucun doute que ces contributions financières visaient à promouvoir les intérêts de la compagnie dans les milieux politiques. En 1905, John A. McCall, président de la New York Life Insurance, fut convoqué devant la commission d'enquête de New York et fit valoir l'idée que la défaite de Byran et la liberté de fondre de la monnaie d'argent étaient pour lui une question *morale*. Selon McCall, "....j'ai consenti à un paiement pour vaincre Free Silver, non pas pour vaincre le parti démocrate, mais pour vaincre l'hérésie de Free Silver, et Dieu merci, je l'ai fait".[325]

Lors de cette même audition, le vice-président de la Mutual Life Insurance a également avancé le concept intéressant selon lequel les entreprises ont le "devoir" de "contrer" les idées et les politiques indésirables. L'histoire du financement de la politique par les entreprises n'a guère préservé les principes de la Constitution et d'une société libre. Plus précisément, il existe une contradiction flagrante entre les principes de coopération sociale et de bienveillance avancés par Perkins et ses collègues hommes d'affaires et le comportement antisocial contemporain de sa propre compagnie d'assurance-vie de New York.

En clair, les principes du socialisme d'entreprise ne sont qu'un mince vernis pour l'acquisition de richesses par quelques-uns au détriment du plus grand nombre.

Nous pouvons maintenant examiner lucidement les prêches de ces financiers plus intimement associés à Roosevelt et au New Deal. Un de ces financiers philosophes qui a exprimé ses idées collectivistes par écrit est Edward Filene (1860-1937). Les Filene étaient une famille d'hommes d'affaires très innovants, propriétaires du grand magasin William Filene's Sons Co. à Boston. Un vice-président des Filene est devenu l'un des trois mousquetaires à la tête de la National Recovery Administration en 1933 ; les deux autres membres du triumvirat étaient Walter Teagle, président de Standard Oil et John Raskob, vice-président de Du Pont et de General Motors.

Dès le début du siècle, Edward Filene s'occupe des affaires publiques. Il a été président de la Metropolitan Planning Commission de Boston, promoteur des banques populaires, et a apporté son aide à divers mouvements coopératifs. Filene a été actif au sein de la Croix-Rouge et de la Chambre de commerce américaine ; il a fondé la League to Enforce Peace (Ligue pour l'application de la paix) ; il a fondé puis présidé la Cooperative League, rebaptisée par la suite Twentieth

325 Cité dans l'ouvrage de Louise Overacker, *Money in Elections*, (New York : Macmillan, 1932), p. 18.

Century Fund ; il est membre de la Foreign Policy Association et du Council on Foreign Relations. À l'époque de Roosevelt, Filene était président du Massachusetts State Recovery Board et a participé activement à la campagne de 1936 pour la réélection de FDR. Filene a écrit plusieurs livres, dont deux, *The Way Out (*1924)[326] et *Successful Living in this Machine Age,* (1932),[327] qui expriment ses penchants philosophiques. Dans *The Way Out,* Filene met l'accent sur le thème de la réduction des déchets et sur l'aveuglement de la concurrence, et souligne la valeur de la coopération entre les entreprises et le gouvernement. Filene résume son argumentation comme suit :

> Deux choses sont claires. La première est que, pour être une bonne entreprise, l'activité doit elle-même être conduite comme un service public. La seconde est que le meilleur service public possible des hommes d'affaires est celui qui est rendu dans et par les entreprises privées du monde.[328]

Ce thème "le service public est une affaire privée" est développé dans un autre de ses livres :

> Ma propre attitude est que les entreprises doivent entreprendre une planification sociale, mais pas dans le but d'étouffer l'apparition de nouvelles théories ni de préserver les anciennes, mais parce qu'il y a eu une révolution sociale. L'ancien ordre a disparu et il est impossible de le rétablir. Nous vivons dans un monde nouveau. C'est un monde dans lequel la production de masse a mis tout le monde en relation avec tout le monde ; et nos projets doivent donc prendre tout le monde en considération.[329]

On trouve également dans Filene l'argument "le chemin de la paix est dans l'équilibre des forces" - une répétition d'une formule du XIXe siècle ressuscitée par Henry Kissinger dans les années 1970 et qui a toujours fini par conduire à la guerre plutôt qu'à la paix. Filene formule sa version comme suit :

> Pas étonnant qu'il y ait eu la guerre. On découvrit bientôt que la paix ne pouvait être maintenue que par un équilibre des forces entre les plus grands concurrents, et cet équilibre des forces était souvent rompu. Finalement, toute cette situation impossible a explosé dans la plus grande guerre de l'histoire de l'humanité. La guerre mondiale n'a pas provoqué le changement mondial que nous constatons depuis peu. Elle a plutôt été l'un des phénomènes de ce changement, tout comme

---

[326] Edward A. Filene, *The Way Out*, (*A Forecast of Coming Changes in American Business and Industry*) (New York : Doubleday, Page, 1924).

[327] Edward A. Filene, *Successful Living in this Machine Age* (New York : Simon & Schuster, 1932).

[328] Filene, *The Way Out*, op. cit. p. 281.

[329] Filene, *Successful Living in This Machine Age*, op. cit. p. 269.

> la Révolution française a été un phénomène de la première révolution industrielle.[330]

Ce thème de la promotion de l'intérêt public en tant que question d'intérêt primordial pour les entreprises elles-mêmes se retrouve chez Myron C. Taylor, président de la United States Steel Company. L'intérêt public, selon Taylor, a besoin de la coopération des entreprises pour une production rationnelle. L'aveuglement des grandes entreprises est évident lorsque Taylor nie que cela constituerait également une restriction au commerce. Taylor omet d'expliquer comment nous pouvons ajuster la production à la consommation sans que ceux qui ne veulent pas coopérer ne soient contraints de le faire. Taylor résume ses propositions comme suit :

> Il s'agit donc de découvrir ce que nous possédons en tant que nation et d'apprendre à l'utiliser plutôt que de partir à la recherche du nouveau uniquement parce qu'il est nouveau. La responsabilité première de l'industrie est de trouver des moyens de promouvoir l'intérêt public et les intérêts de ses propres producteurs, employés, distributeurs et clients, en élaborant et en réalisant tous les plans constructifs autorisés par les lois actuelles, en agissant ouvertement et, dans la mesure du possible, en coopération avec le gouvernement. J'avoue qu'il m'est extrêmement difficile de croire que des plans constructifs et coopératifs entrepris sincèrement par une industrie de base pour ajuster rationnellement la production à la demande dans cette industrie, et qui évitent toute tentative de fixer ou de contrôler artificiellement les prix, puissent être considérés à juste titre comme une entrave aux échanges et au commerce. Car le seul effet serait de supprimer les entraves vitales à la production, aux échanges et au commerce, et de promouvoir les intérêts publics.[331]

La contribution de Standard Oil à cette liturgie est exprimée par Walter C. Teagle, président de la Standard Oil Company du New Jersey et nommé par le président Roosevelt à un poste de haut niveau dans son ARN. Teagle exprime sa version du socialisme d'entreprise comme suit :

> Les maux de l'industrie pétrolière sont propres à cette industrie et nécessitent des remèdes particuliers. Il s'agit de la modification des lois antitrust, de la coopération entre les producteurs et de l'exercice du pouvoir de police des États.[332]

Plus crûment que les autres, Teagle veut que le pouvoir policier de l'État fasse respecter la coopération volontaire :

> La coopération volontaire au sein de l'industrie ne suffit pas pour remédier à ses maux. Elle ne serait pas suffisante même si les restrictions légales à la coopération

---

[330] Ibid, p. 79.

[331] Tiré du livre de Samuel Crowther, *A Basis for Stability*, (Boston : Little, Brown, 1932), p. 59.

[332] Ibid, p. 111.

> étaient supprimées, même si la suppression de ces restrictions entraînait des progrès considérables.
> Pour protéger les droits corrélatifs des producteurs et pour faire respecter les lois de conservation adéquates, il faut faire appel au pouvoir de police de l'État. Il s'agit là d'une question qui relève de l'action des États plutôt que du gouvernement fédéral, mais la coopération entre les différents États et entre les unités opérationnelles de l'industrie sera également nécessaire si l'on veut que la production dans l'ensemble du pays soit limitée aux marchés nationaux.
> La solution du problème dépend donc de la coopération volontaire au sein de l'industrie, de l'exercice du pouvoir de police de l'État, et de la coopération entre les différents États concernés et entre les unités (sic) de l'industrie dans les différents États. Pour permettre cela, les lois antitrust des États et de la Fédération devront être révisées.[333]

Ces extraits reflètent la vision fondamentale de nos philosophes financiers de Wall Street. Ce n'étaient pas des figures mineures issues du monde ouvrier. Au contraire, ils étaient les éléments puissants et influents et, dans des cas importants, associés à Roosevelt et au New Deal. Otto Kahn était un des principaux instigateurs du système de la Réserve Fédérale. Lamont et Perkins étaient des personnages clés dans le domaine des banques et des assurances. L'homme d'affaires Brookings a donné son nom et son argent à l'influent institut de recherche qui a produit les rapports sur lesquels une grande partie de la politique a été fondée. Louis Kirstein, un vice-président de la firme Filene, et Walter Teagle de Standard Oil devinrent deux des trois hommes dominants qui dirigèrent l'Administration nationale du recouvrement sous la direction de Hugh Johnson, le protégé de Bernard Baruch.

Bernard Baruch était probablement le plus prestigieux des membre de Wall Street de tous les temps, dépassant peut-être même en influence Morgan et Rockefeller. Nous allons maintenant examiner le rôle de Baruch et celui des Warburg.

Quelle est la philosophie des financiers décrite jusqu'à présent ? Certainement tout sauf le laissez-faire de la libre concurrence, qui est le dernier système qu'ils souhaitaient voir prospérer. Seul le socialisme, le communisme, le fascisme ou leurs variantes étaient acceptables. L'idéal pour ces financiers était la "coopération", forcée si nécessaire. L'individualisme était inacceptable, et la concurrence était immorale. D'autre part, la coopération était constamment prônée comme étant morale et digne, et nulle part la contrainte n'était rejetée comme étant immorale. Pourquoi ? Parce que, lorsque le verbiage est dépouillé de toutes ces phrases pompeuses, la coopération obligatoire était leur voie royale vers l'obtention d'un monopole légal. Sous le couvert de service public, d'objectifs sociaux et d'un contingent de bonnes intentions, il s'agissait fondamentalement de "laisser la société travailler pour le compte de Wall Street".

---

[333] Ibid, p. 113.

CHAPITRE VI

PRÉLUDE AU NEW DEAL

Quel que soit le parti qui gagne, les tyrans ou les démagogues sont les plus sûrs d'occuper les postes.

Le député Clinton Roosevelt de New York, 1841.

Le récit complet de la construction du socialisme d'entreprise aux États-Unis, tel qu'envisagé par les financiers philosophes identifiés dans le chapitre précédent, dépasse la portée de ce livre, mais nous pouvons ouvrir des perspectives plus larges en examinant brièvement quelques facettes du processus historique : par exemple, le système de Clinton Roosevelt un siècle avant FDR, le War Industries Board de Bernard Baruch et le système de la Réserve Fédérale de Paul Warburg.

En 1841, le lointain cousin de FDR, l'homme d'affaires new-yorkais Clinton Roosevelt, a proposé un plan ressemblant au New Deal pour la planification économique et le contrôle de la société par une minorité. Sous le président Woodrow Wilson, en 1918, Bernard Baruch, socialiste d'entreprise *par excellence,*[334] a suivi les grandes lignes du plan Roosevelt, presque certainement sans le savoir et probablement en raison d'un certain parallélisme inconscient des actions, lorsqu'il a créé le War Industries Board, le précurseur organisationnel de la National Recovery Administration de 1933. Une partie de l'élite des entreprises du WIB de 1918, nommée par Baruch-Hugh Johnson, a par exemple trouvé des niches administratives dans la NRA de Roosevelt. En 1922, Herbert Hoover, alors secrétaire au commerce, et Franklin D. Roosevelt, un futur membre de Wall Street, ont uni leurs forces pour promouvoir les associations commerciales, mettant en œuvre les propositions de planification économique d'après-guerre de Bernard Baruch. Peu de temps après, l'ancien rédacteur socialiste Benito Mussolini a marché sur Rome et a établi - avec l'aide libérale de la société J.P. Morgan - l'État italien des entreprises dont la structure organisationnelle rappelle nettement la NRA de Roosevelt. Aux États-Unis, la glorification de Mussolini et de ses réalisations italiennes a été encouragée par les financiers toujours présents, Thomas Lamont, Otto Kahn et d'autres. Nous ne mentionnerons que brièvement l'implication de Wall Street dans la Russie bolchévique et l'Allemagne d'Hitler - deux États totalitaires gouvernés par une élite autoproclamée - car ces aspects sont

[334] En français dans le texte, NdT.

traités en détail dans d'autres volumes.[335] En bref, la construction de l'Administration nationale de redressement de FDR n'était qu'une facette d'un processus historique plus large - la construction de systèmes économiques où le petit nombre pouvait profiter au détriment du grand nombre constitué par le citoyen-contribuable - et le tout bien sûr promu sous le couvert du bien public, que ce soit la Russie de Staline, l'Italie de Mussolini, l'Allemagne d'Hitler ou le New Deal de Roosevelt.

L'ARN DE CLINTON ROOSEVELT - 1841

Le député new-yorkais Clinton Roosevelt était un cousin du XIXe siècle de Franklin Delano Roosevelt et, incidemment, il était également lié au président Theodore Roosevelt, à John Quincy Adams et au président Martin Van Buren. Le seul effort littéraire de Clinton Roosevelt est contenu dans une rare brochure datant de 1841.[336] Il s'agit essentiellement d'une discussion socratique entre l'auteur Roosevelt et un "Producteur" représentant vraisemblablement le reste d'entre nous (c'est-à-dire le plus grand nombre). Roosevelt propose un gouvernement totalitaire sur le modèle de la société de George Orwell de 1984, où toute l'individualité est submergée par un collectif dirigé par un groupe aristocratique élitiste (c'est-à-dire le petit nombre) qui promulgue toutes les lois. Roosevelt a exigé l'abandon définitif, mais non immédiat, de la Constitution

> **P.** Mais je demande à nouveau : Abandonneriez-vous immédiatement les anciennes doctrines de la Constitution ?
> **A.** Pas du tout. Pas plus que si l'on se trouvait dans un bateau qui fuit, on ne devrait sauter par-dessus bord pour éviter la noyade. C'est un navire qui a été assemblé à la hâte lorsque nous avons quitté le pavillon britannique, et on a alors pensé qu'il s'agissait d'une expérience très douteuse.[337]

Cette première expression du scepticisme de la famille Roosevelt à l'égard de la Constitution rappelle le rejet par la Cour suprême, en octobre 1934 (*Schechter Poultry Corp. v. U.S.*), d'un autre type de changement promu par Roosevelt, un changement "sans entrave" selon la Cour, affranchi des règles d'une société

---

335 Pour Wall Street et les premiers bolcheviks, voir Sutton, *Wall Street et la révolution bolchévique*, op. cit. L'implication de Wall Street dans la montée d'Hitler et du nazisme allemand est le sujet d'un autre volume, *Wall Street et l'ascension de Hitler*.

336 Clinton Roosevelt, *The Science of Government Founded on Natural Law* (New York : Dean & Trevett, 1841). Il existe deux exemplaires connus de ce livre : un à la Bibliothèque du Congrès, Washington D.C. et un autre à la Bibliothèque de l'Université de Harvard. L'existence de ce livre n'est pas consignée dans la dernière édition du catalogue de la Bibliothèque du Congrès, mais a été enregistrée dans l'édition précédente de 1959 (page 75). Une édition en fac-similé a été publiée par Emanuel J. Josephson, dans le cadre de son *Manifeste communiste de Roosevelt* (New York : Chedney Press, 1955).

337 Ibid.

constitutionnelle : le National Recovery Act, lui-même une réplique étrange du programme de Clinton Roosevelt de 1841 en faveur d'une économie collective.

L'ancien système Roosevelt dépendait "d'abord de l'art et de la science de la coopération. Il s'agit de faire en sorte que l'ensemble fonctionne à notre avantage mutuel".[338] C'est cette coopération, c'est-à-dire la capacité à exploiter l'ensemble pour l'intérêt de quelques-uns, qui est, comme nous l'avons vu, le thème général des écrits et des prédications d'Otto Kahn, Robert Brookings, Edward Filene, Myron Taylor et des autres financiers philosophes dont il est question au chapitre 5. Dans le schéma de Roosevelt, chaque homme gravit des échelons précis dans le système social et est nommé à la fonction à laquelle il convient le mieux, le choix de la profession étant strictement limité. Selon les termes de Clinton Roosevelt :

> **P.** Qui sera chargé de désigner chaque classe ?
> **A.** Le Grand Maréchal.
> **P.** Qui sera responsable du fait que les hommes nommés sont les plus qualifiés ?
> **A.** Un collège de physiologistes, de philosophes de la morale, d'agriculteurs et de mécaniciens, qui sera choisi par le Grand Maréchal et responsable devant lui.
> **P.** Contraindriez-vous un citoyen à se soumettre à ses décisions dans le choix d'une vocation ?
> **A.** Non. Si quelqu'un de bonne moralité insiste, il peut essayer jusqu'à ce qu'il trouve la profession la plus adaptée à ses goûts et à ses sentiments.[339]

La production dans le système devait être assimilée à la consommation, et le traitement des "excès et des carences" reflétait les idées poursuivies dans le Plan Swope,[340] la base intellectuelle de la NRA de Roosevelt. Le système est certainement similaire à celui utilisé dans le War Industries Board de Bernard Baruch pendant la Première Guerre mondiale. C'est ainsi que Clinton Roosevelt décrit les devoirs du Maréchal de la Création, dont le travail consiste à équilibrer la production et la consommation :

> **P.** Quel est le devoir du Maréchal de l'Ordre créateur ou producteur ?
> **A.** Il s'agit d'estimer la quantité de production nécessaire pour induire une suffisance dans chaque département en dessous de lui. Lorsqu'il est en fonction, il signale les excès et les insuffisances au Grand Maréchal.
> **P.** Comment va-t-il découvrir ces excès et ces carences ?
> **A.** Les différents commerçants lui feront part de la demande et de l'offre dans chaque secteur d'activité, comme on le verra plus loin.
> **P.** Sous cet ordre se trouvent l'agriculture, les manufactures et le commerce, comme je le perçois. Quel est donc le devoir du maréchal de l'agriculture ?
> **A.** Il devrait avoir sous lui quatre régions, sinon, le commerce extérieur doit combler cette lacune.
> **P.** Quelles sont les quatre régions ?
> **A.** La région tempérée, la région chaude, la région très chaude et la région humide.

---

338 Ibid.

339 Ibid.

340 Voir l'annexe A.

> **P.** Pourquoi les diviser ainsi ?
> **A.** Parce que les produits de ces différentes régions nécessitent des systèmes de culture différents, et sont à juste titre soumis à des organisations différentes.[341]

Il y a ensuite un maréchal de l'industrie qui supervise l'ensemble du système, à l'instar de Baruch en tant que dictateur économique en 1918 et de Hugh Johnson en tant qu'administrateur de l'Administration nationale de redressement en 1933. Les fonctions du maréchal sont décrites par Clinton Roosevelt comme suit :

> **P.** Quelles sont les fonctions du Maréchal des Manufactures ?
> **A.** Il divise les hommes en cinq classes générales, selon le schéma imprimé.
> 1er. Les fabricants de tous les moyens de défense contre les intempéries.
> 2d. Toutes sortes de viandes.
> 3d. Métaux et minéraux.
> 4ème. Produits chimiques.
> 5ème. Machines.
> Tous ces éléments figurent sur les diagrammes imprimés, les bannières, avec une couleur sur un côté et une devise appropriée au verso, montrant l'avantage que chaque classe représente pour toutes les autres : et d'ailleurs, nous remarquons que cela devrait être universellement adopté, pour donner une juste direction à la vanité de l'homme.
> En se référant au tableau et à ce qui a été observé auparavant, les fonctions des agents de ce service seront toutes évidentes.

Les catégories industrielles de 1841 ne sont bien sûr pas précisément les catégories de 1930, mais on peut dégager une similitude généralisée. La 1ère division est celle des vêtements et des tissus, limitée en 1841 au coton, à la laine et au lin, mais étendue aujourd'hui aux matières synthétiques, y compris les plastiques et les fibres. La 2ème division est celle consacrée aux denrées alimentaires. La 3ème division est consacrée aux matières premières, et la 4ème division comprend les médicaments. La 5ème est celle des machines. Aujourd'hui, la 5ème division comprend les nombreuses subdivisions de l'électronique, de la mécanique et du génie civil, mais les cinq catégories pourraient être utilisées pour diviser une économie moderne.

La société de Clinton Roosevelt peut être résumée par sa phrase : "Le système doit régner, et le système doit se préoccuper principalement du bien commun."

LA DICTATURE DE BERNARD BARUCH EN TEMPS DE GUERRE

Si le système de la Réserve Fédérale et son monopole légal privé sur la masse monétaire ont été une source de richesse pour ses opérateurs, l'objectif ultime de faire fonctionner la société au bénéfice de quelques-uns, tel que décrit par Frederick Howe et Clinton Roosevelt, ne peut être atteint que par un contrôle

---

[341] Clinton Roosevelt, *The Science of Government Founded on Natural Law*, op. cit.

planifié de l'ensemble de l'économie, et cela nécessite l'adhésion obligatoire des nombreux petits entrepreneurs aux diktats des quelques personnes qui décident des plans à suivre.

La genèse de la NRA de Roosevelt, un système qui prévoyait l'adhésion obligatoire des petits entrepreneurs à un plan conçu par les grandes entreprises, remonte au War Industries Board américain de Bernard Baruch, créé et élaboré comme une mesure d'urgence en temps de guerre. En 1915, avant l'entrée des États-Unis dans la Première Guerre mondiale, Howard E. Coffin, alors président de General Electric, dirigeait le Comité américain de préparation industrielle. En compagnie de Bernard Baruch et de Daniel Willard de la Baltimore and Ohio Railroad, Coffin était également membre de la Commission consultative du Conseil de la Défense Nationale. En 1915, Bernard Baruch est invité par le président Woodrow Wilson à concevoir un plan pour un comité de mobilisation de la défense. Ce plan Baruch est ensuite devenu le War Industries Board, qui a absorbé et remplacé l'ancien General Munitions Board. Margaret L. Coit, la biographe de Baruch, décrit le War Industries Board comme un concept similaire aux associations commerciales coopératives, un dispositif longtemps souhaité par Wall Street pour contrôler les impondérables de la concurrence sur le marché :

> Des comités d'industrie, de grandes et de petites entreprises, tous deux représentés à Washington, et dotés d'une représentation de Washington chez eux, pourraient constituer l'épine dorsale de toute la structure.[342]

En mars 1918, le président Wilson, agissant sans l'autorité du Congrès, avait doté Baruch de plus de pouvoir que tout autre individu ne l'avait fait dans l'histoire des États-Unis. Le War Industries Board, présidé par Baruch, devint responsable de la construction de toutes les usines et de la fourniture de toutes les matières premières, de tous les produits et de tous les transports, et toutes ses décisions finales relevaient du président Bernard Baruch. En bref, Baruch est devenu le dictateur économique des États-Unis, ou "Maréchal des fabricants" selon le schéma de Clinton Roosevelt. Pourtant, comme le souligne Margaret Coit, "... la création de ce bureau n'a jamais été spécifiquement autorisée par une loi du Congrès."[343]

Ainsi, à l'été 1918, Baruch, doté de pouvoirs extraordinaires et inconstitutionnels, avait, selon ses propres termes, "enfin mis au point un système de "contrôle" positif sur la majeure partie du tissu industriel... Le succès engendra le succès et le commerce fut pris en charge avec une volonté croissante de la part des intérêts concernés".[344]

---

342 Margaret L. Coit, M. Baruch (Boston : Houghton, Mifflin, 1957), p. 147.

343 Ibid, p. 172.

344 Bernard M. Baruch, *American Industry in the War: A Report of the War Industries Board* (mars 1921), avec une introduction de Hugh S. Johnson (New York : Prentice-Hall, 1941) (comprenant "une réimpression du rapport du War Industries Board of World War I, le propre programme de M. Baruch pour la mobilisation totale de la nation tel que présenté à

Au moment de l'armistice, le W.I.B. était composé de Baruch (président), d'Alexander Legge de International Harvester (vice-président), de E.B. Parker et de R.S. Brookings (dont nous avons déjà examiné les idées) qui était chargé de fixer les prix. Les assistants du président étaient : Herbert Bayard Swope, frère de Gerard Swope de General Electric ; Clarence Dillon de la société Dillon, Read & Co. de Wall Street ; Harrison Williams ; et Harold T. Clark.[345]

Le rapport final de Baruch sur l'activité du W.I.B. était bien plus qu'un historique de ses opérations ; c'était aussi un plan spécifique et une recommandation pour la planification économique en temps de paix.

Baruch ne se contentait pas de résumer les leçons à tirer pour la planification en temps de guerre ou pour la préparation industrielle en temps de paix difficile. Au contraire, les conclusions de Baruch s'orientaient, selon ses propres termes, vers les "pratiques industrielles de paix" et à faire des recommandations "relatives aux pratiques commerciales en temps normal". La majeure partie des conclusions concerne le passage d'un système économique planifié en temps de guerre à un système économique planifié en temps de paix, et même les suggestions de pratiques en temps de guerre sont liées aux fonctions applicables en temps de paix. Baruch a suggéré que les "leçons directes les plus importantes à tirer de la guerre" sur le fonctionnement du Conseil des industries de la guerre étaient :

1. La création d'une organisation structurée en temps de paix avec 50 divisions de produits, se réunissant pour suivre le développement de l'industrie et développer l'information. L'idée maîtresse de cette proposition était que les informations nécessaires à la planification du temps de paix soient collectées et que la direction de l'organisation provienne de l'industrie à grande échelle.
2. Que le gouvernement "devrait concevoir un système pour protéger et stimuler la production interne de certaines matières premières utilisées dans la guerre", et
3. Que les industries liées à la guerre devraient être encouragées par le gouvernement à maintenir des organisations structurées pour une utilisation en temps de guerre.

En dehors de ces suggestions assez élémentaires, Baruch s'intéresse exclusivement dans le rapport à la "planification" en temps de paix. On nous présente d'abord le canular que, d'une manière non déclarée, "les processus du

---

la Commission des politiques de guerre en 1931, et des documents actuels sur les priorités et la fixation des prix").

[345] Pour une liste complète du personnel du W.I.B., voir Grosvenor B. Clarkson, *Industrial America in the World War* (New York : Houghton, Mifflin, 1923), annexe III. À la lumière du chapitre 11, ci-dessous, il est intrigant de constater que de nombreux membres du comité du W.I.B. ont des bureaux au 120 Broadway, notamment Murry W. Guggenheim, Stephen Birch (Kennecott Copper), Edward W. Brush (American Smelting and Refining), F. Y. Robertson (United States Metals Refining Co.), Harry F. Sinclair (Sinclair Refining Co.), Charles W. Baker, (American Zinc), et Sidney J. Jennings (United States Smelting, Refining and Mining Co.)

commerce" ont changé et sont maintenant obligés de céder devant "certains nouveaux principes de supervision". Ce non sequitur est suivi de la déclaration :

> Nous avons été progressivement contraints de nous écarter de la vieille doctrine du droit anglo-américain, selon laquelle la sphère du gouvernement doit se limiter à la prévention des ruptures de contrat, des fraudes, des dommages physiques et des atteintes à la propriété, et le gouvernement ne doit exercer sa protection que sur les personnes non compétentes.

Il est nécessaire, écrit Baruch, que le gouvernement "tende la main" pour protéger "les individus compétents contre les pratiques discriminatoires de la puissance industrielle de masse". Si Baruch évoque le contrôle fédéral des chemins de fer et de la flotte marchande, il n'explique pas pourquoi les représentants du grand capital seraient les mieux placés pour exercer ce contrôle. En d'autres termes, il ne dit pas pourquoi le renard est proposé comme l'être le plus compétent pour gérer le poulailler. Baruch s'en prend ensuite aux lois antitrust de Sherman et Clayton au motif que ces lois ne sont que des efforts pour forcer l'industrie à se conformer à des "principes plus simples, suffisants pour les conditions d'une époque révolue", et se félicite de la réussite du War Industries Board parce qu'il a créé des centaines d'associations commerciales contrôlant les prix et les méthodes de distribution et de production :

> De nombreux hommes d'affaires ont fait l'expérience pendant la guerre, pour la première fois de leur carrière, des avantages considérables, tant pour eux-mêmes que pour le grand public, de la combinaison, de la coopération et de l'action commune avec leurs concurrents naturels.

Si ces attributs coopératifs ne sont pas maintenus, affirme Baruch, alors les hommes d'affaires seront tentés "et beaucoup d'entre eux ne pourront pas résister" de mener "leurs affaires pour un gain privé avec peu de référence au bien-être public général". D'un autre côté, les associations commerciales peuvent être d'un grand intérêt public pour atteindre l'objectif souhaité de la coopération, conclut M. Baruch :

> La question est donc de savoir quel type d'organisation gouvernementale peut être conçu pour sauvegarder l'intérêt public tout en préservant ces associations afin qu'elles puissent poursuivre le bon travail dont elles sont capables.

Baruch, comme tout bon socialiste, propose des organisations gouvernementales pour développer ces principes de coopération et de coordination.

Si le lecteur se débarrasse un instant de l'idée d'un antagonisme mutuel entre le communisme et le capitalisme, il verra aisément dans les écrits de Bernard Baruch les objectifs fondamentaux de Karl Marx tels qu'ils sont décrits dans *Le Manifeste Communiste*. Ce qui diffère entre les deux systèmes, ce sont les noms des quelques élitistes qui dirigent l'opération connue sous le nom de planification de l'État ; l'avant-garde du prolétariat chez Karl Marx est remplacée par l'avant-garde du grand capital chez Bernard Baruch.

Qui tirerait profit de la proposition de Baruch ? Le consommateur ? Pas du tout, car les intérêts des consommateurs sont *toujours* protégés par la libre concurrence sur le marché, où les biens et les services sont produits au moindre coût, de la manière la plus efficace, et où le consommateur dispose d'un maximum de choix parmi les producteurs concurrents. Les gagnants des propositions de Baruch seraient les quelques personnes qui contrôlent les principaux secteurs industriels - en particulier le fer et l'acier, les matières premières, les produits électriques, c'est-à-dire les industries déjà bien établies et qui craignent la concurrence de nouveaux venus plus performants. En d'autres termes, les gagnants de sa proposition seraient Bernard Baruch et sa coterie de Wall Street qui contrôle effectivement les grandes entreprises grâce à ses postes de directions imbriquées. La question fondamentale est donc la suivante : à qui profitent ces propositions pour les associations professionnelles et la coordination gouvernementale de l'industrie ? Le principal, voire le seul grand bienfaiteur - en dehors des essaims de conseillers universitaires, de bureaucrates et de planificateurs - serait l'élite financière de Wall Street.

Nous avons donc ici, selon les propres mots et idées de Baruch, une mise en œuvre de l'injonction de Frederic Howe de "faire travailler la société pour vous", le monopoliste. Cela se présente également sous la forme d'une proposition comparable au système de Clinton Roosevelt. Rien ne prouve que Baruch ait entendu parler de Clinton Roosevelt. Il n'était pas nécessaire qu'il le connût ; les avantages de la restriction des échanges et des opportunités ont toujours été évidents pour l'entreprise déjà établie. Il ne sera donc pas surprenant de trouver Bernard Baruch au cœur même de la NRA de Roosevelt, qui elle-même est parallèle à de nombreuses propositions d'après-guerre de Baruch, et qui a investi 200 000 dollars dans l'élection de FDR. Cela explique pourquoi le personnel de Baruch pendant la Première Guerre mondiale souscrit au New Deal. Le général Hugh Johnson, par exemple, a passé les années 1920 à étudier l'organisation industrielle aux frais de Baruch et est devenu en 1933 le patron de la National Recovery Administration. Cela explique également pourquoi Franklin Delano Roosevelt, lui-même membre de l'élite financière de Wall Street pendant une grande partie des années 1920, a été le cofondateur avec Herbert Hoover - un autre Wall Streeter dans les années 1920 - de la première des associations professionnelles proposées par Baruch, l'American Steel Construction Association, dont il est question au chapitre suivant.

Parallèlement aux idées de Bernard Baruch, qui se sont concrétisées au sein de la NRA, il existe un exemple contemporain beaucoup plus réussi de socialisme d'entreprise dans la pratique : le système de la Réserve Fédérale.

PAUL WARBURG ET LA CRÉATION DU SYSTÈME DE LA RÉSERVE FÉDÉRALE

Bien que beaucoup aient contribué, ou pensaient avoir contribué, à l'élaboration de la législation de la Réserve Fédérale, le système était essentiellement le fruit du cerveau d'un seul homme : Paul Warburg, frère de Max Warburg, que nous avons rencontré au chapitre 3. Paul Moritz Warburg (1868-1932) descendait de la famille bancaire allemande d'Oppenheim. Après une formation initiale dans les bureaux de Samuel Montagu & Co. à Londres et de la Banque Russe pour le Commerce Étranger à Paris, Warburg entre dans la maison bancaire familiale de M.M. Warburg & Co. à Hambourg. En 1902, Warburg devient partenaire de la maison de banque new-yorkaise Kuhn, Loeb & Co. tout en continuant à être partenaire de la Warburg de Hambourg. Cinq ans plus tard, à la suite de la panique financière de 1907, Warburg écrit deux brochures sur le système bancaire américain : *Défauts et besoins de notre système bancaire* et *Un plan pour une banque centrale modifiée.*[346]

Dans les années qui suivent 1907, Warburg ne perd pas l'occasion de parler et d'écrire publiquement sur la nécessité d'une réforme bancaire et monétaire aux États-Unis, et en 1910, il propose officiellement la création d'une Banque de réserve des États-Unis. Ce plan est devenu le système de la Réserve Fédérale, et Warburg a été nommé par le président Woodrow Wilson membre du premier conseil de la Réserve Fédérale. Des critiques importantes à l'encontre de Warburg ont éclaté pendant la Première Guerre mondiale en raison du rôle de son frère Max en Allemagne, et il n'a pas été reconduit au Conseil en 1918. Cependant, de 1921 à 1926, après que les critiques se soient atténuées, Warburg est devenu membre du Conseil consultatif du Conseil de la Réserve Fédérale et en a été le président de 1924 à 1926.

Après l'adoption de la loi de 1913 sur la Réserve Fédérale, Warburg et ses associés bancaires ont rapidement commencé à utiliser le monopole bancaire légal à leurs propres fins et objectifs, comme le suggérait Frederic Howe. En 1919, Warburg a organisé l'American Acceptance Council et a été le président de son comité exécutif en 1919-20 et son président en 1921-22. Puis, en 1921, Warburg a organisé et est devenu président de la banque privée International Acceptance Bank, Inc. tout en continuant à siéger au conseil consultatif du conseil de la Réserve Fédérale. En 1925, Warburg a ajouté deux autres banques privées d'acceptation : l'American and Continental Corp. et l'International Acceptance Trust Co. Ces banques étaient affiliées à la Bank of the Manhattan Company, contrôlée par Warburg. En passant, on peut noter que Paul Warburg était également directeur de l'American IG Chemical Corp, la filiale américaine de IG Farben en Allemagne. I.G. Farben a joué un rôle important dans l'arrivée au pouvoir d'Hitler en 1933 et a fabriqué le gaz Zyklon-B utilisé dans les camps de concentration nazis. Warburg a été membre fondateur de la Carl Schurz Memorial

---

[346] Voir aussi Paul Warburg, *The Federal Reserve System, Its Origin & Growth; Reflections & Recollections* (New York : Macmillan, 1930)

Foundation, une organisation de propagande créée en 1930, directeur du prestigieux Council on Foreign Relations, Inc. et administrateur de la Brookings Institution.

Mais c'est grâce à un quasi-monopole de l'International Acceptance Bank Inc. et ses unités affiliées, que Warburg a pu amener la société à travailler pour les Warburg et leurs amis banquiers. L'historien révisionniste Murray Rothbard a examiné les origines de l'inflation des années 1920 qui a conduit à l'effondrement de 1929 et fait cette observation pertinente :

> Si l'achat de titres américains a fait l'objet d'une plus grande publicité, les billets achetés étaient au moins aussi importants et même plus importants que les rabais. Les billets achetés ont mené la parade inflationniste du crédit de la Réserve en 1921 et 1922, ont été considérablement plus importants que les titres lors de la poussée inflationniste de 1924, et tout aussi importants lors de la poussée de 1927. En outre, les billets achetés seuls ont continué à stimuler l'inflation pendant le dernier semestre de 1928, qui fut fatal.[347]

Quels étaient ces "billets achetés" que Rothbard a désigné comme le principal coupable de la dépression de 1929 ? Les billets achetés étaient des acceptations, et presque tous étaient des acceptations bancaires.

Qui a créé le marché de l'acceptation aux États-Unis, largement inconnu avant 1920 ? Paul Warburg.

Qui a gagné la part du lion dans ce commerce d'acceptation à des taux subventionnés artificiellement bas ? L'International Acceptance Bank, Inc.

Qui était l'International Acceptance Bank, Inc. Son président était Paul Warburg, avec Felix Warburg et James Paul Warburg comme co-directeurs. Cependant, un examen plus approfondi de la composition des banques (voir ci-dessous page 95) suggère qu'il s'agissait d'un véhicule représentant l'élite financière de Wall Street.

Les Warburg et leurs amis de Wall Street savaient-ils où leur politique financière allait mener ? En d'autres termes, leur politique financière des années 1920 comportait-elle des éléments de délibération ? Il existe un mémorandum de Paul Warburg qui note clairement que les banques avaient la capacité de prévenir l'inflation :

> Si le gouvernement et les banques des États-Unis étaient des automates impuissants, il faudrait sans doute que l'inflation s'en suive. Mais il est insultant pour nos banques d'avoir l'impression qu'elles ne devraient pas être capables de coopérer à un plan commun de protection tel que, par exemple, le maintien de toutes les réserves de liquidités à un niveau supérieur à celui exigé par la loi, si une telle

[347] Murray N. Rothbard, *America's Great Depression* (Los Angeles : Nash Publishing Corp. 1972), p. 117.

mesure devait effectivement devenir souhaitable pour la plus grande sécurité du pays.[348]

Par conséquent, Rothbard conclut à juste titre :

> Le rôle de premier plan de Warburg dans le système de la Réserve Fédérale n'était certainement pas sans rapport avec le fait qu'il a récolté la part du lion des bénéfices de sa politique d'acceptation.[349]

En bref, la politique de création d'acceptations à des taux artificiels subventionnés n'était pas seulement inflationniste, mais elle était le facteur le plus important, apparemment une politique bancaire délibérée, qui a conduit à l'inflation des années 1920 et à l'effondrement final en 1929, faisant ainsi apparaître le New Deal de FDR ou la planification économique nationale comme nécessaire. En outre, comme le dit Rothbard, "...l'octroi d'un privilège spécial à un petit groupe aux dépens du grand public". En d'autres termes, Wall Street a fait travailler toute la société américaine pour un oligopole financier.

Le plan révolutionnaire de Warburg pour faire travailler la société américaine pour Wall Street était étonnamment simple. Aujourd'hui encore, en 1975, les théoriciens universitaires couvrent leurs tableaux noirs d'équations dénuées de sens, et le grand public se débat dans une confusion déconcertante avec l'inflation et l'effondrement imminent du crédit, alors que l'explication assez simple du problème reste ignorée et presque entièrement incomprise. Le système de la Réserve Fédérale est un monopole privé légal de la masse monétaire qui fonctionne au profit de quelques-uns sous le couvert de la protection et de la promotion de l'intérêt public.

Révolutionnaire ? Oui, en effet ! Mais comme l'a fait remarquer l'un des biographes admiratifs de Warburg :

> Paul M. Warburg est probablement l'homme aux manières les plus douces qui ait jamais personnellement mené une révolution. C'était une révolution sans effusion de sang : il n'a pas tenté de pousser la population à prendre les armes. Il est parti armé d'une simple idée. Et il a vaincu. C'est ce qui est étonnant. Un homme timide et sensible, il a imposé son idée à une nation de cent millions de personnes.[350]

En quoi cette révolution de Warburg diffère-t-elle de la révolution socialiste ? Seulement dans le fait que sous le socialisme, une fois la révolution accomplie et le pouvoir de l'État concentré entre les bonnes mains idéologiques, les récompenses personnelles accumulées ne sont généralement pas aussi substantielles - bien que les fiefs créés par le national-socialisme d'Hitler et les

---

[348] Sénat des États-Unis, Hearings, Munitions Industry, partie 25, op. cit. p. 8103.

[349] Murray Rothbard, *America's Great Depression*, op. cit. p. 119.

[350] Harold Kellock, "Warburg, le révolutionnaire", dans *The Century Magazine*, mai 1915, p. 79.

Soviétiques modernes puissent remettre en question cette observation - et les résultats ne sont pas non plus aussi minces. La dictature monétaire des Soviétiques est évidente. La dictature monétaire du système de la Réserve Fédérale est étouffée et éludée.

Nous devrions ensuite examiner de plus près la Banque Internationale d'Acceptation, le véhicule utilisé pour cette manœuvre d'exploitation révolutionnaire, car elle fournit des signaux valables indiquant que Wall Street avait également un réel intérêt dans la planification économique nationale et un New Deal de type FDR.

THE INTERNATIONAL ACCEPTANCE BANK, INC.

La banque a été fondée en 1921 à New York et est affiliée à la Bank of the Manhattan Company de Warburg. Cependant, le conseil d'administration suggère que les éléments les plus importants de Wall Street avaient également un intérêt et un contrôle significatifs dans l'International Acceptance Bank et en ont profité. En outre, nous constatons un lien frappant entre ses institutions financières affiliées et un plan général visant à établir le socialisme d'entreprise aux États-Unis.

Comme nous l'avons noté, Paul M. Warburg était président du conseil d'administration : son frère Felix, également associé de Kuhn Loeb & Co, et son fils James P. Warburg étaient co-directeurs. Le vice-président du conseil d'administration était John Stewart Baker, également président et directeur de la Bank of Manhattan Trust Co. et International Manhattan Co. ainsi que président du comité exécutif et directeur de la Manhattan Trust Co. Baker était également directeur de l'American Trust Co. et de la New York Title and Mortgage Co. F. Abbot Goodhue a été président et directeur de l'International Acceptance Bank, membre du conseil d'administration des autres banques de Warburg, et directeur de la First National Bank of Boston. Les autres directeurs de l'International Acceptance Bank étaient Newcomb Carlton, directeur de la Chase National Bank contrôlée par Rockefeller, de la Metropolitan Life Insurance Co. contrôlée par Morgan et d'autres grandes sociétés telles que l'American Express Co., l'American Sugar Refining Co. et l'American Telegraph and Cable Co. Newcomb Carlton a également été directeur de l'American Telegraph and Cable et directeur de l'American International Corporation, une société intimement liée à la révolution bolchévique.[351] Un autre directeur de l'International Acceptance Bank qui était également directeur de l'American International Corp. était Charles A. Stone, situé au 120 Broadway et directeur de la Federal Reserve Bank de 1919 à 1932. Bronson Winthrop a également été directeur de l'American International Corp. et de l'International Acceptance Corp. Ainsi, trois directeurs de l'International Acceptance Bank ont eu des mandats d'administrateurs interdépendants avec l'American International Corp, le véhicule clé de l'implication américaine dans la révolution bolchévique.

---

[351] Voir Sutton, *Wall Street et la révolution bolchévique*, op. cit. chapitre 8.

Un autre directeur de l'International Acceptance Bank était David Franklin Houston, qui était également directeur de la Carnegie Corp, de la Guaranty Trust Co. contrôlée par Morgan, de U.S. Steel et d'A.T.&T., ainsi que président de la Mutual Life Insurance Co. Parmi les autres administrateurs de l'I.A.B., on peut citer Philip Stockton, président de la First National Bank of Boston, et administrateur d'A.T.&T., General Electric, International Power Securities, et de nombreuses autres sociétés ; William Skinner, administrateur de Irving Trust Co, Equitable Life Assurance et de l'Union Square Savings Bank ; Charles Bronson Seger, directeur de la société Aviation, de la société Guaranty Trust et de W.A. Harriman ; Otto V. Schrenk, directeur de la société Agfa Ansco, de Krupp Nirosta et de Mercedes Benz ; et Henry Tatnall, directeur de la société Girard Trust. Paul Warburg a également été directeur d'Agfa Ansco, Inc, une société détenue à 60% par I.G. Farben et une "façade" de la société aux États-Unis.

En résumé, les directeurs de l'International Acceptance Bank reflétaient les éléments les plus puissants de Wall Street : les Morgan, les Rockefeller et Harriman, ainsi que les banquiers de Boston.

De plus, Warburg a été associé aux Roosevelt pendant toute sa vie et de façon intime, de l'enfance jusqu'au New Deal. Cette association Warburg-Roosevelt est illustrée par un extrait des mémoires de James P. Warburg :

> "Il se trouve que je connaissais le fils aîné du président élu, James Roosevelt, depuis quelques années, car il vivait dans l'une des maisons de campagne de la propriété de mon oncle Felix à White Plains."[352]

Plus tard, ce même James P. Warburg devient conseiller du président Franklin D. Roosevelt pour les affaires monétaires nationales et internationales. L'intérêt profond de Warburg pour le programme de la NRA se reflète dans un mémorandum de Warburg de 1933 adressé à FDR :

> Mémorandum pour le Président : Problème de monnaie nationale. L'administration n'a, à mon avis, jamais été confrontée à une situation plus grave qu'aujourd'hui. L'ensemble du programme de redressement, qui est au cœur de sa politique, est mis en péril par l'incertitude et le doute dans le domaine monétaire. La loi sur le redressement national ne peut pas fonctionner utilement si l'on craint une dépréciation de la monnaie d'un montant inconnu et si l'on a peur de l'expérimentation monétaire. Il y a déjà eu une formidable fuite de capitaux, et cette fuite se poursuivra à un rythme croissant tant que l'incertitude régnera.[353]

Puis, suite à la propension de Warburg pour le monopole, James Warburg a recommandé à FDR que toutes les idées, actions et décisions monétaires soient centralisées dans le département du Trésor et le Conseil de la Réserve Fédérale.

---

352 James P. Warburg, *The Long Road Home: The Autobiography of a Maverick* (Garden City: Doubleday, 1964), p. 106.

353 Franklin D. Roosevelt et les affaires étrangères, vol. I, p. 325. Mémorandum de James P. Warburg à Roosevelt, 24 juillet 1933

Évidemment, cette proposition garantirait que toutes les décisions monétaires soient prises par le groupe élitiste associé à la Banque Internationale d'Acceptation et au Système de Réserve Fédérale. En juillet 1933, lorsque James Warburg écrivit son mémorandum à FDR, le secrétaire au Trésor était William H. Woodin, qui avait été directeur de la FRB de New York de 1925 à 1931. Nous pouvons également citer les propres associations de FDR avec le Système de la Réserve Fédérale. Son "oncle préféré" Frederic Delano fut nommé vice-président du conseil de la Réserve Fédérale par le président Woodrow Wilson en 1914, et de 1931 à 1936, Delano fut président du conseil d'administration de la Banque de la Réserve Fédérale de Richmond, en Virginie. FDR a nommé Delano président du National Resources Planning Board en 1934.

En 1933-34, les États-Unis ont été confrontés à la plus grande crise financière de leur histoire. Et qu'a fait FDR ? Il a fait appel, en tant que médecins financiers, aux mêmes opérateurs responsables de la crise - une politique aussi sensée que de laisser les fous gérer l'asile.

On trouve donc des associations entre Franklin D. Roosevelt, la famille Warburg et le système de banque centrale inspiré par Warburg, allant de l'enfance à la nomination de Warburg comme conseiller monétaire clé de FDR. Nous verrons plus tard que c'est Warburg qui a déterminé la forme finale de l'Administration nationale de la relance industrielle. D'autre part, la famille Warburg et ses amis de Wall Street contrôlaient la masse monétaire monopolistique privée connue sous le nom de Système de la Réserve Fédérale et, par le biais de la Banque Internationale d'Acceptation, exploitaient ce monopole à leurs propres fins.

Les Pères Fondateurs ont fait preuve d'une profonde sagesse et d'une grande perspicacité quant aux dangers d'une émission monopolistique de monnaie de papier qui se reflète dans l'article I, section 9 de la Constitution américaine :

> "Aucun État ne pourra... émettre autre chose que des pièces d'or et d'argent pour servir d'instrument de paiement de dettes...."

Une contestation constitutionnelle de l'émission des billets de la Réserve Fédérale par un monopole bancaire privé, le Système de la Réserve Fédérale, est attendue depuis longtemps. Il faut espérer que la valeur du dollar n'aura pas à être réduite à zéro, comme c'était le cas dans l'Allemagne de l'après-guerre, avant qu'une telle contestation ne soit lancée et soutenue par la Cour suprême des États-Unis.

CHAPITRE VII

ROOSEVELT, HOOVER, ET LES EFFETS DE COMMERCE

Il est rare que les gens d'un même métier se rencontrent, même pour se divertir, sans que la conversation ne se termine par une conspiration contre le grand public, ou par un stratagème pour augmenter les prix.

Adam Smith, *An Inquiry into the Nature and Causes of the Wealth of Nations* (Londres : George Routledge, 1942), p. 102.

L'idée de faire travailler la société pour un groupe privilégié au sein de cette société n'est née ni chez les socialistes d'entreprise de Wall Street, ni dans la communauté financière en général, ni même chez les socialistes marxistes. En fait, cette notion est antérieure à notre propre société industrielle, et il existe un parallèle intéressant entre les codes du New Deal America (que nous examinerons plus tard) et la législation commerciale du XIIIe siècle en Angleterre.[354]

UN NEW DEAL MÉDIÉVAL

En 1291, les tanneurs de Norwich, en Angleterre, ont été traduits devant le tribunal local chargé d'organiser et de codifier leurs activités de tannage au détriment des citoyens locaux. Deux ans plus tard, en 1293, les cordonniers et les fabricants de selles de Norwich ont été confrontés à des accusations similaires. En "graissant" les législateurs, la structure du pouvoir politique du Norwich médiéval a été amenée à penser que les tanneurs avaient peut-être besoin de protection, après tout.

Cette protection en est venue à intégrer les mêmes principes de base de la planification économique que ceux qui ont été mis en application près de 700 ans plus tard dans le Roosevelt New Deal. Ainsi, en 1307, l'industrie du tannage de Norwich a été légalement codifiée et les salaires et conditions de travail prescrits,

354 Voir Erwin F. Meyer, "English Medieval Industrial Codes" dans *The American Federationist*, janvier 1934. Meyer établit des parallèles fascinants entre les guildes médiévales et la pratique de la NRA sous Roosevelt. À l'époque médiévale, le résultat, comme dans les années 1930, a été de créer "une oligarchie de capitalistes" dans l'économie anglaise.

le tout sous le couvert de la protection du consommateur, mais en pratique en accordant un monopole légal aux tanneurs.

Dans la décennie qui a précédé le New Deal, dans les années 1920, le Wall Streeter Roosevelt a été actif au nom des entreprises pour promouvoir ces mêmes idées de base, à savoir utiliser le pouvoir de l'État pour restreindre le commerce, faire progresser la coopération et utiliser la réglementation gouvernementale pour empêcher la concurrence indésirable d'étrangers plus efficaces. Les associations commerciales des années 1920 étaient plus discrètes dans leurs propositions que les tanneurs de Norwich du XIIIe siècle, mais le principe sous-jacent était le même.

Malheureusement, le rôle de Franklin D. Roosevelt dans le Wall Street des années 1920 a été ignoré par les historiens. Daniel Fusfield observe à juste titre que FDR "a pris une part active dans le mouvement associatif qui allait devenir la N.R.A. du New Deal initial" ;[355] d'autre part, Fusfield, qui offre la seule description détaillée des activités commerciales de FDR, conclut que son attitude envers les affaires relevait d'"un curieux mélange". FDR, dit Fusfield, "insistait sur le fait que les simples profits ne justifiaient pas pleinement l'activité commerciale", qu'un homme d'affaires devait également "avoir la motivation du service public". Pour Fusfield, cela était incompatible avec la participation "à un certain nombre d'entreprises purement spéculatives et aux activités commerciales qui n'avaient pas grand-chose à voir avec le service public".[356]

Fusfield et ses collègues historiens de l'ère Roosevelt ont omis de noter que le "service public" pour un homme d'affaires est absolument cohérent avec la "maximisation du profit" ; en fait, le service public est la voie la plus facile et certainement la plus lucrative vers la maximisation du profit. En outre, plus l'entreprise est risquée et spéculative, plus l'avantage que l'on peut tirer du service public est probablement important.

Si l'on adopte cette vision plus réaliste du bien social, alors l'attitude de Roosevelt à l'égard des entreprises n'est pas du tout "curieuse". Il s'agit en fait d'un programme cohérent de maximisation des profits.

LE CONSEIL AMÉRICAIN DE LA CONSTRUCTION

L'American Construction Council (A.C.C.), créé en mai 1922, a été la première des nombreuses associations commerciales créées dans les années 1920, dispositifs utilisés pour augmenter les prix et réduire la production. La proposition initiale et l'impulsion pour le conseil sont venues du secrétaire au commerce Herbert Hoover, et le conseil a fonctionné sous la direction de Franklin D. Roosevelt, qui commençait alors sa carrière à Wall Street après avoir été secrétaire adjoint de la marine. Les objectifs publics déclarés de l'A.C.C. étaient un "code d'éthique" (un euphémisme pour restriction du commerce libre), l'efficacité et la standardisation de la production. Plus important encore, mais moins connu,

---

[355] Daniel R. Fusfield, *The Economic Thought of Franklin D. Roosevelt and the Origins of the New Deal.*

[356] Ibid.

l'A.C.C. devait donner à l'industrie la possibilité de fixer ses propres niveaux de prix et de production sans craindre des poursuites antitrust par le gouvernement. Le *New York Times* mentionnait :

> Ce sont ces énormes possibilités, dans le dévouement au service public et à l'élimination du gaspillage, qui ont enflammé l'imagination de M. Hoover et de M. Roosevelt et les ont invités à accepter des postes de direction dans le mouvement.[357]

Comme les comités de fixation des prix du conseil des industries de guerre de Baruch, l'A.C.C. était en fait une association industrielle primitive, bien que l'objectif déclaré du conseil soit très ambitieux :

> ... pour placer l'industrie de la construction sur un plan élevé d'intégrité et d'efficacité et pour corréler les efforts d'amélioration réalisés par les agences existantes par le biais d'une association dédiée à l'amélioration du service au sein de l'industrie de la construction ... .[358]

et donc de stabiliser les conditions de profit de l'industrie, des travailleurs et du grand public. Cet objectif était également celui de Baruch pour les associations commerciales en temps de paix : réglementer l'industrie sous le contrôle du gouvernement, tout ça au nom du bien public. Au sein du Conseil Américain de la Construction, le bien public a été prétexté comme l'élimination des scandales découverts par la Commission Lockwood qui enquêtait sur l'industrie du bâtiment à New York.

Cependant, comme ce scandale portait en grande partie sur l'exclusivité et les conditions coercitives similaires imposées aux entrepreneurs et aux monteurs par l'United States Steel Corporation et Bethlehem Steel, le bien public comme justification n'a guère de sens. Ces géants de l'industrie étaient contrôlés par les intérêts de Morgan à Wall Street qui étaient, comme nous le verrons, également à l'origine de la proposition de l'A.C.C. En bref, les prétendues conditions antisociales à résoudre par une association commerciale auraient pu être stoppées beaucoup plus simplement et efficacement par un mémorandum de J.P. Morgan et de ses associés ; il n'était pas nécessaire de promouvoir une association commerciale pour mettre fin à ces abus. Nous devons donc chercher ailleurs la raison d'être des associations professionnelles. La véritable raison, bien sûr, est de protéger l'industrie contre une concurrence indésirable et d'établir des conditions de monopole pour ceux qui sont déjà dans le métier. Comme Howe nous l'a dit, un monopole légal est la voie sûre vers le profit. C'est la formation de ce monopole légal qui a incité Roosevelt et Herbert Hoover à se donner la main contre l'intérêt public, bien que, selon Freidel :

---

[357] *The New York Times*, 15 mai 1922, p. 19.

[358] Cité dans Fusfield, *Economic Thought*, op. cit. p. 102.

> L'ami de FDR, Elliott Brown, l'a mis en garde contre les tendances "socialistes" de ces associations et de Hoover en particulier. Socialistes, parce que dès qu'une association se forme, le gouvernement y porte intérêt par l'intermédiaire d'un employé du ministère du commerce, qui approuve ou désapprouve de nombreuses questions touchant à l'initiative et au bien-être de tous les peuples.[359]

Le rôle de FDR n'est pas vraiment surprenant. Il tentait alors de se lancer dans une carrière commerciale. Il avait des contacts politiques et était plus que disposé, voire désireux, de les utiliser. D'autre part, il existe une étrange dichotomie dans les idées et les pratiques d'Herbert Hoover dans ce domaine de la relation entre le gouvernement et les entreprises. Herbert Hoover a déclaré son adhésion aux principes de la libre entreprise et de l'initiative individuelle et sa suspicion à l'égard de l'intervention du gouvernement. Ces affirmations étaient mélangées à d'autres déclarations contraires encourageant, voire autorisant, l'intervention du gouvernement pour des raisons presque insignifiantes. Malheureusement, les Mémoires d'Herbert Hoover, seule source faisant finalement autorité, ne résolvent pas ces conflits. Le Conseil Américain de la Construction n'est pas mentionné dans les Mémoires de Hoover, bien que le Volume II, "Le Cabinet et la Présidence", souligne les maux de l'intervention gouvernementale dans l'économie, en pointant du doigt le communisme, le socialisme et le fascisme pour commenter, "Ce remède de gauche pour tous les maux des affaires" apparaît maintenant comme "planification nationale". Hoover a ajouté que les "abus" des entreprises étaient seulement "marginaux" et qu'au lieu d'une intervention du gouvernement, "il valait mieux que le monde des affaires coopère pour remédier à ses propres abus".[360]

D'autre part, la correspondance privée de Hoover avec Roosevelt sur le Conseil Américain de la Construction suggère que Hoover, bien que favorable à l'intervention du gouvernement, a pris soin de dissimuler cet intérêt continu de peur de faire tomber l'opposition publique sur sa propre tête et de ruiner la proposition. Une lettre de Hoover à Roosevelt, datée du 12 juin 1923, fait valoir ce point :

> 12 juin 1923
> Franklin D. Roosevelt, vice-président.
> Fidelity and Deposit Company of Maryland 120 Broadway
> New York City
> Mon cher Roosevelt :
> Je suis un peu perplexe quant à votre télégramme du 7 juin. J'avais espéré que le Conseil de la Construction serait uniquement issu des industries sans pression de l'administration. Sinon, il va bientôt se heurter à la même opposition que celle que suscite immédiatement tout ce que le gouvernement touche quant à ce problème.

[359] Freidel, *The Ordeal*, op. cit. p. 152.

[360] *Les Mémoires d'Herbert Hoover*. The Cabinet and the Presidency 1920-1933, (Londres : Hollis and Carter 1952), p. 67.

> Le vaste sentiment du monde des affaires contre l'ingérence du gouvernement tend à détruire même un effort volontaire si l'on pense qu'il est mené sous l'inspiration du gouvernement.
> Je vous prie d'agréer, Monsieur le Président, l'expression de ma haute considération.
>
> Herbert Hoover

En tout état de cause, l'American Construction Council était une association coopérative d'entreprises, de travailleurs et de gouvernements,

> formé à Washington le 19 juin à la suggestion et sous la direction du secrétaire Hoover du ministère du commerce (qui) a fait les premiers pas vers la mise en œuvre d'un programme d'effort de construction qui, on l'espère, éliminera beaucoup des maux qui se sont développés dans l'industrie au cours de la dernière décennie.[361]

Ainsi, c'est l'entrepreneur libre Herbert Hoover qui est devenu le parrain de la première des associations professionnelles, l'American Construction Council, qui a été conçue pour inclure :

> les architectes, les ingénieurs, les ouvriers du bâtiment, les entrepreneurs généraux, les sous-traitants, les fabricants de matériaux et d'équipements, les marchands de matériaux et d'équipements, les intérêts en matière de cautionnement, d'assurance et d'immobilier et les services de construction des gouvernements fédéral, des États et des municipalités.[362]

La réunion d'organisation de l'American Construction Council s'est tenue chez FDR à New York et a réuni une vingtaine de personnes. Ce groupe a discuté du concept du conseil et notamment de la question de savoir s'il :

> devrait être un centre d'échange d'informations pour les différentes associations nationales, un centre d'échange d'informations professionnelles, ou si elle doit être une organisation active, agressive (sic) et militante au service du bien public de l'industrie de la construction.[363]

Il a été décidé à l'unanimité que le conseil devait être une organisation militante agressive et non pas seulement un centre d'information. Ce concept a été discuté avec Dwight Morrow de la firme J.P. Morgan ; avec M. Dick, secrétaire du juge Gary de l'U.S. Steel Corporation ; avec Gano Dunn, président de J.G. White Engineering Corporation ; et avec Stone & Webster. Il est intéressant de

---

[361] *The New York Times*, 9 juillet 1922, VIII 1:3.

[362] *The New York Times*, 15 mai 1922, p. 19, col. 8.

[363] Procès-verbal du conseil d'administration de l'American Construction Council, 20 juin 1922. Dossiers FDR, groupe 14 : Conseil américain de la construction.

noter que la plupart de ces personnes et de ces entreprises sont très présentes dans mon précédent volume, *Wall Street et la révolution bolchévique.*

Après que l'établissement financier ait exprimé son soutien à l'A.C.C., le secteur de la construction dans son ensemble a été approché pour sa réaction. Ce travail préliminaire a abouti à une réunion d'organisation à l'hôtel Washington, Washington D.C., le mardi 20 juin 1922. Franklin D. Roosevelt est élu président du conseil, et John B. Larner, vice-président de l'American Bankers Association, est élu trésorier. Le président du comité des finances était Willis H. Booth de la Guaranty Trust Company. Le comité a ensuite créé ses comités et défini les priorités de ses problèmes.

L'interprétation de Roosevelt des causes des problèmes de l'industrie de la construction a été rapportée par le *New York Times* :

> "La débrouille est la méthode caractéristique utilisée par l'industrie de la construction depuis quelques années. Il n'y a eu aucun système, aucune coopération, aucune planification nationale intensive".

Après avoir souligné qu'un cheminot n'est pas licencié pour cause de mauvais temps, Roosevelt a commenté :

> Dans le secteur de la construction, cependant, nous avons ce grand impondérable dans notre vie économique, le travail saisonnier. Tous les travaux sont concentrés pendant les mois d'été, et aucun n'est effectué pendant l'hiver. Les résultats de cet empilement sont évidents. L'été, la main-d'œuvre se fait rare et les prix montent en flèche, l'hiver, le chômage et les revenus diminuent. La seule chose qui dure toute l'année, c'est l'amertume des hommes engagés dans le travail.[364]

Comment FDR propose-t-il de changer tout cela ?

> Une grande partie du travail peut être étalée sur l'année. Il n'y a aucune raison au monde pour qu'un mécanicien qualifié vivant à New York, par exemple, soit appelé en juin pour participer à la construction d'un bâtiment public en Géorgie. La Géorgie peut construire pendant les saisons de l'année où il est impossible pour New York de construire ; il en va de même pour la Louisiane et tous les États du Sud.

La suggestion de Roosevelt, un non sequitur sans but, était que l'industrie de la construction doit "se concerter sur cette situation : déplacer les matériaux de construction pendant la basse saison et répartir la main d'œuvre". Lors d'une

---

[364] *The New York Times*, 4 juin 1922. On cherche en vain une proposition praticable et réalisable pour résoudre les prétendus problèmes de l'industrie de la construction. Les suggestions les plus valables avancées par Roosevelt et ses collègues planificateurs exigeaient de gagner du temps pour permettre la construction ou le mouvement des hommes et des matériaux tout au long de l'année par "planification". Bien sûr, un système de marché déplace automatiquement les hommes et les matériaux, un point probablement inconnu de FDR.

première réunion du conseil des gouverneurs, tenue au domicile de FDR à New York le 16 mai 1923, FDR a attiré l'attention sur la voie suivie par le conseil :

> "Le Conseil Américain de la Construction était organisé, mais franchement, il n'a pas fait une seule chose depuis cette époque à part collecter les cotisations de quelque 115 organisations différentes, je pense."

FDR a soumis le choix fondamental aux gouverneurs réunis : voulaient-ils continuer à suivre l'ancienne méthode, "Construire tout ce que nous pouvons, en payant n'importe quel prix tant que nous recevons les ordres ? Parce que si c'était le cas, a dit FDR, "Nous pourrions tout aussi bien ajourner." D'un autre côté, poursuit-il, cela ne semble pas être le point de vue de la majorité, et "Nous voulons revenir au véritable objectif fondamental du Conseil, qui était d'empêcher ce genre de choses". Suit alors une série de propositions de résolutions, adoptées à l'unanimité, qui auraient pour effet de ralentir la construction. Le Conseil continua à avoir ses problèmes, résumés dans une lettre du 29 avril 1924 du vice-président exécutif D. Knickerbocker Boyd à Franklin D. Roosevelt, "pour attirer l'attention sur l'état très grave des affaires existant à cette époque". Boyd rappelle à FDR que le secrétaire exécutif, Dwight L. Hoopingarner, a servi "pratiquement" sans salaire, et que 7000 dollars d'arriérés de salaire lui sont dus. Boyd a ajouté : "Ce n'est pas juste et cela ne devrait pas être autorisé à continuer. Il devrait non seulement être remboursé rapidement de tous les arriérés de salaire, mais aussi être assuré d'être payé rapidement à l'avenir - ou alors le travail devrait être arrêté". Ensuite, Boyd a indiqué qu'il s'attendait lui aussi à ce que le temps consacré aux travaux du conseil soit rémunéré, notant que le temps consacré à ce jour s'élevait à 3168,41 dollars, en plus des frais de déplacement. Boyd a suggéré que le conseil fasse face à ses responsabilités, se place sur une base financière adéquate ou se dissolve. Le dernier paragraphe de la lettre de Boyd démontre l'objectif fondamental de ceux qui promeuvent le Conseil Américain de la Construction :

> Si le Conseil devait disparaître, ce serait, à mon avis, une calamité nationale - car je doute qu'après ce deuxième effort de nationalisation de la grande industrie du bâtiment sur des bases humaines, on puisse trouver suffisamment de personnes ayant l'enthousiasme, la foi et la patience nécessaires pour faire une troisième tentative.

Franklin D. Roosevelt, président du Conseil Américain de la Construction, avait plaidé pour une "planification économique" ; aujourd'hui, le vice-président exécutif reconnaît un "effort de nationalisation" de l'industrie de la construction. Cet effort pour organiser l'industrie de la construction sous l'œil somnolent du gouvernement, prétendument pour le bien public, a échoué.

CHAPITRE VIII

WALL STREET ACHÈTE LE NEW DEAL

B.M. [Bernard Baruch] a joué un rôle plus efficace. Le quartier général n'avait tout simplement pas d'argent. Parfois, ils ne pouvaient même pas payer la facture de la radio pour les discours des candidats. Ils n'avaient pratiquement rien pour poursuivre la campagne dans l'État critique du Maine. Chaque fois qu'une crise survenait, B.M. donnait l'argent nécessaire ou allait le chercher.

Hugh S. Johnson, *The Blue Eagle from Egg to Earth*
(New York : Doubleday, Doran, 1935), p. 141.
Sur la campagne de FDR en 1932.

La campagne présidentielle de 1928 a opposé le gouverneur Alfred E. Smith, un catholique soutenu par Tammany Hall et collectiviste de conviction, à Herbert Hoover, un quaker qui se réclame de l'individualisme traditionnel américain et de l'autosubsistance. Herbert Hoover l'a emporté par 21 392 000 voix contre 15 016 000 pour Smith.

Où les banquiers-philosophes de Wall Street ont-ils placé leur soutien et leur influence dans l'élection de Smith-Hoover ? Sur la base de l'interprétation acceptée de la philosophie des financiers, leur soutien aurait dû aller à Herbert Hoover. Hoover a fait la promotion des associations commerciales bien-aimées, bien-aimées, c'est-à-dire par la communauté financière et commerciale. En outre, dans l'*Individualisme américain,*[365] Herbert Hoover a clairement indiqué que le système idéal pour l'Amérique était, selon ses propres termes, "pas de système de libre entreprise" mais, au contraire, une économie réglementée. D'autre part, le membre de l'establishment financier de Wall Street le plus engagé politiquement en 1928 était John J. Raskob, vice-président de Du Pont et de General Motors et administrateur de Bankers Trust Co. et de County Trust Co. Sur l'insistance personnelle du gouverneur Al Smith, Raskob est devenu président de la commission des finances du parti démocrate. Raskob a également été le plus grand donateur individuel, avec plus de 350 000 dollars à la campagne. Quels étaient les objectifs politiques recherchés par Raskob et ses alliés qui rendaient Al Smith si attrayant comme candidat ?

En 1928, John J. Raskob, Bernard Baruch et d'autres membres de Wall Street ont présenté au public les éléments clés de ce qui est devenu le programme de rétablissement national. La promotion de la NRA de Roosevelt date en fait des

[365] New York: Doubleday, page 1922.

discours de Raskob de 1928, prononcés lors de la campagne présidentielle d'Al Smith. Bien qu'Al Smith et Herbert Hoover dépendaient tous deux fortement du "cercle d'or" de Wall Street pour les fonds électoraux, comme nous le détaillerons plus loin dans ce chapitre, l'argent de Du Pont-Raskob-Baruch reposait fortement sur Al Smith.

Smith, bien sûr, a perdu l'élection de 1928 pour les Démocrates, et Herbert Hoover est devenu le président républicain. Malgré la tiédeur de Wall Street, Hoover nomme de nombreux Wall Streeters à ses comités et conseils d'administration. Puis, au milieu de l'année 1932, devant le choix brutal entre un programme de redressement national sous la forme du plan Swope ou des politiques moins fascistes, Hoover refusa d'instituer le socialisme d'entreprise, identifia le plan Swope pour ce qu'il était et fit s'abattre sur lui la colère de Wall Street.

Par conséquent, nous pouvons retracer et nous retracerons dans ce chapitre les propositions de Baruch pour l'ARN et le soutien financier des deux candidats présidentiels à chaque élection par Raskob, Baruch, Du Pont, Rockefeller, et d'autres de l'élite financière. Dans chaque cas, le principal soutien est allé au candidat démocrate désireux de promouvoir le socialisme d'entreprise. En 1928, il s'agissait d'Al Smith, qui était également directeur de la Metropolitan Life Insurance Company, contrôlée par Morgan ; en 1930, il est allé à Roosevelt avec les contributions anticipées à la convention pour le concours Hoover-Roosevelt de 1932. Au milieu de l'année 1932, Herbert Hoover se voit retirer une grande partie du soutien de Wall Street et l'influence et l'argent sont transférés en masse vers l'élection de Roosevelt.

Par la suite, FDR n'a pas abandonné ses partisans. La loi sur le redressement national (National Recovery Act), avec sa capacité intégrée à contraindre les petites entreprises, a été promulguée et est entrée en vigueur en juin 1933. Examinons donc de plus près ces événements et les preuves qui s'y rapportent.

L'INFLUENCE DE BERNARD BARUCH SUR FDR

Selon ses propres déclarations, Hugh Johnson, l'administrateur de la NRA de Roosevelt, a suivi un programme de formation dans les années 1920 sous la tutelle de Bernard Baruch. Johnson relate cette expérience comme suit :

> Je doute que quelqu'un ait eu un accès plus direct ou plus complet aux sources d'information que B.M. et il m'a toujours laissé carte blanche pour la consultation et l'utilisation des scientifiques et experts dont j'aurais pu avoir besoin. Pendant plusieurs années, j'ai été le seul membre du personnel de recherche qu'il a consulté en permanence. Cela et ce qui a précédé étaient une excellente formation pour le service dans la NRA parce que ces études couvraient un segment considérable de

> toute l'industrie américaine et que l'expérience avec le gouvernement reliait les deux.[366]

Johnson lui-même considère les discours de Raskob de septembre et octobre 1928 dans la campagne d'Al Smith comme le début de la NRA de Roosevelt :

> "Il n'y avait rien de particulièrement nouveau dans la substance des principes développés. Nous avions élaboré et exprimé exactement la même philosophie dans la campagne d'Al Smith en 1928...".[367]

Al Smith, le candidat démocrate à la présidence de 1928, était, comme nous l'avons noté, un directeur de Metropolitan Life Insurance, la plus grande compagnie d'assurance-vie des États-Unis, contrôlée par J.P. Morgan, et la majeure partie de ses fonds de campagne provenait du cercle d'or de Wall Street. Bernard Baruch a présenté le plan de la NRA lui-même le 1er mai 1930 - jour propice à une mesure socialiste - dans un discours à Boston. Tout le contenu de la NRA était là, la réglementation, les codes, l'application et la carotte du bien-être pour les travailleurs. Il a été repris dans la plate-forme de Baruch de juin 1932 - celle qu'Herbert Hoover a refusé d'adopter. La NRA a été présentée à nouveau par Baruch lors de son témoignage devant le Sénat et dans des discours devant la Brookings Institution et à l'université Johns Hopkins. En tout, Hugh Johnson compte dix documents et discours, tous présentés avant l'élection de Roosevelt en 1932, dans lesquels "se trouve le développement de la philosophie économique de la campagne de 1928 et de presque tout ce qui s'est passé depuis. D'une partie de cette philosophie, la NRA était une expression concrète".[368]

Les extraits suivants du discours de Baruch du 1er mai 1930 contiennent l'essentiel de ses propositions :

> Ce dont les entreprises ont besoin, c'est d'un forum commun où les problèmes nécessitant une coopération peuvent être examinés et traités avec la sanction constructive et non politique du gouvernement. Il était peut-être judicieux d'interdire par la loi tout ce qui visait à réglementer la production lorsque le monde craignait la famine, mais c'est de la folie publique que de décréter le fonctionnement illimité d'un système qui dégorge périodiquement des masses indigestes de produits non consommables. Aucun bureau répressif, inquisitorial et médiocre ne fera l'affaire - nous devons développer un nouveau concept à cet effet –un tribunal investi comme la Cour suprême, de tant de prestige et de dignité que nos plus grands chefs d'entreprise seront heureux de se défaire de tout intérêt personnel dans les affaires et de servir ainsi le bien commun. Commc la Cour suprême, il doit également être absolument apolitique.

---

[366] Hugh S. Johnson, *The Blue Eagle from Egg to Earth* (New York : Doubleday, Doran, 1935), p. 116.

[367] Ibid, p. 141.

[368] Ibid, p. 157.

> Il ne devrait pas avoir le pouvoir de réprimer ou de contraindre, mais il devrait avoir le pouvoir de convoquer une conférence, de suggérer et de sanctionner ou d'autoriser une coopération de bon sens entre les unités industrielles, afin d'éviter que nos bienfaits économiques ne deviennent des fardeaux insupportables. Son seul pouvoir punitif devrait être de prescrire les conditions de ses licences, puis de les révoquer en cas de violation de ces conditions.
>
> Ses délibérations doivent être ouvertes et doivent être entièrement scientifiques, présentées comme un rapport d'ingénieur et publiées dans le monde entier. Un tel système préserverait l'intérêt public et devrait se substituer aux couvertures inhibitrices des lois Sherman et Clayton...
>
> Ce n'est pas l'ingérence gouvernementale dans les affaires au sens où on l'entend ici qui est condamné. Il s'agit seulement d'un relâchement de l'emprise que le gouvernement a déjà exercée sur les entreprises par les lois antitrust. Il n'y a aucune erreur à limiter une production excessive ruineuse - une politique que le gouvernement fédéral encourage maintenant vigoureusement dans le domaine de l'agriculture. Mais si le changement de concept, qui consiste à passer d'un précédent bureaucratique à un forum ouvert où les entreprises peuvent pratiquer l'autonomie de groupe, agissant de leur propre initiative sous la sanction d'un tribunal apolitique, constructif et utile, n'a rien de pratique, alors l'idée n'est pas réalisable. Mais la possibilité d'une telle autonomie industrielle sous sanction gouvernementale a été clairement démontrée en 1918. De nombreuses difficultés se présentent. En premier lieu, tout ce qui est fait dans l'euphorie et la ferveur de la guerre ne doit être accepté comme critère qu'avec prudence.
>
> Dans la réglementation de la production, le prix n'est qu'un élément de référence. Mais c'est un sujet explosif.
>
> Il y a d'autres réserves évidentes. La réflexion est relancée en ce moment critique parce qu'elle semble digne d'être considérée comme une aide à un développement économique menaçant "d'une ampleur inhabituelle" et comme une alternative à l'ingérence gouvernementale et à la vaste extension des pouvoirs politiques dans le domaine économique - une éventualité qui, en l'absence d'une action constructive des entreprises elles-mêmes, est presque aussi certaine que la mort et les impôts.[369]

Baruch voulait, selon ses propres termes, une résurrection des associations commerciales, un assouplissement des lois antitrust et un contrôle des chefs d'entreprise. Il renvoie le lecteur au War Industries Board de 1918. Certes, Baruch suggère "pas de pouvoir de coercition" et des délibérations "ouvertes", mais de telles protestations de bonne foi ont peu de poids à la lumière de l'histoire économique et des furieux efforts passés de ce même groupe pour établir des cartels et des combinaisons de restriction du commerce. C'est dans ce but qu'un soutien financier a été accordé aux candidats démocrates et républicains ; la majeure partie du financement provenait d'une zone géographique relativement petite de New York.

[369] Ibid, p. 156-7. Italique dans l'original.

WALL STREET FINANCE LA CAMPAGNE PRÉSIDENTIELLE DE 1928

L'orientation du soutien politique peut être mesurée et identifiée par le soutien financier correspondant. Les origines des contributions financières aux campagnes de Smith et Hoover de 1928 peuvent être identifiées, et nous constatons, contrairement aux croyances dominantes, que ce sont les démocrates qui ont reçu la part du lion des fonds de Wall Street ; comme nous l'avons vu, c'est lors de la campagne démocrate que les grandes lignes de la loi sur le rétablissement national ont été promulguées pour la première fois par Baruch et Raskob.

Après l'élection présidentielle de 1928, la commission Steiwer de la Chambre des représentants des États-Unis a enquêté sur les sources des fonds de campagne reçus pour l'élection[370]. Les informations détaillées ont été publiées, mais la commission Steiwer n'a pas enquêté sur les origines et les affiliations des donateurs : elle s'est contentée d'énumérer les noms et les montants des contributions. Le tableau XIII du rapport est intitulé "Personnes ayant contribué des sommes de 5000 dollars et plus au nom du candidat républicain à la présidence". Le candidat républicain à la présidence était, bien entendu, Herbert Hoover. Ce tableau énumère les noms complets et les montants contribués, mais sans l'affiliation des contributeurs. De même, le tableau XIV du rapport est intitulé "Personnes ayant contribué des sommes de 5000$ et plus au nom du candidat démocrate à la présidence". Là encore, les noms complets et les montants sont indiqués, mais l'affiliation de la personne n'est pas précisée.

Ces listes ont été prises et comparées par l'auteur au *Directory of Directors in the City of New York 1929-1930.*[371] Lorsque le contributeur figurant sur la liste du Comité Steiwer était identifié comme ayant une adresse dans un cercle d'un mile du 120 Broadway à New York, le nom et le montant de la contribution étaient notés. Aucune mention n'était faite des personnes ne figurant pas dans l'annuaire et résidant très probablement en dehors de la ville de New York, mais un registre était tenu des sommes d'argent versées par les personnes ne résidant pas à New York. En d'autres termes, deux totaux ont été établis à partir des données du Comité Steiwer : (1) les contributions des personnes inscrites comme administrateurs de sociétés ayant leur siège à New York et (2) les contributions de toutes les autres personnes. En outre, une liste des noms des contributeurs de New York a été établie. En pratique, la procédure de recherche a été biaisée contre l'inclusion des directeurs basés à New York. Par exemple, dans la liste du parti démocrate, Van-Lear Black était inscrit par l'auteur comme un non-résident de New York, bien que Black ait été président de la Fidelity & Casualty Co ; la société

---

[370] Congrès des États-Unis, Comité spécial du Sénat chargé d'enquêter sur les dépenses de la campagne présidentielle, Dépenses de la campagne présidentielle. Rapport en vertu de la résolution 234, 25 février (jour du calendrier, 28 février), 1929. 70e Congrès, 2e session. Rapport du Sénat. 2024 (Washington : Government Printing Office, 1929). Cité ci-après comme le rapport de la commission Steiwer.

[371] New York : *Directory of Directors Co.*, 1929.

avait des bureaux au 120 Broadway, et Franklin D. Roosevelt était leur vice-président à New York au début des années 1920. Cependant, Black était basé à Baltimore et n'était donc pas considéré comme un directeur new-yorkais. Une fois de plus, Rudolph Spreckels, le millionnaire du sucre, était cité dans le rapport du Comité Steiwer pour une contribution de 15 000 dollars, mais n'est pas repris dans le total de New York, car il n'était pas basé à New York. De même, James Byrne a contribué à hauteur de 6500 dollars à la campagne de Smith for President, mais n'est pas répertorié dans le total de New York - il était directeur de la Fulton Savings Bank à Brooklyn et en dehors du cercle d'un mille. Jesse Jones, le banquier texan, a contribué à hauteur de 20 000 dollars, mais n'est pas répertorié comme un directeur new-yorkais parce qu'il était un banquier texan et non new-yorkais. En d'autres termes, la définition d'un contributeur de Wall Street a été établie de manière très stricte et cohérente.

Les principaux contributeurs de Wall Street à Al Smith
Pour la campagne présidentielle - 1928

Nom	Contributions La campagne de 1924 contre le déficit	1928	Contribution au déficit de 1928	Total
John J. Raskob (Du Pont et General Motors)	—	$110,000	$250,000	$360,000
William F. Kenny (W.A. Harriman)	$25,000	$100,000	$150,000	$275,000
Herbert H. Lehman	$10.000	$100.00	$150,000	$260,000
M.J. Meehan (120 Broadway)	—	$50,000	$100,000	$150,000

Source : Adapté de Louise Overacker, *Money in Elections* (New York : Macmillan, 1932), p. 155.

Selon cette définition restreinte, le montant total des contributions des directeurs de Wall Street, pour la plupart liés aux grandes banques, à la campagne présidentielle de 1928 d'Al Smith s'élevait à 1 864 339 dollars. Le montant total des contributions des personnes ne faisant pas partie de ce cercle d'or s'élevait à 500 531 dollars, ce qui donne un total général de 2 364 870 dollars. En bref, le pourcentage des fonds de la campagne présidentielle d'Al Smith provenant de personnes ayant donné plus de 5000 dollars et également identifiées comme étant des directeurs de Wall Street était de 78,83%. Le pourcentage de donateurs hors du cercle d'or n'était que de 21,17%. Si l'on considère le total des contributions d'Al Smith d'une autre manière, les grands donateurs (plus de 5000 dollars) à la campagne de M. Smith, ceux qui sont les mieux placés pour demander et recevoir des faveurs politiques, ont versé près de quatre dollars sur cinq.

L'identité des principaux contributeurs à la campagne Al Smith et au fonds du Comité national démocratique est indiquée dans les tableaux ci-joints.

Contributeurs de 25 000$ ou plus au Comité national démocratique de janvier à décembre 1928 (y compris les contributions énumérées dans le tableau précédent)

			NOTE
Herbert H. Lehman et Edith A. Lehman	Lehman Brothers, et Studebaker Corp.	$135,000	Le conseiller politique en chef de FDR
John J. Raskob	Vice-président de Du Pont et de General Motors	$110,000	Administrateur de l'ARN
Thomas F. Ryan	Président, Bankers Mortgage Co., Houston	$75,000	Président, Reconstruction Finance Corp.
Harry Payne Whitney	Garantie de confiance	$50,000	Voir le chapitre 10 : "L'affaire Butler".
Pierre S. Du Pont	Compagnie Du Pont, General Motors	$50,000	Voir le chapitre 10 : "L'affaire Butler".
Bernard M. Baruch	Financier, 120 Broadway	$37,590	Planificateur de l'ARN
Robert Sterling Clark	Singer Sewing Machine Co.	$35,000	Voir le chapitre 10 : "L'affaire Butler".
John D. Ryan	Banque nationale de la ville, Anaconda Copper	$27,000	—
William H. Woodin	General Motors	$25,000	Secrétaire au Trésor, 1932

Source : *Rapport de la commission Steiwer*, op. cit.

Contributions à la primaire présidentielle démocratique de 1928 par les directeurs* de la County Trust Company.

Nom du directeur	**Contribution à la campagne et au déficit**	**Autres affiliations**
Vincent Astor	$10,000	Great Northern Railway, U.S. Trust Co. Trustee, N.Y. Public Library Metropolitan Opera
Howard S. Cullman	$6,500	Vice-président, Cullman Brothers, Inc.
William J. Fitzgerald	$6,000	—
Edward J. Kelly	$6,000	—
William F. Kenny	$275,000 **	Président et directeur, William F. Kenny Co. Directeur, The Aviation Corp., Chrysler Corp.
Arthur Lehman	$14,000 ***	Associé, Lehman Brothers. Directeur, American International Corp, RKO Corp, Underwood-Elliott-Fisher Co.
M.J. Meehan	$150,000**	61 Broadway
Daniel J. Mooney	—	120 Broadway
John J. Raskob	$360,000 **	Directeur, American International Corp., Bankers Trust Co., Christiania Securities Co. Vice-président, E.I. Du Pont de Nemours & Co. et General Motors Corp.
James J. Riordan	$10,000	—

Alfred E. Smith	—	Candidat à la présidence Directeur : Metropolitan Life Insurance Co.
Total	$842,000	

Notes : *Les directeurs suivants de la County Trust Company n'ont pas contribué (selon les dossiers) : John J. Broderick, Peter J. Carey, John J. Cavanagh, William H. English, James P. Geagan, G. Le Boutillier, Ralph W. Long, John J. Pulleyn et Parry D. Saylor.
**Comprend les contributions au déficit de la campagne.
***Exclut les contributions des autres membres de la famille Lehman à la campagne présidentielle démocratique qui s'élevaient à 168 000$.

En regardant les noms dans ces tableaux, il ne serait ni méchant ni injuste de dire que le candidat démocrate a été acheté par Wall Street avant l'élection. De plus, Al Smith était un directeur de la County Trust Company, et la County Trust Company était la source d'un pourcentage extraordinairement important des fonds de campagne des démocrates.

LES FONDS ÉLECTORAUX D'HERBERT HOOVER

Lorsque nous nous penchons sur la campagne de 1928 d'Herbert Hoover, nous constatons également une dépendance à l'égard du financement de Wall Street, qui trouve son origine dans le carré d'or, mais pas dans la même mesure que dans la campagne d'Al Smith. Sur un total de 3 521 141 dollars de dons importants pour Herbert Hoover, environ 51,4% provenaient de ce carré d'or à New York et 48,6% de l'extérieur du district financier.

Contributions de 25 000$ ou plus au Comité national républicain, de janvier à décembre 1928

La famille Mellon	Banque nationale de Mellon	$50,000
La famille Rockefeller	Pétrole standard	$50,000
La famille Guggenheim	Fusion du cuivre	$75,000
Eugène Meyer	Banque de Réserve Fédérale	$25,000
William Nelson Cromwell	Avocat de Wall Street	$25,000
Otto Kahn	Equitable Trust Company	$25,000
Mortimer Schiff	Banquier	$25,000
	Total	$275,000

Source : *Rapport de la commission Steiwer*, op. cit.

Herbert Hoover a, bien sûr, été élu président ; sa relation avec la mise en place du socialisme d'entreprise a été mal interprétée par la plupart des sources universitaires et médiatiques. La plupart des ouvrages à orientation libérale soutiennent qu'Herbert Hoover était une sorte de laissez-faire néandertalien non reconstruit. Mais ce point de vue est rejeté par les propres déclarations de Hoover : par exemple :

> Ceux qui prétendent que, pendant la période de mon administration, notre système économique était un système de laissez-faire ne connaissent que très peu l'étendue de la réglementation gouvernementale. La philosophie économique du laissez-faire, ou "de la concurrence sauvage", était morte aux États-Unis quarante ans auparavant, lorsque le Congrès a adopté la Commission du commerce interétatique et les lois antitrust Sherman.[372]

Murray Rothbard souligne[373] qu'Herbert Hoover était un partisan important du Parti progressiste de Theodore Roosevelt et, selon Rothbard, Hoover "a contesté de manière néo-marxiste la vision orthodoxe du laisser-faire selon laquelle le travail est une marchandise et que les salaires doivent être régis par les lois de l'offre et de la demande".[374] En tant que secrétaire au commerce, Hoover a fait pression pour que le gouvernement cartellise les entreprises et les associations commerciales, et sa contribution "remarquable", selon Rothbard, "a été d'imposer le socialisme à l'industrie de la radio", alors que les tribunaux travaillaient sur un système raisonnable de droits de propriété privée sur les fréquences radio. Rothbard explique ces incursions dans le socialisme par le fait que Hoover "a été victime d'une maîtrise terriblement insuffisante de l'économie".[375] En effet, Rothbard soutient qu'Herbert Hoover était le véritable créateur du New Deal de Roosevelt.

Bien que les preuves présentées ici suggèrent que Baruch et Raskob avaient plus à voir avec le New Deal de FDR, l'argument de Rothbard a une certaine validité. Les politiques pratiques de Hoover n'étaient pas cohérentes. Il y a quelques actions en faveur du marché libre ; il y a beaucoup de préconisations contre le marché libre. Il semble plausible que Hoover était prêt à accepter une partie, peut-être substantielle, d'un programme socialiste, mais qu'il avait une limite précise au-delà de laquelle il n'était pas prêt à aller.

Au cours des années 1920, dans les années qui ont suivi la formation de l'American Construction Council, plus de 40 codes de pratique compilés par des associations professionnelles ont été adoptés. Lorsqu'il est devenu président, et malgré son association précoce avec l'A.C.C., Herbert Hoover a rapidement mis fin à ces codes industriels. Il a agi ainsi au motif qu'il s'agissait probablement d'associations illégales visant à contrôler les prix et la production et qu'aucun gouvernement ne pouvait les réglementer dans l'intérêt du public. Puis, en février 1931, la Chambre de commerce américaine forma un groupe intitulé "Committee on Continuity of Business and Employment" sous la direction de Henry I.

---

[372] *The Memoirs of Herbert Hoover*: The Cabinet and the Presidency 1920-1923 (Londres : Hollis and Carter, 1952), p. 300.

[373] *New Individualist Review*, hiver 1966.

[374] Ibid, p. 5.

[375] Ibid, p.10.

Harriman. Ce comité a formulé des propositions très proches de celles du New Deal : que la production soit équilibrée pour une consommation égale, que les lois antitrust Sherman soient modifiées pour permettre des accords de restriction du commerce, qu'un conseil économique national soit créé sous les auspices de la Chambre de commerce américaine, et que des dispositions soient prises pour réduire les heures de travail dans l'industrie, pour les pensions et pour l'assurance chômage. Cette proposition a été suivie par un autre comité Hoover, connu sous le nom de "Committee on Work Periods in Industry", sous la direction de P.W. Litchfield, président de la Goodyear Tire and Rubber Company. Puis un autre comité, sous la direction de Walter Teagle, président de la Standard Oil Company du New Jersey, a recommandé le partage du travail, une proposition approuvée par le comité Litchfield. Puis vint le plan Swope en 1931 (voir annexe A). Les plans ont été présentés, mais Herbert Hoover n'a pas fait grand-chose.

Ainsi, sous Herbert Hoover, les grandes entreprises étaient prolifiques dans la publication de plans visant à modifier la loi antitrust Sherman, à permettre l'autorégulation de l'industrie et à établir des codes de restriction du commerce. Le président Herbert Hoover n'a rien fait à leur sujet.

En fait, Hoover a reconnu le plan Swope comme une mesure fasciste et l'a consigné dans ses mémoires, ainsi que ses regrets que Wall Street lui a donné le choix d'adopter le plan Swope - fasciste ou non - et de faire soutenir la candidature de Roosevelt par leur argent et leur influence. C'est ainsi qu'Herbert Hoover a décrit l'ultimatum de Wall Street sous le titre "Le fascisme vient aux affaires - avec de terribles conséquences" :

> Parmi les premières mesures fascistes de Roosevelt figure la loi sur la relance de l'industrie nationale (NRA) du 16 juin 1933. Les origines de ce dispositif méritent d'être répétées. Ces idées ont été suggérées pour la première fois par Gerard Swope (de la General Electric Company) lors d'une réunion de l'industrie électrique à l'hiver 1932. Elles ont ensuite été adoptées par la Chambre de commerce des États-Unis. Au cours de la campagne de 1932, Henry I. Harriman, président de cet organisme, m'a demandé d'accepter de soutenir ces propositions, m'informant que M. Roosevelt avait accepté de le faire. J'ai essayé de lui montrer que ce truc était du pur fascisme, qu'il s'agissait simplement d'une refonte de l'"État corporatif" de Mussolini et j'ai refusé d'accepter tout cela. Il m'a informé qu'au vu de mon attitude, le monde des affaires soutiendrait Roosevelt avec de l'argent et de l'influence. Cela s'est avéré en grande partie vrai.[376]

WALL STREET SOUTIENT FDR POUR SA CANDIDATURE DE GOUVERNEUR DE NEW YORK

Le principal collecteur de fonds de la campagne de réélection de FDR en 1930 était Howard Cullman, commissaire du port de New York et directeur de la County

---

376 Herbert Hoover, *The Memoirs of Herbert Hoover*: The Great Depression 1929-1941 (New York : Macmillan, 1952), p. 420.

Trust Company. Freidel[377] dresse la liste des donateurs de la campagne de 1930, sans indication de leur appartenance à une société. Lorsque nous identifions les affiliations corporatives de ces donateurs, nous constatons une fois de plus que la County Trust Company du 97 Eighth Avenue, New York, avait un intérêt extraordinairement important dans la réélection de FDR. Outre Howard Cullman, les principaux contributeurs suivants à la campagne de FDR étaient également directeurs de la County Trust Company : Alfred Lehman, Alfred (Al) Smith, Vincent Astor et John Raskob. Un autre directeur était le vieil ami de FDR, Dan Riordan, un client de Fidelity & Deposit days au 120 Broadway, et William F. Kenny, un autre supporter de FDR et directeur de County Trust. Pour mettre cette liste en évidence, nous devons nous rappeler que Freidel liste 16 personnes comme principaux contributeurs à cette campagne, et sur ces 16, nous pouvons identifier pas moins de cinq comme directeurs du County Trust et deux autres directeurs non listés comme partisans connus de FDR. Parmi les autres personnalités de Wall Streeters qui ont financé la campagne de 1930 de FDR, citons la famille Morgenthau (avec les Lehman, les plus gros contributeurs) ; Gordon Rentschler, président de la National City Bank et directeur de la Société bancaire internationale ; Cleveland Dodge, directeur de la National City Bank et de la Bank of New York ; Caspar Whitney ; August Heckscher de l'Empire Trust Company (120 Broadway) ; Nathan S. Jones de la Manufacturers Trust Company ; William Woodin de la Remington Arms Company ; Ralph Pulitzer ; et la famille Warburg. En bref, lors de la campagne de 1930, l'essentiel du soutien financier de FDR est venu des banquiers de Wall Street.

Contributions aux dépenses pré-convention de FDR (3 500$ et plus)

Edward Flynn	$21,500	Directeur de la Bronx County Safe Deposit Co.
W.H. Woodin	$20,000	Banque de Réserve Fédérale de New York, Remington Arms Co.
Frank C. Walker	$15,000	Financier de Boston
Joseph Kennedy	$10,000	—
Lawrence A. Steinhardt	$8,500	Membre de Guggenheim, Untermeyer & Marshall, 120 Broadway
Henry Morgenthau	$8,000	Underwood-Elliott-Fisher
F.J. Matchette	$6,000	—
La famille Lehman	$6,000	Lehman Brothers, 16 William Street
Dave H. Morris	$5,000	Directeur de plusieurs entreprises de Wall Street
Sara Roosevelt	$5,000	—
Guy P. Helvering	$4,500	
H.M. Warner	$4,500	Directeur, Motion Picture Producers & Distributors of America
James W. Gerard	$3,500	Financier, 57 William Street
Total	$117,500	

[377] Freidel, *The Ordeal*, op. cit, p. 159.

Peu après la réélection de FDR en 1930, ces bailleurs de fonds ont commencé à collecter des fonds pour la campagne présidentielle de 1932. Ces contributions "précoces" avant la convention ont été décrites par Flynn : "Ces contributeurs, qui ont aidé très tôt quand le besoin était grand, ont tellement gagné la dévotion de Roosevelt que dans la plupart des cas, ils ont finalement reçu des retours substantiels dans les fonctions publiques et les honneurs".[378]

WALL STREET FAIT ÉLIRE FDR EN 1932

En 1932, Bernard Baruch a été l'opérateur clé travaillant en coulisses - et parfois pas tant que ça - pour faire élire FDR, avec l'argent et l'influence des grandes entreprises (voir l'épigraphe de ce chapitre). En outre, Bernard Baruch et Hugh Johnson ont recueilli de nombreuses statistiques et documents au cours de la décennie 1920 pour soutenir leur concept de planification économique nationale par le biais des associations professionnelles. Johnson raconte comment ces informations ont été mises à la disposition des rédacteurs de discours de FDR. Pendant la campagne Roosevelt de 1932 :

> Ray Moley et Rex Tugwell sont venus chez B.M. et nous avons passé en revue tout le matériel que B.M. et moi avions rassemblé et résumé au cours de nos années de travail. Avec Adolf Berle, ils avaient déjà élaboré depuis longtemps les sujets de ce qu'ils pensaient être un schéma idéal de discours économiques pour un candidat à la présidence, mais ils disposaient de peu de faits. À partir de ce moment, nous avons rejoint les forces de Ray Moley et nous nous sommes tous mis au travail pour trouver pour Franklin Roosevelt les idées qu'il a développées dans la très remarquable série de discours exprimés simplement sur l'économie nationale qui a convaincu ce pays qu'il était le leader sur lequel il pouvait compter.[379]

En relisant les discours de la campagne FDR, il devient évident qu'ils manquent de concret et de faits précis. L'équipe de Moley-Tugwell a sans doute exposé le thème général et Baruch et Johnson ont introduit des déclarations de soutien dans des domaines tels que l'expansion du crédit, les conséquences de la spéculation, le rôle du système de la Réserve Fédérale, etc. Il est remarquable, mais peut-être pas surprenant, que ces discours influencés par Baruch aient ramené le lecteur à la Première Guerre mondiale, aient cité l'urgence contemporaine comme étant plus grande que celle de la guerre, puis aient subtilement suggéré des solutions similaires à celles prônées par Baruch. Par exemple, lors du discours du Jefferson Day Dinner du 18 avril 1932, Roosevelt a dit, ou a été incité à dire :

> Comparez cette politique de retard et d'improvisation, frappée de panique, à celle conçue pour répondre à l'urgence de la guerre il y a quinze ans. Nous avons répondu

---

378 John T. Flynn, "Whose Child is the NRA ?" *Harper's Magazine*, septembre 1932, p. 84-5.

379 Hugh S. Johnson, *The Blue Eagle from Egg to Earth*, op. cit., p. 140-1.

> à des situations spécifiques par des mesures réfléchies, pertinentes et constructives. Il y avait le War Industries Board, la Food and Fuel Administration, le War Trade Board, le Shipping Board et bien d'autres encore.[380]

Puis, le 22 mai 1932, Roosevelt s'est penché sur le thème "Les besoins du pays, les demandes du pays, l'expérimentation persistante" et a appelé à une planification économique nationale. Ce discours a été suivi, le 2 juillet 1932, par le premier indice du New Deal.

Enfin, en acceptant la nomination à la présidence à Chicago, FDR a déclaré : "Je vous promets - je m'engage à un New Deal pour le peuple américain".

NOTE : Liste des contributeurs pré-convention de Freidel à la campagne présidentielle de Franklin Delano Roosevelt en 1932.

[381]**Contributeurs à la reconvention de 1932 (plus de 2000$)**	**Affiliations**
James W. Gerard	Gerard, Bowen & Halpin (voir Julian A. Gerard)
Guy Helvering	—
Col. E.M. House, New York	—
Joseph P. Kennedy,1560 Broadway	Ambassadeur à la Cour de St. James New England Fuel & Transportation Co.
Henry Morgenthau, Sr.	Banque de N.Y. & Trust Co. (Contrôleur adjoint)
Underwood-Elliott-Fisher 1133 Fifth Avenue	Banque d'épargne américaine (Trustee)
Dave Hennen Morris	—
Mme Sara Delano Roosevelt, Hyde Park, N.Y.	La mère de FDR
Laurence A. Steinhardt 120 Broadway	Guggenheim, Untermeyer & Marshall
Harry M. Warner 321W. 44th St.	Motion Picture Producers & Distributors of America, Inc.
William H. Woodin Secrétaire au Trésor	American, Car & Foundry ; Remington Arms Co.
Edward J. Flynn 529 Courtlandt Ave.	Bronx County Safe Deposit Co.
James A. Farley s'ajoute à cette liste :	
William A. Julian	Directeur, Central Trust Co.
Jesse I. Straus 1317 Broadway	Président, R.H. Macy & Co. N.Y. Assurance-vie
Robert W. Bingham	Éditeur, Louisville Courier-Journal
Basil O'Connor 120 Broadway	Le partenaire juridique de FDR

[380] *The Public Papers and Addresses of Franklin D. Roosevelt* ; Vol. 1, The Genesis of the New Deal, 1928-1932 (New York : Random House, 1938), p. 632.

[381] Freidel, *The Ordeal*, op. cit. p. 172.

CHAPITRE IX

FDR ET LES SOCIALISTES D'ENTREPRISE

Je pense que c'est aussi révolutionnaire que tout ce qui s'est passé dans ce pays en 1776, ou en France en 1789, ou en Italie sous Mussolini ou en Russie sous Staline.

Le sénateur Thomas P. Gore lors des auditions de la National Recovery Administration, Commission des finances du Sénat américain, 22 mai 1933.

LE PLAN SWOPE

Bien que le New Deal et sa composante la plus importante, la National Recovery Administration (NRA), soient généralement présentés comme la progéniture des éminences grises de FDR, comme nous l'avons vu, les principes essentiels avaient été élaborés en détail bien avant l'arrivée au pouvoir de FDR et de ses associés. Le groupe de réflexion derrière FDR n'a guère fait plus que donner le sceau de l'approbation académique à un plan déjà préparé.

Les racines de la NRA de Roosevelt sont d'une importance particulière. Comme nous l'avons vu au chapitre 6, en permettant de vastes changements dans la structure industrielle, la NRA s'est rapprochée d'un schéma élaboré en 1841 par l'ancêtre de FDR, l'homme d'affaires new-yorkais Clinton Roosevelt.

Nous avons ensuite noté que le dictateur Bernard Baruch préparait un programme de type NRA dans les années 1920 et que lui et son assistant Hugh Johnson faisaient partie intégrante de la planification préliminaire. En outre, la NRA de Roosevelt était dans ses détails un plan présenté par Gerard Swope (1872-1957), président de longue date de la General Electric Company.

Ce plan Swope[382] était à son tour comparable à un plan allemand élaboré pendant la Première Guerre mondiale par son homologue Walter Rathenau, chef de la société allemande General Electric (Allgemeine Elektizitäts Gesellschaft) en Allemagne, où il était connu sous le nom de Plan Rathenau. Examinons donc de plus près le plan Swope.

[382] Voir l'annexe A pour le texte complet.

LA FAMILLE SWOPE

La famille Swope était d'origine allemande. En 1857, Isaac Swope, un immigrant allemand, s'installe à St. Louis comme fabricant de boîtes de montres. Deux des fils de Swope, Herbert Bayard Swope et Gerard Swope, ont ensuite atteint l'apogée de l'entreprise américaine. Herbert Bayard Swope a été longtemps rédacteur en chef du *New York World*, un passionné de courses, un ami proche de Bernard Baruch, et utilisé par FDR comme envoyé non officiel pendant la période du New Deal. Le frère d'Herbert, Gérard, a fait carrière à la General Electric Company. Swope a commencé comme aide à l'usine en 1893, est devenu représentant commercial en 1899, directeur du bureau de St. Louis en 1901, et directeur de la Western Electric Company en 1913. Pendant la Première Guerre mondiale, Swope a été directeur adjoint des achats, du stockage et du trafic au sein du gouvernement fédéral sous le général George W. Goethals et a planifié le programme d'approvisionnement de l'armée américaine. En 1919, Swope est devenu le premier président de l'International General Electric Company. Le succès de la promotion des affaires étrangères de G.E. l'a amené à la présidence de G.E. en 1922 pour succéder à Edwin Rice, Jr. Swope est resté président de G.E. de 1922 à 1939.

General Electric était une société contrôlée par Morgan et avait toujours un ou deux partenaires de Morgan dans son conseil d'administration, tandis que Swope était également directeur d'autres entreprises de Wall Street, notamment International Power Securities Co. et la National City Bank.

Le développement politique de Gérard Swope a commencé dans les années 1890. Le biographe David Loth rapporte que, peu après son arrivée à Chicago, Swope a été présenté aux socialistes Jane Addams, Ellen Gates Starr, et à leur colonie de Hull House. Cet intérêt pour les affaires sociales s'est développé pour culminer avec le plan Swope de 1931 pour la stabilisation de l'industrie, dont 90 pour cent consistait en un plan pour l'indemnisation des travailleurs, l'assurance vie et invalidité, les pensions de vieillesse et la protection contre le chômage. Le plan Swope est un document extraordinaire. Un court paragraphe supprime toute l'industrie des lois antitrust - un objectif industriel de longue date - tandis que de nombreux longs paragraphes détaillent les plans sociaux proposés. En résumé, le plan Swope était un dispositif transparent destiné à jeter les bases de l'État corporatif en désamorçant l'opposition ouvrière potentielle avec une carotte sociale massive.

Le plan Swope et la proposition antérieure et similaire de Bernard Baruch sont devenus la loi Roosevelt sur la relance nationale. Les origines de la NRA à Wall Street ne sont pas passées inaperçues lorsque la loi a été débattue par le Congrès. En témoigne par exemple l'indignation, mais pas tout à fait exacte, du sénateur Huey P. Long :

> Je viens ici maintenant et je me plains. Je me plains au nom du peuple de mon pays, de l'État souverain que je représente. Je me plains au nom du peuple, où qu'il soit connu. Je me plains s'il est vrai, comme me l'ont dit les sénateurs ici présents, qu'en vertu de cette loi, M. Johnson, un ancien employé de M. Baruch, a été chargé de

> l'application de la loi et a déjà appelé comme assistants le directeur de la Standard Oil Co., le directeur de General Motors et le directeur de la General Electric Co.
> Je me plains si M. Peek, qui est un employé de M. Baruch, ou a été, comme on me l'a dit au Sénat, chargé d'appliquer la loi agricole, aussi bon soit-il et quelles que soient ses idées.
> Je me plains si M. Brown, qui, me dit-on dans l'enceinte du Sénat, a été fait un manipulateur influent du bureau du directeur du budget, a été un employé de M. Baruch, et se voit maintenant attribuer cette autorité. Je me plains parce que, le 12 mai 1932, avant que nous nous rendions à Chicago pour nommer un président des États-Unis, je me suis levé ici même, à cet étage, et j'ai dit aux habitants de ce pays que nous n'allions pas avoir l'influence de M. Baruch, à l'époque si puissant avec Hoover, qui manipulait le parti démocrate avant la nomination, après la nomination ou après l'élection.[383]

Huey Long a eu raison de souligner la domination de Wall Street sur la NRA, mais ses identifications sont un peu hasardeuses. Hugh Johnson, associé de longue date de Bernard Baruch, a en effet été nommé à la tête de la NRA. En outre, les principaux assistants de Johnson au sein de la NRA étaient trois chefs d'entreprise : Walter C. Teagle, président de Standard Oil du New Jersey ; Gerard Swope, président de General Electric et auteur du plan Swope ; et Louis Kirstein, vice-président de William Filene's Sons of Boston. Comme nous l'avons vu, Filene était un partisan de longue date du socialisme d'entreprise. Le "chef de General Motors" cité par le sénateur Long était Alfred P. Sloan, sans lien avec la NRA, mais le vice-président de G.M., John Raskob, qui a été le grand collecteur de fonds en 1928 et 1932 et l'opérateur en coulisses qui a promu l'élection de Franklin D. Roosevelt en 1932. En d'autres termes, les postes clés de la NRA et de l'administration Roosevelt elle-même étaient occupés par des hommes de Wall Street. L'explication des relations publiques pour les hommes d'affaires devenus bureaucrates est que les hommes d'affaires ont l'expérience et devraient s'impliquer dans le service public. En pratique, l'intention a été de contrôler l'industrie. Cela ne devrait cependant pas nous surprendre si les socialistes d'entreprise se rendent à Washington D.C. après l'élection de leurs fils préférés pour prendre les rênes de l'administration des monopoles. Il faudrait être naïf pour penser qu'il en serait autrement après les investissements électoraux massifs enregistrés au chapitre 8.

Avant l'inauguration du président Roosevelt en mars 1933, un "brain trust" a été mis en place de manière plus ou moins informelle pour élaborer des plans économiques pour l'ère Roosevelt. Ce groupe comprenait le général Hugh Johnson, Bernard Baruch (voir précédemment pour ses contributions politiques), Alexander Sachs de Lehman Brothers (voir plus loin pour ses contributions politiques), Rexford G. Tugwell et Raymond Moley. Ce petit groupe, trois de Wall Street et deux universitaires, a généré la planification économique de Roosevelt.

Ce lien entre Bernard Baruch et la planification de la NRA a été consigné par Charles Roos dans son volume définitif sur la NRA :

[383] Sénateur Huey P. Long, procès-verbal du Congrès, 8 juin 1933, p. 5250.

> Au début du mois de mars 1933, Johnson et Baruch se lancèrent dans un voyage de chasse et s'arrêtèrent en route à Washington. Moley a dîné avec eux et a proposé que Johnson reste à Washington pour élaborer un plan de relance industrielle... . L'idée séduit Baruch, qui accorde rapidement à Johnson un congé de ses fonctions habituelles. Puis Johnson et Moley, après avoir étudié les différentes propositions jugées valables par ce dernier, entreprirent de rédiger un projet de loi qui organiserait l'industrie pour contrer les effets de la dépression.[384]

Selon M. Roos, le premier projet de la NRA de Johnson était rédigé sur deux feuilles de papier brouillon et prévoyait simplement la suspension des lois antitrust, ainsi qu'un pouvoir presque illimité pour le président Roosevelt de faire presque tout ce qu'il souhaitait avec l'économie, y compris l'octroi de licences et le contrôle de l'industrie. Selon Roos, "cette proposition a bien sûr été rejetée par l'administration, car elle aurait fait du président un dictateur, et un tel pouvoir n'était pas souhaitable".

Ce rejet apparemment accidentel du pouvoir dictatorial non désiré par l'administration Roosevelt peut avoir une certaine importance. Au chapitre 10, nous décrirons l'affaire Butler, une tentative des mêmes intérêts de Wall Street pour installer Roosevelt en tant que dictateur ou le remplacer par une figure de proue plus souple en cas d'objection de sa part. Les premières tentatives de Johnson visaient à mettre en place l'ARN sous une forme compatible avec Roosevelt en tant que dictateur économique, et son rejet par Roosevelt est conforme aux graves accusations portées aux pieds de Wall Street (p. 141). À ce stade de la planification, selon Roos, Johnson et Moley ont été rejoints par Tugwell et plus tard par Donald R. Richberg, un avocat du droit du travail de Chicago. Tous trois ont entrepris de rédiger un projet de loi plus "complet", quoi que cela signifie.

Le général Hugh Johnson, a été nommé à la tête de l'Administration nationale de redressement créée sous le nom de N.I.R.A. et a cru pendant un certain temps qu'il allait également diriger l'Administration des travaux publics. Les plans et schémas élaborés par le général Johnson et Alexander Sachs de Lehman Brothers supposaient que le chef de la NRA dirigerait également le programme de travaux publics.

Par conséquent, c'est dans ce petit groupe de Wall Street que l'on peut trouver les racines du projet de loi de la NRA et de l'administration des travaux publics. Leur effort reflète à la fois les plans de Swope et de Baruch pour le socialisme d'entreprise, avec une première tentative d'organiser une dictature commerciale étatique aux États-Unis.

LES PLANIFICATEURS SOCIALISTES DES ANNÉES 1930

Bien sûr, il y avait beaucoup d'autres plans au début des années 1930 ; en effet, la planification économique était endémique parmi les universitaires, les politiciens et les hommes d'affaires de cette époque. Le poids de l'opinion

[384] Charles F. Ross, *NRA Economic Planning* (Indianapolis: The Principia Press 1937), p. 37.

informée considérait la planification économique comme essentielle pour sortir l'Amérique de la dépression. Ceux qui doutaient de l'efficacité et de la sagesse de la planification économique étaient peu nombreux. Malheureusement, au début des années 1930, aucune expérience empirique n'existait pour démontrer que la planification économique est inefficace, qu'elle crée plus de problèmes qu'elle n'en résout et qu'elle entraîne une perte de liberté individuelle. Certes, Ludwig von Mises avait écrit *Socialisme* et fait des prédictions précises sur le chaos de la planification, mais von Mises était un théoricien économique inconnu à l'époque. Il existe un attrait mystique pour la planification économique. Ses partisans se visualisent toujours implicitement comme des planificateurs, et la psychologie anticapitaliste, si bien décrite par von Mises, est la pression psychologique qui s'exerce en coulisse pour que le plan se réalise. Même aujourd'hui, en 1975, bien après que la planification économique ait été totalement discréditée, nous avons toujours le chant des sirènes de la prospérité par la planification. J. Kenneth Galbraith en est un exemple éloquent, sans doute parce que l'estimation personnelle que Galbraith fait de ses capacités et de sa sagesse est plus grande que celle de l'Amérique en général. Galbraith reconnaît que la planification offre un moyen d'exercer pleinement ses capacités supposées. Le reste d'entre nous doit être contraint à participer au plan par le pouvoir de police de l'État : une négation des principes libéraux peut-être, mais la logique n'a jamais été un point fort chez les théoriciens économiques.

En tout cas, dans les années 1930, la planification économique avait beaucoup plus de partisans enthousiastes et beaucoup moins de critiques qu'aujourd'hui. Presque tout le monde était un Galbraith, et le contenu de base des plans proposés était sensiblement similaire au sien. Le tableau ci-dessous énumère les plans les plus importants et leurs caractéristiques les plus remarquables. L'industrie, toujours soucieuse de trouver un abri contre la concurrence dans le pouvoir étatique, proposa elle-même trois plans. Le plus important de ces plans industriels, le plan Swope, présentait des caractéristiques obligatoires pour toutes les entreprises de plus de 50 salariés, combinant une réglementation continue avec, comme nous l'avons noté, des propositions d'aide sociale extraordinairement coûteuses. Le plan Swope est reproduit dans son intégralité à l'annexe A ; le texte intégral reflète l'absence de propositions administratives bien pensées et la prépondérance de caractéristiques sociales irresponsables. Les premiers paragraphes du plan donnent l'essentiel des propositions de Swope : des associations professionnelles, contrôlées par l'État et dont le pouvoir d'exécution est concentré dans les mains des grandes entreprises par le biais d'un système de votes industriels. Alors que 90% du texte de la proposition est consacré aux pensions de retraite des travailleurs, à l'assurance chômage, à l'assurance vie, etc. En bref, le plan Swope était une carotte pour obtenir ce que Wall Street souhaitait si ardemment : des associations commerciales monopolistiques ayant la capacité d'utiliser le pouvoir de l'État pour faire appliquer dans la pratique la maxime de Frederic Howe "faire travailler la société pour vous".

Plans de stabilisation économique : 1933

Nom du plan	Proposition pour l'industrie	Réglementation gouvernementale	Propositions en matière d'aide sociale
Plan Swope (General Electric)	Plans pour l'industrie Associations professionnelles, adhésion obligatoire après trois ans pour les entreprises de 50 salariés ou plus. Décisions obligatoires	Réglementation continue par la Federal Trade Commission	Assurance vie et invalidité, pensions et assurance chômage
Plan de la Chambre de commerce américaine	Conseil économique national ; pouvoir non obligatoire	Pas de réglementation	Plans individuels des sociétés ; planification des travaux publics
Plan des entrepreneurs généraux associés d'Amérique	Octroi par le Congrès d'un pouvoir accru au Conseil de la Réserve Fédérale. Autorisation d'émettre des obligations pour le fonds renouvelable de la construction ; obligation pour l'augmentation de la construction publique et semi-publique. La Réserve Fédérale doit garantir la solvabilité des banques	Réglementation financière. L'octroi de licences aux entrepreneurs. Création de bureaux de crédit à la construction	Stimulation de l'emploi par une plus grande activité dans le bâtiment et la construction. Obligations d'État pour les bâtiments publics ; développement de la banque de prêts au logement
	Plans de travail		
Plan de la Fédération américaine du travail	Conseil économique national ; pouvoir non obligatoire	Pas de réglementation	Répartition des emplois ; maintien des salaires ; garantie des emplois ; plans de stabilisation à long terme. Semaine de cinq jours et jour plus court immédiatement. Programme de construction publique
	Académique et général		
Plan Stuart Chase	Conseil de la renaissance des industries de guerre utilisant un pouvoir coercitif et obligatoire, limité à 20 ou 30 industries de base	Réglementation continue	Bureaux nationaux de l'emploi ; réduction des heures de travail ; assurance chômage ; augmentation des salaires ; répartition de la main-d'œuvre

Plan national de la fédération civique	"Business Congress" des organisations industrielles. Aucune limitation ou restriction ; pouvoir complet de fixer les prix ou de combiner	Réglementation continue	Régime d'assurance-chômage. Augmenter les salaires
Plan Barbe	Conseil économique national", autorisé par le Congrès, pour coordonner les finances, l'exploitation, la distribution et les entreprises de service public. Chaque secteur est régi par des syndicats subsidiaires	Réglementation continue	Utilisation des chômeurs dans les programmes de logement et les projets publics

Le plan de la Chambre de commerce américaine était similaire au plan Swope, mais n'exigeait qu'une conformité volontaire au code et ne contenait pas les clauses sociales étendues du plan Swope. Le plan de la Chambre de commerce était également basé sur une conformité volontaire, et non sur la réglementation gouvernementale coercitive inhérente à la proposition Swope.

Le troisième plan industriel a été proposé par l'Associated General Contractors of America. Le plan de l'AGC proposait d'accorder des pouvoirs plus importants au système de la Réserve Fédérale pour garantir les obligations des banques pour la construction publique et, sans surprise, la création de bureaux de crédit spéciaux pour la construction financés par l'État, couplées à l'octroi de licences aux entrepreneurs. En bref, l'AGC voulait éviter la concurrence et utiliser les fonds fédéraux (des contribuables) pour promouvoir l'industrie de la construction.

Le plan de la Fédération américaine du travail proposait un Conseil économique national pour diffuser et garantir l'emploi, et entreprendre une planification économique pour la stabilisation. Les syndicats n'ont pas fait pression pour une réglementation gouvernementale.

Les plans universitaires étaient remarquables dans le sens où ils soutenaient les objectifs de l'industrie. Stuart Chase, un socialiste bien connu, proposa quelque chose de très proche des plans de Wall Street : en effet, une reprise du War Industries Board de 1918 de Bernard Baruch, avec un pouvoir coercitif accordé à l'industrie, mais limité à 20 ou 30 industries de base, avec une réglementation continue. Le plan Chase était une approximation du fascisme italien. Le plan Beard proposait également des syndicats sur le modèle italien, avec une réglementation continue et l'utilisation des chômeurs dans les programmes publics inspirés de Marx et de son "Manifeste Communiste". La Fédération civique nationale a défendu le concept de planification totale : le pouvoir total et complet de fixer les prix et les combinaisons, avec une réglementation de l'État et des dispositifs de protection sociale pour apaiser les revendications de la main-d'œuvre.

Presque personne, sauf bien sûr Ludwig von Mises, n'a pointé du doigt les racines du problème pour tirer la conclusion logique de l'histoire économique que la meilleure planification économique n'est pas la planification économique.[385]

LES SOCIALISTES SALUENT LE PLAN SWOPE

Les socialistes orthodoxes ont accueilli le plan de Swope avec une retenue curieuse, bien que peut-être compréhensible. D'une part, ont déclaré les socialistes, Swope avait reconnu les maux du capitalisme sauvage. D'autre part, le système Swope, se plaignaient les socialistes, laisserait le contrôle de l'industrie dans les mains de l'industrie elle-même plutôt qu'à l'État. Comme l'a expliqué Norman Thomas :

> Le plan de régulation de M. Swope est un plan probablement inconstitutionnel visant à mettre le pouvoir du gouvernement à la disposition de puissants syndicats capitalistes qui chercheront à contrôler le gouvernement qui les réglemente et, à défaut, le combattront.[386]

La critique socialiste du plan Swope de General Electric ne s'est pas penchée sur la question de savoir si le système Swope fonctionnerait ou aurait une efficacité opérationnelle, ni sur la façon dont il se proposait de fonctionner ; la critique socialiste orthodoxe s'est limitée à l'observation que le contrôle serait entre de mauvaises mains si l'industrie prenait le relais et non entre les bonnes mains des planificateurs du gouvernement, c'est-à-dire les socialistes eux-mêmes. En résumé, le conflit portait sur la question de savoir qui allait contrôler l'économie : M. Gérard Swope ou M. Norman Thomas.

Par conséquent, la critique de Thomas à l'égard de Swope présente une curieuse dualité, parfois louable :

> Il est certainement significatif qu'au moins un de nos authentiques capitaines d'industrie, un des véritables dirigeants de l'Amérique, ait surmonté la réticence profonde et déconcertée des puissants à aller au-delà des platitudes les plus tristes en nous disant comment réparer les effets de la dépression qu'ils ont tant fait pour causer et si peu pour éviter. De toute évidence, le discours de M. Swope avait ses bons côtés...[387]

D'autres fois, Thomas est sceptique et souligne que Swope "... ne fait plus confiance à l'initiative individuelle, à la concurrence et au fonctionnement

---

[385] Si le lecteur souhaite poursuivre l'explication de cette incapacité omniprésente à voir l'évidence, il ne pourrait pas commencer par un meilleur auteur que Ludwig von Mises, *The Anti-Capitalistic Mentality* (New York ; Van Nostrand, 1956).

[386] "A Socialist Looks at the Swope Plan", *The Nation*, 7 octobre 1931, p. 358.

[387] Ibid, p. 357.

automatique des marchés", mais propose d'orienter le système au profit de "la classe des actionnaires".

Rien ne prouve que Gerard Swope et ses associés aient jamais fait confiance à l'initiative individuelle, à la concurrence et aux marchés libres, pas plus que Norman Thomas. C'est une observation importante, car, une fois que nous abandonnons les mythes de tous les capitalistes en tant qu'entrepreneurs et de tous les planificateurs libéraux en tant que sauveurs de l'homme moyen, nous les voyons tous deux pour ce qu'ils sont : des totalitaires et des opposants à la liberté individuelle. La seule différence entre eux est de savoir qui doit être le dictateur.

LES TROIS MOUSQUETAIRES DE LA NRA

L'Administration Nationale de Redressement, le segment le plus important du New Deal, a ensuite été conçue, construite et promue par Wall Street. La NRA est essentiellement née avec Bernard Baruch et son assistant de longue date, le général Johnson. Dans le détail, la NRA était le Plan Swope, et ses principes généraux ont été promus au fil des ans par de nombreux Wall Streeters éminents.

Il y avait bien sûr des variantes de planification provenant des planificateurs d'influence socialiste et marxiste, mais ces variantes n'étaient pas les versions qui sont finalement devenues la NRA. La NRA était essentiellement fasciste dans la mesure où l'industrie, et non les planificateurs de l'État central, avait le pouvoir de planifier, et ces planificateurs industriels venaient de l'establishment financier de New York. Le bureau de Bernard Baruch se trouvait au 120 Broadway ; les bureaux de Franklin D. Roosevelt (les bureaux new-yorkais de Fidelity & Deposit et les cabinets d'avocats de Roosevelt & O'Connor) se trouvaient également au 120 Broadway. Le bureau de Gerard Swope et les bureaux exécutifs de la General Electric Company se trouvaient à la même adresse. Nous pouvons donc dire, dans un sens limité, que le Roosevelt NRA est né au 120 Broadway, à New York.

Le général Hugh Johnson avait trois assistants principaux à la NRA, et "ces trois mousquetaires ont été en service plus longtemps et ils entraient et sortaient de mon bureau dès qu'ils découvraient quelque chose qui nécessitait de l'attention".[388] Les trois assistants étaient des Wall Streeters des grandes industries qui occupaient eux-mêmes des postes importants dans les grandes entreprises de ces industries : Gerard Swope, président de General Electric, Walter C. Teagle, de Standard Oil du New Jersey, et Louis Kirstein de William Filene's Sons, les commerçants de détail. Grâce à ce trio, un élément dominant des grandes entreprises était aux commandes au plus fort de la NRA. Cette concentration de contrôle explique les milliers de plaintes d'oppression de la NRA qui sont venues d'hommes d'affaires moyens et petits.

Qui étaient ces hommes ? Comme nous l'avons noté, Gerard Swope de General Electric avait été l'assistant du général Johnson au sein du War Industries Board de la Première Guerre mondiale. Alors que la NRA était en discussion, Johnson "suggéra immédiatement son nom au secrétaire Roper". En 1930, General Electric

[388] Hugh S. Johnson, *The Blue Eagle from Egg to Earth*, op. cit. p. 217.

était le plus grand des fabricants de matériel électrique, Westinghouse détenant de nombreux brevets de base dans ce domaine, ainsi qu'une grande participation dans RCA et de nombreuses filiales et sociétés affiliées internationales. À la fin des années 1920, G.E. et Westinghouse produisaient environ les trois quarts des équipements de base pour la distribution et la production d'énergie électrique aux États-Unis. General Electric était cependant l'entreprise dominante dans l'industrie des équipements électriques.[389] Dans le cadre de la NRA, la National Electrical Manufacturers Association (NEMA) a été désignée comme l'agence chargée de superviser et d'administrer le code de l'industrie électrique. La NEMA a agi rapidement et, en juillet 1933, a présenté le deuxième code de "concurrence loyale" à la signature du président.

Le deuxième mousquetaire de Johnson était Walter Teagle, président du conseil d'administration de la Standard Oil du New Jersey. Standard of New Jersey était la plus grande compagnie pétrolière intégrée des États-Unis, et seule la Royal Dutch l'a défiée dans les ventes internationales. La Standard du New Jersey était contrôlée par la famille Rockefeller, dont les avoirs au début des années 1930 ont été estimés entre 20 et 25 pour cent.[390] On pourrait donc dire que Teagle représentait les intérêts des Rockefeller dans la NRA, tandis que Swope représentait les intérêts de Morgan. Il est intéressant de noter au passage que le plus grand concurrent de Standard était Gulf Oil, contrôlé par les intérêts de Mellon, et qu'il y a eu des efforts persistants au début de l'administration Roosevelt pour poursuivre Mellon pour évasion fiscale.

Le troisième des trois mousquetaires de Johnson à la NRA était Louis Kirstein, vice-président de Filene's of Boston. Edward Filene est connu pour ses livres sur les avantages des associations commerciales, la concurrence loyale et la coopération (voir page 81 ci-dessous).

Le sommet de la Roosevelt National Recovery Administration était composé du président de la plus grande société électrique, du président de la plus grande compagnie pétrolière et du représentant du plus important spéculateur financier des États-Unis.

En bref, l'administration de la NRA était le reflet de l'établissement financier de New York et de ses intérêts pécuniaires. En outre, comme nous l'avons vu, puisque le plan lui-même est né à Wall Street, la présence d'hommes d'affaires dans l'administration de la NRA ne peut s'expliquer sur la base de leur expérience et de leur capacité administrative. L'ARN était une créature de Wall Street mise en œuvre par l'élite de Wall Street.

L'OPPRESSION DES PETITES ENTREPRISES

Les partisans de la loi nationale sur la relance industrielle ont montré de façon éclatante que l'ARN protégerait les petites entreprises qui, selon eux, avaient

---

[389] Pour plus d'informations, voir Harry W. Laidler, *Concentration of Control in American Industry* (New York : Crowell, 1931), chapitre XV.

[390] Ibid, p. 20.

souffert dans le passé de l'application inéquitable des lois antitrust ; la suspension des lois antitrust supprimerait leurs caractéristiques les plus indésirables, tandis que l'ARN préserverait leurs dispositions antimonopole bienvenues. Le sénateur Wagner a déclaré que l'ensemble de l'industrie formulerait les codes industriels proposés, et pas seulement les grandes entreprises. Le sénateur Borah, au contraire, a soutenu que le "monopole" était sur le point de recevoir un service qu'il convoitait depuis plus de 25 ans, c'est-à-dire "la mort des lois antitrust" et que les codes industriels de l'ARN "vont être des combinaisons ou des contrats restreignant le commerce, et qu'il ne serait pas nécessaire de suspendre les lois antitrust". Le sénateur Borah a également accusé le sénateur Wagner de trahir l'homme d'affaires légitime au bénéfice de Wall Street :

> Le vieux Rockefeller n'avait pas besoin de droit pénal pour l'aider à s'enrichir. Il a détruit les indépendants partout, il les a dispersés aux quatre vents, il a concentré son grand pouvoir. Mais le sénateur ne donnait pas seulement aux moissonneuses-batteuses tout le pouvoir de rédiger leur code, mais il leur donnait aussi le pouvoir d'accuser et de poursuivre l'homme qui violait le code, même s'il poursuivait une entreprise parfaitement légitime.
> Monsieur le Président, je me fiche de savoir combien nous renforçons, combien nous construisons, combien nous renforçons la loi antitrust ; je m'oppose à une suspension à quelque titre que ce soit, parce que je sais que lorsque ces lois sont suspendues, nous donnons à ces 200 sociétés non bancaires, qui contrôlent la richesse des États-Unis, une puissance prodigieuse, qui ne peut jamais être contrôlée autrement que par les lois pénales appliquées par les tribunaux.[391]

Le sénateur Borah a ensuite cité Adam Smith à cet effet, en soulignant qu'aucune définition de la concurrence loyale ne figurait dans le projet de loi et que les codes de concurrence loyale dégénéreraient en diktats des grandes entreprises. De même, le sénateur Gore a évoqué la possibilité que le président puisse exiger que tous les membres d'une industrie soient titulaires d'une licence et que cela signifie que le président puisse révoquer une licence à son gré, ce qui constitue une violation évidente de la loi et des droits de propriété fondamentaux :

> **SÉNATEUR GORE**. Le Président pourrait-il révoquer cette licence à plaisir ?
> **SÉNATEUR WAGNER**. Oui, pour une violation du code imposée par le gouvernement fédéral.
> **SÉNATEUR GORE**. Sur quel type d'audience ?
> **SÉNATEUR WAGNER**. Après une audition. Il est prévu qu'une audience peut être tenue, avant qu'une licence ne puisse être révoquée.
> **SÉNATEUR GORE**. C'est quelque chose qui affecte réellement la vie et la mort d'une industrie ou d'une entreprise particulière, s'il a le pouvoir de révoquer la licence.
> **SÉNATEUR WAGNER**. Oui, c'est une sanction.
> **SÉNATEUR GORE**. Ce que je voulais vous demander Sénateur, c'est ceci : Pensez-vous que vous pourriez confier ce pouvoir à un cadre supérieur ?
> **SÉNATEUR WAGNER**. Je le fais, en cas d'urgence.

---

[391] Compte rendu du Congrès, 1933, p. 5165.

SÉNATEUR GORE. Pour exterminer une industrie ?
SÉNATEUR WAGNER. Tous ces pouvoirs, bien sûr, sont logés chez un seul individu, et nous devons nous en remettre à lui pour les administrer de manière juste et équitable. Nous avions le même type de pouvoir pendant la guerre.
SÉNATEUR GORE. Je le sais, et M. Hoover, si je peux utiliser ces mots, ce dispositif met les citoyens américains nés libres en faillite sans procès devant un jury.
SÉNATEUR WAGNER. La philosophie de ce projet de loi est d'encourager l'action et l'initiative volontaires de la part de l'industrie, et je doute que ces méthodes obligatoires soient utilisées du tout, sauf en de très rares occasions ; mais si vous voulez relever la norme, vous devez disposer de certaines sanctions afin de faire respecter le code qui pourrait être adopté.
SÉNATEUR GORE. Je comprends, mais si vous voulez mettre en place ce système, vous devez avoir le pouvoir de le faire. Ce que je veux dire, c'est pourquoi, dans un pays libre, un homme libre devrait être obligé de prendre une licence pour s'engager dans une industrie légitime, et pourquoi, dans notre système constitutionnel, quelqu'un devrait avoir le pouvoir de détruire la valeur de ses biens, ce que vous faites lorsque vous créez une situation où il ne peut pas opérer. Il me semble que l'on s'approche du point où l'on s'empare des biens sans procédure légale.[392]

Lorsque nous examinons les résultats de la N.R.A., même quelques mois après l'adoption du projet de loi, nous constatons que ces craintes sénatoriales étaient pleinement justifiées et que le président Roosevelt avait abandonné le petit entrepreneur des États-Unis au contrôle de Wall Street. De nombreuses industries étaient dominées par quelques grandes entreprises, elles-mêmes sous le contrôle des sociétés d'investissement de Wall Street. Ces grandes entreprises ont dominé, par l'intermédiaire des trois mousquetaires, l'établissement des codes de la NRA. Elles avaient le plus de voix et pouvaient fixer des prix et des conditions ruineux pour les petites entreprises.

L'industrie sidérurgique est un bon exemple de la manière dont les grandes entreprises ont dominé le code de la NRA. Dans les années 1930, deux grandes entreprises, United States Steel, avec 39%, et Bethlehem Steel, avec 13,6%, contrôlaient plus de la moitié de la capacité de production de lingots d'acier du pays. Le conseil d'administration de U.S. Steel comprenait J.P. Morgan et Thomas W. Lamont, ainsi que le président Myron C. Taylor. Le conseil d'administration de Bethléem comprenait Percy A. Rockefeller et Grayson M-P. Murphy de Guaranty Trust, que nous retrouverons au chapitre 10.

En 1930, les plus grands actionnaires de U.S. Steel étaient George F. Baker et George F. Baker, Jr, avec des actions combinées de 2000 actions privilégiées et 107 000 actions ordinaires ; Myron C. Taylor, chef du Comité des finances de U.S. Steel, possédait 27 800 actions ordinaires ; J. P. Morgan détenait 1261 actions ; et James A. Farrell avait le titre de propriété de 4850 actions privilégiées. Ces hommes étaient également d'importants contributeurs à la campagne

[392] Sénat des États-Unis, National Industrial Recovery, Audiences devant la commission des finances, 73e Congrès, 1ère session, S.17et H.R. 5755 (Washington : Government Printing Office, 1933), p. 5.

présidentielle. Par exemple, lors de la campagne de Hoover en 1928, ils ont contribué

J.P. Morgan.................................... $5000
J.P. Morgan Company................... $42 500
George F. Baker............................. $27 000
George F. Baker Jr......................... $20 000
Myron C. Taylor............................ $25 000

Au sein de la NRA, nous constatons que U.S. Steel et Bethlehem Steel contrôlaient effectivement l'ensemble de l'industrie en vertu de leurs votes dans les codes industriels ; sur un total de 1428 votes, ces deux entreprises à elles seules ont obtenu un total de 671 votes, soit 47,2%, dangereusement proche du contrôle absolu et avec une capacité incontestable à trouver un allié parmi les entreprises plus petites mais toujours importantes.

La force du vote des ARN dans le code de l'industrie sidérurgique

Société[393]	**Votes au sein de l'autorité du code**	**Pourcentage du total**
Acier américain	511	36.0
Acier de Bethléem	160	11.2
République Acier	86	6.0
Acier national	81	5.7
Jones et Laughlin	79	5.5
Youngstown Sheet & Tube	74	5.1
Acier pour roues	73	5.1
Laminoir américain	69	4.8
Acier intérieur	51	3.6
Acier en creuset	38	2.7
Fer blanc McKeesport	27	1.9
Allegheny Steel	21	1.5
Spang-Chalfant	17	1.2
Sharon Steel Hoop	16	1.1
Continental Steel	16	1.1

393 En outre, les petites entreprises suivantes ont eu des voix : Acme Steel (9), Granite City Steel (8), Babcock and Wilcox (8), Alan Wood (7), Washburn Wire (7), Interlake Iron (7), Follansbee Bros. (6), Ludlum Steel (6), Superior Steel (6), Bliss and Laughlin (6), Laclede Steel (5), Apollo Steel (5), Atlantic Steel (4), Central Iron and Steel (4), A.M. Byers Company (4), Sloss-Sheffield (4), Woodward Iron (3), Firth-Sterling (2), Davison Coke and Iron (2), Soullin Steel (1), Harrisburg Pipe (1), Eastern Rolling Mill (1), Michigan Steel Tube (1), Milton Manufacturing Company (1) et Cranberry Furnace (1).

Source : Rapport de l'ARN sur le fonctionnement du système de points de base dans l'industrie sidérurgique.

Bien que U.S. Steel et Bethléem aient été les principales unités de l'industrie sidérurgique avant l'adoption de la NRA, elles n'ont pas été en mesure de contrôler la concurrence de nombreuses entreprises plus petites. Après l'adoption de la NIRA, ces deux entreprises ont pu, grâce à leur domination du système des codes, dominer également l'industrie sidérurgique.

John D. Rockefeller a organisé le trust Standard Oil en 1882 mais, à la suite d'ordonnances du tribunal en vertu de la loi Sherman, le cartel a été dissous en 33 sociétés indépendantes. En 1933, ces sociétés étaient encore contrôlées par les intérêts de la famille Rockefeller ; la loi Sherman était plus une ombre qu'une substance :

Société	**Revenu net (1930) en millions$.**
Standard Oil du New Jersey	57
Standard Oil of Indiana	46
Standard Oil of California	46
Standard Oil de New York	16

Les bureaux des sociétés "indépendantes" de Standard continuent à être situés au siège de Rockefeller, à cette époque aux 25 et 26 Broadway. Au cours des années 1920, de nouveaux capitaux sont entrés et l'importance des différentes sociétés de Standard Oil a relativement changé.

Au moment du New Deal, la plus grande unité était la Standard Oil du New Jersey, dans laquelle les Rockefeller détenaient une participation de 20 à 25%. Le président de la Standard du New Jersey, Walter S. Teagle, est devenu l'un des trois mousquetaires de la NRA.

Lorsque nous examinons l'industrie automobile en 1930, nous constatons que deux sociétés, Ford et General Motors, ont vendu environ trois quarts des voitures produites aux États-Unis. Si l'on inclut Chrysler, les trois sociétés ont vendu environ cinq sixièmes de toutes les automobiles produites aux États-Unis :

Ford Motor Co.................................... 40 pour cent
General Motors.................................. 35 pour cent
Chrysler Corp..................................... 8 pour cent

Sous la direction de son fondateur, Henry Ford, la Ford Motor Company n'avait guère d'utilité pour la politique, bien que James Couzens, l'un des premiers actionnaires de Ford, soit devenu plus tard sénateur du Michigan. Ford maintint ses bureaux exécutifs à Dearborn, Michigan, et seulement un bureau de vente à New York. Ford était également farouchement anti-NRA et anti-Wall Street, et

Henry Ford se distingue par son absence des listes de contributeurs aux campagnes présidentielles.

D'autre part, General Motors était une créature de Wall Street. La société était contrôlée par la firme J.P. Morgan ; le président du conseil d'administration était Pierre S. Du Pont, de la Du Pont Company, qui en 1933 détenait environ 25% des parts de General Motors. En 1930, le conseil d'administration de General Motors était composé de Junius S. Morgan, Jr. et George Whitney de la firme Morgan, des directeurs de la First National Bank et du Bankers Trust, de sept directeurs de Du Pont et d'Owen D. Young de General Electric.

Un autre exemple est l'International Harvester Company, en 1930 sous la direction de son président Alexander Legge, le géant de l'industrie des équipements agricoles. Legge faisait partie de la NRA. L'association des équipements agricoles a été créée en 1920 par la J.P. Morgan Company et contrôlait environ 85% de la production totale de machines de récolte aux États-Unis. En 1930, la société était encore dominante dans l'industrie :

Société	**Actifs**	**Pourcentage du marché**
International Harvester (11 Broadway)	384 millions de dollars (1929)	60
Deere & Co.	$107	17
Affaire J.I.	$55	8
Autres	$100	15
Total	646 millions de dollars	100

En 1930, au moins 80 grandes entreprises exploitaient le charbon bitumineux aux États-Unis ; parmi elles, deux - Pittsburgh Coal et Consolidation Coal - étaient dominantes. Pittsburgh Coal était sous le contrôle de la famille bancaire de Pittsburgh, les Mellon. Consolidation Coal était en grande partie détenue par J.D. Rockefeller, qui possédait 72% des actions privilégiées et 28% des actions ordinaires. Les Mellon et les Rockefeller sont tous deux de gros contributeurs politiques. De même, la production d'anthracite était concentrée dans les mains de la Reading Railroad, qui exploitait 44% de la houille américaine. Reading était contrôlée par la Baltimore and Ohio Railroad, qui détenait 66% de ses actions, et le président de B&O était E.T. Stotesbury, un associé de la firme Morgan.

Lorsque nous examinons les entreprises de construction de machines aux États-Unis en 1930, nous constatons que la plus grande était de loin General Electric - et le président Swope de G.E. était intimement lié à la NRA.

Grandes entreprises de construction mécanique (1929)

Entreprise	**Actifs en millions**	**Bénéfices (1929) en millions**	**Ventes (1929) en millions**
General Electric, 120 Broadway	$500	$71	$415.3
Radiateur américain & Standard Sanitary, 40 W. 40th St.	$226	$20	
Westinghouse Electric, 150	$225	$27	$216.3

Broadway			
Locomotive Baldwin, 120 Broadway	$100	$3	$40
American Locomotive, 30 Church St.	$106	$7	
American Car & Foundry, 30 Church St.	$120	$2.7	
International Business Machines, 50 Broadway	$40	$6.7	
Ascenseur Otis, 260 11e avenue	$57	$8	
Société Crane	$116	$11.5	

En parcourant la liste, nous constatons qu'American, Car & Foundry (dont le président, Woodin, est devenu secrétaire au Trésor sous Roosevelt), American Radiator & Standard et Crane Company ont tous contribué de manière importante à la carrière politique de FDR.

Compte tenu de cette influence dominante des grandes entreprises au sein de l'ARN et de l'administration Roosevelt, il n'est pas surprenant que l'ARN ait été administrée de manière oppressive pour les petites entreprises. Même pendant la brève existence de l'ARN, jusqu'à ce qu'elle soit déclarée inconstitutionnelle, nous trouvons des preuves d'oppression : voyez les plaintes des petites entreprises dans les secteurs dont nous avons parlé, par rapport à d'autres secteurs dans les petites entreprises ayant beaucoup plus d'unités :

Industrie	**Nombre de plaintes pour oppression (janvier-avril 1934)**
Grande industrie	
Fer et acier	66
Banque d'investissement	47
Pétrole	60
Fabrication électrique	9
Petites entreprises	
Nettoyage et teinture	31
Ice	12
Impression	22
Botte et chaussures	10
Blanchisserie	9

Source : Roos, *NRA Economic Planning*, p. 411, à partir de données non publiées de la NRA.

CHAPITRE X

FDR, LE CHEVALIER BLANC

Dans les dernières semaines de sa vie officielle, le comité a reçu des preuves montrant que certaines personnes avaient tenté d'établir une organisation fasciste dans ce pays. Il ne fait aucun doute que ces tentatives ont été discutées, ont été planifiées et auraient pu être mises à exécution quand et si les bailleurs de fonds le jugeaient opportun....
Cette commission a reçu le témoignage du général Smedley D. Butler (retraité), deux fois décoré par le Congrès des États-Unis ... votre commission a pu vérifier toutes les déclarations pertinentes faites par le général Butler....
John W. McCormack, président de la commission spéciale sur les activités anti-américaines, Chambre des Représentants, 15 février 1935.

Dès Noël 1934, la nouvelle d'un étrange complot visant à installer un dictateur à la Maison Blanche fait surface à Washington et à New York, et l'histoire - d'une importance sans précédent - est rapidement étouffée par le Congrès et la presse de l'establishment.[394]

Le 21 novembre 1934, le *New York Times* a publié la première partie de l'histoire de Butler telle qu'elle a été racontée à la commission des activités anti-américaines de la Chambre des représentants, en lui donnant un traitement de première page et un paragraphe principal intrigant :

[394] Voir Jules Archer, *The Plot to Seize the White House* (New York : Hawthorn Books, 1973) Le livre d'Archer est "le premier effort pour raconter toute l'histoire de l'intrigue dans l'ordre et avec tous les détails". Voir également George Wolfskill, *The Revolt of the Conservatives* (Boston : Houghton, Mifflin, 1962), qui contient de nombreux éléments sur l'intrigue. Le lecteur intéressé devrait également jeter un coup d'œil à George Seldes, *One Thousand Americans* (New York : Honi & Gaer, 1947).
Malheureusement, bien que ces livres aient maintenu la mémoire de l'événement - un effort courageux qui ne doit en aucun cas être sous-estimé - ils reflètent une confusion du fascisme avec la modération. Les partisans de la Constitution rejetteraient bien entendu absolument les efforts dictatoriaux décrits. Certains groupes, comme l'Union conservatrice américaine par exemple, ont depuis une décennie dirigé leurs attaques sur les cibles identifiées par Archer et Seldes. La mauvaise interprétation de ces derniers auteurs est accentuée par le fait que la confusion sur le sens du conservatisme a également empêché ces auteurs d'explorer la possibilité que Wall Street n'ait eu à l'esprit que Franklin Delano Roosevelt comme "l'homme au cheval blanc".

> Un complot des intérêts de Wall Street pour renverser le président Roosevelt et établir une dictature fasciste, soutenu par une armée privée de 500 000 ex-soldats et autres, a été mis en accusation par le major général Smedley D. Butler, officier retraité du corps des Marines...

Le rapport du *New York Times* ajoute que le général Butler "... a dit à ses amis que le général Hugh S. Johnson, ancien administrateur de la NRA, était prévu pour le rôle de dictateur, et que J.P. Morgan & Co. ainsi que Murphy & Co. étaient derrière le complot."

Après cette ouverture prometteuse, le reportage du *New York Times* s'est progressivement effacé pour finalement disparaître. Heureusement, suffisamment d'informations ont fait surface depuis pour démontrer que l'affaire Butler ou le complot pour s'emparer de la Maison-Blanche fait partie intégrante de notre histoire de FDR et de Wall Street.

GRAYSON M-P. MURPHY COMPANY, AU 52 BROADWAY

La figure centrale de l'intrigue était le major général Smedley Darlington Butler, un officier du corps des Marines haut en couleur, populaire et très connu, deux fois décoré de la médaille d'honneur du Congrès et vétéran de 33 ans de service militaire. Le général Butler a témoigné en 1934 devant le Comité McCormack-Dickstein qui enquêtait sur les activités nazies et communistes aux États-Unis qu'un plan pour une dictature de la Maison Blanche lui avait été exposé par deux membres de la Légion américaine : Gerald C. MacGuire, qui travaillait pour Grayson M-P. Murphy & Co, 52 Broadway, New York City, et Bill Doyle, que Butler a identifié comme un officier de la Légion américaine. Le général Butler a déclaré que ces hommes voulaient "déloger la famille royale du contrôle de la Légion américaine lors de la convention qui devait se tenir à Chicago, et [étaient] très désireux de me voir y participer". Un plan a été présenté au général Butler : il devait se présenter à la convention en tant que délégué de la légion d'Honolulu ; il y aurait deux ou trois cents membres de la légion américaine dans le public ; et "ces hommes disséminés devaient commencer à applaudir et à demander un discours, puis je devais me rendre sur la plate-forme et prononcer un discours."

Le discours préparé devait être rédigé par John W. Davis, associé de Morgan. Pour prouver son soutien financier à Wall Street, MacGuire montra au général Butler un livre de banque énumérant des dépôts de 42 000 et 64 000 dollars et mentionna que leur source était le député Grayson. Murphy, directeur de la Guaranty Trust Company et d'autres sociétés contrôlées par Morgan. Un banquier millionnaire, Robert S. Clark, dont les bureaux se trouvent dans le bâtiment de la Bourse au 11 Wall Street, est également impliqué.

Robert Clark était d'ailleurs connu du général Butler depuis sa campagne en Chine. MacGuire et Doyle ont également offert à Butler une somme substantielle pour qu'il fasse un discours similaire devant la convention des vétérans des guerres étrangères à Miami Beach. Selon MacGuire, son groupe avait enquêté sur les antécédents de Mussolini et du fascisme italien, sur l'organisation de Hitler en

Allemagne et sur la Croix de Feu en France et avait laissé entendre qu'il était temps d'établir une organisation similaire aux États-Unis. Le général Butler a témoigné devant la commission du Congrès au sujet de la déclaration de MacGuire en ces termes

> Il a dit : "Le temps est venu maintenant de rassembler les soldats."
> "Oui", ai-je dit, "je le pense aussi". Il m'a répondu : "Je suis parti à l'étranger pour étudier le rôle que joue le vétéran dans les différentes structures des gouvernements étrangers. Je suis allé en Italie pendant 2 ou 3 mois et j'ai étudié la position qu'occupent les vétérans d'Italie dans la structure gouvernementale fasciste, et j'ai découvert qu'ils sont le soutien d'arrière-plan de Mussolini. Ils les maintiennent sur les listes de paie de diverses manières et les gardent heureux et satisfaits ; et ils sont sa véritable colonne vertébrale, la force sur laquelle il peut compter, en cas de problème, pour le soutenir. Mais ce dispositif ne nous conviendrait pas du tout. Les soldats américains n'aimeraient pas cela. Je suis donc allé en Allemagne pour voir ce que faisait Hitler, et toute sa force réside aussi dans les organisations militaires. Mais cela n'aurait pas été possible. Je me suis penché sur les affaires russes. J'ai découvert que l'utilisation des soldats là-bas ne plairait pas à nos hommes. Alors je suis allé en France, et j'ai trouvé exactement l'organisation que nous allons avoir. C'est une organisation de super soldats." Il m'a donné le nom français de cette organisation, mais je ne me souviens pas de ce que c'est. Je n'aurais jamais pu le prononcer, de toute façon. Mais je sais que c'est une super organisation de membres de toutes les autres organisations de soldats de France, composée de sous-officiers et d'officiers. Il m'a dit qu'ils étaient environ 500 000 et que chacun d'eux était à la tête de 10 autres, ce qui leur donnait 5 000 000 de voix. Et il a dit : "Maintenant, c'est notre idée, ici en Amérique, de mettre sur pied une organisation de ce genre."[395]

Quel serait l'objectif de cette super organisation ? Selon le *New York Times*[396], le général Butler aurait déclaré que l'affaire était une tentative de *coup d'État*[397] pour renverser le président Roosevelt et le remplacer par un dictateur fasciste. Cette interprétation est reprise par Archer, Seldes et d'autres écrivains. Cependant, ce n'est pas l'accusation que le général Butler a faite à la commission. La déclaration précise de Butler concernant l'organisation projetée, l'usage qui en sera fait une fois établie et le rôle du président Roosevelt est la suivante ; le général Butler a fait un rapport sur sa conversation avec MacGuire :

> J'ai dit : "Que voulez-vous en faire quand vous le porterez au pouvoir ?"
> "Eh bien", a-t-il dit, "nous voulons soutenir le président".
> J'ai dit : "Le président n'a pas besoin du soutien de ce genre d'organisation. Depuis quand êtes-vous devenu un partisan du Président ? La dernière fois que je vous ai parlé, vous étiez contre lui."

---

[395] Chambre des représentants, Enquête sur les activités de propagande nazie et enquête sur certaines autres activités de propagande, Audiences n° 73-D.C.-6, op. cit. p. 17.

[396] *The New York Times*, 21 novembre 1934.

[397] En français dans le texte, NdT.

Il a dit : "Eh bien, il va nous accompagner maintenant."
"Est-ce qu'il l'est ?
"Oui."
"Eh bien, qu'allez-vous faire de ces hommes, supposez que vous ayez ces 500 000 hommes en Amérique ? Qu'allez-vous faire d'eux ?"
"Eh bien", a-t-il dit, "ils seront le soutien du président".
J'ai dit : "Le président a obtenu l'ensemble du peuple américain. Pourquoi les veut-il ?"
Il a dit : "Ne comprenez-vous pas qu'il faut changer un peu la configuration ? Maintenant, nous l'avons, nous avons le Président. Il doit avoir plus d'argent. Il n'y a plus d'argent à lui donner. Quatre-vingt pour cent de l'argent est maintenant sous forme d'obligations d'État, et il ne peut pas continuer à faire ce racket plus longtemps. Il doit faire quelque chose pour y remédier. Soit il doit nous soutirer plus d'argent, soit il doit changer la méthode de financement du gouvernement, et nous allons veiller à ce qu'il ne change pas cette méthode. Il ne la changera pas".
J'ai dit : "L'idée de ce grand groupe de soldats est donc de l'effrayer, n'est-ce pas ?
"Non, non, non ; pas pour l'effrayer. C'est pour le soutenir quand les autres l'agressent."
J'ai dit : "Eh bien, je n'en sais rien. Comment le président l'expliquerait-il ?"
Il a dit : "Il n'aura pas nécessairement à l'expliquer, car nous allons l'aider. Maintenant, vous est-il venu à l'esprit que le Président est surchargé de travail ? Nous pourrions avoir un président adjoint, quelqu'un à blâmer ; et si les choses ne marchent pas, il peut le laisser tomber".
Il a poursuivi en disant qu'il n'était pas nécessaire de modifier la Constitution pour autoriser un autre membre du cabinet, quelqu'un à prendre en charge les détails du bureau - les retirer des épaules du président. Il a mentionné que le poste serait un secrétaire aux affaires générales - une sorte de super-secrétaire.
PRÉSIDENT [Membre du Congrès McCormack]. Un secrétaire aux affaires générales ?
BUTLER. C'est le terme qu'il a utilisé - ou qu'un secrétaire d'État providence - je ne me souviens plus lequel. Je suis sorti de l'entretien avec ce nom en tête. J'ai eu cette idée en parlant avec les deux, vous voyez. Ils avaient tous les deux parlé du même type de soulagement qui devrait être accordé au président, et il a dit "Vous savez, le peuple américain va avaler ça. Nous avons les journaux. Nous allons lancer une campagne sur le fait que la santé du président est défaillante. Tout le monde peut le dire en le regardant, et les Américains stupides tomberont dans le panneau en une seconde".
Et je pouvais le voir. Ils avaient ce racket de sympathie, qu'ils allaient avoir quelqu'un qui lui enlèverait le patronage de ses épaules et qui lui enlèverait tous les soucis et les détails, et alors il sera comme le président de la France.
J'ai dit : "C'est donc de là que vous tenez cette idée ?"
Il a dit : "J'ai voyagé en regardant autour de moi. Maintenant, à propos de cette super organisation, seriez-vous intéressé à la diriger ?"
J'ai dit : "Cela m'intéresse, mais je ne sais pas si je vais la diriger. Elle m'intéresse beaucoup, parce que vous savez. Jerry, mon intérêt est, mon seul hobby est, de maintenir une démocratie. Si vous obtenez ces 500 000 soldats qui prônent quelque chose qui sent le fascisme, je vais en obtenir 500 000 de plus et vous botter le cul, et nous aurons une véritable guerre chez nous. Vous le savez."
"Oh, non. Nous ne voulons pas cela. Nous voulons que le président soit moins exigeant."
"Oui ; et ensuite vous y mettrez quelqu'un que vous pourrez diriger ; c'est ça l'idée ? Le Président fera le tour des lieux pour baptiser les bébés, inaugurer des

> ponts et embrasser les enfants. M. Roosevelt ne sera jamais d'accord avec cela lui-même."
> "Oh oui, il le fera. Il sera d'accord avec cela."[398]

En d'autres termes, le complot de Wall Street ne visait pas du tout à se débarrasser du président Roosevelt, mais à le mettre à la porte et à installer un président adjoint doté de pouvoirs absolus. La raison pour laquelle il a fallu se donner la peine d'installer un président adjoint n'est pas claire, car le vice-président était en fonction. En tout état de cause, il était prévu de diriger les États-Unis avec un secrétaire aux affaires générales, ce que le public américain crédule accepterait sous le couvert de la protection nécessaire contre une prise de pouvoir communiste.

À ce stade, il est intéressant de rappeler le rôle de ces mêmes financiers et sociétés financières dans la révolution bolchévique - un rôle, soit dit en passant, que le général Butler n'aurait pas pu connaître[399] - et l'utilisation de tactiques de peur similaires de la part des Rouges dans l'organisation des États-Unis de 1922. Grayson M-P. Murphy était, au début des années 1930, administrateur de plusieurs sociétés contrôlées par les intérêts de J.P. Morgan, dont la Guaranty Trust Company, bien connue dans la révolution bolchévique, la New York Trust Company et Bethlehem Steel, et faisait partie du conseil d'administration de l'Inspiration Copper Company, de la National Aviation Corporation, de l'Intercontinental Rubber Co. et des U.S. & Foreign Securities. John W. Davis, le rédacteur de discours du général Butler, était associé dans Davis, Polk, Wardwell, Gardner & Reed du 15 Broad Street. Polk et Wardwell de ce prestigieux cabinet d'avocats, ainsi que Grayson Murphy, ont tous deux joué un rôle dans la révolution bolchévique. En outre, Davis a également été co-directeur avec Murphy dans la société Guaranty Trust contrôlée par Morgan et co-directeur avec l'espoir présidentiel Al Smith dans la société Metropolitan Life Insurance Co. ainsi que directeur de la société Mutual Life Insurance Co., de la société U.S. Rubber Co. et de American Telephone and Telegraph, l'unité de contrôle du système Bell.

Heureusement pour l'histoire. Le général Butler a discuté de l'offre avec une source journalistique impartiale au tout début de ses entretiens avec MacGuire et Doyle. La commission McCormack-Dickstein a entendu le témoignage sous serment de ce confident, Paul Comley French. French a confirmé qu'il était reporter pour le *Philadelphia Record* et le *New York Evening Post et* que le général Butler lui avait parlé du complot en septembre 1934. Par la suite, le 13 septembre 1934, French se rendit à New York et rencontra MacGuire. Ce qui suit fait partie de la déclaration de French au Comité :

> MR. FRENCH. [J'ai vu] Gerald P. MacGuire dans les bureaux de Grayson M.-P. Murphy & Co, au douzième étage du 52 Broadway, peu après 13 heures. Il y a un

398 Chambre des représentants, Investigation of Nazi Propaganda Activities and Investigation of Certain Other Propaganda Activities, Hearings No. 73-D.C.-6, op. cit., pp. 17-18.

399 Voir Sutton, *Wall Street et la révolution bolchévique*, op. cit.

petit bureau privé et je suis allé dans son bureau. J'ai ici quelques citations directes de sa part. Dès que j'ai quitté son bureau, je me suis approché d'une machine à écrire et j'ai noté tout ce qu'il m'a dit. "Nous avons besoin d'un gouvernement fasciste dans ce pays", a-t-il insisté, "pour sauver la nation des communistes qui veulent la démolir et détruire tout ce que nous avons construit en Amérique. Les seuls hommes qui ont le patriotisme pour le faire sont les soldats et Smedley Butler est le leader idéal. Il pourrait mobiliser un million d'hommes en une nuit". Au cours de la conversation, il m'a dit qu'il avait été en Italie et en Allemagne pendant l'été 1934 et le printemps 1934 et qu'il avait fait une étude approfondie du contexte des mouvements nazi et fasciste et de la façon dont les vétérans y avaient joué un rôle. Il disait avoir obtenu suffisamment d'informations sur les mouvements fascistes et nazis et sur le rôle joué par les vétérans, pour en créer un dans ce pays.

Il a souligné tout au long de sa conversation avec moi que tout cela était extrêmement patriotique, que c'était sauver la nation des communistes, et que les hommes avec lesquels ils traitent ont cette idée folle que les communistes vont la démanteler. Il a dit que la seule sauvegarde serait les soldats. Au début, il a suggéré que le général organise lui-même cette tenue et demande à tout le monde de verser un dollar par an de cotisation. Nous en avons discuté, puis il est arrivé au point d'obtenir des fonds extérieurs, et il a dit que ce ne serait pas un problème de réunir un million de dollars.

Au cours de la conversation, il n'a cessé de parler du besoin d'un chevalier blanc, comme il l'appelait, un dictateur qui viendrait au galop sur son cheval blanc. Il disait que c'était la seule façon de sauver le système capitaliste, soit par la menace de la force armée, soit par la délégation du pouvoir et l'utilisation d'un groupe de vétérans organisés.

Il s'est considérablement échauffé après notre départ et il a dit : "Nous pourrions suivre Roosevelt, puis faire avec lui ce que Mussolini a fait avec le roi d'Italie". Cela correspond à ce qu'il a dit au général [Butler], que nous aurions un secrétaire aux affaires générales, et que si Roosevelt jouait le jeu, il serait génial ; et que s'il ne le faisait pas, ils le pousseraient dehors.[400]

ACKSON MARTINDELL, 14 WALL STREET

Le témoignage sous serment du général Smedley Butler et de Paul French lors des auditions de la commission a un fil conducteur. Le général Butler a divagué de temps en temps, et certaines parties de sa déclaration sont vagues, mais il est évident que l'histoire ne se résume pas à un rassemblement innocent de membres de la légion américaine au sein d'une super organisation. Y a-t-il des preuves indépendantes qui confirment la thèse du général Butler et de Paul French ? À l'insu de Butler et de French, Guaranty Trust avait été impliqué dans les manœuvres de Wall Street lors de la révolution bolchévique de 1917, ce qui indique au moins une prédisposition à mélanger affaires financières et politique dictatoriale ; deux des personnes impliquées dans le complot étaient des directeurs de Guaranty Trust. En outre, avant que les audiences ne soient brusquement interrompues, la commission a entendu le témoignage d'une source indépendante,

[400] Chambre des représentants, Enquête sur les activités de propagande nazie et enquête sur certaines autres activités de propagande, Audiences n° 73-D.C.-6, op. cit. p. 26.

qui a confirmé de nombreux détails relatés par le général Butler et Paul French. En décembre 1934, le capitaine Samuel Glazier, commandant du camp du CCC à Elkridge, dans le Maryland,[401]est convoqué devant la commission.

Le 2 octobre 1934, témoigne le capitaine Glazier, il avait reçu une lettre d'A.P. Sullivan, Adjudant général adjoint de l'armée américaine, présentant un certain M. Jackson Martindell, "qui se montrera très courtois avec vous". Cette lettre avait été envoyée à Glazier par le commandement du major général Malone de l'armée américaine. Qui était Jackson Martindell ? Il était conseiller financier et travaillait au 14 Wall Street, auparavant associé à Stone & Webster & Blodget, Inc, banquiers d'affaires du 120 Broadway, et à Carter, Martindell & Co, banquiers d'affaires du 115 Broadway.[402] Martindell était un homme de substance, vivant, selon le *New York Times*, "... au centre d'un magnifique domaine de soixante acres" qu'il avait acheté à Charles Pfizer[403], et était suffisamment influent pour que le général Malone organise une visite guidée du camp du Corps de conservation d'Elkridge, dans le Maryland.

L'association de Martindell avec Stone & Webster (120 Broadway) est importante et justifie à elle seule un suivi de ses associés dans la région de Wall Street.

Le capitaine Glazier a fourni à Martindell la visite du camp demandée et a témoigné devant le comité que Martindell a posé de nombreuses questions sur un camp similaire destiné aux hommes travaillant dans l'industrie plutôt que dans les forêts. Une semaine environ après la visite. Le capitaine Glazier a visité la maison de Martindell dans le New Jersey, a appris qu'il était un ami personnel du général Malone et a été informé que Martindell voulait organiser des camps similaires au CCC pour former 500 000 jeunes hommes. Selon Glazier, cette conversation avait une connotation antisémite et suggérait une tentative de coup d'État aux États-Unis. L'organisation qui parrainait ce renversement s'appelait American Vigilantes, dont l'emblème était un drapeau avec un aigle rouge sur fond bleu à la place de la croix gammée allemande. Il s'agissait en partie d'une vérification indépendante du témoignage du général Butler.

LE TÉMOIGNAGE DE GERALD C. MACGUIRE

Gerald MacGuire, l'un des comploteurs accusés, a été appelé devant la commission et a longuement témoigné sous serment. Il a déclaré qu'il avait rencontré le général Butler en 1933 et que les raisons de sa visite à Butler étaient (1) de discuter du Comité pour un dollar sain et (2) qu'il pensait que Butler serait "un homme bien pour être commandant de la Légion".

---

401 Ibid, parties 1 et 2. Basé sur le témoignage devant la commission McCormack-Dickstein.

402 120 Broadway fait l'objet d'un chapitre dans ce livre et dans un livre précédent, Sutton, *Wall Street et la révolution bolchévique*, op. cit.

403 *The New York Times*, 28 décembre 1934.

MacGuire a admis avoir dit au général Butler qu'il était membre du comité des invités de marque de la Légion américaine ; il avait un "vague souvenir" que le millionnaire Robert S. Clark avait parlé à Butler, mais avait "nié catégoriquement" avoir pris des dispositions pour que Clark rencontre Butler. MacGuire admit avoir envoyé des cartes postales à Butler depuis l'Europe, qu'il avait eu une conversation avec le général à l'hôtel Bellevue-Stratford, et qu'il avait dit à Butler qu'il allait à la convention à Miami. Cependant, lorsqu'on lui demanda s'il avait parlé à Butler du rôle joué par les vétérans dans les gouvernements européens, il répondit que non, bien qu'il ait déclaré avoir dit à Butler qu'à son avis "Hitler ne durerait pas une année de plus en Allemagne et que Mussolini était sur le déclin".[404]

Le témoignage de MacGuire sur sa rencontre avec French diffère sensiblement du récit de French :

> **QUESTION**. Pourquoi M. French a-t-il appelé pour vous voir, M. MacGuire ?
> **RÉPONSE**. Il m'a appelé, selon l'histoire de M. French, pour me rencontrer et faire ma connaissance, car j'avais connu le général Butler, et j'étais un de ses amis, et il voulait me connaître, et c'était principalement l'objet de sa visite.
> **QUESTION**. Rien d'autre n'a été discuté ?
> **RÉPONSE**. Un certain nombre de choses ont été discutées ; oui. La position du marché des obligations, du marché boursier ; ce que je pensais être un bon achat en ce moment ; ce qu'il pourrait acheter s'il avait sept ou huit cents dollars ; la position du pays ; les perspectives de reprise, et divers sujets dont deux hommes discuteraient s'ils se réunissaient.
> **QUESTION**. Rien d'autre ?
> **RÉPONSE**. Rien d'autre, sauf ceci, Monsieur le Président : Comme je l'ai dit hier, je crois, lorsque M. French est venu me voir, il a dit Le général Butler est ou a été approché par deux ou trois organisations - et je crois qu'il a mentionné l'une d'entre elles comme étant un comité de vigilance de ce pays - et il a dit : "Qu'en pensez-vous ?" et je crois que je lui ai répondu : "Pourquoi, je ne pense pas que le général devrait se mêler de ces affaires dans ce pays. Je pense que tous ces gens essaient de se servir de lui, d'utiliser son nom à des fins publicitaires et pour devenir membre, et je pense qu'il devrait se tenir à l'écart de ces organisations.
> **QUESTION**. Rien d'autre ?
> **RÉPONSE**. Rien d'autre. C'était l'essentiel de toute la conversation.[405]

MacGuire a en outre témoigné qu'il travaillait pour Grayson Murphy et que Robert S. Clark avait mis 300 000$ à disposition pour former le Comité pour un dollar sain.

La commission McCormack-Dickstein a pu confirmer le fait que Robert Sterling Clark a transmis de l'argent à MacGuire à des fins politiques :

---

[404] Chambre des représentants, Enquête sur les activités de propagande nazie et enquête sur certaines autres activités de propagande, Audiences n° 73-D.C.-6, op. cit. p. 45.

[405] Ibid, p. 45.

> Il [MacGuire] a en outre déclaré que cet argent lui avait été donné par M. Clark bien après la Convention de Chicago de la Légion, et qu'il avait également reçu de Walter E. Frew de la Corn Exchange Bank & Trust Co. la somme de 1000 dollars, qui a également été placée au crédit du Sound Money Committee.
> MacGuire a ensuite témoigné qu'il avait reçu de Robert Sterling Clark environ 7200 dollars, pour ses frais de voyage à destination, en provenance et à l'intérieur de l'Europe, auxquels s'était ajoutée la somme de 2500 dollars à une autre occasion et de 1000 dollars à un autre moment, et il a déclaré sous serment qu'il n'avait rien reçu de personne d'autre et a en outre témoigné qu'il l'avait déposé sur son compte personnel à la Manufacturers Trust Co. 55 Broad Street.
> MacGuire a en outre témoigné qu'il avait actuellement un compte de retrait 432 dollars par mois, auquel s'ajoutaient quelques commissions. Plus tard, MacGuire a témoigné que les 2500$ et les 1000$ étaient liés à l'organisation du Comité pour un dollar sain.
> Le président McCormack a ensuite posé la question suivante : "M. Clark a-t-il contribué d'une autre manière, outre les 30 000$ et les autres sommes que vous avez énumérées, qu'il vous a données personnellement ?" à quoi MacGuire a répondu : "Non, monsieur, on lui a demandé plusieurs fois de contribuer à différents fonds, mais il a refusé."[406]

Dans son communiqué de presse de New York, la commission a relevé plusieurs divergences dans le témoignage de MacGuire sur la réception des fonds. La section se lit comme suit :

> MacGuire ne pouvait pas non plus se rappeler quel était le but de son voyage à Washington ou s'il avait donné à la Banque centrale de Hanovre treize billets de mille dollars ou qu'il avait acheté une des lettres de crédit avec un chèque certifié tiré sur le compte de M. Christmas.
> Au cours de l'interrogatoire, MacGuire ne pouvait pas se rappeler s'il avait déjà manipulé des billets de mille dollars, et ne se souvenait certainement pas d'en avoir produit treize à la fois à la banque. Il faut se rappeler à ce propos que l'achat de 13 000 dollars avec des billets de mille dollars à la banque est arrivé six jours seulement après que Butler ait affirmé que MacGuire lui avait montré dix-huit billets de mille dollars à Newark.
> De ce qui précède, on peut facilement voir qu'en plus des 30 000 dollars que Clark a donnés à MacGuire pour le Sound Money Committee, il a produit environ 75 000 dollars de plus, ce que MacGuire a admis à contrecœur en étant confronté aux preuves.
> Ces 75 000 dollars figurent dans les 26 000 dollars qui ont été versés sur le compte du Manufacturers Trust, 10 000 dollars en devises au déjeuner, l'achat de lettres de crédit totalisant 30 300 dollars, dont le chèque certifié de Noël était représenté par 15 000 dollars, des dépenses pour l'Europe proches de 8000 dollars. Tout cela reste inexpliqué. Le Comité ne sait pas encore s'il y a eu plus et combien.[407]

La commission a ensuite posé à MacGuire une question évidente : connaissait-il Jackson Martindell ? Malheureusement, une erreur tout aussi évidente dans la

[406] Communiqué de presse. New York City, p. 12.

[407] Ibid, p. 13.

réponse de MacGuire est passée inaperçue. La transcription de la commission se lit comme suit :

> Par le président :
> **QUESTION**. Connaissez-vous M. Martindell, M. MacGuire ?
> **RÉPONSE**. M. Martin Dell ? Non, monsieur ; je ne le connais pas.
> **LE PRÉSIDENT**. C'est son nom ?
> **MR. DICKSTEIN**. Je pense que oui.[408]

Ainsi, en bref, nous avons trois témoins fiables - le général Butler, Paul French et le capitaine Samuel Glazier - qui témoignent sous serment des plans d'un complot visant à installer une dictature aux États-Unis. Et nous avons des témoignages contradictoires de Gerald MacGuire qui justifient clairement une enquête plus approfondie. Une telle enquête était au départ l'intention déclarée de la commission : "Le Comité attend le retour dans ce pays de M. Clark et de M. Christmas. En l'état actuel des preuves, il demande une explication que le Comité n'a pas pu obtenir de M. MacGuire".[409]

Mais le Comité n'a appelé ni M. Clark ni M. Christmas à témoigner. Il n'a pas fait d'effort supplémentaire - du moins, aucun effort supplémentaire n'apparaît dans les archives publiques - pour trouver une explication aux incohérences et aux inexactitudes du témoignage de MacGuire, témoignage qui a été donné à la commission sous serment.

SUPPRESSION DE L'IMPLICATION DE WALL STREET

L'histoire d'une tentative de prise de pouvoir exécutif aux États-Unis a été étouffée, non seulement par les parties directement intéressées, mais aussi par plusieurs institutions habituellement considérées comme protectrices de la liberté constitutionnelle et de la liberté d'enquête. Parmi les groupes qui répriment l'information, on trouve (1) le Congrès des États-Unis, (2) la presse, notamment le *Time* et le *New York Times*, et (3) la Maison Blanche elle-même. Il est également remarquable qu'aucune enquête académique n'ait été menée sur ce qui est certainement l'un des événements les plus inquiétants de l'histoire américaine récente. La répression est encore plus regrettable à la lumière de la tendance actuelle au collectivisme aux États-Unis et de la probabilité d'une autre tentative de prise de pouvoir dictatoriale utilisant comme prétexte de prétendues menaces de la gauche ou de la droite.

La répression exercée par la commission des activités anti-américaines de la Chambre des représentants a pris la forme de la suppression de nombreux extraits concernant les financiers de Wall Street, notamment le directeur de Guaranty Trust, Grayson Murphy, J.P. Morgan, les intérêts de Du Pont, Remington Arms et

---

[408] Chambre des représentants, Enquête sur les activités de propagande nazie et enquête sur certaines autres activités de propagande, Audiences n° 73-D.C.-6, op. cit. p. 85.

[409] Communiqué de presse, New York City, p. 13.

d'autres personnes prétendument impliquées dans la tentative de complot. Même aujourd'hui, en 1975, il est impossible de retrouver une transcription complète des audiences.

Certaines des parties supprimées de la transcription ont été découvertes par le journaliste John Spivak.[410] Une référence à l'administrateur de la NRA Hugh Johnson indiquait le type d'informations supprimées ; la commission a supprimé les mots en italique du témoignage imprimé ; Butler parle à MacGuire :

> J'ai dit : "Y a-t-il encore quelque chose qui bouge ?
> "Oui, dit-il, vous regardez, dans deux ou trois semaines, vous le verrez apparaître dans les journaux. Il y aura de gros bonnets" ... et en deux semaines environ, l'American Liberty League est apparue, ce qui est à peu près ce qu'il a décrit. Nous pourrions avoir un président adjoint, quelqu'un à blâmer ; et si les choses ne marchent pas, il peut le laisser tomber.
> Il a dit : "C'est pour cela qu'il a construit Hugh Johnson. Hugh Johnson a trop parlé et l'a mis dans un trou, et il va le virer dans les trois ou quatre semaines à venir".
> J'ai dit : "Comment savez-vous tout cela ?"
> "Oh," dit-il, "nous sommes tout le temps avec lui. Nous savons ce qui va se passer."[411]

Le témoignage de Paul French a également été censuré par la commission parlementaire. En témoigne l'extrait suivant du témoignage de French qui fait référence à John W. Davis, J.P. Morgan, la Du Pont Company et d'autres personnes de Wall Street et qui corrobore fortement le témoignage du général Butler :

> Au début, il [MacGuire] a suggéré au général [Butler] d'organiser lui-même cette réunion et de demander à tout le monde une cotisation annuelle d'un dollar. Nous en avons discuté, puis il en est venu à obtenir des fonds extérieurs, et il a dit qu'il ne serait pas difficile de réunir un million de dollars. Il a dit qu'il pouvait s'adresser à John W. Davis [avocat de J.P. Morgan & Co.] ou à Perkins de la National City Bank, et à n'importe quelle personne pour l'obtenir. Bien sûr, cela peut ou non vouloir dire quelque chose. C'est-à-dire qu'il fait référence à John W. Davis et Perkins de la National City Bank. Au cours de ma conversation avec lui, je n'ai bien sûr pas engagé le général à quoi que ce soit. Je le sentais juste bien.
> Plus tard, nous avons discuté de la question des armes et des équipements, et il a suggéré qu'ils puissent être obtenus auprès de la Remington Arms Co, à crédit par l'intermédiaire des Du Pont.
> Je ne pense pas qu'à l'époque il ait mentionné les liens de Du Pont avec la Ligue de Liberté américaine, mais il a fait le tour de la question. Autrement dit, je ne pense pas qu'il ait mentionné la Liberty League, mais il a contourné l'idée qu'il s'agissait d'un ultime recours ; l'un des Du Pont fait partie du conseil d'administration de l'American Liberty League et il possèdent une participation majoritaire dans la

---

410 Voir Jules Archer, *The Plot to Seize the White House*, op. cit.

411 George Seldes, *One Thousand Americans*, op. cit, p. 288.

> Remington Arms Co ... Il a dit que le général n'aurait aucun problème à enrôler 500 000 hommes.[412]

John L. Spivak, le journaliste qui a découvert la suppression dans les transcriptions du Congrès, a contesté le témoignage du coprésident de la commission, Samuel Dickstein de New York. Dickstein a admis que :

> la commission avait supprimé certaines parties du témoignage parce qu'il s'agissait de ouï-dire".
> "Mais vos rapports publiés sont pleins de témoignages par ouï-dire." "Ils le sont ?" a-t-il dit.
> "Pourquoi n'a-t-on pas appelé Grayson Murphy ? Votre comité savait que les hommes de Murphy font partie de l'organisation d'espionnage antisémite Order of '76 ?
> "Nous n'avons pas eu le temps. Nous nous serions occupés des groupes de Wall Street si nous avions eu le temps. Je n'aurais pas hésité à aller chercher les Morgan."
> "Vous avez fait citer Belgrano, commandant de la légion américaine, comme témoin. Pourquoi n'a-t-il pas été interrogé ?"
> "Je ne sais pas. Peut-être que vous pouvez demander à M. McCormack de vous expliquer cela. Je n'ai rien à voir avec ça."[413]

Le fait est que la commission n'a pas appelé Grayson Murphy, Jackson Martindell ou John W. Davis, tous directement accusés dans le cadre d'un témoignage sous serment. En outre, la commission a supprimé toutes les parties du témoignage impliquant d'autres personnalités : J.P. Morgan, les Du Ponts, les intérêts des Rockefeller, Hugh Johnson et Franklin D. Roosevelt. Lorsque le membre du Congrès Dickstein a plaidé son innocence auprès de John Spivak, cela était en contradiction avec sa propre lettre au président Roosevelt, dans laquelle il prétend avoir imposé des restrictions même à la diffusion publique des audiences de la commission, telles qu'elles ont été imprimées, "afin qu'elles ne tombent pas entre des mains irresponsables". Le rapport final publié par la commission le 15 février 1935 a enterré l'histoire encore plus profondément. John L. Spivak résume succinctement cet escamotage : "J'ai... étudié le rapport de la commission. Il consacrait six pages à la menace des agents nazis opérant dans ce pays et onze pages à la menace des communistes, ainsi qu'une page au complot visant à s'emparer du gouvernement et à détruire notre système démocratique."[414]

Le rôle des principaux journaux et revues d'opinion dans la couverture de l'affaire Butler est également suspect. En fait, leur traitement de l'événement a l'apparence d'une déformation et d'une censure totales. La véracité de certains grands journaux a été largement mise en doute au cours des 50 dernières

---

[412] Ibid, pp. 289-290.

[413] John L. Spivak, *A Man in his Time* (New York : Horizon Press, 1967), pp. 311, 322-25.

[414] Ibid, p. 331.

années,[415]et dans certains milieux, les médias ont même été accusés de conspiration visant à supprimer "tout ce qui est contraire aux souhaits des intérêts des puissants". Par exemple, en 1917, le membre du Congrès Callaway a inséré dans The Congressional Record la critique dévastatrice suivante du contrôle de la presse par Morgan :

> **M. CALLAWAY**. Monsieur le Président, avec le consentement unanime, j'insère à ce stade dans le procès-verbal une déclaration indiquant la combinaison des journaux, qui explique leur activité dans cette affaire de guerre, dont vient de parler le monsieur de Pennsylvanie (M. Moore) :
>
> En mars 1915, les intérêts de J.P. Morgan, les intérêts de l'acier, de la construction navale et des poudres, et leurs organisations subsidiaires, ont réuni 12 hommes haut placés dans le monde de la presse et les ont employés pour sélectionner les journaux les plus influents des États-Unis et un nombre suffisant d'entre eux pour contrôler de manière générale la politique de la presse quotidienne des États-Unis.
>
> Ces 12 hommes ont résolu le problème en sélectionnant 179 journaux, puis ont commencé par un processus d'élimination, pour ne conserver que ceux nécessaires au contrôle de la politique générale de la presse quotidienne dans tout le pays. Ils ont constaté qu'il n'était nécessaire d'acheter le contrôle que de 25 des plus grands journaux. Les 25 journaux ont fait l'objet d'un accord ; des émissaires ont été envoyés pour acheter l'analyse politique, nationale et internationale, de ces journaux ; un accord a été conclu ; les publications des journaux ont été achetées au mois ; un éditeur a été fourni pour chaque journal afin de superviser et d'éditer correctement les informations concernant les questions de préparation, de militarisme, de politiques financières, et d'autres éléments de nature nationale et internationale considérés comme vitaux pour les intérêts des commanditaires.
>
> Ce contrat existe actuellement et explique que les colonnes d'information de la presse quotidienne du pays soient remplies de toutes sortes d'arguments et de fausses déclarations sur l'état actuel de l'armée et de la marine américaines et sur la possibilité et la probabilité que les États-Unis soient attaqués par des ennemis étrangers.
>
> Cette politique comprenait également la suppression de tout ce qui s'opposait aux souhaits des intérêts servis. L'efficacité de ce système a été démontrée de façon concluante par le caractère des informations publiées dans la presse quotidienne dans tout le pays depuis mars 1915. Ils ont eu recours à tout ce qui était nécessaire pour orienter le sentiment public et pour mettre le Congrès national sur la sellette afin d'obtenir des crédits extravagants et inutiles pour l'armée et la marine sous le faux prétexte que c'était nécessaire. Leur argument de base est qu'il s'agit de "patriotisme". Ils jouent sur tous les préjugés et les passions du peuple américain.[416]

Dans l'affaire Butler, les intérêts accusés sont également ceux identifiés par le député Callaway : la firme J.P. Morgan et les industries de l'acier et des poudres. Le général Butler a accusé Grayson Murphy, un directeur de la Guaranty Trust Company contrôlée par Morgan ; Jackson Martindell, associé à Stone & Webster, allié aux Morgan ; la société Du Pont (l'industrie des poudres) ; et la Remington

[415] Voir Herman Dinsmore, *All the News That Fits*, (New Rochelle : Arlington House, 1969).

[416] Congressional Record, Vol. 55, pp. 2947-8 (1917).

Arms Company, qui était contrôlée par Du Pont et les intérêts financiers de Morgan-Harriman. En outre, les entreprises qui apparaissent dans le témoignage supprimé du Congrès de 1934 sont J.P. Morgan, Du Pont et Remington Arms. En bref, nous pouvons vérifier la suppression par le Congrès en 1934 des informations qui soutiennent les accusations portées en 1917 contre le membre du Congrès Callaway.

Cette suppression s'étend-elle aux grands journaux d'information ? Nous pouvons prendre deux exemples de premier ordre : le *New York Times* et le magazine *Time.* Si une combinaison telle que les accusations de Callaway existait, alors ces deux journaux feraient certainement partie des "25 plus grands journaux impliqués dans les années 1930". Le reportage du *New York Times* sur le "complot" débute par un article en première page du 21 novembre 1934 : "Le général Butler évoque un "Complot fasciste" pour s'emparer du gouvernement par la force", avec le paragraphe principal cité ci-dessus (p. 143). Cet article du *Times* est un assez bon travail de reportage et comprend une déclaration directe du membre du Congrès Dickstein : "D'après les indications actuelles, Butler a les preuves. Il ne portera pas d'accusations sérieuses à moins d'avoir quelque chose pour les étayer. Nous aurons des hommes ici avec des noms plus importants que le sien." Ensuite, l'article du Times indique que "M. Dickstein a dit qu'environ seize personnes mentionnées par le général Butler devant la commission seraient citées à comparaître, et qu'une audience publique pourrait avoir lieu lundi prochain." Le *Times* inclut également des démentis catégoriques et parfois enragés de Hugh Johnson, Thomas W. Lamont et Grayson M-P. Murphy de Guaranty Trust.

Le lendemain matin, le 22 novembre, le *Times* a fait un changement majeur dans sa façon de rapporter l'intrigue. Les révélations ont été publiées sur une page intérieure, bien que le témoignage concerne maintenant Gerald MacGuire, l'un des comploteurs accusés. De plus, on peut discerner un changement décidé dans l'attitude de la commission. Le membre du Congrès McCormack aurait déclaré que "la commission n'a pas décidé d'appeler d'autres témoins. Il a déclaré que le témoin le plus important, à part M. MacGuire, était Robert Sterling Clark, un riche New-Yorkais ayant des bureaux dans le bâtiment de la Bourse".

Alors que le reportage du *Times* était consigné dans une seule colonne, la page éditoriale, sa section la plus influente, comportait un éditorial principal qui donnait le ton des reportages ultérieurs. Sous le titre "Crédulité Illimitée", elle soutenait que l'accusation de Butler était un "récit bancal et peu convaincant". ... Toute l'histoire ressemble à un gigantesque canular ... elle ne mérite pas une discussion sérieuse", et ainsi de suite. En bref, avant que les 16 témoins importants ne soient appelés, avant que les preuves ne soient enregistrées, avant que l'accusation ne soit examinée, le *New York Times* a décidé qu'il ne voulait rien entendre de cette histoire parce qu'il s'agissait d'un canular, qui n'était pas digne d'être publié.

Le lendemain, le 23 novembre, le *Times* a encore modifié ses reportages. Les gros titres portaient désormais sur les rouges et la lutte des syndicats rouges et concernaient les activités présumées des communistes dans les syndicats américains, tandis que le témoignage de Butler et les preuves qui s'accumulaient étaient relégués au plus profond du reportage sur les activités des rouges.

L'histoire qui en résultait était, bien sûr, vague et confuse, mais elle enterrait effectivement les preuves de Butler.

Le 26 novembre, les auditions se sont poursuivies, mais la commission elle-même s'est maintenant montrée frileuse et a publié une déclaration :

> "Cette commission n'a eu devant elle aucune preuve qui justifierait dans la moindre mesure de convoquer des hommes tels que John W. Davis, le général Hugh Johnson, le général James G. Harbord, Thomas W. Lamont, l'amiral William S. Sims ou Hanford MacNider."

Il convient de noter que ces noms sont apparus lors d'un témoignage sous serment, pour être ensuite effacés du registre officiel. Le *Times* a continué à rendre compte de cette évolution sous une forme abrégée sur une page intérieure sous le titre "Le comité Calme sur le "complot" de Butler, n'a aucune preuve pour justifier le témoignage de Johnson et d'autres". Le 27 novembre, le *Times* a réduit son reportage à cinq colonnes sur une page intérieure sous le titre sinistre "l'enquête Butler ne doit pas être abandonnée". Les audiences de décembre ont été rapportées par le *Times* en première page (28 décembre 1934), mais le complot était maintenant qualifié de "complot des rouges pour kidnapper le président, accusations de témoins à l'enquête parlementaire".

En examinant l'histoire de l'affaire Butler dans le *Times* 40 ans après l'événement et en comparant son récit au témoignage officiel imprimé, lui-même fortement censuré, il est évident que le journal, de sa propre initiative ou sous la pression extérieure, a décidé que l'histoire ne devait pas être rendue publique. Conformément à cette interprétation, nous constatons que le *New York Times*, le "journal officiel", omet le témoignage de Butler dans les entrées de son index annuel, dont dépendent les chercheurs et les universitaires. L'index du *Times* pour 1934 comporte une entrée "BUTLER (Maj Gen), Smedley D", mais n'énumère que quelques-uns de ses discours et un portrait biographique. Le témoignage de Butler n'est pas répertorié. Il y a une entrée "Voir aussi : Fascism-U.S.", mais sous cette référence croisée, il n'y a que : "Le Général de division S.D. Butler accuse un complot visant à renverser le gouvernement actuel ; les intérêts de Wall Street et G.P. MacGuire sont impliqués dans l'audience de la Commission du Congrès. Le seul nom significatif de Wall Street mentionné dans l'index est celui de R.S. Clark, qui est signalé comme "perplexe" par les accusations. Aucun des principaux associés de Morgan et Du Pont cités par le général Butler n'est répertorié dans l'index. En d'autres termes, il semble qu'il y ait eu une tentative délibérée de ce journal de tromper les historiens.

Les reportages du magazine *Time* sont tombés dans la fiction à travers ses tentatives de réduire les preuves du général Butler au statut d'absurdité. Si jamais un étudiant veut construire un exemple de reportage biaisé, il y a un exemple de premier ordre dans la comparaison des preuves présentées au Comité McCormack-Dickstein par le général Butler avec le reportage ultérieur publié par le *Time*. Le numéro du 3 décembre 1934 du *Time* présentait l'histoire sous le titre "le complot sans comploteurs", mais l'histoire ne ressemble en rien au témoignage, pas même au témoignage censuré. L'histoire montre le général Butler menant un demi-million d'hommes le long d'une autoroute américaine en criant : "Messieurs, Washington n'est qu'à 30 miles ! Voulez-vous me suivre ?" Butler est ensuite dépeint comme ayant pris de force le contrôle du gouvernement américain par le président Roosevelt. Le reste de l'histoire du *Time* est rempli de références au passé de Butler et d'un assortiment de dénégations de l'accusé. Nulle part on ne tente de rapporter les déclarations du général Butler, bien que les dénégations de J.P. Morgan, Hugh Johnson, Robert Sterling Clark et Grayson Murphy soient correctement citées. Deux photographies sont incluses : J.P. Morgan, le grand-père génial et le général Butler dans une pose qui symbolise universellement la folie - un doigt pointé à l'oreille. Le reportage était un journalisme trash, malhonnête et honteux au possible. Quelles que soient nos pensées sur la propagande nazie ou la déformation de la presse soviétique, ni Goebbels ni *Goslit n'ont* jamais atteint l'expertise hypnotique des journalistes et des rédacteurs du *Time*. Le problème redoutable est que les opinions et les mœurs de millions d'Américains et d'anglophones dans le monde ont été façonnées par cette école de journalisme déformée.

Pour relativiser notre critique, il faut noter que le *Time* était apparemment impartial dans sa poursuite d'un journalisme corrompu. Même Hugh S. Johnson, administrateur de la NRA et l'un des présumés comploteurs dans l'affaire Butler, a été la cible des méfaits du *Time*. Comme Johnson le rapporte dans son livre :

> J'étais dans la tribune lors de ce défilé et je connaissais des centaines de personnes qui saluaient en passant. En bas, il y avait des batteries d'appareils photo, et je savais que si je levais la main plus haut que les épaules, il semblerait que ce soit un "salut fasciste" et que cela soit rendu public. Je n'ai donc jamais levé la main plus haut. J'ai juste tendu le bras et j'ai agité ma main. Mais cela ne m'a pas aidé - *Time* a rapporté que j'avais constamment salué à la manière de Mussolini et qu'il existait même une photo pour le prouver, mais ce n'était pas mon bras sur cette photo. Il portait la manchette à ruban adhésif d'un manteau coupé et une manchette ronde rigide avec un bouton de manchette à l'ancienne et je n'ai jamais porté ni l'un ni l'autre de toute ma vie. Je pense que c'était le bras du maire O'Brien qui se tenait à côté de moi qui avait été superposé sur mon corps.[417]

UNE ÉVALUATION DE L'AFFAIRE BUTLER

Le point le plus important à évaluer est la crédibilité du général Smedley Darlington Butler. Le général Butler a-t-il menti ? Disait-il la vérité ? Exagérait-il pour des raisons de crédibilité ?

Le général Butler était un homme hors du commun au parcours exceptionnel au sein des forces armées : décoré deux fois de la médaille d'honneur, un meneur d'hommes incontesté, avec une bravoure personnelle incontestable, une profonde loyauté envers ses semblables et un sens aigu de la justice. Toutes ces qualités sont admirables. Certes, le général Butler n'était guère le genre d'homme à mentir ou même à exagérer pour une raison mesquine. Son goût pour la dramatisation laisse

[417] Hugh S. Johnson, *The Blue Eagle from Egg to Earth*, op. cit. p.267.

la porte ouverte à l'exagération, mais le mensonge délibéré est très peu probable de sa part.

Les preuves soutiennent-elles sa version ou l'invalide-t-elle ? Le journaliste Paul French du *Philadelphia Record* soutient totalement Butler. Le témoignage du capitaine Glazier, commandant du camp du CCC, soutient Butler. Dans ces deux cas, il n'y a pas de divergence dans les preuves. Les déclarations de MacGuire faites sous serment devant le Congrès ne soutiennent pas Butler. Nous avons donc un conflit de preuves présentées sous serment. De plus, MacGuire a été jugé fautif sur plusieurs points par la commission ; il a utilisé l'évitement de "ne pas se souvenir" à plusieurs reprises et, dans des domaines majeurs tels que le financement par Clark, MacGuire soutient Butler contre son gré. Il y a un noyau dur de plausibilité dans l'histoire de Butler. Il y a une possibilité d'exagération, peut-être pas atypique pour un homme à la personnalité flamboyante tel que lui, mais cela n'est ni prouvé ni réfuté.

Il ne fait aucun doute que le Congrès des États-Unis a rendu un grave service à la cause de la liberté en supprimant l'histoire de Butler. Espérons que certains membres du Congrès ou certaines commissions du Congrès, même à cette date tardive, reprendront le fil et rendront public l'intégralité du témoignage non censuré. Nous pouvons également espérer que la prochaine fois, dans une affaire d'une importance comparable, le *New York Times* sera à la hauteur de sa prétention d'être le journal de référence, un nom qu'il a si admirablement justifié quatre décennies plus tard dans l'enquête sur le Watergate.

CHAPITRE XI

LES SOCIALISTES D'ENTREPRISE AU 120 BROADWAY, NEW YORK CITY

Il [FDR] avait déjà commencé à réapparaître au bureau de la Fidelity and Deposit Company au 120 Broadway. Il ne s'est pas encore rendu à son cabinet d'avocats au 52 Wall Street, en raison de la hauteur des marches de la façade - il ne pouvait pas supporter l'idée d'être porté en public. Au 120 Broadway, il pouvait se débrouiller tout seul pour monter d'un petit pas sur le trottoir.

Frank Freidel, Franklin D. Roosevelt : *The Ordeal*
(Boston ; Little, Brown, 1954), p. 119.

Dans *Wall Street et la révolution bolchévique*, on retrouve bon nombre des personnages principaux (dont FDR) et des entreprises, voire quelques-uns des événements, décrits dans ce livre situés à une seule adresse, l'Equitable Office Building au 120 Broadway, New York City.

Le bureau de Franklin D. Roosevelt au début des années 1920, lorsqu'il était vice-président de la Fidelity and Deposit Company, se trouvait au 120 Broadway. Le biographe Frank Freidel relate ci-dessus sa rentrée dans le bâtiment après son attaque paralysante de poliomyélite. À cette époque, le bureau de Bernard Baruch se trouvait également au 120 Broadway et Hugh Johnson, qui devait plus tard être l'administrateur de la NRA, était l'assistant de recherche de Bernard Baruch à la même adresse.

Les bureaux exécutifs de General Electric et les bureaux de Gerard Swope, auteur du plan Swope qui est devenu l'ARN de Roosevelt, étaient également présents. Le Bankers Club se trouvait au dernier étage de ce même Equitable Office Building et fut le lieu d'une réunion en 1926 des comploteurs de l'affaire Butler. Il est évident qu'il y avait une concentration de talents à cette adresse particulière qui méritait une plus grande description.

LA RÉVOLUTION BOLCHÉVIQUE ET LE 120 BROADWAY

Dans *Wall Street et dans la révolution bolchévique*, nous avons constaté que les financiers liés à la révolution étaient concentrés à une seule adresse à New York, le même Equitable Office Building. En 1917, le siège du district n°2 du Système de la Réserve Fédérale, le plus important des districts de la Réserve Fédérale, était situé au 120 Broadway ; sur les neuf directeurs de la Banque de la

Réserve Fédérale de New York, quatre étaient physiquement installés au 120 Broadway, et deux de ces directeurs siégeaient simultanément au conseil d'administration de l'American International Corporation. L'American International Corporation avait été fondée en 1915 par les intérêts de Morgan avec la participation enthousiaste des groupes Rockefeller et Stillman. Les bureaux généraux de l'A.I.C. étaient situés au 120 Broadway. Ses directeurs étaient fortement imbriqués avec d'autres grands intérêts financiers et industriels de Wall Street, et il est certain que l'American International Corporation a joué un rôle important dans le succès et la consolidation de la révolution bolchévique de 1917. Le secrétaire exécutif de l'A.I.C., William Franklin Sands, à qui le Département d'État avait demandé son avis sur la révolution bolchévique quelques semaines après son déclenchement en novembre 1917 (bien avant qu'une fraction de la Russie ne passe sous contrôle soviétique), a exprimé son soutien ferme à la révolution. La lettre de Sands est citée dans *Wall Street et la révolution bolchévique*. Un mémorandum adressé à David Lloyd George, Premier ministre d'Angleterre, par Dwight Morrow, associé de Morgan, exhorte également à soutenir les révolutionnaires bolchéviques et ses armées. Un directeur de la FRB de New York, William Boyce Thompson, a fait don d'un million de dollars à la cause bolchévique et est intervenu auprès de Lloyd George au nom des Soviétiques en passe de prendre le pouvoir.

En bref, nous avons trouvé un schéma identifiable d'activité pro-bolchévique de membres influents de Wall Street, concentrée à la Banque de Réserve Fédérale de New York et à l'American International Corporation, toutes deux situées au 120 Broadway. En 1933, la banque avait déménagé à Liberty Street.

LA BANQUE DE RÉSERVE FÉDÉRALE DE NEW YORK ET LE 120 BROADWAY

Les noms des directeurs de la FRB ont changé entre 1917 et les années 1930, mais il a été établi que, bien que la FRB ait déménagé, quatre directeurs de la FRB avaient encore des bureaux à cette adresse pendant la période du New Deal, comme le montre le tableau suivant :

Directeurs de la Banque de Réserve Fédérale de New York pendant la période du New Deal

Nom	Mandats d'administrateur pour les entreprises situées au 120 Broadway
Charles E. Mitchell	Directeur de la FRB de New York, 1929-1931, et administrateur de la Corporation Trust Co. (120 Broadway)
Albert H. Wiggin	A succédé à Charles E. Mitchell en tant que directeur de la FRB de New York, 1932-34, et directeur de l'American International Corp, et de Stone and Webster, Inc. (tous deux au 120 Broadway)
Clarence M. Woolley	Directeur de la FRB de New York, 1922-1936, et directeur de la General Electric Co. (120 Broadway), et directeur de la

Owen D. Young	General Electric Co. Directeur de la FRB de New York, 1927-1935, et président de la General Electric Co. (120 Broadway)

Personnes et entreprises situées à :

120 BROADWAY
Franklin Delano Roosevelt
Bernard Baruch
Gérard Swope
Owen D. Young

42 BROADWAY
Herbert Clark Hoover

Autres

American International Corp.
La société The Corporation Trust Co. Empire Trust Co. Inc.
Fidelity Trust Co.
American Smelting & Refining Co.
Armour & Co. (Bureau de New York).
Usine de locomotives Baldwin
Federal Mining & Smelting Co.
General Electric Co.
Kennecott Copper Corp.
Metal & Thermit Corp.
National Dairy Products Corp.
Yukon Gold Co.
Stone & Webster & Blodget, Inc.

Grayson M-P Murphy (52 Broadway)
International Acceptance Bank, (52 Cedar St.)
International Acceptance Trust (52 Cedar St.)
International Manhattan Co. Inc. (52 Cedar St.)
Jackson Martindell (14 Wall St.)
John D. Rockefeller, Jr. (26 Broadway)
Percy A. Rockefeller (25 Broadway)
Robert S. Clark (11 Wall St.)

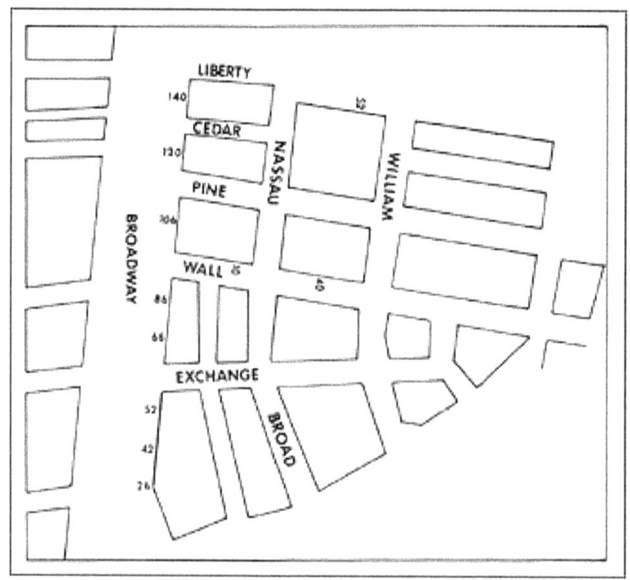

Carte de la région de Wall Street indiquant l'emplacement des bureaux pour les personnes et les entreprises mentionnées dans ce livre.

L'AMERICAN INTERNATIONAL CORPORATION ET 120 BROADWAY

L'American International Corporation (AIC) a été créée en 1915 par une coalition d'intérêts de Morgan, Stillman et Rockefeller ; ses bureaux généraux se trouvaient au 120 Broadway de 1915 à 1920. Le grand enthousiasme de Wall Street pour la formation de l'AIC a entraîné une concentration des éléments financiers les plus puissants au sein de son conseil d'administration - en fait une organisation monopolistique pour le développement et l'exploitation de ressources étrangère.[418] Sur les neuf directeurs du conseil d'administration en 1930, cinq faisaient partie du conseil de l'AIC en 1917, au moment de la révolution bolchévique : Matthew C. Brush, président du comité exécutif de l'American International Corporation et administrateur de l'Empire Trust Company ; Pierre S. Du Pont, membre de la famille Du Pont et administrateur de la Bankers Trust Company ; Percy A. Rockefeller, de la famille Rockefeller et administrateur de la National City Bank ; Albert H. Wiggin, administrateur de la Federal Reserve Bank of New York et de la Rockefeller Chase National Bank ; et Beekman Winthrop, de la Warburg International Banking Corporation et de la National City Bank. Plusieurs financiers de premier plan ont rejoint le conseil d'administration de l'AIC dans les années 1920, notamment Frank Altschul et Halstead G. Freeman de la Chase National Bank, Arthur Lehman de Lehman Brothers et de la Manufacturers Trust Company, et John J. Raskob, vice-président de Du Pont et directeur de General Motors et de la Bankers Trust Company.

Mathew C. Brush, président, directeur et président du comité exécutif d'American International Corporation et président d'Allied Machinery, une filiale, a également été directeur et membre du comité exécutif d'International Acceptance Bank (voir chapitre 6), directeur et membre du comité exécutif de Barnsdall Corporation,[419] directeur d'Empire Trust Company (120 Broadway) et d'Equitable Office Corporation (qui possédait et exploitait le bâtiment du 120 Broadway), directeur de Georgian Manganese Company,[420]et directeur et membre du comité exécutif de Remington Arms Co, identifié par le général Butler dans le dernier chapitre. Matthew C. Brush était en effet à l'avant-garde de Wall Street.

Les contributions politiques de Brush, contrairement à celles des autres directeurs de l'AIC, se sont apparemment limitées à 5000 dollars pour la campagne d'Herbert Hoover en 1928. Brush a été directeur de l'International Acceptance Bank, qui a profité de l'inflation des années 1920, ainsi que directeur de Remington Arms (un nom supprimé dans l'affaire Butler) alors qu'il était

---

418 Voir Sutton, *Wall Street et la révolution bolchévique*, op. cit.

419 La Barnsdall Corporation est la société qui, en 1921, est entrée en Union soviétique pour rouvrir aux Soviétiques les champs de pétrole caucasiens et a ainsi permis à l'Union soviétique de générer les devises nécessaires au développement d'une Russie soviétique ; voir Sutton, *Western Technology and Soviet Economic Development*, 1917 to 1930 (Stanford : Hoover Institution, 1968), Vol. 1.

420 Ibid.

président d'American International, mais il semble avoir été en marge des événements explorés dans ce livre. D'autre part, quatre directeurs d'American International ont été identifiés comme étant d'importants soutiens financiers de Franklin D. Roosevelt : Frank Altschul, Pierre S. Du Pont, Arthur Lehman et John J. Raskob entre 1928 et 1932. La famille Lehman et John J. Raskob ont été, comme nous l'avons vu, au cœur même du soutien de Roosevelt. Il est significatif que l'AIC, le principal vecteur de la participation américaine à la révolution bolchévique, soit également mis au jour, même sous une forme fortuite, dans une étude de l'époque de Roosevelt.

L'AFFAIRE BUTLER ET LE 120 BROADWAY

Le témoignage de la commission des activités anti-américaines de la Chambre des représentants sur la tentative de convertir l'administration Roosevelt en une dictature avec le major général Butler dans un rôle clé de secrétaire aux affaires générales a eu plusieurs liens avec le 120 Broadway. Le comité aurait dû assigner au moins une demi-douzaine de personnes à enquêter sur les déclarations faites sous serment par le général Butler, le capitaine Glazier et Paul French ; quatre d'entre elles se trouvaient au 120 Broadway ou avaient un lien important avec celui-ci.

Selon le conspirateur accusé Gerald MacGuire, la première réunion des participants présumés s'est tenue en 1926 au Bankers Club, 120 Broadway. L'extrait suivant, extrait des audiences de la commission, enregistre la déclaration de MacGuire ; l'auteur de la question était le président McCormack :

> **QUESTION**. Depuis combien de temps connaissez-vous Clark ?
> **RÉPONSE**. Je crois avoir dit que j'ai fait des affaires avec lui et que je le connais depuis 1925 ou 1926.
> **QUESTION**. Vous a-t-il déjà donné ce genre d'argent avant de l'utiliser, comme vous le dites, de la manière dont il voulait que vous le représentiez dans ces transactions ?
> **RÉPONSE**. Dans quelles transactions ?
> **QUESTION**. Dans ces transactions monétaires, depuis ce temps-là ?
> **RÉPONSE**. Dans quelles transactions monétaires ?
> **QUESTION**. Ce que je veux dire, c'est que depuis 1926, à l'époque où vous l'avez rencontré et après ; c'était vraiment la première fois que vous receviez cet argent sans aucun reçu, ni papier, ni rien du tout ?
> **RÉPONSE**. Oui.
> **QUESTION**. Et ce dîner était au Bankers Club, au 120 Broadway, n'est-ce pas ?
> **RÉPONSE**. Oui.
> **QUESTION**. À qui ce dîner a-t-il été donné ; a-t-il été donné à quelqu'un en particulier ?
> **RÉPONSE**. C'était un déjeuner régulier.
> **QUESTION**. Qui était présent à votre table ?
> **RÉPONSE**. Monsieur Christmas.
> **QUESTION**. Et vous ?
> **RÉPONSE**. Oui.
> **QUESTION**. Et M. Clark ?

RÉPONSE. Oui.[421]

Ainsi, bien que la première réunion qui a réuni Robert S. Clark, son avocat Christmas et le vendeur d'obligations Gerald MacGuire se soit tenue au 120 Broadway, et que Christmas et Clark aient été liés de nombreuses façons à MacGuire, ni Christmas ni Clark n'ont été convoqués par le comité. De plus, le capitaine Samuel Glazier du camp CCC d'Elkridge, dans le Maryland, rapporta au comité que Jackson Martindell s'était renseigné sur la formation de 500 000 soldats civils à des fins politiques. Martindell n'a pas été convoqué par la commission pour contester ou confirmer le témoignage l'impliquant dans l'affaire Butler.

La compagnie Du Pont, citée dans la partie supprimée du témoignage, était située au 120 Broadway. Hugh S. Johnson, cité par le général Butler comme un participant probable, se trouvait au 120 Broadway lorsqu'il travaillait comme assistant de recherche pour Baruch ; le bureau de Baruch se trouvait à la même adresse.[422] Clark, MacGuire, et Grayson M-P. Murphy avait des bureaux juste en bas de la rue du n° 120 ; Clark au 11 Wall Street et MacGuire et Murphy au 52 Broadway.

Il est également significatif que les noms supprimés par le comité fussent situés au 120 Broadway : le bureau exécutif de la Du Pont Company et Remington Arms, filiale de Du Pont. Les autres participants nommés, MacGuire, Clark, Christmas, Martindell, Grayson M-P. Murphy (au siège de Rockefeller, 25 Broadway) étaient tous situés à quelques pâtés de maisons du 120 Broadway et dans le cercle d'or décrit précédemment.

FRANKLIN D. ROOSEVELT ET 120 BROADWAY

Nous avons constaté que le bureau préféré de FDR - il en avait deux au début des années 20 - était celui du 120 Broadway. La Georgia Warm Springs Foundation, Inc. de FDR a été créée en tant que société du Delaware en juillet 1926 avec des bureaux au 120 Broadway et est restée à cette adresse au moins jusqu'en 1936. Le rapport annuel de 1934 de la Georgia Warm Springs Foundation indique que son président était Franklin D. Roosevelt, The White House, Washington D.C., et que le siège de la fondation était situé au 120 Broadway. Le vice-président et le secrétaire adjoint étaient Raymond H. Taylor, et le secrétaire-trésorier Basil O'Connor, tous deux présents au 120 Broadway.

Basil O'Connor était un proche associé et partenaire commercial de Franklin D. Roosevelt. Né en 1892, Basil O'Connor a obtenu son diplôme de droit à

---

[421] Chambre des représentants, Enquête sur les activités de propagande nazie et enquête sur certaines autres activités de propagande, Audiences n° 73-D.C.-6, op. cit. p. 80. "M. Clark" était Robert Sterling Clark et "M. Christmas" était l'avocat de Clark.

[422] Sénat des États-Unis, *Digest of Data From the Files of a Special Committee to Investigate Lobbying Activities*, 74e Congrès, deuxième session, première partie : liste des contributions, (Washington, 1936), p. 3.

Harvard en 1915 et a ensuite rejoint le cabinet new-yorkais Cravath and Henderson pendant un an, avant de partir travailler chez Streeter & Holmes à Boston pendant trois ans. En 1919, Basil O'Connor ouvre un cabinet d'avocats à New York sous son propre nom. En 1925, le cabinet de Roosevelt et O'Connor est créé, jusqu'à l'inauguration de FDR en 1933. Après 1934, O'Connor est associé principal du cabinet O'Connor & Farber et en 1944, il succède à Norman H. Davis en tant que président de la Croix-Rouge américaine.

O'Connor a été administrateur de plusieurs sociétés : dans les années 1920, de la New England Fuel Oil Corp., dans les années 1940 de l'American Reserve Insurance Co. et de la West Indies Sugar Corp. De 1928 à sa mort, il a été responsable de l'administration de la Georgia Warm Springs Foundation.

Le Roosevelt New Deal était une mine d'or pour certains des associés de FDR, dont Basil O'Connor. Globe & Rutgers était une compagnie d'assurance recapitalisée avec des fonds publics, et la réorganisation s'est avérée une riche source d'honoraires pour les avocats chargés de la liquidation et de la réorganisation. Parmi ces avocats, l'ancien cabinet du président Roosevelt, O'Connor & Farber, a exigé les honoraires les plus élevés jusqu'à ce que Jesse Jones de la Reconstruction Finance Corporation les réduise. Voici une lettre que Jesse Jones a écrite à Earle Bailie de J. & W. Seligman & Company à propos de ces honoraires :

> 6 octobre 1933. Cher M. Bailie :
> Notre conseil d'administration n'est pas disposé à investir ou à prêter des actions dans une compagnie d'assurance, si nous avons effectivement le droit de le faire, qui envisage de payer des honoraires d'avocats, de procéder à une réorganisation ou autre, comme cela est proposé dans le cas du Globe & Rutgers, qui, d'après les informations dont nous disposons

Basil O'Connor	$200,000
Root, Clark, Buckner & Ballantine	$165,000
Sullivan & Cromwell	$95,000
Prentice & Townsend	$50,000
Cravath, de Gersdorff, Swaine & Wood37.	$500
Martin Conboy	$35,000
Joseph V. McKee	$25,000
Frères Coudert	$12,000

> soit un total de 619 500 dollars. Même la réduction suggérée à un total de 426 000 dollars serait bien plus que ce qui semblerait à cette société être des frais appropriés à payer par une compagnie d'assurance qui est recapitalisée avec des fonds publics.
> Bien à vous, JESSE J. JONES

En vertu d'une ordonnance du tribunal, l'entreprise de M. O'Connor a reçu 100 000 dollars en 1934 et 35 000 dollars de plus l'année suivante.[423]

[423] Jesse H. Jones, *Fifty Billion Dollars* pp. 209-210.

CONCLUSIONS CONCERNANT LE 120 BROADWAY

Il est pratiquement impossible de tirer une conclusion inébranlable sur l'importance du 120 Broadway ; les explications peuvent aller de la conspiration à la coïncidence.

Que pouvons-nous prouver avec des preuves directes plutôt que circonstancielles ?

Tout d'abord, nous savons que l'aide américaine à la révolution bolchévique a pris naissance dans le cercle d'or de Wall Street en 1917 et qu'elle était fortement concentrée à cette adresse particulière. Deuxièmement, lorsque FDR est entré dans le monde des affaires en 1921, l'un de ses deux bureaux se trouvait à cette adresse, tout comme son partenariat juridique avec Basil O'Connor et la Georgia Warm Springs Foundation. Troisièmement, Bernard Baruch et son assistant Hugh Johnson, qui a plus tard participé à la planification et à l'administration de la loi sur la relance de l'industrie nationale, se trouvaient dans le même bâtiment. La NRA était la suite logique des associations commerciales des années 1920, et FDR a joué un rôle de premier plan, avec Herbert Hoover, dans la mise en œuvre des accords d'association commerciale dans les années 1920. Quatrièmement, il y a eu une association entre General Electric et la révolution bolchévique, du moins dans la construction de l'Union soviétique naissante. Les bureaux exécutifs de G.E. se trouvaient à cette adresse, tout comme ceux de Gerard Swope, le président de G.E. qui a rédigé le plan Swope.

Enfin, l'étrange affaire Butler a eu quelques liens avec le 120 Broadway. Par exemple, c'était l'adresse de Du Pont à New York, bien que Remington Arms se soit rendu au siège de Rockefeller, au 25 Broadway. La plupart des comploteurs avaient d'autres adresses, mais toujours dans le cercle d'or.

Rien n'est prouvé par une localisation géographique commune. Si le 120 Broadway était un bâtiment massif, il n'était en aucun cas le plus grand de New York. Mais comment expliquer la concentration à une même adresse de tant de liens vers tant d'événements historiques importants ? On pourrait dire que les oiseaux d'une même plume se rassemblent. D'un autre côté, il est plus que plausible que ces Wall Streeters suivaient la maxime de Frederick Howe et trouvaient plus pratique, ou peut-être plus efficace pour leurs objectifs, d'être à une seule adresse. Le point à retenir est qu'il n'existe aucune autre concentration géographique de ce type et, si nous ignorons les personnes et les entreprises du 120 Broadway, il n'y a aucune raison d'établir un lien entre ces événements historiques et Wall Street. C'est d'ailleurs une excellente raison pour garder son point de vue en acceptant le fait que nous parlons d'une petite fraction de la communauté bancaire, une fraction qui a en fait trahi le centre financier d'une économie libre.

CHAPITRE XII

FDR ET LES SOCIALISTES D'ENTREPRISE

Lors de la première réunion du cabinet après l'entrée en fonction du président en 1933, le financier et conseiller de Roosevelt, Bernard Baruch et son ami le général Hugh Johnson, qui allait devenir le chef de l'administration du rétablissement national, sont venus avec un exemplaire d'un livre de Gentile, le théoricien fasciste italien, pour chaque membre du cabinet, et nous l'avons tous lu avec beaucoup de soin.

Mme Frances Perkins, Secrétaire au Travail de FDR.

Il convient de rappeler à ce stade l'épigraphe du chapitre 1, selon laquelle Franklin D. Roosevelt pensait en privé que le gouvernement américain était détenu par une élite financière. Cette observation n'a bien sûr rien de particulièrement original : elle était courante au XIXe siècle. À l'époque moderne, des écrivains aussi différents que Robert Welch et William Domhoff ont affirmé que l'Amérique était contrôlée par une élite financière basée à New York.

Les Soviétiques, qui n'ont pas toujours tort, ont utilisé ce thème dans leur propagande pendant des décennies, et c'était un thème marxiste avant l'arrivée de Lénine au pouvoir.[424]

C'est sous Roosevelt que des notions keynésiennes pittoresques - les versions modernes du jeu d'escroquerie de John Law avec le papier-monnaie - ont été introduites à Washington, et c'est ainsi que les graines de notre chaos économique actuel ont été jetées au début des années 1930 sous Roosevelt. L'inflation actuelle

[424] Il est peut-être superflu de citer cette littérature, mais par souci d'exhaustivité et pour le bénéfice du lecteur innocent, quelques titres peuvent être inclus : William Domhoff, *Qui dirige l'Amérique ?* (Englewood Cliffs, N.J. : Prentice-Hall, 1967) ; Ferdinand Lundberg, *The Rich and the Super Rich* (New York : Lyle Stuart, 1968), et Gary Allen, *None Dare Call It Conspiracy* (Seal Beach, Californie : Concord Press, 1972) Il est certain que si le poids du papier imprimé a une quelconque influence, le pouvoir de toute élite financière aurait dû s'effondrer depuis longtemps. L'establishment semble avoir une endurance considérable, mais son influence est loin d'être aussi importante que beaucoup le croient. La communauté universitaire est le pilier le plus important qui maintient la crédibilité et donc le pouvoir de l'élite. Ce groupe a, en grande partie, échangé la vérité et l'intégrité contre une partie du pouvoir politique et de l'action financière. Apparemment, les universitaires peuvent être achetés - et pour pas trop cher !

à deux chiffres, un système de sécurité sociale en faillite, une bureaucratie étatique en panne, la hausse du chômage - tout cela et bien d'autres choses encore peuvent être attribués à Franklin Delano Roosevelt et à son tourbillon législatif.

Mais alors que nous payons aujourd'hui le prix de ces politiques malsaines et irresponsables, la désinformation est si répandue que même l'identité des initiateurs du New Deal de Roosevelt et leurs raisons ont été oubliées. Alors que nos économistes couvrent leurs tableaux noirs d'équations statiques dénuées de sens, une opération de pillage dynamique de l'économie est en cours de la part des véritables formulateurs du New Deal libéral.

Alors que les ingénieurs sociaux au cœur tendre ont crié au capitalisme comme étant la cause de la misère du monde, ils ont été béatement inconscients que leurs propres formules sociales émanaient en partie - et ont certainement été discrètement subventionnées - par ces mêmes soi-disant élites capitalistes. La vision étroite de notre monde universitaire est difficile à battre et n'a d'égal que son avidité à toucher des subventions.

Ce que nous constatons, c'est que l'intervention du gouvernement dans l'économie est à l'origine de nos problèmes actuels ; qu'une coterie de Wall Street dispose d'une force substantielle, bien que subtile, au sein de cette structure gouvernementale pour obtenir une législation qui lui soit bénéfique ; et qu'un exemple parfait de cette législation égoïste visant à établir un monopole légal sous le contrôle des grandes entreprises a été le New Deal de FDR et, en particulier, l'Administration Nationale de Redressement.

Le nom de Franklin Delano Roosevelt devrait suggérer, mais c'est rarement le cas, un lien avec Wall Street. Delano et Roosevelt sont tous deux des noms importants dans l'histoire des institutions financières américaines.

Qui était Franklin Delano Roosevelt ?

La carrière pré-politique de Roosevelt ne peut être décrite que comme celle d'un financier. Sa famille et sa carrière avant 1928, ainsi que son élection au poste de gouverneur de New York, étaient toutes deux dans le monde des affaires, plus précisément dans le monde financier. Entre 1921 et 1928, Roosevelt a été directeur de 11 sociétés dont le siège se trouvait dans le cercle d'or de Wall Street et président d'une importante association commerciale. Le Conseil Américain de la Construction.

En outre, Roosevelt n'était pas seulement président de United European Investors, Ltd, créée pour tirer un avantage pécuniaire de la misère de l'hyperinflation allemande, mais il était l'un des organisateurs de l'American Investigation Corporation, un puissant syndicat financier. Les Roosevelt ont formé la société financière Roosevelt & Son à la fin du XVIIIe siècle, et les Delano ont opéré dans l'arène financière à partir du milieu du XIXe siècle au moins.

Les Roosevelt et les Delano n'ont peut-être pas amassé la grande richesse des Morgan et des Rockefeller, mais ils étaient des noms connus et respectés dans les cénacles de la finance internationale. Même dans les années 1920, nous trouvons l'oncle Frederic Delano au conseil de la Réserve Fédérale, et George Emlen Roosevelt comme directeur du Guaranty Trust, la bête noire des gauchistes.

On sait également que le Parti progressiste de Theodore Roosevelt, premier pas vers l'État-providence moderne, a été financé par les intérêts de J.P. Morgan ;

il ne faut donc pas s'étonner que Wall Street ait soutenu Roosevelt en 1928, 1930 et 1932.

En bref, nous avons montré que Roosevelt était un Wall Streeter, descendant de familles importantes de Wall Street et soutenu financièrement par Wall Street. Les politiques mises en œuvre par le régime Roosevelt étaient précisément celles requises par le monde de la finance internationale. Il ne devrait pas être nouveau pour nous que les banquiers internationaux influencent la politique. Ce qui semble avoir été négligé dans l'histoire de l'ère Roosevelt, c'est que non seulement FDR reflétait ses objectifs, mais qu'il était plus enclin à le faire que le soi-disant réactionnaire Herbert Hoover. En fait, Hoover a perdu en 1932 parce que, selon ses propres termes, il n'était pas disposé à accepter le plan Swope, alias NRA, qu'il a qualifié, non sans raison, de "mesure fasciste".

On ne peut pas dire que le Wall Streeter Roosevelt a toujours été un promoteur très éthique dans ses décisions financières. Les acheteurs de ses obligations ont perdu de l'argent, et des sommes considérables, comme le suggère le bref tableau suivant, basé sur les données présentées :

Comment les investisseurs ont profité des mesures de FDR aux commandes

Société associée à FDR	Prix d'émission des actions	Historique des prix ultérieurs
United European Investors, Ltd	10 000 marks (environ 13 dollars)	Entreprise liquidée, les actionnaires se voient offrir 7,50$
International Germanic Trust Company, Inc.	$170	Il est passé à 257$ en 1928, puis a été liquidé en 1930 à 19$ l'action

La perte des fonds des actionnaires peut cependant être liée à un accident ou une mauvaise gestion. De nombreux financiers honnêtes ont échoué. Cependant, l'association avec des personnes de mauvaise réputation connues comme Roberts et Gould dans United European Investors, Ltd. n'était pas accidentelle.

L'association de FDR avec le Conseil Américain de la Construction rappelle l'*obita dicta d'*Adam Smith selon laquelle la loi "... ne peut empêcher les gens du même métier de se réunir parfois, mais elle ne doit rien faire pour faciliter ces réunions, et encore moins les rendre nécessaires".[425] Et pourquoi pas ? Parce que le Conseil Américain de la Construction agissait dans l'intérêt de l'industrie de la construction, et non dans celui du consommateur de services de construction.

L'activité de cautionnement à New York a été faite sur commande pour FDR. En tant que vice-président de la Fidelity & Deposit Company du Maryland, FDR savait précisément comment opérer dans le monde des affaires politisées, où le prix et la qualité des produits sur le marché sont remplacés par des questions telles que "Qui connaissez-vous ?" et "Quelles sont vos politiques ?"

Le coup des Investisseurs Européens Unis était une tentative de tirer profit de la misère de l'hyperinflation allemande de 1921-23. La société opérait sous une

[425] Adam Smith, *An Inquiry Into the Nature and Causes of the Wealth of Nations* (Londres : George Routledge s.d.), p. 102.

charte canadienne, sans doute parce que les conditions d'enregistrement au Canada étaient plus souples à l'époque. L'observation la plus flagrante concerne les associés de FDR à l'U.E.I., dont John von Berenberg Gossler, co-directeur de l'HAPAG du chancelier allemand Cuno, qui était responsable de l'inflation ! Et puis il y a William Schall, l'associé new-yorkais de FDR, qui, quelques années auparavant, avait participé à l'espionnage allemand aux États-Unis - au 120 Broadway. L'élément Roberts-Gould dans United European Investors faisait l'objet d'une enquête criminelle ; FDR savait qu'il faisait l'objet d'une enquête, mais il a continué ses associations d'affaires.

Nous avons ensuite découvert que le fond du New Deal était constellé de financiers de premier plan. Le volet "relance économique" du New Deal était une création de Wall Street - plus précisément de Bernard Baruch et Gerard Swope de General Electric - sous la forme du plan Swope. Dans le chapitre 5, nous avons donc développé l'idée de la politisation des affaires et formulé la thèse du socialisme d'entreprise : la manière politique de gérer une économie est plus attrayante pour les grandes entreprises parce qu'elle évite les rigueurs et l'efficacité imposée d'un système de marché libre. En outre, grâce au contrôle des entreprises ou à l'influence exercée par les organismes de régulation et le pouvoir de police de l'État, le système politique est un moyen efficace d'obtenir un monopole, et un monopole légal conduit toujours à la richesse. Par conséquent, Wall Street s'intéresse intensément à l'arène politique et soutient les candidats politiques capables de maximiser le nombre de décisions politiques, quelle que soit leur appellation, et de minimiser la mesure dans laquelle les décisions économiques de la société sont prises sur le marché.

Wall Street a un intérêt direct dans la politique, car, par le biais de la politique, elle peut faire en sorte que la société travaille pour Wall Street. Elle peut ainsi éviter les pénalités et les risques du marché.

Nous avons examiné une première version de cette idée : La société planifiée de Clinton Roosevelt, publiée en 1841. Nous avons ensuite brièvement discuté de la dictature économique de Bernard Baruch en 1917 et de son intention déclarée de suivre le cours d'une économie planifiée en temps de paix. Nous avons retracé l'histoire de Baruch et de son assistant économique Hugh Johnson jusqu'au cœur même de l'administration de la reprise nationale. Une certaine attention a ensuite été accordée au système de la Réserve Fédérale en tant qu'exemple le plus important de monopole légal privé et au rôle des Warburg par l'intermédiaire de l'International Acceptance Bank et à la manière dont la banque a pu amener la société à travailler pour Wall Street. Dans un dernier regard sur les années précédant le New Deal de FDR, nous avons examiné le fonctionnement de l'American Construction Council, une association commerciale dont le concept est né avec Herbert Hoover, mais dont FDR est le président. Le conseil avait pour objectifs déclarés de limiter la production et de réglementer l'industrie, un euphémisme pour dire que l'industrie contrôlait la maximisation de ses propres profits.

Ensuite, nous avons examiné les contributions financières des élections de 1928, 1930 et 1932 au motif que ces contributions sont une mesure très précise des tendances politiques. En 1928, un pourcentage extraordinaire des contributions les plus importantes, celles de plus de 25 000 dollars, provenait du cercle d'or de Wall Street. Des sommes aussi importantes sont révélatrices, car leurs contributeurs sont plus que probablement identifiables après les élections lorsqu'ils demandent des faveurs en échange de leurs subventions antérieures. Nous avons constaté que pas moins de 78,83% des contributions de plus de 1000 dollars à la campagne d'Al Smith pour la présidence provenaient d'un cercle d'un mile centré sur le 120 Broadway. De même, 51,4% des contributions de Hoover, un chiffre moins élevé mais néanmoins significatif, provenaient de cette même zone. Nous avons ensuite démontré qu'après son élection, Herbert Hoover a reçu un ultimatum de Wall Street : soit il acceptait le plan Swope (la NRA), soit l'argent et l'influence de Wall Street allaient à FDR qui était prêt à mettre en place ce plan. Pour son honneur éternel, Herbert Hoover a refusé d'introduire un tel plan au motif qu'il était équivalent à l'État fasciste de Mussolini. FDR n'était pas si regardant.

Lors de la campagne de 1930 de FDR pour le poste de gouverneur de New York, nous avons identifié une influence majeure de Wall Street. Il y a eu un flux extraordinaire de fonds via la County Trust Company, et John J. Raskob de Du Pont et General Motors est devenu le président du Comité de campagne du partir démocrate et le pouvoir en coulisse déterminant l'élection de FDR. Soixante-dix-huit pour cent des contributions "early-bird" pré-convention pour la candidature présidentielle de FDR en 1932 provenaient de Wall Street.

Le plan Swope était un plan visant à contraindre l'industrie américaine à adhérer à des associations commerciales obligatoires et à l'exempter des lois antitrust. Il a utilisé l'appât d'une carotte sociale massive pour apaiser les craintes des travailleurs et d'autres groupes. L'administrateur de la National Recovery Administration, qui s'est développée à partir du Swope Plan, était l'assistant de Baruch. Le général Hugh Johnson. Les trois mousquetaires, le cercle des assistants de Johnson, comprenaient Gerard Swope de General Electric, Walter Teagle, de la Standard Oil du New Jersey, et Louis Kirstein de Filene's de Boston. L'adhésion aux codes de la NRA était obligatoire pour toutes les entreprises de plus de 50 employés. Le plan Swope NRA a été accueilli favorablement par des socialistes tels que Norman Thomas, dont la principale objection était qu'eux, les socialistes orthodoxes, ne devaient pas gérer le plan.

Heureusement, la NRA a échoué. Les grandes entreprises ont tenté d'opprimer la classe moyenne. Les codes étaient truffés d'abus et d'incohérences. La Cour suprême y a mis un terme dans l'arrêt Schechter Poultry de 1935, bien que son échec ait été évident bien avant la décision de la Cour suprême. En raison de l'échec de la NRA, la soi-disant affaire Butler de 1934 devient d'un intérêt particulier. Selon le témoignage du général Smedley Butler au Congrès, appuyé par des témoins indépendants, il y avait un plan pour installer un dictateur à la Maison Blanche. Le président Roosevelt devait être mis à la porte et un nouveau secrétaire général, le général Butler, s'est vu offrir l'après-guerre pour prendre en charge l'économie au nom de Wall Street. Aussi farfelue que cette accusation puisse paraître, nous pouvons isoler trois grandes déclarations de fait :

1. Les déclarations du général Butler ont été confirmées de manière indépendante et, dans une certaine mesure, l'un des comploteurs n'a pas voulu les confirmer.

2. Wall Street avait un motif pour lancer un pari aussi désespéré : la proposition NRA-Swope était en train de s'effondrer.

3. L'identité présumée des hommes en coulisses est la même que celle des hommes identifiés dans la révolution bolchévique et dans la promotion politique de FDR.

Malheureusement, et pour sa honte éternelle, le Congrès a supprimé l'essentiel du témoignage de Butler. De plus, le *New York Times* a d'abord rapporté l'histoire de manière équitable, mais a ensuite enterré et déformé sa couverture, jusqu'à une indexation incomplète. Il reste une possibilité certaine que l'échec du plan Baruch-Swope-Johnson de la NRA soit suivi d'une prise de contrôle plus secrète et coercitive de l'industrie américaine. Cet événement mérite toute l'attention que des universitaires impartiaux peuvent lui porter. De toute évidence, l'histoire complète n'a pas encore été révélée.

Une fois de plus, comme dans le volume précédent, nous avons trouvé une concentration remarquable de personnes, d'entreprises et d'événements à une seule adresse : 120 Broadway, New York City. C'était l'adresse du bureau de FDR en tant que président de Fidelity & Deposit Company. C'était l'adresse de Bernard Baruch et celle de Gerard Swope. Les trois principaux promoteurs de la National Recovery Administration - FDR, Baruch et Swope - se trouvaient à la même adresse dans les années 1920. Le plus troublant est que la première réunion pour l'affaire Butler s'est tenue en 1926 au Bankers Club, également situé au 120 Broadway.

Aucune explication n'est encore donnée pour cette remarquable concentration de talents et d'idées à une seule adresse. Il est évident qu'il s'agit d'une constatation dont il faudra tôt ou tard tenir compte. Nous avons également trouvé une concentration de directeurs de l'American International Corporation, le véhicule de l'implication de Wall Street dans la révolution bolchévique, et de gros contributeurs à la campagne Roosevelt.

Peut-on envisager cette histoire dans une perspective plus large ? Les idées derrière le Roosevelt New Deal n'étaient pas vraiment celles de Wall Street ; elles remontent en fait à l'époque romaine. De 49 à 44 avant J.-C., Jules César a eu ses projets de travaux publics dans le cadre du New Deal ; en 91 après J.-C., Domitien a fait appel à son équivalent de l'American Construction Council pour arrêter la surproduction. La chute finale de Rome a reflété tous les éléments que nous reconnaissons aujourd'hui : des dépenses publiques extravagantes, une inflation rapide et une fiscalité écrasante, le tout associé à une réglementation étatique totalitaire.[426]

Sous Woodrow Wilson Wall Street a obtenu un monopole de banque centrale, le Système de la Réserve Fédérale. L'importance de l'International Acceptance Bank, contrôlée par l'établissement financier de Wall Street, était que les banques de la Réserve Fédérale utilisaient le pouvoir de police de l'État pour se créer une machine à fabriquer de l'argent perpétuelle : la capacité de créer de l'argent d'un coup de crayon ou en appuyant sur une touche d'ordinateur. Les Warburg,

---

[426] H. J. Haskell, *The New Deal in Old Rome: How Government in the Ancient World Tried to Deal with Modern Problems* (New York : Knopf, 1947), pp. 239-40.

personnages clés de l'International Acceptance Bank - une machine à fabriquer de l'argent à l'étranger - étaient des conseillers de l'administration Roosevelt et de ses politiques monétaires. L'or a été qualifié de "relique barbare", ouvrant la voie à une monnaie de papier sans valeur aux États-Unis. En 1975, au moment où nous écrivons, la monnaie fiduciaire du dollar inconvertible est manifestement en voie de dépréciation ultime.

Wall Street a-t-il reconnu le résultat du retrait de l'or comme soutien à la monnaie ? Bien sûr que oui ! Voici le témoignage de Paul Warburg devant une commission du Congrès :

> "L'abandon de l'étalon-or signifie une fluctuation brutale des taux de change et, par conséquent, la destruction de la libre circulation des capitaux et des affaires étrangères. Les pays faibles répudieront - ou, pour utiliser une expression plus polie, "financeront leurs dettes" - mais il n'y aura pas de démonétisation générale de l'or. À la fin de la guerre, l'or ne vaudra pas moins mais plus."[427]

La conclusion inévitable que nous imposent ces preuves est qu'il existe effectivement une élite financière, comme l'a souligné Franklin D. Roosevelt, et que l'objectif de cette élite est l'acquisition monopolistique de la richesse. Nous avons qualifié cette élite de partisane du socialisme d'entreprise. Elle prospère grâce au processus politique, et elle s'éteindrait si elle était exposée à l'activité d'un marché libre. Le grand paradoxe est que l'influent mouvement socialiste mondial, qui se considère comme un ennemi de cette élite, est en fait le générateur de cette politisation de l'activité économique qui maintient le monopole au pouvoir et que son grand héros, Franklin D. Roosevelt, en a été un instrument à l'efficacité redoutable.

---

[427] Sénat des États-Unis, Hearings, Munitions Industry, partie 25, op. cit. p. 8105.

ANNEXE A

LE PLAN SWOPE

1. Toutes les sociétés industrielles et commerciales (y compris les filiales) employant 50 personnes ou plus et exerçant une activité interétatique peuvent former une association professionnelle qui sera placée sous la supervision d'un organisme fédéral visé plus loin.

2. Ces associations professionnelles peuvent décrire les pratiques commerciales, l'éthique des affaires, les méthodes de comptabilité standard et de calcul des coûts, les formulaires standard de bilan et de compte de résultat, etc. et peuvent collecter et distribuer des informations sur le volume des transactions commerciales, les stocks de marchandises en stock, la simplification et la normalisation des produits, la stabilisation des prix et toutes les questions qui peuvent se poser de temps à autre concernant la croissance et le développement de l'industrie et du commerce afin de promouvoir la stabilisation de l'emploi et de donner le meilleur service au public. Une grande partie de ce type d'échange d'informations et de données est déjà assurée par les associations professionnelles existantes. Un travail beaucoup plus précieux de ce type est possible.

3. L'intérêt public est protégé par la surveillance des entreprises et des associations commerciales par la Commission fédérale du commerce ou par un bureau du ministère du commerce ou par un organe de surveillance fédéral spécialement constitué.

4. Toutes les entreprises relevant de ce plan sont tenues d'adopter des systèmes de comptabilité et de coûts standard et des formes normalisées de bilan et de compte de résultat. Ces systèmes et formulaires peuvent différer selon les secteurs, mais ils suivront un plan uniforme pour chaque secteur, tel qu'adopté par l'association professionnelle et approuvé par l'organe de contrôle fédéral.

5. Toute société dont les participants ou actionnaires sont au nombre de 25 ou plus et qui résident dans plus d'un État, doit envoyer à ses participants ou actionnaires et à l'organe de surveillance, au moins une fois par trimestre, un état de ses activités et de ses bénéfices dans la forme prescrite. Au moins une fois par an, ils envoient aux participants ou actionnaires et à l'organe de surveillance un bilan et un compte de résultat complets dans la forme prescrite. De cette manière, les propriétaires seront tenus informés des conditions de l'entreprise de manière suffisamment détaillée pour qu'il ne puisse y avoir aucune critique d'irrégularité ou de rareté des états ou des méthodes de présentation.

6. L'organe fédéral de surveillance coopère avec le ministère des impôts et les associations professionnelles pour élaborer, pour chaque secteur, des formes normalisées de bilan et de compte de résultat, en fonction de la nature de l'entreprise, afin de rapprocher les méthodes de déclaration des actifs et des revenus avec la base des valeurs et des revenus calculés aux fins de l'impôt fédéral.

7. Toutes les sociétés du type décrit dans le présent document peuvent adopter immédiatement les dispositions de ce plan, mais sont tenues de le faire dans un délai de 3 ans, à moins que ce délai ne soit prolongé par l'organe fédéral de surveillance. Les sociétés similaires constituées après l'entrée en vigueur du plan peuvent entrer en activité immédiatement mais sont tenues de le faire avant l'expiration d'un délai de trois ans à compter de la date de leur constitution, à moins que ce délai ne soit prorogé par l'organe fédéral de surveillance.

8. Pour la protection des salariés, les plans suivants sont adoptés par toutes ces entreprises :

A. **Une loi sur l'indemnisation des travailleurs,** qui fait partie de la législation nécessaire dans le cadre de ce plan, doit, après une étude approfondie, être modelée sur les meilleures caractéristiques des lois qui ont été promulguées par les différents États.

B. **L'ASSURANCE VIE ET L'ASSURANCE INVALIDITÉ**. Tous les employés des sociétés incluses dans ce plan peuvent, après deux ans de service dans ces sociétés, et doivent, avant l'expiration de cinq ans de service, être couverts par une assurance vie et invalidité.

1) La forme de la politique est déterminée par l'association dont la société est membre et approuvée par l'organe fédéral de surveillance. La police appartiendra à l'employé et pourra être conservée par lui et rester pleinement en vigueur lorsqu'il changera d'emploi ou cessera un service particulier comme indiqué plus loin.

2) La valeur nominale d'une police est d'un montant approximativement égal à une année de salaire, mais ne dépassant pas 5000 dollars, à l'exception du fait que l'employé peut, s'il le souhaite, augmenter à ses frais le montant de l'assurance souscrite, sous réserve de l'approbation du conseil d'administration, défini ultérieurement.

3) Le coût de cette assurance vie et invalidité est payé pour moitié par l'employé et pour moitié par l'entreprise pour laquelle il travaille, à l'exception de ce qui suit : le coût de l'entreprise est déterminé sur la base des primes à l'âge réel des employés de moins de 35 ans et sur la base de 35 ans pour tous les employés de 35 ans ou plus et est d'une valeur nominale d'environ une demi année de salaire mais limité à une prime maximale de 2500$ d'assurance. L'employé qui souscrit une assurance à l'âge de 35 ans ou plus paiera la prime excédentaire par rapport au montant basé sur l'âge de 35 ans. Cette mesure supprimera la nécessité de restreindre l'embauche d'employés ou leur transfert d'une entreprise à une autre en raison de leur âge avancé, car elle n'imposera pas à l'entreprise une charge excessive de primes élevées.

4) L'assurance vie et invalidité peut être souscrite par une compagnie d'assurance vie choisie par l'association professionnelle et approuvée par l'organe de contrôle fédéral ou peut être souscrite par une compagnie organisée par l'association professionnelle et approuvée par l'organe de contrôle fédéral, ou une seule compagnie peut être constituée pour servir toutes les associations.

5) L'administration du régime d'assurance de chaque entreprise est placée sous la direction d'un conseil d'administration composé de représentants, dont la moitié est élue par les membres salariés. Les pouvoirs et les devoirs du conseil pour chaque entreprise seront de formuler des règles générales relatives à l'éligibilité des employés, etc., mais ces règles devront être en accord avec le plan général établi par le conseil d'administration général de l'association professionnelle dont l'entreprise est membre, et approuvé par l'organe fédéral de contrôle.

6) Les dispositions relatives à la poursuite d'une police après qu'un employé quitte une entreprise et va dans une autre dans la même association, ou va dans une entreprise dans une autre association professionnelle ; la poursuite de la police après la retraite à la retraite ; les dispositions relatives aux bénéficiaires ; l'invalidité totale ou partielle ; le mode de paiement des primes par retenues sur le salaire ou autrement, hebdomadaire, mensuel ou annuel, doivent être incorporées dans le plan formulé par l'association professionnelle, avec l'approbation de l'organe fédéral de surveillance.

7) Si un salarié quitte une entreprise pour rejoindre une entreprise non membre de l'association professionnelle, s'il s'engage dans une activité commerciale pour lui-même ou s'il se retire d'une activité industrielle ou commerciale, il peut choisir de conserver la partie de la police qu'il a payée, en tout ou en partie, en continuant à payer les coûts des primes intégrales proportionnelles, ou il peut recevoir une police libérée, ou se voir verser la valeur de rachat de la partie pour laquelle il a payé les primes. La valeur de rachat de la partie de la police payée par la compagnie sera versée à la compagnie qui a payé les primes.

C. PENSIONS. Tous les employés des entreprises incluses dans ce plan sont couverts par des plans de pension de vieillesse qui seront adoptés par les associations professionnelles et approuvés par l'organe fédéral de contrôle. Les principales dispositions seront les suivantes :

1) Tout salarié peut, après deux ans de service dans une entreprise entrant dans le champ d'application de ce régime, et doit, avant l'expiration de cinq ans de service, être couvert par le régime de pension de vieillesse.

2) Tout salarié peut, après deux ans de service, et est tenu, après cinq ans de service, de mettre de côté pour le fonds de pension un minimum d'un pour cent de ses revenus, mais pas plus de 50 dollars par an. L'employé peut, s'il le souhaite, mettre de côté un montant plus important, sous réserve de l'approbation du conseil d'administration.

3) La société est tenue de mettre de côté un montant égal au minimum indiqué ci-dessus, à savoir un pour cent des revenus des employés, mais pas plus de 50 dollars par an et par employé.

4) Le pourcentage minimum ci-dessus est le même pour tous les employés qui ont moins de 35 ans lorsque les paiements commencent et le pourcentage minimum pour ces employés reste le même par la suite. Le pourcentage à mettre de côté par les employés qui entrent dans le régime de retraite à 35 ans ou plus est déterminé de telle sorte qu'il leur assure une allocation de retraite à 70 ans, comme s'ils avaient commencé à verser un pour cent à l'âge de 35 ans. Ces dispositions permettent aux salariés de passer d'une entreprise à l'autre dans la même association ou dans des associations différentes à tout âge avec une provision pour les allocations de retraite qui ne sera pas inférieure au taux minimum d'un salarié entré dans le régime de retraite à 35 ans.

5) Les montants mis de côté par l'employé et l'entreprise avec des intérêts composés semestriellement à 5% jusqu'à la retraite à 70 ans, pour un employé moyen typique, donneraient une rente d'environ la moitié du salaire.

6) L'administration du régime de retraite de chaque entreprise est placée sous la direction d'un conseil d'administration, composé de représentants, dont la moitié est nommée par la direction et l'autre moitié élue par les membres salariés. Les pouvoirs et les devoirs du conseil pour chaque entreprise seront de formuler des règles générales relatives à l'éligibilité des employés, aux conditions de retraite, etc., mais ces règles devront être en accord avec le plan général établi par le conseil d'administration général de l'association professionnelle dont l'entreprise est membre, et approuvé par l'organe fédéral de surveillance.

7) Les sommes collectées auprès des salariés et des entreprises sont placées dans le fonds de pension organisé par l'association, dont la gestion est placée sous la direction du conseil d'administration général visé ci-après. En aucun cas, ces fonds ne doivent être laissés sous le contrôle d'une entreprise individuelle.

8) Le fonds de pension doit investir tous les fonds et les placer au crédit des employés individuels, y compris les revenus gagnés par le fonds. Si un salarié passe d'une société à une autre dans la même association, les fonds accumulés à son crédit sont maintenus à son crédit avec un enregistrement de transfert en bonne et due forme. Si un salarié va dans une société d'une autre association, les fonds accumulés à son crédit sont transférés à son crédit dans le fonds de pension de l'association à laquelle il va. Si un salarié va dans une société qui ne relève pas des présentes dispositions ou qui n'est pas membre d'une association professionnelle, s'il se met à son compte ou s'il se retire d'une activité industrielle ou commerciale, le montant de ses versements, majoré des intérêts au taux moyen des fonds, lui est remis. Si un salarié décède avant d'avoir atteint l'âge de la retraite, son bénéficiaire recevra le montant de ses versements, majoré des intérêts au taux moyen acquis par les fonds. Lorsqu'un employé atteint l'âge de la retraite, la totalité du montant accumulé à son crédit, y compris ses propres paiements et ceux de l'entreprise, plus les intérêts accumulés, lui sera donnée sous forme de rente. Si un salarié va dans une entreprise qui ne relève pas de ces dispositions ou qui n'est pas membre d'une association professionnelle, s'il se met à son compte ou s'il se retire d'une activité industrielle ou commerciale, il peut choisir de laisser le montant à son crédit (à savoir ses propres paiements plus ceux de l'entreprise et les intérêts accumulés) à la fiducie de retraite pour le transférer, s'il retourne à l'emploi d'une entreprise relevant des dispositions de ce régime. S'il ne revient pas au service d'une entreprise relevant de ces dispositions, il peut à tout moment par la suite retirer le montant de ses propres versements plus les intérêts au taux moyen gagné par les fonds jusqu'à ce moment. Les cotisations de l'entreprise et les intérêts cumulés crédités aux salariés qui décèdent, ou qui, pour les raisons indiquées ci-dessus, reçoivent ou retirent leurs propres cotisations et intérêts, sont restitués à l'employeur ou aux employeurs qui ont versé les cotisations.

9) Les règles régissant le paiement des pensions de retraite et toutes les autres règles régissant leur maintien sont établies par l'association professionnelle, approuvées par l'organe fédéral de surveillance et observées par le conseil d'administration général et les conseils d'administration des sociétés membres.

D. L'ASSURANCE CHÔMAGE. Tous les employés travaillant à la pièce, à l'heure, à la journée, à la semaine ou au mois, avec un salaire normal de 5000$ par an ou moins (environ 96,15$ par semaine) sont couverts par l'assurance chômage.

1) Tous ces employés peuvent, après deux ans de service dans une entreprise relevant des dispositions du présent régime, et sont tenus, après cinq ans de service, de mettre chacun de leur côté un minimum de 1% de leur salaire, mais pas plus de 50$ par an pour une caisse d'assurance chômage.

2) La société est tenue de mettre de côté un montant égal à celui mis de côté par les salariés, comme indiqué ci-dessus, à savoir un pour cent du salaire de chaque salarié, mais pas plus de 50 dollars par an pour chacun de ces salariés.
3) Si une entreprise régularise et garantit l'emploi d'au moins 50% du salaire normal versé chaque année à ces employés, il n'est pas nécessaire de procéder à l'évaluation de l'entreprise pour les employés couverts par cette garantie, mais les employés verseront un minimum d'un pour cent de leurs revenus, mais pas plus de 50$ par an, dans un fonds spécial à leur propre profit.
Si un tel salarié quitte l'entreprise, décède ou prend sa retraite, le montant de son crédit dans le fonds spécial, majoré des intérêts au taux moyen du fonds spécial, lui est versé ou est versé à ses bénéficiaires ou est ajouté à sa pension.
4) Si une entreprise planifie son travail de manière à pouvoir réduire le chômage, lorsque le montant de son crédit dans la caisse de chômage normale est égal mais non inférieur à 5% des revenus annuels normaux des salariés couverts, l'entreprise peut cesser de verser des cotisations à la caisse. Les versements des salariés continueront.
L'entreprise reprendra ses paiements lorsque son crédit dans la caisse de chômage normale tombera en dessous de 5% des revenus annuels normaux des salariés couverts.
5) Lorsque les versements hebdomadaires effectués par la caisse d'allocations de chômage s'élèvent à 2% ou plus du salaire hebdomadaire moyen des salariés participants, l'entreprise déclare l'urgence du chômage, et les versements normaux des salariés et de l'entreprise cessent. Par la suite, tous les salariés de l'entreprise (y compris les cadres supérieurs) qui perçoivent 50% ou plus de leur salaire moyen à temps plein versent 1% de leur salaire actuel à la caisse de chômage. Un montant similaire est versé au fonds par la société. L'urgence du chômage se poursuit jusqu'à ce que les conditions normales soient rétablies, ce qui est déterminé par le conseil d'administration de chaque société. À ce moment-là, les paiements normaux reprendront.
6) Les principales dispositions relatives à la répartition des fonds suivent ces principes, sauf modification par le conseil d'administration comme indiqué à la section D, paragraphe 7, du présent document. Un certain pourcentage des paiements normaux des salariés et de l'entreprise peut être considéré comme disponible pour aider les salariés participants dans le besoin. Un pourcentage plus important de ces paiements normaux peut être considéré comme disponible pour des prêts aux salariés participants pour des montants n'excédant pas 200 dollars chacun, avec ou sans intérêt, selon ce que détermine le conseil d'administration. Le solde des fonds sera disponible pour les indemnités de chômage. Les indemnités de chômage commencent à être versées après les deux premières semaines de chômage et s'élèvent à environ 50% du salaire hebdomadaire ou mensuel moyen du salarié participant pour un temps plein, mais en aucun cas à plus de 20$ par semaine. Ces versements aux salariés individuels se poursuivent pendant dix semaines au maximum au cours de douze mois consécutifs, sauf prolongation par le Conseil. Lorsqu'un employé participant travaille à temps partiel par manque de travail et reçoit moins de 50% de son salaire hebdomadaire ou mensuel moyen pour un temps plein, il peut prétendre à des versements à partir du fonds, s'élevant à la différence entre le montant qu'il reçoit comme salaire de la société et le maximum auquel il peut avoir droit comme indiqué ci-dessus.
7) La garde et le placement des fonds ainsi que l'administration du régime d'assurance chômage de chaque entreprise sont placés sous la direction d'un conseil d'administration composé de représentants, nommés pour moitié par la direction et élus pour moitié par les membres salariés. Les pouvoirs et les devoirs du conseil d'administration sont de formuler des règles générales concernant l'éligibilité des employés, le délai d'attente avant le paiement des prestations, le montant des prestations et leur durée au cours d'une année, la question de savoir si des prêts doivent être accordés en cas de chômage ou de besoin, si une partie des fonds doit être mise à la

disposition du conseil d'administration pour soulager les besoins découlant de causes autres que le chômage, etc.

8) Si un salarié quitte l'entreprise et va travailler pour une autre entreprise relevant des dispositions de ce plan, le montant proportionnel restant de ses cotisations normales, plus les intérêts au taux moyen des fonds, est transféré à cette entreprise et à son crédit. S'il quitte l'entreprise pour d'autres raisons, s'il décède ou s'il prend sa retraite, la quote-part qui lui reste de ses cotisations normales, majorée des intérêts au taux moyen des fonds, lui est versée, ou à son bénéficiaire, ou est ajoutée à sa pension. Lorsque le crédit de ce salarié est transféré à une autre société, ou versé au salarié ou à son bénéficiaire en vertu de la présente disposition, un montant égal est versé à la société coopérante.

L'ADMINISTRATION GÉNÉRALE. Chaque association professionnelle formera un conseil d'administration général qui sera composé de neuf membres, dont trois seront élus ou nommés par l'association, trois seront élus par les employés des entreprises membres et trois, représentant le public, seront nommés par l'organe de contrôle fédéral. Les membres du conseil général, à l'exception des représentants des travailleurs, exercent leurs fonctions sans rémunération. Les représentants des salariés sont rémunérés au taux normal pour le temps consacré aux travaux du conseil, et tous les membres reçoivent une indemnité de déplacement, dont la totalité est à la charge de l'association professionnelle. Les pouvoirs et les devoirs de ce Conseil général sont d'interpréter les régimes d'assurance vie et invalidité, de retraite et de chômage adoptés par l'association professionnelle et approuvés par l'organe de contrôle fédéral, de superviser les conseils d'administration de chaque société, de constituer et de diriger un fonds de pension pour la garde, l'investissement et les débours des fonds de pension, et en général de superviser et de diriger toutes les activités liées aux régimes d'assurance vie et invalidité, de retraite et de chômage.

ANNEXE B

SPONSORS DES PLANS PRÉSENTÉS POUR LA PLANIFICATION ÉCONOMIQUE AUX ÉTATS-UNIS EN AVRIL 1932.[428]

American Engineering Council, New York.

Fédération américaine du travail, Washington.

Associated General Contractors, Washington.

Charles A. Beard, New Milford, Conn.

Ralph Borsodi, auteur et économiste. New York.

Chambre de commerce des États-Unis, Washington.

Stuart Chase, auteur et économiste. Bureau du travail, New York.

Wallace B. Donham, doyen de la Harvard School of Business.

Ordre fraternel des aigles (Ludlow bill).

Jay Franklin, auteur, *The Forum*.

Guy Greer, économiste, *The Outlook*.

Otto Kahn, banquier. New York.

Sénateur Robert M. La Follette, Sénat américain.

Lewis L. Lorwin, économiste, Brookings Institute, Washington.

Paul M. Mazur, banquier d'affaires. New York.

McGraw-Hill Publishing Co., New York.

Conseil de la Nouvelle-Angleterre, Boston.

Conférence progressiste (projet de loi La Follette).

P. Redmond, économiste, Schenectady, N.Y.

Sumner Slichter, économiste et auteur, Madison Wis.

George Soule, éditeur, *The New Republic*.

C. R. Stevenson, de Stevenson, Jordanie, et Harrison, New York.

Gerard Swope, président de General Electric Co.

---

[428] Liste compilée par le ministère américain du commerce.

Wisconsin Regional Plan, State Legislature, Madison, Wis.

National Civic Federation, New York.

BIBLIOGRAPHIE SÉLECTIVE

SOURCES NON PUBLIÉES

Les archives de Franklin D. Roosevelt à Hyde Park, New York

SOURCES PUBLIÉES

Archer, Jules. *The Plot to Seize the White House,* (New York : Hawthorn Books, 1973)

Baruch, Bernard M., Baruch, *The Public Years,* (New York : Holt, Rinehart and Winston, 1960)

Bennett, Edward W., *Germany and the Diplomacy of the Financial Crisis,* 1931, (Cambridge : Harvard University Press, 1962)

Bremer, Howard, *Franklin Delano Roosevelt,* 1882-1945, (New York ; Oceana Publications, Inc., 1971),

Burton, David H., *Theodore Roosevelt,* (New York : Twayne Publishers, Inc., 1972)

Davis, Kenneth S., *FDR, The Beckoning of Destiny 1882-1928, A History,* (New York : G. P. Putnam's Sons, 1971)

Dilling, Elizabeth, *The Roosevelt Red Record and Its Background,* (Illinois : par l'auteur, 1936)

Farley, James A., *Behind the Ballots, The Personal History of a Politician,* (New York ; Harcourt, Brace and Company, 1938)

Filene, Edward A., *Successful Living in this Machine Age,* (New York : Simon and Schuster, 1932)

Filene, Edward A., *The Way Out, A Forecast of Coming Changes in American Business and Industry,* (New York : Doubleday, Page & Company, 1924)

Flynn, John T., *The Roosevelt myth,* (New York : *The* Devin-Adair Company, 1948)

Freedman, Max, *Roosevelt and Frankfurter,* Their Correspondence- 1928-1945, (Boston, Toronto : Little, Brown and Company, 1967)

Freidel, Frank, *Franklin D. Roosevelt, The Ordeal,* (Boston : Little, Brown and Company, 1952)

Hanfstaengl, Ernst, *Unheard Witness,* (New York : J.B. Lippincott Company, 1957)

Haskell, H.J., *The New Deal in Old Rome, How Government in the Ancient World Tried to Deal with Modern Problems* (New York : Alfred A. Knopf, 1947.)

Hoover, Herbert C., *Memoirs. The Great Depression, 1929-1941,* (New York : Macmillan Company, 1952), Vol. 3.

Howe, Frederic C., *The Confessions of a Monopolist,* (Chicago ; The Public Publishing Company, 1906)

Hughes, T.W., *Forty years of Roosevelt,* (1944...T.W. Hughes)

Ickes, Harold L., administrateur, *National Planning Board Federal Emergency Administration of Public Works,* (Washington, D.C. Government Printing Office, 1934). Rapport final 1933-34.

Johnson, Hugh S., *The Blue Eagle from Egg to Earth,* (New York : Doubleday, Doran & Company, Inc., 1935)

Josephson, Emanuel M., *Roosevelt's Communist Manifesto*. Incorporant une réimpression de *Science of Government Founded on Natural Law,* par Clinton Roosevelt, (New York : Chedney Press, 1955)

Kahn, Otto H., *Of Many Things,* (New York : Boni & Liveright, 1926)

Kolko, Gabriel, *The Triumph of Conservatism, A reinterpretation of American History,* (Londres : Collier-Macmillan Limited, 1963)

Kuczynski, Robert P., *Bankers' Profits from German Loans,* (Washington, D.C. : The Brookings Institution, 1932)

Laidler, Harry W., *Concentration of Control in American Industry,* (New York : Thomas Y. Crowell Company, 1931)

Lane, Rose Wilder, *The Making of Herbert Hoover,* (New York : The Century Co., 1920)

Leuchtenburg, William E., *Franklin D. Roosevelt and the New Deal 1932-1940,* (New York, Evanston, et Londres : Harper & Row, 1963)

Moley, Raymond, *The First New Deal* (New York : Harcourt Brace & World, Inc., n.d.)

Nixon, Edgar B., rédacteur, *Franklin D. Roosevelt and Foreign Affairs,* (Cambridge : The Belknap Press of Harvard University Press, 1969), Volume I : janvier 1933-février 1934. Bibliothèque Franklin D. Roosevelt. Hyde Park, New York.

Overacker, Louise, *Money in Elections,* (New York : The Macmillan Company, 1932)

Pecora, Ferdinand, *Wall Street Under Oath, The Story of our Modern Money Changers,* (New York : Augustus M. Kelley Publishers, 1968)

Peel, Roy V., et Donnelly, Thomas C., *The 1928 Campaign An Analysis,* (New York : Richard R. Smith, Inc., 1931)

Roos, Charles Frederick, *NRA Economic Planning,* (Bloomington, Indiana : The Principia Press, Inc., 1937)

Roosevelt, Elliott and Brough, James, *An Untold Story, The Roosevelts of Hyde Park,* (New York : G.P. Putnam's Sons, 1973)

Roosevelt, Franklin D., *The Public Papers and Addresses of Franklin D. Roosevelt,* (New York : Random House, 1938), Volume One.

Roosevelt, Franklin D., *The Public Papers and Addresses of Franklin D. Roosevelt,* (New York : Random House, 1938), Vol. 4.

Schlesinger, Arthur M., Jr, *The Age of Roosevelt, The Crisis of the Old Order 1919- 1933,* (Boston : Houghton Mifflin Company, 1957)

Seldes, George, *One Thousand Americans,* (New York : Boni & Gaer, 1947).

Spivak, John L. *A Man in His Time,* (New York : Horizon Press, 1967)

Stiles, Leia, *The Man Behind Roosevelt, The Story of Louis McHenry Howe,* (New York : The World Publishing Company, 1954)

Congrès des États-Unis, Chambre des représentants. Commission spéciale sur les activités américaines. *Enquête sur les activités de propagande nazie et enquête sur certaines autres activités de propagande*. 29 décembre 1934. (73e Congrès, 2e session. Audiences n° 73-D. C.-6). (Washington, Government Printing Office ; 1935)

Congrès des États-Unis, Sénat. Commission spéciale chargée d'enquêter sur les activités de lobbying. *Liste des contributions*. Rapport en vertu des Résolutions 165 et 184. (74e Congrès, 2e session). Washington, Government Printing Office, 1936)

Congrès des États-Unis. Sénat. Auditions devant une sous-commission de la commission des affaires militaires. *Mobilisation scientifique et technique.* 30 mars 1943. (78e Congrès, 1ère session. S. 702). Première partie. (Washington, Government Printing Office, 1943)

Congrès des États-Unis. Chambre des Représentants. Comité spécial sur les activités américaines (1934) *Investigation of Nazi and other propaganda*, (74e Congrès, 1ère session. Rapport n° 153) (Washington, Government Printing Office)

Congrès des États-Unis. Sénat, auditions devant la commission des finances. *Reprise industrielle nationale*. S. 1712 et H.R. 5755, 22, 26, 29, 31 mai et 1er juin 1933. (73e Congrès, 1ère session) (Washington, Government Printing Office, 1933)

Congrès des États-Unis. Sénat. Comité spécial chargé d'enquêter sur les dépenses de la campagne présidentielle. *Dépenses de la campagne présidentielle*. Rapport en vertu de la résolution 234, 25 février (jour civil, 28 février), 1929. (70e Congrès, 2e session. Rapport du Sénat 2024). (Washington, Government Printing Office, 1929)

Warren, Harris, Gaylord, *Herbert Hoover and the Great Depression,* (New York : Oxford University Press, 1959)

Wolfskill, George, *The Revolt of the Conservatives, A History of The American Liberty League 1934-1940,* (Boston : Houghton Mifflin Company, 1962)

WALL STREET ET L'ASCENSION D'HITLER

Dédié à la mémoire de Floyd Paxton - entrepreneur,
inventeur, écrivain et Américain, qui croyait et
travaillait pour les droits individuels dans une
société libre selon la Constitution.

PRÉFACE

Le présent ouvrage est le troisième et dernier volume d'une trilogie décrivant le rôle des socialistes d'entreprise américains, également connus sous le nom d'élite financière de Wall Street ou d'establishment libéral de la côte Est, dans trois événements historiques importants du XXe siècle : la révolution de Lénine-Trotsky de 1917 en Russie, l'élection de Franklin D. Roosevelt en 1933 aux États-Unis et la prise de pouvoir d'Adolf Hitler en Allemagne en 1933.

Chacun de ces événements a introduit une variante du socialisme dans un grand pays - le socialisme bolchévique en Russie, le socialisme du New Deal aux États-Unis et le national-socialisme en Allemagne.

L'histoire officielle contemporaine, à l'exception peut-être du *Tragedy and Hope* de Carroll Quigley, ignore ces preuves. D'autre part, on peut comprendre que les universités et les organismes de recherche, qui dépendent de l'aide financière de fondations contrôlées par cette même élite financière new-yorkaise, ne souhaitent guère soutenir et publier des recherches sur ces aspects de la politique internationale. Il est peu probable que le plus courageux des administrateurs morde la main qui nourrit son organisation.

Il est également éminemment clair, d'après les éléments de cette trilogie, que les "hommes d'affaires à l'esprit public" ne se rendent pas à Washington en tant que lobbyistes et administrateurs pour servir les États-Unis. Ils sont à Washington pour servir leurs propres intérêts de maximisation des profits. Leur but n'est pas de promouvoir une économie de marché compétitive, mais de manipuler un régime politisé, appelez-le comme vous voulez, à leur propre avantage.

C'est la manipulation commerciale de l'accession d'Hitler au pouvoir en mars 1933 qui est le sujet de *Wall Street et l'ascension d'Hitler.*

Juillet 1976

Antony C. SUTTON

INTRODUCTION

LES FACETTES INEXPLORÉES DU NAZISME

Depuis le début des années 20, des rapports non fondés ont circulé selon lesquels non seulement les industriels allemands, mais aussi les financiers de Wall Street, ont joué un certain rôle - peut-être un rôle important - dans la montée d'Hitler et du nazisme. Ce livre présente des preuves inédites, dont une grande partie provient des dossiers des tribunaux militaires de Nuremberg, pour étayer cette hypothèse. Cependant, la lecture de ce seul volume ne permet pas de saisir tout l'impact et le caractère suggestif de ces preuves. Deux livres précédents de cette série, *Wall Street* et *la révolution bolchévique*[429] *et Wall Street et FDR*[430], décrivent les rôles des mêmes entreprises, et souvent des mêmes individus et de leurs collègues directeurs, qui ont travaillé dur pour manipuler et aider la révolution bolchévique en Russie en 1917, soutenir Franklin D. Roosevelt pour son accession à la présidence des États-Unis en 1933, ainsi que pour favoriser l'ascension d'Hitler dans l'Allemagne d'avant-guerre. En bref, ce livre fait partie d'une étude plus approfondie sur la mise en place du socialisme moderne par des socialistes d'entreprise.

Ce groupe politiquement actif de Wall Street est plus ou moins le même cercle élitiste généralement connu par les conservateurs comme "l'establishment libéral", par les libéraux (par exemple G. William Domhoff) comme "la classe dirigeante",[431] et par les théoriciens du complot Gary Allen[432] et Dan Smoot[433] comme les "initiés". Mais quel que soit le nom que l'on donne à ce groupe élitiste qui se perpétue, il est apparemment fondamentalement significatif dans la détermination des affaires mondiales, à un niveau bien supérieur à celui des politiciens élus.

---

429 (New York : Arlington House Publishers, 1974)

430 (New York : Arlington House Publishers, 1975)

431 *The Higher Circles: The Governing Class in America*, (New York : Vintage, 1970)

432 *None Dare Call It Conspiracy*, (Rossmoor : Concord Press, 1971). Pour un autre point de vue basé sur des documents "internes", voir Carroll Quigley, *Tragedy and Hope*, (New York : The Macmillan Company, 1966)

433 *The Invisible Government*, (Boston : Western Islands, 1962)

L'influence et le travail de ce même groupe dans l'émergence d'Hitler et de l'Allemagne nazie sont le sujet de ce livre. C'est un domaine de recherche historique presque totalement inexploré par le monde universitaire. C'est un champ de mines historique pour les imprudents et les négligents qui ne sont pas conscients des subtilités des procédures de recherche. Les Soviétiques ont longtemps accusé les banquiers de Wall Street de soutenir le fascisme international, mais leur propre dossier de précision historique ne donne guère de crédit à leurs accusations en Occident, et ils ne critiquent bien sûr pas le soutien de leur propre forme de fascisme politique.

Cet auteur se situe dans un autre camp. Précédemment accusé d'être trop critique à l'égard du soviétisme et du socialisme national, tout en ignorant Wall Street et la montée d'Hitler, ce livre, espérons-le, corrigera un déséquilibre philosophique supposé tout à fait inexact et mettra l'accent sur le véritable élément en cause : quel que soit le nom que vous donniez au système collectiviste - socialisme soviétique, socialisme du New Deal, socialisme d'entreprise ou national-socialisme - c'est le citoyen moyen, le type de la rue, qui est finalement perdant face aux pontes qui dirigent l'opération au sommet. Chaque système, à sa manière, est un système de pillage, un dispositif organisationnel destiné à faire vivre (ou tenter de vivre) tout le monde aux dépens des autres, tandis que les dirigeants élitistes, les chefs et les politiciens, raflent la crème de la crème au sommet.

Le rôle de cette élite du pouvoir américain dans l'accession d'Hitler au pouvoir doit également être considéré en conjonction avec un aspect peu connu de l'hitlérisme qui n'est exploré que maintenant : les origines mystiques du nazisme, et ses relations avec la société de Thulé et avec d'autres groupes conspirateurs. Cet auteur n'est pas un expert en occultisme ou en conspiration, mais il est évident que les origines mystiques, les racines historiques néopaïennes du nazisme, les Illuminati bavarois et la société de Thulé sont des domaines relativement peu connus qui doivent encore être explorés par des chercheurs techniquement compétents. Certaines recherches sont déjà rédigées en français ; la meilleure introduction en anglais est probablement une traduction de *Hitler et la Tradition Cathare de* Jean Michel Angebert.[434]

Angebert révèle la croisade de 1933 d'Otto Rahn, membre de *Schutzstaffel, à* la recherche du Saint Graal, qui aurait été situé dans le fief cathare du sud de la France. La première hiérarchie nazie (Hitler et Himmler, ainsi que Rudolph Hess et Rosenberg) était imprégnée d'une théologie néopaïenne, en partie associée à la société de Thulé, dont les idéaux étaient proches de ceux des Illuminati bavarois. Cette société était une force motrice submergée par le nazisme, avec une puissante emprise mystique sur les fidèles de la S.S.. Les historiens de notre establishment contemporain mentionnent à peine, et encore moins explorent, ces origines

[434] Publié en anglais sous le titre *The Occult and the Third Reich*, (Les origines mystiques du nazisme et la recherche du Saint Graal), (New York : The Macmillan Company, 1974). Voir aussi Reginald H. Phelps, "*Before Hitler Came*" (Avant l'arrivée d'Hitler) *Thule Society and Germanen Orden*" dans le *Journal of Modern History*, septembre 1968, n° 3.

occultes ; par conséquent, ils passent à côté d'un élément tout aussi important que les origines financières du national-socialisme.

En 1950, James Stewart Martin a publié un livre très complet *All Honorable Men*,[435] décrivant ses expériences en tant que chef de la section de guerre économique du ministère de la Justice, qui enquêtait sur la structure de l'industrie nazie. Martin affirme que des hommes d'affaires américains et britanniques ont été nommés à des postes clés dans cette enquête d'après-guerre pour détourner, étouffer et finalement saboter l'enquête sur les industriels nazis et ainsi garder cachée leur propre implication. Un officier britannique a été condamné par la cour martiale à deux ans de prison pour avoir protégé un nazi, et plusieurs officiels américains ont été démis de leurs fonctions. Pourquoi les hommes d'affaires américains et britanniques voudraient-ils protéger les hommes d'affaires nazis ? En public, ils ont fait valoir qu'il s'agissait simplement d'hommes d'affaires allemands qui n'avaient rien à voir avec le régime nazi et étaient innocents de toute complicité dans les conspirations nazies. Martin n'explore pas cette explication en profondeur, mais il est manifestement mécontent et sceptique à ce sujet. Les preuves suggèrent qu'il y a eu un effort concerté non seulement pour protéger les hommes d'affaires nazis, mais aussi pour protéger les éléments collaborateurs des entreprises américaines et britanniques.

Les hommes d'affaires allemands auraient pu révéler beaucoup de faits gênants : En échange d'une protection, ils n'ont pas dit grand-chose. Ce n'est sans doute pas un hasard si les industriels hitlériens jugés à Nuremberg ont reçu moins qu'une tape sur les doigts. Nous nous demandons si les procès de Nuremberg n'auraient pas dû se tenir à Washington - avec quelques hommes d'affaires américains de premier plan ainsi que des hommes d'affaires nazis sur le banc des accusés !

Deux extraits de sources contemporaines introduiront et suggéreront le thème à développer. Le premier extrait est tiré des propres dossiers de Roosevelt. L'ambassadeur américain en Allemagne, William Dodd, a écrit à FDR depuis Berlin le 19 octobre 1936 (trois ans après l'arrivée au pouvoir de Hitler), au sujet des industriels américains et de leur aide aux nazis :

> *Bien que je croie que la paix est notre meilleure politique, je ne peux pas rejeter les craintes que Wilson a soulignées plus d'une fois dans ses conversations avec moi, le 15 août 1915 et plus tard : l'effondrement de la démocratie dans toute l'Europe sera un désastre pour les citoyens. Mais que pouvez-vous faire ? Actuellement, plus d'une centaine de sociétés américaines ont des filiales ici ou des accords de coopération.*
>
> *Les DuPonts ont trois alliés en Allemagne qui apportent leur aide dans le domaine de l'armement. Leur principal allié est la société I.G. Farben, une pourvoyeuse du gouvernement qui donne 200 000 marks par an à une organisation de propagande opérant sur l'opinion américaine. La Standard Oil Company (sous-compagnie new-yorkaise) a envoyé 2 000 000 de dollars ici en décembre 1933 et a gagné 500 000 dollars par an en aidant les Allemands à fabriquer du gaz Ersatz pour les besoins de la guerre ; mais la Standard Oil ne peut sortir aucun de ses*

[435] (Boston : Little Brown and Company, 1950)

> *revenus hors du pays, sauf en marchandises. Elle n'en fait que très peu, déclare ses revenus chez elle, mais n'explique pas les faits. Le président de l'International Harvester Company m'a dit que leurs affaires ici augmentaient de 33% par an (fabrication d'armes, je crois), mais qu'ils ne pouvaient rien retirer. Même les gens de nos avions ont un arrangement secret avec Krupps. General Motor Company et Ford font d'énormes affaires ici par l'intermédiaire de leurs filiales et n'en retirent aucun profit. Je mentionne ces faits parce qu'ils compliquent les choses et ajoutent aux dangers de guerre.*[436]

Deuxièmement, une citation du journal du même ambassadeur américain en Allemagne. Le lecteur doit garder à l'esprit qu'un représentant de la Vacuum Oil Company citée - ainsi que des représentants d'autres entreprises américaines soutenant les nazis - a été nommé à la Commission de contrôle d'après-guerre pour dénazifier les nazis :

> *Le 25 janvier. Jeudi. Notre attaché commercial a fait venir le Dr Engelbrecht, président de la compagnie pétrolière sous vide de Hambourg, pour me voir. Engelbrecht a répété ce qu'il avait dit il y a un an : "La Standard Oil Company de New York, la société mère du Vacuum, a dépensé 10.000.000 marks en Allemagne pour essayer de trouver des ressources pétrolières et construire une grande raffinerie près du port de Hambourg." Engelbrecht continue à forer des puits et à trouver beaucoup de pétrole brut dans la région de Hanovre, mais il n'avait aucun espoir de trouver de grands gisements. Il espère que le Dr Schacht subventionnera son entreprise comme le font certaines entreprises allemandes qui n'ont pas trouvé de pétrole brut. Le Vacuum dépense tous ses revenus ici, emploie 1000 hommes et n'envoie jamais d'argent chez lui. Je ne pourrais pas l'encourager.*[437]

Et plus encore :

> *Ces hommes étaient à peine sortis du bâtiment que l'avocat est revenu pour signaler ses difficultés. Je n'ai rien pu faire. Mais je lui ai demandé : Pourquoi la Standard Oil Company de New York a-t-elle envoyé 1 000 000$ ici en décembre 1933 pour aider les Allemands à fabriquer de l'essence à partir de charbon doux pour les urgences de guerre ? Pourquoi les gens de l'International Harvester continuent-ils à fabriquer en Allemagne alors que leur entreprise ne reçoit rien du pays et qu'elle n'a pas réussi à encaisser ses pertes de guerre ? Il a compris mon point de vue et a convenu que cela paraissait stupide et que cela entraînera des pertes plus importantes si une autre guerre éclate.*[438]

L'alliance entre le pouvoir politique nazi et le "Big Business" américain a pu paraître stupide à l'ambassadeur Dodd et à l'avocat américain qu'il a interrogé. En

---

436 Edgar B. Nixon, éd., *Franklin D. Roosevelt and Foreign Affairs*, Volume III : September 1935-January 1937, (Cambridge : Belknap Press, 1969), p. 456.

437 Édité par William E. Dodd Jr. et Martha Dodd, *Ambassador Dodd's Diary*, 1933-1938, (New York : Harcourt Brace and Company, 1941), p. 303.

438 Ibid, p. 358.

pratique, bien sûr, le "Big Business" est tout sauf stupide lorsqu'il s'agit de promouvoir ses propres intérêts. Les investissements dans l'Allemagne nazie (ainsi que les investissements similaires en Union soviétique) étaient le reflet de politiques plus élevées, avec bien plus qu'un profit immédiat en jeu, même si les bénéfices ne pouvaient pas être rapatriés. Pour retracer ces "politiques supérieures", il faut pénétrer le contrôle financier des multinationales, car ceux qui contrôlent le flux des finances contrôlent en fin de compte les politiques quotidiennes.

Carroll Quigley[439] a montré que le sommet de ce système de contrôle financier international avant la Seconde Guerre mondiale était la Banque des Règlements Internationaux, avec des représentants des sociétés bancaires internationales d'Europe et des États-Unis, dans un arrangement qui s'est poursuivi tout au long de la Seconde Guerre mondiale. Pendant la période nazie, le représentant de l'Allemagne à la Banque des Règlements Internationaux était le bon génie financier d'Hitler et président de la Reichsbank, Hjalmar Horace Greeley Schacht.

HJALMAR HORACE GREELEY SCHACHT

L'implication de Wall Street dans l'Allemagne d'Hitler met en évidence deux Allemands ayant des liens avec Wall Street - Hjalmar Schacht et "Putzi" Hanfstaengl. Ce dernier était un ami d'Hitler et de Roosevelt qui a joué un rôle suspicieusement important dans l'incident qui a amené Hitler au sommet du pouvoir dictatorial - l'incendie du Reichstag en 1933.[440]

Les débuts de l'histoire de Hjalmar Schacht, et en particulier son rôle en Union soviétique après la révolution bolchévique de 1917, ont été décrits dans mon livre précédent, *Wall Street et la révolution bolchévique.* L'aîné des Schacht avait travaillé au bureau berlinois de l'Equitable Trust Company de New York au début du XXe siècle. Hjalmar est né en Allemagne plutôt qu'à New York uniquement à cause de la maladie de sa mère, qui a obligé la famille à rentrer en Allemagne. Le frère William Schacht était un citoyen né aux États-Unis. Pour marquer ses origines américaines, les deuxièmes prénoms de Hjalmar ont été désignés par "Horace Greeley", du nom du célèbre homme politique démocrate. Par conséquent, Hjalmar parlait couramment l'anglais et l'interrogatoire d'après-guerre de Schacht dans le cadre du projet Dustbin a été mené à la fois en allemand et en anglais. Il convient de souligner que la famille Schacht a ses origines à New York, qu'elle a travaillé pour l'importante maison financière de Wall Street, Equitable Trust (qui était contrôlée par la firme Morgan), et que tout au long de sa vie, Hjalmar a conservé ces liens avec Wall Street.[441] Les journaux et les sources contemporaines font état de visites répétées avec Owen Young de General

---

[439] Quigley, op. cit.

[440] Pour plus d'informations sur le "Putzi" Hanfstaengl, voir le chapitre neuf.

[441] Voir Sutton, *Wall Street et la révolution bolchévique*, op. cit. pour les relations de Schacht avec les Soviétiques et Wall Street, et sa direction d'une banque soviétique.

Electric, Farish, président de Standard Oil du New Jersey, et leurs homologues bancaires. En bref, Schacht était un membre de l'élite financière internationale qui exerce son pouvoir dans les coulisses de l'appareil politique d'une nation. Il est un lien clé entre l'élite de Wall Street et le cercle restreint d'Hitler.

Ce livre est divisé en deux grandes parties. La première partie retrace la montée en puissance des cartels allemands à travers les Plans Dawes et Young dans les années 1920. Ces cartels étaient les principaux partisans d'Hitler et du nazisme et ont été directement responsables de l'arrivée au pouvoir des nazis en 1933. Le rôle des entreprises américaines I.G. Farben, General Electric, Standard Oil of New Jersey, Ford et d'autres entreprises américaines est décrit. La deuxième partie présente les preuves documentaires connues sur le financement d'Hitler, avec une reproduction photographique des bordereaux de virement bancaire utilisés pour transférer des fonds de Farben, General Electric et d'autres entreprises à Hitler, par l'intermédiaire de Hjalmar Horace Greeley Schacht.

CHAPITRE I

WALL STREET OUVRE LA VOIE À HITLER

Le plan Dawes, adopté en août 1924, s'inscrit parfaitement dans les plans des économistes militaires de l'état-major allemand. (Témoignage devant le Sénat américain, Commission des affaires militaires, 1946).

La commission Kilgore du Sénat américain de l'après-guerre a entendu des témoignages détaillés de fonctionnaires du gouvernement selon lesquels

> *... lorsque les nazis sont arrivés au pouvoir en 1933, ils ont constaté que de longs progrès avaient été accomplis depuis 1918 pour préparer l'Allemagne à la guerre d'un point de vue économique et industriel.*[442]

La préparation à la guerre européenne avant et après 1933 a été en grande partie due à l'aide financière de Wall Street dans les années 1920 pour créer le système des cartels allemands, et à l'assistance technique de sociétés américaines bien connues qui seront identifiées plus tard, pour construire la Wehrmacht allemande. Alors que cette assistance financière et technique est qualifiée d'"accidentelle" ou due à l'"aveuglement" des hommes d'affaires américains, les éléments présentés ci-dessous suggèrent fortement un certain degré de préméditation de la part de ces financiers américains. Des plaidoyers similaires et inacceptables d'"accident" ont été formulés au nom des financiers et des industriels américains dans l'exemple parallèle de la construction de la puissance militaire de l'Union soviétique à partir de 1917. Pourtant, ces capitalistes américains étaient prêts à financer et à subventionner l'Union soviétique pendant la guerre du Vietnam, sachant que les Soviétiques subventionnait l'ennemi que l'armée américaine combattait de l'autre côté.

442 Congrès des États-Unis. Sénat. Auditions devant une sous-commission de la commission des affaires militaires. Élimination des ressources allemandes pour la guerre. Rapport en vertu des Résolutions 107 et 146, 2 juillet 1945, Partie 7, (78e Congrès et 79e Congrès), (Washington : Government Printing Office, 1945), ci-après dénommé Élimination des ressources allemandes.

La contribution du capitalisme américain aux préparatifs de guerre allemands avant 1940 ne peut être qualifiée que de phénoménale. Elle a certainement été cruciale pour les capacités militaires allemandes.

Par exemple, en 1934, l'Allemagne ne produisait sur son territoire que 300 000 tonnes de produits pétroliers naturels et moins de 800 000 tonnes d'essence synthétique ; le reste était importé. Pourtant, dix ans plus tard, pendant la Seconde Guerre mondiale, après le transfert des brevets et de la technologie d'hydrogénation de la Standard Oil du New Jersey à I.G. Farben (utilisée pour produire de l'essence synthétique à partir du charbon), l'Allemagne a produit environ 6,5 millions de tonnes de pétrole - dont 85% (5,5 millions de tonnes) étaient du pétrole synthétique selon le procédé d'hydrogénation de la Standard Oil. De plus, le contrôle de la production de pétrole synthétique en Allemagne était détenu par la filiale d'I.G. Farben, Braunkohle-Benzin A. G., et ce cartel Farben lui-même a été créé en 1926 avec l'aide financière de Wall Street.

D'autre part, l'impression générale laissée au lecteur par les historiens modernes est que cette assistance technique américaine était accidentelle et que les industriels américains étaient innocents de tout méfait. Par exemple, le Comité Kilgore a déclaré :

> *Les États-Unis ont accidentellement joué un rôle important dans l'armement technique de l'Allemagne. Bien que les planificateurs militaires allemands aient ordonné et persuadé les entreprises manufacturières, d'installer des équipements modernes pour la production de masse, ni les économistes militaires, ni les entreprises ne semblent avoir réalisé dans toute leur ampleur ce que cela signifiait. Leurs yeux se sont ouverts lorsque deux des principales sociétés automobiles américaines ont construit des usines en Allemagne afin de vendre sur le marché européen, sans le handicap des frais de transport maritime et des tarifs allemands élevés. Les Allemands ont été amenés à Detroit pour apprendre les techniques de production spécialisée de composants et d'assemblage à la chaîne. Ce qu'ils ont vu a entraîné une réorganisation et un réaménagement d'autres usines de guerre allemandes importantes. Les techniques apprises à Detroit ont finalement été utilisées pour construire les Stukas .... de bombardement en piqué à une période ultérieure... I.G. Farben dans ce pays a permis à un flot d'ingénieurs allemands de visiter non seulement des usines d'avions mais aussi d'autres usines d'importance militaire, dans lesquelles ils ont appris beaucoup de choses qui ont finalement été utilisées contre les États-Unis.*[443]

À la suite de ces observations, qui soulignent le caractère "accidentel" de l'aide, des auteurs universitaires tels que Gabriel Kolko, qui n'est généralement pas un partisan des grandes entreprises, ont conclu que :

---

[443] Élimination des ressources allemandes, p. 174.

> *Il est presque superflu de souligner que les motifs des entreprises américaines liées à des contrats avec des entreprises allemandes n'étaient pas complètement pronazies...*[444]

Pourtant, Kolko affirme au contraire que les analyses de la presse économique américaine contemporaine confirment que les revues et journaux économiques étaient pleinement conscients de la menace nazie et de sa nature, tout en avertissant leurs lecteurs économiques des préparatifs de guerre allemands. Et même Kolko l'admet :

> *La presse économique [aux États-Unis] savait, dès 1935, que la prospérité allemande reposait sur les préparatifs de guerre. Plus important encore, elle était consciente du fait que l'industrie allemande était sous le contrôle des nazis et était destinée à servir le réarmement de l'Allemagne, et l'entreprise la plus souvent mentionnée dans ce contexte était le géant de la chimie, I.G. Farben.*[445]

De plus, les preuves présentées ci-dessous suggèrent que non seulement un secteur influent des entreprises américaines était conscient de la nature du nazisme, mais qu'il a aidé le nazisme chaque fois que cela était possible (et rentable) - en *sachant parfaitement que l'issue probable serait une guerre impliquant l'Europe et les États-Unis.* Comme nous le verrons, les plaidoyers d'innocence ne correspondent pas aux faits.

1924 : LE PLAN DAWES

Le traité de Versailles, après la Première Guerre mondiale, a imposé une lourde charge de réparations à l'Allemagne vaincue. Cette charge financière - véritable cause du mécontentement allemand qui a conduit à l'acceptation de l'hitlérisme - a été utilisée par les banquiers internationaux à leur propre profit.

L'opportunité d'accorder des prêts rentables aux cartels allemands aux États-Unis a été présentée par le plan Dawes et plus tard par le plan Young. Les deux plans ont été conçus par ces banquiers centraux, qui ont constitué les comités pour leurs propres avantages pécuniaires, et bien que techniquement les comités n'aient pas été nommés par le gouvernement américain, les plans ont en fait été approuvés et parrainés par le gouvernement.

Le marchandage d'après-guerre par les financiers et les politiciens a fixé les réparations allemandes à une redevance annuelle de 132 milliards de marks d'or. Cela représentait environ un quart du total des exportations allemandes de 1921. Lorsque l'Allemagne n'a pas pu effectuer ces paiements écrasants, la France et la Belgique ont occupé la Ruhr pour prendre par la force ce qui ne pouvait être cédé volontairement. En 1924, les Alliés ont nommé un comité de banquiers (dirigé par

---

[444] Gabriel Kolko, "American Business and Germany, 1930-1941", *The Western Political Quarterly,* Volume XV, 1962.

[445] Ibid, p. 715.

le banquier américain Charles G. Dawes) pour élaborer un programme de paiements de réparation. Le plan Dawes qui en résulta fut, selon Carroll Quigley, professeur de relations internationales à l'université de Georgetown, "en grande partie une production de J.P. Morgan".[446] Le plan Dawes a organisé une série de prêts étrangers totalisant 800 millions de dollars dont le produit a été versé à l'Allemagne. Ces prêts sont importants pour notre histoire, car les recettes, collectées en grande partie aux États-Unis auprès d'investisseurs en dollars, ont été utilisées au milieu des années 20 pour créer et consolider les gigantesques combinaisons de produits chimiques et d'acier de I.G. Farben et Vereinigte Stahlwerke, respectivement. Ces cartels ont non seulement aidé Hitler à prendre le pouvoir en 1933, mais ils ont également fourni la majeure partie du matériel de guerre allemand utilisé pendant la Seconde Guerre mondiale.

Entre 1924 et 1931, dans le cadre du plan Dawes et du plan Young, l'Allemagne a versé aux Alliés environ 86 milliards de marks de réparations. Dans le même temps, l'Allemagne a emprunté à l'étranger, principalement aux États-Unis, environ 138 milliards de marks - ce qui représente un paiement net de seulement trois milliards de marks pour les réparations. Par conséquent, la charge des réparations monétaires allemandes aux Alliés a en fait été supportée par les souscripteurs étrangers d'obligations allemandes émises par les établissements financiers de Wall Street - avec, bien sûr, des bénéfices importants pour eux-mêmes. Et, notons que ces entreprises appartenaient aux mêmes financiers qui, périodiquement, enlevaient leur chapeau de banquier et en mettaient de nouveaux pour devenir des "hommes d'État". En tant qu'"hommes d'État", ils ont formulé les plans Dawes et Young pour "résoudre" le "problème" des réparations. En tant que banquiers, ils ont fait circuler les prêts. Comme le souligne Carroll Quigley,

> *Il convient de noter que ce système a été mis en place par les banquiers internationaux et que le prêt ultérieur de l'argent d'autrui à l'Allemagne a été très profitable pour ces banquiers.*[447]

Qui sont les banquiers internationaux de New York qui ont formé ces commissions de réparation ?

Les experts américains du plan Dawes de 1924 étaient le banquier Charles Dawes et le représentant de Morgan, Owen Young, qui était président de la General Electric Company. Dawes était président du Comité d'experts alliés en 1924. En 1929, Owen Young devint président du Comité des experts, soutenu par J.P. Morgan lui-même, avec comme suppléants T. W. Lamont, un partenaire de Morgan, et T. N. Perkins, un banquier des associations de Morgan. En d'autres termes, les délégations américaines étaient purement et simplement, comme l'a souligné Quigley, des délégations J. P. Morgan utilisant l'autorité et le sceau des États-Unis pour promouvoir des plans financiers pour leur propre avantage

[446] Carroll Quigley, op. cit.

[447] Ibid, p. 308.

pécuniaire. En conséquence, comme le dit Quigley, les "banquiers internationaux se sont assis au paradis, sous une pluie de frais et de commissions".[448]

Les membres allemands du comité d'experts étaient tout aussi intéressants. En 1924, Hjalmar Schacht était président de la Reichsbank et avait joué un rôle important dans l'organisation du plan Dawes, tout comme le banquier allemand Carl Melchior. L'un des délégués allemands de 1928 était A. Voegler du cartel sidérurgique allemand Stahlwerke Vereinigte. En bref, les deux pays importants impliqués - les États-Unis et l'Allemagne - étaient représentés par les banquiers Morgan d'un côté et Schacht et Voegler de l'autre, tous deux ayant joué un rôle clé dans la montée de l'Allemagne hitlérienne et le réarmement allemand qui s'en est suivi.

Enfin, les membres et les conseillers des commissions Dawes et Young n'étaient pas seulement associés aux maisons de finance new-yorkaises mais, comme nous le verrons plus tard, ils étaient directeurs d'entreprises au sein des cartels allemands qui ont aidé Hitler à prendre le pouvoir.

1928 : LE PLAN YOUNG

Selon le génie financier d'Hitler, Hjalmar Horace Greeley Schacht, et l'industriel nazi Fritz Thyssen, c'est le plan Young de 1928 (le successeur du plan Dawes), formulé par l'agent de Morgan Owen D. Young, qui a porté Hitler au pouvoir en 1933. Fritz Thyssen affirme que,

> *Je ne me suis tourné vers le parti national-socialiste qu'après avoir acquis la conviction que la lutte contre le Plan Young était inévitable si l'on voulait éviter l'effondrement complet de l'Allemagne.*[449]

La différence entre le Plan Young et le Plan Dawes est que, alors que le Plan Young exigeait des paiements en biens produits en Allemagne financés par des emprunts étrangers, le Plan Dawes exigeait des paiements monétaires et "Selon mon jugement [écrit Thyssen], la dette financière ainsi créée était destinée à perturber toute l'économie du Reich".

Le Plan Young était prétendument un dispositif visant à occuper l'Allemagne avec des capitaux américains et à mettre en gage des biens immobiliers allemands pour une gigantesque hypothèque détenue aux États-Unis. Il convient de noter que les entreprises allemandes affiliées aux États-Unis ont échappé au plan par le biais de la propriété étrangère temporaire. Par exemple, A.E.G. (General Electric allemand), affiliée à General Electric aux États-Unis, a été vendue à un holding franco-belge et a échappé aux conditions du plan Young. Il convient de noter au passage qu'Owen Young était le principal bailleur de fonds de Franklin D. Roosevelt dans l'entreprise européenne unie lorsque FDR, en tant que financier bourgeonnant de Wall Street, s'est efforcé de tirer parti de l'hyperinflation

---

[448] Carroll Quigley, op. cit. p. 309.

[449] Fritz Thyssen, *I Paid Hitler*, (New York : Farrar & Rinehart, Inc., n.d.), p. 88.

allemande de 1925. L'entreprise européenne unie était un véhicule pour spéculer et faire des profits lors de l'imposition du plan Dawes, et est la preuve évidente que des financiers privés (dont Franklin D. Roosevelt) utilisent le pouvoir de l'État pour faire avancer leurs propres intérêts en manipulant la politique étrangère.

L'accusation parallèle de Schacht selon laquelle Owen Young était responsable de l'ascension d'Hitler, bien qu'elle soit manifestement intéressée, est consignée dans un rapport des services de renseignements du gouvernement américain relatant l'interrogatoire du Dr Fritz Thyssen en septembre 1945 :

> *L'acceptation du plan Young et de ses principes financiers a fait augmenter le chômage de plus en plus, jusqu'à ce qu'environ un million de personnes soient au chômage.*
>
> *Les gens étaient désespérés. Hitler a dit qu'il supprimerait le chômage. Le gouvernement au pouvoir à cette époque était très mauvais, et la situation du peuple empirait. C'est la raison pour laquelle Hitler a remporté un énorme succès aux élections. Lors des dernières élections, il a obtenu environ 40%.*[450]

Cependant, c'est Schacht, et non Owen Young, qui a conçu l'idée qui est devenue plus tard la Banque des Règlements Internationaux. Les détails concrets ont été mis au point lors d'une conférence présidée par Jackson Reynolds, "l'un des principaux banquiers de New York", avec Melvin Traylor de la First National Bank of Chicago, Sir Charles Addis, anciennement de la Hong Kong and Shanghai Banking Corporation, et divers banquiers français et allemands.[451] La B.I.S. était essentielle dans le cadre du plan Young, car elle permettait de disposer d'un instrument prêt à l'emploi pour promouvoir les relations financières internationales. Selon ses propres déclarations, Schacht a également donné à Owen Young l'idée qui est devenue plus tard la Banque Internationale pour la Reconstruction et le Développement de l'après-guerre :

> *"Une banque de ce type exigera une coopération financière entre les vaincus et les vainqueurs qui mènera à une communauté d'intérêts qui, à son tour, donnera lieu à une confiance et à une compréhension mutuelles et, ainsi, favorisera et assurera la paix".*
>
> *Je me souviens encore très bien du cadre dans lequel cette conversation s'est déroulée. Owen Young était assis dans son fauteuil, soufflant sur sa pipe, les jambes tendues, ses yeux perçants fixés sur moi. Comme j'ai l'habitude de le faire lorsque je propose de tels arguments, je faisais un "aller-retour" tranquille et régulier de long en large de la pièce. Quand j'ai eu fini, il y a eu une brève pause. Puis tout son visage s'est illuminé et sa détermination a trouvé son expression dans les mots :*

---

450 U.S. Group Control Council (Allemagne), Office of the Director of Intelligence, Intelligence Report No. EF/ME/1, 4 septembre 1945. Voir également Hjalmar Schacht, *Confessions of an Old Wizard*, (Boston : Houghton Mifflin, 1956)

451 Hjalmar Schacht, op cit. p. 18. Fritz Thyssen ajoute : "Même à l'époque, M. Dillon, un banquier new-yorkais d'origine juive que j'admire beaucoup, m'a dit : 'À ta place, je ne signerais pas le plan'".

"Dr Schacht, vous m'avez donné une merveilleuse idée et je vais la vendre au monde entier."[452]

LA B.R.I. - LE SOMMET DU CONTRÔLE

Ce jeu d'idées et de coopération entre Hjalmar Schacht en Allemagne et, par l'intermédiaire d'Owen Young, les intérêts de J.P. Morgan à New York, n'était qu'une facette d'un vaste et ambitieux système de coopération et d'alliance internationale pour le contrôle du monde. Comme le décrit Carroll Quigley, ce système consistait à :

> "... rien de moins que de créer un système mondial de contrôle financier, entre des mains privées, capable de dominer le système politique de chaque pays et l'économie du monde dans son ensemble.[453]

Ce système féodal a fonctionné dans les années 1920, comme il fonctionne aujourd'hui, par l'intermédiaire des banquiers centraux privés de chaque pays qui contrôlent la masse monétaire nationale des différentes économies. Dans les années 1920 et 1930, le système de la Réserve Fédérale de New York, la Banque d'Angleterre, la Reichsbank en Allemagne et la Banque de France ont également plus ou moins influencé indirectement l'appareil politique de leurs pays respectifs par le contrôle de la masse monétaire et la création de l'environnement monétaire. Une influence plus directe a été réalisée en fournissant des fonds politiques aux politiciens et aux partis politiques, ou en leur retirant leur soutien. Aux États-Unis, par exemple, le président Herbert Hoover a imputé sa défaite de 1932 au retrait du soutien de Wall Street et au transfert des finances et de l'influence de Wall Street à Franklin D. Roosevelt.

Les politiciens sensibles aux objectifs du capitalisme financier, et les académies proliférant avec des idées de contrôle mondial utiles aux banquiers internationaux, sont maintenus dans la ligne d'un système de récompenses et de pénalités. Au début des années 1930, la Banque des Règlements Internationaux de Bâle, en Suisse, était le vecteur de ce système international de contrôle financier et politique, que Quigley appelait "le sommet du système". Le sommet de la B.I.S. a poursuivi son travail pendant la Seconde Guerre mondiale en tant que moyen par lequel les banquiers - qui n'étaient apparemment pas en guerre les uns avec les autres - ont poursuivi un échange mutuellement bénéfique d'idées, d'informations et de planification pour le monde de l'après-guerre. Comme l'a fait remarquer un auteur, la guerre n'a fait aucune différence pour les banquiers internationaux :

> *Le fait que la Banque dispose d'un personnel véritablement international présentait, bien entendu, une situation très anormale en temps de guerre. Un président américain traitait les affaires courantes de la Banque par l'intermédiaire*

[452] Ibid, p. 282.

[453] Carroll Quigley, op. cit. p. 324.

d'un directeur général français, qui avait un directeur général adjoint allemand, tandis que le secrétaire général était un sujet italien. D'autres ressortissants occupaient d'autres postes. Ces hommes étaient, bien entendu, en contact personnel quotidien les uns avec les autres.

À l'exception de M. McKittrick [voir infra], les vols étaient bien sûr situés en permanence en Suisse pendant cette période et n'étaient pas censés être soumis aux ordres de leur gouvernement à un moment quelconque. Cependant, les directeurs de la Banque sont restés, bien entendu, dans leurs pays respectifs et n'ont eu aucun contact direct avec le personnel de la Banque. Il est cependant allégué que H. Schacht, président de la Reichsbank, a gardé un représentant personnel à Bâle pendant la majeure partie de cette période.[454]

Ce sont ces réunions secrètes, "... des réunions plus secrètes que toutes celles jamais tenues par les francs-maçons de l'Arche royale ou par tout ordre rosicrucien..."[455] entre les banquiers centraux au "sommet" du contrôle qui ont tant intrigué les journalistes contemporains, bien qu'ils n'aient que rarement et brièvement pénétré ce secret.

LA CONSTRUCTION DES CARTELS ALLEMANDS

Le système allemand des cartels est un exemple pratique de la façon dont la finance internationale opère en coulisses pour construire et manipuler des systèmes politico-économiques. Les trois plus gros prêts gérés par les banquiers internationaux de Wall Street pour des emprunteurs allemands dans les années 1920 dans le cadre du plan Dawes étaient au profit de trois cartels allemands qui, quelques années plus tard, ont aidé Hitler et les nazis à prendre le pouvoir. Les financiers américains étaient directement représentés au sein des conseils d'administration de deux de ces trois cartels allemands. Cette aide américaine aux cartels allemands a été décrite par James Martin comme suit :

> "Ces prêts pour la reconstruction sont devenus un véhicule pour des arrangements qui ont fait plus pour promouvoir la Seconde Guerre mondiale que pour établir la paix après la Première Guerre mondiale."[456]

Les trois cartels dominants, les montants empruntés et le syndicat flottant de Wall Street étaient les suivants :

Le cartel allemand	Syndicat de Wall Street	Montant émis

[454] Henry H. Schloss, *La Banque des Règlements Internationaux* (Amsterdam, : North Holland Publishing Company, 1958)

[455] John Hargrave, *Montagu Norman*, (New York : The Greystone Press, n.d.). p. 108.

[456] James Stewart Martin, op. cit. p. 70.

Elektrizitats-Gesellschaft (A.E.G.) (société allemande d'électricité générale)	National City Co.	$35,000,000
Vereinigte Stahlwerke (United Steelworks)	Dillon, Read & Co.	$70,225,000
Américain I.G. Chemical (I.G. Farben)	National City Co.	$30,000,000

Si l'on considère l'ensemble des prêts accordés[457], il apparaît que seule une poignée d'établissements financiers new-yorkais ont pris en charge le financement des réparations allemandes. Trois sociétés - Dillon, Read Co., Harris, Forbes & Co. et National City Company - ont émis près des trois quarts de la valeur nominale totale des prêts et ont récolté la plupart des bénéfices :

Responsable du syndicat de Wall Street	**Participation aux questions industrielles allemandes sur le marché des capitaux américain**	**Bénéfices sur les prêts allemands*.**	**Pourcentage du total**
Dillon, Read & Co.	$241,325,000	2,7 millions de dollars	29.2
Harris, Forbes & Co.	$186,500,000	1,4 million dollars	22.6
National City Co.	$173,000,000	5,0 millions dollars	20.9
Speyer & Co.	$59,500,000	0,6 million dollars	7.2
Lee, Higginson & Co.	$53,000,000	n.a.	6.4
Guaranty Co. de N.Y.	$41,575,000	0,2 million dollars	5.0
Kuhn, Loeb & Co.	$37,500,000	0,2 million dollars	4.5
Equitable Trust Co.	$34,000,000	0,3 million dollars	4.1
TOTAL	$826,400,000	10,4 millions de dollars	99.9

Source : Voir annexe A

*Robert R. Kuczynski, Bankers Profits from German Loans (Washington, D.C. : Brookings Institution, 1932), p. 127.

Après le milieu des années 20, les deux grands groupes allemands, I.G. Farben et Vereinigte Stahlwerke, ont dominé le système des cartels de la chimie et de l'acier créé par ces prêts.

Bien que ces entreprises n'aient eu une majorité de vote dans les ententes que pour deux ou trois produits de base, elles ont pu - grâce au contrôle de ces produits de base - faire respecter leur volonté tout au long de l'entente. I.G. Farben était le principal producteur de produits chimiques de base utilisés par d'autres fabricants de produits chimiques en combinaison, de sorte que sa position de puissance économique ne peut être mesurée uniquement par sa capacité à produire quelques

[457] Voir le chapitre 7 pour plus de détails sur les prêts de Wall Street à l'industrie allemande.

produits chimiques de base. De même, Vereinigte Stahlwerke, dont la capacité de production de fonte brute est supérieure à celle de tous les autres producteurs allemands de fer et d'acier réunis, a pu exercer une influence bien plus grande sur l'entente sur les produits sidérurgiques semi-finis que ne le laisse supposer sa capacité de production de fonte brute. Malgré cela, le pourcentage de production de ces ententes pour l'ensemble des produits était significatif :

Produits de Vereinigte Stahlwerke	**Pourcentage de la production totale allemande en 1938**
Fer à repasser	50.8
Tubes et tuyaux	45.5
La tôle forte	36.0
Explosifs	35.0
Goudron de houille	33.3
Acier en barres	37.1
I.G. Farben	**Pourcentage du total allemand production en 1937**
Méthanol synthétique	100.0
Magnésium	100.0
Azote chimique	70.0
Explosifs	60.0
Essence synthétique (à indice d'octane élevé)	46.0 (1945)
Lignite	20.0

Parmi les produits qui ont amené I.G. Farben et Vereinigte Stahlwerke à une collaboration mutuelle, on trouve le goudron de houille et l'azote chimique, tous deux de première importance pour la fabrication d'explosifs. I.G. Farben occupait une position de cartel qui lui assurait une position dominante dans la fabrication et la vente d'azote chimique, mais ne possédait qu'environ un pour cent de la capacité de cokéfaction de l'Allemagne. Un accord a donc été conclu en vertu duquel les filiales de Farben spécialisées dans les explosifs se procuraient leur benzol, leur toluol et d'autres produits primaires à base de goudron de houille aux conditions dictées par Vereinigte Stahlwerke, tandis que la filiale de Vereinigte Stahlwerke spécialisée dans les explosifs était dépendante pour ses nitrates aux conditions fixées par Farben. Dans le cadre de ce système de collaboration mutuelle et d'interdépendance, les deux cartels, I.G. Farben et Vereinigte Stahlwerke, ont produit 95% des explosifs allemands en 1957-8 à la veille de la Seconde Guerre mondiale. *Cette production a été réalisée grâce à des prêts américains et, dans une certaine mesure, à la technologie américaine.*

La coopération I.G. Farben-Standard Oil pour la production de pétrole synthétique à partir du charbon a donné au cartel I.G. Farben le monopole de la production d'essence allemande pendant la Seconde Guerre mondiale. En 1945, un peu moins de la moitié de l'essence allemande à indice d'octane élevé était produite directement par I.G. Farben et la majeure partie du reste par ses sociétés affiliées.

En bref, en ce qui concerne l'essence synthétique et les explosifs (deux des éléments de base de la guerre moderne), le contrôle de la production allemande de la Seconde Guerre mondiale était entre les mains de deux conglomérats allemands créés par des prêts de Wall Street dans le cadre du plan Dawes.

De plus, l'aide américaine aux efforts de guerre nazis s'est étendue à d'autres domaines.[458] Les deux plus grands producteurs de chars dans l'Allemagne d'Hitler étaient Opel, une filiale à part entière de General Motors (contrôlée par la firme J.P. Morgan), et la filiale Ford A.G. de la Ford Motor Company de Detroit. Les nazis accordèrent un statut d'exonération fiscale à Opel en 1936, pour permettre à General Motors d'étendre ses installations de production. General Motors a réinvesti les bénéfices qui en ont résulté dans l'industrie allemande. Henry Ford a été décoré par les nazis pour ses services rendus au nazisme. (Voir p. 93.) Alcoa et Dow Chemical ont travaillé en étroite collaboration avec l'industrie nazie en procédant à de nombreux transferts de leurs technologie américaine. Bendix Aviation, dans laquelle la société General Motors contrôlée par J.P. Morgan avait une participation importante, fournissait à Siemens & Halske A. G. en Allemagne des données sur les pilotes automatiques et les instruments de bord. Jusqu'en 1940, pendant la "guerre non officielle", Bendix Aviation a fourni à Robert Bosch des données techniques complètes pour les démarreurs d'avions et de moteurs diesel et a reçu des redevances en retour.

En bref, les entreprises américaines associées aux banquiers d'affaires internationaux de Morgan-Rockefeller - et non, il faut le noter, la grande majorité des industriels américains indépendants - étaient intimement liées à la croissance de l'industrie nazie. Il est important de noter, en développant notre histoire, que General Motors, Ford, General Electric, DuPont et la poignée de sociétés américaines intimement liées au développement de l'Allemagne nazie étaient - à l'exception de la Ford Motor Company - contrôlées par l'élite de Wall Street - la firme J.P. Morgan, la Rockefeller Chase Bank et, dans une moindre mesure, la Warburg Manhattan Bank.[459] Ce livre n'est pas une mise en accusation de toute l'industrie et de la finance américaines. Il s'agit d'une mise en accusation de "l'élite" - ces entreprises contrôlées par une poignée de maisons financières, le système de la Federal Reserve Bank, la Banque des Règlements Internationaux, et leurs accords de coopération internationale et cartels qui tentent de contrôler le cours de la politique et de l'économie mondiales.

---

[458] Voir Gabriel Kolko, op. cit. pour de nombreux exemples.

[459] En 1956, les banques Chase et Manhattan ont fusionné pour devenir la Chase Manhattan.

CHAPITRE II

L'EMPIRE I.G. FARBEN

Farben était Hitler et Hitler était Farben.
(Sénateur Homer T. Bone devant la commission sénatoriale des affaires militaires, 4 juin 1943).

À la veille de la Seconde Guerre mondiale, le complexe chimique allemand d'I.G. Farben était la plus grande entreprise de fabrication de produits chimiques au monde, avec une puissance et une influence politiques et économiques extraordinaires au sein de l'État nazi hitlérien. I.G. Farben a été décrit à juste titre comme "un État dans un État".

Le cartel Farben date de 1925, lorsque le génie organisateur Hermann Schmitz (avec l'aide financière de Wall Street) a créé la giga-entreprise chimique à partir de six entreprises chimiques allemandes déjà géantes - Badische Anilin, Bayer, Agfa, Hoechst, Weilertermeer et Griesheim-Elektron. Ces entreprises ont fusionné pour devenir l'Internationale Gesellschaft Farbenindustrie A.G. - ou I.G. Farben en abrégé. Vingt ans plus tard, le même Hermann Schmitz a été jugé à Nuremberg pour des crimes de guerre commis par le cartel I.G. D'autres directeurs d'I.G. Farben furent jugés, mais les filiales américaines d'I.G. Farben et les directeurs américains d'I.G. elle-même furent tranquillement oubliés ; la vérité fut enterrée dans les archives.

Ce sont ces connexions américaines à Wall Street qui nous préoccupent. Sans les capitaux fournis par Wall Street, il n'y aurait pas eu I.G. Farben en premier lieu et presque certainement pas Adolf Hitler et la Seconde Guerre mondiale.

Parmi les banquiers allemands siégeant au Farben *Aufsichsrat* (le conseil de surveillance)[460] à la fin des années 1920, on trouve le banquier hambourgeois Max Warburg, dont le frère Paul Warburg a été l'un des fondateurs du système de la Réserve Fédérale aux États-Unis. Ce n'est pas un hasard si Paul Warburg était également membre du conseil d'administration d'American I.G., la filiale américaine à part entière de Farben. En plus de Max Warburg et Hermann Schmitz, qui furent les artisans de la création de l'empire Farben, les premiers membres du Farben *Vorstand* étaient Carl Bosch, Fritzter Meer, Kurt Oppenheim et George

[460] Les entreprises allemandes ont un conseil d'administration à deux niveaux. L'*Aufsichsrat* s'occupe de la surveillance générale, y compris de la politique financière, tandis que le *Vorstand* s'occupe de la gestion quotidienne.

von Schnitzler.[461] Tous, sauf Max Warburg, ont été accusés de "crimes de guerre" après la Seconde Guerre mondiale.

En 1928, les holdings américains de I.G. Farben (c'est-à-dire la société Bayer, General Aniline Works, Agfa Ansco et Winthrop Chemical Company) ont été organisés en une société holding suisse, I.G. Chemic (Inter-nationale Gesellschaft fur Chemisehe Unternehmungen A. G.), contrôlée par I.G. Farben en Allemagne. L'année suivante, ces sociétés américaines fusionnent pour devenir l'américaine I.G. Chemical Corporation, rebaptisée plus tard General Aniline & Film. Hermann Schmitz, l'organisateur de I.G. Farben en 1925, est devenu un des premiers nazis importants et un partisan de Hitler, ainsi que le président de la société suisse I.G. Chemic et le président de la société américaine I.G. Le complexe Farben, tant en Allemagne qu'aux États-Unis, est alors devenu une partie intégrante de la formation et du fonctionnement de la machine d'État nazie, la Wehrmacht et la S.S.

I.G. Farben présente un intérêt particulier pour la formation de l'État nazi, car les directeurs de Farben y ont contribué matériellement. Hitler et les nazis au pouvoir en 1933. Nous avons des preuves photographiques (voir page 60) que I.G. Farben a contribué à hauteur de 400 000 RM à la "caisse noire" politique d'Hitler. C'est ce fonds secret qui a financé la prise de contrôle par les nazis en mars 1933. Bien des années auparavant, Farben avait obtenu des fonds de Wall Street pour la cartellisation et l'expansion de 1925 en Allemagne et 30 millions de dollars pour I.G. américain en 1929, et avait des directeurs de Wall Street au sein du conseil d'administration de Farben. Il faut noter que ces fonds ont été collectés et les directeurs nommés des années avant qu'Hitler ne soit promu dictateur allemand.

LA PUISSANCE ÉCONOMIQUE DE I.G. FARBEN

Des observateurs qualifiés ont fait valoir que l'Allemagne n'aurait pas pu entrer en guerre en 1939 sans I.G. Farben. Entre 1927 et le début de la Seconde Guerre mondiale, I.G. Farben a doublé de taille, une expansion rendue possible en grande partie par l'assistance technique américaine et par les émissions d'obligations américaines, comme celle de 30 millions de dollars offertes par la National City Bank. En 1939, I.G. acquiert une participation et une influence de gestion dans quelque 380 autres entreprises allemandes et plus de 500 entreprises étrangères. L'empire Farben possédait ses propres mines de charbon, ses propres centrales électriques, des unités sidérurgiques, des banques, des unités de recherche et de nombreuses entreprises commerciales. Il y a eu plus de 2000 accords de cartel entre I.G. et des entreprises étrangères - y compris Standard Oil du New Jersey, DuPont, Alcoa, Dow Chemical, et d'autres aux États-Unis. L'histoire complète de I.G., Farben et de ses activités mondiales avant la Seconde Guerre mondiale ne pourra jamais être connue, car les principaux documents allemands ont été détruits en 1945 en prévision de la victoire des Alliés.

[461] Extrait de *Der Farben-Konzern* 1928, (Hoppenstedt, Berlin : I928), pp. 4-5.

Cependant, une enquête menée après la guerre par le ministère américain de la guerre a conclu que :

> *Sans les immenses installations de production d'I.G., sa recherche intensive et ses vastes affiliations internationales, la poursuite de la guerre par l'Allemagne aurait été impensable et impossible. Farben n'a pas seulement concentré ses énergies sur l'armement de l'Allemagne, mais aussi sur l'affaiblissement de ses victimes potentielles, et cette tentative à double sens d'étendre le potentiel industriel allemand pour la guerre et de restreindre celui du reste du monde n'a pas été conçue et exécutée "dans le cours normal des affaires". La preuve accablante que les fonctionnaires de I.G. Farben avaient une connaissance préalable complète du plan de conquête du monde par l'Allemagne et de chaque acte agressif spécifique entrepris par la suite.*[462]

Les directeurs des entreprises Farben (c'est-à-dire les "fonctionnaires I.G. Farben" mentionnés dans l'enquête) comprenaient non seulement des Allemands mais aussi d'éminents financiers américains. Ce rapport du département de guerre américain de 1945 concluait que la mission d'I.G., confiée par Hitler dans la période d'avant-guerre, était de rendre l'Allemagne autosuffisante en caoutchouc, essence, huiles lubrifiantes, magnésium, fibres, agents de tannage, graisses et explosifs. Pour remplir cette mission essentielle, I.G. a dépensé des sommes considérables dans des processus d'extraction de ces matériels de guerre à partir de matières premières allemandes indigènes - en particulier les abondantes ressources en charbon allemandes. Lorsque ces procédés ne pouvaient pas être développés en Allemagne, ils étaient achetés à l'étranger dans le cadre d'accords de cartel. Par exemple, le procédé pour l'iso-octane, essentiel pour les carburants d'aviation, a été obtenu des États-Unis,

> *... en fait entièrement [de] l'Amérique et nous l'avons connu en détail dans ses différentes phases grâce à nos accords avec eux [Standard Oil of New Jersey] et nous l'utilisons très largement.*[463]

Le procédé de fabrication du plomb tétraéthyle, essentiel pour l'essence d'aviation, a été obtenu par I.G. Farben des États-Unis, et en 1939, I.G. a acheté pour 20 millions de dollars d'essence d'aviation de haute qualité à la Standard Oil du New Jersey. Avant même que l'Allemagne ne fabrique du plomb tétraéthyle par le procédé américain, elle a pu "emprunter" 500 tonnes à l'Ethyl Corporation. Cet emprunt de plomb tétraéthyle essentiel n'a pas été remboursé et I.G. a perdu la garantie d'un million de dollars. De plus, I.G. a acheté d'importants stocks de magnésium à Dow Chemical pour la fabrication de bombes incendiaires et a stocké des explosifs, des stabilisateurs, du phosphore et des cyanures provenant de l'étranger.

---

[462] *Élimination des ressources allemandes*, p. 943.

[463] Ibid, p. 945.

En 1939, sur les 43 principaux produits fabriqués par I.G., 28 étaient "de première importance" pour les forces armées allemandes. Le contrôle ultime de Farben sur l'économie de guerre allemande, acquis au cours des années 1920 et 1930 avec l'aide de Wall Street, peut être mieux évalué en examinant le pourcentage de la production de matériel de guerre allemand produit par les usines Farben en 1945. À cette époque, Farben produisait 100% du caoutchouc synthétique allemand, 95% du gaz toxique allemand (y compris tout le gaz Zyklon B utilisé dans les camps de concentration), 90% des plastiques allemands, 88% du magnésium allemand, 84% des explosifs allemands, 70% de la poudre à canon allemande, 46% de l'essence à indice d'octane élevé (aviation) allemande et 33% de l'essence synthétique allemande.[464] (Voir le graphique 2-1 et le tableau 2-1).

Tableau 2-1 : Dépendance de l'armée allemande (Wehrmacht) à l'égard de la production de I.G. Farben (1943) :

Produit	Production allemande totale	Pourcentage produit par I.G. Farben
Caoutchouc synthétique	118 600 tonnes	100
Méthanol	251 000 tonnes	100
Huile de lubrification	60 000 tonnes	100
Colorants	31 670 tonnes	98
Gaz toxique	—	95
Nickel	2000 tonnes	95
Plastiques	57 000 tonnes	90
Magnésium	27 400 tonnes	88
Explosifs	221 000 tonnes	84
Poudre à canon	210 000 tonnes	70
Haut indice d'octane (Aviation)	650 000 tonnes	46
Essence		
Acide sulfurique	707 000 tonnes	35

Le Dr von Schnitzler, du I.G. Farben *Aufsichsrat*, a fait la déclaration pertinente suivante en 1943 :

[464] *New York Times*, 21 octobre 1945, section 1, p. 1, 12.

Il n'est pas exagéré de dire que, sans les services de la chimie allemande fournis dans le cadre du plan quadriennal, la poursuite de la guerre moderne aurait été impensable.[465]

Chart 2-1: German Army (Wehrmacht) Dependence on I.G. Farben Production (1943):

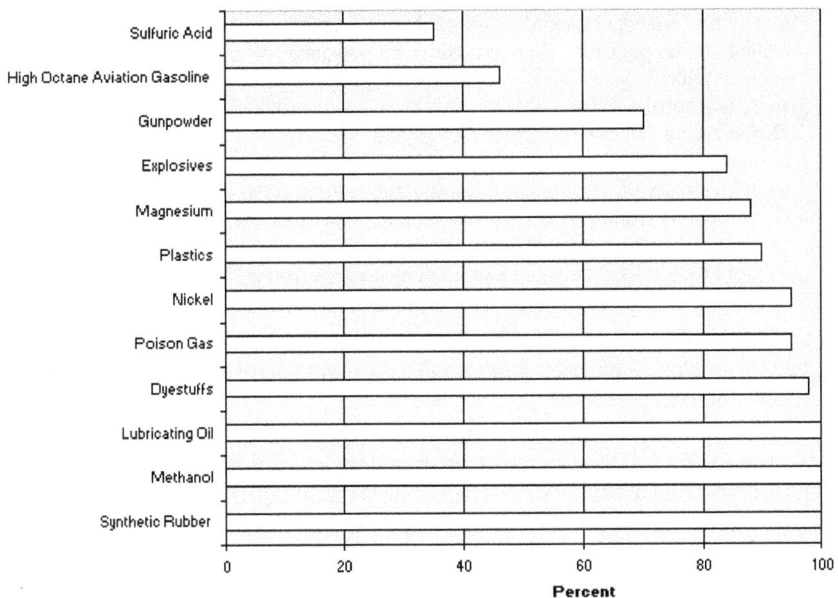

Malheureusement, lorsque nous enquêtons sur les origines techniques des plus importants de ces matériels militaires - outre le soutien financier à Hitler - nous trouvons des liens avec l'industrie américaine et les hommes d'affaires américains. Il y a eu de nombreux accords Farben avec des entreprises américaines, y compris des accords de commercialisation de cartels, des accords de brevet et des échanges techniques, comme l'illustrent les transferts de technologie Standard Oil-Ethyl mentionnés ci-dessus. Ces accords ont été utilisés par I.G. pour faire avancer la politique nazie à l'étranger, pour recueillir des informations stratégiques et pour consolider un cartel chimique mondial.

L'un des aspects les plus horribles du cartel de I.G. Farben était l'invention, la production et la distribution du gaz Zyklon B, utilisé dans les camps de concentration nazis. Le Zyklon B était de l'acide prussique pur, un poison mortel produit par I.G. Farben Leverkusen et vendu par le bureau de vente de Bayer par l'intermédiaire de Degesch, un détenteur de licence indépendant. Les ventes de Zyklon B représentaient près des trois quarts du chiffre d'affaires de Degesch ; suffisamment de gaz pour tuer 200 millions d'êtres humains a été produit et vendu par I.G. Farben. Le rapport du Comité Kilgore de 1942 indique clairement que les

[465] Ibid, p. 947.

directeurs d'I.G. Farben avaient une connaissance précise des camps de concentration nazis et de l'utilisation des produits chimiques d'I.G. Cette connaissance préalable devient significative si l'on considère plus tard le rôle des directeurs américains dans la filiale américaine d'I.G. On peut lire dans l'interrogatoire de 1945 du directeur d'I.G. Farben, Von Schnitzler :

> **Q.** Qu'avez-vous fait lorsqu'on vous a dit que les produits chimiques à base d'azote étaient utilisés pour tuer, pour assassiner les personnes détenues dans les camps de concentration ?
> **A.** J'étais horrifié.
> **Q.** Avez-vous fait quelque chose à ce sujet ?
> **A.** Je l'ai gardée pour moi parce que c'était trop terrible..... J'ai demandé à Muller-Cunradi s'il savait, ainsi qu'Ambros et d'autres directeurs à Auschwitz, que les gaz et les produits chimiques étaient utilisés pour assassiner des gens.
> **Q.** Qu'a-t-il dit ?
> **A.** Oui : tous les directeurs de l'I.G. à Auschwitz le savent.[466]

I.G. Farben n'a pas tenté d'arrêter la production de ces gaz - une façon plutôt inefficace pour von Schnitzler d'exprimer son inquiétude pour la vie humaine, "parce que c'était trop horrible".

Le bureau de Berlin N.W. 7 de I.G. Farben était le principal centre d'espionnage nazi à l'étranger. L'unité fonctionnait sous la direction de Max Ilgner, directeur de Farben, neveu de Hermann Schmitz, président d'I.G. Farben. Max Ilgner et Hermann Schmitz faisaient partie du conseil d'administration de l'I.G. américain, avec leurs collègues Henry Ford de la Ford Motor Company, Paul Warburg de la Bank of Manhattan et Charles E. Mitchell de la Federal Reserve Bank of New York.

Au début de la guerre, en 1939, les employés de VOWI ont été intégrés à la Wehrmacht, mais ils ont continué à effectuer le même travail que lorsqu'ils étaient sous les ordres de I.G. Farben. L'un des plus éminents de ces travailleurs du renseignement de Farben dans le N.W. 7 était le prince Bernhard des Pays-Bas, qui a rejoint Farben au début des années 1930 après avoir accompli une période de 18 mois de service dans le S.S. en uniforme noir.[467]

La branche américaine du réseau de renseignement VOWI était Chemnyco, Inc. Selon le ministère de la guerre,

---

[466] Élimination des ressources allemandes.

[467] Bernhard est aujourd'hui plus connu pour son rôle de président des réunions secrètes, dites "Bilderberger". Voir Congrès américain, Chambre des représentants, Commission spéciale sur les activités anti-américaines, *Enquête sur les activités de propagande nazie et Enquête sur certaines autres activités de propagande.* 73e Congrès, 2e session, Audiences n° 73-DC-4. (Washington : Government Printing Office, 1934), Volume VIII, p. 7525.

Grâce à ses contacts commerciaux habituels, Chemnyco a pu transmettre à l'Allemagne d'énormes quantités de documents allant de photographies et de plans à des descriptions détaillées d'installations industrielles entières.[468]

Le vice-président de Chemnyco à New York était Rudolph Ilgner, un citoyen américain et frère du réalisateur Max Ilgner de American I.G. Farben. En bref, Farben a dirigé VOWI, l'opération de renseignement extérieur nazie, avant la Seconde Guerre mondiale et l'opération VOWI était associée à des membres importants de l'establishment de Wall Street par l'intermédiaire d'American I.G. et de Chemnyco.

Le ministère américain de la Guerre a également accusé I.G. Farben et ses associés américains d'être le fer de lance des programmes de guerre psychologique et économique nazis par la diffusion de la propagande via des agents Farben à l'étranger, et de fournir des devises étrangères pour cette propagande nazie. Les accords du cartel Farben ont favorisé la guerre économique nazie - l'exemple le plus marquant étant la restriction volontaire de Standard Oil du New Jersey sur le développement du caoutchouc synthétique aux États-Unis sur ordre de I.G. Farben. Comme l'indique le rapport du ministère de la Guerre :

En résumé, la détermination de Standard Oil à maintenir un monopole absolu sur le développement du caoutchouc synthétique aux États-Unis a permis à I.G. d'atteindre pleinement son objectif d'empêcher la production américaine en dissuadant les entreprises américaines de caoutchouc d'entreprendre des recherches indépendantes sur le développement des procédés de caoutchouc synthétique.[469]

En 1945, le Dr Oskar Loehr, chef adjoint de l'I.G. "Tea Buro", confirme que I.G. Farben et Standard Oil du New Jersey ont mis en œuvre un "plan préconçu" pour supprimer le développement de l'industrie du caoutchouc synthétique aux États-Unis, au profit de la Wehrmacht allemande et au détriment des États-Unis pendant la Seconde Guerre mondiale.

Le témoignage du Dr Loehr se lit (en partie) comme suit :

Q. Est-il vrai que pendant le retard pris dans la divulgation des procédés de buna [caoutchouc synthétique] aux sociétés de caoutchouc américaines, Chemnyco et Jasco tenaient entre-temps I.G. bien informé du développement du caoutchouc synthétique aux États-Unis ?
A. Oui.
Q. Ainsi, à tout moment, I.G. était pleinement conscient de l'état de développement de l'industrie américaine du caoutchouc synthétique ?
A. Oui.
Q. Étiez-vous présent à la réunion de La Haye lorsque M. Howard [de la Standard Oil] s'y est rendu en 1939 ?
A. Non.

---

[468] Ibid. p. 949.

[469] Ibid. p. 952.

Q. Qui était présent ?
A. M. Ringer, qui était accompagné par le Dr Brown de Ludwigshafen. Vous ont-ils parlé des négociations ?
A. Oui, dans la mesure où ils étaient sur la partie buna.
Q. Est-il vrai que M. Howard a déclaré à I.G., lors de cette réunion, que les développements aux États-Unis avaient atteint un tel stade qu'il ne lui serait plus possible de conserver les informations relatives aux procédés de fabrication du buna auprès des entreprises américaines ?
A. M. Ringer l'a signalé.
Q. Est-ce à cette réunion que, pour la première fois, M. Howard a dit à I.G. que les entreprises américaines de caoutchouc pourraient devoir être informées des procédés et qu'il a assuré à I.G. que Standard Oil contrôlerait l'industrie du caoutchouc synthétique aux États-Unis ? Est-ce bien cela ?
A. C'est exact. C'est la connaissance que j'ai obtenue par l'intermédiaire de M. Ringer.
Q. Dans tous ces arrangements, depuis le début du développement de l'industrie du caoutchouc synthétique, la suppression de l'industrie du caoutchouc synthétique aux États-Unis faisait donc partie d'un plan préconçu entre I.G. d'une part et M. Howard de Standard Oil d'autre part ?
A. C'est une conclusion qui doit être tirée des faits précédents.[470]

I.G. Farben était la plus grande source de devises étrangères de l'Allemagne d'avant-guerre, et ces devises permettaient à l'Allemagne d'acheter des matières premières stratégiques, du matériel militaire et des procédés techniques, et de financer ses programmes d'espionnage, de propagande et ses diverses activités militaires et politiques à l'étranger avant la Seconde Guerre mondiale. Agissant au nom de l'État nazi, Farben élargit son propre horizon à une échelle mondiale qui entretient des relations étroites avec le régime nazi et la Wehrmacht. Un bureau de liaison, la *Vermittlungsstelle W*, a été créé pour maintenir les communications entre I.G. Farben et le ministère allemand de la Guerre :

> *L'objectif de ce travail est la mise en place d'un dispositif pour l'armement qui pourrait être inséré sans difficulté dans l'organisation existante d'I.G. et ses différentes usines. En cas de guerre, l'I.G. sera traité par les autorités concernées par les questions d'armement comme une grande usine qui, dans sa tâche pour l'armement, dans la mesure où il est possible de le faire du point de vue technique, se régulera elle-même sans aucune influence organisationnelle de l'extérieur (le travail dans ce sens a été en principe convenu avec le ministère de la guerre Wehrwirtschaftsant) et à partir de ce bureau avec le ministère de l'économie. Dans le domaine d'activité de la Vermittlungsstelle W, outre l'organisation et la planification à long terme, la collaboration continue en matière d'armement et de questions techniques avec les autorités du Reich et les usines de l'I.G.*[471]

Malheureusement, les dossiers des bureaux de la Vermittlungsstelle ont été détruits avant la fin de la guerre, bien que l'on sache d'après d'autres sources qu'à

---

[470] Ibid p. 1293.

[471] Ibid p. 954.

partir de 1934, un réseau complexe de transactions s'est développé entre l'I.G. et la Wehrmacht. En 1934, I.G. Farben commença à se mobiliser pour la guerre, et chaque usine I.G. prépara ses plans de production de guerre et les soumit aux ministères de la guerre et de l'économie. En 1935, six simulations de guerre ont été organisés dans les usines I.G. Farben et les procédures techniques de guerre ont été répétées.[472] Ces simulations ont été décrites par le Dr Struss, chef du secrétariat du comité technique d'I.G :

> *Il est vrai que depuis 1934 ou 1935, peu après la création de la Vermittlungsstelle W, des simulations de guerre théoriques avaient été organisées pour examiner comment se matérialiseraient les effets des bombardements sur certaines usines. On prenait notamment en considération ce qui se passerait si des bombes de 100 ou 500 kilos tombaient sur une certaine usine et quel en serait le résultat. Il est également vrai que le terme "Kriegsspiele" a été utilisé pour cela.*
>
> *Les Kriegsspiele ont été préparés par M. Ritter et le Dr Eckell, plus tard en partie par le Dr von Brunning sur ordre personnel du Dr Krauch ou sur ordre de l'armée de l'air, je n'en ai pas connaissance. Les tâches ont été confiées en partie par le Vermittlungsstelle W et en partie par des officiers de l'armée de l'air. Un certain nombre d'officiers de tous les groupes de la Wehrmacht (marine, armée de l'air et armée de terre) ont participé à ces Kriegsspiele.*
>
> *Les endroits touchés par les bombes ont été marqués sur une carte de l'usine afin de pouvoir déterminer quelles parties de l'usine seraient endommagées, par exemple un compteur de gaz ou une importante canalisation. Dès la fin du raid, la direction de l'usine a constaté les dégâts et a indiqué quelle partie de l'usine devait s'arrêter de fonctionner ; elle a également indiqué le temps nécessaire pour réparer les dégâts. Lors d'une réunion suivante, les conséquences du Kriegsspiele ont été décrites et il a été établi que dans le cas de Leuna [l'usine], les dommages étaient considérablement élevés ; il a notamment été constaté que les modifications des conduites devaient être effectuées à un coût considérable.*[473]

Par conséquent, tout au long des années 1930, I.G. Farben a fait plus que se conformer aux ordres du régime nazi. Farben a été l'initiateur et l'opérateur des plans nazis pour la conquête du monde. Farben a agi comme un organisme de recherche et de renseignement pour l'armée allemande et a volontairement lancé des projets de la Wehrmacht. En fait, l'armée n'a que rarement eu à s'adresser à Farben ; on estime qu'environ 40 à 50% des projets Farben pour l'armée ont été initiés par Farben lui-même. En bref, selon les mots du Dr von Schnitzler :

> *Ainsi, en agissant comme il l'avait fait, I.G. contracta une grande responsabilité et constitua une aide substantielle dans le domaine chimique et une aide décisive à la politique étrangère de Hitler, qui conduisit à la guerre et à la ruine de l'Allemagne. Je dois donc conclure qu'I.G. est en grande partie responsable de la politique d'Hitler.*

---

[472] Ibid p. 954.

[473] Ibid, pp. 954-5.

SOIGNER LA RÉPUTATION DE I.G. FARBEN

Ce misérable tableau de la préparation militaire d'avant-guerre était connu à l'étranger et a dû être vendu - ou déguisé - au public américain afin de faciliter la collecte de fonds et l'assistance technique de Wall Street au nom de I.G. Farben aux États-Unis. Une importante société de relations publiques de New York a été choisie pour vendre le marchand de la mort I.G. Farben aux États-Unis. La firme de relations publiques la plus connue à la fin des années 1920 et dans les années 1930 était Ivy Lee & T.J. Ross de New York. Ivy Lee avait auparavant entrepris une campagne de relations publiques pour les Rockefeller, afin de redorer le blason des Rockefeller auprès du public américain. La firme avait également produit un livre décousu intitulé *USSR*, entreprenant la même tâche de nettoyage pour l'Union soviétique - alors même que les camps de travail soviétiques étaient en pleine effervescence à la fin des années 20 et au début des années 30.

À partir de 1929, Ivy Lee devient conseiller en relations publiques pour I.G. Farben aux États-Unis. En 1934, Ivy Lee a présenté un témoignage à la commission des activités anti-américaines de la Chambre des représentants sur ce travail pour Farben.[474] Lee témoigna qu'I.G. Farben était affilié à la firme américaine Farben et que "l'I.G. américain est une holding avec des directeurs tels que Edsel Ford, Walter Teagle, un des dirigeants de la City Bank....". Lee expliqua qu'il était payé 25 000 dollars par an en vertu d'un contrat passé avec Max Ilgner d'I.G. Farben. Son travail consistait à contrer les critiques dont I.G. Farben faisait l'objet aux États-Unis. Les conseils donnés par Ivy Lee à Farben sur ce problème étaient suffisamment acceptables :

> *En premier lieu, je leur ai dit qu'ils ne pourraient jamais réconcilier aux yeux du monde le peuple américain avec le traitement qu'il inflige aux Juifs : que cela était tout simplement étranger à la mentalité américaine et ne pouvait jamais être justifié dans l'opinion publique américaine, et qu'il ne servait à rien d'essayer.*
>
> *En second lieu, tout ce qui a trait à la propagande nazie dans ce pays était une erreur et ne doit pas être repris. Notre peuple considère qu'il s'est mêlé des affaires américaines, et c'était une mauvaise idée.*[475]

Le paiement initial de 4500 dollars à Ivy Lee dans le cadre de ce contrat a été effectué par Hermann Schmitz, président de I.G. Farben en Allemagne. Il a été déposé à la New York Trust Company sous le nom de I.G. Chemic (ou "l'I.G. suisse", comme l'a appelé Ivy Lee).

Cependant, le second et principal paiement de 14 450 dollars a été effectué par William von Rath de l'I.G. américain et également déposé par Ivy Lee à la New York Trust Company, au crédit de son compte personnel. (Le compte de la firme

[474] Congrès américain. Chambre des représentants, Comité spécial sur les activités anti-américaines, *enquête sur les activités de propagande nazie* et *enquête sur certaines autres activités de propagande*, op. cit.

[475] Ibid, p. 178.

était à la Chase Bank.) Ce point sur l'origine des fonds est "important si l'on considère l'identité des directeurs de l'American I.G., car le paiement par l'American I.G. signifiait que la majeure partie des fonds de propagande nazie n'était pas d'origine allemande. *Il s'agissait de fonds américains gagnés aux États-Unis et sous le contrôle de directeurs américains, bien qu'ils aient été utilisés pour la propagande nazie aux États-Unis.*

En d'autres termes, la plupart des fonds de propagande nazie gérés par Ivy Lee n'ont pas été importés d'Allemagne.

L'utilisation de ces fonds américains a été mise en cause par la Commission des activités anti-américaines de la Chambre des représentants :

> **M. DICKSTEIN**. Si je vous comprends bien, vous avez témoigné que vous n'avez reçu aucune propagande et que vous n'avez rien à voir avec la diffusion de la propagande dans ce pays ?
> **M. LEE.** Je n'ai pas témoigné du fait que je n'ai rien reçu M. Dickstein.
> **M. DICKSTEIN**. Je vais donc éliminer cette partie de la question.
> **M. LEE**. J'ai témoigné que je n'ai diffusé aucune information.
> **M. DICKSTEIN**. Avez-vous reçu ou votre entreprise a-t-elle reçu à un moment quelconque de la littérature de propagande en provenance d'Allemagne ?
> **M. LEE**. Oui, Monsieur.
> **M. DICKSTEIN**. Et c'était quand ?
> **M. LEE**. Oh, nous avons reçu – cela dépend ce que vous appelez de la propagande. Nous avons reçu une immense quantité de littérature.
> **M. DICKSTEIN**. Vous ne savez pas ce qu'était cette littérature et ce qu'elle contenait ?
> **M. LEE**. Nous avons reçu des livres, des brochures, des coupures de presse et des documents, en grande quantité.
> **M. DICKSTEIN**. Je suppose que quelqu'un de votre bureau les passerait en revue et verrait ce qu'ils étaient ?
> **M. LEE**. Oui, Monsieur.
> **M. DICKSTEIN**. Et ensuite, après avoir découvert ce qu'ils étaient, je suppose que vous en avez gardé des copies ?
> **M. LEE**. Dans certains cas, oui : et dans d'autres, non. Un grand nombre d'entre eux, bien sûr, étaient en allemand, et j'avais ce que mon fils m'avait envoyé. Il m'a dit qu'elles étaient intéressantes et significatives, et que je les avais traduites ou que j'en avais fait des extraits.[476]

Enfin, Ivy Lee a engagé Burnham Carter pour étudier les nouveaux rapports américains sur l'Allemagne et préparer des réponses pronazies appropriées. Il convient de noter que cette littérature allemande n'était pas de la littérature de Farben, mais de la littérature officielle hitlérienne :

> **M. DICKSTEIN**. En d'autres termes, vous recevez ce matériel qui traite des conditions allemandes actuelles : Vous l'examinez et vous les conseillez. Cela n'a rien à voir avec le gouvernement allemand, bien que le matériel, la littérature, soit des publications officielles du régime hitlérien. C'est exact, n'est-ce pas ?

---

[476] Ibid, p. 183.

M. LEE. Une bonne partie de la littérature n'était pas officielle.

M. DICKSTEIN. Ce n'était pas de la littérature I.G., n'est-ce pas ?

M. LEE. Non, c'est I.G. qui me l'a envoyé.

M. DICKSTEIN. Pouvez-vous nous montrer un bout de papier qui est arrivé ici et qui a un rapport avec le G.I. ?

M. LEE. Oh, oui. Ils publient beaucoup de littérature. Mais je ne veux pas poser la question. Il ne fait aucun doute que, sous leur autorité, j'ai reçu une immense quantité de matériel provenant de sources officielles et non officielles.

M. DICKSTEIN. Exactement. En d'autres termes, le matériel envoyé ici par le G.I. était du matériel diffusé - nous appellerions cela de la propagande - par l'autorité du gouvernement allemand. Mais la distinction que vous faites dans votre déclaration est, si je comprends bien, que le gouvernement allemand ne vous l'a pas envoyé directement ; qu'il vous a été envoyé par le G.I.

M. LEE. Bien.

M. DICKSTEIN. Et cela n'a rien à voir avec leurs relations d'affaires de tout à l'heure.

M. LEE. C'est exact.

L'I.G. FARBEN AMÉRICAIN

Qui étaient les financiers de l'establishment de Wall Street qui dirigeaient les activités de l'I.G. américain, la filiale d'I.G. Farben aux États-Unis qui faisait la promotion de la propagande nazie ?

Les directeurs américains de I.G. Farben comptaient parmi les membres les plus éminents de Wall Street. Les intérêts allemands se sont implantés aux États-Unis après la Première Guerre mondiale et ont réussi à surmonter les obstacles destinés à empêcher I.G. d'accéder au marché américain. Ni la saisie des brevets allemands, ni la création de la Fondation Chimique, ni les barrières tarifaires élevées n'ont constitué un problème majeur.

En 1925, la General Dyestuff Corporation est devenue l'agent commercial exclusif des produits fabriqués par Gasselli Dyestuff (rebaptisée General Aniline Works, Inc. en 1929) et importés d'Allemagne. Les actions de General Aniline Works ont été transférées en 1929 à American I.G. Chemical Corporation, puis en 1939 à General Aniline & Film Corporation, dans laquelle American I.G. et General Aniline Works ont fusionné. American I.G. et son successeur, General Aniline & Film, est l'unité par laquelle le contrôle des entreprises d'I.G. aux États-Unis a été maintenu. Le nombre d'actions d'American I.G. était de 3 000 000 d'actions ordinaires A et 3 000 000 actions ordinaires B. En échange de participations dans General Aniline Works et Agfa-Ansco Corporation, I.G. Farben en Allemagne a reçu toutes les actions B et 400 000 actions A. Trente millions de dollars d'obligations convertibles ont été vendues au public américain et garanties quant au principal et aux intérêts par l'Allemand I.G. Farben, qui a reçu une option d'achat de 1 000 000 d'actions A supplémentaires.

Tableau 2-2 : Les directeurs de l'I.G. américain à 1930 : American I,G.

Directeur américain I,G.	Citoyenneté	Autres grandes associations
Carl BOSCH	Allemand	FORD MOTOR CO. A-G
Edsel B. FORD	ÉTATS-UNIS	FORD MOTOR CO. DETROIT
Max ILGNER	Allemand	Dirige le bureau I.G. FARBEN N.W.7 (INTELLIGENCE). Coupable au procès de Nuremberg pour crimes de guerre.
F. Ter MEER	Allemand	Coupable aux procès de Nuremberg pour crimes de guerre
H.A. METZ	ÉTATS-UNIS	Directeur de I.G. Farben Allemagne et BANK OF MANHATTAN (États-Unis)
C.E. MITCHELL	ÉTATS-UNIS	Directeur de la FEDERAL RESERVE BANK OF N.Y. et de la NATIONAL CITY BANK
Herman SCHMITZ	Allemand	Au sein des conseils d'administration de I.G. Farben (Président) (Allemagne), de la Deutsche Bank (Allemagne) et de la BANK FOR INTERNATIONAL SETTLEMENTS. Coupable au procès de Nuremberg pour crimes de guerre.
Walter TEAGLE	ÉTATS-UNIS	Directeur FEDERAL RESERVE BANK OF NEW YORK and STANDARD OIL OF NEW JERSEY
W.H. von RATH	Naturalisé	Directeur de GERMAN GENERAL U.S. ELECTRIC (A.E.G.)
Paul M. WARBURG	ÉTATS-UNIS	Premier membre de la FEDERAL RESERVE BANK OF NEW YORK et de la BANK OF MANHATTAN
W.E. WEISS	ÉTATS-UNIS	Produits en livres sterling

Source : Manuel des investissements de Moody's ; 1930, p. 2149.
Note : Walter DUISBERG (États-Unis), W. GRIEF (États-Unis) et Adolf KUTTROFF (États-Unis) étaient également directeurs de l'Américain I.G. Farben à cette époque.

La gestion de l'I.G. américain (plus tard General Aniline) était dominée par l'I.G. ou d'anciens fonctionnaires de l'I.G. Hermann Schmitz a été président de 1929 à 1936, puis son frère, Dietrich A. Schmitz, citoyen américain naturalisé, lui a succédé jusqu'en 1941. Hermann Schmitz, qui était également directeur de la Banque des Règlements Internationaux, le "sommet" du système de contrôle financier international. Il est resté président du conseil d'administration de 1936 à 1939.

Le conseil d'administration initial comprenait neuf membres qui étaient, ou avaient été, membres du conseil d'I.G. Farben en Allemagne (Hermann Schmitz, Carl Bosch, Max Ilgner, Fritzter Meer et Wilfred Grief), ou avaient été précédemment employés par I.G. Farben en Allemagne (Walter Duisberg, Adolf Kuttroff, W.H. von Rath, Herman A. Metz). Herman A. Metz était un citoyen américain, un démocrate convaincu en politique et un ancien contrôleur de la ville de New York. Un dixième, W.E. Weiss, avait été sous contrat avec I.G.

Les directeurs de l'I.G. américain n'étaient pas seulement éminents à Wall Street et dans l'industrie américaine, mais ils étaient surtout issus de quelques institutions très influentes :

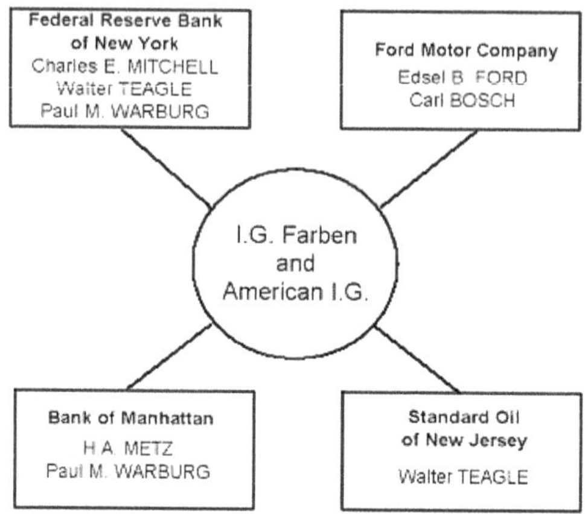

Les quatre autres membres du conseil d'administration de l'I.G. américain étaient des citoyens américains éminents et des membres de l'élite financière de Wall Street : C.E. Mitchell, président de la National City Bank et de la Federal Reserve Bank of New York ; Edsel B. Ford, président de la Ford Motor Company ; W.C. Teagle, autre directeur de la Standard Oil du New Jersey ; et Paul Warburg, premier membre de la Federal Reserve Bank of New York et président de la Bank of Manhattan Company.

Les directeurs de l'I.G. américain n'étaient pas seulement éminents à Wall Street et dans l'industrie américaine, mais ils étaient surtout issus de quelques institutions très influentes. (Voir le tableau ci-dessus).

Entre 1929 et 1939, la composition du conseil d'administration d'American I.G. a changé. Le nombre de directeurs a varié de temps en temps, bien qu'une majorité d'entre eux aient toujours eu des antécédents ou des relations avec des I.G., et le conseil n'a jamais eu moins de quatre directeurs américains. En 1939 - probablement à l'approche de la Seconde Guerre mondiale - un effort a été fait pour donner au conseil un caractère plus américain, mais malgré la démission de Hermann Schmitz, Carl Bosch et Walter Duisberg, et la nomination de sept nouveaux directeurs, sept membres appartenaient toujours au groupe I.G. Cette prédominance du G.I. s'est accrue au cours des années 1940 et 1941, lorsque des réalisateurs américains, dont Edsel Ford, ont pris conscience de la malsaine politique du G.I. et ont démissionné.

Plusieurs observations de base peuvent être faites à partir de ces preuves. Tout d'abord, le conseil d'administration d'American I.G. comptait trois directeurs de la Banque de la Réserve Fédérale de New York, la plus influente des différentes banques de la Réserve Fédérale. American I.G. avait également des liens avec la Standard Oil du New Jersey, la Ford Motor Company, la Bank of Manhattan (qui deviendra plus tard la Chase Manhattan) et l'A.E.G. (German General Electric). Ensuite, trois membres du conseil d'administration de cette société américaine ont été reconnus coupables lors des procès de Nuremberg pour crimes de guerre. Il s'agissait des membres allemands, et non américains. Parmi ces Allemands se trouvait Max Ilgner, directeur du bureau I.G. Farben N.W. 7 à Berlin, c'est-à-dire le bureau de renseignement nazi d'avant-guerre. Si les directeurs d'une société sont collectivement responsables des activités de la société, alors les directeurs américains auraient également dû être jugés à Nuremberg, en même temps que les directeurs allemands - c'est-à-dire si le but des procès était de déterminer la culpabilité de guerre. Bien sûr, si le but des procès était de détourner l'attention de l'implication des États-Unis dans la montée en puissance d'Hitler, ils ont très bien réussi...

CHAPITRE III

GENERAL ELECTRIC FINANCE HITLER

Parmi les premières mesures fascistes de Roosevelt figure la loi sur la relance de l'industrie nationale (NRA) du 16 juin 1933. Les origines de ce dispositif méritent d'être répétées. Ces idées ont été suggérées pour la première fois par Gerard Swope de la General Electric Company ... elles ont ensuite été adoptées par la Chambre de commerce des États-Unis ...

(Herbert Hoover, *Les Mémoires d'Herbert Hoover : La Grande Dépression,* 1929-1941, New York : The Macmillan Company, 1952, p. 420)

La multinationale General Electric a joué un rôle sans précédent dans l'histoire du XXe siècle. La General Electric Company a électrifié l'Union soviétique dans les années 20 et 30, et a répondu à la maxime de Lénine selon laquelle "le Socialisme c'est le pouvoir des soviets + l'électricité".[477] Le plan Swope, créé par l'ancien président de General Electric, Gerard Swope, est devenu le New Deal de Franklin D. Roosevelt, par un processus déploré par l'ancien président Herbert Hoover et décrit dans *Wall Street et FDR.*[478] Il existait une relation intime et durable entre Swope et Young de la General Electric Company et la famille Roosevelt, comme il en existait une entre General Electric et l'Union soviétique. En 1936, le sénateur James A. Reed du Missouri, un des premiers partisans de Roosevelt, a pris conscience de la trahison des idées libérales de Roosevelt et a attaqué le programme Roosevelt New Deal comme une mesure "tyrannique" "menant au despotisme, [et] recherchée par ses commanditaires sous le couvert de l'aspiration communiste à la "justice sociale". "Le sénateur Reed a également accusé au Sénat que Franklin D. Roosevelt était "un homme engagé pour les royalistes économiques" à Wall Street et que la famille Roosevelt "est l'un des plus grands actionnaires de la General Electric Company".[479]

En fouillant dans les coulisses de l'histoire allemande de l'entre-deux-guerres et de l'histoire d'Hitler et du nazisme, nous trouvons Owen D. Young et Gerard

[477] Pour les détails techniques, voir l'étude en trois volumes, Antony C. Sutton, *Western Technology and Soviet Economic Development,* (Stanford, Californie : Hoover Institution Press, 1968, 1971), 1973), ci-après dénommée *Western Technology Series.*

[478] Publié en 1 volume par Le Retour aux Sources, www.leretourauxsources.com.

[479] *New York Times,* 6 octobre 1936. Voir aussi Antony C. Sutton, *Wall Street et FDR,* op. cit.

Swope de General Electric liés à la montée de l'hitlérisme et à la suppression de la démocratie allemande. Le fait que les directeurs de General Electric se retrouvent dans chacune de ces trois catégories historiques distinctes - c'est-à-dire le développement de l'Union soviétique, la création du New Deal de Roosevelt et la montée de l'hitlérisme - suggère à quel point les éléments du Big Business sont vivement intéressés par la socialisation du monde, pour leurs propres buts et objectifs, plutôt que par le maintien du marché impartial dans une société libre.[480] General Electric a largement profité du bolchevisme, du socialisme du New Deal de Roosevelt et, comme nous le verrons plus loin, du national-socialisme dans l'Allemagne hitlérienne.

GENERAL ELECTRIC DANS L'ALLEMAGNE DE WEIMAR

Walter Rathenau était, jusqu'à son assassinat en 1922, directeur général de l'Allgemeine Elekrizitats Gesellschaft (A.E.G.), ou General Electric allemande, et comme Owen Young et Gerard Swope, ses homologues aux États-Unis, il était un éminent défenseur du socialisme d'entreprise. Walter Rathenau s'est exprimé publiquement contre la concurrence et la libre entreprise. Pourquoi ? Parce que Rathenau et Swope voulaient tous deux la protection et la coopération de l'État pour leurs propres objectifs et profits particuliers. (Mais bien sûr pas pour les objectifs et les profits de quelqu'un d'autre.) Rathenau a exprimé leur plaidoyer dans *La nouvelle économie politique :*

> *La nouvelle économie ne sera pas, comme nous l'avons vu, une économie d'État ou gouvernementale mais une économie privée engagée dans un pouvoir de résolution civique qui nécessitera certainement la coopération de l'État pour une consolidation organique afin de surmonter les frictions internes et d'augmenter la production et l'endurance.*[481]

Lorsque nous démêlons la prose emphatique de Rathenau, cela signifie que le pouvoir de l'État devait être mis à la disposition des entreprises privées pour leurs propres besoins, c'est-à-dire ce que l'on appelle communément le national-socialisme. Rathenau s'est prononcé publiquement contre la concurrence et la libre entreprise transmissible par héritage.[482] Non pas à l'égard de leur propre richesse, pour autant qu'on puisse la déterminer, mais en ce qui concernait la richesse de ceux qui ne bénéficiaient pas d'influence politique dans l'appareil d'État.

---

480 Bien sûr, les plaidoyers socialistes des hommes d'affaires sont toujours d'actualité. En témoignent les cris des blessés lorsque le président Ford a proposé la déréglementation des compagnies aériennes et du transport routier. Voir par exemple le *Wall Street Journal* du 25 novembre 1975.

481 Traduction polycopiée dans la bibliothèque de l'institution Hoover, p. 67. Voir aussi Walter Rathenau, *In Days to Come,* (Londres : Allen & Unwin, s.d.)

482 Ibid, p. 249.

Owen D. Young de General Electric était l'un des trois délégués américains à la réunion du plan Dawes de 1923 qui a établi le programme de réparations allemand. Et dans les plans Dawes et Young, on peut voir comment certaines entreprises privées ont pu bénéficier du pouvoir de l'État. Les prêts les plus importants accordés par Wall Street à l'Allemagne dans les années 1920 étaient des prêts de réparation ; c'est finalement l'investisseur américain qui a payé les réparations allemandes. La cartellisation de l'industrie électrique allemande sous l'égide de l'A.E.G. (ainsi que des industries sidérurgiques et chimiques évoquées aux chapitres un et deux) a été rendue possible grâce à ces prêts de Wall Street :

Date de l'offre	Emprunteur	Banque de gestion aux États-Unis	Montant nominal de l'émission
26 janvier 1925	Compagnie générale d'électricité (A. E, G.)	National City Co.	\$10,000,000
9 décembre 1925	Allgemeine National City Co. Elektrizitätsitats-Gesellschaft (A. E.G.)		\$10,000,000
22 mai 1928	Compagnie générale d'électricité (A.E.G.)	National City Co.	\$10,000,000
7 juin 1928	Compagnie générale d'électricité (A. E.G.)	National City Co.	\$5,000,000

En 1928, lors des réunions de réparation du Plan Young, nous trouvons le président de General Electric, Owen D. Young, à la présidence en tant que principal délégué américain, nommé par le gouvernement américain pour utiliser la puissance et le prestige du gouvernement américain afin de décider des questions financières internationales en augmentant les profits de Wall Street et de General Electric. En 1930, Owen D. Young, qui a donné son nom au plan Young pour les réparations allemandes, est devenu président du conseil d'administration de la General Electric Company à New York. Young était également président du comité exécutif de la Radio Corporation of America et directeur de la General Electric (A.E.G.) allemande et d'Osram en Allemagne. Young a également siégé au conseil d'administration d'autres grandes sociétés américaines, dont General Motors, NBC et RKO ; il a été conseiller du National Industrial Conference Board, directeur de la Chambre de commerce internationale et vice-président du conseil d'administration de la Banque de Réserve Fédérale de New York.

Gerard Swope a été président et directeur de la General Electric Company ainsi que de sociétés françaises et allemandes associées, dont A.E.G. et Osram en Allemagne. Swope a également été directeur de RCA, NBC et de la National City Bank of New York. D'autres directeurs d'International General Electric à cette époque reflètent le contrôle de Morgan sur la société, et Young et Swope étaient généralement connus comme les représentants de Morgan au conseil d'administration de G.E., qui comprenait Thomas Cochran, un autre associé de la firme J.P. Morgan. Le directeur de General Electric, Clark Haynes Minor, était président d'International General Electric dans les années 1920. Un autre directeur était Victor M. Cutter de la First National Bank of Boston et une figure des "républiques bananières" en Amérique centrale.

À la fin des années 1920, Young, Swope et Minor d'International General Electric se sont lancés dans l'industrie électrique allemande et ont acquis, sinon le contrôle comme certains l'ont rapporté, du moins un poids important dans les affaires internes d'A.E.G. et d'Osram. En juillet 1929, un accord a été conclu entre General Electric et trois entreprises allemandes - A.E.G., Siemens & Halske et Koppel and Company - qui détenaient ensemble toutes les actions d'Osram, le fabricant d'ampoules électriques. General Electric a acheté 16% des actions d'Osram et a conclu un accord commun pour le contrôle international de la production et de la commercialisation des ampoules électriques. Clark Minor et Gerard Swope deviennent directeurs d'Osram.[483]

En juillet 1929, des rumeurs circulant dans les milieux financiers allemands, selon lesquelles General Electric rachète également A.E.G. et que des pourparlers sont en cours à cette fin entre A.E.G. et G.E.[484] En août, il est confirmé que 14 millions de marks d'actions ordinaires d'A.E.G. seront émis au bénéfice de General Electric. Ces actions, ajoutées aux actions achetées sur le marché libre, ont donné à General Electric une participation de 25% dans A.E.G. Un accord de coopération plus étroit a été signé entre les deux sociétés, fournissant à la société allemande la technologie et les brevets américains. Il a été souligné dans les médias qu'A.E.G. n'aurait pas de participation dans G.E., mais que d'autre part G.E. financerait l'expansion d'A.E.G. en Allemagne.[485] La presse financière allemande a également noté qu'il n'y avait pas de représentation d'A.E.G. au conseil d'administration de G.E. aux États-Unis, mais que cinq Américains siégeaient désormais au conseil d'administration d'A.E.G. Le *Vossische Zeitung* a noté :

> *L'industrie électrique américaine a conquis le monde, et seuls quelques bastions d'opposition restants ont pu résister à l'assaut...*[486]

En 1930, à l'insu de la presse financière allemande, General Electric avait également obtenu un monopole technique effectif de l'industrie électrique soviétique et allait bientôt pénétrer même dans les derniers bastions de l'Allemagne, en particulier le groupe Siemens. En janvier 1930, trois hommes de G.E. furent élus au conseil d'administration d'A.E.G. - Clark H. Minor, Gerard Swope et E. H. Baldwin - et International General Electric (I.G.E.) poursuivit ses efforts pour fusionner l'industrie électrique mondiale en un cartel géant sous le contrôle de Wall Street.

En février, General Electric s'est concentré sur le dernier géant allemand de l'électricité, Siemens & Halske, et bien qu'il ait pu obtenir un important bloc d'obligations émises au nom de la firme allemande par Dillon, Read de New York, G.E. n'a pas pu obtenir de participation ou de directeurs au conseil

---

[483] *New York Times*, 2 juillet 1929.

[484] Ibid, 28 juillet 1929.

[485] Ibid, 2 août 1929 et 4 août 1929.

[486] Ibid, 6 août 1929.

d'administration de Siemens. Bien que la presse allemande ait reconnu que même ce contrôle limité était "un événement économique historique de premier ordre et une étape importante vers la formation d'un futur trust électrique mondial",[487] Siemens a conservé son indépendance vis-à-vis de General Electric - et cette indépendance est importante pour notre histoire. Le *New York Times a* rapporté :

> *Toute la presse souligne le fait que Siemens, contrairement à A.E.G., maintient son indépendance pour l'avenir et précise qu'aucun représentant de General Electric ne siégera au conseil d'administration de Siemens.*[488]

Il n'y a aucune preuve que Siemens, que ce soit par l'intermédiaire de Siemens & Halske ou de Siemens-Schukert, ait participé directement au financement d'Hitler. Siemens n'a contribué à Hitler que légèrement et indirectement par le biais d'une participation dans Osram. En revanche, tant A.E.G. qu'Osram ont financé directement Hitler par l'intermédiaire de la Nationale Treuhand de manière substantielle. Siemens a conservé son indépendance au début des années 1930 alors que l'A.E.G. et Osram étaient toutes deux sous domination américaine et avec des directeurs américains. Rien ne prouve que Siemens, sans directeurs américains, ait financé Hitler. En revanche, nous disposons de preuves documentaires irréfutables que la General Electric allemande et Osram, tous deux pourvues de directeurs américains, ont financé Hitler.

Dans les mois qui ont suivi la tentative de prise de contrôle de Siemens par Wall Street, le schéma d'une confiance du monde au développement dans l'industrie électrique s'est clarifié ; les luttes internationales pour les brevets ont pris fin et la participation de la G.E. dans l'A.E.G. est passée à près de 30%.[489]

Par conséquent, au début des années 1930, alors qu'Hitler se préparait à s'emparer du pouvoir dictatorial en Allemagne - soutenu par certains industriels allemands et américains, mais pas tous - la General Electric (A.E.G.) allemande était détenue par International General Electric (environ 30%), la Gesellschaft für Electrische Unternemungen (25%) et Ludwig Lowe (25%). International General

---

[487] Ibid, 2 février 1930.

[488] Ibid, 2 février 1930.

[489] Ibid, 11 mai 1930. Pour les machinations d'avant-guerre de General Electric, d'Osram et de la société néerlandaise N.V. Philips Gloeilampenfabrieken d'Eindhoven Holland, voir le chapitre 11, "Electric Eels", dans James Stewart Martin, op cit. Martin était chef de la division de guerre économique du ministère américain de la justice et commente que "l'A.E.G. d'Allemagne était largement contrôlée par la société américaine General Electric". L'hypothèse de cet auteur est que l'influence de la G.E. était quelque peu inférieure au contrôle, bien qu'assez importante. En raison de la position officielle de Martin et de l'accès à des documents officiels, inconnus de l'auteur, sa déclaration selon laquelle l'A.E.G. était "largement contrôlée" par la société américaine General Electric ne peut être rejetée à la légère. Cependant, si nous acceptons que G.E. "contrôlait largement" A.E.G., alors les questions les plus sérieuses se posent qui réclament une enquête. A.E.G. était un des principaux financiers d'Hitler et le "contrôle" impliquerait plus profondément la société mère américaine que ne le suggèrent les preuves présentées ici.

Electric détenait également une participation d'environ $16^{2/3}$% dans Osram, ainsi qu'une influence indirecte supplémentaire dans des sociétés liées à German General Electric par l'intermédiaire de Common Electric Directors :

Entreprises liées à German General Electric par l'intermédiaire de directeurs communs de l'électricité	**Directeurs de la société allemande General Electric (A.E.G.)**	**Relation entre l'entreprise liée et le financement d'Hitler**
Accumulatoran-Fabrik	Quandt Pfeffer	Financement direct
Osram	Mamroth Peierls	Financement direct
Deutschen Babcock-Wilcox	Landau	Non connu
Aciéries unies	Wolff Nathan Kirdorf Goldschmidt	Financement direct
Krupp	Nathan Klotzbach	Financement direct
I.G. Farben	Bucher Flechtheim von Rath	Financement direct
Alliance et Association de Stuttgart	von Rath Wolff	Signalée, mais non justifiée
Phoenix	Fahrenhorst	Financement direct
Thyssen	Fahrenhorst	Financement direct
Demag	Fahrenhorst Flick	Financement direct
Dynamit Gelsenkirchener	Flechtheim Kirdorf	Par I.G. Farben
Bergwerks	Flechtheim	Financement direct
International General Electric	Jeunes Swope Minor Baldwin	Par l'intermédiaire de l'A.E.G.
L'Américain I.G. Farben	von Rath	Par I.G. Farben
Banque internationale (Amsterdam)	H. Furstenberg Goldschmidt	Non connu

Osram par l'intermédiaire des directeurs de l'A.E.G. Au sein du conseil d'administration d'A.E.G., outre les quatre directeurs américains (Young, Swope, Minor et Baldwin), on trouve Pferdmenges de Oppenheim & Co. (un autre financier d'Hitler), et Quandt, qui possédait 75% d'Accumlatoren-Fabrik, un important financier direct d'Hitler. En d'autres termes, parmi les membres allemands du conseil d'administration d'A.E.G., nous trouvons des représentants de plusieurs des entreprises allemandes qui ont financé Hitler dans les années 1920 et 1930.

GENERAL ELECTRIC ET LE FINANCEMENT D'HITLER

Les racines du socialisme d'entreprise moderne sont profondément ancrées dans la gestion de deux sociétés multinationales affiliées : General Electric

Company aux États-Unis et ses associés étrangers, dont la General Electric allemande (A.E.G.), et Osram en Allemagne. Nous avons noté que Gerard Swope, deuxième président et président du conseil d'administration de General Electric, et Walter Rathenau de l'A.E.G. ont promu des idées radicales de contrôle de l'État par des intérêts commerciaux privés.

À partir de 1915, International General Electric (I.G.E.), situé au 120 Broadway à New York, a agi en tant qu'organisme d'investissement étranger, de fabrication et de vente pour la General Electric Company. I.G.E. détenait des intérêts dans des entreprises manufacturières étrangères, notamment une participation de 25 à 30% dans la société allemande General Electric (A.E.G.), ainsi que des participations dans Osram G.m.b.H. Kommanditgesellschaft, également à Berlin. Ces participations ont donné à International General Electric quatre directeurs au conseil d'administration d'A.E.G., et un autre directeur à Osram, et une influence significative dans les politiques intérieures de ces sociétés allemandes. L'importance de cette propriété de General Electric est que A.E.G. et Osram étaient des fournisseurs de fonds importants pour Hitler lors de son ascension au pouvoir en Allemagne en 1933. Un bulletin de virement bancaire daté du 2 mars 1933 de A.E.G. à Delbruck Schickler & Co. à Berlin demande que 60 000 Reichsmark soient déposés sur le compte de la "Nationale Treuhand" (Tutelle nationale) pour l'usage d'Hitler. Ce bordereau est reproduit plus loin.

I.G. Farben était le plus important des bailleurs de fonds nationaux d'Hitler, et (comme on l'a noté ailleurs) I.G. Farben contrôlait I.G. américain. De plus, plusieurs directeurs d'A.E.G. faisaient également partie du conseil d'administration d'I.G. Farben - c'est-à-dire que Hermann Bucher, président d'A.E.G., faisait partie du conseil d'administration d'I.G. Farben ; de même que les directeurs d'A.E.G. Julius Flechtheim et Walter von Rath. I.G. Farben a contribué à hauteur de 30% au fonds de la tutelle nationale (ou de la reprise) d'Hitler de 1933.

Walter Fahrenhorst de l'A.E.G. faisait également partie du conseil d'administration de Phoenix A-G, Thyssen A-G et Demag A-G - et tous contribuaient au fonds d'Hitler. Demag A-G contribuait à hauteur de 50 000 RM au fonds d'Hitler. Il avait un directeur au sein d'A.E.G. - le célèbre Friedrich Flick, et premier partisan d'Hitler, qui fut plus tard condamné au procès de Nuremberg. Accumulatoren Fabrik A-G était un contributeur d'Hitler (25 000 RM, voir page 60) avec deux directeurs au sein du conseil d'administration de l'A.E.G., August Pfeffer et Gunther Quandt. Quandt possédait personnellement 75% d'Accumulatoren Fabrik.

ALLGEMEINE ELEKTRICITÄTS-GESELLSCHAFT
FINANZVERWALTUNG

BERLIN NW 40, Friedrich-Karl-Ufer 2/4

Bankhaus
Delbrück Schickler & Co.,
Berlin W.8,
Mauerstr. 61-65.

1933

2. März 1933

Betrifft

Wir überweisen Ihnen per Reichsbankgirokonto

RM 60 000.-

(i. W.: Sechzigtausend Reichsmark)

zu Gunsten des bei Ihnen geführten Kontos: "Nationale Treuhand".

Hochachtungsvoll
ALLGEMEINE ELEKTRICITÄTS-GESELLSCHAFT

Antwort erbeten an Finanzverwaltung

Récépissé bancaire original du transfert daté du 2 mars 1933, de German General Electric vers la banque Delbrück, Schickler à Berlin, avec instruction de payer 60 000 RM au Nationale Treuhand (administré par Hjalmar Schacht et Rudolf Hess) qui fut utilisé pour faire élire Hitler en mars 1933. Source : tribunal militaire de Nuremberg document n°391-395.

Osram Gesellschaft, dans laquelle International General Electric avait une participation directe de $16^{2/3}$, avait également deux directeurs au sein du conseil d'administration de l'A.E.G : Paul Mamroth et Heinrich Pferls. Osram a contribué à hauteur de 40 000 RM directement au fonds Hitler. Le groupe Otto Wolff, Vereinigte Stahlwerke A-G, bénéficiaire de prêts substantiels à New York dans les années 1920, disposait de trois directeurs au conseil d'administration de l'A.E.G : Otto Wolff, Henry Nathan et Jakob Goldschmidt. Alfred Krupp von Bohlen, propriétaire unique de l'organisation Krupp et un des premiers partisans d'Hitler, était membre du Aufsichsrat de l'A.E.G. Robert Pferdmenges, membre du cercle des amis de Himmler, était également directeur de l'A.E.G.

En d'autres termes, presque tous les directeurs allemands de la General Electric étaient des partisans financiers d'Hitler et étaient associés non seulement à A.E.G. mais aussi à d'autres sociétés finançant Hitler.

Walter Rathenau[490] est devenu directeur de A.E.G. en 1899 et, au début du XXe siècle, il était directeur de plus de 100 sociétés. Rathenau a également été l'auteur du "Plan Rathenau", qui présente une remarquable ressemblance avec le "Plan Swope" - c'est-à-dire le New Deal de FDR mais écrit par Swope de G.E. En d'autres termes, nous avons l'extraordinaire coïncidence que les auteurs des plans sur le modèle du New Deal aux États-Unis et en Allemagne aient également été les principaux soutiens de leurs exécutants : Hitler en Allemagne et Roosevelt aux États-Unis.

M. Swope a été président du conseil d'administration de la General Electric Company et de l'International General Electric. En 1932, les directeurs américains de l'A.E.G., étaient très liés aux milieux bancaires et politiques américains comme suit

GERARD SWOPE	Président d'International General Electric et président de la General Electric Company, directeur de la National City Bank (et d'autres sociétés), directeur d'A.E.G. et d'Osram en Allemagne. Auteur du New Deal de FDR et membre de nombreuses organisations Roosevelt.
Owen D. Young	Président du conseil d'administration de General Electric et vice-président de la Banque de Réserve Fédérale de New York. Auteur, avec J. P, Morgan, du Plan Young qui a remplacé le Plan Dawes en 1929. (Voir le premier chapitre).
CLARK H. Minor	Président et directeur d'International General Electric, directeur de British Thomson Houston, Compania Generale di Electtricita (Italie), et Japan Electric Bond & Share Company (Japon).

En bref, nous disposons de preuves solides d'une authenticité incontestable pour démontrer que la General Electric allemande a contribué de manière substantielle au financement politique d'Hitler. Il y avait quatre directeurs américains de l'A.E.G. (Baldwin, Swope, Minor et Clark), qui était détenue à 80% par International General Electric. De plus, I.G.E. et les quatre directeurs américains représentaient le plus grand intérêt et avaient donc la plus grande influence sur les actions et les politiques d'A.E.G. De plus, presque tous les autres directeurs de l'A.E.G. étaient liés à des entreprises (I.G. Farben, Accumulatoren

[490] Fils d'Emil Rathenau, fondateur d'A.E.G., né en 1867 et assassiné en 1922.

Fabrik, etc.) qui contribuaient directement au financement politique d'Hitler. Cependant, seuls les directeurs allemands de l'A.E.G. ont été jugés à Nuremberg en 1945.

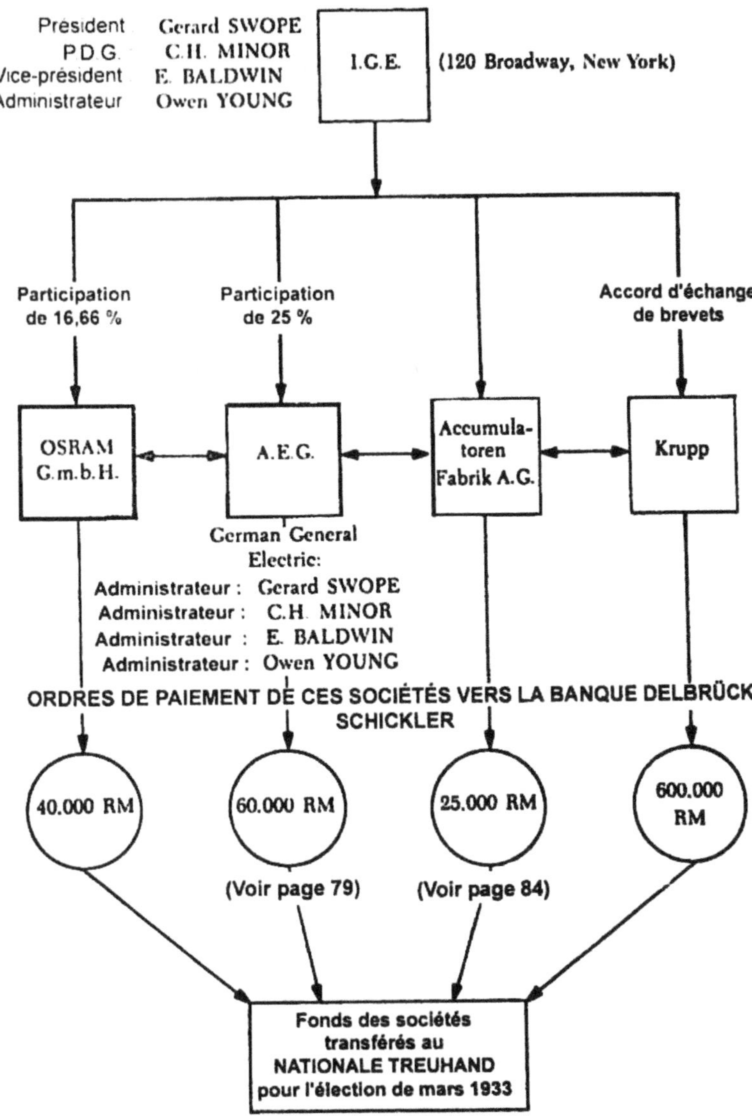

COOPÉRATION TECHNIQUE AVEC KRUPP

En plus de l'aide financière à Hitler, General Electric a étendu son aide aux ententes avec d'autres bailleurs de fonds d'Hitler pour leur bénéfice mutuel et celui de l'État nazi. Le carbure de tungstène cémenté est un exemple de cette coopération G.E.-Nazi. Avant novembre 1928, les industries américaines disposaient de plusieurs sources pour le carbure de tungstène et les outils et matrices contenant cette composition de métal lourd. Parmi ces sources figuraient la société Krupp d'Essen, en Allemagne, et deux entreprises américaines auxquelles Krupp expédiait et vendait alors, la Union Wire Die Corporation et Thomas Prosser & Son. En 1928, Krupp s'est engagée à accorder des licences sur des brevets américains qu'elle détenait à la Firth-Sterling Steel Company et à la Ludlum Steel Company. Avant 1928, ce carbure de tungstène destiné à être utilisé dans des outils et des matrices se vendait aux États-Unis à environ 50 dollars la livre.

Les brevets américains que Krupp prétendait détenir ont été cédés par Osram Kommanditgesellschaft, et avaient été précédemment cédés par la société allemande Osram à General Electric. Cependant, General Electric avait également développé ses propres brevets, principalement les brevets Hoyt et Gilson, couvrant des procédés concurrents pour le carbure de tungstène cémenté. General Electric pensait pouvoir utiliser ces brevets de manière indépendante sans enfreindre ou concurrencer les brevets Krupp. Mais au lieu d'utiliser les brevets G.E. indépendamment en concurrence avec Krupp, ou de tester ses droits en vertu des lois sur les brevets, General Electric a conclu un accord de cartel avec Krupp pour mettre en commun les brevets des deux parties et donner à General Electric le contrôle monopolistique du carbure de tungstène aux États-Unis.

La première étape de cette entente a été franchie par Carboloy Company, Inc, une filiale de General Electric, constituée dans le but d'exploiter le carbure de tungstène. Le prix des années 1920, qui était d'environ 50 dollars la livre, a été porté par Carboloy à 458 dollars la livre. Il est évident qu'aucune entreprise ne pouvait vendre de grandes quantités de carbure de tungstène dans cette fourchette de prix, mais le prix maximiserait les profits de G.E. En 1934, General Electric et Carboloy ont également pu obtenir, par achat, la licence accordée par Krupp à la Ludlum Steel Company, éliminant ainsi un concurrent. En 1936, Krupp a été incité à s'abstenir de toute nouvelle importation aux États-Unis. Une partie du prix payé pour l'élimination du marché américain du carbure de tungstène fabriqué à l'étranger était un engagement réciproque que General Electric et Carboloy n'exporteraient pas à partir des États-Unis. Ces sociétés américaines se sont donc liées par contrat, ou ont permis à Krupp de se lier les mains, et ont refusé les marchés étrangers à l'industrie américaine. La société Carboloy a ensuite racheté l'entreprise de Thomas Prosser & Son, et en 1937, pour près d'un million de dollars, Carboloy a racheté l'entreprise concurrente de la Union Wire Die Corporation. En refusant de vendre, Krupp a coopéré avec General Electric et Carboloy pour persuader Union Wire Die Corporation de vendre.

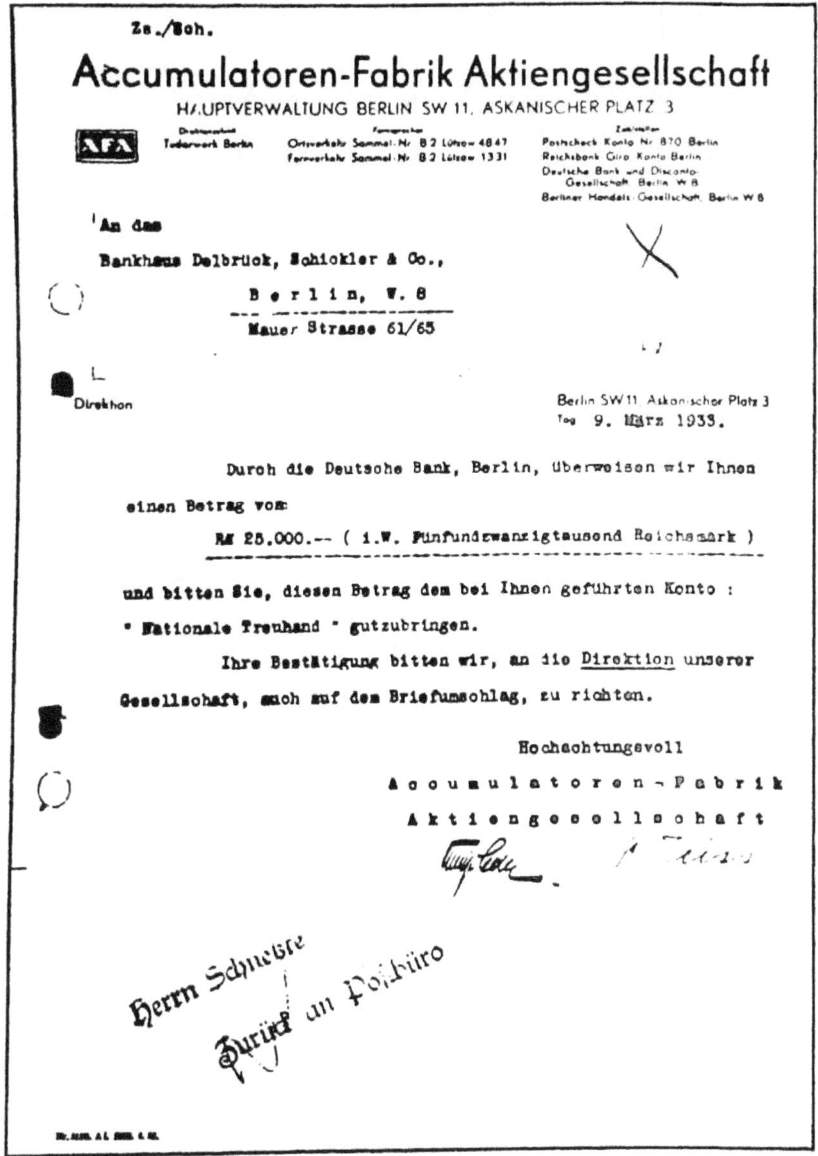

Zs./Boh.

Accumulatoren-Fabrik Aktiengesellschaft

HAUPTVERWALTUNG BERLIN SW 11, ASKANISCHER PLATZ 3

AFA

Drahtanschrift: Tudorwerk Berlin

Fernsprecher: Ortsverkehr Sammel-Nr. B 2 Lützow 4847 — Fernverkehr Sammel-Nr. B 2 Lützow 1331

Zahlstellen: Postscheck Konto Nr. 870 Berlin — Reichsbank Giro Konto Berlin — Deutsche Bank und Disconto-Gesellschaft Berlin W 8 — Berliner Handels-Gesellschaft Berlin W 8

An das

Bankhaus Delbrück, Schickler & Co.,

Berlin, W. 8

Mauer Strasse 61/65

Direktion

Berlin SW 11 Askanischer Platz 3

Tag 9. März 1933.

Durch die Deutsche Bank, Berlin, überweisen wir Ihnen einen Betrag von

RM 25.000.-- (i.W. Fünfundzwanzigtausend Reichsmark)

und bitten Sie, diesen Betrag dem bei Ihnen geführten Konto : " Nationale Treuhand " gutzubringen.

Ihre Bestätigung bitten wir, an die Direktion unserer Gesellschaft, auch auf dem Briefumschlag, zu richten.

Hochachtungsvoll

Accumulatoren-Fabrik Aktiengesellschaft

Zurück an Postbüro

Récépissé du transfert bancaire orignal daté du 9 mars 1933, d'Accumulatoren-Fabrik vers la banque Delbrück Schickler à Berlin, avec instruction de payer 25 000 RM au Nationale Treuhand (administré par Hjalmar Schacht et Rudolf Hess) utilisé pour faire élire Hitler en mars 1933.

Les licences pour la fabrication de carbure de tungstène ont alors été refusées. Une demande de licence de la Crucible Steel Company a été refusée en 1936. Une demande de licence de la Chrysler Corporation a été refusée en 1938. Une licence de la Triplett Electrical Instrument Company a été refusée le 25 avril 1940. Une licence a également été refusée à la General Cable Company. Pendant plusieurs années, la Ford Motor Company a exprimé sa forte opposition à la politique de prix élevés suivie par la Carboloy Company, et à un moment donné, elle a demandé le droit de fabriquer pour son propre usage. Cette demande a été refusée. À la suite de ces tactiques, General Electric et sa filiale Carboloy ont émergé en 1936 ou 1937 avec un monopole quasi total du carbure de tungstène aux États-Unis.

En bref, General Electric - avec la coopération d'un autre partisan d'Hitler, Krupp - obtint conjointement pour G,E. un monopole aux États-Unis pour le carbure de tungstène. Ainsi, au début de la Seconde Guerre mondiale, General Electric avait un monopole à un prix établi de 450 dollars la livre - presque dix fois plus que le prix de 1928 - et l'utilisation aux États-Unis avait été restreinte en conséquence.

A.E.G. ÉVITE LES BOMBARDEMENTS PENDANT LA SECONDE GUERRE MONDIALE

En 1939, l'industrie électrique allemande était devenue étroitement liée à deux entreprises américaines : International General Electric et International Telephone and Telegraph. Les plus grandes entreprises de la production électrique allemande et leurs affiliations étaient classées par ordre d'importance :

Entreprise et type de production	Pourcentage de la production allemande de 1939	Entreprise affiliée aux États-Unis
Industrie des courants forts		
General Electric (A.E.G.)	40 pour cent	International General Electric
Siemens Schukert A.G	40 pour cent	Aucune
Brown Boveri et Cie	17 pour cent	Aucune
Téléphone et télégraphe		
Siemens et Halske	60 pour cent	Aucune
Lorenz A.G.	85 pour cent	I.T.T.
Radio		
Telefunken (A.E.G. après 1941)	60 pour cent	International General Electric
Lorenz	35 pour cent	I.T.T.
Fils et câbles		
Felton & Guilleaume A.G.	20 pour cent	I.T.T.
Siemens	20 pour cent	Aucune
A.E.G.	20 pour cent	International General Electric

En d'autres termes, en 1939, l'industrie allemande de l'équipement électrique était concentrée dans quelques grandes sociétés liées au sein d'un cartel international et par actionnariat à deux grandes sociétés américaines. Ce complexe industriel n'a jamais été une cible privilégiée pour les bombardements de la

Seconde Guerre mondiale. Les usines A.E.G. et I.T.T. n'ont été touchées qu'accessoirement lors de raids ponctuels mais plutôt rarement. Les usines d'équipements électriques bombardées comme cibles n'étaient pas celles affiliées à des entreprises américaines. Ce sont les usines Brown Boveri à Mannheim et Siemensstadt à Berlin - qui n'étaient pas liées aux États-Unis - qui ont été bombardées. En conséquence, la production allemande de matériel de guerre électrique a augmenté régulièrement tout au long de la Seconde Guerre mondiale, atteignant un sommet en 1944. Selon les rapports de l'enquête américaine sur les bombardements stratégiques :

> "Selon les assistants de Speers et les responsables des usines, l'effort de guerre en Allemagne n'a jamais été entravé de manière importante par une quelconque pénurie de matériel électrique".[491]

L'usine A. E.G. située au 185 Muggenhofer Strasse, à Nuremberg, est un exemple de la politique de non-bombardement de la General Electric allemande. L'étude de la production de cette usine pendant la Seconde Guerre mondiale est intéressante, car elle illustre la façon dont la production en temps de paix a été convertie en travail de guerre. L'usine d'avant-guerre fabriquait des équipements ménagers, tels que des plaques chauffantes, des cuisinières électriques, des fers à repasser électriques, des grille-pain, des fours industriels, des radiateurs, des chauffe-eau, des fours de cuisine et des chauffages industriels. En 1939, 1940 et 1941, la plupart des installations de production de l'usine de Nuremberg ont été utilisées pour la fabrication de produits en temps de paix. En 1942, la production de l'usine a été réorientée vers la fabrication de matériel de guerre. Des pièces métalliques pour les équipements de communication et les munitions telles que les bombes et les mines ont été fabriquées. La production de guerre consistait également en pièces pour les projecteurs et les amplificateurs. Le tableau suivant montre de façon très frappante la conversion au travail de guerre :

Année	**Total des ventes en 1000 RM**	**Pourcentage pour la guerre**	**Pourcentage de la production ordinaire**
1939	12,469	5	95
1940	11,754	15	85
1941	21,194	40	60
1942	20,689	61	39
1948	31,455	67	33
1944	31,205	69	31

491 The United States Strategic Bombing Survey, *German Electrical Equipment Industry/Report,* (Equipment Division, January 1947), p. 4.

Les dommages physiques réels causés par le bombardement de cette usine ont été insignifiants. Aucun dommage grave n'est survenu avant les raids des 20 et 21 février 1945, vers la fin de la guerre, et la protection était alors assez bien développée. Les raids au cours desquels les bombes ont frappé la zone de l'usine et les dommages insignifiants qui ont été causés sont énumérés ci-dessous :

Date du raid	Bombes frappant une usine	Dommages causés
8 mars 1943	30 bâtonnets de type I.B.	Une bagatelle, mais trois entrepôts à l'extérieur de l'usine principale ont été détruits.
9 septembre 1944	Aucune (dégâts dus à l'explosion)	Dégâts causés par des bagatelles, des vitres et des rideaux d'occultation.
26 novembre 1944	14000 lb HE en espace ouvert dans les terrains de l'usine	Atelier de bois détruit, conduite d'eau rompue.
20 février 1945	2 HE	3 bâtiments endommagés.
21 février 1945	5 HE, beaucoup d'I.B.	Le bâtiment administratif a été détruit et les travaux d'émaillage endommagés par l'administration centrale.

Un autre exemple de centrale allemande General Electric non bombardée est l'usine A.E.G. de Koppelsdorf qui produit des radars et des antennes de bombardiers. D'autres usines A.E.G. n'ont pas été bombardées[492] et leur production de matériel de guerre l'a été :

LISTE DES USINES QUI N'ONT PAS ÉTÉ BOMBARDÉES PENDANT LA SECONDE GUERRE MONDIALE, PAR EXEMPLE

Nom de la branche	Lieu	Produit
1ère usine de Reiehmannsdoff avec des subdivisions à Wallendorf et Unterweissbach	Kries Saalfeld	Instruments de mesure
2. Werk Marktschorgast	Bayreuth	Démarrage
3. Werk F18ha	Sachsen	Ensembles d'envoi en ondes courtes
4. Werk Reichenbach	Vogtland	Batteries de cellules sèches
5. Travail Burglengefeld	Sachsen/S.E. Chemnitz	Lourds démarreurs
6. Werk Nuremburg	Belringersdorf/ Nuremberg	Petites composantes
7. Werk Zirndorf	Nuremberg	Lourds démarreurs
8. Travail à Mattinghofen	Oberdonau	1 KW Senders 250 mètres et longue vague pour les torpilleurs et les U-boats
9. Unterwerk Neustadt	Cobourg	Équipement radar

Le fait que les usines d'A.E.G. en Allemagne n'ont pas été bombardées pendant la Seconde Guerre mondiale a été confirmé par le Strategic Bombing Survey des États-Unis, dirigé par des universitaires tels que John K. Galbraith et

[492] U.S. Strategic Bombing Survey, Plant Report of A.E.G. (Allgemeine Elektrizitats Gesellschaft), Nuremberg, Allemagne : juin 1945), p. 6.

des Wall Streeters comme George W. Ball et Paul H. Nitze. Leur "German Electrical Equipment Industry Report" daté de janvier 1947 conclut :

> *L'industrie n'a jamais été attaquée en tant que système cible de base, mais quelques usines, comme Brown Boveri à Mannheim, Bosch à Stuttgart et Siemenstadt à Berlin, ont fait l'objet de raids de précision ; de nombreuses autres ont été touchées lors de raids de zone.*[493]

À la fin de la Seconde Guerre mondiale, une équipe d'enquête alliée, connue sous le nom de FIAT, a été envoyée pour examiner les dommages causés par les bombes aux usines de l'industrie électrique allemande. L'équipe chargée de l'industrie électrique était composée d'Alexander G.P.E. Sanders de l'International Telephone and Telegraph de New York, de Whitworth Ferguson de la Ferguson Electric Company, New York, et d'Erich J. Borgman de Westinghouse Electric. Bien que l'objectif déclaré de ces équipes était d'examiner les effets sur les bombardements alliés de cibles allemandes, l'objectif de cette équipe particulière était de remettre l'industrie allemande de l'équipement électrique en production le plus rapidement possible. Whirworth Ferguson a rédigé un rapport daté du 31 mars 1945 sur les A.E.G. Ostland-werke et a conclu que "cette usine est immédiatement disponible pour la production de pièces et d'assemblages métalliques fins.[494]

Pour conclure, nous constatons que Rathenau de l'A.E.G. et Swope de General Electric aux États-Unis avaient tous deux des idées similaires pour mettre l'État au service de leurs propres objectifs. La General Electric a joué un rôle important dans le financement d'Hitler, elle a largement profité de la production de guerre - et pourtant elle a réussi à éviter les bombardements pendant la Seconde Guerre mondiale. Il est évident que l'histoire brièvement étudiée ici mérite une enquête beaucoup plus approfondie - et si possible officielle.

---

493 Par conséquent, "la production pendant la guerre a été suffisante jusqu'en novembre 1944" et "selon les assistants de Speer et les responsables des usines, l'effort de guerre en Allemagne n'a jamais été entravé de manière importante par une quelconque pénurie de matériel électrique". Les difficultés n'ont surgi qu'à la toute fin de la guerre, lorsque l'ensemble de l'économie était menacé d'effondrement. Le rapport conclut : "On peut donc dire que tous les besoins importants en matériel électrique en 1944 ont été satisfaits, car les plans ont toujours été optimistes".

494 Étude américaine sur les bombardements stratégiques, AEG-Ostlandwerke GmbH, par Whitworth Ferguson, 31 mai 1945.

I.G. FARBENINDUSTRIE AKTIENGESELLSCHAFT

Bankabteilung

Firma

Delbrück Schickler & Co.,

Berlin W.8,

Mauerstr. 63/65.

FRANKFURT (MAIN) 20

B./G3. den 27. Febr. 33.

Wir teilen Ihnen hierdurch mit, dass wir die DRESDNER BANK in FRANKFURT/M., FRANKFURT A/M., beauftragt haben, Ihnen morgen vormittag

RM 400.000.--

zu vergüten, die Sie zu Gunsten des Kontos

"NATIONALE TREUHAND"

verwenden wollen.

Hochachtungsvoll

I.G. FARBENINDUSTRIE AKTIENGESELLSCHAFT.

dch. EILBOTEN.

Récépissé du transfert original, daté du 27 février 1933,d'IG Farben vers la banque Delbrück-Schickler à Berlin, avec pour instruction de verser 400 000 RM au Nationale Treuhand (administré par Hjalmar Schacht et Rudolf Hess), utilisé pour faire élire Hitler en mars 1933. Source : tribunal militaire de Nuremberg, document n°391-395.

CHAPITRE IV

LA STANDARD OIL RAVITAILLE LA DEUXIÈME GUERRE MONDIALE

En deux temps trois mouvements, l'Allemagne va produire suffisamment de pétrole et de gaz à partir de charbon pour une longue guerre. La Standard Oil de New York fournit des millions de dollars pour l'aider.

(Rapport de l'attaché commercial de l'ambassade des États-Unis à Berlin, Allemagne, janvier 1933, au département d'État à Washington, D.C.)

Le groupe de sociétés Standard Oil, dans lequel la famille Rockefeller détenait un quart des parts (et le contrôle), a joué un rôle essentiel[495] dans la préparation de l'Allemagne nazie à la Seconde Guerre mondiale. Cette aide à la préparation militaire est née du fait que les réserves relativement insignifiantes de pétrole brut de l'Allemagne étaient tout à fait insuffisantes pour la guerre mécanisée moderne ; en 1934, par exemple, environ 85% des produits pétroliers finis allemands étaient importés. La solution adoptée par l'Allemagne nazie consistait à fabriquer de l'essence synthétique à partir de ses abondantes réserves de charbon nationales. C'est le procédé d'hydrogénation permettant de produire de l'essence synthétique et les propriétés de l'iso-octane dans l'essence qui ont permis à l'Allemagne d'entrer en guerre en 1940 - et ce procédé d'hydrogénation a été développé et financé par les laboratoires Standard Oil aux États-Unis en partenariat avec I.G. Farben.

Les preuves présentées aux comités Truman, Bone et Kilgore après la Seconde Guerre mondiale ont confirmé que Standard Oil avait en même temps "sérieusement mis en péril les préparatifs de guerre des États-Unis". Des preuves[496] documentaires ont été présentées aux trois commissions du Congrès, selon lesquelles avant la Seconde Guerre mondiale, Standard Oil avait convenu avec I.G. Farben, dans le cadre de l'accord dit "Jasco", que le caoutchouc synthétique était dans la sphère d'influence de Farben, alors que Standard Oil ne

[495] En 1935, John D. Rockefeller, Jr. possédait des actions évaluées à 245 millions de dollars dans la Standard Oil du New Jersey, la Standard Oil de Californie et la Socony-Vacuun Company, *New York Times,* 10 janvier 1935.

[496] Élimination des ressources allemandes, op. cit. p. 1085.

devait avoir un monopole absolu aux États-Unis que si et quand Farben autorisait le développement du caoutchouc synthétique aux États-Unis :

> *En conséquence, la norme [du Comité Kilgore] a pleinement atteint l'objectif du gouvernement américain qui était d'empêcher la production américaine en dissuadant les entreprises américaines de caoutchouc d'entreprendre des recherches indépendantes pour développer des procédés de caoutchouc synthétique.*[497]

Malheureusement, les commissions du Congrès n'ont pas exploré un aspect encore plus inquiétant de cette collusion entre Standard Oil et I.G. Farben : à cette époque, les directeurs de la Standard Oil du New Jersey avaient non seulement des affiliations de guerre stratégique avec I.G. Farben, mais aussi d'autres liens avec l'Allemagne de Hitler - jusqu'à contribuer, par l'intermédiaire de filiales allemandes, au fonds personnel de Heinrich Himmler et à être membre du Cercle des amis de Himmler jusqu'en 1944.

Pendant la Seconde Guerre mondiale, la Standard Oil du New Jersey a été accusé de trahison pour cette alliance passée avant-guerre avec Farben, alors même que ses activités continues en temps de guerre au sein du Cercle des amis de Himmler étaient inconnues. Les accusations de trahison ont été niées avec véhémence par Standard Oil. L'une des plus importantes de ces défenses a été publiée par R.T. Haslam, un directeur de Standard Oil du New Jersey, dans le *Petroleum Times* (25 décembre 1943), et intitulée "Des secrets transformés en armes de guerre puissantes grâce à l'accord I.G. Farben".[498] Il s'agissait d'une tentative de renverser la situation et de présenter la collusion d'avant-guerre comme avantageuse pour les États-Unis.

Quels qu'aient pu être les souvenirs de guerre et la défense hâtive de Standard Oil, les négociations et les contrats de 1929 entre la Standard Oil et I.G. Farben ont été enregistrés dans la presse contemporaine et décrivent les accords entre la Standard Oil du New Jersey et I.G. Farben ainsi que leurs intentions. En avril 1929, Walter C. Teagle, président de la Standard Oil du New Jersey, devient directeur de la nouvelle organisation américaine I.G. Farben. Non pas parce que Teagle s'intéressait à l'industrie chimique, mais parce que,

> *Depuis quelques années, elle entretient des relations très étroites avec certaines branches des travaux de recherche de l'I.G. Farben, qui sont étroitement liées à l'industrie pétrolière.*[499]

Teagle a annoncé que des travaux de recherche communs sur la production de pétrole à partir du charbon étaient menés depuis un certain temps et qu'un

[497] Ibid.

[498] *NMT*, affaire I.G. Farben, p. 1304.

[499] *New York Times*, 28 avril 1929.

laboratoire de recherche pour ces travaux allait être créé aux États-Unis[500]. En novembre 1929, cette société de recherche commune Standard-Farben a été créée sous la direction de la Standard Oil Company du New Jersey, et toutes les recherches et tous les brevets relatifs à la production de pétrole à partir du charbon détenus par I.G. et Standard ont été mis en commun. Auparavant, au cours de la période 1926-1929, les deux sociétés avaient coopéré au développement du processus d'hydrogénation, et des installations expérimentales avaient été mises en service aux États-Unis et en Allemagne. Il était maintenant proposé de construire de nouvelles usines aux États-Unis à Bayway, dans le New Jersey, et à Baytown, au Texas, en plus de l'expansion de l'usine expérimentale précédente à Bâton Rouge. La norme est annoncée :

> *... l'importance du nouveau contrat tel qu'il s'applique à ce pays réside dans le fait qu'il garantit que le processus d'hydrogénation sera développé commercialement dans ce pays sous la direction des intérêts pétroliers américains.*[501]

En décembre 1929, la nouvelle société, Standard I.G. Company, est créée. F.A. Howard est nommé président, et ses directeurs allemands et américains sont annoncés comme suit : E.M. Clark, Walter Duisberg, Peter Hurll, R.A. Reidemann, H.G. Seidel, Otto von Schenck et Guy Wellman.

La majorité des actions de la société de recherche étaient détenues par Standard Oil. Le travail technique, le travail de développement des procédés et la construction de trois nouvelles usines de production de pétrole à partir de charbon aux États-Unis ont été confiés à la Standard Oil Development Company, la filiale technique de Standard Oil. Il ressort clairement de ces rapports contemporains que le travail de développement du pétrole à partir du charbon a été entrepris par la Standard Oil du New Jersey aux États-Unis, dans des usines de la Standard Oil et avec un financement et un contrôle majoritaires de la Standard. Les résultats de ces recherches furent mis à la disposition de I.G. Farben et devinrent la base du développement du programme de pétrole à partir du charbon d'Hitler qui rendit possible la Seconde Guerre mondiale.

L'article de Haslam, écrit par un ancien professeur de génie chimique au M.I.T. (alors vice-président de Standard Oil du New Jersey), soutenait - contrairement à ces faits enregistrés - que Standard Oil était en mesure, grâce à ses accords Farben, d'obtenir de la technologie allemande pour les États-Unis. Haslam a cité la fabrication de caoutchouc buna, de toluol et de paratone (Oppanol), utilisés pour stabiliser la viscosité du pétrole, un matériau essentiel pour les opérations de ravitaillement dans le désert et en hiver en Russie. Cependant, cet article, avec ses prétentions égoïstes erronées, a trouvé son chemin vers l'Allemagne du temps de guerre et a fait l'objet d'un mémorandum "secret" I.G. Farben daté du 6 juin 1944, adressé par le défendeur de Nuremberg et le fonctionnaire von Knieriem de l'époque à ses collègues de la direction de Farben. Cette note "secrète" de von

---

[500] Ibid.

[501] Ibid, 24 novembre 1929.

Knieriem expose les faits que Haslam a évités dans son article du *Petroleum Times.* Le mémo était en fait un résumé de ce que Standard n'était pas disposé à révéler au public américain - c'est-à-dire la contribution majeure apportée par la Standard Oil du New Jersey à la machine de guerre nazie. Le mémorandum Farben indique que les accords de Standard Oil étaient *absolument essentiels* pour I.G. Farben :

> *La conclusion d'un accord avec Standard était nécessaire pour des raisons techniques, commerciales et financières :sur le plan technique, parce que l'expérience spécialisée dont seule une grande compagnie pétrolière disposait était nécessaire au développement de notre procédé, et qu'une telle industrie n'existait pas en Allemagne ; sur le plan commercial, parce qu'en l'absence de contrôle économique de l'État en Allemagne à l'époque, IG devait éviter une lutte concurrentielle avec les grandes puissances pétrolières, qui vendaient toujours la meilleure essence au prix le plus bas sur des marchés contestés ; sur le plan financier, parce que IG, qui avait déjà dépensé des sommes extraordinairement importantes pour le développement du procédé, devait demander un allègement financier afin de pouvoir poursuivre le développement dans d'autres nouveaux domaines techniques, comme le buna.*[502]

Le mémorandum Farben a ensuite répondu à la question clé : Qu'est-ce que I.G. Farben a acquis de Standard Oil qui était "vital pour la conduite de la guerre" ? Le mémorandum examine les produits cités par Haslam - c'est-à-dire l'iso-octane, le toluol, l'oppanol-paratone et le buna - et démontre que, contrairement à ce que prétend publiquement Standard Oil, leur technologie provenait en grande partie des États-Unis et non de l'Allemagne.

Sur l'iso-octane, le mémorandum Farben dit, en partie :

> *En raison de leurs décennies de travail sur les carburants, les Américains ont été en avance sur nous dans leur connaissance des exigences de qualité requises par les différentes utilisations des carburants. Ils avaient notamment développé, à grands frais, un grand nombre de méthodes pour tester l'essence pour différentes utilisations. Sur la base de leurs expériences, ils avaient reconnu la bonne qualité antidétonante de l'iso-octane bien avant de connaître notre processus d'hydrogénation. Cela est prouvé par le seul fait qu'en Amérique, les carburants sont classés en fonction de leur indice d'octane, et l'iso-octane a été classé comme le meilleur carburant avec le chiffre 100. Toutes ces connaissances sont naturellement devenues les nôtres grâce à l'accord, qui nous a permis d'économiser beaucoup d'efforts et nous a préservé de nombreuses erreurs.*

I.G. Farben ajoute que l'affirmation de Haslam selon laquelle la production d'iso-octane n'a été connue en Amérique que par le processus d'hydrogénation de Farben n'était pas correcte :

---

[502] NMT, affaire I.G. Farben, volumes VII et VIII, p. 1304-1311.

Dans le cas de l'iso-octane, en particulier, il est démontré que nous devons beaucoup aux Américains, car, dans nos propres travaux, nous pourrions largement nous inspirer des informations américaines sur le comportement des carburants dans les moteurs. En outre, nous avons également été tenus au courant par les Américains de l'évolution de leur processus de production et de son développement ultérieur.

Peu avant la guerre, une nouvelle méthode de production d'iso-octane a été trouvée en Amérique - l'alkylation avec isomérisation comme étape préliminaire. Ce procédé, que M. Haslain ne mentionne pas du tout, provient en fait entièrement des Américains et nous l'avons fait connaître en détail dans ses différentes étapes grâce aux accords que nous avons conclus avec eux, et nous l'utilisons très largement.

Sur le toluol, I.G. Farben souligne une inexactitude factuelle dans l'article de Haslam : le professeur Haslam affirme que le toluol n'a pas été produit par hydrogénation aux États-Unis. Dans le cas de l'oppanol, le mémo de I.G. qualifie les informations de Haslam d'"incomplètes" et en ce qui concerne le caoutchouc buna, "nous n'avons jamais donné d'informations techniques aux Américains, et il n'y a pas eu de coopération technique dans le domaine du buna". Plus important encore, le mémo Farben poursuit en décrivant certains produits non cités par Haslam dans son article :

En conséquence de nos contrats avec les Américains, nous avons reçu d'eux, au-delà de l'accord, de nombreuses contributions très précieuses pour la synthèse et l'amélioration des carburants et des huiles lubrifiantes, qui, à l'heure actuelle, pendant la guerre, nous sont très utiles ; et nous avons également reçu d'eux d'autres avantages. En premier lieu, on peut citer les suivants :

1) Surtout, l'amélioration des carburants par l'ajout de plomb tétraéthyle et la fabrication de ce produit. Il n'est pas nécessaire de mentionner spécialement que sans le plomb tétraéthyle, les méthodes de guerre actuelles seraient impossibles. Le fait que depuis le début de la guerre nous ayons pu produire du plomb tétraéthyle est entièrement dû aux circonstances dans lesquelles, peu de temps auparavant, les Américains nous avaient présenté les plans de production, avec leur savoir-faire. C'était d'ailleurs la première fois que les Américains décidaient d'accorder une licence sur ce procédé dans un pays étranger (outre la communication de secrets non protégés) et ce uniquement sur nos demandes urgentes à Standard Oil pour réaliser notre souhait. Contractuellement, nous ne pouvions pas l'exiger, et nous avons découvert plus tard que le ministère de la guerre à Washington n'avait donné son autorisation qu'après de longues délibérations.

2) Conversion des insaturés de faible poids moléculaire en essence utilisable (polymérisation). De nombreux travaux ont été réalisés dans ce domaine, ici comme en Amérique. Mais les Américains ont été les premiers à mener le processus à grande échelle, ce qui nous a suggéré de développer également le processus à grande échelle technique. Mais au-delà de cela, des usines construites selon des procédés américains fonctionnent en Allemagne.

3) Dans le domaine des huiles lubrifiantes également, l'Allemagne, par le biais du contrat avec l'Amérique, a appris des expériences qui sont extraordinairement importantes pour la guerre actuelle.

À cet égard, nous avons obtenu non seulement l'expérience de Standard, mais aussi, par l'intermédiaire de Standard, l'expérience de General Motors et d'autres grandes entreprises automobiles américaines.
4) Il convient de mentionner un autre exemple remarquable de l'effet avantageux pour nous du contrat entre IG et Standard Oil : dans les années 1934/1935, notre gouvernement avait le plus grand intérêt à rassembler de l'étranger un stock de produits pétroliers particulièrement précieux (en particulier, de l'essence et de l'huile de lubrification pour l'aviation), et à le garder en réserve pour un montant approximativement égal à 20 millions de dollars à la valeur du marché. Le gouvernement allemand a demandé à IG s'il n'était pas possible, sur la base de relations amicales avec Standard Oil, d'acheter ce montant au nom de Farben ; en fait, cependant, en tant que représentant du gouvernement allemand. Le fait que nous ayons effectivement réussi, au moyen des négociations les plus difficiles, à acheter la quantité souhaitée par notre gouvernement à l'American Standard Oil Company et au groupe néerlandais - anglais Royal - néerlandais - Shell et à la transporter en Allemagne, n'a été rendu possible que grâce à l'aide de la Standard Oil Co.

DU PLOMB ÉTHYLIQUE POUR LA WEHRMACHT

Un autre exemple important de l'aide apportée par Standard Oil à l'Allemagne nazie - en coopération avec General Motors - a été la fourniture de plomb éthylique. Le fluide éthylique est un composé antidétonant utilisé dans les carburants pour l'aviation et l'automobile pour éliminer le cliquetis et améliorer ainsi l'efficacité des moteurs ; sans ces composés antidétonants, la guerre mobile moderne serait impraticable.

En 1924, l'Ethyl Gasoline Corporation a été créée à New York, détenue conjointement par la Standard Oil Company du New Jersey et la General Motors Corporation, pour contrôler et utiliser les brevets américains pour la fabrication et la distribution de plomb tétraéthyle et de fluide éthylique aux États-Unis et à l'étranger. Jusqu'en 1935, la fabrication de ces produits n'était entreprise qu'aux États-Unis. En 1935, Ethyl Gasoline Corporation a transféré son savoir-faire en Allemagne pour l'utiliser dans le programme de réarmement nazi. Ce transfert a été effectué en dépit des protestations du gouvernement américain[503].

L'intention d'Ethyl de transférer sa technologie antidétonante à l'Allemagne nazie a été portée à l'attention de l'Army Air Corps à Washington, D.C. Le 15 décembre 1934, E. W. Webb, président d'Ethyl Gasoline, a été informé que Washington avait appris l'intention de "former une société allemande avec l'I.G. pour fabriquer du plomb éthylique dans ce pays". Le ministère de la guerre a indiqué que ce transfert technologique était très critiqué, ce qui pourrait "avoir les plus graves répercussions" pour les États-Unis ; que la demande commerciale de plomb éthylique en Allemagne était trop faible pour être intéressante,

[503] Voir la lettre du ministère américain de la guerre reproduite à l'annexe D.

> *... il a été dit que l'Allemagne s'arme secrètement [et] que le plomb éthylique serait sans doute une aide précieuse pour les avions militaires.*[504]

La société Ethyl a ensuite été informée par le Corps d'aviation de l'armée de terre que "vous ou le conseil d'administration de la société Ethyl Gasoline ne devez en aucun cas divulguer en Allemagne des secrets ou un "savoir-faire" en rapport avec la fabrication du plomb tétraéthyle.[505]

Le 12 janvier 1935, Webb a envoyé au chef du corps d'aviation de l'armée de terre un "exposé des faits", qui était en fait un déni de toute transmission de ces connaissances techniques ; il a proposé d'insérer une telle clause dans le contrat pour se prémunir contre tout transfert de ce type. Toutefois, contrairement à son engagement envers le Corps d'aviation de l'armée, Ethyl a ensuite signé un accord de production conjointe avec I.G. Farben en Allemagne pour former Ethyl G.m.b.H. et avec Montecatini dans l'Italie fasciste dans le même but.

Il convient de noter les directeurs d'Ethyl Gasoline Corporation au moment de ce transfert[506]: E.W. Webb, président et directeur ; C.F. Kettering ; R.P. Russell ; W.C. Teagle, Standard Oil of New Jersey et administrateur de la Georgia Warm Springs Foundation de FDR ; F. A. Howard ; E. M. Clark, Standard Oil of New Jersey ; A. P. Sloan, Jr. ; D. Brown ; J. T. Smith ; et W.S. Parish de Standard Oil of New Jersey.

Les fichiers I.G. Farben saisis à la fin de la guerre confirment l'importance de ce transfert technique particulier pour la Wehrmacht allemande :

> *Depuis le début de la guerre, nous avons été en mesure de produire du tétraéthyle de plomb uniquement parce que, peu de temps avant le déclenchement de la guerre, les Américains avaient mis en place pour nous des usines prêtes à produire et nous avaient fourni tout le savoir-faire. De cette manière, nous n'avons pas eu besoin d'effectuer le difficile travail de développement, car nous pouvions commencer la production immédiatement sur la base de toute l'expérience que les Américains avaient acquise pendant des années.*[507]

En 1938, juste avant le déclenchement de la guerre en Europe, la Luftwaffe allemande avait un besoin urgent de 500 tonnes de plomb tétraéthyle. Un responsable de DuPont a informé l'Allemagne que de telles quantités d'éthyle seraient utilisées à des fins militaires.[508] Ces 500 tonnes ont été prêtées par l'Ethyl

---

[504] Congrès des États-Unis. Sénat. Auditions devant une sous-commission de la commission des affaires militaires. *Mobilisation scientifique et technique,* (78e Congrès, 1ère session, S. 702), partie 16, (Washington : Government Printing Office, 1944), p. 939. Cité ci-après sous le nom de "Mobilisation *scientifique et technique".*

[505] Ibid.

[506] Annuaire du pétrole et des produits pétroliers, 1938, p. 89.

[507] *New York Times,* 19 octobre 1945, p. 9.

[508] George W. Stocking & Myron W. Watkins, *Cartels in Action, (New* York : The Twentieth Century Fund, 1946), p. 9.

Export Corporation de New York à l'entreprise allemande Ethyl G.m.b.H., dans le cadre d'une transaction organisée par le ministère de l'Air du Reich avec le directeur de I.G. Farben, Mueller-Cunradi. La garantie a été arrangée dans une lettre datée du 21 septembre 1938[509] par l'intermédiaire de Brown Brothers, Harriman & Co. de New York.

LA STANDARD OIL OF NEW JERSEY ET LE CAOUTCHOUC SYNTHÉTIQUE

Le transfert de la technologie de l'éthyle pour la machine de guerre nazie a été répété dans le cas du caoutchouc synthétique. Il ne fait aucun doute que la capacité de la Wehrmacht allemande à combattre la Seconde Guerre mondiale dépendait du caoutchouc synthétique - ainsi que du pétrole synthétique - car l'Allemagne ne dispose pas de caoutchouc naturel, et la guerre aurait été impossible sans la production de caoutchouc synthétique de Farben. Farben avait le quasi-monopole de ce domaine et le programme de production des grandes quantités nécessaires était financé par le Reich :

> *Le volume de la production prévue dans ce domaine dépassait de loin les besoins de l'économie du temps de paix. Les coûts énormes impliqués ne correspondaient qu'à des considérations militaires dans lesquelles la nécessité d'autosuffisance sans tenir compte du coût était décisive.*[510]

Comme pour les transferts de technologie de l'éthyle, la Standard Oil du New Jersey était intimement associée au caoutchouc synthétique de I.G. Farben. Une série d'accords de cartel communs ont été conclus à la fin des années 1920 en vue de former un monopole mondial commun du caoutchouc synthétique. Le plan de quatre ans d'Hitler est entré en vigueur en 1937 et en 1938, Standard a fourni à I.G. Farben son nouveau procédé de caoutchouc butyle. D'autre part, la Standard a gardé secret le processus allemand du buna aux États-Unis et ce n'est qu'en juin 1940 que Firestone et U.S. Rubber ont été autorisés à participer aux essais du butyle et ont accordé les licences de fabrication du buna. Même à cette époque, la Standard a essayé d'obtenir du gouvernement américain qu'il finance un programme de buna à grande échelle - en réservant ses propres fonds pour le procédé de butyle, plus prometteur.[511]

Par conséquent, l'aide standard dans l'Allemagne nazie ne se limitait pas au pétrole provenant du charbon, bien qu'il s'agisse du transfert le plus important. Non seulement le procédé pour le tétraéthyle fut transféré à I.G. Farben et une usine construite en Allemagne appartenait conjointement à I.G., à General Motors et aux filiales de Standard ; mais encore, en 1939, la filiale allemande de Standard

---

[509] Pour les documents originaux, voir *NMT*, I.G. Farben case, Volume VIII, pp. 1189-94.

[510] *NMT*, affaire I.G. Farben, volume VIII, p. 1264-5.

[511] Mobilisation scientifique et technique, p. 543.

a conçu une usine allemande pour le gaz d'aviation. Le tétraéthyle fut expédié d'urgence pour la Wehrmacht et une aide importante fut apportée à la production de caoutchouc butyle, tout en gardant secret aux États-Unis le procédé Farben pour le buna. En d'autres termes, la Standard Oil du New Jersey (d'abord sous le président W.C. Teagle, puis sous W..S. Farish) a constamment aidé la machine de guerre nazie tout en refusant d'aider les États-Unis.

Cette séquence d'événements n'était pas un accident. Le président W.S. Farish a fait valoir que ne pas avoir accordé une telle assistance technique à la Wehrmacht "... aurait été injustifié".[512] L'assistance était bien informée, s'étendait sur plus d'une décennie et était si importante que sans elle, la Wehrmacht n'aurait pas pu entrer en guerre en 1939.

LA COMPAGNIE PÉTROLIÈRE GERMANO-AMÉRICAINE (DAPAG)

La filiale de Standard Oil en Allemagne, Deutsche-Amerikanische Petroleum A.G. (DAPAG), était détenue à 94% par la Standard Oil du New Jersey. DAPAG possédait des succursales dans toute l'Allemagne, une raffinerie à Brême et un siège social à Hambourg. Par l'intermédiaire de la DAPAG, la Standard Oil du New Jersey était représentée dans les cercles intérieurs du nazisme - le cercle Keppler et le cercle des amis de Himmler. L'un des directeurs de la DAPAG était Karl Lindemann, également président de la Chambre de Commerce Internationale en Allemagne, ainsi que directeur de plusieurs banques, dont la Dresdner Bank, la Deutsche Reichsbank et la banque privée à orientation nazie de C. Melchior & Company, et de nombreuses sociétés, dont la HAPAG (Hamburg-Amerika Line). Lindemann a été membre du cercle des amis de Keppler jusqu'en 1944 et a ainsi donné à la Standard Oil du New Jersey un représentant au cœur même du nazisme. Un autre membre du conseil d'administration de la DAPAG était Emil Helfrich, qui était un des premiers membres du Cercle Keppler.

En résumé, la Standard Oil du New Jersey avait deux membres du cercle Keppler comme directeurs de sa filiale allemande à 100%. Les versements au Cercle de la part de la filiale de Standard Oil, et de Lindemann et Helffrich en tant que directeurs individuels, se sont poursuivis jusqu'en 1944, l'année précédant la fin de la Seconde Guerre mondiale.[513]

---

[512] Robert Engler, *The Politics of Oil,* (New York : The MacMillan Company, 1961), p. 102.

[513] Voir le chapitre neuf pour plus de détails.

CHAPITRE V

L'I.T.T. AIDE LES DEUX BELLIGÉRANTS

Ainsi, pendant que les avions Focke-Wolfe de l'I.T.T. bombardaient les navires alliés et que les lignes de l'I.T.T. transmettaient des informations aux sous-marins allemands, les radiogoniomètres de l'I.T.T. sauvaient d'autres navires des torpilles.

(Anthony Sampson, *The Sovereign State of I.T.T.*, New York : Stein & Day, 1973, p. 40).

Le géant multinational International Telephone and Telegraph (I.T.T.)[514] a été fondé en 1920 par Sosthenes Behn, entrepreneur né aux îles Vierges. De son vivant, Behn était l'incarnation même de l'homme d'affaires politisé, gagnant ses bénéfices et construisant l'empire I.T.T. par des manœuvres politiques plutôt que sur le marché concurrentiel. En 1923, grâce à son habileté politique, Behn a acquis le monopole téléphonique espagnol, la Compania Telefonica de España. En 1924, I.T.T., maintenant soutenu par la firme J.P. Morgan, a acheté ce qui est devenu plus tard le groupe International Standard Electric, qui regroupe des usines de fabrication dans le monde entier.

Le conseil d'administration de I.T.T. reflétait les intérêts de J.P. Morgan, avec les associés de Morgan, Arthur M. Anderson et Russell Leffingwell. Le cabinet d'avocats Davis, Polk, Wardwell, Gardiner & Reed était représenté par les deux associés juniors, Gardiner & Reed.

DIRECTEURS DE L'I.T.T. EN 1933 :

Directeurs	Affiliation avec d'autres entreprises de Wall Street
Arthur M. ANDERSON	Associé, J.P. MORGAN et New York Trust Company
Hernand BEHN	Banque d'Amérique
Sosthène BEHN	BANQUE NATIONALE DE LA VILLE
F. Wilder BELLAMY	Partenaire de Dominick & Dominicik
John W. CUTLER	GRACE NATIONAL BANK, Lee Higginson
George H. GARDINER	Associé de Davis, Polk, Wardwell, Gardiner & Reed
Allen G. HOYT	BANQUE NATIONALE DE LA VILLE
Russell C. LEFFINGWELL	J.P. MORGAN, associé, et CARNEGIE CORP.

[514] Pour une excellente revue des activités mondiales de l'I.T.T., voir Anthony Sampson, *The Sovereign State of I.T.T.*, (New York : Stein & Day, 1973).

Bradley W. PALMER	Président du Comité exécutif, FRUIT UNI
Lansing P. REED	Associé de Davis, Polk Wardwell, Gardiner & Reed

La National City Bank (NCB) du groupe Morgan était représentée par deux directeurs, Sosthenes Behn et Allen G. Hoyt. En bref, I.T.T. était une société contrôlée par Morgan ; et nous avons déjà noté l'intérêt des sociétés contrôlées par Morgan pour la guerre et la révolution à l'étranger et les manœuvres politiques aux États-Unis.[515]

En 1930, Behn a acquis la société holding allemande Standard Elekrizitäts A.G., contrôlée par I.T.T. (62% des actions avec droit de vote), A.E.G. (81,1% des actions avec droit de vote) et Felton & Guilleaume (6% des actions avec droit de vote). Dans cette opération, Standard a acquis deux usines de fabrication allemandes et une participation majoritaire dans Telefonfabrik Berliner A.G.I.T.T. a également fourni les filiales de Standard en Allemagne, Ferdinand Schuchardt Berliner Fernsprech-und Telegraphenwerk A,G., ainsi que Mix & Genest à Berlin, et Suddeutsche Apparate Fabrik G,m.b.H. à Nuremberg.

Il est intéressant de noter au passage que si l'I.T.T. de Sosthenes Behn contrôlait les compagnies de téléphone et les usines de fabrication en Allemagne, le trafic de câbles entre les États-Unis et l'Allemagne était sous le contrôle de la Deutsch-Atlantische Telegraphengesellschaft (la compagnie allemande Atlantic Cable). Cette société, ainsi que la Commercial Cable Company et la Western Union Telegraph Company, avaient le monopole des communications transatlantiques par câble entre les États-Unis et l'Allemagne. W.A. Harriman & Company a racheté un bloc de 625 000 actions de Deutsch-Atlantische en 1925, et le conseil d'administration de la société comprenait un éventail inhabituel de personnages, dont beaucoup ont été rencontrés ailleurs. Il comprenait, par exemple, H. F. Albert, l'agent d'espionnage allemand aux États-Unis pendant la Première Guerre mondiale, Von Berenberg-Gossler, l'ancien associé de Franklin D. Roosevelt, et le Dr Cuno, un ancien chancelier allemand de l'ère inflationniste de 1923. L'I.T.T. aux États-Unis était représenté au conseil d'administration par von Guilleaume et Max Warburg de la famille bancaire Warburg.

LE BARON KURT VON SCHRODER ET L'I.T.T.

Il n'existe aucune trace de paiements directs effectués par I.T.T. à Hitler avant la prise du pouvoir par les nazis en 1933. En revanche, de nombreux paiements ont été effectués à Heinrich Himmler à la fin des années 1930 et pendant la Seconde Guerre mondiale elle-même par l'intermédiaire de filiales allemandes d'I.T.T. La première rencontre entre Hitler et les responsables de l'I.T.T. - pour autant que nous sachions - a été rapportée en août 1933[516], lorsque Sosthenes Behn et le représentant allemand de l'I.T.T., Henry Manne, ont rencontré Hitler à Berchtesgaden. Par la suite, Behn prit contact avec le cercle Keppler (voir chapitre

[515] Voir également Sutton, *Wall Street et la révolution bolchévique*, op. cit.

[516] *New York Times*, 4 août 1933.

neuf) et, sous l'influence de Keppler, le baron nazi Kurt von Schröder devint le gardien des intérêts de l'I.T.T. en Allemagne. Schröder a servi de canal pour l'argent de l'I.T.T. acheminé à l'organisation S.S. de Heinrich Himmler en 1944, alors que la Seconde Guerre mondiale était en cours et que les États-Unis étaient en guerre contre l'Allemagne.[517]

Par l'intermédiaire de Kurt Schröder, Behn et son I.T.T. ont eu accès à l'industrie allemande de l'armement, très rentable, et ont pris des participations importantes dans des entreprises d'armement allemandes, notamment dans les avions Focke-Wolfe. Ces opérations d'armement ont généré des profits considérables, qui auraient pu être rapatriés dans la société mère américaine. Mais ils ont été réinvestis dans le réarmement allemand. Ces réinvestissement des profits dans les entreprises d'armement allemandes sous prétexte que Wall Street était innocent des méfaits du réarmement allemand - et qu'il ne connaissait même pas les intentions d'Hitler - sont frauduleux. Plus précisément, l'achat par I.T.T. d'une participation substantielle dans Focke-Wolfe signifiait, comme l'a souligné Anthony Sampson, qu'I.T.T. produisait des avions allemands utilisés pour tuer les Américains et leurs alliés - et l'entreprise a réalisé d'excellents bénéfices.

Avec Kurt von Schröder, I.T.T. a eu accès au cœur même de l'élite du pouvoir nazi. Qui était Schröder ? Le baron Kurt von Schröder est né à Hambourg en 1889 dans une vieille famille de banquiers allemands bien établie. Un ancien membre de la famille Schröder s'est installé à Londres, a changé son nom en Schroder (sans le diérèse) et a organisé la société bancaire de J. Henry Schroder à Londres et la J. Henry Schroder Banking Corporation à New York. Kurt von Schröder devient également partenaire de la banque privée de Cologne, J. H. Stein & Company, fondée à la fin du XVIIIe siècle. Schröder et Stein avaient tous deux été les promoteurs, en compagnie de financiers français, du mouvement séparatiste allemand de 1919 qui tentait de séparer la riche Rhénanie de l'Allemagne et de ses troubles. Au cours de cette escapade, des industriels rhénans de premier plan se réunirent chez J. H. Stein le 7 janvier 1919 et, quelques mois plus tard, organisèrent une réunion, sous la présidence de Stein, pour développer le soutien du public au mouvement séparatiste. L'action de 1919 échoua. Le groupe essaya de nouveau en 1923 et fut le fer de lance d'un autre mouvement visant à séparer la Rhénanie de l'Allemagne pour la placer sous la protection de la France. Cette tentative a également échoué. Kurt von Schröder se lia alors à Hitler et aux premiers nazis, et comme dans les mouvements séparatistes rhénans de 1919 et 1923, Schröder représentait et travaillait pour les industriels et les fabricants d'armement allemands.

En échange d'un soutien financier et industriel organisé par von Schröder, il a ensuite acquis un prestige politique. Immédiatement après l'arrivée au pouvoir des nazis en 1933, Schröder est devenu le représentant allemand à la Banque des Règlements Internationaux, que Quigley appelle le sommet du système de contrôle international, ainsi que le chef du groupe de banquiers privés conseillant la Reichsbank allemande. Heinrich Himmler nomme Schroder chef de groupe senior

517 Voir également le chapitre neuf pour les preuves documentaires de ces paiements I.T.T. au S.S.

S.S., et à son tour Himmler devient un membre éminent du Keppler's Circle. (Voir le chapitre neuf).

En 1938, la banque Schroder à Londres devient l'agent financier allemand en Grande-Bretagne, représenté aux réunions financières par son directeur général (et un directeur de la Banque d'Angleterre), F.C. Tiarks. Dès la Seconde Guerre mondiale, le baron Schröder avait ainsi acquis une liste impressionnante de relations politiques et bancaires reflétant une large influence ; il a même été rapporté au Comité Kilgore américain que Schroder était suffisamment influent en 1940 pour amener Pierre Laval au pouvoir en France. Selon la liste établie par le Comité Kilgore, les acquisitions politiques de Schroder au début des années 1940 se présentent comme suit :

Chef de groupe senior SS.	Groupe commercial pour le commerce de gros et le commerce extérieur - Responsable.
Croix de fer de première et de deuxième classe.	Akademie fur Deutsches Recht (Académie de droit allemand) - Membre
Consul général de Suède.	Ville de Cologne - Conseiller.
Chambre de commerce internationale - Membre du comité administratif.	Université de Cologne - Membre du conseil d'administration.
Conseil de la Poste du Reich - Membre du conseil consultatif.	Fondation Kaiser Wilhelm - Sénateur.
Assemblée de l'industrie et du commerce allemands - Membre présidant.	Conseil consultatif des Germano-Albanais.
Membre du Conseil des affaires économiques du Reich.	Bureau de compensation des marchandises - Membre.
Deutsche Reichsbahn - Président du conseil d'administration.	Commission de travail du groupe du Reich pour l'industrie et le commerce - Vice-président[518]

Les relations bancaires de Schröder étaient tout aussi impressionnantes et ses relations d'affaires (non mentionnées ici) prenaient deux pages :

Banque des Règlements Internationaux - Membre de la direction.	Deutsche Verkehrs-Kredit-Bank, A.G., Berlin (contrôlée par la Deutsche Reichsbank) - Président du conseil d'administration.
J.H. Stein & Co, Cologne - Associé (la Banque Worms était correspondante française).	Deutsche Ueberseeische Bank (contrôlée par la Deutsche Bank, Berlin) - Directeur[519]
Deutsche Reichsbank, Berlin. Conseiller du conseil d'administration.	Wirtschaftsgruppe Private Bankegewerbe - Leader.

C'est Schroder qui, après 1933, a représenté Sosthenes Behn de l'I.T.T. et les intérêts de l'I.T.T. dans l'Allemagne nazie. C'est précisément parce que Schroder avait ces excellentes relations politiques avec Hitler et l'État nazi que Behn le nomma aux conseils d'administration de toutes les sociétés allemandes d'I.T.T : Standard Electrizitatswerke A.G. à Berlin, C. Lorenz A.G. de Berlin et Mix & Genest A.G. (dans laquelle la Standard détenait une participation de 94%).

518 Élimination des ressources allemandes, p. 871.

519 Ibid.

Au milieu des années 1930, une autre liaison a été établie entre Wall Street et Schroder, cette fois-ci par les Rockefeller. En 1936, les activités de prise ferme et les activités générales liées aux valeurs mobilières de la J. Henry Schroder Banking Corporation à New York ont été fusionnées dans une nouvelle société de banque d'investissement - Schroder, Rockefeller & Company, Inc. au 48 Wall Street. Carlton P. Fuller de Schroder Banking Corporation devient président et Avery Rockefeller, fils de Percy Rockefeller (frère de John D. Rockefeller) devient vice-président et directeur de la nouvelle société. Auparavant, Avery Rockefeller avait été associé en coulisses à la J. Henry Schroder Banking Corporation ; la nouvelle société l'a fait sortir du placard.[520]

WESTRICK, TEXACO, ET I.T.T.

I.T.T. avait encore une autre voie d'accès à l'Allemagne nazie, par l'intermédiaire de l'avocat allemand Gerhard Westrick. Westrick faisait partie d'un groupe restreint d'Allemands qui avaient fait de l'espionnage aux États-Unis pendant la Première Guerre mondiale. Ce groupe comprenait non seulement Kurt von Schröder et Westrick, mais aussi Franz von Papen - que nous rencontrerons en compagnie de James Paul Warburg de la Banque de Manhattan au chapitre dix - et le Dr Heinrich Albert. Albert, prétendument attaché commercial allemand aux États-Unis pendant la Première Guerre mondiale, était en fait chargé de financer le programme d'espionnage de von Papen. Après la Première Guerre mondiale, Westrick et Albert ont formé le cabinet d'avocats Albert & Westrick qui s'est spécialisé dans les prêts de réparation de Wall Street et en a largement profité. Le cabinet Albert & Westrick s'est occupé de la partie allemande des prêts de la banque J. Henry Schroder, tandis que le cabinet de John Foster Dulles de Sullivan and Cromwell à New York s'est occupé de la partie américaine des prêts Schroder.

Juste avant la Seconde Guerre mondiale, l'opération d'espionnage Albert-Papen-Westrick aux États-Unis a commencé à se répéter, mais cette fois-ci, les autorités américaines étaient plus vigilantes. Westrick est venu aux États-Unis en 1940, soi-disant comme attaché commercial mais en fait comme représentant personnel de Ribbentrop. Le flot de visiteurs à l'influent Westrick en provenance d'éminents directeurs de sociétés pétrolières et industrielles américaines, a attiré l'attention du FBI sur Westrick.

À cette époque, Westrick est devenu directeur de toutes les opérations de I.T.T. en Allemagne, afin de protéger les intérêts de I.T.T. pendant l'implication prévue des États-Unis dans la guerre européenne.[521] Parmi ses autres entreprises, Westrick a tenté de persuader Henry Ford de couper l'approvisionnement de la Grande-Bretagne, et le traitement de faveur accordé par les nazis aux intérêts de Ford en

[520] *New York Times*, 20 juillet 1936.

[521] Anthony Sampson rapporte une réunion entre le vice-président de l'I.T.T., Kenneth Stockton, et Westrick, au cours de laquelle la préservation des propriétés de l'I.T.T. a été planifiée. Voir Anthony Sampson, op. cit. p. 39.

France suggère que Westrick a partiellement réussi à neutraliser l'aide américaine à la Grande-Bretagne.

Bien que la plus importante relation d'affaires de Westrick aux États-Unis pendant la guerre ait été avec International Telephone and Telegraph, il a également représenté d'autres entreprises américaines, notamment Underwood Elliott Fisher, propriétaire de la société allemande Mercedes Buromaschinen A.G., Eastman Kodak, qui avait une filiale Kodak en Allemagne, et l'International Milk Corporation, avec une filiale à Hambourg. Parmi les contrats de Westrick (et celui qui a reçu le plus de publicité), il y avait un contrat pour que Texaco fournisse du pétrole à la marine allemande, qu'il a arrangé avec Torkild Rieber, président du conseil d'administration de la société Texaco.

En 1940, Rieber a discuté d'un accord pétrolier avec Hermann Goering, et Westrick aux États-Unis a travaillé pour la Texas Oil Company. Sa voiture a été achetée avec des fonds de Texaco, et la demande de permis de conduire de Westrick a donné Texaco comme adresse professionnelle. Ces activités ont été rendues publiques le 12 août 1940. Rieber a ensuite démissionné de Texaco et Westrick est retourné en Allemagne. Deux ans plus tard, Rieber est président de South Carolina Shipbuilding and Dry Docks, supervisant la construction de navires de la marine américaine pour plus de 10 millions de dollars, et administrateur de la Barber Asphalt Corporation et de la Seaboard Oil Company de l'Ohio, appartenant à la famille Guggenheim.[522]

I.T.T. EN ALLEMAGNE PENDANT LA GUERRE

En 1939, I.T.T. aux États-Unis contrôlait Standard Elektrizitats en Allemagne, et à son tour Standard Elektrizitats contrôlait 94% de Mix & Genest. Au conseil d'administration de Standard Elektrizitats se trouvaient le baron Kurt von Schröder, un banquier nazi au cœur du nazisme, et Emil Heinrich Meyer, beau-frère du secrétaire d'État Keppler (fondateur du cercle Keppler) et directeur de la General Electric allemande. Schröder et Meyer étaient également directeurs de Mix & Genest et de l'autre filiale I.T.T., la C. Lorenz Company ; ces deux filiales I.T.T. étaient des contributeurs monétaires au Cercle des amis de Himmler - c'est-à-dire à la caisse noire des S.S. nazis. Jusqu'en 1944, Mix & Genest a versé 5000 RM à Himmler et 20 000 RM à Lorenz. En bref, pendant la Seconde Guerre mondiale, International Telephone and Telegraph effectuait des paiements en espèces au leader S.S. Heinrich Himmler. Ces paiements ont permis à I.T.T. de

[522] Les informations selon lesquelles Rieber aurait reçu 20 000 dollars des nazis sont sans fondement. Ces rapports ont fait l'objet d'une enquête du F.B.I. sans qu'aucune preuve ne soit apportée. Voir Sénat des États-Unis, sous-commission chargée d'enquêter sur l'administration du . Internal Security Act, Committee on the Judiciary, *Journal de Morgenthau (Allemagne),* Volume I, 90ème Congrès, 1ère session, 20 novembre 1967, (Washington : U.S. Government Printing Office, 1967), pp. 316-8. Sur Rieber, voir également l'*annexe du procès-verbal du Congrès,* 20 août 1942, p, A 1501-2, remarques de l'honorable John M. Coffee.

protéger son investissement dans Focke-Wolfe, une entreprise de construction aéronautique produisant des avions de chasse utilisés contre les États-Unis.

L'interrogatoire de Kurt von Schröder le 19 novembre 1945 met en évidence le caractère délibéré de la relation étroite et profitable entre le colonel Sosthenes Behn de l'I.T.T., Westrick, Schröder, et la machine de guerre nazie pendant la Seconde Guerre mondiale, et que cette relation était délibérée et bien informée :

> **Q**. Vous nous avez indiqué, lors de votre précédent témoignage, un certain nombre d'entreprises en Allemagne dans lesquelles la Société internationale de téléphone et de télégraphe ou la Standard Electric Company avaient une participation. L'International Telephone and Telegraph Company ou la Standard Electric Company détenaient-elles une participation dans d'autres sociétés en Allemagne ?
> **A**. Oui. La compagnie Lorenz, peu avant la guerre, a pris une participation d'environ 25 pour cent dans la société Focke-Wolfe A.G. à Brême. Focke-Wolfe fabriquait des avions pour le ministère de l'air allemand. Je pense que plus tard, lorsque Focke-Wolfe s'est développée et a pris plus de capital, la participation de la société Lorenz est tombée un peu en dessous de ces 25%.
> **Q**. Cette participation de la société Lorenz dans Focke-Wolfe a donc commencé après que la société Lorenz ait été détenue et contrôlée à près de 100% par le colonel Behn par l'intermédiaire de la Société internationale de téléphone et de télégraphe ?
> **A**. Oui.
> **Q**. Le colonel Behen *[sic]* a-t-il approuvé cet investissement de la société Lorenz à Focke-Wolfe ?
> **A**. Je suis convaincu que le colonel Behn a approuvé la transaction avant que ses représentants, qui étaient en contact étroit avec lui, ne l'approuvent officiellement.
> **Q**. En quelle année la société Lorenz a-t-elle effectué l'investissement qui lui a permis d'obtenir cette participation de 25% dans Foeke-Wolfe ?
> **A**. Je me souviens que c'était peu de temps avant le déclenchement de la guerre, c'est-à-dire peu de temps avant l'invasion de la Pologne. [Ed : 1939]
> **Q** Westrick saurait-il tout sur les détails des participations de la société Lorenz à Foeke-Wolfe, A.G. de Brême ?
> **A**. Oui. Mieux que moi.
> **Q**. Quel a été le montant de l'investissement de la société Lorenz dans l'AG Focke-Wolfe, de Brême, qui lui a donné une participation initiale de 25% ?
> **A**. 250.000.000 RM initialement, et ce montant a été considérablement augmenté, mais je ne me souviens pas de l'ampleur des investissements supplémentaires que la société Lorenz a faits à ce Focke-Wolfe A.G. de Brême.
> **Q**. De 1933 jusqu'au déclenchement de la guerre européenne, le colonel Behn était-il en mesure de transférer les bénéfices des investissements de ses sociétés en Allemagne à ses sociétés aux États-Unis ?
> **A**. Oui. Bien qu'il aurait fallu que ses sociétés prennent un peu moins que la totalité des dividendes en raison de la difficulté à obtenir des devises étrangères, la majeure partie des bénéfices aurait pu être transférée à la société du colonel Behn aux États-Unis. Cependant, le colonel Behn n'a pas choisi de le faire et à aucun moment il ne m'a demandé si je pouvais accomplir cela pour lui. Au lieu de cela, il semblait parfaitement satisfait de voir tous les bénéfices des sociétés en Allemagne, que lui et ses intérêts contrôlaient, réinvestir ces bénéfices dans de nouveaux bâtiments et machines et dans toute autre entreprise de production d'armements.
> Une autre de ces entreprises, Huth and Company, G.m.b.H., de Berlin, fabriquait des pièces de radio et de radar, dont beaucoup étaient utilisées dans les équipements destinés aux forces armées allemandes. La compagnie Lorenz, si je me souviens

bien, avait une participation de 50% dans Huth and Company. La société Lorenz avait également une petite filiale qui faisait office d'agence commerciale pour la société Lorenz auprès des particuliers.
Q. Vous avez été membre du conseil d'administration de la société Lorenz, d'environ 1935 jusqu'à aujourd'hui. Pendant cette période, la société Lorenz et certaines autres sociétés, telles que Foeke-Wolfe, avec laquelle elle détenait des participations importantes, étaient engagées dans la fabrication d'équipements pour l'armement et la production de guerre. Saviez-vous ou avez-vous entendu parler d'une quelconque protestation du colonel Behn ou de ses représentants contre ces entreprises engagées dans ces activités préparant l'Allemagne à la guerre ?
A. Non.
Q. Êtes-vous certain qu'en aucune autre occasion Westrick, Mann [sic], le colonel Behn ou toute autre personne liée aux intérêts de la Compagnie internationale de téléphone et de télégraphie en Allemagne ne vous a demandé d'intervenir au nom de la compagnie auprès des autorités allemandes.
A. Oui. Je ne me souviens d'aucune demande d'intervention dans une affaire importante pour la société Lorenz ou pour tout autre intérêt international en matière de téléphone et de télégraphe en Allemagne.

J'ai lu le procès-verbal de cet interrogatoire et je jure que les réponses que j'ai données à la question de MM. Adams et Pajus sont exactes en toute connaissance de cause. s/Kurt von Schröder

C'est cette histoire de coopération entre l'I.T.T. et les nazis pendant la Seconde Guerre mondiale et d'association de l'I.T.T. avec le nazi Kurt von Schröder que l'I.T.T. a voulu dissimuler - et a presque réussi à dissimuler. James Stewart Martin raconte que lors des réunions de planification de la division des finances de la Commission de contrôle, il a été chargé de travailler avec le capitaine Norbert A. Bogdan, qui, sans son uniforme, était vice-président de la J. Henry Schroder Banking Corporation de New York. Martin raconte que "le capitaine Bogdan s'était vigoureusement opposé à l'enquête sur la banque Stein au motif qu'il s'agissait de "broutilles".[523] Peu après avoir bloqué cette manœuvre, deux membres permanents du personnel de Bogdan ont demandé l'autorisation d'enquêter sur la banque Stein - bien que Cologne ne soit pas encore tombée aux mains des forces américaines. Martin se souvient que "la division des renseignements a bloqué celle-là", mais certaines informations sur l'opération de la banque Stein-Schröder-I.T.T. ont circulé.

---

[523] James Stewart Martin, op. cit. p. 52.

CHAPITRE VI

HENRY FORD ET LES NAZIS

Je voudrais souligner l'importance que les hauts fonctionnaires [nazis] attachent au respect du désir et au maintien de la bonne volonté de "Ford", et par "Ford", j'entends votre père, vous-même et la Ford Motor Company, Dearborn.

(Josiah E. Dubois, Jr, *Generals in Grey Suits*, Londres : The Bodley Head, 1953, p. 250).

Henry Ford est souvent considérée comme une énigme au sein de l'élite de Wall Street. Pendant de nombreuses années, dans les années 20 et 30, Ford était connu comme un ennemi de l'establishment financier. Ford a accusé Morgan et d'autres d'utiliser la guerre et la révolution comme réaliser des profits colossaux et d'user de leur influence dans les milieux sociaux-politiques comme un moyen d'enrichissement personnel. En 1938, Henry Ford, dans ses déclarations publiques, avait divisé les financiers en deux classes : ceux qui profitaient de la guerre et utilisaient leur influence pour provoquer la guerre en vue d'en tirer de grands profits, et les financiers "constructifs". Dans ce dernier groupe, il incluait désormais la Maison de Morgan. Lors d'une interview[524] accordée au *New York Times* en 1938, Ford s'est prononcé en ce sens :

Quelqu'un a dit un jour que soixante familles dirigent les destinées de la nation. On pourrait bien dire que si quelqu'un concentrait les projecteurs sur vingt-cinq personnes qui gèrent les finances de la nation, les véritables faiseurs de guerre du monde seraient mis en relief de façon audacieuse.

Le journaliste du *Times* a demandé à Ford comment il comparait cette évaluation à sa critique de longue date de la maison Morgan, ce à quoi Ford a répondu :

Il y a un Wall Street constructif et un Wall Street destructeur. La Maison Morgan représente le côté constructif. Je connais M. Morgan depuis de nombreuses années. Il a soutenu et appuyé Thomas Edison, qui était aussi mon bon ami...

[524] 4 juin 1938, 2:2.

Après avoir exposé les maux de la production agricole limitée - prétendument provoquée par Wall Street - Ford a continué,

> *... si ces financiers avaient fait ce qu'ils voulaient, nous serions en guerre maintenant. Ils veulent la guerre parce qu'ils font de l'argent à partir d'un tel conflit - à partir de la misère humaine que les guerres apportent.*

D'un autre côté, lorsque nous enquêtons sur ces déclarations publiques, nous constatons que Henry Ford et son fils Edsel Ford ont été à l'avant-garde des hommes d'affaires américains qui tentèrent d'être présents des deux côtés de chaque barrière idéologique à la recherche du profit. Selon les propres critères de Ford, les Ford font partie des éléments "destructeurs".

C'est Henry Ford qui, dans les années 30, a construit la première usine automobile moderne de l'Union soviétique (située à Gorki) et qui, dans les années 50 et 60, a produit les camions utilisés par les Nord-Vietnamiens pour transporter des armes et des munitions destinées à être utilisées contre les Américains.[525] À peu près à la même époque, Henry Ford était également le plus célèbre des bailleurs de fonds étrangers d'Hitler, et il a été récompensé dans les années 1930 pour ce soutien durable par la plus haute décoration nazie pour les étrangers.

Cette faveur nazie a suscité une tempête de controverses aux États-Unis et a finalement dégénéré en un échange de notes diplomatiques entre le gouvernement allemand et le Département d'État. Alors que Ford protestait publiquement qu'il n'aimait pas les gouvernements totalitaires, nous constatons en pratique que Ford a sciemment profité des deux côtés de la Seconde Guerre mondiale - des usines françaises et allemandes produisant des véhicules pour la Wehrmacht, et des usines américaines construisant des véhicules pour l'armée américaine, pour le plus grand profit du groupe Ford.

Les protestations d'innocence de Henry Ford suggèrent, comme nous le verrons dans ce chapitre, qu'il n'approuvait pas le fait que des financiers juifs profitent de la guerre (comme certains l'ont fait), mais si l'antisémite Morgan[526] et Ford lui-même, profitaient de la guerre, c'était acceptable, moral et "constructif".

HENRY FORD : LE PREMIER BAILLEUR DE FONDS ÉTRANGER D'HITLER

---

[525] Une liste de ces véhicules Gorki et de leurs numéros de modèle se trouve dans Antony G. Sutton, *National Suicide: Military Aid to the Soviet Union,* (New York : Arlington House Publishers, 1973), tableau 7-2, p. 125.

[526] La Maison Morgan était connue pour ses opinions antisémites.

Le 20 décembre 1922, le *New York Times* rapporte[527] que le constructeur automobile Henry Ford finance les mouvements nationalistes et antisémites d'Adolf Hitler à Munich.

Simultanément, le journal berlinois *Berliner Tageblatt* a demandé à l'ambassadeur américain à Berlin d'enquêter sur l'intervention d'Henry Ford dans les affaires intérieures allemandes et de la stopper. Il a été rapporté que les bailleurs de fonds étrangers d'Hitler avaient fourni un "quartier général spacieux" avec une "foule de lieutenants et de fonctionnaires très bien payés". Le portrait d'Henry Ford était bien en vue sur les murs du bureau personnel d'Hitler :

> *Le mur derrière son bureau dans le bureau privé d'Hitler est décoré d'une grande photo d'Henry Ford. Dans l'antichambre, il y a une grande table couverte de livres, dont la quasi-totalité est une traduction d'un livre écrit et publié par Henry Ford.*[528]

Le même rapport du *New York Times* commentait que le dimanche précédent, Hitler avait fait une revue,

> *Le Storming Battalion..., 1000 jeunes hommes en uniformes flambant neufs et armés de revolvers et de matraques, tandis qu'Hitler et ses hommes de main se déplacent dans deux puissantes voitures flambant neuves.*

Le *Times* fait une distinction claire entre les partis monarchistes allemands et le parti fasciste antisémite d'Hitler. Henry Ford, a-t-on noté, a ignoré les monarchistes Hohenzollern et a investi son argent dans le mouvement révolutionnaire hitlérien.

Ces fonds Ford ont été utilisés par Hitler pour fomenter la rébellion bavaroise. La rébellion échoua et Hitler fut capturé puis traduit en justice. En février 1923, lors du procès, Auer le vice-président du parlement bavarois témoigna :

> *Le parlement bavarois sait depuis longtemps que le mouvement Hitler a été en partie financé par un chef antisémite américain, qui est Henry Ford. L'intérêt de M. Ford pour le mouvement antisémite bavarois a commencé il y a un an, lorsqu'un de ses agents, cherchant à vendre des tracteurs, est entré en contact avec Diedrich Eckhart, le célèbre panallemand. Peu de temps après, M. Eckhart a demandé à l'agent de M. Ford une aide financière. L'agent est retourné en Amérique et aussitôt l'argent de M. Ford a commencé à arriver à Munich.*
>
> *M. Hitler se vante ouvertement du soutien de M. Ford et fait l'éloge de M. Ford en tant que grand individualiste et grand antisémite. Une photographie de M. Ford*

[527] Page 2, colonne 8.

[528] Ibid.

est accrochée dans les bureaux de M. Hitler, qui est le centre du mouvement monarchiste.[529]

Hitler a reçu une peine de prison douce et confortable pour ses activités révolutionnaires bavaroises. Le reste de ses activités lui a permis d'écrire *Mein Kampf.* Le livre de Henry Ford, *The International Jew,* diffusé auparavant par les nazis, fut traduit par eux dans une douzaine de langues, et Hitler utilisa des sections du livre mot pour mot dans l'écriture de *Mein Kampf.*[530]

Nous verrons plus tard que le soutien d'Hitler à la fin des années 20 et au début des années 30 est venu des cartels de l'industrie chimique, sidérurgique et électrique, plutôt que directement d'industriels individuels. En 1928, Henry Ford a fusionné ses actifs allemands avec ceux du cartel chimique I.G. Farben. Une participation importante, 40% de Ford Motor A.G. d'Allemagne, a été transférée à I.G. Farben ; Carl Bosch de I.G. Farben est devenu le chef de Ford A.G. Motor en Allemagne.

Simultanément, aux États-Unis, Edsel Ford rejoint le conseil d'administration de l'Américain I.G. Farben. (Voir chapitre deux).

HENRY FORD REÇOIT UNE DÉCORATION NAZIE

Une décennie plus tard, en août 1938 - après que Hitler eut atteint le pouvoir avec l'aide des cartels - Henry Ford reçut la Grand-Croix de l'Aigle allemand, une distinction nazie conçue pour les étrangers illustres. Le *New York Times* a rapporté que c'était la première fois que la Grand-Croix était décernée aux États-Unis et qu'elle devait célébrer le 75e anniversaire d'Henry Ford.[531]

La décoration a soulevé une tempête de critiques dans les cercles sionistes aux États-Unis. Ford a reculé au point de rencontrer publiquement le rabbin Leo Franklin de Detroit pour exprimer sa sympathie pour le sort des Juifs allemands :

> *Mon acceptation d'une médaille du peuple allemand [dit Ford] n'implique pas, comme certains semblent le penser, une quelconque sympathie de ma part pour le nazisme. Ceux qui me connaissent depuis de nombreuses années se rendent compte que tout ce qui engendre la haine me répugne.*[532]

---

529 Jonathan Leonard, *The Tragedy of Henry Ford,* (New York : G.P. Putnam's Sons, 1932), p. 208. Voir également le fichier décimal du Département d'État américain, Microcopie des Archives nationales M 336, rouleau 80, document 862.00S/6, "Money sources of Hitler", un rapport de l'ambassade américaine à Berlin.

530 Voir à ce sujet Keith Sward, *The Legend of Henry Ford,* (New York : Rinehart & Co, 1948), p. 139.

531 *New York Times,* 1er août 1938.

532 Ibid, 1er décembre 1938, 12:2.

La question de la médaille nazie a été reprise dans un discours prononcé à Cleveland par le secrétaire de l'intérieur Harold Ickes. Ickes a critiqué Henry Ford et le colonel Charles A. Lindbergh pour avoir accepté les médailles nazies. La partie curieuse du discours d'Ickes, prononcé lors d'un banquet de la Cleveland Zionist Society, était sa critique des "juifs riches" et de leur acquisition et utilisation des richesses :

> *Une erreur commise par un millionnaire non juif se répercute sur lui seul, mais un faux pas fait par un homme juif riche se répercute sur toute sa race. C'est dur et injuste, mais c'est un fait auquel il faut faire face.*[533]

Peut-être Ickes se référait-il tangentiellement aux rôles des Warburg dans le cartel I.G. Farben : Les Warburg faisaient partie du conseil d'administration d'I.G. Farben aux États-Unis et en Allemagne. En 1938, les Warburg ont été chassés d'Allemagne par les nazis. D'autres juifs allemands, comme les banquiers Oppenheim, ont fait la paix avec les nazis et ont reçu le "statut honorifique d'Aryen".

---

[533] Ibid, 19 décembre 1938, 5:3.

New York Times, August 1, 1938

HITLER ACCLAIMED BY 200,000 IN FETE

Wild Scenes of Enthusiasm Mark Parade of Athletes at the Breslau Festival

SUDETENS BREAK RANKS

40,000 Swarm Around Stand of Chancellor and Girls Give Flowers in Homage

HENRY FORD GETTING HIGH HONOR FROM GERMAN GOVERNMENT

The industrialist receiving the Grand Cross of the German Eagle, a decoration for distinguished foreigners, on the occasion of his seventy-fifth birthday. The presentation marked the first time that the award has been made in this country. At the left is Fritz Heiler, German consular representative at Detroit, and at the right Karl Kapp, German consul at Cleveland

New York Times, December 20, 1922

BERLIN HEARS FORD IS BACKING HITLER

Bavarian Anti-Semitic Chief Has American's Portrait and Book in His Office.

SPENDS MONEY LAVISHLY

One German Paper Appeals to the United States Ambassador to Make Investigation.

Copyright, 1922, by The New York Times Company. Special Cable to THE NEW YORK TIMES.

BERLIN, Dec. 19.—A rumor is current here that Henry Ford, the American automobile manufacturer, is financing Adolph Hitler's nationalist and anti-Semitic movement in Munich. Indeed, the Berlin Tageblatt has made an appeal to the American Ambassador in Berlin to investigate and interfere.

Doubtless there is some ground for suspicion that Hitler is spending foreign money, for the paper marks his admirers throughout Germany contribute toward his movement would hardly suffice to pay for such large ... as his personal and business ...

ANTI-SEMITIC RIOTS SPREAD IN RUMANIA

Parade of Jews Broken Up by Students at Jassy and Many Are Beaten.

BUCHAREST, Rumania, Dec. 19 (Jewish Telegraphic Agency).—A large number of Jews at Jassy were severely beaten and three of them were wounded when a mob of students attacked a demonstration yesterday which was arranged by Jews as a protest against attacks on Jews throughout the country.

The object of the parade was to point out the need for Government protection of the Jews, who, the leaders declare, have been made the object of nationwide aggression in order to bring about repeal of the constitutional clauses guaranteeing their complete enfranchisement.

Daily demonstrations against Jews continue in the capital. There also are attacks at Czernowitz and Klausenberg, according to reports from those places, the demonstrations often ending in street fights with the police in their efforts to disperse the mobs.

The offices of liberal newspapers which protested against the anti-Jewish aggression are being guarded by police and the street patrols have been reinforced.

SUNDAY FOR WORLD PEACE.

Federal Council Asks 100,000 Churches to Observe Day.

WASHINGTON, Dec. 19.—The Federal Council of Churches of Christ in America issued today a request to 100,000 congregations in the United States to ... Dec. 28 as "World Peace Sun..."

LA FORD MOTOR COMPANY PARTICIPE À L'EFFORT DE GUERRE ALLEMAND

Une sous-commission du Congrès d'après-guerre qui enquêtait sur le soutien américain à l'effort militaire nazi a décrit la manière dont les nazis ont réussi à obtenir l'aide technique et financière des États-Unis qui était "assez fantastique".[534] Entre autres preuves, la commission a pu voir un mémorandum préparé dans les bureaux de Ford-Werke A.G. le 25 novembre 1941, écrit par le

[534] Élimination des ressources allemandes, p. 656.

Dr H. F. Albert à R. H. Schmidt, alors président du conseil d'administration de Ford-Werke A.G. Le mémorandum citait les avantages d'avoir une majorité de la firme allemande détenue par la Ford Motor Company à Detroit. La Ford allemande avait pu échanger des pièces Ford contre du caoutchouc et du matériel de guerre essentiel nécessaire en 1938 et 1939 "et ils n'auraient pas pu le faire si Ford n'avait pas été détenue par les États-Unis". De plus, avec un intérêt américain majoritaire, German Ford "serait plus facilement en mesure d'intervenir et de dominer les avoirs de Ford dans toute l'Europe". Il a même été rapporté au Comité que deux hauts responsables allemands de Ford s'étaient disputés personnellement pour savoir qui allait contrôler Ford d'Angleterre, à tel point que "l'un d'eux s'est finalement levé et a quitté la pièce avec dégoût".

Selon les preuves présentées au Comité, Ford-Werke A.G. a été techniquement transformée à la fin des années 1930 en une société allemande. Tous les véhicules et leurs pièces ont été produits en Allemagne, par des ouvriers allemands utilisant des matériaux allemands sous direction allemande et exportés vers les territoires européens et d'outre-mer des États-Unis et de la Grande-Bretagne.

Les matières premières étrangères nécessaires, caoutchouc et métaux non ferreux, étaient obtenues par l'intermédiaire de la société américaine Ford. L'influence américaine avait été plus ou moins convertie en une position de soutien *(Hilfsstellung)* pour les usines allemandes de Ford.

Au début de la guerre, la Ford-Werke se met à la disposition de la Wehrmacht pour la production d'armement. Les nazis pensaient que tant que la Ford-Werke A.G. serait majoritairement américaine, il serait possible de mettre les autres sociétés européennes de Ford sous influence allemande - c'est-à-dire celle de la Ford-Werke A.G. - et d'exécuter ainsi la politique nazie de la "Grande Europe" dans les usines Ford d'Amsterdam, d'Anvers, de Paris, de Budapest, de Bucarest et de Copenhague :

> *Une majorité, même si elle n'est que faible, d'Américains est indispensable pour la transmission des derniers modèles américains, ainsi que des méthodes de production et de vente américaines. Avec l'abolition de la majorité américaine, cet avantage, ainsi que l'intervention de la Ford Motor Company pour obtenir des matières premières et des exportations, seraient perdus, et l'usine allemande ne vaudrait pratiquement plus que sa capacité en machines.*[535]

Et, bien sûr, ce genre de stricte neutralité, qui adopte un point de vue international plutôt que national, avait auparavant porté ses fruits pour la Ford Motor Company en Union soviétique, où Ford était considérée comme le nec plus ultra de l'efficacité technique et économique à atteindre par les Stakhanovistes.

En juillet 1942, la société française Ford a fait parvenir à Washington des informations sur les activités de Ford dans le cadre de l'effort de guerre allemand en Europe. Les informations incriminantes ont été rapidement enterrées et même aujourd'hui, seule une partie de la documentation connue peut être retracée à Washington.

---

[535] Élimination des ressources allemandes, p. 657-8.

Nous savons cependant que le consul général des États-Unis en Algérie était en possession d'une lettre de Maurice Dollfuss de la société française Ford - qui prétendait être le premier Français à se rendre à Berlin après la chute de la France - à Edsel Ford concernant un plan selon lequel Ford Motor pourrait contribuer à l'effort de guerre nazi. La Ford française était capable de produire 20 camions par jour pour la Wehrmacht, ce qui [écrivait Dollfuss] est mieux que cela,

> *... que font nos concurrents français moins chanceux. La raison en est que nos camions sont très demandés par les autorités allemandes et je crois que tant que la guerre durera et au moins pendant un certain temps, tout ce que nous produirons sera pris par les autorités ....allemandes ; je me contenterai de vous dire que ... l'attitude de stricte neutralité que vous avez adoptée, avec votre père, a été un atout inestimable pour la production de vos entreprises en Europe.*[536]

Dollfuss révéla que les bénéfices de cette entreprise allemande s'élevaient déjà à 1,6 million de francs, et que les bénéfices nets pour 1941 n'étaient pas inférieurs à 58 000 000 de francs - parce que les Allemands ont payé rapidement la production de Ford. À la réception de cette nouvelle, Edsel Ford a câblé :

> *Ravi d'entendre que vous faites des progrès. Vos lettres sont très intéressantes. Vous réalisez pleinement le grand handicap sous lequel vous travaillez. J'espère que vous et votre famille allez bien.*
> *Salutations.*
>
> *s/ Edsel Ford*[537]

Bien qu'il existe des preuves que les usines européennes appartenant à des intérêts de Wall Street n'ont pas été bombardées par l'armée de l'air américaine pendant la Seconde Guerre mondiale, cette restriction n'est apparemment pas parvenue au commandement britannique des bombardements. En mars 1942, la Royal Air Force a bombardé l'usine Ford à Poissy, en France. Une lettre ultérieure d'Edsel Ford au directeur général de Ford, Sorenson, à propos de ce raid de la RAF, commentait : "Des photographies de l'usine en feu ont été publiées dans des journaux américains mais heureusement, aucune référence n'a été faite à la Ford Motor Company."[538] En tout état de cause, le gouvernement de Vichy a versé 38 millions de francs à la Ford Motor Company en compensation des dommages causés à l'usine de Poissy. Cela n'a pas été rapporté dans la presse américaine et ne serait guère apprécié par les Américains en guerre contre le nazisme. Dubois affirme que ces messages privés de Ford en Europe ont été transmis à Edsel Ford par le secrétaire d'État adjoint Breckenridge Long. C'est ce même secrétaire Long qui, un an plus tard, a supprimé les messages privés par l'intermédiaire du Département d'État concernant l'extermination des Juifs en Europe. La

---

536 Josiah E. Dubois, Jr, *Generals in Grey Suits*, (Londres : The Bodley Head, 1958), p. 248.

537 Ibid, p. 249.

538 Ibid, p. 251.

divulgation de ces messages aurait pu être utilisée pour aider ces personnes désespérées.

Un rapport de renseignement sur les bombardements de l'armée de l'air américaine rédigé en 1943 le note,

> *Les principales activités de guerre [de l'usine Ford] sont probablement la fabrication de camions légers et de pièces détachées pour tous les camions et voitures Ford en service dans l'Europe de l'axe (y compris les Molotov russes capturés).*[539]

Les Molotov russes ont bien sûr été fabriqués par l'usine Ford à Gorki, en Russie. En France, pendant la guerre, la production de voitures particulières a été entièrement remplacée par des véhicules militaires et, à cette fin, trois grands bâtiments supplémentaires ont été ajoutés à l'usine de Poissy. Le bâtiment principal contenait environ 500 machines-outils, toutes importées des États-Unis et comprenant un bon nombre de types plus complexes, tels que les fraises à engrenages Gleason, les automates Bullard et les aléseuses Ingersoll.[540]

Ford a également étendu ses activités en temps de guerre à l'Afrique du Nord. En décembre 1941, une nouvelle société Ford, Ford-Afrique, est enregistrée en France et obtient tous les droits de l'ancienne Ford Motor Company, Ltd. d'Angleterre en Algérie, Tunisie, Maroc français, Équateur français et Afrique occidentale française. L'Afrique du Nord n'étant pas accessible à la Ford britannique, cette nouvelle compagnie Ford - enregistrée en France occupée par l'Allemagne - a été organisée pour combler cette lacune. Les directeurs étaient pronazis et comprenaient Maurice Dollfuss (le correspondant d'Edsel Ford) et Roger Messis (décrit par le consul général des États-Unis à Alger comme "connu de ce bureau, réputé sans scrupules, est déclaré être à 100% pro-allemand")[541]

Le consul général des États-Unis a également indiqué que la propagande était courante à Alger sur :

> *... la collaboration des capitaux franco-germano-américains et la sincérité douteuse de l'effort de guerre américain, [il] pointe déjà un doigt accusateur sur une transaction qui a longtemps fait l'objet de discussions dans les milieux commerciaux.*[542]

En bref, il existe des preuves documentaires que la Ford Motor Company a travaillé dans les deux camps de la Seconde Guerre mondiale. Si les industriels nazis jugés à Nuremberg étaient coupables de crimes contre l'humanité, il doit en être de même pour leurs collègues de la famille Ford, Henry et Edsel Ford. Cependant, l'histoire de Ford a été dissimulée par Washington - apparemment

[539] Ibid.

[540] U.S. Army Air Force, *Aiming point report No I.E.2,* 29 mai 1943.

[541] Fichier décimal du Département d'État américain, 800/610.1.

[542] Ibid.

comme presque tout ce qui pouvait toucher au nom et à la subsistance de l'élite financière de Wall Street.

CHAPITRE VII

QUI A FINANCÉ ADOLF HITLER ?

Le financement d'Hitler et du mouvement nazi n'a pas encore fait l'objet d'une étude approfondie et exhaustive. Le seul examen publié des finances personnelles d'Hitler est un article d'Oron James Hale, "Adolf Hitler: Taxpayer",[543] qui relate les frictions d'Adolf avec les autorités fiscales allemandes avant qu'il ne devienne *Reichskanzler* [Chancelier du Reich], Dans les années 1920, Hitler se présente au fisc allemand comme un simple écrivain appauvri vivant de prêts bancaires, avec une automobile achetée à crédit. Malheureusement, les documents originaux utilisés par Hale ne permettent pas de connaître la source des revenus, des prêts ou du crédit de Hitler, et la loi allemande "n'exigeait pas des travailleurs indépendants ou des professionnels qu'ils divulguent en détail les sources de revenus ou la nature des services rendus".[544] De toute évidence, les fonds pour ses automobiles, le salaire de son secrétaire privé Rudolf Hess, un autre assistant, un chauffeur, et les dépenses encourues par l'activité politique, provenaient bien de quelque part.

Mais, tout comme le séjour de Léon Trotsky à New York en 1917, il est difficile de concilier les dépenses connues d'Hitler avec la source précise de ses revenus.

QUELQUES-UNS DES PREMIERS SOUTIENS D'HITLER

Nous savons que d'éminents industriels européens et américains parrainaient toutes sortes de groupes politiques totalitaires à cette époque, y compris des communistes et divers groupes nazis. Le Comité Kilgore américain en fait état :

> *En 1919, Krupp apportait déjà une aide financière à l'un des groupes politiques réactionnaires qui ont semé la graine de l'idéologie nazie actuelle. Hugo Stinnes a été l'un des premiers à contribuer au parti nazi (National Socialistische Deutsche Arbeiter Partei). En 1924, d'autres industriels et financiers de premier plan, dont Fritz Thyssen, Albert Voegler, Adolf [sic] Kirdorf et Kurt von Schroder, donnaient secrètement des sommes importantes aux nazis. En 1931, les membres de l'association des propriétaires de charbon dirigée par Kirdorf s'engagèrent à*

---

[543] *The American Historical Review*, Volume LC, NO. 4, juillet. 1955. p, 830.

[544] Ibid, note de bas de page (2).

payer 50 pfennigs pour chaque tonne de charbon vendue, l'argent devant aller à l'organisation que Hitler était en train de construire.[545]

Le procès d'Hitler à Munich en 1924 a permis de prouver que le parti nazi avait reçu 20 000 dollars des industriels de Nuremberg. Le nom le plus intéressant de cette période est celui d'Emil Kirdorf, qui avait auparavant servi d'intermédiaire pour le financement de la participation allemande à la révolution bolchévique.[546] Le rôle de Kirdorf dans le financement d'Hitler était, selon ses propres termes :

> *En 1923, je suis entré en contact pour la première fois avec le mouvement national-socialiste ; j'ai entendu le Führer pour la première fois dans la salle d'exposition d'Essen. Son exposé clair m'a complètement convaincu et m'a submergé. En 1927, j'ai rencontré le Führer personnellement pour la première fois. Je me suis rendu à Munich et j'ai eu une conversation avec le Führer dans la maison des Bruckmann. Pendant quatre heures et demie, Adolf Hitler m'a expliqué son programme en détail. J'ai ensuite supplié le Führer de rassembler l'exposé qu'il m'avait donné sous forme de brochure. J'ai ensuite distribué ce pamphlet en mon nom dans les milieux commerciaux et industriels.*
>
> *Depuis lors, je me suis mis entièrement à la disposition de son mouvement. Peu après notre conversation de Munich, et suite au pamphlet que le Führer a composé et que j'ai distribué, un certain nombre de rencontres ont eu lieu entre le Führer et des personnalités de premier plan dans le domaine de l'industrie. Pour la dernière fois avant la prise du pouvoir, les chefs d'entreprise se sont réunis chez moi avec Adolf Hitler, Rudolf Hess, Hermann Goering et d'autres personnalités du parti.*[547]

En 1925, la famille Hugo Stinnes a contribué financièrement à la transformation de l'hebdomadaire nazi *Volkischer Beobachter* en un quotidien. Putzi Hanfstaengl, ami et protégé de Franklin D. Roosevelt, a fourni le reste des fonds. Le tableau 7-1 (voir plus loin) résume les contributions financières actuellement connues et les associations professionnelles des contributeurs des États-Unis. Putzi ne figure pas dans le tableau 7-1, car il n'était ni industriel ni financier.

Au début des années 1930, l'aide financière à Hitler a commencé à circuler plus facilement. Il y eut en Allemagne une série de rencontres, irréfutablement documentées dans plusieurs sources, entre des industriels allemands, Hitler lui-même, et plus souvent les représentants de Hitler, Hjalmar Schacht et Rudolf Hess. Le point critique est que les industriels allemands qui finançaient Hitler étaient principalement des directeurs de cartels avec des associations américaines, la propriété, la participation ou une forme de lien subsidiaire. Les bailleurs de fonds de Hitler n'étaient pas, dans l'ensemble, des entreprises d'origine purement

---

[545] *Élimination des ressources allemandes*, p. 648. L'Albert Voegler mentionné dans la liste des premiers partisans d'Hitler du Comité Kilgore était le représentant allemand à la Commission du Plan Dawes. Owen Young de General Electric (voir chapitre trois) était un représentant américain pour le plan Dawes et a formulé son successeur, le plan Young.

[546] Antony C. Sutton, *Wall Street et la révolution bolchévique*, op. cit.

[547] *Preussiche Zettung*, 3 janvier 1937.

allemande, ni des représentants d'entreprises familiales allemandes. À l'exception de Thyssen et de Kirdoff, il s'agissait dans la plupart des cas de multinationales allemandes - c'est-à-dire I.G. Farben, A.E.G., DAPAG, etc. Ces multinationales avaient été créées grâce à des prêts américains dans les années 1920 et, au début des années 1930, elles étaient dirigées par des Américains et bénéficiaient d'une forte participation financière américaine.

Un flux de fonds politiques étrangers non pris en compte ici est celui rapporté par la Royal Dutch Shell, basée en Europe, le grand concurrent de Standard Oil dans les années 20 et 30, et la gigantesque invention de l'homme d'affaires anglo-néerlandais Sir Henri Deterding. Il a été largement affirmé qu'Henri Deterding a personnellement financé Hitler. Cet argument est avancé, par exemple, par le biographe Glyn Roberts dans *L'homme le plus puissant du monde*. Roberts note que Deterding a été impressionné par Hitler dès 1921 :

> *... et la presse néerlandaise a rapporté que, par l'intermédiaire de l'agent Georg Bell, il [Deterding] avait mis à la disposition d'Hitler, alors que le parti était "encore en gestation", pas moins de quatre millions de florins.*[548]

Il a été rapporté (par Roberts) qu'en 1931 Georg Bell, l'agent de Deterding, a assisté à des réunions de patriotes ukrainiens à Paris "en tant que délégué conjoint d'Hitler et de Deterding".[549] Roberts rapporte également :

> *Deterding a été accusé, comme en témoigne Edgar Ansell Mowrer dans son livre l'"Allemagne remet les pendules à l'heure", d'avoir remis une importante somme d'argent aux nazis, étant entendu que le succès lui donnerait une position plus favorable sur le marché pétrolier allemand. En d'autres occasions, des chiffres allant jusqu'à 55 000 000 de livres ont été mentionnés.*[550]

Le biographe Roberts a vraiment trouvé le fort antibolchevisme de Deterding de mauvais goût, et plutôt que de présenter des preuves solides de financement, il est enclin à supposer plutôt qu'à prouver que Deterding était pro-Hitler. Mais le pro-hitlérien n'est pas une conséquence nécessaire de l'antibolchevisme ; en tout état de cause, Roberts n'offre aucune preuve de financement, et cet auteur n'a pas trouvé de preuves tangibles de l'implication de Deterding.

Le livre de Mowrer ne contient ni index ni notes de bas de page quant à la source de ses informations et Roberts n'a aucune preuve spécifique de ses accusations. Il existe des preuves indirectes que Deterding était pronazi. Il est ensuite allé vivre dans l'Allemagne d'Hitler et a augmenté sa part du marché pétrolier allemand. Il y a donc peut-être eu des contributions, mais elles n'ont pas été prouvées.

---

548 Glyn Roberts, *The Most Powerful Man in the World*, (New York : Covicl, Friede, 1938), p. 305.

549 Ibid, p. 313.

550 Ibid, p. 322.

De même, en France (le 11 janvier 1932), Paul Faure, membre de la Chambre des Députés, a accusé l'entreprise industrielle française Schneider-Creuzot de financer Hitler - et a incidemment impliqué Wall Street dans d'autres circuits de financement.[551]

Le groupe Schneider est une célèbre firme de fabricants d'armement français. Après avoir rappelé l'influence de Schneider dans l'établissement du fascisme en Hongrie et ses vastes opérations internationales d'armement, Paul Fauré évoque Hitler et cite le quotidien français *Le Journal,* indiquant "qu'Hitler avait reçu 300 000 francs or suisses" provenant de souscriptions ouvertes en Hollande au nom d'un professeur d'université nommé von Bissing. Paul Fauré déclare que l'usine Skoda de Pilsen était contrôlée par la famille française Schneider, et que ce sont les directeurs de Skoda, von Duschnitz et von Arthaber, qui ont effectué les souscriptions à Hitler. Fauré conclut :

> *... Je suis troublé de voir les directeurs de Skoda, contrôlés par Schneider, subventionner la campagne électorale de M. Hitler ; je suis troublé de voir vos entreprises, vos financiers, vos cartels industriels s'unir au plus nationaliste des Allemands...*

Là encore, aucune preuve concrète n'a été trouvée pour ce prétendu flux de fonds hitlériens.

FRITZ THYSSEN ET LA W.A. HARRIMAN COMPANY DE NEW YORK

Un autre cas insaisissable de financement d'Hitler est celui de Fritz Thyssen, le magnat allemand de l'acier qui s'est associé au mouvement nazi au début des années 20. Interrogé en 1945 dans le cadre du projet Dustbin,[552] Thyssen se souvient qu'il a été approché en 1923 par le général Ludendorff lors de l'évacuation française de la Ruhr. Peu après cette rencontre, Thyssen a été présenté à Hitler et a fourni des fonds aux nazis par l'intermédiaire du général Ludendorff. En 1930-1931, Emil Kirdorf approcha Thyssen et envoya ensuite Rudolf Hess négocier un nouveau financement pour le parti nazi. Cette fois-ci, Thyssen a arrangé un crédit de 250 000 marks à la Bank Voor Handel en Scheepvaart N.V., située au 18 Zuidblaak à Rotterdam, en Hollande, fondée en 1918 avec H.J. Kouwenhoven et D.C. Schutte comme associés directeurs.[553] Cette banque était une filiale de la August Thyssen Bank of Germany (anciennement von der Heydt's

[551] Voir *Chambre des Députés - Débats,* 11 février 1932, p. 496-500.

[552] Conseil de contrôle du groupe américain (Allemagne0 Bureau du directeur du renseignement, Agence d'information sur le terrain, technique). Rapport de renseignement n° EF/ME/1,4 septembre 1945. "Examination of Dr. Fritz Thyssen," p, 13, ci-après cité comme "Examination of Dr.

[553] La banque était connue en Allemagne sous le nom de Bank *fur Handel und Schiff.*

Bank A.G.). C'était la banque personnelle de Thyssen, et elle était affiliée aux intérêts financiers de W. A. Harriman à New York. Thyssen a rapporté à ses interrogateurs du Projet Dustbin que :

> *J'ai choisi une banque néerlandaise parce que je ne voulais pas être confondu avec les banques allemandes dans ma position, et parce que je pensais qu'il était préférable de faire des affaires avec une banque néerlandaise, et je pensais avoir les nazis un peu plus entre les mains.*[554]

Le livre de Thyssen, *I Paid Hitler*, publié en 1941, est censé avoir été écrit par Fritz Thyssen lui-même, bien que Thyssen en nie la paternité. Le livre affirme que les fonds destinés à Hitler - environ un million de marks - provenaient principalement de Thyssen lui-même. *I Paid Hitler* avance d'autres affirmations non fondées, par exemple que Hitler descendait en fait d'un enfant illégitime de la famille Rothschild. La grand-mère d'Hitler, Frau Schickelgruber, aurait été une servante de la famille Rothschild et serait tombée enceinte :

> *... une enquête ordonnée par le défunt chancelier autrichien Engelbert Dollfuss a donné des résultats intéressants, car les dossiers du service de police du monarque austro-hongrois étaient remarquablement complets.*[555]

Cette affirmation concernant l'illégitimité d'Hitler est entièrement réfutée dans un livre d'Eugène Davidson, plus solidement étayé, qui implique la famille Frankenberger, et non la famille Rothschild.

En tout état de cause, et c'est plus pertinent de notre point de vue, la banque de façade August Thyssen aux Pays-Bas - c'est-à-dire la Bank voor Handel en Scheepvaart N.V. - contrôlait l'Union Banking Corporation à New York. Les Harriman avaient des intérêts financiers dans cette Union Banking Corporation, dont E. Roland Harriman (le frère d'Averell) était l'un des directeurs. L'Union Banking Corporation de New York était une opération conjointe de Thyssen et Harriman avec les directeurs suivants en 1932[556]:

E. Roland HARRIMAN	Vice-président de W. A. Harriman & Co, New York
H.J. KOUWENHOVEN	Banquier nazi, associé gérant de la August Thyssen Bank et de la Bank voor Handel Scheepvaart N.V. (la banque de transfert des fonds de Thyssen)
J. G. GROENINGEN	Vereinigte Stahlwerke (le cartel de l'acier qui a également financé Hitler)
C. LIEVENSE	Président, Union Banking Corp, New York City
E. S. JAMES	Partenaire Brown Brothers, puis Brown Brothers, Harriman & Co.

---

[554] Examen du Dr Fritz Thyssen.

[555] Fritz Thyssen, *I Paid Hitler*, (New York : Farrar & Rinehart, Inc., 1941). p. 159.

[556] Tiré de *Bankers Directory*, 1932 édition, p, 2557 et Poors, *Directory of Directors*. J.L. Guinter et Knight Woolley étaient également directeurs.

En liquidant ces affaires russes en 1929, Averell Harriman a reçu un bénéfice inattendu d'un million de dollars de la part des Soviétiques, réputés pour avoir la dent dure et ne rien donner sans contrepartie. Parallèlement à ces succès dans la finance internationale, Averell Harriman a toujours été attiré par le service dit "public". En 1913, le service "public" d'Harriman a débuté par une nomination à la Commission du Parc des Palissades. En 1933, Harriman est nommé président du Comité de l'emploi de l'État de New York et, en 1934, il devient administrateur de la NRA de Roosevelt - une création mussolinienne de Gerard Swope de General Electric.[557] Il s'ensuit un flot de postes "publics", d'abord dans le cadre du programme de prêts-bails, puis comme ambassadeur en Union soviétique, puis comme secrétaire au commerce.

[557] Voir Antony C. Sutton, *Wall Street et FDR*. Chapitre neuf, "Le plan Swope", *op. cit.*

TABLEAU 7-1 : LIENS FINANCIERS ENTRE LES INDUSTRIELS AMÉRICAINS ET ADOLF HITLER

Date	Banquiers américains et les industriels	Entreprise affiliée aux États-Unis	Source allemande		Intermédiaire pour les fonds/agent
1923	Henry FORD	FORD MOTOR COMPANY	—		—
1931	E.R. HARRIMAN	UNION BANKING CORP	Fritz THYSSEN	250.000 RM	Bank voor Handel en Scheepvaart N.V. (Filiale de la August Thyssen Bank)
1932		Flick (un directeur de l' AEG)	Friedrich FLICK	150.000 RM	Directement vers le NSDAP
		AUCUNE	Emil KIRDORF	600.000 RM	"Nationale Treuhand" a/c à la Delbrück Schickler Bank
Février-mars 1933	Edsel B. FORD C.E. MITCHELL	AMERICAN I.G.	I.G. FARBEN	400.000 RM	"Nationale Treuhand
Février-mars 1933	Walter TEAGLE Faul M. WARBURG	AUCUNE	Reichsverband der Automobilindustrie	100.000 RM	"Nationale Treuhand
Février-mars 1933	Gérard SWOPE Owen D. YOUNG C.H. MINOR	INTERNATIONAL GENERAL ELECTRIC	A.E.G.	60.000 RM	"Nationale Treuhand
Février-mars 1933	E. Arthur BALDWIN	AUCUNE	DEMAG	50.000 RM	
Février-mars 1933	Owen D. YOUNG	INTERNATIONAL GENERAL ELECTRIC	OSRAM G.m.b.H.	40.000 RM	"Nationale Treuhand

Février-mars 1933	Sosthène BEHN	I.T.T.	Telefunken	35.000 RM	"Nationale Treuhand
Février-mars 1933		AUCUNE	Karl Herrman	300.000 RM	"Nationale Treuhand
Février-mars 1933		AUCUNE	A. Steinke (Directeur de BYBUAG)	200.000 RM	"Nationale Treuhand
Février-mars 1933		AUCUNE	Karl Lange (Industrie des machines)	50.000 RM	"Nationale Treuhand
Février-mars 1933		AUCUNE	F. Springorum (Hoesch A.G.)	36.000 RM	"Nationale Treuhand
Février-mars 1933	Edsel B. FORD	Ford Motor Co.	Carl BOSCH (I.G. Farben & Ford Motor A.G.)		
1932-1944	Walter TEAGLE J.A. MOFFETT W.S. FARISH	Standard Oil de N.J.	Emil HELFFRICH (German-American Petroleum Co)		Heinrich Himmler S.S. via le cercle de Keppler
1932-1944	Sosthène BEHN	I.T.T.	Kurt von SCHRÖDER Mix & Genest Lorenz		Heinrich Himmler S.S. via le cercle de Keppler

En revanche, E. Roland Harriman a limité ses activités aux affaires privées dans le domaine de la finance internationale sans s'aventurer, comme le faisait son frère Averell, dans le service "public". En 1922, Roland et Averell ont créé la société W. A. Harriman & Company. Plus tard encore, Roland devient président du conseil d'administration de l'Union Pacific Railroad et administrateur du magazine *Newsweek,* de la Mutual Life Insurance Company of New York, membre du conseil des gouverneurs de la Croix-Rouge américaine et membre de l'American Museum of Natural History.

Le financier nazi Hendrik Jozef Kouwenhoven, co-directeur de Roland Harriman à l'Union Banking Corporation à New York, était directeur général de la Bank voor Handel en Scheepvaart N.V. (BHS) de Rotterdam. En 1940, la BHS détenait environ 2,2 millions de dollars d'actifs dans l'Union Banking Corporation, qui à son tour faisait la plupart de ses affaires avec la BHS.[558] Dans les années 1930, Kouwenhoven était également directeur de la Vereinigte Stahlwerke A.G., le cartel de l'acier fondé avec des fonds de Wall Street au milieu des années 1920. Comme le baron Schroder, il était un partisan important d'Hitler.

Un autre directeur de la New York Union Banking Corporation était Johann Groeninger, un citoyen allemand ayant de nombreuses affiliations industrielles et financières avec Vereinigte Stahlwerke, le groupe August Thyssen, et un poste de directeur de August Thyssen Hutte A.G.[559]

Cette affiliation et cet intérêt commercial mutuel entre Harriman et les intérêts de Thyssen ne suggèrent pas que les Harriman aient directement financé Hitler. En revanche, cela montre que les Harriman étaient intimement liés aux nazis Kouwenhoven et Groeninger et à une banque de façade nazie, la Bank voor Handel en Scheepvaart. Il y a tout lieu de croire que les Harriman étaient au courant du soutien de Thyssen aux nazis. Dans le cas des Harriman, il est important de garder à l'esprit leur relation intime et durable avec l'Union soviétique et la position des Harriman au centre du New Deal de Roosevelt et du Parti démocratique. Les preuves suggèrent que certains membres de l'élite de Wall Street sont liés à, et ont certainement de l'influence sur tous les groupements politiques importants du spectre socialiste mondial contemporain - le socialisme soviétique, le national-socialisme d'Hitler et le New Deal socialiste de Roosevelt.

LE FINANCEMENT D'HITLER LORS DES ÉLECTIONS GÉNÉRALES DE MARS 1933

En mettant de côté les affaires Georg Bell-Deterding et Thyssen-Harriman, nous examinons maintenant le noyau du soutien d'Hitler. En mai 1932, la rencontre dite du "Kaiserhof" a eu lieu entre Schmitz de I.G. Farben, Max Ilgner de l'Américain I.G. Farben, Kiep de la ligne Hambourg-Amérique et Diem du Trust allemand de la potasse. Plus de 500 000 marks ont été levés lors de cette

[558] Voir Élimination des ressources allemandes, p. 728-30.

[559] Pour d'autres liens encore entre l'Union Banking Corp. et les entreprises allemandes, voir Ibid, pp. 728-30.

réunion et déposés au crédit de Rudolf Hess à la Deutsche Bank. Il est intéressant de noter, à la lumière du "mythe de Warburg" décrit au chapitre 10, que Max Ilgner de l'Américain I.G. Farben a contribué à hauteur de 100 000 RM, soit un cinquième du total. Le livre de "Sidney Warburg" revendique l'implication de Warburg dans le financement d'Hitler, et Paul Warburg était un directeur de l'américain I.G. Farben[560] alors que Max Warburg était un directeur de I.G. Farben.

Il existe des preuves documentaires irréfutables d'un autre rôle des banquiers et des industriels internationaux dans le financement du parti nazi et du *Volkspartie* pour les élections allemandes de mars 1933. Au total, trois millions de Reichsmarks ont été souscrits par des entreprises et des hommes d'affaires de premier plan, convenablement "lavés" par un compte à la Delbruck Schickler Bank, puis remis entre les mains de Rudolf Hess pour être utilisés par Hitler et le NSDAP. Ce transfert de fonds a été suivi par l'incendie du Reichstag, l'abrogation des droits constitutionnels et la consolidation du pouvoir nazi. L'accès au Reichstag par les incendiaires se faisait par un tunnel depuis une maison où logeait Putzi Hanfstaengl ; l'incendie du Reichstag lui-même a été utilisé par Hitler comme prétexte pour abolir les droits constitutionnels. En bref, quelques semaines après le financement majeur de Hitler, une série d'événements majeurs se sont succédés : la contribution financière de banquiers et d'industriels de premier plan aux élections de 1933, l'incendie du Reichstag, l'abrogation des droits constitutionnels et la prise de pouvoir ultérieure par le parti nazi.

La réunion de collecte de fonds s'est tenue le 20 février 1933 dans la maison de Goering, qui était alors président du Reichstag, avec Hjalmar Horace Greeley Schacht comme hôte. Parmi les personnes présentes, selon von Schnitzler de I.G. Farben, se trouvaient :

> *Krupp von Bohlen, qui, au début de 1933, était président du Reichsverband der Deutschen Industrie Reich Association of German Industry ; Dr. Albert Voegler, le dirigeant des Vereinigte Stahlwerke ; Von Loewenfeld ; Dr. Stein, chef de la Gewerkschaft Auguste-Victoria, une mine qui appartient à l'IG.*[561]

Hitler a exposé ses opinions politiques aux hommes d'affaires réunis dans un long discours de deux heures et demie, en utilisant à bon escient la menace du communisme et d'une prise de pouvoir communiste :

> *Il ne suffit pas de dire que nous ne voulons pas du communisme dans notre économie. Si nous continuons sur notre ancienne voie politique, alors nous périrons. ....C'est la tâche la plus noble du dirigeant que de trouver des idéaux plus forts que les facteurs qui rassemblent le peuple. J'ai reconnu, même à l'hôpital, qu'il fallait chercher de nouveaux idéaux propices à la reconstruction. Je les ai trouvés dans le nationalisme, dans la valeur de la personnalité, et dans le refus de la réconciliation entre les nations...*

---

[560] Voir le chapitre 10.

[561] *NMT*, Volume VII, p. 555.

> *Nous sommes maintenant à la veille des dernières élections. Quel que soit le résultat, il n'y aura pas de recul, même si les prochaines élections n'entraînent pas de décision, d'une manière ou d'une autre. Si l'élection ne décide pas, la décision doit être prise par d'autres moyens. Je suis intervenu afin de donner une fois de plus au peuple la possibilité de décider de son sort par lui-même ....*
>
> *Il n'y a que deux possibilités, soit de repousser l'adversaire pour des raisons constitutionnelles, et à cette fin encore une fois cette élection ; soit une lutte sera menée avec d'autres armes, ce qui peut exiger de plus grands sacrifices. J'espère que le peuple allemand reconnaîtra ainsi la gravité de l'heure.*[562]

Après l'intervention de Hitler, Krupp von Bohlen a exprimé le soutien des industriels et des banquiers assemblés sous la forme concrète d'un fonds politique de trois millions de marks. Ce fonds s'avéra plus que suffisant pour acquérir le pouvoir, car 600 000 marks restèrent inutilisés après les élections.

Hjalmar Schacht a organisé cette rencontre historique. Nous avons déjà décrit les liens de Schacht avec les États-Unis : son père était caissier pour la branche berlinoise d'Equitable Assurance, et Hjalmar était intimement lié à Wall Street presque tous les mois.

Le plus grand contributeur au fonds a été I.G. Farben, qui s'est engagé à hauteur de 80% (ou 500 000 marks) du total. Le directeur A. Steinke, de BUBIAG (Braunkohlen-u. Brikett-Industrie A.G.), une filiale de I.G. Farben, a personnellement contribué à hauteur de 200 000 marks supplémentaires. En bref, 45% des fonds pour l'élection de 1933 proviennent de I.G. Farben. Si nous regardons les directeurs de l'entreprise américaine I.G. Farben - la filiale américaine d'I.G. Farben - nous nous rapprochons des racines de l'implication de Wall Street dans Hitler. Le conseil d'administration d'American I.G. Farben comptait à cette époque certains des noms les plus prestigieux parmi les industriels américains : Edsel B. Ford de la Ford Motor Company, C.E. Mitchell de la Federal Reserve Bank of New York, et Walter Teagle, directeur de la Federal Reserve Bank of New York, de la Standard Oil Company du New Jersey et de la Georgia Warm Springs Foundation du président Franklin D. Roosevelt.

Paul M. Warburg, premier directeur de la Federal Reserve Bank of New York et président de la Bank of Manhattan, était un directeur de Farben et en Allemagne, son frère Max Warburg était également directeur de I.G, Farben. H. A. Metz, de I.G. Farben, était également directeur de la Warburg's Bank of Manhattan. Enfin, Carl Bosch, de l'Américain I.G. Farben, a également été directeur de la Ford Motor Company A-G en Allemagne.

Trois membres du conseil d'administration de l'Américain I.G. Farben ont été reconnus coupables lors du procès pour crimes de guerre de Nuremberg : Max Ilgner, F. Ter Meer et Hermann Schmitz. Comme nous l'avons noté, les membres américains du conseil d'administration - Edsel Ford, C. E. Mitchell, Walter Teagle et Paul Warburg - n'ont pas été jugés à Nuremberg et, d'après les archives, il semble qu'ils n'aient même pas été interrogés sur leur connaissance du fonds Hitler de 1933.

---

[562] Josiah E. Dubois, Jr, *Generals in Grey Suits*, op. cit. p. 323.

LES CONTRIBUTIONS POLITIQUES DE 1933

Qui sont les industriels et les banquiers qui ont mis des fonds électoraux à la disposition du parti nazi en 1933 ? La liste des contributeurs et le montant de leur contribution sont les suivants :

CONTRIBUTIONS FINANCIÈRES À HITLER : 23 février-mars. 13, 1933 :
(Le compte Hjalmar Schacht chez Delbruck, Schickler Bank)

Contributions politiques des entreprises (avec certains directeurs affiliés)	Montant promis	Pourcentage du total de l'entreprise
Association pour les intérêts miniers (Kitdorf)	$600,000	45.8
I.G. Farbenindustrie (Edsel Ford, C.E. Mitchell, Walter Teagle, Paul Warburg)	400,000	30.5
Salon de l'automobile, Berlin (Reichsverbund der Automobilindustrie S.V.)	100,000	7.6
A.E.G., German General Electric (Gerard Swope, Owen Young, C.H. Minor, Arthur Baldwin)	60,000	4.6
Demag	50,000	3.8
Osram G.m.b.H. (Owen Young)	40,000	3.0
Telefunken Company pour la télégraphie sans fil	85,000	2.7
Accumulatoren-Fabrik A.G. (Quandt of A.E.G.)	25,000	1.9
Total de l'industrie	1,310,000	99.9

Plus les contributions politiques des hommes d'affaires individuels :

Karl Hermann	300,000
Directeur A. Steinke (BUBIAG- Braunkohlen-u. Brikett - Industrie A.G.)	200,000

Vous. Karl Lange (membre directeur du conseil d'administration du Verein Deutsches Maschinenbau-Anstalten)	50,000
Dr. F. Springorum (Président : Eisen-und Stahlwerke Hoesch A.G.)	36,000

Source : Voir l'annexe pour la traduction du document original.

Comment pouvons-nous prouver que ces paiements politiques ont réellement eu lieu ? Les paiements à Hitler dans cette dernière étape sur la route du nazisme dictatorial ont été effectués par la banque privée de Delbruck Sehickler. La Delbruck Schickler Bank était une filiale de la Metallgesellschaft A.G. ("Metall"), un géant industriel, la plus grande entreprise de métaux non ferreux en Allemagne, et l'influence dominante dans le "commerce" mondial des métaux non ferreux. Les principaux actionnaires de *"Metall"* étaient I.G. Farben et la British Metal Corporation. On peut noter incidemment que les directeurs britanniques du "Metall" *Aufsichsrat* étaient Walter Gardner (Amalgamated Metal Corporation) et le capitaine Oliver Lyttelton (également au conseil d'administration d'Amalgamated Metal et, paradoxalement, plus tard au cours de la Seconde Guerre mondiale, pour devenir le ministre britannique de la production).

Il existe parmi les pièces du procès de Nuremberg les originaux des bordereaux de virement de la division bancaire de I.G. Farben et d'autres sociétés énumérées à la page 110 vers la Delbruck Schickler Bank à Berlin, informant la banque du transfert de fonds de la Dresdner Bank, et d'autres banques, vers leur compte de la Nationale Treuhand (tutelle nationale*)*. Ce compte a été utilisé par Rudolf Hess pour les dépenses du parti nazi pendant les élections. La traduction du bordereau de virement de I.G. Farben, choisi comme échantillon, est la suivante

Traduction de la lettre de I.G. Farben du 27 février 1933, conseillant le transfert de 400 000 Reichsmarks sur le compte de la Tutelle nationale :
I.G. FARBENINDUSTRIE AKTIENGESELLSCHAFT
Département de la Banque

> Ferme : Delbruck Schickler & Cie, BERLIN W.8
> Mauerstrasse 63/65, Francfort (Main) 20
> Notre référence : (mention dans la réponse)
> 27 février 1933 B./Goe.
> Nous vous informons par la présente que nous avons autorisé la Dresdner Bank de Francfort-sur-le-Main à vous payer demain matin : RM 400.000 que vous utiliserez en faveur du compte "NATIONALE TREUHAND" (Tutelle nationale).
> Respectueusement,
> I.G. Farbenindustrie Aktiengesellschaft par ordre :
> (Signé) SELCK (Signé) BANGERT
> Par livraison spéciale.[563]

[563] *NMT,* Volume VII, p. 565.

À ce stade, nous devrions prendre note des efforts qui ont été faits pour détourner notre attention des financiers américains (et des financiers allemands liés à des sociétés affiliées aux États-Unis) qui étaient impliqués dans le financement d'Hitler. Habituellement, la responsabilité du financement d'Hitler a été exclusivement attribuée à Fritz Thyssen ou Emil Kirdorf. Dans le cas de Thyssen, cette accusation a été largement diffusée dans un livre dont l'auteur présumé était Thyssen au milieu de la Seconde Guerre mondiale, mais qu'il a par la suite répudié.[564] La raison pour laquelle Thyssen a voulu se démettre avant la défaite du nazisme reste inexpliquée.

Emil Kirdorf, qui est mort en 1937, a toujours été fier de son association avec la montée du nazisme. La tentative de limiter le financement d'Hitler à Thyssen et Kirdorf s'étendit jusqu'aux procès de Nuremberg en 1946, et ne fut contestée que par le délégué soviétique. Même le délégué soviétique n'était pas disposé à produire des preuves d'associations américaines ; cela n'est pas surprenant, car l'Union soviétique dépend de la bonne volonté de ces mêmes financiers pour transférer en URSS la technologie occidentale avancée dont elle a tant besoin.

À Nuremberg, des déclarations ont été faites et autorisées à ne pas être contestées, qui étaient directement contraires aux preuves directes connues présentées ci-dessus. Par exemple, Buecher, directeur général de la General Electric allemande, a été exonéré de toute sympathie pour Hitler :

> *Thyssen a avoué son erreur comme un homme et a courageusement payé une lourde peine pour cela. De l'autre côté se trouvent des hommes comme Reusch de la Gutehoffnungshuette, Karl Bosch, le défunt président du I.G. Farben Aufsichtsrat, qui aurait très probablement connu une triste fin s'il n'était pas mort à temps. Leurs sentiments étaient partagés par le vice-président du Aufsichtsrat de Kalle. Les sociétés Siemens et AEG qui, à côté d'I.G. Farben, étaient les plus puissantes entreprises allemandes, étaient des opposants déterminés au national-socialisme.*
>
> *Je sais que cette attitude hostile de la part de Siemens à l'égard des nazis a eu pour conséquence un traitement assez brutal de la firme. Le directeur général de l'AEG (Allgemeine Elektrizitats Gesellschaft), Geheimrat Buecher, que j'ai connu lors de mon séjour dans les colonies, était tout sauf un nazi. Je peux assurer au général Taylor qu'il est certainement faux d'affirmer que les grands industriels en tant que tels ont favorisé Hitler avant sa prise de pouvoir.*[565]

Pourtant, à la page 56 de ce livre, nous reproduisons un document émanant de General Electric, qui transfère des fonds de General Electric sur le compte de la National Trusteeship contrôlé par Rudolf Hess au nom d'Hitler et utilisé lors des élections de 1933.

---

[564] Fritz Thyssen, *I Paid Hitler,* (New York : Toronto : Farrat & Rinehart, Inc., 1941).

[565] *NMT,* Volume VI, pp. 1169-1170.

De même, von Schnitzler, qui était présent à la réunion de février 1933 au nom d'I.G. Farben, a nié les contributions d'I.G. Farben à la Nationale Treuhand de 1933 :

> *Je n'ai plus jamais entendu parler de toute cette affaire [celle du financement d'Hitler], mais je crois que le bureau de Goering ou de Schacht ou le Reichsverband der Deutschen Industrie avait demandé au bureau de Bosch ou de Schmitz le paiement de la part d'IG dans le fonds d'élection. Comme je n'ai pas repris l'affaire, je ne savais même pas à l'époque quel montant avait été payé par le GI. Selon le volume de l'IG, je devrais estimer la part de l'IG à quelque 10% du fonds électoral, mais pour autant que je sache, il n'y a aucune preuve que I.G. Farben ait participé aux paiements.*[566]

Comme nous l'avons vu, les preuves sont irréfutables en ce qui concerne les contributions politiques en espèces à Hitler au moment crucial de la prise de pouvoir en Allemagne - et le précédent discours de Hitler aux industriels a clairement révélé qu'une prise de pouvoir coercitive était l'intention préméditée.

Nous savons exactement qui a contribué, combien et par quels canaux. Il est à noter que les plus gros contributeurs - I.G. Farben, German General Electric (et sa société affiliée Osram), et Thyssen - étaient affiliés aux financiers de Wall Street. Ces financiers de Wall Street étaient au cœur de l'élite financière et ils occupaient une place importante dans la politique américaine contemporaine. Gerard Swope de General Electric était l'auteur du New Deal de Roosevelt, Teagle était l'un des principaux administrateurs de la NRA, Paul Warburg et ses associés à l'American I.G. Farben étaient les conseillers de Roosevelt. Ce n'est peut-être pas une coïncidence extraordinaire que le New Deal de Roosevelt - appelé "mesure fasciste" par Herbert Hoover - ait ressemblé si étroitement au programme de Hitler pour l'Allemagne, et que Hitler et Roosevelt aient pris le pouvoir le même mois de la même année - mars 1933.

[566] *NMT*, Volume VII, p. 565.

CHAPITRE VIII

PUTZI : AMI D'HITLER ET DE ROOSEVELT

Ernst Sedgewiek Hanfstaengl (ou Hanfy ou Putzi, comme on l'appelait plus souvent), comme Hjalmar Horace Greeley Schacht, était un autre Allemand-Américain au cœur de la montée de l'hitlérisme. Hanfstaengl est né dans une famille bien connue de la Nouvelle-Angleterre ; il était un cousin du général de la guerre de Sécession John Sedgewiek et un petit-fils d'un autre général de la guerre de Sécession, William Heine. Présenté à Hitler au début des années 1920 par le capitaine Truman-Smith, l'attaché militaire américain à Berlin, Putzi est devenu un ardent défenseur d'Hitler, a parfois financé les nazis et, selon l'ambassadeur William Dodd, "... il aurait sauvé la vie d'Hitler en 1923".[567]

Par coïncidence, le père du leader S.S. Heinrich Himmler était également l'entraineur de Putzi au gymnase royal bavarois Wilhelms. Les amis de Putzi à l'université de Harvard étaient des "futures personnalités remarquables" comme Walter Lippman, John Reed (qui a joué un rôle important décrit dans *Wall Street et la révolution bolchévique)* et Franklin D. Roosevelt. Après quelques années à Harvard, Putzi a créé l'entreprise artistique familiale à New York ; c'était une délicieuse combinaison d'affaires et de plaisir, car comme il le dit, "les noms célèbres qui m'ont rendu visite étaient légion, Pierpont Morgan, Toscanini, Henry Ford, Caruso, Santos-Dumont, Charlie Chaplin, Paderewski, et une fille du président Wilson".[568] C'est également à Harvard que Putzi s'est lié d'amitié avec le futur président Franklin Delano Roosevelt :

> *Je prenais la plupart de mes repas au Harvard Club, où je me suis lié d'amitié avec le jeune Franklin D. Roosevelt, à l'époque un sénateur de l'État de New York en pleine ascension. J'ai également reçu plusieurs invitations à rendre visite à son cousin éloigné Teddy, l'ancien président, qui s'était retiré dans sa propriété de Sagamore Hill.*[569]

---

[567] William E. Dodd, *Ambassador Dodd's Diary, 1933-1938,* (New York : Harcourt, Brace & Co., 1941), p. 360.

[568] Ernst Hanfstaengl, *Unheard Witness,* (New York : J.B. Lippincott, 1957), p. 28.

[569] Ibid.

De ces amitiés variées (et après avoir lu ce livre et ses prédécesseurs, *Wall Street et FDR* et *Wall Street et la révolution bolchévique*), le lecteur peut considérer que l'amitié de Putzi se limitait à un cercle particulièrement élitiste, Putzi est devenu non seulement un ami, un bailleur de fonds et un financier de Hitler, mais un de ses premiers partisans. Il était " ... presque la seule personne qui pouvait se permettre de franchir les limites parmi ses connaissances (d'Hitler)".[570]

En bref, Putzi était un citoyen américain au cœur de l'entourage d'Hitler du début des années 20 à la fin des années 30. En 1943, après avoir perdu la faveur des nazis et avoir été interné par les Alliés, Putzi a été libéré sous caution des misères d'un camp de prisonniers de guerre canadien par son ami et protecteur, le président Franklin D. Roosevelt. Lorsque les actions de FDR menacèrent de devenir un problème politique interne aux États-Unis, Putzi fut à nouveau interné en Angleterre. Comme s'il n'était pas assez surprenant de voir Heinrich Himmler et Franklin D. Roosevelt jouer un rôle important dans la vie de Putzi, nous découvrons également que les chants de marche des sections d'assaut nazies ont été composés par Hanfstaengl, "y compris celui qui a été joué par les brigades de chemises brunes lorsqu'elles traversèrent la porte de Brandebourg le jour où Hitler a pris le pouvoir.[571] Pour couronner le tout, Putzi a déclaré que la genèse du chant nazi "Sieg Heil, Sieg Heil", utilisé dans les rassemblements de masse nazis, n'était autre que "Harvard, Harvard, Harvard, rah, rah, rah".[572]

Putzi a certainement contribué au financement du premier quotidien nazi, le *Volkische Beobachter*. Il est moins facile de vérifier s'il a sauvé la vie d'Hitler des communistes, et bien qu'il ait été tenu - à son grand regret - à l'écart du processus d'écriture de *Mein Kampf* Putzi a eu l'honneur de financer sa publication, "et le fait qu'Hitler ait trouvé un personnel en état de marche lorsqu'il a été libéré de prison est entièrement dû à nos efforts".[573]

Lorsque Hitler est arrivé au pouvoir en mars 1933, simultanément avec Franklin Delano Roosevelt à Washington, un "émissaire" privé a été envoyé de Roosevelt à Washington D.C. pour rencontrer Hanfstaengl à Berlin, avec un message indiquant que, comme il semblait que Hitler allait bientôt prendre le pouvoir en Allemagne, Roosevelt espérait, au vu de leur longue connaissance, que Putzi ferait de son mieux pour éviter toute précipitation et toute initiative précipitée. "Pensez à votre jeu de piano et essayez d'utiliser la pédale douce si les choses deviennent trop bruyantes", tel était le message de FDR. "Si les choses commencent à devenir gênantes, veuillez contacter notre ambassadeur immédiatement.[574]

---

[570] Ibid, p. 52.

[571] Ibid, p. 53.

[572] Ibid, p. 59.

[573] Ibid, p. 122.

[574] Ibid, pp. 197-8.

Hanfstaengl est resté en contact étroit avec l'ambassadeur américain à Berlin, William E. Dodd - apparemment à son grand désarroi, car les commentaires enregistrés de Putzi sur Dodd sont nettement peu flatteurs :

> *À bien des égards, il [Dodd] était un représentant insatisfaisant. C'était un modeste petit professeur d'histoire du Sud, qui dirigeait son ambassade avec un minimum de moyens et essayait probablement de faire des économies sur son salaire. À une époque où il fallait un millionnaire robuste pour rivaliser avec la flamboyance des nazis, il se balançait avec effacement comme s'il était encore sur le campus de son université. Son esprit et ses préjugés étaient mesquins.*[575]

En fait, l'ambassadeur Dodd a tenté de refuser la nomination de Roosevelt au poste d'ambassadeur. Dodd n'avait pas d'héritage et préférait vivre de sa solde au Département d'État plutôt que du butin politique ; contrairement à l'homme politique Dodd était exigeant envers ceux dont il recevait de l'argent. En tout cas, Dodd commentait tout aussi sévèrement Putzi, "... il a donné de l'argent à Hitler en 1923, l'a aidé à écrire *Mein Kampf*, et était en tout point familier avec les motifs d'Hitler"...

Hanfstaengl était-il un agent de l'establishment libéral aux États-Unis ? Nous pouvons probablement écarter cette possibilité, car, selon Ladislas Farago, c'est Putzi qui a dénoncé la pénétration britannique de haut niveau du commandement hitlérien. Farago rapporte que le baron William S. de Ropp avait pénétré les plus hauts échelons nazis avant la Seconde Guerre mondiale et que Hitler s'était servi de lui "... comme consultant pour les affaires britanniques ".[576] De Ropp n'était soupçonné d'être un agent double que par Putzi. D'après Farago :

> *La seule personne... qui l'ait jamais soupçonné d'une telle duplicité et qui ait mis en garde le Führer à son sujet est l'erratique Putzi Hanfstaengl, le chef du bureau d'Hitler, formé à Harvard, qui traite avec la presse étrangère.*

Comme le note Farago, "Bill de Ropp jouait le jeu dans les deux camps - un agent double au sommet".[577] Putzi était tout aussi diligent pour mettre en garde ses amis, comme Hermann Goering, contre des espions potentiels dans leur camp. En témoigne l'extrait suivant des mémoires de Putzi, dans lequel il pointe le doigt accusateur d'espionnage sur le jardinier des Goering...

> *"Herman", ai-je dit un jour, "Je parie n'importe quel argent que ce Greinz est un espion de la police." "Putzi", Karin [Mme Herman Goering] est entrée par*

575 Ibid, p. 214.

576 Ladislas Farago, *The Game of the Foxes*, (New York : Bantam, 1973), p. 97.

577 Ibid, p. 106.

> *effraction, "c'est un type si gentil et un merveilleux jardinier." "Il fait exactement ce qu'un espion doit faire", lui ai-je dit, "il s'est rendu indispensable."*[578]

En 1941, Putzi n'était plus en faveur auprès d'Hitler et des nazis, il a fui l'Allemagne et a été interné dans un camp de prisonniers de guerre canadien. L'Allemagne et les États-Unis étant maintenant en guerre, Putzi a recalculé les chances et a conclu : "Maintenant, je savais avec certitude que l'Allemagne serait vaincue."[579] La libération de Putzi du camp de prisonniers de guerre a eu lieu grâce à l'intervention personnelle de son vieil ami, le président Roosevelt :

> *Un jour, un correspondant de la presse de Hearst nommé Kehoe a obtenu l'autorisation de visiter Fort Hens. J'ai réussi à avoir quelques mots avec lui dans un coin. "Je connais bien votre patron", lui ai-je dit. "Vous me rendrez un petit service ?" Heureusement, il a reconnu mon nom.*
>
> *Je lui ai donné une lettre qu'il a glissée dans sa poche. Elle était adressée au secrétaire d'État américain, Cordell Hull. Quelques jours plus tard, elle était sur le bureau de mon ami du Harvard Club, Franklin Delano Roosevelt. J'y proposais d'agir en tant que conseiller politique et psychologique dans la guerre contre l'Allemagne.*[580]

La réponse et l'offre de "travailler" pour la partie américaine ont été acceptées. Putzi a été installé dans un environnement confortable avec son fils, le sergent de l'armée américaine Egon Hanfstaengl, également présent en tant qu'assistant personnel. En 1944, sous la pression d'une menace républicaine de dénoncer le favoritisme de Roosevelt pour un ancien nazi, Egon est envoyé en Nouvelle-Guinée et Putzi se précipite en Angleterre, où les Britanniques l'internent rapidement pour la durée de la guerre, Roosevelt ou pas Roosevelt,

LE RÔLE DE PUTZI DANS L'INCENDIE DU REICHSTAG

Les amitiés et les manipulations politiques de Putzi purent ou non avoir de grandes conséquences, mais son rôle dans l'incendie du Reichstag est significatif. L'incendie du Reichstag le 27 février 1933 est l'un des événements clés des temps modernes. L'attentat a été utilisé par Adolf Hitler pour revendiquer une révolution communiste imminente, suspendre les droits constitutionnels et s'emparer du pouvoir totalitaire. À partir de ce moment, il n'y a plus eu de retour en arrière pour l'Allemagne ; le monde a été mis sur la voie de la Seconde Guerre mondiale.

À l'époque, l'incendie du Reichstag fut imputé aux communistes, mais il ne fait guère de doute, d'un point de vue historique, que le feu a été délibérément mis

---

[578] Ernst Hanfstaengl, *Unheard Witness, op.* cit. p. 76.

[579] Ibid.

[580] Ibid, pp. 310-11.

par les nazis pour fournir une excuse à la prise du pouvoir politique. Fritz Thyssen a fait ce commentaire lors des interrogatoires de Dustbin après la guerre :

> *Lorsque le Reichstag a été brûlé, tout le monde était sûr que cela avait été fait par les communistes. J'ai appris plus tard en Suisse que tout cela n'était qu'un mensonge.*[581]

Schacht déclare avec force :

> *De nos jours, il est clair que cette action ne peut être rattachée au parti communiste. Il sera difficile d'établir dans quelle mesure les différents nationaux-socialistes ont coopéré à la planification et à l'exécution de cet acte terroriste, mais compte tenu de tout ce qui a été révélé entre-temps, il faut admettre que Goebbels et Goering ont chacun joué un rôle de premier plan, l'un dans la planification, l'autre dans l'exécution du plan.*[582]

L'incendie du Reichstag a été délibérément déclenché, probablement à l'aide d'un liquide inflammable, par un groupe d'experts. C'est là que Putzi Hanfstaengl entre en scène. La question clé est de savoir comment ce groupe, déterminé à mettre le feu, a pu accéder au Reichstag pour faire son travail. Après 20 heures, une seule porte du bâtiment principal était déverrouillée et cette porte était gardée. Un peu avant 21 heures, une visite du bâtiment par les gardiens a indiqué que tout allait bien ; aucun liquide inflammable n'a été remarqué et rien n'était à signaler dans la salle des séances où l'incendie a pris naissance. Apparemment, personne n'aurait pu accéder au bâtiment du Reichstag après 21 heures, et personne n'a été vu entrer ou sortir entre 21 heures et le début de l'incendie.

Il n'y avait qu'une seule façon pour un groupe de personnes avec des matériaux inflammables d'entrer au Reichstag - par un tunnel qui reliait le Reichstag et le Palais du Président du Reichstag. Hermann Goering était président du Reichstag et vivait dans le Palais, et on sait que de nombreux hommes des S.A. et des S.S. se trouvaient dans le Palais. Selon les mots d'un auteur :

> *L'utilisation du passage souterrain, avec toutes ses complications, n'était possible qu'aux national-socialistes, l'avancée et la fuite de la bande incendiaire n'était possible qu'avec la connivence d'employés haut placés du Reichstag. Tous les indices, toutes les probabilités pointent de façon accablante dans une direction, pour conclure que l'incendie du Reichstag était l'œuvre des National-Socialistes.*[583]

---

[581] Rapport *Dustbin* EF/Me/1, interview de Thyssen, p. 13.

[582] Hjalmar Horace Greeley Schacht, *Confessions of "The Old Wizard"*, (Boston : Houghton Mifflin, 1956), p. 276.

[583] George Dimitrov, *The Reichstag Fire Trial*, (Londres : The Bodley Head, 1934), p. 309.

Comment Putzi Hanfstaengl s'inscrit-il dans ce tableau d'incendie criminel et d'intrigue politique ? Putzi - de son propre aveu - se trouvait dans la salle du Palais, à l'autre bout du tunnel menant au Reichstag. Et selon le procès pour incendie du Reichstag, Putzi Hanfstaengl se trouvait en fait dans le Palais lui-même pendant l'incendie :

> *L'appareil de propagande se tenait prêt, et les chefs des troupes d'assaut étaient à leur place. Les bulletins officiels étant planifiés à l'avance, les ordres d'arrestation préparés, Karwahne, Frey et Kroyer attendant patiemment dans leur café, les préparatifs étaient terminés, le schéma presque parfait.*[584]

Dimitrov l'affirme également :

> *Les dirigeants national-socialistes, Hitler, Goering et Goebbels, ainsi que les hauts fonctionnaires national-socialistes, Daluege, Hanfstaengl et Albrecht, étaient présents à Berlin le jour de l'incendie, bien que la campagne électorale ait atteint son apogée dans toute l'Allemagne, six jours avant le scrutin. Goering et Goebbels, sous serment, ont fourni des explications contradictoires pour leur présence "fortuite" à Berlin avec Hitler ce jour-là. Le national-socialiste Hanfstaengl, en tant qu'"invité" de Goering, était présent dans le palais du président du Reichstag, juste à côté du Reichstag, au moment où l'incendie a éclaté, bien que son "hôte" n'y soit pas à ce moment-là.*[585]

Selon le nazi Kurt Ludecke, il existait un document signé par le dirigeant de la S.A. Karl Ernst - qui aurait mis le feu et aurait été assassiné par la suite par d'autres nazis - qui impliquait Goering, Goebbels et Hanfstaengl dans la conspiration.

LE NEW DEAL DE ROOSEVELT ET LE NOUVEL ORDRE D'HITLER

Hjalmar Schacht a défié ses interrogateurs de Nuremberg d'après-guerre en faisant remarquer que le programme *New Order* (Nouvel Ordre) de Hitler était le même que celui du *New Deal* (Nouvelle Donne) de Roosevelt aux États-Unis. Les interrogateurs ont examiné et rejeté cette observation, ce qui est compréhensible. Cependant, quelques recherches suggèrent que non seulement les deux programmes sont assez similaires dans leur contenu, mais que les Allemands n'ont pas eu de mal à observer les similitudes. Il y a dans la bibliothèque Roosevelt un

---

[584] Ibid, p. 310.

[585] Ibid, p. 311.

petit livre présenté à FDR par le Dr. Helmut Magers en décembre 1933.[586] Sur la page de garde de cet exemplaire de présentation est inscrite l'inscription :

> *Au président des États-Unis, Franklin D. Roosevelt, en profonde admiration pour sa conception d'un nouvel ordre économique et avec dévotion pour sa personnalité. L'auteur, Baden, Allemagne, 9 novembre 1933.*

La réponse de FDR à cette admiration pour son nouvel ordre économique a été la suivante[587]:

> *(Washington) 19 décembre 1933*
> *Mon cher Dr Magers : Je tiens à vous remercier pour l'exemplaire de votre petit livre sur moi et le "New Deal". Bien que, comme vous le savez, j'aie fait mes études en Allemagne et que j'aie pu parler allemand avec une aisance considérable à une époque, je lis votre livre non seulement avec beaucoup d'intérêt, mais aussi parce qu'il va m'aider à améliorer mon allemand.*
> *Très sincèrement,*

Le New Deal ou le "nouvel ordre économique" n'est pas une créature du libéralisme classique. C'était une créature du socialisme d'entreprise. Les grandes entreprises, telles qu'elles étaient représentées à Wall Street, s'efforçaient de mettre en place un ordre étatique leur permettant de contrôler l'industrie et d'éliminer la concurrence, et c'était là le cœur du New Deal de FDR. La General Electric, par exemple, est très présente dans l'Allemagne nazie et dans le New Deal. La General Electric allemande était un important financier d'Hitler et du parti nazi, et A.E.G. a également financé Hitler directement et indirectement par l'intermédiaire d'Osram.

International General Electric à New York a été un participant majeur dans la propriété et la direction d'A.E.G. et d'Osram. Gerard Swope, Owen Young et A. Baldwin de General Electric aux États-Unis ont été directeurs d'A.E.G. Cependant, l'histoire ne s'arrête pas à General Electric et au financement d'Hitler en 1933.

Dans un livre précédent, *Wall Street et la révolution bolchévique,* l'auteur a identifié le rôle de General Electric dans la révolution bolchévique et la localisation géographique des participants américains au 120 Broadway, New York City ; les bureaux exécutifs de General Electric se trouvaient également au 120 Broadway. Lorsque Franklin Delano Roosevelt travaillait à Wall Street, son adresse était également le 120 Broadway. En fait, la Georgia Warm Springs Foundation, la fondation FDR, était située au 120 Broadway. Le principal bailleur de fonds d'une des premières entreprises Roosevelt de Wall Street du 120

---

[586] Helmut Magers, *Ein Revolutionar Aus Common Sense,* (Leipzig : R. Kittler Verlag, 1934).

[587] Nixon, Edgar B., rédacteur, *Franklin D. Roosevelt and Foreign Affairs,* (Cambridge : The Belknap Press of Harvard University Press, 1969), Volume 1 : janvier 1933-février 1934. Bibliothèque Franklin D. Roosevelt. Hyde Park, New York.

Broadway était Gerard Swope de General Electric. Et c'est le "plan de Swope" qui est devenu le "New Deal" de Roosevelt - le plan fasciste qu'Herbert Hoover ne voulait pas imposer aux États-Unis. En bref, le Nouvel Ordre d'Hitler et le New Deal de Roosevelt étaient tous deux soutenus par les mêmes industriels et leur contenu était assez similaire - c'est-à-dire qu'il s'agissait de plans pour la formation d'un État corporatif.

Il y avait alors des ponts, à la fois corporatifs et individuels, entre l'Amérique de FDR et l'Allemagne d'Hitler. Le premier pont était celui de l'Américain I.G. Farben, filiale américaine de I.G. Farben, la plus grande entreprise allemande. Paul Warburg, de la Banque de Manhattan et de la Banque de Réserve Fédérale de New York, siégeait au conseil d'administration de l'américain I.G. Farben. Le deuxième "pont" était entre International General Electric, une filiale à 100% de la General Electric Company et sa filiale en partie allemande, A.E.G. Gerard Swope, qui a formulé le New Deal de FDR, était président d'I.G.E. et membre du conseil d'administration d'A.E.G. Le troisième "pont" était entre Standard Oil du New Jersey et Vacuum Oil et sa filiale allemande à 100%, Deutsche-Amerikanisehe Gesellschaft. Le président de la Standard Oil du New Jersey était Walter Teagle, de la Banque de Réserve Fédérale de New York. Il était administrateur de la Georgia Warm Springs Foundation de Franklin Delano Roosevelt et a été nommé par FDR à un poste administratif clé de la National Recovery Administration.

Ces sociétés ont été profondément impliquées dans la promotion du New Deal de Roosevelt et dans la construction de la puissance militaire de l'Allemagne nazie. Le rôle de Putzi Hanfstaengl dans les premiers temps, jusqu'au milieu des années 1930 en tout cas, était un lien informel entre l'élite nazie et la Maison-Blanche. Après le milieu des années 1930, lorsque le monde s'est mis sur la voie de la guerre, l'importance de Putzi a décliné - tandis que les grandes entreprises américaines continuaient d'être représentées par des intermédiaires tels que le baron Kurt von Schroder, l'avocat Westrick, et l'adhésion au Cercle des Amis de Himmler.

CHAPITRE IX

WALL STREET ET LE PREMIER CERCLE NAZI

Pendant toute la période de nos contacts d'affaires, nous n'avions aucune idée du rôle de complice de Farben dans la politique brutale d'Hitler. Nous offrons toute l'aide que nous pouvons apporter pour que la vérité complète soit mise en lumière et qu'une justice impartiale soit rendue.

(F. W. Abrams, président du conseil d'administration, Standard Oil of New Jersey, 1946).

Adolf Hitler, Hermann Goering, Josef Goebbels et Heinrich Himmler, le groupe intérieur du nazisme, étaient en même temps les chefs de fiefs mineurs au sein de l'État nazi. Des groupes de pouvoir ou des cliques politiques étaient centrés autour de ces dirigeants nazis, et surtout, après la fin des années 1930, autour d'Adolf Hitler et d'Heinrich Himmler, le chef du Reich des S.S. (le redoutable *Schutzstaffel).* Le plus important de ces cercles intérieurs nazis a été créé sur ordre du Führer ; il a d'abord été connu sous le nom de "Cercle Keppler", puis de "Cercle des amis de Himmler".

Le Cercle Keppler a été créé par un groupe d'hommes d'affaires allemands soutenant la montée au pouvoir de Hitler avant et pendant 1933. Au milieu des années 1930, le Cercle Keppler est passé sous l'influence et la protection du chef des S.S. Himmler et sous le contrôle organisationnel du banquier de Cologne et de l'éminent homme d'affaires nazi Kurt von Schroder. Schroder, on s'en souviendra, était à la tête de la banque J.H. Stein en Allemagne et affilié à la L. Henry Schroder Banking Corporation de New York. C'est au sein de ces cercles les plus intimes, le noyau même du nazisme, que nous trouvons Wall Street, y compris la Standard Oil du New Jersey et I.T.T., représentée de 1933 à 1944.

Wilhelm Keppler, fondateur du premier Cercle des amis, illustre le phénomène bien connu de l'homme d'affaires politisé - c'est-à-dire un homme d'affaires qui arpente l'arène politique plutôt que le marché libre pour réaliser ses profits. Ces hommes d'affaires s'intéressent à la promotion des causes socialistes, car une société socialiste planifiée offre une possibilité de contrats plus lucratifs grâce à l'influence politique.

Sentant de telles possibilités de profit, Keppler rejoint les national-socialistes et est proche d'Hitler avant 1933. Le Cercle des amis est né d'une rencontre entre Adolf Hitler et Wilhelm Keppler en décembre 1931. Au cours de leur conversation - c'était plusieurs années avant que Hitler ne devienne dictateur - le futur Führer a exprimé le souhait d'avoir des hommes d'affaires allemands fiables à disposition pour des conseils économiques lorsque les nazis prendront le pouvoir. "Essayez d'obtenir quelques dirigeants économiques - ils ne doivent pas nécessairement être membres du Parti - qui seront à notre disposition lorsque nous prendrons le pouvoir.[588] C'est ce que Keppler s'est engagé à faire.

En mars 1933, Keppler est élu au Reichstag et devient l'expert financier de Hitler. Cela n'a duré que brièvement. Keppler fut remplacé par l'infiniment plus compétent Hjalmar Schacht, et envoyé en Autriche où il devint en 1938 commissaire du Reich, mais put encore utiliser sa position pour acquérir un pouvoir considérable dans l'État nazi. En quelques années, il s'empare d'une série de postes de direction lucratifs dans des entreprises allemandes, dont celui de président du conseil d'administration de deux filiales d'I.G. Farben : Braunkohle-Benzin A.G. et Kontinental Oil A.G. Braunkohle-Benzin était l'exploitant allemand de la technologie de Standard Oil of New Jersey pour la production d'essence à partir du charbon. (Voir le chapitre quatre).

En bref, Keppler a fait la guerre au président de la même entreprise qui a utilisé la technologie américaine pour l'indispensable essence synthétique qui a permis à la Wehrmacht d'entrer en guerre en 1939. Ce fait est significatif, car, associé aux autres preuves présentées dans ce chapitre, il suggère que les profits et le contrôle de ces technologies fondamentalement importantes à des fins militaires allemandes ont été conservés par un petit groupe de sociétés et d'hommes d'affaires internationaux opérant au-delà des frontières nationales.

Le neveu de Keppler, Fritz Kranefuss, sous la protection de son oncle, s'est également fait connaître en tant qu'adjudant du chef S.S. Heinrich Himmler et en tant qu'homme d'affaires et opérateur politique. C'est le lien de Kranefuss avec Himmler qui a conduit le cercle Keppler à s'éloigner progressivement d'Hitler dans les années 1930 pour se rapprocher de l'orbite de Himmler, où en échange de dons annuels aux projets S.S. de Himmler, les membres du cercle recevaient des faveurs politiques et une protection non négligeable de la part des S.S.

Le baron Kurt von Schroder était, comme nous l'avons noté, le représentant de l'I.T.T. dans l'Allemagne nazie et un des premiers membres du Cercle Keppler. Le premier cercle Keppler était composé de

LES MEMBRES ORIGINAUX (AVANT 1932) DU CERCLE KEPPLER

Membre du cercle	Principales associations
Wilhelm KEPPLER	Président de Braunkohle-Benzin A.G., filiale d'I.G. Farben (exploitée par Standard Oil of N.J., technologie du pétrole tiré du charbon)
Fritz KRANEFUSS	Neveu de Keppler et adjudant de Heinrich Himmler. Sur le stand de BRABAG
Kurt von SCHRODER	À bord de toutes les filiales internationales de téléphonie et de télégraphie en Allemagne
Karl Vincenz KROGMANN	Maire de Hambourg
Août ROSTERG	Directeur général de WINTERSHALL
Otto STEINBRINCK	Vice-président de VEREINIGTE STAHLWERKE

[588] Extrait de la déclaration sous serment de Wilhem Keppler, *NMT*, Volume VI, p. 285.

	(cartel de l'acier fondé avec des prêts de Wall Street en 1926)
Hjalmar SCHACHT	Président de la REICHSBANK
Emil HELFFRICH	Président du conseil d'administration de GERMAN-AMERICAN PETROLEUM CO. (détenue à 94% par Standard Oil du New Jersey) (voir ci-dessus sous Wilhelm Keppler)
Friedrich REINHARDT	Président du conseil d'administration COMMERZBANK
Ewald HECKER	Président du conseil d'administration d'ILSEDER HUTTE
Graf von BISMARCK	Président du gouvernement du STETTIN

LE CERCLE DES AMIS DE LA S.S.

Le premier Cercle des Amis a rencontré Hitler en mai 1932 et a entendu une déclaration des objectifs nazis. Heinrich Himmler participa alors fréquemment à ces réunions et, par son intermédiaire, divers officiers S.S. ainsi que d'autres hommes d'affaires se joignirent au groupe. Ce groupe s'est élargi au fil du temps pour devenir le Cercle des amis de Himmler, Himmler agissant comme protecteur et facilitateur pour ses membres.

Par conséquent, les intérêts bancaires et industriels - étaient fortement représentés dans le cercle restreint du nazisme, et leurs contributions financières d'avant 1933 à l'hitlérisme, que nous avons énumérées précédemment, ont été amplement remboursées. Parmi les "cinq grandes" banques allemandes, la Dresdner Bank avait les liens les plus étroits avec le parti nazi : au moins une douzaine de membres du conseil d'administration de la Dresdner Bank occupaient un haut rang nazi et pas moins de sept directeurs de la Dresdner Bank faisaient partie du cercle élargi des amis de Keppler, qui n'a jamais dépassé 40.

Lorsque l'on examine les noms comprenant à la fois le cercle Keppler d'origine d'avant 1933 et le cercle Keppler et Himmler élargi d'après 1933, on constate que les multinationales de Wall Street sont fortement représentées - plus que tout autre groupe institutionnel. Prenons chaque multinationale de Wall Street ou son associé allemand à tour de rôle - ceux identifiés au chapitre sept comme étant liés au financement d'Hitler - et examinons leurs liens avec Keppler et Heinrich Himmler.

I.G. FARBEN ET LE CERCLE KEPPLER

I.G. Farben était fortement représenté au sein du cercle Keppler : pas moins de huit des 40 membres du cercle rapproché étaient des directeurs d'I.G. Farben ou d'une filiale de Farben. Parmi ces huit membres figuraient, outre le baron Kurt von Schroder, Wilhelm Keppler et son neveu Kranefuss, décrits précédemment. La présence de Farben a été soulignée par le membre Hermann Schmitz, président de I.G. Farben et directeur de Vereinigte Stahlwerke, deux cartels construits et consolidés par les prêts de Wall Street des années 1920. Un rapport du Congrès américain a décrit Hermann Schmitz comme suit :

> *Hermann Schmitz, l'une des personnalités les plus importantes d'Allemagne, a remporté des succès remarquables simultanément dans les trois domaines distincts que sont l'industrie, la finance et le gouvernement, et a servi avec zèle et dévouement tous les gouvernements au pouvoir. Il symbolise le citoyen allemand qui, à partir des ravages de la Première Guerre mondiale, a rendu possible la Seconde.*
>
> *Ironiquement, on peut dire que sa culpabilité est d'autant plus grande qu'en 1919, il était membre de la délégation pour la paix du Reich et que, dans les années 1930, il a été en mesure d'apprendre aux nazis ce qu'ils devaient savoir concernant la pénétration économique, les utilisations des cartels, les matériaux synthétiques pour la guerre.*[589]

Friedrich Flick, créateur du cartel de l'acier Vereinigte Stahlwerke et directeur d'Allianz Versicherungs A.G. et de German General Electric (A.E.G.), était un autre membre du Keppler Circle au sein du conseil d'administration d'I.G. Farben.

Heinrich Schmidt, directeur de la Dresdner Bank et président du conseil d'administration de Braunkohle-Benzin A.G., filiale d'I.G. Farben, était dans le cercle ; tout comme Karl Rasehe, autre directeur de la Dresdner Bank et directeur de la Metallgesellschaft (société mère de la Delbruck Schickler Bank) et des Accumulatoren-Fabriken A.G. Heinrich Buetefisch était également directeur d'I.G. Farben et membre du cercle Keppler. En bref, la contribution d'I.G. Farben à la Caisse nationale de Rudolf Hess - la caisse noire politique - a été confirmée après la prise de pouvoir de 1933 par une forte représentation dans le cercle intérieur nazi.

Combien de ces membres du Keppler Circle dans le complexe I.G. Farben étaient affiliés à Wall Street ?

LES MEMBRES DU PREMIER CERCLE DE KEPPLER ASSOCIÉ AUX MULTINATIONALES AMÉRICAINES

Membre du Cercle Keppler	I.G. Farben	I.T.T.	Standard Oil du New Jersey	General Electric
Wilhelm KEPPLER	Président de BRABAG, filiale de Farben		—	
Fritz KRANEFUSS	Sur Aufsichrat de BRABAG		—	
Emil Heinrich MEYER		Présent au sein de toutes les filiales allemandes de I.T.T : Standard/Mix & Genest/Lorenz	—	Conseil d'administration de l'A.E.G.
Emil HELFFRICH			Président de la DAPAG (détenue à 94% par le Standard du New Jersey	

[589] Élimination des ressources allemandes, p. 869.

Friedrich FLICK	I.G. Farben	—	—	Conseil d'administration de l'A.E.G.
Kurt von SCHRODER		À bord de toutes les filiales I.T.T. en Allemagne		

De même, nous pouvons identifier d'autres institutions de Wall Street représentées dans le premier cercle des amis de Keppler, confirmant leurs contributions monétaires au Fonds de Tutelle National géré par Rudolf Hess au nom d'Adolf Hitler. Ces représentants étaient Emil Heinrich Meyer et le banquier Kurt von Schroder au sein des conseils d'administration de toutes les filiales I.T.T. en Allemagne, et Emil Helffrich, le président du conseil d'administration de la DAPAG, détenue à 94% par la Standard Oil du New Jersey.

WALL STREET DANS LE CERCLE S.S.

Les grandes multinationales américaines étaient également très bien représentées dans le futur Cercle d'Heinrich Himmler et ont apporté des contributions en espèces aux S.S. (au Sonder Konto S) jusqu'en 1944 - alors que la Seconde Guerre mondiale était en cours.

Près d'un quart des contributions faites au Sonder Konto S de 1944 provenaient des filiales de International Telephone and Telegraph, représentées par Kurt von Schröder. Les versements de 1943 des filiales de l'I.T.T. au compte spécial ont été les suivants :

Mix & Genest A.G.	5.000 RM
C. Lorenz AG	20.000 RM
Felten & Guilleaume25.	25.000 RM
Kurt von Schroder	16.000 RM

Et les paiements de 1944 l'ont été :

Mix & Genest A.G .	5.000 RM
C. Lorenz AG	20.000 RM
Felten & Guilleaume20.	25.000 RM
Kurt von Schroder	16.000 RM

Sosthenes Behn, de International Telephone and Telegraph, a transféré le contrôle de Mix & Genest, de C. Lorenz, et des autres intérêts de Standard Telephone en Allemagne à Kurt von Schroder - qui était un membre fondateur du Keppler Circle et l'organisateur et le trésorier du Cercle des Amis de Himmler. Emil H. Meyer, S.S. Untersturmführer, membre du Vorstand de la Dresdner Bank, A.E.G., et directeur de toutes les filiales d'I.T.T. en Allemagne, était également membre du Cercle des Amis de Himmler - donnant à I.T.T. deux puissants représentants au cœur de la S.S.

Une lettre du baron von Schroder à son confrère Emil Meyer, datée du 25 février 1936, décrit les objectifs et les exigences du cercle Himmler et la nature ancienne du compte spécial "S" avec des fonds dans la propre banque de Schroder - la J,H. Stein Bank de Cologne :

> Au Prof. Dr. Emil H. Meyer
> Berlin, 25 février 1936 (écriture illisible)
> S.S. (Untersturmführer) (sous-lieutenant) Membre du conseil d'administration (Vorstand) de la Dresdner Bank
> Berlin W. 56, Behrenstr. 38
> Personnel !
> Au Cercle des Amis du Leader du Reich SS,
> À l'issue de la tournée d'inspection de 2 jours à Munich à laquelle le Chef du Reich SS nous avait conviés en janvier dernier, le Cercle des Amis a accepté de mettre - chacun selon ses moyens - à la disposition du Chef du Reich sur le "Compte spécial S" (Sonder Konto S), à établir auprès de la société bancaire J.H. Stein à Cologne, des fonds qui doivent être utilisés pour certaines tâches en dehors du budget.
> Cela devrait permettre au chef du Reich de s'appuyer sur tous ses amis. À Munich, il a été décidé que les soussignés se rendraient disponibles pour la création et la gestion de ce compte. Entre-temps, le compte a été ouvert et nous voulons que chaque participant sache que s'il souhaite apporter des contributions au Leader du Reich pour les tâches susmentionnées - soit au nom de son entreprise, soit au nom du Cercle des Amis - il peut effectuer des paiements à la société bancaire J.H. Stein, Cologne (compte de compensation de la Banque du Reich, compte de chèques postaux n° 1392) sur le compte spécial S.
> Heil Hitler !
>
> (Signé) Kurt Baron von Sehroder
> (Signé) Steinbrinck[590]

Cette lettre explique également pourquoi le colonel Bogdan de l'armée américaine, anciennement de la Schroder Banking Corporation à New York, était soucieux de détourner l'attention des enquêteurs de l'armée américaine de l'après-guerre de la banque J. H. Stein à Cologne vers les "grandes banques" de l'Allemagne nazie. C'est la banque Stein qui détenait les secrets des associations des filiales américaines avec les autorités nazies pendant la Seconde Guerre mondiale. Les intérêts financiers new-yorkais ne pouvaient pas connaître la nature précise de ces transactions (et en particulier la nature des documents qui auraient pu être conservés par leurs associés allemands), mais ils savaient qu'il pourrait bien exister des traces de leurs transactions en temps de guerre - suffisamment pour les embarrasser auprès du public américain. C'est cette possibilité que le colonel Bogdan a tenté sans succès d'écarter.

---

[590] *NMT*, Volume VII, p. 238. "Traduction du document N1-10103, pièce à conviction 788." Lettre de von Schroder et de l'accusé Steinbrinck au Dr Meyer, fonctionnaire de la Dresdner Bank, le 25 février 1936, notant que le Cercle des Amis mettrait des fonds à la disposition de Himmler "pour certaines tâches en dehors du budget" et avait créé un "compte spécial à cet effet".

La General Electric allemande a largement profité de son association avec Himmler et d'autres nazis de premier plan. Plusieurs membres de la clique Schroder étaient directeurs de l'A.E.G., le plus éminent étant Robert Pferdmenges, qui était non seulement membre des cercles Keppler ou Himmler mais aussi partenaire de la maison bancaire aryanisée Pferdmenges & Company, le successeur de l'ancienne maison bancaire juive Sal. Oppenheim de Cologne. Waldemar von Oppenheim a obtenu la distinction douteuse (pour un Juif allemand) de "Aryen honoraire" et a pu poursuivre l'activité de son ancienne maison bancaire établie sous Hitler en partenariat avec Pferdmenges.

MEMBRES DU CERCLE D'AMIS DE HIMMLER QUI ÉTAIENT ÉGALEMENT DIRECTEURS DE SOCIÉTÉS AFFILIÉES AUX ÉTATS-UNIS :

	I.G. Farben	I.T.T.	A.E.G.	Standard Oil du New Jersey
KRANEFUSS, Fritz	X			
KEPPLER, Wilhelm	X			
SCHRODER, Kurt	X			
Von BUETEFISCH, Heinrich		X		
RASCHE, Dr. Karl	X			
FLICK, Friedrich	X		X	
LINDEMANN, Karl				X
SCHMIDT, Heinrich	X			
ROEHNERT, Kellmuth			X	
SCHMIDT, Kurt			X	
MEYER, Dr. Emil		X		
SCHMITZ, Hermann	X			

Pferdmenges était également directeur de l'A.E.G. et a utilisé son influence nazie à bon escient.[591]

Deux autres directeurs de la General Electric allemande étaient membres du Cercle des amis de Himmler et ont fait des contributions monétaires au Sonder Konto S en 1943 et 1944 :

Friedrich Flick 100.000 RM

Otto Steinbrinck (un associé de Flick) 100.000 RM

Kurt Schmitt était président du conseil d'administration de l'A.E.G. et membre du cercle des amis de Himmler, mais le nom de Schmitt n'est pas inscrit sur la liste des paiements pour 1943 ou 1944.

Standard Oil du New Jersey a également apporté une contribution importante au compte spécial de Himmler par l'intermédiaire de sa filiale allemande, Deutsche-Amerikanische Gesellschaft (DAG), qu'elle détient à 94%. En 1943 et 1944, la DAG a apporté les contributions suivantes :

Le conseiller d'État Helfferich de German-American Petroleum A.G.	10.000 RM
Le conseiller d'État Lindemann de German-American Petroleum A.G	10.000 RM
et personnellement	4.000 RM

591 Élimination des ressources allemandes, p. 857.

Tableau 9-1 : Représentation de Wall Street dans les cercles de Keppler et de Himmler, 1933 et 1944

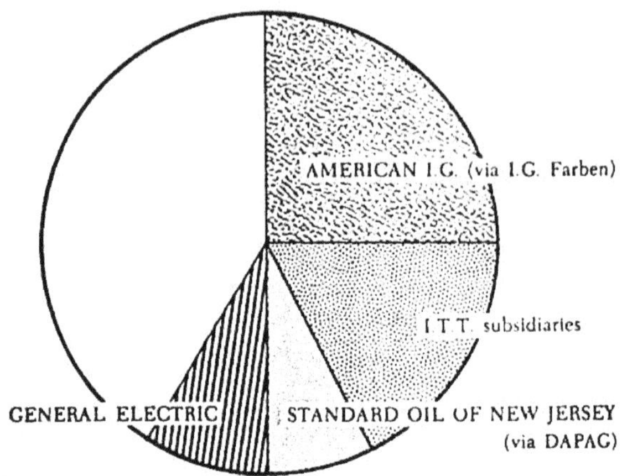

REPRESENTATION DE WALL STREET DANS LE CERCLE D'AMIS DE KEPPLER
(basée sur la déclaration de Keppler en 1933, relative aux membres)

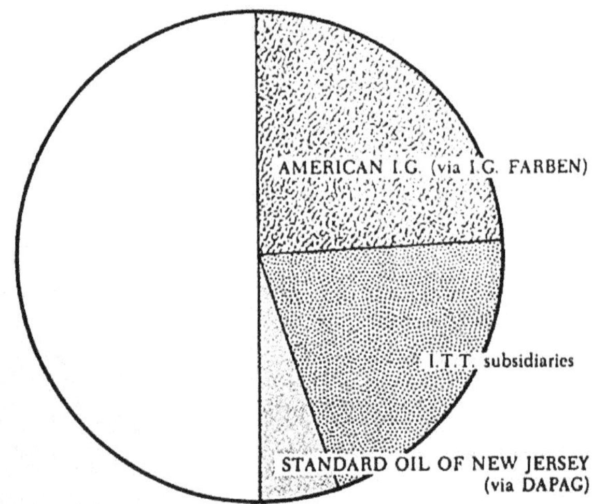

REPRESENTATION DE WALL STREET DANS LE CERCLE D'AMIS DE HIMMLER
(basée sur les contributions faites à Himmler en 1944)

Il est important de noter que le Staatsrat Lindemann a apporté une contribution personnelle de 4000 RM, faisant ainsi une distinction claire entre la contribution de 10 000 RM de la filiale à 100% de Standard Oil of New Jersey et la contribution personnelle du directeur Lindemann. Dans le cas du Staatsrat Hellfrich, la seule contribution a été celle de Standard Oil de 10 000 RM ; il n'y a pas de don personnel enregistré.

I.G. Farben, société mère d'American I.G. (voir chapitre 2), a également contribué de manière significative à la Sonder Konto S de Heinrich Himmler en la dotant de quatre administrateurs : Karl Rasehe, Fritz Kranefuss, Heinrich Schmidt et Heinrich Buetefisch. Karl Rasche était membre du comité de direction de la Dresdner Bank et un spécialiste du droit bancaire international. Sous Hitler, Karl Rasche est devenu un directeur éminent de nombreuses sociétés allemandes, dont Accumulatoren-Fabrik A.G. à Berlin, qui a financé Hitler, la Metallgesellschaft et Felten & Guilleame, une société de technologie de l'information. Fritz Kranefuss a été membre du conseil d'administration de la Dresdner Bank et administrateur de plusieurs sociétés, outre I.G. Farben. Kranefuss, neveu de Wilhelm Keppler, était avocat et jouait un rôle important dans de nombreuses organisations publiques nazies. Heinrich Schmidt, directeur de I.G. Farben et de plusieurs autres sociétés allemandes, était également directeur de la Dresdner Bank.

Il est important de noter que ces trois personnes - Rasche, Kranefuss et Schmidt - étaient les directeurs d'une filiale d'I.G. Farben, Braunkohle-Benzin A.G. - le fabricant allemand d'essence synthétique utilisant la technologie Standard Oil, résultat des accords I.G. Farben-Standard Oil du début des années 1930.

En bref, l'élite financière de Wall Street était bien représentée dans les premiers cercles Keppler et dans les cercles Himmler ultérieurs.[592]

[592] La nature significative de cette représentation est reflétée dans le graphique 8-1, "Représentation de Wall Street dans les cercles Keppler et Himmler, 1933 et 1944".

CHAPITRE X

LE MYTHE DE "SIDNEY WARBURG"

La question vitale, qui n'est que partiellement résolue, est de savoir dans quelle mesure l'accession d'Hitler au pouvoir en 1933 a été aidée directement par les financiers de Wall Street. Nous avons montré, à l'aide de documents originaux, qu'il y a eu une participation et un soutien indirects des Américains par l'intermédiaire de sociétés allemandes affiliées et (comme par exemple dans le cas de I.T.T.) qu'il y a eu un effort conscient et délibéré pour bénéficier du soutien du régime nazi. Ce financement indirect a-t-il été étendu au financement direct ?

Après l'arrivée au pouvoir d'Hitler, des entreprises et des particuliers américains ont travaillé au nom du nazisme et ont certainement profité de l'État nazi. Nous savons, grâce aux journaux intimes de William Dodd, l'ambassadeur américain en Allemagne, qu'en 1933, un flot de banquiers et d'industriels de Wall Street se sont présentés à l'ambassade américaine à Berlin, exprimant leur admiration pour Adolf Hitler - et désireux de trouver des moyens de faire des affaires avec le nouveau régime totalitaire. Par exemple, le 1er septembre 1933, Dodd rapporte que Henry Mann de la National City Bank et Winthrop W. Aldrich de la Chase Bank ont tous deux rencontré Hitler et "ces banquiers estiment qu'ils peuvent travailler avec lui".[593] Ivy Lee, l'agent des relations publiques de Rockefeller, selon Dodd, "s'est montré à la fois capitaliste et favorable au fascisme".[594]

Nous pouvons donc au moins noter un accueil sympathique à la nouvelle dictature nazie, qui rappelle la manière dont les banquiers internationaux de Wall Street ont salué la nouvelle Russie de Lénine et Trotsky en 1917.

QUI ÉTAIT "SIDNEY WARBURG" ?

La question posée dans ce chapitre est l'accusation que certains financiers de Wall Street (les Rockefeller et Warburg ont été spécifiquement désignés) ont directement planifié et financé la prise de contrôle d'Hitler en 1933, et qu'ils l'ont fait depuis Wall Street. Sur cette question, le soi-disant mythe de "Sidney

---

[593] William E. Dodd, *Journal de l'ambassadeur Dodd*, op. cit. p. 31.

[594] Ibid, p. 74.

Warburg" est pertinent. L'éminent nazi Franz von Papen a déclaré dans ses *Mémoires*[595]:

> *... le récit le plus documenté de l'acquisition soudaine de fonds par les nationaux-socialistes est contenu dans un livre publié en Hollande en 1933, par l'ancienne maison d'édition d'Amsterdam Van Holkema & Warendorf, intitulé De Geldbronnen van Het Nationaal-Socialisme (Drie Gesprekken Met Hitler) sous le nom de "Sidney Warburg".*

Un livre portant ce titre en hollandais par "Sidney Warburg" fut en effet publié en 1933, mais ne resta sur les étals de livres en Hollande que quelques jours. Le livre fut détruit et retiré des ventes.[596] L'un des trois exemplaires originaux survivants a été traduit en anglais. La traduction a été déposée à un moment donné au British Museum, mais elle est maintenant retirée de la circulation publique et n'est pas disponible pour la recherche. On ne sait rien de l'exemplaire original néerlandais sur lequel cette traduction anglaise était basée.

Le deuxième exemplaire néerlandais appartenait au chancelier Schussnigg en Autriche, et on ne sait rien de son emplacement actuel. Le troisième exemplaire néerlandais a été acheminé en Suisse et a été traduit en allemand. La traduction allemande a survécu jusqu'à nos jours dans les archives sociales suisses à Zurich, en Suisse. Une copie certifiée conforme de la traduction allemande authentifiée de ce survivant suisse a été achetée par l'auteur en 1971 et traduite en anglais. C'est sur cette traduction anglaise de la traduction allemande que se fonde le texte de ce chapitre.

La publication du livre de "Sidney Warburg" a été dûment rapportée dans le *New York Times* (24 novembre 1933) sous le titre "on redoute un canular sur les nazis". Un bref article signale qu'un pamphlet de "Sidney Warburg" a été publié en Hollande, et que l'auteur n'est pas le fils de Felix Warburg. Le traducteur est J. G. Shoup, un journaliste belge vivant en Hollande. Les éditeurs et Shoup "se

---

595 Franz von Papen, *Mémoires*, (New York : E.P. Dutton & Co., 1953), p. 229.

596 Le texte anglais de ce chapitre est traduit d'une traduction allemande authentifiée d'un exemplaire de l'édition néerlandaise de *De Geldbronnen van Het Nationaal-Socialisme (Drie Gesprekken Met Hitler)*, ou *Les sources financières du national-socialisme (Trois conversations avec Hitler*. L'auteur néerlandais original est donné comme "Door Sidney Warburg, vertaald door I.G. Shoup" (Par Sidney Warburg, tel que raconté par I.G. Shoup).

La copie utilisée ici a été traduite des Pays-Bas par le Dr Walter Nelz, Wilhelm Peter et René Sonderegger à Zurich, le 11 février 1947, et la traduction allemande porte une déclaration sous serment selon laquelle "Les trois témoins soussignés vérifient que le document d'accompagnement n'est autre qu'une traduction fidèle et littérale du néerlandais vers l'allemand du livre de Sidney Warburg, dont un exemplaire a été constamment mis à leur disposition pendant tout le processus de traduction. Ils attestent qu'ils ont tenu cet original entre leurs mains, et qu'ils l'ont lu au mieux de leurs capacités, phrase par phrase, en le traduisant en allemand, comparant ensuite le contenu de la traduction d'accompagnement à l'original en toute conscience jusqu'à ce qu'un accord complet soit trouvé".

demandent s'ils n'ont pas été victimes d'un canular". Le compte-rendu du *Times* ajoute :

> *Le pamphlet répète une vieille histoire selon laquelle des Américains de premier plan, dont John D. Rockefeller, ont financé Hitler de 1929 à 1932 à hauteur de 32 millions de dollars, leur motif étant "de libérer l'Allemagne de l'emprise financière de la France en provoquant une révolution". De nombreux lecteurs du pamphlet ont fait remarquer qu'il contient de nombreuses inexactitudes.*

Pourquoi l'original néerlandais a-t-il été retiré de la circulation en 1933 ? Parce que "Sidney Warburg" n'existait pas et qu'un "Sidney Warburg" était revendiqué comme auteur. Depuis 1933, le livre de "Sidney Warburg" a été présenté par diverses parties comme un faux ou comme un document authentique. La famille Warburg elle-même s'est donné beaucoup de mal pour prouver sa fausseté.

Que dit le livre ? Selon le livre, que s'est-il passé en Allemagne au début des années 1930 ? Et ces événements ont-ils une quelconque ressemblance avec des faits que nous savons être vrais d'après d'autres preuves ?

Du point de vue de la méthodologie de recherche, il est préférable de supposer que le livre de "Sidney Warburg" est un faux, à moins que nous ne puissions prouver le contraire. C'est la procédure que nous allons adopter. Le lecteur pourrait bien se demander - alors pourquoi prendre la peine d'examiner de près une éventuelle contrefaçon ? Il y a au moins deux bonnes raisons, en dehors de la curiosité académique.

Tout d'abord, les Warburg prétendent que le livre est un faux et ce par quoi il justifie leur dénégation présente une curieuse défaillance. Les Warburg qualifient de faux un livre qu'ils admettent ne pas avoir lu ni même vu. La dénégation des Warburg se limite spécifiquement à dénoncer qu'il ait pu être rédigé par un Warburg. Cette négation est acceptable, mais elle ne nie ni ne rejette la validité du contenu. La dénégation ne fait que répudier la paternité du livre.

Deuxièmement, nous avons déjà identifié I.G. Farben comme un financier et un bailleur de fonds clé d'Hitler. Nous avons fourni des preuves photographiques du bordereau de virement bancaire de 400 000 marks de I.G. Farben sur le compte de la caisse noire politique "Nationale Treuhand" de Hitler, géré par Rudolf Hess. Il est maintenant probable et presque certain, que "Sidney Warburg" n'existait pas. D'autre part, il est de notoriété publique que les Warburg étaient étroitement liés à la gestion d'I.G. Farben en Allemagne et aux États-Unis. En Allemagne, Max Warburg était un directeur de I.G. Farben et aux États-Unis, le frère Paul Warburg (père de James Paul Warburg) était un directeur de l'américain I.G. Farben. En bref, nous avons des preuves irréfutables que certains Warburg, dont le père de James Paul, le dénonciateur du livre "Sidney Warburg", étaient des directeurs de I.G. Farben. Et I.G. Farben est connu pour avoir financé Hitler. "Sidney Warburg" était peut-être un mythe, mais les dirigeants de I.G. Farben, Max Warburg et Paul Warburg, étaient eux, bien réels. C'est une raison suffisante pour aller plus loin.

Résumons d'abord le livre que James Paul Warburg prétend être un faux.

SYNOPSIS DU LIVRE DE "SIDNEY WARBURG" SUPPRIMÉ

Les sources financières du national-socialisme[597] s'ouvre sur une prétendue conversation entre "Sidney Warburg" et le co-auteur/traducteur I.G. Shoup. "Warburg" raconte pourquoi il remettait à Shoup un manuscrit en anglais pour traduction en néerlandais et publication en Hollande, selon les termes du mythique "Sidney Warburg" :

> *Il y a des moments où je veux me détourner d'un monde où règnent l'intrigue, la ruse, l'escroquerie et la manipulation de la bourse... Savez-vous ce que je ne pourrai jamais comprendre ? Comment il est possible que des personnes de bonne et honnête moralité - pour lesquelles j'ai de nombreuses preuves - participent à des escroqueries et à des fraudes, sachant pertinemment que cela touchera des milliers de personnes.*

Shoup décrit ensuite "Sidney Warburg" comme "le fils d'un des plus grands banquiers des États-Unis, membre de la société bancaire Kuhn, Loeb & Co. de New York". "Sidney Warburg" dit ensuite à Shoup qu'il ("Warburg") veut témoigner pour l'histoire sur la manière dont le national-socialisme a été financé par les financiers de New York.

La première partie du livre s'intitule simplement *"1929"*. Elle relate qu'en 1929, Wall Street avait d'énormes crédits en cours en Allemagne et en Autriche, et que ces créances avaient, pour la plupart, été gelées. Alors que la France était économiquement faible et redoutait l'Allemagne, elle recevait également la "part du lion" des fonds de réparation qui étaient en fait financés par les États-Unis. En juin 1929, une réunion a eu lieu entre les membres de la Banque de la Réserve Fédérale et les principaux banquiers américains afin de décider de ce qu'il convenait de faire au sujet de la France, et en particulier d'appuyer son recours aux réparations allemandes. Cette réunion a réuni (selon le livre "Warburg") les directeurs de la Guaranty Trust Company, les "présidents" des banques de la Réserve Fédérale, ainsi que cinq banquiers indépendants, le "jeune Rockefeller" et Glean de la Royal Dutch Shell. Carter et Rockefeller ont, selon le texte, "dominé les débats. Les autres ont écouté et se sont contenté de hocher la tête".

Le consensus général lors de la réunion des banquiers était que la seule façon de libérer l'Allemagne des griffes financières françaises était une révolution, soit communiste, soit nationaliste allemande. Lors d'une réunion précédente, il avait été convenu de contacter Hitler pour "essayer de savoir s'il était prêt à recevoir un soutien financier américain". Or, Rockefeller aurait vu plus récemment un tract germano-américain sur le mouvement national-socialiste d'Hitler et le but de cette deuxième réunion était de déterminer si "Sidney Warburg" était prêt à se rendre en Allemagne comme messager pour prendre contact personnellement avec Hitler.

En échange d'un soutien financier, Hitler devait mener une "politique étrangère agressive et susciter l'idée d'une vengeance contre la France". Cette

---

[597] La version anglaise est éditée par Omnia Veritas Ltd, sous le titre *Hitler's Secret Backers, the Financial Sources of National Socialism*. www.omnia-veritas.com.

politique, pensait-on, devait déboucher sur un appel de la France aux États-Unis et à l'Angleterre pour obtenir leur aide dans "les questions internationales concernant l'éventuelle agression allemande". Hitler ne devait pas connaître le but de l'assistance de Wall Street. Il serait laissé "à sa raison et à son ingéniosité de découvrir les motifs de la proposition". "Warburg" accepta la mission proposée et quitta New York pour Cherbourg sur le paquebot Île de France, "avec un passeport diplomatique et des lettres de recommandation de Carter, Tommy Walker, Rockefeller, Glean et Herbert Hoover".

Apparemment, "Sidney Warburg" a eu quelques difficultés à rencontrer Hitler. Le consul américain à Munich n'a pas réussi à prendre contact avec les nazis, et finalement Warburg s'est adressé directement au maire Deutzberg de Munich, "avec une recommandation du consul américain", et un appel à orienter Warburg vers Hitler. Shoup présente ensuite des extraits des déclarations de Hitler lors de cette première rencontre. Ces extraits comprennent les habituelles divagations antisémites hitlériennes, et il faut noter que toutes les parties antisémitiques du livre "Sidney Warburg" sont prononcées par Hitler. (Ceci est important, car James Paul Warburg prétend que le livre de Shoup est totalement antisémite). Le financement des nazis a été discuté lors de cette réunion et Hitler aurait insisté sur le fait que les fonds ne pouvaient pas être déposés dans une banque allemande mais seulement dans une banque étrangère à sa disposition. Hitler a demandé 100 millions de marks et a suggéré que "Sidney Warburg" fasse un rapport sur la réaction de Wall Street par l'intermédiaire de von Heydt à Lutzowufer, 18 Berlin.[598]

Après avoir fait son rapport à Wall Street, Warburg a appris que 24 millions de dollars étaient une somme trop élevée pour les banquiers américains ; ils ont offert 10 millions de dollars. Warburg contacte von Heydt et une nouvelle rencontre est organisée, cette fois avec un "homme à l'allure peu distinguée, qui m'a été présenté sous le nom de Frey". Des instructions ont été données pour mettre 10 millions de dollars à la disposition de la société Mendelsohn & Co. Bank à Amsterdam, en Hollande. Warburg devait demander à la banque Mendelsohn d'établir des chèques en marks à l'ordre de nazis nommés dans dix villes allemandes.

Par la suite, Warburg s'est rendu à Amsterdam, a accompli sa mission avec Mendelsohn & Co. puis s'est rendu à Southampton, en Angleterre, et fut ramené à New York par le navire *Olympia* où il rendit son rapport à Carter de la Guaranty Trust Company. Deux jours plus tard, Warburg transmit son rapport à l'ensemble du groupe de Wall Street, mais "cette fois, un représentant anglais était assis à côté de Glean de la Royal Dutch, un homme nommé Angell, l'un des dirigeants de l'Asiatic Petroleum Co. Warburg fut interrogé sur Hitler, et "Rockefeller montra un intérêt inhabituel pour les déclarations d'Hitler sur les communistes".

Quelques semaines après le retour de Warburg d'Europe, les journaux de Hearst ont montré un "intérêt inhabituel" pour le nouveau parti nazi allemand et

---

598 Notez que "von Heydt" était le nom original de la Dutch Bank voor Handel en Seheepvaart N.V., une filiale des intérêts de Thyssen et dont on sait maintenant qu'elle a servi d'entonnoir pour les fonds nazis. Voir "*Élimination des ressources allemandes*".

même le *New York Times* a publié régulièrement de courts reportages sur les discours d'Hitler. Auparavant, ces journaux n'avaient pas montré un intérêt trop marqué, mais cela a changé.[599] De plus, en décembre 1929, une longue étude sur le mouvement national-socialiste allemand parut "dans une publication mensuelle de l'université de Harvard".

La deuxième partie de l'ouvrage supprimé *Les sources financières du national-socialisme* est intitulée "1931" et s'ouvre sur une discussion de l'influence française sur la politique internationale. Elle affirme qu'Herbert Hoover a promis à Pierre Laval de France de ne pas résoudre la question de la dette sans consulter au préalable le gouvernement français et [écrit Shoup] :

> *Lorsque Wall Street a découvert cela, Hoover a perdu d'un seul coup le respect de ce cercle. Même les élections suivantes ont été affectées - beaucoup pensent que l'échec de Hoover à se faire réélire peut être attribué à cette question.*[600]

En octobre 1931, Warburg reçoit une lettre d'Hitler qu'il transmet à Carter de la Guaranty Trust Company, puis une autre réunion de banquiers est convoquée dans les bureaux de la Guaranty Trust Company. Les avis étaient partagés lors de cette réunion. "Sidney Warburg" rapporta que Rockefeller, Carter et McBean étaient pour Hitler, tandis que les autres financiers étaient incertains. Montague Norman de la Banque d'Angleterre et Glean de la Royal Dutch Shell soutinrent que les 10 millions de dollars déjà dépensés pour Hitler étaient trop importants et qu'Hitler ne passerait jamais à l'action. Les participants à la réunion se mirent finalement d'accord sur le principe d'aider davantage Hitler et Warburg entreprit à nouveau une mission de messager et retourna en Allemagne.

Au cours de ce voyage, Warburg aurait discuté des affaires allemandes avec "un banquier juif" à Hambourg, avec un magnat de l'industrie et d'autres partisans d'Hitler. Il a notamment rencontré le banquier von Heydt et un certain Luetgebrumm. Ce dernier déclara que les troupes d'assaut nazies étaient incomplètement équipées et que les S.S. avaient grandement besoin de mitrailleuses, de revolvers et de carabines.

Lors de la réunion suivante entre Warburg et Hitler, Hitler a fait valoir que "les Soviétiques ne peuvent pas se passer de nos produits industriels. Nous leur donnerons du crédit, et si je ne suis pas capable d'affaiblir la France moi-même, alors les Soviétiques m'aideront". Hitler a dit qu'il avait deux plans de prise de contrôle en Allemagne : (a) le plan de révolution, et (b) le plan de prise de contrôle légale. Le premier plan serait une question de trois mois, le second une question

---

599 L'examen de l'index du *New York Times* confirme l'exactitude de la dernière partie de cette déclaration. Voir par exemple la soudaine ruée d'intérêt du *New York Times*, le 15 septembre 1930 et l'article de fond sur "Hitler, force motrice du fascisme allemand" dans le numéro du 21 septembre 1930 du *New York Times*. En 1929, le *New York Times* n'a publié qu'un seul bref article sur Adolf Hitler. En 1931, il publia une vingtaine d'articles importants, dont pas moins de trois "Portraits".

600 Hoover a déclaré qu'il avait perdu le soutien de Wall Street en 1931 parce qu'il ne voulait pas suivre son plan pour un New Deal : voir Antony C. Sutton, *Wall Street et FDR, op. cit.*

de trois ans. Hitler aurait dit : "la révolution coûte cinq cent millions de marks, la prise de contrôle légale coûte deux cent millions de marks - que décideront vos banquiers ? Après cinq jours, un câble de Guaranty Trust est arrivé à Warburg et est cité dans le livre comme suit :

> *Les montants suggérés sont hors de question. Nous ne voulons pas et ne pouvons pas. Expliquez à l'homme qu'un tel transfert vers l'Europe va bouleverser le marché financier. Absolument inconnu sur le territoire international. Attendez-vous à un long rapport, avant qu'une décision ne soit prise. Restez sur place. Poursuivez l'enquête. Persuadez l'homme que ses exigences sont intenables. N'oubliez pas d'inclure dans le rapport votre propre opinion sur les possibilités d'avenir de l'homme.*

Warburg a télégraphié son rapport à New York et trois jours plus tard, il a reçu un second télégramme :

> *Rapport reçu. Préparez-vous à livrer dix, au maximum quinze millions de dollars. Aviser l'homme de la nécessité d'une agression contre un pays étranger.*

Les 15 millions de dollars ont été acceptés pour la voie de la prise de contrôle légale, et non pour le plan révolutionnaire. L'argent a été transféré de Wall Street à Hitler via Warburg comme suit : 5 millions de dollars à Mendelsohn & Company, Amsterdam ; 5 millions de dollars à la Rotterdamsehe Bankvereinigung à Rotterdam ; et 5 millions de dollars à la "Banca Italiana".

Warburg s'est rendu dans chacune de ces banques, où il aurait rencontré Heydt, Strasser et Hermann Goering. Les groupes se sont arrangés pour que les chèques soient identifiées par des noms différents dans différentes villes d'Allemagne. En d'autres termes, les fonds ont été "blanchis" dans la tradition moderne pour dissimuler leurs origines en provenance de Wall Street. En Italie, le groupe de paiement aurait été reçu dans le bâtiment principal de la banque par son président et, en attendant dans son bureau, deux fascistes italiens, Rossi et Balbo, auraient été présentés à Warburg, Heydt, Strasser et Goering. Trois jours après le paiement, Warburg est rentré à New York depuis Gênes sur le *Savoya*.

Là encore, il fit son rapport à Carter, Rockefeller et aux autres banquiers.

La troisième section de *Sources financières du national-socialisme* s'intitule simplement "1933". La section relate la troisième et dernière rencontre de "Sidney Warburg" avec Hitler - la nuit où le Reichstag a été incendié. (Nous avons noté au chapitre huit la présence de l'ami de Roosevelt, Putzi Hanfstaengl, au Reichstag). Lors de cette réunion, Hitler informa Warburg des progrès des nazis vers une prise de contrôle légale. Depuis 1931, le parti national-socialiste avait triplé sa taille. Des dépôts massifs d'armes avaient été effectués près de la frontière allemande en Belgique, en Hollande et en Autriche - mais ces armes nécessitaient des paiements en espèces avant d'être livrées. Hitler demandait un minimum de 100 millions de marks pour assurer la dernière étape du programme de prise de contrôle. Guaranty Trust fit parvenir à Warburg une offre de 7 millions de dollars au maximum, à verser comme suit : 2 millions à la Renania Joint Stock Company à Düsseldorf (la branche allemande de la Royal Dutch), et 5 millions à d'autres banques. Warburg a rapporté cette offre à Hitler, qui a demandé que les 5 millions de dollars soient envoyés à la Banca Italiana à Rome et (bien que le rapport ne le dise pas) on peut supposer que les 2 autres millions ont été versés à Düsseldorf. Le livre se termine par la déclaration suivante de Warburg :

> *Je me suis acquitté de ma mission dans les moindres détails. Hitler est le dictateur du plus grand pays européen. Le monde l'a maintenant vu à l'œuvre depuis plusieurs mois. L'opinion que j'ai de lui ne compte pas à présent. Mais je reste persuadé que ses agissements prouveront qu'il est mauvais. Pour le bien du peuple allemand, j'espère du fond du cœur que j'ai tort. Le monde continue de souffrir sous un système qui doit se plier à un Hitler pour se maintenir en vie. Pauvre monde, pauvre humanité.*

Tel est le résumé du livre supprimé de "Sidney Warburg" sur les origines financières du national-socialisme en Allemagne. Certaines des informations contenues dans le livre sont maintenant de notoriété publique - bien qu'une partie seulement ait été généralement connue au début des années 1930. Il est extraordinaire de constater que l'auteur inconnu a eu accès à des informations qui n'ont fait surface que bien des années plus tard - par exemple, l'identité de la banque von Heydt en tant que circuit financier d'Hitler. Pourquoi le livre a-t-il été retiré des librairies et mis au pilon ? La raison invoquée pour le retrait était que "Sidney Warburg" n'existait pas, que le livre était un faux et que la famille Warburg prétendait qu'il contenait des déclarations antisémites et diffamatoires.

Les informations contenues dans le livre ont été ressuscitées après la Seconde Guerre mondiale et publiées dans d'autres livres dans un contexte antisémite qui n'existe pas dans le livre original de 1933. Deux de ces livres d'après-guerre étaient *Spanischer Sommer* de René Sonderegger et *Liebet Eure Feinde* de Werner Zimmerman.

Plus important encore, James P. Warburg de New York a signé une déclaration sous serment en 1949, qui a été publiée en annexe dans les *Mémoires* de von Papen. Cette déclaration sous serment de Warburg niait catégoriquement l'authenticité du livre de "Sidney Warburg" et affirmait qu'il s'agissait d'un canular. Malheureusement, James P. Warburg se concentre sur le livre antisémite *Spanischer Sommer* de Sonderegger de 1947, et non sur le livre original écrit par "Sidney Warburg" supprimé et publié en 1933 - où le seul antisémitisme provient des prétendues déclarations de Hitler.

En d'autres termes, la déclaration sous serment de Warburg a soulevé bien plus de questions qu'elle n'en a résolu. Nous devrions donc nous pencher sur la déclaration sous serment de Warburg en 1949 qui nie l'authenticité des sources financières du national-socialisme.

DÉCLARATION SOUS SERMENT DE JAMES PAUL WARBURG

En 1953, le nazi Franz von Papen publie ses *Mémoires.*[601] C'est ce même Franz von Papen qui avait été actif aux États-Unis pour le compte de l'espionnage allemand pendant la Première Guerre mondiale. Dans ses *Mémoires,* Franz von Papen aborde la question du financement d'Hitler et rejette la faute sur l'industriel Fritz Thyssen et le banquier Kurt von Schröder. Papen nie avoir financé Hitler, et en effet, aucune preuve crédible n'a été apportée pour lier von Papen aux fonds d'Hitler (bien que Zimmerman dans *Liebert Eure Feinde* accuse Papen d'avoir fait don de 14 millions de marks). Dans ce contexte, von Papen mentionne *Les sources financières du national-socialisme* de Sidney Warburg, ainsi que les deux livres plus récents de Werner Zimmerman et de René Sonderegger (alias Severin Reinhardt), publiés après la Seconde Guerre mondiale.[602] Papen ajoute que :

> James P. Warburg est en mesure de réfuter toute falsification dans sa déclaration sous serment... Pour ma part, je suis très reconnaissant à M. Warburg d'avoir éliminé une fois pour toutes cette calomnie malveillante. Il est presque impossible de réfuter des accusations de ce genre par une simple négation, et son démenti autoritaire m'a permis de donner corps à mes propres protestations.[603]

L'annexe II du livre de Papen comporte deux sections. La première est une déclaration de James P. Warburg ; la seconde est l'affidavit, daté du 15 juillet 1949.

Le premier paragraphe de la déclaration indique qu'en 1933, la maison d'édition néerlandaise Holkema et Warendorf a publié *De Geldbronnen van Het Nationaal-Socialisme. Drie Gesprekken Met Hitler*, et ajoute que :

> Ce livre aurait été écrit par "Sidney Warburg". Un associé du cabinet Warburg & Co. d'Amsterdam a informé James P. Warburg de l'existence de ce livre et Holkema et Warendorf ont été informés que "Sidney Warburg" n'existait pas. Ils ont alors retiré le livre de la circulation.

James Warburg fait ensuite deux déclarations successives et apparemment contradictoires :

> ... le livre contenait une masse de matériel diffamatoire contre divers membres de ma famille et contre un certain nombre de banques et de personnes importantes à

[601] Franz von Papen, *Mémoires,* (New York : E.P. Dutton & Co., Inc., 1958). Traduit par Brian Connell.

[602] Werner Zimmerman, *Liebet Eure Feinde,* (Frankhauser Verlag : Thielle-Neuchatel, 1948), qui contient un chapitre, "Les soutiens financiers secrets de Hitler" et René Sonderegger, *Spanischer Sommer,* (Afroltern, Suisse : Aehren Verlag, 1948).

[603] Franz von Papen, *Mémoires, op.* cit. p. 23.

New York - je n'ai jamais vu à ce jour une copie du livre. Apparemment, seule une poignée d'exemplaires a échappé au retrait de l'éditeur.

Or, d'une part, Warburg prétend n'avoir jamais vu un exemplaire du livre de "Sidney Warburg", et d'autre part, il dit que ce livre est *"diffamatoire"* et procède à une déclaration sous serment détaillée phrase par phrase pour réfuter les informations prétendument contenues dans un livre qu'il prétend ne pas avoir vu ! Il est très difficile d'accepter la validité de l'affirmation de Warburg selon laquelle il n'a "jamais vu à ce jour un exemplaire du livre". Ou s'il ne l'avait pas fait, alors la déclaration sous serment est sans valeur.

James Warburg ajoute que le livre de "Sidney Warburg" fait preuve "d'un antisémitisme évident", et l'idée maîtresse de la déclaration de Warburg est que l'histoire de *"Sidney Warburg"* est de la pure propagande antisémite. En fait (et Warburg aurait découvert ce fait s'il avait lu le livre), les seules déclarations antisémites dans le livre de 1933 sont celles attribuées à Adolf Hitler, dont les sentiments antisémites ne sont guère une grande découverte. Hormis les divagations d'Hitler, il n'y a rien dans le livre original de "Sidney Warburg" qui soit lié de près ou de loin à l'antisémitisme, à moins que nous ne classions Rockefeller, Glean, Carter, McBean, etc. comme juifs. En fait, il est à noter que pas un seul banquier juif n'est nommé dans le livre - à l'exception du mythique "Sidney Warburg" qui est un intermédiaire, et non l'un des prétendus bailleurs de fonds. Pourtant, nous savons de source authentique (par l'ambassadeur Dodd) que le banquier juif Eberhard von Oppenheim a effectivement donné 200 000 marks à Hitler[604], et il est peu probable que "Sidney Warburg" ait manqué cette observation s'il faisait délibérément de la fausse propagande antisémite.

La première page de la déclaration de James Warburg concerne le livre de 1933. Après la première page, Warburg présente René Sonderegger et un autre livre écrit en 1947. Une analyse minutieuse de la déclaration de Warburg et de la déclaration sous serment montre que ses démentis et ses affirmations se réfèrent essentiellement à Sonderegger et non à Sidney Warburg. Or, Sonderegger était antisémite et a probablement fait partie d'un mouvement néo-nazi après la Seconde Guerre mondiale, mais cette affirmation d'antisémitisme ne peut pas s'appliquer au livre de 1933 - et c'est là le nœud du problème. En bref, James Paul Warburg commence par prétendre discuter d'un livre qu'il n'a jamais vu mais qu'il sait être diffamatoire et antisémite, puis, sans avertissement, il déplace l'accusation vers un autre livre qui était certainement antisémite mais qui a été publié une décennie plus tard. Ainsi, la déclaration sous serment de Warburg confond si complètement les deux livres que le lecteur est amené à condamner le mythique "Sidney Warburg" avec Sonderegger.[605] Examinons certaines des déclarations de J.P. Warburg :

---

604 William E. Dodd, *Journal de l'ambassadeur Dodd*, op. cit. pp, 593-602.

605 Le lecteur peut examiner la déclaration complète de Warburg et la déclaration sous serment ; voir Franz von Papen, *Mémoires, op. cit.* p. 593-602.

Déclaration sous serment de James P. Warburg New York City, 15 juillet 1949	**Commentaires de l'auteur sur l'affidavit de James P. Warburg**
1. Concernant les allégations totalement fausses et malveillantes faites par René Sonderegger de Zurich, Suisse, et autres, comme indiqué dans la partie précédente de cette déclaration, je, James Paul Warburg, de Greenwich, Connecticut, États-Unis, dépose ce qui suit :	Notez que l'affidavit concerne René Sonderegger, et non le livre publié par J.G. Shoup en 1933.
2. Aucune personne telle que "Sidney Warburg" n'existait à New York en 1933, ni ailleurs, à ma connaissance, à l'époque ou à une autre époque.	On peut supposer que le nom "Sidney Warburg" est un pseudonyme, ou qu'il est utilisé à tort.
3. Je n'ai jamais donné de manuscrit, de journal, de notes, de câbles ou d'autres documents à quiconque pour traduction et publication en Hollande et, plus précisément, je n'ai jamais donné de tels documents au présumé J.G. Shoup d'Anvers. Pour autant que je sache et que je me souvienne, je n'ai à aucun moment rencontré une telle personne.	L'affidavit se limite à l'octroi de documents "pour la traduction et la publication en Hollande".
4. La conversation téléphonique entre Roger Baldwin et moi-même, rapportée par Sonderegger, n'a jamais eu lieu et est une pure invention.	Rapporté par Sonderegger, pas "Sidney Warburg".
5. Je ne suis pas allé en Allemagne à la demande du président de la Guaranty Trust Company en 1929, ni à aucun autre moment.	Mais Warburg s'est rendu en Allemagne en 1929 et 1930 pour l'International Acceptance Bank, Inc.
6. Je suis allé en Allemagne pour affaires pour ma propre banque, The International Acceptance Bank Inc. de New York, en 1929 et 1930. À aucune de ces occasions, je n'ai eu à enquêter sur l'éventuelle prévention d'une révolution communiste en Allemagne par la promotion d'une contre-révolution nazie. Je suis en mesure de prouver qu'à mon retour d'Allemagne après les élections du Reichstag de 1930, j'ai averti mes associés qu'Hitler arriverait très probablement au pouvoir en Allemagne et que le résultat serait soit une Europe dominée par les nazis, soit une seconde guerre mondiale - peut-être les deux. Cela peut être corroboré ainsi que le fait que, suite à mon avertissement, ma banque a procédé à une réduction de ses engagements allemands aussi rapidement que possible.	Notez que Warburg, par sa propre déclaration, a dit à ses associés bancaires qu'Hitler arriverait au pouvoir. Cette affirmation a été faite en 1930 - et les Warburg ont continué à diriger I.G. Farben et d'autres entreprises pronazies.
7. Je n'ai eu de discussions nulle part, à aucun moment, avec Hitler, avec aucun responsable nazi, ou avec qui que ce soit d'autre sur l'octroi de fonds au parti nazi. Plus précisément, je n'ai eu aucune relation de ce type avec Mendelssohn & Co, ni avec la Rotterdamsche Bankvereiniging ou la Banca Italiana. (Cette dernière est probablement destinée à lire Banca d'Italia, avec laquelle je n'ai pas non plus eu de telles transactions).	Il n'y a aucune preuve qui contredit cette affirmation. Pour autant que l'on puisse remonter, Warburg n'avait aucun lien avec ces sociétés bancaires, sauf que le correspondant italien de la Banque de Manhattan de Warburg était la "Banca Commerciale Italiana" - qui est proche de la "Banca Italiana".

8. En février 1933 (voir pages 191 et 192 du Spanischer Sommer), lorsque j'aurais apporté à Hitler le dernier versement de fonds américains et que j'aurais été reçu par Goering et Goebbels ainsi que par Hitler lui-même, je peux prouver que je n'étais pas du tout en Allemagne. Je n'ai jamais mis les pieds en Allemagne après l'arrivée au pouvoir des nazis en janvier 1933. En janvier et février, j'étais à New York et à Washington, travaillant à la fois avec ma banque et avec le président élu Roosevelt sur la crise bancaire qui sévissait alors. Après l'investiture de M. Roosevelt, le 3 mars 1933, j'ai travaillé avec lui en permanence à la préparation de l'ordre du jour de la Conférence économique mondiale, à laquelle j'ai été envoyé comme conseiller financier au début du mois de juin. Il s'agit d'une affaire de notoriété publique.	Il n'y a pas de preuves qui contredisent ces déclarations. "Sidney Warburg" ne fournit aucune preuve à l'appui de ses affirmations. Voir *Wall Street et FDR*, pour plus de détails sur les associations allemandes du FDR.
9. Les déclarations qui précèdent devraient suffire à démontrer que l'ensemble du mythe de "Sidney Warburg" et l'identification fallacieuse de moi-même avec l'inexistant "Sidney" qui s'ensuit sont des fabrications de mensonges malveillants sans le moindre fondement dans la vérité.	Non. James P. Warburg déclare n'avoir jamais vu le livre original "Sidney Warburg" publié en Hollande en 1933. Par conséquent, sa déclaration sous serment ne s'applique qu'au livre de Sonderegger, qui est inexact. Sidney Warburg est peut-être un mythe, mais l'association de Max Warburg et Paul Warburg avec I.G. Farben et Hitler n'en est pas un.

JAMES WARBURG A-T-IL EU L'INTENTION D'INDUIRE EN ERREUR ?

Il est vrai que "Sidney Warburg" pourrait bien avoir été une invention, dans le sens où "Sidney Warburg" n'a jamais existé. Nous supposons que le nom est un faux ; mais quelqu'un a écrit le livre. Zimmerman et Sonderegger ont peut-être ou non diffamé le nom de Warburg, mais malheureusement, lorsque nous examinons la déclaration sous serment de James P. Warburg publiée dans les *Mémoires* de von Papen, nous sommes laissés dans le noir comme jamais. Il y a trois questions importantes et sans réponse :

(1) pourquoi James P. Warburg prétendrait-il qu'un livre qu'il n'a pas lu est faux ?

(2) pourquoi la déclaration sous serment de Warburg évite la question clé et détourne la discussion de "Sidney Warburg" vers le livre antisémite Sonderegger publié en 1947 ? et

(3) pourquoi James P. Warburg serait-il si insensible à la souffrance des Juifs pendant la Seconde Guerre mondiale pour publier sa déclaration sous serment dans les *Mémoires* de Franz von Papen, qui était un nazi éminent présent au cœur du mouvement hitlérien depuis les premiers jours de 1933 ?

Non seulement les Warburg allemands ont été persécutés par Hitler en 1938, mais des millions de Juifs ont perdu la vie à cause de la barbarie nazie. Il semble élémentaire que toute personne ayant souffert et ayant été sensible aux souffrances passées des Juifs allemands évite les nazis, le nazisme et les livres néo-nazis comme la peste. Pourtant, nous avons ici le nazi von Papen qui agit comme un hôte bienveillant pour l'anti-nazi autoproclamé James P. Warburg, qui semble se réjouir de cette opportunité. De plus, les Warburg auraient eu amplement l'occasion de publier une telle déclaration sous serment et de lui donner une large publicité sans avoir à le faire par le biais de canaux néo-nazis.

Le lecteur gagnera à réfléchir à cette situation. La seule explication logique est que certains des faits présentés dans le livre de "Sidney Warburg" sont soit vrais, soit proches de la vérité, soit gênants pour James P. Warburg. On ne peut pas dire que Warburg ait eu l'intention d'induire en erreur (bien que cette conclusion puisse sembler évidente), car les hommes d'affaires sont des intellectuels et des raisonneurs notoirement illogiques, et il n'y a certainement rien qui puisse exempter Warburg de cette catégorisation.

QUELQUES CONCLUSIONS DE L'HISTOIRE DE "SIDNEY WARBURG".

"Sidney Warburg" n'a jamais existé ; en ce sens, le livre original de 1933 est une œuvre de fiction. Toutefois, nombre des faits peu connus à l'époque et consignés dans le livre sont des faits avérés et vérifiables ; et la déclaration sous serment de James Warburg ne vise pas le livre original mais plutôt un livre antisémite diffusé plus de dix ans plus tard.

Paul Warburg était un directeur de l'American I.G. Farben et donc lié au financement d'Hitler. Max Warburg, un directeur de l'allemand I.G. Farben, signa - avec Hitler lui-même - le document qui nommait Hjalmar Schacht à la Reichsbank. Ces liens vérifiables entre les Warburg et Hitler suggèrent que l'histoire de "Sidney Warburg" ne peut être rejetée comme une contrefaçon totale sans un examen approfondi.

Qui a écrit le livre de 1933, et pourquoi ? I.G. Shoup dit que les notes ont été écrites par un Warburg en Angleterre et lui ont été données pour qu'il les traduise. Le motif de Warburg était supposé être un véritable remord pour le comportement amoral des Warburg et de leurs associés de Wall Street. Cela semble-t-il être un motif plausible ? Il n'est pas passé inaperçu que ces mêmes Wall Streeters qui complotent la guerre et la révolution sont souvent dans leur vie privée de véritables citoyens décents ; il n'est pas à exclure que l'un d'entre eux ait changé d'avis ou ait éprouvé des remords. Mais cela n'est pas prouvé.

Si le livre était un faux, alors par qui a-t-il été écrit ? James Warburg admet qu'il ne connaît pas la réponse, et il écrit : "Le but original de la contrefaçon reste quelque peu obscur même aujourd'hui. [606]

Un gouvernement pourrait-il falsifier le document ? Certainement pas les gouvernements britannique ou américain, qui sont tous deux indirectement impliqués par le livre. Certainement pas le gouvernement nazi en Allemagne, bien que James Warburg semble suggérer cette possibilité improbable. Serait-ce la France, ou l'Union soviétique, ou peut-être l'Autriche ? La France, peut-être parce

[606] Franz von Papen, *Mémoires, op.* cit. p. 594.

que la France craignait la montée de l'Allemagne nazie. L'Autriche est une possibilité similaire. L'Union soviétique est une possibilité parce que les Soviétiques avaient également beaucoup à craindre d'Hitler. Il est donc plausible que la France, l'Autriche ou l'Union soviétique aient joué un rôle dans la préparation du livre.

Tout citoyen qui forge un tel livre sans disposer de documents internes au gouvernement devrait être remarquablement bien informé. La Guaranty Trust n'est pas une banque particulièrement connue en dehors de New York, mais il existe un degré extraordinaire de plausibilité quant à l'implication de Guaranty Trust, car il s'agit du véhicule que Morgan a utilisé pour financer et infiltrer la révolution bolchevique.[607] Celui qui a désigné Guaranty Trust comme le véhicule de financement d'Hitler en savait beaucoup plus que l'homme de la rue, ou disposait d'informations gouvernementales authentiques. Quel serait le motif d'un tel livre ?

Le seul motif qui semble acceptable est que l'auteur inconnu savait qu'une guerre était en préparation et espérait une réaction publique contre les fanatiques de Wall Street et leurs amis industriels en Allemagne - avant qu'il ne soit trop tard. Il est clair que, quel que soit l'auteur du livre, son motif était presque certainement de mettre en garde contre l'agression hitlérienne et de pointer du doigt sa source à Wall Street, car l'assistance technique des sociétés américaines contrôlées par Wall Street était encore nécessaire pour construire la machine de guerre d'Hitler. Les brevets d'hydrogénation de Standard Oil et le financement du pétrole issu du charbon, les installations, les viseurs de bombes et les autres technologies nécessaires n'avaient pas encore été entièrement transférés au moment de la rédaction du livre de "Sidney Warburg". Par conséquent, ce livre aurait pu être conçu pour briser le dos des partisans d'Hitler à l'étranger, pour empêcher le transfert prévu du potentiel de guerre des États-Unis et pour éliminer le soutien financier et diplomatique de l'État nazi. Si tel était le but, il est regrettable que le livre n'ait atteint aucun de ces objectifs.

[607] Voir Antony C. Sutton, *Wall Street et la révolution bolchévique*, op. cit.

CHAPITRE XI

COLLABORATION ENTRE WALL STREET ET LES NAZIS PENDANT LA SECONDE GUERRE MONDIALE

À l'arrière-plan des affrontements sur les divers fronts de la Seconde Guerre mondiale, grâce à des intermédiaires en Suisse et en Afrique du Nord, l'élite financière de New York a collaboré avec le régime nazi. Les dossiers saisis après la guerre ont fourni une masse de preuves démontrant que pour certains éléments du Big Business, la période 1941-1945 se déroulait "comme d'habitude". Par exemple, la correspondance entre les entreprises américaines et leurs filiales françaises révèle l'aide accordée à la machine militaire de l'Axe - alors que les États-Unis étaient en guerre avec l'Allemagne et l'Italie. Les lettres entre Ford de France et Ford des États-Unis entre 1940 et juillet 1942 ont été analysées par la section de contrôle des fonds étrangers du département du Trésor. Leur rapport initial concluait que jusqu'à la mi-1942 :

> (1) l'activité des filiales Ford en France s'est considérablement accrue ; (2) leur production était uniquement au profit des Allemands et des pays sous son occupation ; (3) les Allemands ont "clairement montré leur volonté de protéger les intérêts de Ford" en raison de l'attitude de stricte neutralité maintenue par Henry Ford et feu Edsel Ford ; et (4) l'activité accrue des filiales Ford françaises pour le compte des Allemands a reçu les éloges de la famille Ford en Amérique. [608]

De même, la Rockefeller Chase Bank a été accusée de collaborer avec les nazis en France pendant la Seconde Guerre mondiale, alors que Nelson Rockefeller occupait un poste de pantouflage à Washington D.C. :

> Le bureau parisien de la Chase Bank a adopté le même comportement pendant l'occupation allemande. L'examen de la correspondance entre Chase, New York, et Chase, France, de la date de la chute de la France à mai 1942, révèle que (1) le directeur du bureau de Paris a apaisé et collaboré avec les Allemands pour placer les banques Chase dans une "position privilégiée" ; (2) les Allemands avaient une estime toute particulière pour la banque Chase - en raison des activités

[608] Journal de Morgenthau (Allemagne).

internationales de notre siège social (Chase) et des relations agréables que la succursale de Paris a entretenues avec nombre de leurs banques (allemandes) et leurs organisations locales et hauts fonctionnaires (allemands) ; (3) le directeur de Paris a "appliqué très vigoureusement les restrictions à l'encontre des biens juifs, allant même jusqu'à refuser de débloquer des fonds appartenant à des Juifs en prévision de la publication prochaine par les autorités d'occupation d'un décret comportant des dispositions rétroactives interdisant ce déblocage" ; (4) le bureau de New York, malgré les informations susmentionnées, n'a pris aucune mesure directe pour écarter le directeur indésirable du bureau de Paris, car il "pourrait réagir contre nos intérêts (Chase), car nous avons affaire non pas à une théorie mais à une situation." [609]

Un rapport officiel adressé au secrétaire au Trésor de l'époque, M. Morgenthau, concluait que :

Ces deux situations [c'est-à-dire celles de Ford et la Chase Bank] nous convainquent qu'il est impératif d'enquêter immédiatement sur place sur les activités des filiales d'au moins certaines des grandes entreprises américaines qui opéraient en France pendant l'occupation allemande.[610]

Les fonctionnaires du Trésor ont insisté pour qu'une enquête soit ouverte avec les filiales françaises de plusieurs banques américaines - à savoir Chase, Morgan, National City, Guaranty, Bankers Trust et American Express. Bien que Chase et Morgan aient été les deux seules banques à maintenir des bureaux français pendant toute la durée de l'occupation nazie, en septembre 1944, toutes les grandes banques de New York faisaient pression sur le gouvernement américain pour obtenir l'autorisation de rouvrir les succursales d'avant-guerre.

Une enquête ultérieure du Trésor a produit des preuves documentaires de la collaboration entre la Chase Bank et J.P. Morgan avec les nazis pendant la Seconde Guerre mondiale. La recommandation d'une enquête complète est citée dans son intégralité ci-après :

COMMUNICATION INTERNE DU DÉPARTEMENT DU TRÉSOR

Date : 20 décembre 1944
Pour : Secrétaire Morgenthau
De : Monsieur Saxon
L'examen des dossiers de la Chase Bank, à Paris, et de Morgan and Company, en France, n'a progressé que suffisamment pour permettre de tirer des conclusions provisoires et de révéler quelques faits intéressants :

CHASE BANK, PARIS

[609] Ibid.

[610] Ibid.

a. Niederman, de nationalité suisse, directeur de Chase, Paris, était sans conteste un collaborateur ;
b. Le siège de Chase à New York a été informé de la politique collaborationniste de Niederman mais n'a pris aucune mesure pour le faire sortir. Il existe en effet de nombreuses preuves que le siège social de New York considérait les bonnes relations de Niederman avec les Allemands comme un excellent moyen de préserver, sans l'altérer, la position de la Chase Bank en France ;
c. Les autorités allemandes étaient soucieuses de maintenir la chasse ouverte et ont d'ailleurs pris des mesures exceptionnelles pour fournir des sources de revenus ;
d. Les autorités allemandes souhaitaient "être amies" avec les grandes banques américaines, car elles s'attendaient à ce que ces banques soient utiles après la guerre en tant qu'instrument de la politique allemande aux États-Unis ;
e. Le Chase, Paris s'est montré très soucieux de satisfaire les autorités allemandes de toutes les manières possibles. Par exemple, la Chase a tenu avec zèle le compte de l'ambassade allemande à Paris, "car chaque petite chose compte" (pour maintenir les excellentes relations entre la Chase et les autorités allemandes) ;
f. L'objectif global de la politique et du fonctionnement de Chase était de maintenir la position de la banque à tout prix.

MORGAN AND COMPANY, FRANCE

a. Morgan and Company se considérait comme une banque française et était donc tenue de respecter les lois et réglementations bancaires françaises, qu'elles soient d'inspiration nazie ou non, et elle l'a effectivement fait ;
b. La société Morgan and Company était très soucieuse de préserver la continuité de sa maison en France et, pour y parvenir, elle a élaboré un modus vivendi avec les autorités allemandes ;
c. Morgan and Company jouissait d'un grand prestige auprès des autorités allemandes, et les Allemands se vantaient de la splendide coopération de Morgan and Company ;
d. Morgan continua ses relations d'avant-guerre avec les grandes entreprises industrielles et commerciales françaises qui travaillaient pour l'Allemagne, dont les usines Renault, confisquées depuis par le gouvernement français, Peugeot [sic], Citroën et bien d'autres.
e. Le pouvoir de Morgan and Company en France n'a rien à voir avec les faibles ressources financières de la firme, et l'enquête en cours sera d'une réelle utilité en nous permettant pour la première fois d'étudier le modèle Morgan en Europe et la manière dont Morgan a utilisé son grand pouvoir ;
f. Morgan and Company a constamment cherché ses fins en jouant un gouvernement contre un autre de la manière la plus froide et la plus peu scrupuleuse.
M. Jefferson Caffery, ambassadeur des États-Unis en France, a été tenu informé de l'évolution de cette enquête et m'a apporté à tout moment son soutien et ses encouragements, en principe et en fait. En effet, M. Caffery lui-même qui m'a demandé comment les filiales Ford et General Motors en France avaient agi pendant l'occupation, et a exprimé le souhait que nous nous penchions sur ces sociétés une fois l'enquête bancaire terminée.

RECOMMANDATION

> Je recommande que cette enquête, qui, pour des raisons inévitables, a progressé lentement jusqu'à présent, soit maintenant menée de toute urgence et que le personnel supplémentaire nécessaire soit envoyé à Paris dès que possible.[611]

L'enquête complète n'a jamais abouti, et aucune investigation n'a jamais été menée sur cette activité présumée de trahison jusqu'à aujourd'hui.

L'IG AMÉRICAIN PENDANT LA SECONDE GUERRE MONDIALE

La collaboration entre les hommes d'affaires américains et les nazis dans l'Europe de l'Axe a été parallèle à la protection des intérêts nazis aux États-Unis. En 1939, American I.G. a été rebaptisé General Aniline & Film, General Dyestuffs étant son agent de vente exclusif aux États-Unis. Ces noms dissimulaient en fait le fait que American I.G. (ou General Aniline & Film) était un important producteur de matériel de guerre important, notamment d'atrabine, de magnésium et de caoutchouc synthétique. Des accords restrictifs avec sa société mère allemande I.G. Farben ont réduit les livraisons américaines de ces produits militaires pendant la Seconde Guerre mondiale.

Un citoyen américain, Halbach, est devenu président de General Dyestuffs en 1930 et a acquis le contrôle majoritaire en 1939 de Dietrich A. Schmitz, un directeur de American I.G. et frère de Hermann Schmitz, directeur de I.G. Farben en Allemagne et président du conseil d'administration de American I.G. jusqu'au déclenchement de la guerre en 1939. Après Pearl Harbor, le Trésor américain a bloqué les comptes bancaires de Halbach. En juin 1942, l'Alien Property Custodian saisit les actions de Halbach dans General Dyestuffs et reprit l'entreprise en tant que société ennemie en vertu de la loi sur le commerce avec l'ennemi. Par la suite, l'Alien Property Custodian a nommé un nouveau conseil d'administration pour agir en tant que fiduciaire pendant la durée de la guerre. Ces actions étaient une pratique raisonnable et habituelle, mais quand on fouille sous la surface, une autre histoire tout à fait anormale apparaît.

Entre 1942 et 1945, Halbach est nominalement consultant auprès de General Dyestuffs. En fait, Halbach dirigeait la société, à raison de 82 000 dollars par an. Louis Johnson, ancien secrétaire adjoint à la guerre, a été nommé président de General Dyestuffs par le gouvernement américain, pour lequel il recevait 75 000 dollars par an. Louis Johnson a tenté de faire pression sur le Trésor américain pour débloquer les fonds gelés de Halbach et lui permettre de développer des politiques contraires aux intérêts des États-Unis, alors en guerre avec l'Allemagne. L'argument utilisé pour obtenir le déblocage des comptes bancaires de Halbach était que ce dernier dirigeait la société et que le conseil d'administration nommé par le gouvernement "aurait été en mauvaise posture sans les avis de M. Halbach".

Pendant la guerre, Halbach a intenté un procès à l'Alien Property Custodian, par l'intermédiaire du cabinet d'avocats Sullivan and Cromwell, pour évincer le

---

[611] Ibid, pp. 800-2.

gouvernement américain de son contrôle des sociétés I.G. Farben. Ces poursuites n'ont pas abouti, mais Halbach a réussi à maintenir les accords du cartel Farben intacts tout au long de la Seconde Guerre mondiale ; l'Alien Property Custodian n'est jamais allé devant les tribunaux pendant la Seconde Guerre mondiale pour les poursuites antitrust en cours. Pourquoi ? Leo T. Crowley, chef du bureau du gardien des biens étrangers, avait John Foster Dulles comme conseiller, et John Foster Dulles était un associé du cabinet Sullivan and Cromwell mentionné ci-dessus, qui agissait au nom de Halbach dans sa poursuite contre le gardien des biens étrangers.

Il y a eu d'autres situations de conflit d'intérêts qu'il convient de noter. Leo T. Crowley, le gardien des biens étrangers, a nommé Victor Emanuel aux conseils d'administration du General Aniline & Film et du General Dyestuffs. Avant la guerre, Victor Emanuel était directeur de la J. Schroder Banking Corporation. Schroder, comme nous l'avons déjà vu, était un important financier d'Hitler et du parti nazi - et à cette époque même, il était membre du Cercle des amis de Himmler, apportant des contributions substantielles aux organisations S.S. en Allemagne.

À son tour, Victor Emanuel a nommé Leo Crowley à la tête de Standard Gas & Electric (contrôlée par Emanuel) à 75 000 dollars par an. Cette somme s'ajoutait au salaire de Leo Crowley versé par l'Alien Property Custodian et à 10 000 dollars par an en tant que directeur de la Federal Deposit Insurance Corporation du gouvernement américain. En 1945, James E. Markham avait remplacé Crowley en tant qu'A.P.C. et avait également été nommé par Emanuel comme directeur de Standard Gas à 4850 dollars par an, en plus des 10 000 dollars qu'il tirait du Alien Property Custodian.

L'influence de General Dyestuffs en temps de guerre et cette confortable coterie gouvernement-entreprises au nom de I.G. Farben est illustrée par l'affaire du cyanamide américain. Avant la guerre, I.G. Farben contrôlait les industries de la drogue, des produits chimiques et des colorants au Mexique. Pendant la Seconde Guerre mondiale, il a été proposé à Washington que l'entreprise American Cyanamid reprenne cette industrie mexicaine et développe une industrie chimique "indépendante" avec les anciennes entreprises I.G. Farben saisies par le gardien mexicain des biens étrangers.

En tant que fondés de pouvoir du banquier Schroder Victor Emanuel, Crowley et Markham, qui étaient également des employés du gouvernement américain, ont tenté de régler la question de ces intérêts d'I.G. Farben aux États-Unis et au Mexique. Le 13 avril 1943, James Markham a envoyé une lettre au secrétaire d'État Cordell Hull pour s'opposer au projet de transaction sur le cyanamide, au motif qu'il était contraire à la Charte de l'Atlantique et qu'il interférerait avec l'objectif d'établir des entreprises indépendantes en Amérique latine. La position de Markham a été soutenue par Henry A. Wallace et le procureur général Francis Biddle.

Les forces liguées contre l'accord sur le cyanamide étaient Sterling Drug, Inc. et Winthrop. Sterling et Winthrop risquaient tous deux de perdre leur marché de la drogue au Mexique si l'accord sur le cyanamide était conclu. Le général Aniline et le général Dyestuffs de I.G. Farben, dominés par Victor Emanuel, ancien associé du banquier Schröder, étaient également hostiles à l'accord sur le cyanamide.

D'autre part, le Département d'État et le Bureau du coordinateur des affaires interaméricaines - qui se trouve être le bébé de guerre de Nelson Rockefeller - ont soutenu le projet d'accord sur le cyanamide. Les Rockefeller s'intéressent bien sûr aussi aux industries pharmaceutiques et chimiques en Amérique latine. En bref, un monopole américain sous l'influence de Rockefeller aurait remplacé un monopole nazi d'I.G. Farben.

I.G. Farben a remporté cette manche à Washington, mais des questions plus inquiétantes se posent lorsque nous examinons le bombardement de l'Allemagne en temps de guerre par l'U.S.A.A.F. On a longtemps entendu des rumeurs, mais jamais prouvé, selon lesquelles Farben a bénéficié d'un traitement de faveur - c'est-à-dire qu'il n'a pas été bombardé. James Stewart Martin commente comme suit le traitement de faveur reçu par I.G. Farben lors du bombardement de l'Allemagne :

> Peu après que les armées eurent atteint le Rhin à Cologne, nous roulions sur la rive ouest, en vue de l'usine I.G. Farben de Leverkusen, qui n'avait pas subi de dommages, de l'autre côté du fleuve. Sans rien savoir de moi ni de mes affaires, il (le conducteur de la jeep) a commencé à me tenir des propos sur I.G. Farben et à me montrer du doigt le trajet entre la ville de Cologne bombardée et le trio d'usines intactes en périphérie : l'usine Ford et l'usine United Rayon sur la rive ouest, et l'usine Farben sur la rive est...[612]

Bien que cette accusation soit une question très ouverte, nécessitant de nombreuses recherches spécialisées sur les archives des bombardements de l'U.S.A.A.F., d'autres aspects du favoritisme pour les nazis sont bien connus.

À la fin de la Seconde Guerre mondiale, Wall Street s'est installée en Allemagne par l'intermédiaire du Conseil de contrôle pour protéger ses anciens amis du cartel et limiter la ferveur de dénazification qui porterait atteinte aux anciennes relations d'affaires. Le général Lucius Clay, le gouverneur militaire adjoint pour l'Allemagne, a nommé des hommes d'affaires qui s'opposaient à la dénazification des postes de contrôle du processus de dénazification. William H. Draper de Dillon-Read, la société qui a financé les cartels allemands dans les années 1920, est devenu l'adjoint du général Clay.

Le banquier William Draper, en tant que général de brigade, a constitué son équipe de contrôle à partir d'hommes d'affaires qui avaient représenté les entreprises américaines dans l'Allemagne d'avant-guerre. La représentation de General Motors comprenait Louis Douglas, un ancien directeur de G.M., et Edward S. Zdunke, un chef de General Motors d'avant-guerre à Anvers, nommé pour superviser la section d'ingénierie du Conseil de contrôle. Peter Hoglund, un expert de l'industrie automobile allemande, a reçu un congé de General Motors. La sélection du personnel du Conseil a été effectuée par le colonel Graeme K.

---

[612] James Stewart Martin, *All Honorable Men*, op. cit. p. 75.

Howard - ancien représentant de G,M. en Allemagne et auteur d'un livre qui "fait l'éloge des pratiques totalitaires [et] justifie l'agression allemande...".[613]

Le secrétaire au Trésor Morgenthau, profondément troublé par les implications de ce monopole de Wall Street sur le destin de l'Allemagne nazie, prépara un mémorandum à présenter au président Roosevelt. Le mémorandum complet de Morgenthau, daté du 29 mai 1945, se lit comme suit :

MEMORANDUM
29 mai 1945
Le lieutenant-général Lucius D. Clay, en tant qu'adjoint du général Eisenhower, dirige activement l'élément américain du Conseil de contrôle pour l'Allemagne. Les trois principaux conseillers du général Clay au sein de l'état-major du Conseil de contrôle sont :

1. L'ambassadeur Robert D. Murphy, qui est en charge de la Division politique.
2. Louis Douglas, que le général Clay décrit comme mon conseiller personnel pour les questions économiques, financières et gouvernementales". Douglas a démissionné de son poste de directeur du budget en 1934 ; et pendant les huit années suivantes, il s'est attaqué aux politiques budgétaires du gouvernement. Depuis 1940, Douglas est président de la Mutual Life Insurance Company, et depuis décembre 1944, il est directeur de la General Motors Corporation.
3. Le brigadier-général William Draper, qui est le directeur de la division économique du Conseil de contrôle. Le général Draper est un associé de la société bancaire Dillon, Read and Company. Le *New York Times* de dimanche a publié l'annonce de la nomination de membres clés du personnel par le général Clay et le général Draper à la division économique du Conseil de contrôle. Ces nominations sont les suivantes :

1. R.J. Wysor est chargé des questions métallurgiques. Wysor a été président de la Republic Steel Corporation de 1937 jusqu'à une date récente, et avant cela, il était associé à la Bethlehem Steel, à la Jones and Laughlin Steel Corporation et à la Republic Steel Corporation.
2. Edward X. Zdunke doit superviser la section d'ingénierie. Avant la guerre, M. Zdunke était à la tête de General Motors à Anvers.
3. Philip Gaethke sera responsable des opérations minières. Gaethke était auparavant lié à Anaconda Copper et était responsable de ses fonderies et de ses mines en Haute-Silésie avant la guerre.
4. Philip P. Clover sera chargé de traiter les questions relatives au pétrole. Il était auparavant représentant de la Socony Vacuum Oil Company en Allemagne.
5. Peter Hoglund doit s'occuper des problèmes de production industrielle. Hoglund est en congé de General Motors et on dit qu'il est un expert de la production allemande.
6. Calvin B. Hoover sera responsable du groupe de renseignement du Conseil dc contrôle et sera également conseiller spécial du général Draper. Dans une lettre adressée au rédacteur en chef du *New York Times* le 9 octobre 1944, Hoover écrit ce qui suit :

La publication du plan du secrétaire Morgenthau pour traiter avec l'Allemagne m'a profondément troublé ... une telle paix carthaginoise laisserait un héritage de haine qui empoisonnerait les relations internationales pour les générations à venir

613 Journal de Morgenthau (Allemagne), p. 1543. Le livre du colonel Graeme K. Howard était intitulé, *America and a New World Order*, (New York : Scribners, 1940).

... le vide dans l'économie de l'Europe qui existerait par la destruction de toute l'industrie allemande est une chose difficile à envisager.

7. Laird Bell sera le conseiller juridique principal de la division économique. Il est un avocat bien connu de Chicago et en mai 1944, il a été élu président du *Chicago Daily News*, après la mort de Frank Knox.

L'un des hommes qui ont aidé le général Draper dans la sélection du personnel de la division économique était le colonel Graeme Howard, vice-président de General Motors, qui était en charge de leurs affaires à l'étranger et qui était un représentant important de General Motors en Allemagne avant la guerre. Howard est l'auteur d'un livre dans lequel il fait l'éloge des pratiques totalitaires, justifie l'agression allemande et la politique d'apaisement de Munich, et reproche à Roosevelt d'avoir précipité la guerre.

Ainsi, lorsque nous examinons le Conseil de contrôle pour l'Allemagne du général Lucius D. Clay, nous constatons que le chef de la division des finances était Louis Douglas, directeur de la General Motors contrôlée par Morgan et président de la Mutual Life Insurance. (Opel, la filiale allemande de General Motors, avait été le plus grand producteur de chars d'assaut d'Hitler). Le chef de la division économique du Conseil de contrôle était William Draper, un associé de la firme Dillon, Read, qui avait tant à voir avec la construction de l'Allemagne nazie en premier lieu. Les trois hommes étaient, sans surprise à la lumière de découvertes plus récentes, membres du Council on Foreign Relations.

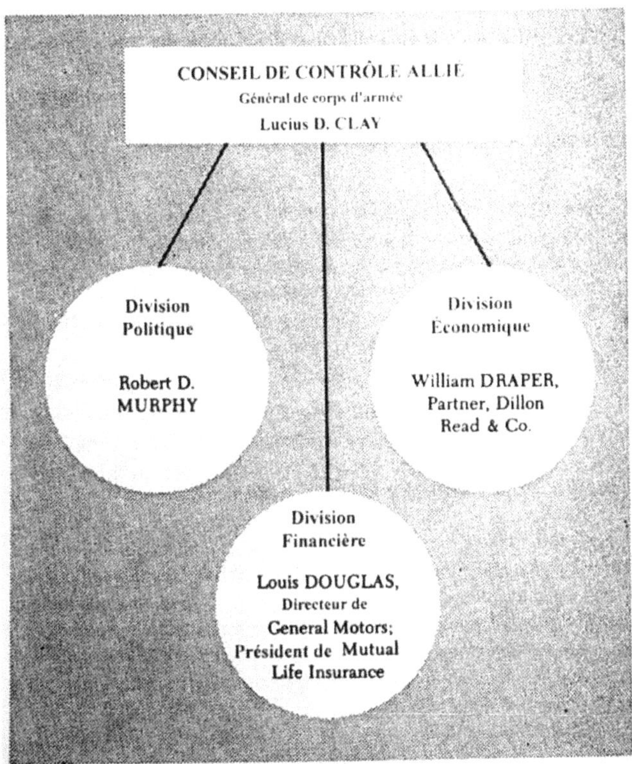

LES INDUSTRIELS ET LES FINANCIERS AMÉRICAINS ONT-ILS ÉTÉ COUPABLES DE CRIMES DE GUERRE ?

Le procès de Nuremberg pour crimes de guerre a proposé de sélectionner les responsables des préparatifs et des atrocités de la Seconde Guerre mondiale et de les traduire en justice. La question de savoir si une telle procédure est moralement justifiable est discutable ; il est justifié de considérer que Nuremberg était une farce politique très éloignée des principes juridiques.[614] Cependant, si nous supposons qu'il existe une telle justification juridique et morale, alors tout procès de ce type devrait sûrement s'appliquer à tous, quelle que soit leur nationalité. Qu'est-ce qui devrait par exemple exempter Franklin D. Roosevelt et Winston Churchill, mais pas Adolf Hitler et Goering ? Si l'infraction est une préparation à la guerre, et non une vengeance aveugle, alors la justice devrait être impartiale.

Les directives préparées par le Conseil de contrôle américain en Allemagne pour l'arrestation et la détention des criminels de guerre font référence aux "nazis" et aux "sympathisants nazis", et non aux "Allemands". Les extraits pertinents sont les suivants :

> *a. Vous rechercherez, arrêterez et détiendrez, en attendant de recevoir de nouvelles instructions quant à leur sort, Adolf Hitler, ses principaux associés nazis, d'autres criminels de guerre et toutes les personnes qui ont participé à la planification ou à l'exécution d'entreprises nazies impliquant ou entraînant des atrocités ou des crimes de guerre.*

Suit alors une liste des catégories de personnes à arrêter, dont :

> *(8) Nazis et sympathisants nazis occupant des postes importants et clés dans (a) les organisations civiques et économiques nationales et locales ; (b) les sociétés et autres organisations dans lesquelles le gouvernement a un intérêt financier majeur ; (c) l'industrie, le commerce, l'agriculture et les finances ; (d) l'éducation ; (e) le système judiciaire ; et (f) la presse, les maisons d'édition et autres agences diffusant des nouvelles et de la propagande.*

Les principaux industriels et financiers américains cités dans ce livre sont couverts par les catégories mentionnées ci-dessus. Henry Ford et Edsel Ford ont respectivement contribué à Hitler et profité de la production allemande en temps de guerre. Standard Oil of New Jersey, General Electric, General Motors et I.T.T. ont certainement apporté des contributions financières ou techniques qui constituent une preuve *prima facie de* "participation à la planification ou à l'exécution d'entreprises nazies".

Il y a, en bref, des preuves qui suggèrent :

---

[614] Le lecteur devrait examiner l'essai *The Return to War Crimes* (Le retour aux crimes de guerre), dans James J. Martin, Revisionist Viewpoints, (Colorado : Ralph Mules, 1971).

a) la coopération avec la Wehrmacht (Ford Motor Company, Chase Bank, Morgan Bank) ;

b) l'aide au plan quadriennal nazi et la mobilisation économique pour la guerre (Standard Oil of New Jersey) ;

c) la création et l'équipement de la machine de guerre nazie (I.T.T.) ;

d) le stockage de matériel essentiel pour les nazis (Ethyl Corporation) ;

e) l'affaiblissement des ennemis potentiels des nazis (l'Américain I.G. Farben) ; et

f) la poursuite de la propagande, du renseignement et de l'espionnage (l'Américain I.G. Farben et l'homme de relations publiques de Rockefeller, Ivy Lee).

Il existe au moins suffisamment de preuves pour exiger une enquête approfondie et impartiale. Cependant, comme nous l'avons déjà noté, ces mêmes entreprises et financiers ont joué un rôle important dans l'élection de Roosevelt en 1933 et ont donc eu une influence politique suffisante pour étouffer les menaces d'enquête. Des extraits du journal de Morgenthau démontrent que le pouvoir politique de Wall Street était suffisant même pour contrôler la nomination des officiers responsables de la dénazification et de l'éventuel gouvernement de l'Allemagne d'après-guerre.

Ces entreprises américaines étaient-elles au courant de leur assistance à la machine militaire d'Hitler ? D'après les entreprises elles-mêmes, il est clair que non. Elles clament l'innocence de toute intention d'aider l'Allemagne d'Hitler. En témoigne un télégramme envoyé par le président du conseil d'administration de la Standard Oil du New Jersey au secrétaire à la Guerre Patterson après la Seconde Guerre mondiale, alors que l'enquête préliminaire sur l'aide de Wall Street était en cours :

> Pendant toute la période de nos contacts d'affaires, nous n'avions aucune idée du rôle de complice de Farben dans la politique brutale d'Hitler. Nous offrons toute l'aide que nous pouvons apporter pour que la vérité complète soit mise en lumière et que justice soit rendue de manière impartiale.
>
> F.W. Abrams, président du conseil d'administration

Malheureusement, les preuves présentées sont contraires aux affirmations télégraphiées d'Abrams. La Standard Oil du New Jersey a non seulement aidé la machine de guerre d'Hitler, mais elle avait connaissance de cette assistance. Emil Helfferich, le président du conseil d'administration d'une filiale de Standard of New Jersey, était membre du Cercle Keppler avant l'arrivée d'Hitler au pouvoir ; il a continué à apporter des contributions financières au Cercle Himmler jusqu'en 1944.

Par conséquent, il n'est pas du tout difficile de visualiser pourquoi les industriels nazis étaient perplexes face aux "enquêtes" et supposaient à la fin de la guerre que leurs amis de Wall Street allaient les renflouer et les protéger de la colère de ceux qui avaient souffert. Ces attitudes ont été présentées au Comité Kilgore en 1946 :

Vous serez peut-être également intéressé de savoir, Monsieur le Président, que les dirigeants d'I.G. Farben et d'autres, lorsque nous les avons interrogés sur ces activités, étaient parfois très indignes. Leur attitude générale et leurs attentes étaient que la guerre était terminée et nous devrions maintenant les aider à remettre I.G. Farben et l'industrie allemande sur pied. Certains d'entre eux ont dit ouvertement que cet interrogatoire et cette enquête n'étaient, selon eux, qu'un phénomène de courte durée, car dès que les choses se sont un peu tassées, ils s'attendaient à ce que leurs amis des États-Unis et d'Angleterre reviennent. Leurs amis, disaient-ils, mettraient un terme à des activités telles que ces enquêtes et veilleraient à ce qu'ils reçoivent le traitement qu'ils considèrent comme approprié et à ce qu'une aide leur soit apportée pour rétablir leur industrie.[615]

[615] Élimination des ressources allemandes, p. 652.

CHAPITRE XII

CONCLUSIONS

Nous avons démontré par des preuves documentées un certain nombre d'associations critiques entre les banquiers internationaux de Wall Street et la montée d'Hitler et du nazisme en Allemagne.

Premièrement : que Wall Street a financé les cartels allemands au milieu des années 20 qui, à leur tour, ont procédé à l'arrivée d'Hitler au pouvoir.

Deuxièmement : que le financement d'Hitler et de ses S.S. provenait en partie de filiales ou de sociétés affiliées à des entreprises américaines, dont Henry Ford en 1922, de paiements par I.G. Farben et General Electric en 1933, puis de la Standard Oil du New Jersey et de paiements de filiales d'I.T.T. à Heinrich Himmler jusqu'en 1944.

Troisièmement : que les multinationales américaines sous le contrôle de Wall Street ont largement profité du programme de construction militaire d'Hitler dans les années 1930 et au moins jusqu'en 1942.

Quatrièmement : que ces mêmes banquiers internationaux ont utilisé leur influence politique aux États-Unis pour dissimuler leur collaboration en temps de guerre et, pour ce faire, ont infiltré la Commission de contrôle américaine pour l'Allemagne.

Nos preuves pour ces quatre grandes affirmations peuvent être résumées comme suit :

Dans le premier chapitre, nous avons présenté des preuves que les plans Dawes et Young pour les réparations allemandes ont été formulés par des membres éminents de Wall Street, portant temporairement le chapeau d'hommes d'État, et ces prêts ont généré une pluie de profits pour ces banquiers internationaux. Owen Young de General Electric, Hjalmar Schacht, A. Voegler et d'autres personnes intimement liées à l'accession d'Hitler au pouvoir avaient été auparavant les négociateurs des parties américaine et allemande, respectivement. Trois maisons de Wall Street - Dillon, Read ; Harris, Forbes ; et, National City Company - ont géré les trois quarts des prêts de réparation utilisés pour créer le système de cartel allemand, y compris les dominants I.G. Farben et Vereinigte Stahlwerke, qui ont produit ensemble 95 pour cent des explosifs pour le camp nazi pendant la Seconde Guerre mondiale.

Le rôle central d'I.G. Farben dans le coup d'État d'Hitler a été examiné dans le chapitre deux. Les directeurs de l'entreprise américaine I.G. (Farben) ont été identifiés comme des hommes d'affaires américains de premier plan : Walter Teagle, un associé et bailleur de fonds de Roosevelt et un administrateur de la

NRA ; le banquier Paul Warburg (son frère Max Warburg était au conseil d'administration d'I.G. Farben en Allemagne) ; et Edsel Ford. Farben a versé 400 000 RM directement à Schacht et Hess pour les élections cruciales de 1933 et Farben a ensuite été à l'avant-garde du développement militaire dans l'Allemagne nazie.

Un don de 60.000 RM a été fait à Hitler par la General Electric allemande (A.E.G.), qui avait quatre directeurs et une participation de 25-30% détenue par la société mère américaine General Electric. Ce rôle a été décrit au chapitre trois, et nous avons constaté que Gerard Swope, un des initiateurs du New Deal de Roosevelt (son segment de l'Administration nationale de redressement), ainsi qu'Owen Young de la Banque de la Réserve Fédérale de New York et Clark Minor d'International General Electric, étaient les personnages dominants de Wall Street de A.E.G. et l'influence unique la plus significative.

Nous n'avons également trouvé aucune preuve permettant d'inculper la société allemande d'électricité Siemens, qui n'était pas sous le contrôle de Wall Street. En revanche, il existe des preuves documentaires que tant A.E.G. qu'Osram, les autres unités de l'industrie électrique allemande - qui avaient toutes deux une participation et un contrôle américains - ont financé Hitler. En fait, presque tous les directeurs de la General Electric allemande étaient des bailleurs de fonds d'Hitler, soit directement par l'intermédiaire d'A.E.G., soit indirectement par l'intermédiaire d'autres entreprises allemandes. G.E. a complété son soutien à Hitler par une coopération technique avec Krupp, visant à restreindre le développement américain du carbure de tungstène, qui a fonctionné au détriment des États-Unis pendant la Seconde Guerre mondiale. Nous avons conclu que les usines A.E.G. en Allemagne ont réussi, par une manœuvre encore inconnue, à éviter les bombardements des Alliés.

Un examen du rôle de la Standard Oil du New Jersey (qui était et est contrôlée par les intérêts de Rockefeller) a été entrepris au chapitre quatre. Standard Oil n'a apparemment pas financé l'accession d'Hitler au pouvoir en 1933 (cette partie du "mythe propagé par Sidney Warburg" n'est pas prouvée). En revanche, des paiements ont été effectués jusqu'en 1944 par la Standard Oil du New Jersey, pour développer de l'essence synthétique à des fins de guerre pour le compte des nazis et, par le biais de sa filiale à 100%, au Cercle des amis S.S. de Heinrich Himmler à des fins politiques. Le rôle de Standard Oil était d'apporter une aide technique au développement nazi du caoutchouc et de l'essence synthétiques par le biais d'une société de recherche américaine sous le contrôle de la direction de Standard Oil. L'Ethyl Gasoline Company, détenue conjointement par Standard Oil du New Jersey et General Motors, a joué un rôle essentiel dans la fourniture de plomb éthylique vital à l'Allemagne nazie - malgré les protestations écrites du ministère américain de la Guerre - en sachant clairement que le plomb éthylique était destiné à des fins militaires nazies.

Dans le chapitre cinq, nous avons démontré que l'International Telephone and Telegraph Company, l'une des multinationales les plus connues, a travaillé des deux côtés de la Seconde Guerre mondiale par l'intermédiaire du baron Kurt von Schroder, du groupe bancaire Schroder. I.T.T. détenait également 28% des parts de la société Focke-Wolfe, qui fabriquait d'excellents avions de chasse allemands.

Nous avons également découvert que Texaco (Texas Oil Company) était impliquée dans les entreprises nazies par l'intermédiaire de l'avocat allemand Westrick, mais qu'elle avait renoncé à son président du conseil d'administration Rieber lorsque ces entreprises ont été rendues publiques.

Henry Ford a été un des premiers (1922) partisans d'Hitler et Edsel Ford a poursuivi la tradition familiale en 1942 en encourageant la Ford française à tirer profit de l'armement de la Wehrmacht allemande. Par la suite, ces véhicules produits par Ford ont été utilisés contre les soldats américains lors de leur débarquement en France en 1944. Pour sa reconnaissance précoce et son aide opportune aux nazis, Henry Ford a reçu une médaille nazie en 1938. Les archives de French Ford suggèrent que Ford Motor a reçu des nazis un traitement particulièrement favorable après 1940.

Les pistes du financement d'Hitler sont rassemblées dans le chapitre sept et répondent avec des noms et des chiffres précis à la question : qui a financé Adolf Hitler ? Ce chapitre met en accusation Wall Street et, incidemment, personne d'autre d'importance aux États-Unis, à l'exception de la famille Ford. La famille Ford n'est pas normalement associée à Wall Street mais fait certainement partie de "l'élite du pouvoir".

Dans les chapitres précédents, nous avons cité plusieurs associés de Roosevelt, notamment Teagle de Standard Oil, la famille Warburg et Gerard Swope. Dans le chapitre huit, le rôle de Putzi Hanfstaengl, un autre ami de Roosevelt et un participant à l'incendie du Reichstag, est retracé. La composition du cercle intérieur nazi pendant la Seconde Guerre mondiale, et les contributions financières de la Standard Oil du New Jersey et des filiales de l'I.T.T. sont retracées au chapitre neuf. Des preuves documentaires de ces contributions financières sont présentées. Kurt von Schröder est identifié comme l'intermédiaire clé dans la gestion de cette "caisse noire" de la S.S.

Enfin, au chapitre 10, nous avons passé en revue un livre supprimé en 1934 et le "mythe de Sidney Warburg". Le livre censuré accusait les Rockefeller, les Warburg et les grandes compagnies pétrolières d'avoir financé Hitler. Si le nom "Sidney Warburg" était sans aucun doute une invention, le fait extraordinaire reste que l'argument du livre supprimé écrit par un certain "Sidney Warburg" est remarquablement proche des preuves présentées ici. Il reste également à savoir pourquoi James Paul Warburg, quinze ans plus tard, voudrait tenter, de manière plutôt transparente et glissante, de réfuter le contenu du livre de "Warburg", un livre qu'il prétend ne pas avoir vu. Il est peut-être encore plus difficile de comprendre pourquoi Warburg a choisi les *Mémoires* du nazi von Papen pour présenter sa réfutation.

Enfin, au chapitre 11, nous avons examiné le rôle des banques Morgan et Chase dans la Seconde Guerre mondiale, et plus particulièrement leur collaboration avec les nazis en France alors qu'une guerre majeure faisait rage.

En d'autres termes, comme dans nos deux précédents examens des liens entre les banquiers internationaux de New York et les grands événements historiques, nous constatons un schéma avéré de subvention et de manipulation politique.

L'INFLUENCE PRÉPONDÉRANTE DES BANQUIERS INTERNATIONAUX

En examinant le large éventail de faits présentés dans les trois volumes de la série Wall Street, on constate la récurrence persistante des mêmes noms : Owen Young, Gerard Swope, Hjalmar Schacht, Bernard Baruch, etc. ; les mêmes banques internationales : J.P. Morgan, Guaranty Trust, Chase Bank ; et le même endroit à New York : généralement le 120 Broadway.

Ce groupe de banquiers internationaux a soutenu la révolution bolchevique et a ensuite profité de la création d'une Russie soviétique. Ce groupe a soutenu Roosevelt et a profité du socialisme du New Deal. Ce groupe a également soutenu Hitler et a certainement profité de l'armement allemand dans les années 1930. Alors que le Big Business aurait dû mener ses activités commerciales chez Ford Motor, Standard of New Jersey, etc., nous le trouvons activement et profondément impliqué dans les bouleversements politiques, la guerre et les révolutions dans trois grands pays.

La version de l'histoire présentée ici est que l'élite financière a sciemment et avec préméditation assisté la révolution bolchevique de 1917 de concert avec les banquiers allemands. Après avoir largement profité de la détresse hyperinflationniste allemande de 1923, et avoir prévu de faire porter le fardeau des réparations allemandes sur le dos des investisseurs américains, Wall Street a découvert qu'elle avait provoqué la crise financière de 1929.

Deux hommes ont alors été soutenus en tant que leaders pour les principaux pays occidentaux : Franklin D. Roosevelt aux États-Unis et Adolf Hitler en Allemagne. Le New Deal de Roosevelt et le plan de quatre ans de Hitler présentaient de grandes similitudes. Les plans Roosevelt et Hitler étaient des plans de prise de contrôle de leurs pays respectifs par les fascistes. Alors que la NRA de Roosevelt a échoué, en raison des contraintes constitutionnelles en vigueur à l'époque, le Plan de Hitler a réussi.

Pourquoi l'élite de Wall Street, les banquiers internationaux, voulaient-ils Roosevelt et Hitler au pouvoir ? C'est un aspect que nous n'avons pas exploré. Selon le "mythe de Sidney Warburg", Wall Street voulait une politique de vengeance, c'est-à-dire une guerre en Europe entre la France et l'Allemagne. Nous savons, même par l'histoire de l'establishment, que tant Hitler que Roosevelt ont mis en œuvre des politiques menant à la guerre.

Les liens entre les personnes et les événements dans cette série de trois livres nécessiteraient un autre livre. Mais un seul exemple indiquera peut-être la remarquable concentration de pouvoir au sein d'un nombre relativement restreint d'organisations, et l'utilisation qui fut faite de ce pouvoir.

Le 1er mai 1918, alors que les bolcheviks ne contrôlaient qu'une petite partie de la Russie (et allaient même faillir perdre cette partie durant l'été 1918), la Ligue américaine d'aide et de coopération avec la Russie fut organisée à Washington pour soutenir les bolcheviks. Ce n'était pas un comité du type "Pas touche à la Russie" formé par le parti communiste américain ou ses alliés. C'était un comité créé par Wall Street avec George P. Whalen de la Vacuum Oil Company comme trésorier et Coffin and Oudin de la General Electric, ainsi que Thompson du Système de la Réserve Fédérale, Willard de la Baltimore & Ohio Railroad, et divers socialistes.

Lorsque nous regardons la montée d'Hitler et du nazisme, nous trouvons Vacuum Oil et General Electric bien représentés. L'ambassadeur Dodd en Allemagne a été frappé par la contribution monétaire et technique de la Vacuum Oil Company, contrôlée par Rockefeller, à la construction d'installations militaires d'essence pour les nazis. L'ambassadeur a tenté de mettre en garde Roosevelt. Dodd croyait, dans son apparente naïveté concernant la conduite des affaires mondiales, que Roosevelt interviendrait, mais Roosevelt lui-même était soutenu par ces mêmes intérêts pétroliers et Walter Teagle de la Standard Oil du New Jersey et de la NRA était au conseil d'administration de la Fondation Warm Springs de Roosevelt. Ainsi, dans un exemple parmi tant d'autres, nous trouvons la Vacuum Oil Company, contrôlée par Rockefeller, qui a joué un rôle important dans la création de la Russie bolchevique, le renforcement militaire de l'Allemagne nazie et le soutien du New Deal de Roosevelt.

LES ÉTATS-UNIS SONT-ILS DIRIGÉS PAR UNE ÉLITE DICTATORIALE ?

Depuis une dizaine d'années, et certainement depuis les années 1960, un flux constant de littérature a présenté la thèse selon laquelle les États-Unis sont dirigés par une élite non élue et qui se perpétue elle-même. En outre, la plupart de ces livres affirment que cette élite contrôle, ou du moins influence fortement, toutes les décisions de politique étrangère et intérieure, et qu'aucune idée ne devient respectable ou n'est publiée aux États-Unis sans l'approbation tacite, ou peut-être le manque de désapprobation, de ce cercle élitiste.

De toute évidence, le flux même de la littérature anti-establishment témoigne en soi du fait que les États-Unis ne peuvent être entièrement sous la coupe d'un seul groupe ou d'une seule élite. D'autre part, la littérature anti-establishment n'est pas pleinement reconnue ou raisonnablement discutée dans les cercles académiques ou médiatiques. Le plus souvent, elle consiste en une édition limitée, produite à titre privé et diffusée presque de main à main. Il y a quelques exceptions, certes, mais pas assez pour contester l'observation selon laquelle les critiques anti-establishment n'entrent pas facilement dans les canaux d'information/distribution normaux.

Alors qu'au début et au milieu des années 60, tout concept de domination par une élite conspiratrice, ou même par n'importe quelle sorte d'élite, était une raison suffisante pour rejeter d'emblée son promoteur comme un "cinglé", l'atmosphère pour de tels concepts a radicalement changé. L'affaire du Watergate a probablement apporté la touche finale à un environnement de scepticisme et de doute qui se développait depuis longtemps. Nous en sommes presque au point où quiconque accepte, par exemple, le rapport de la Commission Warren, ou croit que le déclin et la chute de M. Nixon n'ont pas eu d'aspects conspirateurs, est suspect. En bref, plus personne ne croit vraiment au processus d'information de l'establishment. Et il existe une grande variété de présentations alternatives des événements désormais disponibles pour les curieux.

Plusieurs centaines de livres, couvrant tout l'éventail du spectre politique et philosophique, ajoutent des bribes de preuves, des hypothèses et des accusations. Ce qui était il n'y a pas si longtemps une idée farfelue, dont on parlait à minuit derrière des portes closes, dans des chuchotements feutrés et presque conspirateurs, est maintenant ouvertement débattu - non pas, bien sûr, dans les journaux de l'establishment, mais certainement dans des talk-shows radio hors réseau, dans la presse clandestine, et même de temps en temps dans des livres de maisons d'édition respectables de l'establishment.

Posons donc à nouveau la question : Y a-t-il une élite de pouvoir non élue derrière le gouvernement américain ?

Une source d'information substantielle et souvent citée est Carroll Quigley, professeur de relations internationales à l'université de Georgetown, qui a publié en 1966 une histoire moderne monumentale intitulée *Tragédie et Espoir.*[616]Le livre de Quigley se distingue des autres dans cette veine révisionniste, du fait qu'il est basé sur une étude de deux ans des documents internes d'un des centres de pouvoir. Quigley retrace l'histoire de l'élite du pouvoir :

> ... les pouvoirs du capitalisme financier avaient un autre objectif de grande envergure, rien de moins que de créer un système mondial de contrôle financier entre des mains privées capables de dominer le système politique de chaque pays et l'économie du monde dans son ensemble.

Quigley démontre également que le Council on Foreign Relations, la National Planning Association et d'autres groupes sont des organes de décision "semi-secrets" sous le contrôle de cette élite au pouvoir.

Dans la présentation tabulaire suivante, nous avons énuméré cinq ouvrages de ce type, dont celui de Quigley. Leurs thèses essentielles et leur compatibilité avec les trois volumes de la série "Wall Street" sont résumées. Il est surprenant que dans les trois grands événements historiques notés, les supputations de Carroll Quigley ne soient pas du tout compatibles avec les preuves présentes dans la série "Wall Street". Quigley fait beaucoup pour prouver l'existence de l'élite au pouvoir, mais ne pénètre pas les opérations de cette dite élite.

Il est possible que les documents utilisés par Quigley aient été expurgés et qu'ils ne contiennent pas d'éléments probants sur la manipulation élitiste d'événements tels que la révolution bolchevique, l'accession d'Hitler au pouvoir et l'élection de Roosevelt en 1933. Il est plus probable que ces manipulations politiques ne soient pas du tout consignées dans les dossiers des groupes de pouvoir. Il se peut qu'il s'agisse d'actions non enregistrées d'un petit segment *ad hoc* de l'élite. Il est à noter que les documents utilisés par nous proviennent de sources gouvernementales, enregistrant les actions quotidiennes de Trotsky, Lénine, Roosevelt, Hitler, J.P. Morgan et des différentes entreprises et banques impliquées.

---

[616] Carroll Quigley, *Tragedy and Hope, a history of the World in our time*, op. cit.

D'autre part, des auteurs tels que Jules Archer, Gary Allen, Helen P. Lasell et William Domhoff, écrivent à partir de points de vue politiques très différents[617], sont en accord avec les preuves présentées dans la trilogie "Wall Street". Ces écrivains présentent l'hypothèse d'une élite au pouvoir manipulant le gouvernement américain. La série "Wall Street" démontre comment cette "élite du pouvoir" hypothétique a manipulé des événements historiques spécifiques.

Il est évident que tout exercice d'un tel pouvoir sans contrainte et supra-légal est inconstitutionnel, même s'il est enveloppé dans le cadre d'actions respectueuses de la loi. Nous pouvons donc légitimement soulever la question de l'existence d'une force subversive opérant pour supprimer des droits garantis par la Constitution.

L'ÉLITE DE NEW YORK COMME FORCE SUBVERSIVE

L'histoire du XXe siècle, telle qu'elle est consignée dans les manuels et les revues de l'establishment, est inexacte. C'est une histoire qui se fonde uniquement sur les documents officiels que diverses administrations ont jugé bon de mettre à la disposition du public.

Table : **LES PREUVES DE LA SÉRIE "WALL STREET" SONT-ELLES COHÉRENTES AVEC LES ARGUMENTS RÉVISIONNISTES CONNEXES PRÉSENTÉS AILLEURS ?**

(1) New York : MacMillan, 1966.
(2) New York : Hawthorn, 1973.
(3) Seal Beach : Concord Press, 1971.
(4) New York : Liberty, 1963.
(5) New Jersey : Prentice Hall, 1967.

[617] Il y en a beaucoup d'autres ; l'auteur a choisi plus ou moins au hasard deux conservateurs (Allen et Lasell) et deux libéraux (Archer et Domhoff).

Auteur et titre :	Thèse essentielle :	La thèse est-elle cohérente avec : (1) Wall Street et la révolution bolchevique	(2) Wall Street et FDR	(3) Wall Street et la montée d'Hitler
Carroll QUIGLEY : *Tragedy and Hope* (1) l'establishment "semi-secret" de la côte Est	L'établissement de la côte Est "semi-secret" et les verrouillages jouent un rôle dominant dans la planification et la politique aux États-Unis.	Quigley n'inclut pas les preuves présentées dans *Wall Street et la révolution bolchevique* (pp. 385-9)	Non : L'argument de Quigley est totalement incompatible avec ce qui précède (voir p. 533)	Le récit de Quigley sur la montée d'Hitler (pp. 529-33) ne contient pas de preuves de l'implication de l'establishment.
Jules ARCHER : *Plot to seize the White House* (2)	En 1933-4, il y a eu une conspiration de Wall Street pour supprimer FDR et installer une dictature fasciste aux États-Unis.	Pas pertinent, mais les éléments de Wall Street cités par Archer étaient impliqués dans la révolution bolchevique.	Oui : en général, les preuves d'Archer sont cohérentes, sauf que le rôle de FDR est interprété différemment.	Les parties d'Archer portant sur Hitler et le nazisme sont conformes à ce qui précède.
Gary ALLEN : *None Dare Call It Conspiracy* (3)	Il existe une conspiration secrète (le Council on Foreign Relations) visant à installer une dictature aux États-Unis et, en fin de compte, à contrôler le monde.	Oui, à l'exception de variations mineures sur le financement.	Non inclus dans Allen mais cohérent.	Non inclus dans Allen mais cohérent.
Helen P. LASELL : *Power Behind the Government today* (4)	Le Council on Foreign Relations est une organisation subversive secrète qui se consacre au renversement du gouvernement constitutionnel aux États-Unis.	Les preuves de Lasell sont conformes à ce qui précède.	Les preuves de Lasell sont conformes à ce qui précède.	Les preuves de Lasell sont conformes à ce qui précède
William DOMHOFF : *Who Rules America?* (5)	Il existe une "élite du pouvoir" qui contrôle toutes les grandes banques, les entreprises, les fondations, le pouvoir exécutif et les agences de régulation du gouvernement américain.	La série ci-dessus étend l'argumentation de Dombolls à la politique étrangère.	La série ci-dessus étend l'argumentation de Domhoff aux élections présidentielles.	La série ci-dessus étend l'argument de Domhoffs à la politique étrangère.

Mais une histoire précise ne peut pas se baser sur une diffusion sélective des archives documentaires. L'exactitude exige l'accès à tous les documents. En pratique, à mesure que sont acquis les documents précédemment classés dans les dossiers du Département d'État américain, du ministère britannique des Affaires étrangères, des archives du ministère allemand des Affaires étrangères et d'autres dépositaires, une nouvelle version de l'histoire apparaît ; la version de l'establishment qui prévaut est considérée comme non seulement inexacte, mais aussi conçue pour dissimuler un tissu omniprésent de tromperie et de conduite immorale.

Le centre du pouvoir politique, tel qu'autorisé par la Constitution américaine, est constitué d'un Congrès et d'un Président élus, travaillant dans le cadre et sous les contraintes d'une Constitution, telle qu'interprétée par une Cour suprême impartiale. Par le passé, nous avons supposé que le pouvoir politique était par conséquent soigneusement exercé par les pouvoirs exécutif et législatif, après délibération et évaluation des souhaits de l'électorat. En fait, rien ne pourrait être plus éloigné de cette hypothèse. L'électorat soupçonne depuis longtemps, mais sait maintenant que les promesses politiques ne valent rien. Le mensonge est à l'ordre du jour pour les responsables de la mise en œuvre des politiques. Les guerres sont lancées (et arrêtées) sans la moindre explication cohérente. Les discours politiques ne sont jamais assortis d'actes correspondants. Pourquoi en serait-il autrement ? Apparemment parce que le centre du pouvoir politique a été déplacé ailleurs au détriment des représentants élus et apparemment compétents de Washington, et que cette élite au pouvoir a ses propres objectifs, qui sont incompatibles avec ceux du grand public.

Dans cette série de trois volumes, nous avons identifié pour trois événements historiques que le siège du pouvoir politique aux États-Unis - le pouvoir en coulisses, l'influence cachée sur Washington - comme celui de l'établissement financier à New York : les banquiers privés internationaux, plus précisément les maisons financières de J.P. Morgan, la Chase Manhattan Bank contrôlée par Rockefeller et, dans les premiers temps (avant la fusion de leur Manhattan Bank avec l'ancienne Chase Bank), les Warburg.

Les États-Unis sont devenus, malgré la Constitution et ses prétendues contraintes, un État quasi totalitaire. Si nous n'avons pas (encore) les signes extérieurs de la dictature, les camps de concentration et le fait de frapper à la porte à minuit, nous avons très certainement des menaces et des actions visant la survie des critiques qui ne sont pas de l'establishment, l'utilisation de l'Internal Revenue Service pour mettre les dissidents au pas, et la manipulation de la Constitution par un système judiciaire politiquement inféodé à l'establishment.

Il est dans l'intérêt pécuniaire des banquiers internationaux de centraliser le pouvoir politique - et cette centralisation peut être réalisée au mieux à travers la mise en place d'une société collectiviste, telle que la Russie socialiste, l'Allemagne nationale-socialiste ou les États-Unis socialistes sous la planification de la Fabian Society.

On ne peut pas comprendre et apprécier pleinement la politique américaine du XXe siècle et la politique étrangère sans se rendre compte que cette élite financière monopolise effectivement la politique de Washington.

Dans tous les cas, les documents récemment publiés impliquent cette élite et confirment cette hypothèse. Les versions révisionnistes de l'entrée des États-Unis dans les Première et Deuxième guerres mondiales, de la Corée et du Vietnam révèlent l'influence et les objectifs de cette élite.

Pendant la plus grande partie du XXe siècle, le système de la Réserve fédérale, en particulier la Federal Reserve Bank of New York (qui échappe au contrôle du Congrès, non auditée et non contrôlée, avec le pouvoir d'imprimer de la monnaie et de créer du crédit à volonté), a exercé un quasi-monopole sur la direction de l'économie américaine. Dans le domaine des affaires étrangères, le Council on Foreign Relations, qui est en apparence un forum innocent pour les universitaires, les hommes d'affaires et les politiciens, contient dans sa coquille, peut-être inconnue de beaucoup de ses membres, un centre de pouvoir qui détermine unilatéralement la politique étrangère américaine. Le principal objectif de cette politique étrangère submergée - et manifestement subversive - est l'acquisition de marchés et de pouvoir économique (de profits, si vous voulez), pour un petit groupe de multinationales géantes sous le contrôle virtuel de quelques sociétés d'investissement bancaire et de familles qui les contrôlent.

Par le biais de fondations pilotées par cette élite, les recherches d'universitaires dociles et sans scrupules, "conservateurs" comme "libéraux", ont été conduites vers des directions utiles aux objectifs de l'élite essentiellement pour maintenir cet appareil de pouvoir subversif et anticonstitutionnel.

Par le biais de maisons d'édition contrôlées par cette même élite financière, des livres malvenus ont été écartés et des livres utiles ont été promus ; heureusement, l'édition comporte peu de barrières à l'entrée et parvient presque toujours à rester dans le cadre d'une saine compétition. Grâce au contrôle d'une douzaine de grands journaux, dirigés par des éditeurs qui pensent tous de la même façon, l'information du public peut être orchestrée presque à volonté. Hier, le programme spatial ; aujourd'hui, une crise énergétique ou une campagne pour l'écologie ; demain, une guerre au Moyen-Orient ou une autre "crise" fabriquée.

Le résultat total de cette manipulation de la société par l'élite de l'establishment a été quatre grandes guerres en soixante ans, une dette nationale paralysante, l'abandon de la Constitution, la suppression de la liberté individuelle et des opportunités offertes à l'exercice des talents naturels, et la création d'un vaste fossé de crédibilité entre l'homme de la rue et Washington, D.C. Alors que le dispositif transparent de deux grands partis clamant des différences artificielles, avec ces conventions se changeant en foire d'empoigne et le cliché d'une "politique étrangère bipartite" n'est plus crédible et que l'élite financière elle-même reconnaît que ses politiques ne sont pas acceptées par le public, elle est manifestement prête à faire cavalier seul sans même chercher un soutien public nominal.

En bref, nous devons maintenant examiner et débattre pour savoir si cet establishment élitiste basé à New York est une force subversive opérant délibérément pour supprimer la Constitution et empêcher le fonctionnement d'une société libre. Telle sera la tâche qui nous attend au cours de la prochaine décennie.

LA VÉRITÉ RÉVISIONNISTE QUI ÉMERGE LENTEMENT

L'arène de ce débat et le fondement de nos accusations de subversion sont les preuves fournies par l'historien révisionniste. Lentement, au fil des décennies, livre par livre, presque ligne par ligne, la vérité de l'histoire récente a émergé au fur et à mesure que les documents étaient publiés, sondés, analysés et placés dans un cadre historique plus valable.

Examinons quelques exemples. L'entrée des États-Unis dans la Seconde Guerre mondiale aurait été précipitée, selon la version de l'establishment, par l'attaque japonaise sur Pearl Harbor. Les révisionnistes ont établi que Franklin D. Roosevelt et le général Marshall étaient au courant de l'attaque japonaise imminente et n'ont rien fait pour avertir les autorités militaires de Pearl Harbor.

L'establishment voulait la guerre avec le Japon. Par la suite, l'establishment s'est assuré que l'enquête du Congrès sur Pearl Harbor serait conforme à la politique de Roosevelt. Selon les mots de Percy Greaves, expert en chef de la minorité républicaine au sein de la commission parlementaire mixte chargée de l'enquête sur Pearl Harbor :

> Les faits complets ne seront jamais connus. La plupart des soi-disant enquêtes ont été des tentatives pour supprimer, tromper ou confondre ceux qui cherchent la vérité. Du début à la fin, les faits et les dossiers ont été dissimulés afin de ne révéler que les éléments d'information qui profitent à l'administration faisant l'objet de l'enquête. On dit à ceux qui cherchent la vérité que d'autres faits ou documents ne peuvent être révélés parce qu'ils sont mêlés à des journaux intimes, qu'ils concernent nos relations avec des pays étrangers ou ne contiennent aucune information de valeur.[618]

Mais ce n'était pas la première ni la dernière tentative de faire entrer les États-Unis en guerre. Les intérêts de Morgan, de concert avec Winston Churchill, ont essayé d'entrainer les États-Unis dans la Première Guerre mondiale dès 1915 et y sont parvenus en 1917. L'ouvrage *Lusitania* de Colin Thompson implique le président Woodrow Wilson dans le fameux naufrage - un stratagème d'horreur destiné à générer une réaction publique pour entraîner les États-Unis dans la guerre contre l'Allemagne. Thompson démontre que Woodrow Wilson savait quatre jours à l'avance que le Lusitania transportait six millions de munitions plus des explosifs, et donc que "les passagers qui se proposaient de naviguer sur ce navire naviguaient en violation des lois de ce pays".[619]

La commission d'enquête britannique dirigée par Lord Mersey a reçu l'instruction du gouvernement britannique "qu'il est considéré comme politiquement opportun que le capitaine Turner, le capitaine du *Lusitania*, soit désigné comme le principal responsable du désastre".

---

618 Percy L. Greaves, Jr, "The Pearl Harbor Investigation", dans Harry Elmer Harnes, *Perpetual War for Perpetual Peace,* (Caldwell : Caxton Printers, 1953), p, 13-20.

619 Colin Simpson, *Lusitania,* (Londres : Longman, 1972), p, 252.

Rétrospectivement, compte tenu des preuves de Colin Thompson, il est plus juste d'attribuer la faute au président Wilson, au colonel House, à J.P. Morgan et à Winston Churchill ; cette élite conspiratrice aurait dû être jugée pour négligence délibérée, voire pour trahison. C'est à l'honneur éternel de Lord Mersey qu'après avoir accompli son "devoir" selon les instructions du gouvernement de Sa Majesté, et en faisant porter le blâme au capitaine Turner, il a démissionné, rejeté ses honoraires et, à partir de cette date, refusé de s'occuper des commissions du gouvernement britannique. À ses amis, Lord Mersey disait du naufrage du *Lusitania* qu'il s'agissait d'une "sale affaire".

Puis, en 1933-34, la firme Morgan a tenté d'installer une dictature fasciste aux États-Unis. Selon les termes de Jules Archer, il était prévu qu'un putsch fasciste prenne le contrôle du gouvernement et "le dirige sous la direction d'un dictateur au nom des banquiers et des industriels américains".[620] Une fois de plus, un seul individu courageux a émergé - le général Smedley Darlington Butler, qui a dénoncé la conspiration de Wall Street. Et une fois de plus, le Congrès se distingue, en particulier les membres du Congrès Dickstein et MacCormack, par son refus lâche de ne faire que mener une enquête symbolique de blanchissage.

Depuis la Seconde Guerre mondiale, nous avons assisté à la guerre de Corée et à la guerre du Vietnam, des guerres inutiles, longues et coûteuses en dollars et en vies humaines, qui n'ont d'autre but que de générer des contrats d'armement de plusieurs milliards de dollars. Il est certain que ces guerres n'ont pas été menées pour endiguer le communisme, car pendant cinquante ans, l'establishment a entretenu et subventionné l'Union soviétique qui fournissait des armes aux autres parties belligérantes au cours des deux guerres - la Corée et le Vietnam. Notre histoire révisionniste montrera donc que les États-Unis ont directement ou indirectement armé les deux parties, au moins en Corée et au Viêt Nam.

Dans l'assassinat du président Kennedy, pour prendre un exemple national, il est difficile de trouver quelqu'un qui accepte aujourd'hui les conclusions de la Commission Warren - sauf peut-être les membres de cette Commission. Pourtant, des preuves essentielles sont encore cachées aux yeux du public pendant 50 à 75 ans. L'affaire du Watergate a démontré, même à l'homme de la rue, que la Maison-Blanche peut être un nid d'intrigues et de tromperies.

De toute l'histoire récente, l'histoire de l'opération Keelhaul[621] est peut-être la plus dégoûtante. L'opération Keelhaul a été le rapatriement forcé de millions de Russes sur ordre du président (alors général) Dwight D. Eisenhower, en violation directe de la Convention de Genève de 1929 et de la longue tradition américaine de refuge politique. L'opération Keelhaul, qui contrevient à toutes nos idées de décence élémentaire et de liberté individuelle, a été entreprise sur les ordres directs du général Eisenhower et, nous pouvons maintenant le présumer, faisait partie d'un programme à long terme visant à nourrir le collectivisme, qu'il s'agisse du nazisme d'Hitler du communisme soviétique ou du New Deal de FDR. Pourtant, jusqu'à la récente publication de preuves documentaires par Julius Epstein,

---

620 Jules Archer, *The Plot to Seize the White House,* (New York : Hawthorn Book, 1973), p. 202.

621 Voir Julius Epstein, *Operation Keelhaul,* (Old Greenwich : Devin Adair, 1973).

quiconque osait suggérer qu'Eisenhower trahirait des millions d'individus innocents à des fins politiques était vicieusement et impitoyablement attaqué. [622]

Ce que cette histoire révisionniste nous apprend réellement, c'est que notre volonté, en tant que citoyens individuels, de céder le pouvoir politique à une élite a coûté environ la vie à deux cents millions de personnes dans le monde entre 1820 et 1975. Ajoutez à cette misère indescriptible les camps de concentration, les prisonniers politiques, la répression et l'oppression de ceux qui tentent de faire éclater la vérité.

Quand tout cela va-t-il s'arrêter ? Cela ne s'arrêtera pas tant que nous n'aurons pas agi sur la base d'un simple axiome : le système de pouvoir ne continue que tant que les individus le souhaitent, et il ne continuera que tant que les individus tenteront d'obtenir quelque chose pour rien. Le jour où une majorité d'individus déclarera ou agira comme si elle ne voulait rien du gouvernement, déclarera qu'elle s'occupera de son propre bien-être et de ses intérêts, alors ce jour-là, les élites au pouvoir seront condamnées. L'attrait de "suivre" les élites du pouvoir repose sur le fait d'obtenir quelque chose pour rien. C'est une forme d'appât. L'establishment offre toujours quelque chose pour rien ; mais ce quelque chose est pris à quelqu'un d'autre, sous forme d'impôts ou de pillage, et attribué ailleurs en échange d'un soutien politique.

Les crises et les guerres périodiques sont utilisées pour alimenter d'autres cycles de pillage et de récompense qui, en fait, resserrent le nœud coulant autour de nos libertés individuelles. Et bien sûr, nous avons des hordes de larves universitaires, d'hommes d'affaires amoraux et de simples parasites, qui sont les bénéficiaires improductifs du pillage généralisé.

Mettons un terme à ce cercle vicieux du pillage et de la récompense immorale et les structures élitistes s'effondreront. Mais la tuerie et le pillage ne cesseront pas tant qu'une majorité n'aura pas trouvé le courage moral et la force intérieure de rejeter le jeu de l'escroquerie et de le remplacer par des associations bénévoles, des communes volontaires ou des sociétés locales décentralisées.

[622] Voir par exemple Robert Welch, *The Politician,* (Belmont, Mass. : Belmont Publishing Co., 1963).

ANNEXE A

PROGRAMME DU PARTI OUVRIER NATIONAL-SOCIALISTE ALLEMAND

Note : Ce programme est important, car il démontre que la nature du nazisme était connue publiquement dès 1920.

LE PROGRAMME

Le programme du parti des travailleurs allemands est limité dans le temps. Les dirigeants n'ont pas l'intention, une fois les objectifs annoncés dans ce programme atteints, d'en créer de nouveaux, simplement pour accroître artificiellement le mécontentement des masses et assurer ainsi la pérennité du parti.

1. Nous demandons l'union de tous les Allemands pour former une Grande Allemagne sur la base du droit à l'autodétermination dont jouissent les nations.
2. Nous demandons l'égalité des droits du peuple allemand dans ses relations avec les autres nations et l'abolition des traités de paix de Versailles et de Saint-Germain.
3. Nous demandons des terres et des territoires (colonies) pour nourrir notre peuple et pour installer notre population superflue.
4. Seuls les membres de la nation peuvent être citoyens de l'État. Seuls ceux qui sont de sang allemand, quelle que soit leur croyance, peuvent être membres de la nation. Aucun Juif ne peut donc être membre de la nation.
5. Toute personne qui n'est pas citoyenne de l'État ne peut vivre en Allemagne qu'en tant qu'hôte et doit être considérée comme étant soumise à des lois étrangères.
6. Le droit de vote sur le gouvernement et la législation de l'État doit être exercé par le seul citoyen de l'État. Nous exigeons donc que toutes les nominations officielles, de quelque nature qu'elles soient, que ce soit dans le Reich, dans le pays ou dans les petites localités, soient accordées aux seuls citoyens de l'État.
7. Nous nous opposons à la coutume corruptrice du Parlement qui consiste à pourvoir des postes uniquement en fonction de considérations partisanes, sans référence à la personnalité ou aux capacités.
8. Nous exigeons que l'État se donne pour premier devoir de promouvoir l'industrie et les moyens de subsistance des citoyens de l'État. S'il n'est pas possible de nourrir toute la population de l'État, les ressortissants étrangers (non-citoyens de l'État) doivent être exclus du Reich.
Toute immigration non allemande doit être empêchée. Nous exigeons que tous les non-allemands entrés en Allemagne après le 2 août 1914 soient immédiatement obligés de quitter le Reich.
9. Tous les citoyens de l'État sont égaux en droits et en devoirs.

10. Le premier devoir de chaque citoyen de l'État doit être de travailler avec son esprit ou avec son corps. Les activités de l'individu ne doivent pas entrer en conflit avec les intérêts de l'ensemble, mais doivent se dérouler dans le cadre de la communauté et être destinées au bien général.
Nous exigeons donc :
11. Suppression des revenus non gagnés par le travail.

L'ABOLITION DE LA SERVITUDE D'INTÉRÊT

12. Compte tenu de l'énorme sacrifice de vies et de biens exigé d'une nation par chaque guerre, l'enrichissement personnel dû à une guerre doit être considéré comme un crime contre la nation. Nous demandons donc la confiscation impitoyable de tous les gains de guerre,
13. Nous demandons la nationalisation de toutes les entreprises qui ont été jusqu'à présent constituées en sociétés (Trusts).
14. Nous demandons que les bénéfices du commerce de gros soient répartis.
15. Nous exigeons un développement important de l'offre pour la vieillesse.
16. Nous exigeons la création et le maintien d'une classe moyenne saine, la communalisation immédiate des locaux commerciaux de gros et leur location à un tarif bon marché aux petits commerçants, et qu'une extrême considération soit accordée à tous les petits fournisseurs de l'État, des autorités de district et des petites localités.
17. Nous demandons une réforme foncière adaptée à nos besoins nationaux, l'adoption d'une loi sur la confiscation sans compensation des terres à usage communal, la suppression des intérêts sur les prêts fonciers et la prévention de toute spéculation foncière.
18. Nous exigeons des poursuites impitoyables à l'encontre de ceux dont les activités sont préjudiciables à l'intérêt commun. Les sordides criminels contre la nation, les usuriers, les profiteurs, etc. doivent être punis de mort, quelles que soient leurs croyances ou leur race.
19. Nous demandons que la loi romaine, qui sert l'ordre mondial matérialiste, soit remplacée par un système juridique pour toute l'Allemagne.
20. Dans le but d'ouvrir à tout Allemand capable et travailleur la possibilité de faire des études supérieures et d'obtenir ainsi un avancement, l'État doit envisager une refonte en profondeur de notre système national d'éducation. Le programme d'études de tous les établissements d'enseignement doit être adapté aux exigences de la vie pratique. La compréhension de l'idée d'État (sociologie de l'État) doit être l'objectif de l'école, à partir de la première aube de l'intelligence chez l'élève. Nous exigeons le développement des enfants doués de parents pauvres, quelle que soit leur classe ou leur profession, aux frais de l'État.
21. L'État doit veiller à élever le niveau de santé de la nation en protégeant les mères et les nourrissons, en interdisant le travail des enfants, en augmentant l'efficacité corporelle par la gymnastique et les sports obligatoires prévus par la loi, et en soutenant largement les clubs engagés dans le développement corporel des jeunes.
22. Nous demandons l'abolition d'une armée rémunérée et la formation d'une armée nationale.
23. Nous demandons une guerre juridique contre le mensonge politique conscient et sa diffusion dans la presse. Afin de faciliter la création d'une presse nationale allemande, nous exigeons :
a) que tous les rédacteurs en chef de journaux et leurs assistants, employant la langue allemande, doivent être membres de la nation ;
b)qu'une autorisation spéciale de l'État est nécessaire pour la parution de journaux non allemands. Ceux-ci ne sont pas nécessairement imprimés en langue allemande ;

(c) que la loi interdit aux non-Allemands de participer financièrement à des journaux allemands ou de les influencer, et que la sanction pour infraction à la loi est la suppression de tout journal de ce type et l'expulsion immédiate du non-Allemand concerné.
Il doit être interdit de publier des documents qui ne contribuent pas au bien-être national. Nous demandons que soient poursuivies en justice toutes les tendances artistiques et littéraires susceptibles de désintégrer notre vie en tant que nation, et que soient supprimées les institutions qui vont à l'encontre des exigences susmentionnées.
24. Nous demandons la liberté pour toutes les confessions religieuses dans l'État, dans la mesure où elles ne constituent pas un danger pour lui et ne militent pas contre les sentiments moraux de la race allemande.
Le parti, en tant que tel, est en faveur d'un christianisme positif, mais ne s'engage pas en matière de croyance à une confession particulière. Il lutte contre l'esprit juif-matérialiste en nous et hors de nous, et est convaincu que notre nation ne peut atteindre une santé permanente que de l'intérieur sur le principe : L'INTÉRÊT COMMUN AVANT LE SIEN
25. Pour que tout cela se réalise, nous demandons la création d'un pouvoir central fort de l'État. Autorité incontestée du Parlement politiquement centralisé sur l'ensemble du Reich et son organisation ; et formation de Chambres des classes et des professions en vue de l'exécution des lois générales promulguées par le Reich dans les différents États de la confédération.
Les dirigeants du Parti jurent d'aller de l'avant - si nécessaire en sacrifiant leur vie - pour assurer l'accomplissement des points précédents. Munich, le 24 février 1920.

Source : Traduction officielle en anglais par E. Dugdale, réimpression de Kurt G, W. Ludecke, *I Knew Hitler* (New York : Charles Scribner's Sons, 1937),

ANNEXE B

DÉCLARATION SOUS SERMENT DE HJALMAR SCHACHT

Moi, Dr. Hjalmar Schacht, après avoir été averti que je serai passible de sanctions pour avoir fait de fausses déclarations, déclare sous serment, de mon plein gré et sans contrainte, ce qui suit :

Les sommes versées par les participants à la réunion du 20 février 1933 chez Goering ont été versées par eux aux banquiers. Delbruck, Schickler & Cie, Berlin, au crédit d'un compte "Nationale Treuhand" (qui peut être traduit par "Tutelle nationale"). Il a été convenu que j'avais le droit de disposer de ce compte, que j'administrais en tant que fiduciaire, et qu'en cas de décès, ou si la tutelle devait être résiliée de toute autre manière, Rudolf Hess aurait le droit de disposer du compte.

J'ai disposé des montants de ce compte en émettant des chèques à l'ordre de M. Hess. Je ne sais pas ce que M. Hess a réellement fait de cet argent.

Le 4 avril 1933, j'ai fermé le compte auprès de Delbruck, Schickler & Co. et j'ai fait transférer le solde sur le "Compte Ic" auprès de la Reichsbank qui portait mon nom. Par la suite, j'ai reçu l'ordre de Hitler directement, qui a été autorisé par l'assemblée du 20 février 1933 à disposer des sommes collectées, ou par l'intermédiaire de Hess, son adjoint, de verser le solde d'environ 600 000 marks à Ribbentrop.

J'ai lu attentivement cette déclaration sous serment (une page) et l'ai signée. J'ai fait les corrections nécessaires de ma propre écriture et j'ai paraphé chaque correction dans la marge de la page. Je déclare sous serment que j'ai dit toute la vérité au meilleur de ma connaissance et de ma conviction.

(Signé) Dr. Hjalmar Schacht
12 août 1947

Dans une déclaration sous serment ultérieure du 18 août 1947 (N1-9764, Pros. Ex 54), Schacht a déclaré ce qui suit à propos de l'interrogatoire susmentionné :

> "J'ai fait toutes les déclarations figurant dans cet interrogatoire à Clifford Hyanning, un enquêteur financier des forces américaines, de mon plein gré et sans contrainte. J'ai relu cet interrogatoire aujourd'hui et je peux affirmer que tous les faits qu'il contient sont vrais, à ma connaissance et selon ma conviction. Je déclare sous serment que j'ai dit toute la vérité au meilleur de ma connaissance et de ma conviction".

Source : Copie de la pièce à conviction 55. *Procès des criminels de guerre devant les tribunaux militaires de Nuremberg en vertu de la loi n° 10 du Conseil de contrôle,*

Nuremberg, octobre 1946-avril 1949, Volume VII, I.G. Farben, (Washington : U.S. Government Printing Office, 1952).

ANNEXE C

LES INSCRIPTIONS SUR LE COMPTE DE "TUTELLE NATIONALE", QUI SE TROUVE DANS LES DOSSIERS DU DELBRUCK, SCHICKLER CO. BANQUE

TUTELLE NATIONALE
PRÉSIDENT DE LA REICHSBANK DR. HJALMAR SCHACHT,
BERLIN-ZEHLENDORF

23 février	Debibk (Deutsche Bank Diskonto-Gesellschaft) Association pour les intérêts miniers, Essen		23 février	200,000.00
24	Transfert sur le compte Rudolf Hess, actuellement à Berlin	100,000.00	24	
24	Karl Herrmann		25	150,000.00
	Salon de l'automobile, Berlin		25	100,000.00
25	Directeur A. Steinke		27	200,000.00
25	Demag A.G., Duisberg		27	50,000.00
27	Société Telefunken pour la télégraphie sans fil Berlin		28	85,000.00
	Osram G.m.b.H., Berlin		28	40,000.00
27	Bayerische Hypotheken-und Wech selbank, succursale de Munich, Kauflingerstr. en faveur de Verlag Franz Eher Nachf, Munich	100,000.00	28	
27	Virement sur le compte Rudolf Hess, Berlin	100,000.00	27	
28	I.G. Farbenindustrie A.G. Frankfurt/M		1er mars	400,000.00
28	Frais de télégraphe pour le transfert à Munich	8.00	28 février	
1er mars	Votre paiement		2 mars	125,000.00
2	Transfert télégraphique à la Bayerische Hypotheken-und Wechselbank, succursale de Munich, Bayerstr.			

	pour le compte de Josef Jung	400,000.00	2	
	Frais de transfert télégraphique	23.00	2	
	Transfert de compte Rudolf Hess	300,000.00		
2	Remboursement du directeur Karl Lange, Berlin		3	30,000.00
3	Remboursement de la part du directeur Karl Lange, compte "Maschinen-industrie		4	20,000.00
	Remboursement de Verein ruer die bergbaulichen Interessen, Essen		4	100,000.00
	Remboursement de Karl Herrmann, Berlin, Dessauerstr. 28/9		4	150,000.00
	Remboursement de la société Allgemeine Elektrizitaetsgesellschaft, Berlin		4	60,000.00
7	Remboursement du directeur général Dr. F. Springorum, Dortmund		8	36,000.00
8	Virement de la Reichsbank : Bayerische Hypotheken-und Wechselbank,			
	succursale Kauffingerstr.	100,000.00	8	
		1,100,031.00		1,696,000.00
		1,100,031.00	8 mars	1,696,000.00
8 mars	Bayerische Hypotheken-und Wechselbank, Munich, succursale Bayerstr.	100,000.00	8	
	Virement sur le compte Rudolf Hess	250,000.00	7	
10	Accumulatoren-Fabrik A.G. Berlin		11	25,000.00
13	Association f.d. intérêts miniers, Essen		14	300,000.00
14	Remboursement Rudolf Hess	200,000.00	14	
29	Remboursement Rudolf Hess	200,000.00	29	

Le 4 avril	Commerz-und Privatbank Dep. Kasse N. Berlin W.9 Potsdamerstr. 1 f. Spécial			
	Compte S 29	99,000.00	4 avril	
5	Intérêts selon la liste 1			
	pourcentage		5	404.50
	Factures de téléphone	1.00	5	
	Affranchissement	2.50	5	
	Balance	72,370.00	5	
	Solde reporté	2,021,404.50		2,021,404.50
			5 avr.	72,370.00

ANNEXE D

LETTRE DU MINISTÈRE AMÉRICAIN DE LA GUERRE À ETHYL CORPORATION

Pièce n° 144
(manuscrit) M. Webb a envoyé des copies pour les autres directeurs
Copie à : M. Alfred P. Sloan, Jr, General Motors Corp, New York City, M. Donaldson Brown, General Motors Corp, New York City.
15 décembre 1934.

M. E. W. Webb,
Président de la société Ethyl Gasoline Corporation, 185 E, 42e rue, New York City.
Cher M. Webb : J'ai appris aujourd'hui par notre division des produits chimiques organiques que la société Ethyl Gasoline Corporation a l'intention de créer une société allemande avec l'I.G. pour fabriquer du plomb éthylique dans ce pays.
Je viens de passer deux semaines à Washington, dont une partie non négligeable a été consacrée à critiquer l'échange avec des sociétés étrangères de connaissances chimiques qui pourraient avoir une valeur militaire. Une telle communication d'informations par une entreprise industrielle peut avoir les plus graves répercussions sur celle-ci. La société Ethyl Gasoline ne ferait pas exception à la règle, en fait, elle serait probablement visée par une attaque spéciale en raison de la propriété de ses actions.
Il semblerait, à première vue, que la quantité de plomb éthylique utilisée à des fins commerciales en Allemagne soit trop faible pour être suivie. Il a été affirmé que l'Allemagne s'arme en secret. Le plomb éthylique serait sans aucun doute une aide précieuse pour les avions militaires.
Je vous écris pour vous dire qu'à mon avis, ni vous ni le conseil d'administration de l'Ethyl Gasoline Corporation ne devez en aucun cas divulguer en Allemagne des secrets ou un "savoir-faire" en rapport avec la fabrication du plomb tétraéthyle.
Je suis informé que vous serez informé par la division des colorants de la nécessité de divulguer les informations que vous avez reçues de l'Allemagne aux fonctionnaires compétents du ministère de la guerre.

Je vous prie d'agréer, Monsieur le Président,
l'expression de ma haute considération,

Source : Sénat des États-Unis, Audiences devant une sous-commission de la commission des affaires militaires, de la *mobilisation scientifique et technique,* 78e Congrès, deuxième session, partie 16, (Washington D.C. : Government Printing Office, 1944), p. 939.

ANNEXE E

EXTRAIT DU JOURNAL DE MORGENTHAU (*ALLEMAGNE*)[623] CONCERNANT SOSTHENES BEHN DE L'I.T.T.

16 mars 1945
11 h 30

RÉUNION DU GROUPE
Bretton Woods - I.T. & T. - Réparations

Présent :
M. White
M. Fussell
M. Feltus
M. Coe
M. DuBois
Mme Klotz

***H.M., Jr** :* Frank, pouvez-vous *résumer* cette affaire sur I.T.&T. ?

***M. Coe** :* Oui, monsieur. I.T. &T. a d'ailleurs transféré ou reçu hier ou il y a quelques jours 15 millions de dollars de leurs dettes en dollars payés par le gouvernement espagnol et qu'ils sont autorisés à faire sous notre licence générale, donc tout va bien. Cependant, c'est en partie dans le cadre de leur représentation auprès de nous, dans le cadre d'un accord pour la vente de la société en Espagne, ils essaient donc de nous forcer la main. La proposition qu'ils nous ont faite depuis quelques années sous différentes formes prend maintenant cette forme. Ils peuvent obtenir le remboursement de leurs créances en dollars, ce qu'ils disent ne pas avoir pu faire jusqu'à présent - soit 15 millions de dollars maintenant et 10 ou 11 millions de dollars plus tard. Ils vont vendre l'entreprise à l'Espagne et recevoir en retour 30 millions de dollars d'obligations - des obligations du gouvernement espagnol - qui doivent être amorties sur un certain nombre d'années et à un rythme d'environ 2 millions de dollars par an. Ils doivent recevoir 90% de ces exportations afin d'amortir les obligations plus rapidement, s'ils doivent les exporter aux États-Unis.

[623] *Morgenthau Diary* (Germany), op. cit.

***H. M. Jr** :* Comme le marchand d'allumettes que j'ai mentionné dans mon discours.

***M. Coe** : C'*est exact. Le gouvernement espagnol. Ils sont prêts, disent-ils - ils sont capables d'obtenir du gouvernement espagnol des assurances, que celles-ci ne le seront pas, que les actions que le gouvernement espagnol a l'intention de revendre n'iront à personne sur la liste noire, et ainsi de suite. Lors de certaines négociations que nous avons eues avec eux ces dernières semaines, ils ont été disposés à aller plus loin sur ce point. Notre hésitation à ce sujet tient à deux choses : premièrement, on ne peut pas faire confiance à Franco, et s'ils en sont capables - si Franco est capable de vendre pour 50 millions de dollars d'actions de cette société en Espagne dans les prochaines années, il pourrait très bien la vendre à des intérêts pro-allemands. Il semble douteux qu'il puisse la céder aux Espagnols, c'est donc la première chose à faire. La deuxième chose que nous ne pouvons pas trop bien documenter, mais je pense qu'elle est plus prononcée dans mon esprit que dans celui des fonds étrangers et des juristes. Je ne pense pas non plus que nous puissions vraiment faire confiance à Behn.

***M. White** :* Je suis sûr que vous ne pouvez pas.

***M. Coe** :* Nous avons ici des enregistrements d'entretiens, remontant à loin, que certains de vos hommes ont eus avec Behn - Klaus en était un - dans lesquels Behn a dit qu'il avait eu des conversations avec Goering avec la proposition que Goering devait tenir I.T. &T. Comme vous vous en souvenez, I.T. &T. a essayé d'acheter le général Aniline et d'en faire une société américaine, et cela faisait partie de l'accord dont Behn a parlé très franchement à l'État et à nos avocats. Il pensait qu'il était parfaitement normal de protéger la propriété : C'était avant que nous n'entrions en guerre.

***H. M., Jr.** :* Je ne m'en souviens pas.

***M. Coe** : L'*homme qui s'occupe maintenant de leurs propriétés est Westrick qui, vous vous en souvenez, est venu ici et a été mêlé à Texaco. Ils ont essayé par tous les moyens de préparer des affaires plus tôt pour s'échapper. Ils sont liés à un groupe allemand de premier plan, etc. D'autre part, le colonel Behn a été utilisé plusieurs fois comme émissaire par le Département d'État et je crois qu'il est personnellement en très bons termes avec Stettinius. Nous avons reçu des représentants du ministère des affaires étrangères une lettre dans laquelle ils affirment n'avoir aucune objection. Nous vous avons proposé tout à l'heure - la lettre que je vous ai envoyée suggérant de demander à State, si compte tenu de nos objectifs de refuge, ils ont toujours dit oui. Je suis convaincu, après avoir parlé avec eux au téléphone ces deux derniers jours, qu'ils répondront par écrit et diront oui, ils pensent toujours que c'est une bonne affaire.

***H. M., Jr** :* C'est la position dans laquelle je suis. Comme vous le savez, messieurs, je suis débordé maintenant et je ne peux pas m'occuper personnellement de cette affaire, et je pense que nous allons devoir la confier au Département d'État, et s'il veut la régler, très bien. Je n'ai tout simplement pas le temps ni l'énergie pour les combattre sur cette base.

M. Coe *:* Alors nous devrions l'autoriser maintenant.

M. White *:* Vous devriez d'abord recevoir une lettre. Je suis d'accord avec le secrétaire sur ce point de vue, à savoir qu'il ne faut pas faire confiance à ce Behn au coin de la rue. Il y a quelque chose dans cet accord qui semble suspect et nous avons eu affaire à lui ces deux dernières années. Cependant, c'est une chose de le croire et une autre de le défendre devant les pressions qui seront exercées ici pour tenter de priver cette entreprise de l'accord commercial, mais je pense que ce que nous pourrions faire, c'est faire savoir au Département d'État que, dans le cadre d'un projet de refuge, il ne pense pas qu'il y ait un danger que l'un de ces actifs - je citerais certains d'entre eux, et j'épellerais la lettre. Mettez-les dans le dossier et faites-les même un peu peur et tenez bon, ou au moins ils auront eu le dossier et vous aurez attiré leur attention sur ces dangers. Ce Behn nous déteste de toute façon. Nous nous sommes interposés entre lui et les marchés depuis au moins quatre ans.

H. M., Jr *:* Suivez ce que White a dit. Quelque chose dans ce sens. "Cher M. Stettinius, ces choses me dérangent en raison des faits suivants, et je voudrais que vous me disiez si nous devrions ou non...."

M. White *:* "Compte tenu du danger que les avoirs allemands soient dissimulés ici, l'avenir -" et qu'il revienne en disant "Non", nous le surveillerons.

M. Coe *:* Nous avons dit que nous voulions donner quelque chose à Acheson lundi.

H. M., Jr *:* Et si vous me préparez ça pour demain matin, je le signerai.

M. Coe *:* O.K.

Source : Sénat des États-Unis, sous-comité chargé d'enquêter sur l'administration de la loi sur la sécurité intérieure. Comité du pouvoir judiciaire, *Morgenthau Diarty (Allemagne)*, Volume 1, 90e Congrès, 1ère session, 20 novembre 1967, (Washington D.C. : U.S. Government Printing Office, 1967), p. 320 du livre 828. (Page 976 de l'impression du Sénat américain).
Note : "M. White" est Harry Dexter White. Le "Dr Dubois" est Josiah E. Dubois, Jr, auteur du livre "*Generals in Grey Suits*" (Londres : The Bodley Head, 1953). "H.M. Jr." est Henry Morgenthau Jr, Secrétaire au Trésor.
Ce mémorandum est important, car il accuse Sosthenes Behn d'avoir tenté de conclure des marchés en coulisses dans l'Allemagne nazie "pendant 4 ans au moins" - c'est-à-dire que pendant que le reste des États-Unis était en guerre, Behn et ses amis faisaient encore des affaires comme d'habitude avec l'Allemagne. Cette note soutient les preuves présentées dans les chapitres cinq et neuf concernant l'influence de l'I.T.T. dans le cercle restreint de Himmler et ajoute Herman Goering à la liste des contacts de l'I.T.T.

BIBLIOGRAPHIE SÉLECTIVE

Allen, Gary. *None Dare Call It Conspiracy.* Seal Beach, California: Concord Press, 1971.

Ambruster, Howard Watson. *Treason's Peace.* New York: The Beechhurst Press, 1947.

Angebert, Michel. *The Occult and the Third Reich.* New York: The Macmillan Company, 1974.

Archer, Jules. *The Plot to Seize the White House.* New York: Hawthorn Books, 1973.

Baker, Philip Noel. *Hawkers of Death.* The Labour Party, England, 1984.

Barnes, Harry Elmer. *Perpetual War for Perpetual Peace.* Caldwell, Idaho: Caxton Printers, 1958.

Bennett, Edward W. *Germany and the Diplomacy of the Financial Crisis, 1931.* Cambridge: Harvard University Press, 1962.

Der Farben-Konzern 1928. Hoppenstedt, Berlin, 1928.

Dimitrov, George, *The Reichstag Fire Trial.* London: The Bodley Head, 1984.

Dodd, William E. Jr., and Dodd, Martha. *Ambassador Dodd's Diary, 1933-1938.* New York: Harcourt Brace and Company, 1941.

Domhoff, G. William. *The Higher Circles: The Governing Class in America.* New York: Vintage, 1970.

Dubois, Josiah E., Jr. *Generals in Grey Suits.* London: The Bodley Head, 1958.

Engelbrecht, H.C. *Merchants of Death.* New York: Dodd, Mead & Company, 1984.

Engler, Robert. *The Politics of Oil.* New York: The Macmillan Company, 1961.

Epstein, Julius. *Operation Keelhaul.* Old Greenwich: Devin Adair, 1978.

Farago, Ladislas. *The Game of the Foxes.* New York: Bantam, 1978.

Flynn, John T. *As We Go Marching*, New York: Doubleday, Doran and Co., Inc., 1944.

Guerin, Daniel. *Fascisme et grand capital.* Paris: Francois Maspero, 1965.

Hanfstaengl, Ernst. *Unheard Witness.* New York: J. B. Lippincott, 1957.

Hargrave, John. *Montagu Norman.* New York: The Greystone Press, n.d.

Harris, C.R.S. *Germany's Foreign Indebtedness.* London: Oxford University Press, 1985.

Helfferich, Dr. Karl. *Germany's Economic Progress and National Wealth, 1888.1913.* New York: Germanistic Society of America, 1914.

Hexner, Ervin. *International Cartels.* Chapel Hill: The University of North Carolina Press, 1945.

Howard, Colonel Graeme K. *America and a New Worm Order.* New York: Scribners, 1940.

Kolko, Gabriel. "American Business and Germany, 1930-1941," *The Western Political Quarterly*, Volume XV, 1962.

Kuezynski, Robert R. *Bankers' Profits from German Loans*, Washington, D.C.: The Brookings Institution, 1982.

Leonard, Jonathan. *The Tragedy of Henry Ford.* New York: G.P. Putnam's Sons, 1932.

Ludecke, Kurt G.W. *I Knew Hitler.* New York: Charles Scribner's Sons, 1937.

Magers, Helmut. *Ein Revolutionar Aus Common Sense.* Leipzig: R. Kittler Verlag, 1934.

Martin, James J, *Revisionist Viewpoints.* Colorado: Ralph Mules, 1971.

Martin, James Stewart. *All Honorable Men*, Boston: Little Brown and Company, 1950.

Muhlen, Norbert. *Schacht: Hitler's Magician.* New York: Longmans, Green and Co., 1939.

Nixon, Edgar B. *Franklin D. Roosevelt and Foreign Affairs.* Cambridge: Belknap Press, 1969.

Oil and Petroleum Yearbook, 1938.

Papen, Franz von. *Memoirs.* New York: E.P. Dutton & Co., 1953.

Peterson, Edward Norman. *Hjalmar Schacht.* Boston: The Christopher Publishing House, 1954.

Phelps, Reginald H. *"Before Hitler Came": Thule Society and Germanen Orden,* in the *Journal of Modern History*, September, 1963.

Quigley, Carroll, *Tragedy and Hope.* New York: The Macmillan Company, 1966.

Ravenscroft, Trevor, *The Spear of Destiny.* New York: G.P. Putnam's Sons, 1973.

Rathenau, Walter. *In Days to Come.* London: Allen & Unwin, n.d.

Roberts, Glyn. *The Most Powerful Man in the World.* New York: Covici, Friede, 1938.

Sampson, Anthony. *The Sovereign State of* I.T.T. New York: Stein & Day, 1975.

Schacht, Hjalmar. *Confessions of "The Old Wizard."* Boxton: Houghton Mifflin, 1956.

Schloss, Henry H. *The Bank for International Settlements.* Amsterdam: North Holland Publishing Company, 1958.

Seldes, George. *Iron, Blood and Profits.* New York and London: Harper & Brothers Publishers, 1934.

Simpson, Colin. *Lusitania.* London; Longman, 1972.

Smoot, Dan. *The Invisible Government.* Boston: Western .Islands, 1962,

Strasser, Otto. *Hitler and I.* London: Jonathan Cape, n.d.

Sonderegger, Rene. *Spanischer Sommer.* Affoltern, Switzerland: Aehren Verlag, 1948.

Stocking, George W, and Watkins, Myron W. *Cartels in Action.* New York: The Twentieth Century Fund, 1946.

Sutton, Antony C. *National Suicide: Military Aid to the Soviet Union.* New York: Arlington House Publishers, 1978.

Wall Street and the Bolshevik Revolution. New York: Arlington House Publishers, 1974.
Wall Street and FDR. New York: Arlington House Publishers, 1975.
Western Technology and Soviet Economic Development, 1917-1930. Stanford, California: Hoover Institution Press, 1968.
Western Technology and Soviet Economic Development, 1980-1945. Stanford, California: Hoover Institution Press, 1971.
Western Technology and Soviet Economic Development, 1945-1965. Stanford, California: Hoover Institution Press, 1973.

Sward, Keith. *The Legend of Henry Ford.* New York: Rinehart & Co., 1948.

Thyssen, Fritz. *I Paid Hitler.* New York : Farrar & Rinehart, Inc. s.d. "Procès des criminels de guerre devant les tribunaux militaires de Nuremberg en vertu de la loi n° 10 du Conseil de contrôle", Volume VIII, affaire I.G. Farben, Nuremberg, octobre 1946-avril 1949. Washington : Government Printing Of-flee, 1953. United States Army Air Force, Aiming point report No. 1.E.2 du 29 mai 1943.

Sénat des États-Unis, auditions devant la commission des finances. *Vente d'obligations ou de titres étrangers aux États-Unis.* 72e Congrès, 1ère session, S. Res. 19, 1ère partie, 18, 19 et 21 décembre 1931. Washington : Government Printing Office, 1931.

Sénat des États-Unis, auditions devant une sous-commission de la commission des affaires militaires. *Mobilisation scientifique et technique.* 78e Congrès, 2e session, S. Res. 107, partie 16, 29 août et 7, 8, 12 et 13 septembre 1944. Washington : Government Printing Office, 1944.

Congrès des États-Unis. Chambre des Représentants. *Commission spéciale sur les activités américaines et enquête sur certaines autres activités de propagande.* 73e Congrès, 2e session, audiences no 73-DC-4. Washington : Government Printing Office, 1934.

Congrès des États-Unis. Chambre des Représentants. Commission spéciale sur les activités américaines (1934). *Enquête sur les activités nazies et autres activités de propagande.* 74e Congrès, 1ère session, rapport n° 153. Washington : Government Printing Office, 1934.

Congrès des États-Unis. Sénat. Auditions devant une sous-commission de la commission des affaires militaires. *Élimination des ressources allemandes pour la guerre.* Rapport en vertu des Résolutions 107 et 146, 2 juillet 1945, Partie 7. 78e Congrès et 79e Congrès. Washington : Government Printing Office, 1945.

Congrès des États-Unis. Sénat. Auditions devant une sous-commission de la commission des affaires militaires. *Mobilisation scientifique et technique.* 78e

Congrès, 1ère session, S. 702, partie 16, Washington : Government Printing Office, 1944.

United States Group Control Council (Allemagne), Bureau du directeur du renseignement, Field Information Agency. Rapport de renseignement technique n° EF/ME/1. 4 septembre 1945.

États-Unis Sente. Sous-comité d'enquête sur l'administration de la loi sur la sécurité intérieure, Comité du pouvoir judiciaire. *Journal de Morgenthau (Allemagne).* Volume 1, 90ème Congrès, 1ère session, 20 novembre 1967. Washington : U.S. Government Printing Office, 1967.

Fichier décimal du Département d'État des États-Unis.

Enquête sur les bombardements stratégiques aux États-Unis. *AEG-Ostlandwerke GmbH,* par Whitworth Ferguson. 81 mai 1945.

Enquête sur les bombardements stratégiques aux États-Unis. *Rapport de l'industrie allemande du matériel électrique.* Equipment Division, janvier 1947.

United States Strategic Bombing Survey, *rapport d'usine de l'A.E.G.* (Allgemeine Elektrizitats Gesellschaft). Nuremberg, Allemagne : juin 1945.

Zimmerman, Werner. *Liebet Eure Feinde.* Frankhauser Verlag : Thielle-Neuchatel, 1948.

DÉJÀ PARUS

OMNIA VERITAS
Omnia Veritas Ltd présente :
EUSTACE MULLINS
L'ORDRE MONDIAL
NOS DIRIGEANTS SECRETS
Une étude sur l'hégémonie du parasitisme
LE PROGRAMME DE L'ORDRE MONDIAL : DIVISER POUR MIEUX RÉGNER

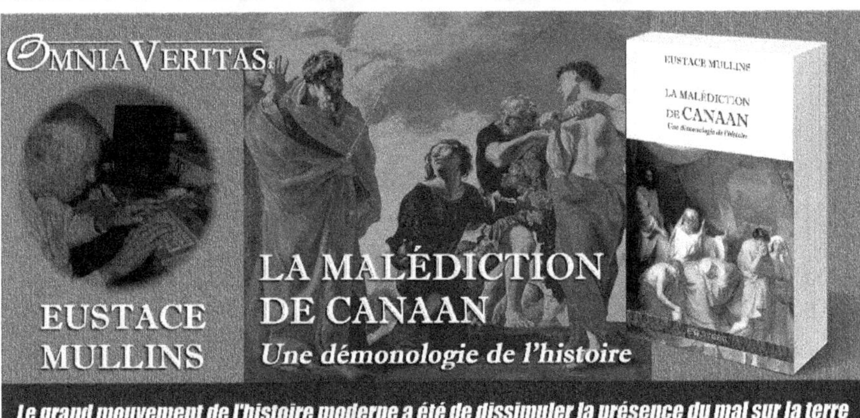
OMNIA VERITAS
EUSTACE MULLINS
LA MALÉDICTION DE CANAAN
Une démonologie de l'histoire
EUSTACE MULLINS
LA MALÉDICTION DE CANAAN
Le grand mouvement de l'histoire moderne a été de dissimuler la présence du mal sur la terre

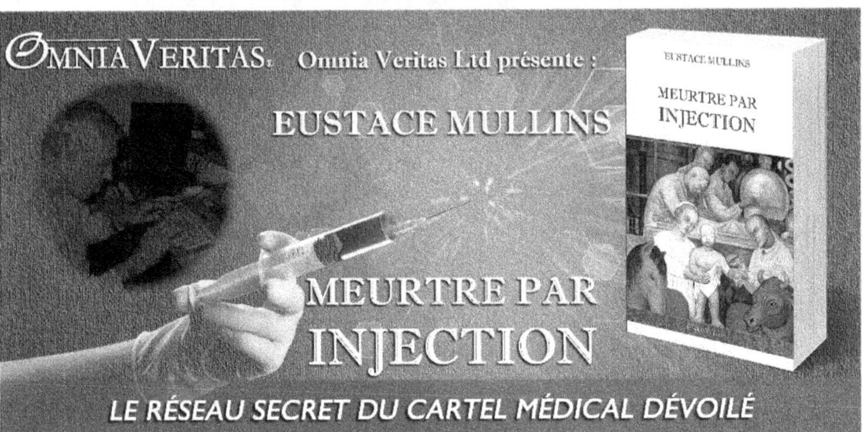
OMNIA VERITAS
Omnia Veritas Ltd présente :
EUSTACE MULLINS
EUSTACE MULLINS
MEURTRE PAR INJECTION
MEURTRE PAR INJECTION
LE RÉSEAU SECRET DU CARTEL MÉDICAL DÉVOILÉ

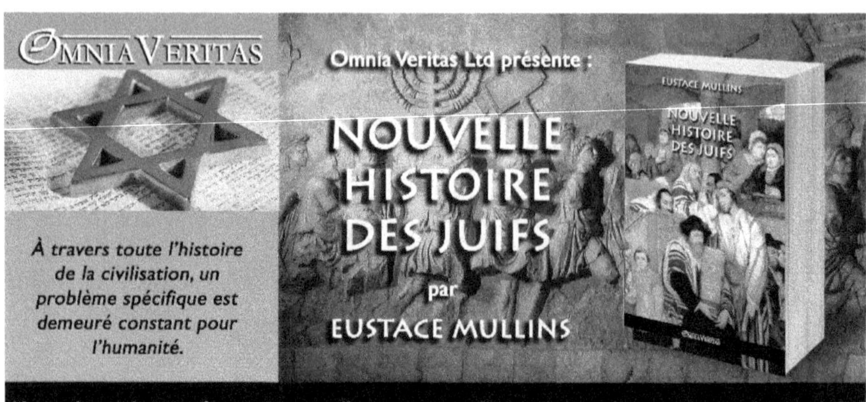
OMNIA VERITAS
Omnia Veritas Ltd présente :
NOUVELLE HISTOIRE DES JUIFS
par
EUSTACE MULLINS
À travers toute l'histoire de la civilisation, un problème spécifique est demeuré constant pour l'humanité.
Un seul peuple irrita les nations qui l'avaient accueilli dans toutes les parties du monde civilisé

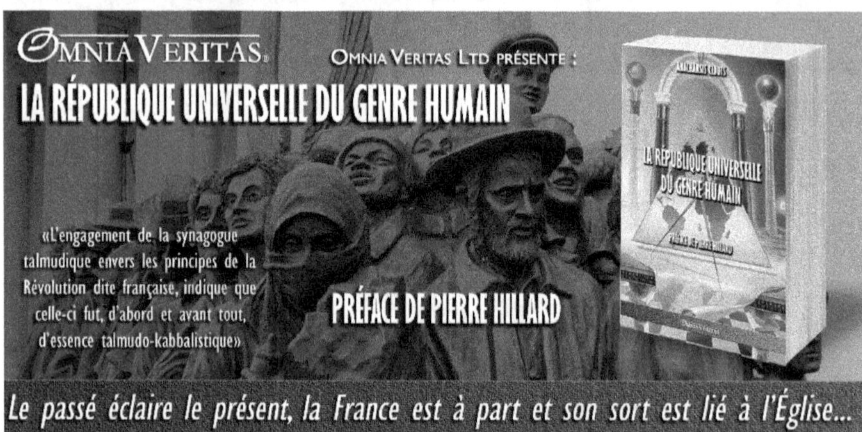
OMNIA VERITAS
OMNIA VERITAS LTD PRÉSENTE :
LA RÉPUBLIQUE UNIVERSELLE DU GENRE HUMAIN
«L'engagement de la synagogue talmudique envers les principes de la Révolution dite française, indique que celle-ci fut, d'abord et avant tout, d'essence talmudo-kabbalistique»
PRÉFACE DE PIERRE HILLARD
Le passé éclaire le présent, la France est à part et son sort est lié à l'Église...

OMNIA VERITAS
OMNIA VERITAS LTD PRÉSENTE :
LE MONDE OCCULTE DES COMIC BOOKS DE DC COMICS À MARVEL
«Le rôle des comics américains Marvel se doit d'être épinglé en raison de leur action délétère sur la psyché de l'enfant.»
PRÉFACE DE PIERRE HILLARD
Les esprits révoltés se construisent un «messie de substitution»...

Et si notre système monétaire n'avait jamais été mûrement réfléchi ?

OMNIA VERITAS
Omnia Veritas Ltd présente :
L'EMPRISE DU MONDIALISME
I CRISE ÉCONOMIQUE MAJEURE ORIGINE - ABOUTISSEMENT
II INITIATION & SOCIÉTÉS SECRÈTES
III LE SECRET DES HAUTES TECHNOLOGIES
IV HÉRÉSIE MÉDICALE & ÉRADICATION DE MASSE
V L'EMPOISONNEMENT GLOBAL
I
II
III
IV
V
Le mondialisme décrypté après sept années d'investigation

OMNIA VERITAS
Omnia Veritas Ltd présente :
LES ŒUVRES DE PAUL RASSINIER
J'avais pensé que, sur un sujet aussi délicat, il convenait d'administrer la vérité à petites doses

OMNIA VERITAS
Omnia Veritas Ltd présente :
2000 ans
de complots
contre l'Église
de
MAURICE PINAY
Aucun autre livre au cours de ce siècle n'a été l'objet d'autant de commentaires dans la presse mondiale.
Une compilation de documents d'Histoire et de sources d'indiscutable importance et authenticité

OMNIA VERITAS
Omnia Veritas Ltd présente :
KEVIN MACDONALD
LA CULTURE DE LA CRITIQUE
LES JUIFS ET LA CRITIQUE RADICALE
DE LA CULTURE DES GENTILS
Ses analyses mettent à jour l'influence culturelle prépondérante des Juifs et leur volonté de miner les nations dans lesquelles ils vivent, pour mieux dominer la société diversifiée qu'ils prônent tout en demeurant eux-mêmes un groupe ethnocentré et homogène, hostile aux intérêts des peuples blancs.
Une analyse évolutive de l'implication juive dans les mouvements politiques et intellectuels du XXe siècle

OMNIA VERITAS
Omnia Veritas Ltd présente :
ISRAËL SHAHAK
HISTOIRE JUIVE
RELIGION JUIVE
LE POIDS DE TROIS MILLÉNAIRES
Rescapé des camps de concentration nazis, il est aussi un auteur et un militant pour la paix, antisioniste radical.
Ses écrits sur le judaïsme ont engendré des controverses...

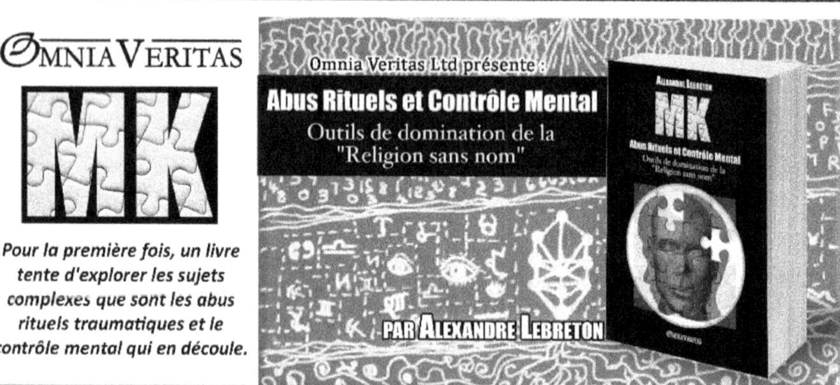
OMNIA VERITAS
MK
Omnia Veritas Ltd présente :
Abus Rituels et Contrôle Mental
Outils de domination de la "Religion sans nom"
PAR ALEXANDRE LEBRETON
Pour la première fois, un livre tente d'explorer les sujets complexes que sont les abus rituels traumatiques et le contrôle mental qui en découle.
Comment est-il possible de programmer mentalement un être humain ?

www.omnia-veritas.com

www.ingramcontent.com/pod-product-compliance
Lightning Source LLC
Chambersburg PA
CBHW060321100426
42812CB00003B/838

* 9 7 8 1 9 1 3 8 9 0 2 5 4 *